A History of the United States, Volume 2: Version 1.0

By

David J. Trowbridge

S-350288-BW-4

9 781453 326091

A History of the United States, Volume 2: Version 1.0

David J. Trowbridge

Published by:

Flat World Knowledge, Inc.
1111 19th St NW, Suite 1180
Washington, DC 20036

Brief Contents

Contents

Image Credits

- Library of Congress

    Figure 1.1, Figure 1.2, Figure 1.5, Figure 1.7, Figure 1.8, Figure 1.9, Figure 1.10, Figure 1.11, Figure 1.13, Figure 1.16, Figure 1.17, Figure 1.18, Figure 2.2, Figure 2.7, Figure 2.12, Figure 2.13, Figure 2.14, Figure 2.17, Figure 2.16, Figure 2.18, Figure 2.19, Figure 2.20, Figure 2.21, Figure 2.22, Figure 2.23, Figure 2.24, Figure 2.25, Figure 2.26, Figure 2.27, Figure 2.28, Figure 2.29, Figure 2.30, Figure 2.31, Figure 2.33, Figure 3.1, Figure 3.2, Figure 3.3, Figure 3.8, Figure 3.10, Figure 3.11, Figure 3.14, Figure 3.15, Figure 3.16, Figure 3.17, Figure 3.18, Figure 3.22, Figure 3.23, Figure 3.24, Figure 3.25, Figure 3.26, Figure 3.27, Figure 3.29, Figure 4.1, Figure 4.2, Figure 4.5, Figure 4.7, Figure 4.8, Figure 4.9, Figure 4.10, Figure 4.14, Figure 4.15, Figure 4.16, Figure 4.17, Figure 4.18, Figure 4.19, Figure 4.21, Figure 4.22, Figure 4.24, Figure 4.26, Figure 4.27, Figure 4.28, Figure 4.33, Figure 4.34, Figure 4.35, Figure 4.37, Figure 5.1, Figure 5.2, Figure 5.3, Figure 5.12, Figure 5.16, Figure 5.18, Figure 5.19, Figure 5.20, Figure 5.21, Figure 5.22, Figure 5.23, Figure 5.27, Figure 5.28, Figure 5.31, Figure 5.32, Figure 6.1, Figure 6.2, Figure 6.3, Figure 6.5, Figure 6.8, Figure 6.9, Figure 6.10, Figure 6.11, Figure 6.12, Figure 6.13, Figure 6.15, Figure 6.18, Figure 6.19, Figure 6.21, Figure 6.22, Figure 6.25, Figure 6.26, Figure 7.1, Figure 7.4, Figure 7.10, Figure 7.11, Figure 7.12, Figure 7.13, Figure 7.16, Figure 7.17, Figure 7.18, Figure 7.20, Figure 7.22, Figure 7.27, Figure 8.1, Figure 8.15, Figure 9.1, Figure 9.15, Figure 9.17, Figure 10.13, Figure 10.21, Figure 10.22, Figure 11.3, Figure 11.4, Figure 11.6, Figure 11.9, Figure 11.15, Figure 11.16, Figure 12.3, Figure 12.12, Figure 12.14, Figure 12.15, Figure 12.16, Figure 13.2, Figure 13.13, Figure 13.14

- National Archives and Records Administration

    Figure 1.3, Figure 1.14, Figure 2.1, Figure 2.3, Figure 2.5, Figure 2.9, Figure 2.10, Figure 3.5, Figure 4.29, Figure 5.9, Figure 5.24, Figure 5.30, Figure 6.4, Figure 6.16, Figure 6.27, Figure 7.2, Figure 7.3, Figure 7.5, Figure 7.6, Figure 7.7, Figure 7.15, Figure 7.24, Figure 8.2, Figure 8.3, Figure 8.4, Figure 8.5, Figure 8.6, Figure 8.7, Figure 8.8, Figure 8.10, Figure 8.11, Figure 8.16, Figure 8.22, Figure 8.25, Figure 9.8, Figure 9.10, Figure 9.12, Figure 9.13, Figure 9.20, Figure 9.21, Figure 9.22, Figure 10.3, Figure 10.11, Figure 10.15, Figure 10.17, Figure 10.23, Figure 11.1, Figure 11.2, Figure 11.12, Figure 11.13, Figure 11.14 (Jack E. Kiplinger, photographer), Figure 11.21, Figure 12.1, Figure 12.2, Figure 12.4, Figure 12.5, Figure 12.7, Figure 12.8, Figure 12.9, Figure 12.10, Figure 12.17, Figure 12.20, Figure 12.22, Figure 13.3, Figure 13.4, Figure 14.10

- *The Freedman's Third Reader.* (Boston: American Tract Society, 1866)

    Figure 1.4

- Courtesy Wikimedia Commons

    Figure 1.6, http://commons.wikimedia.org/wiki/File:Major_Martin_Delany.jpg. Photo: dbking (CC-BY-2.0)

    Figure 1.15, http://commons.wikimedia.org/wiki/File:TheUsualIrishWayofDoingThings.jpg

    Figure 1.19, http://commons.wikimedia.org/wiki/File:Hayes_Civil_War.jpg

    Figure 2.6, http://commons.wikimedia.org/wiki/File:Indian_Land_for_Sale.jpg

    Figure 2.8, http://commons.wikimedia.org/wiki/File:US_Transcontinental_Railroads_1887.jpg. Digital reconstruction and restoration: DigitalImageServices.com (CC-BY-SA3.0 Unported)

    Figure 3.7, http://commons.wikimedia.org/wiki/File:Buffalo_Bills_Wild_West_Show,_1890.jpg

    Figure 3.13, http://commons.wikimedia.org/wiki/File:1892prescountymap.PNG. Author: Tilden76 at en.wikipedia (CC-BY-3.0)

    Figure 3.19, http://commons.wikimedia.org/wiki/File:Bryan,_Judge_magazine,_1896.jpg

    Figure 3.21, http://commons.wikimedia.org/wiki/File:Duluth-lynching-postcard.jpg

    Figure 3.28, http://commons.wikimedia.org/wiki/File:Liliuokalani_of_Hawaii.jpg

    Figure 4.13, http://commons.wikimedia.org/wiki/File:The_Curse_of_California.jpg

    Figure 4.20, http://commons.wikimedia.org/wiki/File:Debs_campaign.jpg

    Figure 4.26, http://commons.wikimedia.org/wiki/File:YellowTerror.jpg

    Figure 4.30, http://commons.wikimedia.org/wiki/File:Maimon_Home.jpg

    Figure 4.31, http://commons.wikimedia.org/wiki/File:Jewish_immigration_Russia_United_States_1901.jpg

    Figure 5.4, http://commons.wikimedia.org/wiki/File:1918_flu_in_Oakland.jpg

    Figure 5.7, http://commons.wikimedia.org/wiki/File:Oscar_Micheaux.jpg

    Figure 5.10, http://en.wikipedia.org/wiki/File:Map_Europe_alliances_1914-en.svg. Authors: historicair, Fluteflute & User:Bibi Saint-Pol (CC-BY-SA-2.5-Generic)

    Figure 5.14, http://commons.wikimedia.org/wiki/File:Lusitania_warning.jpg

    Figure 5.25, http://commons.wikimedia.org/wiki/File:WorldWarI-MilitaryDeaths-EntentePowers-Piechart.png

    Figure 5.29, Figure 10.12, Figure 10.24, Figure 12.11; http://commons.wikimedia.org/wiki/File:Blank_US_Map.svg. Author: User:Theshibboleth. (CC-BY-SA-3.0-Unported)

Figure 7.8, http://commons.wikimedia.org/wiki/File:Fort_Peck_Dam_%28Fort_Peck_Montana%29_Spillway_01.jpg

Figure 7.9, http://commons.wikimedia.org/wiki/File:Sandinoflagusmc.jpg

Figure 7.23, http://commons.wikimedia.org/wiki/File:Bundesarchiv_Bild_183-R69173,_M%C3%BCnchener_Abkommen,_Staatschefs.jpg. Source: Deutsches Bundesarchiv (German Federal Archive), Bild 183-R69173 (CC-BY-SA-3.0-Germany)

Figure 7.26, http://commons.wikimedia.org/wiki/File:Stroop_Report_-_Warsaw_Ghetto_Uprising_06b.jpg

Figure 7.28, http://commons.wikimedia.org/wiki/File:United_China_Relief1.jpg

Figure 8.12, http://commons.wikimedia.org/wiki/File:General_douglas_macarthur_meets_american_indian_troops_wwii_military_pacific_navajo_pima_island_hopping.JPG

Figure 8.19, http://commons.wikimedia.org/wiki/File:Bundesarchiv_Bild_101I-318-0071-16A,_Polen,_bespannte_Einheiten_bei_Fluss%C3%BCberquerung.jpg (CC-BY-SA-3.0-Germany)

Figure 8.20, http://commons.wikimedia.org/wiki/File:Pacific_Theater_Areas;map1.JPG

Figure 8.23, http://commons.wikimedia.org/wiki/File:Troops_advance_in_a_snowstorm.jpg

Figure 8.24, http://commons.wikimedia.org/wiki/File:Ww2-asia-overview.gif

Figure 9.2, http://commons.wikimedia.org/wiki/File:Cold_war_europe_military_alliances_map_en.png. Author: San Jose (CC-BY-SA-3.0-Unported)

Figure 9.3, http://commons.wikimedia.org/wiki/File:EleanorRooseveltHumanRights.png

Figure 9.5, https://commons.wikimedia.org/wiki/File:Germany_location_map_labeled_8_Jun_1947_-_22_Apr_1949-colored.svg. User: WikiNight2 (GNU Free Documentation License, Version 1.2)

Figure 9.6, http://commons.wikimedia.org/wiki/File:Israel-CIA_WFB_Map_%282004%29.png

Figure 9.18, http://commons.wikimedia.org/wiki/File:1950s_%E4%B8%AD%E5%9C%8B%E4%BA%BA%E6%B0%91%E5%86%B3%E4%B8%8D%E8%83%BD%E5%AE%B9%E5%BF%8D.jpg

Figure 9.19, http://commons.wikimedia.org/wiki/File:Location_Map_Asia.svg

Figure 10.2, http://commons.wikimedia.org/wiki/File:CheHigh.jpg

Figure 10.5, http://commons.wikimedia.org/wiki/File:Indochine_fran%C3%A7aise_%281913%29.jpg

Figure 10.6, http://commons.wikimedia.org/wiki/File:French_M24_Chaffee_Vietnam.jpg

Figure 10.7, http://commons.wikimedia.org/wiki/File:John_Kennedy,_Nikita_Khrushchev_1961.jpg

Figure 10.12, http://commons.wikimedia.org/wiki/File:Educational_seperation_in_the_US_prior_to_Brown_Map.PNG

Figure 10.14, http://commons.wikimedia.org/wiki/File:101st_Airborne_at_Little_Rock_Central_High.jpg

Figure 12.21, http://commons.wikimedia.org/wiki/File:Equal_Rights_Amendment_Map.svg

Figure 13.8, http://commons.wikimedia.org/wiki/File:USPlanGrenadaUrgentFury.svg. Authors: Derfel73; NordNordWest; John M. Shalikashvili, Joint Chiefs of Staff, OpenStreetMap contributors (CC-BY-SA-3.0)

Figure 13.10, http://commons.wikimedia.org/wiki/File:Eastn-bloc4.svg. Author: Goldsztajn (CC-BY-SA-3.0-Unported)

Figure 13.16, http://commons.wikimedia.org/wiki/File:HenryCisnerosLibraryHIGHRES.JPG. Author: CityView (CC-BY-SA-3.0 Unported)

Figure 13.17, http://commons.wikimedia.org/wiki/File:Berlin_Blockade-map.svg. Author: User:historicair (CC-BY-SA-3.0-Unported)

Figure 14.12, http://commons.wikimedia.org/wiki/File:Charlotte20DecMakeLeveesGarage.jpg. Author: Infrogmation (CC-BY-2.5-Generic)

Figure 14.15, http://commons.wikimedia.org/wiki/File:US_incarceration_timeline-clean.svg

Figure 14.16, http://commons.wikimedia.org/wiki/File:Dontaskdonttellcredible.jpg

Figure 14.19, http://commons.wikimedia.org/wiki/File:Day_47_Occupy_Wall_Street_November_2_2011_Shankbone_10.JPG. Author: David Shankbone (CC-BY-3.0-Unported)

- *Frank Leslie's Illustrated Newspaper*, 19 January 1867

  Figure 1.12

- *National Atlas of the United States*, US Department of the Interior; nationatlas.gov

  Figure 1.20, Figure 4.4, Figure 4.12, Figure 6.17, Figure 6.28, Figure 9.8, Figure 9.24, Figure 10.16, Figure 11.5, Figure 11.23

- "Little Bighorn Battlefield National Monument, Historical Handbook Number One," 1969. National Park Service, US Dept. of the Interior, http://www.cr.nps.gov/history/online_books/hh/1b/hh1toc.htm

  Figure 2.4

- Courtesy Wikipedia

  Figure 2.11, http://en.wikipedia.org/wiki/File:Invaders.gif

Figure 4.3, http://en.wikipedia.org/wiki/File:Strike1902.JPG

Figure 7.25, http://en.wikipedia.org/wiki/File:Never_was_so_much_owed_by_so_many_to_so_few.jpg

Figure 11.24, http://en.wikipedia.org/wiki/File:My_Lai_massacre.jpg

Figure 13.18, http://en.wikipedia.org/wiki/File:EasternBloc_PostDissolution2008.svg. **Author: Mosedschurte. (CC-BY-SA-3.0)**

Figure 14.18, http://en.wikipedia.org/wiki/File:TeaPartyByFreedomFan.JPG

- Library and Archives Canada / C-029977

  Figure 2.15

- Library of Congress, Rare Book and Special Collections Division, National American Woman Suffrage Association Collection

  Figure 2.17

- *Harper's Weekly*, 20 May 1871

  Figure 2.32

- Courtesy Sears Brands, LLC

  Figure 3.4

- Library of Congress, Music Division

  Figure 3.6, Figure 4.11

- Nebraska State Historical Society [nbhips 10007]

  Figure 3.9

- Kansas State Historical Society, http://www.kansasmemory.org, Copy and Reuse Restrictions Apply

  Figure 3.12

- *The New York Times*, 25 March 1854.

  Figure 3.20

- The History Department at the United States Military Academy, http://www.westpoint.edu/history/SitePages/Our%20Atlases.aspx

  Figure 3.30, Figure 3.31, Figure 3.32, Figure 5.10, Figure 5.11, Figure 5.26, Figure 8.18, Figure 10.4

- Courtesy of http://www.donstivers.com

  Figure 3.33

- Library of Congress, Prints and Photographs Division, "Built in America" Collection.

  Figure 4.6

- Library of Congress, Chronicling America: Historic American Newspapers

  Figure 4.19, *The Evening World*, 08 July 1903

  Figure 4.32, *The Alliance Herald*, 25 February 1909

  Figure 5.32, *Prescott Journal-Miner*, 1917

- National Park Service, Booker T. Washington National Monument

  Figure 4.23

- Women of Protest: Photographs from the Records of the National Woman's Party, Manuscript Division, Library of Congress, Washington, D.C.

  Figure 4.25

- Courtesy of the Lawrence Public Library

  Figure 4.36

- *The Crisis: A Record of the Darker Races*, November 1910. New York: NAACP, 1910. General Collections, Library of Congress. Courtesy of the NAACP. [Digital ID # na0026]

  Figure 5.5

- The Internet Archive, http://www.archive.org/details/dw_griffith_birth_of_a_nation?start=5759.5

  Figure 5.6

- Library of Congress, Serial and Government Publications Division

  Figure 5.13

- "Hell Fighters! Let's Go!" by H. Charles McBarron, http://www.history.army.mil/html/artphoto/pripos/usaia.html

  Figure 5.15

- British Cartoon Archive, University of Kent

Figure 5.17

- *Huntington Advertiser*, 11 September 1921. Courtesy of West Virginia State Archives
    Figure 6.7
- From the Collections of the Washington State Archives
    Figure 6.14
- Courtesy of the University of Kentucky. Louis Edward Nollau Nitrate Photographic Print Collection, circa 1866–1958: 1998ua002
    Figure 6.20
- Library of Congress, Prints & Photographs Division, Carl Van Vechten Collection
    Figure 6.23, LC-USZ62-92598
    Figure 6.25, LC-DIG-van-5a52142
- Courtesy of League of United Latin American Citizens (LULAC) National Office, Washington DC & LULAC National President Margaret Moran
    Figure 7.14
- Photographs in the Carol M. Highsmith Archive, Library of Congress, Prints and Photographs Division
    Figure 7.16, Figure 7.17
- © AP Photo
    Figure 7.21
- Althea Prexeda Semanchik Turlington Collection, Veterans History Project, American Folklife Center, Library of Congress. http://lcweb2.loc.gov/diglib/vhp/story/loc.natlib.afc2001001.33593/
    Figure 8.9
- US Naval History and Heritage Command Photograph; Courtesy of the US Marine Corps History Division
    Figure 8.13
- Library of Congress, Prints & Photographs Division, Visual Materials from the NAACP Records [LC-USZ62-135259]
    Figure 8.14
- Courtesy of the Dwight D. Eisenhower Library
    Figure 8.17, Figure 9.23
- "Overlord Area: 1944" map from "Historical Perspectives on the Operational Art," by Michael D. Krause & R. Cody Phillips, eds. Center of Military History, United States Army. http://www.history.army.mil/books/OpArt/
    Figure 8.21
- Courtesy of The Herb Block Foundation
    Figure 9.4, A 1949 Herblock Cartoon, copyright by The Herb Block Foundation
    Figure 10.10, A 1950 Herblock Cartoon, copyright by The Herb Block Foundation
    Figure 10.20, A 1961 Herblock Cartoon, copyright by The Herb Block Foundation
    Figure 13.9, A 1987 Herblock Cartoon, copyright by The Herb Block Foundation
- Kent State University Libraries, Special Collections and Archives
    Figure 9.7
- Courtesy of the Holt Labor Library
    Figure 9.11
- By permission of the Marcus Family
    Figure 9.14
- *Top Secret*, 1961
    Figure 9.16
- US Naval Historical Center Photograph [NH 96378]
    Figure 9.20
- Robert Knudsen. White House Photographs. John F. Kennedy Presidential Library and Museum, Boston
    Figure 10.1
- Courtesy of NASA; Image Credit: National Space Science Data Center
    Figure 10.8
- Tom Kelley Archive/Retrofile RF/Getty Images
    Figure 10.9

About the Author

David J. Trowbridge (PhD, University of Kansas) is an assistant professor of history and director of African and African American Studies at Marshall University. He teaches graduate and undergraduate courses on civil rights, race and ethnicity, and military and diplomatic history. His favorite course to teach remains the introductory US history survey. In these courses he is able to witness the transformation as students discover their own love of history (much to their surprise). Dr. Trowbridge has published several articles in leading academic journals, including the *Journal of African American History*. He is also the editor of several books about local history and is the author of a forthcoming book entitled *Jim Crow in the Land of John Brown* that explores the origins of racial segregation in the Midwest. In addition to his academic career, Dr. Trowbridge is a veteran of the United States Air Force, a former firefighter, and a true believer in the power of education to enrich lives and strengthen the nation.

Preface

As an academic doctor, books about history are the only thing I can legally prescribe. Over the past decade, I have written almost three thousand prescriptions. But not all patients/students have taken their medicine. A few years ago, I decided that I needed to re-consider exactly what I was prescribing. Was the $80 textbook I used at a community college based on a proper diagnosis of the needs of my students? Was the textbook that was even more expensive (but mostly full of pictures) the right book for my students at a research institution? Clearly not. But where could I find better medicine that would address my patients' chief com-plaint—overpriced textbooks that failed to address their needs?

This search led to the creation of this textbook. We constructed *A History of the United States* by reading and experimenting with each of the textbooks that are on the market. We already knew that many students approach college as if it is a quest to figure out what material is likely to be on an exam. We were surprised to see how savvy students were when they applied this model to textbook reading—many of them simply skip through about a third of a typical US history textbook. It was clear that we could elim-inate lengthy opening vignettes, extended block quotes, and special sections that students assumed were placed in shaded boxes to indicate that they were not going to be on the exam.

We also found that students are allergic to textbooks that only have a few pictures, and they really do learn from images that are presented in a way that teaches an important lesson. However, these same students also admitted that they were easily distracted when they read. When there are too many pictures and when all these images disrupt the flow of the text, they admitted, they catch themselves "browsing" their textbooks as if they were catalogs or popular magazines.

This information led to the creation of a book that has just as many pictures and maps as any other book on the market, but one that is careful to place these images in ways that do not disrupt the narrative. The team of photo researchers and map-makers at Flat World Knowledge worked with historians and reviewers to only select images that had a compelling message. They were also careful to avoid the trap of overloading pages with images that distracted students and turned reading into browsing.

Here's the best part: this allowed the author freedom to include a lot more content and essential background information without making the book any longer than other textbooks. We found that key concepts that are important to understanding his-tory—such as the difference between Socialism, Capitalism, and Communism—could be incorporated into the text. We were able to include examples from labor history beyond Homestead, Haymarket, and Pullman. In so doing, we hope our book communicates the simple truth that the historic conflict between labor and capital was not limited to Chicago and Pennsylvania.

This inclusive approach was applied to every aspect of the book. For example, each section on the Cold War includes examples from Africa and Latin America in addition to Europe and Asia. The civil rights movement includes examples from the Great Plains, the Pacific Northwest, Appalachia, and the Northeast in addition to the Deep South. Women's history, Latino/Latina history, Asian American history, LGBT history, and other important but often-marginalized topics have also been incorporated throughout most of the chapters. And because every book is customizable, instructors can add local and thematic history wherever they believe it is needed.

Because no single prescription can fit every patient, the book can even be customized, abridged, or enlarged. One of the great things about this book is that it can be revised and improved by myself and others. In this regard, I would love to hear from instruct-ors and students alike. I am interested to find the ways this book worked for you and hear your ideas about ways to improve it. All ideas are welcome, as are stories about how this book has made a difference in your experiences as teachers and students.

I have been extremely fortunate to work with so many supportive colleagues who have generously given their time and talents to help shape this book. Thank you to those at the University of Kansas, the University of Illinois, Marshall University, and a host of other institutions who have suggested books and articles and reviewed portions of the manuscript. I would especially like to thank each of the historians who served in a formal capacity as the reviewers of the manuscript. Your counsel and kindly written criticism helped me through each step of the writing and editing process.

- Blaine Browne, Broward College
- Alan Bloom, Valparaiso University
- Shin Bowen, Southeast Missouri State University
- Errol Tsekani Browne, Duquesne University
- Robert Caputi, Erie Community College, State University of New York
- George Carson, Central Bible College
- Andrea DeKoter, SUNY Cortland
- Jamieson Duncan, Ashland University
- Michael P. Gabriel, Kutztown University of Pennsylvania
- Candace Gregory-Abbott, California State University, Sacramento
- Michael Hall, Armstrong Atlantic State University
- Eric Jackson, Northern Kentucky University
- Cherisse Jones-Branch, Arkansas State University

- Andrew Lee, New York University
- Chris Lewis, University of Colorado Boulder
- James Lindgren, SUNY Plattsburgh
- Daniel Murphree, University of Central Florida
- Dennis Nordin, Mississippi State University
- Elsa Nystrom, Kennesaw State University
- Brian Plummer, Azusa Pacific University
- Chris Rasmussen, Fairleigh Dickinson University
- Itai Sneh, John Jay College of Criminal Justice
- Carol Siler, Eastern Kentucky State University

I also want to thank the team at Flat World. Michael Boezi, Vanessa Gennarelli, Alisa Alering, and a host of others stoically endured and tolerated an author who still believes that the phrase "technology in the classroom" refers to a chalkboard and fluorescent lighting.

David J. Trowbridge
david.trowbridge@marshall.edu

WARNING. Instructors who have adopted this textbook have experienced the following side-effects: increased student participation, better grades on exams, and an increased likelihood that students will try to hug their professors for saving them so much money. Students who arrive to class with questions inspired by their reading are advised to consult their doctors of history, as this may be an indication of a rare condition known as curiosity about the past.

CHAPTER 1
What Does Freedom Mean?: Reconstruction, 1865–1877

The Civil War ended in April 1865, but the end of combat did not mean that the nation had resolved all of the issues that had led it to war. After the Confederate surrender at Appomattox, America faced the task of Reconstruction—a broad term referring to the rebuilding of the war-torn South and the political reunification of the nation. For many Americans, Reconstruction was a time of personal reconciliation and rebuilding. Soldiers sought to reconstruct lives as civilians. Black and white farmers who had lost their land or otherwise been displaced during the war did their best to reconstruct lives as urban laborers. Families severed by sectionalism sought reunion while those who had lost husbands and fathers experienced their own version of reconstruction. Veterans and widows found comfort in one another, adopted orphans, and literally reconstructed families that had been destroyed by the war. For tens of thousands of the war's wounded, reconstruction took on a literal meaning as they sought to rebuild their shattered bodies with artificial limbs and resume life as laborers and farmers.

The postwar period was also a time when ideas about race and gender were challenged. Black leaders pushed for full political, legal, and economic equality. Women increasingly formed organizations and lobbied for the recognition of these same rights. Although they were denied the ballot in all but a handful of Western communities during Reconstruction, women who had managed farms, worked as teachers and nurses, directed relief societies, and entered the workforce as laborers during the Civil War continued to challenge traditional ideas about women's roles in society. In so doing, they reconstructed their own identities and the very notion of womanhood.

With the exception of a small but growing number of suffragists and their supporters, issues of gender equality were perceived as being secondary to questions about race and the condition of former slaves. Former slave owners sought to reconstruct plantation agriculture in an era without slavery. They were opposed by 4 million former slaves who attempted to define for themselves the meaning of emancipation and determine their own places within the postwar economy. Of foremost importance to these individuals were the reconstruction of family and community, equal economic opportunity, and the full recognition of political rights. As a result, issues surrounding black suffrage and the economic condition of former slaves occupied the nation's attention throughout Reconstruction.

FIGURE 1.1

Reconstruction was a time of transition from slavery to freedom for both planters and the former slaves. The following political cartoon from the July 29, 1865, issue of *Harper's Weekly* sarcastically presents the perspective of some former owners who claimed that that the end of slavery was actually a time of liberation from the responsibilities of caring for their slaves. Here, the planter exclaims, "My boy, we've toiled and taken care of you long enough—now you've got to work!"

reparation

Payment for a previous
wrongdoing. In the case of
slavery, the victims requested
but never received
compensation for their
unpaid labor and suffering.

While individuals coped with the aftermath of war and the meaning of freedom, the nation faced difficult questions about how the South would transition from plantation slavery to a system of free labor. Americans also debated whether Confederate leaders should face trial for the crime of treason and whether the South should be held responsible for the Union's wartime expenses. Further deliberations regarding the vast sums needed to rebuild Southern cities, harbors, railroads, and levees revealed the continued divisions between Northerners and Southerners. Some Northerners argued that confiscation of the land and property of Confederate rebels would serve as punishment for Southern treason while also providing the government with revenue to settle war debts and fund reconstruction projects. African American leaders argued that Confederate land and property might be redistributed to former slaves as **reparation** for years of unpaid toil. Such resources would provide a degree of material security and economic independence for some of the most vulnerable Southerners. However, most whites simply wished a return to the status quo, minus slavery. They assumed that former slaves would become agricultural wage laborers on the farms and plantations that were owned by their former masters. These individuals believed that redistribution of property was a violation of the limited powers granted to the federal government and might lead to greater political and economic instability.

1. RACE, REUNION, AND THE AFTERMATH OF WAR

LEARNING OBJECTIVES

1. Identify the vision for Reconstruction held by former slaves, white Southerners, and presidents Abraham Lincoln and Andrew Johnson. Identify how each group worked to further their objectives.
2. Describe the provisions of the Black Codes, being sure to explain the intent and the impact of these laws. Explain how African Americans responded to the Black Codes. Explain the role of the Black Codes and violence in the early years of Reconstruction.
3. Describe the differences and similarities of Lincoln's and Johnson's plans for Reconstruction. Identify the top priority for both of these men in framing their policies. Explain how the Republican and Democratic parties differed in their views on the rights of former slaves.

1.1 Aftermath of War in the South

The physical, financial, and emotional toll of both war and emancipation had shaken the core assumptions of the antebellum South. Confederate currency was worthless, as were the bonds purchased by the Southern people to support the Confederate war effort. Cities were in ruins, property values had collapsed, and the fortunes of many Southerners evaporated in the wake of emancipation. A degree of bewilderment, fear, and even anger might be expected from white Southerners after their attempt to defend their "peculiar institution" of chattel slavery had ironically led to its sudden destruction. However, nothing fueled the indignation of white Southerners like efforts of former slaves to reconstruct lives that were independent of white control. The world must have seemed turned upside-down to the former slave masters, many of whom now possessed only enormous debts. The frustration of military defeat, indignation toward Yankees, and racial antipathies toward African Americans blurred together into a single vein as former masters watched those they had once held in bondage leave their declining plantations in search of new lives. While a few thousand Southerners left the country in hopes of developing plantations in South America and the Caribbean, most remained in the country and hoped that the postwar South could somehow reinvent itself. Some hoped to reconstruct Northern success through factories, farms, and free labor. Others clung to the past and vowed to reconstruct the antebellum order by keeping laborers tied to the plantation system even after the demise of chattel slavery.

For former slaves, freedom from plantation labor brought both joy and uncertainty. Freedom loosed the chains of slavery but also brought the possibility of starvation, homelessness, and even arbitrary imprisonment. Former slaves knew that emancipation was only real if they could achieve a degree of economic security through landownership or the acquisition of wealth. They also knew that genuine citizenship was predicated on the recognition of political rights that carried the force of law. Freedom also meant the recognition of one's manhood or womanhood, expressed at this time by addressing an adult as "Mr." or "Mrs." During slavery, black women and men endured diminutive titles such as "uncle" or "aunt" or "boy" or "girl." At best, they were called by their first names—names that could be changed at the whim of their owners.

The first priority of former slaves, however, was to reunite with loved ones and resume or reconstruct family life. Former slaves traveled enormous distances in search of lost family members, investing what little money they might have in newspaper advertisements describing a beloved parent or child they hoped to find. While white planters expected former slaves to spend every waking hour working in their fields for low wages, many black women and men accepted these jobs as a means of financing their continued search. Others devoted their time and resources to helping family members in need. To a planter at harvest, these wanderings throughout the countryside and assistance to others could appear as laziness or improvidence. However, to the former slave this ability to control of one's time and labor represented the first test of their freedom.

After the reunification of family members, the next priority for former slaves was economic security, followed by education, and the recognition of basic civil rights. Former slaves pooled their resources and financed the operation of thousands of schools. Their herculean efforts were matched by hundreds of black and white teachers, many of whom moved to the South and taught for little or no pay. Others formed organizations that petitioned for voting rights and the elimination of discriminatory laws. Most white Southerners viewed each of these actions through the prism of white supremacy. From this perspective, the establishment of schools and demands for equal rights was evidence that former slaves had forgotten their rightful place at the bottom of the social hierarchy. For those who believed in white supremacy, any refusal of employment, no matter the conditions or pay, was proof that former slaves thought emancipation meant freedom from personal responsibility. Furthermore, the assumption that blacks were incapable of intellectual advancement rendered black education pointless and made black citizenship a threat to the well-being of the republic. White supremacy also required that black men and women display **deference** to whites. From this perspective, every manifestation of black agency was a threat to the social order.

As black men and women increasingly demanded their rights and refused to work under the same conditions as had typified chattel slavery, many Southern whites began to argue that a similar system of rigid white supervision was needed to keep black laborers "in their place" for the greater good of society. Former slaves responded by drawing on traditions of protest and collective action. For example, black workers near Montgomery in 1865 collectively negotiated wages and each contributing a portion of his or her salary to care for those in need. Others openly discussed the possibility of insurrection against landowning whites. Similar to the slave rebellions of the past, rumors of armed insurrection led to greater demands for government intervention to uphold white supremacy and restrict the freedoms of black women and men. However, due to the economic concerns of planters who were dependent on the labor of former slaves, these expressions of militancy also forced landowners to concede better conditions for agricultural laborers in the near term.

Shortly after the war had ended, members of Richmond's black community circulated a petition that protested the city's pass system. At this time, the city required African Americans to acquire "passes" from whites before they could travel freely—a practice that had been common during slavery. The petition also highlighted the economic success and self-sufficiency that typified black Richmond. The petition also responded to President Andrew Johnson's mistaken assumption that government aid was being lavishly bestowed on former slaves. The petition addressed the president directly and explained that blacks in Richmond contributed their own funds to care for the orphans and elderly who had been left to fend for themselves by their callous former masters. Contrary to the president's public statements, few blacks sought or had been given the aid that was being distributed by federal agents, the petition exclaimed: "Which have been so bountifully bestowed upon the unrepentant rebels of Richmond."

deference

The act of humbly submitting to another and acknowledging their superiority and/or authority. While deference is appropriate in some relations, during Reconstruction whites expected all black people to demonstrate deference toward them as a manifestation of white supremacy.

FIGURE 1.2

In this contemporary drawing, a Freedman's Bureau agent is seen preventing a possible riot between Southern whites and former slaves. In reality, there was usually less than one bureau agent per county or parish, and agents spent the bulk of their time negotiating labor contracts with wealthy plantation owners on behalf of former slaves or facilitating the efforts of black communities to form schools. *Harper's Weekly*, July 25, 1868.

Freedman's Bureau

A temporary department of the army charged with caring for Southern refugees regardless of race. They were also directed to provide for the welfare of former slaves. Officially known as the Bureau of Refugees, Freedmen, and Abandoned Lands, the Freedman's Bureau was originally intended to finance its operations by selling abandoned land. After Johnson returned this land to the original owners, Congress had to provide funding to the bureau, which led to political controversy.

Ten Percent Plan

President Lincoln's plan for readmitting Confederate states back into the Union during the Civil War. The plan allowed the states to elect delegates who would begin the process of recreating their government as soon as 10 percent of eligible voters swore an oath of allegiance to the United States.

As this petition suggests, many African Americans were able to care for themselves, even in the aftermath of Civil War. For millions of former slaves as well as white Southerners, however, the postwar period was a time of tremendous suffering. Anticipating this condition, the US Congress established the Bureau of Refugees, Freedmen, and Abandoned Lands in the spring of 1865; this bureau distributed food to destitute Southerners regardless of race. The primary mission of the **Freedman's Bureau** quickly changed from administering aid and managing abandoned lands to negotiating labor contracts between former slaves and planters and working to make sure that all former slaves were employed. Former slaves hoped to receive land as compensation for years of unpaid labor, or at the very least, to be allowed to purchase land on credit. As a result, the establishment of a federal agency designed to return black women and men to work on white-owned plantations seemed like a betrayal of the promise of emancipation and their wartime support of the Union. At the same time, black Southerners recognized that bureau agents often sought to represent the interests of former slaves as they sought fair labor contracts. Planters perceived the bureau agents as Northern interlopers, especially when special courts operated by the Freedman's Bureau mandated higher wages and better working conditions for field laborers. The bureau also established schools and provided medical care, each of which earned the enmity of Southern whites who sought a return to a system of labor and life that more closely resembled chattel slavery.

Many white Southerners feared black autonomy and economic progress for a variety of reasons. If most white Southerners were impoverished prior to the war, four years of service in an army that paid its troops in now-worthless Confederate money did little to help. Yet no matter how poor white Southerners became, the region's racial hierarchy assured whites that even the poorest of them could never fall below the 4 million slaves and free blacks of the antebellum South. The end of slavery threatened to end white privilege as poor whites and former slaves now competed for land and labor. Furthermore, black agency and material progress would prove the falsehood of white supremacy, erode the historic justification for slavery and racial discrimination, and disrupt the self-identity of many whites. If former slaves became self-reliant farmers, then those who had justified slavery as a beneficial system that provided structure for a people incapable of governing themselves would be discredited in ways that would have clear implications on the present day as the South transitioned to free labor during Reconstruction.

1.2 Wartime Reconstruction

The process of Reconstruction—rebuilding the political and economic system of the United States—actually began during the war in many parts of the South that were occupied by the Union army along the Mississippi River, the Border States, and even sections of the Atlantic Coast. Abraham Lincoln viewed wartime Reconstruction in these areas as a way to undermine the Confederacy by offering Southerners the possibility of reunification under the most lenient and generous terms possible. Lincoln's plan granted amnesty—an official pardon—for nearly all of the officers and men who had supported the Confederacy if they only accepted reunification under his terms.

In December 1863, President Lincoln offered the residents of the section of Louisiana that were occupied by the Union army the opportunity to be readmitted into the United States under an agreement that became known as the **Ten Percent Plan**. Lincoln stated that once 10 percent of the residents of these communities who were eligible to vote in 1860 agreed to pledge their loyalty to the Union, these residents could hold elections and begin the process of self-government. Governments organized under these terms could even return to full statehood, provided that they rewrite their state constitutions and ban slavery. Louisiana, Tennessee, and Arkansas were each readmitted to the Union in 1864 under these terms, a stinging defeat for the Confederacy. Although the Ten Percent Plan made no mention of political rights or compensation for the former slaves, it represented a triumph for those who wanted to end slavery. Unlike the Emancipation Proclamation of 1863, which explicitly exempted every county and parish under Union control by name from its provisions, Lincoln's Ten Percent Plan demonstrated a commitment to ending slavery.

Many congressmen supported Lincoln's aims but believed that the Ten Percent Plan was too lenient given the treasonous act of secession and the tremendous cost of the war. Republican Senator Benjamin Wade of Ohio and Representative Henry Davis of Maryland proposed what became known as the **Wade-Davis Bill** as an alternative to Lincoln's plan. Congress approved this measure, which required a majority of adult males to take what was known as the Ironclad Oath—a pledge that stated they had never supported the Confederacy. Lincoln believed that this requirement would prevent most Confederate states from ever returning to the Union, thereby undermining his attempt to promote reconciliation and end the war. Because Congress adjourned shortly after the bill's passage, Lincoln's refusal to sign the Wade-Davis Bill prevented it from becoming a law; a strategy known as the pocket veto.

> *Behind the mists of ruin and rapine waved the calico dresses of women who dared, and after the hoarse mouthings of the field guns rang the rhythm of the alphabet…they came seeking a life work in planting New England schoolhouses among the white and black of the South. They did their work well. In that first year they taught 100,000 souls, and more.*
>
> —*W. E. B. Du Bois on the efforts of female school teachers during Reconstruction*

Although their plan outlining the terms for readmission of former Confederate states was derailed by President Johnson, Congress succeeded in passing two important laws regarding Reconstruction. Even before the war ended, Congress proposed the **Thirteenth Amendment** to the Constitution, which outlawed slavery throughout the United States and its territories. Members of the **National Women's Loyal League (NWLL)**, undeterred by their government's failure to recognize their right to vote, presented Congress with a petition of 400,000 signatures in favor of the movement. "Women can neither take the Ballot nor the Bullet," NWLL leader **Susan B. Anthony** exclaimed, "therefore to us, the right to petition is the one sacred right which we ought not to neglect." At least partially due to the efforts of antislavery women such as those who circulated these petitions, the Thirteenth Amendment was ratified before the end of the year. Women were also a leading force in the establishment and operation of schools for former slaves. Women raised funds through a variety of religious and charitable societies, despite the unpopularity of their cause among many white Northerners. Black education was especially detestable to white Southerners. As a result, the hundreds of Northern black and white women who operated schools for former slaves were constantly harassed and even assaulted on occasion.

Wade-Davis Bill

An alternative to Lincoln's Ten Percent Plan that was approved by Congress but never became law. This plan allowed Confederate states wishing to return to the Union to begin the process of readmission once half of the eligible voters swore and oath that they had never supported the Confederacy.

Thirteenth Amendment

An amendment to the Constitution that forbids slavery or involuntary servitude except as the punishment for a crime.

National Women's Loyal League (NWLL)

A national women's political organization established during the Civil War and dedicated to the abolition of slavery. Members collected 400,000 signatures in favor of the Thirteenth Amendment.

Susan B. Anthony

One of the most influential leaders of the nineteenth century, Susan B. Anthony was an opponent of slavery and a teacher in Rochester, New York, prior to her introduction to the women's suffrage movement in 1850. Anthony was the publisher of *The Revolution*, a newspaper that supported the women's movement. She was also a founder of the National Women's Suffrage Association (NWSA).

1.3   Presidential Reconstruction

Andrew Johnson

A United States senator who represented a pro-Union section of eastern Tennessee. Andrew Johnson became the only legislator from a Confederate state who did not resign his seat in Congress during the Civil War. In an attempted display of national unity and bipartisanship, Lincoln selected the Southern Democrat as his running mate in 1864. Johnson would become president following the assassination of Lincoln.

Frederick Douglass

An escaped slave from Maryland whose autobiography and oratorical skills led him to national prominence, Douglass was the leading abolitionist of the 1860s and the most influential black leader during Reconstruction.

Thaddeus Stevens

A leading Congressman from Pennsylvania, Stevens had been an abolitionist prior to the Civil War and would lead the Radical Republicans in Congress during Reconstruction. He advocated legal and civil rights for African Americans and also called for rebel lands to be confiscated and given to former slaves.

The assassination of Abraham Lincoln on April 14, 1865, elevated Vice President **Andrew Johnson** to the presidency less than a week after Robert E. Lee surrendered to Ulysses S. Grant. Lincoln was a Republican who had selected Johnson as his running mate in 1864 for political reasons. Johnson was the only senator from a Confederate state who remained loyal to the Union. He was also a Democrat and a resident of Tennessee. Lincoln hoped placing Johnson on his ticket would help him generate electoral support beyond his Republican base in the North while undercutting the strength of his opponent's campaign of reconciliation with the South. Although Lincoln won reelection in 1864, many Northern Republicans were greatly disturbed by the selection of Johnson. They were especially critical of their new vice president after his performance at the March 1865 inauguration in which Johnson appeared to be under the influence of alcohol. "To think that one frail life stands between this insolent, clownish drunkard and the presidency," declared the *New York World* just one month prior to Lincoln's assassination. "May God bless and spare Abraham Lincoln."

Johnson's rambling acceptance speech may have been more the result of typhoid than whiskey, but his reputation as an intellectual lightweight was well earned. Johnson had risen through Tennessee politics by appealing to the common man in opposition to wealthy slave holders. However, his conception of the common man was limited to whites and his rhetoric was more calculated toward winning votes than bettering the conditions of ordinary farmers and laborers. While both Lincoln and Johnson hoped Reconstruction could return the nation to the antebellum status quo minus slavery, the two men differed dramatically in what that meant for African Americans. For example, Lincoln wrote many letters in favor of extending the right of suffrage to black Union veterans and even supported limited black suffrage in his final address to the nation. Johnson both publicly and privately embraced white supremacy and continued to oppose black suffrage after Congress approved the Fourteenth and Fifteenth amendments. A comparison of Johnson's private letters provides a marked contrast to those of Lincoln. For example, while Lincoln worked behind the scenes to promote black suffrage in Union-occupied Louisiana, Johnson was uncompromising in his defense of white supremacy. In a letter to the governor of Missouri, Johnson declared that America was "a country for white men, and by God, as long as I am President, it shall be a government for white men."

Despite their different views about race, Johnson's goals for Reconstruction mirrored those of Lincoln's during the war. Both sought a return to the political status quo of 1860 and the elimination of slavery. However, one must remember that Lincoln's wartime policies were dominated by the need to keep the residents of the slaveholding Border States from joining the Confederacy and by a desire to end the war as quickly as possible by offering Confederate citizens a path toward reconciliation. With Lee's unconditional surrender, President Johnson was free to demand more sweeping changes such as black suffrage and redistribution of rebel-held lands to former slaves. **Frederick Douglass** was the most prominent black leader during Reconstruction. Douglass had demanded equal suffrage for over a decade and now argued that landownership was key to freedom. Yet even after more than 200,000 black men defended the Union within the army and the navy, only a handful of white liberals, such as Pennsylvania congressman **Thaddeus Stevens**, supported black suffrage and land redistribution in 1865. As an avowed white supremacist, Johnson simply did not believe that African Americans were deserving or capable of citizenship. In contrast to Lincoln who valued the perspectives of Douglass and other black leaders during the war, the views of African Americans were simply not a consideration in Johnson's vision for a new South based on limited government and free white labor.

Congress was in recess from March until December, leaving President Johnson the choice of calling a special session of Congress or simply making decisions regarding Reconstruction himself. Johnson chose the latter option, believing that he was uniquely positioned to understand the challenges of Reconstruction as a Southern Unionist. Johnson was also personally ambitious and politically motivated. He recognized that if he successfully navigated the complicated issue of national reconciliation, he would develop a strong political following in both the North and the South. Understanding that a bullet rather than the ballot had elevated him to the presidency, Johnson recognized that he must use the next few years to develop his own sources of political support. He believed that guiding the nation through Reconstruction would make him the most esteemed public figure in a political system that had been dominated by sectionalism in recent years. If successful, he believed, his strong leadership during Reconstruction would practically guarantee that he would retain the presidency in the election of 1868.

Johnson believed in limited government and took a conservative approach. His efforts mirrored Lincoln's Ten Percent Plan in many ways, such as his willingness to grant a full pardon to nearly all former Confederates who were willing to take an oath of allegiance to the Union. Even those deemed ineligible for amnesty through this pledge—wealthy planters and high-ranking Confederate officers—could personally apply to the president and be restored to full citizenship. In addition, once a state had decided to begin the process of reunification it could elect new state and federal representatives. Before these provisional Southern governments would be considered sovereign, according to Johnson's plan, they would simply have to pass a resolution declaring that secession from the Union was illegal, ratify the Thirteenth Amendment, repudiate all debts of the Confederacy, and modify their state constitutions to ban slavery. By the fall of 1865, all former Confederate states except Texas had fulfilled these requirements and had been readmitted to the Union. Johnson believed that the nation would be better served by simply moving forward rather than attempting to reconcile the unanswered questions about the status of former slaves. Once the former Confederate states agreed to his terms, Johnson declared that the United States had been restored under his leadership. Johnson's use of "restoration" rather than "reconstruction" reflected his belief in limited government and his opposition to using the power of the federal government to impose sweeping changes on the South. For 4 million African Americans, however, sweeping changes were required if the promise of emancipation was to be fulfilled.

1.4   Violence and Black Codes

Southern congressmen elected under Johnson's Reconstruction plan arrived in Washington in December 1865. The first order of business within every session of Congress was a procedural vote where the current membership determined whether each new senator and representative had been properly elected. This vote was usually a simple procedural matter, but Reconstruction was no ordinary time in the nation's history. With the four-year absence of the Confederate states, Congress was dominated by Northern Republicans. These men voted against accepting the Southern delegates because many of them had been high-ranking Confederate officials. For example, the former vice president of the Confederacy, **Alexander Stephens**, was elected to the Senate in 1866 by his home state of Georgia. From the perspective of many Northerners, if the same men who had organized secession and led rebel armies were allowed to resume power, the Civil War had been fought in vain. The Northern public wanted reconciliation but was equally angered by what appeared to be Southern intransigence and believed Johnson's lenient plan for Reconstruction was to blame. Congress refused to allow Alexander Stephens and numerous other former Confederates to take their seats in the House and Senate in 1866, a fact many of these men used to bolster their political support among white voters. From the perspective of these voters, Congress could not represent their interests so long as it was dominated by Northern Republicans who refused to recognize their elected representatives. As a result, white Southerners viewed Stephens as a political martyr for the cause of states' rights until he was allowed to take a seat in the House of Representatives in 1873.

At the state and local level, Southern lawmakers did not need Northern approval before they could meet and pass laws that applied to their cities and states. Beginning with Mississippi and South Carolina, Southern legislatures passed **Black Codes**—a series of laws designed to curtail the freedoms of African Americans. Exact provisions of these laws varied, but they shared a common goal of returning blacks to their "place" as subservient laborers under white authority. The codes limited the kinds of employment that were open to African Americans and required them to sign contracts and work under conditions that often resembled slavery. In many states, if a black person could not prove that she or he was employed by a white person, they could be arrested. They could also be arrested for being "discourteous" to any white person or for owning the same weapons that white men could legally carry openly. Punishment for such "crimes" could include up to a year of work without pay. Black employees who decided to quit their jobs automatically forfeited all pay they had earned up to that point and could also be arrested and fined. Other Black Codes forbade African Americans from holding public

FIGURE 1.3

Frederick Douglass escaped from slavery in 1838 and became one of the leading antislavery orators. During Reconstruction, he continued to speak on behalf of members of his race, leading dozens of black conventions and supporting laws that would have mandated equal rights for all Americans regardless of race or gender.

Alexander Stephens

An influential Georgia politician and vice president of the Confederacy, Alexander Stephens would demonstrate the ability of leading Confederates to regain power during the final years of Reconstruction. Stephens was elected to Congress in 1873 and also became the Governor of Georgia.

Black Codes

Laws passed by Southern governments after the Civil War that explicitly restricted the freedoms of African Americans.

meetings, purchasing land, consuming alcohol, or living in certain neighborhoods unless they were a servant who lived with the white family that employed them.

Most black codes were passed in the interest of restoring the wealth and status of former planters. However, white craftsmen and laborers also sought laws to prevent former slaves from competing with them in the job market. White workers viewed the end of slavery as a potential threat to their status and well-being, especially if they now had to compete with former slaves, many of whom were skilled craftsmen. In response, states like South Carolina levied heavy taxes on any black person who pursued an occupation beyond the servant or plantation laborer. These laws destroyed the opportunity for thousands of black craftsmen to work as they had during the antebellum period. Many states also passed **apprenticeship laws**, which required that black orphans live with white families who would raise the children as "apprentices." The typical white apprentice at this time was a young man who was learning a trade under the tutelage of a master craftsman. However, in the case of these laws passed during the first years of Reconstruction, "apprentice" was merely a euphemism for a black child who was forced to labor in a workshop or field without pay.

Black Codes were explicitly written to apply to African Americans and utilized language reminiscent of slavery. For example, the laws in South Carolina referred to blacks as "servants" and white employers as "masters." The same law also required that a "servant" must work six days a week from sunrise to sunset as had been customary under slavery. Black Codes also carried provisions whereby black workers who tried to leave a plantation prior to the end of their contracts would be pursued by government officials in ways that mirrored the methods used to track down runaway slaves in the past. Cities also passed their own Black Codes that went beyond the state laws. In Louisiana, for example, a local statute specified that "no negro or freedmen shall be allowed to come within the limits of the town of Opelousas without special permission from his employers." The penalty for violators of this municipal Black Code was imprisonment, forced labor, and a fine. Other communities placed laws forbidding blacks from being seen in public at night, unless required to do so by their white employer. Most of the punishments for breaking the Black Codes were monetary fines. If the individual could not pay the fine, the local sheriff would hire them out at public outcry, a degrading spectacle where black prisoners in chains were paraded before white men who bid on the opportunity to settle the outstanding debt. In return for the "generosity" of those who paid their fines, the prisoner was required to repay their debt through an extended term of unpaid labor—a procedure reminiscent of slave auctions in all but name.

1.5   Black Agency and Resistance

African Americans demonstrated agency by resisting the Black Codes through a variety of methods. Those who did so were often the victims of violent attacks meant to intimidate them and "teach a lesson" to others who might also consider resistance. Hundreds and perhaps thousands of African Americans were murdered in each of the former Confederate states during Reconstruction for their refusal to submit to the dictates of local whites. An estimated 2,000 individuals were murdered in the area surrounding Shreveport, Louisiana, during the first years of Reconstruction. In 1866, two dozen black men, women, and children were lynched near Pine Bluff, Arkansas. The mob left the corpses of its victims hanging in trees and burned the homes of others who had sought to resist the Black Codes. A Freedman's Bureau report in Texas stated that violence was occasionally waged against former slaves for no reason at all, a situation confirmed by similar reports throughout the South. While observers may have witnessed what appeared to be random acts of violence, taken collectively, these attacks were clearly intended to send the message that emancipation changed nothing. In most instances, however, violence was focused against those who attempted to resist subjugation. When black men organized a convention in Louisiana in the summer of 1866 to discuss their plight, forty of the delegates were murdered by a mob that enjoyed the assistance of local police.

Black schools were especially likely to be attacked because they were symbols of racial uplift. Black churches were also targeted because they were used for community meetings and classrooms. Freedman's Bureau agents recorded the murder of nearly a thousand black men and women in Texas within three years of the war's end. Highest on the list of alleged provocations that led to these killings were accusations of "insolence" toward whites. The instigating factors included refusal to tip one's hat to a white man, refusing to bow and remove one's hat in the presence of whites, and at least one instance where a black man tipped his hat and bowed his head so dramatically that he appeared sarcastic to his aggrieved white assailant. In South Carolina, one man was shot in church by a white minister after he defended another black man's right to sit in a particular pew. Admittedly, these examples are among the more astonishing examples of racial violence and some of the thousands of reported murders may have been embellished. However, the frequency with which stories like these were reported by both Southern and Northern observers forced millions of Americans to consider whether the Civil War had been fought in vain. They also led Congress to consider using the power of the federal government to intervene to restore order.

---

apprenticeship laws

Children were regularly separated from their parents during slavery. At the conclusion of the Civil War, a significant number of children were either orphans or simply had no parents that could be located by government officials. In response, Southern governments passed laws that were allegedly intended to care for these children. The laws placed the children with white families who were required to raise them and teach them a trade. In practice, many of these children were used as unpaid labor in fields or domestic service.

Southern blacks did not simply wait for Congressional assistance to stop the violence; black Civil War veterans used their soldierly skills to defend their communities. Black women and men also turned to institutions like the church for both uplift and self-defense. During the antebellum period, whites often required slaves to attend churches where masters could control the message their slaves heard. White preachers encouraged their black congregations to follow God's directive by obeying those He had placed in authority over them. By creating thousands of independent black churches throughout the South during Reconstruction, African Americans rejected this message and demonstrated their agency.

The former slaves' desire for autonomy—their own distinctive religious traditions—and the discrimination they had endured in white churches all led to the establishment of the independent black church at the core of Southern black communities during Reconstruction. These churches hosted educational, social, and political activities and administered to the poor. Reconstruction-era churches even served as meeting places for civil rights rallies, political meetings, and the headquarters for black militias who sought to confront police brutality. Even though these activities are more commonly associated with the civil rights struggle of the following century, historians have uncovered dozens of instances where black man and women refused to give up their seats on steamships or in theaters during Reconstruction. They have also found instances where armed black men captured and delivered white men who had verbally or physically assaulted black women or committed some other crime against black citizens. Their decision to turn these men over to law enforcement despite the unlikelihood of conviction demonstrates a desire for law and order among people well acquainted with the dangers of mob justice.

One of the most important demonstrations of black agency after the war was the establishment of schools. Thousands of white teachers from the North joined thousands of black teachers from around the country who traveled throughout the South and taught at various schools that were initiated during the war and its immediate aftermath. For former slaves, obtaining an education was both a political act and a personal repudiation of white supremacy. After years of being punished for any efforts at education, former slaves placed great faith in learning and viewed education as a right of citizenship. Such ideas represented a radical departure from the antebellum South where education was a privilege of the wealthy. The actions of former slaves even influenced white Southerners who increasingly demanded the establishment of public schools.

Many of the schools established by African Americans were the first of their kind in their communities. As a result, they often permitted any white child or adult who wished to attend the opportunity to do so. The Freedman's Bureau soon took the lead in recruiting teachers and building schools. By 1867, more than 4,000 schools were serving nearly a quarter million students. The Bureau and black leaders also founded colleges to train teachers and clergy. In January 1866, a group of African American ministers opened Fisk University in Nashville, Tennessee. The following year, another group of black religious leaders and educators opened Howard University in Washington, DC, with the assistance of the Freedman's Bureau. The faith the former slaves placed in education spread throughout the South, and many whites also established teacher's colleges on their own or with governmental assistance. In a few locations, such as New Orleans, some of the schools were even racially integrated. While many changes that occurred during Reconstruction were temporary, one of its lasting legacies was the belief that the government was obligated to provide an education for all citizens.

Even though their right to vote was not yet recognized, former slaves organized local political organizations, held conventions, circulated petitions, and drafted resolutions calling for an end to the Black Codes and the recognition of their right to vote. These local organizations were commonly known as **Equal Rights Leagues and Union Leagues**—names that reminded the nation of their members' loyalty during the Civil War and their demand for equality. In hundreds of communities, black women and men formed labor organizations that collectively bargained for higher wages. One of the most effective ways of gaining concessions from their would-be employers was to allow rumors of open rebellion to circulate. Whites had lived in constant fear of slave rebellions and were terrified that the end of slavery would lead to violent retribution. Although most former slaves sought only justice and shunned violence, many followed a religious theology that looked forward to a day of deliverance. Whites sensed this belief but failed to appreciate that black liberation theology rejected violence. Although references to a day of reckoning were rhetorical in nature, whites remembered that slaves had launched dozens of violent rebellions in the past. As a result, any rumor of a general black insurrection appealed to the greatest fears of whites and often inspired a newfound desire for fairness among plantation owners.

When former slaves refused to sign labor contracts prior to January 1, 1866—the date whites feared a general insurrection might occur—white plantation owners experienced a collective change of heart and agreed to the demands of black labor leaders. Once fears of insurrection subsided, however, many plantation owners began backing away from the promises they had made. The ever-present fear of retribution was a double-edged sword. On one hand, it could inspire planters to deal fairly with their employees. However, it also led whites to fear black people and black agency. Whites were suspicious of black meetings and lived in quiet trepidation that freedom would unleash years of justified rage. For

FIGURE 1.4

One of the greatest challenges teachers and students faced in the nineteenth century was the cost of textbooks. This image shows a page of a reader produced by a Northern charitable society that operated schools. They also utilized the concept of a customized textbook to include people and events that were excluded from other books, such as this story about the African American poet Phillis Wheatley.

Equal Rights Leagues and Union Leagues

Politically minded organizations within black communities during Reconstruction. These local organizations promoted recognition of civil and political rights and also engaged in community uplift through the establishment of schools and other needed services that were not met by society or the government.

this reason, whites carefully monitored black behavior and viewed even the most trivial outward manifestations of black self-assuredness as an indication that a person had become a threat. Whites only felt safe among blacks who continued to manifest the deference that was required during slavery. If a black woman refused to yield to a white woman on a sidewalk or if a black man failed to doff his cap and bow to whites he passed on the street, they might eventually subscribe to more radical doctrines of black unity and violent retribution. Tolerating any behavior short of deference to whites would encourage blacks to "forget their place," many whites believed, and might even lead to the reckoning they had feared since the earliest days of slavery.

REVIEW AND CRITICAL THINKING

1. Compare Lincoln and Johnson's plans for Reconstruction. Might Lincoln have handled Reconstruction differently after the war was over and Union victory had been secured?
2. What were the Black Codes? What did whites mean when they spoke of the need to keep African Americans "in their place"? How do African Americans respond to the Black Codes?
3. In what ways do former slaves demonstrate agency following the Civil War? What strategies did former slaves employ to define freedom for themselves?
4. Why did some whites use violence against former slaves during Reconstruction? What might this tell us about the actions of former slaves and the relationships between former masters and former slaves during this time period?

---

2. CONGRESSIONAL RECONSTRUCTION

LEARNING OBJECTIVES

1. Identify the ideas of the Radical Republicans and the Moderate Republicans, and explain what the terms *Radical*, *Moderate*, and *Conservative* mean in terms of the history of Reconstruction.
2. Explain the origin and importance of laws such as the Civil Rights Act of 1866, the Reconstruction Acts, and the Fourteenth and Fifteenth amendments. Identify why some women who supported black civil rights could not support the Fourteenth Amendment.
3. Explain the reasons why Andrew Johnson was impeached. Demonstrate how his trial and the presidential election of 1868 reflected the leading political issues of the Reconstruction era.

Radical Republicans

Members of the Republican Party who demanded equal legal and political rights for African Americans and believed that the power of the federal government should be mobilized to preserve these rights.

Moderate Republicans

Members of the Republican Party who hoped to prevent violence against former slaves but did not initially support measures extending legal and political equality to African Americans.

When Congress reconvened in December 1865, the stage was set for conflict between the White House and Capitol Hill. Republicans were angered by the president's handling of Reconstruction, but were divided in their views about how much the federal government should intervene in matters concerning the former Confederate states. A small group of lawmakers, known as **Radical Republicans**, hoped to use the power of the federal government to mandate legal equality for African Americans, including the right to vote. **Moderate Republicans** hoped that the new Southern state governments would treat African Americans more fairly and agreed that violence and the Black Codes were a clear indication that something more must be done. At the same time, they did not believe in racial equality and considered radical plans to use the federal government to mandate full civil and political equality as a dangerous social experiment. The most common complaint of Moderate Republicans was the way Johnson permitted former Confederate leaders to return to positions of power. Before long, Johnson's refusal to compromise and work with Congress in shaping a more meaningful plan for Reconstruction was also viewed as an affront, and the two groups of Republicans began to see themselves as united against "King Andrew." As time went on, the two groups worked together to oppose President Johnson and his plan for reconstruction.

2.1 Radicals and Moderates

The radical wing of the Republican Party earned their name through their consistent advocacy of causes that were unpopular and therefore derisively labeled as "radical." For example, the leading radical cause in the late 1850s was the immediate abolition of slavery. Abolitionists were extremely unpopular among most whites in both the North and the South at this time. Radicals were vilified and abolitionist speakers were frequently attacked until their cause was vindicated by secession and war. Slavery strengthened the Confederacy, while the service of former slaves helped to save the Union—two facts that led to a convergence of interests between the once radical abolitionists and those who sought to preserve the Union.

Radical Republicans also called for greater federal authority both before and after the Civil War. Like abolition, this idea had been unpopular and was even considered dangerous by many Americans until South Carolina took the doctrine of states' rights to its logical conclusion. Secessionists argued that because all power belonged to the states, the federal government had no authority to stop a state from leaving the nation. Secession led many advocates of a weak central government to reconsider their perspective and move closer to the radical perspective of a strong federal government and limited state sovereignty. As Reconstruction began, the Radicals pushed for a third measure that was equally unpopular with most Americans but would also be vindicated by events—equal legal and civil rights for former slaves. Denying these rights and leaving white Southerners to reconstruct their own governments led to Black Codes and violence, the Radicals argued. If former slaves were granted full citizenship and suffrage, however, Radicals believed that black men would vote for political leaders who would protect their interests. Black suffrage, the Radicals explained to a skeptical nation, meant that the South might reconstruct itself.

By adopting this argument, the Radicals were borrowing an idea of early feminist leaders. Suffragists as early as the 1840s tried to convince a skeptical public that women's suffrage, an unpopular and "radical" measure at that time, would actually promote society's best interests. Without the vote, these women argued, half of the population was unable to speak for themselves and the political interests of women and families became an added burden for men. If women could vote, these early suffragists countered, women could protect themselves by voting for men who supported laws that protected women and children. The Radical Republicans modified this argument by replacing notions of chivalry with another gendered idea. Radicals claimed that black male suffrage would cultivate "manhood" among former slaves who could use the vote to protect their families. Black men as voters would topple the Black Codes, the Radicals continued, because black men would demand leaders who defended their freedom and economic opportunity. Radicals believed the solutions to Reconstruction also required using the power of the federal government, and even the army, to assure that former slaves were guaranteed their rights during a transition period. So long as their rights were enforced, the Radicals argued, black men as voters would eventually solve the problems of Reconstruction and stability and prosperity would replace violence and anarchy throughout the South.

FIGURE 1.5

In this 1869 image of Andrew Johnson, the artist criticizes the authoritative style of the departing president. After his first year in office, many Republicans mockingly referred to the president as "King Andrew." The president was later impeached by the House of Representatives and came within one vote of being removed from office by the Senate.

"FAREWELL A LONG FAREWELL TO ALL MY GREATNESS!"

2.2   Former Slaves, Former Masters, and the Former Vice President

It is important to remember that no matter how egalitarian these radical leaders appeared in comparison to other whites of the era, few of them genuinely felt that African Americans were their equals. In general, Radicals shared a paternalistic view that believed in the possibility of equality after generations of educational and economic progress. No one understood the limitations of Radical Republicans more than Southern black leaders who adapted their arguments to accommodate their tenuous political allies. Black leaders acted tactically by framing their messages in ways that stressed the need for active government intervention to safeguard their rights as citizens and provide funding for schools. In general, these moderate black leaders spoke of equality in the future tense.

A handful of black leaders advanced a more radical argument that stressed equality was not conditional. These leaders demanded full recognition of their right to vote. Some also demanded the redistribution of land that had been abandoned by rebel leaders during the war. Many former slaves believed that they had already paid for these lands twice, once as laborers and a second time as soldiers in defense of the Union. For some, like black editor and Union officer **Martin Delany**, even Frederick Douglass was occasionally too conservative. Like many black leaders, Douglass tactically accommodated whites who viewed civil rights and land redistribution as a form of governmental aid on behalf of grateful former slaves. If the laws of the nation were colorblind, Delany argued, civil rights were already guaranteed to the former slave.

Martin Delany

Known as "the father of black nationalism," Martin Delany was an abolitionist, newspaper editor, Civil War officer, physician, and leading black intellectual. His early life was spent in and around Pittsburgh, and he was active in South Carolina politics during Reconstruction.

FIGURE 1.6

Martin Delany is known as "the Father of Black Nationalism" because he was one of the early advocates of racial separatism. Rather than beg for acceptance among whites, Delany hoped black Americans would create an independent nation in Africa or Latin America. Delany also worked to improve the condition of black women and men in the United States as an author, editor, doctor, and judge. Achieving the rank of major, he was also the highest-ranking black officer in the Civil War.

Sea Islands Experiment
Army officials allowed former slaves to continue working land abandoned by rebel planters on the islands off the coast of South Carolina and Georgia. This was considered an "experiment" by those who viewed the successful operation of plantations by former slaves as a model for Reconstruction.

Delany turned the notion of black dependency on its head, arguing that Southern whites were the ones who requested and received special governmental assistance both before and after the Civil War. When slaves escaped during the antebellum period, Delany reminded listeners, the slave asked for no special assistance from the government. When former slaves took control of abandoned rebel lands, Delany continued, they neither asked for nor received assistance from the government. In each of these cases, Delany countered, whites demanded and received government assistance in returning their absconded slaves and abandoned lands. Even those whites who had tried to destroy the Union had requested and received federal government intervention to recover their lands from the very men and women who had worked those lands for generations without pay. As a result, Delany posited that former slaves were the true defenders of the Founding Fathers' vision of limited government. He also argued that black men should not be expected to beg for the rights the Founding Fathers had proclaimed were given to all people by their Creator. Former slaves could fend for themselves so long as they had equal access to land, Delany argued, and they did not need generations, years, weeks, or even a day to prove that their rights were as self-evident as any other group of Americans.

Had Delany enjoyed access to the records used by historians, he could have pointed to over a dozen locations where former slaves had turned a profit on land that had been abandoned by leading Confederates. For example, the slaves of former Confederate President Jefferson Davis divided the abandoned Davis plantation into individual family farms. These men and women even paid the government for these lands with the profits they had made. As Delany suggests, the Davis family sought and received the assistance of the government in taking the land back from their former slaves.

Union generals are often credited with generosity regarding abandoned rebel lands. One such example is the **Sea Islands Experiment**, where Union officers permitted the former slaves to continue working lands that had been abandoned by plantation owners in coastal South Carolina. In this "experiment," 10,000 men and women collectively ran a number of plantations that provided cotton for the Union army. By the end of the war, about 40,000 freed persons had settled on 400,000 acres of land throughout coastal Georgia and South Carolina. In nearly every instance, these black farmers were evicted by the government in late 1865 despite their vital contributions to the war effort. From Delany's perspective, President Johnson's actions showed that he supported land redistribution, but only so long as it benefitted whites. After all, the president permitted the eviction of black men and women and the president also allowed the abandoned lands to be redistributed back to their former owners regardless of their acts of treason. Landownership was key to independence, and former slaves recognized that if their former masters maintained control of the land, they would have little option but to work for them. "Give us our own land and we will take care of ourselves," one former slave counseled, "return the land to the old masters and they will hire or starve us as they please."

Southern planters, like the president, believed the issue of Reconstruction was settled once their lands had been returned, their pardons were signed, and their states were returned to the Union. But in their swift passage of the Black Codes, their sudden attempt to regain political offices, and their toleration of those who committed violence against African Americans, Southern elites nearly derailed their efforts to recreate the antebellum status quo. Few Northerners were deeply concerned enough about the condition of former slaves to tour the South and observe the conditions they faced. However, news of the Black Codes and the horrific violence caused even the most callous Northerner to think twice about the finality of Reconstruction.

Andrew Johnson also did a great deal to undermine the position of those who considered Reconstruction to be a settled issue, vetoing two bills that enjoyed a great deal of support among Moderates. In early 1866, Congress proposed a two-year extension of the Freedman's Bureau. The bill included a modest budget for schools and support for the bureau's mission as a mediator between planters and laborers. Congress also passed the **Civil Rights Act of 1866**. This law granted citizenship to all persons born in the United States regardless of race, color, or previous condition of servitude. The Civil Rights Act of 1866 also specified that all citizens were guaranteed the right to make contracts, utilize the courts, and enjoy equal property rights. The law made no mention of voting as one of the protected rights of citizenship and explicitly excluded Native Americans who lived on reservations from becoming citizens. The law had tremendous implications for Reconstruction because it implicitly voided the Black Codes and other laws that sought to restrict these freedoms. Despite their overwhelming support in Congress, Andrew Johnson vetoed both bills. Congress quickly superseded both of the president's vetoes and reapproved both measures by the two-thirds majority required by the Constitution. It was the first time in American history that Congress had passed any major piece of legislation over a presidential veto. It was also a sign that the balance of power had shifted from the White House to a Congress that was growing more unified in the wake of the president's obstinacy.

Reconstruction also saw the first substantial amendment of the Constitution when the Thirteenth Amendment, which outlawed slavery, was ratified in December 1865. Only two amendments had been passed since the ratification of the Constitution—the first of which applied to lawsuits across state lines and the second clarified the procedures for electing the vice president. For nearly a century, most American political leaders agreed that the federal government did not have the power to ban slavery within states, and so the Thirteenth Amendment was a radical break with the notion of limited governmental powers. Of course, by the end of 1865, emancipation was hardly controversial and the law merely confirmed what had already occurred during the war. The next two amendments Congress would pass during Reconstruction would be much more controversial. The first expanded the definition of citizenship and the second guaranteed the right to vote regardless of race.

2.3 Reconstruction Amendments

Inspired by the resolutions and petitions passed and circulated by dozens of black conventions, Congress proposed the **Fourteenth Amendment** in June 1867. The Fourteenth Amendment declared that all persons born in the United States were entitled to the "privileges and immunities" of national citizenship regardless of race or previous condition of servitude. Similar to the Civil Rights Act of 1866, the amendment specifically excluded Native Americans who lived on reservations. The amendment also addressed the issue of voting rights for former slaves. Due to the controversial nature of black suffrage (only five Northern states recognized the right of African Americans to vote at this time), Northern politicians engineered a method that would practically require the South to grant black suffrage without specifically mentioning race or requiring black suffrage in their own states.

The Fourteenth Amendment encouraged but did not require black suffrage because it connected the number of seats a state was given in the House of Representatives to the number of adult men who were allowed to vote in that state. If the leaders of a state such as South Carolina did not want to recognize the right of black men to vote, they could legally do so. However, in this example South Carolina would forfeit a majority of its seats in Congress because a majority of the adult men in South Carolina were black. Every Southern state had a large black population and stood to lose between a fourth to over a half of their congressional representatives if they denied black suffrage. Most Northern states, however, could continue to bar black men from voting without losing any representation because their percentage of black residents was so small. For example, Pennsylvania specifically limited the vote to white males in 1837 and continued to do so after the passage of the Fourteenth Amendment without losing a single seat in Congress because the black population of the state was below 4 percent.

In many ways, Andrew Johnson deserves some of the credit for the Fourteenth Amendment. Had the president not been so insistent on opposing even the most modest congressional proposals, such as the extension of the Freedman's Bureau, it is unlikely that Moderates would have joined Radicals in pushing for a Constitutional guarantee of equal protection for African Americans. The president alienated more than just Congress in the fall of 1866 when he traveled from New York to Ohio in opposition to the Fourteenth Amendment. This "Swing Around the Circle," as the president called his journey, featured a number of aggressive speeches in which Johnson attacked his Republican opponents in vile and abusive language. On several occasions it also appeared that the president had had too much to drink. At one point the president nearly stumbled off the edge of a platform while suggesting that former slaves were to blame for their own victimization. The president even proposed that the late president's murder was providential because it cleared the way for him to lead the nation. Never a good judge of his audience, Andrew Johnson was in Illinois when he made this statement.

Johnson's ill-advised tour occurred just before the midterm congressional elections of 1866 and backfired in its avowed purpose of reviving the Democratic Party in the North. Far more important

Civil Rights Act of 1866

A law passed by Congress that granted citizenship to all persons born in the United States regardless of race, color, or previous condition of servitude with the exception of Native Americans who lived on reservations. As citizens, these persons were guaranteed access to the courts, which were bound to enforce contracts and protect their rights.

Fourteenth Amendment

A Constitutional amendment that assured the provisions of the Civil Rights Act could not be overturned by Congress or the Supreme Court. The amendment also added language that guaranteed equal protection of law regardless of race or previous condition of servitude. The Amendment also reduced the number of representatives in Congress of any state that denied its male citizens the right to vote.

than the Democrat's association with an unpopular president, news of massacres and race riots convinced many Americans that the federal government had to take a more active role in Reconstruction. News of the postwar massacres were finally circulating throughout the North and the horrid tales of entire families being massacred convinced many Northerners that the Radicals should be permitted to use the federal government to intervene on behalf of Southern blacks. When the votes were all counted, the Republicans had a two-thirds majority in both the House of Representatives and the Senate for the 1867 and 1868 sessions.

Every Southern state except Tennessee rejected the Fourteenth Amendment in 1866 and early 1867. This rejection, along with race riots in Memphis and New Orleans and continued violence against rural black sharecroppers, led Congress to declare that the former Confederacy was in a state of civil disorder. Congress passed the **Reconstruction Acts** over President Johnson's veto in March 1867. These laws dissolved Southern state governments and voided the readmission of the former Confederate states that had occurred during the Lincoln and Johnson administrations. Most significantly, they divided the South into five districts, which were placed under control of military commanders. The Reconstruction Acts contained a list of requirements that must be met before the former states could be readmitted to the nation for a second time. Chief among these requirements was the ratification of the Fourteenth Amendment and the revision of state constitutions to remove all barriers against black suffrage. These state constitutions would be written by delegates chosen in a special election where black men would vote and even run for election. In addition, federal troops would be stationed throughout the South to make sure that black men would be permitted to vote while certain Confederate leaders would be barred from the polls.

Many Northerners perceived the Reconstruction Acts as mild compared to the actions that could be taken against a defeated territory that had initiated a civil war. White Southerners shared a different perspective and deeply resented the indignity of having their statehood stripped from them. They also felt that black suffrage was being forced on them at gunpoint, as soldiers would occupy their states and run their governments until they "voluntarily" accepted black suffrage. Few Northern states acknowledged the right of black men to vote, white Southerners reminded the nation. Believing that the violence against former slaves had largely subsided, they asked why their communities should be occupied by soldiers nearly two years after the war's end. By their perspective, a handful of Northern congressmen were forcing an entire region to accept a political vision that their own constituents did not support. The deployment of soldiers to enforce the will of Northern politicians on the South that still had no voice in Congress seemed the antithesis of democracy to millions of white Southerners.

For 4 million black Southerners, these federal interventions were long overdue. Former slaves recognized that political power was the key to achieving their dream of publicly funded schools, color-blind justice, and real economic opportunity. Armed now with the vote, black men continued to work collectively as they had before the war to press for equal rights. Former slave owners attempted to maintain the authority they had once exercised, yet once the army occupied the region these men could no longer resort to violence without fear of consequence. Now backed by federal laws that invalidated the Black Codes and protected by soldiers sworn to uphold law and order, the Equal Rights Leagues and Union Leagues proliferated. Black communities organized parades and marched openly carrying banners calling for equal rights. Black men even organized armed militias that pledged their loyalty to local army commanders and offered their assistance in preventing further violence against members of their race.

Many white Southerners boycotted the elections of 1867. Given the reluctance of Northern Republicans to embrace black suffrage at home, white Southerners believed that black suffrage was simply a ploy by the Republican Party to reduce the power of the Democratic Party and force Republican rule in the South. There were few white Republicans who lived south of the Mason-Dixon Line, they pointed out, but if black men were granted suffrage they would likely support the "Party of Lincoln." Because many Southern states and counties had black majorities, black suffrage would likely doom the Democrats in many districts. Although they were certainly correct in identifying the chief motivation of many white Republicans—the creation of a viable Republican Party in the South at the expense of the Democrats—the boycott by white Southerners simply guaranteed a Republican landslide in 1867.

Black men voted and were elected to offices throughout the South in these elections, and black delegates would later play a key role in rewriting Southern Constitutions during this phase of Reconstruction. Black women could not vote but still played a key political role by attending mass meetings and constitutional conventions where they let their voices be heard. Black women were active participants in every aspect of Southern politics during Reconstruction. In many localities, black women took the lead in organizing parades and rallies. They attended conventions as delegates and also held their own meetings where they drafted resolutions and circulated petitions.

Reconstruction Acts

A series of four laws passed by Congress that reversed statehood for every Confederate state other than Tennessee. The laws created five military districts that would be administered by the army until each former state permitted black men to vote, ratified the Fourteenth Amendment, and submitted revised constitutions for Congressional approval.

The majority of Southern Republican political leaders during Reconstruction were white, but as many as 3,000 black men were elected to city, county, state, and even national offices. Sixteen black politicians served in Congress during Reconstruction and personified the amazing change that had taken place in only two years. **Hiram Revels**, a Methodist minister, was elected to fill the Senate seat that had been left vacant by Jefferson Davis when he abandoned his office to lead the Confederacy. Blanche K. Bruce, a former slave from Mississippi, was the first African American elected to fill a full six-year term in the US Senate. More African Americans were elected to the US Congress and Southern state legislatures during Reconstruction than any other time in American history, including the present. Yet even during the years when the Reconstruction Acts, the army, Freedman's Bureau, and the Fourteenth Amendment supported black suffrage, tens of thousands of African Americans were still not permitted to vote for a variety of reasons.

Hiram Revels

The first African American to serve in Congress, Revels represented Mississippi in the US Senate. He would later become the first president of Alcorn Agricultural and Mechanical College (Alcorn State University today).

FIGURE 1.7

This 1870 print depicts a Baltimore parade celebrating the ratification of the Fifteenth Amendment, as well as scenes of African Americans exercising their civil rights, teaching, forming militias, and working in their own fields. Maryland did not ratify the amendment until 1973. However, the amendment still had the force of law in Maryland and throughout the country once it was ratified by two-thirds of the states and became part of the Constitution.

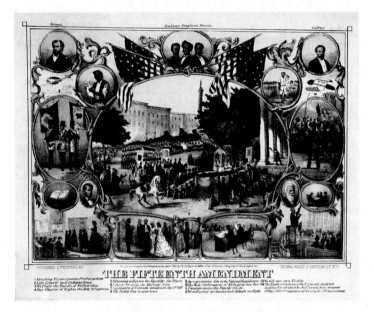

Radical Congressmen were disappointed that the Fourteenth Amendment had not led to black enfranchisement in many Northern states. Furthermore, they were concerned that some white Southerners still opposed black suffrage, regardless of any potential loss of Congressional representation. Still others resorted to fraud and violence to silence black voters. In February 1869, Congress approved the **Fifteenth Amendment**, which explicitly guaranteed the right of citizens to vote regardless of race. The measure was ratified quickly by several Southern states owing to the electoral strength of the black vote. Ironically, the measure was much more contentious in the Northern states.

Nearly an entire year passed before the required three-fourths of states ratified the Fifteenth Amendment. Its eventual passage occurred largely because Congress made its ratification a requirement for readmission for several Southern states. Nevada was the first to ratify the amendment, but only after its legislature was assured that it would not apply to Mexican and Asian immigrants. Similar concerns about other minority groups led to the amendment's failure in Oregon and California. Newspaper columns throughout the West warned readers that the Fifteenth Amendment would lead to "greater oppression" of whites in their communities by enfranchising "Indians and Mongolians." Native American, Asian American, and Mexican American leaders were disappointed that the Fifteenth Amendment did not guarantee universal male suffrage. Although he was not a proponent of extending voting rights to these groups, Charles Sumner was also disappointed in the wording of the law. Sumner hoped the amendment would include language that outlawed the use of poll taxes, property requirements, and literacy tests as prerequisites for voter registration. While such requirements might appear racially neutral, he correctly predicted that white registrars would soon modify these instruments in ways that would disenfranchise black voters.

Fifteenth Amendment

A Constitutional Amendment prohibiting the denial of suffrage the basis of race, color, or previous condition of servitude.

2.4 Women and the Fourteenth and Fifteenth Amendments

Elizabeth Cady Stanton

The leading author of the Declaration of Sentiments—the 1848 document signed by the participants of the first major women's rights convention at Seneca Falls, New York—Stanton would play a leading role in many of the early women's suffrage associations, and would serve as the president of the National Women's Suffrage Association (NWSA) for two decades.

Many prominent supporters of women's suffrage had been leaders in the abolitionist movement, and most of these suffragists were among the earliest advocates of extending the vote to former slaves. However, the Fourteenth Amendment specifically included the word "male" when referring to qualified voters, which led many women's rights advocates to oppose the amendment as it was written. When even the most radical congressmen, such as Wendell Phillips, responded that women's suffrage should be placed on hold, many women's rights activists felt betrayed. Although they might have joined the supporters of the Fourteenth Amendment even if it did not include provisions for women's suffrage, suffragists such as **Elizabeth Cady Stanton** responded that they could not support the amendment because it introduced the word "male" into the Constitution for the first time and implicitly restricted the vote to men. "If that word 'male' be inserted," Stanton cautioned, "it will take us a century at least to get it out." The Fifteenth Amendment extended the right to vote to all regardless of race, but was conspicuously silent about gender—an omission suffragists feared might become a second obstacle in their challenge to combat the idea that voting was an exclusive privilege granted only to men.

Stanton believed that the right to vote should be extended liberally, but she lived in time when many Americans were automatically disqualified from voting because of their race or gender. If the government intended to set restrictions on who was qualified to vote, Stanton argued, these restrictions should at least be based on merits such as education. While supporters believed a provision tying the ballot to formal education would reward intelligence, others believed these kinds of restrictions were elitist. Stanton and other middle-class women enjoyed opportunities for higher education few Americans could obtain regardless of their ambition and aptitude. Other suffragists, such as Lucy Stone who founded the American Equal Rights Association in 1866 alongside Stanton and Susan B. Anthony, believed that women should embrace black suffrage as progress toward their goal of universal suffrage. Stone reminded her contemporaries that public support for women's suffrage was minimal at this time and opposing any extension of the vote would be counterproductive. Recent events had led to a change in public opinion regarding black suffrage, Stone argued, and women should support the extension of suffrage as a matter of justice as well as expediency.

Events in Kansas demonstrated the practicality of Stone's argument. Local suffragists, such as Clarina Nichols, had successfully navigated a provision granting women the right to vote in school elections in the state constitution. In 1867, she and others convinced the legislature to place the issue of women's suffrage on the ballot. The measure's unpopularity among the male electorate resulted in a resounding defeat of the referendum on women's suffrage. It also provided fodder for opponents of black suffrage. Defenders of white supremacy convinced voters that it was not a coincidence that provisions for black suffrage and women's suffrage appeared side by side on the ballot. Black suffrage would lead to women voting, they argued, a gender-based argument that led to the defeat of both proposals in a state many predicted would approve black suffrage.

The issue of whether to support the Fourteenth and Fifteenth amendments and black male suffrage divided some suffragists, but most agreed that Southern violence against former slaves demanded the immediate right to vote as a matter of life and death. Ohio suffrage leader Frances Dana Gage expressed the views of many when she exclaimed that a defeat of the Fifteenth Amendment would prevent millions from exercising their rights while doing nothing to aid the cause of women. Elizabeth Cady Stanton appreciated Gage's argument and understood why many women supported black male suffrage as a tactical concession in an ongoing battle. For Stanton, however, compromise was surrender.

Leading black men such as Martin Delany and Frederick Douglass had supported women's suffrage as early as 1848. In that year, Delany proposed a resolution in favor of women's suffrage at a Cleveland convention of black leaders. Douglass had been one of the leading participants in the first women's rights convention in Seneca Falls that same year. Other black men who were national and state leaders tended to be far more supportive of women's suffrage than their white counterparts. While leading white politicians used female suffrage to mock those who favored black suffrage, even the black leaders who opposed women's suffrage believed the matter at least merited serious discussion. South Carolina was the only state legislature to have a black majority, and it was also the only Southern legislature to endorse women's suffrage. These men invited black women such as Louisa Rollin to address them on the subject in 1869. Three years later, most black delegates voted in favor of a women's suffrage amendment to the South Carolina state constitution.

FIGURE 1.8

Elizabeth Cady Stanton with her daughter Harriet. Together with Lucretia Mott, Stanton planned the first Women's Rights Convention in Seneca Falls, New York, in 1848. Stanton was a prolific writer on behalf of women's rights and served as the president of the National Women's Suffrage Association.

Women's support of black male suffrage was the leading question at the 1869 meeting of American Equal Rights Association. At this meeting, Frederick Douglass expressed his fear that any dissension among women might derail black suffrage. Stanton challenged Douglass to realize that as a black leader, he needed to consider his equal obligation to consider the perspective of the women of his race. As Stanton recognized, black women had a unique perspective on the question. **Sojourner Truth** spoke for many black women in opposing any compromise, even if such a compromise assisted the cause of black male suffrage. Other black women agreed with Douglass and hoped he was correct in predicting that Congress would soon pass a sixteenth amendment that would extend the vote to women. Susan B. Anthony and Elizabeth Cady Stanton disagreed. The two women walked out of the meeting with a small group of supporters who and formed the **National Women's Suffrage Association (NWSA)**. This group continued to challenge disenfranchisement through petitions, lecture tours, and direct protest. Women such as Lucy Stone who supported the Fifteenth Amendment went on to form the **American Women's Suffrage Association (AWSA)**, which followed a slightly more conservative approach. The AWSA believed the best tactic was to work with the male leadership of the Republican Party and promote women's suffrage at the state and local level.

2.5 Impeachment and the Election of 1868

The army was tasked with implementing nearly every aspect of Reconstruction, from overseeing elections to the daily operation of the Freedman's Bureau. As president, Johnson was the military's commander in chief and he used his authority to remove army commanders and bureau officials who supported the Radicals and their vision for a more egalitarian postwar South. In return, the Republicans passed the **Tenure of Office Act** in March 1867. The law forbade the president from removing any federal official whose original appointment had required senate confirmation without first gaining the approval of the Senate. Johnson was outraged and understood that the intent of the law was to prevent him from removing Secretary of War Edwin Stanton. Stanton had become increasingly critical of the president due to his interference with the military and Johnson hoped to replace him with someone who would be more accommodating to his political agenda. Aware of the Tenure of Office Act, Johnson waited until the Senate was in recess before demanding his resignation. When Stanton refused to quit, the president simply appointed another Secretary of War in his place. Congressional Republicans believed that Johnson's actions violated the law and demonstrated criminal contempt for the legislative process. They called for the president's removal, citing Article II, Section 4, of the Constitution, which states that the president "shall be removed from office on impeachment for, and conviction of, treason, bribery, or other high crimes and misdemeanors." Members of the House of Representatives voted along party lines in February 1868, with 126 Republicans voting for impeachment and 47 Democrats opposing the measure.

Impeachment is the first step in the process of removing a president and results in a trial before the Senate. If two-thirds of the Senate votes in favor of conviction, the president will be removed from office. Andrew Johnson was the first president to be impeached, and his trial in the Senate was the leading topic of discussion throughout the nation. Despite their animosity toward President Johnson, some Republicans questioned whether the president had really committed a crime. Edwin Stanton had been appointed by President Lincoln, and the Tenure of Office Act was vague and perhaps unconstitutional given the power it granted the Senate over the president's own cabinet. Others were afraid of who would take over if President Johnson was removed from office. The next in line for the office was the president pro tempore of the Senate, Benjamin Wade, whom a number of Senators did not admire.

Sojourner Truth

Born into slavery in New York as Isabella Baumfree, Sojourner Truth would become one of the leading abolitionists before the Civil War. Selecting the name "Sojourner Truth" for herself, she delivered lectures around the country in defense of civil rights during Reconstruction and suffrage for women.

National Women's Suffrage Association (NWSA)

A national women's rights association that promoted suffrage and other causes. The NWSA was created in 1869 by suffragists who refused to support the Fifteenth Amendment unless it also protected the right of women to vote.

American Women's Suffrage Association (AWSA)

One of the two leading women's suffrage associations in the United States, the AWSA was formed in 1869 when women's rights advocates divided over whether to support the Fifteenth Amendment even if it failed to guarantee women the right to vote. The organization focused on promoting women's suffrage at the state and local level.

Tenure of Office Act

A law that required senate approval before any public official could be removed from office if their original appointment had required the confirmation of the Senate. The law was passed in 1867 and repealed twenty years later.

impeachment

The process of a legislature bringing formal charges against a government official. Impeachment is followed by a trial to determine whether to remove that official from office.

FIGURE 1.9

This scene from Andrew Johnson's impeachment trial demonstrates the spectacle these proceedings became in Washington. Tickets for the few seats in the Senate gallery sold for small fortunes, and Americans across the nation surrounded telegraph offices as they eagerly awaited news from the trial.

Horatio Seymour

An influential New York politician and governor, Horatio Seymour was nominated for the presidency in 1868. He was defeated by the Republican Ulysses S. Grant.

Ulysses S. Grant

A military officer from Ohio who would become the commander of US forces by the end of the Civil War, Ulysses S. Grant was nominated by the Republican Party for the presidency in 1868. He had serves two terms (1869–1877) and generally supported the plans of leading Republicans in Congress regarding the reconstruction of the South.

"Wave the Bloody Shirt"

A phrase used by opponents of the Republican Party to bring attention to the tendency of Republicans to invoke the memory of the Civil War in order to advance their political agenda.

Johnson's trial featured high tensions and dramatic rhetoric, but it was clear to most Americans that the "crime" the president was really being tried for was his opposition to Republican plans for Reconstruction. The Republicans dominated the Senate, yet the attempt to remove Johnson failed by one vote as seven Republicans opposed the measure because they believed removal was both unconstitutional and unwise. Johnson's supporters had secretly assured these senators that the president would no longer oppose their legislation, and Republicans feared actual removal would mean that they were guilty of a similar abuse of power they were accusing Johnson of committing.

During the summer of 1868, both parties held their political conventions to determine who would be their candidate for president. Few Democrats favored Johnson, given his near removal from office. The Democrats instead settled on **Horatio Seymour** who had been an influential governor of New York. The Democrats ran what historian David Blight has called "arguably the most openly white supremacist election campaign in American history." The party adopted the slogan "This Is a White Man's Country, Let White Men Rule," and accused any of their political opponents as being traitors to their race. The Republicans chose the victorious Union commander, **Ulysses S. Grant**. Although Grant was known for holding many paternalistic views about African Americans, he was also associated with the Union victory that led to emancipation. Grant avoided public statements regarding race and the actual campaigning for both candidates was conducted largely by their political supporters. Republicans urged Union men to "vote as you shot" for General Grant, while warning that Seymour and the Democrats were all secret rebels in their hearts. Many predicted that the election would be a referendum on Reconstruction, with a Grant victory symbolizing national support for Republican policies and a Seymour victory demonstrating that the nation wanted to abandon the project and allow the white South to reconstruct itself.

If a Grant victory signaled a continuation of Reconstruction, he and his supporters worked hard to obscure what his policies might be regarding race and reconciliation. His campaign slogan was "Let Us Have Peace," a positive but vague mantra that Grant supporters could use to support a number of perspectives. The slogan might imply the abandonment of controversial programs such as the Freedman's Bureau when talking to conservative audiences, and it could also be spun to imply protection of former slaves from racial violence when talking to Radicals. For example, when campaigning among former slaves and Northerners who were concerned about the conditions they faced, Grant supporters used the slogan to demonstrate the general's devotion to justice and order. Black leaders throughout the South had long called for an increased federal presence for precisely this reason, arguing that an increase in army personnel and Freedman's Bureau agents was required to end the racial violence that had plagued the South.

Although Seymour's vice presidential running mate spoke openly about how a Democratic victory could restore white rule to the South, Seymour himself followed Grant's strategy of avoiding precise statements of policy. Absent of a debate that might have forced a clear discussion of the issues the nation faced, both campaigns quickly denigrated to mudslinging. Democrats publicized Grant's past history of alcoholism while seeking to capitalize on the racial prejudices of the era by branding Grant as a "Negro-Lover." Accusations of affection for American citizens may seem strange politics, but this label was considered one of the sharpest indictments against a white person in 1868 and was tantamount to suggesting that Grant was a traitor to his ancestors. The Republicans were less than virtuous in their campaigns as well. They did not hesitate to **"Wave the Bloody Shirt"**—a phrase that referred to the tendency of Republican candidates to present every election a referendum on whether the Civil War had been fought in vain. While some of their party members had opposed Union participation in the war, Democrats argued that it was both unfair and inaccurate to paint every Democrat with the brush of treason. They also argued that such tactics were intended to distract voters from important political issues. Of course, it did not help Seymour's chances in the North he had been very critical of Lincoln and had shown favor to members of a mob that had attacked Union troops and ransacked a black orphanage during the war.

Union troops supervised the elections in the South to ensure that all men, regardless of race and previous condition of servitude, were permitted to vote. Approximately half a million African Americans went to the polls and historians estimate that at least 90 percent of these votes went to Grant and the Republican Party. Because of the black vote and the fact that Mississippi, Virginia, and Texas had not been readmitted to the Union at the time of the election, Seymour won only two Southern states. The Democratic candidate won Georgia and Louisiana, as well as the Border States of Maryland, Delaware, and Kentucky, his home state of New York, and New Jersey and Oregon. While the election results may give the appearance of a landslide victory for the Republicans, the nation was far from united in support of Grant. Very few Southern whites voted for the former Union commander, a situation reminiscent of Lincoln and the Republican victory of 1860 that led to the Civil War.

Southern whites who supported the Republicans were branded as traitors to the race and the Southern way of life. When the voting results are analyzed, it is easy to see that the greatest area of support for Grant in the South was also the area with the greatest number of African Americans. However, Grant also received support from regions inhabited by poor whites, such as Appalachia. A much smaller percentage of African Americans lived in West Virginia, northern Alabama, and eastern Tennessee, yet these were all areas of support for Grant and the Republican Party. In these regions, whites who were resentful of political domination by wealthy planters found hope in the platform of Republican politicians who promised public schools and government assistance for poor farmers. Because poor whites were the largest voting bloc in the South, followed closely by former slaves, the possibility of political fusion between these groups represented a possible challenge to those seeking a return to the antebellum tradition of small government and low taxes on land. As a result, Democratic leaders worked hard to convince white Southerners that their interests were united as white men and women regardless of their income levels. For the next four years, Democratic leaders worked to convince whites of all economic backgrounds that black suffrage, Yankee domination, and the Republican Party were destroying their beloved communities.

REVIEW AND CRITICAL THINKING

1. Who were the Radicals and the Moderates and what were their goals regarding Reconstruction? To what degree did they pursue equal rights for African Americans? How did different groups of Americans differ in their views on Reconstruction?
2. How did President Johnson's actions help to solidify the Republicans? How might Reconstruction have been different with a Moderate Republican in the White House?
3. How did Southern whites try to limit the ability of freed slaves to have access to the ballot box? How did former slaves respond?
4. Why did Congress pass the Tenure of Office Act in 1867? Was this a legitimate use of congressional power or a violation of the idea of checks and balances? Why did some Republican senators not vote to convict President Johnson?
5. Why did some women oppose the Fourteenth Amendment?
6. What were the major issues of the election of 1868? What did the results of the election show about the unity of the country in 1868?

3.   CHALLENGES OF RECONSTRUCTION

LEARNING OBJECTIVES

1. Identify how sharecropping was a compromise between the desire of former slaves to own farms and the desire of plantation owners to replicate the working conditions of slavery.
2. Summarize the rise of the Republican Party in the South and the role of race in Southern politics. Identify the priorities of Republican leaders and the challenges they faced.
3. Describe how national political scandals hurt the credibility of the Republicans and led to the division of the party. Explain how the rise of the Liberal Republicans demonstrated the way many Americans viewed Reconstruction in the early 1870s.

3.1   Confronting the Klan

Grant owed his election to the recently enfranchised black voters of the South, yet tens of thousands of African Americans were threatened with violence for voting or simply had their ballots discarded by white election officials. These acts of domestic terrorism led to Democratic victories in Georgia and Louisiana during the election of 1868. Despite the presence of Union troops, white-hooded riders of the **Ku Klux Klan** committed acts of violence against the families of black men who attempted to vote. What began as a social club in Pulaski, Tennessee, quickly expanded into a terrorist network dedicated to the preservation of white supremacy through fraud, intimidation, and violence. Klansmen wore white masks, white cardboard hats, and white sheets as they pretended to be ghosts of Confederate soldiers. Klansmen rode throughout the South, torturing and killing African Americans and the few whites who were sympathetic to the challenges they faced.

Ku Klux Klan

Originally a social fraternity in Tennessee, the Klan soon became an organization whose leading purpose was to terrorize African Americans in an effort to keep them from exercising their civil and political rights such as voting.

The Klan's top priority was to stop African Americans from voting. The presence of Union troops at the polls gave rise to a campaign of terror against black civilians rather than direct confrontation with soldiers. Placing a burning cross in front of a black home was a message that the Klan was watching. Those African Americans who were perceived as being too outspoken might be murdered in their beds or dragged from their homes and lynched, their limp bodies serving as an object lesson of what could happen to anyone who did not follow the Klan's "advice." Klan violence was also directed against African Americans who taught schools or established businesses, as both were signs of racial uplift that Klansmen found intolerable. In Georgia alone, dozens of African American men were killed by the Klan in 1868. Similar statistics are evident in states such as Louisiana, Texas, Alabama, South Carolina, and Mississippi.

Despite the potential consequences, black communities held meetings to organize protests and call on the federal government to restore law and order. In 1870, President Grant and the Republicans in Congress responded by ordering an investigation of the Ku Klux Klan. They also passed the **Enforcement Acts**, a series of laws passed in 1870 and 1871 that were aimed at enforcing the provisions of the Fourteenth and Fifteenth amendments. These laws provided for criminal penalties against those who interfered with a citizen's right to vote, banned the wearing of masks and other disguises, placed some elections under direct federal supervision, and authorized the president to suspend habeas corpus and place Klansmen in jail in response to violent crimes. A number of Klansmen were arrested, but few were placed on trial and even fewer were convicted. While some believe the Enforcement Acts were still successful because the Klan slowly disappeared from the scene until the organization's resurgence in the 1920s, others argue that the goals of the Klan—preventing black suffrage and impeding black education and economic progress—were simply achieved by other methods.

3.2 Sharecropping

Black leaders such as Martin Delany and Radical Republicans such as Pennsylvania congressman Thaddeus Stevens repeatedly called on Congress to confiscate land from rebel planters and divide it among former slaves and landless white families. Delany reminded Congress that their original bill creating the Freedman's Bureau was authorized to divide abandoned lands in forty-acre plots among former slaves and poor whites. In the fall of 1865, Thaddeus Stevens responded to these ideas by proposing a bill that would have confiscated land belonging to the wealthiest 10 percent of Southerners. Stevens believed it was these aristocratic men who had led their section into rebellion and his plan called on the federal government to divide their lands into small plots that would be sold on credit to poor Southerners of all races. His proposal would have led 400 million acres changing hands—a radical departure from the concept of limited governmental powers. However, Stevens thought such a departure was necessary if the South and the millions of poor families throughout the region were to become economically stable. Opponents countered that such a massive attempt at land redistribution would lead to greater instability and perhaps even more violence and privation than had occurred during the last four years of war. The role of government was to preserve private property, they reminded Stevens's few supporters, and countered that the region's economy would be best served by a return to plantation agriculture. Small family farms would produce only subsistence crops, they continued, while a return to cotton production would restore the nation's most valuable export and bring money back to the region.

Even Northern Republicans criticized Stevens's plan. They pointed to the vast gulf between the rich and poor in his own state of Pennsylvania and asked whether the senator favored confiscating factories and distributing the property of his wealthy supporters to poor workers. While such scenarios conjured fears of Socialism, the basis of Stevens's idea was less motivated by a desire to redistribute wealth than a belated application of justice. Stevens's proposal was the culmination of ideas posed by dozens of conventions held by black leaders, many of whom were former slaves. The delegates to these meetings believed that they were entitled to the land because of their years in bondage. To a lesser degree, some poor whites also believed they were entitled to some form of reparation for years of limited opportunity in an antebellum political and economic system dominated by planters. Some Confederate veterans pointed out that they had defended chimerical vision of these planters, only to lose their meager property while the wealthy had their lands restored to them after the war.

Not even Thaddeus Stevens fully appreciated the meaning of land to former slaves. He agreed that a small plot of land was an economic asset that could lead to independence. For the emancipated slave, however, land was more than a commodity. Former slaves asked that they be granted title to the land they had lived and worked, land where their ancestors were buried, and land they could pass on to their children. Gaining title to these lands would provide more than just sustenance and stability. Reparation validated years of toil, completed the cycle of justice, sustained their links with the past, and endowed their children's futures. Hundreds of petitions signed by thousands of former slaves were disregarded, however, as the federal government refused to halt the process of returning land held by the federal

government back to its original owners. Few in Congress beyond a handful of Radicals protested this course of action.

The Freedman's Bureau was directed to evict tens of thousands of former slaves who were collectively operating farms and plantations on land that had been seized by the government during the war. Merrimon Howard was among many who wrote letters of protest to military and civilian leaders, pointing out the hypocrisy of army officials who now turned its back on veterans in need. "We were friends on the march…brothers on the battlefield," Howard wrote, "but in the peaceful pursuits of life, it seems that we are strangers."

Despite tremendous hardships, thousands of former slaves were still able to acquire some amount of land and begin the transition from the collectivism of plantation labor to running individual family farms. Even for these fortunate few, landownership was tenuous and any combination of economic downturn, bad luck, or racial injustice could strip them of their property. While thousands lost their land over the next few decades, the vast majority of the 4 million former slaves never achieved their dream of landownership. Few Americans in 1865 possessed the cash reserves needed to start a farm, and this was especially true of former slaves. While many whites were able to get loans to purchase farmland and equipment, this opportunity was rarely extended to African Americans in any section of the country. Many whites who had lost everything during the Civil War were so poor that they were also denied credit. The Homestead Act of 1862 offered 160 acres of free land in the western plains, but even free land required money to build a home and farm. Between the return of land to wealthy planters and the denial of credit, the dream of landownership was deferred for both white and black Southerners.

Although their plight pales in comparison with the former slaves and poor whites of the South, many of the region's plantation owners were also in a difficult position. The war had left many of them with little or no cash to pay laborers. Planters hoped to pay laborers with food and shelter rather than currency. They also hoped to restore the system of gang labor that had prevailed under slavery, with black field hands working under the supervision of white overseers. However, neither former slaves nor white laborers would agree to work under conditions that resembled slavery. Over time, a new system emerged that appeared to be a compromise between the desires of laborers and landowners. Under the **sharecropping** system, laborers worked individual plots owned by planters in exchange for a share of the crop at harvest. Planters provided land, tools, seed, and shelter to the sharecropper on credit.

This system appeared to resolve the most critical issues for landowners—the resumption of agriculture, the control of land and labor, and the ability to postpone cash payments to laborers until after the harvest. Sharecropping promised to pair labor and capital to produce a crop that might stimulate the Southern economy. The system also promised a measure of independence to laborers. Although sharecropping did not provide the same level of independence as landownership, sharecroppers still possessed a degree of autonomy as tenants. At the very least, individual plots of land might feel like one's own land just as a rented house might give a tenant the feeling of home. Unlike slaves, sharecroppers would not be forced to work under the direct supervision of an overseer, and their families would be secure. In addition, sharecroppers could usually maintain gardens and livestock even if the bulk of their crop would be planted according to the dictates of the landowner.

In practice, the system rarely afforded sharecroppers the independence they longed for. Because of widespread poverty, Southern banks only extended credit to those individuals who already owned land. Even these mortgage-backed loans to plantation owners carried high interest rates. Planters used the proceeds to finance planting costs and living expenses of the sharecroppers who lived and worked on their land. Sharecroppers established credit accounts (often in coordination with a local merchant) and promised to repay the costs of tools and seed, along with their rents and the money they owed for food and clothing purchases each year. In theory, the proceeds the sharecroppers earned for their portion of the crop would pay all of these expenses, with money left over that could be saved until they could purchase their own farms. The reality was that most sharecroppers, and some planters and merchants, found themselves in more and more debt each year.

FIGURE 1.11

This photo showing a family of sharecroppers in Alabama in 1939 reveals the poverty that many black and white Southern sharecroppers faced both during and well beyond Reconstruction.

sharecropping

An agricultural system where tenant laborers live and work on land owned by a landlord. The laborers are paid by receiving a share of the crop they raise while the landowner receives the rest of the proceeds.

FIGURE 1.12

In this picture, a black sharecropper is being auctioned off to planters, not as a slave, but as a debtor who was unable to pay his fine. Black sharecroppers were frequently arrested for minor crimes and then forced to work without pay for whoever paid their fines. Trials were usually conducted in such a way that any employer who accused a worker of theft would likely succeed in getting a conviction. As a result, there were many cases where sharecroppers were accused of crimes to avoid paying them or as a way to demonstrate the futility of opposing the planter's will.

debt peonage

A system where laborers are bound to make payments in the form of labor until their obligations are met. The word *peon* refers to a person who has little control over the conditions of their employment.

scalawag

A derisive term used by white Southerners to describe other white Southerners who supported congressional Reconstruction or the Republican Party. The term implies one who is a traitor to their own people.

carpetbagger

A derisive term used by white Southerners to label Northerners whom they believed came to the South during Reconstruction with the intent to profit from their region's misfortune.

Sharecropping contracts usually granted between one-third and one-half of the proceeds from the annual crop to the laborer. From this amount all of the sharecroppers expenses for the season were deducted, with any remaining money being due the sharecropper. Historians have found that many planters and merchants openly robbed the sharecroppers by not paying them their fair share, falsifying the books, or practicing other forms of creative accounting. At the same time, they have also found that many planters and merchants were also in a precarious situation themselves. Due to the scarcity of capital, high interest rates, and declining price of cotton, even honest planters resorted to charging their tenants inflated prices and very high interest rates. When the harvest passed and it came time to settle the account, sharecroppers, especially if they were black, were not permitted to argue with the landowners and merchants. If the family was unable to settle their account, the planter could either extend additional credit or have the sharecropper placed in jail. As the years went by, even the most frugal and industrious sharecroppers fell deeper and deeper in debt. For thousands of former slaves, sharecropping led to the separation of families as black sharecroppers were frequently arrested and forced to work under overseers without pay until their "debt" had been paid in full.

This system of **debt peonage** granted the planters power over their laborers in ways reminiscent of slavery. Planter-dominated assemblies passed laws that made abandonment of one's contract a felony, while eviction of laborers remained the prerogative of landowners. Counties and states also contracted with prison farms where inmates encountered forced labor and corporal punishment for petty crimes they often did not commit. African Americans were especially targeted by Southern courts and were disproportionately sentenced to long prison terms to pay off their "indebtedness."

Whites were usually immune from the most obvious miscarriages of justice. However, the desperation of the sharecropping system led many to commit actual crimes, which also led to a large incarcerated population. One of the leading reasons for the increase in convictions for crimes such as "vagrancy" that were usually unenforced in the past was the creation of the **convict lease system**. For-profit mines, farms, and factories paid cash-strapped Southern governments for each prisoner that was leased to them as unpaid laborers. The convict lease system quickly became a leading source of funds for state governments and saved the government the expense of operating prisons. These for-profit operations were supposed to be regulated by the state, but in practice, inmates were routinely abused and forced to work under dangerous and inhumane conditions. In addition, because the state profited each time an individual was convicted and leased to a privately owned factory or farm, many historians have argued that applying the term *criminal justice system* to the Southern law enforcement at this time is a misnomer. The phrase presumes the guilt of the individuals implies that justice was systematically distributed despite clear indications of racial bias and a predisposition to convict the impoverished.

3.3 Schools and Business Promotion

Republicans hoped to create a strong political party in the South that would help them to maintain control of Congress. This hope would prove a challenge, however, as the Republican Party simply did not exist in most parts of the South. Blacks might be counted on to vote for Republican candidates, but if the Republicans were going to become a sustainable political organization they would need support from whites as well. One likely group that might support the party was the small number of Southerners who had maintained loyalty to the Union. These individuals, labeled by their detractors as turncoats and **scalawags**, were usually small farmers who had long been hostile to the planter elites who dominated the region during the antebellum period.

A small number of Northerners had migrated to the South following the war in hopes of starting businesses that could take advantage of the region's natural resources and low wages. Native white Southerners labeled these individuals as **carpetbaggers**, alluding to the belief that these unscrupulous profiteers arrived only with traveling luggage made from scraps of carpet. While such bags were durable, the derisive term connoted a person who intended to use the South to make a quick profit before returning to his Yankee homeland. Ironically, this stereotype started to backfire as the South became increasingly desperate for any kind of investment. As a result, the insult evolved over time to connote a failed businessman whose poverty was represented by the single carpetbag that carried everything he owned. This brand of Yankee offered nothing to invest, native white Southerners warned, and might even become a public burden or resort to crime.

In actuality, most scalawags maintained a deep commitment to the South that inspired them to stay in the region throughout the war when most Union men migrated north. Likewise, most carpetbaggers were educated women who came to the South as teachers or men with both talent and modest capital to invest. However, some Northerners who came to the region had also been Union soldiers or government agents of the Freedman's Bureau. Although these men were usually motivated by a desire to settle in a region they had come to admire while in the service of the federal government, the notion of former Yankee troops and bureau agents swarming into the region did little to repair the image of the carpetbagger among Southern whites. Suspicion frequently turned to outright hostility when some Northerners became leaders of local Republican Party factions whose electoral strength was based largely on the votes of former slaves. The carpetbaggers and scalawags often advocated reform measures that might have benefitted many Southerners such as publicly funded schools, debt relief, and measures to encourage industrial development. In the end, these policies mattered less than the image the Democrats cultivated of their opponents. The Republicans were the "Party of Lincoln," Southern Democrats reminded all who would listen. Even worse, they continued, the Republicans of the South were an amalgamation of Yankee carpetbaggers, former slaves, local black leaders, Radicals, and scalawags.

Between 1867 and the early 1870s in the South, and even as late as the early 1880s in a few Border States, the Republican Party was able to appeal to enough white voters with a platform promising economic opportunity and education. Republicans dominated every one of the Southern constitutional conventions in the late 1860s. Their revisions led to constitutions that outlawed imprisonment for debt, removed property qualifications for voters and jury members, established publicly funded schools, universities, orphanages, and hospitals, and offered legal guarantees of civil rights regardless of race. State and local governments also revised their tax laws to ease the burden on small landowners while raising taxes on those who owned large plantations. Each of these measures was unpopular with landowners and a break with the Southern tradition of limited government and low taxes for landowners. Nevertheless, the greatest controversy erupted when Republicans used tax revenue and government lands in an attempt to rebuild and expand their infrastructure and provide incentives for businesses development.

Opponents bristled at the imposition of new taxes on large landowners, especially when some former planters were unable to pay and the government seized their land and sold it in small plots at public auction. While these kinds of sales were rarely imposed on the wealthy, rising taxes and unprecedented government spending on public schools were viewed with hostility among the elite. Other Southern whites believed that Reconstruction governments were not content to provide mere legal equality for former slaves. These racial conservatives feared that the real purpose of black conventions was to conspire to take control of the government and grant special privileges for African Americans. After all, they argued, equal rights had already been guaranteed by the Fourteenth and Fifteenth amendments. By this perspective, any new federal or state law specifically aimed at guaranteeing civil rights demonstrated was really intended to grant special privileges for African Americans at the expense of whites. The fear of "social equality"—a phrase that referred to any form of racial integration and often alluded to the possibility of interracial sex—drove white Southerners to oppose any civil rights legislation and fear any challenge to the antebellum racial order.

Economic growth was the best hope for Southern Republican governments as they faced a crisis of legitimacy fueled by racism. Republicans believed that investing in infrastructure and business development plans were key to this kind of growth. They devoted considerable time promoting railroad development, offering rail companies large grants of public land while also partially subsidizing various commercial development schemes. Many of these measures proved effective, but they also placed some Southern governments further into debt. Between 1867 and 1872, the entire Southern rail network was repaired and doubled in size, levees were repaired, and ports and shipyards were modernized. Each of these projects invited opportunities for graft, and critics argued that the new Southern legislatures resembled their Northern cousins when it came to widespread corruption in government. Despite the improvements, Republican dreams of recreating Northern economic success were only partially realized. The Republicans of the South had promised economic development in return for higher taxes, but a global depression that began in 1873 limited their likelihood of success.

The timing could not be worse for Southern Republicans. The depression coincided with a series of national scandals involving Republican leaders in Washington and a division among national leaders that nearly split the Republican Party in two. The depression also accompanied the rise of violence against Southern blacks, most clearly evidenced by the 1873 **Colfax Massacre** in Louisiana. Following a contentious election, vigilantes who were part of the White League—an organization similar to the Ku Klux Klan—decided that they could not accept the Republican victory. These men of the White League armed themselves and attacked black state officials on Easter Sunday. Black men who were members of the state militia attempted to preserve order but were soon overwhelmed and surrendered. The mob later massacred many of their prisoners and murdered a number of black civilians to intimidate the survivors. Federal marshals arrived in time to bury some of the dead but did little to challenge the violent counterrevolution that had just occurred in the town of Colfax.

FIGURE 1.13

African Americans organized local, state, and national conventions throughout Reconstruction to discuss issues and elect leaders. This picture depicts the 1869 National Colored Convention in Washington, DC.

Colfax Massacre

An attack on the local and county government located in Colfax, Louisiana, in April of 1873 by white paramilitary organizations who sought to eliminate the Republican Party in their community. Three whites and an estimated 150 blacks were killed.

Historians know that three white men had been killed in the gunfight, and estimate that 150 black soldiers and civilians were killed by the mob. Three years later, the United States Supreme Court invalidated the indictments of three of the leaders of the mob in *United States v. Cruikshank*. In an infamous decision, the Court ruled that the Fourteenth Amendment only gave the federal government jurisdiction over cases where state governments violated the rights of citizens. Because the mob and paramilitary organizations such as the White League were private citizens, the Court declared, the Fourteenth Amendment did not apply. Ironically, the Fourteenth Amendment had been passed in reaction to similar acts of violence and the refusal of state authorities to prosecute men such as the three mob leaders whose indictments had just been overturned by the Supreme Court.

History and Memory

Courtesy of Wikimedia Commons. http://commons.wikimedia.org/wiki/File:Colfax_Riot_sign_IMG_2401.JPG. Photo: Billy Hathorn (CC-BY-SA-3.0)

The total number of victims in the Colfax Massacre was impossible to determine because a number of bodies had been dumped in a nearby river while others were buried in unmarked graves. Bones of victims have routinely surfaced during various construction projects throughout the city over the past century. The site where sixty of the men had been buried was later disturbed by oil prospectors. In addition to disturbing the grave, the drilling released a stream of natural gas that took the same path as a bubbling spring. A fountain was erected on the site and the gas was lighted, creating a flame that burned above the fountain and attracted curious spectators until 1951 when the eternal flame suddenly stopped burning. According to local residents, the flame was extinguished at the same moment a historical marker was placed near the site of the mass grave. Sanitizing the violence that had taken place, the monument referred to the massacre as the "Colfax Riot" and celebrated that fateful Easter day as "the end of carpetbag misrule in the South."

3.4   Corruption and Division among the Republicans

Credit Mobilier

A fake construction company created by Union Pacific executives to funnel money from government contracts to their own accounts. The company allegedly contracted with Union Pacific to build railroad track. However, the company was actually a fraud and was using the money to purchase Union Pacific stock.

The federal government engaged in unprecedented spending during the Civil War and Reconstruction, and this created unprecedented opportunities for political leaders to accept bribes, profit from insider information, or simply embezzle funds from the public treasury. The most infamous episode of fraud occurred when the directors of the Union Pacific Railroad set up a fake construction company called **Credit Mobilier** in 1867. The government contracted with Union Pacific to build the Transcontinental Railroad, which turned around and subcontracted some of the track building work to Credit Mobilier. Instead of building track, the directors of Credit Mobilier embezzled the money. The scheme might have been less transparent had the directors of Credit Mobilier hid the money instead of bribing congressmen or buying Union Pacific stock.

Similar arrangements led to the disappearance of large sums on the California side of the Transcontinental Railroad that was being built by the Central Pacific Railroad. The Central Pacific was controlled by Collis P. Huntington and a number of other wealthy and influential men. Although they were suspected of fraud, any documentation of that might have proven their culpability was destroyed in a fire. The Credit Mobilier scandal was exposed in 1872, but even with a wealth of incriminating evidence the offenders still escaped prosecution when a second series of bribes derailed the investigation. The public was indignant as reports indicating that $20 million in public money had disappeared. They were also shocked to find that the scandal reached all the way to the vice president. They were positively enraged to find that he and the many congressmen who had received thousands of dollars in cash and Union Pacific stock in exchange for their complicity in the scheme also escaped prosecution.

FIGURE 1.14

This photo depicts the ceremony marking the completion of the Transcontinental Railroad in 1869. Work crews that were building the Central Pacific and Union Pacific railroads met in Utah Territory and commemorated the occasion by driving a golden rail spike. Nearby Ogden, Utah, became the effective terminus for these two rail lines and continues to be an important transportation hub.

While most of the congressmen accused of fraud were Republicans, members of the Democratic Party were no less corrupt. The Democratic Party lacked the national influence of its rivals. As a result, the malfeasance of its members was limited to the states and cities they controlled. Most corruption scandals at this level failed to generate the national headlines of Credit Mobilier, yet the majority of government spending in the 1870s occurred at the state and local level. State and especially city officials awarded contracts for railroads, schools, public buildings, sanitation systems, roads, bridges, and other projects. These same officials often owned stock or were board members of the companies that bid on these projects, creating daily opportunities to use their public authority for personal gain. Other politicians accepted gifts from business leaders with the understanding that they would support a measure that would benefit the donor. Adding to the outright fraud waged by individuals in government was the rise of local political organizations that used their power to reward their supporters. These local political parties were known as **political machines**. The name refers to the machinelike efficiency of the organizations that granted lucrative government contracts to companies that contributed to their party while distributing gifts and government jobs to voters who supported their slate of candidates at the polls.

The most infamous example of a political machine was the political club known as **Tammany Hall** of New York City. Politicians who were members of the Tammany organization awarded millions of dollars in government contracts to companies that agreed to "kick back" some of that revenue to the Democratic Party. This money was then distributed by local party leaders to their constituents, who were made to understand that they were being rewarded for voting the Democratic ticket. Some of the supporters of Tammany Hall and similar political machines in cities across the United States were non-Protestant immigrants from Ireland or Southern and Central Europe. Each of these ethnic groups experienced heavy persecution in nineteenth-century America. Just as Southern whites associated government corruption in their region with black supporters of the Republican Party, the anger of Northern voters was amplified by those who painted a picture of tax dollars being distributed to "the lowest orders of Popish trash." Opponents claimed that these immigrant voters were dangerously "un-American." Catholic immigrants were accused of being loyal only to the Pope.

political machine

A political organization whose leaders dictate the actions of its members, many of whom are elected officials. The machine helps a candidate win election in exchange for that candidate agreeing to use their office to enrich the machine. For example, a machine politician might give a construction company a contract to build a bridge for the city. That company would be expected to "kick back" some of their profits back to the political organization, which could later be used to fund the candidate's campaign.

Tammany Hall

A Democratic political organization in New York City that became a political machine known for corruption under the leadership of "Boss" William Tweed during the 1860s and early 1870s.

FIGURE 1.15

An example of the malicious anti-Irish caricatures of the era. The caption on this cartoon read "The Usual Irish Way of Doing Things" and depicts an animalistic, intoxicated, and violent creature threatening harm unless his every whim is carried out. Such imagery was used to arouse existing anti-Irish prejudice against political machines, as well as local politicians who responded to immigrant concerns and represented immigrant communities.

Calls for reform were not simply the product of racial and ethnic prejudices, even if some of the loudest voices were heavily influenced by bigotry. For many, reform was a moral creed and the reasonable demand of taxpayers who expected efficient and honest government. Businesses that refused to give bribes or simply ended up on the wrong side of a patronage battle, wealthy and middle-class families who wanted lower taxes and greater accountability, and the poor who believed that the real beneficiaries of graft were still the affluent and corrupt all united in a chorus of voices that demanded political reform. A group of Republicans who viewed themselves as the "new abolitionists" sought to respond to these demands. Referring to their faction as **Liberal Republicans**, these men campaigned on a platform pledging emancipation from corruption. They advocated political reform, limited government, and a return to traditional economic policies such as the gold standard and the elimination of barriers to free trade. While they rarely spoke openly about the South, calls for a reduction in government power and spending implied that they also supported a retreat from Reconstruction.

The Liberal Republicans met in Cincinnati, a leading city along the Ohio-Kentucky border that was also symbolic of the new party's desire to unite Northerners with Moderate Democrats who represented the Border States. This new political party was led by a number of former Republicans like **Carl Schurz**—a longtime supporter of abolition and the Republican Party. However, Schurz now believed that the government had done all it could for former slaves and should recall its soldiers, readmit all remaining Southern states, and end Reconstruction. Schurz represented several groups the new party hoped to unite—immigrants, Moderates, political reformers, and residents of the Border States. Schurz was the first German-born person elected to the Senate, a leading Moderate Republican who had supported Reconstruction but was growing weary of the challenges it entailed, a staunch opponent of political corruption, and a resident of Missouri—the crossroads of the North, South, and West. Schurz and his Liberal Republicans promoted a platform that spoke to the frustrations of many Americans. They called for a complete end to federal intervention in the South, the abolition of land grants to railroads, lower taxes, and civil service reform.

3.5 The Election of 1872

The Liberal Republicans had a clear message of what they opposed, but soon divided among themselves over the issues they supported. While the party spoke of civil-service reform and lower taxes, the delegates divided on how best to reduce corruption and govern more efficiently with less revenue. They also disagreed sharply on who should be their presidential candidate. In a compromise that pleased few of their members, the Liberal Republicans elected *New York Tribune* editor **Horace Greeley**. Greeley had been one of the most vocal critics of slavery. As the editor of one of the nation's leading newspapers, he had publicly criticized Lincoln for his unwillingness to push beyond the boundaries of public opinion regarding the issue of slavery. However, as the leader of the Liberal Republicans in 1872, Greeley evidenced a similar caution on matters of race and public opinion. Candidate Greeley claimed that there was simply nothing more the government could do to ensure the freedom of former slaves who must now "root, hog, or die." While this nineteenth-century phrase still connotes the need to defend one's own self, death was a real possibility for Southern blacks who followed this advice by confronting the Klan and other vigilante groups. If the small number of federal troops still stationed in the unreconstructed South left the region, death was almost certain for any black man or woman who stood in defense of their rights.

An even greater irony occurred when the Democratic Party endorsed Greeley as its candidate and adopted the Liberal Republican platform as its own. Greeley had made a name for himself by attacking the Democrats in the most discourteous fashion permissible in the "polite" nineteenth-century print media. Democratic leaders met and chose to endorse their old nemesis because they recognized that fusion with the Liberal Republicans provided their best opportunity to defeat the regular Republican Party and end Reconstruction. These two strange political bedfellows struggled to resolve their differences. The Democrats and Liberal Republicans also failed to divide the regular Republican Party, who rallied behind Grant and won the election of 1872 in a landslide.

Many Southern voters feared that the lower taxes the Liberal Republicans supported would reduce funding for public schools. Black voters recognized that any party that was aligned with the Democrats was unlikely to represent their interests. Some of the delegates to the Liberal Republican convention agreed with this assessment of fusion and spoke of their partnership with the Democrats as if it were a deal with the Confederacy itself. Greeley won only six states and died prior to the meeting of the Electoral College. Although his death had little impact on the outcome of the election, it left presidential electors who had pledged to support the late editor in a quandary. Greeley's delegates voted for several different men, including the late Greeley. More important than this interesting historical side note, the election of 1872 demonstrated that Northerners were growing resentful of the time and money the federal government was devoting to Reconstruction.

FIGURE 1.16

Horace Greeley was the leader of the Liberal Republicans and the founder of the *New York Tribune*, perhaps the most influential newspaper in the mid-nineteenth century.

REVIEW AND CRITICAL THINKING

1. What was the intent of white Southerners who participated in groups such as the Ku Klux Klan? How did the federal government respond to the threat the Klan posed to former slaves and to their plan for Reconstruction?

2. How did slavery compare with sharecropping? How did sharecropping emerge? What system of labor did most landowners desire, and what were the wishes of white and black agricultural workers?

3. Who were the scalawags and the carpetbaggers? Why would many white Southerners use these derisive names to label these individuals, and what role did these individuals play in Reconstruction-era politics?

4. What were the legislative priorities for Southern Republicans once they took control of their states? What were the challenges they faced?

5. How did a political machine like Tammany Hall operate? Why might residents of a city support a political machine? Who would be the most likely to oppose a political machine?

6. Why did many Republicans join the Liberal Republicans? What were the key issues of this party, and did it succeed in pushing this agenda forward? Why or why not?

---

4. RECONSTRUCTION REVERSED

LEARNING OBJECTIVES

1. Summarize the federal government's continuing efforts to provide legal and political equality for former slaves, as well as the shortcomings of these efforts. Explain why laws such as the Civil Rights Act of 1875 failed to end racial discrimination.

2. Explain who the "Redeemers" were and describe the methods they used to seize and maintain political power. Describe the ways the Redeemers effectively reversed recent federal laws regarding universal male suffrage.

3. Summarize the history of the 1876 presidential election and consequences of the Compromise of 1877. Explain why the nation turned away from Reconstruction during the 1870s.

Federal spending on Reconstruction efforts became increasingly controversial as the nation was mired in a depression that began in 1873. Many voters blamed the Republican Party for the hard times, while others simply grew tired of hearing about the conditions former slaves faced in the South when they themselves were experiencing hardship. The Democrats seized on this frustration in 1874, winning control of the House of Representatives, which had been dominated by Republicans since the Civil War. As the Republican Party splintered and its members increasingly turned away from their commitment to Reconstruction, advocating the cause of freedom for former slaves became a political liability in the North as well as in the South.

4.1 The Panic of 1873

Western expansion and economic growth had encouraged railroad construction during and after the Civil War. Investors recognized that transportation would be the key to Western expansion. They also recognized that cities and states were dependent on railroads connecting their communities to the market economy and were offering generous incentives to promote rail construction. At every level of government, officials courted railroad companies and offered large grants of public lands, favorable rates of taxation, publicly financed bonds, and even direct payments of cash. The result was often amazing profits, which fostered the growth of more railroads as well as irrational expectations among investors who subscribed to practically any investment related to railroad construction. These factors conspired to create an environment that encouraged the construction of more railroads than the nation could support. For example, medium-sized towns throughout the rural United States were often serviced by several roads by 1870. Each new road was an unexpected source of competition and made it harder for the other rail companies to earn enough revenue to pay back their loans. Under normal business conditions, unprofitable railroads would have simply ceased operation. But in the booming postwar climate where investors were more likely to buy bonds than ask questions, even the least profitable railroad companies were able to continue daily operations. Some failing companies were even able to build new track with the revenue that poured in from shareholders.

In 1873, this speculation bubble broke as two dozen leading railroads all went bankrupt. Once the news circulated that many of these railroads were losing money, investors stopped buying the bonds that had been used to finance the operation of the unprofitable companies. Without revenue from customers and without continued investment, these railroads could not make payments on their previous loans and were forced into bankruptcy. Even worse, many railroad investors who now owned worthless stocks and bonds had borrowed money to purchase those investments. The result was a general panic that spread through the entire banking system as investors rushed to sell all kinds of railroad bonds—even those issued by profitable companies.

The nation's leading investment bank at this time was operated by railroad magnate Jay Cooke. When Cooke declared bankruptcy in September 1873, what had begun as a panic turned into chaos. Investors rushed to sell any investment, railroad-based or otherwise, to anyone willing to pay cash until the stock market simply closed its doors for two weeks. Even those who had never bought railroad stocks and bonds lost large sums of money because the country's banks were heavy investors in the stock market. Banks in the nineteenth century were not regulated as they have been in recent times, and many had loaned the money they took from depositors to railroads in hopes of cashing in on the boom. Unfortunately, when the bubble burst and the banks lost the money that they had been entrusted with, millions of families lost everything they had deposited.

Economic difficulties usually spell trouble for the political party in power, and the **Panic of 1873** was no exception. As was true with political corruption, both parties were to blame for the economic collapse and both parties blamed each other. In the South, whites had already decided that black politicians and the Republican Party were to blame for the region's troubles. They wasted little time in identifying their scapegoat. Speeches, campaigns, and voting records indicate that many black leaders had been the voice of caution within the Republican Party when it came to railroad promotion. But in the political and economic climate of the South at this time, facts mattered little and most voters had already made up their minds. Had it been otherwise, Southerners might have recognized that black families were the ones most hurt by the Panic of 1873. Among the many banks that lost their depositors' money was the **Freedman's Bank**, a federally chartered bank endowed with the pensions of black soldiers. The Freedman's Bank had received nearly every penny saved by black families through the nation. Believing that the bank was backed by the federal government, black churches, businesses, schools, orphanages, and families deposited $4 million, nearly all of which was lost.

4.2   Civil Rights Act of 1875

African Americans who had been free before the Civil War joined with former slaves in protesting both racial segregation and exclusion from restaurants, hotels, and public transit during Reconstruction. But integration and segregation were complicated issues during these years. Few Southern blacks desired any more contact with Southern whites than was required to complete essential daily tasks. They also recognized that laws and customs mandating racial separation in public spaces were designed to perpetuate white supremacy. They favored integrated schools as a means of breaking down prejudice and ensuring equal educational opportunities. At the same time, they also recognized that their children were not likely to receive fair treatment from white teachers. Black Americans also understood that the issue of raising taxes to support public schools was still controversial, and feared that any requirement of integrated schools might doom the entire system.

Despite all of these obstacles and a desire to build their own institutions, black protest against both formal and informal segregation was common during Reconstruction. The Louisville African Methodist Episcopal church organized a protest against segregation on the streetcars of its city in 1870. When two white men dragged a twenty-year-old teacher from Illinois named Emma Coger from the dining cabin of a steamship in 1873, Coger brought a successful lawsuit against the company. In ruling for Coger, an Iowa court declared that the Fourteenth Amendment and the many references to equality found in the preamble to the Iowa state constitution meant that black passengers were entitled to the same accommodations as white passengers when traveling through their state. Like Coger, dozens of individuals throughout the nation were arrested for such demonstrations during the Reconstruction Era, nearly a century prior to Rosa Parks' iconic stand against segregation in public transit. And like Parks and Coger, some of these women and men prevailed.

Inspired by such courageous activism, Massachusetts senator **Charles Sumner** began a campaign in favor of a strong federal civil rights bill that would outlaw discrimination in schools, hotels, restaurants, churches, and public transportation in the late 1860s. A lifelong abolitionist who suffered debilitating injuries for his passionate oratory about the evils of slavery, Sumner introduced his civil rights bill every year between 1867 and 1874. As he lay dying in the spring of 1874, among his last words to a friend was a desperate plea for Congress to pass his bill. In the November elections of 1874, the Democrats won nearly a hundred new seats in Congress, which meant that the next session of Congress would have a Democratic majority. If the Republicans hoped to honor the late Charles Sumner and use the power of the federal government to outlaw racial discrimination, they all understood that the winter session of 1874–1875 was their last chance.

A handful of white Radicals and the seven black representatives in the House of Representatives faced off against Democrats such as Alexander Stephens. The debate centered on whether the federal government was exceeding its lawful authority by mandating nondiscrimination in schools, churches, and private businesses. Each of the seven black Congressmen related the indignities they had faced on streetcars and in hotels. They also demonstrated how guarantees of civil rights were consistent with the Founding Fathers' vision as expressed in the Constitution, and called on the United States to finally embrace its professed declarations of liberty and equality. Stephens and other Democrats countered that the role of government was to empower local governments to make administrative decisions regarding schools and to protect the rights of individuals to decide how they ran their businesses. For Stephens, proprietors had a right to exclude people of certain races within their own restaurants, hotels, and transportation companies.

Panic of 1873

A depression triggered by global currency fluctuations, the Panic of 1873 was especially severe in the United States due to speculative investments that led to the bankruptcies of many leading businesses and banks.

Freedman's Bank

A federally chartered bank created by Congress to promote thrift and savings among former slaves. The directors of the institution followed the same short-sighted investment strategies of many other banks and were among the hundreds of such institutions to fail in the wake of the Panic of 1873, losing all of the money that thousands of black families had saved.

Charles Sumner

Widely regarded as one of the most ardent white supporters of the abolition of slavery and civil rights for African Americans, Massachusetts politician Charles Sumner would lead the radical wing of the Republican Party in the Senate until his death in 1874.

FIGURE 1.17

Both of these images are from the same magazine that had opposed slavery and called for equal legal and political rights for African Americans throughout the early period of Reconstruction. The first image was published in 1865 and asked readers to consider why a Union veteran would be turned away from the polls. Nine years later, the same magazine depicted black politicians as caricatures rather than men, unfit for political office and the responsibilities of democratic participation.

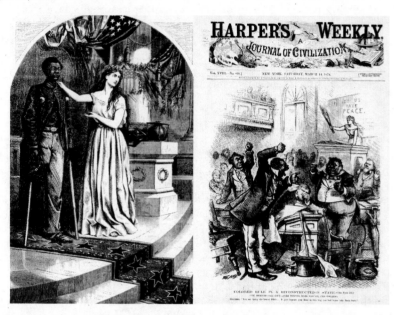

Of all the bill's provisions, the requirement of nondiscrimination in schools and churches were the most controversial. Even Republicans who supported the bill feared that requirements of integrated classrooms would lead to the destruction of the South's nascent public school system. Republican leaders compromised by removing all references to schools and churches from the bill. Once this was accomplished, the bill passed even though no Democrat voted in favor of the measure. Due to public sentiment against the law, the measure proved largely ineffectual. The civil rights law provided the possibility of heavy fines and even jail time for violators, but the law also placed the burden of enforcement on black plaintiffs who would have to hire their own attorneys and sue violators in federal court. Five black litigants financed such cases and won judgments against local hotel, theater, and railroad operators. White defendants appealed these judgments, however, and in 1883, the United States Supreme Court ruled on their behalf and declared the **Civil Rights Act of 1875** unconstitutional. A similar bill outlawing racial discrimination would not pass Congress until 1964.

4.3   Redeemers

The **Amnesty Act of 1872** removed the final set of restrictions against most Confederate leaders and allowed them to run for political office. Liberal Republicans in Congress supported the Amnesty Act because they believed that power should be returned to the South's "natural leaders." They also accepted the argument of Democratic leaders who argued that government corruption had occurred because poor men had risen to power. Men of humble origins would naturally be more tempted to use their power for personal gain than the affluent, they argued, as a man who already owned a vast fortune would have less to gain from accepting a bribe. Liberal Republicans may have resented Southern elites for their Confederate past, yet these men also believed that these men represented the wealth, intellect, and culture of the South. Believing that these men were the region's natural leaders, some Republicans began to agree with Democrats who claimed that the disenfranchisement of Confederate leaders disrupted the natural process of democracy. When combined with elections that were administered by the army, they argued, the results would be contested by the losing side and violence would be more likely. One Northern visitor concluded that violence and corruption had only occurred because the federal government had placed "the control of affairs in the hands of the more ignorant classes," while the natural leaders of the region were barred from holding office.

These arguments about the "ignorant classes" were usually tinged with racism. White Southerners believed that permitting black men to vote and hold public office was intolerable. The majority of black public officials held minor posts at the local level, and South Carolina was the only state where black men held the majority of seats in the state legislature. Yet to many whites, the election of a black sheriff was even more intolerable than a high-ranking political official. From their perspective, victories by

Civil Rights Act of 1875

A law passed by Congress that outlawed racial discrimination in hotels, restaurants, public transportation, and many other public spaces. The law was seldom enforced by the government, even after a number of African Americans sued business owners for discrimination. These cases culminated in a Supreme Court decision in 1883, with the high court declaring that the law itself was unconstitutional.

Amnesty Act of 1872

A law passed by Congress that removed voting restrictions from all former Confederates with the exception of a few hundred high-ranking leaders.

black candidates, many of whom had been slaves only a few years prior, was evidence that Reconstruction had loosed a dangerous revolution. Believing that their government no longer represented their interests, whites began to form their own shadow governments and paramilitary groups. Violence such as the Colfax Massacre became common throughout Louisiana and several other states following nearly every Republican victory during the early 1870s.

White Democrats, many of whom were Confederate leaders, used these prejudices to gain control of the state legislatures of Virginia, North Carolina, and Georgia prior to the Panic of 1873. White Democrats in Texas, Alabama, and Arkansas followed suit and seized control in the next two years. Most of these men ran on a platform that openly called for a return of white power. These politicians and their supporters called themselves **Redeemers**, a name reflecting their belief that a Democratic victory would "redeem" their communities from their present state of "negro domination." Black voters and the few whites who continued to support the Republicans faced violence in each of these states. In Mississippi, the Klan and White League waged a campaign of absolute terror. Because of violence and fraud, even Mississippi counties with large black majorities returned landslide victories for white Democrats in 1875. Republican appeals for protection from Washington fell on deaf ears as Northern politicians increasingly viewed any connection with the South as a political liability.

Whites in surrounding states vowed to replicate the **Mississippi Plan** of open violence and campaigns based on white supremacy to redeem their state. Horace Greeley's call for Southern blacks to stop demanding protection and "root, hog, or die" sounded like stern but fair advice from the Northern white perspective. But for the 4 million former slaves who literally risked their lives by voting, dying was more than a metaphor. When thousands of black men throughout the South stood up to white mobs who sought to seize power by the bullet rather than the ballot, Northern politicians backtracked even further. Massacres of unarmed former slaves had elicited sympathy in the past. Shootouts involving armed black men, even when they were members of state militias and local police forces, provoked the opposite response. From the perspective of many Northern whites, news of any violent confrontation involving black men with guns was evidence that Reconstruction had been a dangerous mistake.

Redeemers

White Southern Democrats who campaigned on a platform of white supremacy insisting on the need to liberate their states from the leadership of black men and those whites who supported the Republican Party.

Mississippi Plan

Is the name given to the use of violence and fraud to prevent African Americans from voting during the 1870s. Although these methods were used throughout the South they were most clearly demonstrated in the state of Mississippi.

FIGURE 1.18

This cartoon depicts collusion between a Wall Street financier, an Irish member of a Democratic political machine, and the founder of the Ku Klux Klan and former Confederate General Nathan Bedford Forest. In this image, the Irish are depicted as subhuman yet are also elevated by their partnership with men who are clearly depicted as "white" against African Americans. Together, these "whites" are crushing a black Union veteran and preventing him from casting his vote, presumably for the Republican Party.

The Redeemers understood that violent repression of black voters could not continue forever. Once they seized power in each of the Southern states, they passed laws that disenfranchised black voters. This took a degree of creativity because the Fourteenth and Fifteenth amendments clearly guaranteed the right to vote irrespective of race. One method the Redeemers concocted was a poll tax in which people had to pay a special tax to cast their ballot. Because most sharecroppers were seldom paid in cash, this provision kept the majority of poor Southerners away from the polls. The Redeemers also required literacy tests—subjective measures evaluated by white registrars who could simply declare that a black registrant failed without further explanation.

If administered evenly, poll taxes and literacy tests would have prevented millions of whites from voting. While many Redeemers represented the elite, they understood that it was important to maintain the support of the majority of Southerners who were poor whites. Redeemer creativity reached its pinnacle with the creation of a special exemption known as the **Grandfather Clause**. This law created an immunity from literacy tests for those men whose fathers or grandfathers were permitted to vote. On its face, the law appeared to guarantee the right to vote as a legacy from one generation to another. African Americans immediately understood the real intent of the law. Decades of enslavement and racial discrimination had prevented their ancestors from voting. As a result, while black men might be barred from the polls by the new requirements, whites could be "grandfathered in" by the Redeemer's laws.

4.4 Compromise of 1877

Corruption scandals kept the Republicans on the defensive throughout the 1870s, even as voters became increasingly concerned about the economy and progressively indifferent to the fate of former slaves. In 1875, the country was absorbed in the **Whiskey Ring** scandal involving government officials who accepted bribes from distillers in lieu of millions in taxes. In this political environment, few Northern politicians supported continued funding to guard the polls and monitor for possible anti-black violence in the South. The Republican retreat from Reconstruction is demonstrated by their refusal to challenge the Redeemers, as well as the nomination of a presidential candidate that opposed federal intervention on behalf of Southern blacks. In the 1860s, the Republican-dominated Congress refused to seat former Confederates, sent soldiers to protect the political rights of former slaves, and even dissolved state governments. Following their crushing defeat in the congressional elections in 1874, Republicans viewed further support for Reconstruction as political suicide and acted as if conditions in the South were not deteriorating.

In 1876, Republicans nominated Ohio Governor and Civil War hero **Rutherford B. Hayes**, largely because he was a Moderate who opposed using the power of the federal government to challenge the Redeemers. As governor, Hayes had confronted political corruption. As a candidate for the presidency, he expressed a desire to end to Reconstruction. Both of these positions appealed to many frustrated white voters. The Democrats responded by nominating a reform governor of their own, **Samuel Tilden** of New York. Tilden took on the infamous Tweed ring of New York City's Tammany Hall. Also similar to Hayes, Tilden vowed to end Reconstruction. Because both men spoke in favor of many of the same issues—limiting federal intervention in the South and eliminating corruption in Washington—the election itself offered little in the way of new ideas and quickly descended into empty slogans and personal attacks. Some Democrats advanced economic and ideological reasons to oppose the Republican-dominated governments of the South. However, their most effective tactic with white voters was their repeated appeal to racial prejudice. These same tactics were equally effective in places like Southern Ohio and Southern Indiana, where Democrats openly ran on platforms of white supremacy and even formed various "Anti-Negro" parties.

When the votes were counted, Tilden had won his home state of New York. He also won New Jersey, Connecticut, Indiana, and appeared to have also swept all of the former Confederate states. He won the popular vote by 250,000 votes and maintained a lead in the electoral vote by the count of 203 to 165. Republicans argued that the electoral results in Louisiana, Florida, and South Carolina—the only three states that were still controlled by the Republican Party—had been tainted by electoral fraud perpetrated by local Democratic leaders. Republicans claimed that Hayes actually won all three of these states, and that the actual result was 185 electoral votes for Hayes and 184 for Tilden.

Republican officials in Louisiana, Florida, and South Carolina disqualified enough Democratic ballots to allow Hayes to win each of these states. They provided strong evidence that the Democrats had indeed used fraud, violence, and intimidation to keep black voters away from the polls. They also found instances where local officials reported election results that provided more votes for the Democrats than the total number of registered voters within their district. If the election was run fairly and if all qualified voters had been permitted to participate, the Republicans argued, the election results throughout the South would have surely mirrored the heavy Republican victories of the last two presidential elections. The Democrats countered by arguing that these previous elections had been dominated by Republican fraud. They believed the original election returns were valid and declared Tilden the winner.

Grandfather Clause

An exemption from voting restrictions such as taxes and literacy tests for those whose grandfathers were able to vote. These laws were intended to disfranchise African Americans whose ancestors were not permitted to vote.

Whiskey Ring

A political scandal involving distillers who evaded taxes by bribing government officials.

Rutherford B. Hayes

A leading Union general during the Civil War and governor of Ohio, Rutherford B. Hayes was the Republican candidate for the presidency in 1876. He had won a contested election after the electoral votes of Louisiana, Florida, and South Carolina were awarded to him in a controversial decision known as the Compromise of 1877.

Samuel Tilden

A Democratic governor of New York who received a majority of popular votes during the presidential election of 1876. Samuel Tilden lost to Republican Rutherford Hayes in the Electoral College after three states that were originally awarded to him were awarded to Hayes instead.

For weeks, both sides dispensed accusations against the other. An official count of the votes needed to be completed in each locality, but the way these counts were administered could be heavily influenced by politics. The Republicans still held a majority in the Senate, and the Democrats held a majority in the House of Representatives. As a result it was unlikely that Congress would ever agree on a winner. Congress appointed a special committee of five Democrats, five Republicans, and five members of the Supreme Court who were expected to be nonpartisan. The committee conducted a formal investigation that uncovered widespread corruption waged by both sides. The Democrats probably had enough ballots claim victory, but it was clear that the Democrats had kept large numbers of African American voters from the polls throughout the South. Three of the Supreme Court justices on the committee were Republicans and two were Democrats, and they ended up voting along partisan lines along with the ten legislators. As a result, the three states in question were awarded to the Republicans.

The Democrats protested the decision, and some feared another civil war might occur. A number of leaders of both political parties held a series of secret meetings to try to resolve the conflict. Historians still do not know exactly what was said at these meetings, but it is clear that a deal was made. It appears that Democrats agreed they would not contest the election of Hayes in return for Republican assurances that the new president would agree to remove all federal troops from the South and declare that Reconstruction was over. It is also likely that Hayes agreed to appoint a Southerner to his cabinet and provide federal support for the construction of a railroad that would connect southern Texas to California.

FIGURE 1.19

A general who was wounded multiple times during the Civil War, Rutherford Hayes was known as a reform governor in Ohio before becoming the nineteenth president following the election of 1876.

FIGURE 1.20

The 1876 presidential election returns were highly contested. Black voters faced fraud and violence throughout the region, so a completely fair election might have resulted in a Republican victory in the contested states and others. At the same time, Democrats pointed out how unusual it was that the solid Democratic vote in the South prevailed in all but three states—the exact states that still had Republican administrations.

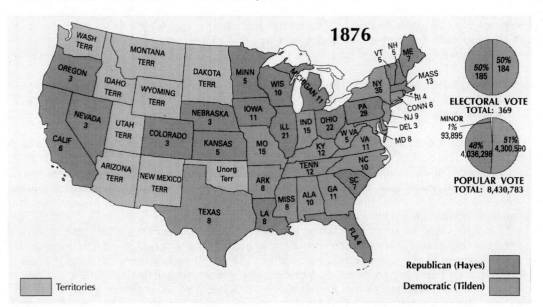

This secret agreement, known as the **Compromise of 1877**, is commonly referred to as the end of Reconstruction. In fact, this is the reason most US history surveys select the year 1877 as their starting or ending point. Students wishing to fully understand history should question the accuracy of precise dates when they involve complex issues. The Republican Party's retreat from Reconstruction occurred before 1877. At the same time, many Republican leaders continued to advocate greater federal intervention to protect former slaves in the years that followed. Others might argue that the election and any secret deal that may have followed had little impact on the removal of federal troops, considering both candidates desired an end to Reconstruction. In the end, perhaps only one conclusion is clear: African Americans were not consulted and did not consider Reconstruction to be settled by the Compromise of 1877. These men and women would continue to fight for a restoration of their rights under the Constitution, while the rest of the nation turned their attention to other matters.

Compromise of 1877

A secret arrangement where Democratic leaders are believed to have agreed not to contest Rutherford Hayes's election to the presidency in exchange for assurances that he would end Reconstruction and promote certain Southern causes.

REVIEW AND CRITICAL THINKING

1. What caused the Panic of 1873? How did economic conditions affect the politics of Reconstruction?

2. What were the provisions of the Civil Rights Act of 1875? Given the passage of this law, how did overt racial segregation persist for nearly a century after the law was passed?

3. Who were the Redeemers, and what did they wish to "redeem" their communities from? What strategies did they use to achieve power? Why did the North increasingly turn its back on the problems of the South and especially the continued injustices that were endured by African Americans?

4. Explain the Compromise of 1877. Some historians argue that Reconstruction demonstrates insincerity in Northern efforts to guarantee legal and political equality for African Americans. What arguments could one make to further this argument? What examples from the reading could be used to support the opposite perspective—that Reconstruction represented a genuine effort to make a transition from slavery to freedom?

5. What were the obstacles in achieving freedom for African Americans during Reconstruction, and how did they meet and/or fail to meet these challenges? How did whites and the federal government help or hinder this progress?

6. Was Reconstruction a success or a failure? How might one's perspective result in different answers to this question?

5. CONCLUSION

Americans considered Reconstruction to be a revolution half completed, although they differed in their beliefs regarding the desirability of the transformation the Radicals and former slaves had hoped to achieve. African Americans were free and legal restrictions against them such as the Black Codes had been removed. Most white Americans thought this was enough change for a dozen years. Some even hoped to reverse these changes and fabricated a mythical past where everyone, including the slaves themselves, were happier under the plantation system of the Old South. Others believed that measures such as the Civil Rights Act of 1875 mandated "reverse discrimination." They were convinced by demagogues that the law guaranteed that black women and men could claim a table in a restaurant or a seat on a train that had been given to a white person.

While few advocated a return to slavery, concerns about lingering issues of racial and economic inequality were harder to define and lacked the emotional certitude of chattel slavery. Black leaders and Northern journalists continued to document the plight of former slaves, but whites who wanted Reconstruction to be over increasingly convinced themselves racial discrimination had been eliminated when slavery ended. Believing otherwise might demand a greater commitment to Reconstruction and the investment of considerable resources. As a result, political leaders who celebrated the end of slavery as the end of the story swept into office, while those who reminded the public of the nation's failure to live up to its professed ideals were usually defeated.

If Reconstruction did not provide lasting freedom for all Americans, it was a time when Americans of diverse backgrounds challenged their second-class citizenship. The period saw the reconstruction of notions about gender as women formed organizations like the National Women's Suffrage Association (NWSA), pursued greater educational and career opportunities, formulated new ideas, and demonstrated on behalf of their right to vote. Immigrants and African Americans formed institutions such as churches, schools, fraternal societies, and political organizations that formed the core of their communities. These institutions built on traditions of extended family as former slaves and people from distant lands became brothers and sisters who accepted responsibility for the welfare of the larger community. The Constitution now embraced the idea of national citizenship, even if many sought to restrict the rights that citizenship conveyed. Lastly, Americans experienced the emergence of a larger, more active, and more powerful federal government. The nation's retreat from Reconstruction in the South did not result in the abandonment of federal influence. Instead, the government transitioned from using its power to promote the expansion of citizenship to promoting Western expansion and industrial growth. And while the federal government retreated from the South and abandoned African Americans, its power was increasingly harnessed along the new frontiers of the American West.

6. FURTHER READING

Butchart, Ronald E. *Schooling the Freed People: Teaching, Learning, and the Struggle for Black Freedom, 1861–1876* (2010).

DuBois, Ellen Carol. *Feminism and Suffrage: The Emergence of an Independent Women's Movement in America, 1848–1869* (1999).

Dudden, Faye E. *Fighting Chance: The Struggle over Woman Suffrage and Black Suffrage in Reconstruction America* (2011).

Foner, Eric. *Reconstruction: America's Unfinished Revolution, 1863–1877* (1988).

Keith, LeeAnna. *The Colfax Massacre: The Untold Story of Black Power, White Terror, and the Death of Reconstruction* (2008).

Richardson, Heather Cox. *West from Appomattox: The Reconstruction of America after the Civil War* (2007).

Schwalm, Leslie. *Emancipation's Diaspora: Race and Reconstruction in the Upper Midwest* (2009).

CHAPTER 2
Western Expansion, the New South, and Industrial America, 1870–1890

The era of Reconstruction was also a time of Western expansion and industrial growth. For some Americans, issues that continued to divide the nation inspired their Western trek. For others, it was the promise of landownership and economic independence that led them to the West. The Homestead Act of 1862 provided free land to help settlers establish farms. However, not everyone who would have liked to take advantage of the Homestead Act had the resources to move their families, build a home, and establish a farm. For these individuals, the growth of industry provided employment and even the potential for modest upward mobility. Migrants from Europe also hoped to establish farms, many seeking what they hoped would be temporary jobs in the great cities of the East before moving on to the Great Plains of the West. For others, it was the Great Lakes and the clusters of ethnic farm communities that inspired their migration. Immigrants also arrived on the West Coast from Asia and established their communities among Anglo and Hispanic settlers. Old prejudices greeted the new Americans on both coasts and throughout the interior. However, the potential of these immigrants as laborers and customers tempered their reception.

Railroads, coal mines, oil refineries, steel mills, and factories recognized that the success of America's industrial revolution was dependent on population growth. Massive corporations emerged during the 1870s and 1880s, each creating national networks of production and finance that forever changed their respective industries. Politics also followed the trend of nationalization. Local and state government remained the focal point of US politics. However, the growing importance of national corporations and national transportation networks led many to call on the federal government to perform some of the regulatory functions that had previously been reserved to the states. The federal government continued its tradition of minimal involvement in the economy at this time. However, a growing chorus emerged from factories and farms, demanding intervention on behalf of workers and small farmers.

For those who viewed the millions of acres of Western land as a commodity to be exploited, the cattle drives, homesteads, and railroad grants were ways of accelerating commercial development. These individuals celebrated the tenacity of homesteaders and cowboys, as well as the audacious spirit of western railroad barons and town boosters. Together, these diverse elements gave shape to the most dramatic population shift in US history. From the perspective of Native Americans who already lived in the West and viewed land as a collective resource, the actions of these individuals constituted an attack on their way of life. The view that land was intrinsically valuable irrespective of "improvements," such as homesteads and railroads, carried little influence in the minds of government and business leaders. As had been the case throughout the nation's past, Native Americans lacked access to the same level of material resources. As a result, they waged a fighting retreat against federal troops and the millions of predominantly Anglo settlers that migrated west. Theirs was a narrative of both victimization and resistance, both a woeful tale and an inspirational story of courage and free agency against overwhelming odds.

1. NATIVE AMERICANS AND THE TRANS-MISSISSIPPI WEST

LEARNING OBJECTIVES

1. Explain the process by which the federal government removed Native Americans to reservations between the 1860s and 1880s.
2. Summarize the ways in which Native Americans resisted removal and assimilation. Explain the obstacles that tribes faced in their struggle to retain sovereignty.
3. Describe the perspective of reformers who sought to promote assimilation. Explain the impact of the Dawes Act on Native Americans and its place within the larger narrative of US history.

1.1 Removal from the Great Plains

The land so coveted—both by those who were arriving in North America during the 1870s and 1880s and by the descendants of earlier immigrants—was part of an ever-shrinking Permanent Indian Frontier. The frontier stretched from the eastern Great Plains to the edge of the West Coast. These lands had originally been guaranteed to Native American tribes in exchange for their acceptance of their forced exclusion from lands east of the Mississippi River. Before the end of the Civil War, however, some of the original treaties with natives were being "renegotiated" to satisfy the wants of land speculators and fulfill the needs of landless farmers. In addition, little effort was made to coordinate the forced migration of Eastern tribes with those tribes that already occupied the Great Plains. As a result, numerous conflicts placed various tribes in opposition to one another in ways that reduced the likelihood of cooperation and Pan-Indian identity.

The Great Plains region was a melting pot long before settlers of Anglo, Asian, and African descent arrived in large numbers following the Civil War. The northern plains were home to a variety of tribes, many of whom were part of the great Sioux nation and spoke similar languages. The tribes of the central plains migrated throughout the region, while the Five Civilized Tribes of the southeast had been driven to reservations in present-day Oklahoma. Most tribes that were native to the Great Plains maintained migratory lifestyles, while some such as the Pawnee built and maintained lodges. Others such as the Cheyenne and Lakota Sioux had adopted the horse centuries before Anglo settlement and were migratory hunters of bison and other game.

FIGURE 2.1

An Oglala Sioux standing in front of his home on the Pine Ridge Reservation in South Dakota. This area was home to a diverse number of tribes, many of whom were not originally from the northern Great Plains.

Few Anglos perceived the differences between the various communities and tribal federations throughout the plains. Many also failed to recognize that groups such as the Pawnee and Lakota each contained many independent tribes. The misperception was not simply an accident. Recognition of the diversity and sovereignty of thousands of tribes stood in the way of the federal government's goal of devising a few treaties that might bind all native peoples to its policy of removal. As a result, the practice of generalizing native life and culture within a given region is tangled within the exploitative practices of the past. While recognizing the liabilities of the task, the historian must still attempt to offer the public a basic overview of life on the plains prior to Western expansion.

Most native societies revolved around communal concepts of life and work that emphasized the tribe as an extended family. Natives constructed their own notions about the separate sphere between male and female roles in society and the family. In general, they established gendered concepts of work with certain tasks being divided among men and women. Many tribes were matrilineal, meaning that men were absorbed into their bride's extended family network and women were recognized as leaders within the home. Women were deeply respected and in charge of many essential aspects of tribal life, such as farming and the home and hearth. Even in matrilineal societies, tribal leadership of religious and political activities was usually dominated by men. One exception was that women often held a prominent role in diplomacy, which was viewed as an extension of kinship.

Tradition, cooperation, and conflict typified native political life and determined the area a particular tribe inhabited. As a result, the idea of legal ownership of the land itself remained a foreign concept to most tribes. At the same time, natives adopted their own notions of land as property when the territories guaranteed to them by agreements with other tribes of treaties with the federal government were in danger. Violence between various groups of Native Americans was not uncommon and opportunities for conflict between tribes increased as more groups were forced westward. The result of each tribal removal led to conflicts between the new arrivals and Native Americans in the West regarding an ever-shrinking amount of resources and land.

The concept of communal rather than personal property, along with frequent migration of Plains Indians, eliminated the drive for acquisition that dominated the lives of Anglo settlers. These tribes had little incentive to plant more crops or kill more animals than they needed to survive. Although trade networks had operated for centuries, the nature of this trade changed rapidly following the arrival of Anglo settlers and modern transportation networks. What appeared as scarcity and privation to Anglos was a lifestyle that allowed natives to spend large portions of their day on their own terms. In fact, many natives considered their lives much richer than those who worked for a wage or spent their entire lives growing wheat for distant cities. Anglo settlers moved to the West in hopes of a better life, yet they enjoyed little time for family and leisure because they replicated the habits of acquisition that dominated their prior lives.

Only belatedly did some settlers recognize that Native American concepts of property and family might have enriched their lives. For example, in the 1920s a former cowpuncher recalled a conversation he had with a Sioux elder in the days before the extinction of the great herds of bison. The men shared a bottle and a fire, exchanging stories of their youths with the occasional nostalgia and creativity that usually accompany old men, whiskey, and campfires. The old ranch hand was deeply impressed by the life his Indian companion described. The days of the Sioux elder had been spent following buffalo herds and enjoying the day's labor of hunting and fishing. The Sioux recalled his life and being full of time with his extended family with "no trouble or worries" beyond their daily needs, which nature provided for them. "I wish I'd been a Sioux Indian a hundred years ago," the ranch hand reflected. "They've been living in heaven for a thousand years and we took it away from 'em for forty dollars a month."

Ranch hands like this cowpuncher were often hired to exterminate the buffalo herds and build fences to clear land for commodity-based agriculture. Because of these actions and the introduction of railroads, settlers, and new species onto the plains, the bison population dwindled from millions to a few hundred by the late 1870s. For native tribes whose economies were based around the bison, depletion of the herds represented an act of extermination. The destruction of bison was perceived as necessary by the government because it had already determined that the Great Plains should be divided and distributed to Anglo farmers. The railroad would connect these farms to the population centers of the East and West, creating a national market economy that was incompatible with roving bison herds and the natives who followed them.

In 1865, chairman of the Senate's Indian Affairs Committee James Doolittle described the options regarding Native Americans as he saw them to a Denver audience. He argued that the best solution was to force natives onto reservations for their own "protection." For Doolittle, the only other possibility was to exterminate the entire native population. As soon as he mentioned this opinion, the audience went wild. "There suddenly arose such a shout as is never heard unless upon some battlefield," an observer recalled. "Exterminate them! Exterminate them!" The creation of such venomous anti-Indian sentiment made nearly any plan short of genocide appear progressive. As a result, the **Bureau of Indian Affairs** was able to present the reservation system as an act of generosity and humanity.

Two major treaties were passed in 1867 and 1868, forcing many tribal leaders to accept the reservation system in exchange for the promise that this land would be theirs forever. The Medicine Lodge Treaty of 1867 forced the relocation of the Plains Apache, Kiowa, Comanche, Arapaho, and Cheyenne to lands in Indian Territory (present-day Oklahoma). The tribes were granted permanent ownership of these lands unless another treaty was made and three-fourths of a tribe's adult male population approved the new treaty. The Medicine Lodge Treaty obligated the government to protect tribal lands from encroachment and provide certain payments and support for the development of schools and farms. In return, the signers (but not necessarily all of the various native tribes affected) pledged to peacefully abandon all claims on their present lands. They also promised to accept the construction of railroads and military posts in their new homelands while abiding by the decisions of federal agents assigned to them.

The Fort Laramie Treaty of 1868 granted ownership of land throughout northern Nebraska, the Dakotas, Wyoming, and Montana to the Lakota, Arapahoe, and Dakota tribes under similar terms. This treaty also obligated the government to provide material support, assistance with the development of agriculture, and resources for schools and other provisions. Unknown to the federal government at the time, the lands "given" to Native Americans in the Fort Laramie Treaty included valuable natural resources including gold. Years later, this discovery would soon test the goodwill of the federal

Bureau of Indian Affairs

An agency of the federal government established in 1824 and charged with the responsibility of managing Native American lands and meeting the treaty obligations of the US government. The bureau was notorious for its treatment of natives in its early history but attempts to be a more progressive organization that promotes tribal sovereignty while providing valuable services.

government regarding their pledge to uphold and protect native title to mineral-rich lands in the Black Hills of South Dakota.

Many natives rejected these treaties, pointing out that they were signed by individuals with no authority to make binding decisions for all native people. Others protested that their leaders signed the treaties under duress and were forced to choose self-preservation over justice. Thousands of natives rejected the treaties and refused to be bound by their terms. However, the majority of natives felt they had no other viable alternative but accept the modest payment the government offered. Unlike treaties with foreign governments, these payments were not in cash. Instead, the government provided annual stipends of basic provisions. Natives were not permitted to control the distribution of these provisions, which made many natives dependent on the government. Many families and tribes vowed to continue their way of life the best they could in their new homes. However, without the resources to recreate their ways of life, many natives became dependent on federal stipends.

President Andrew Johnson cared little for the fate of Native Americans, although some of his successors such as Ulysses S. Grant expressed occasional regret for the crimes committed against "peaceful" tribes who accepted the reservation system. At best, Grant viewed the nation's dealings with natives as dishonorable but could not conceive an alternative to the reservation system. Many of Grant's former colleagues in the military saw Indian affairs from a different perspective. Several of the leading Native American tribes in the central plains had formed an alliance with the Confederacy during the Civil War, believing their goal of sovereignty would be better served by a Confederate victory. These native tribes were among the last to surrender, pointing out that their grievances with the Union were not the same as the Confederate government in Richmond. In addition, a handful of Native Americans in Oklahoma, such as the Cherokees, had practiced slavery. As a result, many officers in the US Army projected their views of the Confederacy on these tribes and on Native Americans in general. Many in the federal government cited the collusion of a handful of native and Confederate leaders as a pretense to justify any policy toward native tribes. For others, the frequent skirmishes between natives and federal troops stationed throughout the West constituted evidence that natives were enemies. By this perspective, native people were the last remnants of a vanquished foe and a permanent threat to the well-being of the United States and its citizens.

FIGURE 2.2

A contemporary artist's rendition of clothing being "given" to natives under the terms of the Medicine Lodge Treaty of 1867. Although this treaty granted permanent ownership of most of the Great Plains, its terms were later altered and its signatories were forced onto smaller sections of land.

ISSUE OF CLOTHING TO THE COMANCHE INDIANS AT TIMBER MOUNTAIN FORK, KANSAS.

1.2 Encroachment and Resistance

Eastern settlers in search of land and mineral wealth soon began to trespass on lands granted to natives by the 1867 and 1868 treaties. In 1871, Congress declared that the federal government would no longer form treaties with natives. Although they guaranteed existing treaties would be honored, the new thinking of congressional leaders and the federal courts reflected the belief that natives were conquered people. In the next three decades, the Supreme Court issued a series of judgments that effectively gave the government the power to modify any treaty with or without the consent of Native Americans. For example, Congress declared that federal agents had jurisdiction over Native American tribal governments in matters of law enforcement—even on tribal lands. This change was justified by the need to "protect" natives by granting federal agents the ability to pursue criminals who crossed into their reservations. Natives protested that the law was actually intended to empower the military to capture native leaders. Before 1885 when this change was made, participants in resistance movements might find asylum on a nearby reservation where the authority of the army and federal marshals was unclear.

The ability of the federal government to unilaterally alter treaties led to wide-scale abuses. The Supreme Court upheld most of these treaty violations, declaring that reservations were now "local dependent communities" instead of "domestic dependent nations," as previously recognized. By the turn of the century, the Supreme Court declared natives to be "dependent wards." This meant that natives were subject to the authority and care of the federal government, much like the relationship of orphaned children to local governments. As a result, any treaty could be altered by Congress without the input of tribal governments. In fact, because those governments represented "dependent communities," whatever authority over their own reservations they enjoyed derived from Congress could be removed at any time.

These court decisions provided the facade of legitimacy for many events that had already occurred. They also legitimized future encroachments on Native American lands. In most instances, the Medicine Lodge and Fort Laramie treaties were simply ignored if they were an inconvenience for land speculators and mining companies. The treaties were especially inconvenient for prospectors who discovered gold in the Black Hills of South Dakota. In response to native claims that white settlers were trespassing on their lands, the federal government sent troops and began to seize the Black Hills through force. The government then demanded that the Lakota Sioux abandon these lands and sent the army to coerce them into accepting the new arrangement. In 1876, a brash junior officer named George Armstrong Custer violated orders in hopes of winning a name for himself. Custer ordered his men to advance on the Lakota rather than await reinforcements. It was a decision that would cost him his life.

If notoriety was Custer's goal, he succeeded at least on that regard. Custer's name remains infamous among scholars of Native American history and students of military tactics. The hasty officer divided his men in hopes of surrounding what he assumed was a small contingent of Lakota Sioux. Separated from his supporting columns, Custer assumed his men were moving in and about to surround the Sioux on all sides. Without adequate preparation for reconnaissance or communication, Custer ordered a fatal charge into what turned out to be a sizable force of warriors led by the Lakota Sioux spiritual leader **Sitting Bull**. Every one of Custer's men who participated in his initial attack was killed. Custer was clearly the aggressor in the Battle of the Little Bighorn and responsible for the slaughter of over 250 US soldiers and Native American scouts who were employed by the army. However, the same collective amnesia that led white Southerners to believe that the Klan had acted in defense led most Americans at this time to blame "Indian savagery" for the resulting massacre. For the first seventy years, the historical interpretation of Little Bighorn was dominated by this perspective. In more recent times, most historians agree with Sitting Bull's contemporary assessment that the Lakota Sioux acted in self-defense while Custer "was a fool who rode to his death."

FIGURE 2.3

"If we must die…we die defending our rights" Lakota Sioux spiritual leader Sitting Bull became a wartime leader under which multiple tribes united to resist forced removal. True to his name, which refers to the strength of an intractable bison, Sitting Bull refused to capitulate until he was killed by authorities who had been sent to arrest him.

Sitting Bull

Lakota Sioux spiritual leader who united multiple tribes and resisted forced removal through a variety of methods, including armed resistance. Sitting Bull is most famous for his leadership in defeating George Armstrong Custer at the Battle of Little Bighorn.

FIGURE 2.4

This map demonstrates Custer's attempt to surround the Sioux at the Battle of Little Bighorn. Because of faulty reconnaissance, Custer's column charged into a superior force of Lakota Sioux warriors without the support of the other two columns of cavalry.

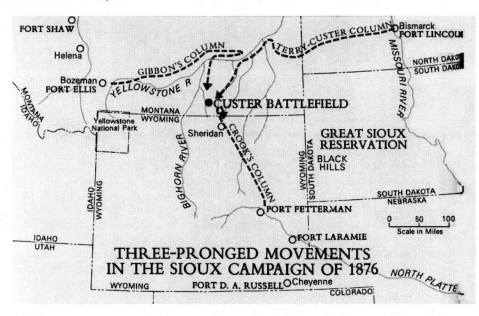

In Northern California, the final act of armed resistance occurred in the Modoc War of 1873. The Modoc people had been forced from their lands and onto a reservation in southern Oregon that was controlled by the Klamath. The two tribes had been rivals throughout their history, which led to numerous conflicts once the Modocs were placed on the Klamath reservation. At several times, groups of Modoc left the reservation and attempted to return to their traditional home in Northern California. Each time they were forced to return. Between the winter of 1872 and spring of 1873, a group of fifty Modoc warriors and their families left the reservation under the leadership of Kientpoos (known to Anglos as "Captain Jack"). The army sent hundreds of soldiers to compel these Modoc to return. However, the unique terrain surrounding Tule Lake provided cover for the Modoc. Moving between caves and trenches formed from ancient lava flows, the Modoc inflicted heavy casualties despite being outnumbered by multiples as large as ten to one.

President Grant intervened in what has been called the Modoc War, believing a peace commission could end the conflict. However, the government refused to consider creating a separate reservation for the Modoc in California—a request the Modoc had made for several decades. Aware that their request for autonomy would continue to be denied, the Modoc ambushed and killed several of the negotiators. In response, the army redoubled its efforts to round up the Modoc and soon captured several tribal leaders who had been responsible for the murder of the negotiators. These men agreed to betray Kientpoos, who was soon captured and executed. The rest of the Modoc were forced to return to the Klamath reservation.

In the Southwest, 8,000 Navajos had been forced to walk four hundred miles to a reservation in New Mexico in 1864. This episode, known as the Long Walk, was soon followed by the forced removal of non-Navajo tribes such as the Hopi onto the same reservation. Similar conflicts between other tribes forced to share land and scarce resources divided other natives in New Mexico against one another. Others, such as the Apaches, directed their efforts against Anglo settlers. After decades of fighting against US and Mexican troops along the present border of New Mexico, Arizona, and the Mexican border, many Apaches accepted an agreement made between an Apache leader named Cochise and the federal government. This agreement led to the relocation of the Apaches to a reservation in southern Arizona. While they recognized the situation that forced Cochise to make such an agreement, other Apache leaders such as **Geronimo** refused to be bound by the agreement. Geronimo was perhaps the most feared of all Apache leaders, but even he was forced to accept the US reservation system after years of relentless pursuit by federal troops.

Geronimo and a small band of his supporters soon found reservation life unacceptable. Chief among their complaints was a long list of unfulfilled promises that federal agents had made to them. In 1885, Geronimo led a group of warriors and their families who escaped the reservation as if breaking free from a prison. The federal government pursued these men, women, and children for over a year. Both the Apaches and federal troops committed dozens of atrocities against civilians during this time. For example, Geronimo's band killed a number of white settlers they encountered out of fear that their hiding places would be revealed. Geronimo soon became the most vilified Indian leader among Anglos, but his style of leadership aroused a variety of reactions among natives. By 1886, Geronimo's band was trapped by federal troops and surrendered peacefully under a promise that they would be granted a new reservation. Instead, these families were placed inside cattle cars and shipped to a federal prison in Florida. Geronimo himself spent most of his remaining years in federal prisons. By the turn of the century, a new perspective on history led to a partial vindication of Geronimo's fight against the federal government. Although never permitted to return to the land he fought for, Geronimo spent the last years of his life as both a celebrity and a curiosity on display at various world's fairs and other exhibitions.

The Nez Perce of the Pacific Northwest also divided on the question of whether to accept the reservation system. Originally inhabiting 13 million acres on land presently belonging to Idaho, Washington, and Oregon, the Nez Perce were forced to accept a reservation that declined in size from the 1850s through the 1870s. In 1877, hundreds of Nez Perce living in the Wallowa River Valley of Oregon rejected their forced relocation to a reservation in present-day Idaho. These Nez Perce traveled in search of other tribes who might join their struggle. They found few who would join them or even offer sanctuary in what would later be named the Nez Perce War. In reality, the "war" was an exodus and a series of strategic retreats as the Nez Perce searched in vain for allies and ultimately decided to flee to Canada. The Nez Perce might have succeeded in forming a significant alliance as they traveled through Idaho, Wyoming, and Montana had it not been for the actions of some of the younger members of the Nez Perce band. After a confrontation led to a shootout, several ranchers were killed and the Nez Perce was pursued by 2,000 cavalry.

Geronimo

An Apache leader who resisted the reservation system by leading a band that left its Arizona reservation and evaded capture until 1886. Few of Geronimo's followers were permitted to return to their original reservation. Geronimo himself was a captive who was vilified until later in his life when he was viewed as a curiosity by Anglo society.

FIGURE 2.5

Geronimo and some of his supporters on their way to prison in Florida in 1886. Geronimo's son is sitting next to his father on the front row in the bottom right corner of this photo.

The cavalry decided that the Nez Perce's escape would present a threat to the reservation system and pursued the tribe. The Nez Perce fought a strategic retreat through 1,100 miles of rugged terrain under the informal leadership of **Chief Joseph**. Together, this small band fought a number of battles as the Nez Perce tried to evade capture by the Seventh Cavalry. Although their Appaloosa horses gave them an advantage in speed over their pursuers, federal troops outnumbered the Nez Perce by a three-to-one margin and the warriors were eventually cornered and surrendered. Chief Joseph recognized that even if his people reached Canada, they would never be permitted to live as they once had. In hopes of discouraging future rebellions, the US Army forcibly removed the surviving Nez Perce to land near Fort Leavenworth and slaughtered the Appaloosa horses. By the time the Nez Perce were permitted to reunite with family members on their reservation in the Northwest, most had perished in what was to them a foreign land.

1.3 The Dawes Act and Assimilation

Henry Knox, the secretary of war during the American Revolution, was part of a group of individuals who were concerned about the welfare of Native Americans. However, he did not believe that the natives' traditional way of life was sustainable and seldom considered native perspectives. These self-appointed reformers believed Native Americans could become "civilized" through **assimilation**—the process of a group adopting the cultural beliefs and norms of the dominant group. While these reformers may have been ethnocentric by modern standards, it is important to remember that most Americans at this time believed natives would simply decline in numbers until they disappeared. At the very least, most believed that efforts to assimilate indigenous people into the dominant culture of Anglo America was an act of kindness based on a naively optimistic view about the capacities and character of natives. Some even subscribed to "scientific" theories about evolution that sanitized the decline of native populations as some sort of "natural" selection. As a result, even though the majority of Americans distanced themselves from rhetoric calling for immediate annihilation of indigenous people, they viewed their extinction as inevitable.

Secretary Knox criticized this view as "more convenient than just" given the desire of Anglos to occupy the lands these tribes occupied. After the Civil War, a small contingent of Anglo reformers such as **Helen Hunt Jackson** agreed. Jackson documented the ways that the federal government had chosen convenience over justice. Jackson's 1881 book *A Century of Dishonor* detailed the long history of the federal government's forcible seizure of native lands. Using archival research, Jackson exposed the government's failure to abide by its own treaties, which it had forced natives to sign when those treaties became inconvenient.

Jackson explained how the reservation system disrupted traditional ways of life for various tribes. However, she was a product of her time and did not support the preservation of native cultures and way of life. Accepting the dominant view of most Anglo reformers, Jackson favored assimilation rather than a return to a lifestyle she equated with barbarism. In fact, Jackson's book criticized the reservation system not only because of the history of injustice surrounding its inception but also because she believed the reservation system perpetuated "uncivilized" traditions and delayed assimilation. In short, Jackson and other like-minded reformers believed the only hope for Native America was to adopt Anglo culture and economic practices such as farming and semiskilled labor. Jackson's book became a national bestseller and more non-Indians began to share her perspective. Eventually, reformers found a way to combine their goals for assimilation with the land hunger of the dominant Anglo majority.

The resulting convergence of interests led to a policy of accelerating assimilation and opening more land for "American" settlement. The **Dawes Act** of 1877 placed Native Americans on small farming plots taken from existing reservations. The law mandated an end to communal property, dividing reservation lands into individual plots that were "given" to each head of household or individual. From the white perspective, the Dawes Act was incredibly generous. Native Americans were being granted free land just as the homesteaders were. Natives would also be given assistance in learning how to adopt "American" methods of farming.

From the native perspective, however, the Dawes Act was the final assault on their way of life. Natives pointed out that dividing the land in this method prevented them from hunting. It also ended their communal lifestyle that was the basis of their social, economic, and religious ways of life. They also demonstrated that the law's methods of distributing land (averaging 160 acres per family) conveniently resulted in millions of acres of "surplus" land. Once the family plots were assigned, the rest of the former reservation would become property of the federal government who would then redistribute the land to Anglo settlers. Within only two years of applying the Dawes Act to a handful of reservations, the government controlled 12 million acres of former Indian lands. The congressmen who approved the law understood the potential benefit of using its terms to acquire more land, but few were as forthright about the Dawes Act as Colorado senator Henry Teller. "The real aim of this bill is to get at the Indian lands," Teller exclaimed. "If this were being done in the name of Greed it would be bad enough; but to do it in the name of humanity is the worst inhumanity."

Chief Joseph

A leader of a band of Nez Perce Indians who resisted forcible relocation from their lands in the Wallowa River Valley of Oregon. In 1877, these Nez Perce traveled through present-day Idaho, Wyoming, and Montana in search of allies while being pursued by the Seventh Cavalry. After a number of battles, the Nez Perce accepted relocation to present-day Oklahoma.

assimilation

The process of making different items similar to one another. In human terms, this refers to the process of members of minority cultures becoming more like the members of the dominant culture.

Helen Hunt Jackson

A leading advocate of reforming the federal government's orientation toward Native Americans, Helen Hunt Jackson detailed the long history of broken treaties and fraud perpetrated against native tribes in her 1881 book *A Century of Dishonor*. She also wrote a novel that was directed toward popular audiences and told the story of the mistreatment of Native Americans in California.

Dawes Act

A law passed in 1887 for the stated purpose of encouraging assimilation among Native Americans. The Dawes Act authorized the government to divide a large number of existing reservations into individual family plots, with the remaining lands being transferred to the federal government.

FIGURE 2.6

A poster advertising "Indian Land" for sale. This circular requests that interested parties contact the supervisor of the nearest school operated by the Bureau of Indian Affairs for more information. In this and many other ways, schools operated on behalf of Native Americans facilitated Anglo settlement.

Natives utilized a variety of strategies to resist allotment. For example, the Prairie Potawatomi of Kansas simply ignored the boundaries of individual plots and continued to live communally on what remained of their former reservation. Various tribes also sought to work collectively to preserve their lands. In 1888, over twenty Indian nations met in a grand council and agreed to form a national tribal government that would represent their interests. The structure of this government permitted collective action in terms of diplomacy and defense of vital interests. It also maintained the independence of each tribe—a political structure not unlike the representation of states within the original federal government. However, the federal government saw such a confederation as a threat and federal agents prevented natives from leaving their reservations to attend future intertribal meetings. The government also responded with a forced sale of the lands belonging to some of the leading tribes of the proposed confederation. Some of these lands were reorganized into the new Territory of Oklahoma. Tribes that resisted allotment found that the federal aid they had been promised in exchange for their acquiescence to previous treaties and forced land sales was also withheld.

The application of the Dawes Act occurred irregularly, and many tribes were not forced to accept allotments for a number of years until their lands were desired by outside interests. This was the situation for the Ute Indians of northeastern Utah. Oil, gas, and other valuable natural resources were discovered on their lands near the turn of the century. As mining companies moved into the area, the Utes were suddenly forced to accept allotment onto the least desirable lands within their reservation. After their protests were ignored, hundreds of Utes simply left the reservation altogether in 1906. They had hoped to find new homes in South Dakota among allied Sioux. However, they found that the Sioux had also been forced to accept allotment, and their lands were disappearing. Now homeless, the federal government responded by negotiating jobs for the displaced Utes. The men were put to work building the railroads that brought settlers to claim the lands they once controlled.

During the debate over the Dawes Act, Senator Teller cited examples through history where natives had been forced to abandon reservations that had been guaranteed to them in favor of small plots of land. He showed that in the majority of these cases, the policy failed and the individuals were forced to sell their nearly worthless land. "When thirty or forty years shall have passed and these Indians shall have parted with their title," Teller predicted, "they will curse the hand that was raised professedly in their defense." Teller's warning seemed clairvoyant in the decades that followed. An estimated 60 percent of natives who were forced to accept allotment lost control of their land within two generations. Tribes in Oklahoma that had been originally exempted from the terms of the Dawes Act soon saw their lands divided and redistributed under its terms.

REVIEW AND CRITICAL THINKING

1. How did Native American life on the Great Plains, the Southwest, and the West Coast change between 1860 and the 1880s? What challenges do academics face when they try to neatly summarize the experiences of native peoples?.

2. What were the legal terms that led to Native American removal and Anglo expansion into the Great Plains? What was the long-term effect of these treaties?

3. What led to conflict between the Lakota Sioux and the US government in the 1870s? How did the historic memory of the "last stand" of George Armstrong Custer change in the past century and a half?

4. Summarize and compare the experiences of various tribes you read about such as the Lakota Sioux, Prairie Pottawatomi, Modoc, Apache, Nez Perce, Utes, and Navajo. What variables might account for the varied experiences of each of these tribes?

5. Explain the perspective of reformers such as Helen Hunt Jackson? What was assimilation, and why might this goal be viewed differently today than it was in her time? Was Jackson genuinely concerned about Native Americans? What might have limited her perspective?

6. What was the Dawes Act, and why did Native Americans share a different perspective regarding its provisions than the dominant society? How did various tribes resist the Dawes Act?

2.   WINNING AND LOSING THE WEST

LEARNING OBJECTIVES

1. Explain the importance of homesteading and railroads in Western history. Describe the importance of cattle drives and barbed wire to the development of agriculture and ranching.
2. Compare the experiences of racial and ethnic minorities in the North and West to the challenges faced by African Americans in the South. How were the strategies used by each of these groups related? Why did whites in these regions discriminate against ethnic and racial minorities while remaining critical of white Southerners for limiting the freedoms of former slaves?
3. Identify the various strategies used by suffragists during the 1870s and 1880s. Analyze the arguments and strategies of leading women's rights advocates. Analyze the reasons that some women sought to work within nineteenth-century notions about gender while others were more radical and sought to overturn these notions.

2.1   Homesteaders and Railroads

The **Homestead Act of 1862** took effect on January 1 of the following year, the same day as the Emancipation Proclamation. For many Americans, both laws seemed to promise liberation. For millions of families, homesteads provided a path to independence through landownership, just as emancipation brought deliverance from bondage and the hope of economic independence. For many, the hardships of life on the Great Plains and a life as a Southern sharecropper offered something less than freedom. The dangers of the Western trek were nothing compared to the trials of former slaves who first tested the Emancipation Proclamation. However, homesteaders who headed west and former slaves who labored in the South shared a common faith that hard work and eventual landownership was the path to achieving the promise of freedom in America.

Horace Greeley was not the first to exhort the young men of his nation to "Go West." However, his voice as editor of the New York *Weekly Tribune* carried the most influence. Both as a journalist and presidential candidate in 1872, Greeley expressed the belief held by millions of Americans that Western expansion would act as a "safety valve" for US cities. The option of leaving the city permitted laborers who could not find decent employment or decent housing the option of starting anew in the "salubrious and fertile West." By removing millions of unemployed and underemployed urban workers, Greeley's **safety-valve theory** suggested, Western expansion would also benefit workers who remained in the cities by reducing the number of workers. As a result, the law of supply and demand would operate in favor of workers who could demand better pay and conditions as employers competed with one another for labor.

Western expansion would succeed where industrial unions and urban reform organizations had failed, many promoters of the West believed. Unscrupulous factory owners would lose their employees and slums would clear themselves, Western boosters predicted. Employers and cities would be compelled to create attractive working and living conditions that would rival the prosperous and "salubrious" life of the homesteader. Eastern businesses would also benefit from Western expansion, Greeley and others argued. Western expansion would create new markets for manufactured goods in America's interior. Believing in this synergistic relationship between rural expansion, urban renewal, and commercial opportunity, national leaders backed legislation that transferred a billion acres of Western land to homesteaders and railroad developers between the 1860s and 1890s.

Of these billion acres, only 30 percent were granted under the terms of the Homestead Act and other government initiatives that provided free land. The most desirable lands were sold or granted to developers. The rest were distributed to homesteaders who were required to build homes and clear fields, thereby "improving" the land. In addition, homesteaders were required to pay a small fee at the land office when they filed for the deed. The other 700 million acres of Western land were purchased, usually by those who had the financial means to secure fertile lands that were near a navigable river or railroad. The federal government relied on these land sales in an era before federal income tax and toleration for large budget deficits beyond financing wars. Given the importance of land sales, many were concerned that the government's practice of granting free land to railroad companies to spur construction was a form of graft.

Homestead Act of 1862

A law encouraging Western migration by granting sections of federal lands that were west of the Mississippi River so long as certain conditions were met. Chief among these conditions was that settlers "improve" the land by cultivating fields and building homes and utility buildings.

safety-valve theory

A name given by historians to the idea that Western expansion would benefit the leading cities and established rural districts of the East by providing an alternative to wage labor. Without such a "safety valve," tensions would grow as farmland and jobs became increasingly scarce.

First Transcontinental Railroad

Financed largely by an 1864 grant of federal lands to the Union Pacific and Central Pacific railroads. The two companies built track between Omaha, Nebraska, and Sacramento, California. San Francisco and Oakland were connected with the East and South when both lines were completed in 1869. Ogden, Utah, served as the connection point between the two rail lines.

In 1864, Congress granted twenty sections of free land for every single mile of track constructed by the builders of the **First Transcontinental Railroad**, which would stretch from Omaha to the California coast. The federal government essentially cosigned the railroad's bonds and also granted the railroad millions of acres of free land that they could sell as they built track. The commercial value of these lands increased significantly as they built the track, providing a constant stream of revenue to the developers as they moved west. In addition to the land sales, the Union Pacific and Central Pacific would completely own and control the track the government subsidized. Although the phrase "corporate welfare" would not come into common usage for another century, it seemed to many as if the federal government had shouldered the risk for the private companies that built the railroads by backing their bonds and then went a step further by giving these companies millions of acres of land. The federal government would eventually grant over 100 million acres to various railroads throughout the West, a fact that concerned many would-be settlers.

Given the state of American finance in the mid-nineteenth century, however, few other ways were available to finance a railroad line of this magnitude. American investors and companies did not have the kinds of resources to finance the construction of a transcontinental railroad. Congress recognized that its land reserves were the only resource the federal government controlled that could be used to finance the completion of such a mammoth project. Without access to a railroad, these lands had little commercial value. In fact, these isolated lands could scarcely be given away as homesteads. However, once a single railroad line connected the West Coast with the East Coast and the Great Plains, the total value of the lands the government still controlled in the vicinity of that railroad line would suddenly become quite valuable. Upon completion of the First Transcontinental Railroad, millions of acres of government land throughout the West would eventually be served by feeder railroads that would connect the hinterlands to the main line. The government's willingness to give away these lands to spur railroad construction also spurred land sales and resulted in far greater revenue for the government in the long run. The railroad network that grew from the First Transcontinental Railroad allowed the government to sell rather than give away the majority of its lands throughout the West.

FIGURE 2.7

This photo of homesteaders in Nebraska in 1886 demonstrates the pride that pioneer families took in the homes and farms that they built.

Those who could afford to purchase land near the railroads had the best chance of creating a financially successful farm. However, the majority of Americans could not afford land near railroads. Free land could still be acquired through homestead grants until the 1880s, but these lands were generally of marginal value and isolated. Those with modest resources developed these fields in anticipation of the day when a railroad might be built in the general vicinity. These farmers joined with boosters of nearby towns and pooled their scarce resources to purchase local railroad bonds under promises of repayment and the construction of feeder lines that would connect their farms to the market economy. In these instances, farm families, local merchants, and real estate boosters mortgaged their futures together in hopes that a railroad would bring wealth to their community.

If successful, farm and real estate values increased dramatically, while the holders of the bonds could look forward to repayment of their investment with interest. In many cases, however, the local railroads were ill-conceived and inadequately financed. In such cases, the result was often bankruptcy for the railroad developers and a total loss for the hopeful investors. In dozens of instances throughout the 1880s and beyond, entire towns were built on the hopes of railroad access. Many of these disappeared nearly overnight when it became clear that the railroad would not be built. Many area farmers were so poor they had no choice but to resign themselves to another season of transporting their grain by wagon. In other cases, buildings and homes were moved by wagon to the nearest town with railroad access. As a result, for every successful city created by the railroad, there were also several ghost towns.

FIGURE 2.8

By 1887, four transcontinental lines connected the West Coast with an expanding rail network throughout the Mountain West and Great Plains.

The workers who built the rails the commercial West was built on may have taken the greatest risks of all. Tens of thousands of construction workers migrated to America from China and Europe with little more than a hope to earn a decent wage and then return to their homelands. Others workers, particularly the Irish and African American laborers who were often recruited by the railroads had lived in the United States for generations. These men were joined by Anglo homesteaders who had lost everything, failed mining prospectors hoping to return home, and orphans barely tall enough to swing a hammer. As a result, the Union Pacific and Central Pacific work camps represented a cross-section of the developing nation. In some ways these camps were both melting pots and the most egalitarian of institutions, establishing pay scales based only on the amount of track built each day. Time-and-a-half bonuses were held as incentive for days when a certain number of miles were completed.

The consequence was both faulty construction and a pace of work that created old men and amputees as quickly as it built track. Under these circumstances, the First Transcontinental Railroad was completed when the westbound Union Pacific crews met with the eastbound Central Pacific on May 10, 1869, at Promontory Point, Utah. Congress soon approved a series of similar land grants that spurred construction of four other major rail lines. The Atchison, Topeka, and Santa Fe line connected Kansas City and the Missouri River Valley to the Southwest in the 1870s. The Southern Pacific linked New Orleans to Southern California in the same decade. The Northern Pacific connected Chicago with Portland in 1883. Ten years later, a fifth transcontinental line was completed even further north, connecting Seattle with the Great Lakes.

2.2   Cattle Drives to Ranching

The plains of South Texas were among the first areas cleared of bison. By the 1860s, they were home to millions of longhorn cattle. By the end of the Civil War, the nation's rail system extended to western Missouri—a distance of about eight hundred miles from the pastures of Texas. Responding to market forces, ranchers initiated cattle drives to transport beef from those pastures to the nearest rail terminus by hoof. A crew of a dozen cowboys could surround and drive several hundred cattle across the open prairie. From the railroad terminus, the cattle were shipped directly to butchers in urban markets. The drives were dangerous and dirty, especially for those cattlemen selected to ride at the back of the herds. As the years progressed, the railroad extended further west creating "cow towns" from Wichita, Kansas, to Greeley, Colorado, and eventually, Cheyenne, Wyoming, and Prescott, Arizona. Eventually, the residents of these towns would demand an end to the cattle drive. Despite the mythology that would later be created, the chief complaint of residents of the cattle towns was not bandits or brothels or any of the other form of human depravity. Instead, what was most dreaded by the farmers and ranchers of the Great Plains was a parasite that infected many of the herds in the Southwest and was transported north by the cattle drives. A quick survey of newspapers printed in Abilene City, Texas, and Dodge City, Kansas, during the 1870s will turn up very few gunfights. In their place will be hundreds of articles about the dreaded Texas cattle fever that infected local herds.

FIGURE 2.9

A cowboy prepares to drive a herd of cattle across the Great Plains. In the horizon, one of his fellow cowboys can be seen among hundreds of cattle.

Infectious bovine diseases failed to capture the imagination of urban America. Perhaps owing to the pervasiveness of human contagion in these communities, city dwellers disregarded these and other real-life dangers that made the West much like the rest of the nation. Instead, Easterners reveled in fictional accounts of high-noon gunfights, bandits, Indian raids, and the mythical cowboy. In reality, cattle town violence was not much different from that of violence in the big cities where most victims were found shot in the back or stabbed by thieves. In the lore created by dime novels, however, shootouts between bandits and sheriffs and the skill of drovers won the West. Over time, Old West fiction became incorporated into the collective memory of the West. The real-life challenges related to weather, disease, fire, commodities markets, bank loans, and mortgages were largely forgotten. In creating a mythical West, the actual lived experience of Westerners was largely discarded. In its place arose a pulp fiction based on epic experiences that appealed to readers seeking a momentary escape from the mundane challenges they faced in their own lives.

Only when discussing the importance of horsemanship and other cowboy skills did the fiction of the West reflect reality. The origins of the rodeo can be found in contests held by cowboys, such as one held in Deadwood, Dakota Territory, in the spring of 1876. The cowboy who most excelled in a number of tasks, such as lassoing a wild horse while demonstrating marksmanship and other skills, would receive the prize money. Half of the dozen contestants were African American, including the legendary cowboy Nat Love, who won the event. Other than these rodeos and the seasonal paydays when herds were brought to market, the reality of the life of a cattle drover was anything but exciting. Cattle drovers also hailed from diverse backgrounds and were very poorly paid. Most were simply itinerant farmhands desperate enough to take a job that mixed hours of tedium with moments of terror. If anything was unique about the cattle drives, it may be the cooperation between black, Hispanic, and European immigrants that composed the workforce.

With the exception of the cattle season, cow towns such as Dodge City were usually quiet places. Prostitution and other forms of vice were more likely to thrive in urban areas where business could thrive year-round. Contrary to popular image, Western prostitutes were scarce, and few of these women ever made much money. They were a diverse lot, bound mostly by tragic stories that led them to this kind of existence. For example, half of the prostitutes in boarding houses from Helena to San Francisco were of Asian origin. With the exception of those who would later run their own bordellos, few women who entered the trade ever made a fortune or even owned property.

The cattle drives were already declining when a new kind of barbed wire was invented in 1874. This commonsensical invention allowed for the inexpensive fencing of large ranches throughout the Great Plains and signaled the decline of the open range. By this time, ranching was becoming big business, and most cattle were processed in huge meatpacking plants in cities such as Kansas City, St. Louis, and Chicago. Reducing their expenses by placing their plants closer to the supply of Midwestern cattle, Philip Armour and Gustavus Swift created mammoth processing facilities that shipped sides of beef in insulated railcars packed with ice. The emergence of the commercial meatpacking industry reduced shipping costs since entire railcars could be packed with meat rather than live animals. This economy came at a high price for local butchers who became increasingly obsolete but greatly lowered the cost of meat and forever altered the American diet.

Once the prairies were fenced, blizzards such as those that occurred in 1887 and 1888 decimated herds of cattle because the fences trapped and confused the animals and kept them from moving together and staying warm. The consequences of the fence were equally devastating on the itinerant ranchers who owned cattle or sheep but no land. The introduction of barbed wire was particularly damaging for Hispanic and other herders who had lived in certain areas of the West for generations. Land speculators and ranch operators claimed huge sections of land and erected fences. The result was that the trails and paths that had provided access to rivers and lakes were severed, and those who did not own land with abundant water supply were suddenly unable to provide water for their animals. Conflicts between ranchers and herders erupted in a series of fence wars throughout Texas in the 1880s. By the fall of 1883, an estimated $20 million in damages had been inflicted on both sides. Commercial ranches erected fences around lands they owned (or merely claimed to own), while neighbors and itinerant herders attacked and destroyed these barriers. Some herders even set deadly prairie fires in retaliation, and property owners responded with their own brand of vigilante justice against the herders. The state government responded by increasing the penalties for fence-cutting while expanding the presence of law enforcement agencies such as the Texas Rangers.

The railroad reached northwest New Mexico in 1879 and with it came tensions between Anglo modes of settlement based on private property and the communal traditions of landownership that had defined the *nuevo Mexicano* way of life. Under the traditional Spanish land system, communal interests such as access to prairies and water had to be respected, regardless of who owned a particular section of land. However, Anglo landowners soon claimed the most valuable lands of the Southwest and forbid sheepherders and others to "trespass" on their lands. By the late 1880s, a vigilante group known as Las Gorras Blancas formed in opposition to the fencing of the lands that had traditionally been open for grazing. This group was known by the white hoods they wore to protect their identities, as well as the use of guerilla tactics that were waged in their attempt to reverse patterns of Anglo settlement in northern New Mexico. These "white caps" as they became known, rode at night to intimidate property owners whose fences they cut to maintain access to water and grass for their herds.

Las Gorras Blancas also attacked the property of railroads as a protest against the low wages paid to the predominantly Hispanic workforce of the region. These groups also recognized that the railroads threatened to disrupt their way of life by transforming the communal-based economy of the region into a Capitalist system based on private ownership of land. These groups mixed ethnic and cultural identity with class consciousness. At the same time, many Hispanic ranchers divided on questions of ethnic solidarity in favor of class consciousness with poor Anglo farmers against land speculators—many of whom were wealthy landowners in Mexico. Some nuevo Mexicano leaders turned to politics, uniting voters of various ethnic groups beyond their class interests but usually failing to enact the legal reforms needed to return the lands to communal ownership. By the 1890s, the many of these political leaders joined the Populist Party and fought for higher wages for Hispanic railroad workers and traditional land and water rights for the areas predominantly Hispanic sheepherders.

The most dramatic fence war occurred in Wyoming in 1892. The **Johnson County War** resembled many of the labor conflicts of the era as large operators formed the Wyoming Stock Growers' Association and hired armed guards who used violence against those who opposed them. Small independent ranchers protested the enclosure of what had been public lands and the theft of "maverick" cattle—calves who belonged to a particular herder but had not yet been marked. "If you stole a few cattle, you were a rustler," and would be jailed, the small ranchers complained. However, "if you stole a few thousand, you were a cattleman." Eventually, the small ranchers used their larger population to their advantage and formed their own associations and bypassed the railroads and cattle pens that catered toward the interests of the large ranches.

FIGURE 2.10

A Chicago stockyard with the Armour and Swift meatpacking plants in the distance.

Johnson County War

An 1892 conflict between small ranchers and large landowners in Wyoming. The large landowners built fences around their lands, which severed the access to water and prairies for many local ranchers. When the local ranchers protested by cutting fences, the large landowners formed the Wyoming Stock Growers' Association and hired armed gunmen, which led to violence.

FIGURE 2.11

A contemporary photo identifying the gunmen hired by the cattle barons in Wyoming as "invaders" during the Johnson County War.

These small ranchers sought to collectively drive their cattle to market as had been the tradition prior to the arrival of the railroad. However, the big ranchers in Wyoming responded by hiring fifty gunmen to intimidate the ranchers and stop the cattle drive. Several of the organizers and cowboys were murdered, leading to an outburst of vigilante justice on all sides. Eventually, the federal government intervened by sending the US Army to restore order. Although these troops helped to prevent bloodshed, they were also ordered to intervene on behalf of the large property owners and put an end to the cattle drives. By the time the troops arrived, most of the witnesses to the murders had also disappeared. The result was an end to the tradition of ranching on the open prairie. Within a generation, many of the small landowners had also vanished. In addition to at least a dozen fatalities, the independent spirit of the open prairie that had defined the West for generations had been lost. In its place was the beginning of the modern cattle industry based on mass production and efficiency.

2.3 Mining, Manufacturing, and Diversity in the West

Mining had led to the rapid growth of communities in California following the 1849 discovery of gold. The same was true a decade later in western Nevada following the discovery of the Comstock Lode and its $300 million worth of silver. By 1870 Virginia City, Nevada, boasted its own stock exchange and hundred saloons. A decade later, the town had been practically abandoned. The story of Virginia City was repeated throughout the West as the discovery of gold, silver, copper, zinc, and lead created boom towns and ghost towns from California to Colorado.

> I have but two or three Lady acquaintances in this country. Ladies are not plenty. There are a great many in the mining towns that take the form of a woman, but oh so fallen and vile.
>
> —A married woman complaining about the absence of women in a mining camp beyond a handful of prostitutes.

Prospectors and miners lacked the resources needed to construct mines. In response financial markets emerged in leading West Coast cities such as Sacramento, as well as all the various subindustries that depended on mining and miners. Once the railroad reached the Southwest in the 1880s, copper mining quickly became the leading industry of southern Arizona. Discoveries of mineral wealth fueled the growth of railroad lines that connected formerly isolated mining camps and led to the growth of new communities. However, the discovery of gold in 1896 along what would become the Alaskan-Canadian border led to the creation of a community that could not wait for railroads. Few of the prospectors in the Klondike ever struck it rich. However, recognizing that these prospectors would require food and supplies, Alaska entrepreneurs like Belinda Mulrooney made a fortune. Mulrooney moved from east Juneau, Alaska, and established a mercantile business, hotel, and restaurant that provided her with enough steady revenue to also engage in the mining business.

Mining towns were the most dangerous and diverse communities in post–Civil War America. Entrepreneurs and laborers from every corner of the globe descended on each discovery of precious metal. The dangers of life in the mines, which killed just over 1 percent of their workforce per year, often paled in comparison with the violence of the mining camps and makeshift towns. Here an army of miners lived among immigrant laborers who processed the ore. These laborers were not prone to organization. However, in a number of mining communities they at least temporarily overcame language barriers and prejudice to collectively bargain for some of the highest wages paid to workers in industrial America. Eventually, these mining towns either disappeared when the mines were exhausted or developed into manufacturing centers such as Boise, Idaho, and Butte, Montana.

The rapid business growth of the West was dependent on immigrant labor and the emergence of the national transportation and communication networks of railroads, telegraphs, canals, and steamships.

Non-English-speaking immigrants from Europe usually settled in clustered groups throughout the West. These communities permitted immigrants to retain language and customs for several generations. Churches and fraternal organizations formed the core of these clusters and helped to maintain a sense of tradition and community. Ethnic clusters created migrant majorities in large areas of North Dakota, Minnesota, and Wisconsin. Mining towns in Wyoming were sometimes known informally by names such as "Little Dublin," indicating the predominance of Irish settlers.

Copper mines surrounding Butte, Montana, even sent dozens of recruiters throughout Ireland leading to a continued predominance of Irish labor. Butte was unique in that it was one of the few mining towns that developed into a major city. The predominance of Irish laborers and absence of preexisting Anglo-owned shops and factories allowed many Irish laborers to become business owners. As a result, the residents of "Little Dublin" achieved a level of independence and stability that was rare among first-generation migrants. In most other areas of the West, the Irish and other minorities were heavily discriminated against much as they were in the cities of the East Coast and Ohio River Valley.

Newcomers from Asia followed similar patterns of migration and community building in the West through schools, churches, and fraternal organizations. Like most European immigrants, Chinese and other Asian immigrants did not intend to live in the United States forever and sought to retain their language and customs. Like the Irish and central Europeans, Asian migrants experienced discrimination. This discrimination was particularly severe for Chinese laborers on the West Coast during the 1870s and 1880s. Some managed to form profitable businesses, arousing the envy of white Americans. For others, the poverty of many Chinese laborers helped to sustain images of newcomers as part of an "Asiatic plague" that harmed commercial growth. The migrants themselves were often viewed as a burden on California and the rest of the West, even though nearly every migrant was self-supporting. Groups such as the California Working Men's Party sought to curtail all Asian migration. These men argued that Chinese and other immigrants competed for "their" jobs and the willingness of these newcomers to work hard for low wages created downward pressure on all wages. These groups lobbied for local and state laws banning immigration.

The efforts of such groups spread beyond the West Coast, culminating with congressional approval of the **Chinese Exclusion Act of 1882**. This was the first law in US history to bar a group of immigrants explicitly because of their race or ethnicity. Its passage was aided by the creative rhetoric of anti-Chinese groups who argued that they opposed "importation" rather than "immigration." While Europeans were "immigrants" who came to America and overcame hardships to secure employment, such language robbed the Chinese of human agency. In addition, Americans new and old were quite aware that theirs was a nation of immigrants. By labeling the Chinese as "imports," these men furthered conspiratorial notions of a Chinese "horde" being "dumped" into the nation. Deprived of free agency and robbed of their status as immigrants, anti-Chinese activists created the notion that these workers were being "imported" by nefarious business syndicates to take jobs away from hard-working Americans.

The 1882 law specifically barred Chinese laborers (but not wealthy Chinese investors) from entering the United States. The law was strengthened or modified twice in the next dozen years before being modified to discourage Korean and Japanese migration. Owing to America's allegiance with China in World War II, the law was finally repealed in the 1940s and replaced with a quota permitting no more than 105 Chinese immigrants per year. Until this time, few Americans questioned the exclusion of Chinese laborers as anything but a progressive measure meant to protect "real Americans" from imagined vices and labor shortages.

FIGURE 2.12

This Alaskan mercantile catered to miners in the Klondike in the late 1890s.

Chinese Exclusion Act of 1882

Banned the migration of Chinese laborers into the United States. Wealthy Chinese citizens could still migrate to the United States, as the law was aimed at appeasing those who believed that Chinese migrants were causing pressure on the employment market in the West Coast. Because the law was explicitly aimed at barring people of Chinese descent, it added to an atmosphere of intolerance toward Asian Americans in the United States.

FIGURE 2.13

This 1882 political cartoon is critical of the Chinese Exclusion Act. It pictures a stereotypical laborer from Asia being excluded while foreign radicals from Europe are apparently welcomed to enter.

In many ways, hostility to Chinese migrants was one of the few unifying measures that brought the diverse groups along the West Coast together. Politicians needing a few extra votes could always count on gaining the support of the working class by blaming the presence of Asian immigrants for whatever difficulties their community was having. Rather than offering real solutions or even identifying the structural causes of poverty and worker discontent, such leaders distracted the population and pandered to existing suspicions that illegal immigration was the cause of a particular problem. The law sanctioned racism in ways that legitimized prejudice against all minorities. It also placed a stigma on all Asian Americans, African Americans, and Mexican Americans, regardless of whether they were citizens. The irony was that many of these "outsiders" had lived in the United States for several more generations than the average white resident of California.

Most historians are just beginning to revise their interpretations of the West to consider the experiences of people of Latin American descent. Just as African Americans faced violence from the Ku Klux Klan, Tejanos and other Westerners of Hispanic descent were frequently the target of ethnic violence. The children of these residents also endured segregated schools in Texas, Arizona, California, and were even forced into crumbling one-room schools in some of the industrial cities of the Midwest. In each case, segregated schools enrolled Mexican American children, regardless of whether they spoke English. Cities such as Los Angeles and San Francisco also maintained separate schools for children of Chinese immigrants. Over time, the question of whether Korean, Japanese, and Filipino children should be sent to the "white" schools or the schools reserved for Chinese children led to local and even international conflicts.

Within urban areas throughout the nation Greek, Italian, Irish, Jewish, and Slavic immigrants were also discriminated against and restricted to the worst jobs and neighborhoods. However, these groups were increasingly regarded as white and therefore eligible to attend the public schools of their choice regardless of whether they spoke English. However, many of these immigrant communities formed their own schools in hopes of perpetuating their language, religion, and culture. For the children of Native Americans, however, education was directed toward the eradication of these cultural elements of their worldview through assimilation. White religious groups and the federal government established boarding schools where native children were sent, sometimes without parental consent. Here, the children were instructed in the religious beliefs, history, culture, and language of their Anglo teachers. These teachers believed that such training was vital to the future success of native children, a perspective that some natives feared was becoming increasingly evident as Western migration made their traditional way of life more and more difficult to maintain.

In 1869, the African American leader Frederick Douglass challenged Americans to consider the extent to which their national character and wealth was connected to its diversity. For Douglass, America's success was related to its incorporation of people from all over the globe into a "composite nation." Douglass repeatedly condemned the discrimination faced by Chinese immigrants. He also denounced those who uncritically presumed that nonwhite migration would somehow lead to the downfall of the nation. He was not alone. Sojourner Truth spoke on behalf of Native Americans, while Sumner pointed out that Asian children in California endured school segregation. Martin Delany often juxtaposed "heathen" members of non-Christian faiths with Protestant blacks who faced discrimination. White liberals who had been part of the abolitionist movement also joined the chorus. In 1870, Charles Sumner attempted and failed for the third time to remove the word *white* from statutes regulating naturalization in hopes of extending citizenship to nonwhite immigrants and Native Americans.

Not all liberal whites or black leaders expressed such open-minded sentiment toward all immigrant groups. Thaddeus Stephens had been a tireless agitator for the rights of African Americans but occasionally expressed anti-Semitic sentiment. Elizabeth Cady Stanton was an abolitionist but frequently contrasted the "lower orders" of immigrants with middle-class white women who were denied suffrage. Poor and illiterate Asians and Hispanics born in the United States and Native Americans who lived outside reservations could enjoy the right to vote, Stanton frequently reminded her listeners. That middle-class and college-educated white women were barred from the polls while these groups could vote often increased the indignity of early white suffragists.

2.4 Women's Suffrage

Historians have often conveyed the image of the West as an all-male preserve. With the exception of a few pioneering women who receive honorable mention, cowgirl-celebrities such as Annie Oakley, and a veritable army of nameless women whose virtue was bartered in saloons and mining camps, the Western woman is nonexistent. Western women are often caricatured rather than studied. This is not because of lack of sources because tens of thousands of letters, diaries, newspaper articles, and other primary sources written by women about their experiences have survived into the present. An honest history of the West must recognize the simple fact that homesteading, ranching, mining, and city building were family enterprises. Women may have been scarce in certain Western communities, such as mining camps and cattle drives, but even in these "male" spheres, women were often present. As colonial scholar Laurel Thatcher Ulrich famously observed, the historical record is biased toward female caricatures of vice and idolatry while the armies of "well-behaved women" are seldom included. Despite the popular growth of sometimes misunderstanding the phrase Ulrich created, "well-behaved" women did make history. In no other region and in no other time is this truth as patently manifested as in the American West.

It was in the West that women settled homesteads, broke horses, and raised crops as well as children. And it was in the West that women first secured the legal recognition of their right to vote. In 1859, Kansas women secured the right to vote in school elections due to a campaign headed by Clarina Nichols. The success of this campaign was largely due to Nichols' ability to frame leadership in the schools within the context of the home and childrearing—two areas that were considered part of women's traditional roles. However, these rights opened the door for future campaigns in Kansas and throughout neighboring states. In 1887, Kansas women successfully lobbied for the extension of their voting rights to include city elections. In response, more than a dozen women were elected as mayors in Kansas alone prior to the turn of the century.

By 1869, the territory of Wyoming included provisions for women's suffrage that were expanded to include all elections by the time of statehood in 1890. Women also secured the right to vote in Utah in 1870. These female voters surprised many by upholding the legality of polygamy until the federal government intervened. Western women succeeded in placing provisions for full recognition of their voting rights in Kansas and Colorado in the 1870s, although these measures were defeated. Washington's Territorial legislature included women's suffrage in their 1883 state constitution. Colorado was the first state to approve women's suffrage in an all-male referendum in 1893. Three years later, the men of Idaho and Utah approved similar measures 1896. By this time, the right of women to vote in city and school elections was recognized by certain communities throughout the West while measures granting full suffrage in state and national elections were placed on the ballot in California, Oregon, and Washington. In each of these instances and hundreds of others, women led the initiative through petitions, parades, speeches, articles, and broadsides.

The successes of the women's suffrage movement during the late nineteenth century are frequently overshadowed by the passage of the Nineteenth Amendment, which guaranteed the right to vote regardless of sex in 1920. However, this victory was only made possible by the efforts of previous generations who secured that right at the local and state level over a period of fifty years. Education was the foundation of the suffrage movement, and by 1870, more women than men graduated from high school. Local women led campaigns to develop public libraries and pooled their resources to build reading rooms for women. Younger women pondered the meaning of novels such as *Little Women* where the principal characters struggle with the conflict between personal fulfillment and the gendered expectations of society. Women soon dominated professions such as teaching and nursing that were largely closed to them prior to the Civil War. There was also a proliferation of women's societies dedicated to a variety of political causes from sanitation to suffrage. The greatest of these issues was temperance, and the largest of these organizations was the **Women's Christian Temperance Union**, which was formed in 1874.

FIGURE 2.14

Pictured here as a Joan of Arc-like heroine, a prohibitionist battles the evils of liquor "In the Name of God and Humanity." The artist conjures the image of women acting politically in the most radical way possible—utilizing the traditionally masculine style of physical combat. Yet the artist combines this radical behavior with the conservative notion of women endeavoring to uphold morality and protect the family. In real life, hundreds of women framed their radical and political acts of smashing saloons within society's accepted role of women as guardians of the family and virtue.

WOMAN'S HOLY WAR.
Grand Charge on the Enemy's Works

Women's Christian Temperance Union

A national women's association originally dedicated to the prohibition of alcohol. The WCTU expanded to take on dozens of issues of importance to women, including the right to vote.

Carrie A. Nation

An infamous prohibitionist known for using a hatchet to smash saloons that violated state and local temperance laws. Carrie Nation defied notions about gender by using physical violence against the property of saloon owners. She also used more conventional methods of protest by delivering hundreds of lectures on topics ranging from women's suffrage to the dangers of child labor.

Lydia Maria Child

A religious-minded reformer who opposed slavery and protested against the unfair treatment of Native Americans. She was also a leader within the early women's suffrage movement until her death in 1880.

Mary Ann Shadd Cary

An abolitionist during slavery, a recruiter of black troops during the Civil War, and a teacher, newspaper editor, and national African American leader during the rest of her life. She occupied both formal and informal positions of leadership within a variety of labor and civil rights organizations during Reconstruction and the 1880s.

Women rallied behind the banner of temperance, often violating the era's notions of a woman's "proper place" by engaging in direct protest. Women held "pray-ins" where they occupied saloons and requested divine assistance in purging their communities of the evil spirits they believed were introduced by the consumption of liquid spirits. If these methods failed, some women completely defied the era's notions of feminine passivity by smashing those saloons to pieces with hatchets. The most famous of these reformers was Carrie Amelia Moore, a former victim of domestic abuse perpetrated by an alcoholic husband. Divorced and remarried, her legal name became **Carrie A. Nation**, which she believed was a divine message that the Lord had called her to "carry a nation" from vice to virtue.

Nation traveled the countryside delivering lectures about the evils of alcohol and selling souvenir "hatchets" she autographed to raise funds. She needed this money to pay for the fines she received after being arrested dozens of times for destroying saloons. In many cases, Nation was able to defend her actions in court and avoid imprisonment because the saloons she chose were operated in dry cities and counties. As a result, even her arrests served her intended purpose of embarrassing the police who often accepted bribes in exchange for permitting saloons to operate in violation of local temperance laws. Although she operated mostly in the Midwest, her fame spread quickly. For example, barrooms from New York to San Francisco placed signs near the door that read "All Nations Welcome, but Carrie."

The WCTU shunned the more aggressive methods of Carrie Nation in favor of moral suasion and political activism. In choosing this moderate view, the WCTU was perceived as the model of middle-class womanhood and quickly expanded into the nation's largest women's organization. The WCTU eventually developed thirty-nine departments, each dedicated to some area of community advancement that was important to its female members. But the organization had its more radical adherents who soon seized the initiative. By the end of Reconstruction, many of these women grew frustrated with asking male political leaders to listen to them and believed that the only way they would be taken seriously is if they could vote. Ironically, this was a conclusion reached by Carrie Nation long ago. Although her audiences paid to see the famed "bar-room smasher," many of her lectures were dedicated to the subject of women's suffrage as a means of purifying the electoral process.

Lydia Maria Child is most remembered for her poem about a journey "over the river and through the woods" that led to someone's grandmother's home. Child's writing reflects another journey, however, as she like many other women increasingly came to believe in the need for women's suffrage. Men argued that women were too innocent and pure to be "tainted" by participation in the corrupt and sometimes violent realm of politics. Child responded by turning this argument on its head. If men were genuinely concerned about corruption in politics, and if women were the guardians of morality, who better to clean up politics than women, she asked. Child took a more direct route when corresponding with constitutional scholars like Charles Sumner. Demonstrating her knowledge of history and constitutional theory, Child demonstrated that true democracy required the consent of all citizens. "Either the theory of our government is false," Child wrote, "or women have a right to vote."

Black women were often the most politically active women during Reconstruction and regularly attended national conventions as delegates. This was especially true in the North where black women had taken the lead in the abolitionist movement for decades. John Mercer Langston, perhaps the most renowned black leader during Reconstruction next to Frederick Douglass, urged his fellow attendees at a black labor conference to tolerate no discrimination of gender in their organization's membership or leadership positions. **Mary Ann Shadd Cary**, a newspaper editor and educator who established racially integrated schools was among the many women in attendance who were appointed to leadership positions. Cary served as the chair of the Colored National Labor Union Committee on Female Suffrage and her speech to that organization led to the adoption of a resolution banning gender discrimination in every form.

Harriet Johnson's attendance as a delegate to the 1869 National Convention of Colored Men demonstrated the connection between Reconstruction politics, region, and gender. Johnson, an administrator at Pennsylvania's Avery College, received strong support from delegates representing Northern urban communities. After a nearly unanimous vote of both Northern and Southern black leaders, she was welcomed to join the otherwise male delegates during an era when few white women were even permitted to observe political conventions led by white men. This difference was largely the result of women's leadership in the abolitionist movement and the high percentage of black men who served alongside black and white women in the long battle to end slavery. In addition, black men had learned from personal experience that even disfranchised people could mobilize and exert political influence through petitions, moral suasion, and appeals to reason.

Partially because one could act politically without voting, not all women believed that suffrage was necessary to promote women's issues during Reconstruction. Many women were already active participants in political auxiliaries and various community organizations that relied on a good relationship with men who were business and political leaders. These women feared that they might lose the power they exerted indirectly through organizations that received male support if they offended male sensitivities by calling for the vote. Women had tremendous political power, one woman explained to the editor of a local black newspaper, by speaking "a word or two, which appeared to be dropped carelessly" into a conversation with a husband or community leader. Using this tactic, women could not only convince male leaders to support their ideas, but they could also convince these men that the idea was their own.

Women who opposed the efforts of suffragists were often very active in community associations and worked tirelessly behind the scenes or within women's "auxiliary" branches of male organizations. These women urged suffragists to compare the results of their indirect approaches with the backlash experienced by women who insisted on equality and demanded the right to vote. Suffragists were branded as unfit mothers, unfeminine, dangerous, immoral, and even mentally deranged. Advocating radical doctrines that had little chance of enactment actually hurt the cause of women's rights, some women argued, by causing a defensive posture among men. Male backlash, they feared, could threaten years of progress by women who delicately advanced their concerns by gently reminding city fathers of their manly obligations to aid their wives, mothers, daughters, and sisters.

FIGURE 2.15

Mary Ann Shadd Cary was born free in the slave state of Delaware. She and her family moved to Pennsylvania and then Canada to escape the conditions African Americans faced including the possibility of being illegally captured and sold into slavery. She was a teacher, author, newspaper editor, and national leader within a variety of black labor, political, and civil rights organizations.

FIGURE 2.16

Anti-women's suffrage cartoons followed the strategy of attacking suffragists as unfeminine and their male supporters as feeble. Rather than confront the ideas of women such as Stanton and Anthony or advance their own arguments, opponents usually chose personal attacks or farcical images of a world turned upside-down where women would attempt to mimic the actions and traits of men while children were left to fend for themselves.

The reaction of men who felt threatened by woman's suffrage paralleled the reaction of those who opposed the expansion of rights for African Americans during Reconstruction. The assumption of unchallenged male authority guaranteed status and privilege to all men in the same way the era's racial assumptions elevated all whites. One might fail in the classroom, the workplace, and be held in low esteem by one's peers, yet they could never lose their race or gender. As a white person or a man in such a society, one enjoyed both security against falling to the lowest rungs of the social order and the exclusive privilege to climb the social ladder to its highest levels.

FIGURE 2.17

An early flyer from upstate New York advocating women's suffrage as a way to promote civic housekeeping. The flyer exclaims that "the ballot is the broom of democracy" and calls on women to yield it to clean up their cities just as they remove filth from their homes.

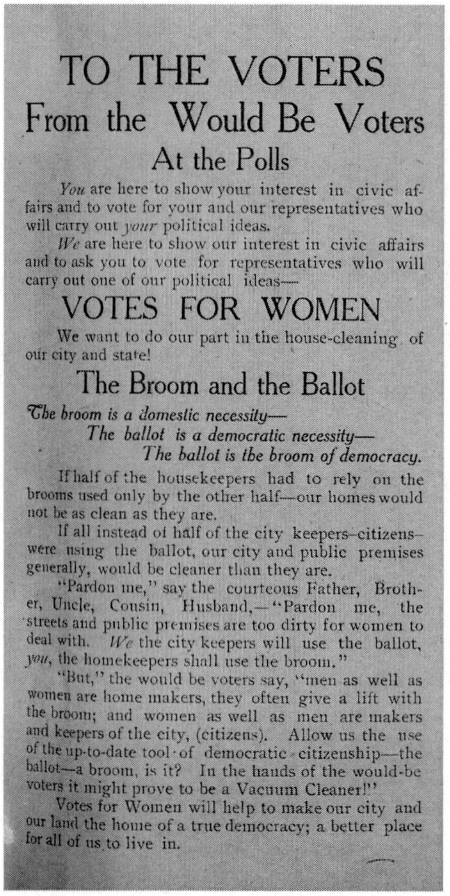

TO THE VOTERS
From the Would Be Voters
At the Polls

You are here to show your interest in civic affairs and to vote for your and our representatives who will carry out *your* political ideas.

We are here to show our interest in civic affairs and to ask you to vote for representatives who will carry out one of our political ideas—

VOTES FOR WOMEN

We want to do our part in the house-cleaning of our city and state!

The Broom and the Ballot

The broom is a domestic necessity—
The ballot is a democratic necessity—
The ballot is the broom of democracy.

If half of the housekeepers had to rely on the brooms used only by the other half—our homes would not be as clean as they are.

If all instead of half of the city keepers—citizens—were using the ballot, our city and public premises generally, would be cleaner than they are.

"Pardon me," say the courteous Father, Brother, Uncle, Cousin, Husband,—"Pardon me, the streets and public premises are too dirty for women to deal with. *We* the city keepers will use the ballot, *you*, the homekeepers shall use the broom."

"But," the would be voters say, "men as well as women are home makers, they often give a lift with the broom; and women as well as men are makers and keepers of the city, (citizens). Allow us the use of the up-to-date tool of democratic citizenship—the ballot—a broom, is it? In the hands of the would-be voters it might prove to be a Vacuum Cleaner!"

Votes for Women will help to make our city and our land the home of a true democracy; a better place for all of us to live in.

It is important to remember that Americans who lived during this era believed that theirs was an egalitarian society, the last vestige of discrimination eliminated by the end of chattel slavery. As a result, counterarguments to black equality and women's rights usually adhered to the following line of reasoning: (1) White male leadership was not artificially imposed but rather a natural consequence of superior intellect, education, and experience in civic affairs; (2) participation in government was best left to the most intelligent and experienced voters and leaders; (3) because of their inexperience, women and minorities could easily be deceived into voting demagogues and tyrants; (4) even if they could not vote, women and minorities were assured "virtual representation" by elected officials who would protect the interests of all Americans. Just as children should not be permitted to vote due to inexperience and immaturity, this perspective concluded, women and minorities should "know their place" and defer to white men whose superior judgment would guarantee that the best interests of all.

The problem for most defenders of the social order was that the holes within this line of reasoning were easy targets for women like Sojourner Truth and Elizabeth Cady Stanton who possessed two of the finest minds among all Americans in the nineteenth century. Sojourner Truth dismantled arguments against women's suffrage and exposed the hypocrisy of men who claimed to oppose women's suffrage for the good of womankind. Elizabeth Cady Stanton used her superior intellect and knowledge of history to turn each of these arguments against her opponents. She countered that the concept of deference to one's "natural superiors" was used to prop up monarchies around the globe and reminded those who would listen that America was founded in protest against virtual representation. She also turned the paternalistic statements of men who defended the separation of the "male sphere" of public life and the "female sphere" of the home with her characteristic wit: "If God has assigned a sphere to man and one to woman, we claim the right ourselves to judge His design in reference to us." After all, Stanton explained, "a man has quite enough to do to find out his own individual calling, without being taxed to find out also where every woman belongs."

2.5 Exodus: The Last Pioneers

Southern black women and men continued to organize after their rights to vote and hold office was effectively nullified by fraud and violence. These Americans increasingly supported a movement that demonstrated the connections between race, region, and the continuing challenge of Reconstruction. When faced with political disenfranchisement and limited economic opportunity, hundreds of thousands of Southern blacks held meetings to investigate the possibility of migration to the North and West. The number of actual migrants who traveled to places such as Kansas and Indiana—the two most popular destinations—were limited to about 20,000 people.

> *Most of us crossed the Mississippi or Missouri with no money but with a vest wealth of hope and courage. Haste to get rich made us borrowers, and the borrower has made booms, and booms made men wild, and Kansas became a vast insane asylum covering 80,000 miles.*
>
> *—Kansas official recalling the vast loans that were made to white settlers wishing to purchase farm land and equipment on credit.*

The implications and possibilities of black migration out of the South were significant, as demonstrated by three months of congressional hearings on the subject. In general, Southern blacks wished the opportunity to become homesteaders on Western lands or find work in Northern cities. However, only a small percentage had enough money to make the trek and support themselves until they could secure productive farms. Southern planters were alarmed at the possibility of losing the sharecroppers who provided the labor their own economic security was built on. Perhaps most revealing aspect of black migration was the way white Northerners and Westerners, despite years of vocal concern for the plight of Southern blacks, sought to prevent these families from migrating to their communities.

In many ways, the 20,000 Southern migrants who were known as "**Exodusters**" might be considered the last pioneers in the history of the American West. Like many of the first immigrants to America, the Exodusters sought deliverance from oppression through migration. They pooled their meager resources into collective migratory ventures and took a leap of faith into an unknown land. Most migrants traveled in small groups that were the result of months of planning and financial sacrifice. Despite the fact that most Western migrants—white and black alike—arrived with little more than a few dollars and faith in providence, most whites in the Great Plains viewed the exodus as a threat to their communities. Resurrecting a Reconstruction-era myth that denigrated black ambition for landownership, Westerners created a fictional account of the exodus that accused the migrants as searching for a land where they would no longer have to work.

Whites also justified their own hostility to the Exodusters by claiming the entire migration was some sort of welfare scheme. According to this view, unscrupulous railroad agents sold tickets to Southern blacks by claiming the "forty acres and a mule" promised to them in the aftermath of the Civil War now awaited them in the West. Even though most white migrants to the West had been the beneficiaries of government aid in the form of subsidized transportation and land in the 1860s and early 1870s, the Exodusters were accused of seeking governmental handouts. Ironically, these migrants arrived too late to take advantage of fertile land under the Homestead Act and most intended to work for wages until they could purchase a farm.

Such a perspective allowed Westerners, most of whom were stalwart Republicans, to oppose the exodus while still claiming to be concerned about the plight of Southern blacks. Even members of the Kansas Freedman's Relief Association, a group of liberal whites who provided limited aid to some of the Exodusters, soon diverted the largest share of relief funds to diverting Exodusters to other communities. They also paid to send agents into the South to see if they could convince Southern blacks that they were better off staying where they were. Southern whites reveled in the hypocrisy of Northerners who quickly changed their tune about conditions former slaves faced in the South. "The 'man-and-brother' theory will do very well," a Southerner wrote of Northern sentiment toward black rights "as long as the 'man-and-brother' is in the South."

These charges of Northern hypocrisy were demonstrated by the cold reception the Exodusters faced from Colorado to Indiana. For example, shortly after a large group of Exodusters arrived in Emporia, Kansas, the stalwart editor of a Republican paper reconsidered his views on Reconstruction. Although his newspaper had denounced the Klan and called for federal troops to be redeployed to the South to protect black voters until 1880, the prospect of black migration to his town led him to exclaim that "a kinder or more humane people" could not be found than Southern plantation owners.

Most Exodusters arrived with enough money to take care of themselves and quickly found work. Those in need of aid were usually housed in black churches and cared for by the black communities, which composed over 10 percent of the population of Kansas in 1880. At the same time, Exodusters did relish a hope that the government might intercede on behalf of former slaves. Some held conferences calling for reparation by reserving lands in the Southwest—the black homeland of which Martin Delany and other leaders had dreamed. Others viewed governmental support for the exodus as the best way to finally settle the issues of Reconstruction. Requests for federal funds to aid the migrants were denied; however, lawmakers devoted three months and $40,000 to a congressional investigation to determine the cause of the migration. While the migrants themselves made their intentions patently clear, the hearings quickly descended into political squabbling. Republican politicians sought to prove that the cruelty of Southern Democrats vindicated their previous attempts at Reconstruction. In return, Democrats argued that black migration to the North was part of a Republican conspiracy to depopulate the South prior to the 1880 census, thereby increasing the number of congressmen and presidential electors allotted to the North. As had been true of Reconstruction itself, the perspective of Southern blacks was ignored.

Had Congress sought the perspective of the Exodusters, they might have listened to local black leaders such as Kansas's John Waller. "This is a Revolution, but a peaceful and quiet one," Waller wrote to his governor. "Do you ask what has caused such a step? Then listen while I answer as only a black man, and former slave, can answer…we are robbed of our freedom in the South; our manhood is not ever respected, our people are murdered without mercy, and our school houses are burned." Waller went on to compare the Exodus to the American Revolution, quoting Patrick Henry and exclaiming, "I care not what course others may take, as for me give me liberty or give me death…this is the sentiment of the colored race today."

Exodusters

Southern black migrants who sought homes in the Great Plains and northern border states such as Indiana in hope of the political, legal, and economic freedom they were denied after Reconstruction. An estimated 20,000 migrants journeyed to Kansas and other western locations, which led to a congressional investigation and efforts to stop the migration by Southern whites who feared the loss of their labor force and Northern whites who opposed black migration to their communities.

FIGURE 2.18

A contemporary rendition of the Exodusters on their way to Kansas. Most images of black pioneers depicted the migrants in a negative light—a sharp contrast to similar images of white homesteaders. Perhaps as an attempt to depoliticize the movement out of the South, the editors of this journal wrote a caption claiming that the Exodusters were fleeing yellow fever.

Congress might have also challenged the notion that the Exodusters were naively traveling in search of a chimerical "land of milk and honey." They might have listened to Georgia state legislator Henry McNeal Turner who exclaimed that "there is not a colored man in a million that has the least idea of getting a mule and forty acres of land by going to Kansas." For Turner, the creation of this myth was part of an effort to blame Southern blacks for the conditions they faced and spread prejudice against those who sought to leave the region. Congress might have also sought the perspective of Sojourner Truth, who traveled throughout the Great Plains and hoped Congress would support the creation of a black state in the West. While speaking in Topeka, Truth pointed out how common it was for government and private aid to be requested and given to white homesteaders. Why then, she asked, was the arrival of hundreds of thousands of poor whites cheered as evidence of American progress while black Americans were assumed to be vagrants and "advised" to seek homes elsewhere?

Far from being naive about the realities of life on the plains or a burden to white Westerners, most Exodusters devoted at least a year to saving money and seeking out information about the West before they began their trek. When they reached their destinations, they organized mutual aid societies and were almost always self-supporting within weeks of their arrival. Hundreds purchased their own farms, many within black farming communities, while others joined preexisting, all-black towns such as Nicodemus, Kansas.

Although some Exodusters were welcomed by companies in need of labor, most found that the color line was drawn tightly against them. For example, Colorado mines spent thousands of dollars recruiting laborers yet reported that they had no openings when several black leaders toured the area in search of jobs. When individual black men sought work in the same mines, however, they were often hired. The same was true of coal mines in Iowa, railroad construction companies in Nebraska, and farmers throughout the region. Individuals might be treated with relative fairness, but when the Exodusters arrived in a large group, they usually met strong opposition. Southern Indiana became so hostile to black labor that white farmers who employed Exodusters were the victims of property damage. Indiana politicians who promised to "defend" their counties against black migration were usually swept into office. Whites in neighboring states such as Illinois, Ohio, and Nebraska each held meetings to determine how best to divert their small numbers of Exodusters to other states. Despite all these challenges, the Exodusters established farms, businesses, and even entire towns from Indiana to Kansas.

REVIEW AND CRITICAL THINKING

1. How did the actions of the federal government affect Western expansion? Summarize the history of Western expansion between 1865 and 1890, with an emphasis on the experience of ordinary Americans from diverse backgrounds. Is the story of Western expansion the story of progress or the story of exploitation? Is it a story of individual or collective action? What are the enduring lessons of the West? Has the story of the West been manipulated or distorted in ways that might distract from these lessons?

2. Summarize the importance of homesteaders, railroads, cattle drive, and mining within the context of Western history. How did these economic activities shape life in the West and the rest of the nation?

3. Why might the mythic West emphasize cowboys and conflict instead of the importance of federal policy and the action of ordinary families? In what ways did the creation of the mythic Old West distort the actual history of the West?

4. In what ways did the challenges of the West reflect the class struggles between the wealthy and the poor in urban America? In what ways might the West been more egalitarian?

5. Summarize the struggle for women's suffrage in the West and the rest of the nation from Reconstruction through the 1880s. Why might women's suffrage have been more successful in the West, and what might this suggest about women's roles within the West itself?

6. How does the exodus demonstrate Northern sentiment regarding Reconstruction? In what ways does the exodus demonstrate black agency? What were the challenges black migrants faced as they moved to the West?

7. The Compromise of 1877 is typically cited as the end of Reconstruction. Might the exodus of 1879–1880 better represent the end of Reconstruction, or does it demonstrate that even Northern whites were never sincere in their expressed concern for the welfare of former slaves?

3. GROWTH OF INDUSTRIAL AMERICA AND THE NEW SOUTH

LEARNING OBJECTIVES

1. Explain how government influenced the development of industry during the 1870s and 1880s. Describe how monetary policy affected the economy and explain how corporations emerged. Describe the methods by which the government attempted to both promote and regulate these enterprises.

2. Describe the methods used by the heads of industry to expand local businesses into national corporations. Also, explain how the nation's economic system was growing increasingly interconnected during this period, as evidenced by the Panic of 1873.

3. Explain the vision of those who sought to create a "New South" and the challenges they faced. Describe the ways that the New South reflected the ideas and challenges of Reconstruction, as well as new challenges related to modernity and the growth of industry.

3.1 Trade and Finance

In July 1873, a group of outlaws loosened a piece of track leading to the derailment of a train near Council Bluffs, Iowa. Jesse and Frank James joined other former Confederate bushwhackers as they removed $2,000 from the train's safe. It was the first of many notorious train robberies conducted by the James gang and similar outfits. Across the plains in Wyoming, the legendary African American cowboy Nat Love explained why many Westerners seemed to be cheering on these outlaws as if they were some sort of modern-day Robin Hood. "If they were robbers," Love explained, "by what name are we to call some of the great trusts, corporations and brokers, who have for years been robbing the people of this country?" Perhaps exaggerating the charity of the James brothers, Love argued that they had stolen "from the rich and gave to the poor, while these respected members of society steal from the poor to make the rich richer."

The story of post–Civil War industrial growth is similar to the development of the West and comes with its own outlaws and pioneers. It is a narrative of rugged individualism aided by government intervention on behalf of industrial development. This development in turn was something that most Americans believed was fuel that kept the engines of progress turning. The story of industrial growth is also a narrative of victimization and agency on the part of those who populated America's great cities on the eve of the **Second Industrial Revolution**. Like many Native Americans, workers fought to preserve the traditions of their artisan ancestors and argued that all development was not necessarily progress. And just as Western development depended on the railroads built with federal support, the growth of industry was only made possible by the loosening of laws regarding incorporation, federal support of railroads and canals, government contracts, and the use of federal and state troops to force striking laborers back to work.

Incorporation permitted entrepreneurs to enjoy the same profit and control of their business as they would under a sole proprietorship but limited their financial and legal liabilities if their business lost money or harmed others. Unlike a sole proprietorship whose failure could result in the loss of one's own home or even jail time, the owners of corporations could take risks without fearing the loss of anything more than the time and money they had put into the business. Defenders of corporations pointed out that these protections were the only way entrepreneurs could find investors and managers with the skills and resources needed to start new industries. Without such laws, few of the companies that fueled industrial growth and created jobs would have developed as quickly.

Corporations also permitted individuals to purchase stock—a certificate granting partial ownership of a company. One of the key benefits of incorporation was that stockholders were not legally liable themselves if a corporation they invested went bankrupt or was sued in court. They could lose everything they invested, but nothing more than they had invested. For other investors, companies needing capital sold bonds—a promise to repay a loan along with an agreed-on percentage of interest each year. The sale of stocks and bonds promised to allow ordinary Americans the ability to share in the profits of corporate America. In practice, however, only a small number of families owned securities until mid- to late twentieth century.

Second Industrial Revolution

A period from the end of the Civil War to the outbreak of World War I that was host to a significant transformation of US industry. Innovations in steel production, the assembly line, and inventions such as the internal combustion engine and the ability to harness the power of electricity were key to the transformation. Equally important was the development of the nation's financial system that facilitated investment and permitted the growth of corporations.

FIGURE 2.19

Steelworkers in Pittsburgh at the turn of the century.

tariffs

Taxes on imported goods. Many nations use these taxes to raise revenue while "protecting" domestic industries by raising the prices of foreign goods.

FIGURE 2.20

A photo showing brokers inside the New York Stock Exchange in 1908. In this image, information about share prices are printed on paper and placed on kiosks. Similar methods were used in the 1880s, but information traveled via the telegraph.

gold standard

A monetary system where currency is exchangeable for a fixed amount of gold.

Like the railroads and Western land speculators, Northern corporations depended on government support and sought to influence public officials in a number of ways. For example, Northern business interests lobbied government officials who agreed to increase **tariffs** on a number of manufactured goods. These taxes protected the developing industries of the United States against cheaper steel and textiles from Europe by requiring importers to pay a tax when they brought their wares into the United States. In effect, these tariffs raised the price of foreign goods, which gave American-made products a competitive advantage. In an era without federal income taxes, tariffs joined Western land sales as the primary source of revenue for the federal government. Together, these two sources of income permitted the federal government to completely pay its debts related to the Civil War within a single generation.

Those who supported tariffs pointed to the revenue they generated and the domestic job creation that depended on protecting US factories from foreign competition. However, the Republican majority that passed these tariff increases soon came under fire as Southern Democrats returned to Congress in larger numbers. Raising the taxes on foreign imports had upset Southerners because Europeans retaliated with their own tariffs against the products America exported, like cotton and tobacco. Because most US factories were still located in the North, Southerners and Westerners seldom benefitted from tariffs, which resulted in higher prices for manufactured goods. More importantly, Britain turned toward India and other cotton-producing colonies within its empire that were exempt from the taxes that importers of American cotton were required to pay.

Competing perspectives regarding the tariff remained a cornerstone of US political debate. Soon this debate included policies regarding monetary policy and laws regulating corporations. America followed Britain and other leading nations in adopting the **gold standard** in 1873. Prior to this decision, American money had been backed by both silver and gold. Anyone with American currency could redeem dollars for silver or gold at a certain percentage tied to the relative value of those precious metals. In addition, the government agreed to buy back the greenback currency it had issued during the Civil War, a currency that was not backed by anything more than the government's promise to back these paper bills.

The adoption of the gold standard gave Americans and foreign investors great faith in the value of the money printed by the federal government. However, it also restricted the nation's currency to the value of the gold held by the federal government. This restriction had upset many Southerners and Westerners because most of the nation's gold and gold-backed currency was located in the East. Westerners were particularly eager to have the nation's currency backed by silver because this would increase the value of recently discovered silver deposits in Western locales such as Nevada. In addition, connecting silver to the nation's currency would benefit Western banks. In 1874, for example, New York and Massachusetts banks held $120 million of gold-backed US currency. Every bank in every state west of Ohio controlled less than half of that amount. The gold standard meant that a Western farmer had to borrow money from middlemen who had access to the money in Eastern banks. As a result, much of the net profit from a successful farm went to satisfy commissions and interest charges. Even worse, a single unsuccessful crop often meant foreclosure and loss of one's farm to a distant East Coast banker.

Approximately half of those who went to the West to establish farms eventually migrated to one of the Eastern or Midwestern cities. Given the frequency with which Western farmers went bankrupt, Eastern financiers took on significant risks each time they sent money out West. As a result, the high interest rates Western farmers were forced to accept were not simply the result of greedy Eastern bankers. In politics and finance, however, perception is reality. These charges, along with the frequency of foreclosure, led to the creation of an East-West divide. In addition, because the amount of money that was printed was tied to a finite amount of gold rather than the increasing value of real estate and factories, banks were not able to make as many loans as they would have if there had been more money in circulation.

Corporations might have had easier access to Eastern money, but the limits of the money supply likewise resulted in high interest payments that cut into their profits. The public seldom sympathized with bankers and businessmen, however, and each farm foreclosure or factory shutdown widened the gulf of distrust between labor and capital. The federal government did not believe that it was proper to increase the money supply by printing more currency. This philosophy was influenced by the tradition of noninvolvement in the economy, a tradition of hands-off management known as **laissez-faire**.

Because currency was scarce, its value increased each year—a phenomenon known as deflation. Deflation benefitted banks and those who already controlled large amounts of currency for the simple reason that the money they held increased in value automatically, while the loans they made were repaid with dollars that were worth more than the original dollars the bank had loaned. For those such as farmers who owed money, however, deflation required them to pay back loans in the future with dollars that were worth more than those they had originally received.

The belief that America's bankers and industrialists were corrupt was evidenced by the rapidity with which a single phrase became the symbol of post-Reconstruction America. Referring to the perception of corporate domination and corruption among government officials, novelist Mark Twain labeled the era the Gilded Age in an 1873 novel. However, Twain's contemporaries understood that greed and corruption were hardly new. Would-be reformers in the 1870s referenced the practices of banks and railroads to the questionable finance and cronyism that had been used to finance canals and other projects in decades past.

However, the size and scope of modern graft was now conducted on a national scale. In addition, the number of journalists had increased along with literacy rates. The result was that dozens of newspapers were printed in nearly every language and every city, with many of these journalists exposing scandals or at least repeating rumors of corruption. Even the most benign business deals were conducted with increasingly ambitious financing schemes that invited speculation—among both financiers in Wall Street and those who gathered on Main Street to discuss politics. Similar themes regarding suspicion of corporations and financiers would continue long past the Gilded Age. However, for the first time, a significant number of Americans debated and understood the impact of tariffs and monetary policy on their own lives.

3.2   Growth of Cities and Titans of Industry

The scale of industrial development expanded dramatically following the Civil War as entrepreneurs such as Andrew Carnegie and John D. Rockefeller used the corporate framework to construct empires. These men, along with innovations as simple as barbed wire or as elaborate as the dynamo, each fueled economic growth and changed the landscape of America. Alexander Graham Bell's telephone revolutionized communications, while Thomas Edison's pioneering work in the uses of electricity would transform US factories. However, each of these inventions of the 1870s, with the exception of barbed wire, would not drastically alter American life until the turn of the century. In the meantime, the proliferation of the steam engine and other previous inventions accelerated the transformation of work on farms and within factories. In addition, new ways of structuring production, such as the assembly line, reduced the need for skilled laborers by breaking down the work of craftsmen into simple motions that could be taught to any able bodied man, woman, or child.

laissez-faire

A phrase that roughly translates to "let it be," laissez-faire refers to a political system that enacts few restrictions on the actions of businesses and maintains low taxes on private property.

FIGURE 2.21

Standard Oil was often presented as an aggressive monopoly in the press. In this image, the company appears as an octopus whose tentacles are wrapped around other industries such as steel and shipping. The beast is also in control of Congress and is reaching for the White House.

John D. Rockefeller

The founder of Standard Oil, John D. Rockefeller revolutionized US industry by organizing a number of nominally independent oil companies into a trust.

trust

A group that controls the stock and therefore effectively owns and controls a number of companies. Trusts were established to get around laws intended to prevent monopolies.

America's industrial output increased 70 percent between the Civil War and 1873, an economic upsurge without precedent in an era of global scarcity. Fueling the rapid growth of US productivity was the labor of a quarter-million immigrants who arrived every year with hopes of finding work in America's cities. Urban life in America was seldom the long-term goal for these immigrants, most of who hoped to earn money and eventually return to their homelands. For this reason, few immigrants saw any reason to learn English or assimilate into what they viewed, at least initially, as a foreign nation. Even those who considered making America their home usually saw urban life as a temporary way station on their way toward saving money and purchasing a farm somewhere in the nation's interior.

Standing between the immigrant's dream of returning home or buying land was the fact that many of these immigrants borrowed money to finance their voyage. Even those who did not enter the nation in debt rarely earned more money than they needed for their daily survival. In this way, many immigrants experienced a state of financial dependency that was not unlike that of the sharecropper. However, the rapid growth of the US economy allowed many of these immigrants the opportunity to eventually escape the cycle of debt that was becoming a permanent feature of the rural South. Unfortunately, low wages and insecurity of employment left most of them trapped in the ethnic enclaves of America's cities where they worked for wages rather than achieving their dream of financial independence.

Along with the creation of corporate finance and the growing landless population of potential laborers, new innovations in corporate management such as the trust permitted the growth of industrial America. By the end of the Reconstruction, **John D. Rockefeller** had run his local competitors out of business and controlled most of the oil refineries in Cleveland. His methods were both ruthless and ingenious, as he made secret deals with suppliers and the railroads that allowed him to lower prices until his competitors agreed to sell their refineries to Rockefeller's Standard Oil Company. Rockefeller now hoped to expand his holdings to become the largest oil company in the United States. Unfortunately for Rockefeller, hundreds of other oil refineries existed at this time. The gasoline-fueled internal combustion engine was just being developed and would not become widespread until the early 1900s. As a result, the oil business at this time produced mostly lubricants and fuel for heating lamps—products that were relatively easy to create from crude oil. In addition to the large number of simple refineries, Ohio and other states prevented those who owned oil refineries in one locality from buying their competitors or expanding their businesses to other states.

Rockefeller designed a method of sidestepping the law by creating a new form of corporate management/ownership called the **trust**. Rockefeller's Standard Oil Trust was simply a group of investors controlled by Rockefeller who bought the stock of various "independent" oil companies in various states. This stock was then held "in trust" for Standard's stockholders. Although it would have been illegal for Rockefeller or Standard Oil to own all of these oil companies directly, it was not illegal to purchase publicly traded stock. As long as Rockefeller's trustees owned the majority of shares, they could control the decisions made by each "independent" oil company and reap the majority of the profits. And it was all completely legal.

Rockefeller used the trust and the methods that had permitted him to corner the refinery business in Cleveland to expand his holdings and control of the oil industry. As Standard Oil grew, it became harder for other oil companies to match Rockefeller's prices because he demanded and received discounts from suppliers and shippers. Rockefeller's competitors were simply too small to demand similar concessions, and shareholders were all too willing to sell their declining stock to Rockefeller's trust at higher-than-market prices. By the 1890s, Standard Oil controlled 90 percent of the nation's oil refineries. Titans within other industries followed suit by creating trusts that soon controlled the stock of many corporations. In addition, many of the trustees who effectively controlled each of these industries sat on dozens of corporate boards and made "gentleman's agreements" with one another to avoid what they believed would be excessive competition.

Steel production required more investment than the early oil refineries, which in turn required government intervention. Railroad development and federal tariffs barring the importation of steel from more developed industrial nations in Europe permitted US entrepreneurs to create a domestic steel industry. Demand for steel was high throughout the nation as the navy expanded and railroad mileage doubled every decade between the Civil War and 1890. A Scottish immigrant by the name of **Andrew Carnegie** had risen through the ranks of corporate America, his talent and ambition being noticed by every supervisor from his boyhood years in a telegraph office. Some of these men even loaned money to the ambitious Carnegie, which he invested wisely. Using these proceeds as collateral, Carnegie began investing in steel production. Between his modest fortune and his exceptional connections, Carnegie financed the creation of a modern steel mill based on new technologies he had observed in Britain. With domestic financing and international technology, Carnegie was soon able to make better steel for lower prices than his competitors.

Rather than attempt to indirectly purchase and control competing firms, as Rockefeller had done, Carnegie believed the secret to the steel industry was to control every aspect of the steel-making process. Rather than pay suppliers for raw materials and transportation companies for shipping costs, Carnegie sought to purchase his own mines and own a controlling interest in shipping companies and railroads. As a result, Carnegie controlled every aspect of steel production and distributions and could offer his products at better prices than any other manufacturer. While Britain had been the birthplace of the Bessemer process on which Carnegie based his production methods, Carnegie's US Steel corporation produced more steel than the entire British Empire by the turn of the century. His methods were just as brutal as Rockefeller's were, but he would later become one of the most beloved men in the nation when he donated most of his personal fortune of $300 million to charitable causes.

3.3 Culture and Politics

Business leaders utilized new ideas from the field of science to study methods of production, as well as develop new technologies. Many began to liken the cutthroat competition of the business world to that of the natural world, a doctrine known as **social Darwinism**. Charles Darwin's *Origin of Species* posited that animals, which were better adapted to their environment, were more likely to survive. More importantly, he argued that nature assigned new traits to animals such as longer legs or thicker fur. If these traits aided their survival, Darwin argued, a process of natural selection occurred in which the animals with these traits would thrive while others would perish. Before long, advocates of all kinds of social theories used Darwin's ideas about animals to justify their preconceived ideas about race, ethnicity, and even the business world.

Although many business leaders (and most defenders of white supremacy) likely never read Darwin's books, they adopted slogans such as "natural selection" and "survival of the fittest" to sanitize their elimination of rivals as "natural." Darwin might not agree that the creation of trusts and the often devious methods business leaders employed to eliminate rivals fit his definition of natural selection. He would especially take exception to the bribes and other methods that corporations used to gain government contracts over their rivals—a process that actually reduced competition. If anything, the creation of trusts and other methods designed to reduce competition actually thwarted the evolution of more efficient business methods. At the same time, the emergence of larger corporations that could take advantage of economies of scale fit Darwinian concepts of evolution within the business world. By consuming their less-efficient rivals, those corporations with superior traits were more likely to survive.

Late in his life, Carnegie sought to mitigate some of the problems inherent in this kind of hyper-competitive business mind-set. Carnegie published *The Gospel of Wealth* in 1889, espousing the idea that the wealthy industrialist had an obligation to care for the less fortunate, including his own workforce. Veterans of Carnegie's business empire responded to their aging employer's book with mixed reactions. Some believed that the steel magnate had provided thousands of well-paying jobs and praised Carnegie's generosity in endowing libraries and charitable projects later in his life. Others argued that Carnegie had been a tyrannical businessman who still accepted many of the evolutionary tenets of social Darwinism. At best he had become paternalistic, they argued, assuming that the wealthy possessed superior intellect and vision, which obligated them to provide for those who were less endowed.

Financiers such as **J. Pierpont Morgan** agreed, although Morgan believed the greatest contribution he could make was by ensuring stability in a financial system he and his banking associates increasingly controlled. Morgan, like most of the nation's wealthy men of the 1870s and 1880s, had avoided service during the Civil War by hiring a substitute to serve in his place after being drafted. He then negotiated a lucrative deal during the war, purchasing and reselling obsolete rifles for a tidy profit. By the 1890s, Morgan controlled the finances of four of the nation's six largest railroads. Morgan would also finance the purchase of Carnegie's US Steel, issuing stock to the public at a price significantly higher than the company was worth. At the same time, Morgan demonstrated that the wealthy people could serve the public interest and their own interests at the same time. Morgan used his influence to calm

Andrew Carnegie

Rose from humble origins to become the leading steel producer in the world, Andrew Carnegie sought to control every aspect of steel production and lower costs by direct ownership of mines, foundries, and railroads. Carnegie became a philanthropist in later life, gifting his enormous fortune to construct libraries, schools, and institutions of higher education.

social Darwinism

Inspired by a loose interpretation of Darwin's theory of evolution, social Darwinism proposes the theory that the human advancement will be facilitated if those who are not able to effectively compete in society are not artificially assisted, therefore becoming less likely to pass on their inferior traits.

J. Pierpont Morgan

The leading financier of the late nineteenth and early twentieth century, J. P. Morgan helped to finance the consolidation of industry and personally negotiated the creation of leading corporations such as General Electric and US Steel.

investors during various financial crises, often using his own money to back a system in danger of collapse.

Despite the fact that bankers such as J. P. Morgan at times controlled more gold than the federal government, corporations recognized that their fortunes remained dependent on the favorable operation of the political system. The government controlled laws and regulations regarding trade and finance, as well as the money supply itself. In addition, business leaders also recognized the importance of winning government contracts. The vast majority of these contracts, as well as laws and regulations governing corporate behavior, were controlled by state and local governments. These elected officials were notorious for expecting political contributions and exchanging financial support for favorable legislation. Urban politics operated within the patronage system, a label referring to the expectation that government jobs and contracts would be awarded to those who contributed the most to the political party in power. This same tendency was sometimes called the "spoils system." This label was an abbreviated form of the phrase "to the victor go the spoils." Under such a system, a victorious mayor would be expected to reward government jobs and contracts, "the spoils of office," to those who had contributed the most to his campaign.

3.4   The New South

The shadow of the Civil War lingered throughout the South during and beyond Reconstruction. Many of the region's railroads, bridges, and factories had been destroyed and were only gradually rebuilt. Major ports like Norfolk and Charleston limped along, while pilots steered around the remains of sunken ships. Both the plantation belt and the up-country remained isolated from the sources of capital that might spur commercial development. Seaports and a handful of cities such as Atlanta, Raleigh, Lexington, and Memphis rebounded more quickly than the interior, and some Southerners even enjoyed a measure of prosperity by the late 1870s. A handful of Southerners even predicted that the destruction of war might lead to sectional rebirth through a more diversified economy. The lesson of the war, they argued, was the fallacy of an economy based only on a few crops, such as cotton, and a political system dominated by wealthy planters. Soon these voices included a group of reformers, investors, and industrialists who called for the creation of a **New South** modeled on individual family farms and industrial prosperity. By merging the finest traditions of the Old South with the profitability of Northern industry and the egalitarianism and independence of the West, they argued, the former Confederacy might reinvent itself and become the leading region of the United States.

Editor **Henry Grady** was among the leading proponents of such a vision. Grady believed that the end of slavery and the decline of the planter aristocracy would permit greater democracy while encouraging immigration and the growth of factories. He also believed the South enjoyed superior advantages of climate, natural resources, and inexpensive labor. He and other New South boosters understood that development was dependent on railroad construction. The South's rail infrastructure before the Civil War was haphazard. Many Southern railroads had been built to connect leading cotton plantations to ports rather than cities. In addition, Southern tracks had been built by a patchwork of private companies that each set their tracks at different widths. The result was that cars and engines could not run on the same tracks as they journeyed throughout the region.

Under the direction of New South promoters, total rail miles increased 400 percent during the 1870s and 1880s. Equally important, the South reconstructed existing track to accommodate national standards and the same train that ran in Manhattan could now operate in Mobile. By the end of the century, the South became the leading producer of cloth and employed more than 100,000 workers within the textile industry. However, this production came at its own price as many mills were owned and controlled by Northerners who viewed Southern poverty as an opportunity to hire Southern women and children at much lower rates.

FIGURE 2.22

An image celebrating the *commercial might* of the United States marching across the ocean and challenging the "divine right" of European monarchs. J. P. Morgan personifies the triumph of American industry and Capitalism with its cornucopia of railroads, telegraph lines, steamships, and factories. The image plays on the contemporary notion that Europe was still dominated by feudal lords.

New South

A progressive vision for the South based on modeling the economic success of the North and West by promoting individual family farms rather than plantations and encouraging the development of industry.

Henry Grady

A Georgia editor and promoter of the New South, Grady valued education and hoped to promote a vision for his region based on both industry and agriculture.

The iron and steel industry was equally important to the New South and usually provided higher wages. Iron ore was taken directly from Appalachian mines to Southern steel cities such as Birmingham. Much of the wealth created by these factories helped spur the construction of additional factories and industries throughout the South. At the same time, most of the original capital to build these enterprises came from Northerners who would continue to control the industry and usually operated Southern mills in a way designed to enrich their own region. As a result, Grady's vision was only partly fulfilled.

Cotton, along with other cash crops such as tobacco and rice, remained the core of the Southern economy. The indebtedness of those who produced these crops kept many Southerners desperately poor. Sharecropping expanded throughout the 1870s and 1880s as small farmers fell deeper into debt and were forced to sell their land and work on the farms of others. These *others* were usually in debt themselves. As a result, they required that hired workers plant cotton—one of the few crops that could reliably be sold for cash each harvest.

By 1890, 40 percent of families in the Deep South were sharecroppers who desperately needed to maximize every acre of land that was available to them if they were to ever escape the cycle of debt. Many sharecroppers turned to fertilizers and used methods that increased short-term yields but depleted the topsoil. Without trees and natural grasses, millions of acres of land had no vegetation at harvest time. Rain and wind finished the process of soil erosion begun by overplanting. Together, this ecologically unsustainable model slowly destroyed the productivity of many Southern farms and deposited silt and fertilizer into Southern rivers.

The poverty of the land and people who lived on it was further exasperated by the **crop lien system**. The landowner and the merchant who provisioned the sharecropper were usually in debt themselves. Influenced by merchants, bankers, and landlords, Southern courts established a hierarchy that determined who would get paid first at harvest time. The laborer occupied the lowest rung—being paid only after merchants, mills, banks, brokers, and the landowner were satisfied. As a result, the crop lien system meant that the sharecropper had to assume the risks and finance many aspects of cotton production, even though they were essentially wage laborers. Sharecroppers bought seed and supplies on their own accounts, for which they were legally liable.

Courts defended the practice of charging high interest rates to laborers for items purchased on credit, even though laborers' wages were withheld during this same period and did not earn interest. Because of these laws, sharecropping transferred much of the risk of running a business on the laborer. In addition, interest rates for laborers ranged "from 24 percent to grand larceny" according to one Southerner. Employees in factories were paid an established amount after each day or week, while the owners of factories were the only ones liable for the loans used to purchase equipment and raw materials. The sharecropper was paid once a season if the crop was successful, and only after satisfying expenses, interest charges, and any other obligations.

The sharecropper was not the only potential victim since many landowners and merchants also lost money. At the root of the problem was the dire economic condition of the South. Without capital or access to the credit required to build factories, Southern elites turned to cotton production at the exact same time that global overproduction lowered cotton prices to one-third of their antebellum levels. While the plight of landlords may pale in comparison to those who worked their fields, many planters were also caught in their own cycle of debt as they borrowed money at high interest rates to produce cotton that kept dropping in price. Planters and merchants enjoyed one tremendous advantage, however, as crop lien laws guaranteed they were paid first when the cotton was sold at market. For this reason, many whites and former slaves who worked the land turned toward their elected representatives in hope of reforming these laws. They also petitioned in favor of public schools and a more progressive tax code. Others hoped their elected representatives would encourage the growth of industries that would provide better job opportunities and an alternative to cotton production.

Tobacco was one of the few growth industries controlled almost exclusively by Southerners. James Duke was the ambitious son of a wealthy tobacco factory owner who may have been the first to fully grasp the potential of marketing within his industry. Americans preferred smoking cigars and pipes, which were considered masculine, especially when compared to the cigarette, which was heavily stigmatized as effeminate. Cigarettes were also associated with despised immigrant groups from central and southern Europe, which further stigmatized their use among most "white" Americans. Duke believed he could change this image. He invested heavily in new machinery that could produce cigarettes faster and cheaper than any other form of tobacco, and sold his products at prices below cost. He also invested heavily in marketing, plastering images of "manly" men enjoying cigarettes that were now readily available and very inexpensive. He even gave free samples to soldiers and

FIGURE 2.23

African Americans at work under white supervision at a tobacco plant in Richmond, Virginia. This photo was part of an international display that meant to show racial harmony.

crop lien system

A system of credit that was common throughout the South, the crop lien system allowed farmers to finance their operations by using their future crops as collateral for loans. Interest rates for these kinds of loans were high, a fact that prevented most borrowers from prospering even when crop yields were high.

FIGURE 2.24

Women at work at the Mollahan mill in South Carolina. In the past, cotton mills had to be located near sources of running water and were therefore more likely to be located in New England.

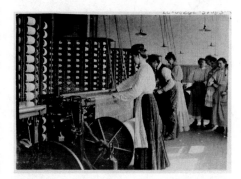

"manly" blue-collar workers. As a result, the image of the cigarette was rehabilitated and working-class men adopted the highly addictive product as part of their culture.

Because of his earlier efforts to eliminate competitors, Duke's American Tobacco Company controlled 90 percent of the tobacco market by the turn of the century. In 1911, Progressives within the federal government ordered the company broken up, not because of well-known health risks, but because they believed Duke had established a monopoly. By this time, Duke had invested in energy and other industries that spurred job construction throughout North Carolina and surrounding communities. He would also donate much of his fortune to various universities in the region. His money might have been better invested in the public schools of the South, as spending per pupil in this region was the lowest in the nation, even before it dropped by 50 percent once the Radical Republicans were purged from office. Fifteen percent of whites could not read, while half of the black population had no public schools open to its members within a child's walking distance.

In fairness, most Southern states devoted a similar percentage of their total tax revenue to public schools, as did other states. Because taxes on land remained low, there simply was not much revenue for education, and efforts to increase taxes were usually rebuffed by the powerful Democratic Party that represented landowners. It should also be pointed out that school segregation was not limited to the South. Virtually every Northern and Western community with a black, Hispanic, or Asian population above 15 percent also maintained schools that were segregated in one form or another. States as far west as Missouri and as far north as Delaware required separate schools by law. Other states, such as Kansas, permitted segregation as long as there were enough black students to justify the added expense of operating two school systems.

Southern educational boosters were on the defensive following Reconstruction, yet were able to develop over a hundred denominational colleges. States also utilized revenue from federal land sales to create universities that would focus on teaching agricultural science and industrial skills they hoped would boost the commercial fortune of their region. The Virginia legislature set aside an entire quarry of what would soon be known as "Hokie Stone" to create Virginia Polytechnic and State University in the hills of Blacksburg. The first public university in Texas opened its doors in rural Brazos County and was likewise dedicated to "practical" educational fields such as agriculture and mechanics. Black politicians and community leaders also petitioned and secured the creation of dozens of agricultural and technical colleges. Savannah State, North Carolina A & T, and Florida A & M were among those founded during the 1880s and 1890s, despite prejudice and tremendous financial obstacles.

FIGURE 2.25

Americans recognized that nicotine was addictive and cigarettes were health hazards during the nineteenth century. This turn-of-the-century product promises to cure one's addiction to nicotine for only five dollars.

Together with white state colleges such as Georgia Tech, North Carolina College of Agriculture and Mechanical Arts (known presently as NC State), and Florida Agricultural College (known today as the University of Florida), the New South embraced the idea that colleges should teach a trade in addition to the liberal arts. These notions of college as a place of vocational training would be criticized by the academy in future generations. However, the idea of college as a place of learning a trade would once again steer the ambitions of college students and administrators by the late twentieth century. Like the late nineteenth century, modern colleges and universities focus more resources toward placing students in specific jobs in business and industry rather than the arts, humanities, and literature.

New South promoters also hoped to encourage foreign immigration to their region. Some boosters even attempted to lure Asian and Hispanic settlers to the region. However, the existence of the crop lien system and the resultant conditions sharecroppers faced discouraged outside immigration. The poverty of the rural South also allowed factories to pay low wages and still attract workers from the hinterlands. Foreign immigration remained negligible in the South at a time when the North and West were attracting millions of new settlers each year. Promoters of the New South wrote thousands of editorials suggesting ways to remedy the imbalance. Many of these editorials blamed the South's failure to attract its share of "honest labor" from Europe on the presence of "shiftless" nonwhite laborers. Others were more forthright, arguing that native white and foreign laborers would not enter the South because they would receive the same starvation wages that were paid to black workers and sharecroppers of all races.

Because of the Republican Party's affiliation with the black vote during Reconstruction, white voters remained loyal to the national Democrat Party between Reconstruction and the civil rights movement of the 1960s. However, a wealth of independent candidates and political parties existed on the local level. As a result, the New South was both a political backwater and the birthplace of the largest grassroots third-party movement in US history during the 1890s. In the near term, a diverse lot of unreconstructed Confederates, New South business promoters, gentlemen planters, backwoods populists, and small farmers constituted a Southern Democratic Party that agreed on little else than the need to prevent former slaves from ever voting or holding office again.

3.5   Immigration, Race, and Ethnicity

Economic growth in the North and South, like the West, was dependent on family labor. Sharecropping forced Southern children to work in cotton fields, but children of all regions were expected to labor on family farms. City life seldom led to an escape from adult work. Nearly one in four urban children held full-time jobs after the Civil War. Immigrants, farmers, and former slaves all shared a reverence for education. At the same time, they faced the crushing reality that the labor of their children was often the difference between starvation and survival. New England mirrored the South in the proportion of urban children who worked in textile mills, while the youth of many children in Appalachia was spent underground in coal mines. Each of these jobs made old women and old men out of their youthful practitioners. Children were estimated to be twice as likely to suffer workplace injuries as their adult coworkers. By 1880, only a half-dozen states had passed laws requiring children to have reached the age of twelve prior to entering the workplace. For some parents, child labor laws threatened to lower the family income to unsustainable levels. As a result, child labor laws were only as effective as parents and factory operators chose to make them.

More than 200,000 immigrants arrived in New York City alone each year following the Civil War, with many more arriving in port cities of the East and West. With the exception of prejudice against Asian immigrants along the West Coast and people of Hispanic descent in the Southwest, assumptions that America's nonwhites and new arrivals were part of a "lower order" were usually most visible in the cities of the East and Midwest. Despite the diversity of enclaves such as New York, Baltimore, and Philadelphia, the ethnically segregated neighborhoods of these seaports prevented the creation of a multicultural "composite nation" advocated by Frederick Douglass during Reconstruction. Anti-immigrant prejudice was pervasive, as was the use of scapegoats for urban problems. For example, an urban legend placed the blame for the Great Chicago Fire of 1871 at the feet of a careless Irish immigrant and the hooves of her filthy cow.

Although the story of the Chicago Fire had in fact no basis, it spread almost as quickly as the fire itself because it bolstered existing assumptions that the Irish were irresponsible and dangerous. Such xenophobic sentiment was also used to sanitize crime and infant mortality rates. Children born in America's ethnic enclaves were three to five times more likely to die in their infancy than children born to the wealthy and middle class. That these statistics aroused little alarm in late nineteenth-century America demonstrated that many saw the death of immigrant children as something less than a national tragedy.

Immigrants were also the targets of violence waged by native whites who resented their presence. In the Border South communities of Cincinnati and St. Louis, emancipation and black migration intensified the ethnic and racial prejudices of white residents. From the perspective of these whites, it seemed that each day, some black workers were "imported" into the city so that a company could replace a white worker for lower wages. River ports from Cincinnati to Pittsburgh experienced decline in traffic during the 1870s and 1880s as railroads replaced riverboats. That this occurred at the same moment former slaves and immigrants arrived in river cities looking for work led to increased racial tension throughout the Ohio River Valley. As a result, both groups were often the scapegoats for a decline in industries that began long before they arrived.

FIGURE 2.26

Cincinnati was once one of the largest cities in America due to its location on the Ohio River. This 1873 image shows scenes from one of the many pork-processing plants in a neighborhood referred to as Pigtown.

PORK PACKING IN CINCINNATI.

The potential for conflict between African Americans and white workers was especially pronounced in port cities in former slaveholding states beyond the Deep South, such as Delaware and Maryland. White Baltimore workers demanded that companies stop hiring blacks in the shipping trades during the 1870s. Although black men dominated several antebellum trades along the waterfront, such as caulkers, many unemployed whites moved to cities like Baltimore and demanded that black men in these fields be fired to provide more jobs for white Americans. Black men in Baltimore fought to maintain their jobs but were eventually forced out by white employers. One group of black men responded by forming the Chesapeake Marine Railway and Dry Dock Company, a black-owned and controlled shipbuilding company that was formed in the immediate aftermath of the Civil War. These men ran very successful businesses in the city's Inner Harbor for two decades.

However, racism limited the ability of this company's officers to obtain loans needed to modernize their facilities. As a result, the company could not afford the needed improvements to work on steel-hulled ships that dominated the industry by the end of the century. For most African Americans in and beyond the Baltimore harbor, the fact whites controlled most industries and only considered black women as domestics and black men for the worst and lowest-paying jobs was the worst aspect of the color line. The same was true of numerous immigrant groups. Some who saw few other options turned away from legitimate work and turned to a subeconomy that featured petty theft, gambling, prostitution, and crime. These shadow communities grew in every American city and eschewed traditional mores and values while also violating racial lines. The alleyways and taverns of these urban environments were home to both interracial cohabitation and conflict, making the inner cities the first racially integrated communities in America. These were no racial utopias, however, as black-white and ethnic-religious conflicts in each of these neighborhoods frequently descended into violence.

REVIEW AND CRITICAL THINKING

1. In what ways did the government influence the emergence of large companies? What were the methods used by men such as Carnegie, Rockefeller, and Morgan? Did these individuals become wealthy by creating superior methods of production and finance, or did they simply eliminate their rivals in ways that damaged the economy?

2. What caused the Panic of 1873? How did the nation's economic system become so interdependent that these factors could spread throughout the country?

3. Explain how stocks, bonds, tariffs, and decisions regarding the issue of government currency affected the nation's economy. What was inflation and deflation, and why did different Americans view inflation in different ways?

4. What, if anything, was "new" about the New South? What were the obstacles New South promoters faced? To what degree did they overcome these obstacles and develop industry and other important resources for sustained growth?

5. Consider the way immigration affected the diversity of America's cities during this period. In what ways might prejudice have benefitted employers and divided workers? Do you think employers were responsible for these attitudes?

---

4. CHALLENGING THE GILDED AGE

LEARNING OBJECTIVES

1. Define the term *Gilded Age*, and describe the way various groups such as the Readjusters, Grangers, and labor unions resisted domination by industrialists and corrupt politicians.

2. Compare the purpose and creation of labor unions and agrarian organizations such as the Grange. Explain their purpose and the way that these organizations demonstrate the agency of "everyday people" during this period.

3. Explain the ideas behind the New Departure. Describe the efforts and ideas of suffragists during this era, as well as the obstacles they faced.

4.1 National Politics and the Gilded Age

The term **Gilded Age** was first coined by novelist Mark Twain as an indictment of the era's greed and corruption. The term itself was a protest against the factors that led to the consolidation of power into the hands of a small coterie of industrialists and politicians. Overreliance on the image of the Gilded Age and its corruption and corporate power may create the false impression that these men (and a few women) dominated life during the late nineteenth century. In reality, half of Americans lived and worked on farms during this era. In addition, at least half of those classified by the US Census as city dwellers lived in towns with only a few thousand residents. Although all Americans were affected by the growth of corporate power, they remained much more independent of national markets and national political parties than any generation that followed. Many historians hesitate to use the label Gilded Age because it may create the false assumption that corruption typified the era. Perhaps more importantly, simple labels deny the complexity of an era that saw personal standards of living expand alongside the growth of industry. The Gilded Age was host to corruption but also grassroots protest against corruption. It saw the expansion of corporate power but also the expansion of democracy for hundreds of thousands of women.

National politics entered a phase of relative equilibrium following Reconstruction. Both parties had roughly equivalent electoral strength on a national level. However, within a particular region and state, one or the other party was usually so dominant that the concerns of voters could be neglected without immediate consequences at the polls. Presidential elections during this time were close, yet stale and predictable as the South supported the Democratic candidate, while the West and North tended to vote Republican. Rutherford B. Hayes remained tainted by the Compromise of 1877 and was despised by many workers for his unprecedented use of military power to curtail the labor strikes later that year. Hayes wisely decided against running for reelection in 1880. Republican James A. Garfield defeated Democrat Winfield Hancock, an election that was already decided by the political affiliation of each state and the Electoral College system, even though the popular vote was extremely close. Garfield swept New England, the Midwest, and most of the West. Although Hancock won California, this state was not yet populous enough to swing the election, and the Democrats struggled to win more than a

Gilded Age

A period of rapid economic growth and expansion between Reconstruction and the turn of the century. The phrase has a negative connotation, as *gilded* refers to an object that is covered in a superficial layer of gold.

few states beyond the South. The major difference between the two parties was that the Republicans supported slightly higher tariffs.

FIGURE 2.27

An artist's rendition of the Garfield assassination. The president was shot at a train depot in Washington, DC. He was on his way to Williams College, the president's alma mater, to deliver a speech.

Leading political figures often spoke out against the dangers of the patronage system. However, it was not until the assassination of President James Garfield in July 1881 that significant measures were taken to reform the way government jobs were distributed. Garfield was killed by a deranged man who was apparently disappointed that the president had not returned his letters or appointed him to an important diplomatic post. The assassination led journalists to investigate the many cases were individuals had received government jobs they were not qualified for simply because they had political connections. These investigations revealed shocking nepotism within political machines, even evidence of graft in the newspapers themselves. For example, office seekers openly advertised their willingness to "kick back" portions of their salary to any political party or politician that could secure them a job.

Pendleton Civil Service Act

A law passed in 1883 that established the Civil Service Commission, a federal agency that administers competitive examinations for those seeking certain government jobs.

Garfield's replacement, Chester A. Arthur, had only been nominated as vice president because of his connections to political machines. In response, Congress passed the **Pendleton Civil Service Act**. Arthur had little choice but to support the new law, which introduced modest reforms. The Pendleton Act prohibited federal officeholders from making contributions to the politicians who had appointed them. In addition, it established the Civil Service Commission. This federal agency administered competitive examinations for those seeking certain government jobs. Most bureaucrats were still appointed rather than selected for merit during the 1880s, and only a small percentage of federal jobs required applicants to pass any examination. However, the Civil Service Commission would expand and influence similar reform in states and cities.

Chester Arthur hoped to win election in his own right in 1884. However, despite his support for the Pendleton Act, he remained associated with the political machines that secured his original nomination to the vice-presidency. With the support of some Republicans who refused to support Arthur, former Buffalo mayor and Democratic candidate Grover Cleveland prevailed in 1884. The tariff remained the prevailing issue of the election, with more Americans favoring the reduction of these taxes due to the growing surplus of the federal treasury. Government spending remained low enough that even without federal income taxes, the loans made during the Civil War could be repaid through tariffs with money left over. Cleveland recommended reducing the tariff, which won the support of the South as well as many others who hoped to start exporting US goods.

While in office, Cleveland deferred to Congress and the states. He believed in limited federal power and hoped to reconcile the continuing cultural divide between the South and the North. The president cited these doctrines and goals in defense of his decision to not intervene in the South, even when a growing number of black men were lynched for attempting to vote, start businesses, or simply refused to abide by new laws mandating racial segregation. Cleveland was much more responsive to the petitions of farmers who felt that they were being crushed by the monopolistic practices of railroads. The president approved the Interstate Commerce Act, which provided limited federal regulation of railroads.

In 1888, Cleveland was defeated by Republican Benjamin Harrison. As President, Harrison raised tariffs even higher in hopes of protecting Northern industry. However, Cleveland would return to the White House four years later, defeating Harrison in 1892. The three presidential elections between 1880 and 1888 were incredibly close contests. The popular vote between the Republican and Democratic candidate in each of these elections was so close that less than 1 percent of the nation's voters preferred one candidate over the other. In 1892, the most important development was not Cleveland's slightly larger margin of victory, but the emergence of a third political party that introduced measures that were much more compelling to most voters than the tariff. In the years leading up to this election, urban and rural reformers practiced a form of activism at the local level that demonstrates that the vitality of local politics during the Gilded Age.

4.2   Readjusters and Reformers

Elections in nineteenth-century America were ripe with corruption, ranging from the free flow of whiskey provided by political parties to outright bribery, fraud, and intimidation of voters. Ballots were printed in advance and distributed to voters who were often pressured by their employers or landlords to vote for a certain candidate. These preprinted ballots did not provide voters the option of "splitting the ticket" by voting for candidates of various political parties. Even worse, these ballots were often printed on colored paper, making it obvious to the dozens of men standing around the ballot box who voted for what party in an era where the secret ballot was unheard of and community members knew everyone by name. Political machines emerged in America's cities and controlled elections by offering small bribes to the impoverished voters of working-class and immigrant neighborhoods. They also formed alliances with business and some labor leaders. These alliances allowed the lieutenants of the machine to reward loyal voters with jobs while providing their larger donors in industry with government contracts. Neighborhood political leaders affiliated with the machine also used some of the money to provide needed social services. As a result, many of the working class viewed the machine politicians as modern-day Robin Hoods and their only friends in politics.

Others turned to monetary policy as a method of redress. The **Greenback Party** emerged during the 1870s and attracted a million voters for its various candidates by 1878. As the name suggests, the Greenbackers promoted the creation of a national currency that was not backed by gold. Greenbackers were usually farmers who were deeply in debt or aspiring entrepreneurs who had been prevented from borrowing money because of the limited money supply tied to gold. Greenbackers recognized that if the government abandoned the gold standard or otherwise created more money, inflation and higher prices/wages would be the result. This prospect terrified those with money in the bank, but for those in debt, inflation would help their situation considerably. Farm prices and wages would increase to keep up with the cost of living, yet the amount owed to a bank would remain the same and actually be much easier to pay back.

When the Greenbackers succeeded in electing over a dozen congressmen in the 1878 election, creditors and the wealthy responded with a broad attack at any attempt to abandon the gold standard as a dangerous Communist plot. While much of the rhetoric was clearly intended to derail discussion of the Greenbackers' ideas, moderates reminded voters that a currency backed by gold was an international standard of most developed nations and the only guarantee of that currency's value. Most Americans agreed that experimenting with fiat currency was a risk they could not afford in a time of peace. However, the ideas of the Greenbackers lasted long after their party disintegrated in the early 1880s.

FIGURE 2.28

Opponents of the Greenbackers attempted to discredit their economic ideas by associating them with political movements that were considered foreign and radical. Here, a Greenbacker embraces supporters of the Socialist and Communist movements. Also pictured is a cross-dressing man holding the banner of women's suffrage.

THE FACTORS OF THE GREENBACK-LABOR-SOCIALIST-WOMAN-SUFFRAGE PARTY.

Greenback Party

A short-lived third-party movement that sought to increase the amount of money in circulation by having the government print legal currency that was not tied to the nation's gold reserves. This action would cause inflation, something that would aid farmers who were usually in debt and struggling with declining crop prices.

National Grange of the Patrons of Husbandry

Known simply as the Grange and composed of local chapters that served as both a social and fraternal organization for farmers. The Grange grew rapidly during the late nineteenth century, and many Grange leaders began turning toward politics to address the concerns of their members.

Despite the near monopoly of Southern Democrats, some of the most interesting and progressive political ideas originated from the South and its various local political groups loosely connected to the **National Grange of the Patrons of Husbandry**. Known as the Grange, the organization grew quickly from isolated chapters of isolated farmers looking for social connections and a measure of economic cooperative activity. Members soon included educational and political events among harvest festivals and other social events. They also began to work collectively to promote their mutual self-interest as farmers, pooling their resources to purchase a tractor or harvester that none could afford on his own. The Grange also sought to pool their resources to purchase grain elevators, start cooperative stores, and even sponsored lawsuits against monopolistic railroads.

The Grange was most successful as a local organization, although its national representatives also secured legislation on behalf of its members. For example, they secured federal regulation of grain elevators they believed were acting as monopolies and charging exorbitant rates. After railroads and grain elevators challenged the legality of government regulation, the Grange even won a Supreme Court decision that was favorable to its members. In 1877, the court ruled in *Munn v. Illinois* that privately owned grain elevators were operated in the public interest much like utility companies and were therefore subject to government regulation. By the 1890s, most local Granges and the local third parties that were loosely affiliated with the Grange had declined or merged with other groups. Like the Greenbackers, the ideas of the Grangers about collective action and politics would live on and inspire a national movement.

Bourbons

The name given to aristocratic leaders of the South. The name comes from a similar label that was given to the large landlords of France that kept their workers in a state of economic servitude.

Readjusters

Progressive reformers in Virginia and other areas of the South that sought to challenge the rule of elite landowners. The name given to these reformers reflects their desire to "reduce" the state debt and "adjust" the amount of money that went toward services such as education.

The most successful third-party movement of the early 1880s emerged in Virginia. Like most former Confederate states, Virginia's state government was saddled with enormous debt. A former Confederate general named William Mahone sought to unite poor whites and poor blacks together against the planter elite who still dominated state politics. These elites were known as **Bourbons** throughout the South by their opponents. The name was a reference to the European aristocracy that dominated France in spite of the will of the agricultural workers and artisans who led to popular revolts and beheadings every other generation. Believing the American Bourbons of the South controlled the Democratic Party, Virginians of diverse backgrounds rallied behind Mahone and a slate of candidates known as **Readjusters**.

FIGURE 2.29

An 1873 promotional poster for the National Grange. Notice the incorporation of various scenes depicting the cooperation of neighbors, harmonious family life, and the bountiful harvest provided by the Grange member.

In 1879, the Readjusters won control of the state legislature and initiated their plan to "reduce" the state debt and "adjust" the amount of money that went to meaningful government services such as education. Faced with a popular challenge that temporarily united white and black voters behind a Progressive vision of economic reform, the Bourbons fought back by exploiting the long-standing prejudice of race. The affiliation of the Readjusters with local and national Republicans provided all the evidence white voters needed to substantiate allegations that the goal of the Readjusters was to return the state to the "bayonet rule" of federal troops during Reconstruction. The racial and regional loyalty of white voters who voted alongside blacks and Northerners was equated with the highest dishonor on the white race. The Readjusters were voted out of office by 1883, and their goals of separate but relatively equal funding for education and the elimination of poll taxes that kept poor people of all races from voting were defeated.

4.3   Rise of Organized Labor

Labor divided along the lines of specific trades at this time, forming unions within each trade in the hopes of higher wages and better working conditions. Just as the Southerners who sought to challenge the power structure faced enormous obstacles, urban workers in the North and West sought to challenge the dominant power structure. In so doing, they faced dire consequences if they failed. Urban workers participating in union organization might be **blacklisted**—a practice where employers maintained and shared "do not hire" lists of suspected labor organizers with one another. A few underground labor organizations such as the **Knights of Labor** emerged as a secret worker's fraternity with utopian goals. The Knights believed in a radical reordering of the economic system with factories being collectively owned and controlled by the workers. In some ways, this was a similar vision offered by those who had advocated collective land redistribution to former slaves following the Civil War. However, like radical ideas about land, the Knights won few converts to their philosophy of collective ownership of factories, although their membership increased in the years that followed.

The Knights attracted a small but devout following in their early years. By 1879, there were 10,000 members when Scranton, Pennsylvania, mayor Terrance Powderly was also selected to lead the Knights. Membership grew exponentially to 700,000 members following a successful strike by some members of the Knights in 1886. About 10 percent of members were women and African Americans—something that made the Knights very unique at this time but also aroused opposition among other labor movements. Ironically, the philosophy of the Knights of Labor was not one based on winning tactical goals such as raises, but rather on mobilizing politically in hopes of winning support for their more radical goals of eliminating child labor, minimum wages and maximum hours, and eventually collective ownership.

Leaders of various trade unions—the kinds of organizations that represented skilled laborers within a specific craft rather than the general laborers the Knights sought to organize—declared a national work stoppage for May 1, 1886. May 1 would soon be known as Labor Day and become an international day of worker solidarity. In the meantime, tens of thousands of workers in various leading cities who were affiliated with various trade unions walked off their jobs to demonstrate the power of workers over management. Most returned the next day, but in Chicago, tensions were already high because of a long-standing disagreement and strike at the McCormick Harvester. Although Powderly believed the strike was a mistake, his union had grown far beyond his control, and some laborers affiliated with the Knights participated in this and other strikes throughout the city. McCormick hired strikebreakers, a practice that had led to small-scale violence between union workers and the new employees who were replacing them. On May 3, the two groups clashed and the police opened fire on the crowd, killing four workers.

FIGURE 2.30

William Mahone of Virginia was a former Confederate general who led the Readjusters against what they believed was Bourbon domination. These reformers hoped to challenge the role of the Southern elite, reduce government debt, and provide more funds for public education.

blacklisted

Occurs when one's name is circulated among employers who maintain a list of individuals who are not to be given a job. The purpose of the blacklist was to isolate labor activists and prevent them from getting jobs where they might encourage other workers to organize.

Knights of Labor

A leading labor union during the 1880s, the Knights advocated worker solidarity and believed that labor (workers), rather than capital (financiers and corporations), were the source of economic development. As a result, this union, which included women and minorities, advocated a greater share of profits and control over factories for workers.

FIGURE 2.31

A contemporary image of the Haymarket Affair depicting the police as being attacked directly by anarchists. *Harper's Weekly* was a leading publication and chose to refer to the event as "The Anarchist Riot." This interpretation typified the view of most newspapers at this time.

Haymarket Affair

Occurred on May 4, 1886, in Chicago's Haymarket Square. At least a dozen participants in a labor demonstration were shot after a bomb exploded among protestors and police. The event polarized Americans, with those who opposed labor activism blaming the demonstrators and union leaders citing the event as evidence that the police only served the interests of large firms.

National Labor Union

A national federation of trade unions founded in 1866 in hopes of promoting arbitration, a new political party based on the interest of laborers, and limiting the working day to eight hours.

The following day, thousands of Chicagoans gathered at the city's Haymarket Square to protest police violence and the intimidation of union workers. An unknown party set off a bomb that injured many in the crowd and killed several policemen. Once again the police fired into the crowd, allegedly in response to armed anarchists who sought to destroy the Capitalist system. Eight known anarchists present that day were arrested, and four were executed with little evidence to connect them to the violence. Most newspapers referred to the event as the Haymarket Riot, emphasizing the lawlessness of many in the crowd whose behavior made an otherwise peaceful labor protest turn violent. Others labeled May 4, 1886, as the Haymarket Massacre, emphasizing the deaths of at least a dozen bystanders and police, most of whom were killed by the undisciplined fire of their fellow officers. Because of the radicalism of some leaders present during the **Haymarket Affair**, radical labor unions such as the Knights of Labor were connected to the violence in the public mind. May 1 would not be celebrated in the United States, as it was in the rest of the world, because government officials viewed labor activism with suspicion. Membership in the Knights and other unions dropped and many Americans began to connect the labor movement to anarchists and Communists who advocated any method to destroy the Capitalist system.

More typical of the labor movement during the 1870s and 1880s was the **National Labor Union** (NLU) whose members hoped the government would use its expanding power to arbitrate disputes between workers and management. Many viewed the establishment of a law limiting the workday to eight hours as a panacea—an instant cure for all problems. Perhaps as many as 700,000 laborers joined the NLU in support of the eight-hour day, believing that a reduction from the ten- to fourteen-hour workdays they experienced would improve the quality of their lives while also requiring employers to hire more workers. In the end, only the federal government established eight hours as the standard for its employees during this period, many of whom faced pay cuts in return for the reduction in hours.

FIGURE 2.32

This cartoon was obviously created by an opponent of organized labor. However, it reveals one of the leading obstacles faced by union organizers. Here, a workingman bypasses the bank and deposits his earnings into the coffers of "The Workingmen's Association." The cartoon plays on images of gender as the artist presents the man as a poor provider. His wife holds an empty shopping basket while his son wears tattered clothing.

Most workers in America did not join the NLU or the Knights of Labor due to the costs of union membership and the potential repercussions by employers. America's reluctance to embrace working-class solidarity was also cultural. America's heritage of independent family farms was different from other nations where peasants worked on farms owned by nobility. Nineteenth-century Americans were fiercely independent and often viewed unions with suspicion because they believed that workers and management shared a mutual heritage and self-interest. Many believed that working for wages was a temporary step on their way to starting their own farm or business and eventually hiring workers themselves. As a result, workers in a factory considered themselves future farmers or shopkeepers and were less likely to develop collective identities as brothers and sisters of labor. The idea of **American Exceptionalism**—the belief that America is unique from all other nations—created a faith that America was a land of economic opportunity unlike any other nation. Both native-born and immigrant laborers subscribed to this idea to different degrees, either as their birthright or as a rite of passage for surviving the arduous Atlantic or Pacific crossing. If one could not rise from poverty to wealth in America, then America was not that different from other nations where fortunes were inherited and seldom earned.

As a result, membership in a group such as the Knights of Labor would have represented a fundamental shift in ideology from believing one could rise from laborer to owner through character and hard work to resigning oneself to a life working for others. If life as a wage laborer was a temporary way station on the road to economic independence, many Americans wondered, why waste one's time and money on behalf of a worker's union? If collectivism was already a foreign concept for many US workers with entrepreneurial ambitions, their suspicion was heightened by world events when French Communards seized property in Paris in the spring of 1871. In contrast to the Old World represented by European workers who sought radical changes to the economic system, most US workers bought into the **free labor ideology**. As free women and men, laborers would choose to work for employers that treated them fairly. The free market regulated both products and producers, they believed, so it was in the best interest of business owners to produce quality merchandise and satisfied workers. The most ambitious members of the working class who might have become labor leaders were even more likely to reject theories about collectivism and redistribution of wealth; their ambition fueling their hunger to become members of the upper classes themselves.

American Exceptionalism appeared naive to some, yet for thousands of Americans, the journey from the bottom to the boardroom was more than some fantasy—it was a history that surrounded them and repeated itself with regularity. Authors such as Horatio Alger capitalized on the very real phenomenon of upward mobility and America's faith in it by authoring popular serial novels that told of young men rising from humble origins. Many of America's wealthiest families had risen from poverty to affluence, each time proving to many that America was different from other countries where it seemed that one was either born wealthy or poor. Ironically for many of the self-made, success

American Exceptionalism

The belief that the United States is completely unique from other nations. The idea can be taken to the point of believing that the study of other nations and people are of little value to understanding US history.

free labor ideology

The belief that Northern progress was based on the freedom of workers to choose their occupations and employers and profit from their labor. Following the end of slavery, this idea evolved into the belief that workers' freedom to choose their employer was a natural source of protection from potentially unscrupulous employers.

simply hardened them to those who were not as fortunate. America during the 1880s was home to the beginning of gentrification as the wealthy lived increasingly insulated lives. They moved away from the city core so they would not have to live among the poor who were relegated to tenements near factories and wharves. New York City expanded to over one million souls by 1880, most of whom lived in increasingly crowded buildings originally designed for a fraction of their current occupants. These neighborhoods were naturally home to higher rates of crime and lower standards of sanitation, factors that helped to reinforce existing prejudices against poor immigrants as unclean and prone to vice.

American Exceptionalism and the nation's suspicion of radicalism resulted in a much narrower range of political reactions to the growth of corporations. Most reformers accepted the basic structure of Capitalism and simply sought to use the power of the government to regulate the free market in the public interest. Over time, it appeared that only the federal government was powerful enough to counter the power of corporate barons who operated in multiple cities and states. These women and men feared that if the government failed to regulate these industries, an oligarchy would soon emerge where power was vested in the hands of a few powerful business leaders. Most Americans retained their suspicion of government during these years, but a growing number began to incorporate a more powerful and active government in their definition of freedom. By the 1890s, their ideas about the role of the federal government began to attract significant attention.

4.4   The "New Departure" in Women's Suffrage

Elizabeth Cady Stanton proudly exclaimed in 1878 that the arguments she and other suffragists had made over the last three decades had yet to be defeated by any man in debate. Yet just as opponents of black freedom avoided discussion with black leaders, opponents of women's suffrage had no intention to take chances in the free marketplace of ideas. The most common and most potent argument against black freedom was violence and race-baiting, while the opponents of women's suffrage launched personal attacks against the character and moral purity of suffragists. Rather than debate whether women could overcome their lack of practical experience in public affairs or whether the time required for such activities would jeopardize their role as mothers—real concerns among many Americans—opponents leveled barrages of insults at suffragists and those who supported them. Most men went to extraordinary lengths to prove their masculinity, and the self-identity of women in the nineteenth century was equally tied to notions of gender. As a result, when suffragists were labeled as unfeminine and accused of abandoning their children, most women naturally sought to distance themselves from the movement. Even those willing to bear the indignity of being shunned by their community also had to consider that their husbands would be ridiculed or even fired from jobs if they persisted in the suffrage movement. A man who was incapable of commanding the proper behavior of his wife, many believed, could certainly not be expected to maintain discipline among men in the workplace.

FIGURE 2.33

Antisuffrage propaganda depicted women's suffrage as a radical doctrine that would lead to negative consequences. This 1880 cartoon features eight caricatures such as women driving ugly women from the polls, dressing as men and drinking in public, and voting for a handsome demagogue.

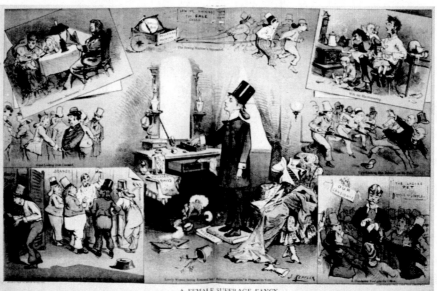

A FEMALE SUFFRAGE FANCY.

As a result, the women's suffrage movement was placed on the defensive in ways that reflected the obstacles the early abolitionist movement faced. Like the abolitionists who divided on whether to seek gradual laws encouraging manumission or to devote all efforts to the total destruction of slavery, early suffragists divided about whether they should focus strictly on suffrage or conduct a broad campaign against gender discrimination in all its varieties. The American Women's Suffrage Association (AWSA) continued to be more conservative, and its members hoped to work with male leaders who could pass women's suffrage laws at the local and state level. This approach had led to a handful of localities approving women's suffrage in school elections even prior to the Civil War. In these cases, women used the era's notion of women's "proper sphere" being the home. If women were responsible for the children, they argued, shouldn't they naturally have a voice in the operation of schools? Similar arguments led to the extension of suffrage in city elections as women needed a voice in community government if they were to be guardians of the home. Women even won the right to vote in Western states such as Wyoming and Utah in 1869 and 1870, respectively. While the AWSA as an organization cannot be credited alone for these victories, their more conservative strategy led to dozens of successful suffrage campaigns throughout the nineteenth century.

Thanks to the efforts of Lucretia Mott and other women who sought to heal the divide between the AWSA and the National Women's Suffrage Association (NWSA), these two organizations frequently worked together. The NWSA continued to be more radical, however, taking on controversial measures such as women's property rights, divorce laws, contraception, and even the very notion of whether marriage and motherhood was the highest station a woman could achieve. Stockbroker and editor **Victoria Woodhull** was even more radical than most members of the NWSA. Woodhull exposed one of the long-standing taboos in US culture—the sexual double standard between women and men. If a single woman chose to engage in sexual relationships with one or even multiple partners, Woodhull argued, she should not be castigated for her choice any more than a bachelor might be.

Rev. Henry Ward Beecher was the most prominent American clergymen at this time. Beecher attacked Woodhull, questioning her integrity and likening the outspoken women's leader to a jezebel. This Biblical caricature assaulted Woodhull's virtue, but it also spread her ideas given Beecher's celebrity-like notoriety. Woodhull did not back down from Beecher's accusations. Instead, she published a report exposing an extramarital affair between the reverend and the wife of one of his leading parishioners. Ironically, the scandal that followed validated Woodhull's ideas about America's sexual double standard. The well-connected Beecher suffered no consequences, but his mistress was excommunicated from the church. Although she was not permitted to vote and therefore was presumably barred from holding public office, Woodhull ran for president of the United States in 1872. She chose Frederick Douglass for her running mate. The image of a white woman and black man campaigning together would have surely created a scandal. However, Douglass was touring internationally at this time and likely never knew about the nomination.

Few women even within the NWSA endorsed Woodhull's candidacy or methods. They did, however, subscribe to her more radical perspective that women were equal to men and therefore already possessed equal rights. By the early 1870s, NWSA leaders pursued a strategy called "the **New Departure**," which was a philosophy of equal rights grounded in the idea that all citizens possessed the right to vote. If voting was a right of citizenship and there were no laws specifically taking that right away from citizens because of gender, followers of the New Departure believed, then no special laws enfranchising women were needed. Others pointed out that the Fourteenth Amendment granted the rights of citizenship to women and added to this their belief that citizens in a democracy automatically possessed the right to vote. These women studied state and federal constitutions and local election laws. They also became experts in history and political theory, often emphasizing that their republic was formed in protest of taxation without representation. Armed with books of law and a cache of tax receipts, hundreds of NWSA members registered to vote—or at least attempted to do so.

Victoria Woodhull

A leader of the early women's suffrage movement, Victoria Woodhull subscribed to the idea that suffrage was a right possessed by all American citizens regardless of gender. She confronted the sexual double standard of Victorian America, published a newspaper, worked in the investment industry, and even ran for president of the United States.

New Departure

An ideology espoused by some of the more radical suffragettes of the 1870s that suggested that because women were citizens they already possessed the right to vote and were entitled to equal protection of this right under the Fourteenth Amendment.

FIGURE 2.34

Victoria Woodhull was one of the most interesting people in the late nineteenth century. Stockbroker, author, editor, presidential candidate, and radical women's rights advocate, Woodhull defied convention and usually got the better of any man or woman who debated her.

Sojourner Truth and Mary Ann Shadd Cary followed the New Departure all the way to the polls where they were turned away like hundreds of other suffragists around the country. Susan B. Anthony arrived at the polls and demonstrated to bewildered registrars that there were no laws barring women from voting in her home of Rochester. Although permitted to cast her vote, the vote was later disqualified and a warrant was made for her arrest. Speaking to a group of supporters at a NWSA meeting years later, Anthony described the peculiarities of her arrest and how the experience reflected the way her actions and the resulting police action against a middle-class white woman violated the conventions of race, social class, and gender in nineteenth-century America. The arresting officer arrived at her home, Anthony recalled, nervously made small talk, and eventually notified her that she was to be arrested. "Is that the way you arrest men?" she asked the officer. After he sheepishly admitted it was not, Anthony demanded that she be arrested "properly" and presented her wrists to be handcuffed. The officer refused and instead of restraining Anthony and taking her to jail, he pulled out his pocketbook and arranged for a carriage to deliver the lady outlaw to the police department.

The trial was equally tense as Anthony's notoriety spread the news of the court's proceedings. The state ruled that citizenship was not a guarantee of suffrage and that even if women were not explicitly excluded by laws regarding suffrage, they did not have the right to vote. Anthony refused to pay her $100 fine, and the police wisely chose not to send another officer to her home to arrest her for nonpayment. The following year, the House of Representatives debated women's suffrage and Missouri's Virginia Minor took her lawsuit against the registrar who had disqualified her vote all the way to the United States Supreme Court. Minor echoed decades of women's rights advocates as she likened suffragists to the nation's founders who confronted taxation without representation. She also challenged the court to consider the arguments of feminist thinkers and the New Departure. In the end, the case of *Minor v. Happersett* mirrored the decision against Anthony as the Supreme Court ruled that voting was not an inherent right of citizenship. Despite the ruling, the publicity both women received and the debate they inspired challenged many to reconsider their assumptions about gender and democracy.

> ### REVIEW AND CRITICAL THINKING
>
> 1. Identify a few early labor unions, and explain the challenges they faced to attract members. Explain American Exceptionalism as it applies to the conflict between labor and capital that was such a driving force in the history of the industrial revolution.
> 2. Consider how the experiences of African Americans were related to discrimination of other groups, such as Native Americans, eastern and southern European immigrants, Latina/Latino peoples, and immigrants from Japan and China. What were the strategies used against these groups by those whites who sought to "keep them in their place"?
> 3. How did the experiences of Northern laborers compare with sharecroppers? What were the strategies used by both in attempting to better their conditions? Why might many Northern workers turn away from labor unions during Reconstruction?
> 4. What were the various strategies used by suffragists during Reconstruction? Identify what arguments were conservative in terms of accepting nineteenth-century notions about gender and which arguments were radical for their time.
> 5. How "new" was the New Departure? In what ways did the protest of women against gender discrimination mirror the fight for civil rights of racial and ethnic groups, and in what ways was it unique?
> 6. What was unique about the experiences of Native Americans compared with other racial and ethnic minorities in America? What was the intent of assimilation, and why might some natives fiercely oppose assimilation while others viewed it with ambivalence?

5. FURTHER READING

Ayers, Edward. *The Promise of the New South: Life After Reconstruction* (1992).

Baker, Jean H. *Votes for Women: The Struggle Revisited* (2002).

Blanke, David. *Sowing the American Dream: How Consumer Culture Took Root in the Rural Midwest* (2000).

Buenger, Walter L. *The Path to a Modern South: Northeast Texas between Reconstruction and the Great Depression* (2001).

Downs, Gregory. *Declarations of Dependence: The Long Reconstruction of Popular Politics in the South, 1861–1908* (2011).

Goldman, Robert. *A Free Ballot and a Fair Count: The Department of Justice and the Enforcement of Voting Rights in the South, 1877–1893* (2001).

Hahn, Steven. *The Roots of Southern Populism: Yeoman Farmers and the Transformation of the Georgia Upcountry, 1850–1890* (2006).

Hine, Robert V., and John Mack Faragher. *The American West: A New Interpretive History* (2000).

West, Elliot. *The Last Indian War: The Nez Perce Story* (2009).

White, Richard. *"It's Your Misfortune and None of My Own": A History of the American West* (1991).

CHAPTER 3
Populism and Imperialism, 1890–1900

Four main developments occurred during the last decade of the nineteenth century. The first was the spectacular growth of cities. The transformation of urban America accelerated in the 1890s as port cities specializing in connecting the countryside with world markets gave way to the development of factories and financial centers throughout the nation. The second was the growth of a third-party movement known as Populism. Farmers and some urban workers united to form a class-based movement because they believed that their interests were not being met by the nation's two political parties. Although the Populists would be a political force for only a brief moment, their ideas would greatly influence ideas about government and the nature of American politics. The third development was the growth of institutionalized racial discrimination. Segregation of white and black Americans moved from custom to law in the 1890s. This development illustrated a hardening of racial prejudice, but also demonstrated that black Americans were becoming wealthier and more assertive. Although segregation had existed in the past, by the 1890s Southern legislatures began passing ordinances that compelled racial separation by law. These laws were a response by racial conservatives who feared that black women and men were progressing in ways that might threaten the racial hierarchy. They were especially concerned that the new generation who had never known the "civilizing" effects of slavery must be compelled to keep "their place" at the bottom of Southern society.

The fourth development was the physical growth of the nation and the acquisition of overseas territories. In 1800, the nation was a loose confederation of sixteen states with a total population of 5 million souls. By 1900, 75 million Americans belonged to a global empire that stretched across the continent and effectively controlled much of Alaska, Cuba, the Philippines, Puerto Rico, Hawaii, and Guam. Ever aware of their own historic struggle against colonialism, American leaders claimed that they had no interest in creating an empire. The history of Western expansion demonstrated otherwise, even if few of the nation's leaders considered the acquisition of land from Native Americans in these terms. In addition, Americans pointed out that the newly acquired islands in the Caribbean and Pacific had requested US assistance in their revolution against Spain. The United States promised that it was unique from all the other world powers. In some ways, America would live up to these promises by granting limited self-government to these areas or incorporating them into the nation and extending citizenship to inhabitants. When it came to the nonwhite peoples of the Caribbean and Pacific, however, the United States believed it could not grant full independence until the inhabitants proved that they were "ready" for democracy. In places like the Philippines, the inhabitants demonstrated an unwillingness to wait for self-government. Perceiving US troops as occupiers rather than liberators, Filipinos rose in armed rebellion. In other places, American imperialism was dominated more by a desire for commercial development and military bases. In these islands, inhabitants enjoyed a higher degree of autonomy even if their claims to national independence remained unfulfilled.

1. URBAN AMERICAN AND POPULAR CULTURE

LEARNING OBJECTIVES

1. Describe the factors that led to urban growth, and explain how US cities were able to accommodate so many new residents. Next, explain how immigration and migration from the countryside changed urban life.

2. Explain why some Americans at this time were concerned about the growth of vice. Also, explain how the marketing of products developed at this time and how it changed US history.

3. Describe the kinds of cultural activities that Americans enjoyed at the turn of the century. Discuss the reasons why activities such as sporting events became popular at this time. Finally, describe the growth of a uniquely American form of music called "ragtime" and the impact of popular culture on life in urban America.

1.1 The Growth of the City

The population of New York City quadrupled between the end of the Civil War and the start of World War I, as 4 million souls crowded into its various boroughs. Chicago exploded from about 100,000 to earn its nickname as the "Second City" with 2 million residents. Philadelphia nearly tripled in this same time period to 1.5 million. Before the start of the Second Industrial Revolution, even these leading cities served the needs of commerce and trade rather than industry. Early factories relied on waterpower, and the location of streams and falls dictated their location. By the 1880s, factories were powered by steam, allowing their construction near population centers. Soon the cityscape was dotted with smokestacks and skyscrapers and lined with elevated railroads.

The skyscraper was made possible by the invention of steel girders that bore the weight of buildings, which could be built beyond the limit of 10 to 12 stories that had typified simple brick buildings. Passenger and freight elevators were equally important. The price of constructing skyscrapers demonstrated the premium value of real estate in the city center. By 1904, Boston and New York completed underground railways that permitted these areas to expand—a marvel of engineering that required few modifications to the rapidly changing city. These early mass transit systems accommodated the proliferation of automobiles in the next two decades by removing trolley lines from the increasingly crowded streets.

These elevated and subterranean railroads (called the "el" or the "subway," respectively) transported residents between urban spaces that were increasingly divided into separate districts. City planners mapped out districts for manufacturing, warehouses, finance, shopping, and even vice. Those who could afford it could purchase a home in the suburbs—outlying residential districts connected to the city by railways and roadways. Unlike the rest of the city, these neighborhoods were limited to single-family homes and included parks and even utilities such as plumbing and electricity. Suburbanites could also enjoy the pastoral trappings of America's rural past with lawns and gardens. The daily commute seemed a small price to pay for the reduction of crime and pollution that was endemic within the city center. A suburbanite might even remain connected to the city through the proliferation of the telephone—still a luxury in the 1890s, but one that expanded to several million users within the next decade. However, the majority of urbanites were crowded into tenements that housed hundreds of people that might not include luxuries such as plumbing, ventilation, or more than one method of egress to escape a fire.

One in six Southerners lived in cities by 1900, and most blocks were occupied by either black or white families. The same phenomenon of residential segregation was still emerging in the North. In sharp contrast to the black population of the South, the majority of whom remained on farms and plantations, the vast majority of African Americans in the North lived in towns and cities. Both Northern and Southern cities contained one or more black-owned business districts. Most black communities with more than a few thousand black residents boasted their own newspaper, numerous doctors, a few attorneys, and a variety of stores and restaurants. Segregation encouraged the growth of these business districts where black shoppers were treated with dignity and at least a few black office clerks, professionals, and sales staff could find steady employment. Lingering prejudices and the desire to maintain language and culture sustained similar ethnic neighborhoods and business districts within Northern cities.

FIGURE 3.1

This 1902 photo shows continuing work being done to construct an underground rail system in New York City.

Swedes and Germans began to constitute the majority of residents in upper-Midwestern cities near the Great Lakes, and nearly every major city had at least a dozen newspapers that were printed in different languages. Although many Americans lumped immigrants together based on their language and nationality, immigrants sought association with those who were from the same region. In many parts of Europe, major cultural differences and old rivalries separated people who were countrymen only due to recent political realignments of Europe. As a result, dozens of fraternal and mutual-aid associations represented different groups of Germans, Italians, Poles, and Hungarians. Jewish residents likewise maintained their own organizations based on their culture and religion. As the migrants moved to smaller cities, Sicilians, Greeks, and northern and southern Italians might set aside old hostilities and see each other as potential allies in a strange land. Ethnic communities, such as San Francisco's Chinatown and Baltimore's Little Italy, might appear homogenous to outsiders. In reality these neighborhoods were actually melting pots where various people of Asian and Italian descent lived and worked.

The growth of cities was also the result of migration from the American countryside. In 1890, the US Census eliminated the category of "frontier"—a designator referring to areas with population densities below two people per square mile, excluding Native Americans. By this time, nearly every acre of fertile public land had already been sold or allotted. In response, historian Frederick Jackson Turner drafted a paper advancing an idea that would soon be labeled the **Frontier Thesis**. Turner argued that the existence of the frontier gave America its distinctive egalitarian spirit while nurturing values of hard work and independence. For Turner, America's distinctiveness was shaped by Western expansion across a vast frontier. At the frontier line itself, Turner argued, Americans were faced with primitive conditions, "the meeting point between savagery and civilization." The result was a unique situation where the West was both a crucible where American character was forged and a safety valve for the overpopulation and overcivilization of Europe. Those who subscribed to Turner's idea questioned how the elimination of the frontier might alter the direction of American history. Others recognized the congruity between Western expansion and urban and industrial life. Modern critics point out that Turner failed to recognize the agency and contributions of Native Americans and argued that his reliance on the mythic frontiersman also neglected the importance of families, communities, government, and commerce within the West.

Frontier Thesis

An idea proposed by historian Frederick Jackson Turner in 1890, which argued that the frontier shaped US history. Turner saw the frontier as "the meeting point between savagery and civilization." At this westward-moving border, Turner believed that American society was constantly reinvented in ways that affected the East as well as the West.

1.2 Vice and the Growth of Urban Reform

To the frontier the American intellect owes its striking characteristics. That coarseness and strength combined with acuteness and inquisitiveness…What the Mediterranean Sea was to the Greeks…the ever retreating frontier has been to the United States….And now, four centuries from the discovery of America, at the end of a hundred years of life under the Constitution, the frontier has gone, and with its going has closed the first period of American history.

—Historian Frederick Jackson Turner

Despite the "closing" of the western frontier in 1890, a new generation of Americans would see new frontiers throughout urban America. During the next three decades, these pioneers sought ways to improve sanitation and healthcare, provide safer conditions for workers and safer products for consumers, build better schools, or purge their governments of corruption. One of the leading urban reform projects was the attempt to eliminate certain criminal behaviors. Every major city and most small towns had their own vice districts where prostitution, gambling, and other illicit activities proliferated. These districts were usually restricted to one of the older and centrally located neighborhoods where upper- or middle-class families no longer resided. For this reason, vice was often tolerated by city authorities so long as it confined itself to these boundaries.

Vice was profitable for urban political machines that relied on bribes and the occasional fines they collected through raids. These limited attempts at enforcement filled city coffers and presented the impression of diligence. Police and the underworld often fashioned an unspoken understanding that vice would be tolerated in certain neighborhoods that were home to racial and ethnic minorities. A Jewish writer recalled playing on streets patrolled by prostitutes who advertised their services "like pushcart peddlers." Innocence was an early casualty of a youth spent on Manhattan's Lower East Side. "At five years I knew what it was they sold," the writer explained. Children in multiethnic neighborhoods from Minneapolis to Mobile experienced similar scenes as the police "protected" brothels and gambling houses in exchange for bribes. In fact, most prostitution dens were located near police stations for this very reason.

Anne "Madame" Chambers of Kansas City provides a model example of the collusion between vice and law enforcement at this time. Chambers used the police to deliver invitations to her various "parties" to area businessmen. The police were also paid to guard the door of her brothel in order to protect the identity of her guests. Most clientele were not residents of the vice districts themselves but middle- and upper-class men who reveled in the illicit pleasures of Kansas City's tenderloin district. Others engaged in the spectator sport of "slumming," observing the degraded condition of inner-city life as a means of reveling in their own superior condition. Whether they partook in or merely observed the illicit pleasures of the red-light district, the physical separation of vice from their own quarantined neighborhoods provided both physical and ideological insulation from the iniquities of the city. A businessman could disconnect himself from the actions committed in the various tenderloin districts of his city and then return to his own tranquil neighborhood. Unlike the immigrant or the nonwhite who could not find housing outside of vice districts, the middle-class client retained the facade of respectability because of the space between his home and the vice district that quarantined deviance in poor and minority neighborhoods.

In many cases, a house of this type is a haven of last resort. The girls have been wronged by some man and cast out from home. It is either a place like this or the river for them…After a while they began to have hopes, and no girl who has hopes wants to stop in a place of this type forever, no matter how well it is run and how congenial the surroundings.

—Madame Chambers, reflecting on her life operating houses of prostitution in Kansas City between the 1870s and 1920s

These underworlds were host to both gay and straight. The legal and social fabric of the late nineteenth century equated homosexuality with deviance and therefore quarantined all public displays of homosexuality to the vice districts. Homosexuals at this time lived closeted lives outside of these spaces, although they described their own experience as living behind a mask rather than within a closet. In fact, historians have not found examples of the phrase "closet" in reference to gay life until the mid-twentieth century. Gay men and women of this era sought to create safe spaces where they could take off those masks. They created code words and signals such as "dropping hairpins"—a phrase referring to certain signals that only other homosexuals would recognize. To recognize and to be recognized by others permitted these men and women to "let their hair down"—another coded phrase referring to the ability to be one's self. Because all homosexual behavior was considered illicit, gay men and women found the vice districts both a refuge and a reminder of the stigma they would face if they ever removed their mask anywhere else.

Although vice neither defined nor typified urban life, the police and political machines concentrated vice in ways that made it more noticeable while furthering America's suspicion of urban spaces. Reformers hoped to do more than simply quarantine these establishments, pressing for tougher enforcement of existing laws while pushing for tougher prohibition measures against alcohol. The Progressive Era of the early twentieth century saw a unified effort to purge the city and all America of vice. In the meantime, a small group of reformers in the late nineteenth century believed that the best way to combat vice was to improve the condition of the urban poor. Most urban communities were already home to collective efforts to start daycares and educational outreach programs, long before the middle-class reformers took an interest in their plight. In many cases, churches provided partial financing for such institutions, while the women of a particular community volunteered their time watching children or teaching classes in English or various job-related skills. By the 1890s, middle- and upper-class women were increasingly involved in such efforts. Deriving their inspiration from European settlement houses that provided homes and/or social services such as daycare for working mothers, a host of American men and women brought the settlement house movement to America. The most famous of these was **Jane Addams**.

Addams was born into a wealthy family who viewed the purpose of college for women as a sort of literary finishing school that would prepare one's daughter for marriage. They were shocked when their daughter returned from college expressing the desire to pursue an advanced degree, fearing that such a path would make it unlikely that their aging daughter would ever find a suitable husband. Undaunted, and refusing to abandon the development of her mind, Jane Addams studied medicine and the burgeoning field of social welfare. She toured the settlement houses of London and resolved to create similar institutions in the United States. In 1889, Addams secured and remodeled a mansion in Chicago called Hull House. Addams lived and worked at Hull House with her intimate friend Ellen Gates Starr and a variety of other women. Together, these women assisted poor mothers and recent immigrants who also resided at Hull House. Some of the social workers, such as Florence Kelley, were committed Socialists. However, most were short-time residents who came from wealthy backgrounds and were studying social work in college. Together, these college women and career reformers taught classes on domestic and vocational skills and operated a health clinic for women and a kindergarten for children. Before long, Hull House had become a community center for the largely Italian neighborhood it served. The Progressive Era of the early 1900s saw the expansion of the number of settlement houses, with approximately 400 similar institutions operating throughout the country.

Other settlement houses in Chicago and throughout the nation were directly affiliated with collegiate social work programs. This was especially true of historically black colleges such as Hampton Normal and Agricultural Institute (known as Hampton University today) in Virginia. Here, alumna Janie Porter Barrett founded the Locust Street Settlement House in 1890, the first of such homes for African Americans. Before this time, local organizations affiliated with the **National Association of Colored Women's Clubs (NACWC)** took the initiative in providing social services within the black community. The NACWC was formed in 1896, but most of the local chapters predated the merger and had been active in creating orphanages, health clinics, schools, daycares, and homes for the elderly African Americans who were generally unwelcome in institutions operated by local and state governments. These women also created homes for black women attending predominantly white colleges throughout the North. For example, the Iowa Federation of Colored Women's Clubs purchased a home where black students attending the University of Iowa and Iowa State University could live. They even discussed the merits of sponsoring special schools to help black women prepare for college. They soon abandoned this plan for fear it might be misunderstood by whites as an invitation to reestablish the state's Jim Crow schools, which had been defeated by three state Supreme Court decisions in the 1860s and 1870s.

Jane Addams

A leader in the emerging field of social welfare, Addams observed settlement houses in London and used this knowledge to found Chicago's Hull House in 1889. Addams also organized against child labor and was an outspoken opponent of the United State's entry into World War I, an unpopular position at the time but one that led to her being awarded the Nobel Peace Prize in 1931.

FIGURE 3.2

Jane Addams was a pioneer of the settlement house movement in America, founding Hull House in Chicago. Addams was awarded the Nobel Peace Prize in 1931.

National Association of Colored Women's Clubs (NACWC)

Organized at a meeting held by Josephine St. Pierre Ruffin in Washington, DC, in 1896, the NACWC was formed as a national organization to promote and coordinate the activities of local African American women's organizations throughout the nation. These activities included personal and community uplift as well as confronting segregation.

1.3 Mail-Order Houses and Marketing

FIGURE 3.3

Activist, educator, writer, and leader, Mary Church Terrell was the first president of the National Association of Colored Women's Clubs. She earned a master's degree and taught at Ohio's Wilberforce College, spoke multiple languages, and was a leader in the fight to desegregate the schools and the restaurants of Washington, DC, where she lived and worked for much of her life.

Advances in transportation and communication created national markets for consumer products that had previously been too expensive to ship and impossible to market outside of a relatively small area. Companies such as the Great Atlantic and Pacific Tea Company opened A&P retail outlets, while Philadelphia's John Wanamaker pioneered the modern department store. Discounters like Woolworth's offered mass-produced consumer goods at low prices at their "nickel and dime" stores. Department stores like Sears soon began marketing some of their smaller and more expensive items, such as watches and jewelry, through mail-order catalogs. By 1894, the Sears catalog had expanded to include items from various departments and declared itself the "Book of Bargains: A Money Saver for Everyone." Isolated farmers and residents of towns not yet served by any department store suddenly had the same shopping options as those who lived in the largest cities. The Sears catalog and the advertisements of over a thousand other mail-order houses that emerged within the next decade shaped consumer expectations and fueled demand. By the early twentieth century, an Irish family in Montana might be gathered around the breakfast table eating the same Kellogg's Corn Flakes as an African American family in Georgia. These and millions of other Americans could also read the same magazines and purchase items they had never known they needed until a mail-order catalog arrived at their doorstep.

Marketers recognized that they could manufacture demand just as their factories churned out products. Trading cards were distributed to children featuring certain products. Newspapers and magazines began making more money from advertising than from subscriptions. Modern marketing became a $100-million-per-year industry by the turn of the century, employing many of the brightest Americans producing nothing more than desire. The distribution of these advertisements extended beyond lines of race, region, and social class. Indeed, aspiration for material goods and the commercial marketplace that fueled this desire may have been the most democratic American institution. For some families, participation in the marketplace also became a reason to take on extra work. For others, the emergence of marketing was just another cruel reminder of their own poverty in a land of plenty.

FIGURE 3.4

Begun as a small circular offering watches and jewelry for sale by mail, the Sears Catalog quickly expanded to include hundreds of items. The catalog stimulated consumer desire, spurred by the advent of free rural mail delivery in 1896 and the company's unique "money-back guarantee." Years after its founding, a company employee predicted the catalog would become a primary source for historians by providing "a mirror of our times, recording…today's desires, habits, customs, and mode of living."

In addition to the retail outlets and mail-order houses, national brands emerged and offered products such as Coca-Cola, Crisco, and Quaker Oats. Traveling salesmen sold many products, from vacuum cleaners to life insurance and investments. The rapid growth of a national market for many of these products meant that many opportunities for miscommunication arose. Many companies simply hired more salesmen in hopes of turning their regional businesses into national empires. Rapid expansion meant that executives in distant home offices could do little more than issue guidelines they hoped their salesmen would follow. These individuals often established their own terms and prices that were designed to increase sales and their own profit margins. For example, salesmen of Captain Frederick

Pabst's beer figured out they could increase their own profit by adding water to the kegs of beer they sold. America's taste for lighter beers was hardly a tragic consequence. For the family who invested all they had in watered-down stock or the widow who purchased a life insurance policy that did not offer the benefits she had been promised, such frauds held dire consequences. As a result, companies that delivered a consistent product and succeeded in protecting their brands from the potential avarice of their own sales staff developed national reputations. Before long, the reputation of such brand names became the most valued asset of a corporation.

1.4   Rise of Professional and College Sports

Like the corporations and mail-order houses that sprang forth during the late nineteenth century, spectator sports expanded from local contests organized around gambling during the antebellum period to become big business by the turn of the century. Boxing remained controversial in the 1890s, but it was also popular—extremely popular. The emergence of international icons such as the first true world heavyweight champion John L. Sullivan helped the sport to enter the mainstream of American culture. The son of Irish immigrants, Sullivan celebrated his heritage at a time when the Irish were heavily persecuted in America. Sullivan's reputation for toughness was forged in the days of bare-knuckle brawls that ended only when one man yielded. These grueling fights were banned by the turn of the century, but stories of the Irish heavyweight champion's grit lasted long after his first major defeat in 1892—an event that corresponded with Sullivan's first use of boxing gloves. Although boxing moved toward respectability with the addition of gloves and rule-making associations, baseball retained its title as the most popular sport in America.

The Cincinnati Red Stockings became the first salaried team in 1869. By 1890, there were three major leagues, dozens of regional and semipro leagues, corporate sponsors, and crowds in excess of 10,000 spectators. The color line was drawn tightly in baseball, boxing, and other sports from the beginning, but it was never complete. Contrary to myth, Jackie Robinson was not the first African American to play in Major League Baseball. That honor belongs to Moses Fleetwood Walker, a catcher for the Toledo Blue Stockings of the American Association in 1884. At least one light-skinned individual of partial African heritage "passing" for white predated Walker, while dozens of players from Latin America who also had African ancestors played throughout the early twentieth century. One of the more elaborate demonstrations of the malleability of the color line occurred in 1901 when legendary Baltimore manager John McGraw signed Charlie Grant. Grant was a star of several African American teams who played in the barnstorming era of black baseball—the period before the formation of the Negro National League in 1920. An informal ban barred black players shortly after Moses Fleetwood Walker left Toledo because of the racism he endured. As a result, McGraw required Grant to adopt the name "Tokahoma" and pretend to be a Native American. The ruse did not last long, however, as Chicago's emerging black neighborhoods within the city's South Side gave such a friendly reception to Tokahoma that Chicago manager Charles Comiskey recognized the deception and refused to play the game if Charlie Grant took the field.

The greatest athlete at this time was likely a Native American who played professional baseball and football in addition to winning the decathlon in the 1912 Olympic Games. Jim Thorpe was born on Oklahoma's Sac and Fox Reservation and was sent to a number of boarding schools. Like most athletes, he played semiprofessional baseball to help pay for his expenses and escape the military discipline and manual labor of the Indian Industrial School in Carlisle, Pennsylvania. This boarding school was designed to assimilate Native Americans into the dominant Anglo culture. Unfortunately, even though Thorpe needed to earn money to support himself while a student at Carlisle, the Olympic committee decided to enforce the ban against "professional" athletes on Thorpe. The Committee stripped Thorpe of his medals, despite the fact that many other Olympians had also played for money. During the 1980s, a campaign waged by historians and college students convinced the Olympic Organizing Committee to restore Thorpe's medal posthumously.

FIGURE 3.5

Jim Thorpe was born on the
Sac and Fox reservation in
Oklahoma and is widely
regarded as the greatest
athlete in the history of
sport.

Thorpe also led Carlisle to victory over most of the top college football programs in the nation. College football was second only in popularity to professional baseball at this time. College football rivalries were legendary by 1902 when Michigan defeated Stanford in the first Rose Bowl. Attendance at this game demonstrated that that the sport had progressed from the first college football matches of the 1870s that were informal challenges by student clubs who played by an ever-changing set of rules. By the 1890s, college football was the topic of conversation each weekend—among both enthusiasts and those who sought to ban the rough game. Early college football lived somewhere on the border between rugby and boxing, with little or no protective clothing. The introduction of the forward pass helped to spread the players across the field and reduced the number of crushed ribs at the bottom of the scrum. However, the rule change also added to the speed of the game, leading to concussions as players hit one another at full stride. In 1891, James Naismith, a physical education teacher in Springfield, Massachusetts, invented a new team sport that resulted in fewer injuries and could be played indoors during the cold winter months. He hung up two bushel baskets and had his students try to throw a soccer ball into the baskets. He would later coach college basketball at the University of Kansas.

The crowds at popular sporting events developed chants and songs to cheer along their team. The most famous song of all was "Take Me Out to the Ball Game," by a Tin Pan Alley composer. Colleges developed fight songs by taking popular melodies and adding their own lyrics or by altering popular fight songs such as "Oh Wisconsin" to include their own mascot and school. The University of Michigan's fight song "The Victors" was also "borrowed" heavily by area rivals. The original lyrics celebrated the team as "Champions of the West"—an indication that the future Big Ten schools were still viewed as "Western" at the turn of the century.

While popular chants were often very similar from college to college, students and community members usually added elements of local flavor. For example, the chalk-rock limestone walls of the buildings that then formed the University of Kansas inspired students to change "Rah, rah, Jayhawk" into "Rock Chalk, Jayhawk." Games with neighboring Missouri rekindled the historic feud where Southern bushwhackers killed antislavery leaders and burned the Free State Hotel of Lawrence. Missourians emphasized that the original Jayhawkers had also crossed into their state, usually liberating more whiskey and horses than slaves despite the historic memory of Lawrence as a Free State stronghold. Professional football failed to draw such community identity and remained on the margins until the mid-twentieth century. By 1900, college football was an institution, basketball was gaining popularity, and baseball in all its forms was the national pastime.

1.5 Popular Culture

ragtime

A uniquely American form of
music that featured "ragged"
rhythms and a strong beat
that compelled its listeners to
dance or at least tap their
feet. Its structure flouted
conventional theories about
music at the turn of the
century. This genre inspired
improvisation and gave birth
to other forms of music such
as jazz.

The New York City neighborhood where the melodies of many of college fight songs and other tunes were written became known as Tin Pan Alley. The name may have derived from the "tinny" sound of the dozens of cheap upright pianos. Or it may be related to the cacophony of sound that resembled the reverberations of tin cans in a hollow alley as the neighborhood's composers and sheet music publishers experimented with different sounds. From these alleys could be heard a new kind of music known as **ragtime**, a genre that blended black spirituals with Euro-American folk music. Made famous by urban composers, ragtime was born in the taboo world of red-light districts and interracial dance halls. In these hidden joints, white and black musicians created a uniquely Southern sound. Ragtime would soon spread to the black-owned halls of the North. Oral histories indicate that these melodies sounded just slightly off whenever whites imposed their presence on the early jazz halls of the upper Midwest. For all of its crushing oppression, ragtime was at home in the Deep South where black and white had always lived in intimate closeness to one another. The region's language, food, and music reflected both the tensions and the bonds that forged generations of creole culture. A distinctly Southern form of expression, ragtime celebrated this fusion without apology and gave birth to the second uniquely American form of cultural expression—jazz music.

Scott Joplin

An African American
composer who was among
the great innovators that
created ragtime music. Joplin
was born in Texas and
traveled throughout the
South, living and teaching
music in Missouri and a host
of other states as well as
Northern cities such as
Chicago.

The most famous composer and performer of the era was **Scott Joplin**, an African American who toured black communities from New Orleans to Chicago years before most of white America discovered ragtime. Thanks to the spread of new technologies, ragtime would be enjoyed in recorded form by many young white Americans, much to the chagrin of their parents. Within a few years, a growing number of white composers and artists added their talents to ragtime and joined traveling black musicians in spreading the new sound throughout the globe. Other white musicians, such as John Phillip Sousa, utilized the tempo of ragtime to create popular band music. Sousa specialized in stirring marches for military bands. The band director of the United States Marine Band, Sousa traveled the nation. Soon his "Stars and Stripes Forever" became one of the most beloved patriotic songs in America.

FIGURE 3.6

"Maple Leaf Rag" was Scott Joplin's first successful composition. Joplin's music was spread by the sale of sheet music and the popularity of this song led to the spread of *ragtime* as a uniquely American genre of music.

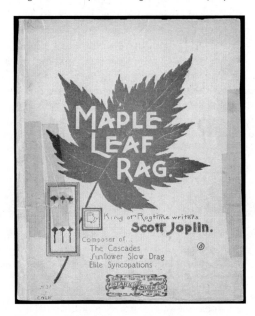

For those who preferred the theater, American audiences were treated to thousands of touring troupes who played several shows per day in every town large enough to draw an audience. The actors of these troupes had to be flexible, performing classical Shakespeare one afternoon and a vaudeville-type variety show a few hours later. The **vaudeville** show included songs, dance, slapstick comedy, and usually a chorus line of dancing women whose outfits left less to the imagination as the evening wore on. The more risqué, the better the chance a troupe would play to a full house each night. The exhortations of those who believed the theater to be the tool of the devil usually inspired more souls to attend these cabarets. The most popular form of entertainment at this time was the melodrama—an exaggerated style of morality play that demonstrated the persistence of Victorian standards of thought. The melodrama featured dastardly villains, damsels who constantly fell into distress, and daring men who never stooped to the antihero's methods to save the day. An even larger-than-life type of live performance was the traveling circus. Most attendees of P. T. Barnum's circus agreed that he delivered on his promise to provide audiences with the greatest show on earth.

vaudeville

A type of variety show that became one of the most popular forms of entertainment at the turn of the century. A vaudeville show might feature sketch comedy, music, and burlesque dancers.

FIGURE 3.7

Buffalo Bill poses with a group of Native Americans who performed in his touring shows that celebrated the "Winning of the West."

Buffalo Bill

William "Buffalo Bill" Cody was a cowboy and scout for the military who also became a leading showman. Buffalo Bill's traveling Wild West shows combined sentimental Western history with vaudeville entertainment that thrilled crowds around the globe.

Traveling circuses and vaudeville shows increasingly sought to present epic stories from US history. No topic was more popular that the fictionalized image of the West. As the last bands of Apaches and Lakota were annihilated or placed onto reservations, a sort of curious nostalgia emerged regarding what most assumed was a "vanishing race" of American Indians. The general public no longer vilified Native Americans once they no longer represented a perceived threat. However, few at this time attempted to understand Native American experience from their own perspectives. Ironically, a man with tremendous respect for native life and culture became the architect of a traveling exhibition that reduced the complexities of Western history into a cabaret. William Frederick "**Buffalo Bill**" Cody's Wild West Show thrilled audiences with displays of horsemanship, sharpshooting, and other rodeo skills by cowboys and cowgirls. But the main attraction and the reason millions in Europe and the United States paid to attend Buffalo Bill's show were the "Indian attacks" on peaceful settlers that brought out the cavalry. For most Americans, Buffalo Bill's sanitized and simplified reconstruction of "How the West Was Won" substituted for the real history of the American West. Audiences cheered as the cavalry gallantly rounded up the "rogue" Indians in a display of showmanship where no one really got hurt.

REVIEW AND CRITICAL THINKING

1. How did the rapid growth of cities affect those who lived in the nation's urban areas, as well as those that continued to live in small towns and the countryside?

2. Describe life within the urban vice districts. Why were these places tolerated by authorities, and what can one learn about urban and social history from studying these kinds of places?

3. How did women like Jane Addams and Janie Porter Barrett make their mark on urban history? How did their participation in the public sphere counter and/or demonstrate notions about a separate sphere of activity for women?

4. How did marketing and the development of national brands and national markets affect American life?

5. Many Americans at this time feared that the character of the nation was being degraded by a culture that placed too much value on material possessions. What kinds of evidence might they have cited to support this view?

6. How did popular culture and entertainment reflect American society at this time in the nation's history? What can one learn from analyzing cultural history?

2.   NATIONAL POLITICS AND THE POPULIST PARTY

LEARNING OBJECTIVES

1. Explain how the Farmer's Alliance spread and led to the development of the Populist Party. Identify the goals and issues of the Populists.
2. Evaluate the effectiveness of the Populists in achieving their goals. Explain the obstacles they faced, such as race and the challenge of uniting urban workers and farmers. Finally, analyze how well the Populists were able to bridge these gaps.
3. Summarize the issues and results of the election of 1896. Explain the fate of the Populists and their ideas and describe how the Populists affected the political history of the United States.

2.1   Rise of the Populist Party

During the 1880s, farmer's collective organizations known as the Grange declined, as did the Greenback Party. However, the twin ideals of monetary reform and legislation beneficial to farmers were carried on by a new organization called the **Farmers' Alliance**. The alliance was similar to the Grange, and in fact, some local chapters of the alliance had previously been affiliated with the Grange. The first alliance chapter was organized in Texas and quickly expanded to include over a hundred chapters by the early 1880s. The alliance had spread so rapidly due to its outreach/education program that contracted with traveling lecturers. These individuals earned commissions when they organized new alliance chapters. The alliance also affiliated with various existing farmer's associations and formed partnerships with nearly a thousand local newspapers, most of which were already in print. By 1888, there were 1.5 million alliance members nationwide. This rapid growth was greatly facilitated by the decision of existing organizations to affiliate with the Farmers' Alliance. For example, the Agricultural Wheel had been formed in Arkansas and attracted half a million members in other Southern states. In this way, the alliance was slightly different from the Grange. Its base of membership was local, and its chapters were autonomous. Perhaps more importantly, the alliance welcomed women over the age of sixteen as full members, as well as white tenant farmers and sharecroppers. The alliance would occasionally work with leaders of the **Colored Farmers' National Alliance**, an organization that grew to a million members and remained independent of white alliances.

Women were especially active in the alliance, a unique feature of the organization when considering the conservatism of the South and rural West. Despite ideas about separate spheres of activity for women and men, female alliance members chaired meetings, organized events, and delivered lectures. A significant number of women held key leadership positions in local and state offices within the alliance from the Deep South to California. Most strikingly, women were full members of most alliance chapters in an age when most women could only participate in "men's" organizations as members of separate female auxiliary chapters. The efforts of female alliance members were usually phrased in conservative terms that stressed traditional roles of protecting the home and children. However, the entities the home needed protection from were banks and railroads. Participation in the alliance placed women in the public realm of political activity, circulating petitions and holding debates in support of new laws.

Because the Grange represented only landowners, their efforts had been largely dedicated to cooperative efforts to create stores, grain elevators, and mills. Alliance chapters engaged in these economic activities as well, and women operated dozens of the alliance cooperative stores. The alliance was even more active than the Grange had been in the political realm. Because its membership was more economically diverse, many of its chapters sought more radical reforms on behalf of poor farmers and landless tenant farmers. For the alliance, securing legislation protecting landowning farmers from the monopolistic practices of banks, commodities brokers, and railroads was only the beginning.

Farmers' Alliance

The Farmer's Alliance was a national federation of autonomous local farmer's organizations that sought to represent the interests of their members. Even more than the National Grange, which preceded them, the Farmer's Alliance had a heavy influence on politics between Reconstruction and the turn of the century.

Colored Farmers' National Alliance

Due to the exclusionary policies of the Farmer's Alliance, black farmers formed the Colored Farmers' National Alliance at a meeting in Texas during 1886. The organization grew quickly and had as many as a million members at its peak.

Interstate Commerce Act

A law demanded by farmers and passed in 1887 that required railroads to establish standard fares and publish these rates. This prevented the informal pricing practices that often discriminated against small farmers who had few options when it came time to ship their grain to the market.

Sherman Anti-Trust Act

A federal law passed in 1890 that gave the government the power to break up corporations that it believed were acting in restraint of free trade by forming monopolies or engaging in other practices that allowed firms to artificially raise prices.

FIGURE 3.8

This satirical "nursery rhyme" depicts the oil trusts as a "modern Bill Sikes," a reference to a fictional villain in Charles Dickens's popular novel *Oliver Twist*.

In 1887, the lobbying efforts of the nascent alliance, along with other farmers' associations, led Congress to pass the **Interstate Commerce Act**. The law required railroads to establish standard rates and publish these prices. It also prohibited railroads from giving free passes or other benefits to try and sway lawmakers and journalists from being favorable to railroad interests. The law also required that these rates be "reasonable and just" and created the Interstate Commerce Commission to regulate the business practices of railroads. These were seemingly commonsensical government reforms from the perspective of farmers, especially given the practices of some unscrupulous railroad operators. Prior to 1887, railroads could arbitrarily raise rates around harvest time or charge different rates to different customers to win the business of large firms. Small farmers had little chance of getting such discounts.

By 1890, a similar reform movement was being waged by small businesses and consumer advocates. These groups lobbied for the passage of the **Sherman Anti-Trust Act**, a law aimed at reducing the power of monopolies. Supporters of the new law believed that businesses, which should naturally be competing with one another, were often secretly working in concert to reduce competition by forming trusts. For example, the Beef Trust was an arrangement between the largest beef packers where members agreed not to bid against one another when purchasing livestock from individual farmers. If each leading purchaser of cattle refused to bid against one another, the price of cattle would be kept artificially low to the benefit of the beef packer and the detriment of the farmer. Dozens of trusts also maintained informal agreements against starting "price wars," where each promised not to lower the price they charged consumers.

Corporations defended themselves from their critics by pointing to the inefficiencies that occurred in the past when there were dozens of beef packers, oil refineries, and other competing businesses in every major city. In many cases, prices had declined when these companies merged or affiliated with the various trusts that controlled their industry. Although there was truth in these claims, there was equal validity to accusations of unfair business practices. The Sherman Anti-Trust Act gave the federal government unprecedented powers and empowered it to break up corporations that had formed "combinations in restraint of trade." This vague phrase was intended to give wide-ranging power to those who sought to enforce the law and dissolve trusts. The new law was hailed as an end to monopoly; however, nearly all of the lawsuits brought under the terms of the law in the next fifteen years were dismissed on technicalities. In fact, corporations actually benefitted from the actions of courts during this time after the Supreme Court redefined the Fourteenth Amendment to defend the rights of corporations against the state.

From the perspective of farmers, the legal system was being commandeered by attorneys representing railroads and trusts. These entities were undermining both the Interstate Commerce Act and Sherman Anti-Trust Act, reformers believed, while the government stood idly by or actively assisted those who represented the trusts. Railroads continued to overcharge small farmers in violation of the Interstate Commerce Act, largely because the law required farmers to initiate a complaint. The understaffed regulatory commission could only investigate a small fraction of these complaints, and even when they believed they had a case they rarely had the resources to match their opposition. The same was true regarding anti-trust acts for ranchers who sold beef or grain to large corporations.

FIGURE 3.9

Alliance leaders met in Ocala, Florida, during December 1890. A number of local alliance chapters had already turned to political action by this time. For example, these alliance members in Columbus, Nebraska, formed their own political party and nominated a ticket of farmers for local and national office in July 1890.

Despite these frustrations, the partial victory of getting these laws passed and securing a handful of convictions also led to increased political activism among alliance members. In addition, the diminishing price of grain in the late 1880s led a number of farmers to view the alliance as a possible source of protection against economic decline. Alliance-sponsored lecturers continued to travel throughout the rural South and West during these lean years, touting the value of collective action. They also resurrected the ideas of rural Greenbackers and spoke against the gold standard and its tight money supply which kept interest rates high and farm prices low. Already influential in state and local politics in over a dozen states, the National Alliance turned to national politics. In 1890 they held a convention in Ocala, Florida. Their goal was to establish a platform that would unite alliance members from coast to coast. Equally important, alliance leaders sought political partnerships with labor unions and various middle-class reform movements representing the growing urban population. Delegates to the Ocala convention hoped their efforts would lay the groundwork for a new political party that would unite farmers and factory workers and represent the majority of working Americans. The degree to which they succeeded is still a subject of debate among historians.

2.2 The Subtreasury Plan and Free Silver

Delegates to the 1890 meeting drafted what became known as the Ocala Demands, a list of proposed changes to the nation's political and financial system that challenged the conservative and laissez-faire policies of the era. The National Alliance dominated the Ocala meeting, and most alliance chapters endorsed the Ocala Demands and supported its vision of federal action on behalf of farmers. Chief among these reforms was a proposal to create federally subsidized warehouses where farmers could store their grain until they decided the market price was favorable. Many local alliance chapters had already tried to provide this service for their members, but most had failed in their objective because their members were in debt and could not afford to store their grain for more than a few weeks. Dubbed subtreasuries, alliance members believed these federal warehouses would solve their dilemma by issuing immediate payment of up to 80 percent of the crop's present value. As a result, buyers would no longer be able to force cash-strapped farmers to sell their grain shortly after harvest. If all farmers participated in subtreasuries across the nation, the alliance argued, brokers and trusts could no longer dictate the price of grain.

subtreasury plan

A proposal that was advocated by farmer's organizations such as local Alliance chapters wherein the federal government would subsidize the construction of grain warehouses where farmers could store their grain in anticipation of better market prices. Farmers believed this would stabilize commodity prices and protect indebted farmers who often had no choice but to sell their grain as soon as it was harvested regardless of market conditions.

free silver

The shorthand nickname given to the idea that the government should print money that was backed by both gold and silver. This would place more money into circulation, which would make it easier to obtain loans and provide a measure of relief for indebted farmers. Opponents believed that abandoning the gold standard would reduce foreign investment and destroy value of the dollar.

The **subtreasury plan** demonstrated a revolution in sentiment among America's farmers away from the concept of limited government that had typified Thomas Jefferson's ideal of rural America. Instead of achieving freedom *from* government via laissez-faire policies and small government, the idea was now freedom *through* government via regulation and the subtreasury plan. In addition to this novel innovation, the Ocala Demands included a host of other ideas that had been proposed by both rural and urban reformers in the previous two decades. The delegates called for lower tariffs and greater regulation of railroads, although they stopped short of advocating direct government ownership of railroads. The platform also recommended the reinstatement of federal income taxes, which had been abandoned since the end of the Civil War. Although the wording of the resolution itself was nonspecific, alliance members intended that only the middle and upper classes would pay taxes, with the wealthiest paying higher rates. The Ocala Demands also supported the notion of governmental reform and direct democracy. The current practice at this time was for state legislators to appoint U. S. senators, but the Ocala Demands called for the direct election of US senators by popular vote. Relatively obscure in its own time, the Ocala convention and its demands would shape American political debate for the next decade.

The platform also supported a monetary policy that would soon be known as **"free silver"**—an abbreviation of the phrase "the free coinage of silver." This phrase simply meant that the US mint would create silver coins and/or print bills redeemable for silver and place them into circulation alongside the existing currency that was backed by gold. The word *free* simply meant "unlimited" in this context and was meant to differentiate their plan from the Sherman Silver Purchase Act of 1890, which will be described later. Because currency was redeemable for a certain amount of gold, the government could only print an amount of money equal to the total value of gold reserves it controlled. While the population and the total amount of wealth increased each year, new discoveries and purchases of gold lagged behind. As a result, the strict application of the gold standard would mean that there would be such a small amount of currency in circulation that the laws of supply and demand would actually cause the dollar to increase in value each year.

Deflation caused the value of currency to increase over time. Although this sounds good in theory it can have disastrous effects on the growth of the economy. Deflation meant that those who wished to borrow money had to pay very high rates for two reasons. First, the relative amount of currency in circulation was shrinking, which meant borrowers faced stiff competition from other borrowers and lenders could practically name their terms. Secondly, because the value of currency increased each year, banks could also make money by simply hoarding their cash. This deflation of the currency was exactly what those with money wanted, and exactly what indebted farmers feared. For those who have more debt than currency, printing more money and causing inflation would actually bring a measure of relief.

The Sherman Silver Purchase Act of 1890 was intended to provide a small measure of that relief to farmers and others in debt. It required the government to purchase a limited amount of silver each month and then increase the amount of money in circulation by creating silver certificates that would be used just like the dollar. However, the plan did not work because consumers and investors preferred gold-backed currency. To make matters worse, the Silver Act financed the purchase of silver by issuing notes that could be redeemed in either silver or gold. Most holders of these notes immediately exchanged the notes for gold, which did nothing to increase the amount of money in circulation. Worse, these redemptions pushed US gold reserves dangerously low. The result was deflation, panic on Wall Street, and banks further restricting the amount of money they were willing to loan.

FIGURE 3.10

A political cartoon showing William Jennings Bryan who backed the idea of free silver on a one dollar bill. The bill bearing the image of his opponent William McKinley, a defender of the gold standard, is worth almost twice as much as Bryan's money. The intended message was that the idea of free silver would cause economic instability. The slogans "We Want No Change" and "Four More Years of the Full Dinner Pail" were meant to support the status quo and the reelection of William McKinley.

Those who favored maintaining the gold standard cited the failure of the Sherman Silver Purchase Act as "proof" that increasing the idea of "free silver" was dangerous. In fairness, the Sherman Silver Purchase Act was not a fair test of the idea because it did not provide for the "free" (unlimited) coinage of silver. More importantly, the Sherman Silver Purchase Act did not treat silver-backed money as regular currency. The Ocala Demands sought to remedy this situation by having US currency backed by both gold and silver. It would create a flexible exchange rate that would eliminate any incentive for speculation or redeeming currency for one metal or the other. It also required the government to issue enough currency backed by silver that at least $50 per capita was in circulation at any given moment.

The alliance also formed partnerships with the Knights of Labor and especially laborers in mining and the railroad industry. Hoping to create a political party representing all productive laborers from the factories to fields, the Populist Party (known officially as the People's Party) was formed after a series of conventions in 1892. National Farmer's alliance president Leonidas L. Polk was nominated as the new party's presidential candidate. Unfortunately, Polk died prior to the party's national convention which was held in Omaha, Nebraska, in July 1892. Delegates at the Omaha convention nominated the former Greenback leader James B. Weaver in his place. Building on the ideas of the Ocala Demands, delegates created the **Omaha Platform**. This Populist statement of policy was drafted in hopes of uniting the demands of labor unions and the Farmer's Alliance.

The Omaha Platform of 1892 may have been the most significant political document of the late nineteenth century, even though the Populist Party itself would dissolve within a decade. Although many of its specific regulations regarding economic and agricultural reform were not adopted, the ideas of the Omaha Platform would shape debate for years to come. In addition, many of its provisions would eventually become law. For example, the Omaha Platform called for immigration restriction (adopted in 1921 and 1924), the establishment of federal income tax (adopted in 1913 with the ratification of the Sixteenth Amendment), and the direct election of US senators (also adopted in 1913 with the ratification of the Seventeenth Amendment). The platform also advocated more direct democracy by granting the people the power to submit laws through referendum and the ability to recall elected officials before their term ended. The Omaha Platform also advocated the eight-hour working day, term limits for politicians, use of secret ballots in all elections, and printing money that was not backed by gold. With the exception of government ownership of railroads and telegraph lines, nearly all of the major goals of the Populist were eventually adopted by law or custom.

Omaha Platform

The formal statement of the policies of the People's Party (also known as the Populists) that was issued at its formative meeting in Omaha, Nebraska, in July 1892.

FIGURE 3.11

Populist candidate for president in 1892 James B. Weaver and vice presidential candidate James G. Field ran under the banner "Equal Rights to All, Special Privileges to None." Field was a former Confederate general from Virginia while Weaver was a former abolitionist from Iowa. The two hoped to demonstrate national unity in an era of continued sectionalism in politics.

FIGURE 3.12

A photo showing armed men who enforced the declaration of a Republican victory in Kansas. A number of Populist leaders had seized control of the statehouse but the doors were broken and these deputized men regained control. Notice that this force included African Americans, who accounted for as many as 20 percent of Republican voters in southeastern Kansas and the state capital of Topeka.

In the near term, however, the Populists struggled to attract supporters. Populists believed that the Republicans and Democrats both represented the *money interest*, a term referring to bankers and wealthy corporations who benefitted from the limited amount of currency in circulation. As a result, their platform advocated many of the ideas of the Greenback Party. However, most industrial workers were not in debt as farmers were. They feared inflation would increase prices faster than wages would rise. They also shared many of the same concerns of their employers and feared that altering the nation's financial system could lead to instability and unemployment.

Workers also tended to support tariffs on foreign imports because these taxes protected domestic production. Tariffs are taxes on imported goods. Without tariffs, overseas factories could sell their products in the United States for lower prices. Farmers tended to oppose tariffs because the nation was an exporter of cotton, grain, and other agricultural commodities. When the United States charged tariffs on foreign manufactured goods, other nations retaliated by imposing taxes on American exports. Farmers hoped reducing America's tariffs would inspire other nations to do the same, reducing the taxes placed on American exports like cotton and grain. In short, farmers and workers may have shared similar experiences, but they often did not share identical financial interests. As a result, the Populist Party struggled to expand from an agrarian movement to one that united both farmers and urban laborers.

Populist presidential candidate James B. Weaver won over a million votes and carried Idaho, Nevada, Colorado, and Kansas in the 1892 election. The Populists also influenced the national election in 1892 when the Democratic candidate Grover Cleveland defeated incumbent Republican Benjamin Harrison—a reversal of the 1888 election in which Harrison had defeated Cleveland. The Republican and Democratic campaigns focused on issues such as the tariff. From the perspective of the Populists, this was only one of many issues and one that distracted from the more meaningful reforms they proposed. On a local level, Democrats and Republicans vied for control of Eastern cities and states, while the rising Populist Party secured numerous victories in the South and West. Populists even claimed victory in a majority of the districts of the Kansas state legislature. However, a three-day "war" between armed Populist and Republican politicians within the state capital led to arbitration and the Republicans ended up claiming a majority of the seats in the legislature.

FIGURE 3.13

A map showing county-by-county results in the 1892 election. Notice the success of the Populists in the West and the pockets of support for the Populists in the otherwise solidly Democratic South.

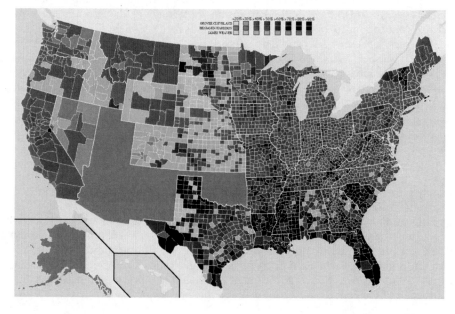

The Populists were a growing political force beyond the West. After the 1892 election, Populists controlled a significant number of seats in state legislatures throughout the South as well as the western plains and mountain states. The party even sent 14 delegates to Congress, while a dozen states selected Populist governors for at least one term during the 1890s. The growth of the People's Party also led to cooperative efforts between members of the two major parties and the Populists. Representatives of the Republicans and Democrats often nominated a single ticket composed of candidates from their party and a handful of Populists. This strategy of two political parties joining together to defeat the dominant party of a particular region became known as **fusion**. In Western states such as Nebraska, where the Republican Party was dominant, Populists and Democrats often joined forces. Pockets of Republicanism managed to survive past Reconstruction in Southern states such as Tennessee, Virginia, and Texas, but the Democrats still dominated state politics. In these states, Populists and Republicans used the strategy of fusion to defeat a number of Democratic candidates. Fusion was most effective in North Carolina where black Republicans and white Populists created a fusion ticket and together swept the 1894 legislative and gubernatorial elections.

fusion

In this context, fusion was the strategy of merging two independent political parties under one ticket in order to increase the likelihood of winning elections.

2.3   Race and Southern Populism

Despite continuing efforts to keep black voters from the polls, over 100,000 black voters cast ballots in each state of the Deep South in the early 1890s. As a result, white Southern Populist leaders from Texas to Virginia worked to mobilize black voters in ways that saw limited cooperation across the color line in politics for the first time since the end of Reconstruction. White Populist leaders agreed on the need to unite farmers and laborers, but they remained hesitant to embrace people of diverse racial and ethnic backgrounds for fear of being labeled as "radicals." This issue was especially problematic in the South. Although some Southern whites recognized that they shared common economic and political interests with African American farmers and sharecroppers, white alliance leaders rarely cooperated with black leaders. In most cases, the failure to cross racial lines proved the Achilles's heel of Southern Populism. At other times, the economic interests of white and black farmers were not identical. For example, some white farmers owned land that was rented to black sharecroppers and tenant farmers.

Excluded from the Southern alliance, black Southerners established the Colored Farmers' National Alliance in 1886. In 1891, a group of black cotton pickers around Memphis who were working on white-owned land organized a strike and demanded higher wages during the harvest season. Whites lynched fifteen leaders of this strike. The local white alliances were silent on the matter despite the fact that each of these men had been members of the Colored Farmers' National Alliance. At other times, white and black farmers shared the same concerns. For example, a boycott against jute producers crossed the color line and spread from Texas to Georgia. Jute was used to produce the sacks that protected cotton bales. When an alliance of jute producers conspired to raise their prices, black and white alliance members throughout the South united and made their own bags from cotton until the "jute trust" backed down.

Historians have often been tempted to exaggerate the degree of cooperation between white Democrats and black Republicans in the South during the 1890s. Georgia's white Populist leader **Tom Watson** spoke forcibly against the methods some Democrats had used to intimidate and disfranchise black voters in the past. He and other white Georgia Populists even defended the life of a black politician from an armed white mob. However, Watson and nearly every other white Populist of the South were firmly committed to white supremacy and saw their partnership with black voters in tactical terms. They opposed the fraud and intimidation of black voters only when it was used against black men who supported the Populist Party. White Populists believed they were "educating" black voters by lecturing them about how voting for the Populist ticket would aid white farmers and landlords, providing benefits that would "trickle down" to black sharecroppers. If landlords could avoid paying high rates to railroads and men who controlled commodities markets, they argued, the landlords could then pay black tenants and sharecroppers higher wages.

From the perspective of black voters, Southern Populists were not much different from Southern Democrats who tolerated black suffrage so long as black voters agreed to vote as instructed. If the Populists spoke out against the knight-riding tactics that were similar to the Klan's, it was largely because those tactics had favored Democrats in the past and were beginning to be used against white Populists. At the same time, the fact that some white Populists in the South sought a degree of cooperation with black political organizations made Southern Populists different from the Democratic Party. As a result, Southern black voters sought to maintain their independence and distance, but also sought tactical partnerships with white Populists.

Tom Watson

A leading Southern Populist, Tom Watson was an editor and Georgia politician who sought to unite poor white Southerners against the elite landowning families he believed still controlled the state through the Democratic Party.

FIGURE 3.14
Marion Butler of North Carolina

Wilmington Race Riot

An outbreak of violence against African Americans and black businesses in Wilmington, North Carolina, following the defeat of the Democratic Party in November 1898. Republicans and Populists had joined together to sweep the elections, but many of the victorious candidates were forced to give up their positions or simply fled the city for their lives.

FIGURE 3.15

The remains of the offices of the *Wilmington Daily Record* in the wake of the 1898 Wilmington Race Riot.

North Carolina's Marion Butler personified the racial tensions and tactics of white Populists. As a leader of his county chapter of the Southern alliance, Butler edited a Populist newspaper called the *Caucasian*. The masthead of Butler's paper originally exclaimed "Pure Democracy and White Supremacy." However, this was removed when the Populists decided they could advance their interests by courting black voters. Butler recognized that the only way to defeat the heavy majority enjoyed by the Democratic Party in North Carolina was to form a partnership with the Republican Party, even if it still contained many political leaders from the Reconstruction Era. Butler agreed to head a fusion ticket in 1894, including a number of white and black Republican leaders among white Populist candidates. Black Republicans and white Populists united behind the ticket, which swept the state. The Populist victory in North Carolina resulted in Butler's election to the US Senate at the ripe old age of thirty-two. It also brought hundreds of local alliance leaders into the Populist-dominated state legislature. The Populist victory also resulted in George Henry White's election to the US House of Representatives. White would be the last black Southerner to serve in Congress until the 1970s.

Progressive for its era and region, race relations in North Carolina would soon implode. The astounded Democrats launched an offensive against Butler and white Populists as traitors to their race. Ironically, Butler's position as a defender of white supremacy should have been clear. Butler and the rest of the white Populist leaders were outspoken in their beliefs that black men and women were inherently inferior to whites. If Populists were different from Democrats in terms of race, Butler explained, it was because they were "not in favor of cheating and fraud" to exclude black voters. The Democrats shared no such reservations and branded Butler as a liberal who favored interracial marriage. They also created Red Shirt clubs that promised to redeem white women from the indignity of purchasing stamps from the handful of black postmasters the Populists had appointed.

The Red Shirts then decided to use force to take control of the local government, much like what white mobs had done in Louisiana during Reconstruction. They destroyed the homes and businesses of black leaders and precipitated a massacre in Wilmington in November 1898. Officially known as the **Wilmington Race Riot**, Red Shirts murdered a dozen black men, ransacked black communities, and burned the office of the African American newspaper the *Wilmington Daily Record*. The violence was anything but random, as Wilmington was the largest city in the state and contained a black majority that had just defeated the Democratic Party's local candidates in the November election. Dedicated to controlling the entire state, white Democrats ran many of the few remaining Republican-Populist officials out of town and took control of the state legislature by force.

Only in the wake of such atrocity could North Carolina Populists be viewed as racial moderates. Populists were willing to give black voters a separate and subservient place in political and economic life. In return, they expected black voters to express their gratitude at the polls by supporting white candidates. In exchange for convincing men of their race to "vote properly," a handful of black leaders might be appointed to minor offices. Black voters understood the limitations of their Populist "allies." From the perspective of many black voters, however, fusion with the Populists could result in tactical gains such as funding for black schools and laws that might encourage fair treatment for sharecroppers.

In the end, even this possibility for limited cooperation and tactical gains was derailed as North Carolina Democrats launched a malicious campaign. Black voters faced lynch mobs, the homes of black leaders were attacked, and white Populists were labeled Yankees and "lovers" of black women and men. Few white Populists were racial liberals, but these racial accusations were repeated with such frequency and intensity that truth became irrelevant. These accusations were also very effective. The Democrats swept the 1898 elections in North Carolina and enacted poll taxes that prevented all sharecroppers and tenants without access to cash from voting.

In 1900, North Carolina followed the pattern of establishing subjective literacy tests as a requirement for all voters. The tests empowered white registrars to disqualify black voters, regardless of their educational level. Given the recent campaigns against him, Butler phrased his opposition to the literacy test very carefully. Between various calls for white supremacy and his newfound desire to eliminate the menace of black suffrage, Butler meekly pointed out that literacy tests might unintentionally disfranchise hundreds of thousands of white voters. In response, the senator was subjected to death threats and labeled as a traitor to the white race. The Democratically controlled North Carolina legislature recognized that Butler's argument was valid even as they excoriated him. They quietly responded by adopting a grandfather clause that effectively exempted whites from the literacy tests.

Populists in various other Southern states were likewise removed from office by many of the same methods. For example, Texas had been one of the leading states for Southern Populists until the adoption of the poll tax in 1902, a law that reduced the ability of poor farmers to vote. In 1923, Texas adopted a new technique to limit the effectiveness of black voters. The state created a system of primary elections in which only members of a particular party could vote. The direct primary was hailed as a progressive measure because it empowered the members of a party, rather than its leaders, to select their candidates. However, the Democratic Party restricted its membership to whites.

Federal law did not permit such distinctions to be made in the general election, but the laws were silent regarding racial restrictions in private political organizations at this time. Even though black men could still legally vote in the general election, it mattered little because whoever won the Democratic nomination would easily defeat any candidate backed by minority voters or the nominal Republican Party of Texas. Black and Hispanic voters protested, but state and federal courts ruled that the Democratic Party could restrict membership however it chose. Attempts to declare the white-only primary a violation of the Fourteenth and Fifteenth amendments failed until 1944.

The decline of Southern Populism effectively ended the last meaningful and independent black participation in Southern public life until the mid-twentieth century. In response to claims of "negro domination" that mirrored the fears expressed by Redeemers during Reconstruction, white Southern Democrats revived and expanded the violence black voters. They also passed "reforms" to voting laws that were intended to bar African Americans. As a result, black voters were marginalized in the South for the next three generations. Poll taxes eventually excluded many white voters as well. However, poor whites and poor blacks continued to oppose one another and plant more cotton. Although they were all trapped in a cycle of downward mobility, the region's elites successfully kept poor people divided against each other. However, these elites struggled with their own dilemmas, victims themselves of a colonialist model of finance that forced them to borrow at high rates. The South continued to grow cotton at depressed prices, a course of action that impoverished nearly everyone in the region and discouraged investment and innovation.

2.4   The Panic of 1893 and Labor Activism

> We are born in a Pullman house, fed from the Pullman shops, taught in the Pullman school, catechized in the Pullman Church, and when we die we shall go to the Pullman Hell.
>
> —Alleged statement of a Pullman resident during the 1894 Pullman Strike.

It would become clear by the late 1890s that fusion with the major political parties was a short-sighted strategy. In 1892, however, the Populists were becoming increasingly influential in state and local politics throughout the West and the South. To capitalize on this momentum and become a significant force in national politics, the Populists would have to do better at attracting urban voters and Northern farmers. This presented a host of challenges given the often-competing economic interests of farmers who owned land and equipment and laborers who worked for wages. In addition, Populist leaders would have to overcome cultural traditions that divided Northerners and Southerners, and transcend the cultural divide between rural and urban America.

Finally, the Populists needed to find a way to resolve tensions between the ethnically, racially, and religiously diverse citizenry and their base within the Farmer's Alliance, which were predominantly old-stock Anglo Protestants. From a strictly tactical point of view, the Populists did not have to secure the support of black voters or any particular ethnic group to become a national political party. However, the People's Party could not succeed if it failed to secure a significant foothold among the workforce of urban America, which was becoming increasingly diverse. These voters tended to support local political machines that provided immediate and tangible benefits to their communities. Most urban dwellers were unenthusiastic about some aspects of the Populist platform that were designed to benefit farmers, especially plans to increase farm prices through federally financed warehouses.

Given these obstacles, the Populists were relatively successful in crafting a class-based message based on the solidarity of all workers and farmers against bankers and Capitalists. This success was partially due to a lingering recession that began in the early 1890s and became a full-fledged depression in 1893. The depression would linger until the late 1890s. Similar to the railroad speculation that triggered the economic problems of the 1870s, the **Panic of 1893** began when leading railroads declared bankruptcy. By the end of the year, 500 banks had failed and unemployment neared 20 percent. Farmers had experienced several years of depression before the Wall Street crash, while industrial workers faced declining pay.

Panic of 1893

A financial crisis that was spurred by railroad speculation. The Panic of 1893 led to high unemployment and a depression that lasted for several years.

FIGURE 3.16

An engraving depicting barges burning during the Homestead Strike, which is listed as the "Homestead Riot" by the publisher of the magazine that printed these images in 1892. Students should consider the implications of referring to the event as either a "riot" or a "strike."

Homestead Strike

Occurred in 1892 when steelworkers in Homestead, Pennsylvania, were locked out of their mills following demands for higher pay. The conflict turned violent in early July when workers clashed with armed guards hired by Carnegie Steel, leaving a dozen people dead and leading to the deployment of National Guard troops.

Coxey's Army

A group of several hundred protesters who marched to the nation's capital in 1894 in support of the ideas of Ohio politician Jacob Coxey. These Ohioans were joined by hundreds of others who believed that the federal government should provide temporary jobs following the Panic of 1893. However, Coxey's ideas were not seriously considered and his "army" was turned away.

The most patent example of labor strife before the Panic of 1893 occurred in the steel mills of Pennsylvania. In the spring of 1892, a plant owned by Andrew Carnegie in Homestead, Pennsylvania, reduced pay just as a hard-won union contract was coming to an end. Management had anticipated the workers' decision to strike and stockpiled warehouses full of finished steel in advance. Management also contracted with the Pinkerton detective agency to escort strikebreakers into the factory. The intent was to crush the union, which had secured the previous contract with a strike. The aging Andrew Carnegie was genuinely distressed about the resulting violence, yet did nothing to intercede with the decisions of the plant managers. After workers armed themselves and seized control of the plant, managers of the Homestead plant hired replacement workers and Pinkerton guards. The striking men clashed with the Pinkertons and sought to keep the replacement workers from entering the plant. Several men died in the conflict which was later crushed by federal troops. Most of the formerly unionized workers that survived the **Homestead Strike** meekly accepted the reduced pay, twelve-hour shifts, and elimination of their union. From the perspective of the workers in Pennsylvania, any tears the distant Andrew Carnegie cried for those who died at his plant were crocodilian.

A businessman in Ohio named Jacob Coxey was outraged by the Homestead Strike. In addition to his sympathy for the laborers, Coxey believed that the federal government should borrow money and provide temporary jobs until the economy recovered. Although this idea would serve as the basis of the New Deal response to the depression of the 1930s, the notion was considered radical during the depression of the 1890s. Coxey was an outstanding promoter, however, and led a group of a hundred workers who marched from central Ohio to the nation's capital to ask for jobs. By the time they arrived, their numbers had grown to several hundred, and they were joined by several thousand other unemployed men who launched their own journeys to Washington, DC, from communities across America. The media dubbed these men **"Coxey's Army."** The federal government treated them as invaders. Coxey was arrested for "trespassing" on what was actually pubic land, and most of his followers returned to their homes.

Coxey's Army inspired Populist supporter L. Frank Baum to write the novel *The Wizard of Oz* based on Coxey's efforts and the Populist message. Although its political meaning was soon forgotten, Baum intended the Scarecrow to represent farmers, the Tin Man to represent industrial workers, and the Cowardly Lion to embody political leaders who often lacked the courage to represent their constituents over powerful outside interests. Overcoming these shortcomings, the three characters unite with Dorothy—a female personification of the purity of the American people and the strength of Populism in the Great Plains. Together, they marched along the yellow-brick road, which symbolized the gold standard as measured by ounces (abbreviated as "oz"). Together, they withstood the sinister plot of the wicked witch. The witch represented the money interests of the East that sought to divide farmers, workers, and political leaders. The four heroes finally reach Oz and meet the Wizard, a small man who hid behind a facade of smoke and mirrors. In the end, the only way home was for Dorothy to click her heels together. Although modern audiences remember those shoes as being ruby red, they were actually silver in the original novel and represented the Populist goal of free silver as a panacea for the nation's economic woes.

The Knights of Labor endorsed the Populist Party, but their numbers had declined substantially following a number of strikes that had been crushed by federal and state governments during the last two decades. Other unions were hesitant to back the Populists. Skilled workers at this time joined craft-specific unions that were affiliates of the **American Federation of Labor (AFL)**, a national confederation of independent unions, which had been founded in 1886 by **Samuel Gompers**. The AFL focused on tactical goals, such as pay increases, through collective bargaining and strikes. The AFL was relatively successful in this regard, and the 250,000 skilled workers it represented by 1892 had enjoyed modest pay increases prior to the start of the depression. However, these wage increases would not last and the majority of laborers were not eligible to join the AFL.

Gompers's union remained more conservative than groups such as the Knights of Labor. The AFL generally excluded women and minorities and rejected ideas such as collective ownership of factories. Many AFL leaders were reluctant to join the Populists, especially Gompers. The AFL leader specifically warned its members about the potential dangers of affiliating with any political party, especially an unknown quantity like the Populists. For a few years in the mid-1890s, however, some AFL members rejected Gompers and his advice and supported the Populists.

A major strike was launched during the depression by a union that was more radical than the AFL, the United Mine Workers (UMW), which was formed in the summer of 1894. The workers had two main demands: First, the return of wages to previous levels, and second, that these wages would be paid in cash. In the wake of bank failures and depression, it was difficult and expensive to finance operations in US dollars. This difficulty led mining companies and some factories to issue their own currency known as **scrip**. This employer-issued currency was not legal tender. As a result, miners and factory workers who were paid in scrip could only redeem their paychecks for goods at company-owned stores. These goods were usually overpriced. Payment in scrip also prevented workers from moving or finding new jobs because they had no cash. Others became dependent on credit accounts that had been opened on their behalf at the company store.

Although the UMW had only 15,000 members, miners were part of a unique culture that stressed brotherhood and mutual aid. These principles were a matter of life and death given the dangers of mining and the importance of teamwork in completing their daily work. This brotherhood inspired solidarity behind the strike and also led miners to march from one mine to another to spread the word of their activities. By May, a strike that began only weeks earlier had grown to include an estimated 250,000 miners nationwide. Many eastern miners in Pennsylvania were subjected to violence from hired men known euphemistically as "detectives." The miners gave as good as they got in skirmishes in West Virginia, Illinois, and Ohio. In the isolated coal fields of Colorado, thousands of miners marched hundreds of miles to spread word of the strike and support one another. However, in the lean times of the depression, the mines still offered better pay than many jobs that were more susceptible to the forces of supply and demand. As a result, the operators successfully resisted union demands in the 1890s. The strikes cost the companies hundreds of thousands of dollars in lost revenue in addition to the expenses of hiring the police force that was used to break the strikes.

A second major strike occurred in 1894 involving the Pullman Palace Car Company near Chicago. Industrialist George Pullman experimented with a theory called **welfare Capitalism**, building a factory town to house the workers who built his passenger railcars. Pullman believed the brutal living conditions and high rents workers endured in cities were a leading cause for their unhappiness. He hoped that by creating a model city and paying for all of his workers' expenses, he would avoid labor strikes and command a loyal workforce. By establishing a factory in the countryside with fresh air and no access to alcohol, Pullman believed, Illinois would be home to a healthy and sober workforce with unparalleled productivity.

The factory town of Pullman featured relatively spacious living quarters, a beautiful library and church, and a store where workers could purchase items on credit. Employee purchases at the store, as well as rent, were deducted from their paychecks. Pullman's welfare Capitalism was less liberal, however, when it came to freedom of expression. He did not tolerate dissent or even independent organizations or meetings in his town. He employed inspectors who watched the employees to make sure they abided by his standards of clean living and were not organizing any kind of labor movement. Although outsiders marveled at the order and cleanliness of this factory town, workers resented the controlling aspects of their employer. Still, as long as wages were high, most at least appeared to agree with middle-class observers who considered industrial workers "lucky" to live in work in a town like Pullman.

American Federation of Labor (AFL)

A national federation of independent craft unions that was formed after a meeting in Columbus, Ohio, in 1886. Leaders of most of the nation's largest unions were present at this meeting and agreed to join the AFL to coordinate their activities and increase their political clout.

Samuel Gompers

Founded the AFL and led that organization from 1886 until his death in 1924, with the exception of a period between 1894 and 1895 when members of the organization revolted against his leadership because of his lack of support for the People's Party.

scrip

Currency that is issued by an employer or some other organization and is not a legal tender.

FIGURE 3.17

An image depicting American Railway Union leader Eugene Debs as "King Debs" during the Pullman Strike. In this anti-union image, Debs is depicted as preventing the movement of railcars that were full of food while factories were forced to sit idle for lack of coal and other supplies.

welfare Capitalism

A system where private employers provide services for the welfare of their workers, such as health care and other benefits.

Eugene Debs

An Indiana politician who
became one of the leading
national figures in labor and
political history from the
1890s to the early 1920s.
Eugene Debs was a founder
of the American Railway
Union and led the Pullman
Strike. He would later grow
more radical in his criticism of
the Capitalist system and
represent the Socialist Party
as its candidate for president
in several elections.

Pullman Strike

In response to a decline in
wages, workers at the factory
town of Pullman, Illinois,
declared a strike in the
summer of 1894. They were
supported by Eugene Debs
and the American Railway
Union, whose members
declared their intention to
make sure no railcar made by
the Pullman Company
moved until the wages of
their fellow workers were
restored. Believing that the
strike was derailing economic
recovery, the federal
government used the army
to end the strike.

The depression reduced the demand for Pullman's luxury railcars, and the factory responded with layoffs and pay cuts. These cuts were not accompanied by reduced rents or prices in the company store. As a result, workers were faced with conditions that resembled what sharecroppers faced—they had little or no pay once their rent and expenses were deducted. Many of Pullman's employees were members of the American Railway Union (ARU) led by **Eugene Debs**. In May 1894, the ARU supported a local strike of Pullman workers. More significant was Debs's nationwide strike of all ARU members who refused to work on any train that included cars made by the Pullman Company. The potential significance of the Pullman Strike was clear: by mobilizing all workers within an entire industry, a strike began by workers at a single company could have national implications.

By July, the nation's rail traffic had slowed substantially due to the large number of Pullman railcars. Even if rail companies agreed to isolate the Pullman Company, its thousands of railcars could not simply be placed on sidetracks. The federal government responded by ordering the strike to end and mobilizing troops to force railroad workers to follow the orders of their bosses. When this gambit failed, the government required trains with Pullman cars to also transport the US mail. If workers refused to work on these trains, they could be charged with the federal crime of interfering with the US mail.

President Grover Cleveland vowed to end the strike by any means possible. "If it takes every dollar in the Treasury and every soldier in the United States Army to deliver a postal card in Chicago," he declared, "that postal card should be delivered." The US attorney general broke the strike by securing a court order demanding an end to the strike because by slowing rail traffic the unions were acting to restrain trade. This was a provision of the Sherman Anti-Trust Act that was originally intended to limit the power of corporations and trusts rather than labor unions. However, because one union—and a controversial union leader such as Debs—had succeeded in disrupting the nation's transportation network, it appeared to many as if the ARU had become too powerful.

With the intervention of the federal government, the **Pullman Strike** was crushed and train traffic resumed its previous volume. The union at the Pullman factory was broken, and ARU and union activism in general suffered a major defeat. Had the Pullman Strike been successful and if unions were permitted to use sympathy strikes such as Debs had intended, the balance of power between workers and corporations might have been drastically altered. Instead, the workers who had participated in the strike were fired. Some were even blacklisted, meaning they were branded as "troublemakers" and their names placed on a list that was circulated to other employers. Debs himself was sent to jail for six months for his violation of an earlier court order. His sentence did not curtail his growing radicalism, as the union leader began envisioning the creation of a utopia in the West. Five years later, Debs turned to Socialism in hopes of fulfilling his dream of worker solidarity.

FIGURE 3.18

This turn-of-the-century illustration proposes the idea that consumers were the victim of conflicts between labor and management. The image depicts conflict between a Capitalist labeled "Commercial Trust" and a worker labeled "Labor Trust" who is wielding a club labeled "Strike." On his knees between the two is a helpless "Consumer" who appears to be begging for mercy.

A small strike in the coal fields of western Missouri and eastern Kansas in 1899 demonstrated the folly of excluding workers of a particular race or ethnicity. Management of the Kansas and Texas Coal Company intentionally recruited only black workers in hopes of convincing their lily-white workforce that all would be permanently replaced if they did not end their strike immediately. Railroad management circulated handbills throughout the South that advertised Missouri and Kansas as "the paradise for colored people." While these circulars urged Southern blacks "to join your friends in the land of plenty," the reception these men received was anything but friendly. The 1,200 black men who arrived in the region on special trains that summer immediately recognized that their reception might be slightly less friendly than promised. Their convoys stopped to pick up armed guards, and management instructed the riders against looking out of their windows. A Midwestern sheriff demonstrated a much stronger prejudice than typified Southern lawmen, threatening to prevent blacks from entering his city "if it takes deputizing every man in Cherokee County [Kansas]." As a result, the miners were housed in stockades guarded by state troops and Pinkerton guards. If western Missouri and eastern Kansas was paradise for black men, one new arrival reportedly exclaimed, this was "as near as [he] ever wanted to get to heaven."

2.5 Fusion and the Decline of the Populists

> *You come to us and tell us that the great cities are in favor of the gold standard. I tell you that the great cities rest upon these broad and fertile prairies. Burn down your cities and leave our farms, and your cities will spring up again as if by magic. But destroy our farms and the grass will grow in the streets of every city in the country…having behind us the producing masses of the nation and the world. Having behind us the commercial interests and the laboring interests and all the toiling masses, we shall answer their demands for a gold standard by saying to them, you shall not press down upon the brow of labor this crown of thorns. You shall not crucify mankind upon a cross of gold.*
>
> —*Speech of William Jennings Bryan at the Democratic convention in Chicago, July 8, 1896.*

The Populists increased their nationwide tally of votes by 40 percent between 1892 and 1894. Their largest percentage gains were in the industrial cities of the Midwest, demonstrating that they were on their way to expanding beyond a purely agrarian movement. A third of the ballots cast in Minneapolis were for Populist candidates, while 20 percent of voters had cast their ballots in Milwaukee, and 12 percent of Chicagoans supported the Populists. Coal-mining districts were even more enthusiastic, with over half of the voters in areas of western Pennsylvania voting for Populist candidates. As encouraging as these results were for those hoping to expand their base beyond Western farmers, national Populist leaders recognized that they had not yet unified Southern agrarians and the nation's workers.

Part of the problem was that Northern urban Populist leaders like Eugene Debs and Wisconsin's Victor Berger were perceived as radicals by many farmers. From the perspective of many farmers, Debs had tried to halt rail traffic simply to prove his power. The endorsement of Populism among radical unionists such as Debs also made the People's Party more susceptible to charges of Socialism, although Debs himself opposed Socialism at this time. From the perspective of urban workers, Populist demands for government control of railroads and the subtreasury plan were vast increases of government power that would only aid farmers. In addition, many of the more radical urban Populists endorsed limited plans for collective ownership of factories that seemed socialistic to farmers who owned land. The Populists, however, could not simply distance themselves from radical labor leaders because they represented many of the unionized workers the Populist's were seeking to appeal to during the lean years of the depression. As a result, the Populists were growing nationwide but were still not a unified national party in 1894.

In 1896, the Democrats held their national convention in Chicago two weeks before the Populist convention. The Democrats adopted the doctrine of free silver, as the "people's currency." They promised voters that free silver would stimulate investment in the cities, raise the fortunes of indebted farmers, and even offer benefits to business interests, although this final provision was left conspicuously unspecific. They also nominated the young and energetic **William Jennings Bryan** of Nebraska, a charismatic politician who would soon earn a national reputation as the "Boy Orator of the Platte." Bryan may have known little at first about how free silver would solve the problems of the nation. "The voters of Nebraska are for free silver and so I am for free silver," he allegedly claimed, promising only "I will look up the arguments later." However, Bryan was likely being facetious as he delivered hundreds of speeches in which he explained how increasing the money supply would benefit workers and farmers. The fiery and homespun manner he used to address crowds demonstrated that politics was as much about personalities as it was platforms. As a result, a more accurate statement might have been

William Jennings Bryan

A charismatic Nebraska politician who became the presidential nominee of both the Populists and the Democrats in 1896. Bryan would be nominated by the Democrats in two subsequent elections but was never able to defeat his Republican opponent in any of these three elections.

that Bryan was for free silver and, therefore, the people were for it as well. Whether his listeners ever looked up the economic arguments Bryan's ideas depended on was anyone's guess.

FIGURE 3.19

A widely circulated cartoon, this image depicts the Populists and William Jennings Bryan as a serpent that is consuming the Democratic Party. Ironically, the Populists were the ones that were swallowed up by their fusion with the Democrats in 1896. Four years later, the People's Party scarcely existed while Bryan headlined the Democratic ticket.

William McKinley

A Republican governor and congressman from Ohio, McKinley was nominated for president in 1896 and defeated the fusion candidacy of William Jennings Bryan in 1896. McKinley represented conservative business interests and the gold standard and convinced many working-class voters that conservative economic policies would benefit them by assuring economic growth.

A sizeable number of Democrats who supported President Cleveland and the gold standard were so upset with their party's choice of Bryan that they walked out of the convention. Many of these conservative, progold Democrats would later support the Republican candidate. The Populists were equally stunned, meeting in St. Louis and debating which of their options was less self-destructive. The Populists could issue a platform and nominate a candidate that was similar to the Democrats—a measure that would almost surely produce a Republican victory. The other option was to endorse Bryan and urge their supporters to vote for the Democratic candidate this election year. The danger of national fusion, of course, was that their fledgling party might be swallowed up by the Democrats. In what may have appeared as a compromise, the Populists chose to endorse Bryan but reject the Democrat's vice presidential candidate. Instead, they nominated Georgia's Tom Watson for vice president. The Democrats refused to snub their original vice presidential candidate, Arthur Sewall of Maine. As a result, Populists voted for Bryan and Watson, while Democrats voted for Bryan and Sewall. As a result, some observers feared a constitutional crisis if the Populists won without a clear vice presidential selection. The issue would become even more clouded if Bryan passed away.

Neither scenario occurred, at least not in 1896. **William McKinley** accepted the Republican nomination and backed a platform built on probusiness policies. Chief among these was the maintenance of the gold standard. McKinley's campaign resonated with bankers and the wealthy who expressed their apprehension with the prospect of a William Jennings Bryan administration by making generous donations to the Republican Party. Bryan tried to make up the difference with an active campaign. The thirty-six-year-old traveled though nearly two dozen states, standing atop a platform on his modified railcar at each rail stop and giving as many as a dozen speeches per day. McKinley ran his campaign through correspondence from his Canton, Ohio, home. The Republicans used their money and influence to spread two messages. The first was a positive one, stressing the soundness of currency backed by gold and the strength of America's international credit because of the nation's adherence to the gold standard. The second was less uplifting, likening Populism to Communism. Other negative propaganda claimed that the only way to ensure "a full dinner pail" was to avoid the destruction of industry and currency that the Populists and the harebrained Bryan would unwittingly introduce.

It had been a few years since the worst economic times of the Panic of 1893. The economy was slowly recovering, and farmers and workers were less inclined to believe the Capitalist system was failing them in the fall of 1896. At the local level, the Populists gained modest support among workers but their growth stalled in the West. The Populists also lost ground in North and South Dakota, Nebraska, Colorado, and Idaho after rejecting fusion with local Democrats. In what would prove to be a harbinger of the future, Republican and Democratic candidates in each of these states swept back into office by adopting some of the most popular aspects of the Populist platform as their own.

The wealthy and the middle class within the Northeast, as well as a slight majority of the laborers and even the farmers of this region, voted for McKinley out of fear of what inflation might do to the national economy. The South and the farmers of the Midwest supported Bryan, but it was not enough. The popular vote was relatively close, but 7.1 million Republican voters indicated the prevailing belief that abandoning the gold standard was a risk the nation should not take during a period of gradual economic recovery. McKinley's message of prosperity through stability had carried the day. On a state and local level, the Populists still controlled many offices. They elected twenty-two men to the House of Representatives and controlled five senate seats. However, the Republican victory despite fusion doomed the Populists as a national party. State and local Populist parties mostly disappeared by 1900. However, Bryan and the ideas of the Populists lived on. Bryan would be the Democratic nominee for president in two of the next three elections. He and other politicians representing the two major parties would adopt many of the goals of the Populists, and many of these ideas would be enacted by a new group of reformers during these twelve years.

1. Describe the rise of the Farmer's Alliance. How was the Grange of the 1870s and 1880s similar to and different from the alliance?

2. Summarize the Ocala Demands and the Omaha Platform. What were the goals of the Populist Party? In what ways did the Populists succeed and/or fail?

3. What was fusion, and how was Southern Populism influenced by race? How did white Democrats eliminate the black vote in the South, and what were the lasting consequences of poll taxes for this region?

4. What were the strengths and liabilities of Pullman's system of welfare Capitalism? Were Pullman workers worse off than other workers under this system? If not, why might they have been so much more upset over their living conditions than other wage laborers at this time?

5. Summarize the major strikes that occurred during the early 1890s. What were the obstacles to unionization, what were the goals of workers, and how successful were workers in achieving those goals? What impact did government have on the union movement during the 1890s?

6. Explain why McKinley won the election of 1896 and what this defeat meant for the Populists and those who favored their ideas. Would you consider the Populists as failures? Explain your answer with specific examples.

3. IMMIGRATION, ETHNICITY, AND THE "NADIR OF RACE RELATIONS"

LEARNING OBJECTIVES

1. Explain who the "new immigrants" were and why many Americans opposed their arrival in the United States. Describe the actions that were aimed at trying to limit migration from Central and Southern Europe during the 1890s.

2. Explain what historians mean when they refer to the 1890s as "the nadir of race relations." List the kinds of evidence that might support this conclusion, as well as ideas and examples that show race relations were no worse, or were even better, than during Reconstruction and the 1880s.

3. Describe the ways that African Americans defended their rights and strengthened their communities during the 1890s. At the same time, explain the significance of lynching on those efforts. Analyze the meaning of lynching and Jim Crow, and describe the ways black Americans faced such injustice.

3.1 The "New" Immigrants

Ellis Island was opened in 1892. This small island within the New York harbor became the port of entry for about half of the immigrants to the United States in the next two decades. Those who were able to purchase regular tickets were entitled to proper sleeping quarters and were met on board by processing agents. These US immigration officials asked a few questions before permitting these immigrants to disembark. Those who could not afford a regular ticket were restricted to the steerage section of the boat and slept among the cargo.

These individuals faced closer scrutiny by immigration agents. Unlike their more affluent shipmates, these immigrants were directed through various checkpoints and holding areas constructed throughout Ellis Island. Among these checkpoints were rapid medical examinations aimed at preventing the introduction of contagious diseases to the country. The worst of these tests was for an eye disease known as trachoma; it required having one's eyelids inverted. After the medical exam, inspectors asked each immigrant a list of questions. If an immigrant's name was too difficult for the inspector to spell, it might simply be changed. The final question was the trickiest and the most dangerous. The immigrants were asked if they had a job waiting for them in the United States. Contract-labor laws prohibited recruiters from "importing" laborers. The law was intended to protect domestic workers from companies who might recruit laborers abroad in an effort to replace their present workforce. As a result, those who answered "yes" might find their last dollar paying for a return journey within the steerage of a cargo ship. For the rest, a ferry transported them to New York City where they hoped to reunite with family members and quickly find a "situation"—the term used at this time to indicate employment.

nativists

Nativists hoped to prevent migration of nonwhites, non-Protestants, Jews, and other "new" immigrants from Central and Southern Europe. Ironically, they also shared prejudices against Native Americans who were not part of their vision for a white, Anglo-Saxon, and Protestant America.

Most white immigrants who arrived in America before 1880 were from Western Europe. The British, French, Dutch, German, and Scandinavian immigrants are often called old-stock Americans for this reason. This moniker also applies to Protestants from Northern Ireland, and the descendants of all these old-stock immigrants. **Nativists** were individuals who hoped to restrict the migration of non-Protestant immigrants who were not part of this old stock. Nativists retained prejudices against the majority of Irish who practiced Catholicism. Some even viewed Catholic immigration from Ireland as a regrettable consequence of Britain's failure to vanquish the island. Oral histories of Irish Catholic immigrants recall signs stating "No Irish Need Apply" in employment offices. Historians have not been able to find any clear evidence of such signs. A complete search of the *New York Times* between the Civil War and 1920 has only found a few anti-Irish provisos in the tens of thousands of help-wanted advertisements. The apparent rarity of actual signs or legally sanctioned discrimination did not make the persecution the Irish faced any less real. In addition, prejudices against people of German origin also remained strong in most areas of the country.

The Wisconsin state legislature passed the Bennett Law in 1889. Among its provisions was a ban on the German language in both public and private schools throughout the state. The old-stock Americans of Wisconsin resented the rapid growth of the German population and especially their cultural traditions related to alcohol. They believed that the public schools could be used to assimilate German children and spread Protestant values and culture, if not Protestant religion directly. Others viewed German schools with suspicion, believing that they were furthering the degradation of American culture and leading the state toward the bilingualism of nearby Canada. German Americans denounced the Bennett Law as a restriction of their freedoms and a Yankee assault on German culture by nativists who forced their values on others. Working with other ethnic Wisconsinites, recent immigrants rallied at the polls and voted for candidates who rescinded the Bennett Law 1891.

FIGURE 3.20

Prejudice against the Irish remained strong but was continuing to decline during the 1890s. This 1854 employment advertisement stating "No Irish Need Apply" is one of only of few of its kind that historians have found. Nevertheless, the impression remains that such signs were common. In reality, the kinds of discrimination most immigrants endured were usually more indirect.

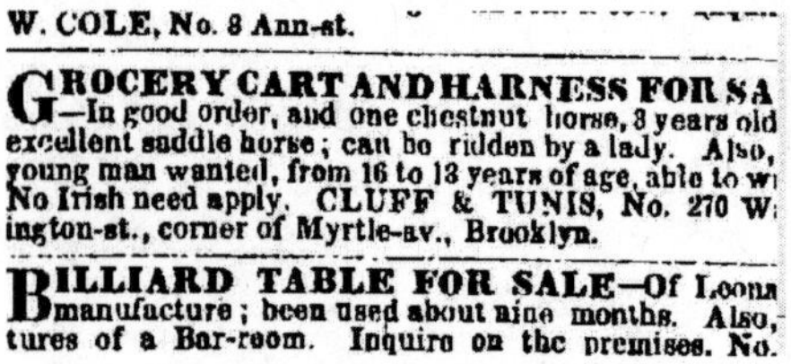

W. COLE, No. 8 Ann-st.

GROCERY CART AND HARNESS FOR SA—In good order, and one chestnut horse, 8 years old excellent saddle horse; can be ridden by a lady. Also, young man wanted, from 16 to 18 years of age, able to wr No Irish need apply. CLUFF & TUNIS, No. 270 W ington-st., corner of Myrtle-av., Brooklyn.

BILLIARD TABLE FOR SALE—Of Leona manufacture; been used about nine months. Also, tures of a Bar-room. Inquire on the premises. No.

Prejudice against Irish and German immigrants declined after the 1890s partially because a new group of "despised" immigrants took their place at the bottom of America's ethnic hierarchy. After 1890, migration from Western Europe slowed considerably and immigrants from Southern and Eastern Europe began arriving in large numbers for the first time. These Jewish, Greek, Italian, Russian, Polish, Slavic, and other immigrants were despised by many throughout Western Europe, and these prejudices were carried across the Atlantic. Old-stock Americans, regardless of whether they were recent immigrants themselves, gave these "new" immigrants something less than a warm welcome to "their" country.

Nativists who opposed "nonwhite" immigration from central and southern Europe, along with other nations beyond Western Europe, formed the American Protective Association in 1887. This group launched hateful campaigns against the Jewish and Catholic migrants who were arriving in larger numbers. A second organization, the Immigration Restriction League, wanted a mandatory literacy test as a requirement for entering the country. In contrast to the English-based literacy tests that future generations of nativists would support, the Immigration Restriction League proposed written exams that were based on an immigrant's native language. Most of the 20 million European immigrants who arrived in the next two decades had been denied the opportunity to attend school and could not read or write in any language. Although Congress approved a law requiring new arrivals to be able to pass a very basic test in the language of their choice, the law was vetoed by President Grover Cleveland. The president phrased his opposition in the language of egalitarianism and presented America as a land of opportunity and refuge for all who were willing to work. However, he was also under heavy pressure to veto the law by business interests who saw the new immigrants as a valuable source of cheap labor.

3.2 Race, Ethnicity, and Disfranchisement

The federal government did not pass mandatory literacy tests for prospective immigrants, but nine Western and Northern states enacted English-based literacy tests for prospective voters. These exams were intended to prevent non-English speaking immigrants from voting. Perhaps recognizing the possible incongruity of their actions, few whites from these states protested as the South passed additional laws aimed at preventing African Americans from voting. As described in a previous section, the fusion of white and black voters in North Carolina and other Southern states had threatened the interests of the Democratic Party and many of the Bourbon elite they represented. Similar measures were adopted by other Southern states much earlier than North Carolina. For example, Florida's 1885 poll tax placed a heavy financial burden on sharecroppers and laborers of all races who desired to participate in elections.

Beginning with Mississippi in 1890, Southern states held special conventions and rewrote their state constitutions to add provisions such as poll taxes. These conventions also added subjective measures designed specifically to keep black voters from the polls. For example, the Mississippi convention added an "understanding clause," requiring voters to interpret a clause of the new constitution to the satisfaction of the registrar, who was presumably white. Despite continued violence and fraud, 130,000 African Americans in Louisiana were still able to cast votes in the 1896 elections. The fusion of white and black voters under the Populist banner threatened the Democratic Party's control of Louisiana. The state legislature responded by adopting a new constitution that included literacy tests and the grandfather clause in 1898. By 1900, there were only 5,000 registered black voters in Louisiana.

Grandfather clauses and poll taxes kept poor voters of all races from the polls and thwarted movements such as Populism that sought to unite voters based on economic issues. Literacy tests reduced the number of eligible voters, but illiteracy was not the real issue in Louisiana and other Southern states. For example, there were only a few thousand registered black voters in Alabama in 1900, even though census records for that year recorded over 100,000 literate black men in state. The adoption of the white primary negated the effectiveness of minority votes in states that were dominated by a political party that explicitly sought to uphold white supremacy. As a result, few black voters were willing to submit themselves to literacy tests and pay poll taxes to participate in general elections that did not matter.

Between 1890 and 1908, every Southern state adopted poll taxes and other measures intended to restrict black suffrage. In many cases, the wealthy viewed the tendency of poll taxes to also reduce the number of poor white voters as a bonus. By emphasizing white supremacy, poor white voters had effectively disfranchised themselves by approving new state constitutions that enacted the poll tax. By 1920, Mississippi had only 60,000 voters participate in its general election. South Carolina recorded almost half this number. Northern states with similar populations recorded five to ten times the number of votes for the same number of presidential electors and representatives in Congress. As a result, wealthy white Southerners found that their votes carried more weight than Northerners (even when compared to the antebellum days when slaves were counted as three-fifths of a person in determining population and congressional apportionment).

Northern states were not immune from prejudice. California voters adopted an amendment to their state constitution in 1894 that allowed registrars to challenge the literacy of any potential voter. In such cases, the voter would have to read a hundred words of the state constitution to the satisfaction of the registrar. Few doubted that the registrar would select individuals to challenge by considering race and ethnicity. Eight other Northern states adopted similar provisions during this era as a deliberate measure to take the vote away from Hispanic citizens and recent immigrants.

In many cities, voting districts were gerrymandered by white Protestants who concocted ways to put nearly every Catholic and minority resident into one district. In other areas, voting districts might be drawn to ensure majorities for a particular party in nearly every district. Gerrymandering could be subtle, but some voting districts contained significantly more residents than others as a means of diluting the electoral power of certain voters. **Gerrymandering** was common in the South but was especially endemic in Northern, Southwestern, and West Coast cities with large immigrant populations. From Mexican Americans in Los Angeles to the sizeable Catholic population of Maine, voting districts were usually drawn in ways that diluted the strength of minority communities.

3.3 Lynching and the Campaign for Legal Justice

"We had to do it!" exclaimed a white Democrat in explaining how his Georgia county with 1,500 registered voters somehow recorded 6,000 votes in 1894. "Those damned Populists would have ruined the country." For many whites, the possibility of "negro domination" was far more than a political concern and justified lawlessness beyond voting fraud. For many, it even justified murder. Lynching—the killing of a person without trial, usually in retaliation for an alleged crime or other infraction—peaked with nearly two hundred lynchings annually between 1890 and 1910.

Lynchings of alleged thieves had occurred in the frontier in the past, but nearly every lynching after the turn of the century was racially motivated. About 10 percent of these racially motivated lynchings occurred outside of the South, meaning that the percentage of black victims in comparison to the total black population was similar throughout the country. Lynchings occurred in a number of "liberal" Northern and Western communities, even those such as Quindaro, a neighborhood of Kansas City, which was founded by abolitionists. Lynchings also occurred in rural areas of the West and cities with small black communities, such as Duluth, Minnesota. However, lynchings were usually rare in cities with a sizeable and well-organized black working class, such as Baltimore and Philadelphia. It is likely that this was related to the likelihood of retribution against the would-be perpetrators in these cities.

gerrymandering

The process of drawing electoral districts or other boundaries in such a way as to favor one group. For example, the potential importance of minority voters could be limited by creating voting districts that placed a small number of minority voters in a number of districts or simply placing them all in one district that still had a white majority.

FIGURE 3.21

Perhaps the most disturbing aspect of this photo of a lynching is that it was used as a postcard, indicating community sanction of the killing that had taken place. This particular lynching of three men occurred in Duluth, Minnesota, a chilling reminder that lynching was not limited to the South.

Ida Wells

Born into slavery during the Civil War and forced to abandon formal education in order to provide for her family, Wells eventually became a teacher, civil rights leader, newspaper editor, and international lecturer. She was arrested for refusing to give up her seat on a Southern railroad in 1883 but was most famous for her tireless but unsuccessful efforts on behalf of a federal antilynching law.

About half of the lynchings during this time period were carried out against men who allegedly raped white women. Although there was occasionally strong circumstantial evidence to suspect the guilt, in many cases the charges were quite unbelievable. Black civil rights activists **Ida Wells** documented the details of lynching cases, demonstrating that in many cases the victim had never even been accused of a crime beyond refusing to kowtow to white supremacy. She also argued that in many instances where interracial sex had actually occurred, it was consensual until the relationship was discovered. Wells argued that the potential community shame led some white women to accuse her lover of rape. In such instances, the outpouring of community support for the "victim" was overwhelming. White women demanded that white men take action to protect the spotless virtue of the alleged victim, many times a lower-class woman who had never been considered for the pedestal she was now placed on. Such women soon found their elevated position a lonely existence, especially when their former lover or any other unfortunate black man the howling mob came across was lynched.

For many angry lynch mobs, it was usually insufficient to simply kill their victim. Crowds of thousands of men, women, and children watched and participated in a symbolic orgy of community-sanctioned violence. An example from a Midwestern city demonstrates how quickly this violence could denigrate into a grisly ritual. Fred Alexander, a man who may have been mentally disabled and had lived his entire life in Leavenworth, Kansas, after being accused of rape was forced to eat his own genitals before his body was riddled with bullets, dragged through the streets, hung from a light pole, and then set on fire. A coroner's jury declared that Alexander had been killed by "persons unknown," although many whites had taken home pieces of his charred flesh for souvenirs. Many times, the body was paraded through the black community, a grizzly reminder that white supremacy must not be challenged. The only evidence against Alexander was that he had been seen by the victim who heard a man whistling just before the crime had taken place. As the local paper explained, everyone in the town knew Fred Alexander "had a habit of whistling."

Ida Wells was born into slavery in 1862 and lost her parents at age sixteen due to yellow fever. She raised her five younger brothers and sisters by working as a teacher, supplementing her abbreviated formal education with a love of books and learning for its own sake. She stood up to segregation, refusing to give up her seat on a railroad in 1883 and then suing the Chesapeake and Ohio Railroad after she was dragged from the car by two men. Wells sued the rail company and won, although the Tennessee Supreme Court later reversed the decision. Years later, the state of Tennessee and the rest of the South passed laws specifically permitting, and in many cases, requiring segregation in public transportation and most other public areas of life. Wells continued her confrontation of the color line, becoming an editor and an owner of the black newspaper the *Memphis Free Speech*, while continuing her work as a mentor of local children and a leading intellectual.

Her new job permitted Wells the resources to research the hundreds of lynchings that occurred each year and to compile statistics. She asked whites to consider why interracial rape, which had been almost unknown in the past, had suddenly become the greatest danger to Southern white women. For Wells, and for most thinking people, lynchings were not really about alleged crimes, but were rather a communal fete of white supremacy. Wells demonstrated how victims were often individuals who refused to abide by the expected racial codes of the South. A black man or woman who attempted to vote or hold office, started a successful business, or simply refused to move out of the way of a white person on a narrow sidewalk could be the next victim.

After a friend of Wells was lynched in 1892, Wells printed an editorial suggesting that interracial sex in the South was neither uncommon nor always rape. That she was correct mattered little. A mob destroyed her printing press and would have likely lynched Wells had she not been in Chicago at the time. She did not return to the South, but instead traveled worldwide and lectured about the problem of lynching. She also led the movement to make lynching a federal crime. Because local courts rarely convicted whites for lynching in the North and seldom even bothered arresting anyone for these murders in the South, Wells and other African Americans demanded that the federal courts intervene. For the next sixty years, all attempts to make lynching a federal crime were defeated by Southern Democrats in the Senate.

3.4   Creating and Confronting Jim Crow

Federal law prohibited racial segregation between the passage of the Civil Rights Act in 1875 and its nullification by the Supreme Court in 1883. The law was seldom enforced in the North or the South. At best, the federal law prevented states from passing laws mandating segregation beyond schools—a kind of separation that was banned from the original draft of the 1875 law but removed before its passage. Almost every federal lawsuit against violators of the Civil Rights Act was either thrown out on technicalities, mired in a maze of delays, or lumped together in the group of cases that were dismissed when the Supreme Court ruled the law unconstitutional in 1883. By the late 1880s, Southern states passed a variety of segregation ordinances that were nicknamed **Jim Crow** laws. By the end of the decade, nearly every form of public activity, from riding a streetcar to attending a theater, was segregated by law. Alabama passed a law forbidding interracial checkers, New Orleans segregated its prostitutes, and Mississippi prohibited any book used by black students to be used in a white school.

The name "Jim Crow" came from the stage name of an antebellum white actor who blackened his face and danced, pretending to be a buffoonish slave who was happy and lucky to be "looked out for" by a caring master. This style of entertainment featuring whites who mocked black men and women was known as **blackface**. A popular variety of blackface featured several white men with blackened faces who performed a comedic routine wherein they could not answer the simplest questions posed to them by a white interlocutor. White audiences enjoyed these shows immensely. Strangers felt a spirit of commonality and superiority with the rest of the white audience who laughed at the hapless "black" minstrel. Just as many enjoy the feeling of inclusion that arises from making someone else the butt of a joke, the minstrel show gave audiences a collective identity that was positive by its exclusion of "the other." Yet behind the black makeup and the red lipstick of the grinning blackface minstrel was something more sinister. Blackface celebrated white racial supremacy in ways that justified segregation and miseducation. Why not bar inferior children from the public school, the minstrel seemed to ask. What was wrong with preventing foolish men from being voters, and why would one not want to separate second-class citizens from first-class accommodations? Blackface entertainment and Jim Crow went hand in hand, and both traveled well beyond the South.

Black women and men challenged each of these laws, braving Southern jails and lynch mobs long before the modern civil rights movement of the 1960s. For example, a group of prominent black leaders in New Orleans organized the Comité des Citoyens (Citizens' Committee) in September 1891. The purpose of the organization was to challenge Louisiana's 1890 law that required separate rail cars or compartments for white and black passengers. The law itself was written to sound innocuous, claiming only "to promote the comfort of passengers." The committee raised more than a thousand dollars and attracted several liberal white attorneys who agreed to represent their case. Before the committee could challenge the law in the courts, someone had to be arrested for violating the law. The committee selected Homer Plessy for the unenviable task, hoping that his very light complexion would further their argument that people should not be separated or excluded because of perceptions about race. The committee also arranged a deal with a local railroad. This particular line opposed the segregation law because it added to their operating costs by requiring additional rail cars with separate compartments. The rail company agreed to have Plessy arrested, while the committee was waiting at the jail with bail money in hand.

FIGURE 3.22

Ida Wells was a leader of the antilynching movement. In 1892 she published a book entitled *Southern Horror: Lynch Law in All Its Phases*, which documented the frequency and consequences of lynching.

IDA B. WELLS.

Jim Crow

A term referring to the practice of racial segregation. The term itself is a derivative of the stage name taken by a popular white actor who mocked African Americans during the antebellum period. As a result, the origins of the phrase are indicative of the intent of "Jim Crow" laws to convey and enforce white supremacy.

blackface

A popular form of so-called entertainment consisting of white actors using soot or makeup to blacken their faces and act buffoonish in a manner that mocked African Americans and conveyed a message of unity and supremacy among white audience members.

FIGURE 3.23

A poster for a minstrel show featuring a white actor in blackface.

Homer Plessy's lead attorney Albion Tourgée also led a national organization that communicated about civil rights issues via the mail. After more than four years of trials and appeals, the case was heard by the US Supreme Court. Tourgée argued that justice was "colorblind" while the Fourteenth Amendment guaranteed all citizens the same right to due process regardless of race. In an infamous decision, the Supreme Court ruled in *Plessy v. Ferguson* (1896) that a segregation law might be valid if it supported established traditions and customs. The court upheld the Louisiana law, arguing that it met this historical criteria and served a positive social good by promoting "comfort and the preservation of the public peace and good order." The court disagreed that segregation implied discrimination or inferiority. "We consider the underlying fallacy of the plaintiff's argument to consist in the assumption that the enforced separation of the two races stamps the colored race with a badge of inferiority," the Supreme Court responded. "If this be so, it is not by reason of anything found in the act, but solely because the colored race chooses to put that construction upon it." John Marshall Harlan was the only member of the Supreme Court who dissented.

The *Plessy* decision would stand until the Supreme Court specifically revoked it in the 1954 case *Brown v. Board of Education*, which outlawed segregation in public schools. In the meantime, the 1896 decision included a provision that would become the basis of hundreds of civil rights lawsuits during the next sixty years. In issuing its defense of legal segregation, the majority decision required separate facilities to also be equal. This requirement led to numerous demands for better equipment and facilities for black schools and other segregated facilities throughout the Jim Crow South.

> Our constitution is color-blind, and neither knows nor tolerates classes among citizens. In respect of civil rights, all citizens are equal before the law…We boast of the freedom enjoyed by our people above all other peoples. But it is difficult to reconcile that boast with a state of law which, practically, puts the brand of servitude and degradation upon a large class of our fellow citizens—our equals before the law. The thin disguise of 'equal' accommodations for passengers in railroad coaches will not mislead anyone, nor atone for the wrong this day done.
>
> —US Supreme Court Justice John Marshall Harlan dissenting in Plessy v. Ferguson, which upheld the constitutionality of Louisiana's segregation law.

Lawsuits against segregation itself would continue after 1896 in many Northern and Western states. This was because many of these states passed their own civil rights laws before or almost immediately after the Supreme Court invalidated the Civil Rights Act in 1883. T. Thomas Fortune, one of the most outspoken black leaders of this era, founded a national civil rights organization called the National Afro-American League in 1887. Four years later, he successfully sued a New York barroom that drew the color line against him. Neither his case nor his victory was particularly unusual. Black plaintiffs sued at least half a dozen restaurants and hotels between 1892 and the turn of the century in the state of Iowa alone. One of these cases included the proprietor of the restaurant inside the statehouse, an instance of discrimination that shows that civil rights laws were only enforced because of the actions of African Americans. Most local civil rights cases were dismissed on lack of evidence, but numerous judgments were issued in favor of black plaintiffs. In most of these cases, however, the judgments were for trifling amounts of money that did not even cover court costs. Many plaintiffs faced threats, and those with white employers or landlords might lose their jobs and homes. The consequences of confronting the color line in less obvious ways were likewise dangerous, even in the North.

Raised beyond the veil of slavery, a new generation of African Americans relished and preserved the stories of their ancestors who confronted the lash with dignity. At the same time, they recognized that they were the heirs of some lesser freedom beset by prejudice and segregation. They passed on the work songs and freedom songs of their slave ancestors, the stories of fathers and grandfathers who served in the Union army, and experiences of legions of women like Harriet Tubman who escaped from slavery in one form or another. For many, their proud history demonstrated a path to freedom through the creation of stronger communities that might serve as a cocoon against the ugliness of the outside world.

Many historians of the black experience have identified the 1890s as "the nadir of race relations." They cite the passage of segregation laws and the second wave of attempts to disfranchise black voters as evidence of their claim. Jim Crow laws, they remind their readers, were not created until a generation after slavery's abolition. Other historians point out that custom rather than law separated white and black following the end of slavery. Few former slaves attempted to dine in restaurants or attend theaters, and those who needed to ride a train usually went to great lengths to avoid whites. With a few notable exceptions, they argue, segregation was as thorough before the enactment of Jim Crow laws in the 1890s as it was in later years. By this perspective, the creation of segregation laws might be evidence that at least some black Southerners were becoming more wealthy and assertive.

These same historians see the turn of the century as a time of limited progress despite the enactment of segregation laws. They cite the growth in the number of black teachers, professionals, entrepreneurs, and black colleges. Legal segregation provided a facade of legitimacy to the constricted freedoms and prejudices of the past, yet it also strengthened the sense of commonality among African Americans who built their own institutions beyond its veil. As a result, the black experience during the 1890s resists sweeping characterizations, just as the people of the era resisted segregation. During the final years of the nineteenth century, most of these protests were more subtle than a civil rights lawsuit.

In 1895, Booker T. Washington gave a famous speech known as "The Atlanta Compromise," which argued that segregation was less important than creating good schools for black children and good jobs for black men. Privately, Washington also worked to aid civil rights activism. Publicly, however, Washington appeared to accept segregation as a tactical compromise. This tactic permitted Washington to have access to a number of white lawmakers and white philanthropists. In exchange for accepting segregation, Washington challenged these whites to make sure that black schools were receiving better support, if not equal support as required by law. Whether Washington's decision was for the best interest of the race would be debated by black leaders during the early decades of the twentieth century.

FIGURE 3.24

This mid-nineteenth century image of a black man being removed from a rail car in Philadelphia reveals a number of truths about segregation. First, the color line was not limited to the South even if actual laws requiring segregation were passed in Southern states in the 1890s. Second, African Americans protested both formal and informal segregation long before the modern civil rights movement of the 1960s.

REVIEW AND CRITICAL THINKING

1. How were the "new" immigrants different from previous groups who came to America, and why did nativists oppose their arrival? What kinds of strategies did nativists propose?

2. Why would some politicians seek to require literacy tests for immigrants, while others would oppose such restrictions? How does the immigration debate of the 1890s compare to that of the present day?

3. How did literacy tests and poll taxes affect Southern politics? What was the impact of the white-only primary? What were obstacles did African Americans who sought to exercise their constitutional right to vote face in the South in the 1890s?

4. In what ways might the late nineteenth century be the *nadir* of race relations? In what ways might it be considered an era of progress? What was the intent of Jim Crow laws, and how did African Americans confront these laws during this era? Explain your answer using historical examples.

4. IMPERIALISM AT HOME AND ABROAD

LEARNING OBJECTIVES

1. Analyze the history of Native Americans within the context of imperialism. Compare the experiences of Native Americans to colonized peoples outside of the United States. Lastly, explain how imperialism can involve more than just physical acquisition of territory.
2. Summarize the way the United States acquired Hawaii, considering various perspectives on whether this acquisition was imperialistic.
3. Explain the causes of American intervention in the Spanish-American War. Summarize America's role in that conflict, explaining the sentiment behind the Platt and Teller Amendments.

4.1 Oklahoma and South Dakota

Imperialism refers to the establishment of dominant and exploitive relationships between a political entity, such as a nation, and another group or political entity such as a colony. The experiences of Native Americans are the clearest example of imperialism in US history. However, they are not often considered in this context because most people think of imperialism as involving foreign countries and they forget that Native Americans lived apart from the United States for most of their history. They also forget that treaties between the US government and Native Americans recognized individual tribes as sovereign nations. As a result, the creation of the reservation system and the acquisition of reservation land in violation of treaties are textbook examples of colonization. Between 1492 and the turn of the century, an estimated population of 7 to 10 million people had declined to just over 200,000 as a result of epidemic disease, massacres, and policies designed to promote either assimilation or extermination. Native lands were taken through conquest and incorporated into US territories, while Native Americans themselves were forced onto reservations and denied citizenship. Given the entire history of humankind, it would be hard to find any example that more perfectly fit the definition of imperialism.

As described in the previous chapter, Native Americans resistance had been rendered legally moot by the federal government and Supreme Court in the late nineteenth century. In addition, the federal government declared that 2 million acres of land in what was then known as "Indian Territory" would be opened for non-Indian settlement on a first-come basis. The government declared April 22, 1889, as the day settlers could enter parts of what eventually became the state of Oklahoma and stake their land claims. A second **Oklahoma land rush** was established on September 16, 1893, in an area formerly known as the "Cherokee Strip." On that day, an estimated 50,000 would-be settlers lined up on the border to begin a race to claim 42,000 homesteads. Advertisements for the land claimed that Native Americans "were rejoicing to have the whites settle up this country."

Oklahoma land rush

A phrase that refers to the dramatic method of the distribution of federal lands that once belonged to Native Americans in Oklahoma. There were several land rushes that corresponded with each distribution of land. In each case, land seekers lined up across a border line and awaited a signal that released them to claim a section of land on a first-come basis. The first land rush occurred on April 22, 1889, and was followed by a second land rush in the Cherokee Strip on September 16, 1893.

Washington took our lands and promised to feed and support us. Now I, who used to control 5,000 warriors, must tell Washington when I am hungry. I must beg for that which I own…My heart is heavy. I am old, I cannot do much more.

—Sioux leader Red Cloud speaking on the effects of the reservation system as recalled by an anthropologist who spoke with Red Cloud during the revival of the Ghost Dance.

The severe depression of 1893 added high stakes to the drama of the land rush, which was signaled by firing a cannon at noon. Those who had promoted the area and hoped to stake claims were known as "Boomers," while those who had illegally snuck into the territory to squat on choice sections of land were called "Sooners." Law and order submitted to the avarice of land speculators and the desperation of the landless. Claimants often used weapons and violence to convince earlier settlers that they had actually arrived on a certain portion of land before the claimants had. As land offices began recording the first claims, thousands of disappointed would-be Boomers turned their wagons north. For many, their last best chance to own land had failed to materialize for want of speed or because they had been convinced by the business end of a revolver to abandon their claim.

For those who lost out on the 1889 and 1893 land rushes, the Curtis Act of 1898 provided a third opportunity to take Indian land. This law removed the restrictions that had protected the Five Civilized Tribes of Oklahoma (Choctaw, Cherokee, Chickasaw, Muscogee, and Seminoles) from allotment in the original Dawes Act of 1887. The Curtis Act opened millions of acres throughout the next two decades. For those who were less interested in farm land, another cottage industry arose in Oklahoma. Practitioners of this trade unapologetically referred to themselves as "grafters." The grafters sought to profit from the poverty of Native Americans by swindling them out of their remaining lands or at least the mineral and oil rights to those lands. In many ways, the discovery of oil and valuable natural resources on reservation land was history repeating itself. After all, the Cherokees had been forcibly removed from Georgia to Oklahoma in the 1830s after gold had been discovered on their lands. The discovery of oil in Oklahoma would have similar consequences.

Previous imperialistic policies divided the Lakota Sioux, now living on a fraction of their original reservation in the recently admitted state of South Dakota. Sioux tribal leader Red Cloud had finally acquiesced to a treaty that ceded the Black Hills to the federal government following the discovery of gold in that region. Another tribal leader named Crazy Horse rejected this treaty. He would later be vindicated by the Supreme Court, which agreed with his interpretation years later. Crazy Horse and his followers revived traditions such as the Ghost Dance, in which participants would vanquish their enemies and revive the spirits of their ancestors. Fearing an uprising, the federal government dispatched soldiers to the area. They also ordered reservation police to arrest Lakota leader Sitting Bull in December 1890. A minor scuffle escalated after they surrounded his home and the police shot and killed Sitting Bull. The followers of Crazy Horse and other leaders who hoped to resist assimilation were encamped next to Wounded Knee Creek at this time. After Sitting Bull had died, federal troops were dispatched to the area to pacify the rest of the Sioux.

On December 29, 1890, federal troops surrounded the native encampment near Wounded Knee Creek with automatic rifles and 42mm Hotchkiss guns—the same weapons that had been used against the Nez Perce in 1877. After the Sioux were disarmed, the soldiers searched the possessions of each tribal member to make sure there were no hidden weapons. A deaf member of the tribe attempted to prevent the loss of his rifle, after which a shot was reportedly fired by an unknown party. The nervous (or revenge-driven, according to some sources) members of the cavalry immediately opened fire on the encampment. An estimated 300 Sioux and two dozen soldiers died in the ensuing firestorm. Despite every indication that nearly every shot was fired by US troops, including those shots that killed their comrades, many of the soldiers were decorated for bravery for their part in the **Wounded Knee Massacre**. For Native Americans, Wounded Knee signaled the final act of physical resistance to the loss of their lands. For non-Indians the massacre was both a shameful reminder of the history of Western conquest and a welcome sign that the Native American question had finally been settled.

FIGURE 3.25

An advertisement promoting lands in what would become Oklahoma. Notice how the poster claims that these lands were purchased by the government a year after the Civil War on behalf of former slaves. In actuality, a treaty was signed requiring the Choctaw and Chickasaw tribes to end slavery and provide land for slaves they had owned. These slaves were not given the land, and the federal government never paid for the land in question.

Wounded Knee Massacre

Occurred on December 29, 1890, in present-day South Dakota after a group of Sioux were surrounded by troops and artillery. As troops took the weapons from the Sioux, someone fired a shot that led to confusion and heavy fire from automatic weapons. An estimated 300 Sioux men, women, and children were killed during the attack. A dozen US troops were also killed, mostly by the fire of their own comrades.

FIGURE 3.26

Following the massacre at Wounded Knee, the corpses of the Lakota Sioux were buried in a mass grave.

4.2 Cultural Imperialism and Native America

A second federal initiative that was allegedly done for the benefit of Native Americans was the creation of boarding schools for Native American children. Like the Dawes Act, many Anglos believed that they were assisting natives through promoting assimilation through compulsory education. Unlike the Dawes Act, the provision of boarding schools was not calculated to bring immediate gain for white settlement. Most of the reformers and instructors were genuine in their belief that their efforts would benefit native children.

For example, Richard Pratt founded Carlisle Indian School at an abandoned military barracks in Pennsylvania. Pratt was a career army officer who had led both black and Native American troops and rejected the era's belief in innate racial inferiority. Pratt believed that native culture was inferior, however, and proposed that it be eradicated through forced assimilation. Pratt and others recognized that it would be much easier to assimilate children rather than adults, and easier still if the government could separate children from their families and tribes. As a result, over 20,000 children were attending boarding schools such as Carlisle by the turn of the century. For a handful of white lawmakers, funding for these schools was viewed as an investment that would discourage any further Native American resistance. "One fourth of the youth of any tribe (attending a boarding school) would be sufficient hostage against an Indian war," explained Massachusetts senator George Frisbie Hoar in 1882.

Pratt was far more sympathetic, but even he bluntly summarized the object of these schools as finding a way to "kill the Indian and save the man." The phrase indicated the belief that eradicating native culture was the only way to "save the savage" from himself. Such were the sentiments of generally well-meaning Anglo reformers who met each year between the 1880s and the outbreak of World War I at Lake Mohonk, New York. The annual Lake Mohonk Conference of the Friends of the Indian shaped the development of a federally controlled system of Native American education. Together with the federal government, these reformers determined that the goal of native education would be the extinction of Native American language, religion, and culture.

We are going to conquer barbarism, but we are going to do it by getting at the barbarism one by one. We are going to do it by the conquest of the individual man, woman and child, which leads to the truest civilization. We are going to conquer Indians by a standing army of schoolteachers, armed with ideas, winning victories by industrial training, and by the gospel of love and the gospel of work.

—Rutgers president and Native American Reformer Merrill Gates at the 1891 Lake Mohonk Conference.

Whether they attended Phoenix Indian School in Arizona; Sherman Institute in California, Chilocco Indian Agricultural School in Oklahoma, or dozens of other boarding schools, Native children were forbidden to speak of their former lives or even speak in their own language. Young men had their long hair shaved, a traumatic experience for many whose culture equated long hair with masculinity. Non-Protestant religions were forbidden, while military discipline and corporal punishment shaped everyday life. Young women were taught domestic skills that could be useful in homemaking or finding jobs as servants. The boys were taught the skills of farming and industrial labor. Each of these skills corresponded with low-paying jobs in manual labor, a future that seemed inevitable as the reservation system was being dismantled. As a result, many native parents grudgingly accepted federal agents' demands that their children attend. If parents resisted, their children were usually taken from them by force through a court system that simply declared the parents unfit guardians.

FIGURE 3.27

A 1908 image of the United States Indian Industrial Training School in Lawrence, Kansas. After years of dynamic change, this institution has become a four-year college for members of federally recognized tribes. Today the institution is known as Haskell Indian Nations University.

Many instructors treated children with kindness, yet even these teachers practiced a form of cultural imperialism that taught children to disparage their own traditions, religion, and language. The rest enforced harsh discipline, operating the school in a way more appropriate for a military camp than a place of learning. The schools were less-than-wholesome places, for reasons beyond corporal punishment. Children who had been relatively isolated from crowd diseases such as tuberculosis and influenza were suddenly surrounded by these microbes. Because school officials believed assimilation would be discouraged by allowing children to be among members of their own tribe, the students were surrounded by children from all over the country. This recipe for infection was perfected by sudden changes of climate, diet, and dress. Children who had spent their whole lives running barefoot were forced to wear flannel shoes, an incredibly traumatic experience that did little to protect one from contagion, as evidenced by oral histories.

Mortality rates have been estimated as high as 30 percent for children in their first year away from home. Few of the Apache children who were captured along with Geronimo in 1886 survived their first years at Carlisle. Many of these deaths were not recorded, and the remains of the children were sometimes placed in mass graves. Eventually, each boarding school built cemeteries as a disproportionately large number of children died of disease and other causes. For example, the United States Indian Industrial Training School in Lawrence, Kansas, included a cemetery with 103 grave markers that had been issued by the army. Today, the school has become Haskell University, a place where Native Americans earn four-year degrees and celebrate their cultural heritage. Occasionally, new remains are discovered at Haskell during construction projects in places beyond the cemetery. These instances are somber reminder of the mixed heritage of the institution's boarding school past and the callous way that some Native American remains were simply discarded when these boarding schools were first established. These cemeteries are among the most potent reminders of the consequences of assimilation. However, they also produce strong emotions among Native Americans, who are understandably hesitant to use the final resting place of their child ancestors as an object lesson in American history. As a result, most cemeteries are preserved in quiet dignity by tribal and school authorities.

4.3 Annexation of Hawaii

Historians in the last few decades have begun their discussion of American imperialism by discussing the conquest of continental America. This change in interpretation is due to the belated recognition that centuries of Western expansion had only been possible by conquest, diplomacy, and deceit. Imperialistic policies and attitudes facilitated the removal of sovereign tribes of Native Americans and permitted a third of Mexico to be acquired by force during the 1840s. Similar to earlier treaties with native leaders, the conquest of Mexico was formalized by an agreement signed by a government in duress. The United States also acquired vast territories of land by purchase and warfare with Spain, Britain, Russia, and France. By the late nineteenth century, the United States began acquiring overseas possessions as well. American classrooms did not contain world maps proudly denoting formal colonies in red, as occurred in England. However, in the 1890s, the United States acquired and administered territories in ways that were often similar to their British cousins.

The native inhabitants of the independent Kingdom of Hawaii were decimated by the same diseases that had killed Native Americans. Although the native population had stabilized in the previous century, Native Hawaiians were a minority by the 1890s as Asian laborers migrated to work the island's sugarcane fields. American investors owned many of these fields and successfully lobbied Congress to eliminate tariffs on sugar exports to the United States in 1876. Eleven years later, the United States responded with its own demand—a naval base at Pearl Harbor. The King of Hawaii accepted this demand under duress. He was later replaced by his sister **Queen Liliuokalani**, who was made of sterner stuff than her brother and sought to reclaim at least a share of self-rule for native Hawaiians. She challenged laws banning the use of the Hawaiian language in public schools and sought to reclaim voting rights for nonwhite laborers. Desperate for revenue, she also sought to legalize and tax illicit drugs such as opium.

The elimination of tariffs on Hawaiian sugar led to a dramatic increase in sugar exports to the United States, from 20 million pounds in the 1870s to over 200 million pounds by 1890. By this time, sugar production had become an important industry in the United States. In addition to sugar cane in Florida and Louisiana, the successful cultivation of the sugar beet from the Great Lakes to the Great Plains had made the domestic sugar lobby increasingly powerful. These domestic producers convinced Congress to offer subsidies for American-made sugar, which once again placed the sugar barons of Hawaii at a competitive disadvantage. The queen introduced a new constitution in 1893 that expanded the rights of native Hawaiians. Sugar planters on the island used the queen's progressive reforms as a pretext to seize power and offer the island to the United States for annexation. Hawaii's pineapple magnate Sanford Dole agreed to lead the new government of the island. US Marines armed with Gatling guns surrounded the queen's palace. Hoping to prevent bloodshed, the queen agreed to abdicate her throne so long as she would be permitted to present her interpretation of events to Congress. If Congress decided to disregard the queen's perspective and accept annexation, the Hawaiian magnates such as Dole and the sugar barons would become domestic producers exempt from tariffs.

Native Hawaiians attempted to resist what they perceived to be the seizure of their independent nation. However, the presence of US soldiers and the decision of the United States to provide military support to the new government meant that armed resistance would likely be suicidal. At the same time, the Senate was so disturbed by the way power had been seized that it delayed the annexation treaty until the representative of the queen was permitted an opportunity to address them. By the time this occurred, the 1893 congressional session had ended and Grover Cleveland was president rather than Benjamin Harrison, who had favored the annexation of Hawaii. Annexation of Hawaii was delayed as a result, but the Republicans championed the acquisition of the island during the election of 1896. Republican William McKinley won the presidential election that year and supported annexation even more than Harrison. In fact, McKinley personally attempted to maneuver the annexation treaty through Congress in 1898.

Opposition to annexation remained high during the first half of 1898. Native Hawaiians presented two petitions signed by nearly every resident of the island. Anti-imperialist senator George Frisbie Hoar led those who opposed the treaty, but failed to win support in the Senate. This changed following the outbreak of war with Spain in 1898. The political climate changed substantially once the war began because Hawaii represented a strategic location halfway between the West Coast and the Spanish-controlled Philippines. Just to be sure, President McKinley withdrew the treaty accepting Hawaii as a US territory and resubmitted it as a resolution. McKinley's maneuver meant that the annexation "resolution" required only a simple majority vote rather than the two-thirds required for treaty ratification. A similar scheme had been used during the 1840s regarding the then-controversial annexation of Texas. With over a quarter of the Senate abstaining, the resolution passed and Hawaii became a US territory in 1900. Its territorial constitution was unique, however, in that it limited suffrage to white male property owners—a provision not included in a state or territorial constitution since before the Civil War.

FIGURE 3.28

Queen Liliuokalani sought to defend the rights of Native Hawaiians and protested against what she believed was imperial aggression against her people.

Queen Liliuokalani

The last monarch of Hawaii was widely respected for her efforts to protect the sovereignty of her nation and the rights of its native inhabitants. Queen Liliuokalani was arrested and imprisoned for resisting an 1895 coup that was backed by the island's wealthy planters and was unable to prevent the annexation of Hawaii by the United States in 1898.

4.4 Spanish-American War in Cuba

In 1890, Naval theorist **Alfred Mahan** published a series of lectures he had delivered at the Naval War College in Rhode Island entitled *The Influence of Sea Power upon History, 1660–1783*. Mahan used history to demonstrate that the great commercial powers of history achieved their status through naval power. He connected these examples with his own ideas about the need to expand and modernize the US fleet. For Mahan, the navy must pursue two goals. First, it must produce faster battleships that could outmaneuver and outgun existing ships. Second, because ships required massive amounts of coal, the navy must acquire refueling stations across the globe where its ships could be resupplied. He recommended acquiring Hawaii, building a canal across Panama or Nicaragua, and creating coaling stations in the Caribbean and Asia. A young man named Theodore Roosevelt had attended some of Mahan's lectures and strongly agreed, as did many in Congress. In the next ten years, the United States would accomplish each of these goals except the canal, which was still under construction in Panama.

Industrialists supported the construction of a modern navy because they sought access to foreign markets where they might trade raw materials for American-made products and produce. Ironically, this was the very model of colonial economics the United States had rebelled against in 1776 and 1812. "We must have new markets," Massachusetts senator Henry Cabot Lodge argued, "unless we would be visited by declines in wages and by great industrial disturbances." Lodge spoke to the concerns of the wealthy and poor, each of which suffered during the early 1890s when warehouses were full of unsold products. The difference between themselves and the British, Americans assured themselves, was that they would still respect the independence of foreign nations while spreading ideas about democracy and freedom. Many of these sentiments were genuine, although they were often tainted by assumptions that the nonwhite people were unprepared for democracy and their "independent" nations would therefore need to be temporarily managed by Americans.

FIGURE 3.29
Naval Officer and
Strategist Alfred Mahan

Alfred Mahan

A naval theorist and historian who argued that naval power was the most important characteristic of powerful and prosperous nations throughout history. Mahan helped to promote the construction of a modern fleet of big ships with big guns that would grant the United States power to regulate commerce and prevail in the Spanish-American War.

FIGURE 3.30

This map demonstrates the success of Cuban rebels in pinning down Spanish troops, whose locations are depicted with red circles.

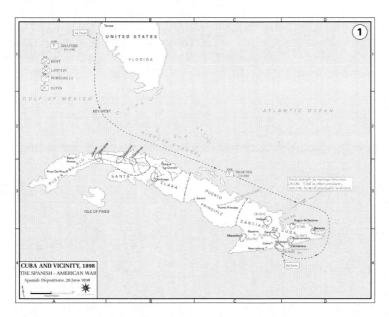

Cuba had long been the most-coveted foreign territory among Americans who desired to expand into the Caribbean. In fact, the United States had tried to purchase Cuba from Spain in 1848 for $100 million. Southerners in Congress made multiple attempts before and after 1848 to acquire the sugar-producing island, but met strong Northern opposition and other obstacles that derailed each of their efforts. Some Southerners fled to Cuba during and immediately after the Civil War because slavery was still legal and would not be formally abolished on the island until 1886. The end of slavery in Cuba was accelerated by several uprisings launched by free and slave rebels. During the 1890s, Cubans continued their struggle for liberation, this time fighting for political independence from Spain. By 1895, Spain and the Cuban rebels were involved in a full-scale war. The Spanish crown offered numerous concessions, but refused to grant the rebels complete independence. From the perspective of the Spanish monarchy, losing Cuba would empower the regime's critics at home and embolden other colonized people to launch similar rebellions against the crumbling Spanish Empire.

FIGURE 3.31

Details of the battle for Santiago in Cuba.

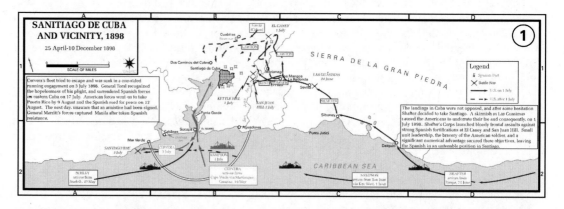

Americans supported the Cubans for four main reasons. First, their rallying cry of *Cuba Libre* was reminiscent of America's own struggle for independence from a European monarch. Second, US businesses hoped to invest in Cuban agriculture. Third, Spain's exit from the Caribbean would further the Monroe Doctrine—the nineteenth-century declaration of American authority regarding matters concerning the Western Hemisphere. Fourth, Spanish commanders resorted to inhumane methods to try and crush the Cuban rebels through fear and intimidation. Suspected rebels were tortured and killed, while entire villages believed to be harboring rebels were relocated to refugee camps where they suffered starvation and disease.

As a result, humanitarian concerns mixed with self-interest and convinced Americans to provide limited aid to the Cubans by the late 1890s. Spain refused to surrender the island, even though it recognized that the crumbling empire could never control Cuba as it had in the past. The fear in Madrid was that Cuban independence would spark other uprisings, especially among the people of Spain who had grown suspicious of the monarchy. Americans had their own concerns, chiefly the possibility that another foreign power might take control of the island. Less than ninety miles from Florida, a Cuba controlled by one of Europe's leading imperial powers could potentially threaten the United States. More realistically, a Cuba controlled by Cubans might lead to the seizure of US-owned plantations and prevent further investment in the region.

FIGURE 3.32

A global map showing US acquisitions throughout the Caribbean and Pacific.

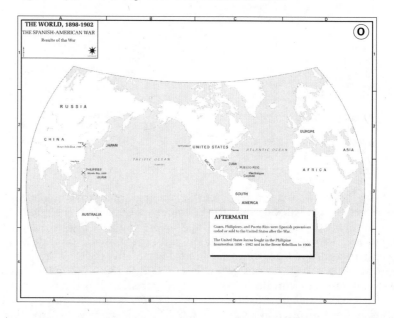

If the United States entered the war, it might change the way a Spanish defeat was perceived. The United States was an industrialized nation adjacent to Cuba, and American intervention provided a way for Spain to honorably retreat in the face of overwhelming force. President McKinley responded to the popular support for Cuban independence and the aspirations of US business interests by sending warships to surround the harbors of Cuba. America had not declared war or even sent troops to the island itself, but this show of "gunboat diplomacy" sent a clear message of US intentions.

On February 15, 1898, the USS *Maine* mysteriously exploded just outside Havana. An underwater exploration of the wreckage nearly a century later showed that the *Maine* was almost certainly sunk by an internal combustion involving the stored fuel the ship carried. In 1898, however, American journalists printed a more spectacular story: a Spanish mine or torpedo had destroyed a US ship stationed off the coast of Havana. The claim soon became that the USS *Maine* had merely been sent to evacuate US investors who lived on the island, making what was actually an accident appear to be an unprovoked act of war. The cause of *Cuba Libre* now mixed with the worst kind of yellow journalism as speculation rather than facts many to demand vengeance for the death of 250 sailors and marines.

McKinley demanded and Congress overwhelmingly complied with a declaration of war. In an effort to appease those who feared American intentions were imperialistic, the declaration of war officially renounced all intentions to control Cuba. Congress passed the Teller Amendment, which tied military funding to a resolution barring the US from annexing Cuba when the war was over. The Teller Amendment declared that Americans had no interest in Cuba beyond assisting the Cuban people secure independence from Spain. Cubans welcomed American military aid in their quest for independence. At the same time, they recognized that America's entry into the war risked the possibility that US troops would simply replace the Spanish. Although the Teller Amendment disclaimed and even outlawed any attempt by the United States to seize Cuba, Cubans understood that America remained committed to its strategic objective of gaining more control over the Caribbean.

The US Army contained fewer than 30,000 troops. Although augmented by the National Guard, these units were still controlled by individual states at this time, which generally refused to send their men overseas directly. Instead, ambitious men within each state nominated themselves for officer positions and organized volunteer regiments. The result was a logistical nightmare. The army had few supplies and fewer troops. Now they were also overwhelmed with about 200,000 untrained and unequipped volunteers commanded by political appointees eager to make a name for themselves.

Fortunately for the US Army, Spain lacked the military resources to station enough troops to patrol the entire island. Cuban rebels controlled the highlands and vast stretches of rural territory. They also conducted guerilla raids, which gave the rebels effective control of the island except its coastal cities. In addition, the Spanish navy was limited to outdated ships and the American navy was in the midst of modernizing its fleet. The US Navy surrounded and captured the Cuban fleet in Santiago Bay with few casualties. The US Army secured the heights of San Juan through the combined efforts of the African American infantry and a volunteer cavalry under the command of Roosevelt. The **Battle of San Juan Hill** catapulted Roosevelt to celebrity status, while the black troops were instantly forgotten by most except the men of Roosevelt's makeshift regiment who attested to their bravery. With the rural highlands controlled by the Cubans and the ports and harbors controlled by the Americans, Spain decided it could surrender with honor before more men died to prevent an inevitable outcome.

Battle of San Juan Hill

The most significant land battle during the Spanish-American War, the Battle of San Juan Hill resulted in the capture of the heights around San Juan in Cuba by US forces.

FIGURE 3.33

This painting by artist Don Stivers depicts the cooperation of white and black soldiers at the battle of San Juan Hill.

What was not inevitable was the status of Cuba following the war. Congress modified the Teller Amendment with the **Platt Amendment**—a measure that limited its original guarantee of Cuban independence. The Platt Amendment gave the United States control of many aspects of Cuba's foreign policy, especially regarding trade and military alliances. The Platt Amendment forbade Cuba to permit any foreign power to build military bases on the island and restricted the ability of Cubans to make diplomatic and commercial decisions that the United States deemed contrary to Cuba's interests. Some of these provisions were more genuinely concerned about maintaining Cuba's independence than others. For example, restrictions on foreign debt were intended to prevent the troubles some recently independent nations had encountered. Others were clearly designed to benefit the United States, such as an agreement to cede land to the United States that would be used as naval base. The result was the creation of the US base at Guantanamo Bay—a source of contention between Cuba and the United States for the next century and beyond.

4.5 Spanish-American War in the Pacific

Knowing that war with Spain was likely, Assistant Secretary of the Navy Theodore Roosevelt had previously sent Commodore George Dewey's Pacific fleet to Hong Kong where it was to refuel and wait further orders. The navy had long desired a base in Asia. When the Spanish-American War erupted, the fleet was sent to "liberate" the Philippines from Spain. Like Cuba, the Philippines had been waging a war for independence against a distant Spanish Empire. On May 1, 1898, the American fleet surrounded and destroyed seven Spanish ships anchored in Manila, losing only one sailor who died of health issues. The Battle of Manila Bay elevated Commodore Dewey to hero status and vindicated the navy's decision to follow Mahan's advice in building a modern fleet.

Filipino leader Emilio Aguinaldo agreed to coordinate his attacks with the 15,000 US troops that arrived in late July. Aguinaldo's guerilla warriors kept the Spanish troops isolated in Manila. As a result, the arrival of US troops was actually a relief for the beleaguered Spanish. Believing that surrendering to the native Filipinos would be dishonorable and would make the Spanish empire appear weak, the Spanish waited to surrender to the newly arrived force of US troops. Honor required a staged display of gunfire by both sides where a handful of soldiers still managed to die prior to the surrender. In signing the Treaty of Paris, which ended the war, the Spanish granted independence to Cuba and sold the Philippines to the United States for $20 million. The US Navy had also captured the former Spanish possessions of Puerto Rico and Guam, hardly firing a shot. The treaty acknowledged that these islands were also US territory.

> *God has not been preparing the English-speaking and Teutonic peoples for a thousand years for nothing but vain and idle self-admiration. No…He has made us adept in government that we may administer government among savage and senile peoples…He has marked the American people as His chosen nation to finally lead in the redemption of the world.*
>
> —*Senator Albert J. Beveridge, 1900*

From the perspective of the Filipinos, they and not the Americans had defeated the Spanish. However, the United States had managed to seize control of their would-be independent nation like some sort of powerful vulture perched off the coast of Hong Kong. The United States felt differently, having defeated the Spanish fleet, paid $20 million for the islands, and accepted the surrender of Spain at a ceremony in which no Filipinos were permitted to participate. Aguinaldo appealed to US leaders, pointing out his belief that the American people did not favor, and the US Constitution did not permit, the acquisition of colonies. He and other Filipinos had held the United States in high esteem prior to this point. After his appeals fell on deaf ears, Aguinaldo called on his people to continue their fight for independence, this time against the imperial rule of the United States. Roosevelt spoke candidly on the subject of Filipino independence, stating that if the United States was "morally bound to abandon the Philippines," as Aguinaldo suggested, they "were also morally bound to abandon Arizona to the Apaches."

In August, Aguinaldo created a revolutionary government; and by February 1899, Filipino guerillas and US troops were engaged in a war of attrition. The entire Spanish-American War had resulted in fewer than four hundred combat deaths, but the conflict between Filipinos and US troops raged on. Major combat operations against the rebels had largely ceased by 1901, when all but a small number of militant Filipino nationalists agreed to end their armed struggle. By that time, an additional 4,000 US troops and several hundred thousand Filipinos had perished. These civilian casualties included a large number of women and children because the United States had utilized a policy designed to starve the Philippines into submission. This campaign was nothing like the scorched earth policy of Sherman's

March to the Sea in the final years of the Civil War. The military drew few distinctions between civilians and belligerents in the Philippines.

The tactical approach was reminiscent to the seventeenth-century warfare between colonists and Native Americans, except this time the newcomers had automatic weapons. The moral justifications were also similar. "It is not civilized warfare," a US journalist reported. "The only thing they know and fear is force, violence, and brutality, and we are giving it to them." To be sure, atrocities occurred on all sides. The desperation of Aguinaldo's forces led to torture of US troops. Those Filipinos who agreed to accept American sovereignty were cared for in refugee camps and provided food. The rest were free to starve as the refugees in a nation whose food source had been destroyed. Some American observers justified the occupation by concluding the Filipinos were not civilized, emphasizing their dependence on US provisions. Others in the United States were quick to point out that the Filipinos had agricultural surpluses until the occupation of their island by US forces.

> *The truth is, I didn't want the Philippines, and when they came to us as a gift from the gods I did not know what to do with them…I went down on my knees and prayed Almighty God for light and guidance more than one night. And one night it came to me…we could not give them back to Spain—that would be cowardly and dishonorable…we could not turn them over to France or Germany—our commercial rivals in the Orient—that would be bad business…we could not leave them to themselves-they were unfit for self-government…there was nothing left to do but take them all, and educate the Filipinos, and uplift and civilize them, and by God's grace do the very best by them as our fellow-men for whom Christ also died. And then I went to bed, and went to sleep and slept soundly.*
>
> *—President William McKinley, explaining what he believed was divine inspiration on behalf of maintaining the Philippines under American rule to Methodist leaders in 1899.*

Antiwar activists and anti-imperialists in America questioned their nation's presence in the Philippines after the Spanish had surrendered. They believed the reason the United States had intervened was to acquire an Asian colony that would serve to force open the door to trade in China. For anti-imperialists, the costs of the war did not justify the human consequences or the moral degradation of a nation that had entered the war for the stated purpose of defending the freedom of Cubans. Anti-imperialists were also shocked by the callous statements of some veterans regarding civilian casualties. "I am growing hardhearted," one soldier wrote home. "I am in my glory when I can sight my gun on some dark skin and pull the trigger." Many other veterans wrote candid reports of the atrocities they witnessed or participated in. Most soldiers hoped to defeat rebel forces without the loss of innocent life. Others began to question their orders, especially when General Jacob Smith gave his infamous order to kill every Filipino that was physically able to shoulder a rifle.

Historians refer to the official war that occurred between Aguinaldo's forces and the United States between 1899 and 1902 by several names, such as the **Philippine Insurrection** or the Philippine War of Independence. The choice of title usually indicates the perspective of the author. Historians are also left with the choice of citing the US Army's estimate of a few thousand civilian casualties (individuals killed by gunfire) or the much higher estimate that includes the hundreds of thousands who died of starvation and disease. The question of casualties is further complicated by the tens of thousands of nationalist Filipinos who continued to fight for independence after the official surrender to US forces in 1902. In addition, a small number of Filipino Muslims sought to maintain control of the Southern Philippines before surrendering in 1913.

Taken together, each of these conflicts eroded the image of the Filipino people as grateful recipients of American freedom. Opponents of imperialism within the United States began to question the inherent goodness of their nation. Journalists documented the torture of captured Filipino rebels through the use of something called the "water cure" (presently called waterboarding) that simulated the sensation of drowning. Many of these atrocities came to light by aging veterans who came forward during the Vietnam War. Haunted by the memories of burning fields and the blurred line between villagers and guerilla warriors in their own youth, the nation's attention to civilian casualties in Vietnam led to renewed interest in the stories of Spanish-American War veterans. Two generations later, Americans would return their attention to the use of torture during war when reports of waterboarding detainees reached the media following the September 11th attacks and Iraq and Afghanistan wars.

Philippine Insurrection

A period of armed resistance by Filipinos between 1899 and 1902 in opposition to US occupation of the Philippines. Many Filipinos perceived the United States as a foreign and imperialistic presence in their country and supported the efforts of revolutionary leader Emilio Aguinaldo, who hoped to secure national independence.

REVIEW AND CRITICAL THINKING

1. To what extent was the United States an imperialistic nation before 1890? How might considering Native American history in the context of imperialism alter our perspective of American history?

2. Construct a critical summary of the history of Oklahoma and South Dakota from two perspectives—that of Native Americans and that of nonnative settlers. Compare the history of Wounded Knee and the Oklahoma land rush to previous events in American history.

3. Did world events play an important role in shaping US history from the time of Reconstruction to the turn of the century, or was the United States an "island nation" unaffected by the rest of the world?

4. Describe the nature of US expansion during the 1890s. Using what you know about world history, compare US imperialism to that of other expansionistic world powers. Was US imperialism unique?

5. Why might interpretations of Native American history and the acquisition of overseas territories have changed dramatically over the past century? What causes historical interpretations to change, and why is it important to understand this process?

4.6 Conclusion

By 1890, the memory of the Civil War had finally started to fade in national politics. In its place were new concerns about the growing power of corporations, the strength of American democracy, and questions about nation's proper international role. For African Americans, the decade brought the growth of public schools and colleges. It also brought Jim Crow laws, lynchings, and disfranchisement. The way Americans made money was also changing. By 1890, less than half of Americans made their living from the land. As a result, the relative economic equality that had typified a nation of small farmers gave way to a modern Capitalist system with all its advantages and liabilities. When times were good and wages were increasing, the Second Industrial Revolution was praised as eliminating scarcity. For most of the 1890s, however, the economy was mired in depression. The Panic of 1893 highlighted the increasingly unequal distribution of wealth. Americans grew increasingly concerned that the majority of wealth in the nation was controlled by only a few thousand families. There had always been a gap between rich and poor in the United States, but the crash of the banking system made it clear that some financiers were taking unacceptable risks with other people's money.

The countryside and cities were full of reformers and agitators, each proclaiming their own gospel of wealth and ways to fix the economy. The polarization and hard times helped to propel the growth of one of these reform movements—Populism. Farmers launched the movement and attempted to join with urban workers to create the People's Party, or Populists. In the South, white Populists tentatively sought the support of black voters and then quickly abandoned them. The Democratic Party continued to represent the interests of landowners in the South and responded to the Populist challenge in ways resembling the final years of Reconstruction. This time, the Democrats completed earlier efforts to disfranchise black voters, transforming Southern politics by becoming the only viable political party. The Populists would disappear as a national party by 1900 but would leave American political culture forever changed. Many Populist ideas would be adopted by the Republicans and Democrats during the Progressive Era.

International affairs began to occupy a much more prominent role in American politics following the acquisition of overseas colonies. Some, like William Jennings Bryan, would condemn America's presence in the Philippines as contrary to America's traditions of liberty. Others, such as William McKinley and his vice presidential running mate in 1900 Teddy Roosevelt, celebrated expansion and wrapped the American flag around the acquisition of empire. From this perspective, the United States had liberated these islands from Spanish oppression and then remained behind to liberate the people of these lands from themselves until they were ready for independence. By 1900 the United States had unofficial control over much of Cuba and directly possessed the island colonies of Hawaii, Guam, and the Philippines in the Pacific, as well as Puerto Rico. Membership in the American Empire was not without benefits, however, even if the people of these islands still preferred independence. Each of these islands provided strategic value in terms of military power and commerce. Whether the United States would extend traditions of democracy to these islands or rule them as conquered territories would be one of the leading questions of the next decades.

---

5. FURTHER READING

Beeby, James M. *Revolt of the Tar Heels: The North Carolina Populist Movement, 1890–1901* (2008).

Giddings, Paula J. *Ida: A Sword Among Lions: Ida B. Wells and the Campaign Against Lynching* (2008).

Hild, Matthew. *Greenbackers, Knights of Labor, and Populists: Farmer-labor Insurgency in the Late-nineteenth-century South* (2007).

Litwack, Leon. *Trouble in Mind: Black Southerners in the Age of Jim Crow* (1998).

McCartney, Paul T. *Power and Progress: American National Identity, the War of 1898, and the Rise of American Imperialism* (2006).

Perez, Louis. *The War of 1898: The United States and Cuba in History and Historiography* (1898).

Pierce, Michael. *Striking with the Ballot: Ohio Labor and the Populist Party* (2010).

Postel, Charles. *The Populist Vision* (2007).

Smith, Robert Michael. *From Blackjacks to Briefcases: A History of Commercialized Strikebreaking and Unionbusting in the United States* (2003).

Warren, Kim. *The Quest of Citizenship: African American and Native American Education in Kansas, 1880–1935* (2010).

Wood, Amy Louise. *Lynching and Spectacle: Witnessing Racial Violence in America, 1890–1940* (2009).

CHAPTER 4
From Populism to the Progressive Era, 1900–1912

The depression of the 1890s seemed a distant memory by the early years of the twentieth century. The economy had rebounded and farm prices stabilized. Some US companies profited handsomely from the expansion of the navy and acquisition of overseas colonies, even if many Americans agreed with Senator George F. Hoar of Massachusetts that ruling these territories without the consent of the people was "contrary to the sacred principles" of the nation. These individuals and a wealth of others hoped to promote social justice and greeted the twentieth century with optimism and energy. Taken together, these predominantly middle-class reformers who emerged during the 1890s are known as the **Progressives**.

The Progressives believed government should be more active in promoting the welfare of the people. However, although they agreed with some of the ideas of the Populists, the Progressives were generally much more conservative. They were often alarmed at the radicalism of the Populists and believed in reforming society and government rather than proposing sweeping changes to the Capitalist system. For example, they rejected the Populist idea of direct government control or ownership of railroads. They also rejected major changes to the monetary system, such as using both gold and silver to back the dollar. Instead, the Progressives believed that government should use its powers to more actively regulate the financial system and prevent the growth of monopolies. They also hoped the government would be more active in promoting social justice and human welfare.

In short, the Progressives were middle-class reformers who believed in the preservation of private property but opposed the laissez-faire policies of the past. They hoped to reduce government corruption and increase efficiency by appointing a new generation of college-educated experts to key government positions. In doing so, the Progressives were optimistic that government regulation could protect all members of society within the existing Capitalist system. They sought reform rather than revolution, and feared that sweeping changes or retreat from Capitalism would disrupt the economic growth of the previous decades.

Despite a number of similarities, the Progressives were as diverse as the issues they championed. Some sought social justice through anti–child labor laws, prison reform, workplace safety regulations, public health programs, or minimum wage laws. Others focused on providing more services, such as public utilities and urban sanitation. Still others believed that the key to reform was to make the political system more democratic. By exposing the misdeeds of corrupt businesses and politicians and empowering voters to have more control over their government, the Progressives believed that voters would naturally support reform candidates and demand more accountability. A small number also fought for more rights for women and minorities, although issues of race and gender often divided the Progressives. Still others championed the developing fields of social and political science, searching for ways to make government and society more efficient.

Progressives

A diverse assortment of reformers who sought to improve the condition of certain groups or society as a whole through government action at the turn of the century. Progressives were typically middle class and well educated. They also opposed Socialism, believing instead that the Capitalist system was efficient but had shortcomings that needed to be addressed by government regulations designed to protect workers and consumers.

Even if they supported a diverse range of goals, the Progressives themselves usually had a few things in common. They were generally well educated and shared a common faith in the power of public education to improve society and reform the political system. They generally supported local government initiatives aimed at providing better schools, sanitation, roads, and municipal services like utilities and public transportation. Progressives rejected Socialism but also rejected the notion that the private sector could regulate itself or that existing charitable organizations were sufficient to provide for the needy.

1. NATIONAL POLITICS DURING THE PROGRESSIVE ERA

LEARNING OBJECTIVES

1. Explain the importance of national Progressive political leaders such as Teddy Roosevelt. Describe Roosevelt's philosophy about the role of the federal government at home and abroad.
2. Describe the way the federal government sought to resolve conflicts between labor and management and prevent monopolies during the Progressive Era. Explain how this strategy compares to the ways government dealt with trusts and labor disputes in the past.
3. Summarize the presidential election of 1912. Explain the reasons for Wilson's victory and the role Roosevelt played as a third-party candidate. Also, explain why nearly a million voters supported the candidacy of Eugene Debs. Explain the ideas and goals of the Socialist Party and how they compared to those of the Progressives.

1.1 The Rise of Teddy Roosevelt and Federal Power

Theodore "Teddy" Roosevelt

The youngest president in American history, Roosevelt was only forty-two when the assassination of William McKinley elevated him to office in September 1901. Roosevelt believed that the federal government should arbitrate conflicts between workers and industry. He also sought to limit the power of trusts, or at least make sure that these large companies operated in the public interest.

The politician who would come to represent the Progressive movement on the national stage was **Theodore "Teddy" Roosevelt**. An asthmatic and sickly child born into affluence, Roosevelt developed his own brand of toughness as he labored to transform his mind and body, often against the warnings of his physicians. Wealth facilitated his metamorphosis, as Roosevelt went from home school to Harvard where he embraced "masculine" activities such as boxing. Affluence allowed him to cultivate a diverse range of talents. However, it was his force of personality and talent that empowered Roosevelt and drove him to try his hand at a variety of careers. Believing the men of his postfrontier generation were becoming "soft," Roosevelt dedicated much of his life to searching for adventure—a way of living he called the "strenuous life." Roosevelt succeeded at most of his activities, publishing a book on naval history, tracking down horse thieves in the Dakotas, leading a contingent of cavalrymen in the Spanish-American War, and serving in the state legislature of New York. And this was just the first four decades of the future President's life.

Roosevelt's family fortune also softened the consequences of his failures. Roosevelt bought and then abandoned a ranch in North Dakota after a blizzard wiped out his herds in 1886. While most men would face ruin after such a disaster, Roosevelt was able to return to his home in New York City where his wealth and connections led to a series of increasingly important political appointments, including commissioner of police. Later appointed to the newly formed US Civil Service Commission, Roosevelt gained a reputation as a reformer who rooted out political corruption. Roosevelt was appointed assistant secretary of the navy in 1897 but resigned his post the following year when the Spanish-American War broke out. Roosevelt saw the war as an opportunity for adventure and personally led a group of volunteers against an entrenched Spanish position. Regarded as a war hero following the successful assault on San Juan Hill, Roosevelt returned to New York and was elected governor on the Republican ticket in 1898. The leaders of the state's powerful Republican political machine feared that Roosevelt's popularity and reform agenda would loosen their grip on local politics. To remove Roosevelt, state politicians encouraged the incumbent President McKinley to select the war hero as his running mate in 1900.

With the popular Roosevelt by his side, McKinley once again faced the Democratic candidate William Jennings Bryan in 1900. Bryan attempted to revive the issue of free silver in this campaign. However, the recent economic recovery greatly reduced the perceived relevance of Bryan's economic ideas. Bryan also ran as an antiwar candidate, a position that appealed to many Americans who were beginning to view the war in the Philippines with suspicion. However, Bryan's anti-imperialist message failed to overcome the belief that McKinley's probusiness policies and overseas acquisitions were promoting the growth of US industry and commerce. With slogans such as "Four More Years of the Full Dinner Pail," the McKinley-Roosevelt ticket prevailed in a close election.

McKinley died only six months into his second term after an assassin shot the president during the 1901 Pan-American exposition in Buffalo. Roosevelt was informed of his pending ascension to the White House while he was on a mountain-climbing expedition. He was soon sworn into office and served as president for the remainder of McKinley's term. Roosevelt also won the election in his own right in 1904. During his seven-and-a-half years as president, Roosevelt's personality and exploits dominated the news as much as his policies. For example, he invited professional boxers to spar with him in the White House—leading to an injury that left him blind in one eye. Roosevelt even rode one hundred miles on horseback in a single day—a feat many considered impossible. His love of the outdoors was legendary and helped to inspire a number of measures designed to preserve areas for sportsmen and the expansion of the national park system.

While in office, Roosevelt rejected the idea that the president should defer to Congress. "It is the duty of the president to act upon the theory that his is the steward of the people," Roosevelt remarked, adding that he believed the president "has the legal right to do whatever the needs of the people demand, unless the Constitution or the laws explicitly forbid him to do it." As president, Roosevelt introduced many of the reform measures sought by the Progressives, and in so doing, created a larger and more active federal government.

During his successful reelection campaign in 1904, Roosevelt promised that he would not seek a second term in 1908. He kept that promise and retired temporarily from public life, only to seek the nomination of the Republican Party in 1912. When the Republicans chose the incumbent William Howard Taft as their candidate, Roosevelt decided to run as the candidate of the Progressive Party. Although many states at this time had various independent third parties that used the term *Progressive* in their name, Roosevelt's decision to run under a national Progressive Party banner in 1912 helped to forge a measure of unity among these various local parties. Like the Populists, however, the Progressive Party would prove short lived, but many of their ideas were incorporated into the platforms and policies of the Republicans and Democrats.

1.2   Business and Politics in the Progressive Era

By the early 1900s, the largest 1 percent of corporations produced nearly half of the nation's manufactured goods. Roosevelt and the Progressives believed that industry and finance were ruled by an **oligopoly**—a system where a small number of individuals exercise almost complete control. In defense of their perspective, nearly all of the nation's railroads were managed by one of six firms. Half of these companies were controlled by the investment bank led by J. P. Morgan. Standard Oil controlled nearly 90 percent of the nation's domestic oil refineries. Trusts controlled most other major industries, while a series of mergers and acquisitions meant that retailers were increasingly affiliated with national chains. Many Americans were concerned by the consolidation of power by these corporations. At the same time, they recognized that most of these corporations had succeeded by engineering more efficient methods than the patchwork of local firms they had replaced. Still, the Progressives believed that too much consolidation in any industry discouraged innovation and invited unfair practices.

Progressive reformers were generally middle-class women and men who had prospered during the second Industrial Revolution. As a result, they sought to reform capitalism rather than incite revolution. Progressive efforts at economic reform were directed at promoting efficiency and stability. The Progressives were deeply concerned by the kinds of class conflict that were erupting in other industrial nations during this time and hoped that governmental regulation of industry and labor might prevent the growth of radical doctrines such as **Socialism** in the United States. At the same time, the Progressives believed that failure to regulate industry would result in a system that favored productivity over sustainability and economy over wages and workplace safety. If wages for workers were too low, the Progressives pointed out, workers would be much more likely to launch strikes and adhere to radical doctrines. As a result, the Progressives had a different perspective than unions. They favored many of the same policies, but did so out of concern for sustained economic growth and stability. For the Progressives, the growing popularity of Socialism overseas and in the United States was a symptom of the government's laissez-faire policies. If government would intervene to prevent the growth of monopolies and mediate labor conflicts, the Progressives argued, the Capitalist system would provide both efficiency and fairness.

FIGURE 4.1

This 1885 photo of Teddy Roosevelt demonstrates both his rugged grit as a rancher in the Dakotas and the wealth that permitted him to pursue a variety of careers. The ornate silver knife Roosevelt is carrying was made for his family by the New York jeweler Tiffany & Company. Despite his affluence and connections, Roosevelt earned the respect of his fellow ranchers in the Dakotas.

oligopoly

a situation when a particular industry is dominated by a small number of powerful firms. In contrast, a monopoly exists when only one firm controls an industry.

Socialism

Because Socialism can refer to a philosophy, a political movement, and an economic and a political system, there are numerous variants of the definition of Socialism. In general, Socialism is a system where productive property such as farms and factories are collectively held and administered.

FIGURE 4.2

Although he was a popular president, many satirized Roosevelt's domineering tendencies. This cartoon depicts Roosevelt as a giant carrying a "big stick," which he was fond of referring to, and peering down at a diminutive figure labeled "the Constitution."

1902 Anthracite Coal Strike

A strike that began in the coal mines of eastern Pennsylvania that was resolved by federal arbitration. The miners received a modest pay increase but failed in their efforts to bar nonunion labor from the mines.

Socialists did not believe that the reforms the Progressives favored would be enough. They argued that Capitalism inherently led to exploitation of workers. The only solution, Socialists believed, was for government to seize control of the means of production (factories, mines, farmland, etc.) and run each of these enterprises in the public interest. From the perspective of middle-class Progressives, Socialism was the antithesis of freedom because it eliminated private property. Progressives believed the role of government was to protect private property and nurture the profit motive that inspired hard work and innovation. However, many workers lacked basic necessities and felt they had little chance to acquire any material security under the present system. For those who believed they were being exploited, and for those who contrasted their poverty with the wealth of the leading capitalists, the idea of equally dividing the nation's wealth and permitting the government to run factories and farms held some appeal.

Progressives recognized the limitations of free market, even if they did not fully appreciate these shortcomings from the perspective of the poor. By enlarging the power and scope of government, the Progressives believed that they could regulate corporate America in a way that would ensure fair competition between businesses and fair conditions for workers. However, some Americans believed that the kinds of government intervention the Progressives sought might inadvertently become the first steps towards Socialism. By creating a powerful central government that had the power to regulate the private sector, they argued, the Progressives might unwittingly be creating a government that might eventually grant itself the power to seize control of businesses and other forms of private property. If the federal government ever became this powerful, opponents of Progressivism feared, political leaders might eventually rise to power by advocating class warfare and the seizure and redistribution of the nation's wealth.

A small number of business leaders viewed Progressive reform as a compromise between Socialism and pure Capitalism. They believed some government regulation was necessary to make the free market operate correctly. They also believed the possibility of government intervention might help mitigate the demands of workers and prevent the popular uprisings that occasionally swept Europe. These business leaders pointed out that the kinds of changes the Progressives supported were usually mild reforms that reflected the shared interests between workers, management, and the public.

The government's actions in negotiating a settlement between 100,000 striking coal miners and management during the **1902 Anthracite Coal Strike** provides an example of this kind of compromise and reform. Miners throughout Pennsylvania demanded a 20 percent raise and provisions forbidding nonunion workers from being employed within the mines. Management refused to consider these demands and argued that permitting a union-only workforce would effectively grant workers control over whom they could hire. As both sides prepared for a long strike, the rest of the nation faced the prospect of a winter without coal. Roosevelt and other Progressive leaders proposed that both sides agree to arbitration by experts in the field of coal mining. The coal unions agreed to this arbitration. Eventually, the government compelled the coal operators to agree as well. Workers' demands that only union workers could be employed in the mines were rejected, but they did receive a 10 percent raise and reforms designed to increase safety and welfare on the job.

Although he was able to promote a compromise, some aspects of Roosevelt's response to the coal strike angered conservatives and business owners. For example, the president threatened to use the military to seize and administer the mines if a solution could not be reached. Roosevelt's intervention demonstrated a new philosophy of federal activism in response to a strike that threatened the public welfare. Rather than sending the military to break up the strike, the military would be used to operate the mines while the government acted as mediator. If mediation failed, both labor and management would suffer. From the perspective of conservative opponents of Progressivism, Roosevelt's threatened seizure of privately owned mines indicated that the government had grown too powerful. The unions countered that the only reason such methods were even contemplated was because management refused to consider the reasonable requests of workers. From the perspective of the Progressives, the 1902 strike demonstrated that a few coal operators had become too powerful and government regulation was necessary to prevent future conflicts from ever reaching the point of a nationwide strike.

Given the political upheaval in other developing nations and the past history of violent strikes in the United States, some business leaders were willing to accept a more active government at the turn of the century. Some believed the government might promote stability and better relations between labor and management. Corporate growth had not been curtailed by previous government regulations such as the Interstate Commerce Act, Sherman Anti-Trust Act, and various state regulations regarding workplace safety. In fact, some business leaders even argued that the existence of government agencies with limited powers over trade and commerce did more to provide the appearance of government regulation than actual reform. The creation of antitrust laws and small regulatory agencies had appeased reformers during the late nineteenth century, they argued, and might help to absorb public criticism and demands for more substantive reforms.

The Progressives of the twentieth century were not content with the mere appearance of reform, however. They became more insistent on breaking up trusts and creating powerful regulatory agencies as the decade progressed. Roosevelt personified this tendency. He began his administration by agreeing to continue the conservative policies of the late William McKinley. Before long, Roosevelt demonstrated his penchant for greater regulation of corporate America. For example, he ordered the Department of Justice to investigate the Northern Securities Company in 1902. Roosevelt believed that the only purpose of this railroad trust was to create a cartel. Northern Securities was a holding company that controlled three of the largest railroads in the country. The purpose of the company, Roosevelt argued, was to conspire against competitors while not competing against one another. Existing laws and the sentiments of their own shareholders prevented these three companies from simply merging into one giant railroad. Through the creation of Northern Securities Company, however, a single board effectively coordinated operations in ways that reduced competition between the three railroads while strangling many of their smaller competitors. After two years in court, the Supreme Court agreed with Roosevelt and ordered a breakup of the giant trust.

FIGURE 4.3

The 1902 Anthracite Coal Strike in Pennsylvania resulted in a ten percent raise and other demands. The victory would prove short-lived as coal companies simply changed the rates they charged miners who were dependent upon supplies and housing controlled by the company.

FIGURE 4.4

Alton Parker swept the South, which was dominated by the Democratic Party by 1904. Roosevelt's Square Deal and moderate Progressive reforms were supported by the rest of the nation.

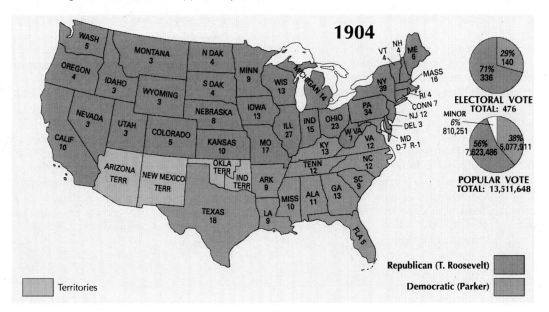

During the 1904 election, Roosevelt promised a "Square Deal" that would protect US workers and farmers from monopolies and unscrupulous businesses. The Democratic candidate Alton B. Parker supported many of Roosevelt's views, especially when it came to the danger of monopolies. However, Parker was far more conservative and opposed the president's goal of expanding the power of the federal government. Parker believed that the states, rather than the federal government, could best act to protect workers and consumers. As a result, it was difficult for Parker to provide positive examples of what he might do if elected to lead a federal government he believed should defer to the states. Parker and his supporters feared that the expansion of federal power was contrary to the interests of the nation and its traditions of limited government. While many agreed with this message, Roosevelt's growing enthusiasm for Progressive reforms allowed him to give positive examples of how he might use the government to address issues of concern to voters.

With the exception of Roosevelt's enthusiasm for overseas expansion—a mainstay of the Republican Party during this era—observers noticed that Roosevelt backed many of the goals that had been associated with the Democrats in recent presidential campaigns. During the 1890s, the Democrats fused with Populists and considered themselves to be the party who defended workers and farmers against the interests of big business. Meanwhile, the Republicans supported more conservative and probusiness policies. Parker's conservatism and support for the gold standard set him at odds with many in the Democratic Party. In some ways, Roosevelt better fit the ideas of Progressive Western Democrats and former Populists, while Parker embodied many of the ideas of the late William McKinley and conservative Republicans. As a result, it was difficult for Parker to win support among Western and Northern Democrats, and he failed to win even one state beyond the Mason-Dixon Line. Parker swept the Democratic South for two reasons. First, he defended the concept of local control over the federal government. Second, the Republican Party had largely ceased to exist in many Southern communities. In the North and the West, however, voters overwhelmingly supported Roosevelt's Square Deal and its promise of more rigorous federal regulation.

After winning the presidency on his own in 1904, Roosevelt began to view his office as a "bully pulpit" from which he could enforce his reform agenda. The Roosevelt administration brought lawsuits against several leading trusts, including Standard Oil, the Du Pont Corporation, and the American Tobacco Company. Roosevelt was soon labeled a "trust buster" by some businessmen who opposed him. Ironically, the mood of the country had changed, and this derogatory label backfired by increasing Roosevelt's popularity among liberal Republicans and Progressives. However, Roosevelt was careful to maintain positive relations with many business leaders, and he continued to receive campaign donations from the usual Republican supporters. Roosevelt also made it clear that he opposed the breaking up of certain "good trusts," even as he avoided precise definition of which trusts were operating in the public interest. During his two terms in office, Roosevelt initiated only twenty-five lawsuits against corporations he believed had violated the law. Roosevelt preferred working with business leaders and convincing them to agree to certain regulations through the Department of Commerce and Labor, which was created in 1903. The majority of corporations agreed to the relatively mild demands of the commerce department and its growing staff of corporate and legal experts. In this way, Roosevelt's White House personified the Progressive faith in the ability of experts within government to resolve problems by meeting with labor and business leaders rather than resorting to the courts or strikes to settle differences.

The federal bureaucracy expanded under Roosevelt and the reform-minded culture of the Progressive Era. Roosevelt secured the passage of the Elkins Act, which forbade railroads from offering rebates to its preferred customers. The Roosevelt administration argued that these rebates were a way of charging different prices to different customers without explicitly violating the Interstate Commerce Act. In 1906, Roosevelt and Congress passed the **Hepburn Act**. This new law expanded the authority of the Interstate Commerce Commission (ICC) which had been created in 1887 to regulate railroads. In the past, the ICC could only investigate complaints of excessive rates and file lawsuits against railroads they believed were in violation of the spirit of fair competition. Under the Hepburn Act, the ICC could actually establish maximum rates that railroads could charge. If a particular railroad believed the ICC's rates were set too low, it was now their responsibility to file suit and prove their case. As a result, the burden of proof and the hassle of initiating lawsuits now belonged to the railroads rather than the consumer and the ICC. Progressives cheered the Hepburn Act as model legislation providing the kind of vigorous government intervention they hoped would expand to other industries. Conservatives believed the new law concentrated too much power into the hands of federal bureaucrats. Business leaders feared that the new law might lead toward a much larger role for government as a regulator of private industry beyond the railroads.

Hepburn Act

A 1906 law that granted the Interstate Commerce Commission (ICC) the authority to establish maximum rates that railroads could charge.

1.3   The West and Conservationism

FIGURE 4.5

President Theodore Roosevelt with conservationist John Muir overlooking California's Yosemite Valley in 1903.

The Hepburn Act signaled an end of laissez-faire policies regarding some of the biggest and most powerful companies in the United States, even if the ICC used its new powers cautiously. ICC officials consulted with the rail companies before establishing maximum rates and other regulations to ensure fairness and continued operation of the nation's infrastructure. Roosevelt also consulted with business leaders in ranching, agriculture, mining, and forestry before drafting laws regarding land use and environmental conservation. Individual states had taken the lead in establishing nature reserves and state parks. Due to the efforts of Sierra Club founder **John Muir** and other conservationists, Congress had also established a number of national parks. Roosevelt was inspired by the efforts of Muir, who hoped to preserve the wilderness for its own sake, even if the President tended to see the purpose of conservation in utilitarian terms.

In many ways, Roosevelt's conservationism was similar to the perspective of **Gifford Pinchot**, chief of the US Forest Service. Pinchot's goal was to promote the scientific management of government lands to ensure the long-term availability of lumber and other natural resources. Pinchot harnessed the power of the federal government to halt the destruction of forests and required lumber companies to plant trees and follow other regulations. His agency promoted the natural reforestation of areas where trees were harvested and also banned the controversial practice of clear-cutting entire forests. Together, Roosevelt and Pinchot quadrupled the nation's total forest reserves to enclose 200 acres.

Roosevelt was a sportsman, and this perspective influenced his policies regarding conservation. He viewed the purpose of conservation largely in terms of preserving lands and species for recreation. In order to prevent overhunting, Roosevelt supported the creation of state agencies that regulated hunting through laws and game wardens. Many of these regulations disrupted the traditional ways of Native Americans and other rural dwellers who depended on hunting for food. At the same time, Roosevelt's creation of fifty wildlife refuges and numerous national parks helped to preserve the wilderness and various species for future generations. Roosevelt also helped to mobilize public support for conservation, leading to the creation of the National Park Service during the Wilson Administration in 1916.

Muir collaborated with Roosevelt and Pinchot, recognizing the delicate status of the Conservationist Movement and his need to work with the federal government to promote his ideas. However, Muir could not abide by Pinchot's decision to support the construction of a reservoir within Yosemite National Park. The purpose of the Hetch Hetchy Reservoir was to provide water to the city of San Francisco. Opponents countered that the reservoir would be disastrous for the ecology of Central California. Roosevelt demonstrated the limits of his belief in conservation, supporting the reservoir as a question of the needs of humanity versus romantic sentiment about the preservation of a picturesque valley. The Sierra Club and its founder John Muir launched a strenuous campaign in opposition to the reservoir project. They could only delay its passage, and construction was finished in 1923. The controversy split the conservation movement between those who sided with Muir about the need to preserve nature for its own sake and those who agreed with Pinchot about the needs to make nature serve the needs of man.

John Muir

The leading conservationist of the early twentieth century, John Muir founded the Sierra Club and documented the importance of preserving California's Sierra Nevada Mountains.

Gifford Pinchot

Led the US Forestry Service and promoted the notion that government should ensure the sustainability of natural resources. Pinchot also increased the number of protected forests and required lumber companies to plant trees while outlawing the destructive practice of clear-cutting entire forests.

> *The American people have evidently made up their minds that our natural resources must be conserved. That is good, but it settles only half the question. For whose benefit shall they be conserved—for the benefit of the many, or for the use and profit of the few?*
>
> —Gifford Pinchot, conservationist and first Chief of the US Forest Service

Newlands Reclamation Act

Officially called the Water Reclamation Act of 1902, the Newlands Act established the federal Reclamation Service. This agency sponsored projects such as dams and irrigation systems that distributed water to arid regions of the West.

Similar to the ways that aridity had defined the patterns of Western settlement and life following the Civil War, questions regarding water usage defined Western history during the early twentieth century. Nevada senator Francis Newlands introduced the Water Reclamation Act of 1902, a law which was often referred to as the **Newlands Reclamation Act**. This law created the Reclamation Service, a federal agency charged with finding ways to spur agricultural and commercial development by distributing water to arid regions of the West. The Newlands Act set aside funds from the sale of federal land for large-scale irrigation projects. For example, the Shoshone Project brought water to the Bighorn Basin of Wyoming, while Arizona's Theodore Roosevelt Dam near Phoenix permitted urban sprawl in the midst of a desert. Original regulations limited the sale of water from the federal government's dams and irrigation networks to cities and individual family farms that were no larger than 160 acres. However, these regulations were increasingly modified or ignored as commercial farming and industry began to dominate the West.

FIGURE 4.6

This 1920 photo shows the commercial development along the Cuyahoga River in Cleveland. This river would later become synonymous with environmental pollution, but the practice of dumping industrial waste into rivers was common throughout the nation at this time.

The federal government largely neglected the most troubling environmental issue of the West—the long-term challenge of sustaining cities and commercial farms within the arid plains. Likewise, the environmental impact of commercial farming, industrial growth, and mining was not addressed. Coal companies were still permitted to abandon mines, even those that left open pits. Mine operators were also permitted to use hydraulic mining techniques that used millions of gallons to blast earth away from ore. The environmental consequences of these mining techniques were rarely considered in an era where cities and factories used rivers as their own dumping ground for sewage and industrial waste. Throughout the nation, most cities simply ignored the inconvenient truth that those who lived downstream depended on the same river for their drinking water. The Cuyahoga River between Cleveland and Akron became forever associated with environmental disaster when it became so polluted that it caught on fire in 1969. However, conflagrations on the surface of this and other American rivers were actually quite common during the early 1900s. During these years, cities emptied their sewage directly into rivers. Refineries dumped oil and industrial waste with little thought of the long-term consequences. Although the Progressives sought to preserve the pristine environment of the vanishing wilderness, few gave much thought to the modern environmental concerns of air and water pollution.

1.4 Progressivism and President Taft

In a moment of jubilance he would later regret, Roosevelt promised that he would not run for reelection on the evening of his 1904 victory. Despite his desire to seek a second full term, Roosevelt remained true to his word and supported Secretary of War **William Howard Taft** as the Republican nominee in 1908. Roosevelt's support helped Taft secure the Republican nomination over Wisconsin senator **Robert La Follette**. Ironically, La Follette had been one of the strongest advocates of Progressivism and was the Republican leader who had initiated many of the Progressive reforms credited to Roosevelt. As governor of Wisconsin, La Follette instituted direct primaries for all major political offices. He also supported a method called "recall" where citizens could remove public officials. La Follette and other Progressives also supported methods of direct democracy, such as initiative and referendum, where citizens could introduce laws through petitions and special elections.

William Howard Taft

An influential judge in Ohio, Taft rose to national prominence after Teddy Roosevelt supported his nomination for president in 1908. Taft served one term and later became the Chief Justice of the Supreme Court.

Robert La Follette

A Republican politician from Wisconsin who was deeply influenced by the Progressive Movement of the early 1900s, La Follette enacted a number of reforms as governor of Wisconsin; these laws were aimed at increasing the power of government to regulate corporations.

Progressives within the Republican Party favored La Follette over Taft. However, La Follette was labeled by some conservative Republicans as a radical who supported Socialism. Although he worked with the leaders of the growing Socialist Party in Wisconsin, La Follette strenuously and vocally opposed Socialism. He believed the key to preventing the kind of worker's rebellion the Socialists were trying to foment was to reform the Capitalist system to be more responsive to the public interest and human rights. This idea was soon known as "the Wisconsin idea," due to La Follette's efforts in his home state. La Follette passed stricter regulations regarding worker safety and child labor. La Follette also favored stronger state welfare programs for women and children, as well as government-mandated pensions for workers. Although he would receive nearly 5 million votes as an independent candidate in 1924, many conservatives within the Republican Party viewed La Follette with suspicion and chose to support Taft in 1908.

FIGURE 4.7

A political cartoon lampooning Bryan's attempts to revive support for ideas such as free silver. Among Bryan's supporters is an aged man beating a drum labeled "dead issues." Following his third defeat in 1908, Bryan moved away from the national spotlight. He would make one final major public appearance during the 1920s debate regarding public education, religion, and the theory of evolution.

THE POPULIST PAUL REVERE.

For the third and final time in 1908, the Democrats selected William Jennings Bryan as their candidate. Once again, the political atmosphere of the early 1900s gave Bryan little room to maneuver and differentiate himself as the defender of the common man. Taft benefitted from his association with Roosevelt, who was hailed as a reformer. Equally important, the Republicans retained the support of corporations as well as many laborers and farmers. Many voters found it difficult to differentiate between the platforms of Bryan and Taft. The Democratic candidate espoused many of the same policies and ideas of the past seven-and-a-half years under Roosevelt—policies the voters believed Taft would continue.

Taft had widespread experience as a public figure through a series of political appointments and diplomatic posts. However, he had never run for political office before his nomination for president in 1908. It mattered little, as Taft's advisors framed the terms of the campaign in ways that likened their candidate to the popular Teddy Roosevelt. Fairly or not, Bryan was portrayed as a perennial second-place candidate, while Taft was presented as the next Roosevelt. For some, Bryan's recent conversion to Progressivism seemed opportunistic. In reality, Bryan may have been more committed to Progressive reform than nearly every Republican except Robert La Follette and a few other Republicans of Yankee conviction who simply could not bear the thought of being a Democrat. Bryan craved the opportunity to enforce antitrust legislation nearly as much as he longed to be president. His campaign called for tougher regulation of Wall Street and federal insurance for bank deposits—two reforms that might have addressed some of the problems that led to the Great Depression. In the end, neither of these reforms occurred, at least not until after the financial panic of 1929.

Taft's victory did not lead to an end to Progressivism. The new president surprised many Republican Party insiders by pursuing antitrust legislation even more vigorously than Roosevelt. Taft made few distinctions regarding the "good" trusts his predecessor had tolerated and trusts that acted in restraint of trade. For example, Roosevelt had defended trusts operated by businessmen like J. P. Morgan, citing several times when the investment banker purchased securities during stock market panics that helped calm other investors. Taft disagreed, taking on companies controlled by the House of Morgan and other "good trusts."

FIGURE 4.8

An image depicting Taft as a nurse caring for Roosevelt's policies, which are being handed by the outgoing president to his hand-picked successor. In reality, Taft was much more aggressive in antitrust legislation but did not share his predecessor's enthusiasm for politics.

Despite these antitrust lawsuits, Taft generally sided with the conservatives of his party when it came to legislation. Only occasionally did the president side with the Progressive wing of the Republican Party, which was led by La Follete in the Senate and the long-serving Nebraska congressman George Norris in the House. Even then, Taft had little appetite for Congressional politics. For example, the president supported an effort to lower tariffs on manufactured goods—a measure that was opposed by many Northern Republicans. By the time the president's bill made it through Congress, Senators who represented manufacturing interests had added hundreds of amendments that kept tariffs quite high in nearly every industry. Progressive Republicans urged their president to veto the bill as a matter of principle, but Taft had no stomach for power politics and went along with the conservative leadership of his party.

As the tariff bill demonstrates, many of Taft's attempts to reform the political system ended in failure because the president refused to go against the conservative majority of his own party. A scandal involving a questionable deal arranged by the secretary of the Interior further reduced the image of the Taft administration. Secretary Richard Ballinger leased federal land in Alaska Territory to men he had once represented as an attorney in Seattle. These men sought to develop coal mines in the Alaska frontier. As head of the Forestry Service, Gifford Pinchot hoped to prevent this from occurring. When his efforts to block the deal failed, Pinchot went behind the president's back and published a number of accusations. The public and Congress took notice, but an investigation revealed no obvious indication of wrongdoing.

It appeared to many that Pinchot had sought to generate a scandal in order to scuttle the Alaska land deal, and Taft felt he had little choice but to fire Pinchot for insubordination. This action greatly diminished the president's record as a conservationist while the impression of scandal and disloyalty created a negative impression of the Taft administration. Although Roosevelt would be remembered as the environmental president of the early twentieth century, Taft placed more land under federal protection in his one term as president than Roosevelt. He also secured legislation that granted the president the authority to block federal land sales. However, Taft would be forever remembered as the man who fired Gifford Pinchot and permitted energy companies to exploit the Alaskan frontier. Roosevelt would also be known as the leading Progressive, despite the fact that Taft signed more Progressive reforms into law. However, most of these reforms were the result of legislation that had reached Congress after years of grassroots campaigns led by local Progressives. Taft supported but did not initiate these Progressive reforms.

1.5 Latin America and Asia

Insular Cases

Refers to a number of US Supreme Court cases that were decided in 1901 and dealt with the rights of inhabitants of the islands the United States controlled after the Spanish-American War. The Supreme Court declared that the Constitution did not apply to territories, nor did its protections extend to the residents of the colonies.

Having agreed to a tentative peace agreement in the Philippines in 1902, the military government that had ruled the island transitioned into one that promised eventual Filipino independence and limited self-government. The Filipinos and the residents of Guam, Puerto Rico, and the American Samoa pressed for greater independence. They also challenged the idea that the people who lived in what became US territories should not be granted the rights of US citizens. In a series of important court decisions known together as the **Insular Cases**, federal judges disagreed with their perspective. The Court ruled that the Constitution did not "follow the flag." In other words, the Constitution did not automatically apply to territories, and its protections did not extend to colonized peoples.

As the leading defender of the growing US empire, Senator Albert Beveridge of Indiana supported the Court's decision. The Constitution "applies only to people capable of self-government," Beveridge explained. Beveridge candidly pointed out that nonwhites in the United States were explicitly or implicitly denied the right of citizenship and self-government and asked why Filipinos and Puerto Ricans should be an exception. African Americans in the South faced disfranchisement and segregation, he reminded his audience, while Native Americans living on reservations and most Asian immigrants were explicitly denied citizenship and the right to vote. If the Progressives were so concerned about the rights of Pacific Islanders and those in the Caribbean, Beveridge asked, why were they usually so reluctant to discuss the condition of minorities within the United States?

Beveridge might have pressed this point further had he not also supported the nativist impulse shared by many Americans. Conceptions of race and the "exotic" among white Americans facilitated the nation's acceptance that nonwhite people in the United States and abroad were simply "different" from them. Attitudes ranging from paternalism to the most virulent forms of racism softened the mercenary aims of land speculators and imperialists by presenting native peoples as the natural losers of a Darwinian contest between civilization and savagery. Paternalists spoke of their desire to uplift the "savage" Indian and Filipino in ways that presented conquest as the first step in assimilation. Others equated native populations to jungle animals whose lives meant little in comparison with more evolved beings such as themselves. Even paternalists such as Theodore Roosevelt, who believed indigenous populations shared a certain exotic vitality, were eager to make more land available for white settlement and provide the United States with the benefits of empire.

While many supporters of the anti-imperialist movement opposed colonization on moral grounds, these liberals were outnumbered by racial conservatives who were motivated by fears of increasing the diversity of the US population. One of the leading concerns of these individuals was that the extension of citizenship rights would permit the migration of Filipinos and Puerto Ricans to the United States. South Carolina senator Ben Tillman was one of the most outspoken racial conservatives in America. He blamed the existence of a black majority on the problems the South faced. From Tillman's perspective, his mission was to warn naive white Progressives who did not fully understand the danger posed by nonwhite migration. Nonwhite Americans countered Tillman's message and presented a different perspective. For example, the author of a letter published in *The Broad Axe*, an African American newspaper published in Salt Lake City, asked why Americans "send tracts and bibles to Africa and India to Christianize the heathen" only to "then…send cannon and dynamite so that the poor native wretches may be blown into eternity if they attempt to defend their homes." "Let us live up to our Constitution and laws and set an example for other nations which we claim are inferior to us," the author concluded.

As this letter indicates, the first years of America's overseas empire saw renewed efforts at missionary work. They also featured racism, intolerance, and even violence against those who opposed the presence of US forces. The majority of fatalities on both sides were due to diseases such as yellow fever. Because whites assumed African Americans were immune to the "jungle" diseases of the Philippines, a high proportion of black troops were stationed overseas and died in larger numbers and percentages than other soldiers. The army's medical service, led by Dr. Walter Reed, eventually pioneered ways of preventing the spread of yellow fever. Within a few years, these methods and vaccines were applied to the civilian population. Numerous US-based charitable associations provided medical supplies, while some Filipino businesses profited from trade. In this way at least, there were some tangible benefits to being part of the American empire.

FIGURE 4.9

This 1899 cartoon depicts Cuba, Puerto Rico, Hawaii, and the Philippines as unruly children who must be compelled to learn their lessons in civilization before they can join the rest of the class. In the corner sits a Native American "dunce" whose book is upside-down, and an African American child must clean the school's windows rather than participate.

The acquisition of the Philippines was intended to open Asian markets to US commerce. China was a declining empire that had been defeated by the rising world power of Japan in the 1890s. However, China remained one of the largest and most important markets. Throughout world history, access to East Asian markets defined the commercial success of Middle Eastern and European empires. China's demonstrated inability to keep foreign traders out of their nation at the turn of the century led to a full scramble among European powers to acquire "spheres of influence" by occupying Chinese ports.

Boxer Rebellion

An uprising that erupted in the summer of 1900 and was centered around Beijing. The "Boxers" feared that their society had been corrupted by the West and protested against their own government's inability or unwillingness to keep Western traders and culture out of China.

Roosevelt Corollary

Expressed by President Roosevelt in 1904, this statement of American foreign policy declared that the United States would intervene in the affairs of independent nations throughout the Western Hemisphere whenever US officials believed those nations needed assistance. As a result, the United States expected European nations with concerns in the Western Hemisphere to work through US officials.

Panama Canal

A canal completed in 1914 that links the Atlantic and Pacific Oceans through a fifty-mile canal across the nation of Panama.

Secretary of State John Hay proposed that each European nation and the United States agree to not restrict one another from trade within these spheres. However, the United States had no ability to enforce such an agreement, and the idea was largely ignored until a nationalist uprising within China sought to remove all foreign influence by force. A group known as the Fists of Righteous Harmony (called the "Boxers" in the United States and Britain) captured the foreign embassies in Beijing (then known as Peking). An international coalition made up of Japanese, Russian, British, German, and US forces soon put down the **Boxer Rebellion** in the summer of 1900. The Boxers had risen up as part of a popular uprising against the failure of their government to keep opium traders and other foreign profiteers out of the nation. Failing to spur a revival of traditional Chinese ways and eliminate foreign influence, the defeat of the Boxers permitted the spread of trade and Western ideas throughout East Asia.

While Americans sought to maintain trade with Japan and compete with Europeans for access to Chinese markets, they expected to maintain a near-monopoly of trade in the Caribbean and Latin America. President Roosevelt offered his own interpretation of the Monroe Doctrine that would be known as the **Roosevelt Corollary**. The Monroe Doctrine had been issued in 1823 and declared that the United States would guarantee the independence of nations in the Western Hemisphere. In 1904, Roosevelt offered his interpretation of the Monroe Doctrine in which he declared that the United States must intervene in the affairs of independent nations throughout the Western Hemisphere whenever US officials believed those nations needed assistance. If one of these nations was experiencing financial instability or political turmoil, for example, Roosevelt believed that assistance from "some civilized nation" was required. Latin Americans protested that the Roosevelt Corollary was nothing more than a fabricated justification of American imperialism. The wording of the president's decree demonstrates the delicacy of the issue, stating that the United States would intervene "however reluctantly…to exercise international police power." In many instances, that police power was used to protect US companies or compel repayment of loans made by European and US banks.

Intervention in Latin America could also be motivated by strategic concerns. The narrow isthmus of Panama was the northernmost region of the nation of Columbia. Prior to 1903, the United States had opposed at least two attempts by Panamanians who sought to declare independence and form their own nation. In 1903, however, Roosevelt sent warships and marines to protect a group of Panamanians who sought independence. The change was motivated by America's desire to build a canal across Panama and the reluctance of Colombian officials to approve the venture.

Politicians in Colombia sought a payment of $25 million before the United States could begin construction of the Panama Canal. In response, Roosevelt made a secret deal to offer military aid to the Panamanians. In exchange for the rights to build the canal, the United States provided military aid to help ensure that Panama's revolution succeeded. A relatively small force of Panamanians would have likely been crushed by the Colombian army had it not been for US aid. When the revolution began, Colombia could not send troops by sea because US warships blocked the ports. A US company controlled the only railroad in the region and permitted the Colombian officers to board the northernbound trains. US forces then arrested the officers upon their arrival in Panama, and the train did not return for the rest of the troops as promised. With this assistance, Panama secured its independence.

Colombia protested and eventually received payment of $25 million for damages suffered due to US intervention in what Colombians believed was a civil war. In addition, the United States also had to compensate Panama for the right to construct and operate the canal in its country. Finally, the United States were also forced to provide partial compensation for a French construction company that had begun work on the canal in the 1880s. In short, Roosevelt's duplicity reduced US prestige in Latin America and cost the United States millions more than would have been necessary had he dealt honestly with Colombia. "I took Panama," the president would later brag. His bravado proved costly in terms of lives and money, and prevented the consideration of other alternatives. For example, building a canal across Nicaragua provided a less politically volatile alternative. Although Nicaragua is much wider than Panama, construction teams could have utilized flatter land and several natural lakes to build a longer but less expensive canal.

Instead, Roosevelt secured the land rights to a ten-mile "canal zone" and began the construction of the **Panama Canal**. The same French company that had built the Suez Canal had spent $200 million and lost 10,000 to 20,000 lives to starvation and disease in a failed attempt to build the canal over a dozen years. US engineers completed the task in less than ten years, but another 5,000 construction workers perished. Once completed, the Panama Canal ranked as one of the most important feats of engineering in world history. Like the Suez Canal, which permitted ships to navigate between Europe and Asia without traveling around Africa, the Panama Canal permitted ships to avoid the journey around South America. Its completion occurred less than a month after the outbreak of World War I and permitted US warships and cargo traveling from one coast to the other to avoid the extra 8,000 mile journey and dangerous waters around Cape Horn.

President Taft believed that investing money in the Caribbean and South America would help to heal the strained relations between the United States and these nations. He called this philosophy "**Dollar Diplomacy.**" The president argued that US investment and management expertise would produce stability and prosperity throughout Latin America. However, US investors usually did little more than purchase existing businesses and plantations, which did little to promote job growth. Equally important, profits from these businesses would now flow to the United States and other foreign investors, leaving Latin America more impoverished and unstable than before.

The Roosevelt Corollary was often cited in justification of US military intervention throughout the region. For example, Taft sent the Marines to Nicaragua in response to political turmoil that threatened US investments in 1912. These troops would occupy Nicaragua almost continuously until they were removed in 1933. Similar political and financial instability threatened US business interests in Haiti, the Dominican, and Cuba between the early 1900s and the 1930s and led to additional deployments of US troops. In several cases, the potential failure of foreign investors to repay American loans convinced US officials to station troops within Latin American customs houses. In these instances, tax revenues from tariffs were redirected to American and European banks that managed the loans. From the US perspective, such measures were necessary to ensure repayment. From the perspective of Latin America, the Roosevelt Corollary was little more than a veil to mask economic imperialism. Puerto Ricans demanded independence, but they were instead granted US citizenship in 1917. This helped provide reform on this island, although Puerto Ricans and others could do little to ensure that US companies paid their fair share of local taxes or promoted businesses that aided the local economy.

1.6   The Election of 1912

Roosevelt's retirement from politics ended as soon as the former president returned from an African safari in 1909. The following year, the former president delivered a high-profile political speech in which he gave his support to a number of progressive Republican candidates in the upcoming congressional election. By the spring of 1912, Roosevelt openly criticized Taft, and few were surprised when he announced his intention to run for president once again. Still popular among many Republicans, Roosevelt's decision to seek the Republican nomination threatened to split an already divided party.

Many wealthy Republicans viewed Teddy Roosevelt as a traitor to his class, especially after a speech in which the former president proclaimed a doctrine he called the **New Nationalism**. Roosevelt's speech occurred during a 1910 ceremony that dedicated a statue in Osawatomie, Kansas, to the memory of John Brown. Although the former president honored John Brown, he chose to not mention Brown's raid on a West Virginia armory or Brown's controversial plan to liberate slaves. Instead, Roosevelt's focused on contemporary politics, arguing that property should be regulated in the public interest. Roosevelt emphasized the importance of protecting personal property and maintaining the profit incentive of free enterprise. However, he believed that these principles should be considered within the larger context of public interest and human welfare. Roosevelt's philosophy of New Nationalism permitted many Progressives to see Roosevelt as a supporter of their own causes, which were dependent on a strong and activist federal government. It also led conservative Republicans to forget their previous reservations about their current president and rally behind the banner of William Howard Taft.

Presidential nominations were still dominated by leading members of a particular party at this time. As a result, influential members of the Republican Party, who tended to be more conservative, enjoyed tremendous leverage over the rank-and-file membership of their party. Only a handful of states had transferred the authority to select nominees from party leaders to party members through primary elections. Roosevelt's victory in the Ohio primary (Taft's home state) demonstrated the likelihood that Roosevelt would fare much better in the 1912 general election. Roosevelt also won nine of the twelve other Republican state primaries. However, Roosevelt had alienated many leading members of the Republican Party, and Taft enjoyed the advantage of being the incumbent. When the Republican delegates met and held their nominating convention, party leaders quickly decided to nominate Taft before many of the delegates from states that had voted for Roosevelt were able to participate. Roosevelt's supporters were indignant and promised to back Roosevelt if he ran as an independent. Far from ending the Progressive challenge within their ranks, the Republicans widened the divisions within their party and alienated their own members in the states that had adopted the primary system.

Dollar Diplomacy

An expression of President Taft's foreign policy regarding Latin America that sought to replace military deployments with efforts to promote economic development. Taft hoped American investments in Latin America would promote stability and improve diplomatic relations between the United States and Latin America.

FIGURE 4.10

This contemporary cartoon plainly indicates its belief that Roosevelt and the federal government backed the Panamanian Revolution in exchange for the right to build a canal across Panama. Most Americans at the turn of the century understood their government's role and supported their president's actions regarding Panama.

New Nationalism

A political doctrine expressed by Teddy Roosevelt in 1910 that demonstrated his acceptance of Progressive ideas. New Nationalism sought the creation of a more powerful federal government that would regulate corporations and the economy in the public interest.

Progressive Party

Also known as the "Bull Moose Party" in response to an expression by its leader, Teddy Roosevelt, the Progressive Party was a short-lived third party movement that supported Roosevelt's presidential campaign in the 1912 election.

FIGURE 4.11

The cover for Teddy Roosevelt's 1912 campaign song. Roosevelt's Progressives were known as the "Bull Moose Party." Supporters utilized the "masculine" image of the bull moose (a nickname for a male moose) in contrast to the less-robust animal mascots of their rivals.

Woodrow Wilson

A historian and college administrator who became governor of New Jersey in 1910, Wilson entered national politics and was nominated for president by the Democrats in 1912. As president, Wilson supported a number of Progressive issues demonstrating the bipartisan support for Progressive ideals at this time.

Although Taft would be the Republican nominee, Roosevelt decided to run as the candidate of the **Progressive Party** and resume his bid for the presidency. Suggesting a more prominent role for women within the newly launched Progressive Party, Jane Addams was given the honorary position of seconding Roosevelt's nomination. However, the Progressive Party had few early supporters beyond Roosevelt and his political allies. Even fewer believed the new organization could prevail against the two major parties. A reporter covering the convention asked Roosevelt for his thoughts on the matter. The ever-enthusiastic Roosevelt laughed off the sparse number of supporters attending the convention and claimed that he felt "as strong as a bull moose." The nickname stuck, and the Progressives were soon known as the Bull Moose Party.

Roosevelt's campaign featured a mixture of his doctrine of New Nationalism and Progressive ideas about how to improve government and the economy. Roosevelt endorsed women's suffrage, an insurance system for injured workers and the unemployed, federal welfare programs for women and children, higher taxes for the wealthy, and more rigorous government regulation of corporations. As a result, Teddy Roosevelt had redefined his political orientation. As president, he had been a liberal Republican who generally sided with conservative interests. As leader of his Bull Moose Party, however, Roosevelt had moved significantly toward the political left.

Labor leader Eugene Debs also reinvented himself, running as the Socialist Party candidate for president in 1912. The journey of Eugene Debs from labor activism to Socialism occurred while he was serving a prison sentence for his support of a nationwide strike on behalf of rail workers. Debs polled 900,000 votes representing 6 percent of the popular vote. Debs and other Socialists believed that their message equating public ownership of property with democracy was gaining strength, and they were optimistic about the future of Socialism in the United States following the election. However, world events and the growing conservatism of US culture and politics meant that the election of 1912 would represent the high-water mark of the Socialist Party in US presidential politics. The existence of Deb's campaign may have taken some votes away from Roosevelt. However, the very existence of an organized Socialist party made it harder for the opponents of the Progressives to present Roosevelt and other Progressive candidates as radicals.

The Democrats nominated a newcomer to the political scene: New Jersey governor and former history professor **Woodrow Wilson**. Wilson had spent most of his time in academia and had not run for any public office until winning the governorship of New Jersey in 1910. The former Princeton administrator backed many of the ideas of the Progressives and had instituted a number of popular reforms as governor, such as regulating public utilities and a workers' compensation law. Wilson also called for breaking up trusts and restoring the competition of small and local businesses. As a result, many powerful interests within the state of New Jersey and the Democratic Party opposed Wilson and his ideas. In fact, many within Princeton had also opposed their former president because of his attempts to change the way their school had operated in the past. These conservatives would be much more supportive of Wilson after he secured the presidency. While in the White House, Wilson remained supportive of Progressive reforms at the state level, but he believed that the federal government should not interfere. While he supported strong labor laws for New Jersey, he believed that attempting to institute the same measures nationwide would violate principles of local control and risk creating an overly "meddlesome" federal government.

Most Progressives had been Republicans prior to 1912. However, Democrats in the South and certain areas of the rest of the nation increasingly supported a number of Progressive reforms. By 1912, leading Democratic politicians such as Woodrow Wilson had adopted many of the Progressives' ideas as their own. Reflecting the division that led to the re-nomination of Taft, few prominent Republican leaders at the state or national level joined the Progressive Party. The former president's own son-in-law even decided to support Taft because he feared that any defection from the Republican fold would destroy his budding political career. However, millions of rank-and-file members of the Republican Party supported Roosevelt, who outpolled Taft by over half a million votes.

> *It is only once in a generation that a people can be lifted above material things. That is why conservative government is in the saddle two-thirds of the time.*
>
> —*Woodrow Wilson*

The divisions between Republican supporters of Taft and Roosevelt were sometimes distasteful. Taft issued an indictment of the former president as egotistical and dangerously radical. Roosevelt responded by presenting Taft as the embodiment of political corruption. At one of the low points of the election, both sides engaged in name calling. Roosevelt won this race to the bottom by calling his former secretary of war a "fathead" whose brain was less developed than that of a guinea pig. The comment did little to enhance Roosevelt's standing, as Taft weighed nearly 300 pounds but was regarded as a kind and honest man. It was a rare low for Roosevelt, who was also well regarded. More characteristic of the Bull Moose leader was his delivery of a rousing speech just moments after being shot in the chest by a would-be assassin. Roosevelt could not use his notes on this occasion, as they were covered in his blood, although they may have saved his life. The bullet passed through the metal case Roosevelt used to hold his trademark round glasses and was nearly stopped by the speech, which had been folded over many times and was nearly as thick as a small book.

Local political meetings were even more volatile, fueled by the whiskey that flowed during such events, regardless of Prohibition laws. Suffragists representing the votes of women argued that the low state of US politics demanded the moral influence of the fairer sex. In seven Western states, women did more than protest their exclusion from politics—they cast ballots and even won election to a number of local and state offices. Despite predictions that women would be easily misled or overly sentimental, the votes of women in these states were usually spread evenly between the candidates in ways that mirrored the overall vote in their communities. Women and men in Utah supported the conservative Taft in equal numbers, while women in more liberal areas of the West were part of the majority that cast their ballots for Roosevelt.

Progressive and Socialist candidates both spoke in favor of immediate federal legislation extending the vote regardless of gender. Democrat Woodrow Wilson was evasive on the subject, at least as a candidate in 1912. His supporters in states where women could vote tended to overstate Wilson's support for female suffrage, while the image of the Democratic candidate was more conservative on the subject in other states. The same was true of Taft. Despite the evasiveness of the Republican and Democratic candidates, the 1912 election saw growing support for women's suffrage. As more and more women secured their right to vote, it became politically dangerous to oppose women's suffrage. Most politicians recognized that even in areas where women could not vote, opposition to equal suffrage would be a poor long-term strategy as the national suffrage movement gained momentum. Once the goal of a constitutional amendment extending suffrage to all women was realized, hundreds of thousands of women would be casting ballots in every congressional district. These voters would remember the men who had opposed their rights in the past.

FIGURE 4.12

This map shows the results of the 1912 election. Wilson's use of popular Progressive campaign issues and the division of Republicans between Taft and Roosevelt helped assure a Democratic victory.

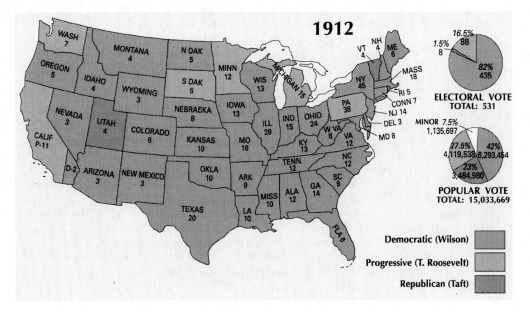

The Democrats benefitted from the defection of Roosevelt from the Republican to the Progressive Party. "Don't interfere when your enemy is destroying himself," Wilson exclaimed as both Taft and Roosevelt competed for Republican support. Wilson received only 42 percent of the popular vote. However, because of the unique system of American presidential elections Wilson appeared to win a landslide victory in the electoral college. Wilson won nearly every state beyond the Great Lakes region, which rallied behind the Progressives. The Democrats also took control of the Senate and added to their numbers in the House of Representatives. After the election, most people who had supported the Progressive Party returned to the Republicans. A number of Progressives were elected at the state and local level, and Progressive ideas had a tremendous influence on President Wilson. However, the Progressives as a political organization quickly faded away, much like the Populists following the election of 1896. Roosevelt remained a leading national figure, while Taft would later be appointed to the Supreme Court where he served as Chief Justice. Given Taft's aversion to elections and politics, he found his new role in the judiciary more suitable to his tastes.

REVIEW AND CRITICAL THINKING

1. How did Roosevelt emerge as the leading political figure of the early 1900s? How do his political views change over time and influence US history?

2. What were the major laws and decisions affecting corporations during these years? How do they reflect changing views about the role of government?

3. Describe the ways that Taft and Roosevelt sought to preserve natural resources. In what ways was the conservation movement of the early 1900s similar to and different from later environmental movements?

4. Was the United States an imperialist nation during these years? Identify US objectives in Latin America and provide examples of the impact the United States had upon various Latin American nations in the early 1900s.

5. What was the significance of the election of 1912? How did Wilson capture the presidency in a landslide without winning a majority of the popular vote?

---

2. THE PROGRESSIVES

LEARNING OBJECTIVES

1. Identify the various methods used by Progressive reformers and list the various issues they supported. Describe the perspectives and ideas that united the Progressives, and evaluate their effectiveness in promoting the reforms they supported.

2. Summarize the campaigns for Prohibition, public education, and other leading Progressive reforms. Describe Progressive efforts to promote more efficient and responsive government at the local and national levels.

3. Describe the ways that Progressives sought to protect children and end child labor. Explain the obstacles they faced, and evaluate the effectiveness of their strategies.

2.1 Muckrakers

By the turn of the century, every American town with more than a few hundred residents had its own newspaper. A city of 50,000 might have a dozen different newspapers, many of which were owned and operated by recent immigrants and were published in German, Yiddish, Italian, or Greek. There were also newspapers that sought to represent the views of labor unions, African Americans, and various political parties and movements. Nearly every town with at least a few thousand residents had two leading newspapers that were usually directly subsidized by the Republican and Democratic Parties. In addition, many of the leading and nationally circulated newspapers were dominated by a handful of powerful newspaper syndicates. Local papers usually reprinted articles written by these syndicates, which were then distributed through the "wire." However, the desire to keep and attract subscribers meant that local newspapers were usually willing to publish a variety of viewpoints. In both cases, articles submitted by readers and wire stories distributed by political parties and national syndicates provided much-needed copy for the tens of thousands of understaffed local newspapers. As a result, a well-written editorial might soon appear in a number of newspapers across the nation. A century prior to the widespread use of the Internet to share ideas, ordinary Americans joined professional journalists in broadcasting their opinions through the print media.

FIGURE 4.13

An artist's view of railroad monopoly as "The Curse of California." The railroad appears as an octopus that controls the money and politics of the state while encouraging foreign migration and strangling local businesses and farms.

Progressives seized this medium to spread their ideas. Journalists who sought to expose injustice and corporate malfeasance were known as "muckrakers." The term itself derived from a speech by President Roosevelt in 1906. Roosevelt described these journalists as armed with a "muckrake" exposing all that was foul and dirty in hopes of motivating others to take action. The president offered both praise and criticism for muckrakers, emphasizing the importance of their work so long as they maintained fidelity to the truth. Many Progressives conducted research to demonstrate the justice of their causes, yet like the caricature of the **muckraker**, they might also become so focused on exposing corruption that they exaggerated its existence. Muckrakers might also conduct research that was calculated to validate a preconceived conclusion and thereby ignore or marginalize facts and perspectives that were contrary to their opinions. Despite the abuses of some muckrakers, the Progressives generally succeeded in exposing dirty secrets of political machines, corporations, and governmental administrations.

Many of the leading muckrakers even published novels intended to bring their observations to a larger audience in hopes of promoting their reform agenda. One of the first muckrakers was California's Frank Norris, who published a novel called *The Octopus: A Story of California* in 1901. The Octopus in this West Coast story was a railroad conglomerate that kept raising rates in an effort to force farmers, such as the novel's protagonist, to sell their land. Like the animal he chose to represent the railroad trust, Norris presented railroad barons as aggressive creatures whose tentacles reached in multiple directions and strangled the independence of ordinary farmers.

New York Tribune reporter Jacob Riis used a different medium to demonstrate the way corporate greed led to the impoverishment of the city. His book, *How the Other Half Lives*, was first published in 1890 and demonstrated the power of photojournalism. Given the state of photography at this time, Riis had to stage his photos, and his subjects had to hold still for a few seconds. As a result, photos of street toughs robbing children of their factory wages were not quite authentic, even if they did communicate a deeper truth about living conditions in neighborhoods like New York's infamous Hell's Kitchen. At the same time, Riis' subjects often resented the way they were forced to look pitiful to elicit the reader's emotions. A keen observer can find elements of the agency of Riis' subjects in much of his work. The same is true of other photojournalists. For example, rural Southerners and Appalachians insisted on wearing their Sunday best in photos meant to depict squalor. As a result, these photos demonstrate both the poverty of the region and the quiet dignity of the laboring people that inhabited these places.

The work of Nellie Bly reflects a similar brand of determination. Bly published *Ten Days in a Mad-House*, based on her experiences as an inmate at a New York asylum for the insane. After faking insanity and being arrest and interned, Bly documented the inhumane conditions she and others endured within the asylum. Many of her readers were outraged and demanded an official investigation of New York's Blackwell Island where Bly was kept. As a result, a significant movement to reform prisons and asylums emerged. **Ida Tarbell** used a less dramatic method, spending years researching court filings and any internal memos she could find regarding the dealings of each company that composed John D. Rockefeller's mammoth empire. Originally published as a serial within a popular magazine, Tarbell's *The History of the Standard Oil Company* was a tour de force that exposed Standard Oil as a monopoly

Muckraker

Meant to be a derogative nickname, a "muckraker" was a journalist that sought to uncover corruption and other hidden threats to the well-being of society.

Ida Tarbell

A talented researcher and journalist from Pennsylvania who exposed the monopolistic practices of John Rockefeller's Standard Oil Company.

and led to its breakup. A similar expose on US Steel by Ray Stannard Baker was also influential, but it failed to disband the company Andrew Carnegie had formed. Baker is best known for his 1908 book *Following the Color Line*, which was one of the few efforts by white journalists to document the conditions faced by African Americans during this era.

In 1906, Upton Sinclair published *The Jungle*, the most famous of all muckraking novels and a heartbreaking tale about a resilient Lithuanian immigrant named Jurgis Rudkus. In the novel, Jurgis responds to each injustice within the workplace by resolving to work harder until he finally discovers Socialism, which promises material security and equality. Sinclair had intended the novel to promote Socialism, but the atrocities most readers recalled were those committed against consumers rather than immigrant workers like Jurgis. Sinclair's protagonist was employed by various meatpackers, and his narrative was packed full of horrific violations of basic sanitation. Most readers missed the political message of the book and remembered only the festering bacteria and vermin that went into the sausage and might also be part of the food they just served their own family. Even today, teachers who receive essays on *The Jungle* that only focus on the author's pro-Socialist message can easily discern that the student must not have read the book's gory description of rats and even human body parts falling into the grinder and becoming part of the tainted sausage Sinclair described.

The Jungle

The most famous of all muckraking novels, Upton Sinclair's *The Jungle* revealed the unsanitary practices of the beef packing industry. The author had hoped his book would inspire readers to challenge the Capitalist system, which he believed exploited the consumers of adulterated beef and also the workers who produced it.

FIGURE 4.14

Ida Tarbell was a Progressive journalist who exposed the monopolistic practices of Standard Oil Company. She disliked the term "muckraker" and its pejorative implications. She referred to herself instead as a historian. Her seminal work was titled *A History of Standard Oil Company* and was based upon Tarbell's skill in finding and interpreting primary sources to chronicle the history of Rockefeller's business practices.

FIGURE 4.15

Many Progressive reformers sought to publicize the unsanitary conditions of beef packing facilities. The small portrait is Reverend J. R. Day, the Chancellor of Syracuse University who presented a different perspective. Day brought attention to the efficiency and economy of the beef industry which made it possible for urban workers to include meat in their daily diets.

The Jungle was published as Progressives were waging a fight for greater regulation of the meatpacking industry. Armed with the public support generated by Sinclair's book, the government passed the Federal Meat Inspection Act and the **Pure Food and Drug Act** in 1906. The former established guidelines regarding sanitation and required federal meat inspectors to be present at all stages of production. The Pure Food and Drug Act required labels that included all ingredients and would lead to regulations restricting the use of narcotics such as opium and cocaine in medicines. The implications of the Socialist brotherhood Sinclair hoped to promote were largely forgotten. "I aimed at the public's heart," Sinclair would later lament, "and by accident I hit it in the stomach."

2.2 Prohibition and the Social Gospel Movement

Prohibition remained one of the leading causes promoted by middle-class Protestant reformers. The **Anti-Saloon League** was formed in 1893 by a group of religious-minded reformers in Ohio. The League began as a local political organization that would only endorse candidates who had pledged their support for Prohibition. Protestant churches, the Anti-Saloon League, the Women's Christian Temperance Union, and various local temperance groups were so effective in Ohio that a candidate's stance on Prohibition became the single leading issue in many elections. The same was true in hundreds of other communities throughout the nation where Protestants utilized the goals and methods of the Progressive Movement, calling on state and local governments to ban the consumption and sale of alcohol.

In many districts throughout rural America, no candidate could win without the endorsement of local prohibition organizations. The movement was especially strong in the Protestant-dominated Bible Belt of the South and the Midwest. By 1905, three states had outlawed alcohol. This number grew to nine states by 1912 and 26 states by 1916. During its 1913 national convention in Columbus, Ohio, delegates celebrated the Anti-Saloon League's twentieth anniversary by dedicating themselves to the passage of a Constitutional amendment banning alcohol throughout the entire country. The success of the Anti-Saloon League as a political organization meant that few lawmakers who represented the growing number of "dry" states would dare to oppose such a measure.

Prohibition demonstrated the Progressive belief in the idea of "applied Christianity," known as the **Social Gospel Movement**. Over 60 percent of Americans were Protestant in the first decades of the twentieth century. Protestant churches led the fight for a number of reforms that sought to influence behavior beyond Prohibition. One of the reasons for the renewed emphasis on Prohibition at this time was concern about the growing number of Catholics, which reached 15 million by 1915. The rise was more the result of increased immigration from southern and central Europe, Mexico, and Latin America. Recent trends in immigration also led to dramatic increases in the numbers of Jews in the US as well as small but growing Hindu, Muslim, and Buddhist communities. Protestants responded by launching a movement to renew their faith and revive missionary zeal through dedication to public welfare.

FIGURE 4.16

An annual meeting of the Anti-Saloon League in Atlantic City, New Jersey. Like all successful movements in the United States, the strength of the Anti-Saloon League was in local chapters who engaged in grassroots campaigns in support of prohibition.

Pure Food and Drug Act

A 1906 law that enacted federal standards of inspection and sanitation on meatpackers. The law also required drug makers to list ingredients. The law was inspired by a number of muckraking exposés about adulterated foods and dangerous patent medicines.

Anti-Saloon League

Began as a local temperance society in Ohio in 1893, the Anti-Saloon League emerged as the leading prohibitionist organization in the country and successfully lobbied for a host of local and state laws banning alcohol by the early twentieth century.

Social Gospel Movement

A movement that emerged during the early twentieth century that sought to apply the principles of Christianity to alleviate major social problems such as poverty, crime, and child labor. Many adherents of the movement were inspired by minister Charles Sheldon who challenged his followers to ask themselves "What would Jesus do?"

Adherents to the Social Gospel Movement were inspired by the Charles Sheldon novel *In His Steps*. This Congregational minister from Topeka, Kansas, challenged his readers to ask themselves "what would Jesus do" when making everyday decisions. The Social Gospel Movement led to a renaissance in charitable efforts and taught that service to the poor was the obligation of those who had been blessed with material wealth. Protestant sects such as the Salvation Army and religious service organizations such as the YMCA and YWCA grew in number and prestige for their emphasis on charitable work. The Social Gospel Movement also motivated campaigns to treat workers more fairly and called into question practices of racial and religious discrimination. At times, the movement also reinforced existing attitudes of paternalism and the uncritical association of poverty with crime and vice. Despite the sometimes paternalistic and condescending attitudes, the urban poor began to return to church in response to the creation of outreach missions in neighborhoods once ignored by the larger Protestant congregations.

2.3 Education and Child Labor

FIGURE 4.17

Young children employed inside a South Carolina textile mill in 1908. These children were often injured by the rapidly moving machinery. In fact, small children were employed as "doffers" specifically for their ability to fit in small spaces and replace bobbins while the machines were operating.

Between Reconstruction and the start of World War I, the percentage of children who regularly attended public schools had more than doubled. The number of public high schools increased from fewer than 100 to more than 6,000 during this same period. Most of these schools focused on the liberal arts, classical languages, and advanced math skills. However, as more and more children attended school, a movement to provide vocational skills emerged with the support of business interests as well as many parental groups. The vocational education movement demonstrated increasing awareness of the value of technical and trade skills in the new industrial economy. Early training programs included courses in scientific agriculture, as well as mechanical and industrial trades. Young women received a different curriculum, largely based on cultivating their skills as homemakers. Colleges also began including courses intended to prepare students for the business world and some specific trades, although the vast majority still focused on the classic model of education based on language, science, and the liberal arts.

Progressives viewed public education as the engine of social mobility. Through public schools and colleges, the children of farmers and common laborers might gain the skills and knowledge that would allow them greater upward mobility. However, the percentage of students attending college remained modest compared to the rapid growth of high schools. College was not an option for most graduates due to the financial difficulty of paying one's full tuition bill in advance. Progressives responded by funding various scholarship programs, while fraternal associations were able to help a handful of their members' children attend college.

Other Progressives focused on reforming Native American boarding schools and developing more educational opportunities for the graduates of these institutions. For example, Murray State School of Agriculture (today Murray State College) in Oklahoma operated as both an agricultural and a community college for its predominantly Native American student population. Progressive reformers also worked to reduce the appalling mortality rates at the boarding schools for young Native Americans. Through reform, more children survived away from home due to a variety of common-sense initiatives to better protect health of the students. The decline was also the result of school officials sending sick children home to recover—not only a salubrious measure for the children who were well enough to travel but also one designed to shelter schools officials from blame if the illness proved fatal.

The most significant Progressive reforms aimed at improving the lives of the young were those that sought to restrict the employment of school-aged children. Thanks in large part to local anti-child labor organizations, at least a dozen states passed laws limiting child labor in the early 1900s. These laws were not always enforced, but they did help to reduce the number of children killed in industrial accidents. In 1880, over one million children under 16 were part of the paid labor force—a disturbing statistic given that nearly half of the nation's children lived on farms where their labor was expected but not recorded. By 1900, only 284,000 children under 16 held jobs beyond the home and farm. The result was a dramatic decline in illiteracy. By 1900, less than half a million children were illiterate and states and communities were passing laws making school attendance mandatory for children under various age limits.

Progressives in Illinois passed a law limiting the workday for children aged sixteen and under. However, business interests within Illinois attacked the law as socialistic and had it repealed in 1895. By this time, the reformer **Florence Kelley** had been attracted to Chicago by the work of Jane Addams. Kelley became one of the leading advocates for stronger laws to protect children. She was later appointed by the governor to inspect conditions affecting children who worked in factories throughout Illinois.

Jane Addams and Josephine Lowell founded the **National Consumers League** (NCL) as an advocacy group that sought to end child labor and other abusive practices by informing consumers about the conditions under which certain products had been made. Florence Kelley became the first general secretary of the group and traveled around the nation documenting the conditions of working women and children. She and other NCL leaders also delivered thousands of public lectures. The NCL certified products that were not made by children and urged consumers to only buy items that displayed the NCL label. A group with a similar acronym, the National Child Labor Committee (NCLC) was organized in 1904. This group focused on legislative efforts and lobbied Congress to outlaw child labor. NCLC leaders testified to Congress that 2 million children under the age of sixteen were at work in America's factories. Other women such as Mary Harris "Mother" Jones led marches of children who displayed banners asking for the opportunity to attend school.

FIGURE 4.18

Two young women participating in a protest march with signs reading "Abolish Child Slavery" in both Yiddish and English.

Florence Kelley

The first general secretary of the National Consumers League, Florence Kelley was one of the most prominent advocates of anti–child labor laws in the United States. She was also a supporter of a host of other progressive causes such as civil rights and was one of the founding members of the NAACP.

National Consumers League (NCL)

Founded in 1899 by Josephine Lowell and Jane Addams, the NCL lobbied for anti–child labor laws and urged consumers to boycott products made by child labor.

FIGURE 4.19

Among the most poignant images of the anti-child labor movement are those of very young children holding signs asking for a few hours per week that they might attend school or play with other children.

Efforts to pass federal legislation banning child labor failed until the midst of the Great Depression when Congress agreed that such laws were needed to protect the jobs of adult males. States that passed child-labor laws found that goods made by young children in other states entered their markets. The result was a net loss of local jobs and no discernible reduction in child labor. In 1916, Congress passed a federal law that made it illegal to ship goods that had been made by children under the age of fourteen out of the state. However, this law was voided two years later by the Supreme Court. The court agreed with a North Carolina mill that the law violated the Tenth Amendment, which grants states the authority over matters that are not explicitly mentioned in the Constitution.

Many believed that the only way to truly outlaw child labor was to pass a Constitutional Amendment. In the meantime, Progressive women under the banner of the NCL, NCLC, and other groups lobbied for the creation of the Children's Bureau as an agency within the Department of Labor. President Taft approved the measure in 1912 and agreed to appoint a woman to the head the new agency out of respect for the efforts of these reformers. Julia Lathrop led the Children's Bureau for the next decade, using her position and celebrity as the first female head of any federal agency to push for stronger measures to protect children. Other Progressives, such as Harvard professor Alice Hamilton, led investigations that publicized the harmful effects of deadly fumes on the bodies of children who labored in various factories. Still other Progressive women and men documented the conditions faced by children who were employed because of their ability to crawl through narrow mine shafts.

Progressives in Ohio boasted that their law prohibiting boys under the age of sixteen and girls under the age of eighteen from working more than forty-eight hours per week was "the best child-labor law in the United States and probably the world." In actuality, most industrialized nations had developed much tougher restrictions against child labor than the United States. The Ohio law was passed in 1908, the result of years of activism by Progressives, and came on the heels of a 1906 attempt to pass a law barring children aged fifteen and younger from working more than nine hours per day. Arkansas led the South with a similar law barring child labor, which was passed a few years later.

> *In the march of time it became necessary to withdraw the children from school, and these machines came to be operated by the deft touch of the fingers of the child....It is not a question of white labor or black labor, or male labor or female or child labor, in this system; it is solely a question of cheap labor, without reference to the effect upon mankind.*
>
> —*Eugene Debs in the Socialist newspaper* Appeal to Reason, *December 1900.*

As support for stronger child labor laws grew, the Progressives recognized that one of their chief obstacles to passing these laws was the ability of legislative committees to prevent their measures from reaching the floor for public debate and a recorded vote. As a result, the Progressives directed much of their later efforts toward promoting reforms such as initiative and referendum. Initiative allowed residents to petition their legislature directly, while referendum required that a proposed law be placed on the ballot. Once these democratic initiatives were approved, state legislatures were no longer able to thwart child labor laws and other reforms through inaction. The result was a dramatic increase in anti-child labor laws in the late Progressive Era.

2.4 Efficiency in Business and Government

Frederick W. Taylor

An engineer from Pennsylvania who advocated "scientific management" of industry, Taylor argued that careful study of every aspect of the production processes could improve efficiency by eliminating unnecessary steps and wasted motions.

Progressives who sought to create a more ordered world were influenced by business leaders such as **Frederick W. Taylor**. Taylor studied the efficiency of steel mills throughout the 1890s, breaking down each of the tasks workers performed into a series of motions. Taylor then analyzed the ways that these motions could be made more efficient. His studies were ridiculed by some business leaders, but others recognized the potential of an idea that became known as "Taylorism"—the theory that scientific study of the production process could reduce wasted time and energy.

Numerous factories paid Taylor and other consultants to study their production processes in hopes of maximizing efficiency. Taylor's 1911 book *The Principles of Scientific Management* inspired managers to more strictly regulate the methods workers used. It also led to the speeding up of assembly lines. As a result, workers sometimes felt as if they themselves had become machines. This feeling was especially pervasive when workers were forbidden to leave the assembly line for any reason, including restroom breaks, because their absence would force the assembly line to stop.

The acceptance of Taylor's theories in business reflected a growing desire to improve the efficiency of organizations through scientific study of operations and by placing experts in charge of management. The same was true of government, especially at the local level where Progressive reformers continued their attack on corruption. Progressives believed that the first key to efficient government was ending the patronage system and awarding jobs to experts. The second step was removing the dictator-like structure of city governments in favor of systems that spread power among specialists who were selected to head specific departments.

Progressive reformers studied various examples of local governments as models. The city of Galveston, Texas, had been decimated by a hurricane in September 1900 that cost the lives of an estimated 8,000 people. Relief funds and rebuilding efforts were thwarted by the inefficiency of the city government until the state legislature intervened by appointing a commission of experts to take control. As a result, this important port city quickly recovered. Experts in city planning and civil engineering constructed storm walls and even raised the low-lying parts of the city that had suffered the worst flood damage. As a result, the city withstood a similar hurricane in 1915 with minimal damage or loss of life.

A major flood in Dayton, Ohio, led to the development of another model of civic reform. Rather than adopting the city commission system of Galveston, Dayton replaced the mayor with a city manager who was an expert in the field of urban management. The city manager was appointed by the city council, a provision which assured voter input and accountability. By 1920, over 1,000 cities were utilizing either the city commission system of Galveston or the city manager system of Dayton.

Hundreds of cities took reform even further, leading to public ownership of public utilities. Leading cities in Ohio such as Toledo and Cleveland, along with dozens of other cities, led the way in what has been labeled "municipal socialism." These city governments built or took control of existing streetcar lines and public utilities. They also created publicly owned water, sewer, and sanitation departments. Milwaukee mayor Emil Seidel was the first of many mayors elected on the Socialist ticket in 1910. Under his administration, Milwaukee developed new departments for public works and city parks. Reforms for municipal electric plants faced larger obstacles, although city and state governments became active in encouraging development of generating stations and distribution systems that would provide their residents with low-cost electricity. Although the idea of direct government ownership in other industries attracted few adherents, the benefits of publicly owned utility companies led many cities to engage in similar programs.

FIGURE 4.20

Debs's running mate was Emil Seidel, Socialist mayor of Milwaukee. In the early 1900s, two congressmen, scores of state legislators, and more than a hundred mayors representing the Socialist Party were elected. Although the Socialists remained weak on the national level, their ideas were very influential in municipal government.

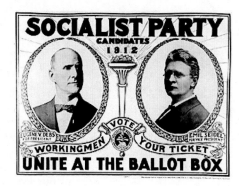

REVIEW AND CRITICAL THINKING

1. Who were the Muckrakers? Why would a Progressive leader such as Teddy Roosevelt offer both praise and criticism for the Muckrakers?

2. How did Progressive reformers influence the political culture of the 1900s? How effective were they in promoting their ideas?

3. Did women have a unique role within the Progressive movement, or were their efforts and contributions similar to those of men? What can we learn about the Progressive movement by considering the history of the early 1900s from the perspective of various women?

4. Summarize the efforts of Progressives in passing child labor laws. What can one learn about the political environment of the early 1900s and prevailing notions about the role of government from these campaigns?

5. Why were new laws permitting citizens to directly submit legislation through referendum and the initiative important? What was "municipal socialism," and why did it attract so many supporters who opposed socialism in general?

3.   RADICALISM AND THE LIMITS OF EGALITARIAN REFORM

3.1   Women's Rights and Birth Control

The typical working woman of the late nineteenth century needed their income for survival and occupied low-status positions as domestic servants. Others endured routine and often physically exhausting jobs in textile manufacturing. As a result, the image of a "working woman" had often been associated with notions of victimization and the failure or absence of a male breadwinner. However, by 1900, half a million women worked in offices as clerks, switchboard operators, and secretaries. As the century progressed, upwardly mobile women increasingly occupied professional careers in teaching and nursing as well as clerical jobs. In response, the image of the working woman began to change.

FIGURE 4.21

Women representing leading women's colleges such as Vassar join with women representing the University of Kansas, Stanford, and the University of Missouri in a protest outside the White House. A new generation of college-educated women led the suffrage movement as it gained momentum in the Progressive Era.

Middle-class women also joined organizations such as the National Association of Colored Women's Clubs and the Women's Christian Temperance Union. As a result, women were becoming engaged in community issues in larger numbers. As more women acquired formal education, entered the paid workforce, and became engaged in public life, they questioned the notion that the home was the only proper place for a woman. These challenges to the status quo were most evident in the growth of the women's suffrage movement. The early 1900s saw a number of victories for the movement that were both a result and a cause of the increased education, upward mobility, and political activism of women during this era.

The final victory of women's suffrage in 1920 was only possible because of thousands of successful campaigns to secure the right to vote in school elections, city and county elections, and elections within a particular state. Women in Wyoming, Utah, Idaho, and Colorado had secured their right to vote statewide by 1900. Women in the state of Washington secured a referendum on women's suffrage that was placed on the ballot in 1910. These women gave lectures and spread flyers throughout the state and convinced a majority of male voters to approve the measure. The following year, a similar effort resulted in the passage of a ballot initiative in California. Recognizing the tendency of male political leaders to jump on the women's suffrage bandwagon once women in their districts could vote, the women of California recalled that after 1911, no male politician could be found in the entire state who had ever opposed the measure.

Many of the women who were drawn to the cause of suffrage had been active in the public sphere for a number of years before becoming suffragists. Like most Progressives, they focused most of their energies on the problems of urban and industrial America. The condition of workers and the urban poor formed the vanguard of the movement, with numerous Progressive organizations pressing for laws that would limit the maximum number of hours women could be required to work. Both the architect and object of these protective laws, women led the rank-and-file membership of these movements. They also led countless local initiatives and were more likely to occupy leadership roles within civic organizations than any previous era in US history.

By 1900, several million women were already active within local suffrage movements. Millions more would join the National American Women's Suffrage Association in the next decade. For most women, however, the road to becoming a suffragist began with a particular reform that placed them in the public sphere. The same was true of men within the Progressive movement, many of whom gradually came to support women's suffrage as a tactical goal to promote a specific reform such as Prohibition. A few years of actively promoting a public cause tended to transform Progressive men and women from relative indifference regarding the suffrage question to supporting votes for women to more effectively pursue their own reform agenda. Before long, Progressive women and men began to support women's suffrage on its own merit as part of the larger crusade for social justice.

Although suffrage remained controversial, Progressives generally avoided social taboos. For example, few Progressives supported the efforts of **Margaret Sanger** to discuss "birth control." Sanger was a nurse who did not invent the methods she discussed, but she was among the first to publicly breach the social taboos regarding the subject of birth control. A handful of Socialist journals were among the first to print her articles. However, by 1914, Sanger was publishing her own serial publication titled the *Woman Rebel*. Because this journal was distributed through the US mail, it was subject to the Comstock Laws, which banned the circulation of "obscene" material. At the time these laws were passed and throughout the early decades of the twentieth century, spreading information regarding contraception was considered indecent. It was even subject to state and local penalties. After fleeing to Europe, Sanger returned to the United States and opened a women's clinic that distributed diaphragms. She also spread information suggesting that a woman should both enjoy sexual relations and control her body's reproductive system.

Arrested for promoting ideas and methods that offended the sensibilities of many social conservatives and Progressives alike, Sanger quickly became notorious as the leading public advocate of birth control. Her infamy led to the spread of information regarding birth control by both her supporters and critics. Newspapers throughout the nation discussed the issue, although her detractors often used creative methods to avoid printing details about the subject. In 1921, Sanger formed the American Birth Control League. Sanger was also active in poor and immigrant communities she identified as being vulnerable to unwanted pregnancies.

Sanger's choice to focus on these communities was influenced by the fact that wealthy women were usually able to secure these same services discreetly. In addition, Sanger's clinics were able to operate beyond the public eye in poor communities. Some immigrants perceived that the efforts of some birth control advocates in their communities were directed at reducing their numbers, a selective form of population control. Scholar Harriet Johnson's provocative book *Medical Apartheid* demonstrates the ways that birth control and other medical experiments regarding fertility were used against African American communities in these years and beyond. For most African American women and men of the early 1900s, however, their most immediate concerns were economic discrimination and the spread of Jim Crow.

FIGURE 4.22

This 1913 photo shows a parade of suffragists in New York City. Leading suffragists in the West began traveling to states such as New York that had not yet approved women's suffrage.

Margaret Sanger

A nurse who was originally from the state of New York, Sanger toured internationally promoting the legalization of contraceptive methods and was the founder of Planned Parenthood.

3.2 Booker T. Washington and W. E. B. Du Bois

Among a number of prominent black leaders at the turn of the century, two men came to represent two different perspectives regarding the challenges faced by black America. **W. E. B. Du Bois** was the first African American to receive a PhD from Harvard University. As a Northerner, and especially as a wealthy and well-educated member of the black upper class, Du Bois advocated for equality of opportunity in education and other endeavors. He believed any accommodation to segregation or white supremacy, even to achieve tactical gains such as better schools or opportunities for black workers, was contrary to the best interests of the race if these concessions required the acceptance of segregation. In 1903, Du Bois published the *Souls of Black Folk*, which included a chapter that challenged the views of the most famous black American at this time, **Booker T. Washington**. Du Bois believed that Washington had no right to speak for all black Americans. He also believed that Washington accommodated white supremacy by accepting segregation in a mistaken attempt to foster goodwill among Southern whites.

FIGURE 4.23

Booker T. Washington was an effective fundraiser for African American schools and colleges in a time period when public funds were directed towards white-only schools. He is pictured here with philanthropist Robert C. Ogden on the far left, Secretary of War and future president William Howard Taft to the left of Washington, and Andrew Carnegie on the right.

Washington had risen from a childhood working in the salt mines of West Virginia to becoming the most famous black educator in America. He transformed a one-room school in Tuskegee, Alabama, into a college that prepared thousands of black women and men for careers in education and industry. Perhaps most impressive, Washington achieved this feat by securing funding from the all-white state legislature of Alabama.

In 1895, Washington was asked by the directors of the Cotton States Exposition in Atlanta, Georgia, to deliver a speech that would demonstrate to the world that race relations in the South were stable. Washington understood that these leading white Southerners were motivated by a desire to attract investment to the region by minimizing the importance of racial discrimination, but he saw the speech as an opportunity to demand fair treatment. Calling on whites to treat black workers with more fairness, Washington offered acceptance of segregation in exchange for humane treatment and a commitment to equal funding for black schools and better job opportunities for black workers. At this time, schools for Southern black children received only a third to a quarter of the funds allocated for white children. African Americans in the South understood Washington's tactical approach, and many applauded his efforts to find any way to increase funding for black schools and greater job opportunities. These individuals were more concerned about building better schools and black-owned businesses than the "privilege" of attending classes alongside white children. Others disagreed, labeling Washington's speech the **Atlanta Compromise** and Washington's willing acceptance of segregation under any terms as accommodation to white supremacy.

The juxtaposition of the ideas and perspectives of Booker T. Washington and W. E. B. Du Bois provides a starting point for understanding the ideas and challenges faced by black leaders at this time.

Early civil rights activists discussed the merits of both conservative and radical ideas and tactics. These debates were printed in scores of black newspapers, providing historians a wealth of primary sources that demonstrate the intellectual vibrancy of the communities they served. Conservatives such as Washington sought gradual change and tactical goals like equal funding for separate schools. Radicals such as Du Bois opposed such tactics in favor of lawsuits challenging segregation.

Radicals and conservatives also differed on topics such as the creation of vocational training schools. Conservatives recognized that such training would prepare men and women for jobs as laborers, but radicals feared that these institutions might discourage black Americans from pursuing other forms of higher education. However, one must remember that someone who was generally radical or conservative could often support both tactical approaches. For example, Washington secretly diverted money to finance civil rights lawsuits from funds he had secured from paternalistic whites who intended to support programs that would train black men for jobs as laborers. At the same time, Du Bois had tremendous respect for the work done by black trade schools and recognized that Washington was very effective as a fundraiser for these kinds of schools.

While Washington looked towards vocational training and practical education programs, Du Bois believed racial equality was predicated upon the leadership of black men and women who had acquired higher education and leadership skills. He referred to these African Americans as "the talented tenth," and emphasized his belief that the advancement of all societies was based on a similar percentage of well-educated innovators and leaders. Du Bois rejected the notion that black colleges should focus only on vocational skills. He worked with other professors to maintain a rigorous academic program at Atlanta University (Clark Atlanta University today) where he taught history and sociology.

In 1905, Du Bois called for a meeting of back leaders to create a national civil rights organization. Many historians believe the group intended to meet in Buffalo, New York, until the hotels of that city refused accommodations to these men. Others question this assumption, pointing out that hotels in Northern cities were usually willing to accommodate wealthy African American leaders when they traveled. The group stayed in nearby Niagara, and their organization became known as the **Niagara Movement**. The group had little difficulty finding accommodations in eastern West Virginia for their second annual meeting at Harper's Ferry, the site of John Brown's historic rebellion against slavery. By 1909, the women and men of the Niagara Movement helped to create the National Association for the Advancement of Colored People (NAACP).

Du Bois also sought to correct the historical image of race and slavery that was created by white scholars during this era. Scouring the archives for primary sources, such as letters written by former slaves to former owners, white historians sought to validate the popular image of the contented slave. The letters of thousands of slaves were scoured for a single sentence that might be cited to prove that they had been well treated or had kind memories of their previous life in bondage. Given the millions of individuals who had been enslaved, the peculiarities of nostalgia and memory, and the power of institutions such as family and community, these historians found many examples of positive memories. They often cited these examples out of context to further their quest to vindicate the "peculiar institution" of American chattel slavery. Du Bois confronted this historical ventriloquism by collecting sources of African Americans along with other black scholars such as Carter Woodson. Together, they and other historians published journals and books that presented the perspectives of African Americans.

The last term of an African American congressman expired in 1901. No black American would serve in Congress again until Chicago's Oscar De Priest in 1929. In most areas of the South, the only way blacks could vote was with their feet. An estimated 200,000 African Americans demonstrated this last measure of agency by migrating to the North between 1890 and 1910. A million and a half more would abandon the South in the next two decades, a phenomenon known as the Great Migration by historians.

Without the right to vote in the South where 90 percent of African Americans still lived in 1910, the opinions of blacks could be ignored with impunity by national political leaders such as Roosevelt or Taft. Roosevelt demonstrated his lack of concern for the perspective of black Americans by issuing a dishonorable discharge of three companies of black infantry after a violent incident that occurred in 1906 between white civilians and a group of black soldiers in Brownsville, Texas. Neither the army nor the president gave the soldiers an opportunity to defend themselves through a court martial. In fact, there was barely any investigation of the incident. The majority of those discharged had no connection to the altercation whatsoever as they had remained on post on the day the conflict occurred.

The black vote was important in many Northern cities and might often make the difference in local and state elections. However, from the perspective of national politics, the black population outside the South represented only 1 percent of the total population at the turn of the century. As a result, neither party felt compelled to make the needs of African Americans a priority if doing so risked losing votes in the white-only elections of the South. Although critical in local elections in many cities, the Republican Party took black electoral support for granted in national elections, and Democrats rarely even bothered meeting with black leaders. In the decades following Reconstruction, the Republican Party shifted from fighting the racism of Southern whites to accommodating it in an attempt to

Niagara Movement

An African American civil rights organization formed along the New York–Canada border by W. E. B. Du Bois and other black leaders in 1905.

FIGURE 4.24

W. E. B. Du Bois believed that Booker T. Washington's acceptance of segregation was unacceptable, even as a tactical maneuver to secure more funds for black schools. Du Bois initiated a national civil rights organization known as the Niagara Movement in 1905.

broaden their electoral base among whites. Although black leaders found few alternatives to supporting the Republicans as long as the Democrats remained the party of white supremacy, in future decades, a new generation of Democratic leaders would begin to court black voters.

3.3 Civil Rights in the Progressive Era

Similar to "liberal" issues such as women's suffrage, Progressives were more likely to support moderate civil rights reforms and antilynching legislation. However, some white Progressives actively supported the enactment of segregation laws because they accepted the tenets of white supremacy and thought such laws would reduce racial friction. Yet to discard the entire Progressive movement as racially conservative would be to ignore the growing black middle class who supported the ideas of the Progressives and worked to frame racial equality within the era's campaigns for social justice.

Although the Fourteenth Amendment was intended to protect African Americans from violations of their rights as citizens, the Supreme Court had declared that segregation was consistent with the amendment and with its 1896 decision in *Plessy v. Ferguson*. In the early 1900s, the court interpreted "due process of law" to protect corporations. Meanwhile, less than a handful of individuals were ever convicted in response to the annual lynching of several hundred African Americans. Black leaders such as Ida Wells lobbied on behalf of a federal antilynching law. Although more than two hundred bills that would have made lynching a federal crime were introduced, only three ever passed the House of Representatives. None of these bills ever became law due to the united opposition of white Southern Democrats.

During the 1930s, singer Billie Holiday recorded a chilling ballad reminding the nation that "Southern trees bore strange fruit." However, few whites North or South chose to speak out on the issue of lynching because of the assumption that most victims of lynch mobs were guilty of committing rape. In this and countless other ways, historians Mary Ritter Beard and Charles Beard observed, any support of even the most basic civil rights for African Americans "had become bad form in the North." While the Beards and others explored race beyond the Mason-Dixon Line, a growing number of black scholars exploded the myth that lynching was connected to crimes against women. Instead, they argued that lynching was a collective display meant to bolster white supremacy and vent feelings of rage against a despised "other." They believed that black victims, whether innocent or guilty of any crime, served as a scapegoat for the personal failures of those who participated in the mob killings.

Expressions of this brand of rage became commonplace, and hundreds of Northern trees were stained by the same blood that ran in the South. Lynchings in the North and West often resulted in a trial, but the perpetrators were seldom convicted of their crimes. North and South were not so different in this regard, nor were they different when it came to a different kind of violence—the daily execution of black ambition. "Why do we send our children to high schools and academies," a black educator asked, only "to earn $1.50/day cleaning the sewers?" By focusing nearly exclusively on the most obvious manifestations of racial violence, historians have sanitized the violence of miseducation. By excluding black perspectives and ignoring the history and culture of nonwhites, schools reinforced the assumption of white supremacy. Equally disturbing is the fact that the creation of the color line in thousands of Northern and Midwestern communities has been expunged from the historical record. Most US communities maintained formal or informal systems of segregated schools. For example, school board records throughout Kansas, Iowa, Nebraska, and Illinois record the existence of "colored schools" in nearly a hundred towns. However, textbooks that teach the history of these states do not include any of these examples beyond the famous Topeka case of *Brown v. Board of Education*. Some even incorrectly assure their young readers that the schools of their states were always racially integrated.

A small but growing number of historians are challenging the notion that black history was limited to the South during these years. They also challenge the notion that civil rights activism was unique to the 1950s and 1960s. Although national leaders such as Booker T. Washington may have at least superficially adopted a strategy of conciliation, historians are now turning the lens of local history to challenge the notion that the other 8 million African Americans who lived during the "nadir of race relations" wore the same mask. This change in perspective from national to local is challenging historic interpretations and revealing the complexity of an era that saw a dramatic rise in black education and entrepreneurial ventures that coincided with an increase in racial violence.

Historians have recently uncovered dozens of civil rights cases involving schools, restaurants, hotels, theaters, riverboats, railroads, and even elevators during every year of the early 1900s. In about a third of the cases that have been discovered in the Midwest, the black plaintiffs won. The number of lawsuits declined over time because the results rarely justified the effort. Penalties for violators were usually minimal, and any compensation paid to the plaintiff was often insufficient to cover the expense of taking the case to court. However, sources indicate that the possibility of being sued for discrimination reduced the tendency for whites in states with civil rights laws to practice at least the most overt forms of discrimination.

FIGURE 4.25

Mary Ritter Beard and her husband Charles Beard were two of the leading historians in the early twentieth century. Mary Ritter Beard was also active in the women's suffrage movement and was a lifelong advocate of social justice and women's education.

3.4 Asian and Mexican Immigration

America's relationship with its empire reflected a variety of competing ideas regarding race, science, and culture. Many Americans embraced **Orientalism**, the practice whereby people in the Western Hemisphere appropriated Eastern art, music, literature, and culture to fit their own preconceived ideas of Asia and Asians as "exotic." Just as some Americans sought to romanticize the meaning of Native American history and experience without truly understanding the perspectives of Native Americans, an imagined "Oriental" culture became fashionable among middle and upper-class Americans seeking authentic experience beyond their own material affluence.

Others tried to prove the existence of innate racial differences using a pseudoscience called **eugenics**. Eugenicists sought to demonstrate that lighter-skinned races were more evolved. They used techniques that appeared to be scientific, such as measuring the size of brains. Of course, the relatively obvious agenda of eugenicists, who conducted "research" to validate their own predetermined conclusions about white supremacy, made most academics doubt the integrity of eugenics as a scientific discipline. Even during the early 1900s, most scientists distanced themselves from the eugenicists, even if they shared many of their racial assumptions.

FIGURE 4.27

Filipinos were placed on display during the 1904 World's Fair in St. Louis. A different US city hosted a World's Fair nearly every other year, and each featured similar exhibits of indigenous peoples. These displays often mixed the paternalism of their organizers with the agency of their "performers." The result was a mixture of genuine displays of indigenous culture and life within a Eurocentric cabaret that assumed the "backwardness" of other civilizations.

This form of scientific racism reached its peak during the 1920s. However, it may have never been more clearly celebrated than at a living display of "primitive" races during the 1904 St. Louis World's Fair. The purpose of the exhibit was to show that the indigenous peoples of the Philippines were progressing under the tutelage of the federal government. When it arrived in the Philippines in 1898, the US military appropriated existing police forces that were then employed to pacify those who resisted American occupation. The 1904 display juxtaposed these uniformed men against various "primitive" peoples such as the "Moros" who practiced Islam and the "monkey-like Negritos" who were practically naked.

The intended message of Filipino inferiority may have worked too well. The federal government, future president William Howard Taft, and even President Roosevelt intervened when it became clear that fairgoers were leaving the "Congress of Races" believing that the Filipinos were too primitive to ever become civilized. A cartoon published in a local newspaper showing President Roosevelt attempting to place trousers on the Filipinos was merely a comic expression of the actual efforts to micromanage the display and present the desired message of the US government regarding its empire. As historian Robert Rydell has shown, correspondence of President Roosevelt's private secretary includes concerns that the appearance of men wearing "a mere G string" did not support the government's message about the Philippines. "If fairgoers perceived the villagers as utterly backward and incapable of progress," Rydell explains, "the displays would actually buttress the racists' arguments used by anti-imperialists to oppose annexation of the islands."

FIGURE 4.26

Many US newspapers utilized a variety of negative stereotypes to depict Asian immigration as a threat to America. While most presented the idea that immigrants would take jobs away from "native Americans," some presented the immigrants themselves as a threat.

Orientalism

The imitation of Eastern art and culture by Westerners.

eugenics

A pseudoscientific field of study that is based on the idea that human evolution can be facilitated by preventing the reproduction of inherently inferior peoples.

FIGURE 4.28

The Southwestern Borderlands were always a melting pot and a center of ethnic and cultural conflict. In this image, an Anglo cowboy plays cards with a Native American and a migrant from Mexico.

FIGURE 4.29

Asian immigrants entering the United States from Angel Island, a processing center in San Francisco Bay that served a similar function as New York City's Ellis Island.

Gentleman's Agreement of 1907

The name given to an informal pact between US and Japanese officials in 1907. The United States agreed to not explicitly ban Japanese migrants from entering the United States (as it had Chinese migrants) so long as Japan prevented its citizens from migrating to the United States.

While Filipinos and most other residents of overseas US possessions would not be eligible to migrate to the United States at this time, migration from Latin America, the Caribbean, and South America was not restricted by law or quotas. The Newlands Act of 1902 spurred migration, as millions of acres of Southwestern land came under cultivation due to federal irrigation projects. In 1904, a railroad connecting Brownsville and the rest of the Rio Grande Valley with Corpus Christi was completed. The railroad signaled a sudden influx of Anglo land speculators and family farms in what had been an area dominated by Mexican *haciendas* (large estates) and the *vaqueros* (cattlemen).

The total population of Texas's Rio Grande Valley quadrupled between 1900 and 1930. The population increase was fueled by the migration of Anglo and African American land seekers as well as field laborers from Mexico. Three hundred thousand Mexicans entered the United States between 1910 and 1920, most fleeing political and economic turmoil during a series of revolutions and civil wars in Mexico. While the vast majority of Mexicans were drawn to the United States by the promise of steady employment, about 20 percent were professionals, landowners, or skilled laborers who feared reprisal for their connection to the former Mexican President Porfirio Diaz. By 1920, recent immigrants from Mexico comprised 12 percent of the California population. A decade later, nearly a million people and approximately 7 percent of the entire population of Mexico had migrated to the United States.

Although nativists were beginning to organize against the migration of Mexican laborers, the strongest nativist opposition in the West was waged against Asian immigrants. In 1905, nativists and local labor unions in San Francisco established the Asiatic Exclusion League. Among the goals of this organization was the expansion the Chinese Exclusion Act of 1882 to prevent the migration of Japanese and Korean families to the United States.

Similar sentiments and the famous 1906 San Francisco earthquake, which destroyed many of the city's schools, led the San Francisco Board of Education to expand their system of segregation. Responding to native sentiment, the board barred students of Japanese and Korean descent from their neighborhood schools and required them to attend separate schools that had previously been established for Chinese students. In addition to the hardships this created for families that lived all over the city, Japanese Americans protested the board's action for its obvious symbolic meaning. Local protests were soon joined by international outrage. In addition to concerns regarding segregation, Japanese leaders protested their children's restriction to schools with Chinese students given the long-standing tensions between the two nations.

Japan had just defeated Russia in the 1905 Russo-Japanese War and believed that the school board's decision was an affront to the international honor of their nation. President Roosevelt had served as the architect of the peace treaty between Russia and Japan, which was signed in New Hampshire. As a result, Roosevelt held the Japanese in high esteem and feared that angering the increasingly powerful nation of Japan would derail US efforts overseas. Because of these geopolitical concerns, the federal government intervened in hopes of maintaining diplomatic relations and trade with Japan.

At the same time, nativist sentiment in the United States demanded that the exclusionary laws barring Chinese immigration be extended to Japan and Korea. In an effort to appease these sentiments without further alienating Japan, diplomats and political leaders agreed to a secret compromise. The federal government agreed it would not ban Japanese migration in exchange for a promise by the Japanese government to deny visas for all Japanese wishing to immigrate to the United States. In addition, the federal government persuaded the San Francisco school board to limit segregation to Chinese children. The key to the agreement was that it was unofficial, allowing the Japanese government to officially proclaim that its citizens were welcome to migrate to the West, and they simply chose not to do so. As a result, the informal pledge was known as the **Gentleman's Agreement of 1907**.

Laws barring Chinese migration allowed sons (but not daughters) of Chinese migrants to also enter the United States. The goal of this law was to permit a small number of family members and laborers to still come to the United States, while preventing the creation of a self-sustaining and permanent Chinese population. A similar but informal agreement allowed the family members of Japanese Americans who already lived in the United States to also migrate to America. Ironically, a fire caused by the San Francisco Earthquake also destroyed many public records. As a result, a significant numbers of migrants arrived claiming to be related to Asian Americans who had arrived earlier and obtained citizenship. Many of the Chinese male immigrants were known as "Paper Sons" because they had arrived bearing records claiming lineage to men that may or may not have been their actual fathers.

3.5   Jewish and Central European Immigration

By 1905, a million immigrants from Italy, Greece, Russia, and the Balkans of South Central Europe were arriving in the United States each year. Many of these immigrants were Jewish refugees who fled the latest wave of **pogroms**—the anti-Semitic attempts at ethnic cleansing in Russia. Some Russian leaders sought to completely purge their empire of its Jewish population during the late nineteenth and early twentieth centuries. These attacks escalated between 1903 and 1905 and resulted in hundreds of thousands of Jewish immigrants entering the United States between these years. By the early 1920s, an estimated 2 million Jews were living in the United States.

pogroms

A series of attacks on Jews in Russia at the turn of the century that were intended to eliminate the Jewish population of Russia. The pogroms led to significant Jewish migration to the Untied States.

FIGURE 4.30

"Back in the Homeland" by Moshe Maimon. Maimon was a Jewish artist whose work often depicted the violent attacks on Jews in Russia which were known as pogroms.

The majority of these migrants lived in major East Coast cities such as New York, Philadelphia, and Baltimore. However, sizeable Jewish communities were also created in Midwestern towns and Southern port cities such as Galveston, Texas. Prominent Jewish leaders such as Jacob Schiff founded the American Jewish Committee as part of a larger movement to confront anti-Semitism and create a support network for the new arrivals. After a mob in Atlanta seized and lynched a Jewish man who had been accused of rape, Jewish activists and supporters in the United States formed the **Anti-Defamation League (ADL)**.

The core membership of the ADL in its early years were leaders and members of a Jewish fraternal organization known as the Independent Order of B'nai B'rith. This organization had been formed in the United States prior to the Civil War. Anti-Semitism had existed in the United States since the colonial period, but the relatively small numbers of Jews prior to the turn of the century had mitigated the expression of these prejudices. Due to the rapid increase in the number of American Jews, as well as the success of several high-profile Jewish bankers and the proliferation of local Jewish merchants, the old stereotypes and prejudices that had plagued Jews in Europe and Russia began to appear with greater frequency and intensity in their new country. During the 1920s, the United States would enact quotas designed to curb the number of Jewish migrants and other groups from central and Southern Europe. By the time of the Holocaust, anti-Semitism was so strong that efforts to temporarily waive these immigration restrictions and provide sanctuary for European Jews were derailed until the final year of World War II.

Anti-Defamation League (ADL)

The leading Jewish civil rights organization in the United States, the ADL was founded in 1913 in the wake of a lynching of a Jewish American man in Atlanta.

FIGURE 4.31

Migration from Europe and Russia to the United States was facilitated by American Jews who provided physical shelter for the immigrants while also shielding the newcomers from anti-Semitism in America.

While Jews faced stereotypes associating them with greed and capitalistic avarice, other immigrants arriving during these years were often typecast as impoverished vagrants. In reality, immigrants were rarely the poorest residents of their homelands due to the prohibitive costs associated with traveling to the United States. Many of the new arrivals settled within ethnic clusters located in major cities—a tendency that was both the product of prejudice and the source of allegations that the newcomers were "clannish" and did not want to learn English or assimilate into the larger society. As a result, immigrants and immigrant communities were frequently portrayed as "un-American." In reality, these communities celebrated their new homes and sought to incorporate American culture into their traditions. These communities functioned as a mediating institution between the two cultures and prevented newcomers from experiencing a sudden and complete break with their own heritage and identity.

The most obvious forms of hostility to the new immigrants were usually motivated by economic concerns. For example, a group of Greek workers were hired in Omaha as strike breakers during a series of labor conflicts involving the city's beef-packing industry. An unrelated killing involving a spurned lover's jealousy against a Greek man who was living with a "white" woman set off an explosion of anger in February 1909. By this time, existing prejudices against the city's expanding Greek community led to a series of editorials blaming low wages and crime on the residents of the Greek neighborhood. A mob of several thousand gathered in favor of a petition to rid Omaha of "filthy Greeks" in the wake of the killing. After an hour of impassioned speeches, including an emotional appeal of the brother of the man who had been shot by a Greek resident during the lover's quarrel, the mob converged on the Greek neighborhood.

The resulting **Anti-Greek Riot of 1909** led to a mass exodus of Omaha's 1,200 Greek residents. It also touched off similar race riots directed against Greek migrants in other communities such as Dayton, Ohio. One observer recalled that the "Americanism" of many mob members was "of recent origin," pointing to the irony that many of the participants were recent immigrants themselves. Regardless of their own status, "all felt the deeper thrill when the eloquence was poured forth," the observer recalled, because "they were not Greeks." "The fact that they were different from the Greeks was enough to make a common bond for that particular brotherhood," the observer concluded, "especially when it became clear that the Greeks were to be attacked and pillaged and that the assailants might enjoy the strength that comes from union."

FIGURE 4.32

One of many newspaper reports of the attacks against Greek workers in the beef-packing district of South Omaha during the anti-Greek Riot of 1909.

REVIEW AND CRITICAL THINKING

1. How did women challenge views about gender during the early years of the Progressive Era? Summarize the fight for women's suffrage between 1900 and 1912.

2. What were the perspectives of Booker T. Washington and W. E. B. Du Bois? What might account for their difference of perspective? How did these two views conflict and complement each other?

3. How did African Americans confront Jim Crow during the early 1900s? If you were to write a book on the Civil Rights Movement, would you include these early years or focus exclusively on the period after World War II?

4. Summarize the experiences of Mexican and Asian immigrants during this era. Why do you think federal policies regarding migration were different for these groups?

5. Compare the discrimination faced by Jews and other "new immigrants" from central and southern Europe to other groups of Americans. How might have the creation of "whiteness" as a racial category mediated these prejudices in later decades?

RIOT AT SOUTH OMAHA

Angry Crowds Make Merciless Attack on Greeks.

Torch is Applied to Several Buildings and Inmates Beaten and Shot by Vengeful Mob—Windows Smashed in Others.

South Omaha Sunday night was the scene of rioting, murderous assault and pillage. More than thirty buildings have been burned, wrecked or badly damaged, and probably a score of persons injured, half that number seriously. By heroic work the police have prevented actual loss of life.

The immediate cause of the trouble was the killing on Friday night of Policeman Edward Lowery by John Masuredes, a Greek whom the officer had placed under arrest. Masuredes was brought to the Douglas county jail at Omaha and for fear an attempt might be made to lynch him he was taken to Lincoln and placed in the penitentiary to await his preliminary hearing.

On Saturday a petition was circulated in South Omaha and signed by hundreds of citizens, setting forth that a large number of Greek residents of the place were of the undesirable class and calling a mass meeting at the city hall for Sunday afternoon to discuss methods of ridding the city of them.

Source: The Alliance Herald. (Alliance, Box Butte County, Neb.), February 25, 1909.

Anti-Greek Riot of 1909

An attack on the entire Greek population of Omaha, Nebraska, that led over a thousand Greek Americans to flee the city and inspired similar attacks on Greek immigrants in other factory and beef-packing towns.

4. LIFE IN "MODERN AMERICA"

LEARNING OBJECTIVES

1. **Summarize the way that popular culture reflected ideas about gender during the early 1900s.**

2. **Evaluate the impact of labor reformers who were to the left of the mainstream political thought of the Progressives. Describe the way that Mother Jones and others sought to empower workers.**

3. **Explain why some Americans supported the American Socialist Party and ideas of its leader Eugene Debs. Second, explain the perspectives of those who opposed the Socialists in the context of US history during these years.**

4.1 Popular Culture

Traveling shows continued to reach even the most isolated rural areas of the United States. By 1900, agricultural commodity prices had become a bit more stable, permitting many rural dwellers to take advantage of special "excursion rates" that offered discounted rail travel to nearby cities. Saloons also sought to attract more customers by offering free food or even a free vaudeville show to thirsty city-goers. By the turn of the century, saloons were the most numerous business in many urban neighborhoods, outnumbering the diverse local purveyors of dry goods, produce, and meat. Saloons even proliferated in "dry" cities and counties, regardless of the efforts of the WCTU and other Prohibitionists.

Baseball continued to grow in popularity, despite a series of scandals involving gambling that ranged from local teams to the major leagues. Allegations that gangsters and bookies had corrupted the integrity of the game would culminate in 1919 when the Chicago White Sox intentionally lost the World Series to the Cincinnati Reds. The scandal led to the growing popularity of local teams, including those composed of African Americans. One of the most interesting traveling teams was an Iowa-based club known as the All Nations. This team traveled on its own rail car and featured players of various racial and ethnic backgrounds. Other sports such as horse racing had been dominated by African Americans but drew the color line by creating rules requiring membership in all-white jockey associations. Although a handful of black sports stars such as cyclist Marshall Taylor and jockey Isaac Murphy would acquire a measure of fame and fortune, most were excluded from both team and individual sports.

Jack Johnson

The first African American to win the heavyweight title in boxing, Jack Johnson angered whites by not only beating the popular Jim Jeffries but emasculating him in the ring in their 1910 bout in Reno, Nevada. Johnson also openly dated white women in violation of a social taboo of the early twentieth century.

FIGURE 4.33

Jack Johnson defeated Jim Jeffries in 1910 in Reno, Nevada. This victory made Johnson the undisputed heavyweight champion. Whites at this time expected black athletes to act with great humility, but Johnson displayed bravado and flouted his wealth.

Boxer **Jack Johnson** was the most notable exception to the general trend of black exclusion from sports. In 1908, Johnson defeated the reigning heavyweight champion Tommy Burns. The fight was held in Australia because no US venue agreed to host the interracial bout. Most white Americans discounted the fight's significance, pointing to the fact that Burns had only been given the title after the undefeated champion Jim Jeffries retired. The backlash against Johnson was so strong that Jeffries agreed to come out of retirement for the sole purpose of putting Johnson "back in his place." Other black boxers had won the championships of other weight divisions, but Johnson's victory was much more disturbing to many whites because of his bravado and tendency to date white women in violation of the era's social mores. Whites were so angry when Johnson defeated Jeffries in 1910 during a highly anticipated fight in Reno, Nevada, that dozens of episodes of racial violence exploded throughout the country.

In Americus, Georgia, a black man was beaten, shot, lynched, and then set on fire by a white mob for failing to hide his pleasure at the way Johnson humiliated Jeffries in the ring. Whites who could not stop the fight or its outcome wanted to send the message that Johnson's victory had changed nothing. The mania with which the mob tore the man's flesh demonstrated a fear that African Americans were advancing—not only in sports but throughout society—despite attempts to maintain white supremacy.

A young African American named James Nabrit walked past the spot where the lynching had taken place on his way to the one-room school reserved for the education of his race in that Georgia town. He withstood a gauntlet of abuse each day on this walk as whites taunted him, attempting to thwart his ambition in ways that paralleled the 1910 mob. They failed. James Nabrit made that walk every day, eventually graduating first in his class at Northwestern Law School. He would later serve as one of the lead attorneys on behalf of the NAACP in *Brown v. Board of Education*, which outlawed school segregation throughout the nation.

4.2 The Cult of Masculinity

The growing popularity of hypermasculine sports such as boxing was partially a reaction to concerns about the influence of modernity on the martial ethic. Teddy Roosevelt became the leading spokesman for those who feared that "overcivilization" had led middle-class men to lose touch with their own masculinity. Prior to the growth of the corporation, middle-class men were prosperous gentlemen farmers and artisans. These men might not have worked with their hands every day, but they were still connected to the hard and substantial productive labor of the farm and shop. Equally important, they were the masters of their domain as independent producers.

After the turn of the century, the majority of middle-class men were midlevel employees who had to submit to the authority of other men. They neither owned nor controlled productive property nor commanded or conducted physical labor. The number of such jobs in corporate offices multiplied tenfold in the decades following the Civil War. The fact that much of their work was being assigned to a growing army of women did little to counter the fears that clerical labor was emasculating a generation of American men.

A secondary concern was that the growing number of female school teachers was leading young men to become "soft" while eliminating masculine role models. American men had always been raised by women, but this new generation of women was seemingly different from the submissive matron of the past, or at least the popular imagination of the past. Women were increasingly demonstrating their ability to compete in the marketplace and agitating for the vote in every community. Women were also clamoring for the eradication of the saloons where men had gathered in the past. Even the boxing ring and gambling houses had been closed following the campaigns of female reformers. These were progressive changes from the perspective of those horrified by the crippling violence and financial ruin that occurred in such "manly" places. For those already convinced that masculinity was on the decline, the growing power of women to influence politics and constrict the separate sphere of manly recreation was further proof that men were under siege in a battle of the sexes.

The solution, it appeared to some, might be found in other kinds of battles. Roosevelt declared that the Spanish-American War had led to national revitalization through cultivating the martial ethic and rekindling the manliness of generations past. "If we shrink from the hard contests where men must win at hazard of their lives," Roosevelt counseled, "the bolder and stronger peoples will pass us by, and will win for themselves the domination of the world." Roosevelt's exhortation contained multiple references to masculinity, his final exhortation a challenge to the new generation of men who must resolve to fulfill their duties "manfully." Behind the nationalistic bluster, Roosevelt's defense of "splendid little wars" as a method of preventing American men from growing soft and effeminate demonstrated that the conception of masculinity could be cited in defense of aggression as well as protection.

For most of the nineteenth century, manliness was based on the notion of paternal duty and obligation. Historians of gender have shown that the concept of masculinity was related to one's success as a patriarch and provider. The worst gender-based insult at this time was to refer to an adult male as a "boy." Whites regularly used this word to emasculate minority men, denying their independence and therefore rejecting their manhood. By the turn of the century, the conception of manliness and the language used to express it had shifted. Perhaps in relation to concerns about the growing power and influence of women in a world where physical labor was becoming less relevant, men began to define masculinity in opposition to female traits and characteristics. As a result, the worst insults for men were those suggesting effeminate traits. In fact, the entire conception of "emasculation" shifted from projecting immaturity to the use of gender-based and often misogynistic insults.

A "cult of masculinity" emerged in twentieth-century America where prize fighters like Jack Dempsey were idolized. Enlisted soldiers and sailors had previously been held in low regard because these ranks were occupied by the lowest social castes. In the past, such soldiers and sailors were often considered "boys" due to their poverty and bachelorhood. The cult of masculinity reversed that view and military men were increasingly admired for their martial prowess. Bodybuilding had also been held as suspect—either as a vain pursuit or one related to the underground world of homosexuality. By the turn of the century, bodybuilding emerged as a manly pursuit that some middle-class men believed might alleviate some of the consequences of sedentary work routines. As a result of this changing definition of masculinity, the concept of heterosexuality emerged in opposition to homosexuality.

Prior to the turn of the century, heterosexuality did not exist as a category and was merely an assumed trait. People who would later be classed as homosexual were simply marginalized in ways that precluded any deep level of analysis by the dominant society. Psychiatrists and physicians who wrote about the subject tended to assume that gay men were simply men who possessed "feminine" brains. Self-identified homosexual men thought of themselves as "queer," a word that connoted uniqueness rather than a negative stigma. The era's hypermasculinity and the absence of concepts of "straight" and "homosexual" meant that straight men could commit homosexual acts without being considered homosexual. As long as they did not demonstrate effeminate mannerisms associated with "fairies"—a derogatory term applied only to effete homosexuals—a man might successfully project his own homosexual urges upon a male sex partner.

A wealth of primary sources demonstrates the widespread acceptance of this seemingly incongruous way of thinking. For example, newspaper articles frequently described the debauchery of soldiers and sailors on leave who visited both male and female prostitutes. In most cases, the authors only considered the makeup-wearing male prostitutes as "deviants" and "fairies" because of their effeminate dress and mannerisms. The soldier and sailor retained their masculinity regardless of their choice of sexual partner as long as they retained the dominant (masculine) sexual role in that liaison and eschewed effeminate behaviors. Sources from prisons and mining camps likewise demonstrate the degree to which this cult of masculinity permitted men to engage in sex with other men without being regarded as homosexual themselves. The social construction of sexual deviance as related to effeminacy created a closet around many male homosexual acts while vilifying homosexuals who displayed effeminate traits.

4.3   The Limits of Progressivism

Labor activists and Progressives joined together to support legislation that would provide minimum wages, maximum hours, and protect workers from industrial hazards. With the exception of state laws that sought to protect society's interest in making sure that mothers were present in the home during the evening, most of these laws were rejected. Even these laws directed toward the "protection" of women were only as strong as the will to enforce them.

In addition, the Supreme Court voided a variety of laws that had been passed as a result of a partnership between reform politicians and laborers. For example, New York had passed a law limiting the work day to ten hours within bakeries. In 1910, that law was struck down in a landmark Supreme Court case that would be applied to dozens of other laws regulating the workday. In *Lochner v. New York*, the Court agreed with the owner of a bakery in Utica who claimed that the state law restricted the right of workers to make their own contracts on their own terms. By proclaiming that no employee could work more than ten hours per day, the Court argued, the law violated the "liberty of contract" that gave laborers and management to right to form agreements without undue interference of the state. The decision was controversial but would stand until 1937.

The *Lochner* decision undermined many Progressive efforts to use the government to regulate private sector conditions, especially those factors including hours and pay. As a result, workers turned once again to labor strikes—a measure that the Progressives had hoped to avoid by passing these kind of protective laws. Mary Harris Jones may have been the most effective labor advocate of this era, earning the trust of the predominantly male workers in coal mines from Pennsylvania to Colorado. She was affectionately known as "Mother" Jones to these miners, while industrialists knew her only as "the most dangerous woman in the world."

FIGURE 4.34

This 1924 photo shows Mary Harris "Mother" Jones with President Coolidge. Jones faced death threats and was arrested on multiple occasions for her efforts promoting labor unions among miners in Pennsylvania, West Virginia, and Colorado.

FIGURE 4.35

New York City police placing the victims of the Triangle Shirtwaist Fire in coffins. Dramatic images such as these and photos of women leaping to their deaths mobilized public support in favor of stricter building codes and tougher regulations regarding workplace safety.

Triangle Shirtwaist Factory Fire

An industrial tragedy in New York City that led to the death of 146 workers, mostly young women, when a fire trapped employees of the Triangle Shirtwaist Company in March 1911. The fire led to calls for tougher laws regulating building codes and workplace safety.

During her long life, Mother Jones was a fearless organizer who led coal strikes throughout the nation by traveling arduous mountain paths to spread her prounion ideas. Jones had first achieved a measure of notoriety in 1903 when she led a protest march of children carrying signs asking for the right to attend school instead of working in factories. As she approached her eightieth birthday, she faced death threats and was arrested numerous times for her support of coal miners during strikes in West Virginia and Colorado between 1912 and 1914, which are discussed in the next chapter.

Conventions respecting age and gender may have shielded Mother Jones against those who would have otherwise ended her life. Notions of protecting women usually proved hollow, however, when applied to the hundreds of thousands of immigrant and minority women who worked as domestics and laborers. Rape and physical abuse were among the dangers African Americans and other women faced as they worked in middle-class homes and raised white children. Others faced grueling working conditions within the garment industry. These jobs featured ten- and twelve-hour shifts, as well as low wages for male workers and even lower wages for the predominantly female workforce. Children hired to replace bobbins within moving machines and women who worked the looms faced fatigue and the constant risk of injury and even death.

In New York City in 1911, a fire at the Triangle Shirtwaist Company led to the deaths of 146 workers. The majority of those killed were young women who had no escape because the company had locked one of the doors to prevent them from taking breaks. Firefighters had no way to reach the women as their ladders could not reach the top floor of the building whose fire escape had collapsed. As a result, rescue personnel looked on helplessly as women leaped to their deaths. The **Triangle Shirtwaist Factory Fire** finally awakened the nation to the dangerous conditions that led to thousands of workplace fatalities each year. It also led to belated revisions in building codes and a renewed effort to improve the skills and equipment of firefighters.

4.4 Socialism and Radical Unionism

A small number of labor leaders at the turn of the century envisioned a much more radical union movement that would include workers of all races and ethnicities, trades, and skill levels. Like the Knights of Labor, labor organizers such as Eugene Debs turned to Socialism and its vision of worker-owned factories and mines. Socialists believed that the government, as the instrument of the people, should control "the means of production." Socialists used this term to describe productive property such as factories and farms.

Socialists viewed the modern-day relationship between business and government as part of a capitalist plot to maintain the power of wealth. For most Americans, however, Socialism was the antithesis of freedom because it sought to abolish private property and restrict free enterprise. Despite all of the hardships workers faced and the crushing poverty of many Americans, most did not believe that they would fare better under a system that would eliminate the profit motive and distribute wealth to all regardless of their talents and accomplishments. From the perspective of Socialists, however, their doctrine provided liberation from a profit motive that led to child labor and hundreds of daily workplace fatalities.

Most political leaders presented Socialism as antagonistic to the freedoms Americans enjoyed and a violation of principles such as the protection of private property on which the government was founded. Some of the nation's founders recognized the possibility that democracy could lead to the redistribution of wealth that Socialism envisioned. In response, many of the founders favored restrictions barring suffrage from those who did not own significant wealth. From the perspective of Socialists, the efforts of these wealthy men to restrict the vote to landowners demonstrated that the class interests of the founders outweighed their vaunted support for democracy. For these individuals, collective ownership of those things that produced wealth was the highest expression of democracy.

Industrial Workers of the World (IWW)

A radical labor union that enrolled all workers regardless of race, ethnicity, gender, or occupation. The IWW were nicknamed "Wobblies" and sought class solidarity among all laborers in hopes of promoting a revolutionary challenge to the Capitalist system.

In 1905, the **Industrial Workers of the World (IWW)** was formed as a union for those who sought to merge the political goals of American Socialists with the vision of radical unionism created by the Knights of Labor. Like the Knights, the IWW sought to enroll both skilled and unskilled laborers regardless of their race, ethnicity, or gender. A leader of a miner's union, "Big" Bill Haywood was elected to lead the members of the IWW who were soon nicknamed "Wobblies" for reasons that are still unclear.

The total number of these Wobblies rarely exceeded 10,000 at any given moment, but the IWW maintained an influence far larger than its numbers due to the efforts of activists such as Mother Jones. The heart of the IWW's influence was its radical message of worker solidarity against Capitalism. "If the workers of the world want to win, all they have to do is recognize their own solidarity," counseled IWW leader Joseph Ettor. "They have nothing to do but fold their arms and the world will stop...with passive resistance, with the workers absolutely refusing to move, laying absolutely silent, they are more powerful than all the weapons and instruments that the other side have for protection and attack."

Ettor defied the conventional logic that suggested women and immigrants would not join the labor movement when he organized multiple strikes in textile mills throughout the country. The most famous of these was the **Lawrence Textile Strike of 1912**. In January of that year, Progressive reformers in Massachusetts passed a state law making it illegal for employers to compel women and children to work more than fifty-four hours per week. Employers responded with immediate reductions in pay that led 20,000 workers to the picket lines. Lawrence was a mill town, and city authorities mobilized on behalf of the owners. Officials in Lawrence even ordered the fire department to spray the women and children on the picket line with fire hoses in the midst of a Massachusetts winter. Authorities defended their actions by pointing out that IWW members had trespassed onto mill property, breaking windows and shutting off power to prevent the mills from operating after hiring strikebreakers.

FIGURE 4.36

One of many handbills circulated during the Lawrence Textile Strike of 1912 to encourage solidarity. A "scab" is someone who crosses a picket line and resumes work during a strike.

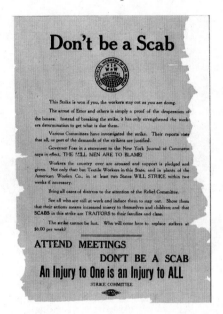

Despite mass arrests and police harassment, the mill workers, with the support of the IWW, succeeded in having their pay restored. This success was due to the efforts of Socialists and IWW supporters throughout the East Coast who established soup kitchens and even agreed to care for the workers' children so that strikers could stay on the picket lines. In making this concession, mill owners secretly planned to reduce wages once IWW organizers left the area. This would become one of the most effective tactics in the arsenal of management and would reverse the short-lived success of numerous strikes during this era.

Ideas about the constitutional protections of political speech were still developing at this time. Socialists such as Emma Goldman advocated violence to destroy the Capitalist system. Goldman also led an organization called the Free Speech League, but her willingness to endorse violence did little to convince Americans of this generation that freedom of speech should be absolute. In fact, numerous local laws were passed barring the right of any political speech in certain areas known for labor radicalism, such as San Diego's "soapbox row."

Lawrence Textile Strike of 1912

A strike of an estimated 20,000 mill workers in Lawrence, Massachusetts, that was supported by the IWW and led to a partial restoration of wages. The mills had reduced the weekly pay of workers in response to a Massachusetts law that reduced the maximum workweek to fifty-four hours.

Karl Marx

A revolutionary German philosopher that viewed the history of every society as a progression of class struggle. Marx believed that once a society became industrialized, workers would eventually rise up against the ruling Capitalist class and create an economic and political system that distributed property among workers.

Although American socialists rarely initiated violence, their ideological support of revolution against capitalism and the violent acts of socialists and other radicals in Europe created a different impression among many Americans. However, mainstream Socialist leaders in the US such as Eugene Debs were seldom as radical as their European counterparts. Most US Socialists hoped to work through the existing political system and did not envision the overthrow of government via an armed revolution of the working class. American Socialist thinkers were also more likely to share working-class backgrounds than European theorists such as **Karl Marx**. Known as the leading figure in Socialist thought at this time, Marx eschewed physical labor, even when his own family was suffering. He also held ironically condescending views toward the working class. The same was true of some American Socialists, although Debs and those affiliated with the IWW were unapologetically blue collar.

FIGURE 4.37

Soldiers with bayonets drawn surround striking workers and guard the entrance to the mills in Lawrence, Massachusetts, during the strike of 1912.

Because of concerns about the growth of Socialism through radical labor unions, IWW members were frequently arrested. Some IWW leaders were committed Socialists who feared that a successful strike that resulted in higher wages would reduce the militancy of their members by discouraging the kind of activism that might lead toward their ultimate goal of collective ownership. The degree to which rank-and-file members of the IWW-affiliated unions shared this goal is difficult to determine. Like the Knights of Labor, many members were likely more concerned with their immediate welfare and wages.

However, unlike the Knights of Labor, which expanded rapidly, the IWW remained a relatively small and tight-knit confederation of unions. As a result, a large percentage of IWW members were involved in the protests and mass arrests that led to the notoriety and infamy of the organization. More than any other labor union, Wobblies shared an ideological commitment to a politically unpopular goal. The IWW was considered radical, even among those who disapproved of the violent methods that were often used to suppress their opinions. In response, the IWW utilized many of the direct action techniques that would later be identified with the civil rights movement of the 1960s. IWW members often endured great hardships by participating in sit-ins, boycotts, and protest marches. They hoped that filling the jails would help to further their goals. At the same time, many IWW members rejected the doctrine of nonviolent resistance that would define the civil rights movement.

> *Your Honor, years ago I recognized my kinship with all living beings, and I made up my mind that I was not one bit better than the meanest on earth. I said then, and I say now, that while there is a lower class, I am in it, and while there is a criminal element I am of it, and while there is a soul in prison, I am not free.*
>
> —*Eugene Debs following his 1918 conviction for violating the Sedition Act*

REVIEW AND CRITICAL THINKING

1. How did women "win the right to vote" in America? How did radical and conservative ideas of gender shape the debate on women's suffrage?

2. What are the implications of the exclusion of women's suffrage beyond the national victory in 1920 from the historical record, and how does the inclusion/exclusion of women affect one's understanding of the nation's history?

3. Who was Mary Harris Jones, and what was her impact on US history? Does knowing she was a Socialist alter your opinion of her life and legacy?

4. What did Socialists in the United States hope to accomplish? Why might Socialism have attracted so many followers at the turn of the century?

5. Why did the predominantly white coal miners of Colorado to burn the company stores during the Ludlow Massacre of 1914? How might this compare with the reasons predominantly nonwhite urban dwellers burned stores and destroyed property in the "race riots" of the late 1960s? How did the national reaction to these events compare?

5. CONCLUSION

Progressivism was a diverse reform movement that emerged in the 1890s and early 1900s and would profoundly influence the next century of American political thought. Whereas conservatives believed that restricting the size and power of the government was the key to liberty, the Progressives believed that certain government regulations could promote efficiency and social justice. Although their critics accused them of starting down a path that would lead to Socialism, Progressives believed they were charting a middle course between complete government control over industry and the laissez-faire practices of the past.

Progressives regarded private property as sacred, but they also believed that some measure of government intervention was necessary to prevent monopolies and protect the vulnerable. They also had a tendency to view the issues they supported in moral and/or religious terms. In some instances, they carried their faith in a particular reform to the point of believing it might be a panacea that would cure most of society's ills. At their best, they selflessly dedicated their lives to causes that provided little or no tangible benefit for themselves or members of their social class. At their worst, they looked down upon those in need of charity and failed to consider the perspectives of the working class and impoverished masses for whom they claimed to speak.

Many business leaders appreciated the Progressive Movement's opposition to radical doctrines, especially when compared to other reform philosophies and the political upheaval of other industrial nations. These conservatives also preferred mild government regulation and stability that the Progressives promoted, if it could prevent the social unrest and radicalism that had occurred during the Populist revolt of the 1890s. However, business leaders still feared that some Progressive reforms might lead toward the creation of powerful government entities that might someday challenge their ability to act with relative impunity. Furthermore, social conservatives feared that these reformers might create a government that would be more progressive in enforcing economic, racial, and gender equality.

6. FURTHER READING

Cole, Peter. *Wobblies on the Waterfront: Interracial Unionism in Progressive-Era Philadelphia* (2007).

Dawley, Alan. *Changing the World: American Progressives in War and Revolution* (2003).

Flanaghan, Maureen A. *Seeing with Their Hearts: Chicago Women and the Vision of a Good City, 1871–1933* (2002).

Gilmore, Glenda. *Gender and Jim Crow: Women and the Politics of White Supremacy in North Carolina, 1896–1920* (1996).

Johnston, Robert D. *The Radical Middle Class: Populist Democracy and the Question of Capitalism in Progressive Era Portland, Oregon* (2006).

Kelley, Blair M. *Right to Ride: Streetcar Boycotts and African American Citizenship in the Era of Plessy v. Ferguson* (2010).

Klein, James E. *Grappling with Demon Rum: The Cultural Struggle Over Liquor in Early Oklahoma* (2008).

McGerr, Michael. *A Fierce Discontent: The Rise and Fall of the Progressive Movement in America, 1870–1920* (2005).

Montejano, David. *Anglos and Mexicans in the Making of Texas, 1836–1986* (1987).

CHAPTER 5
The Late Progressive Era and World War, 1912–1920

On the morning of June 29, 1914, Americans awoke to the news that the heir to the throne of Austria-Hungary had been killed. The news seemed remote to most Americans, but the assassination would soon become the pretext for a global war of attrition. Austrian demands for retaliation mixed with existing tensions, ambitions, and alliances in a way that led a number of nations to declare war on each other. In July and August of 1914, the leading nations of Europe rushed to join what they hoped would be a limited and brief war that would unite their citizens and lead to the acquisition of new territories. While some Europeans leaders attempted to stop the war, once the soldiers of their rivals began to march, they feared that failure to respond in kind would lead to disaster. A system of alliances involving European empires meant that war would have a profound impact on colonized peoples throughout North America, Asia, North Africa, Australia and the Middle East. More than 60 million men served in the armies of the belligerent nations, and 9 million of these soldiers perished. At least this many women and children also died because of famine and disease directly related to the war. Among the casualties of the war was the end of the Progressives' faith that modern technology, democracy, and rationality might lead to a new age in which scarcity and misery would be eliminated.

US businesses sought to profit from the war by selling goods to the belligerents while maintaining neutrality. Prior to this time, Americans congratulated themselves for following the advice of their founders and avoiding "foreign entanglements." Chief among such entanglements were the pledges of mutual defense that formed the basis of European alliances and might have required US mobilization in 1914. Instead, exports of US grain and military supplies led to reduced unemployment and increased corporate profits. The war also brought a sudden halt to European immigration to the United States, which increased domestic demand for labor and resulted in modest wage increases. However, the fact that the bulk of this very profitable trade was conducted with Britain and France led Germany to respond by attacking ships believed to be transporting US-made supplies to its enemies. These vessels often carried US civilians, and when these vessels were sunk, political and business leaders along with the majority of "old-stock" Americans from Western Europe responded with anger. American public opinion increasingly turned against Germany, especially after the discovery of a secret communication by German leaders seeking an alliance with Mexico against the United States. Yet even after the US declaration of war in 1917, most Americans felt grateful that a vast ocean separated their nation from the killing fields of Europe.

FIGURE 5.1

This 1917 poster depicts a US sailor being sent overseas by the goddess of liberty. It reflects the belief among Americans about the purity of their motives in World War I.

The Progressive Era's faith in government regulation had led to a host of domestic reforms under the Wilson administration. Although these reforms had dominated Woodrow Wilson's first administration, they quickly gave way to wartime mobilization. Even as the nation began to prepare for war, the Progressive faith in the positive momentum of history continued. Americans demanded, and Wilson promised, that the United States would not only would turn the tide of war against German aggression but also would ensure that this be the last war of its kind. Women and minorities agreed to support their nation's fight to spread freedom and democracy, but demanded that these principles be applied in their homeland. Despite the hastening of Progressive reforms such as women's suffrage, the nation would retreat from Progressive ideals in the postwar summer of 1919 that was dominated by anti-Communist hysteria and racially motivated violence.

By 1920, the nation returned to its isolationist orientation. Business and political leaders focused on promoting development and only indirectly addressed the difficulties of reconstruction in Europe and the rest of the world. For Europeans, World War I would claim the lives of millions and ignite revolutions in its wake. Even European nations that had not been dissolved politically had been at least partially transformed by the experiences of war at home and abroad. For most Americans, the experiences of the war were far less traumatic. Only directly involved in the conflict for nineteen months, the United States was never under any credible threat of invasion. Ten times as many Americans would lose their lives in an influenza pandemic that occurred at the end of the war than on the battlefields of Europe. Yet for most Americans, the war and the revolutionary changes that occurred in its aftermath forever altered the way they viewed the rest of the world, labor relations, and the role of government. In addition, the moralistic tenor with which many viewed their participation in the war shaped their ideas about America's role in the world and would have a profound effect on the way they viewed a second war that erupted two decades later.

1. THE WILSON ADMINISTRATION AND THE COMING WAR

LEARNING OBJECTIVES

1. Describe the Wilson administration's attempts to regulate industry and the banking system during his first term, and describe the changes to the Constitution during these years.
2. Discuss the different perspectives of labor and management, and summarize the conflicts between workers and operators in the nation's coal mines.
3. Explain the factors that led to the founding of the NAACP and the significance of this organization in its early years. Also, discuss the ways that conflicts regarding race and ethnicity in the American Southwest at this time affected the nation.
4. Summarize the origin and outbreak of World War I.

1.1 Business, Banking, and National Politics

Wilson pledged to make the interests of farmers and laborers a leading priority, promising reforms that would "shield" these groups from the negative consequences of industrialization and the abuses of monopolies. The president supported the Clayton Antitrust Act of 1914, which clarified the definition of illegal business practices. The act declared that any action that reduced competition in the marketplace would be subject to federal penalties, as determined by the newly created **Federal Trade Commission (FTC)**. The FTC was charged with enforcing federal regulations, such as a section of the Clayton Act that prohibited individuals from serving as members of a corporation's board of directors if they had a conflict of interest. For example, if an individual was a member of Ford's board of directors, he could not also serve another automaker in that capacity. In the past, various holding companies had conspired to form trusts by appointing the same individuals to multiple boards as a way of conspiring to eliminate competition. The Clayton Act also required government approval for mergers and acquisitions to prevent the growth of monopolies, and it banned a variety of unfair business practices. For example, a company could no longer require one of its suppliers to refuse the business of its competitors as part of the price of doing business. In the past, courts had interpreted antitrust laws such as the Sherman Act against labor unions. For example, the leaders of the Pullman Strike of 1894 were declared in violation of antitrust laws when their wildcat strike began affecting other rail companies. For this reason, the Clayton Act specifically exempted labor unions from its provisions.

The Clayton Act was inspired by the work of Progressive attorney, author, and later Supreme Court Justice **Louis Brandeis**. Known as "the People's Lawyer," Brandeis authored the influential book *Other People's Money*, which exposed the techniques used by trusts to create monopolies and destroy small businesses. Brandeis showed how men who sat on the boards of banks, as well as various trusts, were able to manipulate the money supply to enrich themselves. The book also demonstrated the artificial limits that were placed on the supply of capital and the way these methods discouraged consumer spending and investment. At their worst, these trusts destroyed innovation by rewarding companies that were less competitive but enjoyed powerful connections. Brandeis also fought on behalf of the right of free speech—a liberal cause that was still gaining acceptance in the early twentieth century. His nomination to the Supreme Court was controversial both because of his liberal politics and because he was Jewish in an era of virulent anti-Semitism. Today, most scholars of legal history consider Brandeis to be one of the most capable justices in US history. In an era when protections of free speech and privacy were considered secondary and conditional to other interests, Brandeis helped to construct the modern legal framework that protected these freedoms as inherent rights of all US citizens.

Federal Trade Commission (FTC)

A federal agency created in 1914 to enforce antitrust legislation and other measures designed to prevent monopolies and unfair business practices. The FTC also seeks to defend consumers from fraud and deceptive business practices.

Louis Brandeis

Author, attorney, and the first Jewish appointee to the US Supreme Court. A leading private university in Massachusetts was named in honor of Brandeis, who was known as a someone who exposed corruption in the financial industry and defended consumers against corporate interests.

FIGURE 5.2

Progressive attorney Louis Brandeis was the first Jewish appointee to the US Supreme Court. A fellow Justice called Brandeis a "militant crusader for social justice whoever his opponent might be."

Federal Reserve Act of 1913

Created the modern central banking system of the United States. The Federal Reserve acts as a central bank for the government and establishes monetary policies that affect the economy such as the federal funds rate—the interest rate commercial banks pay to borrow money.

progressive taxation

A system where the rate of taxation increases for individuals who earn more money. For example, incomes between $50,000 and $80,000 might be taxed at 20 percent, while incomes between $300,000 and $1,000,000 would be taxed at 35 percent.

Wilson recognized that the nation's banking system needed federal support to provide greater stability, especially as a number of prominent banks failed despite the relative financial tranquility of the early 1900s. In each instance, bank failures led to the loss of depositors' money and panicked selling on Wall Street. In an effort to provide greater regulation and stability to the nation's banking system, the **Federal Reserve Act of 1913** created the Federal Reserve and twelve district banks scattered throughout the nation. The Federal Reserve has authority over policies such as the amount of money the government should print. The role of the Federal Reserve also includes authority over monetary policy, including the establishment of interest rates that member banks pay to borrow money from each other. The Federal Reserve can lower this rate to spur investment or raise it to limit inflation.

Some Progressives supported a program whereby the federal government would also require strict regulation of private banks and provide insurance against bank failures. However, these more active government measures would not be approved until after the nationwide panic that helped create the Great Depression. The powers granted to the Federal Reserve expanded during these years, and the institution continues to manage the nation's banking system by regulating the flow of credit to banks. As a result, decisions made by the Federal Reserve have a direct impact on businesses and the general public.

The Populists of the 1890s had sought the enactment of a modest federal income tax that would apply only to the wealthy. Previous attempts to add direct taxes on the wealthy had been challenged in the courts, leading to the decision to seek a constitutional amendment specifically authorizing a federal income tax. With the support of the Progressives, the Sixteenth Amendment was approved by Congress in 1909 and ratified by the states in February 1913. That fall, Congress approved an annual tax on all those who made more than $4,000 per year. Because most workers made about $80 per month, only the wealthiest 5 percent of households paid any federal taxes the following year. In addition, the tax rates were quite modest, ranging from 1 percent for those who made just above $4,000 to a maximum rate of 7 percent for the wealthiest Americans. Conservatives feared that these relatively modest taxes would be the harbinger of more assessments. In 1916, they fought against a proposed tax increase and an additional tax on corporations. They were especially angered by the creation of an estate tax that was levied when property valued above a certain amount changed hands from a deceased individual to his or her children. Even after tax rates increased and the exemption was lowered, most Americans still did not earn or own enough property to come under the terms of the new law. Most believed the feature requiring those with higher incomes to pay higher rates—a feature known as **progressive taxation**—was fair. As the size of the federal government increased in future decades, tax rates also increased while the exemption level declined. As a result, larger percentages of Americans were required to pay federal income taxes, resulting in greater public awareness regarding federal tax policies.

A second goal of the Populist Party of the 1890s was a constitutional amendment requiring direct election of US senators. Although the Populists had failed to pass this measure, their ideas continued to generate support leading to the approval of the Seventeenth Amendment in April 1913. The amendment ended the practice whereby state legislatures selected the delegates to the Senate. Instead, popular elections in each state would determine each senate seat. Other goals of the Populists were realized during the early years of the Wilson administration, such as the Adamson Act establishing the eight-hour day for railroad workers. The federal government also approved a measure providing financial compensation and reimbursement of medical expenses for laborers injured at work, although the measure only applied to federal employees.

1.2 Labor and the Mine Wars in West Virginia and Colorado

Laborers, unions, and Progressive reformers worked at the state level throughout the early 1900s and successfully passed a growing number of mandatory compensation laws that were similar to the protections federal employees enjoyed. States also passed a host of laws mandating maximum hours and minimum wages. However, tens of thousands of employees continued to be injured or even killed at work each year. These industrial casualties led to demands for workers' compensation laws that would apply to private industry much like the federal laws that protected federal workers. In addition to a desire to improve workplace safety, part of the reason Progressives favored these reforms was a desire to thwart the growth of radicalism and the Socialist Party. They also hoped to prevent labor strikes, which continued to increase in number, duration, and intensity. By 1916, the Industrial Workers of the World (IWW) had nearly 100,000 members. Not all of these women and men approved the Wobblies' ultimate goal of a general worker's revolution. However, most at least viewed the IWW as favorable alternative to the more conservative unions such as the American Federation of Labor (AFL).

In many areas where the IWW led strikes, such as the rubber mills of Akron, Ohio, and among the lumberjacks in the Dakotas, the AFL was nonexistent. The IWW sought to organize all workers regardless of race or gender, including the women of the Akron mills. Contrary to the notion that women did not enter the industrial workforce in large numbers until World War II, women represented over 20 percent of workers in the rubber industry at this time. The IWW also organized the men of the lumber camps in Minnesota, as well as the immigrant iron miners of the North Star State. These IWW-sponsored strikes began in 1916 with the sawmill workers and spread into the hinterlands where the men whom the lumber companies pejoratively labeled "timber beasts" lived. Government officials acceded to nearly every demand of the coal companies, mobilizing police to arrest labor leaders and even passing laws against the circulation of pamphlets. Newspapers also agreed to print a variety of stories about lumberjacks hiding caches of weapons and committing acts of terrorism with little effort to verify the accuracy of their reports.

Because some workers, IWW leaders, and Socialist agitators had acquired arms or had advocated violent resistance in the past, nearly every story that was printed became at least somewhat believable in the public mind. The IWW fought back when attacked by sheriffs and representatives of the lumber companies. The result was a number of shootouts, such as one in Washington state that left dozens wounded and seven dead in 1916. After these violent confrontations, the lumber companies received even greater assistance from law enforcement officials, which helped them crush the strikes and the IWW. Minnesota created a Commission of Public Safety that rounded up and arrested the remaining labor leaders. The state legislature even passed a law criminalizing the spread of information by those whose beliefs were considered radical or dangerous by government officials.

The most famous labor strikes of this era occurred in the minefields of Colorado and West Virginia. The Paint Creek-Cabin Creek Strike began in the spring of 1912 when unionized workers in West Virginia demanded a pay increase and coal operators retaliated against the union. The conflict quickly spread to the nonunionized coalfields and soon became a contest to determine whether workers had the right to organize and bargain collectively. A series of skirmishes between miners, state troops, police, hired "detectives" who were employed by the coal company, and men who came to the area as strikebreakers gripped the nation's headlines for an entire year. The federal government would later hold investigations into the actions of two different West Virginia governors who sided with the coal companies. This was the first time the federal government had launched an official investigation of the actions of a state government in US history—a crucial turning point in the history of states' rights versus federal authority. Most investigators believed that the state used heavy-handed tactics to help thwart the unions and the miners. Recent historians have further detailed the way that coal companies instigated violence by men hiring armed detectives to intimidate the workers. More than 200 miners and labor organizers were imprisoned, including the eighty-six-year-old union organizer "Mother" Mary Harris Jones. Many of these labor organizers faced military court-martials, while others had been imprisoned without charges. Although most, including Jones, were eventually released, the state had clearly acted on behalf of the coal operators who successfully prevented the spread of unionization throughout Appalachia.

Jones was ordered by the governor to leave the coalfields of West Virginia. She complied but did not retire from the work of representing miners. The next year, she could be found walking to and from various mining communities in the mountains of Colorado, representing the IWW and spreading news and ideas about labor activism. The Rockefellers owned a variety of mines in central Colorado where immigrant and native-born workers had been used against one another in the past to thwart labor activism. Due to the efforts of Mother Jones and the leaders of the United Mine Workers, the Colorado miners launched one of the most well-organized strikes in US labor history between September 1913 and April 1914. In that month, state troops attacked an encampment of miners and their families. The event is known today as the **Ludlow Massacre** and includes the deaths of an estimated two dozen men, women, and children.

The Colorado miners protested the long hours and low pay they were forced to endure, as well as the practices of the coal companies, which charged high rents and food prices in the mining towns that were ruled by company officials. Jones was denounced in the Senate as the "mother of all agitators." Jones reminded the Senate that at her age, she could only hope to be the "grandmother of all agitators." She countered that the conditions within the coal industry had created the strikes, not her sojourns between the camps. The coal companies convinced the state to arrest Jones and send troops. They also hired hundreds of their own private detectives armed with automatic weapons. Many of the miners had already acquired weapons of their own and vowed to fight back. The nation again watched in horror as men killed for coal, viewing the arrival of the National Guard and other federal troops as the only way to restore order.

At first the miners cheered the arrival of guardsmen, believing the governor had sent the troops to protect them from the hired guns of the coal companies. Instead, the soldiers surrounded coal camps. The result was a series of well-publicized massacres where soldiers set the men's tents on fire to force their compliant surrender. Given the tendency of the miners' families to hide in the tents for safety, this was an effective tactic to control the miners at least in the short term. After the Ludlow tent colony was set on fire, eleven children and two women were burnt to death while a dozen men were killed or wounded trying to escape or turn back to rescue their families.

Ludlow Massacre

The deadliest incident during an extended strike by coal miners, the Ludlow Massacre occurred when Colorado state troops fired on a miner's encampment.

FIGURE 5.3

One of the photos depicting the violence common during the Ludlow Massacre. Here, one of the miners stands next to one of his comrades who was killed.

News of the Ludlow Massacre bred a new spirit of worker solidarity and made the guardsmen question their orders. Area miners began walking off of their jobs and joining the fight, while many National Guard units, themselves composed primarily of working-class men, set down their weapons and denounced the governor. However, federal troops had previously been ordered into the coalfields, and at this critical moment, they arrived and arrested the leaders of the movement. The strike had failed at a tremendous cost to the state and the coal company, while dozens of miners and their families had been killed. Labor leaders and those who opposed unions soon launched a second battle, this time for historical memory. Future activists preserved the memory of the Ludlow Massacre as evidence of corporate-government collusion and the importance of protecting the right of workers to organize. Opponents of unions continued the nineteenth-century tradition of blaming organized labor for the violence that occurred in the wake of yet another strike.

1.3 Birth of the NAACP and *Birth of a Nation*

Support for racial equality remained the most obvious shortcoming of the Progressive movement, although a small number of whites joined or supported organizations dedicated to ending lynching and segregation. The Democrats remained the party of white supremacy in the South. In some areas, such as southern Indiana and Illinois, the Democrats waged local campaigns that channeled the message of Southern Democrats during Reconstruction who swore to take back their government by restoring white rule. In these areas, new patterns of migration led to contested neighborhoods where black workers in cities such as East St. Louis purchased homes in previously all-white neighborhoods and took jobs in previously all-white factories. The 1917 riots in the Illinois suburb of East St. Louis may have been the most deadly of its kind in US history. Official figures list thirty-nine black and nine white citizens as being killed during the East St. Louis Riot, but these figures were questioned at the time, and some historians estimate that at least a hundred more might have been killed. Several thousand black residents simply fled the city while hundreds of homes in black neighborhoods were destroyed. These riots were soon overshadowed by dozens of similar race riots that followed in 1919 and 1921. The nation seemed numb to the violence of these riots, perhaps related to the astounding destruction of World War I and a worldwide influenza outbreak that killed 20 to 40 million between 1918 and 1919.

FIGURE 5.4

Volunteer nurses in Oakland, California, tend to victims of the influenza pandemic who were placed inside a public auditorium and assisted by the American Red Cross.

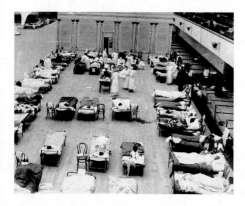

National Association for the Advancement of Colored People (NAACP)

Established in 1909 in the wake of a race riot in Springfield, Illinois, the NAACP quickly became the leading civil rights organization. In its early years, the NAACP sponsored a host of legal challenges against segregation.

A much smaller race riot that occurred nine years prior in a different Illinois community took on a greater symbolic meaning than the carnage in East St. Louis. On August 14, 1908, a white woman accused a black man in Springfield, Illinois, of sexual assault. The facts in the case quickly became immaterial as an angry mob gathered at the prison demanding that the suspect be released to them so that they might immediately lynch him without a trial. When the mob learned that the police had anticipated trouble and transferred the accused man to another jail, the mob decided to set fire to a number of black-owned businesses. Not satisfied, they set the homes of forty black residents on fire and lynched a barber who had attempted to defend his home. The next evening, the mob gathered again and charged a line of police and soldiers who were guarding the now homeless black residents of Springfield. Thwarted again by men with guns, the mob decided to lynch an elderly black man who had lived in Springfield most of his life. The man was singled out because he had married a white woman three decades prior. Fifty black families were suddenly homeless in an attack that demonstrated a mania to attack anyone who was black. Sadly, attacks such as these had occurred in nearby northern cities such as Evansville, Illinois, and Cincinnati, Ohio. However, the Springfield riot shocked the nation as two black men who had been accused of no crime had been brutally murdered in the shadow of Abraham Lincoln's historic home. If something like this could happen in Springfield, most Americans finally recognized, it could happen anywhere.

In response, a group of liberals of various racial backgrounds formed the **National Association for the Advancement of Colored People (NAACP)** in 1909. Hundreds of local, state, and even national civil rights groups had come and gone since Reconstruction. The NAACP was different for a number of important reasons. It attracted a broad and diverse nationwide membership. Although most of its national officers in its formative years were liberal whites, the local chapters of the NAACP were led by officers who were predominantly African American. At the national level, W. E. B. Du Bois was the only black officer appointed to lead the NAACP when it was founded. He was given a "token" position as the editor of the NAACP's publication department, a position that was tantamount to putting together a newsletter that would highlight the actions of the new organization. However, Du Bois soon became the most influential member of the organization when he used this position to establish *The Crisis*—the official publication of the NAACP. Much to the chagrin of some of the more conservative white officers of the NAACP at this time, *The Crisis* was uncompromising in its demand for equality and unconcerned with accommodating the views of those who advocated moderate change. While these national leaders espoused their ideas through correspondence with chapter leaders and concerned themselves mostly with clerical matters and the collection of monthly dues, Du Bois and *The Crisis* became the effective voice of the NAACP.

The strength of the NAACP was in its local chapters. These grassroots organizations won a series of small but important decisions against segregation in various Northern and Western cities during the 1910s. The most significant NAACP victory of this decade occurred in the Border South town of Louisville, Kentucky, in 1917. The city had passed an ordinance that legally mandated residential segregation. Other cities such as St. Louis and Baltimore considered similar measures that won the support of most white voters. Had the Louisville NAACP not challenged the segregation law as a violation of the Fourteenth Amendment, most major cities and hundreds of smaller communities would have likely passed similar ordinances. Racial strife regarding housing exploded in violence that killed nearly forty people in Chicago in 1919. That year, the violence spread to as far north as Connecticut and led to race riots in Western towns such as Omaha where the mayor was nearly lynched in an unsuccessful attempt to protect a black man from a mob of at least 4,000. After riddling the man's body with bullets, the men lynched his corpse, drug his body through the streets, and then set it on fire. Despite dozens of photos clearly showing the faces of the mob, the only men convicted of any crime in Omaha were those accused of damaging the courthouse.

Racial conservatives defended the Louisville segregation law as racially neutral because it forbid whites from living in predominantly black neighborhoods just as it prevented black families from buying homes in white neighborhoods. The leaders of the Louisville NAACP understood that most whites nationwide supported the law and decided to frame their arguments as a violation of property rights. As a result, they tested the law by having one of their leading white members sell a house to the president of the local chapter who was black. When the law prevented the black man from taking ownership of the house he had purchased, he backed out of the contract, leaving the white property owner empty-handed. Even supporters of the law marveled at the genius of the Louisville NAACP to create a situation where a law intended to mandate racial segregation had infringed on the property rights of a white landowner. National NAACP president and constitutional lawyer Moorfield Storey argued the case on behalf of the bereaved white landowner, arguing that his freedom to dispose of his property had been abridged by the segregation law. The Supreme Court agreed that the law was an unconstitutional abridgement of the government's responsibility to protect private property rights, although the justices added their own editorial support for residential segregation in the majority decision. As a result, the 1917 case of *Buchanan v. Warley* outlawed residential segregation laws but did little to confront the idea that white and black Americans should not live in the same neighborhoods.

The NAACP was less successful with its attempts to challenge directly the legal doctrine of separate but equal in the South, although the organization did strike down the legality of the Grandfather Clause that had exempted whites from laws restricting voter registration. NAACP chapters in Maryland and Oklahoma worked together and won a series of legal challenges to their state constitutions, which culminated in the Supreme Court decision in *Guinn v. the United States* (1915). Although the court ruled that the Grandfather Clause violated the Fifteenth Amendment, other provisions restricting black suffrage continued just as other methods of maintaining residential segregation survived *Buchanan v. Warley*.

One of the greatest successes of the NAACP nationwide was the ability of local chapters to prevent or restrict the showing of a racially charged film that became the first Hollywood blockbuster. *Birth of a Nation* was a historically themed drama depicting Reconstruction as a tragic era where former slaves were foolishly permitted to vote and hold office. Along with a coterie of corrupt white liberal carpetbaggers bent on destroying the South, the film suggested that former slaves who were suddenly elevated to positions in government demonstrated incompetence and depravity. The film portrayed white women being ravaged by black men while the would-be heroes of the region, the former Confederates, were barred from their natural role as leaders and protectors by an invading army of Yankee soldiers. In the end, the Ku Klux Klan emerges in the film as the "protectors" of the South, and white Yankees and Southerners experience a rapprochement based on a return to normalcy through mutual recognition of white supremacy as an inherent truth. The silent film began with a screenshot displaying a quote of the sitting president and former professor of history Woodrow Wilson. "The white men were aroused by a mere instinct of self-preservation," viewers were informed, "until at last there sprung into existence a great Ku Klux Klan, a veritable empire of the South, to protect the Southern country." The quote was taken from one of the leading US history textbooks, one that Wilson had authored and that reflected the dominant view of Reconstruction by white historians at this time.

FIGURE 5.5

The very first image of *The Crisis*, the official journal of the NAACP.

Buchanan v. Warley

A lawsuit sponsored by the Louisville NAACP that challenged and defeated the city's residential segregation law. This was a significant victory because a number of other cities such as Baltimore and St. Louis were about to pass similar laws.

FIGURE 5.6

A still image from the film *Birth of a Nation*. This film was the most-viewed movie in Hollywood history and was shown in theaters for several decades. The movie depicted the Klan as heroic, black voters as unprepared for citizenship, and the unification of the North and South based on a common recognition of Aryan supremacy.

FIGURE 5.7 Pioneering Black Filmmaker Oscar Micheaux

African American historians countered this heroic view of the Klan with their own interpretations of the past. In addition, scores of local NAACP chapters protested against the racist implications of the film. In dozens of cities and even a handful of states such as Kansas and West Virginia, white and black members of the NAACP passed special laws barring the showing of films that might incite racial hatred. These small victories united individual chapters and may have accounted for the rapid growth and sustainability of the NAACP in an era when attempts to pass national legislation against Jim Crow and lynching were repeatedly blocked by Southern Democrats. African American author and filmmaker Oscar Micheaux responded to the commercial success of *Birth of a Nation* by directing films that depicted black history from Africa to America. Micheaux directed more than forty movies that employed black actors and actresses and presented the black perspective of African American history. Many of Micheaux's films and books were inspired by his experience as a homesteader in South Dakota. In fact, it was his third novel about a black homesteader in this region that led to his "discovery" by a black-owned film company that was founded in Lincoln, Nebraska, before moving to Los Angeles.

Micheaux also formed his own commercial studio based out of Chicago and produced films such as *The Homesteader* and *Within Our Gates*. These were among the first "race films"—that is, movies made by black filmmakers for black audiences. Micheaux strictly guarded the independence of his projects and created dramatic films that portrayed black history, as well as dramas featuring dignified black women and men who played the roles of heroines and heroes rather than fools or villains. As a result, these early years are sometimes called the "golden era of black cinema." However, experts in black film history, such as modern director Melvin Van Peebles, have also demonstrated the tremendous sacrifices that were made by these early pioneers. Black film producers such as Micheaux surrendered the profits their creative energies might have produced making comedies. The black actors and actresses who rejected the stereotypical roles Hollywood offered also rejected the wealth and fame some black actors achieved. For example, Lincoln Perry earned over $1 million playing the character of Stepin Fetchit. Although Perry was both talented and well educated and could have played a variety of characters, his on-stage buffoonery appealed to racist images at a time when black actors and actresses in Hollywood were limited to roles as cowardly brutes, submissive fools, and contented servants. Race films themselves rarely made money, but from the perspective of black audiences, the sacrifices of these pioneers offered a few precious seconds of humanity on the silver screen.

1.4 Origin of the Great War

Austria-Hungary was a divided and crumbling empire—so much so that its government actually had two different and often competing centers of government. Seeking to reassert its authority over the Balkans, Austria-Hungary seized control of Bosnia and Herzegovina in 1908. This action deeply angered many Slavic people throughout the region. Tensions remained high throughout the Balkans and peaked in June 1914 when Austria-Hungary's Archduke Franz Ferdinand was assassinated by an advocate of Slavic nationhood and independence. The individual who committed the deed was tied to a nationalist movement based out of the independent nation of Serbia. This group and many others supported a growing independence movement among ethnic Serbs within Austria-Hungary. In addition to the Serbs, nearly a dozen other subject peoples representing various ethnic groups sought to free themselves of imperial rule and create their own independent nations. Facing internal revolt that threatened the implosion of their empire, the leaders of Austria-Hungary felt that they must make an example of Serbia. However, the situation was complicated by an alliance between Serbia and Russia that required each nation to come to the other's defense.

FIGURE 5.8

Europe was dominated by a few leading empires, each of which had a number of alliances with other European empires. This map demonstrates the emergence of two alliance systems, the Triple Entente and the Central Powers. It also indicates the divisions within Austria-Hungary among various ethnic groups. Notice the position of Serbia, a small nation that was allied with Russia.

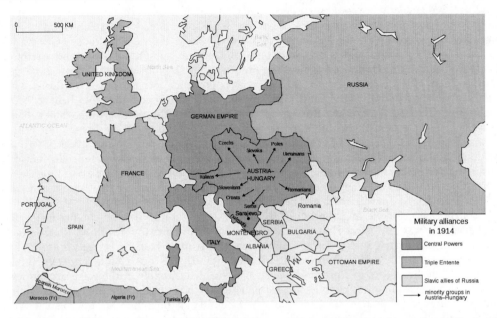

The political and diplomatic situation throughout Europe was equally complex and volatile. Imperial rivalries, territorial conflicts, arms buildups, and a series of military alliances created the possibility that a regional conflict like what was emerging in the Balkans might expand until it involved nearly all of the leading armies of the world. Unresolved conflicts and historic grievances throughout Central Europe framed the tensions. Prussia (the dominant state of what would become modern Germany) had defeated France in 1871 and acquired the formerly French territory of Alsace-Lorraine. Neither of the countries considered the matter settled, and both nations garrisoned an increasing number of troops along their common border. Each nation also formed alliances with neighboring nations. These alliances discouraged either from precipitating a war to seize more territory, yet they also increased the likelihood that any war between the two nations would expand beyond France and Germany.

The forts and troops along the German-French border represented only a fraction of the rapidly expanding armed forces of Europe in early 1900. England, France, Germany, Russia, Italy, Belgium, and other imperial powers sought to expand their global empires. Most of these local battles were waged by and on colonized peoples. European conquest was dependent on exploitation of long-standing political, ethnic, and religious divisions. Even as millions throughout Africa and Asia attempted to maintain their independence, others found themselves fighting on behalf of Europeans for a variety of reasons. Europeans were likewise divided, and imperial competition led to dozens of small conflicts between each of these nations along the contested borders of their overseas colonies. However, in each case, great efforts were made to make sure that warfare did not spread into Continental Europe. The brief Franco-Prussian War was the only war fought in Europe between these nations between Napoleon's defeat in 1815 and the outbreak of World War I ninety-nine years later. From the perspective of Africans, Asians, and many peoples in Southern Europe and the Middle East, historians who refer to this period as a time of peace demonstrate a callous indifference to their struggle. From the perspective of many Europeans, the nineteenth century was one of territorial expansion while avoiding direct armed conflict with other imperial powers.

Diplomacy was key to maintaining the status quo in this imperial conflict, just as naval power was key to expansion. Britain maintained a navy that was more than double the size of its next closest rival. However, surface ships were vulnerable to submarines that were nearly impossible to detect until the development of effective sonar technology in World War II. Germany led the way in developing a modern submarine fleet, but the rapprochement between Britain, France, and Russia was less a response to the growth of German naval power than the economic and military potential of this newly unified nation on the continent of Europe. As the German economy and military modernized and expanded, these three historical rivals formed military alliances intended to neutralize potential German territorial ambitions. From the Germans' perspective, these alliances appeared to be a concerted effort to isolate and perhaps even attack their nation. The Germans responded to what they labeled *einkreisung* (encirclement) by strengthening their alliances with the Ottoman Empire and Austria-Hungary. Unfortunately for Germany, these two allies were both declining empires, while Britain, France, and

Russia were gaining in economic and military power each year. As a result, by the early 1900s, some in the German military were calling for a "preventive strike" that might reduce the territory of rivals such as France before the comparative military strength of Germany and her allies declined any further.

From the perspective of the German chancellor, the conflict in the Balkans seemed like the ideal pretext to launch such an attack under the guise of supporting Germany's beleaguered ally. If Austria-Hungary could be induced to attack Serbia, Russia would be bound by treaty to mobilize its army in defense of tiny Serbia. Germany could then declare war on Russia in the name of defending its own ally. Because France was an ally of Russia, this might also serve as a pretext for a quick German attack on France. This offensive into France was harder to justify; however, France had attacked Germany in the recent past. Given the long-standing grievance between Germany and France, a preventive strike might be vindicated as a necessary defense against the French. After all, France might have viewed the German deployment of troops to the south and east as an opportunity to seize its lost territories. Long before the assassination of Franz Ferdinand, German generals had devised a plan they believed would allow them to defeat both France and Russia. Using a quick strike through Belgium, rather than along the heavily armed German-French border, German forces could outflank the French army and seize Paris within six weeks. The plan was based on the assumptions that Russia's massive army would mobilize slowly and that the attack of France would succeed, allowing Germany to redeploy its victorious troops to the east before the bulk of the Russian army could mobilize against Austria-Hungary. Britain was the wildcard in such a scenario, but the Germans were willing to gamble that Britain would risk its own security to defend France, which had been their chief rival throughout history.

Had it not been for the intervention of Germany, it is doubtful that the conflict in the Balkans would have led to war. If Austria-Hungary invaded Serbia while Germany stood idle, Russia would easily crush Austria-Hungary. Such a defeat would encourage Austria-Hungary's rivals in the Balkans, as well as the various groups within their empire who sought independence. No one understood this situation better than the leaders of Austria-Hungary, who treaded carefully in the wake of their assassinated leader. They felt honor bound to issue a list of demands to Serbia demanding an investigation and various measures to prevent future attacks on their country by anarchists and Serbian nationalists. When Serbian officials agreed to nearly every demand, many believed the conflict would be resolved through diplomacy. After all, dozens of previous conflicts that appeared much more serious had been peacefully resolved in recent decades. However, German leaders pushed Austria-Hungary to declare war on Serbia. German officials promised unconditional military support for Austria-Hungary if Russia or any other nation joined the conflict. From the perspective of Austria-Hungary, this unsolicited German assistance could help them crush their foes in the Balkans and secure their empire against various nationalists and dissidents within their own borders.

From the German perspective, offering this assurance (known by historians as the "blank check theory") was a means by which they might later attack Russia and France in the name of defending Austria-Hungary. Had Germany been victorious, this outcome may have become the official historical interpretation of the origins of the war. Instead, Germany's decision to invade France via neutral Belgium inspired the anger of England and would later be cited as one of the leading justifications for US intervention. After receiving Germany's unconditional support, Austria-Hungary declared war on Serbia on July 28, 1914. Russia responded by mobilizing its forces as expected; Germany then kept its promise by sending troops to aid Austria-Hungary. Germany also launched its secret plan to invade Belgium as a means of attacking France. Unfortunately for Germany, England honored its treaty to aid France. The Ottoman Empire honored its commitment to Germany, as did Bulgaria. Because of these treaties and alliances, German leaders had engineered a situation where a conflict in the Balkans led into a global war. World War I placed the **Central Powers** of Germany, Austria-Hungary, the Ottoman Empire, and Bulgaria against the **Allied Powers** of Britain, France, and Russia. By 1917, the United States also joined the Allied Powers. Italy originally refused to join the conflict, despite its treaty with Germany. Italian neutrality proved short lived, however, as opportunistic Italian leaders later joined the Allied Powers when it became apparent that doing so might lead to territorial acquisition.

The fighting ended in November 1918, and the Treaty of Versailles was signed the following year. One of the provisions of this treaty required the defeated Germans to accept all the blame for starting the war. While it is difficult to find reasons against assigning primary blame to Germany, it is important to consider the culpability of other nations. It is also important not to confuse the aims of Germany in 1914 with those of Hitler in 1939. In World War I, German leaders hoped to fight a quick and limited war against France, similar to the Franco-Prussian War of 1871. They believed they could expand their territory and unite their people in such a conflict. They also believed that failure to take the initiative would leave Germany increasingly vulnerable to an attack by France or another rival power in the future. Germans feared that this attack might come when its own allies (the crumbling empires of Austria-Hungary and the Ottoman Empire) would not be in a position to aid them. The German chancellor did not predict that England would enter the war to defend France or that the United States would join the fight in 1917. Most importantly, no one in 1914 understood that the war would turn into a nightmare of attrition that would leave 9 million dead. As a result, most European leaders and a surprising number of European troops welcomed the news of war during the fall of 1914. Inspired by a

Central Powers

Originally based on the Triple Alliance of Germany, Austria-Hungary, and Italy, the Central Powers were nations that fought together against the Allied Powers during World War I. Italy joined the war on the side of the Allied Powers, while the Ottoman Empire and Bulgaria joined the Central Powers.

Allied Powers

Originally based on the Triple Entente of France, Britain and Russia, the Allied Powers were nations that fought together during World War I against the Central Powers. The Allied Powers grew to include Italy, Japan, Belgium, and the United States.

youth spent playing with toy soldiers and reading dime novels full of sanitized images of war, most men viewed war as a grand coming-of-age adventure and a test of their manhood. Imagining the future glory of their nation and themselves in the fall of 1914, millions of grown men promised their wives and children that they would return home as heroes by Christmas. A third of those who survived returned with crippling injuries, while the rest returned with a chastened perspective about the glory of war.

1.5 Race, Revolution, and War in the American Southwest

The Mexican Revolution began in 1910, leading to the removal of the dictatorial government of President Porfirio Diaz. Many Mexican citizens supported Diaz's successor, Francisco Madero, and his government's support of democratic reforms. Among Madero's supporters was a former outlaw known as **Francisco "Pancho" Villa**, who had received weapons and other assistance from the United States due to his opposition of Diaz. However, Madero was murdered in 1913, and General Vicotiano Huerta seized power. After Madero's death and for the next four years, a civil war raged between the supporters of Huerta and various other political and military leaders. Villa opposed both Huerta and his chief rival, Venustiano Carranza. However, Villa believed that Carranza was the better of the two and agreed to help him seize power from General Huerta in 1914. Carranza held off other challengers and was eventually given the official recognition of the Wilson administration. US officials recognized that Carranza's government was not democratic, but hoped his dictatorship would at least lead to greater stability in Mexico. Villa resolved to continue fight in hopes of ousting Carranza, a decision that led the US government to withdraw its aid to Villa's supporters. The Wilson administration feared the only alternative to Carranza was civil war. From Pancho Villa's perspective, he and those who favored a genuine revolution of the people had been betrayed by both the United States and the new government of Mexico. Villa and his supporters (known as Villistas) vowed to fight on, even though they numbered only a few thousand men with dwindling supplies.

Americans of Mexican descent were keenly aware of the issues facing their homeland. Revolutionary philosopher and leftist political activist Ricardo Flores Magòn had mobilized Mexican Americans against the Diaz regime. After serving a prison sentence for attempting to start an armed anti-Diaz uprising in Tijuana and throughout Baja California, Magòn also began speaking out against the discrimination Mexican Americans faced in their own country. The vast majority of Mexican Americans, from fieldworkers to landowners, rejected most of Magòn's more militant ideas. However, his Los Angeles-based newspaper *Regeneraciòn* inspired a small number of committed followers who dedicated themselves to a revolutionary plot known as **Plan de San Diego**. The original intent of this plan was to support an armed revolution that would lead to the formation of an independent republic from the US states that had once been a part of Mexico. Whites in Texas, New Mexico, California, Colorado, and Arizona would later believe that this revolutionary plot to capture their states had been planned by Germans or other outsiders. However, it is now clear that the declining social and economic condition faced by people of Mexican descent in these states inspired at least 1,000 men to pledge their loyalty to Plan de San Diego.

Many of these revolutionaries were former ranch owners, while others had depended on the dwindling haciendas of the Southwest for their living. Others were drawn to Plan de San Diego by the racism of the Anglo newcomers. Prior to the land rush, most of the Anglos who had chosen to live in the agricultural valleys of South Texas, Arizona, New Mexico, and California either genuinely accepted their neighbors as equals or at least downplayed any feelings of racial or and ethnic prejudice toward the Hispanic majority. In the 1930s, scholar Jovita Gonzalez documented the experiences of these borderlands and found that both Anglos and people of Mexican descent proudly maintained their cultural heritage while respecting one another prior to the great land rushes that brought more Anglos to the region at the turn of the century. Intermarriage was common and even celebrated as a form of diplomacy and synergistic cultural exchange. Although discrimination and quarrels did occur, these conflicts were usually negotiated peacefully, and those who could not abide "the other's" presence either became pariahs or simply chose to leave the region. The land rush and the enclosure of individual farms introduced conflict as the newcomers pledged to make the borderlands "a white man's country." For Anglos, the creation of family and commercial farms that served a market-based economy represented progress. For those of Mexican descent, the Anglo influx threatened to destroy their way of life. The title of one of Jovita Gonzalez's early works, *With the Coming of the Barbed Wire Came Hunger*, reflects that fact that borderland conflict was not simply an ethnic or cultural struggle. For people of Hispanic descent, Anglo colonization had profound economic implications.

Francisco "Pancho" Villa

A leading general during the Mexican Revolution, Pancho Villa received American assistance until the US government officially recognized the government of Venustiano Carranza as the legitimate government of Mexico. In retaliation for what he viewed as betrayal, Villa attacked American citizens and the town of Columbus, New Mexico.

Plan de San Diego

A revolutionary scheme of Ricardo Flores Magòn that called for the recapture of American land that once belonged to Mexico.

FIGURE 5.9

A political cartoon showing a diminutive Pancho Villa fleeing an angry Uncle Sam who is crossing into Mexico. In the background is a smoldering fire, a reference to Villa's attack on Columbus, New Mexico.

Magòn and his followers believed that the Mexican Revolution provided an opportunity to challenge the status quo and spread the revolutionary sentiment of Plan de San Diego. In New Mexico, Mexican and Mexican American vigilante groups launched raids against commercial farms and ranches they believed had stolen land belonging to formerly independent rancheros. They hoped to unite Asians and African Americans and encourage them to join their cause but failed to find much support even among the majority of Mexican Americans in the region. A major reason for the lack of popular support was the violent rhetoric that some revolutionaries espoused. Like Magòn, many of these groups were influenced by the ideas of anarchists. For example, the name of one band of New Mexico vigilantes translates to "The Black Hand"—the name of the Serbian anarchist group that would be blamed for planning the assassination of Austrian Archduke Franz Ferdinand that led to World War I.

The deadly conflicts that erupted in the borderland would also share connections with World War I. The most violent of these occurred in South Texas and near the railroad towns of Columbus, New Mexico, and El Paso, Texas. Several hundred were killed and at least a million dollars of property was destroyed between July 1915 and the end of 1917. The first shots were fired by raiders hoping to seize property and drive white settlers out of the region, but the majority of the killings were committed by the Texas Rangers, various US Army and National Guard units, and armed white vigilantes. Atrocities were committed by both sides, and many peaceful settlers of Mexican descent were killed or jailed in the various roundups that followed each outbreak of violence. About half of the white and Mexican settlers of some farming communities simply fled north or south, while many others who had hoped to avoid the conflict felt their best chance of survival was to join with a particular side or faction. The exodus led to a severe labor shortage and an effort to quarantine "good Mexicans," a euphemism for a laborer who did not support Magòn and other revolutionaries. By September 1915, reports of executions and lynchings of Mexican and Mexican Americans along the border were so commonplace that they were no longer newsworthy. "It is only when a raid is reported, or an [Anglo] is killed, that the ire of the people is aroused," a local commentator explained.

By the spring of 1916, Carranza's government was able to bring most of the raids originating from Mexico to stop. The people of the borderlands remained on guard, however, as supporters of Pancho Villa indicated their desire to retaliate against the United States for its support of Carranza and to capture weapons and supplies. Villa and five hundred of his supporters attacked the town of Columbus, New Mexico, in March 1916. These attacks resulted in the deaths of over a dozen US soldiers and civilians. **General John Pershing** led thousands of US troops into Mexico to pursue the former US ally Pancho Villa. Although the Carranza administration opposed Villa, it demanded that Pershing withdraw and regarded the US military's uninvited presence in Mexico as tantamount to invasion.

Tensions between the two countries regarding US military presence in Mexico had already been high after a deadly clash in the Mexican city of Veracruz that occurred on April 21, 1914. A small group of US sailors had been arrested for entering an area that was off-limits to foreigners. Mexican officials released these men to their commanders, who inexplicably demanded that these Mexican officers salute them and the US flag as a symbolic apology for enforcing the law. Under the pretext of an insult to national honor, US troops responded to the imagined slight by occupying the city of Veracruz. Nineteen US servicemen and perhaps as many as 200 Mexican lives were lost in resulting street battles. As a result, many Mexican citizens viewed Pershing's 12,000 troops with suspicion when they entered Mexico and feared that the tens of thousands of National Guardsmen who were sent to the border might become the vanguard of an invading army. After all, Villa's attack and the insecurity along the border was at least perceived as a compelling reason to start a war as the pretenses cited by the Polk administration when the United States invaded Mexico in 1846. However, Pershing's men failed to locate Villa, who retained his popularity as a Robin Hood figure among the residents of Northern Mexico.

The incident revealed the unpreparedness of the US Army and led to extremely high tensions between the United States and Mexico. These two factors also influenced Germany's later decision to propose an alliance with Mexico. If the United States should later decide to enter World War I on the side of the British and French, German officials pledged to help Mexico recapture various Southwestern states if Mexico would join the war as a German ally. Germany hoped that the United States would be unable to send a sizeable force to Europe if they also had to fight a defensive war along their extended border with Mexico. British intelligence intercepted this communication, known as the **Zimmerman Telegram**, on January 1917. Because Germany and the United States were at peace at this time, revelation of this poorly conceived plot helped influence the US decision to enter the war. Although Mexico immediately declined Germany's offer, the Zimmerman Telegram further inflamed the tensions and fears between Anglos, Mexican Americans, and Mexicans in the Southwest. For the rest of the nation, the failure of the US military to locate Villa played into the arguments of both sides of the growing debate about whether the United States should increase military funding.

General John Pershing

The commander of American forces in Europe during World War I. Because he had once served as a commander of African American troops, he was given the derisive nickname "Black Jack." The 10th Cavalry was one of the finest units in the US military, so the nickname demonstrates the pervasiveness of racism in the military and the nation at this time.

Zimmerman Telegram

A communication sent by a German ambassador to officials in Mexico, offering an alliance against the United States. Although Mexico never seriously considered aiding the German cause, the Zimmerman Telegram led to increased tensions along the US-Mexican border.

REVIEW AND CRITICAL THINKING

1. Explain how efforts to prevent monopolies and regulate the financial sector continued during the late Progressive Era. What was the significance of the laws such as the Federal Reserve Act and the Clayton Anti-Trust Act? What kinds of tax policies did Progressives favor?

2. Describe the differences between labor unions such as the IWW and the AFL. What were the experiences of miners who sought to form unions during these years? What was the significance of violence in these conflicts, and what role did state and federal governments play?

3. What was the significance of the film *Birth of a Nation*, and how did African Americans confront these kinds of negative stereotypes? What led to the formation of the NAACP and how did this organization challenge segregation and racial bigotry in its first decade of existence?

4. How did the assassination of an Austrian leader lead to a global war? Explain the causes of World War I.

5. Why did the United States support Pancho Villa during the early years of the Mexican Revolution? Describe how relations between Mexico and the United States became strained during these years, and how these events affected and were influenced by World War I.

2. THE GREAT WAR AND AMERICA

2.1 The War in Europe and the Russian Revolution

Schlieffen Plan

A strategic German offensive based on attacking France through Belgium rather than their shared border. This plan was drafted long before World War I, a fact that has been cited as proof of German bellicosity. However, most of Europe's leading empires had multiple contingency plans for various offensive and defensive strategies.

The **Schlieffen Plan** had been developed in advance by German military commanders and proposed a way to win a quick and limited war in France by attacking through Belgium rather than the well-defended border between Germany and France. After prevailing over France, German commanders planned to transfer these troops to counter the threat posed by the Russian army in east. Following the strategy laid out by the Schlieffen Plan, German troops entered Belgium on August 3, 1914. They initially encountered much stronger resistance than they had expected, and some of the German commanders responded by ordering cities burned to the ground. The resistance delayed the German advance and allowed France to begin redeploying its troops. On the Eastern Front, Russian forces mobilized much faster than anticipated and threatened East Prussia. The German high command placed General Paul von Hindenburg in charge of the defense of Germany's Eastern Front and shifted some of the troops planned to participate in the invasion of France to the east. At the Battle of Tannenberg in late August, Russian troops were surrounded, and over 70,000 were killed or wounded before the remaining 90,000 surrendered. The Russian defeat temporarily neutralized the threat to Germany in the east, although this success came at the cost of reducing the number of German forces in the west. Due to Belgian resistance and the redeployment of forces, Germany did not secure its hold on Belgium until August 20.

FIGURE 5.10

This map shows the French and German battle plans. The French hoped to cross into Southern Germany while the German Schlieffen Plan was based on a quick offensive through Belgium and Northern France.

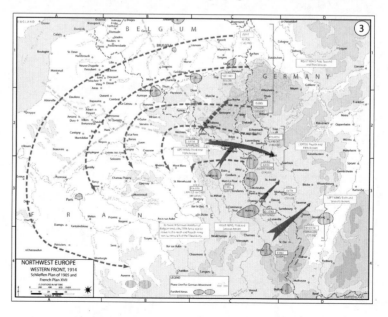

Britain's relatively small land army rushed to eastern France and joined the French in their defense against the German army. In general, this action was a fighting retreat, and by September 5, the Germans had reached France's Marne River. By this time, French troops had been transferred from the southern border with Germany and mounted a fierce resistance in the **Battle of the Marne**. In the next week, a million troops on each side clashed, dug defensive trenches, and attempted to outflank the other's lines of defense. The French stalled the German offensive at the Battle of the Marne and forced the Germans to fall back behind a line of defensive trenches forty miles east of the Marne River. Behind these trenches, the Germans rallied and were able to halt the British and French counterattack.

Each side attempted to go around the other's trenches while rapidly constructing its own line of defensive fortifications, complete with artillery and machine-gun nests. In an era before modern tanks and aircraft, neither side could overrun the other's trenches with infantry and cavalry charges. As a result, whichever side could maneuver around the other's trenches would hold the upper hand. In what has been dubbed "The Race to the Sea," both sides sought to maneuver their forces north before the other could counter. The race was a draw, and the Western Front was transformed into nearly five hundred miles of frontline trenches after neither side was able to outflank and get around the trenches the other was constructing. In front of these networks lay a vast no-man's-land where millions of rounds of ammunition and artillery shells killed every living thing. Behind the trenches was a vast network of miles of secondary trenches. When both sides reached the English Channel, and with nowhere else to maneuver, a deadlock ensued.

The German failure was a result of underestimating Belgium and French resistance, assuming Britain would not send its army to defend France, and underestimating the speed of Russian mobilization. As a result, Germany was forced to fight a war on multiple fronts—the very thing the Schlieffen Plan was designed to prevent. In the next four years, millions died during a series of failed attempts to push the enemy from the relative safety of its disease and vermin-infested trenches. Millions of men lived in these trenches, enduring daily artillery barrages and the constant threat of sniper fire if they ever allowed their head to rise above ground level. Mud and human refuse were constant companions, as were diseases such as trench foot, which could only be cured by amputation.

FIGURE 5.11

This map shows the location of both armies along a long defensive line of trenches after the French stalled the German offensive at the Battle of the Marne in 1914. For the next three years, the bulk of the fighting in the Western Front was along this line of trenches.

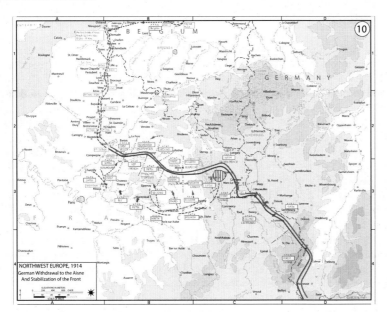

Americans were shocked by the daily carnage of this war of attrition as tens of millions of rounds of artillery shells were launched and frequent attempts were made to overcome hundreds of machine-gun crews by massing thousands of men in deadly frontal assaults. At various points, both sides attempted to overwhelm the other by sending a human tidal wave over the top of their trenches and across no-man's-land. Germany launched just such an offensive in February 1916 in hopes of overwhelming the French fortress city of Verdun. Even though the Germans succeeded in taking Verdun, the French simply constructed more defensive fortifications just past the city, which negated any tactical advantage the Germans might have won. France then responded with its own counterattack against the exhausted Germans, which resulted in the recapture of Verdun. After ten months, over a million men were killed or injured in the battle around Verdun, and neither side had gained any ground. The British launched

Battle of the Marne

A major turning point in World War I, British and French troops stopped the German offensive in a week of heavy fighting in early September 1914. Both sides formed defensive trenches that neither were able to surmount, marking the transition to a war of attrition.

a similar offensive between July and November 1916. Known as the Battle of the Somme, the British advanced only six miles and lost a million casualties.

The Germans had greater success on the Eastern Front, capturing Warsaw and driving Russian troops back from their previous advance, and inflicting 2 million casualties in 1915 alone. Russia's immense army absorbed these losses, while launching its own successful offensives against Austria-Hungary. The Russian advance motivated Romania to enter the war on the side of the Allied Powers, even though it had earlier formed an alliance with Germany. Like Romania, Italy had been aligned with Germany, but it declared neutrality at the start of the war and later joined the Allied Powers in hopes of territorial preservation and expansion. Similar to the experience of Romania, Italy enjoyed modest success against the forces of Austria-Hungary but was unable to defeat the German reinforcements that were later sent to Southern Europe. The greatest suffering in the east was borne by the Russians. An estimated 3.6 million soldiers were killed or missing while 2.1 million men languished in German prisoner-of-war camps. In a nation that was already suffering internal turmoil before the war, Russians turned against their government, who they held responsible for the war and the famine that ravaged the countryside.

The **Russian Revolution** began in February, leading to the abdication and eventual execution of the czar. At first, Russians were optimistic that their provisional government would restore stability. However, the Russian army suffered reverses in the field, while vital resources were diverted from the people of Russia to support the war effort. Worker's councils known as "Soviets" demanded increasing authority over the political affairs of the nation. As the war continued to bring little but suffering to the Russian people, a Socialist Party known as the Bolsheviks emerged as the leading political faction in Russia. The Bolsheviks enjoyed the support of the peasants and workers with their promise to end the war immediately and provide landownership for farmers and collective ownership of factories for urban workers.

The Bolsheviks were led by Vladimir Lenin who seized power in November 1917 and quickly signed an armistice halting the war between Germany and Russia. By March, the cease-fire was permanent with the signing of the Brest-Litovsk Treaty, which declared a formal end to hostilities between Germany and Lenin's Socialist government in Russia. A civil war between Lenin's supporters and his opponents waged for the next two years in Russia, but the supporters of Lenin prevailed against those who sought a return to the czarist government. A small contingent of American troops was deployed to aid those who opposed the Bolsheviks. Although militarily insignificant, the US intervention demonstrated the hostility of many Americans toward Socialism and led to strained relations between the two countries.

Along the Western Front, men who were conscripted into the French army began refusing orders they believed were suicidal. Similar refusals to go over the top were encountered among German and British troops who felt no desire to prove their patriotism by advancing against machine guns in battles that sacrificed the lives of tens of thousands of troops to achieve marginal strategic gains. In January 1917, President Wilson had attempted to capitalize on a nascent but growing peace movement in Europe. He hoped to negotiate an agreement whereby each belligerent nation would agree to return to the territorial status quo before the war. The German Reichstag met in July 1917 and discussed Wilson's idea of "peace without victory." The Catholic Centre Party and the Socialists declared their willingness to discuss peace under these conditions. Although many leftists and moderates throughout Europe likewise favored the idea and the plan actually secured the support of a majority in the German Reichstag, the leaders of Europe rejected the idea. A similar plan brokered by the pope also failed.

Two main reasons account for the failure of these attempted negotiations. First, the leaders of Europe still hoped and believed that they would ultimately prevail. To accept a return to the status quo in the midst of the war would be tantamount to admitting that the decision to enter the war was a mistake and millions of soldiers had died in vain. Second, hostility and fear about the growing power of Socialist parties throughout Eastern and Western Europe made those in power even more hesitant to end the war. The Socialists had grown largely because of their consistent opposition to the war as a Capitalist plot. Regardless of the validity of such a theory, ending the war without declaring a victor would raise grave questions about the lofty pronouncements that were made to justify the war and even more questions about the present leadership of one's nation. Fearful that ending the war would fuel the growth of Socialism, even Wilson sought to thwart the efforts of Socialists who were holding peace conferences throughout Europe. Confident in their eventual victory, while privately candid about the limited value of any potential new territory in comparison to what had been sacrificed to obtain it, the leaders of Europe continued the war. Each believed that only victory might justify the lives of the millions who had already perished.

2.2 From Neutrality to War

As the war waged in Europe, President Wilson counseled Americans to be "neutral in thought as well as action." Even as the nation reasserted its neutrality, neither the president nor the majority of

Russian Revolution

A popularly supported revolution that overthrew the Tsarist government of Russia in February 1917. After a period of civil war, the Bolshevik Party seized power, installed a Socialist government, and signed an armistice with Germany prior to the end of World War I.

FIGURE 5.12

In the wake of the Russian Revolution, both Russia and Romania signed an armistice with Germany. Both nations were forced to accept severe terms by the Germans. In this French image, Germany is crushing a man representing Russia and holding a knife to the neck of a woman representing Russia.

Americans really followed the spirit of this advice. A third of the nation's people were either European immigrants or the sons or daughters of these "new Americans." Many Americans of German descent identified with their homeland, while those from Central Europe had a variety of loyalties and concerns that also outweighed their president's decree. Irish Americans nursed a deep and historic distrust of England. French, British, Belgian, and Russian immigrants understandably favored the Allied Powers. Most American leaders in politics and business were of Western European origins and strongly favored Britain. Sentiment, geography, and the effectiveness of the British naval blockade of German ports in the North Sea led most American businesses to trade with Britain and France. Although neutrality implied that the United States would not act in a manner that favored either side, American farmers provided two-thirds of the food consumed by British soldiers and civilians. Although France had once boasted a productive agricultural system, the loss of labor and the destruction of the French countryside east of Paris created a situation where the French were also increasingly dependent on grain provided by American farmers. American forests, mines, and factories also produced finished goods and raw materials that were essential to the war effort of Britain and France.

FIGURE 5.13

This map from the *New York Times* depicts the war as a contest not only between governments and nations but between various races.

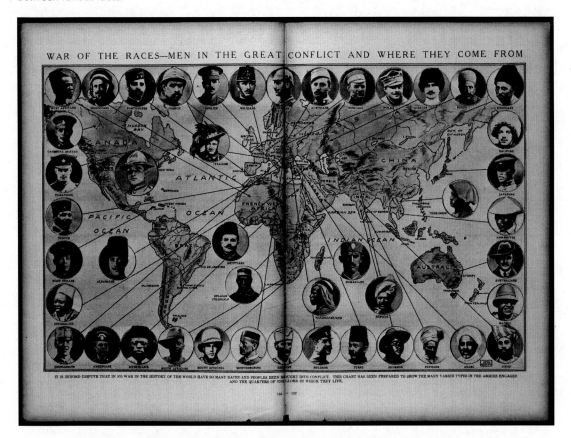

As the war dragged on and the western Allied nations could no longer afford to purchase these vital resources with cash, US banks provided the governments and businesses of Western Europe with billions of dollars of loans and credit. Despite its neutrality, the federal government also provided loans to the Allied Powers. German Americans invested $25 million in German banks, a trifling amount in comparison to the billions that were provided to England and France. However, the existence of aid and investment to all nations provided some substance to American claims of neutrality. Secretary of State William Jennings Bryan feared that the trade and credit imbalance might eventually lead the United States into the war to protect US investments, the bulk of which were tied to the fortunes of Britain and France. As an isolationist, he had spent much of the past decade and a half demonstrating the tendency of American loans and investments in Latin America to lead to military intervention in this region. Bryan eventually resigned his position in protest of America's drift toward the Allied Powers, an occurrence that was welcomed by those favoring greater American intervention and investment. Because America's historic, economic, and cultural ties to England and France were far stronger than Germany, American neutrality strongly favored the Allied Powers.

Germany recognized that the Western Allies were dependent on American food and credit. The Germans hoped that they might counter this threat by unleashing their submarines on British and

French ships that were transporting American-made food and material across the Atlantic. Germany had only 24 submarines in 1914 but had expanded its fleet to 120 submarines by 1917. The German government declared that the sea-lanes leading to Europe and France were war zones and warned Americans that any ship heading toward these ports would be sunk. Americans protested this German declaration as a violation of the rights of neutral nations and a defilement of the international concept of freedom of the seas. Ironically, a similar declaration by the British navy regarding the North Sea—which provided access to German ports—had aroused little concern among most Americans.

On May 15, 1915, a German U-boat sunk the British freighter *Lusitania*. Of the 1,200 lives lost, 128 were Americans. Despite the fact that the *Lusitania* was carrying a billion dollars' worth of war material, including 4 to 6 million rounds of ammunition, most Americans viewed the sinking of the *Lusitania* as an act of unprovoked aggression. Germans defended the measure as an act of self-defense and emphasized that they had even published warnings to civilians about the danger of traveling on British vessels—some of which specifically named the *Lusitania* as a target. However, Germany recognized that the sinking of ships with civilian passengers on board would only unite their opponents and might even lead the United States into the war. As a result, the German navy declared that it would not sink any more civilian vessels without first providing for the safety of those on board.

Despite these assurances, the *Lusitania* sinking had already inspired Congress to approve a dramatic peacetime expansion of the US military. The **National Defense Act of 1916** doubled the size of the army to 175,000 soldiers and authorized $600 million for new ship construction. These expenditures were financed by an expansion of the income tax system to include modest taxes on the middle class and significant taxes on armaments companies that were profiting from the war. When a French passenger ferry named the *Sussex* was also sunk on March 14, 1916, Germany again pledged that it would not attack civilian vessels without first providing for the safety of occupants. This renewed promise was strengthened by some specific guidance and became known as the **Sussex Pledge**. Unfortunately for German naval commanders, the Sussex Pledge neutralized the only advantage submarines enjoyed over other vessels—the element of surprise. Germany promised its submarines would rise to the surface and summon other boats to provide space for passengers. Of course, such an action might prove suicidal for German submarine crews if a suspected civilian vessel turned out to be a British or French warship. As a result, the Sussex Pledge led to a sudden decline in the effective deployment of German submarines in the Atlantic.

By early 1917, German leaders believed that the French and British could not continue the war for long if they were denied access to US supplies. They also recognized that their own ability to supply their armies was dwindling and that civilian support for the war was declining. The Germans calculated that even if the United States entered the war, it would take at least a year to raise, train, and equip a substantial army. The Germans had observed the impotence of the US military in protecting its own border from the ragtag forces of Pancho Villa. Its decision to approach Mexican authorities about a potential alliance proved disastrous, but Germany had already declared that all US ships would be sunk without warning by the time the Zimmerman Telegram was intercepted. Germany announced a new policy of unrestricted submarine warfare on February 1, 1917; this policy led to an immediate end to diplomatic relations between the United States and Germany. In the next two weeks, Americans reacted to the sinking of a half dozen US ships in the Atlantic with rage. The release of the terms of the Zimmerman Telegram to the US public on March 1 added to the sense of rage and produced the sentiment that the United States was honor bound to respond with military force. From the perspective of the Germans, US entry was a calculated risk they were willing to take if it might mean the ability to block at least temporarily the supply routes that were keeping Britain and France in the war.

> *A ship carrying contraband should not rely on passengers to protect her from attack—it would be like putting women and children in front of an army.*
>
> —*US Secretary of State William Jennings Bryan*

Sidebar definitions:

Lusitania

A British ocean liner that traveled between England and New York until it was sunk by a German submarine in May 1915. Among the more than 1,200 passengers who lost their lives were 128 American citizens.

National Defense Act of 1916

A peacetime measure approved by Congress authorizing troop increases and construction of new ships for the US Navy. Although most members of Congress still opposed US entry into World War I at this time, the law demonstrated that government officials believed it was prudent to increase the nation's military preparedness in response to world events.

Sussex Pledge

A promise made by the German government to limit its use of submarine warfare against civilian vessels following the sinking of the French passenger ship in March of 1916.

However, even as more and more Americans agreed that they could no longer be neutral, most were still reluctant to send an army to Europe. They had watched the war transform into the hellish nightmare of trench warfare and remained thankful that they were divided from Europe by a vast ocean. The decision to remain neutral in the conflict had proven the most popular policy of President Wilson in the last four years. However, in addition to the injured honor produced by the sinking of US ships and the Zimmerman Telegram, strategic concerns induced some Americans to favor US entry on the side of Britain and France. The long-term consequences of their neutrality changed in early 1917 as it appeared that Germany might prevail while Bolsheviks might seize power within Russia. If the United States' entry into the war could bolster the sagging morale of Britain and France, some in the United States began to argue that such a declaration might be necessary. Others pointed out that a US declaration of war might also bolster those in Russia who opposed Lenin and were in favor of continuing the war and turning back the Socialist revolution.

Declaring war did not necessarily mean full mobilization of a massive land army, these early supporters of intervention pointed out. The army might simply send a support units and weapons. After all, American foodstuffs and manufactured goods appeared more important to winning the war in early 1917 than the small number of available ground troops. A declaration of war would free the US Navy to escort US merchant ships and attack German submarines and other vessels that had been threatening the Atlantic sea-lanes. In short, a declaration of war did not require a draft or even full mobilization of existing forces. It would bolster the morale of the Western Allies and provide the opportunity for greater security for US products and ships across the Atlantic. In consideration of these options, Wilson issued a declaration of war on March 20, and Congress approved the measure by a large margin during a special session. The president issued the declaration on April 6, thereby ending the United States' official policy of neutrality. Shortly after the declaration, the president and Congress approved dramatic increases in military spending and the construction of dozens of training camps.

Substantial numbers of US troops would not arrive in Europe for another year, but the US declaration of war had an instant and dramatic effect on Allied shipping. The adoption of the convoy system reversed the military success of German U-boats as the US Navy began escorting fleets of cargo ships. By September 1917, the German navy was launching new submarines at a record pace, but these new ships could not make up for the rapid sinking of U-boats by the US Navy. The first divisions of US troops had already arrived in Europe at this time, their safe passage being almost guaranteed by the convoy system. As a result, the calculated risk Germany took in sinking US ships failed in its objective of limiting the shipment of American goods. On June 26, 1917, Allied ships began carrying a different payload that would demonstrate the folly of Germany's decision. Fifteen thousand US soldiers under the command of General John J. Pershing debarked for Europe on this day, the advance guard of an army that transported 2 million men to Europe the next year-and-a-half. However, the Germans had one more calculated risk they planned on taking—a massive offensive that nearly ended the war before more than a handful of US divisions had even arrived in France.

2.3 Creating an Army

Representatives of the Western Allies arrived in the United States immediately following the declaration of war. Like many in the United States, these British and French envoys assumed that the primary contribution of their new American allies would be grain, money, raw materials, and manufactured goods. Congress and US banks provided credit on generous terms to ensure that all of these commodities would be in ready supply. However, Congress also authorized the rapid expansion of the army and navy. Britain and France assumed these troops would be integrated into their own command structure. US military leaders, especially General Pershing, opposed such a plan and refused to consider anything other than an independent US command in Europe. Pershing requested that at least a million men be sent to Europe, where they would be assigned to their own sector of the Western Front and placed under his command. At the same time, Pershing recognized that it would take at least a year before anything resembling an American army might be assembled and trained. As a result, he agreed to send a number of units to assist the British and French. The most famous of these units was the 369th Infantry, respectfully known as the "**Harlem Hellfighters**" by their German opponents. The 369th suffered high casualties and earned the respect of the French, who awarded the entire regiment the Croix de Guerre—one of the highest awards, which is usually reserved for individual acts of heroism. The experience of the 369th contrasted markedly with that of most African Americans who served within the US Army and were placed in labor battalions.

FIGURE 5.14

A warning issued by the German Embassy advising Americans that a state of war existed and any British ship, such as the *Lusitania* advertised here, was liable to be sunk by the German Navy. This warning is dated April 22, 1915, and the *Lusitania* was sunk less than one month later.

Harlem Hellfighters

A nickname given by German troops to members of the 369th US Infantry who fought with the French army during World War I. These African American troops suffered high casualties and were all awarded the Croix de Guerre by France for their valor.

FIGURE 5.15

This painting by H. Charles McBarron Jr. shows the Harlem Hellfighters of the 369th Infantry Regiment in battle. Because of their valor, France awarded the entire regiment the Croix de Guerre.

Although Wilson and other government officials hoped to maintain the tradition of an all-volunteer army, two main concerns led to the use of the draft. Congress believed that volunteer enlistment would be insufficient to increase the size of army from its present strength. After all, the army had not grown significantly despite the National Defense Act, which permitted the army to enlist over 200,000 men. At the time the United States entered the war, the US Army had only 122,000 enlisted men in the regular army. The 180,000 men in various state-run National Guard units might bolster this number, yet these units were largely independent of the federal army. In addition, some states still had special provisions forbidding the deployment of their guardsmen overseas. The second concern was that volunteer enlistment would be haphazard. The government feared that men with vital industrial skills would voluntarily join the military when they would actually be more useful on the home front. Part of this sentiment was related to the continued belief that the United States' most vital contribution would continue to be money and material, along with the mobilization of the navy to guard these shipments on its perilous journey across the Atlantic. American and foreign leaders recognized that modern warfare required the full mobilization of industry, and US allies needed food and equipment more than they needed soldiers—at least in the spring of 1917.

Selective Service System

A system created by the US government requiring mandatory registration for possible conscription into the armed forces for all young men between the ages of twenty-one and thirty. In the present day, all male citizens between the ages of eighteen and twenty-five are required to register.

Congress in May created the **Selective Service System**, which required that all men between the ages of twenty-one and thirty register for the draft. Civilians operated local draft boards that helped to limit organized opposition to the draft. However, local control also led to haphazard enforcement and arbitrary interpretations of service disqualifications and deferments. Draft boards were instructed to rank registrants within categories such as health, wartime value of their civilian occupation, and home responsibilities. A young man without a job in perfect health could expect to be inducted if he was drafted, but a father who was a skilled wielder would likely be granted an exemption. Draft boards operated by white Southerners often granted every possible exemption to black draftees due to concerns that military service would lead to racial equality. Other boards operated by white Southerners took the opposite perspective, granting exemptions for white draftees while ignoring compelling evidence that should have led to exemptions for black men with important jobs and families to support.

Those who opposed the war for moral or religious reasons were likewise vulnerable to the decisions of local draft boards, which became notorious for their arbitrary rulings. Most draftees who could document their long-standing membership in a particular religious order that the federal government recognized as pacifistic were granted exemption from military service. Those who were not members of organized churches were left to the mercy and judgment of the boards that rarely had the time or inclination to really investigate individual cases. Once a local board recognized a man as a conscientious objector, he was to be given an alternative assignment. The military moved slowly in providing these assignments, and the majority of registered objectors spent many months in military camps awaiting orders. That 16,000 of the first 20,000 men registered as conscientious objectors decided to relinquish their combat exclusion while in these camps is indicative of the "persuasive" methods that were used to convince these men to take up arms.

By the end of the war in November 1918, nearly 4 million soldiers had joined the US Army and Navy—about 60 percent of whom were draftees. Eastern port cities swarmed with soldiers, most of who were from rural backgrounds and had rarely been to a large city. The wartime boom was also a tremendous boon to the vice districts of these cities until government regulations and military police created effective methods of quarantining the men. The emphasis on purity was related to the view that many US leaders shared that the war was a moral crusade. Other prominent Americans, such as the aging Theodore Roosevelt, saw war as the ultimate test of manhood. Like most generations before them, American boys spent their youth playing with toy soldiers and listening to the stories of heroism passed down from the veterans of the Civil War. History and memory are often distant cousins and, in most cases, those who claimed to speak on behalf of the wartime generation had never suffered in a Confederate prisoner-of-war camp or endured the brutality of the Wilderness Campaign. Popular journals refused to print stories submitted by amputees and prisoners, leading to a fictionalized account of war as some kind of benign escapade that marked the journey from boyhood to manhood.

Like those who had actually seen years of campaigning in the Civil War and those who were part of the occupying force in the Philippines during the Spanish-American War, the first American volunteers would learn that courage and endurance were often two separate choices rather than character traits. Machine guns and trench-borne diseases made few distinctions based on chivalry and honor. For these survivors, Armistice Day orators who spoke of the "magnificent orchestra of war" must have been far away from the front. Those who knew war chose to remain silent about their time spent living among death. That memory of the Great War was far different in the States than in Europe was directly related to the simple fact that the vast majority of the 4 million Americans who joined the military saw no combat action before the war ended in November 1918. The most thoughtful among them agreed with those who saw the war as a tragedy, even if their own military experience contained moments of adventure.

2.4 Government, Industry, and Military Production

Britain had adopted the slogan "Business as Usual" and opposed the methods of government control over the civilian population and the economy that would become commonplace in other belligerent nations. However, by the time of US entry into the war, even Britain had engaged in unprecedented economic controls and resorted to the draft. US governmental policies were often based on the British model. England belatedly recognized that the war would require full mobilization of all the productive capabilities of their empire. Until that time and especially throughout Europe's nineteenth century, wars were localized and quick, decided by a few pitched battles. However, during World War I, entire societies were enlisted and transformed in the name of victory. Rationing, price controls, the dizzying pace of factory work, and widespread shortages required civilian populations to sacrifice in ways that paralleled the service of those on the battlefield.

The US government recognized that the war effort depended on the development of a united home front to supply and equip its armed forces. To realize this goal, the Wilson administration assumed a greater level of control over the production and distribution of food, fuel, and machinery. The federal government also assumed an active role in controlling the economy by setting prices, standardizing production, and rationing goods. The level of tolerable political dissent was also reduced and millions of young men were conscripted into military service. To win support for these extreme measures and to ensure political support, the government launched a nationwide program aimed at "selling the war." Every sector of the US population, including women and children, were both actively engaged and targeted in these campaigns.

FIGURE 5.16

Many World War I recruiting posters contained gendered messages such as this one. Here, the female embodiment of Liberty asks the men of America to fight on her behalf and defend her honor. The phrase "fight for us" also implies that men are being called on to protect womankind.

FIGURE 5.17

This cartoon depicting conscientious objectors as effete demonstrates some of the prejudices that men who refused to take up arms for moral or religious reasons faced.

Committee on Public Information (CPI)

A federal agency created to manage information related to America's participation in World War I and influence public opinion in favor of the war. Due to constitutionally guaranteed freedoms of expression, many of the CPI's attempts to influence the media became controversial.

FIGURE 5.18

One of the many posters printed by the federal government depicting World War I as a moral struggle and urging Americans to purchase war bonds to back their fighting men and the front. These bonds paid interest and were used to finance a large percentage of the war effort.

War Industries Board (WIB)

A federal agency placed in charge of procuring essential wartime materiel for the government during World War I. Because of the enormity of the task, the WIB ended up managing many aspects of the American economy during the war.

In April 1917, Wilson appointed George Creel to head the **Committee on Public Information (CPI)**. This agency was charged with promoting the war effort in ways that presented the sacrifices of Americans on the home front and the battlefield as something bigger than preventing German expansion or protecting US interests. The CPI presented the war as part of a moral struggle for freedom over tyranny. The CPI printed over 50 million posters, pamphlets, films, and other propaganda materials connecting America's war effort to lofty ideals, while others focused on German aggression in invading France and Belgium. Creel was a former newspaperman and was very reluctant to use the power of the government to censor the press. Although the CPI did censor and even forcibly terminate a number of left-leaning and antiwar newspapers, Creel's agency generally focused more on mobilizing public opinion than censorship. In this way, the US home front was unique from most of the belligerent nations where the government took control of the media.

One of Creel's most successful programs was the creation of a virtual army of Four Minute Men who gave brief prowar speeches at all public gatherings. Whether attending a baseball game, a concert, or a movie, the performance would not begin until the audience sang a patriotic tune, recited the pledge of allegiance, and listened to one of Creel's volunteer orators. The CPI also preached a message of "100 percent Americanism," which called on Americans to back the war effort but could also have more sinister racial and ethnic overtones. African Americans, Jews, Germans, and other racial, ethnic, and religious groups were often challenged by the dominant Anglo Protestant majority to prove their patriotism. Because the default image of a 100 percent American was a white Protestant, all others were considered suspect unless they could prove they were furthering the war effort in some significant fashion. Anti-German sentiments that had been largely discarded since the nineteenth century were suddenly revived in ways that encouraged a degree of vigilantism against some German Americans. Public schools canceled their German-language programs and fired teachers who were suspected of harboring affection for Germany. Concert halls banned music by German composers and hamburgers and German measles became "liberty sandwiches" and "liberty measles." Perhaps most tragic, being seen with a German Shepherd or dachshund became unfashionable, and some of these dogs were abandoned by their owners in an ironic attempt to prove their loyalty.

Wilson's idealism about the war was both related his desire to sell the war effort as well as a reflection of his own idealism. He declared that the United States desired "no material compensation for the sacrifices" his nation would endure. The president promised that the United States would not accept any territorial acquisitions resulting from the war. This did not mean that the United States did not expect greater recognition from the international community. Wilson hoped that US participation in the war would permit him to play a leading role in negotiating the eventual Allied victory and framing the postwar international order. He and other Americans also recognized that the war was creating new opportunities for US businesses. Industries that had once been dominated by European firms were suddenly open to US production. American companies that already enjoyed international positions in steel production, shipbuilding, and automobiles manufacturing were reaping tremendous profits during the war due to foreign and domestic demand. These companies would enjoy even more lucrative contracts as the federal government dramatically increased its orders for raw materials and finished products.

Wilson appointed Bernard Baruch to lead the **War Industries Board (WIB)**, which was created in July 1917. Baruch was charged with coordinating the efforts of private enterprise to maximize efficiency and production of products and raw materials the military needed. The WIB was empowered to seize factories, mines, and other private enterprises if the government felt that they were not being used efficiently. For example, in July 1918, workers at the Smith and Wesson gun factory in Springfield, Massachusetts, declared a strike. Chief among their complaints was the mandatory requirement that newly hired workers sign a statement promising that they would never join a labor union. These agreements became known as "yellow-dog" contracts for reasons that are still not fully understood. Rifles were crucial to the war effort, and the federal government ordered the factory to rehire the discharged workers and end its practice of requiring workers to sign antiunion contracts. When the company refused, the WIB seized the entire plant. In a similar strike involving workers at the Remington gun factory in Bridgeport, Connecticut, the government sided with management by threatening to draft all workers who did not return to work. In both instances, the government used coercive power to ensure sustained production of vital war material.

As indicated by the Smith and Wesson and Bridgeport strikes, the WIB regarded labor stoppages within vital industries as potentially treasonous and responded by either seizing the plants or issuing "work or fight" orders for workers. Had these seizures or threats occurred in larger numbers or over several years, many Americans would have likely protested these actions as contrary to the nation's tradition of limited governmental, freedom of contract, and protection of private property. However, Baruch used his coercive powers sparingly. Instead, he compelled corporations to produce the things the military needed by offering higher-than-market prices. To ensure the full and rapid participation of US industry, the WIB even approved contracts guaranteeing profit by paying expenses related to creating new factories or converting existing facilities from civilian to military production. Finally, the WIB worked with labor unions and often supported workers' claims for higher wages. The result was an estimated 100 percent increase in corporate profits and a 20 percent increase in the average income of workers during the war.

FIGURE 5.19

This crew of four men armed with a Maxim gun could wipe out an entire regiment in seconds. Early machine guns required a crew to feed ammunition and circulate water through the weapon to prevent it from overheating.

2.5 Women and the War

As indicated by the swift reaction of the WIB, weapons were among the most important items the government ordered as its military sought to equip nearly 4 million recruits. At the time of America's declaration of war, the federal government owned 600,000 service rifles. US gun manufacturers were convinced to reduce production of rifles for other nations, and the firms of Remington and Winchester were contracted to come up with a design that would replace the 1903 Springfield rifle. Based largely on the British Enfield rifle, the new US service rifle contained a five-round magazine and fired a .30-06 round. Owing to the postwar surplus, veterans were permitted to keep their rifles leading to the widespread adoption of .30-06 cartridge among hunters and sportsmen. Although Americans copied the British design, an American named Hiram Maxim developed the first truly automatic weapon that used its own recoil to load, fire, and extract used cartridges. Many military leaders throughout the world derided the wastefulness of these "machine guns." The defensive nature of the war led to a rapid reconsideration of the usefulness of these weapons, and the machine gun quickly became the dominant weapon of the trenches. The use of automatic weapons also led to a belated reconsideration by military commanders about the wisdom of offensive charges against even the smallest foe if that enemy was well entrenched and armed with automatic weapons. At the beginning of the war, most of France's 2,500 machine guns were left in storage. At the end of the war, France alone had acquired over 300,000 machine guns.

The most important military innovation may have been the development of extremely accurate and rapid-firing artillery pieces. Artillery accounted for the majority of combat deaths and major battles such as Verdun saw over 20 million artillery shells being fired. By the end of the war, the tank had made its combat debut and proved its usefulness both as a mobile artillery unit and as a moving shield for advancing infantry. However, only a few hundred tanks were ever put into operation and none of the fifteen tanks that were produced in the United States and transported to Europe ever saw action. Trucks, tanks, and airpower would prove decisive in World War II. However, these innovations were never available in significant numbers or were not yet utilized in a manner that created a significant tactical advantage during World War I.

FIGURE 5.20

The Women's Land Army of America borrowed from a British idea and trained women for careers in agriculture. Similar courses to those advertised by this poster at the University of Virginia were offered throughout the nation and were intended to help offset the loss of productivity caused by farmers and agricultural workers who joined the army.

FIGURE 5.21

Overall, female employment did not increase as dramatically during World War I as it would in World War II. However, as this poster indicates, women entered a number of jobs that had been almost completely restricted to men, which challenged ideas about gender.

FIGURE 5.22

A US Navy recruiting poster for women. In addition to those employed by the military as civilians, approximately 12,000 women enlisted in the navy during World War I.

Approximately 1 million American women entered jobs that had previously been closed to them owing to their gender. However, overall female employment increased only 6 percent during the war and the vast majority of working women in America continued to work in a small number of professions that were considered appropriate for women. The same was not true of America's European allies, where greater wartime demand and higher percentages of men in uniform led to unprecedented burdens and opportunities for women. In Germany, two out of every five munitions workers were female, while more than 5 million women were engaged in industrial labor in Great Britain.

Although it paled in comparison to the shifting patterns of employment in Europe, the war reconfigured the nature of employment for many American women who were already in the workforce. Approximately 1 million women entered professions that were generally reserved for men between 1917 and 1919. Women understood that they were needed in the industrial workforce, and they raised their expectations and demands accordingly. American women also had greater opportunities to organize formally under the banner of a union. In addition, the demand for labor allowed women to form networks and use information to regarding pay and benefits to their advantage. For example, when black women found that they were being paid less than their white counterparts many protested the differential and often succeeded in securing equal pay.

Although the international conflict created an unprecedented number of employment opportunities for women of all races, these opportunities were still greatly limited, and wages for women were often significantly less than that of their male counterparts. Far from replacing the hierarchical relation of labor organized by categories of race and gender, these new opportunities were still generally limited to the most menial tasks and the lowest wages. Perhaps the most significant impact of the temporary increase in the number of women who labored outside of the home was the sudden demand on the state to provide services for children some working mothers could no longer provide. These new demands that were placed on the wartime government raised issues such as child welfare and public education to areas of national concern.

A small number of women served the military in every US conflict, but World War I saw the first official recognition of women as service members. The Naval Reserve Act of 1916 did not specify gender, which led to the enlistment of nearly 12,000 women in the US Navy and Marines. These women were given the unique rank of Yeoman (F). The grade and classification were a combination of the lowest enlisted rank in the navy and an indication of gender, which connoted the expectation that an individual would be assigned to perform clerical work. While women had been employed by the military to perform these kinds of jobs in the past, they had never been permitted to join the military. Female enlistment went against tradition, which led to immediate demands to halt the practice. However, these yeomen (or "yeomanettes" as they were often called) were granted military pay and benefits. They were also considered veterans when the war was over. Several hundred of these women died while in the service, mostly of diseases that spread rapidly aboard ships and military bases.

Most women that served in military capacities were simply hired as contract laborers. Among the most famous female military laborers were the hundreds of "Hello Girls" who worked on behalf of, but not as members of, the Signal Corps. Although they traveled overseas and were subject to military discipline, these multilingual telephone switchboard operators were not given the same pay and benefits of soldiers and sailors who performed similar linguistic and clerical labor. More than 1,500 female nurses served overseas within the navy, and 10,000 women served as nurses on army bases in Europe. Several hundred of these women did not return home, victims of the dangerous nature of their work among infectious patients. Because they were not official members of the military, these nurses were not eligible for military benefits or given the honor of a military funeral. Even larger numbers of women served in various capacities on US bases, and these women were also ineligible for military rank or pay because of their gender.

As indicated by their service as workers in both civilian and military capacities, most women, as well as advocates of women's suffrage, followed the general trend of public opinion and rallied behind the war effort. However, some women within the women's suffrage movement were divided regarding their nation's decision to enter the war in the spring of 1917. For example, Jane Addams was outspoken as a pacifist and continued to oppose US entry into the war despite being severely chastised for her position. In 1931, Jane Addams's efforts were finally rewarded with the Nobel Peace Prize, but she was often vilified in her own time. In 1915, Addams was among the founders of Woman's Peace Party. She was also a leader in the April 1915 International Congress of Women, which approved resolutions calling for an immediate armistice. Despite some violent threats, she continued to travel and lead efforts to provide supplies for refugees.

Montana congresswoman **Jeannette Rankin** used her status as the first woman in Congress to do more than protest the war—she voted against it in 1917. "You can no more win a war than you can win an earthquake," Rankin famously remarked. Rankin, along with forty-nine of her male colleagues in the House of Representatives, voted against US entry into the war. By the end of the year and owing largely to political pressure, most of her colleagues had reversed course. Rankin held firm to her pacifist convictions, even though it cost her any chance at reelection.

2.6   Over There: America and the End of the War

Optimism grew stronger among German military leaders during the spring of 1918 than at any point in the preceding three years of trench warfare. Largely due to German assistance, Austria-Hungary had stabilized the war in Southern Europe while the Russian Revolution had ended the war in the east. The United States was mobilizing for war, but nothing resembling an independent US Army would arrive in Europe until the summer of 1918. In fact, only three US divisions were in Europe in October 1917, and only two more divisions would arrive in the next five months. US training camps were not at full capacity until early spring; a quarter million troops arrived each month throughout the summer and fall of 1918. Germany had anticipated that the United States would eventually shift the balance of power to the Allies. As a result, Germany directed its efforts to ending the war before these men could see action. It nearly succeeded.

Pershing had hoped that his new recruits would be given at least a year of training before seeing action. However, the transfer of German troops to the Western Front following the Brest-Litovsk Treaty and the devastating German offensive led to the abbreviation of his idealized training schedule. Between March and July 1918, Germany concentrated its forces in a coordinated offensive along the Western Front. The German army advanced forty miles west and nearly succeeded in capturing Paris. However, Pershing deployed 70,000 newly arrived US troops that helped stem the German advance in the battles of Cantigny in May 1918. US troops also contributed to the battles of Chateau-Thierry and Belleau Wood the following month. By July, the familiar challenge of maintaining supply lines against an enemy counteroffensive doomed the German attack. The Germans then began a fighting retreat back to positions that were nearer to their original trenches and supply lines and awaited the American onslaught. By this time, the United States had twenty-five divisions in France, and the Allied Powers seized the initiative.

FIGURE 5.23
Montana Congresswoman Jeannette Rankin

Jeannette Rankin

A field worker of the National American Women's suffrage Association who helped to achieve victories for women's suffrage in North Dakota and Montana, Rankin later became the first female member in Congress. She was also a devoted pacifist and opposed US entry into World War I.

FIGURE 5.24

American troops firing a French-made mobile artillery piece in Germany. US troops and military supplies shifted the balance of the war, although most artillery pieces and shells were not manufactured in America. Large and small artillery pieces such as this gun were incredibly accurate and had a range of over a mile. For these reasons, artillery was the leading killer of men in World War I.

Meuse-Argonne Offensive

A combined offensive by the Allied Powers during the final months of World War I. The Meuse-Argonne Offensive featured the most significant battlefield contribution by American troops and led to the German surrender in November 1918.

Despite nearly three years of trench warfare, the notion that a well-supplied and entrenched machine-gun crew could negate the courage and skill of hundreds of soldiers remained unfathomable to Pershing. The US commander thought he might enjoy greater success than his British and French counterparts. US troops would pay dearly for their general's overly optimistic assessment of their capabilities in the **Meuse-Argonne Offensive**. US troops advanced only ten miles in forty-seven days, failing to reach their objective while suffering thousands of needless casualties. Even when the valor of US troops overcame the terrain and entrenched positions of the enemy, faulty supply and communications converted triumph into tragedy. For example, the infamous "Lost Battalion" advanced far into enemy territory within the Argonne Forest and suffered 70 percent casualty rate until it was eventually rescued by slower units.

Fortunately for the green American troops, they would not face the same fate as the millions of German, French, and British troops who were ordered to advance against machine-gun fire. The Germans had already initiated a strategic withdrawal behind what their leaders hoped would be an impenetrable line of defense. Because this line was further east than the Argonne forest objective in the Meuse-Argonne offensive, US casualties were only a fraction of what had been sacrificed by the British in the Battle of the Somme. However, Pershing had correctly determined that the stalemate of 1917 had been ended. By November, the United States had forty-two divisions in France, and together with the more experienced British and French veterans, the Allies had pushed the center of Germany's line fifty miles east. Recognizing that continuing the war would only result in more killing, Germany's military leaders requested an armistice, which was signed on November 11, 1918. The German army was near its breaking point, and civilian leaders feared that Germany would face a revolution similar to what Russia had just experienced if the war continued much longer. However, the German army was still on French and Belgian soil when the armistice was signed, and many German civilians had been led to believe that the offensive of the spring and summer of 1918 had succeeded. As a result, many Germans would later search for alternative interpretations to explain their defeat.

REVIEW AND CRITICAL THINKING

1. How did Germany nearly defeat France in the first months of World War I? What led to a stalemate on the Western Front and a war of attrition by the end of 1917? Describe the early battles and their significance.

2. How was the Eastern Front different from the fighting in Western Europe? What led to the Russian Revolution, and how did this event affect the war?

3. Most Americans and American leaders strongly opposed involvement in World War I in 1914. What led Congress and the president to declare three years later?

4. How did World War I affect the home front? Explain the ways that the government sought to control industrial output and public opinion.

5. Describe the experiences of women and minorities within the military. How did women challenge notions of gender during the war, and in what ways were their options restrained during the war because of gender?

6. Summarize the military history of America's participation in World War I. How significant was the US declaration of war in determining the outcome of the conflict? How much of an impact did American troops make on the Western Front?

3.   ARMISTICE AND AFTERMATH

LEARNING OBJECTIVES

1. Evaluate the impact of the Wilson administration's impact on the Treaty of Versailles and the strengths and shortcomings of these peace accords.
2. Describe the ways that the United States changed during the war, especially in terms of equality for women and diverse groups of Americans. Evaluate the impact the war had on these changes, as well as the impact of women and minorities on the US war effort.
3. Describe the social and political climate in the United States following the end of the war, paying particular attention to the Red Scare and the outbreak of race riots.

3.1   Demobilization and the Treaty of Versailles

America's demobilization occurred so rapidly that many soldiers spent less time overseas than they had spent training and awaiting assignment in Europe. The nation practically "beat plowshares into swords" in 1917 and 1918 with the sudden conversion to a wartime economy. After the armistice, the nation returned to civilian production in an even shorter amount of time. Days after the war ended, the federal government canceled $4 billion worth of contracts for weapons and other military items. Although the government offered various payments to ensure that US companies did not lose money for these broken contracts, the sudden end of the war resulted in high levels of turnover within wartime industries. These jobs were lost just as soldiers were returning from Europe and seeking employment. Pent-up consumer demand led to the creation of new jobs creating consumer goods and within the construction industry. However, the war had also created high inflation, which reduced the buying power of consumers. Organized labor had often secured contracts that alleviated these forces during the war, but most of these modest wage gains were eliminated once workers were no longer in high demand.

FIGURE 5.25

As this chart indicates, the 116,000 Americans who lost their lives in World War I were but a fraction of the total number of combat deaths suffered by the Allied Powers. In addition to the other costs of battle, many Europeans felt that Americans such as Woodrow Wilson were in no position to dictate the terms of the postwar settlement for this reason.

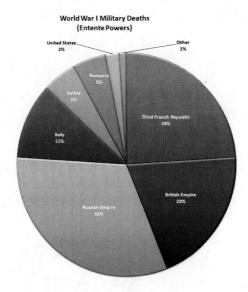

One of the most significant effects of the rapid demobilization was the removal of women from industrial jobs and other positions that had previously been regarded as male occupations. Women's employment in these fields had not occurred in large enough numbers or with the duration needed to fully challenge traditional views about the nature of gender and labor. The shift from home labor to factory labor meant that the small number of young women who found jobs in industry might enjoy larger amounts of discretionary income. However, many male and female reformers worried about the effect of physical labor on women's bodies. Some even predicted that wearing trousers might disrupt gender relations and may even cause damage to reproductive organs. More common were concerns that the proliferation of female labor jeopardized the male position of breadwinner and would place downward pressure on the higher wages male labor had commanded in the past. If the war created job opportunities for some women, peace had the opposite effect. The brief experience of these women in industry and the continuing importance of women as clerks, telephone operators, secretaries, teachers, nurses, and other professional positions did lead to some changes for women. Combined with their growing political power as voters, women convinced the federal government to create a permanent Women's Bureau in the Department of Labor.

The war officially ended when Germany signed the **Treaty of Versailles**, although the US Senate rejected its provisions. President Wilson had high hopes that he could shape the treaty in a manner that would reduce the conditions that had led to the war. A year before the war ended, Wilson proposed a blueprint for a peace based on fourteen principles. The first five of **Wilsons' Fourteen Points** attempted to promote free trade, encourage arms reduction, and reduce the number of overseas colonies. The next eight provisions dealt with self-determination for Southern and Central Europe—areas that had previously been claimed various empires but that might be used to create a patchwork of independent nations. Wilson's fourteenth point was the linchpin of the entire plan, or at least its goal to "end all wars" in the future. It sought to create a "concert of nations" by creating an international organization that would mediate disputes between nations and prevent aggressor nations from attacking others.

Republicans and a number of conservative Democrats feared that the United States would surrender its sovereignty if they joined Wilson's proposed **League of Nations**. In addition, Wilson failed to include or even seek the advice of leading senators regarding the peace process that was discussed at Versailles—a critical error that left him open to charges of acting unilaterally. Many of Wilson's ideas were incorporated into the final version of the Treaty of Versailles; one example is the creation of nine new nations in Eastern Europe. Liberals hoped that these new nations would reduce ethnic conflicts and promote democracy, while conservatives in Europe and the United States hoped that these states would serve as a buffer and insulate Western Europe from Communism.

In exchange for accepting many of Wilson's ideas and creating the League of Nations, representatives of the Allied Powers demanded and received harsh territorial and financial concessions from Germany. One of the most significant of these concessions was the agreement to pay $33 billion in reparations to the Allied Powers to compensate for their losses in the war. Germany was also forced to agree it had started the war and was alone in the blame for the war's consequences. Germany was forced to surrender the territories of Alsace-Lorraine to France, abandon its colonies, and reduce the size of its army; it was prohibited to develop offensive weapons, such as submarines or military aircraft in the future. The result of these penalties crippled the new German state. It also angered many Germans, and this anger facilitated the rise of Adolf Hitler during the 1930s. In addition, the United States never joined the League of Nations due to its rejection of the Treaty of Versailles and a return to isolationism.

FIGURE 5.26

A map of Europe showing the national boundary realignment following World War I and the Treaty of Versailles.

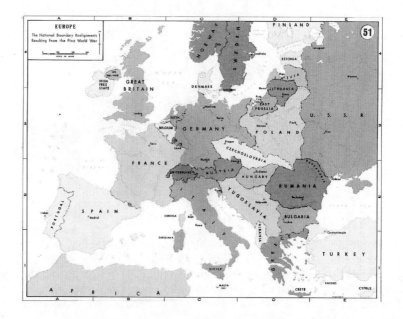

Treaty of Versailles

Was signed between Germany and the remaining Allied Powers on June 28, 1919. In addition to officially ending World War I, the Treaty of Versailles required Germany to admit guilt for starting the war and pay reparations to compensate many of the nations it fought against.

Wilsons' Fourteen Points

Based on a speech given by President Woodrow Wilson to Congress, the Fourteen Points were various provisions intended to prevent wars in the future by promoting free trade, diplomacy, national self-determination, and disarmament.

League of Nations

An international organization formed after World War I to promote global security and prevent future wars through collective actions of its member nations. The United States never joined the League of Nations, which was largely ineffective in preventing conflicts between nations in the years leading up to the Second World War.

In addition to the Treaty of Versailles, policies affecting the future of the Middle East were determined in the aftermath of World War I. England had issued the **Balfour Declaration** during the war. Named after the foreign secretary who framed the document, the Balfour Declaration expressed the support of the British government toward the creation of a Jewish homeland in Palestine. After the war, Britain was assigned the responsibility to administer Palestine, and Jewish residents throughout Palestine and throughout the world called on Britain to make good on these sentiments. However, the British had received Arab support in World War I and recognized that the Arab majority in the Middle East would strongly oppose anything that might lead to a Jewish state. The British were especially concerned about the stability of the oil-rich countries of the Middle East. As a result, the British had also declared during the war that they would support Arab nationalism and ensure that the rights of all peoples in the Middle East would be protected. Because the British had invested millions in oil exploration, they wanted assurance that any actions would not jeopardize their standing with local Arab leaders.

Statements of support for Arab control of Palestine and the Balfour Declaration contradicted with one another and were easy to make when Britain had no control of the region. However, at the conclusion of World War I, the Allies dissolved the Ottoman Empire, and the French took control of Syria and Lebanon. Other Middle Eastern states such as Iraq were placed under the control of the British who were also appointed as the administrators of Palestine. In each of these "mandates," the British and French were responsible for supervising the transition from part of the Ottoman Empire to full independence. This proved especially difficult, as British leaders had promised Palestinian leaders that they would provide aid for the creation of a sovereign Arab nation. Complicating the matter was that Jews and Arabs, along with the small number of Christians in the area, all considered Palestine as sacred land. Nationalist forces in each of these areas felt betrayed as they had supported the British and French in World War I. Jews throughout the British Empire shared similar feelings as Britain failed to act on the Balfour Declaration. Instead, Britain sought to administer in these areas in ways that secured access to oil. The British sought to prevent conflict rather than resolve what many believed was an irreconcilable struggle between Jews and Arabs over the future of Palestine.

> **Balfour Declaration**
>
> A communication by British Foreign Secretary Arthur Balfour during World War I that expressed his belief that the British government should support the creation of a Jewish state in Palestine.

3.2   The Final Triumph of Women's Suffrage

Even in communities where black and white women worked together to promote suffrage, most black women formed their own organizations and the rank-and-file membership of these groups lived separate lives. White National American Woman Suffrage Association (NAWSA) members were often more liberal regarding the color line, yet they also hoped to attract a larger following in the South and often catered to the racial prejudices of some of their members. For example, 5,000 suffragists from across the country met in Washington, DC, under the auspices of the NAWSA in 1913. The white leadership declared that representatives of black women's organizations should march in their own separate columns behind the whites.

Ida Wells had been a member of NAWSA for many years, and although she had formed an organization for black suffragists in Chicago, her presence in Washington, DC, was as part of the integrated Illinois chapter of NAWSA. As a result, the decision that Wells must march in the back of the column angered her and several other Illinois women who vowed to march alone with Wells between the members of various black suffrage associations and the NAWSA. The rest of the white suffragists worried that the presence of white and black women marching in the same column might offend Southerners at the very moment when the suffrage movement was beginning to gain ground in that area of the country. As the march began, the insults hurled from the men who had lined the streets led few to notice that Wells had joined the otherwise white procession. Despite her willingness to stand by them as they crossed a gauntlet of jeers and taunts, most whites would have preferred that Wells and other black women would have not participated at all. As had been the case with other movements for social justice, the failure to overcome racial prejudice would reduce the effectiveness of the suffrage movement. For example, the Southern States Women's Suffrage Conference was dedicated to promoting state laws that would explicitly limit the vote to white women despite the obvious contradiction with the Fifteenth Amendment.

The suffrage movement also remained divided between those who accepted society's notions of gender and those who sought to challenge those conventions. The conservative wing of the women's suffrage movement stressed the compatibility of voting within the unique character and responsibilities of women in society. Others were more radical, advocating not only suffrage but also complete gender equality in all aspects of society. These two ideas about suffrage were evident in a debate between sociologist Charlotte Perkins Gilman and NAWSA president Anna Howard Shaw. Shaw emphasized the ways that voting was consistent with women's roles in the home. She advanced the more conservative

FIGURE 5.27

The strength of the movement continued to be local organizations such as this one in Cleveland, Ohio. Male politicians came to understand that continued opposition to female suffrage would likely cost them their jobs as more states revised their voting laws in response to grassroots campaigns organized by women such as these.

idea that women could purify politics and promote reform in ways that were compatible with the notion of a separate sphere of activity for women and men. Gilman saw the vote more as a step toward emancipation from the separate sphere, eliminating one of the ways that women's confinement to the home had been perpetrated and justified in the past. Radicals such as Gilman represented a small minority even within the suffrage movement. However, their ideas would have a profound impact as they represented the vanguard of the feminist movement during this era.

FIGURE 5.28

The artist who produced this 1915 image entitled "The Awakening" depicts the goddess of liberty marching from the west, where women had secured the right to vote, to the east. The image challenges the contemporary notion that the vector of American progress moved westward.

Alice Paul and Lucy Burns were radicals who also understood the tactical value of conservative arguments in favor of suffrage. They also were unsatisfied with the state-by-state strategy of the NAWSA and convinced the leadership of that organization to establish an organization dedicated to promoting a constitutional amendment extending the vote to all citizens regardless of gender. Paul led this organization, which was known as the Congressional Union. While the NAWSA grew to 2 million members, Paul's organization was a small group of determined activists who lobbied on behalf of a federal amendment. The NAWSA continued to push for local reform using the successful tactic of minimizing feminist ideas and promoting the vote as a reform measure. Eventually, Paul would abandon the NAWSA for this reason. Her Congressional Union became the National Woman's Party (NWP) and was free to celebrate women's equality as the heart of the suffrage issue after leaving the more conservative NAWSA. NWP members held protest marches and directly confronted male leaders who continued to oppose suffrage. Paul and her supporters even picketed the White House and chained themselves to the gates when they were ordered to leave. Their arrest was scandalized by many mainstream suffragists in NAWSA who believed that the NWP was alienating moderate men and women who might otherwise support suffrage. However, the conditions these women faced while in prison generated sympathy and led many undecided women and men that the opponents of women's suffrage were not genuinely concerned about the plight of women. The arguments and the tactics of the NWP also convinced many on the fence that groups such as the NAWSA were not so radical after all.

By 1912, ten states and/or territories recognized women's right to vote. In 1913, Illinois granted partial suffrage for women voting in presidential elections, becoming the first state east of the Mississippi to do so. Iowa's Carrie Chapman Catt took over the NAWSA in 1915 and renewed the effort to pass a constitutional amendment; she also pushed for state-by-state reform. Catt and other NAWSA leaders also began to promote suffrage as both as a natural right belonging to all citizens and as a means of promoting reform, healing the divisions between more radical and conservative ideas within the movement. She and other NAWSA leaders continued to oppose the demonstrations of radicals, yet strongly opposed the violence these women sometimes faced from male hecklers and police. Reports that Alice Paul and other women had been beaten and force-fed after waging a hunger strike put those who opposed suffrage on the defensive. Claiming to oppose suffrage as a matter of "protecting" women from the filth and corruption of the outside world, these beatings of women exposed the hollowness of this brand of "chivalry."

In 1917, Arkansas and New York become the first Southern and East Coast states to approve suffrage, although Arkansas law restricted the vote to white women in primary elections. The battle continued throughout the South and the East, but even states such as Maine that had strong Progressive tendencies voted down a 1917 women's suffrage referendum by a two-to-one margin. The failure in Maine reflected the ways that the war had divided voters. Antisuffragists in Maine defeated the measure, largely by arousing populist hostility toward national feminist figures and antiwar leaders. These same campaign methods derailed the rapid progress the suffrage movement had enjoyed and threatened to split the entire movement. However, NAWSA adapted by throwing its support toward the war effort, and the majority of suffragists distanced themselves from leading pacifists. Many women who had opposed America's entry rallied behind the war effort in ways that "proved" their patriotism. With millions of women in the workforce and tens of thousands serving overseas in various nursing and military auxiliaries, even President Wilson decided it was time to end his opposition to women's suffrage.

In 1918, a proposed constitutional amendment granting universal suffrage passed Congress with the support of Jeanette Rankin of Montana, the first and only woman in Congress at this time. Even though President Wilson declared the measure vital to the US war effort, conservatives in the Senate defeated the amendment. NAWSA redoubled their efforts to win popular support for the measure, while the NWP and other more radical women increased the political pressure on male politicians who had opposed the measure. Others pointed out that women in most European countries had been granted the right to vote, including Russia in 1917, Britain in 1918, and Germany and Austria by 1919.

Within the United States, thirty states and territories had approved women's suffrage in at least some elections by 1919, and half of those states recognized the right of women to vote in all elections. As a result, members of the NWP could potentially mobilize women voters against any opponent of women's suffrage in nearly half of the congressional and senatorial elections that would be held in the future. This single fact more than a gradual recognition of gender equality convinced two-thirds of the

Senate to approve a women's suffrage amendment on June 4, 1919. The next step was the required ratification by at least three-fourths of the states (thirty-six states at this time). After fourteen months of daily activism, Tennessee became the thirty-sixth state to ratify the amendment in August 1920.

FIGURE 5.29

This map showing states that had granted full or partial female suffrage by 1919 demonstrates that the success of the Nineteenth Amendment was directly related to activism at the local and state level.

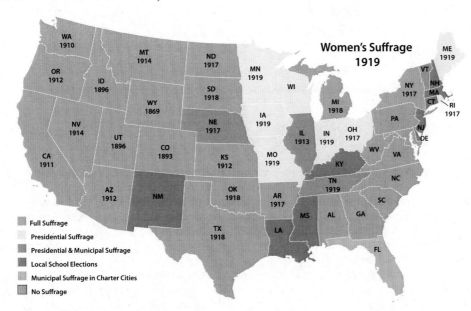

Of all the former Confederate states, only Texas, Arkansas, and Tennessee voted in favor of the Nineteenth Amendment. Conservatives in the South defeated women's suffrage by comparing it to the expansion of the electorate during Reconstruction. "The southern man who votes for the Susan B. Anthony amendment votes to ratify the Fifteenth Amendment," declared South Carolina senator Ellison Smith. However, when nearly every state outside of the Deep South voted for ratification, the intrepid efforts of Southern suffragists who had faced down mobs in their failed attempts to secure their rights were finally rewarded. From the perspective of hindsight, it is clear that NAWSA's calculated sacrifice of its African American members and its explicit rejection of racial unity did little to promote suffrage among white Southerners. In addition, states could still require poll taxes and literacy tests that limited the impact of suffrage for many white and black Southern women. The vote was also withheld from many nonwhite women when federal courts ruled that the Nineteenth Amendment (and the rest of the Constitution) did not apply in overseas colonies. Ironically, women suffrage was adopted by Spain in 1931—just after the women of Puerto Rico secured their right to vote, but prior to women's suffrage in the Philippines.

By 1920, suffrage had attracted the support of relatively conservative women, leading the more radical and early supporters of suffrage to use a new term to identify themselves and their reformist agenda. Small but influential groups such as a New York women's organization known as Heterodoxy promoted **feminism**—a word to describe complete gender equality. For many middle-class women, the privilege of choosing between male candidates once per year was hardly a reprieve from the suffocating comforts of their domestic spheres. The women of Heterodoxy and hundreds of other women's groups included scientists, scholars, ministers, and businesswomen. They sought equal educational and employment opportunities, an end to gendered assumptions about sexual freedom, and an end to prohibitions against spreading information about birth control. "All feminists are suffragists," these women explained, "but not all suffragists are feminists."

A small number of feminists employed as professors and scientists during this era used their skills and training to discredit earlier "scientific" assertions that women were inherently lacking in mental facilities. While other feminists employed logic and rhetoric to argue that women enjoyed all of the talents and capabilities of men, these scholars used the scientific method to debunk myths and demonstrate the scientific veracity of gender equality. For these and other feminists, equality began rather than ended with the ballot box. They argued that women must no longer be defined in ways that assumed that selfless devotion to husband and family was the only aim of womanhood. Many differed, however, when it came to discussing the unique capacities and roles of women in society. While some feminists yearned to abolish traditional gender roles, the majority accepted the basic premise of marriage as a partnership and hoped to give women the freedom to accept or reject traditional gender roles in their own lives.

feminism

Feminism is a term that has evolved into a variety of meanings. Among American feminists at the turn-of-the-century, the term *feminism* referenced one's belief in complete gender equality beyond tactical gains that might be achieved through specific movements for equal employment, suffrage, or property rights.

3.3 Race and Ethnicity

By the God of Heaven, we are cowards and jackasses if now that the war is over, we do not marshal every ounce of our brain and brawn to fight the forces of hell in our own land.

We return.

We return from fighting.

We return fighting!

Make way for Democracy! We saved it in France, and by the great Jehovah, we will save it in the United Stated of America, or know the reason why.

—W. E. B. Du Bois, The Crisis, May 1919

W. E. B. Du Bois organized a conference attended by Africans and African Americans from fifteen nations that met in Paris during the Treaty of Versailles. These delegates presented their demand that Germany's African colonies be granted self-determination to form their own independent nations. The demand was consistent with Wilson's Fourteen Points and the provision in the Treaty of Versailles that granted independence and self-determination to the former residents of Austria-Hungary. However, Wilson and the other delegates ignored these demands, and Germany's African colonies were simply transferred to the European victors. Americans displayed similar disregard toward the perspectives of women and minorities during and after the war. Committee on Public Information (CPI) propaganda portrayed the United States as an all-white nation where white men served as protectors and white women were virtuous guardians of the home front.

African American men and women shared high expectations that the experiences of war might reorder society along more egalitarian lines. Progressive reformers had speculated that the trials of war would also serve as a crucible for social change, thereby validating the sacrifice of a generation. However, War Department policy still restricted African Americans to segregated units commanded by white officers above the company level. Native Americans were permitted to serve in "white" battalions, but were often grouped together and given the most dangerous assignments. As a result, the mortality rate for Native American troops was more than twice as high as the average for the rest of the military. One of these unofficially segregated units, the 142nd Infantry, was drawn largely from separate units of Native Americans within the Oklahoma and Texas National Guard. The 600 Native Americans of this unit distinguished themselves in combat, and many members were awarded medals by the French for their uncommon valor. Several Native Americans such as the Choctaw were highly valued soldiers within the American Signal Corps, using their indigenous language to send coded messages that only native speakers could decipher. These "code talkers" would become even more crucial to the US war effort in the Second World War.

African Americans experienced severe discrimination in every aspect of the military. After being denied enlistment opportunities when the war began, black men were almost twice as likely as other men to have their request for draft exemption rejected. Review boards attempted to present these statistics as the result of factors other than race. Although they were exaggerated, some aspects of their defense were valid, but even these were simply the result of historic discrimination. For example, because many blacks had been excluded from skilled trades, they were less likely to be eligible for deferments based on the importance of their civilian jobs. Furthermore, many black husbands and fathers were so poor that the low pay enlisted men received would actually increase their family income. Southern review boards often cited this tendency when dismissing exemptions requested by black husbands and fathers, although white men who had dependents were usually granted exemption. One of the most infamous cases of discrimination involved the War Department itself rather than the local draft boards. Claiming that he was medically ineligible, the army attempted to force **Lieutenant Colonel Charles Young** to retire. As the army's highest-ranking black officer, Young was in a position to command an independent black regiment and would likely be appointed over white officers. However, Young exposed the scheme by riding his horse hundreds of miles to personally oppose the military's decision and publicly demonstrate his fitness for duty. The army responded by delaying the issue. Young was eventually promoted but was assigned to a segregated training camp in Illinois where he would not be in a position to command white soldiers or officers.

Lieutenant Colonel Charles Young

The highest-ranking African American officer at the outbreak of World War I, Charles Young confronted efforts by military officials to force him into retirement.

The military also intended to prevent black officers from commanding these segregated units until protests by black communities and the National Association for the
Advancement of Colored People (NAACP) led to a compromise. The War Department
declared that black men could serve as lieutenants and captains, but white officers
would occupy the higher ranks even within all-black battalions, brigades, and divisions.
In addition, the army at first intended to appoint relatively few black officers at any
level. White military officials predicted that it would be unlikely that more than a select
few men of color would ever prove themselves capable of serving as officers, and even
fewer that might make them reconsider their position against promoting black men as
field-grade officers.

The War Department established a training school for black officers at Fort Des
Moines in June 1917. Whites in Des Moines initially protested against the quartering of
black troops near their town; however, area black reporters proudly declared that after
a few months, the decorum of the men as well as the economic benefits of the camp had
led to a much friendlier atmosphere between the townsfolk and the camp leaders. "The
people of Des Moines felt at first that they would have to be on their guard against the
men at the Negro training camp, and several instances of discrimination were shown,"
the African American press of Kansas City reported, "but the camp has won Des
Moines." The camp brought to Iowa and the Great Plains future black leaders such as
James B. Morris Sr., a graduate from Howard Law School. After completing officer
training and serving in the war, he returned to Des Moines where he served as deputy
county treasurer and purchased Iowa's leading black newspaper, the *Iowa Bystander*.

Morris was one of nearly half a million African Americans who settled in Northern and Western
cities during the war years. This movement was known as the **Great Migration** and was especially
pronounced in large cities such as St. Louis, Chicago, Cleveland, Detroit, and a host of smaller manufacturing cities as Gary, Indiana, and Youngstown, Ohio. Black workers faced enormous discrimination while their families had limited options for housing in these segregated Northern and Midwestern cities. However, the opportunity to work in a factory provided upward mobility for these men and
their families. Black women were seldom hired in the better-paying jobs that were open to women.
However, most who sought work were able to find jobs in domestic service and other fields that were
being abandoned by white women. That so many families would move halfway across the country so
that a male breadwinner might occupy the toughest and lowest-paid factory jobs demonstrated the
continued hardships and limited job opportunities blacks faced in the South. However, a significant
number of black men found that the war had also created better job opportunities in leading Southern
industrial cities such as Birmingham and Atlanta.

Some black workers were able to secure federal government jobs or positions as laborers in the defense industry, and wages were monitored by the War Industries Board. Within the government's wartime arsenal, labor contracts made no distinction of race. Unlike white women, black women seldom
had the opportunity to change jobs and were limited to taking positions that were previously held by
white women or young boys. In many cases, only white women were able to replace white men in the
labor force, even within unskilled jobs. As white women entered the war industries, black women back-
filled the vacancies left in domestic and industrial service. Although they were often given the oldest
and hardest machines to operate, industrial work was welcomed as a change of pace from domestic service by those black women who were able to secure positions. Black women were often segregated from
other employees and placed in basements or other undesirable parts of the factories. However, the fact
that they were separated encouraged them to develop strong networks of support. Many of these women insisted on and received black supervisors. They registered complaints collectively, and when they
felt they were being mistreated, or when they discovered better work elsewhere, they often abandoned
their jobs together.

Contemporary observers of black women in industry often failed to recognize these assertive traits
as such. Reflecting the narrow-mindedness of their times, critics portrayed black women as ignorant,
lazy, unaccountable, and unprepared for wage labor. Recent historians have challenged this interpretation and explained why such a narrow and prejudiced view might have persisted for so many years. In
short, racist explanations that assumed black shortcomings were the result of innate character differences justified the status quo and presented the comforting fiction that racism was a problem of the
past. This lack of investigation perpetuated the widely held assumption that blacks were denied equal
opportunity during and after the war because they were simply a different caste of people. By ignoring
an era in which blacks were actively contributing to the nation's war effort, historians perhaps uncon-
sciously defended a society that continued to deny black citizens equal rights.

FIGURE 5.30

These African American soldiers from New
York were among those who were awarded
medals by the French government for heroism
during World War I.

Great Migration

Refers to the movement of
1.5 million African Americans
out of the American South
between 1910 and 1930.
Approximately half a million
of these individuals migrated
during World War I in order to
take advantage of wartime
employment in Northern
factories.

3.4   Dissent and Disloyalty

Many historic accounts of the home front tell of a homogenous and optimistic nation that was part of a "great pull together" to defeat tyranny abroad. In many ways, these accounts accurately portray the view of many Americans toward the war effort. Contemporary accounts record the collective actions of nearly every aspect of society. Scout troops organized relief drives, while families participated in meatless and wheatless days. The public celebrated the importance of work and dignity of labor. By framing the war as a moral struggle and by viewing labor as an essential contribution to the war effort, citizens on the home front forged a culture that ennobled their work and gave meaning to their sacrifices.

A deeper investigation reveals that the war also created a xenophobic hysteria that led to the creation of internment camps for some resident aliens and suspected enemy sympathizers. Community organizations and even private businesses formed their own investigation bureaus and encouraged citizens and employees to report any disparaging and "un-American" comments or behaviors they observed among their neighbors and fellow workers. The possibility of disloyalty and sabotage created a situation where individual liberty, collective security, and the interests of the government were weighed against one another. In most instances, the rights of the individuals were respected. However, from the perspective of pacifists, Socialists, and other dissenting groups, the war was a time where their views were brutally repressed.

Sedition Act of 1918

A notorious law that criminalized speeches that sought to discredit the US government or the US war effort during World War I.

In 1917, Congress passed the Espionage Act, which criminalized a number of behaviors such as seeking to disrupt military recruitment or otherwise hinder the war effort or assist the enemy. A provision that would have enforced government censorship was removed from the bill before it was passed, yet some still believed the law violated principles of individual freedom. Although controversial, the law was repeatedly upheld by federal courts. Fewer would defend the **Sedition Act of 1918**, which extended the Espionage Act and made criticizing the federal government during a time of war a criminal offense. Largely owing to the short amount of time before the passage of the law and the end of the war, very few were convicted under the terms of the Sedition Act. However, the newly appointed Attorney General A. Mitchell Palmer called on Congress to extend the provisions of the law even after the war ended.

Red Scare

A period of increased fear and even widespread paranoia regarding potential threats posed by anarchism and Communism between 1919 and 1920.

Palmer's tenure as attorney general coincided with a period of increased concern about the possible spread of Socialism that is today known as the **Red Scare**. During this period, hundreds of leftists and Socialist leaders were arrested with little concern for due process of law. During the war, some Socialists had criticized America's war effort as an action that merely propped up one group of imperialists against another. From perspective of Lenin and many others, World War I was being waged "to decide whether the British or German group of financial marauders [was] to receive the most booty." American Socialists generally viewed war as merely a continuation of historical quest for expansion to bolster Capitalism from its own decline. Although few Americans actually joined Socialist organizations, many workers shared their reservations about the sincerity of their government's claims that the war was being waged on behalf of their freedom. They were especially suspect about those within industry that called on them to work harder and sacrifice more while members of the upper classes drew the greatest profits.

FIGURE 5.31

J. Edgar Hoover was only twenty-nine years old when this photo was taken in 1924, but he had recently been appointed to head the Bureau of Investigation within the Justice Department.

A small percentage of workers registered as conscientious objectors and sought military deferments. These young men actively challenged widely held assumptions about gender roles and patriotism, adopting in their place a position of pacifist nonconformity that placed them at odds with the society around them. Some of these men lost their jobs, were imprisoned, or were even physically beaten for expressing opinions that were not supported by the government or the majority of Americans. The Bureau of Legal Advice was an organization formed during the war as an advocacy group that sought to protect a wide range of political dissent. While most Americans believed that these individuals had the right to their own opinions, the actions of many dissenters led to difficult decisions about the line between dissent and disloyalty. For example, Emma Goldman and her lover Alexander Berkman were sentenced to two years in jail for conspiring to "induce persons not to register" for the draft. Both had a history of supporting violent anarchism and Berkman had even conspired to murder the president of US Steel.

Berkman's advocacy of violence was not typical of those on the left, although a wave of bombings by self-styled anarchists in the summer of 1919 furthered the impression of Socialists and other radicals as intrinsically violent. The actions of a rightwing vigilante group that called itself the American Protective League (APL) was also atypical. The APL harassed, spied on, and occasionally assaulted pacifists and Socialists. Attorney General Palmer at first sought to neutralize the potential threat of all radicals who advocated violence, but not long before his Justice Department began to mirror the tactics of the APL. An ambitious twenty-four-year-old recent law school graduate named J. Edgar Hoover was hired to lead a new branch of the Justice Department charged with domestic surveillance of suspected radicals. Hoover's new agency would eventually expand and become its own bureau—the Federal Bureau of Investigations (FBI).

Hoover and Palmer responded to the perceived threat of Socialist labor leaders, as well as black civil rights leaders who were beginning to sound more militant by conducting quasi-legal raids, illegal surveillance operations, and unconstitutional mass arrests where individuals were detained for simply being a member of a particular leftist organization. The mass arrests became known as the **Palmer Raids** and remain one of the most dramatic examples of the potential excesses of federal law enforcement in American history. Although Palmer originally enjoyed the support of Congress and the public, his department's illegal surveillance methods and mass arrests soon led to greater skepticism about the actual danger of black radicals and political dissidents. Although Palmer made efforts to limit some of his department's excesses and even recommended the pardon of the increasingly radical Eugene Debs, Palmer's declaration that militant Socialists were planning to launch a nationwide revolution on May 1, 1919, made many Americans reconsider their fears of anarchists and radicals when no violence occurred on that day.

FIGURE 5.32

This collage of newspaper reports describes the labor conflict leading up to the Bisbee Deportation. The mining companies and local government officials herded striking miners onto cattle cars destined for Columbus, New Mexico, the same community that had recently been sacked by Pancho Villa.

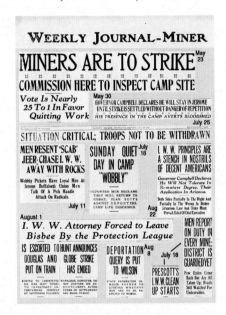

Palmer Raids

A series of legal and extralegal raids on suspected labor organizers, leftists, and political dissidents in the United States after World War I. US attorney general A. Mitchell Palmer was convinced that such methods were necessary to prevent the spread of dangerous radical ideas and organizations. He approved the use of controversial surveillance tactics by Department of Justice officials, including a young assistant named J. Edgar Hoover.

The Red Scare was more than an overzealous response by the federal government to the threats and deeds of a few militant radicals. It also had important economic ramifications as the Justice Department moved to isolate union leaders by labeling them as "Reds" who were anti-American and loyal only to Russia. Using loosely constructed allegations of political disloyalty, Palmer used the power of the federal government to halt a nationwide strike of coal miners in November 1919. Two years prior to Palmer's action on behalf of coal operators, state officials in Arizona had used similar accusations of disloyalty to justify their intervention on behalf of the operators of copper mines. The International Workers of the World (IWW) had organized thousands of copper miners in and around Bisbee, Arizona, and were waging an effective strike in the summer of 1917. Their opponents declared that the leaders of the IWW were part of a Communist and/or pro-German conspiracy to spread labor discontent. City and state authorities sided with the mining companies and rounded up the leaders of the movement along with a thousand IWW supporters. In what became known as the Bisbee Deportation of 1917, these former copper miners were effectively kidnapped and abandoned at a railroad depot in the New Mexico dessert. Had it not been for the intervention of local residents and the US Army, which built a refugee camp for the workers, the government's deportation order might have become a death sentence.

One of the most significant labor strikes in US history erupted in February 1919 and was likewise influenced by the anti-Ccommunist hysteria of the era. Shipyard workers throughout Seattle had long been promised that they would receive pay raises once the government ended its wartime price controls. Because companies could not charge market prices for a number of goods, employers explained, workers would not receive the kinds of pay raises that would naturally occur during a wartime boom. When the war ended and the government ended its policy of price controls, however, the long-expected raises failed to materialize. In response, nearly 40,000 workers in the region's shipyards went on strike. These men and women were joined by an additional 25,000 union members throughout the city who engaged in what became known as a "sympathy strike." Until the shipyard workers received the raises they had been promised, most members of the city's 110 local unions vowed that they too would not report for work.

The Seattle General Strike of 1919 had profound implications regarding the potential impact of strikes and worker solidarity. If successful, labor advocates and opponents both predicted, other cities would experience similar strikes and the balance of power between labor and capital might forever be altered. Those who opposed the strikes predicted that a wave of general strikes would destroy the foundation of America's modern economy and open the door to anarchy. However, conditions in Seattle during the strike were remarkably calm. Because most stores and streetcars were no longer being operated, thousands of union members voluntarily provided essential services such as food delivery and garbage collection. Whether these informal measures would have been adequate in preventing civil unrest and hardship is unknown. The mayor effectively declared martial law and threatened to use federal troops to arrest those who refused his order to go back to work. As dozens of labor leaders were arrested and the prolabor newspaper was seized by local police, the strike quickly ended. Federal troops were not sent to Seattle, as the strike itself lasted less than a week. Most Americans believed that the government's heavy-handed methods were justified in order to prevent "Bolshevism" from spreading to America. This reaction was representative of the change in public opinion from Progressivism to a more conservative political orientation that would typify the 1920s.

REVIEW AND CRITICAL THINKING

1. Asses the strengths and weaknesses of the Treaty of Versailles and League of Nations. What role did President Woodrow Wilson play in the peace process? Why did some in Congress not support Wilson's actions?

2. Why were suffragists successful in passing a constitutional amendment guaranteeing the right to vote regardless of gender in 1920? The women's suffrage movement was entering its eighth decade, so what made the movement different in these later years from the early attempts you have read about?

3. Describe the experiences of African Americans during World War I, both as soldiers and on the home front. What was the significance of the Great Migration?

4. What led to race riots and the Red Scare in 1919? What were the Palmer Raids, and how did fears about the spread of radical doctrines affect American history at this time?

4. CONCLUSION

Many of the labor strikes that occurred during and immediately after World War I were crushed by state and federal agencies. However, continued activism demonstrated that working-class Americans did more than experience a significant increase in their income during the war—they also raised their expectations and were more willing to demonstrate on behalf of their rights as workers. The wartime boom also initiated a rising economic standard that would expand during the 1920s, survive the Great Depression, and continue after World War II. Government involvement during the war had lasting consequences in convincing employers to recognize worker's demands before strikes occurred. That the government might also intervene on behalf of workers demonstrated the importance of mobilizing the political potential of union members. During the war, business leaders were forced to recruit workers; recruitment helped to establish new trends favoring the spread of employee benefits and Progressive reforms such as the eight-hour day. Although the end of the war reduced the advantage some workers and unions had enjoyed, many business leaders had concluded that a degree of voluntary reform could bring greater efficiency and higher output. They also recognized that these reforms might help to prevent the spread of labor unions—something that became one of the leading goals of business leaders in the decades that followed.

The war put new stresses on US institutions and challenged notions of race and gender. Discrimination based on race, class, and gender was largely unaffected by the war although the expectations of women, workers, and minorities were not left unchanged. The result was both an increase in civil rights activism and an intensification of alienation and despair among those who continued to endure discrimination. While government propaganda masked the separateness of experience based on race, class, and gender, the realities of life for most Americans were still largely determined by these categories. By placing greater stresses on unity as a form of patriotic expression, however, the government helped to further the image that discrimination was contrary to the ideals the nation was fighting to defend.

In a number of instances, white and black women came together to advance their common interest in promoting suffrage. However, most women failed to bridge the racial divide in ways that reflected the culture of the early twentieth century. Race would prove to be the most significant obstacle limiting the unity of the suffrage movement since white and minority women generally belonged to separate organizations that only occasionally and tentatively worked together. However, through the efforts of a diverse range of local and national suffrage organizations and groups such as the National Association of Colored Women's Clubs, women would secure their right to vote through the Nineteenth Amendment to the Constitution in 1920. In the meantime, cities and states were the front line in the battle for votes for women. Although the Progressives focused many of their efforts at reform through the federal government, the lives of Americans were still more impacted by the decisions of state and municipal governments. As a result, these early suffrage victories were significant both in their own right and in influencing male political leaders of these states to support women's suffrage on a national scale. The Nineteenth Amendment was passed and ratified by men only after women had secured the right to vote locally in many communities. While some male Progressives supported the Nineteenth Amendment as a matter of equality, most did so only to avoid alienating large and empowered groups of women who cast votes in local elections.

The Western Allies might have been able to win the war without US troops, but they could not have even continued the war into 1918 without the food US farmers produced. Once they finally arrived in France, US troops were equally dependent on foreign-made artillery and other materials, as well as support provided by the British and French. After a failed German offensive in the spring of 1918 and the arrival of over a million US troops, the Allied Powers seized the momentum and began pushing German forces eastward. German propaganda and government-censored newspapers made light of these developments, leading many Germans to wonder why their armies surrendered, even as the bulk of German forces were still in Belgium and France. Adolf Hitler was a soldier in the German army at this time and would later espouse the belief that his nation had somehow been betrayed by cowardly or even traitorous leaders. In reality, German military leaders had expended their supplies in the failed offensive of 1918. The most thoughtful among them recognized that the best they could hope for by November 1918 was to somehow form a line of defensive fortifications that was too deep for the Western Allies to ever overrun. If successful, this combat operation would return to the status quo of 1917, and the war of attrition would continue indefinitely even as millions of US troops entered the fight. As a result, the decision to surrender, even though Germany still held enemy territory, was one that prevented further suffering and the continuation of a war that Germany might prolong indefinitely but never win.

5.   FURTHER READING

Andrews, Thomas G. *Killing for Coal: America's Deadliest Labor War* (2008).

Early, Frances H. *A World Without War: How US Feminists and Pacifists Resisted World War I* (1997).

Ellis, Mark *Race, War, and Surveillance: African Americans and the United States Government During World War I* (2001).

Farwell, Byron. *Over There: The United States in the Great War, 1917–1918* (1999).

Feurer, Rosemary, *Radical Unionism in the Midwest, 1900–1950* (2006).

Greenwald, Maurine Weiner. *The Impact of World War I on Women Workers in the United States* (1980).

Johnson, Jeffrey A. *"They Are All Red Out Here": Socialist Politics in the Pacific Northwest, 1895–1925* (2008).

Kennedy, David M. *Over Here: The First World War and American Society* (1980).

McGerr, Michael. *A Fierce Discontent: The Rise and Fall of the Progressive Movement in America, 1870–1920* (2005).

Murphy, Kevin. *Political Manhood: Red Bloods, Mollycoddles, and the Politics of Progressive Era Reform* (2010).

Recchiuti, John Louis. *Civic Engagement: Social Science and Progressive-Era Reform in New York City* (2006).

CHAPTER 6

Roaring Twenties to the Great Depression, 1920–1932

The 1920s were a period of economic growth and transition. Real wages for most workers increased, while stock prices advanced as much during the 1920s as they had in the previous three decades. The US census of 1920 revealed that, for the first time, a majority of Americans lived in cities and towns with at least 2,500 residents. The 1920s also boasted a uniquely modern culture that celebrated the fast pace of cosmopolitan life. Yet in many ways, the United States was still mired in the past. Progressive reformers sought to publicize the tragedy of preventable diseases and child mortality among the poor. However, it was not until after the discovery that millions of draftees in World War I were malnourished and medically unfit for military service that these reformers had the attention of the federal government. Despite recent advances in medicine, childbirth remained the second-leading cause of death among women.

The emergence of modern medicine permitted child mortality rates to decline significantly among the wealthy, but few other Americans enjoyed regular access to physicians. For the urban poor and many rural dwellers, an average of one in three children died before their fifth birthday. Progressives attempted to counter these trends through federal action. However, conservatives perceived these attempts as symptomatic of the excessive growth of government during the previous two decades. The contest regarding federal support for health care programs for women and infants personifies the transition from Progressivism to more conservative ways of thought regarding the role of government. This transition from Progressivism to conservatism was one of the leading dynamics of the 1920s.

Although the middle and late 1920s saw a resurgence of conservative thought, Progressive ideas about reform would continue into the early 1920s. Grassroots campaigns by the newly formed League of Women Voters, along with a variety of other women's clubs and Progressive organizations, seized the message of military preparedness. They sought to convince voters that prenatal care and other health programs were vital to the nation's well-being. Even conservative groups such as the Daughters of the American Revolution joined the chorus of voices calling for federal intervention to improve prenatal and early childhood care. In response, Congress approved the **Sheppard-Towner Act** in 1921. The Sheppard-Towner Act was based on a bill introduced by Montana congresswoman Jeanette Rankin in 1919. The law provided federal matching grants for state-operated women's health clinics and other programs designed to safeguard the health of women and infants. The Sheppard-Towner Act was the first federally funded program in the nation's history designed to promote social welfare. The law was hardly radical, however, as it provided only modest funding through matching grants to states and communities. These entities were required to provide at least 50 percent of the funding for the health clinics and prenatal programs. They were also responsible for administration and operation of these programs. The availability of federal subsidies spurred the construction of several thousand health clinics in cities and small towns. The greatest impact may have

Sheppard-Towner Act

The first federally funded program encouraging social welfare, the Sheppard-Towner Act provided matching grants for communities to develop women's health clinics and other programs designed to reduce infant mortality.

occurred in isolated rural areas served by traveling nurses and distance-learning programs that trained community midwives.

The Sheppard-Towner Act suggested a new partnership between government, technology, and privately owned hospitals and medical practices. It also reflected growing expectations by citizens toward the federal government. In 1920s America, nearly all federal revenue was dedicated to national defense and repayment of wartime loans. Social welfare was regarded as an obligation of state and local government. Sensing the possibility that success of the Sheppard-Towner Act might lead to more government intervention in their industry, the American Medical Association (AMA) attacked the federally subsidized women's clinics as "socialized medicine."

The AMA launched a campaign against the growth of the federal government into the private sector. The AMA also attempted to cut off funding for the clinics and eliminate further government subsidies for medical services, even those for women and infants. Attorneys representing the AMA pointed out that the Tenth Amendment designated all powers not specifically enumerated in the Constitution to the states. As a result, they argued, providing federal funds for women's clinics was unconstitutional. When the US Supreme Court rejected this argument, the AMA continued its attack against "Socialism" in the private sector of medicine.

The AMA continued to lobby against the Sheppard-Towner Act throughout the 1920s. Meanwhile, the political climate continued its drift away from the liberalism of the Progressives and towards more conservative views regarding the proper role of government. As a result, Congress eliminated federal appropriations for the clinics in 1929. Although the law had been popular, many began to view its provisions as undue interference within the private sector. Later that same year, a financial crisis led many Americans to reconsider the need for federal government activism. Ironically, the federal government was called upon to intervene on behalf of the private sector as the health of the nation's financial system was on the verge of collapse.

1. PROSPERITY AND ITS LIMITS

LEARNING OBJECTIVES

1. **Summarize the major issues of the Harding administration. Explain why Harding was able to enjoy considerable public support during his lifetime but would later be regarded by many as one of the least effective presidents in US history.**
2. **Explain the ways that industry and labor changed in the 1920s. Explain why union membership declined even as the nation experienced an increase in the number of jobs.**
3. **Describe the growth of the consumer culture during the 1920s. Explain how consumerism affected the United States during this decade.**

1.1 A Probusiness Orientation and Scandals in Washington

Warren Harding

The twenty-ninth president of the United States, Harding was a conservative publisher from Ohio whose administration is best known for a series of scandals involving several of his cabinet members.

The federal government intervened on behalf of business throughout the nineteenth century, especially in matters of promoting infrastructure and development. At the same time, the federal government sought to regulate business to prevent monopoly and exploitation of consumers. Many observers argued that the government's track record in this regard was mixed at best. Following the wartime partnership between government and industry, and the anti-Socialist hysteria of the Red Scare, the Republican administration of **Warren Harding** adopted an unapologetically probusiness orientation. Most government officials agreed with Harding's Vice President Calvin Coolidge, who reputedly declared that "the business of America was business." The attempted trust-busting of the Progressive Era gave way to toleration of oligarchy—a term that in this context refers to control of an entire industry by a handful of large corporations.

Progressives continued to compile statistics showing how US Steel, Standard Oil, General Electric, and other firms dominated their respective industries and used their positions to control workers and prices. For many Americans, the prosperity of the era seemed out of place with such an indictment of corporate America. Unemployment was at historical lows, wages were at historic highs, and it seemed that scarcity was becoming a problem of the past as Wall Street and Main Street appeared to be prospering together. Equally important, Wall Street was losing its pejorative image as investment firms hired traveling brokers that peddled investments door to door and coast to coast. For the first time, significant numbers of middle-class Americans were purchasing stocks. As a result, statistics about the wild profits of these corporations were just as likely to stimulate investment as indignation.

The new probusiness climate facilitated the rise of trade associations and professional organizations that represented the interests of particular industries and professions. In the past, corporate executives traveled directly to Washington to advocate their interests. By the 1920s, some of these new organizations established offices near the nation's capital and were able to employ specialists who dedicated themselves to advocacy among lawmakers on the behalf of their clients. Some Americans complained that the power and influence of these lobbyists constituted a nefarious "fourth branch" of government. Others argued that lobbyists circumvented the concept of democracy and introduced new opportunities for corruption. After all, they argued, these advocacy groups provided funding for congressional campaigns that appeared to many as bribes. In some cases, cash was distributed directly to the lawmakers themselves.

Several dishonest legislators were exposed in the early 1920s, and some of the biggest scandals were tied to the Harding administration itself. The first scandal was the discovery that the head of the Veterans Bureau was accepting kickbacks from government contractors and even looting medical supplies that were supposed to be used for injured veterans. Harding's attorney general was later indicted for fraud regarding "irregularities" with the disposition of German assets that had been seized during World War I. He was also accused of receiving kickbacks from bootleggers.

The biggest scandal of the 1920s involved Secretary of the Interior Albert Fall who was believed to have accepted $400,000 in bribes. In exchange, Fall permitted private oil companies to drill on public land in Wyoming. These oil reserves, such as the massive Teapot Dome reserve, were supposed to be left undeveloped as an emergency resource for the military so that the United States would never be dependent on foreign oil during war. The incident was soon labeled the **Teapot Dome Scandal**, a phrase that became synonymous with government corruption throughout the next generation. The public was even more enraged when Albert Fall was only ordered to pay a $100,000 fine and serve one year in jail.

Harding was not directly connected to any of these scandals and remained a popular president prior to his sudden death in August 1923. Calvin Coolidge replaced Harding as president and continued the probusiness policies favored by Harding and the Republican Party. Both of these presidents typified the profile of what many Americans expected of their presidents: a dignified leader and a model citizen. Later revelations would demonstrate that despite their images as devout Christians and family men, neither was above the temptations that ensnared many other men of wealth and power. More damaging, at least to the reputation of the late President Harding, was the revelation that he likely knew many of the details about the scandals within his administration but had failed to prevent them. Though he knew them to be incompetent or unethical, Harding delegated authority to several cabinet officials because they supported his administration and/or were personal friends from his days in Ohio politics. Known as the "Ohio Gang," even though many of the members of Harding's cabal were not from the Buckeye State, these Republican leaders became infamous for corruption. Many also were known to be gamblers and had numerous extramarital affairs that conflicted with their public image and espoused Christian living.

Despite the revelations of corruption, most of the legislation that was favorable to business interests during the early 1920s also promoted economic growth that provided some benefits to the nation's overall welfare. For example, the automotive and oil industries lobbied Congress to approve the Federal Highway Act of 1921. This law provided matching grants for states to build highways and bridges. Although the interstate system would not be developed until after World War II, this program required recipients to coordinate their efforts with neighboring states to create a nationwide grid of roads.

FIGURE 6.1

In reference to the Teapot Dome Scandal, the US Capitol is presented as a boiling teapot. The leasing of Wyoming oil reserves had a tremendous impact on the development of the mountainous West, while the revelation of cash bribes greatly reduced the public's trust in the federal government.

Who Says a Watched Pot Never Boils?

Teapot Dome Scandal

Erupted when news that Secretary of the Interior Albert Fall had arranged to lease the US Navy's Oil Reserves at Teapot Dome, Wyoming, to a private oil company. Fall had received hundreds of thousands of dollars in bribes to permit drilling on publicly owned lands containing oil that had been reserved for use by the navy.

FIGURE 6.2

Andrew Mellon placing a wreath at the foot of a statue honoring Alexander Hamilton. Mellon was an influential Secretary of the Treasury who supported many of the conservative views of Hamilton, a Founding Father and the first Secretary of the Treasury. Mellon was also a wealthy philanthropist who donated millions to the University of Pittsburgh, his alma mater.

Secretary of the Treasury Andrew Mellon was staunchly conservative and supported the era's deep tax cuts for the wealthy. He also resurrected one of the Progressive goals by creating the General Accounting Office, which audited the government's budgets and expense reports. Mellon advocated low taxes for corporations and the wealthy—a condition he believed was a prerequisite for economic expansion. Harding also appointed four conservative and probusiness appointees to the Supreme Court. Bolstered by the inclusion of these conservatives, the Supreme Court repealed federal child labor laws and upheld numerous injunctions ordering unions to halt strikes and return to work.

The Republican-controlled Congress and White House of the 1920s approved three policies that favored business interests, wealthy individuals, and some members of the middle class. Fearful that a European recovery would result in US businesses once again being forced to compete with foreign goods, Congress raised tariffs. These taxes helped to protect US businesses by making foreign goods more expensive, but the law also kept consumer prices artificially high. Second, Congress enacted a series of laws that reduced the tax rate for the wealthiest Americans from over 70 percent to just over 20 percent. Congress also raised the exemption level, which meant that a larger number of middle and upper-middle-class families were no longer required to pay any federal tax. Congress also reduced estate taxes that were assessed on large fortunes passed down to the next generation. Lastly, Congress approved reductions in government spending that resulted in balanced budgets but also led to reduced enforcement of the already-lax regulations on businesses and financiers.

Wealthy individuals and corporations benefitted from each of these decisions, at least in the short run. The tariffs led to increased profits for manufacturers, while the tax reductions permitted entrepreneurs to finance new businesses. Because some of these profits were reinvested in ways that led to job creation, a portion of the economic benefits of lower taxes for businesses and the wealthy likely benefitted the rest of the nation. It would later be apparent, however, that the majority of Americans were not earning enough money to sustain the economic rally of the 1920s, which had been built largely on consumer spending.

The tariffs made it difficult for European nations to repay their debts, and Congress was forced to permit a series of extensions on loans that would eventually default. Progressives argued that the tax reductions Andrew Mellon recommended led to concentrated wealth in the hands of the few. These individuals would later claim that the stock market crash was the result of the wealthy using their revenues to speculate in real estate and the stock market rather than invest in new businesses. By this perspective, lowering the tax rates for the wealthy might reduce stability rather than spur productive investment and job creation.

1.2 Prohibition and Enforcement

After the 1916 Congressional election, two-thirds of the House and Senate were pledged supporters of prohibition. However, many of these lawmakers were not yet convinced that a Constitutional amendment banning the production and sale of alcohol was an appropriate measure for the federal government to take up. World events and local campaigns in support of a prohibition amendment eventually overcame this reservation.

Eighteenth Amendment

A Constitutional Amendment that outlawed the manufacture, transport, and sale of intoxicating liquors. The Eighteenth Amendment would later be repealed by the Twenty-First Amendment in 1933.

The importance of preserving grain as war gripped Europe combined with the moralistic tenor of the nation and a growing hostility to all things German. Prohibition supporters argued that the "Hun's" brewing tradition was dangerously un-American and threatened to weaken the moral fiber of the nation. Over time, politics and religiosity mixed in ways that turned support for prohibition into a litmus test of one's patriotism. In such a political environment, few in Congress wanted to oppose the **Eighteenth Amendment**. The amendment outlawed the manufacture, transport, and sale of intoxicating liquors. Congress approved the measure in December 1917, and the states quickly ratified the amendment, which took effect in January 1919.

State laws had proven ineffective in preventing the manufacture and consumption of liquor, and many critics believed the Eighteenth Amendment would prove equally ineffective. These kinds of laws, critics argued, attempted to legislate morality and impose religious views about alcohol that many Americans rejected. In their failure, these critics added, prohibition laws did little more than inspire disregard for the laws of man. Despite the passage of the Volstead Act which provided federal enforcement for the new Constitutional amendment, enforcement was lax. Bootleggers and speakeasies became more and more abundant as people looked for alternate sources of alcohol.

The resilience of the saloon was partially due to its importance as a cultural space that was important to various subcommunities throughout both rural and urban America. The saloon was where men gathered for political meetings, and local pubs usually doubled as the headquarters of a variety of fraternal organizations. Through these connections, men found that fellowship meant access to information and markets as well as references for jobs. Men who did not drink soon formed their own fraternal organizations and lodges to provide a similar space for meetings and fellowship. The same was true of women. The turn of the century saw the greatest proliferation of women's clubs, both as separate organizations led by women and as auxiliaries of fraternal organizations for men. For most Americans, membership in these groups and local churches provided opportunities for fellowship and recreation and served as their connection to the larger world.

The Eighteenth Amendment empowered Congress to pass laws banning the production, transportation, and sale of alcoholic beverages. Congress passed the Volstead Act in the fall of 1919 over outgoing President Wilson's veto. The law outlawed the production of any beverage with an alcohol content higher than 0.5 percent, although it was later amended to permit the production of wine for home use. The law left enforcement largely to states and local police for most of the 1920s. Penalties for violators of the Volstead Act were usually fines that did little to discourage those willing to break the law from doing so.

State and local ordinances that permitted doctors to prescribe "medicine" containing alcohol, including whiskey and other spirits, also continued. Historians estimate that 1 million gallons of whiskey, among other forms of alcohol, were prescribed each year. Disregard for the law reached all the way to the White House, which maintained an impressive selection of liquor for entertaining official guests. The rest of the nation simply purchased spirits from local bootleggers.

The Volstead Act did little to end the production, sale, or consumption of alcohol, but it did add significantly to the cost of alcohol for consumers. Although it was not the intent of reformers to merely reduce alcohol consumption, the obstacles one had to overcome to obtain alcohol at inflated prices ended the practice of daily consumption for many working class Americans. At the same time, the toleration of those who violated the law and the rarity of severe punishment led many Americans to lower their regard for law enforcement. Before long, criminal groups began making outrageous profits by supplying alcohol. Some of these groups became crime syndicates, using their liquor revenue to purchase weapons while seeking to control other vice trades such as gambling, narcotics, and prostitution.

"Organized crime" expanded significantly during the Prohibition Era. Crime bosses such as Chicago's Al Capone created their own underground empires by committing robberies, selling illicit goods, and using fraud and intimidation to force local businesses to pay "tribute" for protection. Capone directed some of these funds to charitable groups, leading many Chicagoans to obstruct police efforts. Other police officers found Capone's bountiful offerings of cash bribes even more persuasive.

Before Prohibition, organized crime relied more heavily upon the sale of illicit drugs and prostitution. Although these activities continued, the popular image was that Capone and others were making their wealth by providing alcohol to a thirsty nation. As a result, some Americans sympathized with Capone's claims that he was merely providing a service that people wanted. However, Capone's dealings with rival gangs and the police were notoriously violent. Capone and others were careful to conceal the source of their income by laundering their revenue through dozens of businesses. This made it difficult for the FBI to provide clear evidence of what everyone knew was the source of Capone's income. Eventually, the FBI decided to try a different tactic, focusing on the front businesses that were laundering Capone's profits but had neglected to pay taxes.

FIGURE 6.3

New York policemen watch as hundreds of gallons of whiskey are poured into the sewers. Raids such as this failed to halt the flow of alcohol during the 1920s but did create new opportunities for bootleggers and others willing to risk the consequences of breaking prohibition laws.

FIGURE 6.4

The signed verdict convicting Chicago's Al Capone of tax evasion.

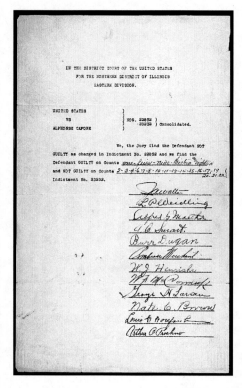

Henry Ford

Entrepreneur who founded Ford Motor Company, which applied assembly line techniques to the production of automobiles. Ford was hostile to unions and a difficult taskmaster, yet he paid his employees more than prevailing wages, intending to command their loyalty and create more consumers for his products.

Prohibition revealed the different standards of law enforcement for the wealthy and the poor. Wealthy Americans reveled in their private cocktail parties, which were seldom disrupted by police. Those with money could avoid dealing with gangsters and purchase their spirits from pharmacies or other sources. When a group of reformers sought to close this loophole by at least limiting the quantity of whiskey a physician might prescribe, the American Medical Association lobbied in opposition. While most doctors questioned the health benefits of "medicinal whisky," they opposed any law that might open the door for other government regulations of what doctors could prescribe for their patients. Critics countered that the AMA was simply hoping to continue a lucrative practice that accounted for tremendous profits among some of its members.

1.3   Technology and Innovation

Radio technology had proven its value in wartime and would revolutionize communications during the early 1920s. By the end of the decade, the first commercial radio networks were born, leading to the syndication of popular programs that could be heard across the nation. The aviation industry also demonstrated the potential of fixed-wing aircraft during the war. US companies quickly expanded from producing a few hundred airplanes each year to 5,000 per year by the end of the decade. By the late 1920s, dozens of major cities were connected by a network of locally owned passenger lines that began offering scheduled flights. Few Americans were able to take advantage of this new mode of air transportation. By the end of the decade, however, one in five Americans owned an automobile. The proliferation of the automobile heralded the beginning of a veritable revolution from public to private transportation. The utility of the automobile was limited in the first years of the new century by prohibitive costs and the lack of roads that were suitable for cars. Once considered the plaything of the super rich, by the late 1920s the automobile became the symbol of middle-class life. Personal ownership of automobiles also altered the way city people thought about urban spaces. With the proliferation of the automobile, cities were planned and constructed around modes of transportation rather than the other way around. The automobile also allowed for the expansion of suburbs beyond the reach of streetcar lines.

Henry Ford did not invent the automobile or the assembly line. Instead, he was the most successful at marrying these two technologies together in ways that increased efficiency and reduced costs. Small household goods were manufactured on assembly lines and canned meats were made by stripping meat from carcasses on "disassembly" lines. Prior to the early 1900s, automobile chassis were placed on blocks, and workers brought the parts to the cars to be assembled one at a time. In 1901, Ransom E. Olds of Lansing had shown that the assembly line could be made to work for automotive production, despite the size and weight of the product. However, the Oldsmobile factory burned to the ground, and Henry Ford invested in a much larger factory that built upon Olds' methods. Ford's heavy steel rails and conveyer belts moved a car's chassis down a line. As a result, workers could stand in one place and complete one simple task, such as securing a specific bolt or adding a headlamp as cars moved along the line.

Ford's newest assembly line, complete with its massive moving belts, was up and running in 1913. Ford produced 250,000 Model T automobiles that year. This was thirty times as many cars as Ford had produced a few years prior; it was also more cars than Oldsmobile and over eighty other competing automakers based primarily out of Ohio, Michigan, and Illinois had ever made. A decade later, Ford was producing 2 million Model Ts, which were nearly identical to the earlier models except for the price. Ford was able to take advantage of economies of scale through mass production; consequently, the price of the Model T dropped from over $800 to under $300. Other automakers produced more diverse offerings, and many competing automakers produced better or cheaper cars. However, in 1913 no one could match the quality of the Model T for the price Ford was charging. As for the monotony of mass production, Ford quipped that his customers could have his vehicle in any color they chose so long as that color was black.

The work was routine and could be completed by anyone with minimal training. As a result, Ford no longer needed to hire workers with mechanical expertise. Instead, he hired unskilled workers but offered better wages than they might make on other assembly lines. Ford famously introduced the Five Dollar Plan, a daily wage that was roughly double the $2–$3 pay rate that was typical for factory work. Ford employees were required to submit to investigations by Ford's Social Department. Ford desired only sober workers who shunned cigarettes and fast lifestyles. By the mid-1920s, the investigators no longer made home visits to determine whether factory workers drank alcohol or engaged in other behaviors their paternalistic boss considered a vice. Instead, they were more likely to investigate a worker's political beliefs. Anyone who embraced Socialism or even considered starting a union would be terminated.

The high wages Ford workers earned permitted most employees to purchase their own automobile. These workers were required to make that purchase a Ford automobile or else they would share the fate of those who attempted to start a union in a Ford plant. Given the high wages Ford offered, most workers tolerated Ford's demands and shunned unionization as Socialistic or even un-American. Ford himself wrapped his techniques of mass production, low prices, and high wages in the language of Americana. The 23 million automobiles on the road in 1929 satisfied Ford that he had democratized the automobile by bringing car ownership to the masses.

Ford's assembly line methods were studied by the emerging business colleges and perfected to maximize efficiency of movement. Older methods of production that required skilled craftsmen largely disappeared, as did the level of job satisfaction workers expressed once they no longer felt connected to the products they produced. Instead of seeing a finished product or working closely with a team, workers stood in one place and performed repetitive tasks. The system was tremendously efficient, and it did provide the opportunity for more jobs among nonskilled workers. Worker productivity in most industrial fields increased by about 50 percent while real wages for the average factory worker also increased. However, these wages usually grew by no more than 10 percent over the decade. The average workweek declined to just over forty hours in some fields—a long goal of the labor movement. However, the typical workweek for industrial workers remained six days of forty-eight hours of labor. In addition, upward mobility was hindered by the elimination of most skilled positions, and a new generation of factory worker was even more disconnected from his labor than in the past.

FIGURE 6.5

Ford automobiles being produced on a Detroit assembly line in 1923.

FIGURE 6.6 Real Average Weekly or Daily Earnings for Selected Occupations, 1920–1930

Year	(1) Weekly Skilled and Semi-Skilled Male Production Workers in 25 Manufacturing Industries	(2) Weekly Unskilled Male Production Workers in 25 Manufacturing Industries	(3) Weekly: Female Production Workers in 25 Manufacturing Industries	(4) Farmworkers Daily Wage Rate
1920	29.16	22.28	15.14	2.82
1922	28.73	20.74	16.9	2.04
1924	30.61	22.45	16.78	2.40
1926	30.60	22.47	16.72	2.32
1928	31.94	23.89	17.15	2.30
1930	29.93	22.47	16.40	2.21

Previous generations of farmers and craftsmen had been able to see tangible evidence of their labor. The only workers in factories with assembly lines who even saw the finished product were those who worked on loading docks, and they usually did not participate in the production of goods. Factory work had always featured monotony, a contest between one's will and the time clock. But workers could at least identify the products they had made before the adoption of the assembly line. Consequently, workers no longer identified themselves in terms of their jobs, as farmers and craftsmen had in the past. No celebration of the harvest took place; no trade or skill provided a sense of identity and union. Unskilled workers were much more likely to change employers and industries many times throughout their lives. As a result, the urban worker sought satisfaction and meaning outside of their jobs in ways that led to the proliferation of recreational activities and the celebration of consumption rather than production.

1.4   Labor and the Limits of Prosperity

The labor movement's postwar gains were quickly neutralized within the climate of the Red Scare. The conservative orientation of the federal government throughout the three Republican administrations of the 1920s likewise created an environment that was hostile toward organized labor. Employers rallied around a strategy they branded the **American Plan**, a series of ideas and tactics that sought to challenge the legitimacy of unions and outlaw provisions that required workers to join unions.

As the name indicates, the American Plan sought to portray any provision requiring a worker to join a union as contrary to "American" principles, such as freedom of choice. Some manufacturers even placed American flags on products that had been made by nonunion labor in hopes of branding organized labor as something that was foreign to the ideals and values of the nation. Central to this tactic were attempts to casually equate unions with Socialism. Because both organized labor and Socialist parties were growing in popularity throughout Europe, supporters of the American Plan simply had to create the impression that these two trends were intrinsically connected.

Businesses lobbied government officials to outlaw collective bargaining throughout the 1920s. They based their argument on the idea that individual workers should be completely free to contract independently rather than be bound by a single contract negotiated on their behalf. Labor leaders contended that the intent of the American Plan was simply to reduce the collective power of unions. They argued that employers were disingenuous in claiming that they were motivated by a desire to liberate workers from union contracts. Reminding the public of the violence used against workers who tried to start unions in the past, union leaders sarcastically asked what had suddenly made modern corporations so very concerned with the freedoms of their workers.

American Plan

The name coined by antiunion industrialists who pledged to never negotiate with union leaders. The American Plan sought to create the image that the "open shop" was synonymous with freedom and other American values, while the "closed shop" forced workers to join unions. Critics argued that this was simply a devious method of spinning antiunion activities that harmed workers.

Labor leaders also sought to explain the difference between collective bargaining and the collective ownership of Socialism. However, without the access to the media and the financial resources enjoyed by many industrialists, labor leaders found themselves on the outside and on the defensive. The conservative political climate that followed in the wake of the Red Scare and the continued notion that unionization was a gateway to Socialism plagued the labor movement throughout the 1920s. Despite the growth of industry and creation of millions of new jobs, union membership declined from 5 million to below 3.5 million by the late 1920s.

The overall percentage of workers who were members of unions also declined from 18 percent to 10 percent in the 1920s. Part of the reason for organized labor's trouble was the slight decrease in the percentage of workers employed in blue-collar jobs due to technology and automation. The emergence of the modern corporation created tens of thousands of new jobs in clerical fields, but these usually remained impervious to organization. Despite the decline in percentages and overall numbers of union workers, labor strikes remained the most potent weapon in the arsenal of labor activism. One of the largest and most radical strikes occurred in a location that had been least welcoming to unions in the past—the South. Northern textile mills had moved to the South in previous decades for precisely this reason. During the 1920s, some of these southern mills were paying workers less than $10 per week at a time when the national average wage for such work exceeded $20. In addition, southern textile mills in the 1920s were the first to experiment with the "stretch-out"—a technique where employers simply fired a large number of workers and required those who remained to make up the slack by working faster. The stretch-out and low pay led to strikes in Tennessee, the Carolinas, and even in a handful of textile mills in the Deep South.

A biracial union backed by the Communist Party emerged in Gastonia, North Carolina, in the late 1920s. This new Southern radicalism threatened to build and maintain worker solidarity across the racial divide by focusing on social class rather than race. In 1929, the union led its white and black workers to the picket lines in protest of wages that failed to provide even the basic necessities of life. Area mills recognized the potential threat of class consciousness in a region where black and white workers had been played against one another for generations. With the support of competing mills, management brought in replacement workers and sought to divide the white and black strikers.

The specter of Communism and "racial amalgamation" led to increased tensions throughout Gastonia until a gun battle left the chief of police and at least one union supporter dead. Seven workers were given extended prison sentences for their possible roles in the death of the police chief. There was barely any investigation into the death of the black union supporter. Shortly thereafter, a female strike leader was shot and killed by mill guards. Together with increased police harassment of the unions and their leaders, populist appeals to racism, and the replacement of striking workers, interracial union activism was only a temporary feature in the South during the 1920s.

Contrary to the Communist propaganda that spread throughout the textile mills, business owners did not always personify the caricature of the greedy Capitalist. In fact, many industrialists tested new ideas from a common belief that humane treatment of workers would lead to increased productivity. "Welfare Capitalism" became the new buzzword in the emerging business colleges and throughout Wall Street. Some business leaders hoped to forestall labor militancy by offering certain perquisites such as profit sharing, pensions, and paid vacations. These kinds of benefits would still be rare for at least another generation, yet more employers than ever before provided limited funding for workers' recreation and social clubs. In each case, the goal was to reduce turnover and labor activism. However, some employers convinced themselves that they were beloved by their workers who completely trusted their well-being to the care of their benevolent employer.

FIGURE 6.7

In August 1921, these West Virginia miners clashed with federal troops in the Battle of Blair Mountain. As many as fifteen thousand miners marched to southern West Virginia to rescue men who had been imprisoned for trying to form labor unions. After a million rounds were fired by both sides, federal troops and even a bomber squadron forced the men to return to their own mining camps. Union leaders were arrested while mine owners enlisted the paranoia surrounding the Red Scare to attack the culture of union activism as "un-American."

FIGURE 6.8

Supporters of the Gastonia, North Carolina, strike called on all mill workers to stand together in solidarity behind fellow workers that had been charged with murder. However, those workers who supported the strike were evicted from their homes, which were owned by the mill. Together with economic pressure and armed guards who shot and killed a female strike leader, the 1929 strike was broken.

Workers took advantage of these services but remained suspicious of welfare Capitalism, largely due to repeated failure of management to live up to its own lofty rhetoric. Some of these employer-sponsored organizations were designed to replace unions or eliminate working men's fraternal organizations. Employers continued to intentionally mix and then separate workers of various ethnicities and regional identities in hopes of keeping them divided and suspicious of one another. With the exception of nonwhite workers who continued to experience discrimination, efforts to exploit Old World animosities became less effective as the twentieth century progressed. For example, descendants of Irish and English immigrants were less likely to view one another as natural enemies than their parents had been. New immigrants from regions such as Northern and Southern Italy found that when they arrived in America, they were simply considered "Italians." Because they faced the same discrimination and prejudice, immigrants put aside their regional rivalries and began to see themselves as Italian-Americans rather than Romans, Neapolitans, Venetians, or Sicilians. Over time, US factories would encourage assimilation and the creation of a common "white" identity among immigrants and old-stock Americans alike.

Other companies experimented with procedures for soliciting workers' concerns in ways that were similar to unions, but they did not charge membership fees. These groups had little power beyond what management allowed but often secured modest reforms or one-time bonuses. Management often used these "company unions" to discredit actual unions by agreeing to negotiate only with the representatives of the company union. For example, if the steelworker's union pressed for a pay raise, the company might grant a one-time bonus to forestall a possible strike. Just to make sure the union did not receive credit for the increase, the company would announce the bonus through the representatives of the company-controlled union. As a result, they hoped workers would perceive the company union as more effective than the independent union that deducted fees from their paychecks.

The decline of labor activism during the 1920s was the result of two leading factors: the conservative political climate of the decade and the general prosperity that led to low unemployment and slightly higher wages. Conservative legislatures continued to vote down anti–child labor laws, and the Supreme Court reversed a handful of provisions that would have limited the number of children in the workforce. Farm and business lobbies became so powerful during the 1920s that a proposed Constitutional amendment banning child labor was approved by only six state legislatures. Unions lobbied on behalf of the amendment but were overwhelmed by the resources of industry. In addition, unemployment dropped to below 5 percent during the mid-1920s, which eliminated some of the financial threat that children's labor posed to working men and women. Similar to periods of low unemployment in the past, however, workers could expect their jobs to be eliminated if the economy began to slow.

1.5 Culture of Consumption and Popular Entertainment

Sell them their dreams. Sell them what they longed for and hoped for and almost despised of having....Sell them dreams—dreams of country clubs and proms and visions of what might happen if only. After all, people don't buy things to have things. They buy things to work for them. They buy hope—hope of what your merchandise will do for them. Sell them this hope and you won't have to worry about selling them goods.

—Advice to participants in a 1923 convention of marketers

The increased production of consumer goods following World War I required an equal commitment to consumption. Manufacturers and merchants rose to the challenge by embracing the burgeoning field of marketing to convince potential customers that they needed the new products that were pouring off US assembly lines. More than previous generations, marketers in the 1920s sought to manipulate the emotions of prospective customers by convincing them that the good life and a life of goods went hand in hand.

To succeed, it was not enough for advertisers to simply sell products as they had in the past. Instead, the new marketing courses taught advertisers how to sell a vision of what a product might do for the customer. Before the turn of the century, the Wharton School at the University of Pennsylvania was nearly alone in its professional training programs in the field of business. Soon, colleges across the country created professional business degree programs to attract students as well as to meet political demands of business leaders and conservative lawmakers who began questioning the value of liberal arts degrees. By the end of the decade, advocates of traditional fields of learning were on the defensive as the United States spent more money on marketing than on education.

In the burgeoning fields of finance and marketing, "making money" was far removed from making products. The beauty industry was created by marketing, convincing women that they might be beautiful if only they purchased a particular product. A generation prior, women seldom looked at themselves in the mirror more than a couple times a day. By 1920, women began carrying purses that contained an arsenal of beauty products, some of which actually had mirrors built into their carrying cases. Marketers labored to eliminate the negative stigma of make-up, which had once been a calling card of the streetwalker.

Soon it was not enough simply to sell a few facial cosmetic products. "The average American woman has sixteen square feet of skin," a promoter of the beauty industry remarked during the 1930s. As a result, he was confident that the $2 billion spent on cosmetics was only a fraction of the possibility if women could be convinced that they needed lotions, perfumes, and accessories to accompany seasonal wardrobes and other invented fashions. Accompanying each of these products was a new science designed to examine the effectiveness of storefront displays, interior designs, and the use of light and space to direct a shopper's attention and manipulate emotions.

What was true of emerging fields such as the beauty industry was doubly true in established markets of consumer goods. The agrarian producer culture of the nineteenth century was giving way to a more transient urban culture where work was valued primarily as a means of providing income. Shopping had been both a masculine venture and a community event, a rare break from work on the farm and a time when men traveled to nearby towns to conduct business among other men they knew personally. By the 1920s, shopping was transforming into an individual task usually performed by married women on behalf of their families and in the company of strangers. Urban shopping districts emerged as feminized spaces in downtown districts that had previously not even included public restrooms for women. And for those who could afford it, shopping was becoming a pleasurable experience in a culture that increasingly glorified consumption.

If notions of autonomy and material security through land ownership no longer defined the American Dream, the rising standard of living did. Pleasure and acquisition came to be viewed as the reason for labor, and both were achieved by shopping. Through the calculated actions of business leaders and the willing acquiescence of the middle-class consumer, a new culture was formed that prized consumption as the ultimate expression of happiness and success. Little noticed at the time, the democratization of desire had encouraged many to value luxury over security. Well over half of the automobiles that were purchased at this time were bought with credit. Perhaps even more revealing, a small number were making impulse purchases with something new called a "personal line of credit." For most workers, these purchases were made under the assumption that their future earnings would increase. What they did not realize was that consumer credit was a response by business leaders who were becoming increasingly aware that the number of consumers who could afford to buy their products with cash was beginning to peak.

Eventually, even the supply of consumers who could buy merchandise on credit would also begin to crest. In the meantime, more and more Americans enjoyed slightly higher wages and a workweek that had declined from over fifty hours per week to just over forty-five hours. The entertainment industry emerged in response to the increase in disposable income and time more workers enjoyed during the 1920s. These diversions also sought to fill a void left by the disconnect between employees and their jobs. Workers might not find their time on the factory floor or at their desks meaningful and satisfying, but they could use their time away from work to pursue pleasure.

FIGURE 6.9

Storefront displays were studied by marketers who sought to manipulate a shopper's emotions and create the image that a product would confer status and enhance a customer's life beyond that product's explicit utility.

FIGURE 6.10

Although athletes such as boxers had achieved international fame, Babe Ruth emerged as the first global icon of team sports during the 1920s.

Babe Ruth

Arguably the greatest hitter in Major League Baseball, Ruth was a pitcher for the Boston Red Sox prior to a controversial trade to the archrival New York Yankees. Ruth was the cultural icon of his day, famous for both his legendary swing and his fast lifestyle that for many was emblematic of the excesses of the 1920s.

By the late 1920s, motion pictures had advanced from the novelty of nickelodeons and scratchy silent pictures to feature films with synchronized sound. Spectator sports proliferated to include tennis, golf, and professional football, alongside perennial favorites such as college football, boxing, and horseracing. However, baseball remained the American pastime and defined American popular culture as nothing else had. Athletes such as **Babe Ruth** transcended sport and celebrity to become an international symbol of the United States. One of only two survivors out of seven children, Ruth was raised by the streets of Baltimore and the Sisters of St. Mary's. Undeniably talented yet susceptible to vice, Ruth possessed more than his share of that uniquely American gregariousness that horrified and charmed at the same time. Because of his talent, Ruth became baseball during the era when baseball was America.

History and Memory

Jack Trice became the first African American football player at the college now known as Iowa State University. He was more known for his desire to study animal husbandry than his football skills, and his desire to share his knowledge with Southern black farmers reminded his classmates of the famous African American botanist and Iowa State alum George Washington Carver. Trice played his first and only game on October 6, 1923, breaking his collarbone on the second play of the game. Trice insisted he was uninjured and returned to the game where some believe opposing players intentionally sought to reinjure him because of his race. Trice was taken to the emergency room and released, only to die two days later of internal injuries. Trice's service to the team was memorialized throughout 1923, after which he was forgotten until a local history project coincided with a new football stadium in 1973. ISU students were active in the civil rights movement and demanded that the new stadium be named after Trice. Administration and alumni opposed the plan, pointing out that Trice had only played one game. A decade later, students finally won the right to name the field after Trice, but many were not satisfied and raised funds to build a statue to commemorate Trice. In 1997, after a quarter century of petitions and letters by students, a new generation of alumni and administrators consented. Iowa State now plays all of its home games at Jack Trice Stadium.

Consider the ways that history and memory change over time as reflected by this story.

1.6   Baseball as America

By October 1928, the question of the color line in towns like Baltimore had seemingly been answered. The schools were segregated by law, while churches, theaters, and neighborhoods were segregated by custom. Black and white residents ate at different restaurants, slept in different hotels, and even visited their loved ones in separate hospitals. Children played at segregated YMCA branches. Adults attended social and political functions of segregated clubs. But at least one event during that month demonstrates that race relations were never quite as simple as they may appear. That month, the Baltimore Black Sox of the Eastern Colored League defeated an all-white All-Star team composed of some of the best players in the major leagues. Ten thousand fans witnessed the game, and there were no reports of racial violence. Despite efforts to prevent black fans from attending by raising gate prices throughout the day, several thousand black fans witnessed their team prevail.

FIGURE 6.11

The Negro National League was the first commercially successful African American baseball league. In 1924, the champion of this league, the Kansas City Monarchs, defeated the champion of the Eastern Colored League, Pennsylvania's Hilldale club and claimed the title as the champion of what became known as the "Colored World Series."

The victory of the Black Sox was not an uncommon scene throughout the 1920s. In fact, Negro League teams had a winning record against the all-white major leaguers that challenged them. The record was ironically aided by organized baseball's attempt to prevent these games from happening. Following a series of victories by teams like the St. Louis Stars, New York Black Yankees, and Homestead Grays of Pennsylvania over their local major league teams, Commissioner Kenesaw Mountain Landis ruled that major league clubs could no longer challenge black teams. However, these contests were the most popular exposition games of the season, and they sold tickets and filled ballparks. As a result, white major leaguers simply assembled their own teams of "all stars" composed of players from area teams. Given the desire of players to maximize their share of the gate receipts, these all-star teams often lacked the depth of regular season pitching rosters. As a result, Landis's ruling increased the tendency of the Negro League teams to prevail over whites.

One must be careful not to exaggerate these symbolic victories over Jim Crow. Placed in a larger context, these baseball games pale in comparison with the progress that was forged in classrooms and courtrooms. Yet for the thousands who attended these games, especially those laboring behind the color line, these victories had profound meaning. For example, in 1925, an all-black, semipro team in Wichita, Kansas, defeated a team representing the local Ku Klux Klan. The schools of Wichita remained segregated the next morning, but surely those who witnessed the game thought about the larger meaning of the afternoon's events.

> *From a sociological point of view, the Monarchs have done more than any other single agent in Kansas City to break down the damnable outrage of color prejudice that exists in the city…[When]…both races sit side by side and root for their particular favorite and think nothing of it, then after a while the same relation may be carried to the workshop, and the ball grounds may be the means of causing someone to be employed where he would not otherwise have been considered, just because "he sat next to me out at the ball park Sunday—he's a pretty good fellow."*
>
> —Kansas City Call (African American newspaper), October 27, 1922

As a touring exhibit demonstrated nearly a century later, baseball was America in the 1920s. The national pastime mirrored the diversity of the nation and any town with more than a few hundred residents sponsored a team that was the pride of the community. On any given Sunday afternoon, nearly as many Americans could be found at the local ballpark as had attended church in the morning. The teams mirrored the diversity of the congregants. German immigrants in North Dakota and Jewish immigrants in New York City commemorated each Fourth of July by playing the American game, a celebration of their new nation and a proud display of their ethnic unity as they challenged teams from other immigrant groups.

Women's teams had been competing since Vassar College's first team took the field in 1866, most famously as part of the touring "Bloomer Girls" teams of the turn of the century. Native American teams toured as well, blurring the lines of sport, showmanship, and accommodation to the expected stereotypes of the white audiences. Japanese American teams like the Fresno Athletics defeated the best college and semipro teams on the West Coast. When not playing for the Yankees, Babe Ruth toured the nation throughout the 1920s as his team of all-stars took on all of these diverse local players. "Organized baseball" consisting of the Major League and its Minor League affiliates had drawn the color line since the late nineteenth century, but barnstorming teams such as Ruth's were more concerned about revenue than the regulations of their commissioner. As a result, Ruth welcomed the competition of African American baseball greats such as **Josh Gibson**, who many believe was the greatest slugger of the era. Ruth also played alongside Japanese American stars such as Kenichi Zenimura, the founder of the Fresno Athletics.

Josh Gibson

Sometimes referred to as the "black Babe Ruth," Gibson compiled the most impressive career statistics in the history of the sport, leading some scholars of the Negro Leagues to argue that Ruth should be called the "white Josh Gibson." Gibson played among many of the greatest ballplayers of all races in the United States, the Caribbean, and Latin America, but owing to race he was excluded from the Major Leagues.

FIGURE 6.12

Asian Americans on the West Coast formed competitive baseball teams. This 1913 poster advertises a touring team composed of Asian Americans who lived in Hawaii and played against college teams throughout the American West.

In addition, thousands of white and black players from the Major Leagues and Negro Leagues played in Cuba, the Dominican Republic, Mexico, and various Caribbean and Latin American countries each summer. These tours resulted in the discovery of hundreds of great Latino ballplayers, many of whom traveled and played in the United States on international touring teams or as players on Negro League teams. These ballplayers were role models, ambassadors, leading men in their community, and some of the first and most visible activists against segregation as they traveled through the nation.

The celebrity status of a team might erode racial barriers. At other times, black players confronted segregation directly by demanding respect and equal accommodations. However, one must remember that these men were ballplayers, managers, and owners above all else. Team members were most concerned with their ability to play the game they loved, and owners had a vested interest in minimizing racial conflict. They could not afford to take chances with alienating white spectators or demand equal accommodations at the risk of being placed in jail during an important road trip. As a result, the teams worked to avoid confrontation by planning their trips along familiar routes, patronizing black-owned businesses, and staying with black families in small towns without black-owned restaurants and hotels.

A handful of African American teams sought refuge from America's binary color line by choosing names such as the Cuban Stars, thereby blurring the line between Afro-Caribbean and Afro-American. About fifty Latino players with light complexions and surnames that reflected the European Spanish heritage of many Caribbean islanders were even deemed "racially eligible" to play for Major League teams. The inclusion of foreign and American-born players of Latino heritage further demonstrated the middle ground between black and white. The complexion of most Caribbean islanders was usually too dark to pass as "Castilian" or any of the other creative euphemisms managers sought to apply to a talented ballplayer they wanted to convince the rest of the world was a descendent of European conquistadors. The existence of these charades, as well as several attempts to "pass" a black player as Native American, demonstrated that race was a social construction rather than a scientifically identifiable category.

REVIEW AND CRITICAL THINKING

1. How does the Sheppard-Towner Act reflect the political environment of the 1920s and government expectations at that time? Why might the AMA choose to oppose such measures, and why would this organization present social welfare programs for women and children as analogous to Socialism?

2. Ford became infamous for his negative views of the working class. Why might someone with such views voluntarily pay such high wages?

3. Why did labor union membership decline during the 1920s? What were the arguments for and against union membership during this era?

4. How did the emerging field of marketing affect the United States during the 1920s? What were the goals of marketers, and how were their tactics different from the ways goods were promoted in previous generations?

5. How did baseball reflect American life and culture during the 1920s? How do the Negro Leagues and the experiences of racial and ethnic minorities in sport demonstrate the opportunities and challenges faced by nonwhites at this time?

2.   IMMIGRATION AND CLOSING THE GOLDEN DOOR

LEARNING OBJECTIVES

1. Analyze the significance of the rebirth of the Ku Klux Klan during the 1920s. Explain why the Klan was able to attract a mainstream following only to lose its members by the end of the decade.
2. Evaluate the influence of nativism on America's immigration policy during the 1920s.
3. Explain the way that immigrant groups were discriminated against by Americans and how many Americans could deny that the conditions recent immigrants and nonwhite Americans faced were inspired by prejudice.

2.1   The Second Klan

The Ku Klux Klan (KKK) reemerged in 1915 as a nativist organization based on white supremacy. Similar to the original Klan that emerged during Reconstruction, the new Klan sought to return African Americans to a condition resembling slavery. The new Klan also sought to prevent the immigration of nonwhite and non-Protestant families to the US. The emergence of the new Klan coincided with the release of D. W. Griffith's *Birth of a Nation*, a film that debuted in 1915 and presented the late nineteenth-century Klan in a heroic light. The next year, the eugenicist Madison Grant's *The Passing of the Great Race* warned white Americans that new immigration from Southern and Eastern Europe threatened to fill the United States with inferior races. Influenced by this and other eugenicist works that blended racism with pseudoscience, some Klan members even believed that nonwhites should be sterilized.

The new Klan officially shunned violence and attracted a mainstream following, even if Klan beliefs often led to acts of violence against minority communities. The new Klan emerged during a period of anti-immigrant and antiblack hysteria, as evidenced by the Red Summer of 1919. In that year, mob violence was perpetrated against black communities in both the North and South. The same year, whites on the West Coast attacked Chinese neighborhoods, Midwesterners participated in riots that destroyed black and Hispanic neighborhoods, and whites on the East Coast sought to halt Jewish migration altogether.

The new KKK grew rapidly during the 1920s, spreading a message that nonwhites and non-Protestants were not "100 percent Americans." The new Klan attracted a large number of followers, many of whom paraded openly without masks. Leading public figures usually hid their identity when participating in Klan rallies, but it was hardly a secret that a substantial number of the members of state legislatures in Colorado, Indiana, Texas, Oklahoma, and Oregon were also members of the secret order. Oregon lawmakers sanctioned a referendum that voters approved, outlawing private schools—a blatantly unconstitutional attack on the Catholic Church. Klan members held rallies in neighboring Washington State that were attended by 20,000 to 70,000 participants. More sinister indications of West Coast Klan activity were the violent intimidation campaigns against Japanese Americans from the Yakima Valley of Washington to San Diego.

The Klan was especially powerful in Indiana, with an estimated membership of 350,000. The Klan soon became so influential throughout the Midwest that journalist William Allen White of Emporia, Kansas, entered the 1924 race for the governorship and made opposition to the Klan the leading issue of his platform. White became a national figure during the 1890s with his conservative attack on the Populists he feared were creating an antibusiness climate in his beloved state. That White and most other conservatives would speak so forcefully against the Klan was an important factor in the Klan's decline.

FIGURE 6.13

The new Klan of the 1920s did much more than march in hoods and sheets to spread their message. This Beaumont, Texas, chapter produced a play titled "The Awakening," which sought to present US history as part of an Aryan struggle against inferior races.

Second Ku Klux Klan

Formed in 1915, the Second Klan was less secretive than its predecessor had been, and the majority of its estimated 4 million members lived in the Midwest and Border South. The Second Klan believed that the United States was in danger of losing its white and Protestant heritage due to the influence of Jews and Catholics, along with the growing presence of nonwhite immigrants from Europe, Latin America, and Asia. Klansmen were also threatened by the growing African American population of the North.

Many historians have been tempted to discount the **Second Ku Klux Klan** of the 1920s as a reactionary element of lower-class whites alienated by the growth, prosperity, and increasing acceptance of nonwhite and non-Protestant Americans. However, the Klan had more than 4 million members at its peak in 1925 and attracted middle-class men and women as equally as it attracted other groups. The Klan was also a fraternal organization complete with a women's auxiliary that gave many members a sense of identity and belonging with its social gatherings, rituals, and honorary titles. Its rallies were steeped in hypernationalistic worship of the flag and celebration of a mythical past where old-time religion and family values guided America.

Because it did not need to unify its members behind a specific platform or policy, the Klan could represent many things to its members. The Klan could be mainstream and extremist. It could be reactionary and hateful at one moment, only to warmly embrace tradition and family values the next. The hollowness of its rhetoric and the willingness of its members to surrender critical thinking allowed its leaders to express hatred toward unions, impoverished strikebreakers, and big business in the same sitting. It could speak to legitimate social concerns such as crime and government corruption. It could even advocate progressive causes before scapegoating the nation's problems on a particular ethnic or religious group. Most importantly, the Klan's restrictive membership meant that venomous accusations against immigrants, Jews, Catholics, minorities, Socialists, or any other group that fell short of their 100 percent Americanism reminded its members of the commonalities they shared.

The Klan grew in membership because of this sense of brotherhood and sisterhood. Equally important, most whites in the 1920s shared some of the basic assumptions of the Klan even if they recoiled from the ways Klansmen expressed their intolerance. Mainstream religious leaders called for Protestant solidarity, while most native-born whites demonstrated assumptions of racial superiority, intolerance for immigrants, distrust of government, and suspicion regarding the loyalties of Jews and Catholics. Klansmen spoke the language of the disaffected and those who felt their way of life was under attack. They also spoke to religious communities by appealing to the preservation of traditional family values. The Klan also demonstrated the ease with which reactionary politics could enter mainstream society during a time of anxiety about rapid social change and the growth of a nonwhite and non-Protestant population.

The significant growth of the Klan's female auxiliary, the Women of the Ku Klux Klan (WKKK), challenges the notions of many historians who suggest, at least by implication, that reactionary politics was an exclusively male domain. In states such as Indiana, women were equally attracted to the Klan's message and joined in roughly equal numbers. One historian estimates that as many as one-third of native-born, white Indiana women joined the WKKK. For these women, the WKKK provided a source of community that was ideologically consistent with many of their political and social beliefs. Many of these women had been active in relatively progressive organizations such as the Young Women's Christian Association. Others were veterans of the fight for women's suffrage. Because the Klan taught that the rights of white Americans were under assault by foreigners, Jews, and nonwhites, Klan activism was viewed by these women as a continuation of their earlier efforts promoting the welfare of the disaffected.

The WKKK often acted like any other women's organization, organizing charitable fundraisers for schools, hosting picnics, and joining parades. However, the WKKK also organized boycotts of Jewish businesses, ran attorneys who defended minorities out of town, and devised strategies to unseat school board members who supported integration. Some women even joined secret organizations such as the Queens of the Golden Mask, which conducted some of the Klan's dirty work. The Indiana Klan leader David Stephenson referred to these women as his "poison squad" and counted on them to spread malicious falsehoods against the families of anyone who dared oppose him or the Klan. However, the WKKK was not merely an adjunct to male leadership. Despite the tendency of Klansmen to celebrate their "protection" of white women, women and men in the Klan sustained female suffrage as a weapon that could help them restore and preserve the values they espoused.

The Klan's blatant celebration of white supremacy might have led to official condemnation from presidents, but these men generally avoided any action that could leave them open to criticism by white voters. Warren Harding was an avowed segregationist, at least when speaking to white Southerners. Calvin Coolidge argued that the federal government should not interfere with "local issues" involving race and religion. He did little to support antilynching legislation and tolerated the continued segregation of federal government employees. Herbert Hoover spoke out against lynching but did little to support antilynching legislation. Instead, he supported the creation of an all-white Republican Party in the South. By preventing black membership, some members of the Republican Party hoped that they could finally end the association between their party and memories of emancipation and Reconstruction. Although he had spoken in opposition to racial segregation while a politician in Wisconsin, even progressive Republicans such as Robert La Follete avoided addressing racial issues once they became candidates for national office.

The Klan declined quickly in 1925 due to three factors. First and most importantly, mainstream conservatives and local officials began to join liberals in denouncing the Klan and its bigotry as un-American by 1923. Second, the hollowness and negativity of their message led many members to lose enthusiasm over time. Finally, local and national Klan leaders became the target of investigations that revealed irregularities regarding the tens of millions of dollars Klan members donated to the organization. The secrecy of the Klan allowed leaders to embezzle its untraceable funds for several years. The result was that many individual klaverns were near bankruptcy, while a coterie of Klan leaders began to display their newfound wealth in ways that aroused suspicion and jealousy among other members.

A series of national scandals in the mid-1920s also led many to question the Klan's espoused support for Christianity, chivalrous protection of white women, and Protestant family values. Indiana Klan leader David Stephenson was convicted in 1925 of embezzlement and second-degree murder after his secretary, whom he had previously raped and assaulted, was found dead. The Indiana Klan had been the largest in the nation with 350,000 members. By the end of 1926, Klan membership in the Hoosier State plummeted to 15,000. Meanwhile, two leading Southern Klansmen were found together in a hotel bedroom with no clothing or women in sight. These and countless other allegations and indictments against Klan leaders made many members question whether they had been deceived by demagogues. The negative attitudes toward non-Protestants and nonwhites remained through the late 1920s and 1930s. However, the downfall of the Klan led many to question these beliefs. Others simply expressed them in more cautious ways.

FIGURE 6.14

"The Watcher on the Tower" was one of the monthly publications of the Washington State Ku Klux Klan. Uncle Sam is pictured wearing a Klan robe. During the conservative political environment of the 1920s, few leading politicians or presidents dared to publicly criticize the Klan, which grew to include as many as four million members.

2.2   Quotas and Unwelcome Americans

The rebirth of the Klan also led to greater activism among Jewish organizations, the NAACP, and immigrant rights groups. For example, NAACP chapters across the nation secured injunctions against the *Birth of a Nation*, an action that energized local chapters. Civil rights groups that defended the rights of immigrants also expanded in response to anti-Klan sentiment. However, because 24 million immigrants entered the United States between 1880 and 1920, many began to fear that the nation was growing too fast. By way of comparison, the total US population at the turn of the century was only 76 million. Many of these newcomers were treated poorly because of their ethnic background. Their reception only grew more hostile as the postwar recession accelerated through 1921. Unemployment soared to nearly 9 percent, and many out-of-work individuals blamed recent immigrants for their misfortune.

Congress responded by passing the Emergency Quota Law of 1921. As the name suggests, the law was meant to enact temporary restrictions on immigration to curb the number of newcomers that might compete for jobs. However, immigration was always a sensitive topic in the US. After all, nearly all Americans were immigrants or the descendants of people who came to America through coercion or free will. As a result, America wrestled with both the heightened nativist impulse of the era and the desire to create a fair law that did not discriminate against any particular ethnicity.

The 1921 law limited the number of immigrants who could be admitted into the United States from any particular country to a number no greater than 3 percent of the total number from that country who were living in the United States in 1910. For example, if there were 1 million Irish living in the United States in 1910, up to 30,000 might legally enter the United States each year. On its face, the law appeared to be racially and ethnically neutral. However, the bulk of the US population in 1910 was from Britain and Western Europe, and most of the migrants who were trying to enter the United States were from nations in Southern and Eastern Europe. These migrants tended to be Jewish, as well as Polish, Italian, Slavic, Greek, and other groups that were severely discriminated against.

FIGURE 6.15

Native Americans and immigrants faced continued discrimination during the early twentieth century. This photo was taken in South Dakota, which was home to a number of Native Americans, some of whom were economically distressed and coping with alcoholism. While some believed that signs like this were evidence of trying to "protect" natives, the negative assumption that all natives were alcoholics and undesirable patrons is also apparent.

National Origins Act of 1924

A law that attempted to curtail immigration from central and southern Europe by creating quotas based on the national origins of immigrants listed in the 1890 census. Because most American immigrants were "white" Europeans from Western Europe in 1890, the law effectively limited immigration of Jews, Italians, Czechs, Poles, Russians, and other groups. The law also implicitly banned immigration of Asians by its provision against any group who was ineligible for citizenship.

The economy recovered in the next few years, but nativist sentiment remained a strong political force. With support of groups ranging from the Klan to mainstream labor unions, Congress approved the **National Origins Act of 1924** with only a handful of dissenting votes. This law was clearly intended to restrict migrants from Southern and Central Europe, but it cunningly obscured this objective by issuing quotas that made no mention of race, nationality, or ethnicity. Instead, the National Origins Act created quotas that were based on the 1890 census. Although three more recent census records were available, 1890 was the most recent census taken prior to the arrival of large numbers of Jews and Southern Europeans.

The law established a quota limiting the number of immigrants from a particular nation to no more than 2 percent of the total number of immigrants who were living in the US prior to 1890. As a result, the law limited the new immigrants from Southern and Eastern Europe to a few thousand per year while permitting far more "white" Europeans from Britain, France, and Germany than actually desired to migrate to the United States. The law was even less subtle regarding those from India and Asia who were excluded entirely by a provision barring the immigration of persons who were ineligible for citizenship. At this time, a variety of laws prohibited anyone of Asian origin from becoming a citizen, while many localities had passed other discriminatory laws that applied specifically to Chinese immigrants.

President Coolidge expressed the view held by many Anglo-Americans that associated whiteness as one of the defining characteristics of what it meant to be an American. "America must be kept American," Coolidge exclaimed upon signing the 1924 act into law. Others such as New York congressman Fiorello LaGuardia argued that the law and the sentiment it produced were contrary to the best interests and finest traditions of the United States.

LaGuardia was the son of an Italian father and Jewish mother. As such, he and his family represented precisely the kind of "un-American" amalgamation the 1924 law sought to prevent. LaGuardia spoke at rallies sponsored by his constituents from the racially and ethnically diverse melting pot of East Harlem. LaGuardia joined tens of thousands of New Yorkers and millions of immigrants across the nation in declaring that they would not be treated as strangers in their own land. Similar protests were held on the West Coast, including legal challenges to California's Alien Land Law of 1920, which prohibited Asian Americans from owning land. Although the California law was framed as a law intending to limit foreign ownership of the nation, the intent was to prevent Californians of Asian descent, who by law could not be citizens, from being anything but landless peasant laborers.

Congressman Emanuel Celler sought to remove the façade of racial neutrality these laws constructed. He also sought to present immigration as a positive good for the nation, challenging his opponents to explain why the eight states with the highest numbers of recent immigrants were also the states that featured the greatest economic growth. Celler represented New York City in Congress for five decades and sponsored a bill that abolished these quotas in 1965.

Despite the protests of many nativists, neither the 1921 nor the 1924 law established quotas or restrictions against immigrants from the Western Hemisphere. Officially, the US government permitted immigration from these nations as part of its commitment to stewardship of the Western Hemisphere, as expressed in the Monroe Doctrine. In actuality, the unrestricted legal immigration from Mexico and other nations was a political compromise demanded by congressmen who represented industry and agribusiness in Texas and the rest of the Southwest. World War I and the subsequent restrictions against migration resulted in Western and Midwestern farms and industries depending on Mexican immigration. Hundreds of thousands of Mexican nationals would enter the nation legally each year until the start of the Great Depression, paying $18 in taxes and fees to receive a visa and work permit. Some of this revenue offset the expense of the US Border Patrol that was also established in 1924. However, at this time, the Border Patrol was one of the smallest federal agencies, and little political pressure existed to prevent those who crossed the border without obtaining legal documentation.

In 1924, the federal government also passed a law permitting Native Americans to become citizens. The law included the federal territory of Alaska where natives had long been fighting for the right to become citizens. For example, the Alaska Native Brotherhood and the Alaska Native Sisterhood had been advocating for citizenship for over a decade before the law was passed. In 1915, the Alaskan government approved a law opening the door for citizenship for natives. However, this process required five whites to testify that an applicant had renounced all traditional ways and was fully assimilated. Much like the Jim Crow South, Alaskan establishments displayed signs indicating that no natives would be served in restaurants. Similar messages appeared in advertisements for laborers specifying that only "white" workers need apply.In the late 1920s, the Brotherhood and Sisterhood joined together using both moral suasion and other more direct methods to protest establishments that discriminated against Alaskan natives. The campaign for civil rights in Alaska peaked during World War II when natives were forcibly removed and arrested for violating the policies of segregated theaters. Efforts of activist Elizabeth Peratrovich and many others would ultimately lead to the passage of an Alaskan law banning segregation in 1945. However, both formal and informal segregation within establishments would persist until statehood, especially in areas where natives lacked economic power precisely because of their exclusion from employment opportunities.

2.3   Nativism and National Security

Nicola Sacco and Bartolomeo Vanzetti were arrested in May 1920 following an attempted robbery of a Massachusetts factory that had left two men dead. Although very little evidence linked them to the crime, both men were radicals who had expressed support for anarchist violence in the past. And they were also Italians, part of the despised group of "new immigrants" whose desperate conditions in Southern Europe had led them to the United States. Convicted in 1921 of both robbery and murder, Sacco and Vanzetti's case attracted the attention of Italian American groups such as the Order Sons of Italy in America who sought to publicize what they believed had been a miscarriage of justice.

Each of these immigrant groups had grown increasingly concerned by the reactionary climate of the 1920s. They sought to demonstrate how the convictions of these two men demonstrated the injustice of the criminal justice system for immigrants and radicals. Over the next six years, these groups filed a number of appeals that raised serious doubts about the guilt of the two men but failed to reverse their death sentences. Several witnesses described the burglars in ways that conflicted with the appearance of both Sacco and Vanzetti. In addition, police could not link either man's fingerprints to the crime, and neither was found in possession of the $15,000 that had been stolen.

However, these appeals and subsequent trials publicized the extremism of some of Sacco and Vanzetti's political beliefs. Both men were supporters of Italian anarchists who advocated anti-Capitalist revolution through violent tactics such as bombings and assassinations. Equally important, the two men had ties to known anarchists who were atop the Department of Justice's most-wanted list for several attempted assassinations. The trials also demonstrated the unlikelihood that either man would have been convicted of the original burglary had it not been for their radical beliefs.

FIGURE 6.16

New York congressman Fiorello LaGuardia pictured with Franklin Delano Roosevelt, who is seated in his car. LaGuardia defended the rights of immigrants in Congress along with fellow New Yorker Emanuel Celler.

Despite international protest ranging from Buenos Aires to Rome, both men were executed on August 23, 1927. Most "white" Americans believed the two men were either guilty of this crime or likely to commit another because of their radical beliefs. Most recent immigrants from central and southern Europe, along with other minority groups who were no strangers to police discrimination, were less likely to sustain the decision of the court. As a result, the **Sacco-Vanzetti Trials** demonstrated that the Red Scare extended throughout the 1920s and also revealed that Americans of different racial and ethnic backgrounds perceived the same events quite differently. It also renewed questions about whether the US justice system tried defendants for their actions or their political beliefs and background.

2.4   Election of 1924

FIGURE 6.17

The 1924 election featured a solidly Democratic South. La Follette carried only his home state of Wisconsin and the Republican Calvin Coolidge easily won a second term.

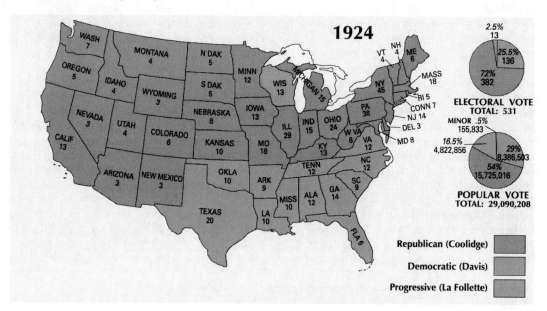

Calvin Coolidge became president following the death of Warren G. Harding in 1923. Coolidge was perhaps the most enigmatic leader of the early twentieth century. Many conservatives spoke out against the growing power and size of government yet sought to expand certain aspects of government authority. However, Coolidge was consistent in believing the federal government should defer to the states. He also demonstrated deference to the Supreme Court and Congress, believing that a president should not be too involved in the day-to-day business of government. At other times, Coolidge demonstrated support for progressive goals. For example, Coolidge outlined a broad legislative agenda full of specific goals, such as child-labor laws, improvements in health care, and environmental protection during one of his addresses to Congress.

Most other times, Coolidge lived up to his nickname of "Silent Cal." As president, Coolidge rarely dominated a conversation and delivered speeches that often lasted only a few minutes. And yet it was Coolidge and not Franklin Delano Roosevelt (FDR) who was the first to use regular radio addresses to the nation, even if FDR would later be credited with originating the idea. Coolidge would also decline running for reelection in 1928, despite the near certainty of victory. A leading biographer suggests that Coolidge may have suffered from clinical depression. Although it is tempting to apply this explanation to his decision to leave public life as well as his insistence on sleeping twelve hours per day while president, no one really understood what drove Coolidge to abandon the hard work and ambition of his earlier years.

Coolidge conducted most of his 1924 reelection campaign from the White House through correspondence. His vice presidential candidate, Charles Dawes, was an enthusiastic campaigner and attacked the third-party candidacy of **Robert La Follette** as promoting socialism. The Democrats nominated a corporate attorney named John W. Davis after several days of balloting. Southern conservatives and northern progressives vied for control of the Democratic Party in ways that ensured a Republican victory short of some major scandal or economic disaster. The Democrats of the North tended to be urban, recent immigrants, Catholic or Jewish, supporters of progressivism, and opponents of Prohibition. The Democrats of the South were white Protestants, old-stock Americans opposed to immigration, and supporters of Prohibition. As long as Coolidge stayed in the White House and the economy did not implode, the election had already been decided unless the Democrats could find a way to unite.

Instead, Northern Democrats were angered by the party's compromise selection of Davis, who might have been mistaken for a Republican in most states beyond his native West Virginia. Meanwhile, La Follette entered the race under the banner of the Progressive Party. His platform demonstrated that Progressive ideas about governmental reform had not been forgotten during the relative prosperity of the 1920s. Ironically, the conservative Coolidge may have gained from La Follete's more liberal campaign, as the Progressive Party likely took more votes away from Davis than Coolidge. Yet even if every one of the nearly 5 million supporters of La Follete had joined with the Democrats, Coolidge would still have won the election of 1924 in a landslide.

FIGURE 6.18

As a three-term senator through the early 1900s, Robert La Follette led the Progressive wing of the Republican Party. He was governor of Wisconsin and would later poll nearly 5 million votes as a third-party candidate for the presidency in 1924.

Robert La Follette

A Republican politician from Wisconsin who was deeply influenced by the Progressive Movement of the early 1900s, La Follette enacted a number of reforms as governor of Wisconsin; these laws were aimed at increasing the power of government to regulate corporations. La Follette ran for president in 1924 as a third-party candidate and received one in six votes, despite the fact he had little chance of winning the general election. As a result, La Follete's candidacy demonstrates that Progressive ideas continued to influence government into the 1920s.

REVIEW AND CRITICAL THINKING

1. How was the Klan of the 1920s similar and different from its Reconstruction-era predecessor? What accounts for the rapid growth and equally rapid demise of the Klan during the 1920s?

2. Explain how nativism influenced US immigration policy during the 1920s. Why might immigration restrictions have been controversial despite the widespread nature of nativist impulses?

3. How did the trial of two Italian immigrants galvanize America during the 1920s? Who were Sacco and Vanzetti? How did their political beliefs affect the trial and challenge the impartiality of the judicial system? Are there any other instances in US history where an individual's political beliefs were placed on trial?

4. Consider the connection between US anxiety regarding anarchists in the 1920s with the Cold War's efforts against Communists in later decades. Or could it be that US concern with anarchism in the 1920s was more similar to that of terrorism in modern times? In what ways are such comparisons valid, and in what ways might they oversimplify or distort the past?

5. Why did Calvin Coolidge win reelection so easily in 1924? What issues divided the Democratic Party? How might these divisions be overcome in future elections?

3. POPULAR CULTURE AND A RENAISSANCE IN HARLEM

LEARNING OBJECTIVES

1. Explain the ways that popular culture influenced ideas about gender and the lives of young women during the 1920s. Also describe the way culture, religion, and science intersected during these years.
2. Evaluate the ways that the rise of the Garvey Movement and the Harlem Renaissance reflected African American culture and life.
3. Describe the popular culture of the 1920s. Analyze the impact of consumerism upon this culture, and describe the ways the United States was becoming more secular.

3.1 A More Secular Culture

The failure of Prohibition led to greater toleration for lawbreakers and demonstrated that American culture was moving away from traditional views. The rise of consumerism had an even greater influence on the culture of the 1920s with its celebration of worldly values such as acquisition and consumption. Americans had always longed for material security and even a few luxuries; the difference was that during the 1920s, the balance between luxury and security had become skewed. Generations of farmers and artisans had viewed credit as a necessary evil, a partial surrender of one's independence that was permissible only in the acquisition of productive property such as land and equipment. The use of credit for any other purpose, especially luxury items such as appliances and automobiles, was nearly unthinkable. By the 1920s, credit was no longer viewed as a surrender of one's liberty but rather as a vehicle by which to enjoy the fruits of modernity. For some, creditworthiness was next to godliness—a symbol that one had been judged as successful and trustworthy.

For others, credit appeared to offer the promise of liberation from a life of living paycheck to paycheck. Mass production meant that goods once regarded as luxury items became more readily available at much more favorable prices. Most urban families by the end of the 1920s owned an automobile. Nearly everyone could afford a radio, and those who could not could at least purchase a homemade radio kit that permitted one to receive signals. Mass marketing spurred mass consumption, democratized desire, and convinced more and more Americans that a life of more goods was indeed the good life. As a result, Americans' suspicion of the wealthy declined during the 1920s, and money increasingly became the principal measure of value in a more secular society. As consumer culture replaced traditional mores in the economic realm, a faster and more secular culture even began to alter notions of gender and sexual morality.

Although changes in gender relations and sexual expression during the 1920s seems modest when viewed from the perspective of the twenty-first century, contemporaries perceived these changes as revolutionary. The increasing agency expressed by women and the changing fashions of the era were certainly not new, as Victorian modes of behavior had always been challenged. Young men and young women had long engaged in sexual exploration, short of and including intercourse. What was new about the 1920s is that "respectable" young women were no longer willing to pretend as if these behaviors and the desires behind them did not exist. New words such as "petting" entered polite society, even if the behaviors they described had long existed behind a veil of Victorian discretion.

For most women, gendered notions of modesty remained the highest expression of their virtue. The difference was that the 1920s were host to public acknowledgment that a mutually satisfying sexual connection was a sign of a healthy relationship rather than a warning sign of female insatiability. At the same time, modern attitudes regarding sex cohabited with antiquated notions about hymeneal purity in ways that continued to reinforce misogynistic attitudes and practices.

FIGURE 6.19

Alice Joyce was a leading actress of the 1920s. Her dress in this image demonstrates the use of straight lines among flappers. The term "flapper" was originally pejorative and based on a gendered perception of a pitiable young bird that tried to show its independence from its mother and nest as it flapped its wings.

The fashions of the 1920s were also a continuation of earlier trends toward simpler and more practical attire. This process was accelerated by the need for metal during the war, which led patriotic women to donate their corsets just as they had in the Civil War. Apparently, these metal and leather contraptions were not missed by many women in the 1920s, and corset sales never recovered. By the 1920s, popular dresses were still quite modest, extending just below the knee. What was novel about the style of the "**flapper**" was that these women adhered to a new standard of beauty based around straight lines and shorter hair. Flappers enjoyed new dance moves that encouraged movement and a few sparks of flirtatious suggestion. Whereas the dresses worn by the idealized Gibson Girl of the turn of the century emphasized the female form, the flapper's gown minimized her hips. Some flappers even attempted to minimize their bust with tightly woven fabric.

Young women were increasingly likely to leave home and experience at least a few years of independence at college prior to marriage. Only 2 percent of young adults attended college at the turn of the century, but only two decades later, that number increased to 7 percent. Colleges doubled in size and then doubled again in this short time, creating virtual cities of youths complete with dormitories and a rapid proliferation of fraternities and sororities. A quarter of students belonged to one of these Greek organizations.

While it was socially acceptable for young men to live alone or with their peers, young women were expected to room with a respectable married family who would also become their chaperones and surrogate parents. By 1920, young women were attending college in nearly equal numbers as young men, leading to a shortage of boarding opportunities for young women. In response, many of the first dormitories were reserved for women. College dormitories provided a home for unmarried female students known as "coeds." Colleges employed older women to live in the dormitories and serve as surrogate mothers for these coeds, each enforcing a strict set of rules and curfews. The perceived need for these "dorm mothers" was spread by contemporary novels such as *Flaming Youth,* which created the stereotype of college life as a time of rebellion and sexual adventure. However, most college students in the 1920s rejected styles of "fast living" that college would later be associated with.

For most college women of the 1920s, the fashionable lifestyle of the flapper was exciting but little more than a temporary diversion from their goal of marriage and motherhood. A flapper could express her independence through wearing makeup, smoking, drinking, and other behaviors once considered "unladylike." Each of these behaviors might have appeared as a minor scandal among a college-aged woman's middle-class family, but they were not the most enduring symbol of gender liberation.

Flappers and the newly independent generation of college women lived in a space between the patriarchy of their father's home and the domestic realm they would create with her future husbands. These women were even known to go out at night with other women, eschewing the once-obligatory male chaperone. These formative years of at least temporary liberation from the constant "supervision" of men was perhaps the most obvious assertion of female independence. This independence was more than a rite of passage for future generations. Women's experiences in college encouraged greater assertiveness among well-educated women and demonstrated that the new "independent woman" of the era was compatible with middle-class respectability.

At the same time, the 1920s and colleges were conservative institutions that reflected the political and economic orthodoxy of the era. Women were steered toward a handful of majors and discouraged from direct competition with men in the classroom or in extracurricular activities. By the mid-1920s, women were even discouraged from competition with one another. Intercollegiate women's athletics had grown from the 1880s to the 1920s, and audiences rivaled men's sports outside of football. By the mid-1920s, reformers argued that strenuous athletic activity was both unfeminine and dangerous to reproductive health. Women's competitive leagues were disbanded and replaced with "play days" where women from various colleges participated in noncompetitive games. The participants were even barred from forming teams that represented their institutions. Instead, the women were divided evenly among other schools to prevent an "unfeminine" spirit of aggressive competition.

flapper

Intended as a condescending label for the young women who embraced the new fashions and lifestyles of 1920s popular culture, "flappers" were women who sought to express their independence from Victorian notions of gender. Known for wearing slightly shorter and looser dresses, applying darker shades of makeup, and engaging in behaviors previously considered "unfeminine," such as smoking, flappers also sought to embrace their views about sexuality rather than simply being the object of male lust.

FIGURE 6.20

The University of Kentucky women's basketball team was one of the best in the nation during the early 1920s. The team in this photo enjoyed an undefeated season. In 1924, however, the University followed the trend of disbanding their women's teams believing that competitive team sports was not appropriate for women.

3.2   Culture War and the Scopes Trial

Scopes Monkey Trial

A highly publicized trial of high school teacher John Scopes who violated a Tennessee law that forbade the teaching of evolution. The trial would become emblematic of the culture wars of the early twentieth century between conservative Christian fundamentalists and modernists who tended to be more secular and liberal.

A trial in the heart of Tennessee came to represent the changing culture of the 1920s, as well as those who sought to preserve traditional views. John Scopes, a recent graduate of the University of Kentucky, was teaching biology in Dayton, Tennessee, when he was found in violation of a state law that prohibited the teaching of Charles Darwin's theory of evolution. Darwin's theories were taught throughout the United States at the time, but they raised the ire of conservatives and evangelicals who believed that evolution ran counter to deeply held religious beliefs about the divine creation of man. In 1925, leading public figures such as William Jennings Bryan arose to defend the state law of Tennessee. Clarence Darrow agreed to defend Scopes's right to academic freedom. The resulting trial, known as the **Scopes Monkey Trial**, quickly descended into a media circus. As news reporters covered the trial's proceedings via live radio, Americans everywhere tuned in to listen as the academics squared off against the defenders of tradition and old-time religion.

One of the reasons Bryan agreed to defend the Tennessee law was that Darwin's theories about evolution were also being used to support eugenicists who advocated sterilization of minorities, which Bryan felt was un-American. However, the bulk of Bryan's argument was based on the idea that the teaching of evolution and the increasingly secular nature of public education threatened the values of rural America. The actual violation of the state law itself was hardly denied, and the trial soon became more of cultural debate than an investigation of the validity of the Tennessee law. Scopes himself was found guilty and fined $100, although he was never required to pay upon appeal.

The notoriety surrounding the trial led most Americans to hold their own debates about the separation of church and state. Most urban reporters believed that the brilliant attorney Clarence Darrow humiliated the devoutly religious Bryan. However, for many Americans, Bryan's declared belief in the literal translation of the Bible was nothing to be ashamed of. Even if the trial resulted in a moral victory for the forces of modern science and secular education, rural Americans, especially rural Southerners, often relished lost causes. For them, the attack upon a law they believed defended their children from heretical theories represented the way urban America, liberals, the federal government, and an increasingly worldly culture threatened their way of life. For the rest of the nation, liberal condescension toward evangelicals and rural Southerners appeared inconsistent with values such as toleration for others that supposedly guided American liberalism.

Although the trial was portrayed as a battle of reason and science versus religion and city versus the countryside, most Americans did not draw lines quite so cleanly. Most Americans believed in both evolution and creationism. Many rural Americans feared that banning evolution for religious reasons violated principles that were supposed to separate the church from the government. In addition, many academics rose to defend traditional views and ways of life against the superficiality of modern culture.

In 1930, a dozen Southern historians published an edited collection of articles called *I'll Take My Stand: The South and the Agrarian Tradition*. The historians sought to defend both the South and rural conservatism. They argued that an agricultural economy was naturally disposed toward more humane, egalitarian, and leisurely societies than that of urban industry. The book mixed an impassioned defense of community, the satisfaction of hard work, and a longing for an Edenic paradise lost. However, these white Southerners also demonstrated some of the most disturbing features of the white South when discussing race. Demonstrating their own misguided ideas about Africa as a land of savagery, several chose to include a nonhistorical defense of slavery as a positive good for the enslaved.

3.3 Pan-Africanism and Marcus Garvey

Black scholars responded to the racial bigotry found within *I'll Take My Stand* by celebrating black life and history in ways that reflected a new attitude of self-awareness and self-assertiveness. Scholar Alain Locke referred to this orientation as "The New Negro," an expression that came to embody the 1920s, even if the phrase itself had been used for over a generation. An African American journalist writing for the *Cleveland Gazette* may have coined this phrase in 1895. Five years later, Booker T. Washington used the phrase for the title of his book *A New Negro for a New Century*. However, the phrase took on a new meaning beyond self-help when Locke began to use it in the 1920s. The "New Negro" he described demanded respect and fair treatment. The "New Negro" might be an artist, an intellectual, a professional, or a common laborer. What they had in common was the refusal to kowtow to those who failed to recognize the dignity of their person or their labor.

W. E. B. Du Bois demonstrated this new spirit of willful confrontation to white supremacy by publishing essays that exposed white power organizations. These reports were based on the investigations of the biracial and blue-eyed Walter White who infiltrated these groups. White's "passing" was in this instance a daring expression of the new militancy among some African Americans. At the same time, it was a reminder that some other black women and men were still fleeing from their true racial identity.

Du Bois and the NAACP also demonstrated the spirit of the "New Negro" by supporting dozens of civil rights lawsuits and demanding an end to the colonization of Africa. Du Bois believed that the second-class citizenship of African Americans reflected this colonial orientation and remained the prominent voice of the NAACP and black intelligentsia throughout the 1920s. However, Du Bois and the NAACP were overshadowed during the early 1920s by a Jamaican named **Marcus Garvey** who advocated a different brand of Pan-Africanism.

Garvey came to America in 1916 and toured Tuskegee Institute, an Alabama teacher's college which was founded by the late Booker T. Washington. While there, he accepted an invitation to tour Harlem and was particularly impressed with the new attitude of self-reliance he saw in hundreds of small businesses throughout the predominantly black New York neighborhood. For Garvey, these economic enterprises that were independent of white money and white control represented the key to racial advancement. Garvey believed that lawsuits demanding integration were wrongheaded because he did not believe that white Americans would ever consent to sharing economic and political control with blacks. Furthermore, Garvey thought that the NAACP was foolish to launch civil rights lawsuits to force white businesses to treat black customers the same as white customers when the result would only mean more business for the white proprietor. He also did not approve of what he perceived as a cringing attitude among some black leaders who "begged" white government leaders to permit them to vote without fear of lynching or to sit in a white-owned theater among other whites.

Instead, Garvey believed the goal was to create black-owned theaters that showed films made by and for black people. He wanted black-owned restaurants and stores that would provide jobs for black employees and outlets for the products made by black artisans. He also wanted black voters to select black candidates, but doubted this would ever happen in the predominantly white political world. As a result, Garvey called for people of African descent to create independent black nations in the Caribbean, South America, and Africa where equality of rights would be recognized in law and deed.

In support of this goal, Marcus Garvey created the **Universal Negro Improvement Association (UNIA)** in Jamaica in 1914. Garvey established the first UNIA branch in the United States three years later, which was aimed at promoting racial pride and developing black-owned businesses; he hoped this would ultimately lead to black economic and political independence, which formed the foundation of his Pan-African vision. Although Illinois's Oscar De Priest would win election to the US Congress in 1928, those who subscribed to the ideal of black nationalism would point out that De Priest was placed on the ballot to secure black support for the lily-white machine politicians that controlled Chicago. De Priest himself advocated civil rights causes, but those who supported black nationalism would also point out that he was the only black American elected to Congress since the late nineteenth century.

FIGURE 6.21

This 1923 photo of Marcus Garvey demonstrates his flair for drama but also the pride that Garvey and his followers took in their movement. UNIA chapters included various ranks and positions which gave members a feeling of importance and belonging.

Marcus Garvey

A Jamaican advocate of Pan-African unity, Garvey created the Universal Negro Improvement Association (UNIA) in New York. The goal of the UNIA was to promote black pride and economic self-sufficiency in the near term while working toward creating independent black republics in Africa, Latin America, or the Caribbean.

Universal Negro Improvement Association (UNIA)

Created by Marcus Garvey in 1917, the UNIA was a fraternal organization that sought to promote pride, economic independence, and a common identity among people of African descent. The UNIA's newspaper *The Negro World* had a circulation that reached millions, while individual UNIA chapters started many successful cooperative economic ventures. The economic ventures of Garvey, however, proved to be epic failures, and the UNIA declined after its national leader was arrested and deported.

FIGURE 6.22

Illinois congressman Oscar De Priest was born to former slaves in Alabama. His family were Exodusters who moved to Ohio in the late 1870s. De Priest eventually settled in Chicago where he was a local politician before winning election to Congress.

Garvey's charisma and message of economic independence resonated with the masses of black Americans. His supporters resented the way their labor was exploited by white bosses while their earnings enriched white store owners and landlords who were often disrespectful. Garvey was unrivaled as a promoter, and he established dozens of businesses that produced products black men and women could be proud of, such as black dolls for children and uniforms for black nurses. Independent UNIA chapters launched dozens of economic cooperatives—stores run by black consumers who pooled their money to purchase goods directly and share profits equally. Together, black Americans rallied under Garvey's goal of "Negro producers, Negro distributors, Negro consumers," which he promised would end the neocolonial power structure that turned black labor into white profit.

Garvey's newspaper *The Negro World* was produced in several languages and had a circulation of nearly 200,000 around the world. The paper included uncompromising editorials about the white power structure and the need for a Pan-African independence movement. It also called for an end to colonialism, in both Africa and the United States. Garvey's militancy attracted the attention of federal agents who feared the charismatic leader of the UNIA might encourage a revolution among black Americans. The federal government tracked Garvey's movements and sought out complaints among his investors in hopes of deporting Garvey back to Jamaica. By 1923, they had enough evidence to imprison the black leader for fraud.

Garvey's most ambitious project was an international passenger and freight company called the *Black Star Line*. The purpose of this company was to promote trade and travel with Africa. Garvey received hundreds of thousands of stock subscriptions and purchased several large but aging ships that turned out to be poorly suited for international travel. For example, the first ship Garvey purchased ended up being worth only a fraction of its price. A touring ship Garvey purchased called the *SS Shadyside* had a leak in the side of its hull and sank. The irony of this disaster did little to improve the financial condition of the *Black Star Line*. After several voyages, most of the ships were in disrepair, and nearly every black leader had turned against Garvey for the loss of nearly every dollar entrusted to him by working-class men and women.

Black leaders were also angered by Garvey's calculating effort to solicit donations from the Ku Klux Klan to further his plans to create an independent black republic. Garvey hoped the Klan's desire to eliminate nonwhites would lead to financial assistance for his dream of creating an independent black republic outside of the United States. In the end, it was the failure of the *Black Star Line* and several duplicitous promises to his investors that destroyed Garvey's movement. After serving a brief jail sentence for investment fraud, Garvey was deported back to Jamaica in late 1927. Despite the poor management of his shipping company, the Garvey movement encouraged black pride. It also facilitated a number of local collective and economic ventures that fared much better than Garvey's ambitious but poorly operated shipping line. At the same time, Garvey's failures also drained precious financial resources from the black community and discouraged investment among those who purchased stock in Garvey's *Black Star Line*.

3.4 The Harlem Renaissance

Langston Hughes

An African American writer and poet who was raised in the Midwest but lived most of his adult life in Harlem. Hughes's poetry became a vehicle for assailing racism while communicating the dignity of African American life and culture.

The African American poet **Langston Hughes** personified the militancy and diversity of the New Negro. His mother had defeated segregation in Topeka, Kansas, five decades before the famous *Brown v. Board* decision that originated in this Midwestern state capitol. The agreement she secured permitted Hughes to attend the school nearest his home. His treatment in this school and the "integrated" schools of nearby Lawrence would leave a lasting impression on the young Hughes about the shortcomings of integration in the North. Langston Hughes's grandfather had been among the martyrs of John Brown's raid in West Virginia. His grandmother kept the bullet-ridden shawl her late husband wore when he was killed at Harper's Ferry and told young Langston stories about his family's long fight for justice. His grandmother was the first black woman to attend Oberlin College in Ohio. His granduncle had been a US congressman representing Virginia. The Hughes ancestry also included Native Americans and people of European descent. His distant relatives even included leading men such as Senator Henry Clay.

Hughes attended Columbia University in 1921, but his real education took place in the adjacent community of Harlem. Hughes immediately recognized that the spirit of his poetry was alive in this mecca of independent black art and culture. In 1926, Hughes and several notable writers, such **Zora Neale Hurston** and Countee Cullen, teamed with artist and fellow Kansan Aaron Douglas to create a literary magazine called *Fire!!* This journal was not well received by the mainstream black press. Few middle and upper-class black readers were prepared for the journal's honest depiction of black life and were deeply troubled by its inclusion of a piece about homosexuality. In fact, the reviewer from the *Baltimore Afro-American* declared that the journal deserved to be thrown into the fireplace. Ironically, a warehouse fire would later destroy many of the unsold copies. Surviving copies of the journal and the work of its contributors and hundreds of other writers and artists demonstrate that the **Harlem Renaissance** represented a new attitude among black intellectuals. We "intend to express our individual dark-skinned selves without fear or shame," Hughes exclaimed. "If the white people are pleased, we are glad. If they are not, it doesn't matter. We know we are beautiful, and ugly too."

This new spirit contrasted sharply with the work of most African American artists, musicians, and writers who, prior to the 1920s, mirrored European styles. Because most white Americans also sought to produce art and literature that reflected European standards, the Harlem Renaissance would inspire the creation of uniquely American art, music, and literature in future generations. Zora Neale Hurston would later become one of the most well-known writers of the era, although her most famous novel, *Their Eyes Were Watching God*, was not published until 1937. Hurston's work acknowledged the poverty and conditions faced by rural blacks and celebrated black dialogue. Her style set Hurston apart during an era when many black newspapers scolded the masses for speaking too informally and too loudly on trains because it created a negative impression in the minds of white passengers. Hurston's work was seldom appreciated in its own time, however, and most artists that participated in the Harlem Renaissance still wrote from the perspective of the black middle class.

Zora Neale Hurston

A controversial figure in her own lifetime for her use of black vernacular in her work, Hurston's prose is renowned today for its drama and authenticity. Hurston's work described the conditions many Southern blacks faced and dealt candidly with controversial topics affecting black communities.

Harlem Renaissance

A cultural movement centered around the black neighborhood of Harlem that produced a wealth of uniquely American art, literature, poetry, music, and plays. While previous generations of African Americans had usually sought to mirror European culture, black artists from around the country joined those in Harlem in creating uniquely American and African American styles of cultural expression.

FIGURE 6.23

Langston Hughes was one of the most prolific writers of the Harlem Renaissance.

FIGURE 6.24

Like many Harlem Renaissance artists, Hale Woodruff was born in the Midwest. He left his hometown of Cairo, Illinois, studied art at Harvard, and taught at Atlanta University as well as Spellman College and Morehouse. His art depicted a variety of topics, including a series of famous murals depicting the slave revolt aboard the *Amistad*.

Despite its middle-class pedigree, the work of the Harlem Renaissance was still daring and uniquely American. Its poetry, prose, music, and art reflected the unique struggles of those who achieved a high level of education and economic security yet were denied the respectability granted to others whose journeys were less burdened. Hughes wrote poems inspired from his own life. For example, he wrote about the loneliness of being the only black student in an "integrated" school and being ridiculed by teachers when he expressed his ambitions to become a writer. No matter how successful one rose to be, even those whites that called themselves friends of the race acted differently among other whites, Hughes explained. Others practiced segregation with little regard for its consequences upon the self-perception of black children. "They send me to eat in the kitchen when company comes," Hughes wrote in his poem *I Too Sing America*, "but I laugh, and eat well, and grow strong." The poem *If We Must Die* by Claude McKay was more direct, counseling violent resistance to the violence of racism in the midst of the race riots of 1919.

The independence of black writers was reflected by the works of black musicians in Harlem and throughout the United States in the 1920s. No longer content to mirror the styles of European classical music or the sedate melodies of the era's Big Bands that excluded them, black musicians created a new style of music that reflected the highs and lows of life in black enclaves like New Orleans. Jazz featured an up-tempo beat with improvised solos bound together by a bolder rhythm and harmony than could be found anywhere else. A phalanx of traveling musicians transferred different styles of music, such as blues with its unique chords and "blue" notes. None of these styles and forms of music was invented by any one person, although W. C. Handy is often known as "the Father of the Blues" for his role in capturing the rhythms he observed throughout black America and transferring them to sheet music.

On any given night in 1920s America, one might go in search of the blues as it moved from its birthplace in the Mississippi Delta north to Chicago and all points east and west. If one knew where to look, they might even find it in the factory towns of New England and the mining camps of Appalachia. However, if a musical style could ever be said to have an address, during the 1920s, the home of jazz was Harlem. The machine politics of Kansas City's Tom Pendergast and other city bosses permitted the growth of tenderloin districts where liquor and jazz flowed. However, none of these compared to Harlem's Savoy Ballroom or Apollo Theater, a melting pot where the Chicago style of Louis Armstrong mixed with the St. Louis Blues and Charlie "Bird" Parker's Kansas City Jazz.

Wealthy and middle-class whites seldom visited Harlem's jazz clubs, despite the rising popularity of jazz and blues worldwide. Most whites preferred the "plantation atmosphere" of Manhattan's Cotton Club, where black musicians performed but were never allowed to partake. At hundreds of similar venues throughout the nation, black musicians, light-skinned dancing girls, and white-gloved waiters offered a taste of black culture to a white America that was not yet ready for the New Negro of Harlem. Despite its hypocrisy in drawing the color line against black patrons, The Cotton Club provided an authentic portrait of US culture and all its contradictions. Scholar Alain Locke wrote that before the Harlem Renaissance, black Americans were expected to follow a formula created by white Americans of the "good negro" who was docile and childlike, hardworking but incapable of independent thought.

> …there would be no lynching, if it did not start in the schoolroom. Why not exploit, enslave, or exterminate a class that everybody is taught to regard as inferior?
>
> —Historian Carter G. Woodson explaining the importance of teaching the culture, language, perspectives, and history of diverse peoples

As evidenced by Locke and many other scholars, such as historian **Carter G. Woodson**, the 1920s also saw a renaissance in black scholarship. Woodson rose from the coal mines and segregated schools of West Virginia to become the second African American to receive a PhD from Harvard University. Woodson started what became black history month. More impressively, Woodson transformed black history from a branch of Southern history practiced by Southern whites to its own scholarly discipline. Woodson's life work was the inclusion of black perspectives and the incorporation of African American history within the larger narrative of US history.

Woodson lived in a time when scholars accepted slavery as a positive good for the slave with a few unfortunate exceptions and a few unkind masters. The standard work on the subject, *American Negro Slavery* (1918) by U. B. Phillips claimed that slaves "were by racial quality submissive rather than defiant, light-hearted instead of gloomy, amiable and ingratiating instead of sullen, and whose very defects invited paternalism rather than repression." Woodson discovered hundreds of firsthand accounts of slavery from the perspective of the slave that forever altered America's perception of American slavery and antebellum history. Woodson also explained how the miseducated views of these historians justified and perpetuated racist ideas in the minds of both white and black Americans.

3.5   The New Woman of the 1920s

Leaders of the suffrage movement began to speak of a "New Woman" who, like the "New Negro," was better educated and more assertive. During the 1920s, one in four Americans in the paid workforce were women. One in twenty married women was engaged in paid employment outside of the home at the turn of the century, but by the 1920s, that number had increased to one in ten. The increase in the number of women in the workforce alone was not evidence of advancement for women, however, since 90 percent of women were employed in only one of ten "female" jobs that featured routine work, low status, and low pay.

The emergence of nursing, and especially teaching, opened new positions for educated women. The teaching field grew exponentially during the early decades of the twentieth century as mandatory school attendance laws finally began to be enforced nationwide. Entering this field was an army of well-trained women, as female high school graduates outnumbered their male counterparts, and 47 percent of college students were women. Men and women were also graduating college in equal numbers during the 1920s. A glass ceiling remained for educators, however, as 80 percent of teachers were women, while only a handful of women had been appointed as principals.

Echoing this imbalance, only a handful of college faculty positions were held by women beyond a few dozen women's colleges that were usually led by male administrators. The discrepancy was not the result of a lack of female candidates, as one in six PhD degrees was awarded to a woman during the 1920s. Owing to the vast number of well-qualified women, the academy began its reluctant march toward gender equality. In many ways, universities were more progressive than the rest of the professions in this regard. Women during the 1920s were also more likely to achieve professional degrees, even if their opportunities to practice law and medicine were even more severely limited than academia. In addition, nine women served in the US Congress during the late 1920s, and thousands of women were appointed or elected to positions in state and local governments nationwide.

The battle for the right to vote had at least partially unified women of diverse backgrounds. With suffrage achieved, the already tenuous cooperation of these groups was threatened. Absent a common cause, the lines of race, ethnicity, region, and social class once again threatened to divide women. The potential threat of disintegration was manifest at the first convention of the National Women's Party (NWP) in 1921. A group of black women rose to address the convention regarding the refusal of some Southern states to recognize their right to vote. NWP leader Alice Paul argued that this was a racial and regional issue best handled by Southern black women separately. African American delegate and NAACP field secretary Addie Hunton protested that this was precisely the kind of issue the NWP must address. "No women are free," Hunton explained, "until all women are free." Paul and other leading white women had a long history of being more liberal in their support of racial equality than the general population. However, it was clear to the black delegates that their interests were secondary concerns to Paul and most whites within the NWP. From Paul's perspective, support for black voting rights would likely split the NWP along racial and regional lines in ways that would derail the women's movement.

Instead, Paul hoped to capitalize on the inertia of that movement and use the voting power of women to pass a law that would forever outlaw gender discrimination. To this end, Paul and the National Women's Party introduced the Equal Rights Amendment in 1923. The amendment was elegant in its simplicity, prohibiting any legal distinctions regarding gender. Paul believed that the amendment would require equal employment and educational opportunities. It would also open new opportunities for entrepreneurial women who needed equal access to bank loans. However, most restrictions upon women in business and the professions were by custom rather than law and would therefore be more difficult to challenge.

Carter G. Woodson

Known as the "Father of Black History," Woodson was an educator in West Virginia who earned a PhD from Harvard and founded what eventually became African American History Month. Equally important, Woodson studied topics such as the history of slavery from the perspective of black Americans during an era when academic studies of slavery were dominated by Southern whites.

FIGURE 6.25

Unappreciated by most Americans during her life, many of Zora Neale Hurston's books are among the best-selling novels. Her most famous novel is semi-autobiographical, detailing life in the all-black town of Eatonville, Florida.

Many women outside the NWP argued that the Equal Rights Amendment threatened to invalidate a number of state laws that women had lobbied for in the past. This included "protective" legislation limiting the number of hours a woman could be required to work and the kinds of physical labor she could be compelled to perform. Other states had created welfare programs known as mother's pensions that provided limited benefits for mothers and widows. In addition, the Sheppard-Towner Act specifically provided funding for women's health clinics. As a result, many women's groups expressed opposition to the Equal Rights Amendment throughout the 1920s for fear that these laws might be invalidated. This division among women would become especially pronounced during the 1970s when the Equal Rights Amendment passed Congress and was sent to the states for ratification.

REVIEW AND CRITICAL THINKING

1. Explain the ways that college life reflected the cultural changes of the 1920s. In what ways were the 1920s a more liberal decade, and in what ways was the decade more conservative?

2. What was the significance of the Scopes trial? How does the trial reflect the cultural divides of US life in the 1920s?

3. What was the Harlem Renaissance? How was the message of black America as expressed by artists and writers in the 1920s relevant to all Americans? Why might few history surveys written prior to the 1970s include any mention of the Harlem Renaissance?

4. What was the significance of the work of historian Carter G. Woodson? Might his argument about the danger of miseducation be applied to other fields of inquiry?

5. What was new about the "new woman" of the 1920s? In what ways did life for American women change during this decade?

---

4. THE CRASH: FROM DECADENCE TO DEPRESSION

LEARNING OBJECTIVES

1. Explain the various causes of the Great Depression. Analyze the reasons for the stock market's decline, the banking crisis, and the decline of consumer demand.

2. Evaluate the response of the Hoover administration to the growing economic turmoil of the early 1930s. Explain how customs of limited government restrained this response, while at the same time exploring the ways that Hoover sought to expand the role of government to meet the crisis in new ways.

3. Summarize the issues of the election of 1932. Explain how Roosevelt was able to win by a landslide while previous Democrats had been defeated by Republicans by equally large margins in previous elections.

4.1 Election of 1928 and the Stock Market Crash

In 1928, Republican presidential candidate Herbert Hoover declared that the United States was "nearer to the final triumph over poverty" than any nation in the history of the world. This kind of rhetoric was expected from presidents and would later be used to make it appear as though Hoover had not anticipated the challenges of the next four years. The criticism is only partially valid. Hoover, more than most political leaders of his day, understood that some of the era's affluence was based on speculation. As secretary of commerce under Harding and Coolidge, Hoover understood these challenges as well as most Americans and had long cautioned about the dangers of stock market speculation.

As a candidate in the 1928 presidential election, however, Hoover's strategy was to connect his leadership of the Commerce Department with the decade's prosperity. The strategy paid dividends as Hoover easily defeated Democrat Al Smith with the support of 21 million voters to Smith's 15 million supporters. The only consolation for the Democrats was that they were successful in mobilizing immigrant voters, although a large part of this growth was simply a reaction to the nativist rhetoric of many within the Republican Party. Smith was the first Catholic to secure the nomination of any major political party. Although the Klan and others who subscribed to anti-Catholic sentiment had declined, Smith's campaign was still tormented by nativist detractors. These efforts backfired, at least in the long term because they brought Catholic voters into the Democratic fold. These two groups—Catholics and immigrants—would prove essential components of the future Democratic coalition that would provide large majorities for their party in future elections.

Part of Hoover's appeal in the 1928 election was the connection in voters' minds between the prosperity of recent years and the Republican Party. His cabinet was composed of business leaders and reflected the confidence of years of financial success. The stock market had been encouraged by nearly a decade of increasingly positive earnings results. There were certainly signs of decline within major industries and real estate, but this was true even during the most robust periods of economic growth. Some of the positive signs were unique to the US. For example, American finance and industry had gained globally in the wake of World War I. US banks and the federal government were receiving millions each year in interest payments from loans made to their Western allies during and after World War I. The United States also enjoyed a favorable balance of trade and a domestic market that was the envy of the rest of the world.

In retrospect, at least, the global signs of economic decline were obvious. Germany was saved from delinquency in its reparation payments only by a series of temporary reprieves that delayed repayment. US banks had invested heavily in Germany both before and after the war. Had it not been for US money that was still flowing to Germany, German banks would have defaulted on their obligations to Western Europe long ago. Even worse, Western Europe's interest payments to US banks and the federal government were dependent upon the receipt of German payments. In other words, America's leading position in world affairs obscured the fact that it stood atop a delicate house of cards that depended on US capital to shuffle the deck. If US banks were unable to provide continued loans to their international creditors, these foreign governments and banks might default. This could start a cycle of defaults that would leave US banks to face their own precarious liquidity issues at home.

FIGURE 6.26

The stock market crash of October 1929 led to bank failures that caused many Americans to lose their life savings as well as their jobs. State and private charities had cared for individuals in the past, but these entities were quickly overwhelmed by the magnitude of the Great Depression.

These US banks had invested their own depositor's money, loaning money to corporations that were also low on cash reserves. Domestic consumer purchases of homes, automobiles, and appliances were declining for two important reasons. First, consumers who could afford these items had already purchased them, while others had purchased them on credit. Neither group could be expected to make the same level of discretionary purchases indefinitely. Second, the distribution of wealth in the nation was dangerously uneven. Corporations had borrowed billions to produce factories that could churn out consumer goods, but there simply were not enough middle-class consumers who could afford their products. The wealthiest 1 percent of Americans controlled over a third of the nation's wealth, and the bottom 50 percent had almost no personal savings whatsoever. The middle class had grown slightly wealthier, but few people could truly be considered middle class. This group of consumers was simply not large enough to sustain the new economy, which was based largely upon consumer spending.

The most obvious sign of financial crisis came in October 1929 when the average valuation of every publicly traded US company dropped by nearly 40 percent. Although this decline merely returned most stocks to the prices of the mid-1920s, the **Stock Market Crash of 1929** was not merely a setback. Hundreds of millions of shares had been purchased with borrowed money with only the stock itself as collateral. When these stock prices fell, the loans could not be repaid. As a result, thousands of banks failed, and millions of depositors lost their life savings.

Even banks that had not made risky loans or speculated in the stock market were punished because depositors did not want to take chances that their bank would be the next to fail. At this time, it is important to remember, the US government did not provide insurance for bank deposits. The result was that banks no longer had money to lend to individuals or businesses to keep the economy going. To make matters worse, banks also began to call in their loans early, which forced businesses to sell their own stock, lay off workers, or simply declare bankruptcy.

This incredibly risky strategy of buying stock with borrowed money was known as "buying on margin." The practice remains legal in the modern era, although it is more heavily regulated. Buying on margin allowed individuals to "leverage" their money to buy more stock than they normally could by using existing stock as collateral. For example, someone with 500 shares of General Electric valued at $100 per share would have an investment valued at $50,000. The use of leverage and margin could permit the investor to use those shares as collateral for a loan of another $200,000, which he would use to purchase another 2,000 shares of GE stock. If GE stock increases in value, the individual stands to make a substantial profit. However, if the stock declines by 40 percent, as most stocks did, the individual's 2,500 shares at $60 each would be worth only $150,000. Because he still owes the bank $200,000 and has only $150,000 in stock to pay it back, he and the bank might be in serious trouble. During the 1920s, many private citizens, corporations, investment firms, and even banks found themselves in precisely this situation. Had the investor simply bought the 500 shares with money he owned, he would still have $30,000 worth of stock even after the 40 percent decline.

It may be easy in hindsight to see the folly of such an investment strategy, but the stock market's unprecedented rise during the 1920s enticed many investors to become gamblers. The era's prosperity had led to dramatic increases in stock prices, partially due to genuine corporate profits but also because

Stock Market Crash of 1929

Refers to a series of days in October 1929 when the aggregate value of publicly traded companies listed on the New York Stock Exchange declined by as much as 10 percent. Although similar panics had led to declines like this over the course of a few days, the stock market crash saw multiple trading sessions in a row, where prices declined rapidly despite the efforts of leading bankers to bolster the market. Because many investors had bought stock with borrowed money, these declines led many individuals, banks, and corporations to go bankrupt. By 1933, the stock market was down by over 80 percent.

many other speculators were also buying stock with money they did not actually have. Eventually, there were not enough new investors to keep buying stocks, and the prices began to decline.

However, these stock price declines were not the only cause of the Great Depression. Stock prices had doubled in the final two years of the 1920s and were overdue for a correction. The greatest significance of the stock market was its effect upon the banking system. The economy's decline had actually begun sector by sector in the mid- to late 1920s in response to declining consumer demand. It was only after the crash of Wall Street that investors started paying attention to the years of declining consumer demand. Prior to the crash of October 1929, investors were happy to purchase stock at inflated prices. Afterwards, the realization that corporate profits lagged behind stock prices led to three consecutive years of stock market declines.

These declines erased the wealth of many potential entrepreneurs and led to the near-collapse of the banking system. It also shook the confidence of credit markets in ways that would prevent economic recovery. Recovery was also prevented by the unequal distribution of wealth in an economy based on consumer spending. When consumers could no longer afford to act as consumers are expected to act, sales declined, and the downward pressure on all financial markets continued. Between bank failures, the stock market crash, massive unemployment, and the complete erosion of consumer demand, it became increasingly clear that the economy would not recover on its own as quickly as it had in the past.

4.2 Hoover's Response

Smoot-Hawley Tariff of 1930

Placed taxes on imported goods during the Depression. The tariff was intended to spur domestic production by limiting foreign imports. However, the tariff encouraged foreign countries to place reciprocal tariffs on US exports, leading many historians to argue that the tariff was counterproductive.

Hoover recognized that the economy risked slowing due to overproduction that had produced glutted markets, especially in agriculture. Hoover believed the solution was higher tariffs for imports and a cooperative effort between businesses and government to expand into foreign markets. The **Smoot-Hawley Tariff of 1930** increased tariffs to record highs in hopes of limiting foreign imports to the United States. Economists predicted that the tariffs would backfire by leading foreign governments to raise tariffs on US products sold abroad. Because the United States was a net exporter of both manufactured goods and agricultural products, the danger of damaging the export trade was greater than the possible benefit of reducing imports. Unfortunately for farmers and industry, the tariff took effect just as a global depression led other nations to place similar tariffs on foreign goods, and international trade fell by two-thirds by 1932. Many in government recognized that raising the tariff was a poor long-term strategy, yet by 1930, most politicians were simply hoping to provide a quick boost to the domestic economy.

The stock market crash led to tighter credit and a suspension of loans from US banks abroad. As a result, only a controversial deal brokered by Hoover granting a one-year suspension of payments on wartime loans prevented an immediate collapse of the international banking system. However, the instability and unlikelihood that European banks could resume payments to the United States when this temporary moratorium ended led private citizens and companies to withdraw their money from European banks. The panic soon spread to the United States where bank runs led to the failure of a few thousand banks between 1931 and 1933. Because US banks had loaned the money that had been deposited to US businesses, real estate developers, and international banks, none of whom could immediately pay back their loans, there was no money to repay all of the depositors who were presenting themselves by the hundreds at the door of US banks.

Great Depression

A period of high unemployment and low economic development between the Wall Street Crash of 1929 and US entry into World War II. The Depression was not limited to the United States, as Europe and the rest of the industrialized world experienced severe declines in their material well-being.

The years 1932 and 1933 were the worst of the **Great Depression**, as bank failures wiped out life savings and discouraged those who still had money from spending or investing it. One-fourth to one-third of Americans who sought jobs were unemployed at any given moment. Private charities that had been somewhat effective at caring for America's poor in years past found themselves in the unenviable position of trying to determine who was in the greatest danger of starvation. Diseases associated with malnutrition that had not surfaced since the leanest years of the Civil War began to reemerge. Several million families were evicted from their homes and lived in the growing shanties that surrounded most cities. That many Americans called these clusters of makeshift shelters "Hoovervilles" indicated that Americans' expectations of the federal government had changed since the crises of the 1870s and 1890s. During those years, most Americans turned to state and local governments for assistance. However, the magnitude of the crisis appeared to be beyond the ability of these institutions and private charity to mitigate.

Instead of Coxey's Army, which had demanded federal jobs during the crisis of the 1890s, more than 15,000 veterans converged on Washington in the summer of 1932. These former World War I soldiers requested early payment of their retirement bonus. Congress and President Hoover debated the matter, but determined that it was more important to maintain a balanced budget. Few of the veterans left the city after their measure was defeated. For many of these men and their families, obtaining an early payment of their bonus was their last best hope. Calling themselves the Bonus Army, these men and their families established their own Hoovervilles throughout the city and resolved to stay until the federal government reconsidered.

On July 28, an enraged President Hoover ordered the military to prevent these men from continuing their protest in front of the White House or US Capitol. Not for the last time in his career, General Douglas MacArthur exceeded a president's orders. He sought to evict the veterans and their families from the nation's capitol by force if necessary. Hoover likely did not fully understand the tactics that the military used on these veterans' families, believing that he had preserved law and order from a trespassing "mob" as he called the men. The media told a different story complete with pictures of tanks under the command of MacArthur and perhaps the last cavalry charge in US military history led by a major named George S. Patton. The troops used poisonous gas that led to the death of an infant, while local police ordered the shacks set on fire. Among the dozens of injured veterans was a former private from Camden, New Jersey, who had been decorated for valor in saving Patton's life during World War I.

Following the government's response to the Bonus Army, the public perceived Hoover as remarkably insensitive to the plight of ordinary Americans. It helped little that Hoover believed that keeping up the regal appearances of the White House might help to demonstrate his confidence in recovery. Hoover had never relished the trappings of office in the first place and might have been better served by communicating a bit of his own history instead of being photographed with white-gloved White House waiters. Hoover rose from poverty as an orphan to become a wealthy engineer. Actually, Hoover had succeeded at nearly everything he tried. He had also demonstrated a capacity for helping others in times of dire need as the head of an international agency that provided relief for Belgians during World War I. Hoover had also coordinated America's remarkably successful humanitarian efforts throughout Europe at the war's conclusion.

However, Hoover also viewed the creation of a large and powerful central government as the first step toward the tyranny that led to World War I. He and most other leading men of his era had come to believe that economic fluctuations were simply part of the business cycle and should be endured with stoic resolve. Hoover also believed in the importance of balanced budgets and ensuring a strong dollar based on the gold standard. While some of his critics suggested that printing more money would help to alleviate the credit crisis, limit bank failures, and perhaps encourage investment, Hoover followed orthodox economists who believed intentionally causing inflation was heresy. Hoover's economic advisers also rejected new ideas such as raising money by selling government bonds to fund public works projects that would provide jobs. In fact, Hoover vetoed a law sponsored by his Democratic opponents that would have done this as the 1930 congressional elections approached.

FIGURE 6.27

The US Capitol appears in the backdrop of burning shacks, the temporary home of veterans who were part of the Bonus Army. These men had traveled to Washington, DC, in hopes of convincing Congress and President Hoover to pay World War I enlistment bonuses early due to the hardships of the Depression. As the photo indicates, that request was denied.

4.3 Election of 1932

It is easy in hindsight to blame Congress for its failure to effectively regulate banks and financial markets. It is also tempting to blame Hoover for not embracing deficit spending, public works projects, and deliberate inflation to try to spur the economy. However, the total federal budget for non–defense-related expenditures was barely more than what some of the larger states spent each year. The expectations of the federal government were limited, and previous recessions and depressions had been dealt with by allowing the business cycle to right itself. From the perspective of history and Treasury Secretary Andrew Mellon, the role of the federal government was to stoically permit the natural workings of the market to "purge the rottenness out of the system."

The Democrats believed that this depression was different, and they began their attack on Hoover and Republican members of Congress during the Congressional elections of 1930. Many of their allegations were less than objective and even unfair. However, partisan attacks against the party in power during times of economic decline was a time-honored strategy among both parties. Democrats used the science of marketing to brand the president and the Republicans as the architects of ruin. The empty pockets of an unemployed worker turned inside out were labeled "Hoover flags," and the newspaper that covered him at night was referred to as a "Hoover blanket" by the Democrats.

After the Democrats gained over fifty seats in the House of Representatives during the 1930 elections, Hoover belatedly agreed to fund some public works projects. He also agreed to provide unprecedented loans to keep banks and other financial firms from going bankrupt. Despite Hoover's activism, sincerity of purpose, and a work schedule that allowed him only a few hours for sleep, the economy continued to decline throughout the election year of 1932. The Democrats successfully branded the federal bailouts of banks—a strategy they had actually recommended to the president—as evidence to support their claims that Hoover cared more about the bankers who allegedly caused the Depression than the people who were suffering from it.

The perception was both unfair and inaccurate, as Hoover had agreed to numerous bipartisan relief efforts that would alleviate conditions in the next few years. For example, the Emergency Relief Act of July 1932 authorized up to $2 billion in loans to states to finance direct relief to those most in need and public works projects to provide jobs. These loans would pale in comparison to the massive federal programs of the next few years. However, these loans and other programs also initiated the process of using the federal government and monetary policy to steer the economy. They also provided funding for the first federal welfare program beyond the Sheppard-Towner Act which had offered limited subsidies for women's health clinics.

In politics, as in most other fields, perception is reality and Hoover was continually branded as insensitive and unwilling to help those in need. Despite Hoover's belated acceptance of what would later be known as Keynesian economics, he would be remembered as a president that did nothing in the face of crisis. He would also be portrayed as someone who believed in "trickle-down" theories of economic growth and recovery. This theory argues the best way to aid the economy is to secure the fortunes of the wealthy and the solvency of banks. Historians have recently argued that this comparison is inaccurate, especially when considered within the context of 1920s America. These times were about to change quickly, however, as Hoover's successor used a variety of new strategies on such a massive scale that most Americans would forget Hoover's limited attempts to use the power of the federal government to address the crisis.

FIGURE 6.28

As this map indicates, the Democratic candidate Franklin Delano Roosevelt easily prevailed over the incumbent Herbert Hoover in the 1932 presidential election.

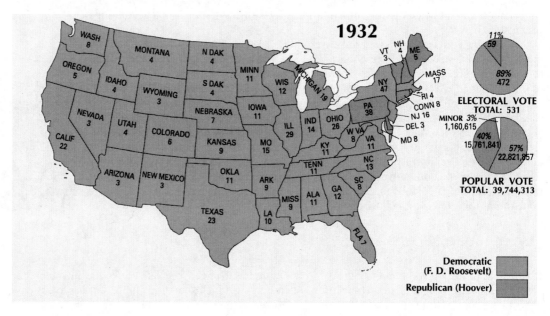

That man was **Franklin Delano Roosevelt (FDR)**, a man of privilege who was born into an affluent family and used his connections to become governor of New York. Roosevelt was a lifelong politician who had been crippled by polio in 1921. With the aid of steel braces and his own indomitable will, he managed to "walk" by throwing his weight forward and bracing himself on the arm of a sturdy companion. For the rest of his life, that companion was his wife Eleanor. Also from a prominent family, the talented and well-educated Eleanor Roosevelt became his public face while her desk-bound husband dispatched armies of letters that kept him connected to the political world.

In the same year that New York's Al Smith lost in a landslide to Hoover, Smith had convinced Roosevelt to enter the gubernatorial race in New York. Roosevelt's victory and rising influence within the Democratic Party in the next four years ironically led to his selection over Al Smith during the 1932 Democratic convention. Hoover was nominated by a dispirited Republican Party but did not campaign in an election that many believed had already been decided by the state of the economy. Roosevelt spent most of 1932 campaigning for office by attempting to reconcile the various elements of his party rather than attempting to confront Hoover. By November 1932, industrial production had declined by 50 percent, and even business interests were abandoning Hoover and the Republicans. Everyone in America knew that whoever won the Democratic nomination had effectively won the presidency by default. What Roosevelt might do to halt the Depression and spur recovery, however, remained anyone's guess.

Franklin Delano Roosevelt (FDR)

A New York governor who became the 32nd president of the United States, Roosevelt would be elected to an unprecedented four terms between 1932 and his death in 1945. Although born and raised in affluence, Roosevelt communicated empathy for those Americans struggling through the Great Depression. As president, Roosevelt used his political power to create a number of federal programs that would later be known as the New Deal. He also sought to intervene on behalf of the Western Allies prior to the official US declaration of war against Japan and Germany in December 1941.

REVIEW AND CRITICAL THINKING

1. How did speculation and debt lead to the stock market crash? Did the stock market crash cause the Great Depression? If you believe it did, why would the market partially recover in 1930?

2. Explain the role of the stock market, banking, international affairs, and declining consumer demand in causing the Great Depression.

3. Most Americans were angered by the Hoover administration and blamed the president for the state of the economy by the time of the 1932 election. Was this criticism fair? Answer this question in context of both the causes of the Depression and the traditions of limited government up to this time.

4. Did Roosevelt unite the various competing factions of the Democratic Party in 1932, or was his landslide more a reflection of another factor?

5. Socialists argued that the Depression revealed the true nature of Capitalism and its insatiable drive for maximizing profit that led to instability. What do you think? Did the Great Depression show the need for government intervention to prevent the downfall of the Capitalist system?

5. CONCLUSION

The 1920s saw dramatic economic growth as factories churned out consumer goods that were marketed and distributed throughout the nation. Local economic control gave way to a national consumer market as business mergers consolidated industries and fueled a meteoric rise in the stock market. Americans were increasingly likely to wear the same clothing and listen to the same radio programs, even drink the same beer and eat the same processed meats. Technology spurred the popularity of the new and uniquely American jazz music, while the burgeoning US film and fashion industry spread the uniquely American image of the "flapper." Americans were increasingly likely to celebrate their new identities as consumers, especially those wealthy enough to enjoy the prosperity of the decade. Popular books such as the *Great Gatsby* protested the hollowness of material wealth but seldom converted its readers to disdain their quest for it. By the end of the decade, the Depression reminded Americans that material goods might bring temporary pleasure, but material security was simply too important to leverage.

Prohibition symbolized the contradictions of the decade: a conservative power structure reflected in the affairs of business and government and a rebellious popular culture that flourished behind this façade. The ease with which the affluent flouted laws meant to curb their power reflected the selective enforcement of Prohibition laws, which created one system of justice for the rich and one for the poor. Women and minorities were allowed a rare glimpse of these power structures as they labored in the background of resorts, largely unnoticed and undisturbed as long as they kept their "place." For the men of the middle class and a fortunate few laborers, there were the speakeasies with their mixture of jazz, liquor, and the promise of fast times and faster women. Jazz was not invented in these resorts or hidden haunts, but these places offered a sample of the era's celebration of sexual liberation and its fusion of black and white musical traditions. This culture arose from the collective experiences of people who traveled the nation in search of work, and its improvised music reflecting the improvised lives of its creators.

6. FURTHER READING

Blee, Kathleen. *Women of the Klan: Racism and Gender in the 1920s* (1992).

Chapman, Erin D. *Prove It On Me: New Negroes, Sex, and Popular Culture in the 1920s* (2012).

Chauncey, George. *Gay New York: Gender, Urban Culture, and the Making of the Gay Male World, 1890–1940* (1994).

Foglesong, David S. *America's Secret War against Bolshevism: US Intervention in the Russian Civil War, 1917–1920* (2001).

Foley, Neil. *The White Scourge: Mexicans, Blacks, and Poor Whites in Texas Cotton Culture* (1999).

Frystak, Shannon. *Our Minds on Freedom: Women and the Struggle for Black Equality in Louisiana, 1924–1967* (2009).

Hewitt, Nancy A. *Southern Discomfort: Women's Activism in Tampa, Florida, 1880s–1920s* (2001).

Lears, Jackson. *Fables of Abundance: A Cultural History of Advertising in America* (1994).

Moran, Jeffrey. *The Scopes Trial: A Brief History with Documents* (2010).

Payne, Phillip G. *Dead Last: The Public Memory of Warren G. Harding's Scandalous Legacy* (2008).

Rolinson, Mary G. *Grassroots Garveyism: The Universal Negro Improvement Association in the Rural South, 1920–1927* (2007).

Simmons, Christina. *Making Marriage Modern: Women's Sexuality from the Progressive Era to World War II* (2009).

CHAPTER 7
The New Deal and Origins of World War II, 1932–1939

Franklin Delano Roosevelt (FDR) inherited a banking system on the verge of collapse and an economy where 12 million job-seekers could not find work. The stock market had declined by over 80 percent, while average household income was just above half of what it had been in the late 1920s. The scale of human suffering was particularly devastating for the 2 million families who lost homes and farms and the 30 million Americans who were members of households without a single employed family member. Perhaps most frustrating was that one in five children was chronically malnourished, while US farms continued to produce more food than the nation could possibly consume. Prices for some farm goods remained so low that millions of tons of food were wasted because it cost more to transport certain items than they would generate in revenue if sold. A similar tragedy existed in the form of warehouses that remained full of coats and other necessities, while millions of Americans lacked the ability to purchase them at nearly any price.

The nation wondered how their new president would fulfill his promise to relieve the suffering and get the nation back to work. Roosevelt had promised a "New Deal" but offered few details of how that deal would operate. In May 1933, a small group of veterans of the Bonus Army decided to return to Washington and see for themselves if the new president would be any more supportive of their request for an early payment of their WWI bonuses. He was not. In fact, three years later, Roosevelt would veto a bill providing early payment, a bill Congress eventually passed without his signature.

FIGURE 7.1

World War I veterans returned to the nation's capitol as Roosevelt took office, seeking early payment of their enlistment bonus. Although neither President Hoover nor Roosevelt agreed to meet with the men, Eleanor Roosevelt and a number of congressmen did. In this photo, Texas congressman Wright Patman and Mississippi's John Rankin collect petitions from members of the Bonus Army.

Eleanor Roosevelt

A leading public figure who
assisted her husband's rise
through New York and
national politics, Roosevelt
also transformed the position
of presidential spouse. She
traveled and advocated a
number of liberal causes from
women's rights to civil rights.
The president supported
some of these causes, but
feared his direct advocacy of
controversial subjects such as
civil rights would jeopardize
his electoral support. Because
of her popularity, Eleanor
Roosevelt's conferences were
covered by every major news
outlet and her decision to
only admit female reporters
to these conferences created
many new opportunities for
women in journalism.

However, in 1933, Roosevelt's treatment of the men and their families showed a degree of compassion and respect that demonstrated Roosevelt had at least learned from the public outrage regarding Hoover's treatment of the Bonus Army. Rather than call out the army, Roosevelt provided tents and rations. **Eleanor Roosevelt** met with the men and promised that the administration would eventually find them jobs. She kept her promise, as World War I veterans were recruited for jobs in new government programs such as the Civilian Conservation Corps. Although this particular program was limited to those below the age of twenty-five, veterans were exempt from the age requirement. One of the veterans was said to have offered a simple comparison that reflected the difference between the two presidents. "Hoover sent the army," the oft-quoted remark began, "Roosevelt sent his wife." Those who know Eleanor Roosevelt understand that she likely met with the veterans on her own initiative. On this and many occasions, the president demonstrated his wisdom by at least partially deferring to the judgment of his most talented advisor.

1. THE FIRST NEW DEAL, 1933–1935

LEARNING OBJECTIVES

1. Explain how President Roosevelt stabilized the banking sector. Identify the changes to the banking and investment industry that occurred between 1933 and 1935.

2. Summarize each of the leading New Deal agencies that were created in the first years of the New Deal. Explain how the role of the federal government changed between 1933 and 1935, using these programs as examples.

3. Analyze the federal government's attempts to create a more ordered economy through the National Recovery Administration. Explain how the government sought to mitigate conflicts between industry and labor, as well as the reasons why the Supreme Court declared the NRA to be unconstitutional.

1.1 The Banking Crisis

The provisions of the Twentieth Amendment to the Constitution shortened the time period between the November election and inauguration of the president from March 4 to January 22. This interim was known as the "lame duck" period and featured several months where the outgoing president remained in office. Because the Twentieth Amendment would not take effect until 1933, Hoover continued to preside over a nation whose banking system was teetering toward collapse.

An assassin's bullet just missed president-elect Roosevelt in February of that year, instead killing Chicago mayor Anton Cermak while the two men were talking. Cermak's death was mourned by Chicagoans and supporters of Progressivism nationwide. The Czech immigrant had risen through Chicago politics and defeated the Republican machine that was operated by city boss "Big Bill" Thompson. Thompson's political machine had dominated the city in previous decades and was allegedly connected to organized crime figures such as Al Capone. Cermak reportedly turned to Roosevelt after the bullet hit him and said that he was glad the new president had been spared. While this mythical expression of the nation's support for their president-elect became legend, most Americans were skeptical that their future leader was up to the challenge before him.

The new president still had not offered many specific details of how he planned to combat the Depression, and news of political gamesmanship between the outgoing and incoming presidents concerned the nation. Communications between Hoover and Roosevelt were full of posturing and intrigue. Hoover insisted that any meeting be held at the White House—a not-so-subtle reminder that he was still the president. Roosevelt wanted Hoover to meet him outside of the White House for similar prideful reasons. Hoover sought Roosevelt's endorsement of several of his plans, a defensible request given the impending transfer of power. However, Roosevelt was suspicious that Hoover's apparent goodwill was really an attempt to transfer responsibility for any consequences onto the new president. By Hoover's perspective, Roosevelt's intransigence was a political calculation based on making sure the nation's economy did not turn the corner until he took office. The tragic result was that little was accomplished in the months between the election and Roosevelt's inauguration.

Bank foreclosures and bank failure did not wait for Inauguration Day. Every state placed restrictions preventing depositors from withdrawing more than a certain amount or a percentage of their holdings each day. Some areas suspended banking operations completely in an attempt to keep the entire system from imploding. Upon assuming office, the president declared his first priority was to restore order in the banking system. He announced that all banks would close for a four-day "holiday" while Congress met in an emergency session. Roosevelt assured the American people that the "nameless, unreasoning, unjustified terror" that gripped the nation was the only thing they needed to fear. The nation's factories and farms were still productive, the president reminded his listeners. These productive centers had fueled the growth of America and would continue to do so if only they could recover from the financial instability that was born of uncertainty rather than any fundamental flaw in their design, the nation's infrastructure, or the national character.

The president's **Emergency Banking Relief Bill** helped to restore confidence by pledging federal backing of the nation's banking system. The bill was passed by unanimous consent in the House and by an overwhelming margin in the Senate on March 9, 1933. Due to the pervasive sense of emergency at that time, there was very little debate on the bill and most legislators never even read the legislation. However, most legislators understood and supported the fundamental changes to the banking system that would result. The new law granted the government the power to evaluate the financial strength of each bank. Those banks that passed inspection were allowed to receive unsecured loans from the federal government at low interest rates to help them through the crisis. The law also granted the federal government the authority to reorganize and reopen banks. Most importantly, Roosevelt committed the federal government to provide loans to banks to prevent them from failing.

The emergency law did not yet create the explicit guarantee of federal insurance for banks, although this guarantee would be part of legislation that would be passed later in Roosevelt's term. However, the president delivered a well-conceived speech that was broadcast throughout the country. In this address, Roosevelt explained how the emergency law would prevent bank failures in the near term. The president's radio address succeeded as banks reopened to long lines of depositors—a welcome sight given the recent history of panicked crowds waiting outside banks to withdraw funds. Conservatives and business interests were relieved that the president had used the power of the federal government to bolster the existing financial system rather than seek more radical change. Consumers were equally pleased to find that the government would take steps to protect the money they deposited in banks. The sudden wave of depositors also demonstrated the trust most Americans still had in government and the basic infrastructure of America's financial system. Roosevelt would continue to use radio addresses, which he later dubbed "fireside chats," to explain his policies directly to the people.

At the same time, Congress's ready acceptance of a sweeping law that effectively gave the Roosevelt administration control over the fate of every private bank in the nation alarmed some observers. Even those who favored the banking bill worried that the balance of power between the executive and legislative branches had shifted in ways that could lead to unintended consequences. In addition, over one hundred members of the legislature were newly elected Democrats unaccustomed to Washington politics and perhaps overly eager to support the Roosevelt administration. Roosevelt's unassuming personality and apparent sincerity helped to reduce this criticism, but not all in Washington or in the nation supported the new president. Others who were more skeptical had grown so frustrated by the perceived inaction of the previous years that they seemed willing to let Roosevelt and the Democrat-controlled Congress try anything.

Roosevelt enjoyed Democratic majorities in both the Senate and the House, and so in 1933, his critics could do little but warn of the possibility that the new president might abuse his powers. This message of warning and dissent remained largely in the background until 1937 when the economic recovery of the president's first term crumbled in the midst of a second Wall Street crash. Until that time, Roosevelt sought to create goodwill among the various interests of labor and capital by inviting representatives of unions and businesses to help shape legislation. Throughout his first four years in office, Roosevelt enjoyed widespread popular support. Although he was able to pass nearly every one of the laws his advisors recommended during these years, securing lasting economic recovery would prove more difficult for the new president.

FIGURE 7.2

Hoover and Roosevelt sit together on Inauguration Day. As the photo indicates, the two men shared reservations toward each other and did not work together during the period between the election and Roosevelt's inauguration.

Emergency Banking Relief Bill

A law granting federal examiners the authority to examine the records of banks and determine which institutions were financially sound. All banks that passed this examination were permitted to reopen with the added security of the federal government's commitment to provide additional funds if needed to ensure the financial stability of the bank.

FIGURE 7.3

President Roosevelt sought to explain his policies directly to the public through a series of radio addresses he called "fireside chats."

1.2 The First Hundred Days

New Deal

A series of economic reforms and programs that were supported by the Roosevelt administration and approved by Congress during Roosevelt's first term. These programs sought to stabilize the banking industry and monetary and agricultural markets and provide temporary jobs.

Harold Ickes

Secretary of the Interior and one of the most influential members of the Roosevelt administration, Ickes was overseer of various federal works projects and supported greater autonomy for Native American tribes.

FIGURE 7.4

Frances Perkins was an influential member of Roosevelt's cabinet and one of the architects of the New Deal as the secretary of labor.

Frances Perkins

The longest-serving Secretary of Labor and the first woman in the cabinet, Perkins skillfully represented the concern of labor leaders within the administration. Although she often worked to secure the support of business leaders, she was consistent in her belief of the right of workers to bargain collectively with their employers.

The emergency banking bill was merely the first of many sweeping changes the Roosevelt administration guided through Congress in the one hundred days between March 9 and June 16, 1933. Together with other bills passed during the subsequent sessions of Congress between 1934 and 1936, Roosevelt created the basis of what would later be known as the **New Deal**. For the first one hundred days of his administration, and for his first three years in office, nearly every proposal Roosevelt endorsed and sent to the floor of Congress was passed by large majorities. Not since George Washington had a US president enjoyed such influence over his nation's government. For some, even the depths of the Great Depression could not justify the concentration of so much power into the hands of one man.

Part of the reason Congress went along with Roosevelt was that the changes his administration introduced were not as radical as his critics had feared. Roosevelt refused to consider having the federal government take direct control of banks or factories—a strategy known as nationalization that would become common in Socialist nations and dictatorships. Roosevelt sought advice from a rather conservative-minded group of well-educated and successful individuals. Known informally as the "Brains Trust," Roosevelt's informal advisers shared the perspective and background of other influential leaders in business and hoped to reform rather than replace the nation's economic system.

Representing the best and the brightest in many fields, Roosevelt's advisers offered a variety of ideas. The president tried nearly all of them in one form or another. In addition to this informal advisory team, Roosevelt appointed a number of well-qualified individuals to his cabinet. Secretary of Labor *Frances Perkins* and Interior Secretary **Harold Ickes** were two of the most influential cabinet members, and many of the strategies the president attempted were those supported by Perkins and Ickes.

Frances Perkins was able to secure the support of organized labor behind the president's plans while also finding support among the leading business men of her day. Ickes administered the public face of the New Deal—government-funded construction projects meant to provide jobs while developing the nation's infrastructure. Although each of the New Deal Programs Roosevelt's advisers championed represented a fundamental change in the expectations of the federal government, many of them were also similar to those being considered by the Hoover administration in the year before Roosevelt's inauguration. The crucial difference was that under Roosevelt, federal programs to stimulate the economy operated on a much more ambitious scale.

By the mid-1930s, the federal government was borrowing hundreds of millions of dollars each year. One-third of the federal budget was spent on public employment projects and relief for the poor. At the same time, federal budget deficits still represented a relatively small percentage of the GDP (gross domestic product)—the total market value of all goods and services produced each year. Federal spending during the Depression was certainly greater than any peacetime period in the nation's history, but it still represented only a fraction of what the government spent during World War I. In addition, the US government would spend more in one year fighting World War II than was spent funding every New Deal program combined.

However, throughout its history the nation had tolerated large deficits and the expansion of government power during wartime and expected contraction and thrift during peacetime. The idea that the government should borrow money and provide direct employment during recessions and depressions had been raised since the 1830s but had never been seriously considered by federal leaders until the beginning of the Great Depression. For example, during a recession at the turn of the century, a group of men called Coxey's Army marched to Washington asking the government to borrow money to provide jobs for the unemployed. These men were branded as radicals, and leaders such as Jacob Coxey were arrested. Keeping this background in mind, one can see why each of the following programs approved during Roosevelt's first one hundred days reflected a very different way of viewing the role of the federal government.

- March 20: The **Economy Act** sought to reduce the budget deficit by reducing government salaries by an average of 15 percent and also enacted cuts to pensions of federal employees including veterans.

- March 22: The **Beer and Wine Revenue Act** amended the Volstead Act by permitting the production and sale of wine and beer that possessed alcohol content no greater than 3.2 percent. These products were subjected to special taxes, thereby increasing government revenue and decreasing the expense related to federal enforcement of prohibition. Congress also approved the Twenty-First Amendment, which repealed the Eighteenth Amendment and officially ended prohibition when the last state required to ratify the amendment did so in December 1933.

- March 31: The **Emergency Conservation Work Act** created the Civilian Conservation Corps (CCC), which provided a total of 2 million jobs for young men from 18 to 25 between its creation and America's entry into World War II. The CCC usually employed 250,000 men at any point in its history and developed state and national parks. CCC workers also worked on hundreds of conservation projects and planted an estimated 3 billion trees. Many participants were able to take vocational courses or earn their high-school diplomas. The men earned wages of $30 per month and most expenses associated with room and board. Of their wages, $25 was sent directly home to their families.

- April 19: The United States temporarily abandoned the gold standard, which permitted more money to be circulated. This action helped to stabilize commodity prices, which pleased farmers and helped to ensure stability in food production and distribution. At the same time, critics suggested that abandoning the gold standard would reduce domestic and international faith in the strength of the dollar and lead to inflation. However, consumer prices remained low throughout the Depression.

FIGURE 7.5

Young men at work building a trail as part of a Civilian Conservation Corps project. The CCC employed young men between the ages of eighteen and twenty-five, as well as a number of veterans of all ages who needed work.

- May 12: The **Federal Emergency Relief Act** created the Federal Emergency Relief Administration (FERA), which increased the funds available to states under Hoover's plan. It also altered these funds from loans that must be repaid to federal grants. Although some FERA funds were used for direct cash payments, most of the $3 billion that was provided to the states was used to provide jobs in various public works projects. Roosevelt and those in Congress hoped to avoid creating a regular schedule of direct cash payments to individuals, a practice that was known as "the dole" in the states and cities that offered such payments. The dole was similar to modern welfare payments and carried the same negative stigma during the 1930s as it would in modern times. However, creating jobs required a much larger initial investment, and it would not be until the creation of the Works Progress Administration of 1935 (WPA) that the federal government would offer substantial funding for public works projects as the primary source of direct relief to the unemployed. FERA operated between 1933 and 1935.

- May 12: The **Agricultural Adjustment Act (AAA)** farm income had declined substantially between 1929 and 1932 as a result of overproduction and declining prices. The AAA sought to stabilize prices by offering payments to farmers who agreed to not maximize their production. The funds for these payments were to be raised by a tax on processors of agricultural commodities such as cotton gins or mills. Congress also passed the Emergency Farm Mortgage Act, which facilitated the refinancing of farm loans.

- May 18: The **Tennessee Valley Authority Act** created the Tennessee Valley Authority (TVA) and authorized federal funds for the creation of hydroelectric dams and other projects meant to provide employment and promote development within one of the most economically distressed regions.

- May 27: The **Federal Securities Act** established legal standards for disclosure of information relevant to publicly traded securities such as stocks and bonds. Together with subsequent legislation, the federal government established the Securities and Exchange Commission, which regulated the investment industry.

- June 13: The **Home Owners' Loan Corporation Act** established the Home Owners' Loan Corporation, which provided refinancing for home mortgages much like the government offered to farmers. This agency refinanced one in five US homes, providing lower interest rates and lower monthly payments that permitted millions of American families to avoid foreclosure and possible homelessness.

- June 16: The **Glass-Steagal Banking Act** established the Federal Deposit Insurance Commission (FDIC) that regulated the banking industry and provided federal insurance for many kinds of bank deposits. The act also separated commercial banking, investment banking, and insurance by prohibiting any single company from providing all of these services and prohibiting officers of an investment firm to also have a controlling interest in a bank or insurance company. These conflict of interest provisions were repealed in 1999.

- June 16: The **National Industrial Recovery Act** was a two-part law creating the Public Works Administration (PWA) and the National Recovery Administration (NRA). The PWA allocated a total of $6 billion in private contracts to build bridges, dams, schools, hospitals, and vessels for the navy during the Depression. The NRA was much more controversial as it established trade unions in various industries that drafted their own rules regarding prices and production. These trade unions often operated as cartels that were controlled by the largest corporations in each industry, despite the ostensible government regulation and participation of labor representatives. The Supreme Court declared the NRA to be an unconstitutional use of government power in May 1935.

1.3 Industry and Labor

The New Deal, like all major legislative reforms, was not simply concocted by members of the Roosevelt administration. Its provisions were the result of hundreds of grassroots initiatives by union workers and the unemployed who created the New Deal through participation in local, state, and national politics. For example, rank-and-file workers in Chicago created and participated in many organizations that communicated their ideas to local government leaders. For the first time in the city's history, the majority of these organizations were not based around ethnicity or a particular craft. Instead, they represented ideas and perspectives that crossed these fault lines that had divided workers in the past.

Support for the federal government directly providing jobs for the unemployed or arbitrating conflicts between labor and management had been building for several generations. The Great Depression led to an increased level of activism among workers who believed that the federal government must intervene on behalf of the common citizen. Local political machines had failed to insulate cities and states from the Depression, while the paternalism and generosity of welfare Capitalism displayed its limits. For example, in 1931, Henry Ford blamed the Depression on the character faults of workers. "The average man won't really do a day's work unless he is caught and cannot get out of it," Ford declared. Later that same year, Ford laid off 60,000 workers at one of his most productive plants.

Private industry and banks were unable to stimulate recovery, and many leading businessmen beyond Henry Ford seemed indifferent to the plight of workers. In response, the Roosevelt administration became more willing to consider the perspectives of the unemployed and the poor. At the same time, Roosevelt was a member of the upper class and shared many of the same conservative beliefs regarding the role of government, as did business leaders and previous presidents. Like Hoover, Roosevelt was an outspoken opponent of expanding the dole—the epithet applied to state and local welfare programs that distributed food and money directly to the needy. He was also sensitive to the ideas of industry and believed that the only way out of the Depression was to create a more favorable business environment through government intervention.

The Roosevelt administration looked toward the War Industries Board of the previous decade as a model for how to achieve both greater prosperity and increased production. Government planning had worked during World War I, Roosevelt's advisers believed, arguing that government intervention could also help revive several industries where prices had declined below the point of profitability. Representatives of workers and the unemployed also convinced Roosevelt that public works projects were necessary to provide immediate employment until the economy and the private sector recovered.

As a result, the New Deal sought to promote two objectives. First, it would provide "workfare" rather than welfare by offering short-term employment in public works projects. Second, it would seek to create a more well-ordered economic system that encouraged the recovery of the private sector in the long run. Key to the operation of this system would be the incremental termination of federal public works programs once private industry began to recover. If government employment continued too long, they believed, these federal programs would compete for workers and prevent America's factories from fully recovering and resuming full production.

Public Works Administration (PWA)

Created by the National Industrial Recovery Act, the PWA was a federal works program that generally worked with private contractors to create major public works projects.

Representing these twin goals of relief through public employment and recovery through economic planning, the National Industrial Recovery Act (NIRA) created two massive agencies. The **Public Works Administration (PWA)** would oversee Roosevelt's "workfare" relief program with a budget of $3 billion in its first year. The PWA contracted with private construction firms to build a variety of public works projects. Among the projects of the PWA were the Grand Coulee Dam in Washington State, the Lincoln Tunnel connecting New Jersey with New York City, the Overseas Highway connecting the Florida Keys, and the San Francisco-Oakland Bay Bridge. Although many doubted the usefulness of air power at the time, the PWA's decisions to build the aircraft carriers *Enterprise* and *Yorktown* would later prove to be two of the most important decisions made during the New Deal.

The second provision of NIRA soon became both the most ambitious and most controversial program of the entire New Deal. The **National Recovery Administration (NRA)** created planning councils that established codes governing each industry. For example, the automotive trade council was led by representatives of major car manufacturers, labor unions, and government officials. Together, this council would determine how many and what types of automobiles would be built, the prices of these vehicles, minimum wages, and other provisions that would guarantee both profitability and the well-being of workers.

The central idea behind the NRA was that without these quotas and minimum standards, car manufacturers (and other businesses) would continue to engage in cutthroat competition with one another. This was important because the Depression decreased the number of consumers to the point that manufacturers were forced to sell their products at or below cost. NRA supporters believed that industry-wide coordination and planning would ensure that manufacturers only produced the number of products that would sell at a predetermined price. Included in this price was a reasonable profit that would permit employers to pay their workers a better wage. In return, employees of these companies could enjoy a measure of financial security and once again become consumers whose discretionary spending had fueled the growth of the 1920s.

Although this kind of central planning might be well-intentioned, many Americans feared that unintended consequences would occur. They feared that planning councils would be controlled by a few corporations within each industry, thereby creating cartels that could operate without any fear of competition. Such a system would permit manufacturers to keep production so low that prices could be increased dramatically. If this occurred, the result would be large profits for industries that intentionally limited production in ways that prevented job growth. Others feared the government would control these planning councils, promoting the growth of Socialism. Defenders of the NRA argued that neither cartelization nor Socialism would develop so long as each council shared power between heads of industry, labor unions, and government regulators. Government planning had worked in World War I, they argued, while the ruinous competition of the unregulated free market had led to the excesses of the 1920s and would likely prolong the current Depression. Equally important, NRA defenders argued, was the fact that participation in the NRA was voluntary. The decisions of planning councils were merely codes rather than law, and businesses were still free to practice free market principles if they did not like the codes in their industry. However, refusal to participate in the NRA was not without its own consequences. Only those businesses that participated could display the NRA's Blue Eagle in their storefronts and on their products. Failure to participate in the NRA was considered unpatriotic, and the government suggested consumers boycott any business that rejected the NRA's codes.

Volunteerism could only be effective if the majority of businesses in any given industry participated in or at least abided by the decisions of the NRA's planning councils. In the first years of the NRA, most industries did participate. However, this level of participation was only achieved by allowing the largest companies in any industry to draft codes allowing them to reduce production and increase prices. While this might encourage stability, critics argued that the NRA was actually preventing economic recovery while violating free market principles. In 1935, the Supreme Court agreed with the critics of the NRA, who argued that the agency violated principles of limited government and free enterprise and placed too much power in the hands of the federal government.

Although the NRA was ruled unconstitutional, it inspired a number of important changes. To provide more jobs for heads of households, the NRA prohibited child labor and set the workweek at forty hours. The NRA also included minimum wages and required companies to pay 150 percent of a worker's normal hourly wage for every hour he or she worked beyond forty hours. Each of these measures had long been goals of the labor movement. Although the forty-hour week and overtime pay were merely codes and not laws, they were now supported by the federal government. The main reason the government supported these measures was to encourage businesses to hire more workers as a means of reducing unemployment.

Subsequent legislation in Roosevelt's first year included the creation of the Civil Works Administration (CWA). The CWA provided federal jobs for 4 million Americans between its creation in November 1933 and its termination only four months later. The majority of CWA workers were employed in small-scale construction and repair jobs, but the CWA also hired teachers in economically depressed areas. Critics charged the CWA with providing needless jobs, such as raking leaves in parks. Given the speed with which the CWA payroll grew and the lack of a bureaucratic structure to secure the needed planning and resources for meaningful projects, such criticism was often well placed. The program's expenses grew faster and larger than the Roosevelt administration had anticipated until the CWA was eliminated in March 1934. However, the CWA would serve as a model for future projects by directly employing workers rather than operating through private contractors. At the same time, it provided a cautionary tale about the need for planning and direction before launching a nationwide public works program.

National Recovery Administration (NRA)

Also created by the National Industrial Recovery Act, the NRA sought to create trade unions representing various industries that would create codes regulating wages, prices, and production. The goal was to provide a more ordered economy and eliminate overproduction that led to unnaturally low prices and low wages. Critics suggested that the NRA created cartels controlled by the largest firms to reduce production while increasing prices. The NRA was declared unconstitutional by the US Supreme Court in 1935.

FIGURE 7.6

Participation in the NRA was voluntary, but only businesses that followed the codes in their industry could display the Blue Eagle Emblem on their products or in their stores.

1.4   The New Deal in the South and West

> *The white and black workers in the South cannot be organized separately as the fingers on my hand. They must be organized altogether, as the fingers on my hand when they are doubled up in the form of a fist.…If they are organized separately they will not understand each other, and if they do not understand each other they will fight each other, and if they fight each other they will hate each other, and the employing class will profit from that condition.*
>
> —A. Phillip Randolph

Tennessee Valley Authority (TVA)

A regional New Deal agency that sought to bring low-cost electrical power to one of the most depressed areas of the country by constructing hydroelectric dams. The TVA also sponsored a number of infrastructure projects, as well as health and educational initiatives.

FIGURE 7.7

A family near Knoxville that was displaced by one of the Tennessee Valley Authority (TVA) projects.

The Roosevelt administration created several programs that were aimed at providing targeted relief within a particular region, but none was as ambitious as the **Tennessee Valley Authority (TVA)**. Inspired by the president's emotional visit to an economically depressed region of the South, the TVA sought to provide direct employment through the construction of roads, buildings, bridges, and other projects. Most importantly, the TVA built hydroelectric dams to bring low-cost electricity to the area that would encourage commercial and industrial development. Many critics were understandably concerned about the environmental consequences of building dams all along the Tennessee River. In addition, many rural families who lived in the river valley were displaced in the process of construction. However, the TVA succeeded in spurring the growth of factories that brought modest prosperity to an area that had been among the most economically depressed regions of the country.

Not all residents of the Tennessee River Valley shared equally in the progress. Only 1 percent of TVA employees were black, and these individuals faced segregation while at work. Later New Deal public works programs such as the WPA would fare better, expanding from a workforce that was 6 percent black to one that was just over 13 percent. Few of these workers had any opportunities for advancement, as only eleven out of the 10,000 Southern WPA supervisors were African Americans. However, for the small number of black families who found work with the TVA, as well as the thousands of white families, the TVA was nothing short of a godsend. It was also a political boon for Roosevelt. Northern progressives hoped the government would launch similar projects around the country, while Southern conservatives cheered their president's economic support for their region. The creation of the TVA represented the first federal support for development of the South outside of Virginia or the Atlantic Coast. After generations of opposing the growth of the federal government, Southerners welcomed federal intervention once it was directed at the development of their infrastructure and economy.

The TVA would prove enormously successful and was one of the most popular programs of the New Deal. Nevertheless, it would take many years for dams to generate electricity that would fuel an industrial revolution throughout the Tennessee River Valley. For those living in the Deep South who were still largely dependent on cotton, the TVA offered little assistance. The price of cotton declined to half of its 1920 price at the start of the Depression. For farmers and sharecroppers in the South, as well as the millions of farmers in the Great Plains and Far West, immediate relief was imperative.

One of Roosevelt's first programs was the creation of a federal agency that provided refinancing for the millions of farm families who could no longer afford their mortgages. Roosevelt's next challenge was to alter the fundamental problem that had led to the mortgage crisis—the rapidly declining prices for agricultural commodities. Roosevelt's solution was the Agricultural Adjustment Act (AAA). This agency offered direct payments to farmers who agreed to reduce their production. For example, an Iowa farmer who grew corn on 200 acres would be offered an amount equal to the profit he might expect to receive on 50 acres if he simply agreed to plant only 150 acres the next year.

Because the AAA was not approved until May 1933, farmers had already planted their crops, so the AAA paid them to plow their crops. For millions of starving Americans, the federal government's decision to pay farmers to destroy crops and slaughter millions of pigs was the cruelest irony. In fairness, the AAA quickly adjusted its tactics and purchased crops and meat which were distributed to needy families. However, the AAA's payments proved devastating for those who worked the land but did not own it. Landowners were effectively being paid to evict tenants, sharecroppers, and other farm laborers whose labor was no longer needed as a result of reduced production.

The AAA resulted in an immediate stabilization of farm prices, an important goal considering that a third of the nation depended on farm prices for their livelihood. The Supreme Court declared a few provisions of the law that rendered the AAA unconstitutional, but this action merely led to relatively minor modifications in the way the AAA was funded and administrated. Although the AAA was favored by farmers and is generally considered a success, one of the leading reasons for the increase in farm prices was the result of an ecological disaster that reduced crop yields on 100 million acres of farmland.

Irrigation permitted farmers to develop nearly every acre of flat soil in the Southern Plains. An extended drought in the mid-1930s turned much of this topsoil to dust. The natural vegetation of the Southern Plains had deep root structures, which had secured the topsoil from erosion for centuries, even during similar times of drought. However, several decades of commercial farming had altered the ecological balance of the Plains in ways that left it vulnerable. Winds blew across the treeless prairies, taking the dusty topsoil with it and creating the ecological disaster known as the **Dust Bowl**.

The crisis of the Dust Bowl was so severe for farmers and those in cities who depended on the business of farmers that one in six Oklahoma residents abandoned the state during the 1930s. About 800,000 farmers and others who were dependent upon the farming industry were displaced as these lands were no longer productive. Most of these individuals headed to the West due to rumors of available jobs in California. However, jobs were also scarce along the West Coast, and the arrival of new job seekers led to tensions between these predominantly white refugees and Asian and Hispanic farm workers. The new arrivals were derisively labeled as "Okies," regardless of what state they had migrated from, while nonwhite Californians were derided as un-Americans, regardless of how long they or their families had lived in the area.

These dams and aquifers also created the possibility of irrigation, which could open millions of acres of previously arid land to farming. Cautious that such a course of action would further depress farm prices and possibly recreate the environmental disaster of the Great Plains, government policy restricted the use of water for farming and ranching in some areas of the West. However, many of these restrictions were ignored or modified. Before long, federal projects were directed toward facilitating the growth of industry and cities in some regions of the West. The result was rapid growth of the urban West in the next few decades that would encourage the most significant population shift in US history since the Homestead Act of 1862.

As the Dust Bowl demonstrated, aridity continued to define the American West. However, some New Deal initiatives sought to alter the region's ecology and transform the West through the creation of massive dams that would provide both electricity and water for certain areas. Much like the TVA, the New Deal of the West placed its hopes in commercial development through damming rivers. The federal government demonstrated the almost limitless possibilities of American labor and engineering by constructing the Boulder Dam, which was later renamed in honor of President Hoover. The Hoover Dam spanned the Colorado River and was instrumental to the urban growth of Las Vegas, Phoenix, and Southern California. Similar dams were built in Washington State and across the Sacramento River.

Dust Bowl

An ecological catastrophe during the mid-1930s within the Southern Great Plains. The Dust Bowl featured windstorms that removed the topsoil of 100 million acres of farmland. This topsoil had largely turned to dust as a result of drought and erosion.

FIGURE 7.8

Montana's Fort Peck Dam was a Public Works Administration project that created one of the largest man-made lakes in the world when it was completed in 1940.

1.5   Diplomacy and the Good Neighbor Policy

The Great Depression bolstered isolationism within the United States and likely influenced the decision to withdraw troops from Haiti and Nicaragua in the early 1930s. Roosevelt put an end to the Platt Amendment's provisions granting US sovereignty of Cuban affairs, with the exception of the US naval base at Guantanamo Bay. These changes signaled the beginning of Roosevelt's **Good Neighbor Policy**, which would mark a new age in US foreign policy in the Caribbean and Latin America.

In contrast to the frequent military interventions and economic imperialism that had typified the last few decades of America's relations with the region, Roosevelt declared that no nation "has the right to intervene in the internal or external affairs" of their neighbors. Humanitarian concerns mixed with economic self-interest in forming Roosevelt's new policy, as many Americans suspected that their tax money was being squandered abroad. Others believed that America's foreign policy was aimed at exploiting the land and labor of Latin American nations when it should be used to fund projects that spurred development at home.

Good Neighbor Policy

A policy aimed at improving relations with Latin American and Caribbean nations by removing US soldiers from these areas and demonstrating greater respect for the right of these nations to govern themselves. The policy was supported by Roosevelt, although many Latin American historians disagree about the sincerity of US commitment to nonintervention in Latin American affairs during the 1930s and beyond.

FIGURE 7.9

The United States Marine Corps in Nicaragua in 1932. Shortly after taking office, Roosevelt recalled these soldiers and many others deployed in Latin America as part of his "Good Neighbor Policy."

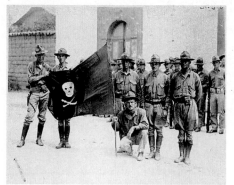

Perceptions of self-interest likewise drove the decision to grant eventual independence to the Philippines, as long as the United States could maintain its naval bases in the region. The agreement granting Filipino independence also created a proviso that stripped Filipinos of the opportunity to work in the United States. This provision subjected any would-be migrants to the provisions of the 1924 National Origins Act, which placed quotas on the number of foreigners who could immigrate to the United States. Despite the fact that the Philippines would remain a US territory for another twelve years, by applying the terms of the 1924 law, only fifty Filipinos were permitted to enter the United States each year.

A different brand of isolationism led the Roosevelt administration to reconsider his earlier commitment to actively participate in the London Economic Conference of 1933. Partially as a result of non-US support, the conference failed to resolve international currency problems. Although it may be unfair to blame the Roosevelt administration for its unwillingness to actively devote itself to the stabilization of European currency, the rapid inflation of the 1920s and 1930s would contribute to the ease by which dictators seized power in central Europe. However, the Roosevelt administration would demonstrate great foresight in seeking to provide aid to England and the other nations willing to stand up to those dictators during his third term in office.

In the meantime, Roosevelt shocked many with his decision to open diplomatic and trade relations with the Soviet Union for the first time since the Russian Revolution of 1917. In addition to the desire to open US goods to new markets, Roosevelt hoped diplomacy would help to counter the growing menace of Japan and Germany. Humorist Will Rogers would comment that Roosevelt would have likely agreed to open diplomatic relations with the devil himself if only he would agree to purchase some American-made pitchforks. History would provide a kinder assessment, as Roosevelt's overtures to the Soviets helped to thaw relations between the two leading nations in ways that would have a profound impact on the outcome of World War II.

REVIEW AND CRITICAL THINKING

1. How did Roosevelt stabilize the banking system? What were the positive and negative consequences of the federal government's much more active role in the economy?

2. Briefly summarize each of the major New Deal programs. In what ways were these programs related? Might any of these programs conflicted with other New Deal initiatives?

3. In what ways did politics—both local and national—influence the direction of the New Deal?

4. How did the New Deal seek to develop the West and South? What were the leading crises of these two regions, and how were they similar and different from one another? What was the long-term consequence of the New Deal for the South and the West?

5. Roosevelt had once agreed with the internationalist perspective of fellow Democrat Woodrow Wilson, who had hoped the United States would take a leading role in the League of Nations. What might have led to the change of perspective a decade later?

6. What was the Good Neighbor Policy? Do you think Roosevelt's commitment to Latin American autonomy was influenced by a desire to reduce the cost of US commitments and investment overseas?

2. LAST HIRED, FIRST FIRED: WOMEN AND MINORITIES IN THE GREAT DEPRESSION

LEARNING OBJECTIVES

1. Describe the challenges women faced during the Depression and the way that the New Deal affected women.
2. Analyze the extent to which the Roosevelt administration provided a "new deal" for nonwhites. Identify the challenges for African Americans, Asian Americans, and Hispanics during the 1930s.
3. Describe the way Native Americans were affected by the New Deal and the programs of the New Deal. Explain why some Native Americans might support the efforts of John Collier while others opposed him.

Kelly Miller, an African American sociologist at Howard University labeled the black worker during the Depression as "the surplus man." African Americans were the first to be fired from jobs when the economy slowed, Miller argued, and they were the last to be hired once the economy recovered. Miller's description was accurate not only for black Americans but also for women, Native Americans, Asian Americans, and Hispanics. For the first time, each of these groups had a voice in the White House. However, that voice was not the president. While Franklin Roosevelt focused his efforts on securing the electoral support of white Southerners and the cooperation of conservative Southern Democrats in Congress, Eleanor Roosevelt spoke for the "surplus" men and women.

Eleanor Roosevelt demonstrated her commitment to unpopular causes at the 1938 Southern Conference for Human Welfare in Birmingham, Alabama. The conference was an interracial coalition of Southern progressives founded the previous year. The group was dedicated to finding ways to provide greater economic opportunities for Southerners. Although they were not necessarily civil rights activists, for the first two days of the conference, members refused to abide by Birmingham law, which forbade interracial seating. When notified of the violation, police chief Bull Connor arrived and notified the participants that they would be arrested if they did not separate themselves into "white" and "colored" sections.

> *No woman has ever so comforted the distressed or so distressed the comfortable.*
>
> —*Connecticut Congresswoman Clare Boothe Luce describing Eleanor Roosevelt.*

Bull Connor would become notorious during the 1960s for his use of police dogs and other violent methods of attacking those who defied the city's segregation ordinances. When Connor ordered the segregation of the 1938 meeting, the predominantly male audience rushed to comply. At that moment, Eleanor Roosevelt picked up her chair and sat in the aisle between the two sections, defying the segregationist police chief to arrest the First Lady of the United States. For this and dozens of other small acts of wit and courage, Eleanor Roosevelt was daily maligned by journalists who assaulted her character and integrity in gendered terms. Later interpretations of history would offer a different perspective on her character and integrity. While Eleanor Roosevelt adopted many of the conservative ideas about race and gender that typified those of her racial and economic background, she also challenged ideas about race, social class, and gender in ways that made her one of the most courageous and important Americans of her time.

2.1 Women and the New Deal

The New Deal reinforced existing gendered assumption about the family and paid labor. The Economy Act of 1933 established procedures requiring government agencies that were reducing their workforce to first establish which of their employees had spouses who already worked for the government and fire these employees first. Although the law made no mention of gender, it was understood that married women were the ones that were to be let go. A 1936 survey revealed that most Americans believed such measures to be fair given the scarcity of jobs for male breadwinners. When asked if married women whose husbands were employed full-time should work for wages, 82 percent said no.

FIGURE 7.10

This WPA poster advertised the availability of maids who had completed training programs and were ready for domestic labor. Women were not encouraged to enter manufacturing fields as they would be during World War II due to the belief that doing so would take away a job from a male head of household.

The public also tended to approve of the practice of paying men higher wages for the same jobs. For example, male teachers were usually paid at least 40 percent more than women; in addition, principals and administrators were nearly always male. In fact, many times when a woman acted as the lead administrator in a school with all-female faculty, she was not listed as the principal, despite the clear expectation that she would perform these duties. In addition, married female teachers were often expected to quit their jobs—a traditional view that had eroded in recent decades but was revived as policy in some school districts during the Depression.

Single women without children might find work in schools but were often ineligible for other government jobs during the Depression. These gendered policies diverged significantly from programs such as the CCC, which employed millions of young men, and the jobs of the National Youth Administration, which were almost exclusively male. Women's leaders such as Eleanor Roosevelt protested the inherent gender bias in these programs and were able to secure some work camps for nearly 10,000 young women.

Gendered notions of family and work made it especially difficult for women seeking jobs through the PWA, TVA, and the rest of the "alphabet soup" of federal programs. Only the WPA directed any specific action toward providing jobs for women, although these were usually in low-paying clerical and service positions. Even at its peak in 1938, only 13 percent of WPA workers were women. In addition, federal and state government policies encouraged private-sector employers to hire male heads of households first.

Those fortunate enough to find a job in the private sector found that the labor codes established by the NRA endorsed gender-specific pay scales that restricted women to certain kinds of jobs and still paid them less than men in many of those positions. The WPA itself did not permit explicit pay differentials, so men and women who worked the same jobs in WPA programs received the same pay. However, most women who worked for the WPA were relegated to low-paying clerical or "domestic" fields, such as preparing meals or sewing uniforms for male workers.

The Depression saw little advancement for the women's movement. The pay differential between men and women working the same job remained at 60 percent, while the average salary for women was half that of men. The percentage of women in the paid workforce, which had steadily been rising, stalled at one in four workers. However, the number of careers open to women and the pay they received would expand in future decades, thanks to the number of women who joined the labor movement during the 1930s. The number of union women grew 300 percent during the decade as 800,000 women joined organizations such as the International Ladies Garment Workers' Union.

Feminists also continued to advocate for legal equality for married women. Prior to the 1920s, American women surrendered their citizenship if they married a man who was not a US citizen. The same was not true for US men, who could become dual citizens if they went abroad, while marriage led to automatic citizenship for their wives and dependents who chose to come to the United States. In the 1920s, the Cable Act provided a way for married women to retain their American citizenship as long as their partners were at least eligible to become citizens—a provision that was partially directed at discouraging American women from marrying Asian immigrants. In 1931, women secured an amendment to the Cable Act that permitted women to retain their citizenship regardless of their husband's status. Although the provision affected very few women, it was a symbolic victory and helped to further efforts of feminists who sought to protect the legal identity of married women.

A much more overt symbol of women's advancement during the 1930s was the proliferation of women in leadership roles in government, women such as Frances Perkins and Mary McLeod Bethune. Perkins was raised in relative comfort and excelled in college with degrees in both the physical and social sciences. She chose to keep her name in marriage and was one of the first women to identify herself as a feminist during a meeting of women's leaders in 1914.

Although Perkins also identified herself as a supporter of revolutionary change for women, she also believed that fundamental differences between men and women needed to be considered in the labor market. She favored laws specifically designed to protect women by limiting the maximum hours they might legally work, a perspective that put her at odds from many other feminists who supported the Equal Rights Act. Perkins is best known as the first woman to serve in the cabinet, and it is in that capacity that her legacy as a women's rights activist remains. Perkins was the second longest-serving and perhaps the most influential member of Roosevelt's cabinet, gaining the trust and support of labor and business leaders in the nearly exclusive male world of 1930s industry.

Roosevelt relied so heavily on the advice and support of **Mary McLeod Bethune** that he considered her the leading member of his "Black Cabinet," an unofficial group of black leaders who advised the president on matters of race. The fifteenth of seventeen children of rice and cotton farmers in South Carolina, Bethune rose to become one of the premiere educators of the 1930s. The only school that was available to Bethune and her siblings in her youth was operated by a church several miles from her home. With the support of her family and neighbors, Bethune was able to attend this school. She quickly developed a love of books and an appreciation of education as the key to empowerment for her people.

In 1904, Bethune turned her home in Daytona, Florida, into a school for young black women. This school expanded into a teacher's college and is today known as Bethune-Cookman College. Bethune also used her home as a headquarters for courses to prepare adults to pass the various exams that were required of African Americans who sought to register to vote. Despite physical threats by dozens of Klansmen, Bethune helped to register hundreds of black voters for the first time in South Florida. In 1935, Bethune founded the National Council of Negro Women and also served as President Roosevelt's advisor on race relations. The following year, Roosevelt appointed her as Director of the Division of Negro Affairs of the National Youth Administration, making Bethune the first African American to head a federal agency.

During the 1930s, Bethune emerged as the most revered black educator since the death of Booker T. Washington. Like Washington, Bethune transformed a one-room school into a college. However, Bethune was far more assertive about her belief in black equality and even directly challenged Klansmen. Bethune also had experience leading schools from the Southern cotton fields to the Chicago slums. As her prestige increased, she traveled the nation as Washington once did, but did so in her own unique style. Not only was she known for her flair for fashion and her strong sense of racial pride, Bethune also refused to accommodate racial slights; her manner disarmed those who might be offended by a powerful black woman. When a white Southerner who was also a guest visiting the White House referred to her as Auntie—a carryover from the paternalism of slavery—Bethune smiled and inquired which of her many brothers and sisters were his father or mother.

2.2 A New Deal for Black America?

The majority of black voters shifted their loyalty from the Republicans to the Democrats during the 1930s. The shift was both a reaction against the Republican Party and a result of Roosevelt's tentative support for civil rights, which would become evident only during the crisis of war. In addition, various New Deal agencies offered limited job opportunities for African Americans. Roosevelt himself can best be described as both compassionate and paternalistic about the plight of black America. He met with but refused to be photographed next to black leaders until his second term in office due to concerns that even one photo with a black leader might alienate white voters. Roosevelt's New Deal programs were usually progressive in terms of race in the North and West, but deferred to the views of white Southerners by permitting racial segregation while limiting the number and types of jobs available for Southern blacks. Eleanor Roosevelt would become an outspoken advocate for equal rights and a federal law against lynching. Although Roosevelt also supported these measures, he refused to back either even following his many landslide victories.

The panic of the Depression lifted the façade of racial fair-mindedness from the New South, as white workers cheered and pledged to boycott any business that employed black men beyond wages equal to whites. Some whites met with political leaders both within and beyond the South to try to create provisions requiring companies to only lay off white workers after first firing nonwhites. In Atlanta, a group of whites organized the "Black Shirts" in 1930 and marched with banners reading "No Jobs for Niggers until Every White Man Has a Job!" As a result, the Depression reversed decades of black economic progress and left 50 percent of black men unemployed at its peak.

In the wake of such catastrophe and economic hardship, the NAACP declined from 90,000 paid members following World War I to fewer than 20,000. Black leaders argued about whether to accept racial separatism; segregation, even if it is accommodationist, might be used as a tactical maneuver to win greater opportunities in the near-term for black workers. As a result, organizations like the NAACP were hardly able to mount a nationwide defense of civil rights and instead fought a rearguard action to protect black workers who were the first to be laid off when companies started downsizing due to the Depression.

The result of these campaigns and previous traditions of discrimination meant that even those few nonwhites who found work within New Deal agencies would receive only the lowliest jobs. Although many of the framers of the New Deal were progressive in terms of race, ethnicity, and gender, these

FIGURE 7.11

Mary McLeod Bethune emerged from poverty in South Carolina to become one of the most influential women in US history. She advised President Roosevelt on matters regarding race, led the National Council of Negro Women, and founded a college in Florida.

Mary McLeod Bethune

A leading educator and founder of Bethune-Cookman College, Bethune advised Roosevelt on matters of importance to African Americans and coordinated meetings of national black leaders known as the "Black Cabinet."

FIGURE 7.12

One of the WPA projects involved the documentation of folk music throughout the nation. This African American musician was photographed as part of this work, although few black musicians and artists were hired by the WPA directly.

FIGURE 7.13

This New York City WPA
Poster offering classes to
teach children how to swim
depicts white and black
children separately. The
poster demonstrates the
existence of informal
segregation that was
pervasive in the North.

redlining

In this context, redlining is
the process of designating
entire neighborhoods as
unacceptable credit risks
based on their racial
demographics. The term itself
comes from the FHA maps,
which designated minority
neighborhoods with a red
line. The FHA was created to
assist homebuyers in need of
credit and did not overtly
make any distinction of race.
However, the FHA refused to
back loans in minority
neighborhoods in an era of
residential segregation,
effectively denying credit to
minority applicants.

agencies relied on the support of white political leaders. The New Deal's primary goal was relief rather than reform, and each agency operated within a system that tolerated racial and gender discrimination.

Agencies such as the WPA determined pay by paying slightly less than prevailing wages as a means of preventing competition with private employers. The WPA also contained a provision that forbade the employment of anyone who had rejected an offer of private employment. Because the "prevailing wage" for Hispanic and African American women was often less than a fourth of what white men might be paid for manual labor, programs such as the WPA often denied employment to women and nonwhites who were seeking jobs beyond those that the discriminatory local market offered. That many New Deal agencies still offered better opportunities for employment should be viewed both as an indication of the progressive intent of many supervisors as well as a gauge of the opportunities for women and minorities within the private sector.

Many of the most progressive events of the 1930s demonstrated the limits of egalitarianism during the Great Depression. For example, the American Federation of Labor (AFL) finally accepted A. Philip Randolph's union of black railroad porters in 1935. At the same time, the AFL refused to support measures that would have required the integration of workers within its various unions. With the exception of Randolph, the nation's most prominent labor leaders also continued to at least unofficially support "white first" hiring policies. New Deal programs also discriminated against black families in subtle but significant ways.

For example, one of the main purposes of the newly created Federal Housing Administration was to provide federally guaranteed home loans for families who might not otherwise be eligible for home ownership. FHA loan applications did not inquire about an applicant's race or ethnicity, which made it appear as though loan decisions were based only on other factors. However, the FHA's underwriting manual indicated the belief that property values deteriorated when black families moved into neighborhoods. As a result, the FHA evaluated a loan based on the location of a house. Administrators consulted neighborhood maps that contained red lines around black neighborhoods and rated other ethnic clusters as credit risks. Because minorities could seldom obtain a house outside of a segregated neighborhood, even if they could pay cash, the FHA practice of "**redlining**" minority neighborhoods effectively meant that the FHA would only support white families buying homes in white neighborhoods.

Despite the crushing discrimination in housing and employment, nothing demonstrated the persistence of racial inequality as starkly as the judicial system of the Deep South. Communist labor leader Angelo Herndon was arrested after leading a peaceful and biracial protest march in Atlanta. Although the participants had simply sought to draw attention to the plight of the unemployed, Herndon was arrested under an obscure statute permitting the death penalty for those leading an insurrection against the government. An African American graduate of Harvard law school defended Herndon and reduced his sentence to twenty years of hard labor on a Georgia chain gang. Many other black Communists found themselves in similar situations as federal and state authorities increased their attack against leftists once the Communist Party added racial equality as part of its agenda.

In neighboring Scottsboro, Alabama, nine adolescent black youths were arrested and charged with raping two white women on a freight train. The young men had jumped aboard a train in search of any work they could find when they found themselves in an altercation with a group of white boys in a similar situation. The white boys were outnumbered and thrown from the train, after which the white youths decided to "get even" by fabricating the charges of rape.

After eight of the young men were sentenced to death, some of the whites came forward and revealed the truth. However, two all-white Southern juries still recommended the death sentence in a series of mistrials and appeals that demonstrated the potential injustice of a white-only jury. A third trial included one black juror—the first to sit on a grand jury in Alabama since Reconstruction. However, under the laws at that time, an indictment could still be made with a two-thirds majority. The white-majority jury voted in favor of a guilty verdict and the death sentence.

Each of these lawsuits was funded by the NAACP, but the bulk of financial and legal support came from the Far Left. Communist organizations had taken the lead in financing civil rights cases and attempts to register black voters during the 1930s, and they likewise took the lead in defending the **Scottsboro Boys**. Although the US Supreme Court twice ruled that these nine young men had been denied fair trials, it would take over a decade to secure the release of many of the defendants.

2.3 Latinos and Asian Americans

The Depression unleashed the hostility against Asian immigrants that was endemic in the 1924 National Origins Act and various state laws that limited the economic opportunities of Asian migrants in California, Oregon, and Washington. Much of this anger was directed at Filipino immigrants who were still legally permitted to enter the United States as citizens of an American colony. In October 1929, a mob of several hundred whites attacked a camp of Filipino laborers near Exeter, California. Angered by the decision of growers to employ Filipinos, the mob clubbed the workers and burned the makeshift homes where their families lived. An even larger anti-Asian race riot attacked a dance hall rented by Filipino workers near Santa Cruz in 1930, leading to hundreds of injuries. These attacks only escalated the violence against Asian workers, including several instances where sleeping quarters and community centers were dynamited. In addition, California amended its laws against interracial marriage to include a prohibition against "whites" marrying Filipinos in 1933.

Even those who were alarmed by the recent discrimination and violence tended to support the efforts of Western state legislatures who attempted to pass special laws barring Filipino migration. The federal government refused to approve these resolutions as long as the Philippines remained US territory. However, in 1934, Congress approved the **Tydings-McDuffie Act**, which granted Filipino independence by 1944. Although the Philippines would still be a US territory until 1946, all Filipinos were immediately classified as noncitizen aliens and were unable to legally live or work in the United States. Although the law stopped short of requiring the immediate deportation of Filipinos already in the United States, Congress approved a measure in 1935 that encouraged voluntary repatriation. Many white Californians were even less subtle in expressing their encouragement that Filipinos return to their native lands. Anti-Filipino prejudice remained high until the United States required the assistance of the Philippines and Filipino-Americans in World War II.

The issue of barring Mexican immigration presented no such legal and diplomatic challenges, even though the Monroe Doctrine was often used to justify colonial practices toward Mexico and Latin America. State governments and federal officials conducted raids that led to the forced deportation of an estimated half a million Mexican Americans. Many of these individuals were placed in sealed boxcars and returned to Mexico in such an emaciated condition that the Mexican government was compelled to send millions of dollars in humanitarian aid to their northern border. Due to the nature of the mass arrests and deportation, many of those who were forcibly sent to Mexico were legal citizens born in the United States who simply lacked documentation at the time of their arrest. A high percentage of those deported were children who had most likely also been born in the United States.

Hostility against Mexican American laborers was not restricted to the Southwest. The 1930 US census was the first and only census that recorded Americans of Mexican descent as a separate race. Eugenicists attempted to use the façade of science to convince others of innate racial inferiority and backed a number of failed efforts to pass laws that would prevent anyone of Mexican descent from entering the United States. Given the high unemployment of white workers in the Midwest, the governor of Kansas wrote personal appeals to the six largest railroads in his state asking that they dismiss all Mexican laborers and hire whites in their place. Similar requests were made of railroads in neighboring Colorado, while farmers in Nebraska who continued to hire Mexican Americans were ostracized by their white neighbors.

Scottsboro Boys

Nine African American boys aged twelve to nineteen who were accused of raping two white women on a freight train in Alabama in 1931. All but the youngest member of the group were sentenced to death in an infamously corrupt set of trials. The NAACP and the Communist Party provided legal defense, and one alleged victim and a witness both admitted that they had lied, yet the all-white juries kept returning guilty verdicts. Most of the young men spent years in prison until they were finally released.

Tydings-McDuffie Act

In response to Filipino activists, this 1934 law granted independence to the Philippines in 1944. Some believe that the law was inspired more by a desire to keep Filipinos from entering the United States, as the law also classified them as noncitizen aliens. Before the law, Filipinos were citizens of a US territory and legally permitted to live and work in the United States.

FIGURE 7.14

The League of United Latin American Citizens (LULAC) was founded in 1929. This photo shows the first LULAC meeting in Corpus Christi, which brought various fraternal and civil rights organizations from around the Rio Grande Valley.

League of United Latin American Citizens (LULAC)

Created by the merger of several civil rights organizations, LULAC was formed in 1929 and remains the oldest and largest advocacy group for the rights of Hispanics in the United States.

The 1930s also saw increased efforts by Mexican Americans to defend their civil rights. For example, college students of multiple races in Southern California joined a protest led by Mexican American students against Chaffey College. The administration had restricted Mexican Americans from using the college's pool but soon agreed to end its policy of segregation. The activism of the students soon spread to the city of San Bernardino, who likewise ended its policies of segregation.

Protests against segregated schools also gained momentum in the 1930s. Ninety percent of Mexican American students in South Texas attended segregated schools during the Great Depression. The 1876 Constitution of Texas explicitly permitted separate schools for white and black children but was silent regarding other minorities. Despite the lack of specific legal guidance, white school officials had created a system where most Mexican American children were educated in separate schools taught by predominantly white teachers who spoke little or no Spanish. Mexican Americans in Del Rio challenged the separate and unequal facilities of their community in 1930.

The Del Rio movement was only possible because of a fundraising campaign that raised thousands of dollars from members of the **League of United Latin American Citizens (LULAC)**. LULAC chapters from McAllen and Harlingen north to San Angelo joined chapters of larger cities such as San Antonio in supporting the lawsuit. Although the Texas Supreme Court refused to hear *Del Rio Independent School District v. Salvatierra*, the lawsuit spurred the development of active LULAC chapters throughout Texas. The refusal of the Texas Supreme Court to hear the case may have been a tacit recognition that LULAC would win its appeal. Diplomatic agreements with Mexico and the US Census Bureau both required that people of Mexican descent be classified as citizens without any distinction of race.

The lawsuit and the refusal of state officials to address their concerns spurred a statewide movement challenging segregation. LULAC also worked with other organizations to form *La Liga Pro-Defensa Escolar* (the School Improvement League), which publicized the inferior conditions and unequal funding of separate schools. These campaigns were rewarded in 1948 when a federal court declared that the segregation of Mexican American children violated the Fourteenth Amendment. However, the court refused to consider whether the same conclusion would apply equally to African Americans who remained segregated under Texas law.

2.4 Native Americans

The Great Depression transformed the poverty of many Native Americans into an unbearable condition. As a result, many within the federal government supported the notion of increasing the funds that were available to the Bureau of Indian Affairs. Secretary of the Interior Harold Ickes had been active in the American Indian Defense Association, a group formed by John Collier in the 1920s that sought to protect the property and preserve the culture of several Native tribes. Ickes appointed Collier as the Commissioner of the Bureau of Indian affairs, a controversial nomination given that Collier's activism on behalf of the Pueblos of New Mexico seemed radical to some. In addition, some Native leaders saw the non-Indian Collier as an outsider and were angered by methods they considered domineering. As Commissioner, Collier rejected notions of simply increasing aid to the destitute in favor of a plan he hoped would restore tribal sovereignty and eventually lead to self-sufficiency.

Indian Reorganization Act (IRA)

Known informally as "The Indian New Deal," the law fundamentally changed the way the Bureau of Indian Affairs operated. The law reversed the strategy of the Dawes Act, which was based on converting communal land into private property, restoring both land and self-government to Native American reservations.

Collier demonstrated elements of the high-handedness that angered his critics in drafting the **Indian Reorganization Act (IRA)** with little initial consultation of Native leaders. However, Collier also did something no other BIA Commissioner had done in the past by holding a series of meetings with tribal leaders around the nation to explain the provisions of his plan as well as listen to concerns and suggestions.

The essence of the plan was to reverse the spirit and letter of the Dawes Act of 1887, which sought to assimilate Native Americans by dividing their land. The IRA restored tribal ownership and provided $10 million of government loans to help tribes establish businesses in agriculture and manufacturing. The law also provided funds to help tribes purchase some of the lands they lost in the past and provided for greater self-government. Collier's plan was criticized by many Native Americans because many of the decisions of the newly empowered tribal governments would be subject to the approval of the BIA and the Secretary of the Interior. In one of the most important provisions, the IRA directed funds from boarding schools to local public schools that would be controlled by the tribes. The IRA also provided funds to facilitate the study of Native American history, language, art, culture, and other subjects.

The IRA sustained tribal opposition among many Native tribes that had already surrendered most of their land and feared they would have little to gain from the plan. In addition, some Native Americans accepted the goals of assimilation and felt the BIA would "turn back the clock" on the progress that had been made toward this goal. Given the long history of BIA programs that failed to live up to their promises, many understandably feared that the IRA was yet another trick to reduce Native lands under the guise of reform.

Largely due to Collier's history of activism and his efforts to solicit feedback, approximately two-thirds of Native tribes approved the measure. Convincing Congress proved equally difficult as the IRA was denigrated by many ethnocentric non-Indians as encouraging a return to "primitive tribalism." Others saw the IRA as a reversal of the federal government's long policy of assimilation many still defended as the most humane policy. However, Congress ultimately approved a watered-down version of Collier's original IRA bill.

Many of the funds that were supposed to be directed toward businesses and schools were never received. Even with these severe shortcomings, the IRA helped reverse five decades of assimilationist policies and restored Native pride and culture on many reservations. In addition, most of the $10 million that was loaned to tribal governments was repaid. Tribal income from various agricultural enterprises alone increased from $2 million to $50 million, partially as a result of these IRA loans.

Collier is still vilified by some Native Americans and scholars for the often high-handed methods he used to secure Native support of his plans. In addition, the BIA's style of elective government conflicted with the traditional methods of self-government of many tribes. Rather than winner-take-all elections, these tribes were governed by councils who sought to establish a consensus based on the input of each member. These are important criticisms that limited the effectiveness of the IRA. At the same time, Collier is also revered for his intent to restore Native sovereignty in ways that reversed hundreds of years of federal policy based on extinction and assimilation. Collier also secured the creation of the Indian Emergency Conservation Program (IECP), which employed 80,000 Native Americans within a branch of the Civilian Conservation Corps. In addition, Collier also put an end to the practice of forcing Christianity upon Native children at boarding schools against their parent's wishes.

REVIEW AND CRITICAL THINKING

1. How were women affected by the Great Depression in ways that were different than men? In what ways does the fight for gender equality move forward and/or backward during the 1930s?

2. In what ways did African Americans benefit from the New Deal? What were the New Deal and Roosevelt's shortcomings from the African American perspective? How did black America change during the 1930s?

3. Describe the experiences of Asian Americans and Mexican Americans during the Great Depression. Most white Americans who lived at this time believed that efforts to deport these groups were not inspired by racism but merely economic self-interest for US citizens. What do you think?

4. Explain why some Native Americans disapproved of Collier's plans and leadership. What do you think? Are these fair criticisms, or did Collier do the best that might be expected given the limited resources of government and the perspectives of the public?

3.   SECOND NEW DEAL AND ITS OPPONENTS, 1935–1939

LEARNING OBJECTIVES

1. Explain the intent behind major programs of the Second New Deal, such as the WPA, Social Security Act, and Wagner Act. Describe the provisions of each.

2. Identify the leading critics of the New Deal, and summarize their arguments. Explain how certain individuals were able to attract a mass following yet were unable to challenge Roosevelt or the two-party system in the election of 1936.

3. Summarize the reasons why many Americans who voted for Roosevelt and still supported the president were becoming increasingly critical of his administration in 1937. Detail the sources of opposition to the New Deal and the reaction of the Roosevelt administration in response to those concerns.

3.1   The Second New Deal

As the 1935 legislative session began, the US economy was more stable than it had been when Roosevelt took office. However, there had not been any significant economic recovery, and unemployment levels remained near their 1932 peak. Roosevelt and Congress agreed it was time to move beyond the limited federal jobs programs that were created in 1933 and 1934. The short-lived CWA had created the number of jobs needed to spur recovery, but it had been dismantled due to the haphazard nature of the program and escalating costs which expanded well beyond the CWA's anticipated budget. In contrast, job growth had been slow within the PWA due to the planning required before beginning major construction projects. In addition, the PWA was under the management of the frugal Harold Ickes. Although he used PWA funds efficiently, critics believed Ickes moved too slowly in creating jobs.

In April 1935, Congress approved a massive spending bill that authorized over $4 billion in new projects. Among the programs this bill created was the National Youth Administration. This agency provided part-time work for college students and was designed to both finance student education and delay the entry of young adults into the full-time labor market. Funds were also allocated for the creation of the Rural Electrification Administration, an agency that financed publicly owned electric co-operatives that provided power to most rural communities for the first time. The flagship program of the "big bill," as Roosevelt called it, was the **Works Progress Administration (WPA)**, which together with future allocations would spend $11 billion over the next eight years.

The first priority of the WPA, the president declared, was to transfer an estimated 3.5 million Americans from the relief roles to the payroll of federal works projects. Roosevelt declared that the government "must and shall quit this business of relief." Offering direct cash payments was "to administer a narcotic," Roosevelt believed. In contrast to the purpose-driven citizens who spent each day engaged in honest labor, Roosevelt suggested that the dole created "a spiritual and moral disintegration fundamentally destructive to the national fiber."

The goal of the WPA was to fund only useful projects that provided wages large enough to offer material security but not so large as to draw workers away from employment in the private sector. The WPA employed 3 million people in its first year and over 8 million during its eight years in existence. During that time, the WPA built 600,000 miles of roads and highways and tens of thousands of buildings and bridges as well as many other projects.

The WPA was not without its critics. The decision to pay lower wages limited the number of experienced foremen, while many of the workers feared that completion of their present project might mean unemployment. Eager to not work themselves out of a job, workers dallied; the WPA was lampooned as standing for "We Poke Along" or "We Putter Around" by those who observed WPA crews taking breaks on the side of a road.

Works Progress Administration (WPA)

A federal jobs program created in 1935 and administered by Harry Hopkins. The WPA spent an estimated $12 billion and employed over 8 million people during its eight years of existence, although usually only about 1.5 million were employed at any given time. The goal of the WPA was to be an employer of last resort for those who otherwise would not have jobs and would presumably find their way onto relief roles. Most WPA workers were engaged in construction projects, although the WPA also employed writers, musicians, artists, and actors through various programs.

FIGURE 7.15

Eleanor Roosevelt visits a WPA worksite in Des Moines, Iowa, in 1936.

Others argued that WPA contracts and jobs were being used as a political football by the Democratic Party. With the exception of New York and a few other cities with Republican administrations, Democratic politicians were usually the ones that decided what projects were built and by whom. Machine politics often controlled these decisions and sometimes led to brazen abuses. For example, the Democratic mayor of Memphis required WPA workers to make political contributions, while Chicago's notorious Democratic machine exacted tribute with little more finesse than the notorious crime bosses that influenced Chicago politics. New Jersey received over $400 million in WPA contracts, but workers in the Garden State were expected to contribute 3 percent of their weekly pay to the Democratic Party. In many of these cases, expectations that government workers kick back some of their pay to local political machines were different primarily in that these paychecks were being funded by taxpayers across the nation rather than city or state treasuries.

The WPA also received criticism from some individuals who believed that four smaller WPA programs designed to employ writers, musicians, actors, and artists were not a wise use of federal revenue. Others defended these programs as ensuring the preservation of history and the arts. The Federal Writers Project supported literature and the humanities and commissioned hundreds of historical research projects, as well as a popular series of state and local guidebooks. One of its most ambitious programs sought to document the history of every state and territory. Another noteworthy project was the preservation of history through over 2,000 interviews with individuals who had grown up in slavery. The research for these two projects remains the largest and most significant collection of primary source material on state and local history and the history of slavery.

FIGURE 7.16

This mural by Charles Wells depicts scenes from the New Deal and is one of more than 100,000 pieces of public art that were sponsored by the WPA. This particular mural can be found in a federal building in Trenton, New Jersey. Similar works can be found in nearly every US city.

The Federal Music Project provided over 200,000 performances and created archives of uniquely American music from Native American reservations to the hills of Appalachia. The Federal Theater project sponsored performances in major cities and created traveling troupes that brought musicals, comedies, and dramas to millions throughout rural America. Perhaps the most famous of the four, the Federal Art Project, commissioned over 100,000 paintings, murals, and sculptures. It also administered an outreach program that funded community art centers and subsidized art classes in public schools. Among its most memorable creations were hundreds of posters promoting various WPA programs that soon became the public face of the entire agency.

Eleanor Roosevelt and others within the president's circle of advisers supported these projects because they were concerned that the Depression had eliminated many of the jobs once available to artists and musicians. If left entirely to the dictates of the free market during a prolonged depression, the defenders of the WPA programs believed, an entire generation of writers, researchers, artists, actors, and musicians would be lost. They argued that the long-term consequences of such an occurrence would be catastrophic because there would be no one to teach the next generation of artists and musicians once the economy recovered.

Roosevelt also backed the **Social Security Act** in August 1935; the act created a government insurance program for the elderly, the temporarily unemployed, and the permanently disabled. Payments were set to begin in 1940 and were financed by a special fund that drew money from a modest tax paid by employers and workers. Initial benefits were also modest. The Roosevelt administration did not intend for Social Security payments to be the primary source of retirement income; rather, the program was designed to provide a guaranteed minimum level of security and the foundation of an individual's retirement fund.

Later generations would increase the benefit from the initial average of $20 per month in ways that indicated a different interpretation of the program. The result of these increases and the growing number of retirees in comparison to workers has created challenges in modern times, yet Social Security remains the most popular welfare program initiated during the New Deal. However, because the plan withdrew money from workers and employers for several years before making payments to beneficiaries, Social Security did not stimulate economic recovery until the first payments were made. In addition, Social Security did not cover domestic or agricultural workers, which left many women and minority families without protection.

Social Security Act

A federal law creating old-age pensions for certain retired workers and their dependents that was financed through taxes paid by employers and employees. The act also provided matching federal grants for states to create unemployment insurance, a system of financial compensation for injured workers, and direct financial aid for impoverished families with children.

FIGURE 7.17

This mural in the Cohen building in Washington, DC, depicts harmony between industry and labor. During the 1930s, the federal government took an unprecedented role in the economy, which often included attempts to negotiate labor conflicts. In 1935, Congress passed the Wagner Act which guaranteed workers the right to organize and bargain collectively.

Wagner Act

The common name given to the National Labor Relations Act due to its sponsorship by New York senator Robert Wagner. The law protected the right of workers to create unions and bargain collectively with employers. The law also created the National Labor Relations Board to enforce its provisions.

A third major provision of the Second New Deal of 1935 was the National Labor Relations Act, more commonly known as the **Wagner Act**. The NRA had included provisions that guaranteed the right of workers to join unions that would collectively negotiate wages and other terms of employment with their employer. Most employers disregarded these provisions, and the NRA itself had been declared unconstitutional for unrelated reasons. In response, the Wagner Act reinstated the principle of government support for workers who sought to bargain collectively. The law prohibited discrimination against union members and required employers to recognize the legitimacy of a union if the majority of their workers were members. The act also prohibited employers from firing workers after a strike and other common actions that had been used to intimidate workers and union members in the past. Equally important, the Wagner Act created the National Labor Relations Board (NLRB) to arbitrate disagreements between unions and employers.

Some labor leaders feared the Wagner Act was still too ambiguous in some regards and, the NLRB lacked the power to do more than facilitate arbitration between employers and union representatives. "All the bill proposes to do is escort [labor leaders] to the door of their employer and say 'here they are, the legal representatives of your employees,'" explained Massachusetts senator David Walsh. Ironically, Walsh's somewhat tongue-in-cheek remark would later be cited by attorneys representing business interests who sought to limit the collective-bargaining provisions of the Wagner Act. In the next two decades, however, the law bolstered both unions and the Democratic Party. Partially due to the popularity of the Wagner Act among union members, the Democrats would enjoy the support of organized labor for the next half century.

John L. Lewis

Perhaps the most influential and controversial labor leader in US history, Lewis led the United Mine Workers and helped create the Congress of Industrial Organizations. Lewis proved extremely effective at winning higher wages for miners, but drew the ire of most Americans for his willingness to call labor strikes during World War II.

The Wagner Act provided federal support for unions and the concept of workers' right to bargain collectively. As a result, union membership expanded rapidly. In some fields, the number of strikes and other protests also increased. United Mine Workers leader **John L. Lewis** demonstrated the new spirit of labor militancy by challenging the AFL and its reluctance to organize the unskilled or semiskilled workers. Although these laborers constituted a majority of the US workforce, they were not members of craft unions and therefore not likely to be represented by any of the various unions belonging to the AFL. Lewis believed that because the nature of labor had changed, mechanization was challenging the importance of the craft unions. As a result, he believed that no laborer would be protected as long as only skilled workers were organized. In response, Lewis organized a federation of unions that sought to represent all workers within a particular sector, such as mining or steel production.

Lewis and other labor leaders created the **Congress of Industrial Organizations (CIO)**, which soon emerged as a rival federation of the AFL. Many unions that were part of this new federation were also much more aggressive in their tactics. For example, the United Auto Workers launched a sit-down strike in which they occupied several General Motors factories. Unlike previous strikes of this nature, federal and state governments did not send military forces to crush the strike, and GM was soon forced to negotiate with UAW leaders. Similar activism led to a union contract providing higher pay and benefits for employees of US Steel.

Congress of Industrial Organizations (CIO)

A federation of unions representing primarily unskilled and semiskilled laborers that was created in 1935. United Mine Workers leader John L. Lewis led these unions out of the American Federation of Labor in 1938, although the two labor federations would merge during the 1950s.

FIGURE 7.18

Although the number of strikes declined during the first years of the Depression, unions were strengthened by the Wagner Act. Workers pictured in this 1937 photo are participating in a sit-down strike in a Chevrolet plant in Flint, Michigan.

With workers throughout various industries belonging to the CIO, union leaders attempted to force other steel plants in Chicago to accept a similar contract for their workers. Members of various unions within the CIO who were not workers at the steel plants in question joined with their fellow steelworkers in a mass demonstration. Tensions were high, and several Chicago police fired upon the unarmed crowd, killing ten and severely injuring thirty. Labor leaders referred to the May 30, 1937, tragedy as the Memorial Day Massacre, while most media accounts presented the crowd as lawless and sympathetic to Communism. The two opposing perspectives reflected unresolved views about the limits of police authority and worker solidarity.

The New Deal was not only popular with union workers. In fact, it proved so popular with various other groups that the American two-party system would be fundamentally transformed during the 1930s. The **New Deal Coalition** referred to the combined electoral strength Democrats enjoyed among various groups until divisions regarding the civil rights movement led white Southerners to embrace the Republican Party. Between the 1930s and the 1960s, however, white Southerners who had traditionally voted for the Democratic Party and rallied behind job-producing projects such as the WPA and TVA were even more likely to produce reliable Democratic majorities.

New Deal Coalition

A term referring to the tendency of union workers, Southern whites, Northern blacks, Catholics, liberals, and Jews to support the Democratic Party in the wake of the New Deal.

Northern workers were equally loyal to the Democrats due to the Wagner Act and subsequent support for prolabor legislation. Northern African Americans increasingly switched their support from the Republican Party of Reconstruction to the Democratic Party of the New Deal, which provided federal jobs that officially offered equal wages regardless of race. Working-class women's leaders also backed the Democrats due to their tentative support for equality in the labor market and the inclusion of women in leadership positions. Jews and Catholics likewise voted Democratic for many of the same reasons. Finally, liberals and the intelligentsia tended to support the New Deal Coalition due to the Democratic Party's tendency to be more supportive of programs that bolstered federal spending for education and the welfare state. The New Deal Coalition did not eliminate divisions of race, ethnicity, religion, region, or social class. As a result, these tensions regularly threatened to split the Democratic Party. However, for the next thirty years, the nation experienced unprecedented material prosperity and Democratic leaders generally avoided any controversial positions that might divide their supporters.

3.2 Dissidents and Demagogues

Like many throughout the nation who were able to cling to some type of employment, the problem of the Depression was not simply the abject poverty that grabbed headlines. The expectations and aspirations of a middle class way of life had also been shattered, and even those lucky enough to cling to their jobs faced declining wages. For the newly poor, Roosevelt's programs had inspired hope but now seemed insufficient to solve the crisis of the Depression. The wealthy were also concerned by the direction of the Roosevelt administration, although they feared that the president had moved too aggressively and in ways contrary to their interests. The Revenue Act of 1935 enacted significant tax hikes for the wealthiest Americans and seemed a harbinger of more radical measures that would seek nothing less than a complete redistribution of wealth.

As the election of 1936 neared, however, Roosevelt still received the support of most Americans and seemed likely to defeat any opposing candidate in a landslide. The Republicans nominated **Alf Landon** in response to Roosevelt's popularity, a decision based on the hope that the popular governor of Kansas might attract the support of moderates without alienating their conservative base. Landon was one of the more liberal members of the Republican Party who had supported many aspects of the New Deal. As Roosevelt's opponent in the election of 1936, Landon hoped to represent voters who supported the basic idea of federal intervention but believed that Roosevelt had extended federal power beyond its proper and Constitutional limits.

Many of those opponents were listeners to a radio program featuring the politically-ambitious commentator **Charles Coughlin**. Father Coughlin was appointed to a working-class parish just outside Detroit in 1926. Coughlin won the support of Catholics throughout the city by his refusal to be cowed by the Klan, which had once burned a cross in front of his parish. Coughlin was personally ambitious and sensed the potential of radio to increase his fame long before many radio stations had the capacity to broadcast signals beyond a few miles. By the time the Columbia Broadcasting System (CBS) was established and looking for a popular and charismatic priest for a weekly show, dozens of local radio stations throughout Detroit were already loyal listeners to Coughlin. CBS soon established Coughlin as one of the leading radio personalities, attracting a loyal network of more than 10 million listeners.

Coughlin soon did more than preach the gospel, including commonsensical suggestions for politicians in his weekly sermons. His ferocious attacks against Communism, the corruption of the banking system, and corporate greed won him a growing audience among non-Catholics. As a result of his popularity, FDR received the endorsement of Coughlin, who soon linked support of Hoover to support for "international bankers" and other enemies of America. Coughlin's rhetoric grew increasingly angry, and his references to moneylenders and international bankers—a code word for anti-Semitic conspiracy theories—grew increasingly vile.

Alf Landon

A well-respected and relatively progressive governor of Kansas, Landon is best known for his landslide defeat in the election of 1936. Landon won the electoral votes of only two states, neither of which was Kansas. Landon supported many aspects of the New Deal but argued that the federal government needed to do more to support private industry rather than creating jobs outside of the private sector.

Charles Coughlin

A Detroit priest who had once stood up for the rights of his Catholic parishioners against the Klan, Coughlin rose to prominence with his nationally syndicated radio program. Over time, Coughlin's rhetoric became angrier and openly anti-Semitic, causing his influence to decline.

Even if Coughlin could have overcome anti-Catholic prejudice and become a mainstream politician, his Canadian birth meant that the "Radio Priest" could never become president. Instead, Coughlin sought political influence through his popular broadcasts and even presented Roosevelt with lists of possible appointees. Roosevelt quickly distanced himself from the explosive rhetoric of Coughlin once the election was over. In retaliation, Coughlin turned from the New Deal, which he had once labeled "Christ's deal," and accused Roosevelt of being in league with the imagined Jewish syndicate who sought to bring gentile America to its knees.

Coughlin's rage soon alienated many of his more educated and open-minded supporters and brought mild condemnation among church leaders. By the late 1930s, some of Coughlin's more enthusiastic supporters took his anti-Semitic rhetoric to their logical conclusion by attacking Jewish leaders and expressing support for Hitler. While Coughlin himself later sought to distance himself from such sentiment, his long history of anti-Semitic remarks had helped to create a climate of anger and fear. As a result, more and more Americans turned away from Coughlin, and his radio programs were cancelled.

As monumental as Coughlin's fall from grace would be, he still enjoyed millions of supporters as Americans prepared for the elections of 1936. Several million older Americans, many of whom had seen their life savings disappear, rallied behind the ideas of Francis Townsend. The Townsend Recovery Plan called on the federal government to provide $200 per month for all persons over sixty years of age who promised not to work and to spend the entirety of their money every thirty days. Townsend believed his plan would provide security for older Americans while stimulating the economy.

The plan sounded appealing and led to the growth of Townsend's followers to 2 million members, few of whom recognized that the math behind the plan was completely faulty. Providing $200 per month for nonworkers would have been nearly impossible at a time when the average monthly income of workers was about $100 per month. Townsend claimed that all benefits could be financed by a federal tax of 2 percent on every business transaction. However, the total cost of his program would have been more than half of the total income of every US worker combined. While encouraging early retirement for workers over sixty years old would create more jobs for younger Americans, the Townsend Plan would merely transfer the purchasing power of most workers to retirees. Not only would millions of workers be unable to support themselves, many of the retirees would likely set some of their money aside despite the law. As a result, the plan would have vastly reduced consumer spending and created extreme hardships for nonretirees.

Another critic of the president was the ambitious Louisiana politician **Huey P. Long**. Political machines were not exclusive to the industrial cities of the North, as demonstrated by Long, who used his position as governor of Louisiana to extort funds that he used to solidify voter loyalty. Posing as a modern-day Robin Hood, Governor Long increased taxes on corporations and used the revenues for much-needed improvements to the state's infrastructure. Although these taxes proved popular among voters, the long-term consequence of Long's antibusiness measures would become problematic as some firms avoided doing business in Louisiana.

FIGURE 7.19

This Detroit WPA Theater production was an adaptation of a 1935 novel by Sinclair Lewis. It featured the rise of a demagogue in the United States who used many of the same techniques as Hitler to win election and then seize power. Perhaps due to traditions of public education, free speech, and democracy, US demagogues were not able to retain public support for more than a few years.

Huey P. Long

A popular Louisiana politician who relied heavily on patronage, rising to the governorship and using his power to appoint state jobs to solicit political donations. Long's popularity stemmed from his willingness to take on planters and corporations. Long rose to national prominence by touting a plan that would confiscate and redistribute wealth. Long made extravagant promises about his plan that were based more on his political ambition than the actual merits of such a scheme. Long also made several enemies, and he was assassinated before the 1936 election.

FIGURE 7.20

Residents of Louisiana usually had strong opinions about politician Huey P. Long. Long was accused of corruption and cronyism, but as this poster demonstrates, he was also effective at providing a number of tangible benefits to voters. He modernized the state's infrastructure and secured funding for Louisiana State University and other colleges throughout the state. His government even provided free textbooks for public school students.

In the near-term, the charismatic Long was beloved by his Louisiana supporters, who even agreed to call him "the Kingfish"—a nickname the egomaniacal Long had invented for himself. Long once humbly supported then-Governor Roosevelt's bid for the presidency in 1932. However, Long soon became a vocal critic of the New Deal after FDR disrupted the Kingfish's ability to appoint his political supporters to federal jobs in Louisiana. Long also hoped that FDR would adopt his approach of using tax policy to redistribute wealth and used his recent election to the US Senate to criticize the president as becoming the tool of bankers and corporations.

Long reached out to the supporters of Coughlin, who blamed bankers for the nation's financial problems. Long's "Share Our Wealth Plan" promised to make "every man a king" by guaranteeing the heads of every US household a check for as much as $5,000, a salary of at least $2,000, and a free college education for all eligible students. The plan was to be funded by a 100 percent tax on all incomes over $1 million. In addition, the government would seize personal assets that exceeded several hundred times the average national net worth of households and limit inheritances to about $5 million.

It mattered little that the revenue generated from what most assumed to be an unconstitutional seizure of property would be insufficient to provide more than a fraction of the promised wealth. It also mattered little that demagogues who railed against Communists were now proposing a plan more radical than anything the Left proposed. The popularity of Coughlin and Long was based more on the volatile mixture of anger, fear, and ignorance than any ideological consistency. In the midst of economic crisis, more than 10 million Americans rallied behind charismatic demagogues who created scapegoats and promised that they alone cared for the fate of the common man. Not for the last time in US history, the ability of the Far Right and the Far Left to appeal to millions of Americans simultaneously demonstrated the potential shallowness of electoral politics. That Coughlin and Long's supporters were willing to subscribe to the angry designs of would-be autocrats revealed the importance of public education and free speech within a democracy.

In the end, most voters turned away from these demagogues and toward the candidates of the two-party system in the 1936 election. Long himself recognized that he could never defeat Roosevelt and may have based his entire electoral scheme on attracting enough voters to make sure that neither Roosevelt nor Landon could win election outright. In the event no candidate received a majority of electoral votes, the election would be decided by Congress and whichever candidate received the support of Long's electoral votes would likely become president. As a result, the Kingfish would get to play the role of kingmaker and could demand his share of the spoils of office. Instead, Long was killed by the relative of one of his local political rivals a year before the election.

It is doubtful that the 1936 election would have resulted in the election of anyone other than Roosevelt, even if Long had entered the race. His followers joined those of Townsend and Coughlin in creating the Union Party. The Socialist and Communist Parties also ran in opposition to the New Deal, arguing that Roosevelt was representing the interests of corporations in a plot to save Capitalism from its natural demise. Conservatives and business interests countered that the New Deal was introducing Socialism. Supporters of Coughlin and the late Long offered a combination of all of these theories, but they mostly continued their populist rants against a litany of straw men and scapegoats. Eventually, many Americans turned away from the politics of accusation. Some even joked that FDR or any other political leader who could arouse so much anger from both the extreme Left and extreme Right must be on the right track. Despite all of the intrigue and speculation about possible third-party candidates, the election of 1936 would become one of the most lopsided presidential elections in US history. The Republican Alf Landon won only two states and 8 electoral votes to FDR's 523.

3.3   Court-Packing Scheme and Reverses of 1937

Roosevelt misinterpreted his stunning electoral victory as a mandate for greater expansion of executive power. Most voters supported the New Deal and believed that its programs had at least prevented more suffering. However, most Americans rallied behind Roosevelt in 1936 for the same reasons they had in 1932—they did not believe the Republicans offered a better alternative. Roosevelt failed to recognize that most of his fellow citizens remained wary of the expanding power of the executive branch and the federal government in general. As a result, the president interpreted several Supreme Court decisions as attacks upon the will of the people rather than a reflection of growing sentiment that parts of the New Deal were indeed unconstitutional.

By the 1936 election, the Supreme Court issued seven decisions reversing various aspects of New Deal laws because they delegated too much authority to the executive branch. Roosevelt was angered by each of these cases but shrewdly made little mention of his designs to redirect the power of the judicial branch until after the election. Secure that he had the support of the people and Congress, the president unveiled the **Judicial Procedures Reform Bill of 1937** only weeks after his second inaugural address. The rest of the nation referred to the bill as Roosevelt's "court-packing scheme." It would soon prove to be the president's most controversial and poorly conceived plan of his entire four terms in office.

Roosevelt characterized the Supreme Court as "nine old men" who were out of touch with the modern interpretation of Constitutional law. Although the true motive had nothing to do with the age of the justices, he declared that his intent was to make the court more efficient by providing help to the overworked court system by adding a new judge for every federal judge above the age of 70. Federal and Supreme Court justices are not known for their youth. Six of the nine Supreme Court justices were over the age of 70, which meant Roosevelt's plan would permit him to appoint six justices at once and increase the size of the Court to fifteen members.

Even Roosevelt's supporters saw through the president's stated intent to improve efficiency and vigor. That Roosevelt submitted the plan to Congress without any prior consultation added to the appearance that the president had become the dictator his critics had warned about. Many leading Democrats joined the opposition to Roosevelt's proposed changes, and the president quickly reversed course. The Supreme Court may have been somewhat chastened by the public reaction to its mode of operation, as well. The court generally sought to avoid further conflict with the executive branch, and several of the more aged justices soon retired. The unprecedented longevity of Roosevelt's tenure permitted the president to make several appointments that were favorable to his administration in the late 1930s.

Roosevelt had criticized Hoover for tolerating budget deficits, but the costs of his New Deal programs resulted in similar deficits throughout Roosevelt's first term. Despite the persistence of high unemployment, a wealth of economic data provided the impression that the nation was slowly clawing its way out of the Depression. As a result, Roosevelt declared his intentions to reduce government spending and present a balanced budget for 1937.

FDR believed that the only true measure of recovery was the ability to provide both economic growth and a balanced budget. As a result, the president reversed earlier inflationary measures, while simultaneously reducing the budgets of emergency programs such as the WPA. In addition, $2 billion in Social Security taxes were set aside for benefit payments that would not begin for another few years. In hindsight, it appears that the slow recovery was largely dependent upon inflation and government spending.

Many of FDR's supporters were rejoicing that the New Deal had ended the Great Depression in the fall of 1937. At this moment, a wave of bad economic news ruined their celebration and revealed rising unemployment and declining productivity. That fall, Wall Street experienced a second crash that was nearly equal to the severity of the crash of 1929. By the end of 1937, the market declined by nearly 50 percent. Unemployment, which had been slowly declining, rose to 18 percent.

Roosevelt was stunned by the suddenness of the decline and likewise scrambled to revive government spending. The president also returned to the airwaves and attempted to reassure the nation that recovery would soon resume. But this time, the President's voice seemed to many Americans to resemble the hollow optimism that had typified Hoover's addresses to the nation during the crisis of 1929. Republicans offered a competing interpretation of the recent decline. They labeled the 1937 decline the "Roosevelt Recession." Just as the Democrats had gained seats in 1930 by pinning the Depression on Hoover, Republicans seized the bad economic news and recaptured over eighty seats in the House and Senate during the 1938 elections.

3.4   From New Deal to Wartime Economy

As Roosevelt's critics gained momentum, the president's advisers debated the cause of the reversal. Business leaders suggested that increased taxes for the wealthy and corporations reduced the amount of money that would have been available for investment. Most of Roosevelt's advisers believed that programs such as the WPA were working and should be renewed with greater vigor, arguing that budget deficits were less of a threat than prolonged depression. Many on the left argued that the Depression was simply self-perpetuating until the nation's wealth was more evenly balanced and more Americans could afford to stimulate the economy by making discretionary purchases. Secretary of the Treasury Henry Morgenthau Jr. had been the strongest advocate of balancing the budget and remained steadfast

Judicial Procedures Reform Bill of 1937

Dubbed the "court-packing scheme" by its opponents, the bill would have allowed the president to appoint an additional judge to serve alongside any federal judge above the age of seventy. Most Americans recognized this as an attempt by President Roosevelt to control the judiciary, which had recently issued a number of decisions unfavorable to various New Deal programs.

FIGURE 7.21

A political cartoon lampooning FDR's Judicial Procedures Reform Bill of 1937. If passed, this law would have given FDR the authority to appoint numerous federal judges, including as many as five Supreme Court Justices.

that the downturn was the result of low investor confidence due to the ruinous debt that kept mounting and the inflationary policies of the past few years.

Elements of each of these competing perspectives overlapped in ways that showed at least some fundamental agreement that the lack of consumer spending was thwarting recovery. Each perspective also agreed that the nation's economic policy must create a favorable business environment, although each differed on the best method to encourage investment. John Maynard Keynes, a relatively unknown economist from England, had been providing unsolicited advice to the president for several years. Although Roosevelt only partially subscribed to Keynes's ideas, the economist believed that the New Deal had created a laboratory that would validate his ideas about the ability of government to use fiscal policy and deficit spending to promote economic growth.

Keynes argued that if the government placed more currency into circulation via projects such as the WPA and permitted banks to borrow at lower interest rates, the economy would recover much quicker. Following this **Keynesian economic theory**, Congress approved an additional $3.5 billion for the WPA and other New Deal programs. Followers of Keynesian theory believed that the government needed to borrow and spend on a much larger scale given the severity of the Depression, arguing that short-term deficits to "prime the pump" of the nation's economy would pay off in the long run by creating millions of jobs. Once these workers were confident again in their ability to purchase discretionary items, Keynesians argued, consumer demand would recover, leading to prosperity for US businesses.

The political Left and Right continued to disagree about the causes of the Great Depression, as well as the legacy of the New Deal. Those on the Right believed that Roosevelt's meddling prevented the natural recovery by enacting higher taxes and discouraging investment by favoring unions. The mainstream Left found myriad examples to support their allegations that the New Deal actually favored big business at the expense of smaller companies and consumers. Those on the Far Left believed that the Capitalist system should have been allowed to collapse in favor of a planned economy operated by the government. Dissident groups such as the American Communist Party gained members during the Depression. However, the 1939 announcement of a partnership between Hitler and Stalin led to a crisis of faith among most fellow travelers.

Most Americans would rally behind their president as the war neared America's shores. In the years between 1936 and 1941, however, Roosevelt would struggle to keep his own party from splintering along the fault lines of race and region. For many wealthy Americans, Roosevelt betrayed his own patrician class by propping up labor unions and supporting taxes designed to redistribute wealth. For white Southerners, Roosevelt also betrayed his race by meeting with black leaders and seeking the support of Northern black voters. Conservatives in the South did not abandon the Democratic Party; instead, they sought to reclaim it. By their perspective, Roosevelt had violated the long-standing gentleman's agreement that provided solid Democratic counties in exchange for an understanding that Democratic leaders would permit the white South to police its own race relations.

Roosevelt offered only the most timid support for the basic rights of African Americans to participate in his New Deal. However, from the perspective of whites inside and beyond the South who believed no black man or woman should be hired by government programs if there were still jobless white applicants, FDR appeared to be promoting a dangerous brand of change. Demagogic politicians combined racial fearmongering with lingering suspicions about the growth of federal power over state's rights to create a conservative coalition that would block all future efforts to expand the New Deal. For example, in 1938, Georgia's Walter George labeled FDR's supporters as "scalawags" and likened federal intervention in the South to Sherman's March. He and other Southern Democrats called on all loyal whites to resist the "liberal" FDR just as their Confederate forefathers had resisted Yankee invaders.

The wartime rhetoric reflected the current mood of the nation, even if it was completely out of touch with reality and deeply conflicted with the economic self-interest of many of George's followers. By 1937 and 1938, international affairs increasingly dominated the president's agenda. Adolf Hitler had seized control of the German government in 1933 and was leading an expansionistic campaign that threatened the security of Europe. Further east, the Japanese invaded China as the first step in the creation of a Pacific empire.

The kind of deficit spending Keynesian economists recommended did not occur until the invasion of Poland led European governments to cry out for American grain and manufactured goods. Before this time, governments around the world feared the consequences of borrowing money, while those who controlled access to credit were chastened by the worldwide depression of the 1930s. Only the emergency of war, and the short-term perspective it fostered, altered these attitudes in ways that would lead to increased borrowing and spending. The United States

---

Keynesian Economic Theory

A school of economic thought based on the work of John Maynard Keynes, which recommends utilizing the power of the federal government to influence the economy. Keynes himself proposed that the US government should borrow money to create jobs programs, thereby placing more money into the hands of consumers who would stimulate economic growth.

FIGURE 7.22

This 1939 sign advertises the availability of credit for consumer purchases—one of many ways that retailers sought to increase the number of customers. Once the United States entered the war in December of 1941, rubber became a scarce item.

likewise abandoned all restraint and borrowed heavily to create its own arsenal of democracy. The wartime spending spurred economic growth but also created unprecedented deficits and saddled the nation with a postwar debt many feared might bankrupt the nation.

REVIEW AND CRITICAL THINKING

1. What was the Second New Deal, and how were its leading programs similar and/or different from the programs enacted during Roosevelt's first one hundred days?

2. Why did many Americans criticize the Works Progress Administration? Imagine you are the president, and construct various arguments to counter these criticisms using specific examples.

3. Why might many historians consider Huey Long, Father Coughlin, and Francis Townsend to be demagogues? Is this a fair criticism? Explain the basis of their mass following and the reason their popularity proved to be so short lived.

4. Had Roosevelt's court-packing scheme passed Congress, would it have been declared constitutional by the Supreme Court? What are the possible implications of a fifteen-member Supreme Court?

5. Why might Social Security be one of the most popular programs of the New Deal? Explain how Social Security is funded and how its creation affected the Great Depression.

6. Most historians are quick to point out that the war, not the New Deal, ended the Great Depression. Does this statement lead one to casually connect war with economic stability? What might be the consequences of such a belief? Might the US government have also ended the Great Depression by spending its money in other ways? What would be the political and social consequence of such a peacetime government spending program in both the long and short term?

4. AMERICA'S ENTRY INTO WORLD WAR II

LEARNING OBJECTIVES

1. Utilizing both diplomatic and military history, explain the outbreak of World War II in Europe. Detail the role of both aggression and appeasement in the origins of the war.

2. Explain how Adolf Hitler was able to conquer France and why he decided to invade Russia. Also explain why Britain decided against an armistice with Hitler following the fall of France. Briefly summarize the military history of World War II (both the eastern and western fronts) before the US declaration of war in December 1941.

3. Summarize American-Japanese relations during the late 1930s up to the attack on Pearl Harbor. Explain how events in Asia influenced America's changing orientation toward Japan.

Asian historians typically cite the Japanese invasion of China in 1937 as the start of World War II. Western Europeans usually select the German invasion of Poland in 1939 as the beginning of the war, while Russians emphasize the German invasion of their nation in 1941. US history textbooks concur with their Western European colleagues but usually offer few details regarding the military history of the conflict until the December 7, 1941, attack against Pearl Harbor. Each of these choices tells us a great deal about the perspectives and priorities of those who produce, assign, and consume history books. Yet these same choices may also distort the global aspects of the war and marginalize the way World War II and its reconstruction shaped the second half of the twentieth century. No textbook could ever cover the entire global scope of the war. As critical thinkers, students should be aware of these choices and consider why some aspects of the war are emphasized over others. Why might the Eastern Front be marginalized in favor of other theaters? How might this same chapter be different in a French, British, German, Russian, Chinese, or Japanese textbook? How might a historian in a former British colony such as India or South Africa view the conflict?

4.1   Appeasement and the Fall of Poland

The Treaty of Versailles ended World War I and sought to prevent future wars. Believing Germany to be the aggressor, the framers of the treaty decided to limit the German military to a small force capable only of defending their nation against a small invading army. The treaty also declared that the German-French border would become a demilitarized zone where no German troops could be stationed. In 1935, German dictator **Adolf Hitler** defied these provisions of the treaty by rebuilding a modern army capable of mounting an offensive campaign. Hitler increased his forces by introducing compulsory military service—allegedly as a measure to provide employment for German men.

The German government also funded the construction of offensive weapons that had been banned by the Treaty of Versailles, such as submarines and tanks. The following year, he violated the treaty's provisions regarding the demilitarized zone by placing troops near the border of France. Many of these programs were kept secret, and Hitler defended each of the obvious violations of the treaty as part of a program of national defense. The armies of Europe had become much more powerful, Hitler explained, and Germany was a landlocked nation surrounded by rivals. As a result, he concluded, following the exact provisions of the Treaty of Versailles would leave his people vulnerable on all fronts.

France and Great Britain doubted the Fuhrer's sincerity, but did little more than verbally protest as Hitler continued to expand his forces and further violate the provisions of the treaty. Those world leaders who did not want to confront Hitler pointed out that many elements of Hitler's explanations were true. Some of the provisions of the Versailles Treaty did seem excessive, they reasoned, and each time they brought their concerns to Hitler's attention, he was quick to respond with an explanation proclaiming his peaceful intentions. Other voices throughout Europe warned that Hitler was bent on conquest and predicted a second world war. The leaders of Europe hoped otherwise and followed a program of appeasement.

Hitler engineered the **annexation** of Austria into Germany in March 1938. Austrian Nazis followed the annexation with an election where the people of that nation overwhelmingly expressed their support for becoming part of his Germany. The support of both the people and the government of Austria was heavily influenced by the actions of Austrian Nazis and the German army that occupied Austria. Given the methods of fraud and intimidation of their new rulers, few in or outside of Austria wished to challenge what had just occurred. Hitler soon demanded that the region of Czechoslovakia known as the Sudetenland, which was home to many people of German origin, also become part of his nation.

FIGURE 7.23

European leaders meet at the 1938 Munich Conference. From left to right, British Prime Minister Neville Chamberlain, Prime Minister of France Édouard Daladier, Adolf Hitler, and Italian dictator Benito Mussolini.

In September 1938, the leaders of France and Britain called a conference in Munich, Germany, to discuss their concerns with the rapid expansion of Hitler's Germany. France and Britain were each imperial powers with colonies all over the globe held in place by military force, so it was difficult for the leaders of these nations to object to German expansion and not appear hypocritical. German expansion had so far included mostly people of German descent and occurred peacefully with the official if not genuine support of the leaders of the involved areas. The two nations agreed to not interfere with Hitler's plans in Czechoslovakia in exchange for his promise that he had no further plans for expansion.

Most Europeans and Americans were satisfied and cheered British Prime Minister Neville Chamberlain's announcement that the Munich Conference had ensured "peace for our time." Of course, Czechoslovakia was not invited to the Munich Conference and was in no position to resist Germany alone. The Germans annexed the Sudetenland in October 1938 and proceeded to threaten Czech leaders until they capitulated to Hitler's forcible annexation of the rest of Czechoslovakia the following spring.

Hitler and Soviet Premier **Joseph Stalin** signed the **German-Soviet Non-Aggression Pact** in August 1939 with both nations pledging that they would not attack each other. They also promised to remain neutral in any war involving the other. Although Hitler used this treaty as evidence of his peaceful intentions, Western European leaders understood the potential threat that Hitler's promise of peace represented for the people of Europe. By making a pact with Stalin, Hitler would not have to face the Russian army if a war broke out in Europe. Hitler had also formed an alliance with Italian dictator **Benito Mussolini**.

Because of these two treaties, Germany would not face enemies to the east and south as they had in World War I if a general war were to erupt. Still, the consequences of the last war were so terrible for Germany that most observers assumed that another general war would not break out as long as diplomacy continued. After all, World War I only occurred after multiple nations declared war instead of working out a diplomatic solution to the invasion of Serbia. So far, none of Hitler's actions qualified as an invasion because he had engineered formal capitulation by the leaders of each nation he annexed.

The next nation Hitler set his sights on refused capitulation. Poland rejected German attempts at annexation and declared its intention to defend itself from an invasion. France and England felt they could do little to forcibly prevent Hitler's previous actions because they had all been officially sanctioned by the leaders of the affected nation. Polish resistance meant that a line had been drawn in the sand that, if crossed, would prove his intentions malignant and demand military intervention. For this reason, the leaders of both nations pledged to support Poland and believed their ultimatum would force Hitler to reconsider further territorial acquisitions. Instead, the Fuhrer ordered his own troops to burn houses near the border of Poland, blame the Polish for attacking German-held territory, and launch an attack to "defend" German territory from "Polish Aggression."

On September 1, 1939, the German Luftwaffe launched massive attacks that quickly overwhelmed the nation's defenses. German infantry and armored divisions simultaneously invaded Poland, while a handful of motorized infantry units raced into the Polish countryside from every direction. The Germans called this strategy of rapid coordinated attacks by ground and air forces "blitzkrieg." The goal was a rapid offensive that could immediately destroy a nation's air force and simultaneously overrun and encircle its major armies stationed near the nation's borders. The name of this strategy roughly translates to "lightning war," a moniker the overwhelmed Polish defenders could have coined as their large armies were quickly enveloped and forced to surrender.

France and Great Britain responded by declaring war on Germany on September 3 but did nothing to help Poland. The Soviet Union had just signed a pact not to fight Germany and would later invade Poland from the east as part of a secret provision of that agreement. Despite the verbal support of Western Europe, Poland was left to face the combined onslaught alone. The next three weeks brought fierce resistance on the part of the Polish people, despite the tremendous odds against them and indifference of their proclaimed allies in Western Europe. This apathy, the agreement between Hitler and Stalin, and a merciless offensive against both military and civilian targets led to Polish surrender in just over a month.

World War II was initiated by blitzkrieg on Poland, but following this initial German storm, the guns fell silent as each nation mobilized for a war many hoped would not come. Outside of Germany, civilians did not celebrate the outbreak of war as they had in 1914. German troops participated in a few offensives in Northern and Eastern Europe, while the main force prepared for an invasion. The French frantically continued work on the **Maginot Line**, an impressive network of fortifications stretching from Belgium to the southernmost limit of France along their common border with Germany.

The Germans would later refer to this time as *sitzkrieg*, "the sitting war," while most of Europe hoped against hope that history was not about to repeat itself. There was no sitzkrieg in Eastern Europe, however, as Hitler consolidated and expanded his position in western Poland while Stalin attacked the eastern portion of that nation in concert with Hitler. The Soviets also launched attacks on Estonia, Latvia, and Lithuania, conquering these former Russian-held lands with minimal resistance. Finland surrendered to Stalin after three months. The rest of the world watched and wondered if Stalin was any different from Hitler.

Joseph Stalin

A Bolshevik revolutionary that emerged as the leader of the Soviet Union by the outbreak of World War II. Stalin ruled as a dictator until his death in 1953 and dealt ruthlessly with rivals and opponents.

German-Soviet Non-Aggression Pact

An agreement between Germany and the Soviet Union declaring that neither would attack the other. Secretly, Hitler and Stalin also made an agreement dividing up Eastern Europe between the two nations.

Benito Mussolini

The leader of Italy's National Fascist Party, Benito Mussolini became the dictator of Italy in the 1920s. He later formed an alliance with Adolf Hitler. Until he was deposed by the Italian people in 1943, Italy fought against the Western Allies and on the side of Hitler's Germany. However, Hitler was able to reinstall Mussolini as a puppet ruler almost immediately after he had been deposed. Afterwards, Italy was effectively ruled by the German military until just before the end of the war in 1945.

Maginot Line

The French line of defensive fortifications stretching from the southern limit of the German-French border to Belgium. Because the German army bypassed this line of fortification, the Maginot Line proved ineffective in World War II.

4.2 Fall of France

In April 1940, German troops launched attacks on Denmark and Norway. Hitler claimed that his actions were necessary to protect the people of these regions from corrupt regimes. He would claim the same benevolent intentions for the Netherlands, Belgium, and Luxembourg, which he invaded the following month. Within a month, German armies had conquered most of these areas and even trapped the small British and French forces that had deployed to these regions in a poorly managed attempt to halt the German advance.

The French had constructed an "impregnable" system of fortifications known as the Maginot Line along the German-French border. The Maginot Line is regarded as one of the classic examples of military unpreparedness, not because it was too thin, but because the Germans simply sidestepped this well-defended border by attacking Belgium and Luxembourg. The French had prepared for this possibility and deployed troops to Belgium, but the Germans launched a second offensive south of these forces in the Ardennes Forrest. The French had planned for this possibility but believed that the armies of these nations would be able to hold the German advance long enough to redeploy their armies to meet the threat. However, the German advance moved so rapidly that even German commanders were surprised. Moving faster than anticipated and even beyond their supply lines, German armies crossed the border into France.

TABLE 7.1 World War II Alliances

Allied Powers 1939–1940	Britain, France, Poland
Allied Powers 1941–1945	Britain, Soviet Union, United States, China, France
Axis Powers	Germany, Italy, Japan
Other Nations with Allied Powers	Australia, Belgium, Brazil, Canada, Czechoslovakia, Ethiopia, Greece, India, Mexico, Netherlands, New Zealand, Norway, Poland, South Africa, Yugoslavia
Other Nations with Axis Powers	Hungary, Romania, Bulgaria

British and French forces rushed to Northern France to meet the German offensive, much as they had during the early stages of World War I. However, German tanks and motorized infantry moved rapidly through the Ardennes Forest to the south of their positions, continued westward, and then turned north. Allied commanders in Northern France had not prepared for this tactic, largely because they assumed that the Ardennes was impassable for a large invading army. As a result, the Germans were able to flank the Allied position in Northern France, cut their supply lines, and pin the British and French between German forces and the northern coast of France. Nearly the entire British army in France, known as the British Expeditionary Force, was vulnerable to attack by German warplanes as they retreated toward the French port city of Dunkirk. Many feared that these men and the French armies with them would surrender or be annihilated unless they could somehow escape back to England.

The British were especially alarmed at the prospect of losing such a large portion of their army, especially given the probability that Hitler would invade their nation next. Military officials and local people worked together to ferry over 300,000 British and French troops to England using any boat that could cross the English Channel. This effort became known as the **Dunkirk Evacuation**. The British were relieved that their army had not been surrounded as many had predicted. British Prime Minister **Winston Churchill** reminded his nation that "wars are not won by evacuation." He pointed out that Britain had succeeded only in abandoning their weapons and equipment to the Nazis. Meanwhile, France was left to face the German onslaught alone.

The situation was quickly deteriorating for the bulk of the French army, still fighting but the victim of crippling early losses. Half of their army had been captured or were still manning the defenses along the shared border of Germany and France when the bulk of the German army descended upon Paris. On June 10, an opportunistic Benito Mussolini declared that his nation of Italy was prepared to aid Germany and invade France from the south. French World War I hero Marshal Henri Petain believed the situation was hopeless and urged his nation to accept a deal with Hitler. On June 22, the leaders of France concurred and agreed to Hitler's terms.

The armistice declared that Germany would control Northern France while Petain would lead a nominally independent French government in the south. The new capital of France was located in the small resort town of Vichy in southern France. Hitler promised that this "independent" French state would be free to make its own decisions and maintain its global empire. However, Petain increasingly found himself choosing between doing the Fuhrer's bidding or risking further bloodshed. French general Charles de Gaulle escaped to England and established a rival French government in exile that opposed the Nazi-accommodating regime in Vichy. Tens of thousands of French citizens vowed to continue the war by joining underground resistance movements throughout the nation. The French soldiers who had escaped to England continued training in anticipation of the opportunity to liberate their homeland. They would not get that chance until 1944.

Much has been made of the rapid defeat of France in World War II. The French army was a large, well-trained, modern army. Its leaders had prepared for a German attack through Belgium, and there was no shortage of valor among the French troops. The crucial error was not only a failure to prepare for an attack similar to the German strategy in World War I but also being unprepared for the German attack through the Ardennes Forest. The Maginot Line was very thin in this area because the French believed the heavily wooded terrain of the forest served as a natural barrier.

The Maginot Line itself was an impressive line of defense, but the French could not build this type of fortification across the entire length of Eastern France due to the high water table that prevented underground construction in many areas. Political and diplomatic considerations also dictated the French defensive effort. From the Belgium point of view, had France extended the Maginot Line all the way north through the Ardennes and to their common border, this would indicate that the French did not intend to assist them in the case of a German invasion but rather intended to hide behind their fortifications. Instead of alienating their ally, the French hoped to quickly deploy troops to a line of forts in Belgium. This plan failed because German paratroopers captured these forts. As a result, the greatest French military blunder was not the construction of the Maginot Line but France's inability to match the speed of German mobilization.

4.3   Battle of Britain

As Hitler moved to consolidate his power throughout Europe, Mussolini offered to negotiate a truce in exchange for England's acceptance of Axis domination throughout continental Europe. Britain still maintained a formidable navy and air force but was nearly defenseless on land after their retreat from Dunkirk. Many British leaders considered Mussolini's offer and recommended that newly appointed Prime Minister Winston Churchill begin negotiation with Hitler through the Italian leader. In the longest hour of his nation's darkest day, Churchill convinced his advisers that surrender was not an option. "If this long island story of ours is to end at last," Churchill counseled his minsters, "let it end only when each of us lies choking in his own blood upon the ground."

Hitler responded to Churchill's refusal to negotiate with an attack intended to test British resolve. Aerial bombardment of English cities began in earnest in July 1940. The Luftwaffe's objective was to break the British will to resist and to destroy the British Royal Air Force (RAF). Even if the island continued to fight, by controlling the skies over Britain, the German navy could land ground troops on the island without fear of being attacked from both the air and ground. The Luftwaffe conducted nightly bombing raids with as many as 1,000 planes targeting airfields, aircraft factories, coastal defenses, and eventually, major cities in hopes of breaking the British will to resist. The **Battle of Britain** had begun.

The British had fewer pilots and aircraft but had the advantage of new technology called radar that could track enemy aircraft. This innovation allowed British pilots to intercept German bombers en route to their targets and launch counterattacks that would harass German fighters. Because the battles occurred over the skies of Britain, RAF pilots were usually rescued after ejecting from planes damaged

FIGURE 7.24

Adolf Hitler poses in front of the Eiffel Tower in June of 1940.

in battle, while German pilots were killed or captured. In addition, German aircraft were already low on fuel by the time they crossed the English Channel.

By August, RAF pilots were shooting down significantly more German planes than they were losing. The RAF's success was partially due to the acquisition of experienced pilots who had escaped from Nazi-occupied France and Poland, as well as pilots from Canada, South Africa, India, Australia, and other British colonies. By mid-September, Hitler postponed the planned invasion of Britain. The Germans continued to bomb military installations and cities throughout Britain, but the threat of imminent invasion had passed for the moment.

The Germans had been stopped but not defeated. The Battle of Britain was the first major battle waged by air forces and, although technically a draw, the first strategic defeat of German forces. Moreover, the battle demonstrated the importance of air power in modern warfare. British Prime Minister Winston Churchill united his country and convinced the nation's leaders to reject Hitler's truce at a moment many predicted that Britain would be invaded.

Churchill himself had a flair for hyperbole that often led to him being caricatured in the years before the war. With his nation on the brink of destruction, Churchill's dramatic speeches now seemed appropriate, and his eulogy of the airmen who sacrificed their lives inspired his countrymen and many throughout the world. "Never in the field of human conflict was so much owed by so many to so few," Churchill exclaimed, connecting the heroic stand of the RAF to the continued freedom of Europe and the United States. His American cousins across the Atlantic greeted his speech and the RAF victory with enthusiasm and relief, yet the majority of Americans did not yet believe that the United States was in jeopardy. Even as the battles over the skies of Britain continued through the next year, the majority of Americans opposed direct military intervention.

4.4 Eastern Front

Hitler's actions against the Soviet Union soon demonstrated Churchill's wisdom in rejecting a deal with Hitler. Despite a nonaggression pact that was not yet two years old, Hitler invaded Russia in June 1941. His objectives were strategic, political, and personal. He wanted to seize control of oil fields and gain access to the Black Sea in the south, seize the industrial cities and fertile Russian plains in the center, and push his hated Bolshevik rival all the way west to Siberia. The Russian army occupied a large portion of Eastern Europe because their 1939 pact with Hitler secretly included the promise that the two nations would divide this territory, in addition to not fighting each other.

As Germany conquered Western Poland, Soviet Armies invaded the Baltic countries and Eastern Poland. Neither of these regions could defend itself against Germany or Russia. As long as the two rivals honored their pact, they could easily dominate Eastern Europe. But neither trusted the other, and both had ambitions beyond sharing control of the region. Hitler recognized that Stalin shared his ambitions regarding Eastern Europe and viewed his surprise attack on Russia as a defense on the new territory he had just acquired. His decision to postpone the invasion of Britain due to the continued success of the RAF freed his land forces to launch the attack he hoped would quickly eliminate his main continental rival.

Hitler sent 3.5 million troops into Russia, believing that a rapid offensive across a broad 1,000-mile front could quickly lead to that nation's collapse. He hoped to deploy his forces so rapidly that he could surround and capture Russian armies and Eastern Russian cities without much of a fight. He also hoped to overwhelm Stalin's forces in the south and cut off Russia's access to the oil fields from the Russian border to the Middle East.

Hitler considered his recent success in Poland and France, as well as Russia's quick exit from World War I, in support of this strategy. Although it is clear in hindsight that the invasion was poorly conceived, many predicted he would defeat Russia within three months. In World War I, the Russian people waged a rebellion, and the nation descended into civil war as a result of the hardships the nation faced as it tried to repel the German offensive, Hitler reasoned. Had he gone further back in history he might have considered Napoleon's ill-fated attempt to conquer Russia. Stalin followed the same strategy that led to Napoleon's defeat, ordering a scorched earth policy where Russian commanders destroyed farms and cities as they retreated to prevent the Germans from seizing food and supplies. Hitler's plans were based on the assumption that Russia would fall before the winter of 1941. With no food or shelter along a 1,000-mile front, it soon seemed that Hitler's troops might share the fate of Napoleon's forces in the harsh Russian winter. That is, if Russia could survive the initial German onslaught.

As German troops advanced through Russia, Hitler's storm troopers waged a campaign of terror in Eastern Europe. Millions of Jews, as well as gypsies, homosexuals, resistance fighters, and people with disabilities, were terrorized and murdered by specialized Nazi units. Jews throughout Poland and Eastern Europe were first ordered to

FIGURE 7.25

A British poster honoring the pilots of the Royal Air Force that defended their nation during the Battle of Britain.

"NEVER WAS SO MUCH OWED BY SO MANY TO SO FEW"

FIGURE 7.26

Polish Jews being rounded up by German troops inside the Warsaw Ghetto in the summer of 1943. Over 300,000 Polish Jews who were sent to the Warsaw Ghetto were killed, most in Nazi extermination camps such as Treblinka.

walled-in ghettos in the center of cities like Warsaw. One of the greatest stories of resistance came from a counterattack of Polish Jews in the Warsaw ghetto when faced with evacuation to the concentration camps in 1943. The attack was heroic in spirit but failed to stop the Holocaust.

Poland was the site of the majority of the Nazi extermination camps, with some of the largest camps such as Auschwitz consisting of a network of many smaller camps. Historians estimate that 6 million Jews were killed by German soldiers in the Holocaust. Although the Warsaw ghetto uprising was quickly crushed, its participants and the thousands of Jews and their allies who resisted the Nazis demonstrated their humanity and contributed to hundreds of thousands of survival stories against a seemingly unstoppable force that desired nothing less than total genocide of an entire race.

4.5   German Aggression and the American Response

The American people were alarmed by Hitler's aggressive posture in the 1930s but wanted assurance that their nation would not become involved in another European war. Many believed that US involvement in trade with the warring nations of Europe in World War I had led to the nation's increasing involvement and eventual entry into that war. In response, Congress passed the **Neutrality Act** of 1935 that banned the sale of weapons to nations at war. The law was first applied to the Italian invasion of Ethiopia and later expanded to include the Spanish Civil War.

Some observers criticized US isolationism for what they viewed as a failure to aid victims of aggression. Few Americans favored intervention in Ethiopia or Spain, however, and US isolationism later included a desire to avoid involvement within the escalating conflicts in Europe and Asia during the late 1930s. Roosevelt publicly favored strict neutrality, but his private communications indicated a growing desire to aid Britain and France should a war with Germany occur. Although the law clearly forbade US businesses from trading with nations at war, Roosevelt assured British and French leaders that the might of US industry stood ready to assist them if Germany ever attacked them.

In 1937, Roosevelt called Congress into a special session to reconsider the wisdom of strict enforcement of the Neutrality Act. The president was in daily contact with Winston Churchill and did not believe that Western Europe would be able to defeat Germany should a war occur unless these nations had access to US markets. He proposed an amendment to the act that was soon nicknamed "**cash and carry.**" This provision altered the Neutrality Act and permitted the United States to sell armaments to any nation if two conditions were met. First, they must pay in full for their merchandise at the time of purchase (cash). Second, they must transport those items back to their own nations on their own ships (carry). The policy appeared neutral but clearly favored the Western Allies as German ships could not reach the United States without first passing through waters controlled by the British and the French. The law also banned US civilians from traveling to nations that were at war—an attempt to prevent a recurrence of the *Lusitania* sinking that had pushed the nation toward intervention in World War I.

The advantages of "cash and carry" for US businesses still mired in the Great Depression led many political leaders to tentatively support the idea. Unlike the US policy of selling merchandise on credit and loaning money during the First World War, US banks and businesses would not be tied to the fortune of the nations that were indebted to them. Equally important, US ships would not have to cross the perilous Atlantic and risk being sunk by German U-boats. Others disagreed, pointing out that "cash and carry" would make America's professed neutrality a farce and was simply one step closer to a declaration of war.

Congress debated these arguments for over a month. The Democratically-controlled legislature ultimately sided with Roosevelt, passing the Neutrality Act of 1937 and legalizing cash-and-carry trade. By the outbreak of war in 1939, Congress also suspended the provisions that banned the sale of military equipment to belligerent nations. Before this decision, Roosevelt privately entertained creative suggestions on ways to circumvent the law, such as US companies sending airplane parts to Canada that could then be assembled and shipped to England.

Neutrality Acts

A series of laws passed between 1935 and 1939 that regulated the sale and transportation of weaponry to nations that were at war with one another. The 1935 Act banned the sale and transport of weapons in hopes of preventing America from becoming involved in another foreign war. The Neutrality Acts of 1937 and 1939 amended the 1935 law by permitting the sale of weapons under certain circumstances as a means of aiding the opponents of Hitler and Japan while boosting the US economy.

cash and carry

The name given to a provision amending the Neutrality Act of 1935 to permit US companies to sell supplies to nations at war as long as those nations paid immediately in cash and arranged to transport those materials on their own ships.

FIGURE 7.27

Tanks and warplanes were not the only thing transferred to the Western Allies by the Lend-Lease Act. In this photo, Wisconsin cheddar cheese is being loaded and shipped to Great Britain to help feed its soldiers.

Wendell Willkie

A former Democrat, Wendell Willkie accepted the 1940 presidential nomination of the Republican Party against the incredibly popular Franklin Delano Roosevelt. Willkie ran on a platform opposed to the massive spending of New Deal programs and accused the president of pushing the nation toward war. Following Roosevelt's victory, Willkie reversed course regarding events in Europe and became one of the leading supporters of FDR's requests to provide military aid to Britain.

Lend-Lease

A program initiated in March 1941 that provided Britain, France, China, and the Soviet Union $50 billion in military aid to continue their fight against Germany and Japan. In return for the use of US military equipment, the recipients agreed to lease portions of their territory for use by the US military. The primary purpose of the law from the US perspective was to ensure that the recipient nations were able to continue the war and provide weaponry that would be used against their mutual enemies.

Churchill and Roosevelt communicated regularly, and by the time of the German invasion of France, both men believed that a genuine US policy of neutrality would doom the Allies. Churchill's dispatches to Roosevelt on this subject became more direct as the Nazi advance continued, warning the US president that a successful German invasion of Britain would threaten US security. If such a scenario occurred, Britain would be forced to sign an armistice that might lead to the British navy and air forces falling into Hitler's hands, the Prime Minister explained. These powerful weapons might soon be unleashed on US shores.

Ironically, Churchill's dire "worst-case scenario" could also be used by those who opposed sending military aid to Western Europe. Isolationists voiced the concern that military aid to Britain might simply fall into German hands. Many military analysts predicted that Britain would soon share France's fate, and Germany's swift victories in Poland and France had resulted in Germany capturing the majority of Polish and French munitions. In addition, America's own army was training with limited supplies of ammunition, while its air force lacked enough planes to train pilots. Rather than ship vital military equipment to Britain that might be captured by the Germans, isolationists argued, the United States should concentrate first on building up its armed forces.

Roosevelt shared many of these concerns but believed the British could defend their island empire if they were provided with US munitions. Throughout the summer of 1940, the Roosevelt administration declared trainloads of weapons and ammunition belonging to the army as "military surplus" that was then sent to assist the British. Roosevelt also instituted a peacetime draft to increase the size of the military. Perhaps most controversial of all his decisions, the president exchanged fifty destroyers for a British promise to lease military bases throughout their empire to the US Navy. These were bold moves given the fact that 1940 was an election year and the majority of Americans still wanted to maintain neutrality. Even as Roosevelt maintained his opposition to entering the war, it was apparent that he was steering the nation away from genuine neutrality.

As the presidential election of 1940 neared, Roosevelt decided not to follow the tradition started by George Washington, who declined reelection after serving two terms. Roosevelt believed that the situation in Europe was reason for him to seek an unprecedented third term as president. His campaign supporters devised an ingenious, if not devious, scheme at the Democratic National Convention in Chicago. Their goal was to make it appear as if the nation demanded that Roosevelt remain in office through the crisis. The Democratic mayor of Chicago filled the convention hall with Roosevelt supporters who chanted "we want Roosevelt" on cue. He allegedly even had a Roosevelt supporter hidden in the building with a microphone and loudspeaker, adding to the noise. Together, Roosevelt's supporters made it appear that a majority of delegates would accept no other candidate. Roosevelt accepted the nomination he likely conspired to achieve and defeated Republican candidate **Wendell Willkie**. Key to Roosevelt's victory was the President's promise to not send US troops into any foreign war.

Roosevelt believed the key to keeping his promise was to dramatically increase the amount of military aid that was being sold and given to England. The cash-and-carry policy was insufficient to meet this demand given the dwindling gold reserves of the British government. In January 1941, Roosevelt proposed the **Lend-Lease** program, which gave the President of the United States the authority to lend, lease, or sell military supplies on credit to any nation the president deemed vital to the defense of the United States.

The RAF had just won a temporary victory against the Luftwaffe that would at least stall any German invasion of the British Isles. This convinced many Americans that the British might be able to withstand the Nazis for another year with US aid. However, isolationists protested that the Lend-Lease program was just one step away from a declaration of war. By lending weapons to Britain, isolationists argued, the United States was not only repeating the actions that led to its eventual participation in World War I but doing so at its own expense.

Members of the isolationist America First Committee believed their country was once again being deceived by business and political leaders who wanted the United States to enter the war for their own personal gain. The **America First Committee** had more than six hundred chapters and hundreds of thousands of members, yet more and more Americans were beginning to agree with the president. Lend-Lease seemed to many Americans as the only way to prevent complete Nazi takeover of Europe, and it would also create jobs in wartime industries. Congress was still overwhelmingly Democratic and passed Roosevelt's bill in March, despite Republican opposition. The law would eventually lead to transfers of $50 billion in military aid to England and other allies.

4.6   Japanese Aggression and the American Response

By 1940, Japan emerged as one of the world's leading industrial nations. Japan's military had also defeated both Russia and China in small wars, and the Japanese Empire expanded its territory in Eastern Asia, including a portion of the Korean peninsula. The nation became more democratic in 1925 when its leaders approved a proposal granting universal male suffrage, but Japan was not a democracy in the Western sense. Japan's laws still conferred great power to the emperor and his military leaders. These men recognized that military power was key to securing access to oil. They also recognized the importance of mobilizing troops quickly in modern warfare.

Although they patterned their military and industry after the West, the Japanese also resented Western influence and believed that the United States, Britain, and France had not dealt fairly with their nation following its contribution to Allied victory in World War I. The Japanese were also angered by the disrespect that the United States demonstrated in passing laws prohibiting Japanese immigration. However, Japan's focus was not on the United States, at least not initially. Instead, Japanese leaders were dedicated to uniting their people behind an ambitious plan to establish their nation as the dominant power in the East. Japanese leaders viewed relations with the United States in the context of their expansionistic plans. They valued diplomacy and trade with the United States to the extent that these activities might further this aim.

For centuries, China had been the leading power in East Asia. Japanese officials recognized that China's ongoing civil war and the imperialistic designs of Europe had divided and weakened their ancient rival. Japanese military leaders believed China's turmoil represented an opportunity for Japanese expansion. An alleged terrorist attack on a Japanese-controlled railroad inside of the Chinese province of Manchuria in September 1931 resulted in Japanese forces being deployed to the area to investigate and protect other Japanese investments. Many around the world believed that the Japanese agents set off the blast as a pretext by which they might justify the resulting military occupation of the region. China made this same point when it asked the League of Nations to intervene on China's behalf. Members of the League protested the actions of Japan in violating the sovereignty of Manchuria, but they offered no assistance to China. Conflicts between Japan and China escalated from this incident, known as the Manchurian Crisis, until the formal declaration of the Second Sino-Japanese War in 1937.

Even as Japanese forces invaded their nation in 1937, the Chinese people remained divided between Socialists and conservatives who sought a restoration of monarchy. The Chinese Civil War continued despite the invasion, and both sides feared that sending their own troops to fight the Japanese would leave their armies vulnerable to each other. As a result, Japanese forces quickly occupied most of China's eastern coast. The war was extremely brutal. Japanese leaders preached that they were members of a master race, similar to the Nazi worldview. Severe atrocities against Chinese civilians became commonplace. The most infamous model of the war's inhumanity occurred in December 1937 when Japanese soldiers raped, tortured, and murdered an estimated 100,000 to 200,000 civilians in the former capital city of Nanking. To this day, some Japanese historians argue that this infamous atrocity known as the Rape of Nanking was little more than Chinese propaganda.

The United States responded with shock and dismay at the brutality of the war in Asia. However, the US government did little to intervene, even after Japanese aircraft attacked and destroyed a US naval vessel while in port near Nanking. Even after a film of the sinking of the USS *Panay* showed Japanese fighter planes gunning down survivors, the majority of Americans believed that recent events demanded withdrawal from the region rather than sending more military forces.

America First Committee

Formed in 1940 to represent those Americans who feared their nation was drifting toward war, the America First Committee claimed a membership of 800,000 and mobilized in opposition to FDR's Lend-Lease program. The organization disbanded following the Japanese attack on Pearl Harbor.

FIGURE 7.28

This World War II propaganda poster calls on Americans to donate funds to assist China's continued fight against Japan. Due to a desire to avoid conflict with Japan, the US offered little assistance to China until after Pearl Harbor.

Greater East Asia Co-Prosperity Sphere

World War II–era Japanese vision of a united Asian continent composed of nominally independent nations that each accepted the leadership of Japan in many aspects of international and domestic affairs. The concept stressed liberating Asian nations from Western colonialism, but many critics saw Japan as merely seeking to replace Western rule and create their own Empire.

In many ways, the situation in Asia resembled that of Europe. Japan believed that its people were racially superior to the various people of mixed ancestry living throughout Asia. They not only sought to increase their territory but also hoped to establish something they called the **Greater East Asia Co-Prosperity Sphere**, which would feature Japanese domination over former European colonies and independent Asian nations alike.

Rather than send troops, US and European leaders called for economic sanctions and warned that harsher steps would follow if Japan continued its aggression. President Roosevelt banned the exports of some armaments and aircraft parts to Japan in 1940 after its leaders formed a military alliance with Germany and Italy. Of all the products Japan imported from the United States, petroleum, especially aviation fuel, was the most important given Japan's limited access to oil fields.

Americans were hesitant to end all trade with Japan, as US forces in the Philippines were vulnerable to attack. As long as the oil-exporting United States maintained trade relations with Japan, the US forces in the region were safe and both nations could maintain neutrality in the affairs of the other. However, as Japan increased its brutal attacks throughout Asia in 1940, the United States moved away from neutrality. Roosevelt decided that the United States could not sell oil that would fuel the Japanese war machine. By late summer, Japan and the United States were no longer trading partners.

REVIEW AND CRITICAL THINKING

1. How did European and United States leaders respond to the rise of Hitler and his increasingly aggressive actions in Central Europe?

2. How was France defeated so quickly? Was the British decision to evacuate their forces once the Germans flanked their position a wise decision? How might the French view the Dunkirk evacuation?

3. What might have happened had Churchill agreed to peace terms with Hitler? Why was the Battle of Britain a significant turning point? What was Hitler's strategic objective, and what might have occurred had he succeeded?

4. Why did the Germans invade the Soviet Union despite their pact with Stalin? What were their strategic objectives?

5. Compare the actions of Japan in Asia during the years leading up to America's entry into World War II with the actions of Germany in Europe.

6. Explain why many opposed military action against Germany throughout the late 1930s. Describe the perspective of those in the United States who opposed intervention until the attack on Pearl Harbor.

7. Why did the United States restrict trade of certain items with Japan?

---

5. CONCLUSION

Compared to the massive borrowing and spending of the war years, the New Deal may appear little more than a "holding action" that prevented conditions from deteriorating beyond the nadir of 1933. The president himself was hardly a radical, and most of the provisions of the New Deal borrowed from previous ideas about monetary policy and earlier programs such as the War Industries Board. In addition, the New Deal only reluctantly embraced Keynesian ideas, and budget deficits remained relatively small until the outbreak of war.

However, the idea that the federal government could and should use its power to regulate private industry during peacetime represented a fundamental shift away from the laissez-faire traditions of the past. Programs such as the WPA offered direct employment when the private sector faltered, signaling a radical change in the expectations of the federal government. Some federal programs such as Social Security were completely new and represented a transfer of responsibility for the care of the elderly and the infirm from individual families and cities and states to the federal government. For the first time in US history, the powers and size of the government expanded significantly during a time of peace. As a result, many New Deal programs continued after World War II ended in 1945.

The United States would officially remain neutral in that war until the Japanese attack on Pearl Harbor. Between 1939 and 1941, this neutrality was a thin façade as Roosevelt believed America must use its potential industrial might to aid Britain and other Allies in their fight against the totalitarian regimes of Germany and Japan. By the end of 1939, unemployment had dropped to its lowest level of the decade as US workers began constructing the "arsenal of democracy" that would supply the armies of America's allies. Roosevelt hoped that selling weapons and food would solve the two biggest crises of the late 1930s: the dual invasion of Europe and Asia and the lingering economic stagnation throughout America. In so doing, the United States would prosper, and the world would be able to defend itself without direct US military intervention. To this end, the United States tolerated the deficits and intervened in the economy as never before.

Perhaps ironically, Roosevelt promised to deal with the Depression as if it were "an invading foe" upon taking office in 1933. In 1941, the United States was attacked, and the federal government received nearly unlimited power to manage the economy. In hindsight, the same methods used to transform the economy would have likely ended the Depression much sooner. At the same time, one must consider whether such extraordinary governmental power would have been tolerated in a time of peace.

6. FURTHER READING

Brinkley, Alan. *The End of Reform: New Deal Liberalism in Recession and War* (1995).

Cohen, Lizabeth. *Making a New Deal: Industrial Workers in Chicago, 1919–1939* (1990).

Grieve, Victoria. *The Federal Art Project and the Creation of Middlebrow Culture* (2009).

Maher, Neil A. *Nature's New Deal: The Civilian Conservation Corps and the Roots of the American Environmental Movement* (2007).

Sitkoff, Harvard. *A New Deal for Blacks: The Emergence of Civil Rights as a National Issue* (1978).

Sklaroff, Rebecca. *Black Culture and the New Deal: The Quest for Civil Rights in the Roosevelt Era* (2009).

Smith, Jason Scott. *Building New Deal Liberalism: The Political Economy of Public Works, 1933–1956* (2009).

Vapnek, Lara. *Breadwinners: Working Women and Economic Independence, 1865–1920* (2010).

Welky, David. *Everything Was Better in America: Print Culture in the Great Depression* (2008).

Worster, Donald. *Dust Bowl: The Southern Plains in the 1930s* (1979).

CHAPTER 8
America and World War II, 1941–1945

In response to Japanese aggression throughout Asia, the United States placed a trade embargo on the Japanese Empire. President Roosevelt hoped that halting Japan's access to oil would cripple Japan's military and halt its aggression in Asia. Instead, it led to a surprise attack by the Japanese against the US naval base at Pearl Harbor in Hawaii on December 7, 1941. America responded with a declaration of war against both Japan and Germany. The declaration revealed that the nation was not yet prepared for a global war. As had been the case in World War I, American leaders quickly sought to mobilize all of the nation's resources in support of the war effort. For the next four years, American industry concentrated on maximizing production of war materiel while 11 million women and men joined the armed forces.

The American way of war was based on developing an overwhelming force that could defeat an enemy with the minimum loss of life among its own troops. This required a superior amount of weaponry and support material and was also based on training and logistics. As a result, the United States was slow to mobilize and its allies in Europe and Asia were left to fight much of the war on their own until American troops arrived. Once those soldiers arrived, however, the tide of war shifted decisively toward the Western Allies.

The war would have an equally dramatic impact on the American home front. Japanese Americans were forced into internment camps until it was shown that such prejudices did nothing to advance the security of the American homeland. Other forms of discrimination were equally slow in being surmounted, with prohibitions against the service of women and minorities being only partially removed in the face of military necessity. As America raced to maximize its human resources to increase industrial production, it also decided that the price of prejudice was too high and began to celebrate its increasingly diverse workforce.

Ideas about limited government were also tested by the crucible of war. In response to the need to coordinate production and maximize efficiency, the federal government expanded its authority over the private sector. Although some feared that central planning might lead the nation to become more like the socialist and fascist nations of Europe, the American way of preparing for war was also unique. Although the government maintained the coercive power to seize factories it rarely did so, offering instead the possibility of high profits and high wages for those who produced the equipment and weapons it needed. By 1945, the US home front produced approximately half of the world's weaponry and the empires of Germany and Japan surrendered.

1. PEARL HARBOR AND THE ARSENAL OF DEMOCRACY

LEARNING OBJECTIVES

1. Explain why Japan took the calculated risk of attacking the US Pacific Fleet at Pearl Harbor. Summarize their tactical and strategic thinking, and evaluate what other options the Japanese military might have considered.
2. Detail the transition from civilian to military production. Explain the federal government's role in managing the economy and the lasting changes that wartime mobilization brought to US society.
3. Describe how the United States financed the war effort. Explain the importance of civilian opinion regarding the war and the role of the general public in making the transition from peacetime to war.
4. Explain how the United States was able to create a large army and navy within a year of the attack against Pearl Harbor. Describe how the emergency of war challenged prevailing notions of race, gender, and sexual orientation, as well as how these notions affected wartime mobilization.

1.1 Pearl Harbor

Few Americans were willing to consider military action against the Japanese in 1940 and 1941, and most considered Asian affairs to be of secondary importance to the events in Europe. To the Japanese, however, the United States embargo was an act of aggression that would make its empire vulnerable at the very moment it was expanding throughout Asia. From this perspective, there appeared little reason to maintain diplomatic relations with the United States. The Japanese now viewed the US-controlled Philippines much in the same context as the Dutch, French, and British colonies in Southeastern Asia. Hitler's war on these European powers could not have occurred at a better time for Japanese imperialists. They convinced the Japanese emperor that their alliance with Germany provided an opportunity for Japanese expansion into Southeastern Asia. With these European nations fighting for their very survival, Japan attacked their colonies throughout the region and seized control of raw materials and trade routes. Before these attacks were launched, however, Japanese officials launched a surprise attack on the United States they believed was necessary to prevent US interference.

Pearl Harbor

A surprise attack launched by the Japanese navy on the American Pacific Fleet anchored at Pearl Harbor in Hawaii on December 7, 1941. The attack resulted in the deaths of over 2,000 US servicemen and servicewomen and greatly reduced the effectiveness of the fleet. However, the attack failed to destroy US aircraft carriers and resulted in the US declaration of war against Japan, Germany, and Italy.

With China and the Europe fighting for survival, Japan expected little resistance in Southeastern Asia. In fact, the Japanese recognized that only one major naval power stood in their way of conquest—the United States. Japanese planners recognized that further aggression in Asia might lead to a more aggressive response than a trade embargo. (Historians now know that US military and civilian leaders had already determined not to intervene with military in Asia, even if Japan attacked US bases in the Philippines.) The Japanese fully recognized the industrial power of the United States; however, they believed a sudden and devastating attack on America's Pacific Fleet at **Pearl Harbor** would cripple the US navy for at least a year. During the interim, Japan planned to complete its conquest of Southeast Asia and build impenetrable defenses throughout the region. America's first opportunity to launch a counterattack would not occur until the summer of 1943, and by this time, the Americans would be ill-advised to send their newly rebuilt navy into the Japanese stronghold for its second slaughter.

By the winter of 1941, US leaders determined that they would no longer trade with Japan unless they ended their expansionistic campaign. In November, the United States demanded that Japan withdraw from China before any resumption of trade could commence. The talks quickly stalled on this point since the leading reason the Japanese sought oil from the Americans was to facilitate the expansion of their empire. By this time, Japanese forces had been secretly preparing for an attack against Pearl Harbor for over a year. In fact, US intelligence officers intercepted messages warning of the possibility of an attack should trade negotiations fail. Given the proximity of the US-controlled Philippines to Japan, many predicted that any attack would occur on these islands. While the military leaders debated on how to respond to a potential attack on the Philippines, all Pacific bases were ordered to increase their internal security. While officials at Pearl Harbor were on alert for potential acts of sabotage, few even considered the possibility of a carrier-based attack 4,000 miles from the Japanese mainland.

Just before 8:00 a.m. on Sunday, December 7, 350 Japanese warplanes launched in two waves from six aircraft carriers attacked America's Pacific Fleet anchored at Pearl Harbor. Each of the eight battleships that were present that morning was damaged, while half of them were destroyed. The attack also sunk a dozen other warships and destroyed nearly 200 aircraft. Of the 2,402 US servicemen who perished that day, nearly half were aboard the USS *Arizona* when a bomb caused its forward ammunition magazines to explode. The Japanese lost only a handful of aircraft in the attack. Their commanders recognized that despite the apparent success of their mission, it had failed to achieve its primary objective of crippling the US Pacific fleet. Although US losses were high, all three of the fleet's aircraft carriers escaped destruction at Pearl Harbor because they had been out to sea for various reasons.

FIGURE 8.1

The USS *West Virginia* burns in the background while a crew saves a navy seaman who was able to escape the destruction.

Hours after the attack at Pearl Harbor began, Japanese warplanes began an assault on US forces stationed in the Philippines. For reasons that are still unclear, General Douglas MacArthur failed to mobilize in preparation for this attack, and Japanese aircraft destroyed most of United States' Far East Air Force, which was still on the ground. Roosevelt addressed Congress on December 8. The president declared the attack at Pearl Harbor to be a "date which will live in infamy" and requested a declaration of war. Congress agreed, and the United States officially declared that a state of war existed with Japan, as well as Germany and Italy.

The American people overwhelmingly supported their president's request for war following the attack on Pearl Harbor. Even former isolationists agreed; they could be found among those who joined the military or otherwise helped their nation prepare for the impending struggle. Indignation at the attack soon turned to fear as Japan defeated French, British, and Dutch colonial forces throughout Southeastern Asia. America's own position in the Pacific was equally perilous. US bases on Guam and Wake Island surrendered to the Japanese. By early 1942, many predicted that a second attack on Pearl Harbor would lead to the capture of Hawaii. Americans on the West Coast feared that a Japanese-controlled Hawaii would be used to stage an invasion of the US mainland.

1.2 Becoming the Arsenal of Democracy

Following his declaration of war in December 1941, Roosevelt sought ways to convert the United States into "the arsenal of democracy" that supplied America and its European allies with the weapons needed to defeat Hitler's armies. This vision embodied both the idealism and economic might of the nation. It also demonstrated his belief that the United States was unique in its capacity for both representative government and industrial production. However, America was still mired in the Depression in 1939. Perhaps worse, a vast gulf existed between the desire of Americans to take the war to Japan and Germany and the present state of their army and navy. Roosevelt and Congress responded to the emergency by enlarging the military and expanding the government's role in the economy in ways never before imagined, even at the height of the New Deal. In the next few years, the United States became the arsenal Roosevelt described. Section 3 examines the expansion of the military and the transition to a wartime economy. Whether this arsenal was truly democratic largely depends on the perspective one considers. Section 4 follows with a review of this question from the perspective of women and minorities.

Even in the Depression year of 1937, America produced ten times as many automobiles as Germany and Japan combined produced. However, two decades of isolationism kept US military spending low, and few US companies produced combat aircraft, tanks, or other munitions so desperately needed by the United States and its allies. If US factories could quickly transition from producing consumer goods such as automobiles to tanks, ships, aircraft, and trucks for its armed forces, the Allies would quickly enjoy an abundance of military equipment. The revision of the Neutrality Act in 1937 and the abandonment of its restrictions on wartime trade between 1939 and 1941 had already led to increased military production by US companies. In addition, Congress appropriated nearly $2 billion in defense spending in 1940 and another $6 billion the following year. Still, ensuring that most US companies shifted from producing vacuum cleaners to machine guns required more than an increase in military purchase orders. Given the sudden transition back to civilian production after World War I, US companies were hesitant to invest the money needed to convert their factories from building refrigerators to machine guns. Any number of events could lead to the sudden cancellation of military purchase orders, they reasoned, and their companies would then be stuck producing goods that were no longer demanded.

The government also had to contend with the long-term effects of the Great Depression. In 1940, 8 million workers were still unemployed, and half of the nation's manufacturing plants were producing below half of their maximum capacity. As a result, the federal government took even greater control of the economy than it had during World War I to make sure that its factories were at peak capacity. For example, the federal government ordered the end of civilian auto production in 1942 as a means of ensuring that more military vehicles were built. The government also created a New Deal–like alphabet soup of programs charged with overseeing the transition to full wartime production.

As the war raged in Europe, Roosevelt announced production goals few thought possible. The federal government worked to ensure US businesses met these goals by using a carrot-and-stick approach. Very lucrative contracts became the carrot as the federal budget increased tenfold during the war. These expenditures allowed government purchasing agents to offer lucrative deals to US business leaders, convincing nearly all leading industries to convert to wartime production. The government paid top dollar for all manner of goods from food to flamethrowers while occasionally seizing manufacturing facilities it felt were not being fully utilized.

The Roosevelt administration's solution to underproductivity thus demonstrated a uniquely American approach that blended free enterprise with unprecedented government intervention. The **War Production Board** offered tax incentives, loans, and even guaranteed profits to businesses that were now understandably eager to produce the goods the military desired. Other government agencies seized control of commodities markets to make sure that these businesses would have access to the raw materials they needed. The **Office of Price Administration** regulated the cost of these raw materials, as well as the prices of consumer goods, to reduce inflation and prevent price gouging of ordinary consumers.

As a result, corporate profits more than doubled between 1941 and 1945. US business leaders could have never dreamed of such a favorable contract, with nearly every expense related to building or converting existing factories being tax deductible. Other contracts offered guaranteed profits on each item produced for the military. Workers benefited as unemployment became a problem of the past, while wages jumped by 30 percent. Because virtually all segments of the population stood to profit from the government's economic programs, criticism was limited to those who opposed the principle of government-imposed economic planning and management. Economist **Friedrich Hayek** authored *The Road to Serfdom* in 1944, arguing that complete control of the economy by government was a trademark of dictatorship.

Influenced by Hayek, many Americans were uncomfortable with the sudden expansion of their government's authority. The War Production Board utilized economic planning that seemed to share similarities with the totalitarian governments of Japan, Germany, and the Soviet Union. At the same time, Americans could point to important differences. Private enterprise still prevailed in nearly every sector of the economy. The federal government rarely used its coercive power to seize a plant or halt a strike, and Americans enjoyed average incomes that were larger than those of German, Italian, and Japanese workers combined. Perhaps most important, the federal government's plan succeeded in increasing military production without creating major hardships on the home front. Even if certain items like nylons were no longer available to civilians, America's total output of consumer goods actually increased during every year of the war. If America's economy could no longer be categorized as free enterprise, it seemed to many that it could not be considered Socialistic either.

Critics who bemoaned the rise of government interference in the economy could offer little rebuttal against the overwhelming statistics of America's wartime production. As early as 1942, the United States was producing more military equipment than any other nation. By 1945, US factories were responsible for nearly half of the world's armaments and had out-produced the factories and farms of England, France, Russia, Germany, Italy, and Japan combined. In total, America produced more than 300,000 aircraft, 100,000 tanks and armored vehicles, 22 aircraft carriers, 8,000 transport ships, and 1,000 armed vessels for the navy. Armament plants churned out 40 billion bullets that could be fired by the 20 million rifles that were made. US factories produced a new all-purpose military vehicle known as the jeep every minute, while a new plane took off from runways adjacent to US factories every five minutes. Massive cargo ships that used to take one or two years to complete were now produced in a matter of weeks. Dubbed "liberty ships," these cargo vessels were indispensable to the American way of war that relied upon overwhelming material supremacy.

US factories were not only more productive than their rivals, but they were also more innovative. Funding for research and development led to the effective military application of technologies such as radar, sonar, proximity fuses, computers, and jet aircraft. The most important new military technology was the realization of an atomic bomb that had only been theorized about by a small number of physicists in the past. The federal government spent more than $300 billion to achieve this mix of production and innovation—more than double the entire federal budget for the last 150 years of the nation's existence. The result was an undeniable superiority of equipment that would allow US troops to quickly win the war while suffering only a fraction of the casualties of their Russian and Chinese allies. Ill-trained and poorly equipped, tens of thousands of Russian and Chinese soldiers perished each week while awaiting the arrival of US forces.

War Production Board

A federal agency directed with procuring all military supplies and armaments and managing the conversion of factories from civilian production to military production. The board sought to achieve peak efficiency by offering lucrative contracts to businesses producing material considered vital to the war effort while restricting or banning the production of nonessential items.

Office of Price Administration

A federal agency tasked with limiting inflation and profiteering during the war by imposing price limits on scarce items such as oil and tires. The agency also froze prices on food items and rent to prevent speculators from buying up large quantities of vital resources and selling them for much higher prices in a time of national emergency.

Friedrich Hayek

Austrian economist who argued that central planning could never be as efficient as the free market. *The Road to Serfdom* argued that complete governmental control of the economy, including central planning over decisions regarding production, distribution, and consumption that typified a Socialist state, would lead to increased governmental control of all aspects of life and eventually lead to totalitarianism. Hayek believed that a free market system with limited governmental regulation of certain functions such as banking provided the best economic results while safeguarding the freedom of the individual.

In retrospect, it is clear that Hitler's decision to invade Russia bought the United States time to make this amazing economic transition. Russia did not fold as many had predicted, but instead kept the German army occupied for the duration of the war. Few understood the disastrous potential of a stalled Russian offensive more than Hitler did. The Fuhrer's advisers cautioned Hitler that he would have but one year to defeat Russia. After this time, the combination of US industrial production and Russian manpower might negate the initial momentum and superiority of equipment the Germans enjoyed. Japanese Admiral **Isoroku Yamamoto** made a similar prediction regarding his nation's war against the United States. Yamamoto argued that a successful attack against Pearl Harbor would buy the Japanese navy a year of unchallenged supremacy in the Pacific. If the war continued for a second and third year, he warned, America's industrial would negate its inertia and put the Japanese empire on the defensive. As a result, both Japan and Germany based their 1941 decisions to attack the United States and Russia on their belief that the war would end quickly. Every day that the Russians and Chinese held out against German and Japanese forces provided US factories and military planners with more time to prepare.

1.3   Financing the War and Selling the War

America's military production and preparation was facilitated by massive government spending. Given the dire necessity of building a military and the benefits to workers and industry alike, few criticized the government's use of borrowed money to finance the war effort. The greatest concern at the time was not the government's ability to repay this money, but whether the sudden influx of federal spending would lead to inflation. The methods of financing the war, however, absorbed most of the extra money that was moving into the economy.

The **Revenue Act of 1942** doubled the amount of money the government received from individual tax returns and forever changed the nature of income tax in America. The law reduced to $1,200 the amount of money that was exempt from federal taxation for families. Since the average income of an American family was just over $1,200, most full-time wage-earners had not paid any federal tax prior to 1942. The following year, the government mandated that employers withhold taxes from each worker's paycheck. By taking out small amounts from each check rather than presenting families with a large bill at year-end, this provision helped to ensure that federal taxes were collected. The number of Americans required to file and pay federal taxes jumped from 4 million to 45 million by the end of the war.

Roosevelt and Congress fought a fierce battle regarding these changes to the tax code, with the increasingly conservative House of Representatives and Senate rejecting many of the president's requests for even steeper tax increases. Roosevelt favored taxation because he feared the consequences of too much borrowing. However, tax increases were a bitter pill for members of the House of Representatives who faced two-year election cycles. Because of these political considerations, the government followed the tradition of financing wars through heavy borrowing. Corporate and personal income taxes financed 45 percent of the war's cost. The government made up the difference by borrowing nearly $200 billion, 20 percent of which was held by private citizens who had purchased war bonds.

As had been the case in previous conflicts, these sales once again served the purpose of mobilizing Americans behind the war effort. Similar to the efforts of George Creel and others during World War I, the government recruited celebrities and athletes to headline bond drives. Purchasing a government bond was more than just a patriotic gesture; bonds represented a secure investment that provided guaranteed repayment with interest. The revenue from these bonds would help many families purchase more goods once the war was over and ensured that civilian production of items such as automobiles and new homes would resume. At the same time, repayment of these bonds decreased the likelihood that federal income tax rates would return to their prewar levels once the war was over.

Contrary to World War I, few Americans questioned the necessity of America's involvement in the Second World War. The government's Office of Censorship was limited to monitoring soldiers' letters and preventing the release of sensitive information that might be of value to the nation's enemies. The **Office of War Information (OWI)** was tasked with mobilizing the already favorable public opinion of the war effort into support for various government initiatives. The transition from censorship in World War I to a more tolerant view of dissent is demonstrated by a 1943 Supreme Court ruling that tolerated those who refused to salute the flag for religious or personal beliefs. The decision illustrated a departure from the state-mandated displays of nationalistic support in Germany and Japan, a theme that was often featured in OWI releases lauding America's toleration for dissent in contrast to the totalitarianism of her enemies. In general, OWI propaganda sought to portray the war as a moral struggle between freedom and totalitarianism. Most OWI posters and films were upbeat, praising America's industrial workers and soldiers and encouraging them to continue their efforts, rather than demonizing the enemy. Yet when it came to the war in the Pacific, OWI propaganda pandered to existing prejudices against the Japanese. Posters and films alternated between portraying the Japanese as diminutive monkeys or rats and hulking ape-like beasts. The imagery was increasingly violent, such as a poster advertising war bonds that depicted a caricatured Japanese head being decapitated from a rat's body. Critics pointed out that anti-German posters were restricted to demonic images of Nazi leaders, while the war against Japan was increasingly presented as a war against a subhuman race.

The OWI employed a few thousand writers and artists who tended to favor not only the war effort but also the ideas of New Deal liberals. Most OWI publications promoted noncontroversial subjects such as general support for the troops, conservation of materials, and a partnership between industrial workers and the troops on the front line. Some OWI publications also sought to promote more liberal ideas, such as the notion that fair pay, medical care, and full employment were rights for which Americans were fighting. As a result, the OWI budget was vastly reduced by an increasingly conservative Congress.

The government granted wider latitude to conscientious objectors and dissenters than in previous wars, largely because so few Americans doubted the basic premise of their nation's participation in the war. Contrary to World War I, America had been attacked and faced a clear moral decision to intervene in both Asia and Europe against the rise of totalitarian regimes. Even reducing the funding for the OWI did little to reduce prowar propaganda as private entities also sought to promote the war. Newspapers were full of daily editorials on the need to fight the Germans and Japanese, and Hollywood produced a litany of films eulogizing the valor of soldiers. While most of this propaganda focused on support for soldiers and celebration of industry, some of this propaganda played to the anger of Americans after Pearl Harbor and even pandered to ethnic and racial hatred.

1.4   Women in Industry and Organized Labor

As America prepared to enter the war, Roosevelt indicated that the nation would not simply match the production of its enemies but instead would crush those enemies with overwhelming material superiority. At its peak, the nation rolled out a new tank and airplane every five minutes. This superiority of equipment kept US casualties low compared with Russia, China, and the Axis Powers. Such production could only be achieved by the addition of 15 million new workers entering US factories for the first time during the war years. Women represented half of these new employees and one-third of the total civilian work force. Many women continued to work in service, clerical, education, and nursing fields, but many of the 6 million women who joined the paid workforce for the first time took up manufacturing jobs traditionally held by men. For many women, entrance into the paid workforce was both ennobling and exhilarating, opening new opportunities and providing a measure of financial independence. Even if only 10 to 20 percent of working women were employed within the defense industries, the can-do image of **Rosie the Riveter** both represented and inspired many women, whether they donned overalls and "manned" the assembly lines or worked more traditional jobs. Minority women seldom experienced the same opportunities for direct upward mobility, yet for many, the war provided the first time a US factory would consider hiring a woman of color for any position at any wage.

BUY WAR BONDS

Office of War Information

A government agency tasked with improving morale and managing the public image of the war effort. The attack against Pearl Harbor resulted in few Americans opposing the war itself, freeing the Office of War Information to mobilize public opinion in support of various government initiatives rather than engaging in censorship. The OWI made films, radio broadcasts, pamphlets, and other forms of wartime advertisements, but it is most remembered for its colorful and creative posters. A division of the OWI created pamphlets and other materials distributed overseas designed to reduce the morale of enemy troops and civilians.

Rosie the Riveter

A mythical female steelworker who came to represent the millions of American women who entered jobs in factories during World War II. A cultural icon whose name derived from popular song lyrics, real life "Rosies" were women who worked jobs previously open only to men.

FIGURE 8.5

One of many real-life "Rosie the Riveters," this woman built military aircraft at a Lockheed plant in Burbank, California.

Despite the entrance of approximately 2 million women into jobs traditionally held by men, wartime propaganda minimized the challenge this trend represented to traditional images of gender. Women's work in defense factories was portrayed as falling within the larger role of women as guardians of the home and family. The war temporarily redefined the domestic sphere to include the home front as well as the household. Men were still in charge and the defenders of the nation, Americans were assured by the prevailing culture, as women entered factories only to assist the men who performed the more difficult and essential tasks. Female production of armaments that were used by men to defend the nation was viewed as compatible with prevailing labor arrangements where women assisted men. A woman on a bomber assembly line performed simple, mindless tasks in support of a skilled pilot flying over enemy territory, this line of reasoning suggested, just as a female secretary might perform routine tasks in support of her male boss, who skillfully navigated the cutthroat world of business. The internal contradictions of this reasoning were evident to many, yet the culture and limited duration of the war conspired to minimize wartime challenges to American notions of work and gender.

Despite the unprecedented number of women in the workforce, American men and women alike were reluctant to abandon traditional lines between male and female labor. The majority of women between the ages of eighteen and sixty-five did not enter the paid workforce at any time during the war. The majority of women who did indicated repeatedly in editorials and opinion polls that they agreed with prevailing notions insisting that female labor in factories was a temporary necessity due to the 16 million men and women who served in the armed forces between 1941 and 1945. These female laborers averaged only 65 percent of the wages paid to men for the same work. They were also usually expected to quit these jobs after the war, although some businesses reasoned that continuing to employ women might provide significant cost savings. Most of the women in these fields voluntarily left their jobs. However, societal expectations and the likelihood that most women would be fired from industrial jobs if they did not resign makes it difficult to determine how voluntarily American women retreated from the factory to the home.

National War Labor Board (NWLB)

A federal agency established in World War I and reestablished by President Roosevelt in World War II to arbitrate disagreements between labor and management. As was the case in World War I, the primary objective of the NWLB was to prevent work stoppages that might derail production of essential wartime supplies and munitions.

Labor unions had benefitted from the enrollment of female workers, yet they were still dominated by men and supported the idea that returning veterans should replace their former sisters of toil. During the war years, however, the unions actively sought to adapt to the changes around them by forming partnerships with government and management. Labor leaders recognized the need to maximize wartime production as a national defense issue and as a means of benefiting their members. As a result, nearly every union leader pledged not to support labor strikes and resolved to work with the **National War Labor Board (NWLB)** to arbitrate disputes with employers.

In return for labor's pledge to avoid strikes, the government agreed to regulate consumer prices to ensure that inflation did not dilute worker wages. The federal government even purchased food directly from farmers and sold it to retailers at a financial loss to keep consumer prices down. More importantly to labor leaders, the government also passed a "maintenance of membership" rule that required all new employees in factories represented by a union to join that union. This arrangement satisfied most labor leaders as their membership rolls expanded. Due to rising wages and the resulting power of the unions, most union members enjoyed significant pay increases and even new benefits, such as pensions and health insurance.

Workers in some industries felt that their pay increases failed to keep pace with corporate profits. Others cited mandatory overtime, assembly line speed-ups, and the occasional wage freezes in some industries as mandated by NWLB agreements. John L. Lewis, head of the United Mine Workers, believed that the NWLB cared little for the miners of his organization. Lewis argued that his miners were not enjoying their proportional share of wartime prosperity given the higher prices of coal, steel, and other mining commodities. Lewis ordered a strike that halted mining operations throughout the country and threatened to halt defense production. As a result, the miner's strike sent panic through the nation and led many to equate labor activism with treason. Given the nation's immense need for coal, iron ore, copper, and other metals, Lewis won significant concessions for his members. The fallout from this strike, however, caused the entire labor movement to lose public support. Congress also responded by passing several laws that limited the power of unions for the duration of the war.

1.5   Creating an Army

Even before the United States joined the war, Congress approved the Selective Service Act of 1940 to address concerns that the army might not be able to defend itself if the war spread from Europe to North America. The law required young men between the ages of twenty-one and thirty-five to register for the draft. The law also classified registrants into four categories. Those who were deemed physically and mentally fit who were single and not employed in an occupation deemed "critical" by the War Department were placed into Category I. Those so placed could expect a draft notice and often chose to enlist rather than wait to be called by their Uncle Sam. Deferments for married men proved temporary, especially after the government noticed a sudden spike in weddings that seemed curiously related to the arrival of draft notices. Fatherhood was the next deferment to succumb to military necessity. However, during the first years of the war, so few dads were drafted that newborns were occasionally nicknamed "weatherstrips" because they insulated families by keeping their fathers out of the draft.

The nation had only 1.6 million soldiers and sailors at the time of the attack on Pearl Harbor, half of whom had enlisted after Roosevelt's enactment of a peacetime draft in 1940. This number would increase nearly tenfold by the end of the war, with 150,000 recruits entering one of 250 training camps set up around the country each week. Most of these recruits had never been far from home but were now sharing bunks and foxholes with others of different ethnic and religious backgrounds. As a result, the war led many to broaden their horizons and shed their prejudices, while others simply became more distrustful of those who seemed different from themselves.

African American troops were the only soldiers explicitly required to endure segregation. However, many West Coast units were composed entirely of Mexican Americans, Japanese, or Filipinos. Puerto Rican recruits were often grouped together in places such as Florida and New York. Elsewhere, informal segregation usually prevailed as Jewish, Asian, Native American, and other groups usually banded together given shared experiences and the prejudices they encountered from others. A large percentage of military members were first- or second-generation immigrants, many of whom were not yet fluent in English. As a result, the war accelerated the assimilation of many soldiers and helped to break down prejudices against immigrants from other parts of the world. A similar breakdown of racial prejudice was prevented by the War Department's decision to maintain separate units for black troops. The US Marines, Coast Guard, and Army Air Corps refused to enlist black troops while the US Navy relegated black sailors to service positions until after Pearl Harbor. After the attack, these branches often assigned black servicemen to labor positions such as cook or cargo loader.

Emblematic of the mentality of the armed forces at this time, the Red Cross recorded the race of blood donors. Military officials segregated "white" and "black" blood, even though scientists and medics alike understood that plasma and blood cells did not recognize their arbitrary categories of race. The NAACP waged a campaign of education that ended this practice, as well as ending some instances of segregation on military facilities. Most campaigns for equality were aimed at increasing the number of black officers while calling on each branch of the military to create or expand black combat units. The most famous of these units were the Tuskegee Airmen and the 761st Tank Battalion, which are detailed in a later section.

The most historic change to the armed services during the war was the authorization of female service, first as civilian members of a women's army auxiliary in 1942 and then as officers and enlisted women entitled to military pay and benefits. Women had worked for the military in World War I as civilians performing many of the same tasks as enlisted men in various noncombat positions. The navy even enlisted 13,000 women to perform these duties during that war, an action that quickly prompted Congress to amend its laws regulating enlistment by adding the word "male" as a requirement instead of an unwritten assumption. Wartime necessity and the activism of women led to the creation of the **Women's Auxiliary Army Corps (WAAC)** and the Women Accepted for Voluntary Emergency Service (WAVES) of the navy, as well as other women's units.

The use of labels such as "voluntary emergency service" and "auxiliary" connote the ways the military tried to qualify its acceptance of female members. However, the navy granted women the status of military members, and the army changed the name of its female branch to the Women's Army Corps (WAC) when its members were granted military status in 1943. Some 350,000 women served in the military as noncombatants filling "female" jobs in clerical and nursing fields, but many also served as mechanics and other traditionally "masculine" jobs. Other units repaired weapons and radios, while a small number of women on the West Coast instructed male pilots how to use their navigational equipment. Nearly 1,000 women flew cargo planes and towed targets for live antiaircraft drills as part of the Women Airforce Service Pilots (WASP). Despite the danger of their job, which led to the mission-related deaths of over three dozen women, the WASPs were denied military benefits and veterans' benefits.

The women stationed at these pilot-training facilities in California contributed to the rapid growth of West Coast cities. Military contracts doubled the size of cities such as Albuquerque, while naval bases doubled the already rapidly expanding population of San Diego. Hundreds of small and middle-sized towns throughout the country experienced wartime booms as nearby soldiers flooded area towns to spend weeks of earnings before their leave expired. The recreational ambitions of some soldiers inspired Congress to pass the May Act in 1941. The law granted military officials the power to close businesses and even restrict entire cities from military personnel if local authorities did not satisfactorily combat prostitution. As a result, more than seven hundred US cities closed down their red-light districts while military police (MP) and the navy's shore patrol watched over vice districts near military installations.

FIGURE 8.8

This college-aged member of Women's Army Corps (WAC) repaired aircraft during World War II. She also had a pilot's license. Other women with similar credentials served as civilian pilots in the Women's Air Force Service Pilots (WASP) program.

Soldiers on leave were required to wear uniforms so that MPs could easily spot military members and regulate their behavior. Servicemen sought to evade these restrictions by utilizing underground "locker clubs" that rented civilian clothes and secured a serviceman's dress uniform until he was ready to return to base. While the behavior of female service members was heavily scrutinized, the military tolerated a certain degree of rule breaking by men on leave. However, one of the businesses that military authorities were especially vigilant in patrolling were bars known to cater to homosexual men.

Although the US military had a long history of discharging soldiers convicted of homosexual acts, World War II saw the first significant attempt to prevent homosexuals from entering the armed services. All potential enlistees were required to undergo brief psychological examinations that included questions about their sexual orientation. The military interviewed 18 million potential service members but only disqualified 4,000 to 5,000 potential enlistees for homosexuality. Historian Allan Berube has demonstrated that this low number was the result of gay men becoming well accustomed to hiding their personal life during this era. For example, Berube has even found that the celebrity musician Liberace was drafted and only disqualified because of a physical injury.

Homosexual men had learned to mask their sexual orientation and casually answered the questions about their attraction to women as heterosexual men were expected to answer them. Few of the 350,000 women who served in the military were directly questioned about their sexual orientation, largely because women's service branches were already battling stereotypes about female soldiers being both unfeminine and sexually aggressive—both characteristics stereotypically attributed to homosexual women. Despite limited attempts to prevent gay servicemen and women from joining the ranks, historians estimate that between 300,000 and 1.2 million of the nation's 15 million women and men who joined the armed services during World War II were homosexuals.

These attempts can accurately be described as limited because most Americans assumed that young men and women deemed fit for service were heterosexual. In addition, the top priority of military psychiatrists was not to screen against homosexuality, but rather to identify those most likely to become psychiatric casualties. Military officials believed proper screening could greatly reduce the number of these psychiatric cases, which accounted for half of the patients in veterans' hospitals twenty years after World War I. Military necessity likewise drove the informal and often reluctant toleration of gay soldiers by their peers and commanders. In 1940 and 1941, most reported cases of homosexuality led to trials and imprisonment. However, by 1942, most of these men were quietly discharged from the service or simply transferred to another unit. After 1942, most commanders, especially those on or near the front lines, were informally counseled to try and "salvage" those under their command who were known to be homosexual, as long as their lifestyle and behavior did not "threaten" others. As one combat medic in the Battle of the Bulge recalled, "No one asked me if I was gay when they called out Medic!" Thousands of openly gay men and women served during World War II, although the vast majority continued to hide their sexual orientation. Among this group were future celebrities such as Rock Hudson, recipients of the Navy Cross and Silver Star, and dozens of high-ranking officers. Gay veterans recall service to their country as their leading concern. For many others, the war was a personal quest against the forces of persecution and intolerance. For gay Americans and the hundreds of homosexuals who fled Europe and enlisted in the US armed forces, the brutal murder of homosexuals in Nazi concentration camps inspired their distinguished service.

REVIEW AND CRITICAL THINKING

1. Why did Japanese leaders decide to attack Pearl Harbor? What did they hope to gain? Did they believe the United States would respond, and if so, why were they willing to take this risk?

2. Some might argue that the governmental control of the economy Friedrich Hayek warned about in *The Road to Serfdom* typified not only a Socialist state but also the powerful central government of the United States during World War II. What do you think? Were the federal government's efforts to direct the economy and wartime production similar to Socialism? If so, why did the United States not become a Socialist nation? Or, do you believe that the growth of the government in World War II put the United States on the road to Socialism Hayek warned of?

3. How did gender affect the nation's industry and military as it mobilized for war? What were the expectations of men and women at this time, and how might the war have challenged the gendered differences of those expectations?

4. How significant was the labor of real-life "Rosie the Riveters" during World War II? Do you think the greater significance is the total material output of these laborers or the way these women challenged prevailing notions of gender? Could the United States have won the war without an increase in female laborers?

5. The military would not authorize homosexual service in the military until the twenty-first century. Why might so many homosexual service members have been tolerated by the military during World War II? What might account for the lack of concern regarding this issue among military leaders and the general public?

2. DOUBLE V: FREEDOM ABROAD, FREEDOM AT HOME

LEARNING OBJECTIVES

1. Detail the reasons for the creation of women's service units within the military and the unique history of these organizations. Explain how these units reflect America's notion of gender at the time and how women's service in the military challenged those assumptions.
2. Explain how Native Americans, Asian Americans, Japanese Americans, and Mexican Americans served their nation despite the discrimination they faced. Compare the experience of these groups to that of African Americans.
3. Compare the experiences of African Americans in the military during World War II to the efforts of black leaders to promote racial equality in the United States. Explain the connection between black military service, the Double-V campaign, and civil rights activism in the twentieth century.

2.1 Women in the Military

Edith Nourse Rogers

A Massachusetts congresswoman who served her district from 1925 to 1960, longer than any woman in history. During her time, she sponsored not only legislation benefitting women, such as bills ensuring that women serving in military positions were granted military status and benefits, but also legislation benefitting all veterans such as the GI Bill.

Women Accepted for Voluntary Emergency Service (WAVES)

The women's branch of the navy during World War II. Unlike the army, the navy immediately recognized women who joined the WAVES as members of the military. Some 100,000 women served within the WAVES of the navy, while another 40,000 served in the marines and coast guard. Approximately 75,000 women served in the nursing corps of the various armed services.

Women's Army Corps (WAC)

Begun as a civilian auxiliary to the all-male army, the Women's Army Corps enlisted 140,000 American women who served in various noncombat positions ranging from clerical work to mechanical and communications fields.

Republican congresswoman **Edith Nourse Rogers** of Massachusetts introduced a bill authorizing the creation of a Women's Auxiliary Army Corps (WAAC) in May 1941. Nourse was motivated by her desire to obtain military benefits for the nearly 60,000 women who were already performing the same job as male soldiers in a variety of clerical and other fields. These women were hired by the military, but because they were not in the military, the women were ineligible for benefits and often paid far less than male soldiers.

Rogers's bill passed in May 1942, by which time each branch of the armed services was creating similar opportunities for female service. For example, the navy organized the **Women Accepted for Voluntary Emergency Service (WAVES)** in August 1942. One important distinction between the two organizations is that women in the WAVES were part of the navy, while the WAACs were considered civilians until 1943. At this time, the WAAC became the **Women's Army Corps (WAC)**, and like the WAVES, WAC members held the same rank and were given the same pay as men. In practice, however, few women were granted promotion past the lowest enlisted ranks. The result was the continued discrimination against women in terms of rank and pay that was typical in civilian employment.

This inequity in promotion was related to the military's perception of female service as an "auxiliary" to the more important work of male soldiering. Most women at this time at least partially accepted the notion that women's service was secondary to that of men. Even women who had more radical ideas about gender usually sought to convince others that female military service was consistent with more widely accepted views about women's roles. For example, Americans viewed British women serving in their nation's various military auxiliaries as heroines forced from their homes by the extraordinary threat of invasion. Americans generally admired the way the British women responded to their nation's call for service and recognized that total warfare required full mobilization of all resources. As a result, advocates of female service in the United States argued that the emergency of war made it permissible for US women to temporarily serve in military roles, just as women in Britain had done.

The public reaction to women's service was skeptical at first, as evidenced by letters to the editor of hundreds of local and national newspapers that questioned the likelihood that women would be effective as soldiers. These letters frequently contrasted the "male" characteristics of discipline, intelligence, and strength with the belief that women were naturally disposed to be overly emotional, illogical, chatty, and obsessed with trivial things like shopping. Others predicted that women's service would lead to a breakdown of the home as well as military discipline. Over time, these objections became less frequent, especially as military officials embraced the idea of women's service and praised the efforts of early recruits.

Despite the nation's growing acceptance of female soldiers and sailors, Americans also reveled in political cartoons, which played on their earlier assumptions that women and military service were incompatible. Newspapers produced hundreds of images of women falling in for revile in curlers, struggling to salute an officer while holding a purse, and falling behind on a march due to high heels and a pesky slip that kept showing underneath their military-issued skirts. Popular cartoons such as *Winnie the WAC* featured the misadventures of an affable but stereotyped blonde who daydreamed about shopping and men while her more serious and soldierly brunette and red-haired bunkmates adjusted easily to army life. These cartoons may have seemed both humorous and good-natured to many readers, especially considering the many mean-spirited portrayals of WACs as unattractive, unpleasant, and unfeminine. Other artists simply poked fun at their society's fears that female service would reverse gender roles. A popular cartoon sarcastically featured the new model of American masculinity at home in an apron, knitting while pining away for his wife as he waited for his protector and provider to send him his monthly allowance as a military "wife."

Surveys of public opinion demonstrate that these cartoons were popular because most Americans reconsidered their initial concerns about limited wartime service leading to the breakdown of traditional gender roles and at least tentatively approved of women serving as WAVES, WAACS, military nurses, and other female service branches. Addressing these initial concerns was the leading task of many advocates of female service, such as Ohio congresswoman Frances Bolton. Bolton and other women worked to minimize the potential threat female service might represent to some men. Women were not joining the military to compete with male soldiers, Bolton explained, but rather assist them with their job of protecting the country during wartime. If the presence of women in nursing and secretarial positions in the civilian sector was considered acceptable work, women asked, why should they be barred from performing these same tasks in the military? The military would still be "a fighting world for you," Congresswoman Bolton assured her male listeners, "and an assisting one for us."

Bolton and other proponents of women's service stressed that female enlistment provided a means by which thousands of male soldiers could be "freed up" to serve in combat operation, just as female factory workers had permitted more men to join the military. Declining enlistments motivated even the most conservative male military leaders to consider this point of view. By 1942, each branch of the military launched a propaganda campaign aimed at convincing Americans that women's service was not a radical departure from other modes of female employment. For example, one poster juxtaposed the image of a civilian woman taking the place of a man on an assembly line with a military woman taking place of a male soldier at a typewriter. In both instances, the man in the poster seemed taller and stronger as well as more confident and happy as he abandoned "women's work" and assumed his proper masculine role as a soldier on the front lines. Such wartime propaganda helped to win support for women's service. However, these images likely had a debilitating effect on the hundreds of thousands of male soldiers employed in clerical and service positions.

Eleanor Roosevelt took a slightly more radical view of women's military service. Roosevelt was an early proponent of the WAAC and worked to secure her husband's support for a number of suggestions she sent to the War Department throughout 1941. After years of work to convince military leaders of the usefulness of female enlistment and its consistency within traditional notions of gender, female service advocates launched offensive campaigns of their own against those who opposed their ideas. Armed with the full support of military leaders, women's rights advocates were able to place opponents of female service on the defensive. Wrapping "GI Jane" in the flag, women's service advocates challenged the patriotism of those who still opposed female service in the later years of the war. If every woman who joined meant that one more rifleman could serve on the front, they asked, how could any loyal American still oppose female enlistment?

Advocates of women's military service also presented wartime service as a way patriotic women could aid the war effort, utilizing emotional images such as sisters and wives of deceased veterans honoring fallen brothers and husbands through their service. By placing opponents of female service on the side of America's enemies, these women engineered a reversal of fortune where opponents of female service were now placed on the defensive. For example, one congressman who opposed women's service complained that he and others would not dare vote against measures to expand women's service for fear of being accused of hindering the war effort.

Women's rights advocates were also able to turn paternalistic arguments about the need to "protect" women against those who opposed equality in the ranks. If the men who opposed granting full military status to women were acting out of concern for these women, they asked, why did those men insist that women work the same clerical jobs as male soldiers but be denied the protection of veterans' benefits? Over time, most Americans recognized the valuable service women provided and supported the decision of each branch and the War Department to grant women full military status and benefits such as the GI Bill. However, many hoped that after the war was over, the military would return to the status quo with women working as civilians for the military rather than soldiers and sailors within it. They feared that changing the military's institutional gender structure would forever alter society's ideas of masculinity and traditional gender roles. Men were expected to fight as part of their role as defenders of the nation and the home according to this traditional model. Under this ideal, women were expected to support the men and play the role of the girl back home for whom each man was fighting. Female soldiers reversed the traditional image of women as the recipient of protection and likewise threatened to challenge the notion of men as protectors. For this reason, many hoped that female membership in the armed services would be limited to the war years.

FIGURE 8.9

Many images from this time period poked fun at the notion of women in the military. Winnie the WAC featured an affable but stereotypical "blonde" whose comical misadventures also poked fun at the army's inclusion of women.

The notion that women's service would be a temporary expedient originated from the initial arguments of women such as Edith Nourse Rogers. She and others who led the fight for female service were radical in their acceptance of women as members of the military who should receive equal pay and benefits. However, many of these women also accepted notions of female service as temporary, separate, and subordinate. Most advocates utilized conventional notions of gender as they tried to win over opponents, assuring them that women would be only temporary workers in auxiliary positions in a chain of command that ultimately reported to male leaders. These women generally avoided any argument that likened women's service to women's rights, and few would have considered themselves as feminists, at first. However, the service and sacrifice of 150,000 WACs, 100,000 WAVES, nearly 40,000 women within the marines and coast guard, and 75,000 military nurses convinced women's advocates and military authorities to agree that women's service was instrumental to the war effort and should continue. In 1948, Congress passed the Women's Armed Service's Integration Act, authorizing female service in all branches of the military during both peacetime and war. However, negative perceptions of female service remained long after women were permanently integrated into the military.

2.2 Japanese Americans American Internment and Military Service

FIGURE 8.10

Japanese American families awaiting baggage inspection upon arrival at an assembly center located near to the present-day campus of California State University–Stanislaus in Turlock, California.

Executive Order 9066

Issued by President Roosevelt in 1942, Executive Order 9066 granted the military the authority to remove persons of Japanese descent from the West Coast. The order also led to the arrest of 5,000 Italian and German immigrants. However, the order was primarily aimed at Japanese Americans and led to the legal internment of an estimated 120,000 people in camps from Arkansas to the West Coast.

The attack on Pearl Harbor and subsequent US defeats spread fear along the West Coast. For Japanese Americans, the news of Pearl Harbor produced a different kind of fear. In addition to sharing the concerns of their countrymen regarding the impending war and those who had lost their lives, they also feared the discrimination they had endured would now take the form of violent retribution for the attack. The FBI immediately conducted mass arrests of Japanese newspaper editors, civil rights and community leaders, even Buddhist priests. Within weeks, the government expanded its dragnet from leaders of Japanese organizations to all persons of Japanese ancestry convinced that the Japanese military were planning additional attacks with the assistance of informers within the United States. Even worse, many Americans and government officials believed that if Japan launched a full attack on the West Coast, most American residents of Japanese ancestry would welcome the invaders and take up arms against their former countrymen.

The FBI also arrested over 10,000 immigrants from Germany and Italy for similar reasons, but these investigations were based on suspicion of membership within pro-Nazi and fascist organizations, unlike the Japanese, who were arrested for association within a Japanese community organization or Buddhist church. Given the millions of Americans of Italian and German descent scattered throughout the nation, there was hardly any consideration of investigating or detaining these groups. In contrast, Japanese Americans were a much smaller minority who tended to live within 100 miles of the West Coast. Italians and Germans continued to face discrimination in America, but decades of migration combined with the common European heritage of other Americans had eroded most of the hostility these groups faced. In contrast, Japanese Americans in 1940 experienced the same racial prejudice that had led to laws restricting their entrance into the nation, including stereotypes that suggested that the Japanese were deceptive by nature. As a result, the military forced 120,000 Japanese Americans to live in detainment camps. Most of the detainees would remain in these camps for the duration of the war.

President Roosevelt issued **Executive Order 9066** on February 19, 1942, authorizing the military to designate sections of the country from which "any and all persons" might be removed. The law did not specify what everyone already understood—that this was a measure granting wide authority to officials in the War Department to force Japanese Americans to leave the West Coast. A number of Roosevelt's advisers believed that the plan was a clear violation of the civil rights of US citizens of Japanese descent and unjustified because despite the mass arrests, not one person had been proven guilty of treasonous crimes. Roosevelt instead chose to follow the advice of his military leaders and accommodate the demands of numerous West Coast politicians who aroused the angry passions of anti-Japanese prejudice in demanding the immediate removal of all persons of Japanese ancestry no matter their age, gender, or length of time as US citizens. Rumors that dozens of Japanese pilots who participated in the raid on Pearl Harbor had been US citizens were reported as fact. Americans were also surrounded by false reports that Japanese residents of Hawaii had worked behind the scenes to prevent early detection of the raid. Surrounded by fear and misinformation, few Americans questioned the military necessity of detainment or challenged the assumption that anyone of Japanese descent should be considered a suspect.

The government's removal and detainment of Japanese Americans followed a three-step process. At first, the military simply ordered Japanese Americans living on the West Coast to migrate east on their own and at their own expense. Voluntary relocation failed because few Japanese Americans agreed to leave and because residents and political leaders of various Western states protested that this would simply make their communities "vulnerable" to Japanese treachery. The government then served notice that all Japanese Americans must register and prepare to be sent to a variety of "assembly centers" operated by the War Relocation Authority (WRA). Few had more than a week to prepare for this second phase of relocation, and as a result, many were forced to sell homes and businesses for a fraction of their value. After arrival at one of eighteen assembly centers, usually fairgrounds surrounded by barbed wire where internees slept in horse stalls, people were forced to wear luggage tags indicating the internment camp to which they would be sent. Transfer to one of ten camps marked the final step of the process.

Life in the internment camps was difficult, especially for the first arrivals in May 1942 who found that their new homes were not ready for habitation. Internees were tasked with building their own camps, even building watchtowers and repairing the barbed wire that surrounded them. Most internees lived in camps in the deserts of California, Utah, and Arizona where temperatures varied from well over 100 degrees to below freezing in the same month. Others lived in swamp-like conditions near the Mississippi river or other inhabited lands. They also faced military discipline including strictly regimented schedules and inspections, a near total lack of privacy, and the arbitrary justice of armed soldiers who guarded the camps. Despite the conditions and injustice that led to their internment, Japanese Americans joined together to improve the quality of life within the camps. Of particular importance were schools, cultural activities, and recreation. Traditional Japanese sports alternated with basketball and baseball, a game played by generations of Japanese immigrants in California. Internees at the Gila River camp in Southern Arizona constructed a modern ballpark and formed several different leagues under the direction of California Kenichi Zenimura, a baseball legend who had once played with Babe Ruth; Zenimura had been detained with his family in the camp. The camp's top teams competed against and defeated army teams, as well as local high schools and colleges.

Most Americans defended this practice as vital to the defense of the nation and denied that the measure was the result of racism. African American leaders were among the strongest critics of relocation as a denial of civil rights. Native Americans shared a unique perspective as the victims of centuries of forced relocation and likewise challenged the alleged racial neutrality claimed by defenders of relocation. Others, such as General John DeWitt who administered the internment program, emphatically believed that race was the basis of the entire program. Dewitt's original memo recommending removal referred to the Japanese as "an enemy race." When questioned about why no person of Japanese ancestry had been found guilty of disloyal acts in the months that followed Pearl Harbor, he insisted that this fact merely confirmed the treachery of the Japanese, who, he contended, were simply hoping America would lower its guard. "I don't want any of them (persons of Japanese ancestry) here," he exclaimed to Congress. "They are a dangerous element.... There is no way to determine their loyalty.... It makes no difference whether he is an American citizen, he is still a Japanese...but we must worry about the Japanese all the time until he is wiped off the map."

FIGURE 8.11

The Hirano family was among the 18,000 people sent to the Poston, Arizona, internment camp. They are pictured here with a photo of a family member who served in the military. The Poston camp was located in the Sonoran Desert and was so isolated that guard towers were not constructed, although the camp was surrounded by fences.

Korematsu v. United States

A US Supreme Court Case in late 1944 in which the Court declared that the internment of Japanese Americans was justified to protect national security. Three of the nine justices dissented, viewing internment as a form of racial discrimination and a violation of the Fourteenth Amendment.

Fred Korematsu

The son of Japanese immigrants, Korematsu was born in Oakland at the end of World War II. He refused the government's order to report to a relocation center and was arrested and jailed. With the assistance of the American Civil Liberties Union, Korematsu appealed his arrest all the way to the Supreme Court, which determined in 1944 that the internment order was justified by the existence of Japanese American spies. Provided with new information detailing the absence of any Japanese American spies, however, a federal court reversed Korematsu's conviction in 1983.

442nd Infantry Regimental Combat Team

An all-Japanese American unit composed of men who had joined the military prior to the attack on Pearl Harbor that was augmented by recruits who had been living in internment camps throughout the West Coast and volunteers from Hawaii and other areas. The 442nd served with distinction in military campaigns throughout Europe, including the liberation of the Dachau concentration camp.

Thousands of Japanese Americans protested their internment from within their camp walls. The strategies they utilized varied from those who sought to demonstrate their loyalty by volunteering for military service to those who renounced their citizenship. Others followed the precedent of Native Americans by protesting forced relocation in dozens of court cases. In *Korematsu v. United States*, the Supreme Court upheld the legality of Japanese internment under the Fourteenth Amendment on December 18, 1944. The court declared that the WRA had not singled out the Japanese American defendant **Fred Korematsu** because of his race and that the exclusion of Japanese citizens from the West Coast was legal. In a second case decided on the same day, the court limited the powers of the War Relocation Authority to detain citizens whose loyalty to the United States had been proven. The wording of this second decision was intentionally vague, allowing the government to selectively release some internees long after Japan's ability to attack the United States had been eliminated.

Like other minority groups before them, Japanese Americans used logic and moral suasion to demonstrate that the discrimination they faced hurt the war effort. Among the many letters and petitions calling for their release were detailed estimates of the total cost of relocation in contrast with the potential contribution Japanese Americans could make to the war effort. Others pointed out the propaganda value the WRA provided the enemy in convincing Asian peoples to support the war effort against the Unites States. Japanese American leaders also sought to make Americans question their leaders' assurances that detainment was needed to protect their safety. If Japanese were such a threat, they reasoned, why were only a few thousand of more than 100,000 persons of Japanese descent in Hawaii detained? Hawaii was the most likely and most vulnerable target, yet the military continued to employ thousands of Japanese who were not US citizens on the very military bases that were so vital to the nation's defense. Had military officials responded to these letters, they would have tacitly admitted that these bases could not operate without the employment of persons of Japanese descent, who represented a third of the islands' population. That persons of Japanese descent continued to work on military bases throughout the Pacific while only a handful of people were ever convicted of spying for the Japanese (most of whom were Caucasian) became a powerful argument to force Americans to reconsider internment.

More than 30,000 Japanese Americans joined the war effort, the majority of whom had been forced from their homes following the attack on Pearl Harbor. Several hundred internees refused induction into the military and were soon transferred from detainment camps to prison. Those who chose to serve the nation that had detained their families joined regiments such as the 100th Battalion, which had been created earlier in the war. Prior to the inclusion of the internees, the 100th Battalion consisted primarily of second-generation Japanese who lived in Hawaii. More than 1,000 young men who were detained on the West Coast volunteered for service in late 1943 when given the opportunity and joined the **442nd Infantry Regimental Combat Team**. Together, the 14,000 men who served within this unit became some of the most highly decorated soldiers in US military history, earning more than 9,000 Purple Hearts. More than 700 Japanese American soldiers were declared missing or killed in action. The medals earned by these men were delivered to surviving family members, many of whom were still detained as "enemy aliens." Military service did not exempt one's family from internment, and so hundreds of soldiers of various backgrounds whose spouses were of Japanese origin also fought to defend a nation that detained their families.

For the 80,000 Americans of Chinese descent and the more than 100,000 who migrated from Korea, Vietnam, the Philippines, and other nations in Southeastern Asia, the attack on Pearl Harbor meant that their new home was now allied with their ancestral home against the Japanese. California residents of Filipino origin were especially motivated to defend both their homelands and formed two regiments of infantry. Thousands of other Filipinos served in various "white" regiments. Women such as Hazel Ying Lee, who had been trained as a pilot in China, flew civilian missions for the army before a mechanical failure caused a crash that ended her life. What might have led to greater acceptance of these Asian Americans and immigrants quickly turned into a nightmare as few white Americans made any effort to distinguish between people of various Asian ancestries. Tens of thousands of Asian Americans from China, Korea, and the Philippines joined the military, yet they and their families faced anti-Japanese taunts from a racially charged and misinformed public. Civilians wore Chinese flags or placed signs in their shops identifying their Korean ancestry to little avail. Even participation in anti-Japanese race-baiting did little to convince some whites that an individual was not simply masking his or her true ancestry and loyalty. Tragically, hundreds of American citizen-soldiers of various Asian ancestries learned that their families had been the targets of racially motivated crimes in letters they received while enlisted in the US military.

2.3 Native Americans

More than 25,000 residents of Native American reservations and another 20,000 Native Americans enlisted in the US armed services, a number representing nearly a third of those native men who were eligible to enlist. The Six Nations (also known as the Iroquois Confederacy) issued their own declaration of war against the Germans and Japanese. This action both demonstrated support for the American cause and emphasized the principle of Native American sovereignty and the importance of tribal governments. Just as the Choctaw had sent secret messages during World War I, Native American soldiers in World War II demonstrated the value of their cultural traditions by using their languages to send messages to one another. Navajo members of the Marine Corps are the most famous example because their complex language was understood by only a handful of non-Navajo people in the world. This complexity allowed the Navajo Marines to speak freely to one another over radio channels with little fear of the enemy deciphering their messages.

These **Code Talkers**, as they became known, adapted many of their words to represent terms used during modern warfare as they sent secret messages on behalf of Allied commanders. For example, "iron fish" represented "submarine," while individual locations could be spelled out with their own unique version of a phonetic alphabet. The Navajo language does not consist of a formal alphabet, so the code talkers would use Navajo words whose English meaning corresponded with the first letter they were trying to communicate. For example, if a code talker wanted to communicate the word "Japan," he might say "jacket-apple-planet-ant-night." German and Japanese intelligence officers knew that the military was once again using indigenous American languages as code, but failed in their efforts to recruit a single member of any of the tribes whose languages were used as code.

The 1930s were host to a number of programs aimed at restoring Native American culture, language, history, and community life within the reservations. The code talkers and the large number of well-educated young men and women who entered the military demonstrated the value of these programs. Yet these individuals and the tens of thousands of others who left the reservations to take wartime jobs in the nation's cities were a bittersweet pill for those seeking to restore native life and culture. The demands of the war reduced funding for further cultural and educational programs, while many of the would-be reservation leaders of the next generation enlisted or found wartime jobs in large cities. Many native veterans decided to take advantage of their military benefits to attend college, and some of these young folks decided to take better-paying jobs in cities throughout the country. The success of these individuals seemed to many Americans as evidence that other natives must also be "liberated" from the reservations. In the next decade, many Americans supported plans designed to close reservations in hopes of completing the process of assimilation. Most of these advocates had positive intentions, but many demonstrated a lack of respect for the agency of native people by their failure to consider the opinions of natives regarding plans for the termination of reservations.

2.4 Hispanic Americans

Military enlistment and the migration of millions from farms to cities created an emergency labor shortage for US farmers at the exact moment the nation needed to increase food production to feed its army and allies. After a decade of discouraging Mexican immigration during the Depression, the federal government now requested assistance from the Mexican government to help the US farmers recruit agricultural laborers. The Mexican government was skeptical of US intentions and worked to gain assurances that Mexican nationals working in US fields would be treated fairly and not drafted or otherwise coerced into military service. The government responded in 1942 by creating the **Bracero Program**, which recruited Mexican laborers in both agriculture and railroad construction to come to the United States.

Under the program, the federal government provided transportation for the braceros (Spanish term for manual laborers) who agreed to have 10 percent of their pay withheld and placed into an account that was to be given to them when they returned to Mexico. Government officials hoped that these deductions would provide an incentive for Mexican laborers to voluntarily leave the country after their services were no longer desired. However, many of the workers either stayed in the United States or never received their money upon return to Mexico. Furthermore, the majority of farmers in border states such as Texas rejected the terms of the Bracero Program because it mandated a minimum wage many farmers refused to pay. As a result, Texas farmers simply encouraged illegal and undocumented immigration because they felt the Bracero program was too restrictive and its terms too expensive for farmers to comply with. Historians estimate that several hundred thousand illegal immigrants entered Texas each year, in addition to an estimated 4.5 million Braceros who legally entered the United States between the war and the termination of the program in 1964.

code talkers

A generic term referring to Native Americans who utilized their indigenous languages to communicate top-secret messages for the US military during World War II. The term usually refers to Navajo members of the marines operating in the Pacific whose ability to speak directly with each other without the time-consuming use of encryption machines gave US commanders the advantage of nearly instant communication without fear of the enemy intercepting their messages.

FIGURE 8.12

General Douglas MacArthur is pictured with members of a unit composed entirely of Native American soldiers. The five troops in this photo are each from different tribes and locations throughout Arizona and Oklahoma. In this way, the unit was both segregated and a melting pot for people of diverse backgrounds.

General Douglas MacArthur, Commander-in-Chief of the Allied Forces in the Southwest Pacific Area, on an inspection trip of American battle-fronts, met representatives of five different American Indian tribes in one United States Army unit. Left to right: S/Sgt. Virgil Brown (Pima) Phoenix, Arizona; First Sergeant Virgil F. Howell (Pawnee) of Pawnee, Oklahoma; S/Sgt. Alvin J. Vilcan (Chitmatcha) of Charenton, La.; General MacArthur; Sgt. Byron L. Tsingine (Navajo) of Fort Defiance, Arizona; Sgt. Larry L. Dekin, (Navajo) of Copper Mine, Arizona. (US SIGNAL CORPS PHOTO)

Bracero Program

A federal initiative aimed at encouraging Mexican nationals to come to the United States as agricultural laborers on temporary contracts between 1942 and 1964.

FIGURE 8.13

One of many Hispanic Americans who were awarded the Medal of Honor posthumously, United States Marine Eugene Obregon used his body to shield his comrades.

More than 300,000 US officers and enlistees of Mexican descent served in World War II. The heroism of many of these men is evidenced by the awarding of more Congressional Medals of Honor to Mexican Americans than any other racial minority. Given the refusal of military officials to bestow this award on men such as **Guy Gabaldòn**, this achievement is all the more remarkable. Gabaldòn grew up in a multiethnic neighborhood in Los Angeles and was partially raised by a Japanese family who were interned during the war. Gabaldòn joined the marines and single-handedly captured hundreds of Japanese prisoners of war during the battle for Saipan in 1944. Gabaldòn used his military training to approach enemy caves and pillboxes, often sniping the guards and then calling on those inside to surrender. Few Japanese ever surrendered to US troops, but Gabaldòn's ability to speak their language helped persuade many that they were trapped and that they would not be harmed if they laid down their weapons. The navy later awarded Gabaldòn the Silver Star and the Navy Cross after a movie based on his heroics debuted in 1960. The film's success led to public demand that Gabaldòn be given the proper military recognition denied to him for sixteen years, but it also featured a white actor in the lead role.

Other Mexican Americans who grew up in Los Angeles faced discrimination of a different sort. Following a series of altercations between white servicemen and Mexican American youths early June 1943, soldiers and sailors openly roamed the streets of Los Angeles for nearly two weeks attacking any young man who appeared to be of Latino heritage. Most California newspapers inflamed the issue through sensational reporting that portrayed Mexican American youths as gang members who were attacking servicemen. Most reports neglected to mention that as many as 5,000 sailors and soldiers had entered the city with clubs and other weapons to "avenge" those who had been hurt in previous altercations. Most historians refer to the event as the **Zoot Suit Riot** due to the popular style of baggy and "flashy" clothing worn by some Mexican American youths. Others believe that because the servicemen were the leading antagonists and the Zoot Suiters were often the targets of their violence, the entire affair should be known by a different name.

Due to negative stereotypes and the criminal record of a few Zoot Suiters, the Los Angeles Police Department (LAPD) arrested hundreds of Mexican American youths throughout the week based only on their choice of clothing. In contrast, thousands of soldiers and sailors who were brandishing weapons were simply ordered back to their barracks. The riots were finally halted when area commanders declared the city off limits to military personnel. The city of Los Angeles responded by passing an ordinance that banned residents from wearing zoot suit. Despite the injunction, Mexican American youths were ordered to stand trial wearing the same baggy clothing in which they had been arrested. The mayor defended the police in a statement declaring that all young men on the streets wearing the now infamous zoot suit would be arrested. Eleanor Roosevelt cautioned Americans that the problem of Los Angeles was much deeper than clothing and deplored the conditions surrounding the trials of the convicted youths. Although her editorial was praised by many as an eloquent and thoughtful analysis, others deplored her use of the term *race riot* and felt her criticism of the LAPD was evidence that the first lady was a Communist sympathizer.

2.5 African Americans and World War II

Many of the soldiers who attacked Mexican American youths also terrorized young black men as they roamed through Los Angeles and San Diego. Each of the various sociological explanations for the violence in California—racial profiling by police, job competition, immigration of racial minorities, segregated neighborhoods, and housing shortages—were problems faced by African Americans in most of the nation's leading cities. Fifty-thousand black residents moved to Detroit within a few short years, but the city's pattern of residential segregation had not changed. Black newcomers typically sought homes in neighborhoods where they felt welcome, and even those willing to integrate white neighborhoods seldom found housing outside established black neighborhoods. These neighborhoods were quickly overwhelmed as millions of black families moved north and west to take advantage of wartime jobs.

Those black families who sought homes outside the "black" areas of town were frequently attacked. In 1942, a new housing project in Detroit named after Sojourner Truth sparked violence when area white residents vowed to prevent black families from moving into "their" neighborhood. The following year, the city exploded in racial violence that led to the deaths of nine whites and twenty-five blacks after a series of altercations in the city park turned several inner-city neighborhoods into battlegrounds. Six blacks were killed in similar racially motivated violence in Harlem. Meanwhile, a white mob in Beaumont, Texas, murdered two residents as they rampaged through the black section of town in an effort to enforce the informal border between a white and black neighborhood.

America was quickly becoming an arsenal, but for millions of African Americans who were still out of work in 1939 and 1940, this arsenal was anything but democratic. For example, in 1940, only a few hundred black workers were employed in the aircraft industry, which employed 100,000 whites. In response to the thousands of companies engaged in defense production that still refused to hire African Americans or relegated them to the lowest-paying jobs, black labor leader A. Philip Randolph proposed a different kind of strike. "Black people will not get justice until the administration leaders in Washington see masses of Negroes—ten, twenty, fifty thousand—on the White House lawn." Randolph predicted that a massive protest march at the nation's capital would expose the hypocrisy of a government claiming to support free-market principles and democracy. The march would reveal that the United States did not follow its own principles of equality concerning employment. The march threatened Roosevelt's desired international image for America as the defender of freedom and democracy by exposing segregation and discrimination at home. In exchange for Randolph's promise to cancel the march, Roosevelt issued **Executive Order 8802** outlawing racial discrimination by any employer who received defense contracts. The order created the Fair Employment Practices Committee (FEPC) to ensure compliance. Although this agency was severely underfunded and discrimination in private industry continued, Roosevelt's was the first significant presidential order prohibiting racial discrimination since Reconstruction.

Randolph's fight for equal opportunity in employment was a leading example of the **Double V** campaign—a call by black leaders to make World War II a battle for freedom at home and abroad. Black soldiers were fighting for victory against Fascism abroad, the African American newspaper the *Pittsburgh Courier* explained. The national black press echoed the *Courier*'s call to arms and called on their readers to ensure victory against tyranny in America. The NAACP expanded from 30,000 members to nearly half a million members. Black suffrage had been curtailed since Reconstruction due to violence as well as laws and practices that effectively prohibited black voting, yet voter drives helped to increase registration in the South from 2 percent to 12 percent of eligible black voters.

Despite these efforts, the voices of most Southern blacks and even some of these registrants were still effectively silenced at the polls. One of the most subtle but pernicious ways blacks were disenfranchised was that some Southern political parties restricted membership to whites. In Southern states where most residents were members of one political party (usually the Democratic Party at this time), the winner of that party's primary election almost always prevailed in the general election. With the assistance of the NAACP, civil rights attorneys convinced the Supreme Court in 1944 that denying blacks the vote in primary elections violated the Fourteenth and Fifteenth Amendments in the landmark case *Smith v. Allwright*.

This new militancy also led to the formation of the **Congress of Racial Equality (CORE)**, the first national, interracial civil rights organization since the formation of the NAACP. Unlike the NAACP, however, CORE was largely composed of young adults who attended Northern and Western colleges. These young people believed that direct action rather than lawsuits was the key to challenging racial segregation. CORE members launched sit-ins in Northern cities such as Chicago, border cities such as Cincinnati, and smaller towns such as Wichita and Lawrence, Kansas. In each instance, black students went to restaurants known for refusing service to African Americans and sat down until they were arrested, beaten, or served.

Proprietors in most of these cities could seldom have the students arrested because Illinois, Ohio, and Kansas, like many other Northern states, had passed civil rights laws in the 1870s and 1880s that outlawed racial discrimination in places of public accommodation. At the same time, law enforcement generally refused to do anything to enforce the civil rights laws. As a result, the students occupied booths for days until each owner finally decided it was in their best financial interest to change their policy and follow the existing but seldom enforced state civil rights laws. Sit-ins also occurred in former slaves states such as Missouri and Kentucky during World War II but resulted in only limited concessions until the 1950s.

African Americans attempted boycotts and others forms of consumer protest to force white-controlled businesses to end segregation and hire black workers throughout the first half of the twentieth century with little success. However, with unemployment nearing its all-time low as wages surpassed record highs, black communities enjoyed a new level of consumer prosperity during World War II. This prosperity, combined with the wartime assertiveness of the Double-V campaign, the creation of local civil rights groups affiliated with CORE, and the exponential growth of the NAACP, led to renewed campaigns to force companies that did business in black communities to end discrimination against black customers and prospective black employees. From Harlem to Houston, black consumers refused to shop at stores located within black communities until they agreed to hire black workers.

Public transportation and utility companies that refused to hire African Americans were especially targeted by civil rights groups due to their regulation by local government and their dependence on black customers. For example, St. Louis residents protested against the refusal of Southwestern Bell to hire African Americans in 1943. The protest began with petitions and letters and later expanded to protest stickers affixed to customer's monthly payments. These stickers highlighted the irony of a

Executive Order 8802

Issued by President Franklin Delano Roosevelt in response to a campaign waged by black labor leaders such as A. Philip Randolph, Executive Order 8802 banned racial discrimination among employers and contractors who did business with the federal government.

Smith v. Allwright

Lonnie Smith of Houston sued local election official S. S. Allwright in 1940 for the latter's refusal to permit Smith to vote in the Democratic primary. The Democratic Party of Texas claimed that its explicit restriction against black voting did not violate the Fifteenth Amendment because the party was a private organization. The Supreme Court disagreed because primary elections were regulated by the state and therefore must follow Constitutional provisions banning racial discrimination. As a result, the Supreme Court's decision guaranteed the right to vote in primary elections regardless of race.

Congress of Racial Equality (CORE)

An interracial civil rights organization founded in 1942 by James Farmer and others who sought to utilize the same nonviolent protest methods employed by Gandhi in India. CORE sponsored major protests beginning with the 1947 Freedom Ride that tested a recent court decision banning segregation on buses traveling from one state to another.

FIGURE 8.14

This poster by a Chicago National Association for the Advancement of Colored People (NAACP) branch demonstrates the way African Americans sought to connect the nation's war against fascism abroad with their ongoing fight against discrimination at home.

FIGURE 8.15

African American fighter pilots attending a briefing in Italy. These men were known collectively as the "Tuskegee Airmen" due to the location of the training school for black pilots at Tuskegee University in Alabama.

nation fighting for democracy abroad yet denying its own citizen jobs at home, protesting the company's "undemocratic, un-American and pro-Hitler employment policy."

The protest that followed illustrated the creativity of many civil rights protests. Hundreds of black customers marched to the Southwestern Bell's St. Louis headquarters and declared that they would start paying their phone bills in pennies until management started employing black workers. Local college students helped coordinate the protest, which required thousands of pounds of pennies and special redemption centers where bill payers could exchange their cash for more pennies. Before long, businesses and banks throughout the city were running out of pennies and protesters appealed to family and friends in neighboring cities for assistance. The protest soon crippled Bell's billing center, and the company relented and began hiring African Americans.

While each of these sit-ins and "pay-ins" were small and local victories, the deeper significance of what was at stake is best expressed by a returning World War II veteran who experienced Jim Crow while on his way home from the war. Traveling through Texas, Lieutenant Lacey Wilson stopped for a meal and was ordered to go to the back door of the restaurant. As he walked back to the train, he noticed a number of captured German soldiers en route to a prison farm who were in the restaurant with their military police escorts. Wilson was shocked to see that these German troops were sitting at one of the same tables where he had just been refused service. "It sickened me so I could not eat a bite after ordering," Wilson recalled. "I was a citizen soldier in the uniform of my country and I had to go through an alley to the back door while some of Hitler's storm troopers lapped up the hospitality of my country." A similar incident occurred when German POWs were seated in front of black soldiers at a concert by Lena Horne until the singer protested and military authorities corrected the situation.

In 1944, three hundred black seamen were killed while loading ammunition in San Francisco due to the failure of a white officer appointed over these men to follow basic safety regulations. Incidents such as these made black men and women question for whose freedom they were fighting. Thousands of black men returning from the war experienced severe discrimination while still in uniform, and at least a dozen veterans were lynched by whites who felt black military service threatened white supremacy.

Perhaps no black leader expressed both hope and disillusionment better than the aging W. E. B. Du Bois who had called on members of his race to "close ranks" and support America's war effort in 1917. A generation later, Du Bois challenged the notion that defeating Germany would promote freedom for people of African descent throughout the world. "If this is a war for freedom," Du Bois exclaimed after defining what freedom meant to people of color in America and Africa, "my gun is on my shoulder." Those who best knew the seventy-four-year-old Du Bois understood that his offer to join a military that fought for an end to racism and colonialism was as genuine as his attempt to become an officer in World War I at age fifty. Du Bois also embraced Socialism by this time and increasingly viewed the war as America assisting Capitalist and imperialistic nations like Britain and France in its fight against the imperialistic powers of Germany and Japan.

The US military continued its policy of segregated units throughout both world wars. Similar to the first war, black leaders demanded and eventually received the commitment of military leaders to commission black officers to lead black units. Black women joined segregated units of women's branches, and like black men, were often relegated to service positions regardless of previous training or skill. Only a campaign led by **Mabel K. Staupers** convinced the military to accept black women as nurses, a decision also influenced by white officials who feared white nurses among black soldiers could lead to interracial dating. However, the two most famous black military units were the 99th Pursuit Squadron, commonly known as the **Tuskegee Airmen**, and the 761st Tank Battalion.

Black leaders pushed the army to make good on the "equal" portion of its separate-but-equal philosophy by training black men for the most respected combat positions as tank drivers and fighter pilots. The military set up flight schools at several historically black institutions, such as Howard University and West Virginia State College, with graduates moving on to train at Tuskegee before earning their wings and fighting German pilots. These men flew more than 1,500 missions escorting bombers. The Tuskegee Airmen shot down or destroyed nearly three hundred enemy aircraft and lost more than one hundred of their own men in combat.

An article in the *Chicago Defender* toward the end of the war made the claim that none of the bombers these men escorted was ever shot down. This seemingly impossible feat has been repeated as fact since it was printed in 1945. Historians have been reticent to challenge this claim because the story of the Tuskegee Airmen has so convincingly demonstrated the bankruptcy of contemporary theories of black inferiority. The fact that a small number of bombers were indeed lost, either from enemy aircraft or from antiaircraft fire that came from the ground and could not be prevented by fighter pilots, does nothing to tarnish the record of the Tuskegee Airmen. Both military records and oral histories attest that the men of this unit were among the most elite fighter pilots in the service.

Likewise, the valor and skill of the 761st Tank Battalion proved critical in rescuing the trapped 101st Airborne in the Battle of the Bulge. Yet despite the service of a million black women and men, discrimination and segregation permeated nearly every aspect of military life. Even UCLA sports star turned US Army officer Jackie Robinson faced daily slights from white servicemen. White personnel denied Robinson's request to play baseball for the otherwise all-white Fort Riley baseball team and court-martialed Robinson in Texas after he refused to move to the back of a bus, which was contractually obligated to be integrated in the first place. Robinson, like the other million black veterans of World War II, resolved that he would not stop fighting tyranny once his military service was complete.

Black servicewomen likewise vowed to fight racism when they returned home. Although black women eventually comprised about 10 percent of female recruits, their service was actively discouraged by military officials throughout the war. Southern newspaper publisher Oveta Hobby served as the first director of the WAC. The NAACP and National Council of Negro Women led by Mary McLeod Bethune opposed her appointment because Oveta Hobby was the wife of a Texas governor who had a poor track record regarding race. Hobby hoped to win the support of black critics and thought that her announcement that black women might comprise as much as 10 percent of the first WAAC recruits would demonstrate her commitment to equality. However, her acceptance of the army's policy of segregation and announcement of what appeared to be racial quotas received heavy criticism in the black press.

Hobby and other WAC leaders were actually open to the possibility of racial integration, but they feared that such a stand might jeopardize their entire program. They also feared that large numbers of black recruits would discourage white women from enlisting. The WACs refusal to be more progressive on matters of race proved a major lost opportunity for the WAC and the military as a whole. Research into the opinions black newspapers throughout the nation expressed demonstrate that African Americans were more favorably disposed to women's service in the military than whites were. However, after the WAC and other women's service branches announced that they would not challenge the military's segregation policies, the support these women enjoyed within the black community was greatly reduced.

Mabel K. Staupers

President of the National Association of Colored Graduate Nurses, the leading professional organization for black nurses during the era of segregation, Staupers led the successful fight to open the nursing corps of the armed services to black women.

Tuskegee Airmen

African American combat pilots belonging to the 332nd Fighter Group and the 447th Medium Bombardment Group trained near Tuskegee University in Alabama. In an era when many white Americans assumed that few African Americans possessed the skill, courage, leadership, and intelligence required to be officers and fighter pilots, the Tuskegee Airmen battled both racism and Fascism by compiling an exemplary record in combat operations in Europe during World War II.

FIGURE 8.16

Black officers inspect their troops in England. This was the first unit of African American WACs assigned overseas.

2.6   Jewish Americans and the Holocaust

FIGURE 8.17

Jewish refugees aboard the SS *St. Louis* were permitted to leave Hitler's Germany in 1939. They intended to seek asylum in Cuba but were denied. They later appealed to the United States but were also denied asylum due to strict quotas in the number of Jewish migrants that were permitted to enter the nation at this time. After being denied asylum in the United States they were forced to return to Europe where many were later sent to concentration camps.

War Refugee Board

Established by the federal government in 1944, the War Refugee Board worked with international Jewish organizations and foreign governments to help rescue Jews and others who were at risk of being sent to German concentration camps.

Jewish Americans also experienced discrimination in and out of the military. For many, theirs was a personal fight against Hitler's attempt to exterminate the Jews of Europe. By early 1942, German military officials had transformed concentration camps into death camps. An estimated 6 million European Jews were murdered in poison chambers and crematoriums throughout Poland and Eastern Europe. Others were subjected to medical experiments to test the reaction of the human body to extreme temperatures, biological weapons, fire, radiation, and rapid altitude changes. Children and pregnant women were special victims of experiments designed to test fertility and childhood diseases because Hitler hoped to use these scientific experiments to study the body's ability to recover from wartime injuries and promote fertility and childhood immunity among members of his "master race."

As Russian troops liberated the survivors of Nazi concentration camps in Eastern Europe throughout 1945, reports confirming the suspected brutality of the Final Solution produced strong reactions of outrage and denial in Americans. For the last decade, Americans had demonstrated a different kind of denial, relegating news of German atrocities against Jewish citizens to the back pages of newspapers. Thanks to the efforts of Jewish organizations such as the American Jewish Committee, intelligence reports confirming Hitler's intention to exterminate the Jews remained in front of the US public throughout the war.

With few exceptions, Americans supported the continuation of immigration quotas and other restrictions that prevented tens of thousands of Jewish refugees from entering the country during the 1930s and throughout World War II. After newspapers stopped printing these reports as news, Jewish leaders purchased full-page advertisements detailing the killing with headings such as "How Well Are You Sleeping? Is There Something You Could Have Done to Save Millions of Innocent People from Torture and Death?" Congresswoman Edith Nourse Rogers and others failed in their attempts to modify immigration restrictions to allow Jewish refugees to enter the United States until 1944. At this time, Jewish leaders convinced Rogers's peers in Congress and President Roosevelt to lift immigration restrictions against Jewish refugees and create the **War Refugee Board**. Other Americans donated money to international Jewish groups who waged secret operations in Nazi-held territory.

REVIEW AND CRITICAL THINKING

1. It has been said that armies usually reflect the societies they defend. Was the military a progressive organization in terms of race, ethnicity, and gender, or did it simply mirror the larger society? How did the personnel demands of the military influence the experiences of women, homosexuals, and minorities?

2. In what ways might World War II be viewed as the origin of the civil rights movement? How did various racial and ethnic groups attempt to connect wartime service and the rhetoric of US leaders to their fight for equal rights?

3. Explain the reasons why the US government chose to intern Japanese Americans. Review the government's handling of the issue of "enemy aliens" in Hawaii and the West Coast and how it affected the war.

4. Referring to the way that wartime demand led many US companies to hire black women for the first time, one African American woman responded to a question about the meaning of the war by saying that "Hitler was the one that got us out of white folks' kitchens." How does this oral history source explain the importance of the war to black economic mobility? What else does this quote tell us about the importance of job opportunities for black women beyond domestic service?

3.   D-DAY TO VICTORY

LEARNING OBJECTIVES

1. Explain how Soviet forces were able to halt the German advance and capture a large German army at the Battle of Stalingrad. Explain the strategic importance of this battle.
2. Explain why the United States invaded North Africa instead of directly attacking the German-occupied beaches of Europe. Describe the impact of the North African campaign on the war.
3. Survey the military history of the Western Front from D-Day to the surrender of Germany. Explain the German strategy and why Allied forces prevailed.
4. Summarize the Pacific Theater of the war. Explain the purpose of the "Island-Hopping" campaign. Explain why aircraft carriers and securing airfields were important, and discuss Truman's decision to drop atomic bombs on Hiroshima and Nagasaki.

3.1   Stalingrad and the Eastern Front

Hitler's strategy was based largely on attacking in places German enemies did not expect attack. As a result, German offensives against Moscow and Leningrad were secondary to the German offensive at the **Battle of Stalingrad**. Hitler focused his efforts on Stalingrad for three main reasons. First, it was named after his archrival and the leader of the Soviet Union. Second, the city was a leading industrial center. Last and most importantly, its location between the oil reserves of the Caucasus and the Volga River meant that control of the city meant access to oil. Control of the city would secure access to the oil-rich regions south of Stalingrad as well as the Volga River from just south of Moscow to Stalingrad.

Battle of Stalingrad

One of the major turning points of World War II, the Battle of Stalingrad began in August 1942 when the German army sought to seize control of the city of Stalingrad. Although they controlled much of the city, Soviet forces launched a counteroffensive that surrounded Stalingrad and forced 100,000 German troops to surrender.

FIGURE 8.18

Stalingrad was strategically located on the Volga River between the Black Sea and the Caspian Sea. As this map indicates, German troops approached from the west and hoped to capture the city and control this vital gateway to the oil-rich Caucasus region Southwestern Asia.

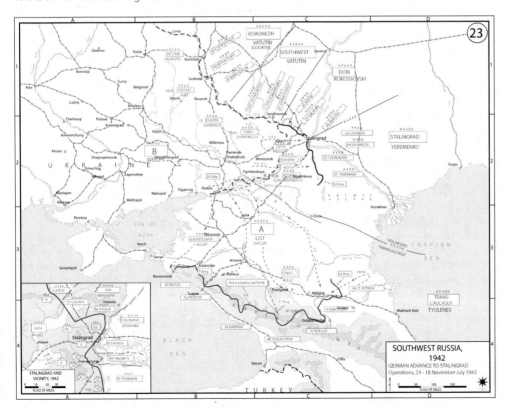

The German offensive began in the summer of 1942 with artillery attacks and bombing raids that destroyed most of the buildings. Believing that preventing civilians from leaving the city was critical to preventing his officers from surrendering the town that bore his name, Stalin positioned troops across the river with orders to fire upon soldiers and civilians who sought to flee east. Stalin meanwhile sent increasingly frustrated dispatches to Roosevelt, asking when US forces might open a second front in Europe to aid his overwhelmed armies. Although the first US bombing raid on German-held territory occurred in August 1942, these bombs caused minimal damage and US troops would not enter France until the summer of 1944.

As a result, the Russians continued to endure the brunt of the Nazi offensive throughout 1942. By October, the Germans controlled the majority of the city. Despite what appeared to be an inevitable German victory, German success actually played to the Russian strategy. Understanding that they could not defeat the Germans in the open, Russian commanders welcomed an urban battle where the battle lines between the two armies would be blurred. Historians have labeled the strategy as "hugging the enemy," as Russian commanders realized that an urban war where Germans and Russians fought hand to hand among a civilian population neutralized the advantages of the technologically superior German forces. The Luftwaffe and German artillery could not fire upon the city if German troops occupied the majority of Stalingrad, thereby allowing Russian fighters disguised as civilians to move throughout the destroyed city and fire upon German troops.

With the majority of the German army inside of the city, the Soviets launched a massive counterattack with fresh divisions of Russian troops storming in from all directions to surround the German army inside the city. Hitler ordered his troops to fight to the last man; but given the cold weather and their increasingly untenable situation, nearly 100,000 Germans surrendered. The Soviets lost more than a million lives in the entire campaign, but the German surrender proved to be the turning point of the Eastern Front. Following the German defeat at Stalingrad, Hitler's momentum was halted as winter set in. Germany's supply lines were perilously thin and the Russian winter made it difficult to transport supplies. Most important, German forces failed to quickly overwhelm the much larger Russian army that now prepared for a counterattack along the 1,000-mile front from Stalingrad to St. Petersburg in the north.

3.2   Bataan to the Battle of Midway

Bataan Death March

A forced march of 75,000 US and Filipino prisoners of war across the Bataan Peninsula. The Japanese captors had little food or water that they could provide to the prisoners. The march is considered a war crime because many of the captors chose to beat or bayonet their prisoners, a practice that may have killed as many as a quarter of the men to die before reaching their destination.

Doolittle Raid

A small-scale bombing raid against the island of Japan launched from an aircraft carrier in retaliation for the attack on Pearl Harbor. The Doolittle Raid was so named not because of the minimal damage of sixteen bombers that carried more auxiliary fuel tanks than bombs, but rather because of the intrepid spirit of the mission's commander James Doolittle and his men.

Both before and after the attack on Pearl Harbor, Japan captured many areas on the coast of Asia, such as Vietnam, as well as numerous islands throughout the Pacific. In the Philippines, US and Filipino troops were surrounded by Japanese invaders and retreated to Corregidor Island. The situation went from desperate to nearly hopeless by March 1942. Ten thousand men had perished, and Washington predicted that the entire US garrison might soon be captured. The navy had no method to evacuate such a large force given Japan's control of the South Pacific at this time, and so President Roosevelt ordered General Douglas MacArthur to abandon his men in the Philippines and reestablish a command post in the safety of Australia. The navy could not provide escape for the 70,000 US and Filipino soldiers who were subsequently captured and forced to walk eighty miles without food or water. Although many of the Japanese troops also lacked supplies on this journey, the actions of many Japanese who bayoneted and clubbed US soldiers during what would soon be known as the **Bataan Death March** demonstrated the cruelty that had been inflicted by the Japanese on their enemies. Nearly a third of the survivors of the march perished in prisoner of war camps due to malnutrition and torture.

There was little that Americans could do in response to Bataan given the state of the Pacific fleet. Attacks on Japanese-held territory could only be launched from aircraft carriers, but America could not send these ships near Japan or any island controlled by the Japanese or they would easily be destroyed. In April 1942, the navy commander James Doolittle engineered a small-scale surprise attack on Tokyo that was later named the **Doolittle Raid**. The navy modified sixteen bombers so they could fly all the way to Japan. There was just one problem: to keep the aircraft carrier out of range of Japanese carriers, the pilots would have to fly halfway across the Pacific, crash land in China, and fend for themselves. Doolittle and his men also understood that bombers were not designed to take off from aircraft carrier decks. Understanding all these risks, these men successfully flew over Japan and dropped a few small bombs that damaged little more than Japan's sense of invulnerability. Given the disastrous events of the Pacific war up to this time, the Doolittle Raid at least let Americans know that their navy had responded to Pearl Harbor with an attack of their own.

FIGURE 8.19

Despite modern impressions of fully mechanized German Panzer units that combined tanks and armored infantry units, very few of Germany's infantry units were motorized in 1939. German supply trains were dependent on horses and mules, as were the British, French, and Russian armies at this time.

By May 1942, Americans had more substantial news to celebrate when US carriers forced the Japanese to retreat in the Battle of the Coral Sea. The victory was bittersweet, however, as the United States lost more ships including an aircraft carrier. Japanese naval officers hoped to destroy the remaining carriers and complete their initial objective against Pearl Harbor of crippling the Pacific Fleet. Unknown to them, however, American intelligence had broken one of the Japanese codes and were able to communicate many of their battle plans to **Admiral Chester Nimitz**. In May 1942, Nimitz learned that the Japanese carriers were among a fleet of nearly two hundred ships that were heading toward the tiny but strategic US base on Midway Island. If Japan succeeded in taking Midway, the Japanese could use the island to launch attacks against Hawaii, which the Japanese believed would force the Americans to end the war on their terms.

Admiral Chester Nimitz

Commander of the US Pacific fleet during World War II, Nimitz became the highest-ranking officer in the navy when he was promoted to Fleet Admiral and would later accept the surrender of Japanese forces aboard the USS *Missouri*.

FIGURE 8.20

The red line in this map depicts the extent of territory controlled by the Japanese prior to the American victory at Midway. After nearly eliminating the Japanese aircraft carrier fleet, the US Navy and Marine Corps began their offensive.

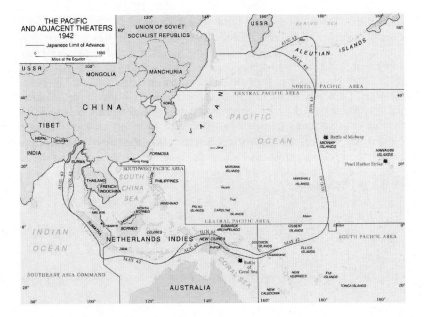

Battle of Midway

A major turning point in the Battle of the Pacific, US forces sunk four Japanese aircraft carriers and defended their airfield on the small island of Midway. US forces had been forewarned of the Japanese attack against Midway due to code-breakers, and the US Navy lost only one carrier.

Nimitz only possessed two undamaged aircraft carriers, which were in the South Pacific. In addition to the *Yorktown*, a third carrier that was heavily damaged, there was also *Saratoga*, which was undergoing major repairs and would not be available. Crews raced to repair the *Yorktown* while Nimitz ordered the scattered US fleet to intercept the Japanese force. Given the numerical superiority of the Japanese fleet, an offensive was risky as it meant the two or three US carriers would both be outnumbered. Nimitz had the advantage of knowing Japan's plans, however, while his Japanese counterparts believed that the US carriers were likely not in the area. During the **Battle of Midway**, the additional planes launched from the three US carriers surprised the Japanese fleet and sunk all four of its carriers, while the Americans lost only the *Yorktown*. The Japanese fleet now only possessed two aircraft carriers, and the Americans still held three. Midway proved the turning point in the Battle of the Pacific as the Japanese fleet could no longer threaten US bases in the central Pacific. Yamamoto's hope that the war with America would be quick was now dashed. He was forced to retreat to within Japan's defensive perimeter and prepare for a long war against an industrial power that launched seventeen large and eleven medium carriers in the next two years.

3.3 North Africa to D-Day

In the first year of the war, German submarines had an easy time sinking Allied ships in the Atlantic. This greatly limited America's ability to provide supplies for Britain and Russia and increased the dangers of sending troops across the Atlantic. As they had done during World War I, US forces utilized the convoy system, which grouped many ships together escorted by fleets of destroyers armed with depth-charges. These convoys would prove even more effective due to the British and American invention of sonar, which was able to detect submarines from miles away. Sonar and the convoy system combined to allow US warships to destroy more German submarines than German factories could produce. In addition, supply and attack vessels were rolling off American assembly lines at astonishing rates that gave the Americans supremacy in this ongoing **Battle of the Atlantic**. The 2,700 Liberty Ships America built between 1941 and 1945 represented three times more cargo-carrying capacity than all of the 3,500 merchant ships the Germans sank during the entire war. By 1943, the US Navy effectively controlled the Atlantic Ocean, allowing US military officials to concentrate men and material in Britain and North Africa in preparation for major offensives against Germany and Italy.

Battle of the Atlantic

An ongoing contest between the German navy and Allied convoys throughout World War II, the Battle of the Atlantic featured tens of thousands of Allied cargo ships and troop transports that were escorted across the Atlantic Ocean. The goal of the German navy was to sink as many of these ships as possible and, by so doing, force the island nation of Britain to surrender for lack of supplies and/or convince Americans that the war was too costly.

Italy entered World War II after Hitler had nearly completed his conquest of France, yet in many ways, Italian aggression helped to initiate World War II and spread the conflict from Europe to Africa. In 1934, Italian dictator Benito Mussolini initiated a confrontation between his forces in the Italian colony of Somaliland and border guards in neighboring Ethiopia. Ethiopia had successfully defended itself against a previous invasion by Mussolini and remained the only independent African nation besides Liberia, which had been established as a refuge for former American slaves. The League of Nations condemned Italy and attempted to negotiate a peaceful resolution, yet the League had no military force. Mussolini used the border clash as a pretense to invade Ethiopia in 1935, and the League offered little more than verbal support for Ethiopian leader Haile Selassie's attempts to defend his nation. The League eventually recommended that its members refuse to trade with Italy. Had these nations and others such as the United States applied economic sanctions against Italy, Mussolini might have been forced to reconsider the Italian invasion. Instead, the only significant aid came from African Americans who raised money for weapons and medical supplies.

Atlantic Charter

An agreement made between Franklin Delano Roosevelt and Winston Churchill prior to America's entry into World War II. The agreement articulated the goals of the United States and Britain in their conflict against Germany and stipulated that neither nation would seek to increase its territory once Germany was defeated.

After Italy and Germany sealed their alliance in 1940, the Axis powers controlled North Africa. Given the immense coastline and vast deserts of North Africa, the anti-Nazi sentiment of the local population, and the fact that the French still controlled the African colonies of Morocco and Algeria, many military planners believed North Africa provided the best opportunity to land Allied troops and open a second front against the Germans. In August 1941, Roosevelt and Churchill met aboard a US naval vessel and discussed this strategy. They also composed a list of eight principles they hoped the world would follow should Nazi Germany be defeated to prevent future conflicts. This agreement was referred to in the following years as the **Atlantic Charter** and called free access to markets, disarmament, and democracy and self-determination for those lands presently occupied by the Axis Powers. Critics pointed out that these principles were not extended to British overseas colonies or the US-controlled areas such as the Philippines.

Churchill and Roosevelt met regularly once America joined the war against Germany, and both agreed in 1942 that their militaries were not yet prepared to launch an attack on German-occupied France. The US military settled upon **Operation Torch**, an invasion of French North Africa under the command of **General Dwight D. Eisenhower**. The goal of this operation was not to defeat the officially neutral French, but to land troops on the continent and push east against German forces on the northeastern corner of Africa. More than 100,000 US and British troops landed in Morocco and Algeria in November 1942. The landings were poorly executed and would have led to horrific casualties had they not been initiated against French colonial commanders who ordered token resistance so as not to violate the orders of Hitler's puppet government in Vichy. The French actually viewed the Allied troops as potential liberators and did what they could to covertly help the British and the Americans as they moved east in pursuit of Germany's Afrika Corps commanded by **Erwin Rommel**. US troops continued to arrive in North Africa, and they vastly outnumbered Italian and German armies until what remained of the Afrika Corps surrendered in May of 1943.

The Allied victory in North Africa resulted in US and British forces holding Tunisia, just south across the Mediterranean, from Mussolini's Italy. Allied forces were hesitant to attack the strongly entrenched German army in France and believed that Italian forces would be much easier to defeat. Roosevelt understood that his arsenal of democracy was still under construction and believed that a direct offensive against German-occupied France would lead to unacceptably high casualties. Instead, he and Churchill planned an attack against Italy, which they derisively labeled "the soft underbelly of the Axis." The Allies began with a successful attack against Sicily but failed to spread their invasion to Italy as quickly as they had planned due to German reinforcements. However, as US troops began to arrive in Sicily in large numbers, the Italian people rebelled against the leadership of Mussolini and his alliance with Hitler. The Italians forced Mussolini into exile, and the new Italian government aligned itself with the United States and Britain as US troops entered Italy in September 1943. Now that the Italians were fighting against the Germans, Hitler treated Italy like conquered territory. He rushed more troops southward to prevent the Allies from advancing through Italy and toward Germany. The "soft underbelly" of Europe featured difficult mountain terrain, which greatly aided the Nazi defenders. The Allies finally liberated Rome in June 1944. However, German troops continued their resistance, and it quickly became clear that the Allied path to Berlin would have to go through France rather than the narrow mountain corridors of Italy.

3.4   D-Day to Victory in Europe

The Western Allies had repeatedly assured Stalin that they would attack German-occupied France, which would relieve pressure from the Soviet Red Army by requiring Hitler to transfer troops away from the Eastern Front. Given the codename Operation Overlord, the campaign to land US and British troops on the French coast presented US forces with the greatest challenge of the war. The landing would be heavily opposed by German defenders throughout the Atlantic Wall. This line of coastal defenses featured fortifications manned by artillery, machine guns, tanks, antiaircraft guns, and divisions of well-rested German soldiers. As a result, the Allies built up a massive invasion force and even a second "dummy" invasion force to distract the Germans from the actual invasion. Double agents, false radio transmissions, and an armada of hollow wooden models resembling ships, tanks, and planes convinced the Germans that the main attack would occur at Calais. The ruse worked because Calais was the most logical choice given its proximity to Britain and the narrowness of the British Channel at this point. In addition, US paratroopers landed behind enemy lines to destroy communication lines, spread misinformation regarding the attack, and soften the German defenses.

The much-anticipated cross-channel invasion from Britain to German-occupied France occurred on **D-Day**, June 6, 1944. The invasion occurred in a region of France known as Normandy and involved thousands of landing craft, 600 warships, and 12,000 planes. Paratroopers belonging to the 82nd and 101st Airborne Divisions landed behind enemy lines the night before to disrupt communications and prevent or delay German reinforcements. The entire weight of the British and US navies and air forces unleashed a constant barrage of fire on the German defenders, while wave after wave of infantry stormed five beaches. These men ran directly into the teeth of the German army and the million rounds of ammunition fired by entrenched defenders.

Operation Torch

The British and US invasion of French North Africa in November 1942. The intent of the campaign was to land forces on the French colonies of Morocco and Algeria in preparation for an attack against Axis forces in Tunisia.

General Dwight D. Eisenhower

Five-star general and Supreme Commander of Allied forces in Western Europe during World War II. Eisenhower directed the Normandy Invasion on D-Day and the subsequent Allied campaigns in France and Germany. Regarded as a war hero, Eisenhower became president of Columbia University before agreeing to join the Republican Party and accepting their nomination for US president. He and running mate Richard Nixon defeated Democrat Adlai Stevenson in the 1952 and 1956 elections.

Erwin Rommel

German Field Marshal who led North African forces to several victories against Allied forces despite tremendous disadvantages. His ability to delay the Allied victory over his Afrika Corps led to the nickname "The Desert Fox," and he is widely regarded as one of the ablest military commanders during World War II. Many believe that Rommel was ordered to commit suicide after the war turned against Germany and after he was implicated in a 1944 plot to kill Hitler.

D-Day

An amphibious landing of US and British forces along a fifty-mile coastline in Normandy, France, on June 6,1944. German defenders enjoyed fortified positions, but Allied forces quickly overwhelmed the German defenders and secured a beachhead that was used to land more troops and heavy equipment.

FIGURE 8.21

The D-Day invasion took place in the highlighted region of Normandy. Numerous efforts were made by US forces to convince the Germans that the attack would take place near Calais, France, which seemed a logical choice given its location near the British coast.

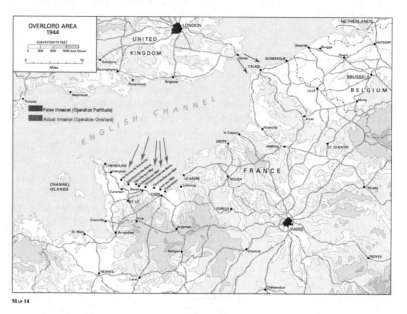

Map 14

General George S. Patton

A leading US general during the Allied campaigns in North Africa and Sicily, Patton led the US Third Army in its rescue of the US troops surrounded during the Battle of the Bulge. Patton is most remembered for speaking his mind and his aggressive style of personal leadership.

The success of the operation was due to the heroism and sacrifice of these first waves of troops who secured the beach against mines and German machine guns. Given the overwhelming superiority of men and equipment, the Allies could now land at Normandy; US and British soldiers were able to break through the German defenses and push inland. By the first day, 150,000 men had cleared a tiny strip of the coast and prepared to confront the German reinforcements that were en route. In the next two months, a million US and British troops would arrive in France and enter the fight against the retreating German line. In August 1944, US soldiers under **General George S. Patton** reached Paris. The Allies controlled most of France by October. The US advance also reduced the number of troops Hitler could deploy against the Soviets, who continued their advance toward Germany from the East.

Americans were elated to hear of the tremendous success of D-Day. But, for the families of those soldiers who paid the ultimate price, the invasion was bittersweet. The news also influenced the 1944 election. Roosevelt hid his declining health and nominated the conservative Democrat Harry Truman as his vice president to help balance the ticket and attract moderates. The Republicans responded by nominating the popular New York governor Thomas Dewey. Dewey was a popular governor who had risen to fame as a lawman who secured convictions against several leading figures in organized crime. Many voters favored Dewey and had increasingly grown frustrated with the domestic policies of Roosevelt, especially his unpopular attempts to raise taxes. However, given the overwhelming success of America, both economically and militarily, and the continuing uncertainty of the war, many undecided voters chose to keep Roosevelt in office. Roosevelt won the election with 53 percent of the popular vote, a much closer election than his three previous landslide victories had been. The 1944 election demonstrated a conservative shift of US politics that would continue after the war was over. Yet most Americans in 1944 still supported Roosevelt and the New Deal.

FIGURE 8.22

Soldiers in the first waves of the Normandy Landing faced gunfire from entrenched German positions on D-Day. This famous photo gives a first-person view of what troops saw when the door to their landing crafts opened on the morning of June 6, 1944.

As the election results were calculated, Allied troops were approaching the German border. Hitler responded with a counterattack designed to break through the Allied line. Hitler believed that if his forces could somehow slice through the Allied line and then turn north, he might isolate, surround, and capture several US and British divisions. Hitler recognized that this action alone would not break the Allied juggernaut, but he would plan on using the hundreds of thousands of men as hostages. With the lives of so many men at risk, Hitler planned on using these prisoners of war as a bargaining chip to force the Allies to end the war and allow Germany to keep some of the lands it had conquered. Due to the rough terrain and harsh weather in the Ardennes, the Allies were surprised by and unprepared for the German counterattack. Allied forces rallied and waged a fighting retreat, holding the line against the German onslaught. At their furthest point of penetration, German forces pushed fifty miles west in the center of the battlefield, which created a bulge in that line. As a result, the Ardennes Offensive became known as the **Battle of the Bulge**.

But the Germans did not control the entire bulge. In the very center of German-captured territory, near the small Belgian city of Bastogne, the men of the 101st Airborne among other units had formed a defensive perimeter and were still holding out. The German commander expected that these men would recognize the futility of their position and surrender. In the boldest move of the army's darkest hour, these soldiers refused the German commander's guarantee of safe quarter as prisoners. Instead, the men, who would soon earn the nickname "Battered Bastards of Bastogne," held their position against the much larger force that surrounded them. Their backs against the wall, black and white troops fought shoulder to shoulder for the first time in the war. Harsh weather prevented aircraft from reaching the men, but hundreds of soldiers and physicians volunteered to be dropped into the beleaguered combat zone by glider, carrying with them vital medical supplies and ammunition. By January, Patton's army reached the trapped US Army and flattened the bulge.

Battle of the Bulge

A German counteroffensive in December 1944 meant to pierce Allied lines in the dense terrain of the Ardennes in Belgium. The Germans failed to cut through the line; instead, they merely pushed the Allies backward, which created a "bulge" along the front. By late January, Allied forces had successfully pushed back east and resumed their offensive toward Berlin.

FIGURE 8.23

Soldiers belonging to the 82nd Airborne Division advance in a snowstorm during the Battle of the Bulge.

Hitler gambled on halting the Allied advance through a counteroffensive. The failure of this attack left his forces depleted and low on fuel and supplies. Allied forces quickly resumed their momentum and crossed the German border in March 1945. Within six weeks, Russian forces were closing in on Berlin from the east while the United States, Britain, and the reconstructed French army approached from the west. In late April, the two armies met, and their leaders apparently decided that the Russians should have the honor of taking the city of Berlin given the millions of casualties they had endured prior to America's entry into the war. Hitler committed suicide rather than surrender, leading German civilian officials to accept the Allied demand for unconditional surrender on May 8, 1945. The day was celebrated across America as Victory in Europe Day or **V-E Day**. US forces reveled with the British and French allies before redeploying forces and focusing the entire might of their arsenal in the continuing war against Japan.

3.5 War without Mercy in Asia

The Pacific front was unique in the way that racism colored the views of Americans and Japanese toward one another. Most American GIs maintained respect for Germans, Italians, and the French throughout the duration of the war. This did not prevent atrocities on either side, nor did it prevent aerial attacks against cities. Yet neither side expressed the desire to annihilate one another as a people—a common theme of both US and Japanese rhetoric in regard to "the other." Propaganda and popular opinion on both sides frequently portrayed the enemy as subhuman, even nonhuman. The Japanese viewed themselves as members of a pure and superior race in contrast to the hedonistic Americans who they believed were devoid of their own culture and heritage. Like leeches, many Japanese believed, Americans absorbed the worst traits of their composite races. As greedy Capitalists, Americans had also profited from the blood of Europe and Asia in each previous war. Americans portrayed the Japanese as animals or vermin, primitive and pitiable while simultaneously devious and malevolent. Hitler and Nazism, rather than the German people, became the symbol of evil in the war in Europe. However, the Japanese as a race was the enemy in the minds of many Americans.

The Pacific theater was also unique because of the vastness of the ocean in which it was fought. Japanese troops had established airbases on islands throughout the Pacific. As a result, US forces could not simply hope to capture one island near Japan because their invading fleet would become an easy target for thousands of aircraft from neighboring islands. The only way to proceed was to capture, or at least isolate, each of the islands Japan controlled one by one, from east to west. The overall US strategy was called "island hopping," moving ever westward and closer to the main island of Japan. Each new island and airfield they possessed could be used to stage an invasion of the next island until the US forces reached mainland Japan.

Following this strategy, 19,000 marines stormed Guadalcanal and two smaller isles within the Solomon Islands in August 1942. Guadalcanal was strategically located at the furthest extent of Japan's island possessions, and seizing control of it would provide the US military with a base of operations from which it could launch future offensives. The battle for Guadalcanal became one of attrition against the resolute Japanese defenders. Due to the estimated losses of taking every island in this manner, the navy modified its strategy. Some of the better-defended islands could be skipped, or "leap-frogged" as General Nimitz called the modified island-hopping plan. If the Japanese maintained control of one island but each of the nearby islands was captured, the navy could simply surround that island with battleships to prevent any supplies from arriving. This strategy preserved US lives by starving the Japanese defenders into submission or death. Even when the Japanese persisted and survived, the strategy of isolation simply made the islands they held irrelevant. Using each newly captured island as a base, the US military launched additional attacks on other islands across the Pacific as it moved steadily toward Japan throughout 1943 and 1944.

FIGURE 8.24

This battle map of the entire Pacific shows the US strategy of "island hopping." The navy and marines moved westward toward Japan, capturing islands from entrenched and determined Japanese soldiers as they went.

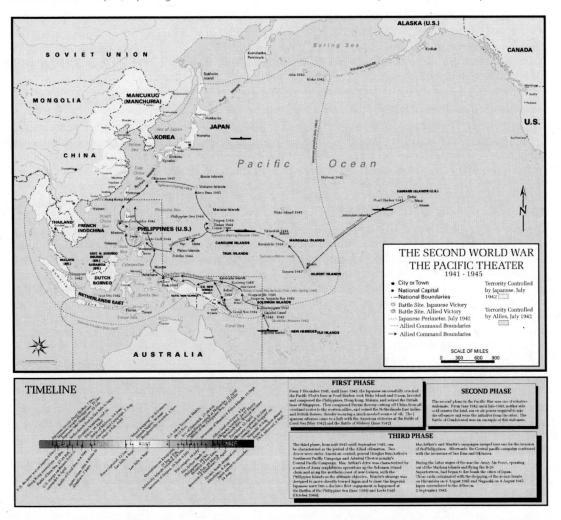

US forces regained control of the Philippines in October 1944 during the Battle for Leyte Gulf. By this time, the Japanese had resorted to suicidal "kamikaze" missions where pilots flew planes loaded with bombs directly into US ships. As a result, Americans needed more than just aircraft carriers; they needed island-based airfields that could not be sunk by kamikaze attacks. They also needed large supply bases that could be used to stage the eventual ground invasion of Japan.

Iwo Jima was one of the islands nearest to Japan. As a result, it was heavily defended by Japanese forces who recognized that surrendering the island to the Americans would provide the US Navy with a strategic location from which they could launch attacks on their homeland. Six thousand US Marines were gunned down as they stormed the beaches of Iwo Jima. Of the estimated 25,000 Japanese defenders at Iwo Jima, only 200 survived. The carnage was repeated with larger numbers on the island of Okinawa in June. Okinawa was the last of the large islands near Japan, and its defenders fought nearly to the last man. More than 1,000 kamikaze pilots flying all manner of aircraft flew their planes into US naval vessels and landing craft. Hundreds of US sailors were killed by these attacks, and 10,000 perished on the beaches of Okinawa before the island was secured.

FIGURE 8.25

The aftermath of the Battle of Tarawa. Tarawa is
a Pacific atoll that was host to some of the
fiercest fighting in 1943.

President Roosevelt suffered a massive stroke on April 12, 1945, and died later that afternoon. Vice President **Harry S. Truman**, a man that Roosevelt selected largely based on political concerns, assumed the presidency. Truman was no stranger to politics, having risen through the ranks of the Pendergast political machine of Kansas City. Truman quickly agreed with his predecessor that the invasion of Japan would cost hundreds of thousands of American lives. The following month, Truman was advised of the success of the **Manhattan Project**, a top-secret operation where US physicists had created the atomic bomb. More than 100,000 Americans had been involved with the project in some manner as construction workers who created the mines and other facilities needed to produce enough uranium to create the bomb.

The bomb was inspired by the work of Jewish refugees to America, such as Albert Einstein, and was assembled and tested in New Mexico by physicists who worked under the leadership of **J. Robert Oppenheimer**. Following a successful test of the bomb in July 1945, Oppenheimer's team reflected on the destructive force it had just unleashed. Three years, $2 billion, and millions of hours of grueling manual and intellectual labor all invested in what many feared was a quixotic fantasy had just resulted in the most unqualified success in the history of scientific and military research. And yet, no one present at the test sight felt like celebrating. "Few people laughed, few people cried, most people were silent," Oppenheimer recalled. "I remembered the line from the Hindu scripture, the *Bhagavad-Gita*...'Now I am become Death, the destroyer of worlds.' I suppose we all thought that, one way or another."

Military leaders and President Truman assembled an advisory committee to discuss how to utilize this new weapon. Some suggested a warning, followed by a demonstration on an uninhabited island. Others believed that only direct military use of the bomb would be effective in forcing the Japanese to surrender, warning that the United States only had a couple bombs ready and could not guarantee that the bomb would detonate properly. While the issue of the bomb's morality remains highly controversial, it is clear that the decision to use the bomb militarily had been made once the Manhattan Project began. This decision was renewed daily by the combined militaries of the world as American, British, German, Soviet, and Japanese air forces alike carpet-bombed cities. Recent bombings of Tokyo alone had killed as many civilians as the two atomic bombs together, and few military or civilian advisers disagreed with Truman's decision to proceed.

The war's racial overtones caused many leaders to underestimate the Japanese's ability to comprehend the implications of the atomic bomb. Japanese and German scientists both understood the possibilities of fusion and advised their military and civilian leaders to conduct similar programs. However, the military strategy of both nations was premised on a quick war, and the United States alone possessed the luxury of time and resources to develop the bomb. As had been the case with the dozens of firebombings that preceded the use of atomic weapons, US officials provided no warnings when they sent a B-29 bomber to drop an atomic bomb on the city of Hiroshima on August 6, 1945.

The bombing of Hiroshima instantly leveled one of Japan's largest cities; 140,000 men, women, and children would perish instantly or within the next few months as their burns and radiation took a toll on their bodies. Japan's leaders refused to surrender, hoping that the United States had not developed enough radioactive material to repeat the attack. If the Americans had more of these bombs, they reasoned, why were US forces still conducting firebombing raids using napalm and conventional explosives? A second attack on the city of Nagasaki three days later convinced Emperor Hirohito that further attacks could be sustained. Word of Japanese surrender arrived in the United States on August 14. An official ceremony marking the surrender of Japan followed two weeks later, with the firebombing of Japanese cities continuing in the interim.

4.   CONCLUSION

The United States greeted the news of Japan's surrender with celebration. Millions of military personnel still stationed in the United States were instantly reunited with family, and those overseas were soon released from duty or at least given temporary furloughs to return home. Truman declared a two-day holiday, and every American city held ticker-tape parades. San Francisco merchants gave free ice cream to soldiers in uniform, then merchant marines and other dockworkers, and eventually to anyone walking by. Jewelers sold every engagement ring they had in stock, and a photographer in Times Square captured a sailor and nurse in a spontaneous embrace, an image forever associated with this day of jubilation. And in a small apartment in Brooklyn, a mother sat quietly clutching a tear-stained telegram from the War Department, informing her that her son would not be coming home.

Similar scenes occurred more than 400,000 times throughout the war as American mothers learned that their sons and daughters had been killed in defense of their country. An additional 700,000 Americans were wounded in a war that killed an estimated 60 million people, the majority of whom were civilians. The death and destruction of the war was contrasted against the victory of democracy over the forces of Fascism. Whether democracy and freedom would spread throughout Europe and Asia, however, was still yet to be seen. For many Americans, the same question about the ultimate triumph of democracy and freedom applied equally to their own nation.

REVIEW AND CRITICAL THINKING

1. In what ways might Stalingrad be one of the major turning points of World War II? Why might so few Americans know about the Battle of Stalingrad and the Eastern Front compared with the Normandy Invasion and other battles on the Western Front?

2. How were the Allies able to successfully invade German-occupied France with so few casualties compared to the major battles of the Eastern Front? What factors account for the difference in casualties between the British, French, and Americans and the Soviets?

3. Evaluate America's response to the Holocaust. How might the United States have done more to lessen the severity of the Holocaust? Would diverting troops to liberate concentration camps have saved lives or merely prolonged the war?

4. Compare the fighting that occurred during the battles of Iwo Jima and Okinawa to those of the Western Front between Germany and the United States and Britain. Why did the United States use atomic weapons against Japan? Did race affect this decision?

5. Given the atrocities committed against many US troops captured in the Philippines by Japanese soldiers, some Americans called for Japanese POWs to be treated with equal brutality. Had the US military followed that advice, how might the war have been more difficult for US marines in the Pacific?

5. FURTHER READING

Atkinson, Rick. *An Army at Dawn: The War in North Africa, 1942–1943* (2002).

Berube, Allan. *Coming Out Under Fire: The History of Gay Men and Women in World War Two* (1990).

Davies, Norman. *No Simple Victory: World War II in Europe, 1939–1945* (2008).

Dower, John W. *War Without Mercy: Race and Power in the Pacific War* (1986).

Keegan, John. *The Second World War* (1990).

Kennedy, David M. *Freedom From Fear: The American People in Depression and War, 1929–1945* (1999).

Kessler-Harris, Alice. *Out to Work: A History of Wage-Earning Women in the United States* (1982).

Longerich, Peter. *Holocaust: The Nazi Persecution and Murder of the Jews* (2010).

Lukacs, John. *Five Days in London: May 1940* (2001).

Meyer, Leisa D. *Creating GI Jane: Sexuality and Power in the Women's Army Corps During World War II* (1996).

Murray, Williamson and Allan Reed Millett. *A War to Be Won: Fighting the Second World War* (2001).

Rosenberg, Rosalind. *Divided Lives: American Women in the Twentieth Century* (1992).

Weinberg, Gerhard L. *A World at Arms: A Global History of World War II* (1994).

CHAPTER 9
The Cold War at Home and Abroad, 1945–1953

The **Cold War** refers to the economic and political rivalry between the United States and the Soviet Union between 1945 and 1991. The conflict was based on the two nations' competing political and economic systems: the Communist system of the Soviet Union and its allies and the democratic Capitalism of the Unites States and its allies. These years featured intense political and economic rivalry as well as diplomatic and military posturing between the two nations. The period was also host to dramatic increases in military spending, hyperbolic rhetoric by leaders of both sides, high tensions, and millions of casualties in proxy wars throughout Latin America, Africa, and Asia.

Both sides viewed their economic and political system as superior to the other and interpreted nearly every world event as part of an ongoing confrontation that would determine whether Capitalism or Communism would become the prevailing ideology throughout the globe. The Soviets tried to spread the economic and political system of Communism to other nations, while the United States promoted its vision of democracy and free enterprise. This competition led to dozens of small-scale military conflicts and several major wars involving the armed forces of both nations. However, as the term "Cold War" suggests, there was no direct military engagement between the two nations.

> **Cold War**
>
> The persistent tension between the United States and its Western supporters against the Soviet Union and other Communist nations between the end of the Second World War and the dissolution of the Soviet Union in 1991. The Cold War featured political, military, and economic rivalries between the West and the international supporters of Communism that led to dozens of wars, even if the United States and the Soviet Union never directly fought one another.

1. POSTWAR EUROPE, ASIA, AND THE MIDDLE EAST

LEARNING OBJECTIVES

1. Explain the origins of the Cold War in terms of diplomatic, political, and military history.
2. Using examples from Europe, Asia, and the Middle East, explain how the Cold War affected global history in the years following World War II.
3. Describe the creation of the United Nations and outline its organizational structure.

The motivation behind Soviet and US attempts to spread their economic and political systems to other nations is heavily debated by historians. What is clear is that both nations came to view the other as aggressive and committed to global domination by the early 1950s. For example, in 1950, officials within the Department of Defense worked with foreign-policy experts to create a report to the National Security Council. This sixty-page document was known by its shortened name, **NSC-68**, and later typified the view of both nations toward the other. NSC-68 explained that the Soviet Union sought "to impose its absolute authority over the rest of the world." The stakes could not have been higher, the report continued, as Soviets threatened not only "destruction of this Republic but of civilization itself."

Many Americans had their doubts about the extent to which the Soviet Union and international Communism really posed a threat to their nation. It also appears that many Soviets at least privately expressed doubts about the potential threat Americans represented to their well-being in these early years. However, the victory of Communist forces in China, the outbreak of the Korean War in 1950, and the political climate that emerged within the United States by 1950 created a situation where few political leaders wanted to be seen as soft on Communism. Within the Soviet Union, a similar political environment emerged, and there was even less tolerance for those who doubted the "hard-liners" that

> **NSC-68**
>
> A lengthy document issued by the National Security Council in 1950 that demonstrated the belief that the Soviet Union represented a direct threat to the American way of life. The document and its core assumptions influenced US foreign policy throughout the Cold War.

dominated the Kremlin. The result was that only five years after their defeat of Hitler, the one-time allies began to evaluate nearly every foreign and domestic-policy decision within the context of a Cold War that seemed increasingly impervious to the ideas and perspectives of those outside of each government's inner circle.

Recent scholarship based on previously closed Soviet archives tends to challenge Cold War perceptions of the Soviet Union as dominated by an ideology of aggression toward the United States and its allies. Instead, what emerges from recently declassified documents is the image of a nation driven primarily by concerns of its own security and stability. At the same time, these documents confirm the existence of massive human rights violations and contempt for democracy and free discussion within the Soviet Union and throughout its sphere of influence. These documents also demonstrate that many of the leaders and people of Eastern Europe enjoyed a higher level of historical agency in shaping the histories of their nations than was previously assumed. Although it remains clear that the Soviet Union dominated military and foreign-policy decisions in each of these nations, the notion that all decisions and all communication flowed downward from the Kremlin is being revised to account for the agency of the people and leaders of Eastern Europe.

1.1   Postwar Diplomacy and Reconstruction of Europe and Asia

The origins of the Cold War can be seen while America and the Soviet Union were still allies in World War II. The two nations had a history of mutual suspicion, and both maintained very different ideas about how postwar Europe should be administered. Each nation wanted to recreate Europe in their own image by forming Western-style democracies or Soviet-aligned Communist governments. In addition, the Soviets wanted to create a pro-Russian "buffer zone" that would insulate them from potential attacks in the future. These conflicting visions were clearly manifest during the meetings of American, British, and Soviet diplomats at the Yalta and Potsdam Conferences in 1945.

Yalta Conference

February 1945 meeting in the Soviet Union between President Franklin Delano Roosevelt, British Prime Minister Winston Churchill, and Soviet Premier Joseph Stalin. The three leaders discussed wartime strategy, the creation of the United Nations, and the reconstruction of Europe.

In February 1945, Churchill, Roosevelt, and Stalin met at the **Yalta Conference**. Yalta was a popular resort city in the Ukraine where the three leaders discussed the future of Germany and Eastern Europe while their armies continued to close in around Hitler. Stalin believed that the defense of his nation depended on creating a Russian sphere of influence in Poland and other Eastern European nations because Poland and Eastern Europe had been used as a corridor to attack Russia several times in the past two centuries. Stalin promised to create a coalition government made up of representatives of the democratic Polish government exiled in London. Churchill and Roosevelt correctly suspected that he would instead create an interim government led by pro-Soviet Communists.

The allies had reason to be concerned about how democratic this process would be given the actions of the Red Army in Poland the previous year. For example, Stalin halted his offensive against Nazi-occupied Warsaw for two months while the German army killed thousands of Polish fighters who opposed Communism. Even though the Western Allies feared that Stalin would turn Poland into a Communist puppet state, they were hardly in any position to demand otherwise considering the Red Army's complete occupation of Eastern Europe. Likewise, the Western Allies recognized that Stalin's army would occupy Eastern Germany. Hoping to keep their tentative alliance alive, Churchill and Roosevelt agreed that each nation would be responsible for occupying and reconstructing the section of Germany and Central Europe that corresponded with the position of their armies.

Potsdam Conference

July 1945 meeting in Germany between new President Harry Truman, new British Prime Minister Clement Attlee, and Soviet Premier Joseph Stalin. The three leaders discussed the reconstruction of Europe and decided to divide Germany and Berlin into American, British, French, and Soviet sectors.

By the time these nations met again in Allied-controlled Germany for the **Potsdam Conference** in July, Churchill would be replaced by Clement Attlee as prime minister and Truman replaced the deceased Roosevelt. Like their predecessors, Attlee and Truman recognized the futility of a military challenge to Stalin's position in Eastern Europe. Instead, they focused their efforts on determining how Eastern Europe might be divided and administered by the Soviets in a way that would foster reconstruction and genuine independence. They hoped that the Soviet Army's presence would be temporary and that new national boundaries might be established throughout Eastern Europe, which might prevent future conflicts.

As had been the case following World War I, those present at the Potsdam Conference attempted to divide Europe into individual nations according to the doctrine of self-determination. Unfortunately, tremendous ethnic and political strife throughout Eastern Europe derailed the process. The dominant peoples of Eastern Europe each sought to remove national and ethnic minorities. In addition, all of these areas were also divided among a host of political factions, each vying for control of regions that had been completely destroyed by war and military occupation. Before long, this economic, ethnic, and political strife spread to Southern Europe in places such as Greece, Italy, and even Western nations such as France.

The postwar settlement was also similar to that of World War I in the way the victorious allies debated the fate of Germany. In addition to dividing Germany into four zones, the German military was disbanded and the National Socialist Party was permanently abolished. The nation's infrastructure was in shambles following the combined onslaught of Western and Soviet armies, so a special council was created to administer humanitarian aid. Each of the four nations created interim governments in their respective zones and prepared for special elections the world hoped would lead to stable and democratic governance to avoid the previous instability of the post–World War I period.

Given the extreme hardships their country endured, Russian leaders also sought reparations as a method of punishing Germany while building up their military. This led to conflict between the four occupying powers as the West sought to rebuild a democratic Germany that could stand on its own and refused Soviet demands for reparations from their sectors of Germany. Within the Soviet sector of Eastern Germany, the provisional government also worked to reconstruct the German economy, but its military also seized many of the nation's economic assets as war reparations, which hindered efforts at reconstruction.

While many Americans shared the desire of Russian leaders to punish their attackers, the United States had prospered during the war and its highest priority was to promote global recovery and avoid the economic and political instability that led to the rise of totalitarian governments. Rather than seeking reparations within its German sector, the United States launched a massive program to aid war-torn Germany and later Japan in hopes of promoting stable democratic governments. In both Asia and Europe, the US perspective was influenced by humanitarian concerns but also guided by self-interest. Business leaders hoped to resume trade with these nations while political leaders feared economic instability might lead Europe and Asia toward Communism. As a result, US aid was aimed at ensuring Japanese and German reconstruction in the American image of democracy and free enterprise. US aid to these former adversaries was rewarded by the close political and economic ties that developed as West Germany and Japan became two of the strongest US allies in their ensuing conflict with the Soviet Union.

US forces occupied Japan from 1945 until 1952, overseeing the transition to a democratic government while also seizing military assets, holding military tribunals for accused war criminals, and overseeing reparations payments. Given the horrific nature of the war in the Pacific, the peacetime transition of Japan from a militaristic dictatorship to a prospering democracy was remarkable. As was the case in Germany, the reconstruction of Japan mirrored the developing Cold War rivalry between the Soviet Union and the United States. The Soviets created their sphere of influence in Manchuria while the Americans occupied Japan. With the help of the newly created United Nations, Korea was temporarily partitioned into US and Soviet sectors and installed with rival governments.

General **Douglas MacArthur** was placed in charge of Japan's reconstruction and created a constitutional democracy similar to the United States. Early years of Japanese reconstruction focused on reducing the power of that nation's military and converting factories from creating munitions to producing consumer goods. Many Americans feared that promoting too much industrial growth might lead to Japan becoming a major power once again. However, as Communism began to spread throughout China and Southeastern Asia, US leaders shifted their orientation and invested resources to ensure Japanese economic growth under a pro-American government. Many of MacArthur's democratic reforms such as female suffrage proved unpopular with the Japanese people at first, but by 1950, America and Japan had transformed from bitter enemies to allies. The basis of this friendship was US economic aid, mutual trade, and hostility to the growth of Communism in neighboring China and North Korea.

The reconstruction of Eastern Europe offers a sharp contrast to that of Japan and West Germany. The people of Eastern Europe had suffered tremendously and now demanded that German residents of the region leave their countries. After all, they reasoned, Hitler had justified his actions in the region based on reuniting all peoples of German origins. For this reason, authorities in Eastern Europe demanded that Germans living in Poland, Czechoslovakia, and Hungary return to Germany. The Potsdam Conference followed this line of reasoning in declaring its intention to create nations along ethnic lines. Poland was to be occupied by people of Polish origins, the Czechs were to live in Czechoslovakia, and Hungary would be for Hungarians, and so on.

FIGURE 9.1

Britain's Clement Attlee, President Harry Truman, and the Soviet Union's Joseph Stalin seated together in Germany following the end of World War II.

Douglas MacArthur

Commander of US forces in the southwest Pacific in World War II, MacArthur was also placed in charge of the Reconstruction of Japan. MacArthur also served as commander of US and UN forces in the Korean War. MacArthur was relieved of duty after making unauthorized remarks calling for an attack against Communist China.

FIGURE 9.2

This map demonstrates the division of Europe that corresponded to the positions of the armies of the Soviet Union and the Armies of the Western Allies. The Soviet Union would dominate the reconstruction of Eastern Europe, with the nations of this region forming socialist governments that were allied with Moscow.

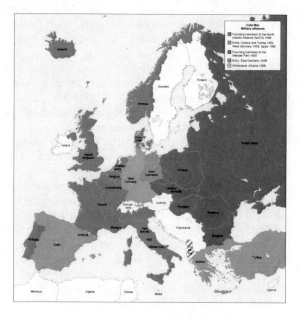

As had been the case after World War I, this plan failed to recognize the vast ethnic diversity of the region and the impossibility of drawing national boundaries that would accomplish its goal without creating millions of refugees. In addition, millions of other ethnic minorities would also be forced to leave their homes if such a plan was universally enforced. Each government partially attempted to purge their nation of various minorities, usually enforcing the provisions of exclusionary schemes on those most vulnerable—the poor. Eastern Europe had scarce resources to feed or transport the millions of refugees created by the expulsion of ethnic minorities, and historians estimate that as many as 2 million people perished in refugee camps in the resulting disorder.

In addition to the atrocities resulting from expulsion, the people of Eastern Europe suffered under various totalitarian governments created under the influence of Stalin's authoritarian régime. Some historians have blamed the "appeasement" of Stalin at the Yalta and Potsdam Conferences for the abandonment of Eastern Europe to Soviet domination. However, the Western Allies were hardly in any position to dictate the reconstruction of Eastern Europe under Soviet terms given the position of the Red Army throughout the region. In addition, the Allies wanted to recreate the area west of Berlin in their own image.

The official declarations at Yalta and Potsdam mandated democratic elections and constitutional government. Indeed, many elections were held and both Communist and non-Communist leaders were democratically elected throughout Eastern Europe in the immediate postwar years. Before long, however, Communist groups throughout the region seized power with Soviet military backing. Shortly after the end of World War II, Hungary, Poland, Romania, Bulgaria, and East Germany all had Communist governments that were backed by the Soviet Red Army.

Yugoslavia liberated itself from Nazi rule, which meant that it was never occupied by the Soviet Army. As a result, Yugoslavian leader **Josip Tito** was able to maintain independence from the Soviet bloc because the Red Army neither liberated nor occupied Yugoslavia. Tito's Communist regime jailed dissenters as had other Soviet-backed regimes yet provided an alternative to Soviet leadership for leftists throughout the globe. By 1948, Europe was divided between democratic and Communist states along a line that corresponded to the orientation of the two superpowers whose armies had liberated Europe from the Nazis. Democracy and Capitalism ruled in the Western nations liberated and occupied by US troops, while the eastern nations liberated by the Soviet Red Army formed Communist governments.

Josip Tito

Leader of Communist Yugoslavia. Tito was significant in world history because he fiercely defended the independence of his nation, despite the attempts of Stalin to dictate the affairs of all Communist states.

1.2   United Nations

Despite the tensions between the United States and the Soviet Union, the postwar period ushered in an era of hope for lasting world peace through better communication and collective action. As the war came to an end, representatives from around the globe met to discuss ways to prevent future conflicts. These diplomats authored a provisional charter for the **United Nations**, a new organization that would replace the ineffectual League of Nations established after the first World War. "Big Three" leaders Winston Churchill, Franklin Delano Roosevelt, and Joseph Stalin discussed the idea throughout the war and even decided some of the early details about how the organization would be structured. Delegates representing various member nations met in San Francisco in April 1945 and discussed various ideas about the postwar world order as well as the best method of structuring the United Nations to meet these challenges. Although the United States had rejected the terms of membership of the League of Nations after World War I, it took the lead in its support of the United Nations. However, because participation in a collectivist organization such as the United Nations requires commitment to decisions one cannot control and may strongly disagree with, US membership in, and relationship with, the United Nations has always been controversial.

The United Nations charter avowed principles of peace through communication and collective action, autonomy and self-determination for people around the world, and respect for human rights irrespective of race, religion, gender, and ethnicity. The charter also established a governmental structure led by the General Assembly, **Security Council**, and the administrative body of the UN called the Secretariat. Each member nation was permitted one representative and one vote within the General Assembly*. Membership on the Security Council, on the other hand, was restricted to fifteen nations. Ten of these seats are nominated on a rotating basis every two years, with the remaining five seats being permanently granted to the five leading Allied Powers (the United States, Great Britain, the Soviet Union [Russia today], China, and France). Any one of these five permanent members can exercise its veto power, effectively blocking any measure regardless of the votes of the other fourteen members of the Security Council.

The Security Council is required to work with the General Assembly* and the Secretary-General, who serves as a chief administrator and executive over the UN. The Secretary-General oversees the Secretariat—an administrative body composed of thousands of professionals who manage the daily operations of the UN. Among the responsibilities of the Secretariat are the operations of dozens of special agencies such as the United Nations Children's Fund (UNICEF), the World Health Organization (WHO), and the United Nations Educational, Scientific, and Cultural Organization (UNESCO). With the aid of the Secretariat, the General Assembly* and Security Council negotiate all international conflicts and attempt to promote common understanding and support basic standards of human rights upon which all nations can agree. For example, a measure drafted by a special committee led by **Eleanor Roosevelt** was presented and approved by the General Assembly* in 1948. Known as the Universal Declaration of Human Rights, this document placed all UN members on record as supporting basic human rights, racial and ethnic equality, freedom of speech, religious toleration, and economic opportunity.

1.3   American-Soviet Conflict

In March 1946, former British Prime Minister Winston Churchill was invited to speak at Westminster College in Fulton, Missouri. Churchill sought to draw US attention to the line dividing Europe between democratic and Communist nations, an "**iron curtain**" he portrayed as dividing the continent between freedom and totalitarianism. While most Americans did not yet view Europe or the rest of the world in such unequivocal terms, recent events were pushing many toward Churchill's perspective.

United Nations

An international organization headquartered in New York City that attempts to mediate global conflicts and disagreements between member nations as a means of promoting worldwide peace, human rights, and economic development and stability.

Security Council

One of the major bodies of the United Nations composed of five permanent members and ten rotating members. The council is charged with maintaining global peace and stability and has the power to make binding decisions.

FIGURE 9.3

Eleanor Roosevelt holds a ceremonial copy of the Universal Declaration of Human Rights, which was approved by nearly every member nation in 1948. The apartheid government of South Africa was among the nations that did not approve the document.

iron curtain

A phrase first expressed by Winston Churchill referencing the dividing line between Communist-dominated Eastern Europe and the West. The phrase was used by Western leaders to denote their belief that something menacing or sinister existed on the other side of the ideological divide.

George Kennan

A Princeton-trained historian who advised Truman regarding Soviet affairs. He viewed the Soviet Union as an aggressor state that sought to expand its doctrines and influence at the expense of US security and prosperity. His ideas helped to frame the American policy of containment.

containment

A strategy to minimize the threat that US policymakers believed Communism and the Soviet Union represented to US interests by preventing the spread of Communism and Soviet influence throughout the globe.

Truman Doctrine

Influenced by the rise of significant Communist parties in Greece and Turkey, Truman announced in the spring of 1947 that the United States would support "free peoples who are resisting attempted subjugation by armed minorities or by outside pressures." In practice, the Truman Doctrine suggested that the United States intervene to prevent the spread of Communism.

In February 1946, Stalin claimed that there could be no long-term peace between Communism and Capitalism and pledged that his Soviet Union would create and maintain the world's most dominant military. In this same month, US adviser **George Kennan** sent his "Long Telegram" from Moscow with a dire warning based on his interpretation of the Soviet worldview. Kennan recognized that Stalin's rhetoric about the perpetual war between Communism and Capitalism did not mean that the Soviets actually desired armed confrontation with Capitalist nations. Instead, he explained that the Soviets desired to promote and expand Communism throughout the world.

Kennan's advice to Truman was to respond by promoting Capitalism and democracy while maintaining a policy of **containment** regarding Communism. Truman agreed that Communism must not spread from those nations that were already in Stalin's sphere of influence to the rest of the world. In other words, the Truman administration recognized that the United States could do little to affect the outcome in Eastern Europe given the postwar agreements between the two nations. Instead, they believed the nation should direct efforts throughout the rest of the world to make sure Communism did not spread beyond the "iron curtain" of which Churchill had spoken. With Europe divided between East and West, the two superpowers soon began a competition to win influence throughout the globe. For both sides, the development of a powerful military was a key element of political and diplomatic influence.

Economic aid was also a key ingredient of the Cold War contest between Western and Soviet influence. European and Asian nations experienced tremendous economic instability in the wake of World War II. Unemployment and inflation were extremely high, and millions were suffering from food shortages. US leaders feared that Communist supporters throughout Europe would capitalize on the instability and fear of the immediate postwar period to spread their ideas. Although US leaders believed that Capitalism was a superior economic system, they recognized that Soviet rhetoric about sharing farmland equally would appeal to landless peasants who worked the land of the wealthy. At the same time, the concept of cooperative ownership of factories would attract supporters among the impoverished workers in the cities. Americans could reflect on their own history to see how Socialism attracted supporters in times of economic crisis. These concerns about the spread of collectivist theories escalated throughout 1946 as Socialist and Communist parties started to garner significant support in nations such as Czechoslovakia, Italy, Finland, and even France. As a result, the United States announced that it would step up its efforts to provide economic aid to these nations as a means of jump-starting a return to Capitalist prosperity. At the same time, the United States also declared that it would keep troops in Europe as a peacekeeping force.

Two nations that were especially important to US policymakers were Greece and Turkey where Communist forces were fighting civil wars for control of their nations. The British traditionally considered this region of the Mediterranean as their sphere of influence, but their own economic struggles forced them to reconsider the costs of this worldview. President Truman wanted to take Britain's place in the region by providing military aid to the monarchies of Greece and Turkey, but he recognized that his own nation's history of isolationism and hostility to monarchy stood in the way. As a result, he addressed the American people in March 1947 in a successful attempt to convince a skeptical nation that the United States must intercede against Communist forces in the Mediterranean. "It must be the policy of the United States," Truman exclaimed, "to support free peoples who are resisting attempted subjugation by armed minorities or outside pressures." This expression of US intervention against any expansion of Communism was to become the central aspect of the **Truman Doctrine**. The president's ability to phrase Cold War containment in terms of protecting freedom resonated deeply with the American people and placed those who opposed his policies on the defensive.

The popular acceptance of the Truman Doctrine and the concern that Communist victories in Greece and Turkey would lead to the expansion of Communism in Europe and the Middle East led to congressional appropriations of $400 million in military aid to the right-wing monarchies of Greece and Turkey. These funds were key to the defeat of Communist forces in both nations. In addition, Congress created the National Security Council and the Central Intelligence Agency (CIA) to gather information about potential threats to the nation. Before long, the CIA was empowered to conduct secret military operations based on this information. In retrospect, it is clear that Truman's advisers exaggerated the extent of Soviet-backing these forces received. It is also apparent that US action in the Mediterranean set the precedent of supplying military aid to any government—democratic or otherwise—that was fighting the spread of Communism. For the next three decades, the containment of Communism was the highest priority and guiding spirit of US foreign policy.

1.4 Marshall Plan and Berlin Airlift

The Soviet Union had a similar perspective regarding foreign policy, although the Soviets hoped to contain the influence of the West throughout the globe. This was especially true regarding Eastern Europe. Russia had endured exponentially more damage and casualties than the United States, Britain, and France combined. Most of its leading cities were destroyed. In addition, the Soviet Union believed that the instability of Eastern Europe threatened its own internal security. As a result, the Soviet Union hoped to reconstruct Eastern Europe in its own image, creating numerous Soviet-controlled Communist nations between the Capitalist nations of Western Europe and its own border.

Stalin ordered his military and political leaders to back the communist parties of Poland, Czechoslovakia, Hungary, and Romania. The result was that each of these nations formed communist governments. These nations had each been devastated by the war, so many of the people of these nations were hopeful that an alliance with a powerful nation like the Soviet Union would provide stability and future economic growth. However, the Soviet Union was hardly in position to offer much assistance following the war, and Stalin ordered the seizure of some of the nations' resources to finance the operations of the Red Army.

The US economic experience during the war was nearly the opposite of Europe, Asia, and the Soviet Union, as no American city had been attacked. (A few of the Alaskan islands were occupied by the Japanese, while the attack on Hawaii triggered the war. Alaska and Hawaii were territories rather than US states at this time, but what is more important is the fact that the civilian populations of these territories were not the target of the attacks, which is in sharp contrast to the experiences of Europe and Asia). The US economy had experienced unprecedented growth. As a result, those nations who were not occupied by Soviet troops turned toward the United States for assistance. By 1947, nations throughout the world recognized that the United States was committed to fighting the expansion of Communism and was willing to provide economic assistance to any nation that shared its political orientation. Yet even with the billions of dollars of US aid that had already been committed, most of Europe and Asia remained mired in economic depression. Communist political parties were continuing to gain new supporters among the impoverished and unemployed. Communist leaders pointed out the vast differences of wealth between the rich and poor in each nation and assured all who would listen that their doctrine of equal distribution of wealth and government ownership of factories would eradicate poverty and provide full employment. In response, the United States implemented the **Marshall Plan**.

The brainchild of the immensely popular George C. Marshall, who was the army's chief of staff during World War II and now served as Truman's secretary of state, the Marshall Plan provided over $12 billion in economic aid to participating nations. The goal was to demonstrate convincingly that America's generosity and prosperity as a Capitalistic democracy could restore European progress better than "hollow" Communist theory and rhetoric. Advocates of the Marshall Plan were equally prone to long-windedness about the supremacy of their economic and political system, but the plan's sudden influx of US currency backed up this rhetoric and immediately restored economic stability. Billions of dollars flowed from the United States to the banks and governments of various European nations to reverse inflation, revive European manufacturing, and provide emergency food and supplies to the desperate population. The United States also provided military aid to nationalist forces battling the Communists in Greece and Italy, even though US leaders had serious reservations about the long-term desirability of propping up the leaders of these forces.

Most US officials downplayed America's support of any regime battling Communism, regardless of whether that regime had the support of the people or subscribed to US democratic ideals. Marshall's own rhetoric tended to emphasize the humanitarian intent of the aid in a way that was often divorced from politics altogether. "Our policy is directed not against any country or doctrine," Marshall exclaimed, "but against hunger, poverty, desperation, and chaos." Each of these conditions existed in the Communist nations of Europe and was especially rampant in the war-torn regions of the Soviet Union. As a result, the Soviet Union was among the sixteen nations that met with US diplomats in Paris in July 1947 to determine what form the US aid would take.

Soviet Foreign Minister Vyacheslov Molotov recognized that the US offer, which had been extended to all European nations, was not intended to include governments such as the Soviet Union that remained committed to Communism. Many historians believe Molotov's attendance was a well-calculated ploy to expose the limits of the Marshall Plan's humanitarian intentions. However, Stalin quickly ordered Molotov to return to Russia, thereby allowing the United States to maintain that they were not motivated by politics while only contributing to non-Communist nations.

The remaining participants requested $29 billion in aid, which Truman quickly reduced to $17 billion before requesting the money from Congress. Although the United States had already distributed over $10 billion in aid in the last few years, the Marshall Plan alarmed many Americans, who deeply opposed such large amounts of foreign aid. Many in Congress agreed, pointing out that the United States had already provided billions in aid both before and after the war. Some members of Congress visited Europe and told heart-breaking stories of widespread starvation. Others mixed this humanitarian impulse with a message of self-interest as they predicted that the United States would be the leading beneficiary of Marshall Plan aid because the money would create stable democracies that would be

Marshall Plan

A program of US financial aid aimed at promoting the reconstruction of Europe. The plan was motivated by a desire to prevent the economic disorder that often facilitated the growth of Communist parties as well as restoring global trade.

FIGURE 9.4

American political cartoonist Herb Block critically compares the state of the Soviet-dominated nations of Eastern Europe with the aid provided to non-Socialist nations under the terms of the Marshall Plan.

reliable anti-Communist allies. In addition, US business interests recognized that European recovery would lead to new markets for their products.

Ironically, Stalin provided the strongest argument in favor of the Marshall Plan. Soviet officials engineered a farcical election in Hungary in August 1947 that resulted in a Communist landslide. Even more alarming, Stalin ordered Soviet forces to invade Czechoslovakia in February 1948. The takeover of pro-Soviet forces in both nations ended the debate in Congress and convinced most of the opponents of the Marshall Plan that Communism would spread throughout Europe unless the United States took proactive measures to repair the European economy.

FIGURE 9.5

Germany was divided into four different sectors. Each sector was assigned to either Britain, France, the United States, or the Soviet Union. Berlin was also divided into four sectors but was in the Soviet sector in the east.

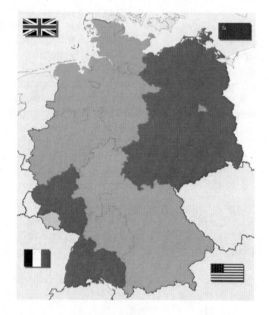

Most historians agree that distributing aid through the Marshall Plan was essential to preventing suffering and the spread of Communism. Together with the efforts of the European people themselves, US aid provided the temporary assistance needed to prevent destitution and the long-term capital investment required for industrial recovery. By the early 1950s, Western Europe was again prospering and Communist parties had lost most of their supporters. The success of the Marshall Plan was most obvious in Germany, which had been divided into American, French, British, and German sectors.

Berlin was located in the Soviet sector in eastern Germany but was also divided into four sectors. While the sectors of Berlin and the part of Germany under Western control were starting to recover by 1948, conditions improved little in the Soviet-controlled eastern sectors. The US, British, and French sectors of Germany moved toward a single currency in preparation for uniting these sections as an independent nation. The plan alarmed Stalin, who responded by ordering a blockade of all land and water routes to Berlin in June 1948. This meant that nothing would be allowed to enter the US sector of Berlin from the west, even much-needed humanitarian aid. Stalin gambled that the Western nations would be unable to provide for the 2 million residents in their sectors of Berlin and would have to abandon their control of the city.

Some of Truman's advisers recommended sending an armored column of tanks and soldiers against the Soviet blockade to demonstrate US commitment to the city of Berlin. Instead, Truman demonstrated America's ingenuity and immense material resources by simply flying all supplies into the city. US planes landed every three minutes during the ensuing **Berlin Airlift**, with more than 1,000 daily flights carrying 2,500 tons of fuel and supplies to the isolated residents of Western Berlin for nearly an entire year. America's ability to simply fly over the Soviet blockade to provide humanitarian aid made Stalin appear both malicious and feeble. Likewise, the incredible logistical success and generosity of the Berlin Airlift provided the world with a contrasting vision of the two superpowers. After it became clear that the Americans could maintain the airlift indefinitely, Stalin lifted the blockade in May 1949. That same month, the Western powers united their three sections and created the Federal Republic of Germany (West Germany) as a constitutional democracy. Five months later, a provisional Communist government was established in the Soviet sector; this section would be known in the United States as East Germany, although its official name was the German Democratic Republic.

Berlin Airlift

A massive US Air Force mission between June 1948 and May 1949 that provided the Western sector of Berlin with vital supplies via cargo planes. The airlift was necessitated by Stalin's decision to cut off all land routes to the city.

1.5   NATO and the Warsaw Pact

With the creation of East Germany, Europe was almost completely divided between Soviet-backed Communist nations in the Eastern- and Western-aligned nations of the Mediterranean and Western Europe. The United States was still reveling in its symbolic victory over the Soviet Union in the Berlin Airlift when the news of Russia's successful test of an atomic bomb reached the states in August 1949. Months later, China established a Communist government. The United States responded to these events by continuing to provide economic aid to non-Communist states, increasing military spending, and forming the **North Atlantic Treaty Organization (NATO)**. NATO was a defensive alliance in which the United States, Canada, and the original ten Western European nations that joined in 1949 promised to join forces against any nation that attacked a NATO member. NATO represented the first peacetime military alliance in US history, yet was overwhelmingly supported by the Senate, which ratified the NATO treaty with an 82–13 vote. By 1951, US troops were assigned to NATO forces in Europe. While the numbers of troops were relatively small, the US role as the leader of NATO symbolized the end of American isolationism and prompted a similar response from the Soviet Union. In May 1955, Russia responded by calling a meeting in Poland, where it would create a similar alliance for the Communist nations of Eastern Europe. Josip Tito declined to join the Soviet-dominated **Warsaw Pact**, leading many US leaders to consider the possibility of forming some type of mutual agreement with the nonaligned Communist leader. However, Yugoslavia's primary role in the emerging Cold War was to demonstrate the possibility of remaining independent of both the American and Soviet orbit.

The Soviet Union also attempted to create their own version of the Marshall Plan to aid the economies of the Communist Eastern bloc nations. The Council for Mutual Economic Assistance (COMECON) provided some aid to its member nations despite the relative weakness of the Soviet economy, which was saddled with disproportionately large expenditures in military and space programs. The Cold War intensified in Asia in 1949 as Stalin held meetings with Chinese Communist leader **Mao Zedong**. Mao's Communist rebels defeated the US-backed nationalist forces of China. The Soviet Union's alliance with the new People's Republic of China seemed to prove the wisdom of the Truman Doctrine. US political leaders and pundits alike spoke of containment in terms of a "domino theory" in which one nation "falling" to Communism appeared to endanger their neighbors. Others spoke of Communism as a contagious disease whose victims must be quarantined to prevent the spread to "healthy" nations.

Truman and his advisers rarely considered China on its own terms, choosing instead to view events in Asia in the context of Europe and the Cold War. The same is true of the American media in the 1940s. As a result, most Americans assumed that the actions of Asian leaders were the product of American and European foreign policies. As a result, Truman came under heavy scrutiny for the "loss" of China to Communism. The criticism discounts the agency of people in China who supported Communist leaders over the alternative, but few in the United States considered events from this point of view. Instead, the perception spread that the Truman administration allowed the Communists to take power in China and the president became increasingly vulnerable to accusations that his administration was "soft" on Communism. Dozens of Republican politicians seized this perception and swept to office in the 1950 and 1952 Congressional elections. Under Truman's watch, the United States had squandered its atomic monopoly, they argued, while watching idly by as their democratic ally in China was defeated by Communist forces.

In reality, the nationalist forces Mao had defeated represented an extremely undemocratic and unpopular dictatorship. There was likely very little America could have done to prevent the defeat of Chiang Kai-shek, the corrupt leader of nationalist forces who was exiled to Taiwan in 1950. However, the perception that Truman was "soft" on Communism soon drove the president to respond in ways that assumed US foreign policy could determine events abroad. Truman responded to the "loss" of China and the increased political pressure by escalating and expanding his containment policy from Europe and Asia to Africa, Latin America, and the Middle East. The United States also formalized an alliance with Japan, Thailand, the Philippines, and Australia that provided these nations with US aid in return for military bases throughout the Pacific. In 1950, Truman also committed US forces to a war in Korea and began providing economic and military aid to French forces fighting in Vietnam.

1.6   The Middle East

The British had pledged support for a Jewish homeland during World War I under the Balfour Declaration, and similar promises regarding a Jewish homeland were made during World War II. However, neither Jewish Zionists (advocates of an independent Jewish state in Palestine) nor the region's Arabic inhabitants had been granted control of Palestine. Tensions rose between Jews and Arabs in the region as Britain sought a plan that would be acceptable to all parties while promoting stability in the region. Arabs were especially concerned by the arrival of Jewish settlers in the early 1930s. Many of these

North Atlantic Treaty Organization (NATO)

A military alliance originally formed in 1949 between the United States and other nations in North America and Europe in response to the perceived aggression of Communist nations. Today, NATO has expanded to twenty-eight members.

Warsaw Pact

A military alliance between the Soviet Union and the Communist nations of Eastern Europe between 1955 and the dissolution of the Soviet Union in 1991.

Mao Zedong

Communist revolutionary who defeated the nationalist forces of Chiang Kai-shek in 1949 to become the leader of the People's Republic of China.

settlers had succeeded in escaping Nazi persecution prior to Britain's ban against Jewish immigration from Europe to Palestine. In 1939, the British again tried to negotiate an agreement between Zionists and Palestinians regarding shared use of the region. However, even the diplomats selected to represent Zionist and Palestinian perspectives refused to acknowledge the existence of the other.

The horrors of the Holocaust and British guilt for blocking the escape of European Jews to Palestine led to renewed support for a Jewish homeland in Europe. Great Britain still controlled Palestine but sought to avoid any settlement that might anger either side. As a result, Britain announced they would follow the advice of the United Nations. In 1947, the UN voted to partition Palestine into separate Jewish and Arab states, with Jerusalem becoming the capital of both nations. The plan appeared reasonable to outsiders, but neither side considered the issue settled. Part of the problem was that there was no way to create an all-Jewish or all-Palestinian nation without forcing tens of thousands of people from their homes.

FIGURE 9.6

Israel was created as a new nation in 1947 with the intention of setting aside certain areas for Palestinians. The new nation was surrounded by Arabic countries that sought to challenge its existence, leading to a series of wars and territory disputes. Conflicts involving the Palestinian Territories known as the Gaza Strip and West Bank were especially turbulent.

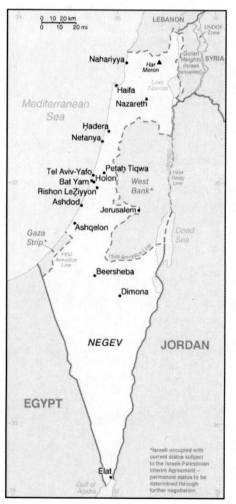

Standard Oil and other US companies were increasingly competing with the British and Dutch for access to Middle Eastern oil. The outbreak of World War II and the expanding commitments of the military increased the importance of the region to the US government, while US oil companies recognized the need to expand production. The US and British governments had promised to consult with Arabic leaders prior to making or supporting any major policy affecting the Middle East. Both Roosevelt and his successor Truman fully understood the importance of Palestine for both Jews and Arabs. Like the British leaders, the US leaders were wary of any action that might promote instability in the region. However, Truman and other US leaders were also deeply influenced by the Holocaust. They knew that the death toll was exacerbated by British and American refusal to allow Jewish refugees into their nations. Likewise, Truman viewed Britain's refusal to allow Jewish refugees into Palestine as indefensible. After all, Britain had declared that Palestine would become a Jewish homeland under the Balfour Declaration.

The situation grew tense as nearly a quarter-million Jewish refugees, many of whom were Holocaust survivors, were living in camps throughout Europe waiting for permission to immigrate to Palestine or other locations. Truman sought to eliminate the restrictions that had prevented Jews from coming to the United States during Hitler's reign. Even after Americans were made aware of the full dimension of the Holocaust, Truman's proposition met significant opposition. Many Americans hoped that the existence of a Jewish nation in Palestine would settle the issue and there would be no need to alter US immigration policies. Others feared that backlash of the Palestinian majority would lead to instability in the region and jeopardize the business relations between US oil companies and the Arab world.

While many viewed their nation's support for Israel as atonement for US inaction regarding the Holocaust, the leading reason for US and international support for the creation of an independent Jewish state may have been the continued reluctance of all nations to accept large numbers of Jewish refugees into their own countries. Although most commended the action as a way of preventing future atrocities against Jews around the globe, some historians believe that US support of Israel was largely influenced by the fact that its creation helped to discourage Jewish migration to the United States.

The United States was the first to extend diplomatic recognition to Israel when it became an independent nation in May 1948. However, Israel was also surrounded by hostile states that pledged to attack it as soon as British troops left. As predicted, once the British mandate had expired and its troops returned to the island, Israel was immediately invaded by several neighboring Arab countries. The attackers failed to effectively combine their forces, and Israel not only defeated these forces but also expanded its territory. The Israeli victory and its resulting territorial gains resulted in 750,000 Arab refugees fleeing from these lands and an ongoing controversy regarding the status of these lands. Although the priority of US policymakers in the Middle East following World War II remained focused on oil exploration and containment of Communism, America would increasingly view Israeli-Palestinian relations as a leading issue of concern.

Tens of thousands of American Jews also migrated to Palestine following its creation in 1948. These were not the only Americans who traveled to the Middle East during this era, as dozens of American and British enclaves were created as oil companies expanded throughout the region. Kirkuk, Iraq; Abadan, Iran; and Dhahran, Saudi Arabia, and other centers of oil exploration became home to tens of thousands of Americans. In the case of Dhahran, a virtual American suburb was constructed to house the nearly 5,000 Americans employed by the Arabian American Oil Company (ARAMCO). The company was formed from an agreement between Standard Oil and a regional Arabian leader named Ibn Saud. The partnership resulted in record profits for the US investors, access to Middle Eastern oil for the US Navy, and the wealth needed for Saud to take over the Arabian Peninsula and create the nation of Saudi Arabia.

The US camp at Dhahran was literally a city within a city, as the Arabic workers were not allowed in the walled American compound, which featured air-conditioned shopping centers and modern hospital facilities. While the Americans lived in relative luxury, the Arabic workers lived in makeshift shanties and were paid less than a dollar per day. The wealth of the oil industry did little to improve the conditions for the majority of King Saud's subjects. The monarch used his share of oil revenues to consolidate both religious and secular authority, replacing a variety of more liberal Islamic sects that had existed throughout Arabia. Saud believed in the literal interpretation of the Koran and instituted Sharia law. Despite the fact that his views were considered by Westerners as violations of human rights and especially the rights of women, US business and political leaders embraced the Saudi leadership.

In neighboring Iran, **Muhammad Reza Shah Pahlavi** (known to Americans as the shah of Iran, with the word "shah" being a word synonymous with "ruler" in that region of the world) had been placed in power by Soviet and British forces that invaded the oil-rich nation in 1941. The shah's policies that were friendly to foreign oil interests were challenged by his prime minister, Muhammad Mossadeq. Mossadeq introduced a number of progressive reforms such as public housing and social security. He had hoped to pay for these programs through the **nationalization** of Iran's oil fields. This greatly concerned both US and British business interests who used both political intrigue and a joint CIA and MI-6 operation to overthrow Mossadeq and reinstall the shah of Iran.

After being placed back in power with the aid of the West, the shah of Iran maintained strong ties to the United States and governed the country in ways favorable to Western oil companies. The shah received a share of the profits from the oil industry and US economic and military aid in exchange for his political support. From the US and British perspective, the shah promoted a stable business environment in a historically volatile region of the world. However, many of the Iranian people resented the way the shah squandered the nation's oil revenues. They strongly resented Western influence and believed that oil revenue should be more equally distributed among the people of their nation. As a result, the shah frequently resorted to the use of his army and secret police to silence dissenters. He would remain in power until 1979 when the popular albeit fiercely anti-American Islamic religious leader Ayatollah Khomeini seized power.

Muhammad Reza Shah Pahlavi

A secular Muslim and pro-Western leader of Iran between 1941 and the Iranian Revolution of 1979. He was temporarily expelled from Iran in 1953 but was placed back in power by a coup supported by the CIA and the British Secret Intelligence Service.

nationalization

Occurs when a government takes control of economic assets such as land or an entire industry. Although previously under private ownership, the entity in question becomes publicly owned. This may occur with or without financial compensation for the original owner.

REVIEW AND CRITICAL THINKING

1. What were the causes of the Cold War? To what degree were the interests of the United States and Soviet Union incompatible? Could the Cold War have been avoided? If so, how?

2. What motivated the United States to establish the Marshall Plan? Why might Stalin have insisted that Eastern European nations reject US aid?

3. What was the immediate and the long-term impact of covert CIA operations around the globe?

4. The shah of Iran embraced the West, while King Saud sought to spread puritanical Islam and Sharia law. Why would the United States form alliances with both of these leaders? What motivated them to form alliances with the United States?

2.   POSTWAR AMERICA

LEARNING OBJECTIVES

1. Explain why the United States did not experience financial turmoil when the war ended. Summarize the impact of the sudden demobilization on the US economy and society.

2. Describe the ideas about gender roles that were prevalent among most Americans during the postwar era. Explain the expectations of men, women, and the family and how some women started to challenge these notions.

3. Summarize the history of the 1948 election. Briefly detail each of the four leading candidates and their leading issue. Explain what Truman promised voters when he called for a Fair Deal and assess how successful he was at achieving his domestic agenda.

Of all the leading participants in World War II, only the United States prospered economically during the conflict. Throughout Europe and Asia, Axis and Allied nations alike were physically devastated and now faced financial catastrophe. Formerly mired in the most severe depression in its history, the United States emerged from the war with full employment, new technologies, dominance in banking and international trade, and the strongest military, and it was the only nation possessing the atomic bomb. While Europe and Asia faced reconstruction, the United States could concentrate its efforts on more construction. Within a decade, the majority of Americans owned their own homes, and over half of the world's manufactured goods were made in the United States. The American dollar replaced the British pound sterling as the world's standard currency, and US companies spread nearly as quickly across the globe as greenbacks. As Americans enjoyed this affluence, they also faced a number of domestic challenges, including the demobilization of the armed services, the question of women's role in the postwar economy, and whether New Deal programs and wartime economic controls should continue in an era of peace and material prosperity.

2.1 Demobilization

Although the United States established worldwide military bases under the terms of the Lend-Lease Act, the nation rapidly scaled down the size of its forces following Japan's surrender. From a wartime high of 12 million men and women, the military shrank to 1 million soldiers by the end of 1947. The United States granted Filipino independence in 1946 and maintained numerous bases on its commonwealth, the euphemism Americans used in place of the word "colony" when referring to the Philippine islands. By 1950, the military had been reduced to 600,000 personnel. The rapid demobilization led military officials to cancel orders for manufactured goods, which caused great concern among workers and factory owners. America's wartime economy was largely based on defense spending, and demobilization also meant that most of the 12 million Americans serving in the armed forces would quickly return to civilian life. With the government cancelling its orders, what would become of the millions of veterans as they searched for civilian employment?

Economists estimated that the sudden influx of these men and women into the labor force combined with the end of wartime production would lead to unemployment rates similar to the latter years of the Great Depression. Other economists believed that these ominous forecasts underestimated personal savings and the immense pent-up demand for consumer products. They pointed out that US families had worked longer hours for higher wages and saved a higher percentage of their pay than at any time in history.

The demands of wartime production meant that US factories had produced tanks instead of automobiles and machine guns instead of sewing machines. As a result, millions of Americans had put their money in savings bonds and savings accounts in eager anticipation of the day they could purchase all of the items they dreamed about during the lean years of the Great Depression and the demanding years of the war. These more optimistic predictions proved correct as the United States enjoyed a postwar boom that rivaled the economic growth of the war years. Unemployment remained negligible as construction companies went back to work building homes, and US factories churned out a wide array of consumer goods for an eager public with cash to spend.

Montgomery GI Bill

A postwar program providing money for veterans so they could attend college or a trade school. The GI Bill also provided certain limited unemployment benefits and a loan program to help veterans purchase a home.

One of the reasons why unemployment did not spike was the Serviceman's Readjustment Act of 1944, popularly known as the **Montgomery GI Bill**. Veterans groups such as the American Legion lobbied Congress for its passage using a mix of moral suasion and economic self-interest. After World War I, they reminded Congress, veterans received little more than a final paycheck and a boat ride home. The result was a catastrophic shock to the labor market as millions of veterans sought jobs at the same moment the War Department stopped purchasing factory products. To prevent another Bonus March and perhaps the unemployment that caused it, the American Legion called on Congress to ease the shock on the labor market by providing returning veterans with college or vocational training. The GI Bill also provided modest unemployment pay of $20 per week for up to one year.

More than 6 million veterans took advantage of the GI Bill's educational benefits, which covered tuition and books at most colleges and technical schools as well as a modest living allowance. The law revolutionized the US university system as schools rushed to accommodate veterans and the revenue they brought with them. The majority of these veterans would have likely never had the opportunity to attend college because they were not the children of wealthy and upper-middle-class families. Many of the veterans were not children at all, and the GI Bill inspired many colleges to build their first housing for married students. Veterans programs also reversed the trend toward female dominance in higher education as women represented only 3 percent of GI Bill recipients. Many colleges that had slight female majorities returned to Victorian-era gender ratios as thousands of veterans took up residence in army surplus tents on campus quads and eagerly awaited new dorms and their turn for a date with an overwhelmed coed.

While over half of those receiving educational benefits attended technical schools, the number attending college was equally vast. In 1947, roughly half of all new college students were veterans, and schools such as the University of Michigan tripled in size from 10,000 to 30,000 students. Most of these veterans hoped that their degrees would make them more competitive on the job market, which led colleges to reconsider their traditional liberal arts focus in favor of career-oriented programs and degrees. Many of the established leaders in academia feared that these changes would lead to a gradual abandonment of their mission to produce well-rounded graduates with strong analytical and communication skills.

A handful of critics even feared that the influx of nonwealthy students might lead to a reduction in academic rigor. Admission standards were not the only concern, as colleges rushed to hire new professors to meet the demand. Colleges in the California state system, for example, had to nearly double the number of instructors from 8,000 to 13,000 in 1946 alone. However, concerns about "dumbing down the curriculum" proved largely groundless as GIs performed so well in the classroom that traditional students referred to them as DARs—an acronym for "Damned Average Raisers." Most university personnel welcomed the opportunity to serve veterans and viewed the GI Bill as a means by which a college education might become more accessible to those from less-affluent backgrounds. Perhaps most significantly, the GI Bill led to a dramatic increase in the education level of the US workforce, resulting in higher levels of productivity.

More than 2 million veterans also took advantage of the GI Bill's home-loan program. In combination with other federal home-loan guaranty programs, millions of American families went from being urban renters to suburban homeowners in the postwar period. The GI Bill made no distinctions of race or ethnicity, but the climate of the 1940s meant that nonwhite veterans found it difficult to use the program to find a home. The same practices of redlining and restrictive covenants that prevented black, Latino, Asian, and Jewish homeowners from obtaining loans under the terms of New Deal programs also limited the ability of many veterans to use their GI Bill benefits to purchase a home.

In large cities, black realtors and black mortgage companies met the needs of black veterans, but even these businesses were unable to help veterans purchase homes beyond the handful of vacancies in ever-congested black neighborhoods. Members of other ethnic groups faced similar challenges in finding housing as Asian and Latino residents were frequently unable to find homes in "white" neighborhoods at any price. As a result, ethnic neighborhoods, barrios, and black communities expanded in the postwar period, while newer suburban communities became exclusively white. Neighborhood segregation emerged from individual choices, yet the process was anything but organic. Residential developers throughout the country mandated racial exclusion and then used the "whiteness" of their new suburban communities as a selling point to attract white homebuyers.

FIGURE 9.7

Three members of different service branches pose in front of Kent State University in Ohio. These men were among 6 million veterans who took advantage of the GI Bill's educational benefits after World War II.

2.2 Truman and the Fair Deal

FIGURE 9.8

Many predicted that Truman would lose the election of 1948 to the popular reformer Thomas Dewey. The Chicago Tribune even projected Dewey as the victor after the election, although an actual count of the votes showed a different outcome. The early headline was famously lampooned by Truman himself.

Progressive Party

Composed of Democrats who believed that Harry Truman was too conservative in both foreign and domestic politics, the Progressive Party emerged in 1948 under the banner of presidential candidate Henry Wallace. The Party called for an end to segregation, equal rights for African Americans, an end to the Cold War, and universal health insurance.

Republicans attacked President Truman during the congressional elections of 1946 with slogans such as "To err is Truman." That these tactics helped win control of the House and Senate reflected the frustrations of voters who believed the new president was either too similar to FDR or had strayed too far from the principles of the New Deal. In the next two years, Truman attempted to demonstrate that he was a genuine heir of FDR by sponsoring bills that would have raised the minimum wage, provided health care to the elderly, extended social security to more Americans, and increased funding for job creation and education programs. However the increasingly conservative Congress rejected each of these bills.

Truman responded in the presidential election of 1948 by using a strategy similar to what the Republicans had used against him. Truman sought to mobilize frustrated voters and asked the nation if they desired a change from the "do nothing" politicians in Washington and highlighting many of the New Deal-like programs he had supported but they had blocked. This strategy of appealing to the frustration of voters worked for the Republicans in 1946, and it also worked for Truman in 1948. However, these negative campaign tactics also left the victorious parties saddled with the burden of higher expectations from an increasingly discouraged electorate.

The situation appeared bleak for Truman in the months leading up to the 1948 election. Two blocks of voters bolted from his Democratic Party, one because they felt the president was too conservative in his domestic policies, and the other because they felt Truman was too liberal regarding civil rights. In 1946, Truman had fired Secretary of Commerce Henry Wallace, a popular leader within the left wing of the Democratic Party. At that time, Wallace openly challenged the president's views about the Soviet Union and the necessity of the emerging Cold War. Wallace's removal hurt Truman's reputation with liberals in the following years.

When Henry Wallace accepted the candidacy of the new **Progressive Party**, many predicted that millions of more liberal Democrats would abandon Truman in favor of Wallace. However, most Democrats recognized that Wallace had little chance of winning the presidency in 1948 and feared voting for Wallace's Progressive Party would do nothing but ensure a Republican victory. Perhaps more importantly, Wallace's unambiguous support for racial equality, universal health insurance, and peaceful coexistence with the Soviet Union made it difficult for Republicans to paint Truman as a liberal. The president only mildly supported civil rights and was an ardent cold warrior, qualities that made him appear a safer choice with many moderates. Truman responded by waging an aggressive campaign aimed at appealing to voters who had supported the New Deal coalition of his predecessor and still equated Republican candidates with the interests of bankers and corporations.

FIGURE 9.9

The election of 1948 was closely contested between Harry Truman and Thomas Dewey. South Carolina's Strom Thurmond ran on a prosegregation ticket under the banner of the States' Rights Democratic Party, better known as the Dixiecrats.

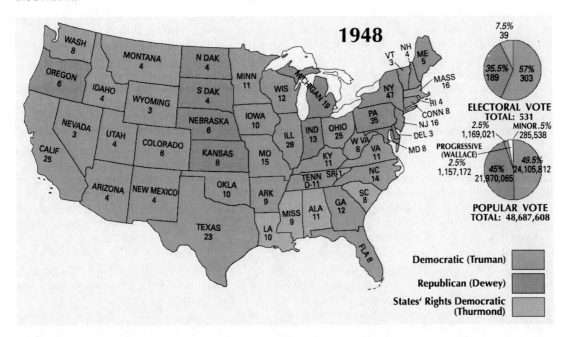

The second group of voters that abandoned Truman was the States Rights Democratic Party, also known as the **Dixiecrats**. Northern delegates approved a moderate statement in support of civil rights reform during the 1948 Democratic National Convention. In an episode reminiscent of the splintering of the Democratic Party prior to the Civil War, thirty-five Southern delegates led by South Carolina's **Strom Thurmond** protested and walked out of the meeting under the banner of "state's rights." The Dixiecrats feared that the federal government had become too powerful and was imposing a liberal agenda upon the nation, which would lead to racial integration. Dixiecrat politicians also spoke to the frustration many hardworking Southern whites felt on issues beyond race. The Dixiecrats swept four Southern states in the election—mostly because Dixiecrat candidate Strom Thurmond was declared the official Democratic candidate in Louisiana, Mississippi, Alabama, and his home state of South Carolina. The intense popularity of Thurmond among Southern whites demonstrated to many conservatives that a platform built on homespun rhetoric, opposition to racial integration, and suspicion of Northern liberals polled well with many voters. As Truman and other Democrats displayed support for moderate civil rights reforms, conservative white Republicans and Democrats alike appealed to populist suspicion of liberal elites and race-baiting to poll large majorities throughout the 1950s and early 1960s.

Dixiecrats

Composed of Southern Democrats and others who believed that Harry Truman was too liberal in terms of race, the Dixiecrats seceded from the national Democratic party in 1948 under the banner of Strom Thurmond, a South Carolinian who favored the continuation of racial segregation.

Strom Thurmond

A senator representing South Carolina for fifty years, Thurmond is most remembered outside of his native South Carolina for his leadership of the Dixiecrat Party in 1948. Thurmond ran for president on a platform calling for the maintenance of racial segregation, a cause he would support until the later years of his life. Thurmond was a Democrat who switched to the Republican Party in 1964 in response to the Democrat's support of the 1964 Civil Rights Act.

Thomas Dewey

An attorney and special prosecutor that secured the conviction of leading gangsters like Lucky Luciano, Dewey rose to prominence and pursued a life in politics. A popular governor in New York, most predicted incorrectly that he would defeat Harry Truman in the 1948 election.

Fair Deal

A term used by President Harry Truman to promote a number of his progressive domestic policies such as national health insurance for the poor and elderly, public housing, and federal support for education and job training.

Executive Order 9981

Issued July 1948 in response to demands by black leaders, President Truman issued this order declaring an end to segregation in the military. The order also required that all members of the military be given equal opportunity regardless of their race, ethnicity, religion, or national origins.

Given the apparent disintegration of the Democratic Party, Republicans predicted an easy victory under the banner of their candidate **Thomas Dewey**. Dewey had risen to prominence as a special prosecutor who took on organized crime and was a popular governor of New York. Dewey received 46 percent of the popular vote against the seemingly unstoppable FDR in 1940, and many predicted he would easily defeat the much less popular Truman in 1948. *Life* magazine ran a picture of Dewey on its cover with the caption "The Next President," while the *New York Times* advised the Democrats to surrender to the inevitable and save everyone the trouble of a campaign. Truman disagreed and ran a vigorous campaign touring over half of the states via train. Ironically, it was Dewey who seemed to follow the *Times* campaign advice. A fiscal conservative, Dewey believes a small, dignified, and noncontroversial campaign was the best way to ensure victory. Truman gained in the polls by calling Congress back into session weeks before the election where he promoted popular measures such as increases to the minimum wage. Still, the *Chicago Tribune* ran the headline "Dewey Defeats Truman" on the evening of the election. The next morning when the votes had actually been tallied, Truman had received 49.5 percent of the popular vote and 57 percent of the Electoral College.

The Democrats also recaptured the House and Senate in 1948. This Democratic Congress proved more conservative than those under FDR, failing even to repeal the antilabor provisions of the Taft-Hartley Act described in the next section. Given the inability of the Democrats to unite in favor of labor's highest priority, it was doubtful that other traditionally Democratic priorities would fare well. However, Truman prodded Congress to enact universal health insurance, increase federal aid to schools, extend Social Security, expand public housing programs, and increase the minimum wage. Truman lumped these and dozens of other programs into something he called the **Fair Deal**. Truman succeeded in passing major legislation creating public housing projects in 1949 and expanding Social Security to cover domestic and farm laborers in 1950. He also issued **Executive Order 9981**, which ordered an end to racial segregation in the military *during* the election of 1948. However, the majority of his proposals met conservative opposition, even within his own party.

Seeking to both associate with and expand the popular programs of FDR's New Deal, Truman's Fair Deal sought a dramatic expansion of federal power during a time of peace and economic prosperity. In addition to public housing and Social Security, he was able to raise the minimum wage to 75 cents per hour, and pass limited funding for flood control and irrigation. However, the president's attempts to expand the welfare state beyond existing New Deal programs were unsuccessful. For example, Truman's health insurance plan granted the federal government the power to set prices. This led not only to a massive increase in the size and scope of the federal government but also to powerful interests in the medical field to oppose the bill. Doctors and hospitals united with conservatives to block Truman's health care bill by raising doubts that it would reduce costs and raising concern that the quality of care would decrease. Others simply sought to smear the plan by claiming it resembled the kind of totalitarianism practiced by Hitler.

2.3   Economic Growth and Labor

The government had imposed price controls and other measures to control inflation during World War II. These controls remained until the summer of 1946, after which prices rose dramatically. Some items doubled in price, while a general index of consumer goods indicated an average price increase of nearly 20 percent. Inflation also rose, so bank deposits and wartime bonds that workers had purchased were worth less than before, while paychecks bought less than they had during the war years. Congress passed a few measures to reestablish price controls on certain items and rents. Within a couple years, the forces of supply and demand eliminated most of the worst cases of price increases, yet most goods were still substantially more expensive than they had been just a few short years ago. The falling value of the dollar made US goods seem less expensive overseas, and the Marshall Plan helped foreign markets recover further enabling the purchase of American-made goods. Although the rapid price increases alarmed many Americans, the postwar period was still one of material progress.

However, in the immediate wake of the end of price controls, many workers were angered by dramatic price increases that they believed vastly exceeded wage increases. One-third of the labor force (excluding those in agriculture and domestic labor) were union members and nearly 5 million workers participated in strikes in 1945 and 1946. Entire industries such as mining saw the majority of their workers on strike. More than 700,000 steelworkers participated in the largest strike in US history, demanding wage increases that kept pace with rising steel prices. Truman feared that strikes of this magnitude could seriously disrupt the postwar economic progress and even threaten national security if permitted to continue. Truman addressed Congress asking for a measure permitting him to draft striking workers into the military that might have passed had steel workers and management not settled their strike.

FIGURE 9.10

Saturday afternoon street scene in Welch, McDowell County, West Virginia, August 24, 1946. The population and local economy of Welch was directly tied to coal mining and steel production, which boomed during the early twentieth century. Today the population of McDowell County has dropped to just over one-fifth of the nearly 100,000 residents that made this the largest coal-producing county in America during the 1950s.

Hostility toward the growth of labor unions and powerful leaders such as John L. Lewis of the United Mine Workers led to a growing movement to modify the terms of the 1935 Wagner Act. Congressmen Robert Taft and Fred Hartley drafted legislation that did more than modify the Wagner Act; it completely reversed the legislative advances made by labor unions in the first half of the twentieth century. The **Taft-Hartley Act** banned closed shops and union shops, arrangements that required employees to either belong to a union prior to being hired or join the union as a condition of employment. The law also banned secondary boycotts where other union members refused to purchase the goods of a particular company. The law also required union leaders to sign affidavits disclaiming any affiliation with the Communist organizations—a measure union leaders protested as an attempt to unfairly connect labor unions with leftists and radicals. The law also limited the use of union funds in political campaigns and permitted states to pass "right-to-work" laws that limited the organizational methods used by unions. Perhaps most importantly, the law also granted presidential authority to postpone any strike that might affect national interests for up to eighty days.

Although President Truman had just fought a personal battle with Lewis and resented the power of many union leaders, he believed that the provision of Taft-Hartley was too severe. Despite the president's veto, Taft-Hartley became law in 1947. The immediate effect on labor unions was not nearly as severe as labor leaders feared, although unions no longer enjoyed 100 percent membership through the enforcement of union and closed shops. Perhaps the most significant consequence of Taft-Hartley was the decline of smaller unions and the failure to organize new unions in the expanding service and technology fields, as well as the continued failure of unionization in the American South. Leading unions waged a campaign known as **Operation Dixie** in the late 1940s aimed at organizing unions in the South. Business interests prevailed against the would-be organizers, largely by threatening to employ black workers if whites joined unions.

Taft-Hartley Act

Passed by Congress over President Truman's veto in June 1947, the Taft-Hartley Act restricted many of the powers of unions. Among the provisions are the elimination of rules mandating that workers join unions and requirements that labor leaders give advance notice before they can call a strike.

Operation Dixie

An unsuccessful campaign by the Congress of Industrial Organizations (CIO) and other labor leaders to organize more unions in the American South following the end of World War II. The South was important to labor as more companies established factories in the region precisely due to the region's political conservatism and hostility to labor unions.

FIGURE 9.11

Leaders of national and local unions alike mobilized against the Taft-Hartley Act. These leaders produced hundreds of posters and flyers, each drawing attention to the potential consequences of the new law upon workers' right to bargain collectively.

2.4 Housing and the Suburbs

Few new homes were constructed between 1941 and 1945 as the nation concentrated its efforts constructing weapons and machines to deliver men and material to the battlefield. The subsequent rapid demobilization combined with pent-up demand and wartime consumer savings created the perfect storm for a severe housing crisis. In response, many developers began to mass-produce homes using assembly line tactics. The new homes were often lacking in terms of architectural originality and craftsmanship, but residential developers had waiting lists of customers who eagerly awaited the opportunity to buy any new home. The most successful of these developers was **William Levitt**, who rapidly converted farmland on the outskirts of Long Island into Levittown, a planned community of 17,000 homes.

Levitt built the homes faster and more efficiently than any other developer did by dividing his nonunion laborers into specialized teams. Each team had a specific task that they performed using preassembled parts of the home. For example, one team nailed drywall while another installed preconnected plumbing components. Once the team had completed its task, they simply walked to the next house and repeated the process. Every house was nearly identical, while every street featured the same landscaping, with identical trees planted every twenty-eight feet. Owners agreed to make only minor modifications to the home and follow a standard maintenance plan that would protect property values. "No man who owns his house and lot can be a Communist," Levitt claimed, "he has too much to do." Cold warrior or not, the owner of a Levitt home certainly demonstrated the benefits of free market Capitalism mixed with the welfare state. With the assistance of Federal Housing Administration loans, new homes could be secured with down payments of less than $100 and monthly payments of about $60. However, not all Americans were eligible for these deals. Not only were the homes nearly identical, but the residents of Levittown were equally homogenous. Racially restrictive covenants limiting who could buy or rent were built into the contracts of Levitt's housing developments throughout New York, New Jersey, and Pennsylvania. The same was true of most suburban developments. Levitt explained his refusal to sell or rent to any African American family as a business decision. According to Levitt, the vast majority of whites would refuse to buy or rent homes in an integrated neighborhood.

William Levitt had plenty of examples to support his theory. The wartime housing shortage placed enormous pressure on existing black and ethnic neighborhoods. Several million black and Mexican American families migrated North and West in search of jobs and racial tolerance. They rarely found either, being the last hired and given the lowest wages. Even those that managed to find good jobs had difficulty finding decent housing, settling instead for apartments created by dividing existing rentals in black and ethnic neighborhoods. As Levitt predicted, even those who were permitted to purchase homes in previously "white" neighborhoods soon found that their presence would not be tolerated by their would-be neighbors. From Chicago to St. Louis to Los Angeles, black and Mexican American homeowners saw their homes destroyed as white fire companies sprayed water on adjacent buildings to ensure that the flames observed racial boundaries.

Housing for the poor of all races was limited but was especially desperate in the West as the populations in many cities doubled in less than a decade. Nearly 200,000 Mexican Americans lived in crowded barrios throughout San Antonio. The situation was even worse in Los Angeles when one of the largest Latino neighborhoods was acquired by the city through eminent domain legislation. The city intended to replace the single-family homes with public housing that would be both low-cost and accommodate more residents. However, after existing housing was razed, area whites protested against the construction of the housing project. The land stood empty for years until acquired by the owner of the Brooklyn Dodgers who agreed to bring his team west in exchange for the city building the team a new stadium.

Even as thousands of suburbs sprouted across Texas and California, racial minorities found fewer and fewer homes that they could buy or rent outside of inner city slums. Many cities hoped that a new program called Urban Renewal might help to remove these slums and replace them with decent housing in neighborhoods with less crime. The National Housing Act of 1949 supported cities with funds for "slum clearance" with the hope that new construction in those areas would somehow fix the structural issues that had led to the decline of those urban neighborhoods. However, as had been the case in Los Angeles, those who were displaced usually ended up on their own with even fewer housing options. In the city, some of the land ended up being used to build overpasses and parking lots. In addition, housing projects quickly became new slums with conditions often aggravated as cities crammed more people into smaller spaces.

The situation on the West Coast was similar for the thousands of Japanese families who had lost their homes because of their forced relocation. Even the "white" soldiers who had married women of Asian descent during their time overseas found that their new families were not welcome in their old neighborhoods. Chinese American veterans who married overseas were not permitted to bring their wives back to the United States until a congressional amendment was made to the War Brides Act nearly two years after the surrender of Japan. Even then, it was not until 1948 that the Supreme Court declared that California laws barring the marriage of Asians and Caucasians were unconstitutional.

2.5   Gender and the Baby Boom

Even before the war was officially over, the government began scaling back and eventually canceled hundreds of military contracts for billions of dollars of supplies and equipment. Within days of the surrender of Japan, these companies laid off over a million workers. A disproportionate amount of these workers were women, the last to be hired in many defense industries and now the first to be fired. In most cases, companies made no attempt to hide the fact that female workers were losing their jobs because they were women. Furthermore, many women viewed their labor as temporary and considered it their duty to give up their jobs for returning male veterans. Postwar surveys determined that the vast majority of men and women in the United States agreed that female workers should be replaced with male workers. A 1946 survey asked if "an efficient woman whose husband could support her" should be discharged and her job given to "an inefficient man who had a family to maintain." Seventy-five percent of men and 70 percent of women reportedly agreed with that statement. Even though most women indicated that they would like to keep their jobs, notions of gender and the fear that continued female employment in "male" jobs would lead to the unemployment and emasculation of veterans led most women to accept their termination without protest.

Millions of women voluntarily left their jobs or were laid off, but the predicted postwar recession never occurred due to a massive increase in consumer spending and the provisions of the GI Bill. Unemployment remained low during the postwar boom, yet the nation still returned to prewar notions about gender and the workplace. For many women, however, wartime employment provided both income and a sense of pride. For most, their new roles as mothers and wives filled the void, yet as later studies would demonstrate, many women felt that their lives were still missing something. However, the culture of the postwar period celebrated motherhood and featured a dramatic increase in the number of children born each year, a phenomenon called the **Baby Boom**. Millions of soldiers eagerly embraced the notion of returning to family life. US women bore more children per capita between 1946 and 1964 than at any time in history. In fewer than twenty years, the nation's population increased by nearly one-third as young couples began families. The increase was due not only to the returning veterans but also to the economic security of the era that convinced many families that they could finally afford another child. The era also witnessed an unprecedented number of divorces as unexpected pregnancies led to hasty marriages that soon failed.

FIGURE 9.12

This aerial photo of a new suburban housing area demonstrates the growth of residential areas beyond the city core as well as the homogeneity of many suburban neighborhoods.

Baby Boom

A period between the end of World War II and the mid-1950s when birthrates suddenly increased due to the return of military personnel, the desire of young Americans to start families, and the economic security allowing established couples to have more children. An estimated 80 million Americans were born in these years.

The sudden increase in divorces suggests that the popular imagination of love and sex in the post-war era needs to be reconsidered. Contrary to the historical image of the era, sex and marriage in the 1950s did not follow a script as predictable as the sitcoms of the age. In 1948 and 1953, Indiana University professor Alfred C. Kinsey published two studies on male and female sexuality, often collectively referred to as the **Kinsey Report**. These publications shocked the nation with their statistics and charts that indicated that 50 percent of men had committed adultery and that nearly as many women had engaged in premarital sex. However, the most shocking revelation was that two of the cultural taboos associated by most Americans with sexual deviance at this time—homosexuality and marital infidelity by married women—were not uncommon. The report indicated that one-third of men had committed at least one homosexual act and nearly a quarter of women had cheated on their husbands. While many criticisms regarding Kinsey's methods and accuracy later led many to discredit the accuracy of his statistics, over a quarter million Americans purchased his books. Kinsey's conclusions may have been inaccurate, but they helped to spread awareness of homosexuality and challenge the notion that only men were having extramarital affairs.

2.6 Popular Culture in Postwar America

Following World War II, more Americans enjoyed more disposable income and more leisure time than at any other time in history. Between labor-saving devices, a gross national product that doubled each decade, and the labor movement's successful push for paid vacations and forty-hour workweeks, Americans had more choices for leisure and cultural activities than ever before. For the first time, Americans embraced professional sports teams in football and basketball. But baseball remained king. And in 1947, the color line in the Major Leagues that had barred African American players since Moses Fleetwood Walker's 1884 season was broken by **Jackie Robinson**.

Robinson was acquired by the Brooklyn Dodgers by a coach who recognized that integration would make his team better and immediately boost gate receipts in a diverse city such as New York. Branch Rickey offered no compensation to the Kansas City Monarchs, the legendary Negro League team for whom Robinson had played. Yet his act in breaking the color line demonstrated a commitment to racial equality few in the Major Leagues shared. The on-field success and selfless demeanor of Robinson led the Dodgers to the pennant in his rookie season and inspired several other teams to integrate in the next three seasons.

Perspectives on the Past

> By applauding Robinson, a man did not feel that he was taking a stand on school integration, or on open housing. But, for an instant, he had accepted Robinson simply as a hometown ball player. To disregard color even for an instant, is to step back away from the old prejudices, the old hatred. That is not a path on which many double back.
>
> —Author and former Dodger announcer Roger Kahn in his introduction to The Boys of Summer

Robinson's entry into the Major Leagues was the culmination of decades of protest against the color line in baseball by black newspapers, Jewish sportswriters, and left-wing activists. Despite the staunch support for integration by socialist journals and organizations, Capitalism proved to be the driving force behind the rapid integration that followed Robinson's debut. Even if the Dodgers had won the pennant, the increase in ticket sales would have led more teams to consider integration. Robinson was the National League's Rookie of the Year, and Dodger home attendance broke records as thousands of curious whites, African American families, and supportive ethnic minorities flocked to see Robinson play.

Rickey's timing was fortunate as millions of Americans had more spare time and disposable income than at any other time in history. As unemployment continued to stay low and wages continued to increase, advertisers took advantage of the affluence and transitioned from selling the war to selling consumer goods. Corporations that had little to advertise during the war suddenly produced an array of products that marketers now sold to an American public eager for the good life, or at least a life of more goods. Television was not a large part of this renewed emphasis on marketing until the mid-1950s, when over half of the population owned a television set. By this time, the television had become such a staple in American life that *TV Guide,* a magazine listing what shows would be broadcast, became one of the best-selling magazines in the nation.

New media technology gave rise to a dominant culture that celebrated consumption and affluence, but it also helped to spur a counterculture movement that rejected the materialism of the era. Critics of the dominant culture have always existed in America, especially during periods of increased consumption. Arthur Miller's *Death of a Salesman* (1949) forced Americans to confront the character of Willy Loman, an aging salesman who bought in fully to the economic orthodoxy of the era. Loman worked hard and developed an identity based on his job. Conscious of his decline but confident that he had achieved success through hard work, Loman is confronted with the hollowness of materialism when his boss shatters his self-created illusion that he was a business success.

British writer George Orwell's *1984* was even more critical of modern society. Set in the futuristic dystopia of the 1980s, Orwell depicted a society that had surrendered its ability to think critically to a centralized government that controlled nearly every aspect of life. The protagonist in Ralph Ellison's *Invisible Man* (1952) experienced a different brand of totalitarianism as an African American man searching for a meaningful existence in a white-dominated city. "You ache with the need to convince yourself that you do exist in the real world…you strike out with your fists, you curse and swear to make them recognize you. And alas, it's seldom successful."

As popular as these books were, the counterculture message of the 1950s ironically reached a broader audience due to improvements in transportation and communication. Neighborhoods such as Greenwich Village in New York were home to artists and writers who helped to create a counterculture known as the **Beat Movement**. The Beats, or beatniks as they were often called, disdained Capitalism and its conspicuous materialism in an often-quixotic search for some higher form of expression and experience. They viewed themselves as nonconformists, often shunning work and other societal expectations to search for higher consciousness. The beat lifestyle valued daily meditation, alternative music and poetry, and displayed an unapologetic tolerance for those who experimented with psychotic drugs. The beatniks revered the ideas of authors and poets such as Allen Ginsberg, a brilliant mind who frequently found inspiration in mind-altering drugs. Ginsberg railed against materialist conformity in favor of authentic experience through impulsive action. Many Americans viewed the beatniks as degenerates and slackers who were self-absorbed and nihilistic. Others were intrigued by the notion of an alternative to their daily routine, even if they refused to abandon its comforts and security. However, due to the prominence of television and radio, most Americans were at least aware of these new self-styled hipsters, just as the nation would be aware of the hippies a generation later.

While the beatniks searched for a higher existence, another group of Americans was creating a new and uniquely American form of expression. Rock 'n' roll was born from a union of amplifiers, electronics, and traditional rhythm and blues. Because it had grown from churches and had its roots in West African call-and-response traditions, the pioneers of this new rhythm and blues sound were African Americans. White musicians like **Elvis Presley** followed their lead and enjoyed both instant celebrity as well as controversy. If imitation is a form of flattery, Presley was deeply impressed by the style of rhythm and blues performed by traveling black musicians. For this reason, white parents feared Presley's "black" music and style might start their daughters down the aisle of interracial marriage. Some attempted to ban certain musicians and albums, while others protested against rock 'n' roll concerts in their community. Frank Sinatra simply thought the music itself was terrible, if in fact rock 'n' roll could even be considered music at all. He referred to the new genre as "the most brutal, ugly, desperate, vicious form of expression" to ever be unleashed on the American airwaves. Like generations before them, teenagers defied their parents and embraced this uniquely American form of music. Few of these children were taking a stand on civil rights by listening to white musicians who rejected the notion that good music recognized the color line. However, the growth of rock 'n' roll increasingly brought white suburbanites and the music of black America together, if only through the airwaves. US businessmen responded to the demand as Capitalists usually do, producing 600 million rock albums by the end of the decade. It was not yet clear if rock 'n' roll was here to stay, but it certainly made its mark on the 1950s.

Both the controversy and profitability of rock 'n' roll personifies the youths of the 1950s. Like all young people, the teenagers of the 1950s craved excitement and sought their own identity beyond the inherited worldview of their parents. Affluence and technology propelled their search for authentic experience as millions of white youths cautiously embraced "black" music from the comfort of their suburban homes and malt shops. Rock 'n' roll offered a temporary escape from the domination of parents and the sanitized culture of affluent white America. Yet the affluence of white America was the very reason the genre spread beyond Southern juke joints and Harlem nightclubs. Technology allowed music to be recorded, reappropriated, and redistributed by white musicians such as Elvis Pressley. Moreover, while few whites would venture to the black neighborhoods of Detroit, the sounds of Motown could be purchased at the local record shop. By the middle of the decade, white and black artists alike were pushing the boundaries of rock 'n' roll. The new generation eagerly bought up the music and its association with rebellion against the monotony of the adult world they each knew would soon become their reality.

Elvis Presley

A native of Mississippi and Tennessee, Presley was inspired by country music and rhythm and blues and merged these styles into a new genre of music that became known as rock 'n' roll.

REVIEW AND CRITICAL THINKING

1. How did the GI Bill affect postwar America? What might have led to such a sweeping and progressive bill being passed during a relatively conservative era in US history?

2. Why might so many working women have accepted the notion that they should quit their jobs to create more employment opportunities for men? What were the strategies some women used to challenge discrimination by employers? Would you consider these efforts radical or conservative?

3. Why did Truman win the election of 1948, and why would so many reporters who covered the election believe that Dewey would win instead? What does the election reveal about leading issues such as race, the Cold War, and the nation's view regarding labor and progressive social programs?

4. Labor leaders predicted that the Taft-Hartley Bill would destroy organized labor. Were they correct? What were the arguments for and against the Taft-Hartley Act, and how has the law affected unions, employers, and workers in the United States?

5. How did popular culture reflect the postwar era? Is studying popular culture useful to understanding the past, or should historians focus more effort on other aspects of history?

3. RED SCARES, LAVENDER SCARES, AND THE QUEST FOR EQUALITY DURING THE EARLY COLD WAR

LEARNING OBJECTIVES

1. Explain how the development of atomic weapons affected the relationship between America and the Soviet Union. Examine the ways that the military and diplomatic concerns about nuclear proliferation affected US culture and society.

2. Describe the Red Scare and the Lavender Scare in the context of the Cold War. Explain why the government feared that leftists and homosexuals threatened the security of the nation. Finally, explain the impact of the Lavender Scare on the later Gay Rights Movement.

3. Place the importance of the integration of the military and *Brown v. Board* within the larger narrative of the black freedom struggle. Explain the role of African Americans in these events, and explain why the government decided to end segregation in two of its leading institutions after years of enforcing racial separation.

Even as America embraced its new role as the global industrial leader and entered an era of unprecedented abundance, scarcity continued to dominate the lives of one in five Americans living below the poverty line. For many of these, racial and ethnic discrimination compounded the problems of poverty. However, more and more Americans directly confronted the violations of their civil rights through direct action and the courts. The early Cold War period also witnessed the worst persecution of homosexuals since the colonial era and the second major attack on the extreme left in the last two generations. For cultural critics such as Arthur Miller, America's attack on the left resembled the Salem Witch trials. And perhaps most ironic of all, the new military technologies that provided America's global supremacy seemed to intensify existing concerns regarding global security.

3.1 Nuclear Age

Americans enjoyed their monopoly of power that came with being the sole possessor of atomic weapon technology, but they also recognized that the Soviet Union and other leading nations would soon achieve nuclear capabilities. As a result, many politicians and scientists considered the possibility of having the United Nations or some other international organization regulate the development of atomic weapons. At the same time, the creation of such an institution might limit the options of leading scientific nations such as the United States. In addition, limits on the types and numbers of weapons member nations could develop might provide an opportunity for rogue states and those who might secretly violate the treaties. Before any such organization was created, the Soviets stunned the world by successfully testing their first atomic weapon in August 1949. Because this was several years earlier than US scientists had predicted, many suspected that the Kremlin had somehow stolen America's atomic secrets.

Americans were already aware that the Soviets had spies operating throughout the United States. In 1948, one of those spies identified the State Department's Alger Hiss as a coconspirator. The spy led officials and reporters to a hollow gourd on his farm that was filled with microfilmed documents Hiss had allegedly typed and passed on to his Soviet contact. It was impossible to prove that these "pumpkin papers" as they became known were created by Hiss. In addition, the alleged incident had occurred so many years ago that Hiss could not even be tried for the crime of espionage. However, the nature of the accusations led to a trial to test Hiss's loyalty, and the jury convicted Hiss of **perjury**.

Even more alarming to most Americans, **Ethel and Julius Rosenberg** were found guilty of facilitating the transfer of nuclear secrets to Soviet physicists. The couple was executed together in the electric chair following a controversial and emotional trial that divided many Americans. For many, the nature of their crime warranted the punishment, while the couple's membership in the American Communist Party validated the postwar persecution of Communists. For others, the association between the Rosenbergs and the Soviet Union was unclear and the charge of treason a willful exaggeration. For some, the government overstated the crimes of these minor figures to justify their actions in the Cold War. "The death sentence is not surprising," Julius Rosenberg wrote his attorney. "There had to be a Rosenberg case because there had to be an intensification of the hysteria in America to make the Korean War acceptable to the American people."

President Truman responded to the successful Soviet test by announcing plans to develop the hydrogen bomb, an atomic weapon utilizing an even more powerful second-stage explosion. American physicists had been secretly exploring the possibility of multiple-stage weapons as early as the first successful test of the original atomic bomb. Even those scientists that feared the incredible destructive power of the hydrogen bomb equally feared the consequences if the Soviet Union developed the weapon before the United States did. These individuals were relieved when Americans conducted the first fusion test in the South Pacific in November 1952, creating a crater one mile wide and 160 feet deep. The Soviet Union responded in August 1953 with its own successful test, after which the United States responded with a deliverable hydrogen bomb dropped on the Bikini Atoll in the Pacific. Remembered for the overwhelming bombshell to which it yielded, the devastated Atoll soon shared its name with an equally persuasive two-piece item altering life on American beaches in the summers to come.

US military strategists debated the implications of their powerful new weapon. They determined that the awesome destructiveness of the hydrogen bomb created its own disincentive against use in war. Theorists proposed that by building up a large nuclear arsenal, the United States could be relatively ensured against a nuclear attack through a theory known colloquially as **Mutually Assured Destruction (MAD)**. The idea behind MAD was the assumption that if one or more nations possessed the ability to destroy one another and were completely committed to launching these weapons in the case of an attack, that neither side would ever attack the other because the consequence would be the annihilation of both nations. As a result, MAD contains a relied-on idea that possession of a nuclear arsenal provides defense through deterrence.

Americans were understandably concerned with ways to protect themselves should their leaders' theories about deterrence prove overly optimistic. The Federal Civil Defense Administration established the Alert America campaign, partially to study methods of early detection of possible threats, and partially to reassure Americans that their government was doing everything in its power to protect them. Short films provided children with advice on how they could survive a Soviet nuclear attack. Schools were provided with comic books and cartoon characters to help them learn methods of self-protection.

Critics believed that the real intention of these cartoons was to scare children and parents in ways that would prevent Americans from questioning the assumptions of the Cold War. While there are reasons to support this analysis, there is also evidence that few Americans in the 1950s took these cartoons and their Saturday morning advice very seriously. Modern audiences still enjoy watching a cartoon turtle named Bert advise white children in a black-and-white film to "duck and cover" using desks and their own limbs to fend off nuclear blasts. However, more representative of the ways Americans sought to protect themselves are the efforts of local organizers to create thousands of community bomb shelters. Others got busy with shovels in their own backyards, creating their own shelters hidden by secret passageways so that unprepared neighbors would not swarm their refuge and its can-based supplies.

perjury

A criminal offense of lying while under oath to tell the truth.

Ethel and Julius Rosenberg

An American couple of Jewish origins, the Rosenbergs were accused of passing on atomic secrets through a family member who was a confessed spy for the Soviet Union. The execution of the couple, who steadfastly denied any espionage, sharply divided many Americans.

FIGURE 9.13

US soldiers observe a test explosion of a nuclear device in 1951. The army continues to maintain this nuclear test site in the Nevada desert about an hour's drive from Las Vegas.

Mutually Assured Destruction (MAD)

A theory of nuclear deterrence that posited that no nuclear power would attack another nuclear power because of the likely consequence that any such attack would lead to the launch of enough nuclear weapons to destroy both nations.

3.2 Second Red Scare

As the Soviet Union bore the brunt of the Nazi attack in the early years of World War II, the American Communist Party enjoyed its greatest popularity with approximately 80,000 members. Although this number rapidly declined following the war and was a microscopic percentage of the 150 million other citizens, some feared that these individuals might commit actions that could jeopardize the security of the nation. Recently declassified Soviet archival sources reveal the existence of more than one hundred spies operating in the United States. Few of these individuals were ever apprehended, but in 1945, federal officials discovered that a pair of State Department workers collaborated with an intelligence officer to pass classified information to Communist supporters. Later that year, an employee of the Soviet Embassy in Canada revealed the existence of espionage within the Manhattan Project. In reaction, a number of the president's political opponents accused Truman as "soft on Communism" despite his administration's increasingly severe language about the threat posed by the Soviet Union in Europe.

Truman increasingly believed that the actual threat of Communism spreading in ways that threatened the United States was often exaggerated. He also believed that the CIA, military, and other government agencies were acting effectively to promote both internal and external security against any potential Communist threat. However, for political reasons, he also went along with demands for stricter surveillance of government employees, issuing an executive order authorizing Loyalty Review Boards to investigate and dismiss any employee they deemed untrustworthy. The Attorney General's office created a list of organizations that it deemed subversive and investigated any government employee it believed had ever been associated with any group on that list. In 1950, Patrick McCarran, a Democratic senator from Nevada, proposed a law requiring all members of the American Communist Party to register with the federal government. Believing restrictions on political affiliation violated constitutional standards of freedom of speech and assembly, Truman vetoed the law. "In a free country," Truman famously responded, "we punish men for the crimes they commit, but never for the opinions they hold." Congress passed the law over the president's veto, with support from both Republican and Democratic legislators.

In February 1950, amid news of Alger Hiss's conviction and reports of a former Soviet spy's arrest, Wisconsin Senator **Joseph McCarthy** addressed a Republican women's group in Wheeling, West Virginia. The senator played to his audience's legitimate concerns about possible Soviet spy networks by alleging that he had compiled a list of 205 "card-carrying Communists" who worked for the State Department. In reality, he had no such list, and when pressured to disclose names, McCarthy stalled, hedged, revised the number to 57, and then claimed that America's enemies had changed his more vague assertion that Communists were working in the State Department into something they knew could not be proven. The experience taught the senator two things: (1) accusations work best when they are nonspecific and (2) allegations of this sort were political gold. McCarthy's technique of accusation without evidence typified the methods of many during this era. As a result, historians use the term **McCarthyism** to refer to the unsubstantiated accusations of disloyalty issued by McCarthy and other demagogues throughout the Cold War period.

McCarthy's sudden prominence led to his appointment to the **House Committee on Un-American Activities (HUAC)**. McCarthy and HUAC rose from obscurity in 1947 when they launched an investigation into charges of Communist influence in Hollywood. Scores of actors, writers, and directors were required to testify. Ten believed they were being forced to appear before a witch trial and refused to cooperate. These members of the "Hollywood Ten" thought they could defend their refusal to testify under the Fifth Amendment, but they were still sent to prison on various charges. A much larger number actors and writers were blacklisted based on expressions of sympathy for Communists, previous political associations, and in some cases, gossip spread by others. Among the blacklisted were Orson Welles and Leo Penn, father of actor Sean Penn. Americans were encouraged to boycott films by British actor Charlie Chaplin, who was forbidden to enter the United States for nearly two decades.

McCarthyism

A blanket term referring to both the anti-Communist hysteria of the postwar period and the techniques used by Wisconsin senator Joseph McCarthy. The senator repeatedly issued accusations of disloyalty against numerous individuals and government agencies without providing any evidence of his claims.

House Committee on Un-American Activities (HUAC)

A congressional committee tasked with investigating alleged instances of subversion and disloyalty among federal employees. After World War II, the committee investigated a number of Hollywood actors, writers, poets, athletes, and other influential private citizens. Although relatively few of those called before the committee were imprisoned, the possibility of being investigated tended to restrict criticism of the government during the postwar era.

FIGURE 9.14

This political cartoon portrays Senator McCarthy as being "cornered" by his own unsubstantiated accusations. McCarthy regularly accused individuals of being disloyal or of being members of the Communist Party but was rarely able to provide evidence of such claims.

African American actor **Paul Robeson** suffered the reverse fate, having his passport revoked in 1950 to prevent him from leaving the United States. While some sharing his point of view were deported, Robeson was forbidden to leave the country because when he traveled abroad, he spoke candidly about US race relations. Robeson's blistering but factual accounts of lynching and Jim Crow were utilized by Soviet agents as they sought to demonstrate the hypocrisy of America and win converts to their doctrines throughout the globe.

Robeson defended socialism partially because he believed that a more equal distribution of wealth would help to erode racism, and partially because many leading socialists were also supporters of civil rights initiatives. Many black leaders in the early twentieth century believed that the communal values of socialism and its enforced economic egalitarianism would help to promote racial and class equality in the United States. When members of the HUAC investigating committee demanded to know his political membership, the former pro football player extended a challenge for the congressmen to follow him into the voting booth and see for themselves. And, unlike many of Robeson's friends who distanced themselves from the accused performer, Robeson made a point of defending his friends even while being investigated by HUAC.

Paul Robeson

A multisport star athlete and top student at Rutgers University, Robeson went on to graduate law school at Northwestern, play football in the NFL, and star in Shakespearean drama. Most famous for his singing, Robeson toured the world and spoke forcibly about American race relations. These comments and his embrace of Communism led to numerous investigations and restrictions being placed on him by the US government.

After being questioned about the loyalty of Benjamin Davis, a Morehouse and Harvard graduate who wrote for the socialist newspaper the *Daily Worker*, Robeson responded that he was proud of his friendship with the often-controversial Davis. "I say that he is as patriotic an American as there can be, and you gentlemen belong with the Alien and Sedition Acts," Robeson exclaimed, likening the prosecution of communists to the late eighteenth century law that criminalized dissent. "You are the nonpatriots," Robeson continued, "and you are the un-Americans, and you ought to be ashamed of yourselves."

Few Americans were willing to express their opinions as forcefully as Robeson and Davis. While many historians today celebrate their impassioned defense of free speech, it is important to remember that these men often infuriated even the most liberal Americans of their day with their continued defense of Joseph Stalin and others who are now considered tyrants. As a result, it is often difficult to arrive upon simple conclusions about the meaning of McCarthyism in American history. Clearly one of the long-term consequences of McCarthy's and Hoover's actions was the blurring of dissent and disloyalty in the minds of many Americans. The idea of questioning the assumptions of the Cold War seemed "un-American" to many, which led to an era of consensus that encouraged short-sighted decisions. McCarthyism also discouraged a number of politicians from sponsoring progressive legislation for fear they might possibly be labeled as "socialist." While European and developing nations embraced programs of state-sponsored health insurance, similar measures repeatedly failed, even during periods when Democrats controlled the White House and Congress.

African American poet and author **Langston Hughes** was called to defend himself before the House Committee on Un-American Activities in 1953 for similar reasons. Hughes only mildly confronted his accusers compared with a later HUAC trial of Robeson. Hughes tried to explain to the committee that his poetic yet critical lines about freedom in America were inspired by his childhood experiences in Lawrence, Kansas, rather than on Communist ideology. Had the committee read Hughes poetry and learned the story of his childhood, they would have learned how he had been discouraged and even belittled by his white teachers. They would have also found that black children endured informal segregation within the supposedly integrated restaurants, theaters, and even classrooms of the North.

Historians estimate that over tens of thousands of artists, teachers, and journalists were fired or otherwise harassed due to their political views or affiliations during the Cold War. Hollywood studios attempted to forestall government criticism by financing production of explicitly anti-Communist films. Movies such as *I Married a Communist* and *The Red Menace* lacked artistic merit and lost money at the box office. Their plots were stale, but they did help to convince government officials of a director's and studio's loyalty to the nation. Even the great American pastime suffered, with Jackie Robinson being forced to publicly disown his friend and fellow black athlete Paul Robeson for the latter's political beliefs. The Cincinnati Reds likewise felt compelled to distance themselves from any possible association to "Red" Communism. They temporarily changed their team name to the "Redlegs" and removed the word "Red" from their uniforms during the late 1950s.

3.3 Lavender Scare

In 1948, university professor Alfred Kinsey published a dense, eight-hundred-page scientific tome called *Sexual Behavior in the Human Male* that became a bestseller as Americans struggled to learn that an estimated 5 percent of the men he interviewed acknowledged that they were homosexuals and even more admitted that they had committed at least one homosexual act in their lives. Although his study demonstrated that homosexuality was far more common than previously assumed, the public reaction was not one of acceptance. In fact, persecution of homosexuals intensified and gay, lesbian, bisexual, and transgender (GLBT) individuals were increasingly forced on the defensive against the widespread association as "deviants." Whereas the subject of gender orientation was rarely breached before the World War II, the climate of the Cold War fostered internal investigations of the most personal aspects of individuals' lives.

Although it has received far less attention than the Red Scare, more federal government employees lost their jobs during the **Lavender Scare**. Between 1947 and 1950, internal investigations of State Department employees led to the removal of ninety individuals based on suspicion that they were homosexual. These purges were intensified in the early 1950s, and historians estimate that several thousand federal employees were fired on grounds of sexual orientation between the end of World War II and the 1970s. The exact number of purged employees is impossible to determine because many individuals chose to voluntarily resign and spare themselves and their families from a governmental investigation. When faced with the commonly used inquisition, "Information has come to the attention of the Civil Service Commission that you are a homosexual. What comment do you care to make?" only a handful of individuals chose to confront their accusers.

The argument for terminating these accused homosexuals was not that they were a threat in and of themselves, but rather that they lived a dishonest and immoral lifestyle. Even more importantly, most homosexuals in the 1950s sought to hide their gender orientation to avoid persecution. "Outed" individuals might be physically assaulted, forced out of their neighborhood, disowned by their families, and as these purges demonstrated, fired from their jobs. As a result, many Americans believed, homosexuals would be susceptible to blackmail by enemy agents who could coerce them into doing their bidding or revealing government secrets. A 1950 government report casually linked negative homosexual stereotypes with inherent character defects that Soviet spies might be able to exploit. "The lack of emotional stability which is found in most sex perverts (a code name for homosexuals in the 1940s and 1950s) and the weakness of their moral fiber, makes them susceptible to the blandishments of the foreign espionage agent." The report also considered it a fact that homosexuals "seldom refuse to talk about themselves" and would therefore be even more likely to volunteer sensitive information to enemy agents.

Years of congressional hearings and FBI investigations have yet to reveal a single instance where a homosexual government employee was blackmailed by an enemy agent. Some historians argue that the blackmail explanation was little more than window dressing used to vindicate what was essentially a witch-hunt. Others view both the Red Scare and the Lavender Scare as populist venting for those who looked toward Washington with suspicion. For many, Washington, DC, was an immoral town filled with bureaucrats, career-driven women, and men who no longer commanded the respect and obedience of the larger world. According to this view, the image of the State Department as a haven for a disloyal fifth column of "commies and queers" provided both a means of protest against social change and government growth and an explanation for the seeming impotence of the United States abroad. Still others have argued that the Lavender Scare appealed to men increasingly concerned with the advances of women and seeking a return to notions of gender that equated masculinity with the roles of provider and protector. By this perspective, attacks on homosexuals served as a proxy for attacks on changing notions of gender and a politically acceptable rebellion against social change.

Fewer Americans were willing to be associated with openly racist ideas or organizations following World War II, yet attacks on homosexuals were permissible within mainstream society. The American Psychiatric Association classified homosexuality as a disease until 1973. Likewise, most Americans viewed statements about the inherent immorality and character weaknesses of homosexuals as common ground for more serious discussions about what might be done to cure or quarantine such persons. If a Communist was someone who was psychologically weak and had surrendered his will to the Kremlin, homosexuals were presented as people lacking self-control of moral fiber. Both were viewed as deviants who worked to indoctrinate others into their underground cliques. As a result, when President Eisenhower issued Executive Order 10450 in 1953, which declared that homosexuality was grounds for dismissal from federal employment, few questioned the soundness of his decision. Even if they had, Eisenhower's proclamation merely confirmed what the government had already been doing behind closed doors.

The action of the federal government would have a number of unintended consequences. Eisenhower's announcement sanctioned the firing of homosexuals in private industry. It also left the State Department with a severe deficit of qualified experts in a number of fields. In addition to losing their jobs, the federal government withdrew the security clearances of suspected homosexuals, which often prevented these experts from finding work in academia or private industry. The atmosphere created by constant internal investigations resulted in creating a climate where few individuals were willing to question the assumptions of the more militaristic members of the administration for fear of being viewed as effete. As a result, some historians believe that the Lavender Scare resulted in many State Department officials adopting a hypermasculine posture. The result, they believe, is that some officials may have uncritically celebrated the escalation of the Vietnam War as a way to either mask their own homosexuality or simply conform to the organizational culture irrespective of their true opinions about events on the ground in Southeastern Asia.

FIGURE 9.16

Although there was far less press coverage on the Lavender Scare than the anti-Communist Red Scare, some Americans feared that America's enemies would blackmail homosexuals into revealing sensitive information.

A second unintended consequence of the Lavender Scare was a growing sense of solidarity among homosexuals. In 1950, Harry Hay founded the **Mattachine Society** in California with three others willing to confront the negative stereotypes and actions the government took against homosexuals. While the Mattachine Society was certainly not the first organization dedicated to the promotion of equal rights for GLBT people, it quickly became a model for similar organizations throughout the nation. Like the Mattachine Society, these early gay-rights organizations operated in secret to protect their members. Even though their secrecy was only necessitated by persecution, the clandestine nature of these groups seemed to provide further proof that homosexuals were secretly plotting something nefarious. And though McCarthyism subsided in the late 1950s, the purges of suspected homosexuals in government would continue for another two decades.

3.4 Two Americas, Separate and Unequal

To celebrate America's victory in World War II and commemorate the 160th anniversary of the Constitution, the National Archives worked with a number of private foundations to create a traveling exhibit of historical archives and documents. In September 1947, the Freedom Train began its travels to more than three hundred cities. The train contained priceless artifacts such as the Mayflower Compact and the Declaration of Independence.

A number of important documents such as the Fourteenth and Fifteenth Amendments were removed from the train by the conservative American Heritage Foundation, which helped to fund the exhibit. In fact, the only one of the three Reconstruction Amendments that was permitted to be displayed alongside the hundreds of other documents was the Thirteenth Amendment, which had ended slavery. In 1947, civil rights lawyers were challenging racial segregation and voting restrictions as incompatible with the Fourteenth Amendment's guarantee of equal protection and the Fifteenth Amendment's unambiguous ensurance of universal suffrage regardless of race. For this reason, the leaders of the conservative American Heritage Foundation felt that displaying these documents would cause controversy that would distract from the celebration of freedom. Langston Hughes responded by asking if the directors would likewise ensure that the Freedom Train had a Jim Crow section when it traveled through Southern cities.

Representative of the Jim Crow system Langston Hughes wrote about, whites and blacks lived separate and often unequal lives. They largely ignored one another in the larger community, as long as both adhered to an unwritten script that dictated the terms of racial relations in a particular place. As long as individuals did not deviate from these protocols—separate seating in theaters, restaurant service at the kitchen door, taking the seat in the back of the bus—they might remain invisible until they safely returned to the haven of the black community. Because those who lived through segregation knew when and where they should expect the indignity of Jim Crow, they could also prepare and even insulate themselves from the experience.

Oral histories of African Americans who lived through the era of Jim Crow frequently talk about segregation as something they and most everyone else in the black community found ways to endure. Many are quick to point out how self-sufficient black communities were, how they had "their own" stores and restaurants where they were always treated with dignity. They describe with great pride the strength of black institutions such as the school and the church. The faculty in many all-black high schools typically held more advanced degrees than some white colleges, largely due to the latter's unwillingness to hire black professors. In these larger cities, African Americans seldom ventured outside the black community except when absolutely necessary. Many use descriptive words such as "haven" or "cocoon" to describe the insulating refuge against Jim Crow their black communities provided. While most oral histories emphasize that segregation was something African Americans tolerated and even accommodated themselves to, they also often painfully recall very specific events in their lives when they were humiliated and degraded.

Oral histories and personal recollections by African Americans at this time reveal that the most painful instances of discrimination occurred at times when it was unexpected. For example, a Houston resident recalled with great anguish an incident that occurred on his ninth birthday. On most days, he and his father would have waited until they returned to their neighborhood before ending their evening with ice cream. However, this day was so perfect that they spontaneously entered a downtown parlor, where his father was then humiliated in front of his young son. A snub from a white person one thought was a friend, an incident involving one's children, or any number of unscripted incidents could turn an inhuman but impersonal system of caste and privilege into a moment of personal degradation. On a day-to-day basis, one could navigate the gauntlet of Jim Crow with the detached calm of a soldier whose armor deflected each of the enemy's rounds. The deepest wounds, as evidenced by oral histories, were those inflicted when one expected to be treated with dignity and thus lowered his or her guard.

But Jim Crow was much more than emotionally painful. Segregation prevented millions from reaching their potential or even finding decent jobs and living conditions. Even black veterans armed with the GI Bill were frequently denied admission to universities and denied financing for home loans. Although the GI Bill itself contained no provisions regarding race, the Veterans Administration only offered financial assistance to those who were able to sign a housing contract or to be admitted to a college. Because most neighborhoods were covered by restrictive covenants, special language in the deed of a home specifying that owners and renters must be white, bank financing was not the largest obstacle for black veterans searching for a home. Likewise, GI Bill benefits did not reverse the informal racial quotas of many Northern universities or the absolute exclusion of black students in most Southern colleges.

Dozens of **Historically Black Colleges and Universities (HBCUs)** did everything in their power to admit as many veterans as possible. Many set up temporary housing in area black churches and held classes day and night. Yet many of these schools had limited offerings beyond specialties in education, theology, and applied sciences. Of the estimated 100,000 black veterans who attempted to use their college benefits, only 5,000 were admitted in northern colleges. HBCUs grew rapidly following the Lanham Act of 1946, which provided additional funding to black colleges. In 1940, enrollment at HBCUs represented only 1 percent of the total United States enrollment. By 1950, it had increased to 3.6 percent. Unfortunately, this growth came too late for most black veterans. Those who were able to attend college, however, soon formed the core of the civil rights movement of the 1950s and 1960s.

3.5   School Segregation

In 1951, high school student Barbara Johns led more than four hundred of her classmates in a protest against the conditions of the black high school in Farmville, Virginia. Johns lured administrators and teachers from the building and announced an assembly where she explained to her fellow students the separate and unequal conditions they faced. The white high school was a modern and spacious facility with an auditorium, gymnasium, and up-to-date classrooms. Their school was an aging facility surrounded by tar paper shacks that passed as classrooms. Johns led her classmates on a walk-out and protest march with signs demanding a new school. The students refused to return to school for two weeks and convinced NAACP attorneys to file a lawsuit that demanded an end to racial segregation in public education.

After three years of proceedings, the US Supreme Court agreed to hear the students' case, along with four similar lawsuits from Washington, DC, Delaware, New Jersey, and Kansas. Because the last name of the lead plaintiff in the Kansas case preceded the others alphabetically, the case is known as *Brown v. The Board of Education of Topeka, Kansas.* In this landmark case, the Supreme Court agreed that separate schools, even if they received equal funding, were inherently unequal and therefore were a violation of the equal protection clause of the Fourteenth Amendment. Unfortunately for Barbara Johns, she was not able to participate in any of the proceedings. Due to threats on her life, her family sent her to live with family members outside of the state.

In areas with large Mexican American communities, such as California and Texas, separate public schools were also maintained for Hispanic children. School officials often utilized "language deficiency" regardless of a child's ability to speak English as a method to perpetuate separate schools for Mexican American children irrespective of law. While non-English speaking "white" immigrant children were permitted to attend schools of their choice, children of Mexican origin were often assigned to separate schools.

In communities where there were only "white" and "black" schools, the complexion of a Hispanic child might be heavily scrutinized and used to assigning children on an individual basis. In many communities, Mexican American children were informally expected to attend separate "Mexican" schools that were financed and operated by Catholic Mexican American parishioners. For example, the school leaders in Emporia, Kansas, refused to create a separate school for black children (despite the demands of some white parents) but expected the growing Hispanic population to attend a "Mexican School" which was operated by the Sacred Heart church. As was the case in most communities, school records provide no evidence that Mexican American children were formally banned from the public schools of Emporia.

Historically Black Colleges and Universities (HBCUs)

Institutions of higher education formed to serve black communities prior to the integration of colleges in the mid-twentieth century. As of 2011, there are just over one hundred HBCUs in the United States, all of which admit students of any race, although enrollments in nearly every HBCU outside of the border South continue to have predominantly black student populations.

Brown v. The Board of Education of Topeka, Kansas

The landmark US Supreme Court case of 1954 declaring that racial segregation in public schools violated the Fourteenth Amendment, regardless of whether those schools were equal in every other aspect. The case was created by consolidating five separate lawsuits that were each sponsored by the NAACP.

FIGURE 9.17

Mendez v. Westminster was a landmark case overturning California's segregation of Hispanic children in its public schools.

Mendez v. Westminster

A 1946 federal court case that reversed the practice of segregating Mexican American students in absence of a state law permitting the practice.

This kind of informal segregation was difficult for parents to fight and remains challenging for historians to document. However, it is clear that Mexican American communities challenged and defeated more obvious forms of discrimination. During World War II, Gonzalo Mendez leased a farm belonging to an interned Japanese American family in a primarily white area of Orange County. When his children were denied enrollment in the neighborhood school, Mendez and other Mexican American residents of Orange County sued the school board of Westminster in 1946. The board's defense argued that separation was not based on ethnicity or national origins, categories that would indicate discrimination as Mendez claimed, but instead on their inability to speak English. In *Mendez v. Westminster*, the board argued that its practice of providing separate schools for Spanish-speaking children until they were able to speak and read English was based on the best interests of the children. However, neither the federal district nor the circuit court of appeals agreed that language was the basis of board policy. Many of the children spoke English, and the court ruled that the board's practice of assigning children to separate schools based on their national origins could not continue.

While the district court believed that separation of children based on national origins was a violation of the Fourteenth Amendment—the same logic that led to *Brown v. Board of Education*—the Ninth Circuit Court of Appeals decided the case on more narrow grounds. While the case is still significant in striking down segregation for Mexican American children, the court avoided any ruling on the Fourteenth Amendment. Instead, it focused on whether California could legally exclude Mexican American children when the educational laws of the state made no such provision.

The laws of California did allow for separate schools for Native American children, as well as those of "Chinese, Japanese, or Mongolian" heritage. The laws made no provision for or against the separation of other minorities. Shortly after this case, however, California governor Earl Warren supported the repeal of the laws permitting segregation for Native American and Asian children. In 1948 in Texas and 1950 in Arizona, Mexican American plaintiffs secured federal court decisions declaring that separate schools for Mexican American children violated the Fourteenth Amendment. Warren would later serve as Chief Justice of the United States Supreme Court and secure a unanimous decision against school segregation in the landmark 1954 case *Brown v. Board of Education*.

REVIEW AND CRITICAL THINKING

1. How did the Cold War impact the domestic political climate within the United States? Describe the development of nuclear arsenals and the way nuclear weapons changed strategic military planning.
2. Compare the Red Scare to the Lavender Scare. Explain how both reflected the culture of the time period, and how both were related to the Cold War. Describe the way both affected various individuals.
3. Describe the way that African Americans and Mexican Americans confronted segregation in the postwar period. Describe the major legal case of this time period related to school segregation.

4. CONTAINMENT AND THE KOREAN "CONFLICT"

LEARNING OBJECTIVES

1. Explain the origins of the Korean War. Explain why the United States and other nations intervened.
2. Summarize the military history of the Korean War. Explain why South Korean and UN forces were able to rally after being pinned down in Pusan, and why they were ultimately beaten back to the 38th Parallel.
3. Explain how the Korean War was affected by domestic issues inside the United States. Explain how the war affected US politics.

The Korean War is often called "The Forgotten War" due to its marginalization in the historical record. However, the war would have a dramatic effect on the United States and its foreign policy in future decades. At the time, a number of prominent US leaders feared that events might spiral out of control as had occurred in 1914 and 1939. At one point, President Truman himself believed that events in Korea might lead to global warfare. Among those who predicted that Korea would spark World War

III were isolationists who believed that America had no business in Asia. Others believed that the fate of "the free world" hinged on whether Communist forces succeeded in their effort to gain control of the Korean peninsula. In the end, the Korean War resulted in a return to the status quo for North and South Korea, but several important precedents were established. The United States determined that it would use military force to stop the spread of Communism. In addition, the president was able to wage war without direct Congressional approval. To this day, the three-year war that cost the lives of 35,000 US soldiers and an estimated 2 to 3 million Koreans is officially known as "the Korean Conflict" in government records.

4.1 Origins of the Korean War

Although both sides tentatively worked together to defend their nation against Japanese forces during World War II, the Chinese civil war resumed in 1945. In May 1949, Communist leader Mao Zedong emerged victorious and declared the People's Republic of China. The United States had backed the nationalist Chiang Kai-shek who now fled to Taiwan. The United States refused to recognize the authority of Mao's government and declared that Chiang's exiled government in Taiwan was the legitimate government for mainland China for the next two decades. Concern by the Western members of the United Nations about allowing Communist China to occupy one of the powerful permanent seats on the UN Security Council also led to Chiang's small government representing China in the United Nations until 1971.

FIGURE 9.18

A Chinese propaganda poster showing American General Douglas MacArthur murdering a mother and child, while American bombers expand the war into China by attacking its civilians.

The Communist victory came despite $2 billion in US aid because of the popular support for Mao and the corruption and inefficiency of Chiang Kai-shek's regime. The message of Mao and other Communist leaders appealed to the majority of landless and poor farmers of China because it promised equal distribution of land and wealth. In contrast, Chiang Kai-shek used deadly force against peasants who were protesting the rising cost of food. Truman's administration argued that there was little more the United States could have done to prevent the Communist takeover of China and that direct military intervention would have been a tragic mistake. However, more and more Americans were beginning to believe the accusations of Republican leaders that the Democrats were to blame for the spread of Communism in Asia. Despite their misgivings with the autocratic Chiang Kai-shek, the United States continued to recognize his government in exile as the official government of China. Meanwhile, the Communist government of Mao Zedong worked to consolidate its power and promote the spread of Communism throughout the continent.

Korea was experiencing a similar civil war between nationalist and Communist forces following the end of World War II. Korea was occupied by Japan until the end of World War II when a diplomatic agreement required Japanese forces north of the **38th Parallel** to surrender to the Soviets, while those south of the parallel surrendered to the Americans. Just as Germany was divided into different sectors, Korea was soon divided in half along the 38th Parallel. Both the United States in the South and the Soviet Union in the North established governments favorable to their own political orientation.

In South Korea, the United States called for elections to replace a popular Communist leader who had led that nation's resistance to Japan in World War II. His replacement, Syngman Rhee, was not nearly as autocratic as Chiang Kai-shek. However, like the exiled Chinese nationalist leader, Syngman Rhee never enjoyed the popular support of the people and had little respect for democracy. In the North, the Soviets supported a Communist government led by **Kim Il Sung**, who displayed even less concern for the opinions of the Korean people whose ideas were different from his own. Historians estimate that as many as 100,000 Koreans perished between 1945 and 1950 as both Rhee and Kim Il Sung sought to reunite Korea under their rule. In addition, both sides (especially the authoritarian Kim Il Sung) used force to silence their opponents in their respective sections of the Korean peninsula.

After four years of occupation, US and Soviet forces left Korea. Both Rhee and Kim Il Sung declared that they were the legitimate rulers of Korea, and both pledged to unite the peninsula under their governments. The North Koreans under Kim Il Sung had the advantage of being supplied with Soviet tanks and other technically advanced equipment, while the Americans were hesitant to provide similar aid to South Korea. There were two main reasons for this reluctance, the first being the corruption of Syngman Rhee's government and the second being that most US leaders were focused much more heavily on Europe than Asia. That would change dramatically on June 25, 1950, when North Korean troops invaded South Korea.

President Truman, already under fire from a growing Republican contingent in Congress for being "soft on Communism," was determined to prevent the Communists from seizing South Korea. Truman ordered naval and air support for South Korea. Most Americans at the time believed that Stalin had masterminded the North Korean attack, and both Congress and the public overwhelmingly approved of Truman's later commitment of US ground forces. Although later critics would accuse the

38th Parallel

Latitude line passing midway through the Korean Peninsula that was used as the dividing line between the Soviet and US sectors during Korea's postwar reconstruction. The line soon became the frontier between the Communist North Korea and the non-Communist South Korea.

Kim Il Sung

Korean nationalist who fought against Japanese occupation of Korea and was appointed by Soviet officials to lead the Communist provisional government for North Korea. In 1948, Kim became the head of North Korea's Communist government.

president of waging a war without specific authorization of Congress, House appropriations for increased military budgets met almost no opposition. In addition, only a few senators even pointed out that the president had not sought a declaration of war. The American people were even more supportive of Truman's actions, believing that waiting for Congressional approval might have caused critical delays. After the war became stalemated, more Americans began to oppose their nation's actions in Korea, and neither Truman nor Eisenhower returned to Congress to seek a formal declaration of war.

In retrospect, had the North Korean invasion been part of a Red Army scheme, Truman's decisive but unilateral action might have led to direct military conflict with the Soviet Union. North Korea continued to receive Soviet supplies and Stalin's blessing throughout the war, but it seems that Kim Il Sung favored the invasion of South Korea and was not simply the puppet of Stalin. America's primary concern was Europe, the North Korean leader recognized, and his invasion was based on his belief that the United States would not use its military to defend Rhee's regime in the South. However, South Korea had been the United States' responsibility after World War II, and so Truman believed its invasion by a Communist regime would cause many to question the United States' commitment to those fighting Communism around the globe. In addition to a perceived challenge of US credibility, the Korean situation occurred just one year after the Communist takeover of neighboring China. The rapid course of events seemed to many Americans as proof of the Domino Theory and its warning about the inertia of one Communist victory quickly spreading throughout an entire region. Americans who had little knowledge of Korea in 1949 anxiously anticipated each day's newspaper, eager to find that US forces had turned back the Communist wave they feared threatened to envelop all of Southeast Asia.

4.2 Invasion to Stalemate

Those Americans watching the news from Korea in June and July of 1950 found little to raise their spirits. Nearly 100,000 troops, many of whom had fought for Mao's Communist forces in China, descended upon the unprepared army of South Korea and quickly occupied the capital of Seoul. The United Nations condemned the North's aggression, but the only UN members to commit significant numbers of troops to fight the armies of Kim Il Sung were the United States and South Korea. The former would not arrive in significant numbers until August, leaving South Korean troops to what could only be called a "fighting retreat" by the most generous observers.

By August and with US assistance, the South Koreans formed a stable defensive perimeter in the far southeastern corner of their country around the port city of Pusan. With UN forces pinned down behind the **Pusan Perimeter**, US General Douglas MacArthur formulated a daring offensive based on an attack where the North Koreans least expected it. Rather than resupply Pusan, he launched an amphibious invasion of the coastal city of Inchon, which was located on the eastern side of the country. The North Koreans had advanced too quickly, the seventy-year-old general surmised, leaving the bulk of their forces in the southern end of the peninsula and their supply lines in the middle of the nation vulnerable to attack. If the marines could somehow overcome the immense tides that led to the construction of fortress-like seawalls around Inchon, US forces could drive a wedge through the North Korean supply lines and trap the invading army between Seoul and Pusan.

On September 15, 1950, 12,000 marines surprised and overwhelmed the North Korean troops during the **Inchon Invasion** and established a secured city as a safe landing zone for US troops. Less than two weeks later US and UN forces pushing east and south liberated the South Korean capital of Seoul. Tens of thousands of North Korean troops were able to escape to the north before MacArthur's forces, now advancing north from Pusan as well as south and east from Inchon, could trap the entire force. Still, the Inchon landing proved to be the turning point in the early phase of the Korean War as half of the North Koreans surrendered and the other half fled back to North Korea. MacArthur's success enhanced his already legendary status among the US public and led many to support his previously unthinkable plan to attack North Korea itself. After some debate among US and even UN leaders, MacArthur was given authorization to pursue the fleeing Communist army into North Korea in the hopes of reuniting Korea into one non-Communist nation.

Pusan Perimeter

A defensive line in the southeastern corner of the Korean Peninsula around the port city of Pusan. UN and South Korean troops were forced to retreat to this corner in the early stages of the Korean War.

Inchon Invasion

An amphibious assault launched by US forces under Douglas MacArthur in the Korean War. Rather than resupply UN and South Korean troops holding out in the Pusan Perimeter, MacArthur directed the bulk of his forces to take Inchon and move east, cutting North Korean supply lines and trapping the North Korean troops between his forces and those at Pusan.

FIGURE 9.19

North Korean troops pushed south across the 38th Parallel, which was intended to be a temporary dividing line. They drove UN and South Korean troops all the way back to Pusan until US forces launched a counteroffensive at Inchon that split the North Korean supply lines and forced them to retreat back across the 38th Parallel.

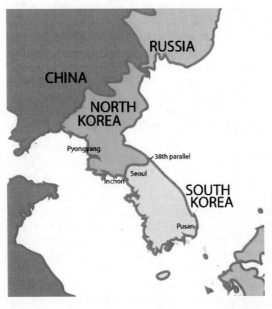

Turning the war from a defense of their South Korean ally to an attack on Communist North Korea was both a daunting task and a delicate political issue. Mao repeatedly warned that Chinese forces would intervene if US troops came close to the Chinese–North Korean border. MacArthur dismissed these warnings as propaganda and predicted that his forces would occupy all of North Korea by Thanksgiving. At first, it looked as though MacArthur's bold action would again be vindicated as US and South Korean troops continued their advance on the beleaguered North Korean force. By late November, the North Koreans were relegated to defensive positions near the Chinese border.

General MacArthur's estimation of Chinese intentions proved as short-sighted as Kim Il Sung's earlier belief that the United States would not send troops to Korea. On November 25, several hundred thousand Chinese soldiers crossed into North Korea and forced US and South Korean forces to retreat southward. The rapid conquest of US troops, like that of their North Korean enemy in the first month of the war, meant that US supply lines were stretched thin and vulnerable to the Chinese counterattack. By Christmas of 1950, Chinese troops had driven US and South Korean forces out of North Korea. By January 1951, North Koreans recaptured Seoul and it looked as if the Chinese and North Koreans might drive UN forces all the way back to Pusan.

FIGURE 9.20

US troops involved in street fighting during the liberation of Seoul in September 1950. The city would change hands several times during the war, leading to a high number of civilian casualties.

Matthew B. Ridgway

Commander of the 8th Army in the Korean War, which led a successful counteroffensive against North Korean positions in the winter of 1950–51. Ridgeway succeeded Douglas MacArthur as commander of US forces after the latter was removed by President Truman in April 1951.

US and South Korean forces were successful in halting the Korean advance; however, a stalemate soon occurred as the two armies dug in, advancing and retreating within a narrow strip of land near the 38th Parallel. This situation deeply frustrated General MacArthur, who suggested that the United States unleash its arsenal of atomic bombs and even called on President Truman to extend the war into China. MacArthur also wanted to aid the forces of exiled Chinese nationalist Chiang Kai-shek if they agreed to attack the Communist Chinese troops. Truman recognized that the Chinese would view any invasion originating from US-supported Taiwan as tantamount to a US declaration of war on their nation. Instead, the president increased troop levels and launched a counteroffensive in Korea. **Matthew Ridgeway** assumed command of this counterattack and quickly regained control of Seoul. By spring, the North Koreans were forced back across the 38th Parallel. South Korea being secure once again, Truman sought an armistice and a return to the prewar status quo of a divided Korea. MacArthur viewed Truman's plans as cowardly and tantamount to Communist victory. As a result, he tacitly worked against the president's peace plan by sending a message to the Chinese demanding unconditional surrender. MacArthur's message hinted that US forces might invade China and even use nuclear weapons if they refused his offer.

4.3 Stalemate to Armistice

Truman believed that MacArthur's actions not only violated the constitutional principle of civilian control of the military but also were nothing short of treason, as they threatened to rekindle a war he had hoped to end. General Omar Bradley believed an attack on China would be "the wrong war, in the wrong place, at the wrong time, with the wrong enemy." The greatest danger, Truman believed, was that an attack against the Chinese would lead to Soviet intervention. The two nations were the leading Communist powers in the world and maintained a mutual assistance pact. As a result Truman and his advisers feared that MacArthur's unauthorized comments might lead America into World War III. However, politics forced Truman to proceed cautiously against his rogue general. MacArthur was still viewed as a hero and military genius, while Truman's approval numbers hovered near 30 percent. Republican politicians won victories by associating the president with the recent Communist surge in Asia.

FIGURE 9.21

A photographer juxtaposes a war-weary Korean with child against the backdrop of an American tank. The war was especially trying for the civilian population.

As the 1950 congressional elections approached, more and more Americans viewed Truman and other Democrats as being "soft" on Communism. Republicans made deep inroads into the previously solid Democratic majority in these elections as a frustrated electorate questioned why the most powerful nation in the world could not prevail against a "backward" nation such as North Korea. Expressions of racial prejudice against Asians that had become commonplace during World War II returned in the form of calls for the use of atomic weapons against civilian populations. Others asserted the federal government was infested with Communists. Why else, they asked, would the great General MacArthur be restricted from pushing forward against other Communist forces? Each day the war continued seemed to confirm the worst of these accusations—US armed forces were being stabbed in the back by their own government and commander in chief.

MacArthur's insistence on total war in Asia progressed from private conversations and secret communications to nearly insubordinate messages in US newspapers. Popular or not, President Truman recognized that MacArthur's actions were both insubordinate and potentially dangerous. A general who wrote his own orders violated the sacred American principle of civilian control of the military. For this reason, the Joint Chiefs of Staff supported the president's decision to relieve MacArthur of command. Many Americans responded with anger upon hearing that the popular general had been so ingloriously removed. Opinion polls demonstrated that the vast majority of Americans backed MacArthur, while Truman's approval ratings explored new depths. The general returned triumphant, touring the East Coast like a conquering hero complete with marching bands and ticker-tape parades. In an emotional address that made even his detractors weep, the old general thanked the American people for the honor of serving them in the last three wars. "Old soldiers never die," he concluded, "they just fade away."

Truman wisely avoided any public statements and allowed MacArthur to enjoy his perhaps long-overdue praise for his decades of military leadership. Only later did Truman explain his decision to replace MacArthur with Ridgeway, detailing to Congress how MacArthur had sought to escalate the war. Truman's argument demonstrated the wisdom of limited war, and Congress responded with a statement thanking MacArthur for his service but concurring with the president's decision. Within weeks, the press and US public continued to discuss the issue, the majority likewise agreeing that any expansion of the Korean War beyond the Korean Peninsula would have been a tragic mistake. President Truman's public image was at least partially restored while those who favored MacArthur's invasion faded away.

The United Nations attempted to negotiate an armistice throughout the next two and a half years, but talks bogged down on three major controversies. The first was the location of the border between North and South Korea. Second, the UN wanted to create a demilitarized zone that would discourage future invasions, a provision that also discouraged the prospects of later Korean reunification. Finally, the United States insisted that Chinese and North Korean prisoners of war should have the choice of returning to the nations they had served or staying in the Western-backed South Korea.

This later point was especially important to Truman for both humanitarian and political reasons. Nearly half of the more than 100,000 North Korean and Chinese prisoners indicated a desire to live in Taiwan or South Korea. Truman believed that living conditions were significantly better in Taiwan and South Korea and likewise predicted that the world would interpret the abandonment of North Korea and China by their own soldiers as a powerful message about the superiority of the US-backed Taiwan and South Korea. For this reason, the Chinese and North Koreans refused peace terms until July 1953. By this time, the World War II hero **Dwight D. Eisenhower** was president.

The former Supreme Allied Commander approved the treaty, which did little more than provide for a ceasefire and the exit of US troops. Truman was at least partially vindicated as half of the Communist prisoners of war chose to stay in Korea. However, the armistice essentially demonstrated the futility of the last three years of fighting. A line near the 38th Parallel became the southern border between Communist North Korea and the non-Communist South. Both sides maintain large military forces along their common border, and neither signed any kind of treaty. In fact, both nations are still technically at war with one another—one of many lasting consequences of the global Cold War.

The war took an incredible toll on the people who lived on both sides of the Korean Peninsula. US troops dropped 650,000 tons of explosives on North and South Korea, following a "scorched earth" strategy devised during the Pacific Campaign of World War II but now unleashed on a peninsula home to 20 million Koreans. **Napalm** and US bombing destroyed more than a thousand villages and nearly eliminated the entire agricultural production of both nations by deliberately attacking irrigation systems. These attacks did cut supply lines and eliminate the ability of enemy troops to live off the land, but not until the ability of peasants to similarly provision themselves had been destroyed. An estimated 4 million Koreans lost their lives. Starvation, more than weapons of all armies combined, accounted for the devastating casualties that reduced the population of both North and South Korea by 10 percent in four years. No US war has ever taken the lives of such a high proportion of a nation's civilian population. In addition, for the 35,000 US soldiers who lost their lives and the more than 100,000 who were wounded, the Korean War was equally devastating.

4.4 Eisenhower and the Election of 1952

Truman's come-from-behind victory in 1948 seemed unlikely to reoccur as the 1952 presidential election neared. His approval ratings dipped below 30 percent during the Korean War, which was increasingly labeled "Truman's War." The United States would spend $21 million fighting the armies of North Korea and China, and by 1951, it was clear it would not result in the quick and decisive victory Americans expected. As a result, Truman declined to run for reelection, and the Democrats nominated **Adlai Stevenson** at their convention in Chicago. Stevenson was a former attorney and governor of Illinois and was a well-respected member of the party. However, his reputation paled in comparison to his Republican opponent, former Allied Supreme Commander Dwight D. Eisenhower.

Eisenhower had never been a member of either the Republican or Democratic parties. In fact, he hadn't even voted for two decades. Yet because of his immense popularity, leaders of both parties tried to convince the former Supreme Allied Commander of Europe to run under their banner. Truman and Eisenhower shared mutual admiration and similar political views on international affairs; however, Eisenhower was deeply conservative when it came to domestic policies. He opposed any expansion of New Deal initiatives and viewed civil rights as an issue the federal government should avoid. As a result, the Republican offer was the only one to which he gave serious consideration.

Stevenson and Eisenhower had similar political views. Neither favored expansive government programs like public housing, and both viewed civil rights as a matter best left to individual states and were ardent cold warriors who supported containment of Communism, nuclear deterrence, and a strong military. Both sought to end the Korean War and reduce defense spending but agreed that the nation must be prepared to confront Communist expansion throughout the globe. Stevenson and the Democrats avoided statements on civil rights like those that led to the "Dixiecrat secession" of their Southern delegates at the 1948 Democratic convention. Ironically, Stevenson's avoidance of civil rights ensured him the vote of the Deep South but did little to help his electoral prospects in Florida, Texas, Virginia, and Tennessee, which, like the rest of the nation, chose the war hero Eisenhower.

FIGURE 9.22

Disputes regarding prisoner exchanges and repatriation led the war to continue into 1953. This photo shows a tent where American prisoners of war were processed before being welcomed back into camp.

Dwight D. Eisenhower

Five-star general and Supreme Allied Commander in World War II. After seven years of avoiding politics, Eisenhower accepted the Republican nomination and defeated Adlai Stevenson in the presidential election of 1952.

Napalm

An incredibly flammable substance formed by turning gasoline into a jelly-like form that is then mixed with other incendiary agents.

Adlai Stevenson

Illinois governor who secured the Democratic nomination for president in 1952 and 1956. Stevenson lost both elections to Eisenhower. In 1961, President Kennedy appointed Stevenson US ambassador to the United Nations where he served until his death in 1965.

FIGURE 9.23

Dwight Eisenhower was greeted by large crowds during his campaign for president, such as this enthusiastic throng in Baltimore.

Richard Nixon

Shrewd politician and vice presidential running mate under Eisenhower, Richard Nixon sought to transform the image of the Republican Party from its association with promoting the interests of business leaders to the defender of the common man. Ruthless in his attacks against political rivals, Nixon was equally skilled in using populist language to appeal to the masses—a skill that catapulted him into the White House in the 1968 presidential election.

With both candidates holding similar views on most of the leading issues, the election became a contest of popular perceptions about the personality of the candidates themselves. Given the already high public approval of Eisenhower, Republican campaign managers keyed in on the image of the war hero and contrasted "Ike" with the wealthy and intellectual Stevenson. Eisenhower's running mate **Richard Nixon** had risen to fame through his enthusiastic pursuit of alleged subversives as a member of the House Un-American Activities Committee. In 1950, Nixon defeated Helen Gahagan Douglas in a vicious California senatorial campaign in which Nixon accused Douglas of being a Communist who was "pink down to her underwear."

Nixon's chief contribution to the presidential campaign was to raise similar doubts as to the political orientation of Stevenson. Nixon was prone to "accidentally" referring to his running mate's opponent as "Alger" instead of Adlai. He corrected himself each time, but it was clear that Nixon was hoping to connect Stevenson with recently convicted Soviet spy Alger Hiss. Other members of the right joined the fray, as McCarthy labeled the last two decades of Democratic administrations as "twenty years of treason." Eisenhower found these attacks distasteful but did little to stop them. And while Stevenson purchased time on television and radio programs to deliver lengthy speeches, Eisenhower was featured in carefully staged television advertisements. These brief commercials anticipated modern campaign ads by featuring the candidate as a courageous war hero, loving family man, and trustworthy advocate of the working class. They conveyed little information and oversimplified complex issues, but they were also remarkably upbeat.

FIGURE 9.24

Dwight Eisenhower won the presidential election of 1952 with over 80% of the electoral vote. The former Supreme Allied Commander even won a handful of Southern states that had not voted Republican since the early years of Reconstruction.

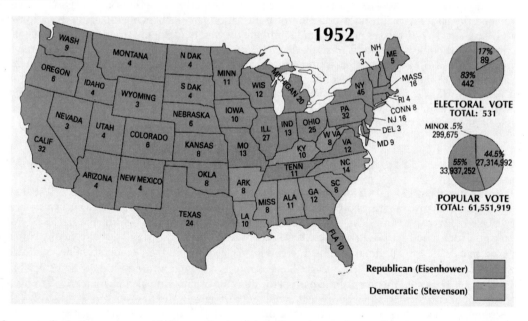

There was little Stevenson could do to counter either Nixon's attacks or Eisenhower's sentimental advertisements. Any denial of the charges of Communist sympathies would serve only to reinforce the McCarthy-inspired tactics of his detractors by further associating words like "Communism" with his own image in the public mind. Eisenhower's television advertisements, like his promise to personally visit Korea, were likewise difficult to counter. These strategies combined with the overwhelming popularity of Eisenhower explain why he won more than 55 percent of the popular vote. Once the election was over, however, many Americans realized that they had no clear idea of what their new president would actually do while in office. Eisenhower gave neither an indication of how his visit to Korea would improve the situation nor did he explain what he meant when he promised an "honorable end" to the conflict.

Even more troublesome to some political observers was the use of vague slogans such as "I like Ike," which to them seemed more appropriate for a merchandising campaign than a presidential election. A leading newspaper editor accused Eisenhower's campaign managers of "selling the president like toothpaste." However, the slogan proved effective due to the overwhelmingly positive public perception of Eisenhower. The former five-star general had led the United States to victory in Europe, and many Americans were confident he would find a way to prevail in Korea. Eisenhower's presence on the ticket lifted the entire Republican Party, who seized control of both the Senate and the House of Representatives. Republicans now controlled both houses of Congress and the presidency for the first time in over two decades.

REVIEW AND CRITICAL THINKING

1. Why did the United States decide to intervene in Korea? Was MacArthur's strategy of directing US forces to Inchon a bold or a reckless strategy? What other military options did the commander have?

2. Why did President Truman fire General MacArthur? If Truman had higher approval ratings, should he have made the change of commander sooner? Why did so many Americans support MacArthur's call to expand the war into China, and what do you think might have happened had the United States followed this strategy?

3. Why were Americans so frustrated with Truman that he did not even run for reelection in 1952? Explain the reason for Eisenhower's victory in 1952.

5. FURTHER READING

Cohen, Lizabeth. *A Consumer's Republic: The Politics of Mass Consumption in Postwar America* (2003).

Gleason, Abbot. *Totalitarianism: The Inner History of the Cold War* (1997).

Harrison, Cynthia. *On Account of Sex: The Politics of Women's Issues, 1945–1968* (1988).

Jackson, Kenneth T. *Crabgrass Frontier: The Suburbanization of the United States* (1985).

Johnson, David. *The Lavender Scare: The Cold War Persecution of Gays and Lesbians in the Federal Government* (2004).

May, Elaine Tyler. *Homeward Bound: American Families in the Cold War Era* (1996).

Patterson, James. *Grand Expectations: The United States, 1945–1974* (1996).

Schrecker, Ellen. *Many are the Crimes: McCarthyism in America* (1999).

Self, Robert O. *American Babylon: Race and the Struggle for Postwar Oakland* (2003).

Stueck, William. *The Korean War: An International History* (1997).

Sugrue, Thomas. *Origins of the Urban Crisis: Race and Inequality in Postwar Detroit* (1996).

CHAPTER 10
The Cold War and the Affluent Society, 1954–1963

American and Soviet leaders focused increased attention on the affairs of nations in Latin America, Asia, and Africa as Cold War tensions increased during the 1950s and spread throughout the globe. The United States and the Soviet Union increasingly viewed that globe as a backdrop upon which their high-stakes contest of ideas and influence was being waged. As a result, these officials often projected a global Cold War framework upon local events and discounted the agency and ideas of the actual participants.

For example, both the United States and the Soviet Union might view the rise of a left-leaning political group in one African nation as evidence of increased Soviet influence throughout the entire continent. In reality, the explanation was usually something connected with local conditions and political opinions that the Kremlin or the US State Department were responding to rather than initiating. Because the State Department or the Kremlin usually consulted few area experts and ignored the perspectives of those who lived in these nations, such misperceptions were rarely challenged. The results were often tragic, both for peoples in these nations and for many Soviet and American soldiers and citizens. The parameters of the Cold War extended into the domestic sphere, where civil rights advocates, union leaders, and any others who espoused messages that were critical of the United States and its political leaders were accused of disloyalty. At the same time, the federal government's desire to improve their nation's international image led the State Department to support a number of civil rights initiatives.

1. THE GLOBAL COLD WAR DURING THE EISENHOWER ADMINISTRATION

LEARNING OBJECTIVES

1. Explain how the actions of people in developing nations (commonly referred to at this time as the "Third World") had an impact upon the history of the Cold War. Discuss the ways that leaders of developing nations demonstrated agency, and explain how their options were influenced and limited by the United States and Soviet Union.
2. Evaluate the increasing US presence in Vietnam between World War II and the end of the 1950s. Explain why US forces chose to support France and ultimately decided to replace the French in the fight against the forces of Ho Chi Minh.
3. Explain US strategy in the Cold War during the Eisenhower administration. Demonstrate the importance of events in Africa, Asia, and Latin America, as well as the role played by science and technology in the Cold War.

1.1 Decolonization and Developing Nations

By the mid-1950s, both the United States and the Soviet Union had adopted a strategy they hoped would limit the influence of their rival. The Soviet Union, for example, backed the repressive North

Korean regime of Kim Il Sung, despite the fact that Kim rejected many of the core principles of Marxism. At the same time, the United States compromised its own democratic ideals by propping up the autocratic Syngman Rhee in South Korea.

Rhee and other leaders of **Third World** nations (referred to today as "Developing Nations") recognized that both US and Soviet leaders feared that the other's political and economic system would spread if not contained. As a result, they created their own strategies aimed at manipulating Cold War tensions for their own gain. To secure economic and military aid from Moscow or Washington, these leaders sometimes adopted the role of pawns in constant danger of being toppled by the forces of Capitalism or Communism. If the Soviet Union wanted to prevent the spread of Capitalism, Kim Il Sung warned, it would have to provide generous support to North Korea else it fall to Syngman Rhee's South Korea, which was backed by the United States. Syngman Rhee likewise convinced the United States to support his repressive but anti-Communist regime by playing to American fears about the imminent spread of Communism. This same pattern appeared throughout the Developing World.

Even developed nations found that they could utilize the Cold War to further their own objectives. For example, French leaders demanded that the United States support its efforts to reconquer its former colony of Indochina (Vietnam). If the United States refused, the French threatened to withdraw their support of NATO. For leaders in Korea and Vietnam who were dependent on US or Soviet military support for their very existence, this brand of high-stakes blackmail might be recognized as a bluff. In addition, gamesmanship was a dangerous strategy for both aligned and nonaligned leaders. In dozens of instances, US and Soviet forces worked covertly to have leaders of developing nations removed by aiding their political opponents or even by backing violent regime change. For example, the United States covertly aided a number of violent coups in Africa that were based on the often exaggerated fears that a particular government or leader might promote Communism.

Such fears were rarely based on credible research. The problem was especially severe in Vietnam, where few US officials who oversaw the distribution of economic and military aid spoke Vietnamese or French. Most had never even been to Vietnam. For this reason, many emerging nations of the "Third World" rejected the pressure to affiliate with Washington or Moscow. For people in these nations, alignment meant willingly becoming a pawn in the superpowers' game. People in these nations understood that US and Soviet aid came at the cost of internal sovereignty, and they were unwilling to sacrifice their newly won independence even if they desperately needed economic aid or military support.

These sentiments culminated in actions taken in 1955 at the Bandung Conference in Indonesia. There, dozens of developing nations resolved to stay out of the Cold War. Together they created a new force—the Non-Aligned Movement. Led by African leaders such as Kwame Nkrumah of Ghana and Gamal Nasser of Egypt, as well as Asian leaders like Jawaharlal Nehru of India, the Non-Aligned Movement encouraged nations to resist the influence of both superpowers, reject military alliances, and refuse to permit the construction of foreign military bases on their lands. Leaders at the Bandung Conference cited recent American intervention in Latin America as a cautionary tale about the dangers of alignment. In 1954, an American-supported coup toppled the popularly elected but leftist government of Guatemala and installed a military junta that would be responsible for the deaths of hundreds of thousands of civilians over the next three decades.

As various former colonies won their independence in Africa, Asia, and Latin America, US officials were determined to prevent any of these "new" nations from "falling" to Communism. They believed that early intervention could prevent another conflict similar to the Korean War. However, many in these nations resented the generous bestowment of American aid to their imperial oppressors through the Marshall Plan following World War II. Because of the massive aid given to Europe, which helped to prop up their empires, it mattered little to residents of developing nations that the United States proclaimed and maintained neutrality in most of their postwar struggles for independence. For the millions of former colonists who fought for and secured independence from Britain, France, the Netherlands, and other European powers during the 1950s and 1960s, the United States could not be trusted because it had been the leading ally of those who opposed their freedom.

It might have been otherwise. Most Americans supported measures that transferred domestic sovereignty to Filipinos during the 1930s and celebrated the creation of an independent Philippines on July 4, 1946. In addition, many Americans made common cause with the people of India and Indonesia and cheered when both became independent nations in 1947 and 1949, respectively. In areas such as French Indochina, however, the United States actively thwarted independence,

Third World

A term referring to economically underdeveloped nations. Most of these nations were not aligned with either the United States or the Soviet Union during the Cold War. The term was used heavily during the second half of the twentiethth century, often in ways that implied backwardness and even inferiority. Today, scholars only use the term "Third World" in the context of contemporary perspective, preferring to use terms such as "developing nations" in most other contexts.

FIGURE 10.1

Kwame Nkrumah was the first Prime Minister of independent Ghana and an influential African leader. Nkrumah is pictured with President Kennedy. However, most communications between Ghana and the United States were conducted by American diplomatic officials such as Ralph Bunche. Bunche advised the State Department on Africa and the Middle East and became the first person of color to win the Nobel Peace Prize.

even after French forces abandoned the region in 1954 due to concerns about the possible spread of Communism.

In other cases, Americans reacted with disinterest as dozens of nations won their independence. Although African Americans sent millions of dollars to aid independence movements in various African nations, few white Americans or white political leaders were supportive of these efforts. For example, black Americans actively assisted the **Mau Mau Revolution**, which began in British East Africa in 1952. After eight years of costly battles, the British finally abandoned their former colony and recognized the independent nation of Kenya. While millions of African Americans related African decolonization with their own freedom struggle, US officials and leading media outlets usually ignored the African independence movement or denigrated the efforts of Africans in overtly racist terms. At best, US officials expressed interest in African affairs only as they affected business interests and the Cold War balance of power.

The same was true in southern and central Asia. Few Americans called for intervention in the violence that killed hundreds of thousands along the India-Pakistan border following British withdrawal from the region. Even when the State Department sponsored aid and antipoverty programs throughout the world, these efforts were often directed against the spread of Communism. However, US diplomats were also guided by genuine humanitarian concerns that were sometimes independent of geopolitical calculations. In each instance, recipients of aid were made to understand that it would be discontinued if a nation turned toward Communism or formed alliances with Communist nations. This was especially true of nations located in the Western Hemisphere.

1.2   Castro and the Cuban Revolution

Preventing rival nations from gaining control of Cuba had driven US foreign policy in the Caribbean since the declaration of the Monroe Doctrine in the early nineteenth century. Cuba's location just ninety miles from the US mainland meant that Cuban affairs could impact national security. The United States tolerated the undemocratic rule of Fulgencio Batista because the Cuban dictator opposed popular Communist movements that sought to replace his regime. From the perspective of most Cubans, however, Batista was a foreign-backed dictator who was more concerned with profiting from his cozy relationships with American business leaders and organized crime bosses than with addressing the nation's problems. Many Americans were horrified by the way Batista brutally suppressed dissent. Others argued that the United States should "look the other way" so long as most of his victims were members of left-wing groups. By 1958, however, US officials decided they could no longer support Batista's brutal and dictatorial regime. At the same time, however, they feared that supporting Batista's removal would result in his replacement by a young Communist revolutionary named **Fidel Castro**.

The thirty-two-year-old Castro led a revolution against Batista and seized power on New Year's Day 1959. Castro's victory was welcomed by many in Cuba—especially the poor. The energetic young leader's popularity was rooted in his promises to improve conditions for workers and restore democratic rule. Yet Castro also faced many opponents. Landowners who had thrived under Batista feared that Castro's support for Marxist doctrines would lead to their property being confiscated by the new government. In response to their protests, Castro executed hundreds of Batista's supporters. Even Castro's idealistic lieutenant Che Guevara, an iconic and globally revered Marxist revolutionary, sometimes assisted in the brutal elimination of Castro's opponents. Castro also launched a failed offensive against the Dominican Republic, resulting in international condemnation.

Mau Mau Revolution

A prolonged and violent anticolonial struggle waged by Kenyan nationalists seeking independence from Britain during the 1950s. Native Kenyans protested the policies of the British government and eventually won independence in 1963.

FIGURE 10.2

Che Guevara was a physician who became one of Castro's revolutionary leaders. Killed at an early age in support of the spread of revolutions throughout Latin America, Che soon became an international icon representing both machismo and Marxism.

Fidel Castro

Cuban revolutionary leader who overthrew the regime of Fulgencio Batista in the winter of 1958 to 1959. Castro would lead Cuba until 2008.

FIGURE 10.3

President Truman and his wife greet the shah of Iran during one of his many visits to the United States. The Shah had been placed back in power by the United States and made a number of policies that favored Western interests. As a result, he was opposed by many Iranians and later removed from power once again.

Despite these abuses of power, Castro retained the support of most Cubans. He justified his actions as necessary to prevent a counterrevolution and bolstered his support among poor Cubans by promoting several wealth redistribution plans. For example, Castro passed a law prohibiting foreign investors and corporations from owning land on the island—a measure that resonated with landless farmers because the majority of Cuban farmland was controlled by US sugar companies. Castro's laws required foreign-owned lands to be redistributed equally among the people of Cuba who would collectively run their own farms. Castro also forced the American owners of the island's resorts and casinos to leave the country, citing their reputed connections with organized crime syndicates.

Castro had spoken out against Communism, which convinced US leaders to officially recognize Castro's revolutionary government in 1959. However, Castro's actions soon convinced Americans that his leadership was harmful to US business interests. Castro, they feared, was leading Cuba down the road to Communism. Congress responded with sanctions restricting travel to Cuba and banning the importation of sugar and other Cuban products. Cuba had been America's sugar bowl and vacation spot since the Spanish were forced from the island in 1898. Now, US economic sanctions were wreaking havoc upon the Cuban economy, thereby threatening popular support for the new leader.

Castro understood that Cuba's long-term economic progress was dependent upon trade with more prosperous nations. He also believed that he needed to build a powerful military that could defend his nation from internal and/or external enemies. When US officials blocked weapons sales between Europe and Cuba, Castro looked toward the Soviet Union. Cuba's growing alliance with the Soviet Union provided a lifeline to the island and an outlet for trade. However, it also alarmed US officials who began to ponder ways that Castro might be removed from power. Meanwhile, Castro's popularity with the Cuban people started to decline as the US embargo led to economic stagnation. Many people also opposed his brutal intolerance of dissent. Some of Castro's original supporters even felt that he had betrayed their revolution and began to question whether they had replaced one authoritarian regime with another. Some of these critics, and especially those with connections to the former landowners who had benefitted from Batista's rule, migrated to the United States with the aid of the CIA.

The CIA encouraged the arrival of Castro's opponents because the agency was planning a secret mission to train and arm ex-Cubans for an invasion of the island. The CIA believed that a small and lightly armed force could overthrow Castro's regime. Similar plans had worked in the past against the leftist government of Jacobo Guzman in Guatemala. In addition, a recent CIA-backed coup in Iran had successfully removed a leader who appeared hostile to US financial and strategic interests. Because of these apparent successes, US officials increasingly viewed covert operations as expedient, simple, and cost-effective. The CIA launched similar campaigns in the Congo, Brazil, and Ghana. However, as events in Cuba and Iran would later demonstrate, covert actions did not always work and often led to unintended consequences.

1.3 The Middle East

Demand for oil mixed with Cold War rivalry and the long-standing conflict between Israel and its Arab neighbors to produce a series of crises in the Middle East during the 1950s. In 1948, Israel had repulsed an attack by Egypt and Syria. In 1956, Egyptian leader Gamal Abdal Nasser resumed the offensive against Israel. Although the attack stalled, Egypt seized control of the Suez Canal from the British and French. However, the combined forces of Israel, Britain, and France quickly overwhelmed Egyptian fighters and threatened to invade Egypt and remove Nasser from power. The resulting conflict became known as the **Suez Canal Crisis**.

Americans recognized that Nasser maintained the support of the Arab world. If the United States chose to come to the aid of France, Britain, and especially Israel, it risked losing Arab support throughout the oil-rich Middle East. Eisenhower was particularly concerned about Nasser's ties to the Soviets, fearing that armed conflict in the Middle East would lead to Soviet intervention on Egypt's behalf. If this happened, Eisenhower believed, the Arab world would view the Soviet Union as an ally, and the West might lose access to Middle Eastern oil.

FIGURE 10.4

A battle map showing the British, French, and Israeli forces moving westward across the Sinai Peninsula toward the Suez Canal. The canal was in Egypt but had long been controlled by the West.

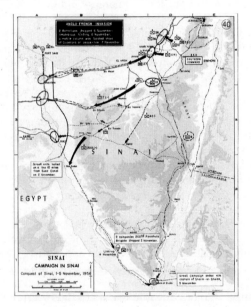

> **Suez Canal Crisis**
>
> A 1956 conflict between Egypt and Israel and their allies following the seizure of the Suez Canal by Egyptian forces under Gamal Abdel Nasser. In response, Britain, Israel, and France threatened to invade Egypt. Eisenhower feared that this would draw the Soviet Union into the region and pressured these nations to withdraw troops. Control of the canal largely returned to the status quo. However, the resolution of the crisis made it clear that the United States had taken the place of Britain and France as the leading outside power in the Middle East.

Eisenhower was especially angry because he believed that the use of force by Britain and France increased the volatility of the crisis and betrayed earlier assurances from both nations that they would act in consultation with the United States. The United States supported Israel's defensive maneuvers, but it opposed Israel's later march into Egyptian territory. The president also shared the concerns of both Israeli and European leaders regarding the seizure of the Suez Canal. Eisenhower believed that diplomacy could best resolve the crisis. But he also relied upon nuclear deterrence by scrambling US forces in the region. In the end, the Soviet Union decided not to intervene, and each of the leading parties permitted Eisenhower and the United Nations to broker a deal that led to the withdrawal of forces and the reopening of the Suez Canal.

Eisenhower Doctrine

A foreign policy statement by President Eisenhower in response to the Suez crisis. Eisenhower promised to send economic and military aid to any nation resisting attack by "any nation controlled by international Communism." The intent was to assure Middle Eastern leaders that the United States would be their ally so long as they opposed Communism.

Ho Chi Minh

A nationalist committed to the independence of his native Vietnam, Ho Chi Minh led forces against the French, Japanese, and United States. During World War II, he received assistance from the United States because both he and the United States were fighting against the Japanese. Due to his support of Communism, however, the United States opposed Ho Chi Minh's later efforts to unite Vietnam under his leadership. He died in 1969.

Geneva Accords

A 1954 agreement ending the war between France and the Vietnamese nationalists led by Ho Chi Minh. Although the Vietnamese hoped for full independence, they accepted a temporary division of the nation with the understanding that an election would be held in 1956. Under the Geneva Accords, the party that won this election would unify all of Vietnam under its leadership.

The Suez Crisis resulted in subtle, but significant, changes in the region. For example, the resolution of the crisis demonstrated that the United States had replaced Britain and France as the dominant Western power in the Middle East. Increased Arab hostility toward the Europeans for their direct military support of Israel allowed the United States to take a larger role in the region. Finally, although US financial support for Israel continued, the Soviet Union's pledge to support Nasser against Israel and the West led many in the Arab world to move closer to the Soviet Union. In response, the United States increased military and economic aid to a number of nonaligned Middle Eastern nations. In addition, the President issued a statement that came to be known as the **Eisenhower Doctrine**. Ratified by Congress in 1957, the President's statement declared that the United States would intervene militarily against any aggressive Soviet action aimed at spreading Communism in the Middle East.

1.4 Vietnam

France governed Vietnam, known then as French Indochina, as one of its colonies from the late 1800s until Japan seized control of the region during World War II. In 1930, a young Vietnamese nationalist named **Ho Chi Minh** formed a Communist resistance group that sought independence and greater economic opportunities for landless farmworkers. After fleeing French Indochina for his life, Ho Chi Minh led the Vietnamese independence movement in exile until 1941, when the Japanese seized control of the region. He then returned to his homeland and, with US aid, formed a nationalist group called the Vietminh. The Vietminh fought for Vietnamese independence against the Japanese during World War II.

The United States supported the Vietminh at this time because the Americans were also fighting the Japanese. Once the Japanese surrendered in 1945, Ho Chi Minh declared Vietnam an independent nation and sought recognition and support from the United States. Ho's top priority was to prevent the French from regaining control of their former colony. However, the United States refused to consider supporting a Communist leader against one of their most important Western allies. Instead, the United States ended its support of Ho Chi Minh and began to provide military aid to France. In exchange, the French promised to support American anti-Communist efforts in Europe. Equipped with supplies purchased by millions of American dollars and armed mostly with American-made weapons, French troops slowly drove the Vietminh north.

Eisenhower took control of the White House in 1952. The new president subscribed to Truman's Domino Theory regarding Communism and decided to continue US efforts to aid the French against Ho Chi Minh. During this time, South Korea was able to stand fast against Communist North Korea only because of US aid. Eisenhower believed that the situation in Vietnam was similar. The President steadily increased support for France—so much so that Washington was eventually financing 80 percent of the French war effort. Despite this aid, Ho Chi Minh's forces were prevailing over the French and maintained popular support. The French desperately appealed to Eisenhower, asking the former Allied Supreme Commander to use US bombers to attack Vietminh positions. However, Eisenhower opposed the idea of sending US troops to fight a war to restore French colonial rule. At the same time, he and other US leaders continued to provide military aid to the French because they feared the alternative was the spread of Communism under the leadership of Ho Chi Minh. In 1954, a major Vietminh offensive decimated French forces at Dien Bien Phu, near the Laotian border. Shortly after this defeat, the French began to remove their troops from the region.

At first, it appeared that Eisenhower would have to either send US forces to fight Ho Chi Minh or accept a Communist victory in Vietnam. Instead, the United Nations brokered an agreement that temporarily divided the nation. This agreement, known as the **Geneva Accords**, placed the former French-backed emperor of Vietnam in charge of the southern portion of the country. Ho Chi Minh was placed in charge of the northern portion. Similar to the agreement that established a truce between North and South Korea, the Geneva Accords designated a line of latitude as a border between the two sides. Vietnam's 17th Parallel was recognized as the temporary border until UN-supervised elections could be held in 1956.

Despite the often brutal tactics used by Ho Chi Minh and his lieutenants to compel both soldiers and civilians to submit to the will of the Vietminh, many Vietnamese revered Ho Chi Minh as a freedom fighter. In their view, Ho Chi Minh had dedicated the last three decades of his life to securing Vietnamese independence from both the French and the Japanese. In contrast, many viewed South Vietnam's president, Ngo Dinh Diem, as a corrupt dictator who had conspired with the French. Ho Chi Minh also favored collective land ownership. This idea appealed to many landless peasants who were forced to work on land that was owned by a small number of wealthy families who had conspired with the French during the colonial era. At the time of the Geneva Accords, many of the landowners and the bureaucrats who helped to keep these families in power were Catholics who had also supported the French. The majority of Vietnamese were impoverished Buddhists.

Given the unpopularity of Diem and all other French-aligned leaders in the southern portion of Vietnam, American officials feared the majority of Vietnamese would vote to join both sections of the country together under Ho Chi Minh's leadership. Diem recognized this and responded by thwarting the scheduled 1956 election. The Eisenhower administration recognized that, if an election were held in 1956, Ho Chi Minh would easily defeat Diem and supported this decision. Hoping to create a prosperous, non-Communist alternative to Ho Chi Minh in the north, the United States sent millions of dollars to assist Diem's government. However, Diem squandered this aid and continued to preside over a government that was as oppressive as it was ineffectual. Nevertheless, the United States continued to send military advisers and equipment to help build up the South Vietnamese army. The hope was that Diem's regime could somehow create a stable and prosperous economy that would provide the people of Vietnam with an attractive option to Ho Chi Minh's Communist government based in the northern city of Hanoi. Instead, most of the funds went to Diem's supporters, thereby increasing the alienation of the people of South Vietnam.

In 1957, Communist guerilla warriors struck targets throughout South Vietnam. Americans referred to these fighters—Communists who supported the North but lived in the non-Communist South—as the **Vietcong**. Ho Chi Minh viewed the Vietcong as a vital part of his strategy to capitalize on popular resentment toward Diem's government in Saigon. As a result, Ho provided the insurgents with virtually all of their weapons and supplies. Delivering those supplies to the South, however, was no easy task given the narrow border between North and South Vietnam. To reach the Vietcong, Communist forces used a secret network of trails that twisted around mountains and valleys of Laos, Cambodia, and Vietnam. This supply network eventually became known as the **Ho Chi Minh Trail**.

Guerilla attacks continued to chip away at Diem's support, but the United States had decided that it must either support Diem, despite his liabilities, or install another leader in his place who opposed Communism. While privately wishing that leaders within the South Vietnamese military would replace Diem with a more effective and democratic leader, US officials continued to provide aid to Diem's government. By the end of Eisenhower's presidency, US leaders had declared they would "sink or swim with Diem." The federal government hoped that Diem's government could somehow resist the increasing attacks by Ho Chi Minh's Communist supporters while ending the corruption and oppression that had turned so many South Vietnamese against his regime.

FIGURE 10.5

Vietnam had a long history of colonial rule by outside powers. This 1913 map was made when Vietnam was a French colony known as Indochina.

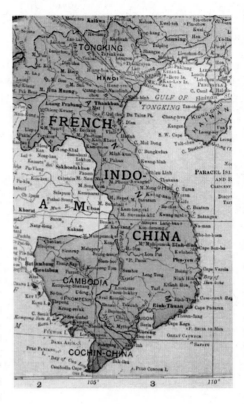

FIGURE 10.6

French troops manning an American-made tank in Vietnam during the early 1950s. Many Vietnamese were skeptical about American intentions in Vietnam during the next two decades due to the American support of the French at this time.

Vietcong

Guerilla warriors in South Vietnam who supported the Communist army of North Vietnam and its leader, Ho Chi Minh, against US forces and the army of South Vietnam during the Vietnam War.

Ho Chi Minh Trail

A network of paths and tunnels connecting North Vietnam and South Vietnam that was used to supply and transport Vietcong and North Vietnamese soldiers. Many of the paths in this network wandered into Laos and Cambodia, and none of them was visible from the air. As a result, it was very difficult for US and South Vietnamese forces to stop the movement of enemy troops and supplies.

1.5 Cold War Europe

Nikita Khrushchev

A Soviet official who emerged as the leader of the Soviet Union shortly after Stalin's death. As Soviet premier, Khrushchev tried to modernize the economy and reduce the widespread human rights abuses that had occurred under Stalin. In 1964, after the Cuban Missile Crisis, opponents in the Soviet Union forced his resignation.

The Soviet Union encountered a crisis of succession following the death of Joseph Stalin in 1953. After a number of internal disputes, **Nikita Khrushchev** emerged in 1955 as the new Soviet premier. The following year, Khrushchev gave a speech that detailed the internal corruption and violent purges that had occurred under Stalin. The speech shocked many Communists, both within and outside of the Soviet Union. Khrushchev's attempts to lift restrictions on intellectuals and artists, however, were cheered by many throughout the globe. Khrushchev also disbanded the secret police, which had been notorious for tormenting dissenters.

Some Americans welcomed these reforms as evidence that the Cold War might thaw under Khrushchev. However, the Soviet premier soon came under fire from some leaders in his country who criticized him as being too "soft" on the West. Khrushchev responded with a series of speeches that reaffirmed his status as a critic of the United States, including a statement that he intended to "bury" the West. When challenged by Western leaders to clarify his incendiary remarks, Khrushchev indicated that it was not the Russians whom Westerners should fear. Instead, Khrushchev predicted that members of the working class would revolt against the Capitalist system. "Of course we will not bury you with a shovel," the Soviet premier explained, "your own working class will bury you."

Over the next decade, the new Soviet government under Khrushchev experienced dramatic increases in industrial productivity and scientific advancement. For many residents of Eastern Europe, however, these Soviet advances did little to ameliorate their condition. Hyperinflation continued to take its toll on the economies of Eastern Europe. Although many had hoped that the death of Stalin would end the brutal repression of dissenters, the Communist governments of Eastern Europe rejected political reforms. Conditions in Hungary were among the worst in Eastern Europe. Hungary had been a part of Hitler's Axis Powers, and its government had been forced to make annual reparation payments to the Soviet Union after the war. Between these payments and economic stagnation, conditions in Hungary steadily declined.

Hungarian Revolution of 1956

A 1956 national uprising by Hungarians seeking an end to Soviet domination. The Soviet Union utilized garrisons of soldiers stationed in Hungary as well as additional troops to crush the uprising, remove the upstart Hungarian government, and reinstall a Communist régime that followed the leadership of the Soviet Union.

Throughout the 1950s, the Soviet-backed Hungarian Communist Party ran unopposed in elections and brutally attacked intellectuals and others who dared to criticize the regime. In the summer of 1956, a revolt in Poland inspired students and workers in Hungary to also demonstrate in favor of democratic reform in their nation. Despite an initial crackdown by the Soviet-backed Polish government, a number of modest reforms had been passed in Poland. Seeking similar results, college students in Hungary launched what became known as the **Hungarian Revolution of 1956**. That October, protesters took to the streets and attacked symbols of Soviet authority, such as a massive statue of Stalin. Soviet forces, which had been garrisoned throughout Hungary since the end of World War II, were quickly besieged by Hungarian revolutionaries in nearly every city and negotiated a ceasefire. In the next ten days, Hungarian leaders established their own provisional government and disbanded the secret police. The new government immediately withdrew from the Warsaw Pact and sought new partnerships with the West.

Many Hungarians hoped that their new government might follow the example of nonaligned nations such as Austria. Hungary's new leaders directed their diplomatic efforts toward seeking help from the United Nations to maintain their newly won and precarious independence. The provisional government pointed out that thousands of Soviet troops remained in their nation, despite Moscow's promise of a total withdrawal. However, the United Nations recognized the volatility of the situation and refused to take action. Eisenhower's advisers cautiously suggested that the President mobilize US troops to demonstrate support for Hungary's attempted escape from the Communist Bloc. Instead, Eisenhower followed the course of the United Nations and refused to intervene. With tensions between the United States and Soviet Union already high due to the Suez Crisis, Eisenhower was reluctant to send troops into Soviet-dominated Eastern Europe.

Eisenhower feared that US intervention would force a tougher Soviet response. Perhaps if the United States and the UN had remained neutral, some advisers believed, Soviet leaders would not feel compelled to intervene, either. Khrushchev might permit Hungary to hold special elections if it could appear as though the Soviets were in control of the situation, US leaders believed. Intervention would destroy such a façade and might convince the Kremlin that a harsh demonstration of Moscow's resolve was needed.

While American leaders debated strategies, Eisenhower's window of time to support Hungary quickly closed. After just ten days, more than twenty armored divisions from the Soviet Union entered Hungary and surrounded the capital. The interim government was overpowered and replaced by a pro-Soviet government that immediately rejoined the Warsaw Pact. Thousands of Hungarians had perished during the attempted revolution, and more than 10,000 were imprisoned. Another 200,000 fled the country. The violent response that ended the Hungarian Revolution served as a warning for other Eastern European nations that might seek independence. It also demonstrated that the death of Stalin would not result in greater political autonomy for the peoples of Eastern Europe.

Soviet leaders had made it clear that they would not permit Hungary—or any other Eastern European country—to leave its sphere of influence. Shortly afterward, however, Khrushchev began to signal possible changes in foreign policy. In subsequent years, he gave several speeches in which he called for "peaceful coexistence" with the West. Eisenhower responded in 1959 by sending Vice President Richard Nixon to visit Moscow—the first official visit of any presidential administration to the Soviet Union since the beginning of the Cold War.

The occasion of Nixon's journey was the opening of the American Exhibition—a display of numerous American cultural artifacts and manufactured goods. A highlight of the exhibit was a model home designed to showcase the comfort and affluence Americans enjoyed. Nixon and Khrushchev toured the home together while cameras recorded their conversation. Historians have labeled the exchange between the two men the "Kitchen Debate," because most of their polite but tense conversation took place in the model home's kitchen.

FIGURE 10.7

President Kennedy meets with Nikita Khrushchev in Vienna, Austria, in 1961. Although relations remained tense, the "Kitchen Debate" in Moscow between Khrushchev and Nixon opened the door for better communication between the leaders of the United States and the Soviet Union.

Although the American exhibit featured numerous works of art and culture, Khrushchev keyed in on the ways the model home emphasized materialistic values he believed were typical of the Capitalistic West. Nixon, too, said little about American contributions to art and culture, responding instead by lauding his nation's material affluence in ways that hinted his belief that Soviet families endured a lower standard of living. In the end, the famed debate featured little in the way of substantive deliberation. However, both leaders emphasized their desire to continue the conversation and improve relations between their countries.

The Soviets sent an exhibit to New York that same summer. Nikita Khrushchev traveled to the United States for a thirteen-day tour in August. The Soviet premier visited a number of cities on the east and west coasts and briefly toured Pittsburgh and an Iowa farm. Although Khrushchev's request to tour Disneyland was denied for security reasons, his trip went smoothly and inspired hope that the two nations might move beyond anxious pleasantries and move toward more substantive matters. Chief among these issues was concern over the growing nuclear arsenals that both nations possessed.

1.6 The Space Race and Nuclear Strategy

The highlight of the 1959 Soviet exhibit in New York was a replica of a small satellite named *Sputnik*. In October 1957, *Sputnik* became the first man-made satellite to orbit the globe. US scientists had made several attempts to launch a satellite that same year, but none of these early spacecraft managed to make it outside the atmosphere. In fact, many spiraled dangerously out of control. The fledgling US space program was increasingly criticized when Soviet scientists successfully launched a second satellite, *Sputnik II*. This satellite weighed more than 1,000 pounds and carried a live passenger—a dog named Laika. Americans expressed indignation that Soviet scientists did not provide a way for Laika to survive her entire space journey, but their own launch attempts were even shorter-lived. One rocket did little more than lean over and fall from its launch pad. The media dubbed this US satellite the "Stayputnik." Finally, on the last day of January 1958, US scientists successfully launched a satellite named *Explorer* into orbit.

> **Sputnik**
>
> The first satellite launched into space. Launched by the Soviet Union on October 4, 1957, *Sputnik* successfully orbited Earth and ushered in the space race—a scientific competition for supremacy in space exploration between the United States and the Soviet Union.

The American media expressed mild panic when the Soviets demonstrated such a commanding early lead in the space race. Some feared that Soviet satellites armed with nuclear bombs would soon be hovering in orbit above American cities. Recognizing the scientific limitations of using satellites as bombers, and believing that American initiative would soon outpace his Soviet rivals, Eisenhower counseled that Moscow's space program had set an important precedent that could actually benefit US strategists. By being the first to launch a satellite that orbited the globe, the Soviets had effectively agreed that national borders did not extend to the heavens. While sending US spy planes into Soviet airspace might be considered an act of war (an issue that would soon increase tensions between the two nations), the fact that the Soviets had launched a satellite that orbited the globe without consulting the United States meant that US scientists could do likewise. Eisenhower envisioned satellites capable of tracking Soviet naval vessels and even spying directly on the Soviet homeland.

FIGURE 10.8

The canine cosmonaut Laika became the first casualty of space exploration after being launched inside of the *Sputnik II* satellite.

Congress responded to the Soviet space program by increasing funding for research and development programs. Further action was taken to consolidate existing aeronautical research programs into the National Aeronautics and Space Administration (NASA). Congress also passed the National Defense Education Act. This law provided direct funding for colleges to promote math, science, and engineering as well as foreign languages and area studies. The name of the law signified the government's view that maintaining the world's premiere system of higher education was vital to national security. A relatively small amount of funding was also included to provide loans for students

who needed financial assistance to attend college. Little noticed at the time, the National Defense Student Loan Program inspired the much larger federal loan programs that presently assist millions of students who otherwise could not afford to attend college or purchase textbooks.

Though significant, government funding for education and many other domestic programs was overshadowed by annual expenditures for defense. President Eisenhower, a military hero and staunch advocate of national defense, viewed the nation's skyrocketing military spending as a threat to the continued economic well-being of the nation. In an era of Cold War fears, those who called for reductions in military spending were often accused of being "soft on Communism." As a result, it was significant that a leader of such unimpeachable military credentials as Eisenhower took the lead on this issue.

The President reasoned that it would be much cheaper to maintain a nuclear arsenal strategically located around the globe than match the size of the massive Red Army with its millions of soldiers. Secretary of State John Foster Dulles agreed. However, the Secretary of State also pointed out that for nuclear deterrence to work, the world had to believe that the United States really would respond to an attack of conventional forces by launching nuclear weapons. As a result, Dulles publicly announced that any attack against the United States would be met with an immediate and direct nuclear assault on that nation. In theory, this strategy of "massive retaliation" was little more than a public acknowledgement of Eisenhower's existing strategy of nuclear deterrence.

second-strike capability

The ability of a nation to launch a significant number of nuclear weapons at an aggressor in retaliation for a nuclear attack, no matter how severe that first attack might have been. It stood as a significant measure of a nation's nuclear deterrence.

Another key piece of the nuclear deterrence strategy was to make it apparent that the Soviets could not launch a first strike that would destroy America's ability to retaliate. Eisenhower and Dulles committed the nation to massive retaliation by constructing an elaborate system based on maintaining **second-strike capability**. By 1960, the United States had decreased overall military spending, but it had increased its number of nuclear warheads to 18,000. The United States also expanded its capacity to instantly deliver those warheads to targets around the globe.

The Strategic Air Command (SAC) of the US Air Force maintained squadrons of bombers armed with nuclear missiles in the skies twenty-four hours a day. The navy deployed fleets of submarines on secret missions throughout the globe—all armed with nuclear missiles and capable of hiding underwater for months at a time. Finally, the United States built top-secret nuclear silos hidden deep underground throughout the nation and on US military bases around the world. Such actions made it clear that even if the Union of Soviet Socialist Republics (USSR) launched its entire arsenal of nuclear weapons (which soon exceeded 20,000 warheads), it could not hope to neutralize the thousands of missiles that were in the skies, underwater, and hidden deep underground. Defenders of massive retaliation argued that such mutually assured destruction would prevent any nuclear attack. Eisenhower's critics labeled the President's reliance on nuclear deterrence as a policy of "brinksmanship." These critics argued that Eisenhower's willingness to rely on nuclear deterrence increased the likelihood that any war, or even a mishap, could lead to the extermination of all life on earth.

The possibility of global annihilation became an increasing concern as both nations developed massive nuclear arsenals composed of weapons that were hundreds of times more powerful than the bombs dropped at Hiroshima and Nagasaki. To maintain their arsenals, both nations performed hundreds of nuclear tests underground, underwater, and even on the ground. Each of these atmospheric tests spread nuclear fallout, and scientists documented spikes in radiation levels that spread far beyond the isolated test sites.

Committee for a SANE Nuclear Policy (SANE)

The leading organization calling for an end to atmospheric testing of nuclear weapons and global disarmament. It was formed in 1957 in response to increased levels of radiation resulting from nuclear tests.

Civilian protests and international condemnation led both sides to consider limiting atmospheric tests. In the United States, activists formed the **Committee for a SANE Nuclear Policy (SANE)** in 1957. SANE's goal was to raise awareness of the dangers of nuclear proliferation and atmospheric testing. These activists were aided in their cause by increased diplomatic communications between the United States and the Soviet Union during the late 1950s. In 1958, the United States, Great Britain, and the Soviet Union agreed to a temporary ban on atmospheric testing. Plans were also made to discuss mutual reductions in the number of nuclear weapons each nation possessed. However, this apparent thaw in the Cold War would prove short-lived.

In 1960, the Soviet Union shot down a US spy plane that had violated its airspace. President Eisenhower initially denied that the United States sponsored spy missions over Soviet territory. However, the President was soon forced to admit culpability when Moscow produced photographs of the captured pilot. Ironically, Eisenhower had considered ending all surveillance flights over the Soviet Union to prevent such a possibility, only to be convinced otherwise by his subordinates. After the incident, relations between the two nations quickly declined. Even an agreement to exchange the pilot for a captured Soviet agent did little to reduce these tensions. Criticized by many in his nation for what they perceived as weakness on the part of the Soviet premier, Khrushchev responded with a bellicose denouncement of the United States for its violation of Soviet airspace and refused to consider any future discussions about nuclear disarmament.

The thaw in relations that many had hoped would take place following Stalin's death was no longer in the forecast. Instead, both nations resumed atmospheric tests in the fall of 1961, which prompted macabre meteorologists to include radiation levels among their weather predictions. The change prompted SANE and an army of celebrities and activists to rally behind the cause of limiting nuclear testing. Because of their efforts, the United States, Britain, and the Soviet Union agreed to the 1963

Partial Test Ban Treaty, which once again banned atmospheric tests. The treaty remains in effect, with only France, China, and North Korea conducting tests beyond the underground experiments the treaty permits.

REVIEW AND CRITICAL THINKING

1. Why did the United States support Ho Chi Minh during World War II, only to later aid France as it tried to retake Vietnam from the Vietminh?

2. Even today, Cold War histories in the United States usually present people of developing nations as passive victims or pawns of the United States and Soviet Union. In what ways might this perspective limit the accuracy of the Cold War narrative? How did the leaders of developing nations determine the course of their own actions, and in what ways did these actions shape the history of the Cold War?

3. How were events in the Middle East influenced by the Cold War? Why did the United States hesitate to provide military aid to assist the Hungarian Revolution? How were the risks that the United States was trying to avoid similar in these two examples?

4. How did science and technology affect the Cold War? What actions did the United States take to promote scientific advancement, and what motivated these policies?

5. Because he was a military leader, many predicted that Eisenhower would increase the use of America's armed forces around the globe. What do you think? Was President Eisenhower more likely to use the military than other presidents? Did his established reputation as a military hero play a role in his decisions regarding national defense?

2.   AMERICA DURING THE EISENHOWER YEARS

LEARNING OBJECTIVES

1. **Explain the reasons why support for Senator McCarthy declined by the end of 1954. Detail the impact of McCarthyism after the Senator faded from the national scene.**

2. **In his farewell address, Eisenhower warned about the potential dangers of the Military-Industrial Complex. Explain what Eisenhower meant, and evaluate the effectiveness of the United States in balancing the role of the military within the framework of a democratic society during this period.**

3. **Detail the transition of the Civil Rights Movement from legal cases under the NAACP to direct action by black communities and college students. Explain how the Cold War had an impact upon the Civil Rights Movement.**

Historians have frequently applied the label "The Affluent Society" to 1950s America. The moniker is both a reference to the increasing material wealth many Americans enjoyed and a tongue-in-cheek jab at the shortsightedness that led few to challenge the notion that all Americans were sharing equally in this prosperity. In 1958, Harvard economist John Galbraith's book *The Affluent Society* aimed to explain the perpetuation of crushing poverty in a nation that enjoyed such vast wealth. Other scholars pointed out that despite the tendency of most Americans to describe themselves as "middle class," the gap between the rich and the poor continued to expand.

Even if many Americans who considered themselves members of the middle class were actually part of the working poor, America's standards of poverty and affluence were still exceptional compared to other nations. By 1960, a majority of American families owned their homes. Luxury items such as cars and televisions were increasingly considered necessities. With the exception of major purchases, Americans also continued to avoid debt. For many Americans, references connecting affluence and egalitarianism carried no ironic overtones as the problems of poverty and racial injustice seemed distant from their reality.

FIGURE 10.9

Representative of the faster pace of life and material affluence, Americans began consuming large numbers of frozen meals that were precooked and individually packaged. These kinds of meals were seldom enjoyed by a family that sat around a table and became known as "TV dinners."

2.1 End of McCarthyism

Despite the atmosphere of prosperity, concerns about internal security continued to plague the nation throughout the 1950s. Senator Joseph McCarthy's techniques were such that very few Americans were willing to challenge his attacks else they became his next target. Even President Eisenhower, a man who detested McCarthy and enjoyed global acclaim, avoided any confrontation with the bellicose senator from Wisconsin. However, a handful of prominent Americans at least indirectly challenged McCarthy's techniques and the hysteria from which they had spawned. Journalist Edward Murrow used his nightly program to investigate the plight of an Air Force veteran who was discharged because he came from a family of Communist sympathizers. Playwright Arthur Miller wrote *The Crucible*, a 1953 drama ostensibly centered on the Salem Witch Trials. Those who read Miller's work in these years clearly perceived the author's purpose of exposing the parallels between Cold War hysteria and the Puritanical fear-mongering and wild accusations that erupted in seventeenth-century Massachusetts.

The characters in Miller's play who sought evidence before convicting those accused of crimes soon found that they were among the defendants. Miller utilized these events in his drama to make his audience consider the tactics of misdirection and guilt by association used by McCarthy. Just as those called to defend themselves on charges of witchcraft had no way to prove their innocence, charges of disloyalty proved equally elusive. These accusations also placed critics of both witch hunts on the defensive by equating dissent with treachery. The indirect nature of the methods Murrow and Miller used to criticize McCarthy helped spare these two from the fate of The Hollywood Ten and others who challenged anti-Communist hysteria in less veiled ways. However, Murrow's television show was later cancelled by its network while Miller was investigated by Congress and subject to harassment by demagogues.

The Crucible debuted in 1953, the same year that Joseph Stalin died and the Korean War ended. These two events helped to reduce the weight of McCarthy's accusations. Perhaps more importantly, more and more Americans were already growing tired of the Wisconsin Senator's wild accusations that were still not substantiated by any credible evidence. Even some of McCarthy's strongest supporters began advising the Senator to stop talking about lists of "card-carrying Communists" in favor of more subjective accusations about the government being soft on Communism. Instead, McCarthy continued to make accusations that even his supporters knew were based on exaggerated or faulty information.

In 1954, Edward Murrow aired an exposé revealing the hollowness of McCarthy's unsubstantiated accusations. The Wisconsin Senator could only respond with insults against the host. McCarthy then expanded his accusations to include members of the army. Military officials refused to be cowed by the senator's bullying techniques and arranged a televised hearing. Millions watched live as McCarthy failed to provide any evidence of disloyal military officers. Instead, he himself became the subject of an inquisition for an earlier attempt to secure a draft deferment for one of his supporters. McCarthy responded with a personal attack on a young army officer he claimed was a Communist. McCarthy had attacked this particular young man before and had promised not to do so again. The army's chief counsel, Joseph Welch, cut the Senator off with the now-famous line "Have you no sense of decency, sir, at long last?" Later that year, the Senate officially censured McCarthy for "unbecoming conduct." He died three years later from an alcohol-related illness.

Senator McCarthy had surrendered all credibility, yet McCarthyism lived on. J. Edgar Hoover continued to use the FBI to monitor, discredit, infiltrate, and otherwise harass left-leaning political groups and civil rights organizations for the next two decades through a program known as **COINTELPRO**. An acronym for "Counter Intelligence Program," the FBI launched COINTELPRO in 1956 to infiltrate and disrupt Communist organizations in the United States. The program quickly escalated to using wiretaps and other forms of illegal surveillance techniques against a variety of organizations from the Ku Klux Klan to Vietnam protesters and the Black Panthers.

Eisenhower recognized the dangers of openly criticizing Hoover and the FBI. He went along with the Bureau chief's demands to expand the various surveillance operations on thousands of Americans from Martin Luther King Jr. to college students and Native American leaders. Even J. Robert Oppenheimer, the "father of the atomic bomb" was targeted for speaking words of caution against the government's plan to expand its arsenal of nuclear weapons. Oppenheimer was fired from his job after the government removed his security clearance, the result of an investigation that made it clear that the FBI had bugged his phone conversations for many years. Fellow scientists refused to speak with the unfairly disgraced physicist for fear they might share a similar fate. Meanwhile, various loyalty programs continued to investigate the personal lives of government employees, with hundreds of workers being fired based on little more than vaguely suspicious behaviors observed by unnamed sources.

2.2   Government and Labor

Eisenhower and most of his Republican colleagues continued to support the expansion of popular New Deal programs such as Social Security. Under his administration, the program expanded to include three-quarters of employed workers and their beneficiaries and the total amount of payments increased tenfold between 1950 and 1960. The idea of a federally mandated minimum wage also continued to receive support by both parties, with the main partisan division being Democratic efforts to expand its provisions to include domestic and farm workers. These liberals found few adherents and these laborers, usually women and minorities, were not covered by the new minimum wage that guaranteed all workers at least one dollar per hour of labor. The two parties also differed on the extent to which the federal government should become involved in labor relations, its power to regulate private businesses, and the size and scope of the welfare state. However, neither Eisenhower nor his Republican colleagues in Congress sought to end entitlement programs such as Social Security or Medicare, meaning that these New Deal initiatives would continue regardless of which party controlled Washington.

Labor unions in the 1950s represented just over a third of workers beyond those in agriculture and domestic service, who were not unionized at all. The industrial unions of the 1950s were both bigger and more conservative than many of the early twentieth century. Nearly all focused on wage and benefit increases, and very few challenged the Capitalist system or advocated collective ownership. The American Federation of Labor (AFL) and Congress of Industrial Organizations (CIO) merged in 1955, yet the new **AFL-CIO** experienced steady declines in the overall percentage of workers who were part of their organization. Part of this decline was structural and reflected overall trends in the economy. The total number of white-collar workers outpaced those who worked with their hands in the late twentieth century. Another challenge for the AFL-CIO was that many corporations were transferring their operations to states that had been hostile to unions and even to overseas locations.

Another reason for the decline was that some union members believed the leadership of the AFL-CIO was becoming complacent. Major strikes declined during the 1950s, and much of the work that was previously carried out by union leaders was now contracted to law firms and arbitration specialists. These hearings were often successful in terms of winning concessions for union members, but they lacked the apparent drama of previous labor activism. Many business leaders believed the opposite—that the leading unions were still too active and too powerful. They viewed the outcome of the most dramatic labor stoppage in the late 1950s, a nationwide strike by half a million steelworkers, as evidence that labor unions had a dangerous amount of control over the private sector. At issue was the conflict between utilizing new technology and reducing the workforce. Union contracts specified the number of workers that should be assigned to certain tasks, but steel companies sought to lower those numbers and save labor costs through automation. After four months, the unions prevailed. The outcome of the 1959 Steel Strike may have been a pyrrhic victory for the unions, however, as many Americans perceived the unions as opposing innovation and efficiency. Even worse for steel workers, American businesses turned to overseas firms during the strike, and domestic steel production never recovered.

Perhaps the greatest setback for the union movement during this era was the growing perception of corruption among union leaders. A 1957 Senate investigation exposed connections between a number of union leaders and organized crime. The investigation led to **Jimmy Hoffa** of the Teamsters Union becoming a household name. The investigation detailed sensational criminal allegations, from starting fake unions to laundering mafia money and an attempt to seize control of the entire shipping industry. In the end, the Senate secured little more than indictments against Hoffa. From that point forward, most Americans associated the Teamsters and numerous other leading unions with corruption. Senator Robert Kennedy rose to prominence as a leading member of the investigation, but he also alienated many working-class Americans who believed he was motivated by an agenda to exaggerate corruption as a means of furthering his own career.

Jimmy Hoffa notwithstanding, the late 1950s was a banner period for those in the domestic shipping industry. In 1956, Congress approved the Federal Highway Act, a national defense initiative that facilitated the movement of troops and equipment while also facilitating private and commercial transportation. The measure led to the construction of the federal interstate system and its 40,000 miles of highways. The Federal Highway Act received its strongest support among automobile and oil companies, but it worried many residents and business owners in smaller cities. Because these new interstates were designed to move traffic at high speeds without stopping, the roads bypassed small towns and directed traffic away from older commercial centers such as downtowns. The result was a drastic improvement in the ability to travel across the nation by automobile as well as the devastation of many small towns and businesses that were bypassed by the new roads.

One of the justifications for interstate construction was to provide civilians with a rapid means of egress in the case of nuclear attack. Defense remained the top budgetary priority of the federal government, with defense spending increasing from $13 billion at the start of the Korean War to more than $50 billion in 1953. The size and expense of America's armed forces had contracted sharply following every war in American history up to this time. However, following the Korean War, the United States decided to maintain a large military and spent more than $40 billion each year through the end of the decade. President Eisenhower was skeptical about the wisdom of this course of action, and chose to highlight the potential danger of escalating military budgets in his January 1961 farewell address.

Military-Industrial Complex

A phrase utilized by outgoing President Dwight Eisenhower to describe what he believed was collusion between the representatives of the munitions industry, the military, and elected officials.

Eisenhower reminded Americans that the nation had only recently developed a permanent armaments industry. The outgoing president believed that this was a necessary development given the changing nature of warfare that placed greater importance on rapid mobilization. However, Eisenhower cautioned against the possibility that those representing the armaments industry might develop "unwarranted influence" in the halls of Congress. He labeled this potential problem the **Military-Industrial Complex**, a name connoting Eisenhower's belief that military and government leaders were often guilty of doing the bidding of defense contractors. In the years that followed, Americans became increasingly aware that lobbyists representing corporations that produced military equipment were donating millions of dollars to political campaigns. These donations were clearly intended to influence politicians who might return the favor by purchasing their products or voting for overall increases in military budgets. Eisenhower believed that the potential harm was not only wasteful spending but also declining accountability among lawmakers to represent the views of their constituents.

2.3　New Americans and Native Americans

Fidel Castro's nationalization of the Cuban sugar fields led US companies to expand their operations in Puerto Rico. This expansion led to the eviction of hundreds of thousands of Puerto Ricans, many of whom were recruited to migrate to American cities by US firms. Between 1945 and 1953, 40,000 to 70,000 Puerto Ricans migrated to New York City each year. By 1960, Puerto Ricans represented nearly 10 percent of the city's inhabitants. In fact, there were more Puerto Ricans living in East Harlem, Chicago, and Miami than lived in the Puerto Rican capital of San Juan. Although all Puerto Ricans were US citizens, most white Americans viewed the newcomers as outsiders. Signs explicitly barred Puerto Ricans from restaurants, while several attempts were made to legally prevent the newcomers from voting in local elections.

US companies continued to recruit Mexican nationals to come to the United States through the Bracero Program. Unlike Puerto Ricans, their lack of citizenship made Mexican workers even more vulnerable. About 450,000 Braceros signed temporary labor contracts in 1959. These contracts permitted the migrants to legally live and work in the United States for a specified period of time and withheld a percentage of their pay until they returned to Mexico. Mexico encountered severe internal conflict during this period, leading many Braceros to choose to stay in the United States and forfeit their withheld pay. Some Americans were alarmed by the growing number of unlawful migrants, leading to the arrest of thousands of undocumented aliens under the terms of the 1950 McCarran-Nixon Internal Security Act. This law had been passed to permit the government to deport "subversives" such as Communists, but was now utilized against Mexican migrants. In 1954, the federal government supported police raids on private homes and areas where migrants were known to gather. The dragnet resulted in a million deportations in only one year. The name the federal government chose for this program, "Operation Wetback," led many to believe that racism was a leading factor in the way the raids were conducted.

A growing cadre of Mexican American scholars and activists documented the frequent use of unlawful tactics among police and immigration agents against persons suspected of being illegal aliens. They also protested the mass deportations and publicized the conditions Mexican laborers faced. Former union organizer Ernesto Galarza completed a PhD at Columbia University and published *Strangers in Our Fields* in 1956. Galarza's study brought national attention to the conditions faced by migrant farm workers. Writer Americo Paredes earned a PhD from the University of Texas at Austin and countered negative stereotypes by publishing a history of South Texas from the perspective of a Mexican American folk hero. Paredes presented an alternative to the dominant narrative by writing history from the perspective of Texans—the original inhabitants of what had only recently become the state of Texas. By this perspective, the Anglo founders of the state were illegal immigrants and the original Texas Rangers were imperialist mercenaries.

In 1952, the **McCarran-Walter Act** removed race as a barrier to citizenship and ended the almost total ban against Asian migration. However, the law reflected continuing prejudice against Asian Americans and merely modified the nation's immigration quota system. After the law passed, no more than 105 Chinese and 185 Japanese immigrants could become citizens each year. Immigration historian Oscar Handlin was among the many who protested these quotas as tantamount to racial exclusion. However, included in the language of the act was a permissive statute granting relatives of current citizens the ability to migrate to the United States beyond these numerical limits. Little-noticed at the time, more than 100,000 people of Asian and African descent immigrated to the United States in the next decade under this provision. President Truman shared the criticisms of Handlin and others who thought the new law was racist. However, the president's veto was overturned by the Democrat-controlled Congress.

FIGURE 10.11

This 1963 story in the *Los Angeles Times* revealed allegations by a bookkeeper who testified that her former employer falsified the records of Braceros in order to withhold some of the worker's pay.

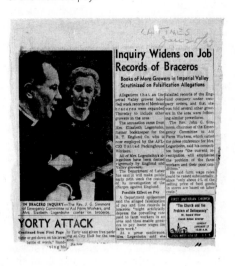

McCarran-Walter Act

An amendment revising the immigration policies of the United States, the McCarran-Walter Act represented a shift from quotas based on national origin to a system based on promoting skilled immigrants and prohibit migration of individuals whose political views were viewed as dangerous. Although many of the national origins provisions were removed or modified, the McCarran-Walter Act still limited the migration of nonwhite peoples from Asia to Africa.

termination

The process of removing federal recognition of a Native American tribe. Termination was proposed as a means to encourage assimilation by offering a final settlement to Native American tribes that its proponents believed would lead to full integration of tribal members into American society. Opponents countered that termination was nothing more than an attempt to withdraw Native American sovereignty. These programs were abandoned after several well-publicized failures, and the government later rerecognized many of the terminated tribes.

Increased immigration led to new attempts to promote assimilation, especially regarding Native Americans who lived on reservations. The Truman administration appointed the same person who was in charge of operating the Japanese internment camps to lead the Bureau of Indian Affairs. The Eisenhower administration sought to reduce funding for reservations. And in 1953, a joint congressional resolution called for the gradual end to all special programs and funding for Native Americans, with the goal of rapid and complete assimilation. **Termination**, as the policy soon became known, led to the end of federal recognition of fourteen tribes between 1954 and 1960. Many Native Americans contrasted the massive government aid that was given to Europe without any conditions with the federal government's policy of termination. They believed the requirement that natives surrender tribal sovereignty was part of a flawed plan to incorporate natives into the US mainstream. The high-profile failure of the policy to improve the lives of two leading tribes, the Menominee of Wisconsin and the Klamath of Oregon, led to a successful campaign to end termination in favor of new programs aimed at strengthening Native American self-governance and revitalizing life on the reservations.

Prior to an 1864 treaty, the federal government had granted the Klamath more than 20 million acres. By the 1950s, that reservation had been reduced to 1.3 million acres in Oregon. However, the tribe was still largely financially independent due to the reservation's natural resources of farmland and timber. Tribal members shared revenue from the use of their land and lived modestly. Previous treaties had guaranteed annual payments to the tribe in exchange for their acceptance of provisions reducing the size of their reservation as well as hunting and fishing rights on area lands. As a result, most Klamath had grown financially dependent on the federal government and the distributions of income paid from the use of their lands. Termination threatened to end the reservation system completely in favor of a lump-sum payment to tribal members. Advocates of termination pressured the Klamath and even spread misinformation asserting that they might lose everything if they did not accept the lump-sum payment.

In 1954, the government agreed to purchase the reservation for $90 million and end federal recognition of the tribe and cease all future payments to tribal members. This proved to be a financially shrewd move on the part of the government, given revenues in excess of $200 million the federal government received for the use of these lands in subsequent years. Some of the Klamath invested their share of the federal payoff wisely. Many others had little knowledge of finance and quickly spent or were swindled out of their money. The result was a tremendous increase in alcoholism, juvenile delinquency, and abject poverty. For many historians, termination represented the modern-day equivalent to the Dawes Act and its destruction of native communities and transfer of native lands to the federal government and land speculators.

2.4   *Brown v. Board* and School Integration

In the late 1930s, black plaintiffs won decisions that secured their right to attend public universities that had previously excluded them. By 1950, the NAACP decided to challenge segregation in public schools. At this time racial separation was required by law in seventeen states and the District of Columbia. In 1954, five lawsuits challenging the constitutionality of school segregation were consolidated under the name *Brown v. The Board of Education of Topeka, Kansas*. The reason the NAACP's case took on the name of the Topeka case was because its plaintiff's name preceded the others alphabetically. However, the selection of a Midwestern city helped to demonstrate that segregation was not simply a Southern phenomenon. Kansas officials were in the process of outlawing segregation but did not move quickly enough to avoid the dubious distinction of being forever associated with racial discrimination. Instead the state's case was assigned to a recent law school graduate who was personally opposed to segregation.

FIGURE 10.12

At the time of the *Brown* decision, seventeen states had laws requiring racial segregation while a number of others had no laws on the subject. States such as Kansas permitted segregation if there was a large number of black students that would allow a separate school to be operated economically.

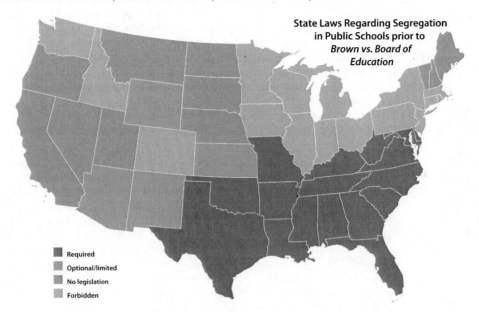

State Laws Regarding Segregation in Public Schools prior to *Brown vs. Board of Education*

- Required
- Optional/limited
- No legislation
- Forbidden

The young attorney would find that he was opposed by the State Department, in addition to the NAACP and a host of liberal organizations. This was because the 1954 case, like everything else at this time, was deeply influenced by the Cold War. Soviet agents had made extensive use of US school segregation in their global propaganda, so much so that the State Department wrote a number of legal briefs in support of the NAACP's position. Diplomats and bureaucrats alike lobbied the Supreme Court and helped convince the justices to unanimously declare that the maintenance of separate schools would no longer be permissible. Over a hundred local courts had made similar rulings beginning in Iowa in 1868. The 1954 decision was historic, however, because the Supreme Court ruled that segregation violated the Fourteenth Amendment of the Constitution. It also explicitly overturned the doctrine of "separate but equal" by declaring that even if schools received equal funding, the simple act of segregation alone violated the doctrine of equal protection. And because the case was decided by the Supreme Court, the decision applied to schools throughout the nation.

The court's decision prompted mixed reactions throughout Border South states that still explicitly required or permitted racial segregation by law. In Missouri, Oklahoma, Delaware, Maryland, and West Virginia, state education officials promised to adhere to the ruling. Many stated that segregation would end with little trouble as long as the change was implemented slowly. The governor of Texas also indicated that his officials would comply with the ruling, but hedged his remarks by indicating that it would take many years before school officials in his state could even develop a plan to start the process.

Those who hoped to stall the process of integration were encouraged by many of the events that followed. President Eisenhower avoided any statement on the matter, and most school districts continued to maintain separate schools. More than ninety Southern congressmen issued a statement they dubbed the *Southern Manifesto*; it denounced the *Brown* decision and urged government officials to ignore it "by all lawful means." State officials throughout the Deep South promised total resistance to any effort to "force" the desegregation of their public schools. For example, Georgia governor Herman Talmadge promised that he would find a way around the court's decision and "insure permanent segregation of the races."

FIGURE 10.13

Not all Southern communities actively resisted integration. Many cities in the Border South peacefully integrated their schools despite resistance by some parents. This photo depicts an integrated classroom in Washington, DC, in 1955.

Urban school districts on the border between North and South, like Baltimore, Lexington, and St. Louis, pursued a different strategy. In predominantly white neighborhoods, a handful of middle-class black students attended formerly all-white schools, while inner-city districts remained almost completely segregated. Some school districts in rural and smaller cities throughout the Border South integrated immediately, but most simply chose to do nothing and see what the courts and federal government would do next. They soon found that black communities would not wait. Local NAACP chapters throughout these communities gathered petitions and filed lawsuits demanding an immediate and unconditional end to segregation.

In 1955, the Supreme Court issued what has become known as *Brown* II, a legal brief that was supposed to contain legal guidelines on how desegregation must proceed. Hoping to bridge the controversy and demonstrate sensitivity to the concerns of Southern whites, the Court declared that public schools must proceed "with all deliberate speed" toward integration. While the court intended that this would demonstrate an understanding of the logistical difficulties of reassigning pupils and teachers, this second *Brown* decision was interpreted by many whites as a loophole they could exploit. In the absence of presidential or congressional support for integration, decisions regarding integration were determined at the state and local level and within the federal courts. In addition, the Brown decision did not yet apply to private schools.

The failure of *Brown* II to provide any timetable for compliance sent a clear message that the government wished to counter Soviet propaganda by outlawing school segregation but would not actively enforce the measure. If black communities desired to end segregation, they would still have to initiate lawsuits and secure court orders forcing each individual school board to integrate. In other words, integration was required by law, but the burden of enforcement fell on those citizens who desired compliance with the law.

FIGURE 10.14

Federal troops were deployed to Arkansas to protect the nine African American students as they attended school during an entire academic year. When faced with future integration cases, many schools in Arkansas and throughout the Deep South simply closed.

Such was the situation in Arkansas in 1957 after the black community secured a court order demanding the integration of Little Rock's Central High School. Nine students with outstanding academic credentials were selected to be the first to integrate the school. Arkansas governor Orval Faubus responded by calling out the Arkansas National Guard to prevent the children from entering the building. This action by a governor to use state troops to prevent a federal court order provoked a constitutional crisis and forced President Eisenhower to end his silence on the matter. Eisenhower summoned Faubus to Washington, where the two agreed that they both opposed the court's decision but had no choice but to follow the law. When Faubus returned to Arkansas, however, he played to the white supremacist majority and once again sought to thwart integration. Eisenhower responded by placing the Arkansas National Guard under federal orders and sending the 101st Airborne to enforce the court order mandating integration. For the rest of the school year, federalized troops escorted the nine students to school. Leading Southern politicians appealed to the populist anger of many whites, likening the use of federal troops as a "second invasion" of the South and promising to hold the line against further Yankee efforts to force integration on their communities.

2.5   Violent Resistance in the Deep South

The desegregation of the buses of Montgomery, Alabama, was one of the few clear victories for the Civil Rights Movement in the Deep South during the 1950s. However, numerous community organizations and the courage of activists such as Mississippi's **Medgar Evers** continued to challenge segregation throughout the decade. After returning to his native Mississippi following World War II, Evers and other veterans marched to the courthouse to cast their votes. They were forced to flee for their lives by an armed mob inside the courthouse. After graduating with honors from the historically black Alcorn A&M (today Alcorn State University), Evers attempted in 1954 to enroll in the all-white law school at the University of Mississippi. His application was denied on a technicality. In the meantime, he accepted a position as the NAACP's first field secretary in Mississippi. It took university officials nearly a year to come up with a reason to reject the academically talented Evers. While his application was still pending, the young Evers attended to his ailing father. Evers recalled that his last moments with his father were marred by the screams of a lynch mob outside the basement window of the segregated hospital. Later that same year, Medgar and his wife Myrlie Evers opened the first NAACP office in Mississippi.

Racial violence thrust Medgar Evers into the national spotlight in 1955 when he led the fight to convict the murderers of fourteen-year-old Emmett Till. The young man was killed in retaliation for allegedly whistling at a young white woman. Although Till's murderers bragged about the crime, they were never convicted. The very fact that Mississippi held a trial, however, was evidence that the Evers had forced a change in the attitudes of both blacks and whites in the Deep South. Blacks in Mississippi defied white mobs outside the trial, openly brandishing weapons as a warning against future attacks. Till's mother requested that her son's casket be left open so that everyone would have to see the beaten and disfigured body of her son. "I wanted the world to see what they did to my baby," she explained. Photos of Till's mutilated face were published in newspapers throughout the world. While Till was one of hundreds of African Americans whose murders escaped justice despite eyewitness reports, the mutilated face of Emmett Till mobilized blacks and some whites behind the growing civil rights movement.

In 1956, segregationists formed the Mississippi Sovereignty Commission. This was but one of many state-funded organizations that used millions of taxpayer dollars to fight integration and spy on civil rights leaders. Recently declassified records include thousands of pages detailing how the Mississippi Sovereignty Commission funded the White Citizens Council, illegally spied on black leaders, worked to persuade private employers to fire black workers connected with civil rights, and was even responsible for some of the information used by Klansmen to murder civil rights activists during its twenty-year existence.

In spite of the daily threat of violence, civil rights activism continued in Mississippi and beyond. Students at HBCUs like Florida A&M initiated a bus boycott in 1956 that led to the desegregation of buses in Tallahassee. The following year, students at the University of Texas lobbied for racial integration. In 1958, black students protested segregation in the public schools of Washington, DC, with the help of Jackie Robinson. Martin Luther King Jr. and a coalition of black clergy responded to the demands of their parishioners and formed the **Southern Christian Leadership Conference (SCLC)** in 1957. The SCLC was a coalition of preachers who viewed desegregation as part of the mission of the black church. This organization remained rather conservative compared to later civil rights groups. However, students and others prodded SCLC leaders such as King to support their direct action campaigns such as sit-ins. Before long, King even agreed to join the students and share their hardships.

2.6   Emergence of Grassroots Activism

Black communities throughout the North and West secured civil rights gains through direct action, court challenges, and by petitioning state legislatures throughout the decade. In 1953, black activists in the state of Washington succeeded in passing an ordinance banning racial discrimination in employment. Two years later, blacks in New Mexico secured a civil rights law banning segregation in restaurants, hotels, and all other public places. Nationally, the NAACP sought similar legal change through federal courts. Between 1938 and 1961, the NAACP took thirty-two cases to the US Supreme Court and won twenty-nine of them. In 1946, for example, the courts banned segregation on buses traveling through multiple states (buses operating in only one state were subject only to the laws of that state). In 1947, members of the Congress of Racial Equality (CORE) launched the Journey of Reconciliation, a collection of white and black activists who traveled together and sought to enforce the court's ban on

Medgar Evers

A civil rights leader in Mississippi who was assassinated on June 12, 1963. Despite the viciousness of those who opposed him, Evers followed the doctrine of nonviolence. However, he also carried a gun with him every day and left multiple weapons around his home to defend his family. After her husband's murder, Myrlie Evers continued to run the local NAACP office that she and her husband had operated since its founding; she later became one of the organization's national leaders.

Southern Christian Leadership Conference (SCLC)

Formed by Martin Luther King Jr. in 1957, the SCLC was an organization led by black ministers who supported the civil rights movement. Although the SCLC was more conservative than many other civil rights groups, the participation of ministers and churches provided the civil rights movement with institutional support, and most civil rights meetings would be held in black churches throughout the nation.

segregation in interstate travel. However, CORE's efforts went largely unnoticed among whites as well as some African Americans.

Less than a decade later, however, a protest against bus segregation would spur a renaissance in CORE's philosophy on direct action. Whereas interstate travel was not an everyday experience, Southern blacks relied on city bus systems for transportation. Segregation on city buses was more personal than interstate travel because riders on a particular route usually knew one another. Birmingham, Alabama, and many other Southern bus systems required that black patrons follow a humiliating daily ritual by entering the front of the bus, paying the fare to the white bus driver, and then exiting the bus and walking to the back door. Once they reentered, a black patron could select an open seat in the back of the bus if it was available. If at any point a white rider did not have a seat, the nearest black patron was expected to silently leave his or her seat and stand in the back.

> *What is too big for one person to handle can be figured out by all of us together…We will have a new kind of school—not a school for teaching reading, writing, and arithmetic, but a school for addressing problems.*
>
> —*Myles Horton, Founder of Highlander Folk School in Monteagle, Tennessee*

Rosa Parks

A Montgomery seamstress and leader within the Montgomery NAACP, Rosa Parks is best known for her refusal to give up her seat on a segregated bus in 1955. Parks worked with other local leaders such as Jo Ann Robinson and Martin Luther King Jr., who together led a movement that successfully forced the integration of the Montgomery bus system.

Highlander Folk School

A nontraditional school in the Appalachian foothills of Tennessee that taught adult learners and served as a place for these adults to discuss and find solutions to the problems their community faced. By 1950, Highlander became a center of activity for civil rights activists throughout Appalachia and the South.

Her challenge of this system would make **Rosa Parks** a household name. Parks was a seamstress and also the secretary of the Montgomery chapter of the NAACP. Months prior to her heroic stand for civil rights, she attended a workshop in the Appalachian foothills of Tennessee at a place called the **Highlander Folk School**. Here she met with white and black activists who had begun holding interracial workshops in anticipation of school desegregation around 1950.

Myles Horton and other Appalachian whites recognized that racism had been used to divide poor whites and poor blacks for decades. They feared that similar prejudices might jeopardize the public school system once the courts mandated integration. Instead, they hoped to unify Appalachians and Southerners of all races and demand that public schools continue to receive funding. If Southerners would stop being divided by race, Horton believed, a movement might be forged that would finally force the wealthy to respond to the demands of working people.

In the fall of 1955, Rosa Parks attended Highlander and participated in a workshop on the power of nonviolent protest. Parks and others from Montgomery, Alabama, left Highlander with doubts that people in their community would go along with anything as radical as school or bus desegregation. But when she returned to Highlander in March 1956, one hundred days into what would become a 381-day boycott, 50,000 people in Montgomery were sticking together and would eventually force the city to integrate the buses.

Rosa Parks was not the first to refuse to give her seat to a white person in Montgomery. Months prior to Parks' arrest, a high school student named Claudette Colvin had been arrested for her refusal to move to the back of the bus. Leading black clergy and community members vowed to stand by Colvin until it was found that she was pregnant and unmarried. At least one other student was arrested prior to Parks. The difference was that Parks was a respected member of the black community whose arrest sparked action by Montgomery NAACP leaders. Jo Ann Robinson recruited students who worked around the clock to distribute flyers publicizing Parks' arrest and calling a mass meeting to decide on a response.

Robinson and E. D. Nixon, president of the local NAACP chapter, had long been preparing for a direct action campaign against the city bus system. Together with a new preacher named **Martin Luther King Jr.** the black community formed the **Montgomery Improvement Association (MIA)** and decided to boycott the buses until the city agreed to a compromise. A committee representing the black community first requested a compromise measure. Black patrons would continue to sit in the back of the bus but would no longer enter the bus through the back door after paying the driver. The city refused. Black patrons represented over half of the people who rode the bus in Montgomery. When 50,000 customers suddenly stopped using the bus, the city faced financial peril. For the next 381 days, the black community of Montgomery taught the nation a lesson in the power of community and the power of consumers. Halfway into the boycott, city leaders agreed to the MIA's original demands. However, members of the community now demanded a complete end to segregation. Together with a court challenge that culminated in a November 1956 Supreme Court decision banning bus segregation, the city of Montgomery agreed to a complete end to all forms of racial discrimination on city buses.

The success of the movement was attributed to the leadership of Jo Ann Robinson, Rosa Parks, E. D. Nixon, and Martin Luther King Jr. King quickly rose to national prominence. The real history of the movement, however, was the story of the power of community activism. With no sign that their protest would ever be rewarded with anything more than arrests and harassment, 50,000 black people walked each day to and from work and school for 381 days. Black and white college students and church groups around the country sent money and even a few used cars to help MIA volunteers provide rides for those whose jobs were too far from their homes to walk. Black-owned taxis reduced their fares and often operated at a financial loss.

In response, white city officials contacted the automotive insurance companies who agreed to cancel policies of all vehicles operated on behalf of the boycott. When this failed to derail the movement, the Montgomery police arrested the volunteers and revoked the licenses of the taxi drivers. The protesters responded by taking the funds they were using for their share of gasoline to purchase more shoes. Members of the city's White Citizens' Council used firebombs and death threats, yet the boycott continued. When some of the participants complained they were too exhausted to continue, the example set by other participants inspired them to endure. "My feets are tired," an elderly woman had declared during one of the many mass movements, "but my soul is rested."

FIGURE 10.15

This is the original report filed by the Montgomery, Alabama, police after they arrested Rosa Parks for refusing to move from the white section of a bus operated by the city. The organizational drive of local leaders such as Parks, Jo Ann Robinson, Martin Luther King Jr., and E. D. Nixon led to a 381-day boycott of the city buses until the city of Montgomery ended its segregation policy.

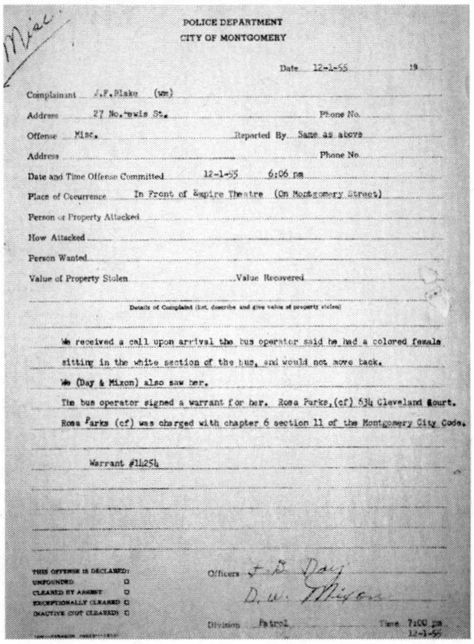

Misc

POLICE DEPARTMENT
CITY OF MONTGOMERY

Date 12-1-55 19

Complainant J.F.Blake (wm)
Address 27 No. Lewis St. Phone No.
Offense Misc. Reported By Same as above
Address Phone No.
Date and Time Offense Committed 12-1-55 6:06 pm
Place of Occurrence In Front of Empire Theatre (On Montgomery Street)
Person or Property Attacked
How Attacked
Person Wanted
Value of Property Stolen Value Recovered

Details of Complaint (list, describe and give value of property stolen)

We received a call upon arrival the bus operator said he had a colored female sitting in the white section of the bus, and would not move back.
We (Day & Mixon) also saw her.
The bus operator signed a warrant for her. Rosa Parks,(cf) 634 Cleveland Court.
Rosa Parks (cf) was charged with chapter 6 section 11 of the Montgomery City Code.

Warrant #14254

THIS OFFENSE IS DECLARED:
UNFOUNDED ☐
CLEARED BY ARREST ☐
EXCEPTIONALLY CLEARED ☐
INACTIVE (NOT CLEARED) ☐

Officers

Division Patrol Time 7:00 pm 12-1-55

Martin Luther King Jr.

Son of a prominent Baptist minister, King would follow in his father's footsteps and rise to national prominence as a clergyman and leader of the Montgomery Bus Boycott. As the leading national civil rights activist, King inspired, led, and participated in dozens of nonviolent protests against discrimination in the workplace and racial segregation until his assassination in 1968.

Montgomery Improvement Association (MIA)

Inspired by Rosa Parks' 1955 refusal to give up her seat on a bus, the black community of Montgomery formed the MIA to pressure the city to end segregation. For 381 days, 50,000 African Americans in Montgomery refused to ride the city buses until segregation was abolished.

REVIEW AND CRITICAL THINKING

1. In a time when anyone questioning the need for massive defense spending was accused of being soft on Communism, President Eisenhower reduced the military budget and called for even greater cuts as he left office. Why was he not accused of being soft on Communism?
2. What accounts for the rapid decline of Senator McCarthy after his meteoric rise to fame in the early 1950s? Did McCarthyism end in 1954? Explain your answer.
3. Why did the *Brown* decision not lead to the end of school segregation? How did African Americans and other minorities confront the persistence of racial segregation in their schools?
4. Which was more important in the ultimate success of the Montgomery Improvement Association—the actions of leaders such as Rosa Parks and Martin Luther King or the actions of MIA members? How did the actions of the MIA lead Montgomery officials to agree to integrate the buses?

3. AMERICA AND THE WORLD DURING THE KENNEDY YEARS

LEARNING OBJECTIVES

1. Summarize the election of 1960, explaining why Kennedy won by the closest of margins.
2. Explain why so many Americans remember Kennedy as a liberal on issues such as Vietnam and civil rights, and discuss how accurately this reflects his record during his short presidency.
3. The history of the modern civil rights movement emphasizes the actions of charismatic leaders such as Martin Luther King Jr. Explain how the incorporation of students and community members enhances our historical understanding of the movement.

3.1 1960 Election

The historic image of President Kennedy demonstrates the frequent gulf between history and memory. Remembered as the quintessential liberal and civil rights supporter, Kennedy actually considered domestic matters as secondary to international affairs. He cared even less for the more liberal wing of his party. He avoided issues of civil rights until his last year in office and was reluctant to advocate the expansion of the welfare state, especially when compared to other the leaders of the Democratic Party.

Kennedy entered the 1960 Democratic primaries as the least popular Democratic contender among blacks and liberal Democrats. His nomination disappointed many Democrats who pointed out that even Richard Nixon had a stronger civil rights record due to a handful of supportive statements he had made while vice president. Richard Nixon had also backed a controversial attempt to introduce a civil rights plank into the Republican Party platform.

In general, both candidates appeared very similar in terms of issues and platforms. Many voters were ambivalent regarding the two candidates after several radio debates. Kennedy's poise and princely appearance has been credited for throwing many votes his way after Nixon refused makeup during an infamous televised debate. However, there is little evidence by which to measure the importance of Kennedy's physical appearance, the importance of which may have been embellished by the latter mystique surrounding the glamour of Camelot and the Kennedy White House.

The Kennedy campaign focused almost exclusively on issues of national security, attacking the Eisenhower administration, and Vice President Nixon by implication, of being too soft on Communism. For example, in one debate with Nixon, he accused the Eisenhower administration of permitting Communists to infiltrate America's own backyard in Cuba and proposed that if he were president, he would support the overthrow of Fidel Castro. Nixon had been quietly planning a secret operation to do just that and could only meekly respond else he risk exposing the plot.

red-baiting

The use of allegations to create the impression that a political rival is a supporter of Communist ideas without specifically making such a claim.

As a politician who won election to the House and Senate by **red-baiting** his opponents and speaking to populist frustrations, Nixon could do little to respond now that he had been in the nation's second-highest office for nearly eight years. Instead, he attempted to connect himself to the popular president under whom he had served. This tactic was derailed by a single comment Eisenhower had made when asked by a reporter for an example of how Nixon had contributed to his eight years in office. "Give me a week," quipped Eisenhower who made few attempts to hide his ambivalence toward the vice president, "and I might think of one."

As the general election neared, many of Nixon's advisers suggested that the Republican candidate issue some kind of mild statement in favor of civil rights. Nixon's refusal to do so helps to explain why he lost his lead in the polls among northern black communities. The other reason why Kennedy won more than 70 percent of the black vote in the general election was that JFK and his brother Robert Kennedy worked behind the scenes to secure the safety and release of Martin Luther King after he was sentenced to four months hard labor in Georgia for a minor traffic citation. The agreement was reached in private since Kennedy recognized that association with civil rights would spell disaster for his campaign among the majority of whites in America who still despised King in 1960.

FIGURE 10.16

The election of 1960 was an incredibly close contest. The third individual to receive electoral votes was Harry F. Byrd, a prominent Virginia politician and advocate of massive resistance to integration. Byrd was not an official candidate, meaning that presidential electors representing Mississippi and Alabama disregarded the votes that were cast in their state and voted for Byrd as a protest against what they believed were the liberal policies of both Nixon and Kennedy.

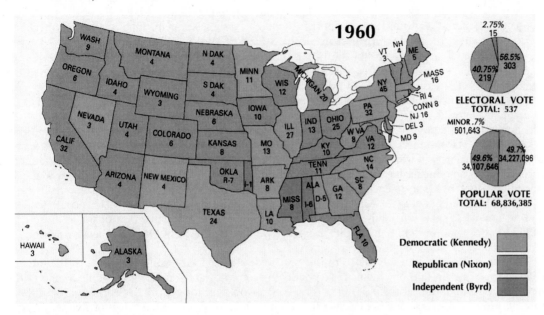

Martin Luther King Sr. responded to the news of his son's release by reportedly exclaiming that it was time he and all other black Americans "take off their Nixon buttons" and support Kennedy. A last-minute campaign to spread the word about JFK's intervention spread through black communities (but remained invisible to whites) and meant the difference in several key states like Illinois and Maryland where Kennedy won by the narrowest of margins. Nationally, Kennedy received only 0.2 percent more votes than Nixon, and had it not been for the urban vote in cities such as Chicago and Baltimore with black majorities, Nixon would have prevailed. Whether Kennedy actually owed his election to African American leaders and their last-minute campaign is a matter of debate; yet black leaders made sure to remind Kennedy of this possibility throughout his term.

3.2   The New Frontier

President Kennedy entered the White House with great energy and electrified the public with his stirring inaugural address in which he challenged listeners to ask how they might serve their nation instead of asking what that nation might do for them. As a candidate, Kennedy exuded youthful vigor and optimism. As a president, he and his young family fascinated the American public. Students and adults alike took speed reading courses to try to match the President's ability to read and comprehend ten pages per minute. Women mirrored the elegant style of Jackie Kennedy while men saw images of Kennedy with his young children, the first ever to grow up in the White House, as a reminder that they too could balance career and fatherhood. Balance would prove to be a difficult goal for the young president, however. The same inaugural that inspired a nation to service also committed the United States to "bear any burden" to contain the Communist threat. Although it would not yet be apparent in 1960, balancing domestic issues with global commitments would become the leading challenge of the decade.

As a candidate, Kennedy had challenged Americans to renew the nation's pioneer spirit and spoke of the new decade as a **New Frontier**. As president, Kennedy would refer to his domestic programs as the New Frontier—a phrase that inspired hope for new possibilities and was vague enough for supporters to envision their own ideas. (Given the historic experiences of Native Americans, the phrases such as "frontier" and "pioneer spirit" had completely different connotations.) Liberals envisioned the New Frontier as the quest to end racial injustice and poverty, fulfilling the nation's promise of liberty and prosperity. Kennedy supported modest spending for antipoverty programs and even began to speak in favor of civil rights, at least in vague terms calculated to lose few votes among white voters.

As President, Kennedy only agreed to meet privately with controversial black leaders such as Martin Luther King Jr. At one of these private meetings, the president asked King to draft a Second Emancipation Proclamation. He told King he would read and sign this document on January 1, 1963, one hundred years after Lincoln outlawed slavery throughout the Confederacy. King obliged, but

Kennedy quickly recognized that such an overt sign of support for King—still hated among most Southern whites and a controversial figure throughout the rest of America—would cost him votes. JFK avoided the civil rights leader until New Year's Day had passed without any statement from Kennedy. For African Americans, if Kennedy was not even willing to honor Lincoln and commemorate the historic end to slavery, it was doubtful that the New Frontier would challenge contemporary barriers of racial prejudice.

Kennedy also avoided women's leaders who sought the president's support for the Equal Rights Amendment, which they had introduced each year beginning in the 1920s. Pressed by Eleanor Roosevelt to offer at least moderate support for women's issues, Kennedy appointed the former First Lady to lead a **Presidential Commission on the Status of Women** in December of 1961. Roosevelt passed away the following year, but the Commission continued to reflect the relatively conservative stance of the older generation of women and men who led the proceedings. Kennedy interpreted the committee's findings as a validation of traditional gender roles.

By 1920, women had attended college in roughly equal numbers as men and were nearly as likely to graduate. By mid-1950s, however, the percentage of women in college had dropped significantly. The number completing a degree was even lower as more and more women were encouraged to think of college as a place to meet a husband. Women represented less than one-fourth of college graduates in 1950. The majority of women in coeducational schools was pursuing degrees in home economics or enrolled to become medical assistants or secretaries. Even though the nation believed it was waging a war to best the Soviets in science and engineering, women who pursued careers in these fields were sometimes accused of being un-American. These women pointed out that the Soviets encouraged women to pursue science and math, challenging Americans to reconsider the patriotism of those who would limit the nation to only half of its human resources. By the early 1960s, women were again attending college in numbers comparable to men.

A major part of Kennedy's New Frontier was dedicated to space exploration. In April 1961, the Soviets placed a man in orbit. Kennedy responded by committing the nation to sending a man to the moon by the end of the decade. Astronaut John Glenn would orbit the earth in February 1962, and on July 20, 1969, Neil Armstrong became the first human to land on the moon. Most of Kennedy's New Frontier programs were quite terrestrial in comparison to his aggressive funding for space exploration. Kennedy was cautious in his support for increasing federal aid for education and provided only limited support for plans to provide universal health care. The most significant liberal measure that passed Congress during the Kennedy administration was an increase in the minimum wage to $1.25 an hour.

The failure of the Democrats to pass a number of liberal domestic programs was at least partially due to Kennedy's belief that domestic issues were secondary to the threat of Communism. At one point, Kennedy openly scoffed at the notion that minimum wage was an increasingly important issue compared to the Cold War in Cuba with an infamous and profanity-laced remark to Richard Nixon. Publicly, however, Kennedy maintained the support of the working class by cultivating his image as an ally of labor.

A handful of liberal programs the Kennedy administration backed, such as public housing, likely did more to aid contractors and union workers than the poor. These urban renewal programs replaced working-class neighborhoods with overpasses and highway projects, often intensifying ghettoization by concentrating the poor in blighted areas of the city. Kennedy also backed funding to aid economically depressed rural areas such as Appalachia. Direct aid for rural Appalachians passed Congress while relief for the urban poor found few supporters, something that demonstrated Congressional aid for the poor was more likely to pass if the American public believed the recipients of that aid were white. Although coal mining communities were home to numerous African Americans and recent immigrants, dictionaries included the word "white" in their definition of "Appalachian" until the 1980s.

Liberals tended to view the establishment of the Peace Corps as the most significant domestic program of the Kennedy administration. The program conciliated some of the more liberal members of the Democratic Party, especially once Sargent Shriver was appointed as the head of the new organization. Shriver was a relative of Kennedy's through marriage and a popular figure within the liberal wing of the Democratic Party. Under Shriver's guidance, the program matched young Americans with humanitarian programs in developing nations. Utilizing recent college graduates, the program cost relatively little and aided the image of the United States abroad while providing young Americans with the opportunity to travel the world and encounter new perspectives. The Kennedy administration also supported environmental legislation protecting forests and wetlands as well as federal aid for public schools, but these programs failed in Congress. While Kennedy's youthful image and public persona did much to inspire Americans, there were few domestic programs beyond mild increases in public housing, Social Security, and the minimum wage for which the president could take credit.

The problem for liberals was that Kennedy was a politician first, a moderate second, and a liberal only when speaking to solidly Democratic audiences. Perhaps more importantly, Kennedy's Congress

FIGURE 10.17

President Kennedy greets young men and women who were among the first volunteers for the Peace Corps.

had a Democratic majority in name alone. The Democrats were fractured among Northern liberals and Southern conservatives. The latter group disdained the expansion of liberal government programs almost as much as they loathed civil rights legislation. Southern Democrats regularly sided with Republicans on domestic issues, and this division proved fatal to Kennedy's proposals for medical insurance for seniors, public housing, and federal aid for education. In each case, the same coalition of conservative Southern Democrats and Republicans who had blocked Truman's more liberal policies also derailed Kennedy's ideas. In the end, this fracture even proved fatal to Kennedy himself. The purpose of his ill-fated trip to Dallas in 1963 was to try to bridge the divide between conservative Texas Democrats who opposed civil rights and other liberal initiatives and the progressive wing of the local party who favored such measures.

3.3 Students and Civil Rights

FIGURE 10.18

Civil rights activists were trained to protect their head and vital organs to prevent paralyzing damage from those who used violence against them. This photo shows an individual who protested segregation in Knoxville, Tennessee, surrounded by a hostile crowd.

As demonstrated during the Double-V campaign of the 1940s, the younger generation was more inclined to utilize direct confrontation to promote civil rights. In 1960, four black freshmen at the historically black North Carolina A&T in Greensboro decided one night that they had enough of legal challenges by the NAACP and white judges counseling patience with the deliberate delays that resulted in declarations of "all deliberate speed." The next morning, the young men went across the street to the local Woolworth drug store where they were only permitted "sack service." The students sat at the counter declaring they would not leave until they were arrested or served. Neither of these things occurred.

The young men occupied the lunch counter and then returned to their dorm where news of their action spread and attracted other students. That night, the students began planning what would become the **Greensboro Sit-Ins**. They coordinated class and work schedules around times when they could occupy each of the seats at the Woolworth counter. If they all stuck together, they reasoned, they could effectively shut down the lunch counter until it ended its discriminatory policy or went out of business. What made Greensboro so different from the dozen-and-a-half previous lunch counter demonstrations waged across the country prior to this time was that this demonstration spread to over one hundred cities within a few months. Before long, white and black students at campuses that had only recently admitted black students, such as the University of Texas at Austin, were holding sit-ins together.

Greensboro Sit-Ins

A sit-in launched by students at North Carolina A&T that quickly spread to over one hundred cities and led to the formation of the Student Non-Violent Coordinating Committee.

The original Greensboro sit-in was ironically also much less organized than many previous campaigns. In Nashville, organizers had first created lists of more than five hundred volunteers and secured a network of vehicles and a map of targeted restaurants and lunch counters. Veteran NAACP organizer and the unofficial leader of King's SCLC, **Ella Baker** recognized the spontaneous nature of the Greensboro sit-ins and the dozens of others launched by students and recognized that the new generation had started something special. The sit-ins were simple and direct; they spread rapidly because they needed less organization than boycotts of essential services like transportation. However, they also incurred greater danger as participants put their bodies where they were not wanted rather than withdrawing them from segregated bus seats where they were needed as customers. Black newspapers were cautious in their reporting of these protests; SCLC leaders expressed skepticism and even discouraged students given the use of violence against the students and the mass arrests in many cities. The NAACP Legal Defense Fund initially refused to defend the first students arrested, for fear of encouraging more students to participate. But Baker supported the students and called a meeting where she facilitated the founding of the **Student Non-Violent Coordinating Committee (SNCC)**.

SNCC was unique because students served in every leadership position. Baker recognized students needed adult leaders to facilitate their meetings, especially given the demanding and transitory schedule of college life. But Baker also recognized that even the most well-meaning adult leaders would crush the independent spirit these young adults brought to the movement. The students were fearless, even reckless at times. While adults usually deferred to the conservative leadership of clergy and black civic officials, the students even challenged Martin Luther King Jr. himself. King was immediately impressed and recognized that the students were taking the initiative he and others had only spoken of taking. After some good-natured cajoling, King decided to participate in a student demonstration in Atlanta. This was King's first deliberate step toward prison, and his arrest brought the Atlanta protest to the attention of the nation. After several arrests, King became a household name and even a celebrity following a fundraising concert held by Frank Sinatra at Carnegie Hall in New York.

In 1961, the union of college students and adult organizers hit its peak when **James Farmer** became the leader of CORE and organized a series of Freedom Rides. In December 1960, the federal courts extended the prohibition against segregation in interstate travel to include waiting rooms and restaurants in bus terminals. Farmer organized groups of white and black students who were willing to test this court decision by sitting and eating together on buses and at terminals throughout the heart of Dixie. Dozens of Freedom Rides occurred throughout 1961, and hundreds of participants were jailed in violation of federal law.

FIGURE 10.19

Students from Florida A&M join CORE and others in protesting racial segregation at a Tallahassee movie theater in 1963.

The most famous of these Freedom Rides traveled through South Carolina and Georgia where local whites vowed the Freedom Riders would never make it through their communities with their lives. Officials in Rock Hill, South Carolina, where a dozen students had just been sentenced to hard labor for participating in a sit-in, actually defended the riders against violence and enforced their legal right to have a meal in the local bus station. A second mob greeted them at their first stop in Alabama and chased them all the way until Birmingham, when the bus suffered a flat tire. The driver of the bus parked and ran for his life while the mob firebombed and brutally attacked the Freedom Riders to the point that some of the young people were permanently disabled. Law enforcement belatedly arrived on scene and halted the violence, an arrangement that an FBI informant within the Birmingham Klan revealed was part of a deal made with local police wherein the mob would be given fifteen minutes of uninterrupted freedom to beat the Freedom Riders until they made their obligatory appearance.

Not satisfied with the damage they had done, members of the angry mob converged on the hospital where the Freedom Riders were taken and might have killed many of the participants had it not been for the efforts of hospital workers and a convoy of local blacks who had taken no oath of nonviolence. Although the police kept their distance, reporters from leading national newspapers trailed each of the Freedom Rides, and photos of burning Greyhound buses made worldwide news. Even Southern newspapers expressed dismay at the violence and some white Southerners began to question the morality of their worldview for the first time. For many liberal whites, the violence was disturbing and forced them to consider stronger measures to protect civil rights. At the same time, Kennedy and others resented the way these activists forced the issue and intruded upon their rosy image of America.

3.4 Albany and Birmingham

President John F. Kennedy called for Southern governors to assure "a friendly and dignified reception" for foreign diplomats of color visiting the United States. The governor of Virginia, where "massive resistance" to desegregation originated, promised to provide Southern courtesy to these guests. He paired his response with the suggestion that nonwhite diplomats identify themselves, else they be mistaken for nonwhite American citizens. College students at Baltimore's Morgan State University and Towson University responded by challenging segregation in restaurants along the highways connecting the United Nations in New York City with the nation's capital in Washington, DC. While the federal government did nothing to confront the discrimination faced by its own citizens, they ordered proprietors to treat all foreign delegates with the utmost courtesy. These sit-ins soon led to the integration of restaurants in Maryland and Delaware.

White leaders quickly learned that as long as they did not commit overt acts of violence, especially violence against middle-class college students, the media and nation would pay little heed to the protesters. Late in 1961, Albany, Georgia, became the epicenter of a SNCC campaign against segregation and prohibitions against black voters. White Southerners blamed the handful of white college students and other "Yankee agitators" on hand for creating the trouble. For the historian, it was a scene reminiscent of antebellum slaveholders who blamed Northern abolitionists for making slaves yearn for freedom. Albany, however, was a homegrown movement led and conducted by Southern blacks. But just as Northern abolitionists had only been "moved to wrath and tears" by the most horrible episodes of violence, whites in Albany recognized that if they refused to follow their scripted role as perpetrators of violence, white Northerners would tire of the issue. After all, Albany whites reasoned, segregation was widespread throughout the North.

By using restraint in arresting protesters and releasing prominent civil rights leaders such as Martin Luther King Jr. after they vowed to stay in jail, Albany demonstrated to the rest of white America how to defeat nonviolence with nonviolence. The media followed a sales-based formula where civil rights news stories only "sold" if they contained sensational violence and national leaders with whom the public was familiar. When the violence was not forthcoming and King was forcibly removed from the jail, the media left town. Albany whites were then free to deal with local activists in any way they pleased.

Fortunately for the health of the civil rights movement, if not for civil rights protesters, Birmingham police chief Bull Connor failed to absorb the lesson of Albany and embraced the aggressor's role when King and SCLC leaders came to his town in 1963. King was arrested and placed in solitary confinement, where he wrote his famous *Letter from a Birmingham Jail*, which chastised local white religious leaders who counseled patience rather than justice. King challenged the notion that white Southerners would eventually decide to integrate on their own if only civil rights protests would stop.

While King wrote letters from prison, a white postal worker from Baltimore named William Moore declared that he would walk from Chattanooga to the state capital of Mississippi where he hoped to ask the governor to reconsider his opposition to civil rights. One hundred miles into his solitary march, Moore was killed. In response, black schoolchildren continued Moore's march from the point where he was slain. The success of this Children's March inspired leaders in Birmingham to recruit middle and high school students to fill their declining ranks as adults were increasingly tiring of being harassed and arrested. Bull Connor responded by blasting the children with high-pressure truck-mounted water turrets. Images of young bodies being torn apart by fire hoses, beaten and arrested by armed police, and bitten by police dogs became the most salient image of the entire movement. Connor's police and firefighters began to refuse his orders, but not before the image of Birmingham galvanized Americans in support of a federal law banning segregation. Business leaders in Birmingham agreed to negotiate an end to segregation because they were concerned that the world's negative image of their city would damage the economy. Even Kennedy decided that he had enough and spoke plainly about the moral bankruptcy of segregation in a nationally televised speech.

FIGURE 10.20

Cartoonist Herb Block pointed out the hypocrisy of a nation that would not accommodate people of color unless they were foreign visitors. "It's all right to seat them," the restaurant manager informs his staff in this 1961 cartoon, "They're not Americans."

"It's All Right To Seat Them. They're Not Americans"

FIGURE 10.21

James Meredith was escorted to all his classes by federal Marshalls during his one year at the University of Mississippi. Meredith integrated "Ole Miss" in 1962 despite violence and a number of death threats that necessitated federal troops to restore order. He completed most of his coursework at Jackson State University, needing only one year to complete his degree at Ole Miss in 1963.

Medgar Evers

A civil rights leader in Mississippi who was assassinated on June 12, 1963. Despite the viciousness of those who opposed him, Evers followed the doctrine of nonviolence. However, he also carried a gun with him every day and left multiple weapons around his home to defend his family. After her husband's murder, Myrlie Evers continued to run the local NAACP office that she and her husband had operated since its founding; she later became one of the organization's national leaders.

Flexible Response

The term Kennedy used to describe his plan to build up conventional forces to give the United States more options beyond nuclear deterrence. Kennedy believed that Eisenhower had relied too heavily on the threat of nuclear war and wanted a large and mobile military that could deploy instantly around the world.

In Jackson, Mississippi, civil rights advocate **Medgar Evers** rushed home to his family so they could celebrate the president's speech. His children were waiting up for him and rushed outside, only to see their father shot in the back by a white supremacist who had been hiding across the street. An all-white jury refused to convict the assassin, even though he privately bragged that he was the one who killed the civil rights leader. In fact, it was not until 1994 that confessed murderer Byron de la Beckwith was convicted and sentenced for killing Medgar Evers.

In life, as well as death, Evers was a symbol of the challenges faced by civil rights workers in the Deep South. Due to the discrimination he faced when he attempted to enroll at the University of Mississippi in 1954, Medgar Evers never attended law school. However, Evers led the fight on behalf of James Meredith against the University of Mississippi in 1962. In June 1962, Evers secured an order by the US Court of Appeals that required the university to admit Meredith. Mississippi governor Ross Barnett referred to the possible admission of James Meredith as "the greatest crisis since the War Between the States" and promised to defy the order by force if necessary.

President Kennedy viewed the governor's use of state police to defy a federal court order as a constitutional crisis and sent three hundred federal marshals to uphold the court's decision. Encouraged by the governor and local police, thousands of whites participated in anti-integration riots that led to more than two hundred arrests and the deaths of two people. Yet Meredith was admitted and graduated the following year despite daily harassment. In 1963, history seemed to repeat itself as the Kennedy administration again used federal marshals to force the integration of the University of Alabama. Governor George Wallace famously stood and blocked the doors of the admissions building with state troopers on the day two black students were expected to enroll. Once again, Kennedy federalized state troops to enforce the desegregation order.

3.5 Bay of Pigs and Cuban Missile Crisis

As a presidential candidate, Kennedy spoke frequently about the need to close the "missile gap," a phrase indicating a shortfall of US nuclear weapons in comparison to the Soviet Union. Although Kennedy himself recognized that no such gap existed, regardless of how many more nuclear weapons the Soviet Union may have produced, Kennedy continued to raise the issue for reasons that are not completely clear. In general, however, Kennedy advocated an approach that was less dependent upon nuclear deterrence he called the **Flexible Response**. Building up conventional forces, especially Special Forces, Kennedy hoped to provide the US military with options beyond nuclear retaliation.

The need for such options became apparent in Berlin during 1961 when the Soviets again threatened to block access to the American sector of the city. Kennedy hinted at the use of "tactical" nuclear weapons until Khrushchev backed down. To Kennedy, the lesson of Berlin was clear: "We intend to have a wider choice than humiliation or all-out nuclear action," the President explained. However, Kennedy agreed with the basic doctrine of nuclear deterrence he inherited from Eisenhower, and the size of the US nuclear arsenal nearly tripled alongside Kennedy's increases in the number of ground troops and other conventional forces.

As a candidate, Kennedy had accused Eisenhower and Nixon of carelessly allowing Cuba to become Moscow's private island. In a televised debate with candidate Nixon, Kennedy suggested that Eisenhower should have armed Cuban exiles and sent them to overthrow Fidel Castro and his pro-Soviet regime. Nixon had secretly been working with the CIA, which was ironically planning the exact mission Kennedy had just suggested. In a rare moment of forbearance, Nixon decided against revealing these plans because they were dependent upon the element of surprise and the denial of American involvement. In a prophetic but disingenuous statement he himself did not believe, Nixon responded by stating that his brash forty-three-year old opponent had just recklessly suggested a plan that would fail miserably, harm the international reputation of the United States, and draw Cuba and the Soviet Union even closer together.

Just days into his administration, the CIA notified Kennedy of its plan to arm Cuban rebels and requested permission to proceed. Kennedy modified the plan by cancelling US air strikes and naval support in hopes of further concealing the US role in the invasion. In April 1961, the navy delivered 1,500 American-trained ex-Cubans to the Bay of Pigs in Southern Cuba. Without further assistance, however, their invasion was crushed by Castro's military. The United States denied any participation in the **Bay of Pigs Invasion** and quietly paid $50 million for the return of the survivors to prevent Castro from using the prisoners to implicate the United States in the failed attack. These efforts made little difference, however, as even America's strongest allies denounced the covert action to topple the government of the small island nation.

The Bay of Pigs Invasion failed, not because Kennedy and his advisers believed 1,500 rebels would prevail over Castro's armies, but because they naively believed that the Cuban people would view these men as liberators and rise up against Castro in a popular revolt. Area experts cautioned against the likelihood of such a revolution in 1961 as Castro still enjoyed popularity among the majority of Cubans. Even those Cubans who opposed the leftist leader viewed the United States with suspicion given US support for the island's previous dictator, Fulgencio Batista. Few Cubans were likely to rally behind the small rebel army because they sought a return to a similar US-backed regime. In response to the failure of the Bay of Pigs Invasion, Kennedy worked to prevent all weapons sales to the Cuban military and even supported a CIA plan to assassinate Castro. Already hostile to Washington, Castro contacted the Soviet Union and requested military protection.

In October 1962, a US spy plane flying over Cuba discovered the construction of Soviet missile silos throughout Cuba. Castro and Khrushchev had engineered a mutually beneficial arrangement. The Soviet Union would place soldiers and nuclear missiles on the island, thereby minimizing the likelihood of another US-sponsored invasion. The arrangement also provided the Soviet Union with a strategic base near the Florida coast. Khrushchev argued that the measure was defensive in nature—a way to counter the presence of US nuclear missiles in Turkey and other American military bases near leading Soviet cities.

Believing that none of the nuclear missiles had yet been delivered to the island, US military officials advised the president to strike Cuba by air and land before such missile silos became operable. Kennedy instead announced the discovery of the missile silos on television and declared a quarantine zone around the island. The US Navy surrounded the island and declared its intention to use force to prevent any Soviet ship from landing any military equipment on the island. The world waited in anticipation of possible nuclear war as Soviet ships armed with nuclear weapons continued West across the Atlantic.

Bay of Pigs Invasion

A failed 1961 covert operation planned by the Eisenhower administration and authorized by President Kennedy with the goal of supporting a coup that would replace Castro's government in Cuba. The United States armed and equipped Cuban refugees, many of whom were supporters of the previous regime under Batista, and hoped that Castro's overthrow would lead to the creation of a Cuban government that was more agreeable to US interests on the island.

FIGURE 10.22

Nearly a thousand women participate in a demonstration urging Kennedy and other world leaders to use restraint during the Cuban Missile Crisis.

Cuban Missile Crisis

A tense diplomatic confrontation in October 1962 between the United States, the Soviet Union, and Cuba regarding an agreement between Khrushchev and Castro to install nuclear weapons throughout Cuba. Khrushchev and Kennedy both agreed remove nuclear missiles that were near the border of each other's nations, and a situation that might have led to nuclear war was peacefully resolved.

During the thirteen days that would be known as the **Cuban Missile Crisis**, US spy planes and fighter jets armed with nuclear missiles flew over Cuba and the Soviet Union. Two of these aircraft were shot down, which might have signaled the intention by either to launch a preliminary attack. US and Soviet naval vessels also armed with nuclear weapons met on the high seas. A single miscommunication could have led to a deadly confrontation and possible nuclear war. The public would have certainly been more anxious had they known that tactical nuclear missiles were already in Cuba and Russian commanders had the authority to launch these weapons in case of attack.

Instead, the world watched as the Soviet ships reversed course. Khrushchev agreed to remove the missile sites from Cuba while Kennedy promised that the United States would also remove its missiles from Turkey. The promise to remove American missiles was made in secret, a fact that made it appear as though Khrushchev had backed down from a situation he had engineered. In the United States, the Secretary of State expressed the feelings of many in likening the episode to a contest of will. "We were eyeball to eyeball," Rusk exclaimed, "and the other guy blinked." Khrushchev's prudence was interpreted as a sign of weakness by many, but possible nuclear war had been averted for the second time in three years.

3.6 Global Containment in Africa, West Germany, and Vietnam

Joseph Mobutu

An authoritarian dictator who presided over the Democratic Republic of Congo (also known as Zaire) following a coup that was supported by the United States because of Mobutu's opposition to Communist groups throughout Africa.

The State Department and the CIA tried to influence the outcome of a number of elections across the globe and even sponsored several efforts to topple leftist governments in Latin America, Africa, and Asia. As dozens of nations transitioned from colonialism to independence, US officials worried that popular Communist leaders in each of these new states might gain control of the newly formed governments. For example, the former Belgian colony of Congo was home to rich natural resources and a popular leftist leader named Patrice Lumumba. Fearing that Lumumba might turn toward either Socialism or nationalizing the assets of foreign mining companies, the federal government supported a coup by **Joseph Mobutu**. Lumumba was arrested and later executed, while Mobutu established a corrupt and authoritarian government that committed numerous crimes against the Congolese people. By Washington's perspective, however, Mobutu ensured stability for Western corporations and his leadership provided a bulwark against Communism in Central Africa.

Kennedy understood the shortcomings of his administration's support of Mobuto and other unpopular and undemocratic leaders in Chile, Argentina, and Haiti. US efforts to contain Communism in Western Europe followed a different path. Instead of indiscriminately sending military aid to any non-Communist, the United States invested heavily in rebuilding the economy of West European nations. In West Germany, for example, the United States provided loans and humanitarian aid and insisted on democratic elections. By 1960, West Germany was a booming industrial democracy and a solid ally of the United States and its global effort to contain Communism.

Berlin Wall

A militarized barrier that completely severed East and West Berlin. Built under Soviet direction in 1961, the Berlin Wall was effective in its purpose to halt the migration of East Germans to the West, but it became a powerful symbol for the United States and its allies who portrayed Communist East Germany as a land of oppression from which its own citizens hoped to escape.

The Soviet Union followed a different approach in neighboring East Germany, insisting on continued reparation payments and crushing political dissent. The same was true in Berlin where Soviet-backed East Berlin stagnated while West Berlin prospered. For this reason, an estimated 2 million residents of East Berlin abandoned the Soviet section of the city for the West. Those who left were usually skilled laborers and professionals whose departure added to the economic malaise of East Berlin. In response, the Soviets ordered the construction of the **Berlin Wall**, a massive concrete barrier built to prevent East Berliners from abandoning the Soviet-dominated portion of the city.

The wall immediately ended the East-West migration. However, it led most observers to question the efficacy of the Soviet system. The West seized the image of the wall as a symbol of the superiority of the Capitalist system, where barbed-wire and machine guns were not needed to keep residents from "escaping" to the other side. Soviet attempts to present the wall as a defensive measure against the West attracted few supporters. Although a handful of government-subsidized commodities were cheaper in East Berlin, few believed that machine guns were really needed to prevent West Berliners from crossing into the Soviet sector and back to purchase discount groceries.

Tensions remained high throughout West Berlin, given the city's location in the Soviet-controlled East Germany. Between 1961 and 1963, Khrushchev issued numerous veiled threats, and many feared that he would use West Berlin as a pawn during the Cuban Missile Crisis. In 1963, Kennedy traveled to Berlin to offer his assurance to the people of West Berlin that the United States would support them at any cost. "Ich bin ein Berliner," Kennedy famously remarked, explaining in a language no one could misinterpret the president's belief that all freedom-loving people stood in solidarity with those in West Berlin. Standing resolute with America's most vulnerable ally, the speech was one of the highlights of Kennedy's presidency.

In contrast to the aid bestowed upon Europe, the Kennedy administration tended to view non-European foreign affairs from a colonialist perspective. Europe demanded patient study, mutually beneficial investments, and even personal visits. Affairs in developing nations, however, were viewed as peripheral. US and Soviet officials made fewer attempts to consult regional experts, instead acting impetuously to prop up any non-Communist rival regardless of the potential consequences for the nation in question. From the perspective of residents in developing nations, their relationship with Moscow and Washington resembled their colonial past in that both superpowers sought to extract some kind of benefit from their relationship without investing the kinds of resources that would provide a mutual benefit for those living in those countries. Vietnam would serve as the perfect example of the consequences of such a mentality for the United States.

Even after the Bay of Pigs fiasco, Kennedy continued to believe that small units of elite commandos might remove and install foreign governments as cleanly as a surgeon replaces a defective organ. US officials who shared this perspective failed to recognize the importance of completing a thorough diagnosis before beginning an operation. Just as a physician requests and considers a patient's past pertinent history before beginning treatment, many scholars suggest the State Department should have more carefully considered a particular nation's history, internal conflicts, and economic problems before resorting to the knife.

In the short term, it seemed to most US officials that their quick surgical operations in Iran, Guatemala, and Central Africa had succeeded and might only result in mild complications. Kennedy believed that by building up US Special Forces, similar operations might succeed in Vietnam. At the least, he hoped these **Green Berets** might prevent a Communist takeover long enough to secure his reelection. "We don't have a prayer of staying in Vietnam," Kennedy remarked in 1963. "But I can't give up a piece of territory like that to the Communists," the President continued, "and then get the people to reelect me." As a result, Kennedy continued Eisenhower's policy of aiding South Vietnamese forces and sending more soldiers to the region. Some of these troops served as military advisers, while others participated in covert operations the White House denied existed until the war was ending.

Those who believe that Kennedy would have ended US involvement in the war in Vietnam before it began in earnest under Lyndon Johnson have numerous reasons to support their conclusions. At the same time, those who subscribe to this point of view must account for Kennedy's belief that Asia represented "the next Europe" in terms of global containment. Perhaps a Kennedy-led Vietnam War would have simply been more reliant on Special Forces and covert operations. For example, in 1962, Kennedy approved secret bombing raids in Laos through a CIA-owned airline known informally as "Air America." Kennedy also approved a program that secretly enlisted members of the Hmong minority in Laos to participate in guerilla raids against the North Vietnamese. The Hmong also fought against communist forces in the Laotian Civil War. Following US withdrawal from Southeast Asia and the victory of Laotian communist forces in 1975, the Hmong became refugees and many eventually migrated to communities in Wisconsin and Minnesota.

FIGURE 10.23

This photo depicts construction of the Berlin Wall. The city's most famous historic landmark, the Brandenburg Gate, is visible in the background.

Green Berets

Members of the US Army Special Forces known for their distinctive headgear that is part of their military dress uniform, the Green Berets were elite commandos that President John F. Kennedy hoped could carry out special missions that might reduce the need to send larger military units into combat.

FIGURE 10.24

The Hmong are an ethnic minority from Southeastern Asia. This map shows the location of sizeable Hmong communities in states such as California, Minnesota, Wisconsin, and North Carolina.

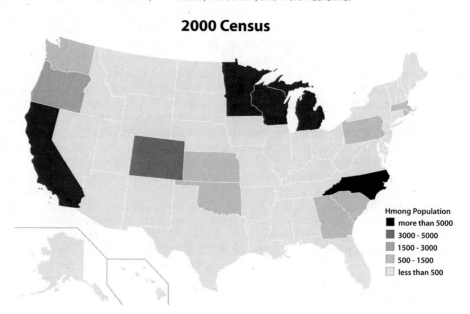

3.7   Chinese-Soviet Split

The Hmong were among many political and economic refugees who fled Southeastern Asia amid rising tensions and numerous undeclared civil wars that were influenced by the geopolitical struggle between East and West. In 1950, the People's Republic of China and the Soviet Union formed the Sino-Soviet Alliance based largely on their shared belief in Karl Marx's **Historical Materialism**. Tensions between these neighboring countries remained as neither had forgotten the long and often contentious history between them.

Stalin recognized the strategic importance of China's embrace of Communism, but he maintained doubts about whether this nondeveloped nation was ready for a true worker's revolution. Marx had predicted Communism would emerge only after a nation evolved from feudalism to Capitalism, after which industrial workers would revolt. Until recently, China was a feudal society of peasants and landowners, Stalin believed, and so he feared China was not yet ready for Socialism. As a result, Stalin invested heavily in an attempt to modernize the Chinese economy in ways that mirrored US goals in Europe under the Marshall Plan. Ironically, this investment may have laid the foundation for China's recent transformation toward Capitalism.

The Chinese appreciated the material aid of their new Soviet ally, but they resented the way Moscow dictated the terms of its acceptance. Following Stalin's death in 1953, Chairman Mao became increasingly critical of Khrushchev's tactical negotiation with non-Communist nations. Mao reacted with anger when the Soviet leader called for "peaceful coexistence" with the West, believing that the Soviet Union was experiencing a counterrevolution and becoming more similar to the United States. During a tense trip to Moscow, Mao rattled Khrushchev and many others with his virulent rhetoric. "No matter what kind of war breaks out—conventional or thermonuclear—we'll win," Mao counseled. "As for China, if the imperialists unleash war on us, we may lose more than 300 million people. So what? War is war. The years will pass, and we'll get to work producing more babies than ever before."

Believing that he alone had the courage to push the sacrifices needed to transform his nation toward the utopian vision of Marx, Mao announced a program he called the **Great Leap Forward** in 1958. The goal was a complete transformation of China from a rural farming society to an industrial superpower led by the proletarian workers. The result, however, was an abandonment of agriculture that led to widespread famine and the death of 20 to 40 million people. By 1960, China and the Soviet Union had become increasingly hostile toward one another, and Soviet aid to China was halted. Even North Korean dictator Kim Il Sung declared the Great Leap Forward a dismal failure. The North Koreans would label similar programs launched by Chairman Mao in future years as "unbelievable madness."

The Chinese were not the only Communists angered by Khrushchev's talk of "peaceful coexistence" with the West. Khrushchev attempted to convince Soviet hardliners in his own nation that his efforts to improve US-Soviet relations were an intelligent tactical maneuver rather than an abandonment of the global struggle against Western Capitalism. Castro was particularly angered by Khrushchev's talk about peaceful coexistence, and he reminded the Soviet premier that the United States had sent troops and assassins against him. Khrushchev responded in his typically direct fashion. "What did you expect them to send you?" he asked the Cuban leader, "presents?" Mao shared Castro's criticism that the Soviet Union was gradually becoming more like the West, but available documents demonstrate that Mao was more concerned with economic affairs and dissidents in his own nation. He believed that the failure of the Great Leap Forward was due to internal opponents who wanted China to follow the Soviet model instead of Mao's more revolutionary schemes. By 1960, Soviet advisers had left China, and Khrushchev believed that Beijing was posturing to replace Moscow as the leader of the Communist world.

Khrushchev's fears were exaggerated, yet the two nations entered an era of competition with one another. This Cold War between China and the Soviet Union was especially pronounced in a number of developing nations. By 1963, Chinese representatives were deployed throughout Asia and Africa with the goal of severing ties between local Communist leaders and the "European" Soviet Union. Given the much higher standard of living in the Soviet Union than most developing nations, as well as the expansionistic tendencies of the Soviet Union and its tight rule over Eastern Europe, many revolutionaries in developing nations became skeptical about the authenticity of Soviet Communism.

Mao's message about the revolutionary struggles of colonized peoples against European imperialists appealed to many who saw parallels in the ways China, another developing nation, had battled imperialist nations over the past century. Leaders of leftist movements throughout the "Third World" were also inclined to support Chinese views about the proletariats of the world battling against the forces of imperialism. The Chinese became active in Africa, but their greatest influence remained in Southeastern Asia. In the end, leaders of developing nations sought to gain from Chinese benefactors but remain independent and steer their own course, just as they accepted American and Soviet aid but jealously guarded their independence.

Great Leap Forward

The attempt of the Chinese Communist Party to transform China from a nation of peasant farmers to an industrialized nation. Tens of millions perished in the resulting decline in agriculture, leading many to doubt the wisdom of central economic planning.

REVIEW AND CRITICAL THINKING

1. The 1960 televised debate between Nixon and Kennedy is frequently portrayed as a contest between a young and vibrant Kennedy and a menacing-looking Nixon who refused to wear makeup. However, those who study the actual reaction of Americans to the debate point out that most Americans did not respond to the debate in such terms. Why might Kennedy be remembered as young and vibrant? Were the two candidates more alike or different, and how has the historical image of the two men altered our understanding of the election of 1960?

2. What were the successes and limitations of the New Frontier? What accounted for Kennedy's limitations in passing more significant domestic legislation given his high approval rating and Democratic majority in Congress?

3. Which was more important: the activism of college students or the leadership of national figures such as Martin Luther King Jr.?

4. Ella Baker ran King's SCLC for a number of years, both as the interim president between the resignations of male clergymen and as the coordinator of most SCLC campaigns. How might the civil rights movement have been different if women were granted full equality within the movement?

5. Do you believe that Kennedy would have handled Vietnam differently than Lyndon Johnson had he been president between 1963 and 1968? What evidence do you have to support your conclusion?

6. Knowing that China and the Soviet Union were increasingly hostile to one another, why might the Kennedy administration continue to portray international Communism as a united front?

4. CONCLUSION

Most historians within and beyond the United States are very critical of the actions of US foreign policymakers when it comes to developing nations during the Cold War era. However, even these critics point out that US aid was often generously bestowed for humanitarian reasons, while US intervention was sometimes directed against an oppressive regime, regardless of how it might affect the Cold War. In most cases, however, historians agree that the leading concern behind America's major foreign policy decisions was the containment or elimination of Communism. The same American officials who authorized humanitarian aid could also display callous indifference to the conditions faced by the people of other nations when concerns about the spread of Communism were involved.

While leaders in Washington exerted tremendous resources aimed at promoting global stability by fighting Communism, their inclination to view developing nations as pawns in a geopolitical chessboard destroyed the goodwill of their humanitarian efforts and alienated the people of many nations. Critics of US foreign policy believe that the failure of US officials to consider the perspectives of developing nations may have thwarted their own efforts to prevent the spread of Communism more effectively than any action taken in Moscow.

The global Cold War affected the domestic civil rights movement in two important ways that often worked against one another. First, it prodded the federal government to end segregation as a means of improving America's global image. Second, the Cold War led to the creation of a political environment that was suspicious of all dissident groups. Anti-Communist witch hunts spread beyond differences of opinions regarding political and economic systems. As a result, civil rights leaders were among those charged with disloyalty. McCarthyism and hysteria rose and fell, but over time fewer Americans were taken in by demagogues who sought to harness fear for their own political gain.

A similar phenomenon occurred in the fight for civil rights, as groups such as the White Citizens Council found fewer adherents after their methods were exposed. Photographs showing violence against activists led to growing support of the civil rights movement, while grassroots campaigns led to both local and national victories against segregation. But as the Albany Movement showed, public support for civil rights might not be forthcoming without patent evidence showing violent injustice. As activists celebrated the Civil Rights Act of 1964 and Voting Rights Act of 1965, a growing number of white Americans were beginning to believe that the problem of race in America had been solved.

5. FURTHER READING

Adelson, Bruce. *Brushing Back Jim Crow: The Integration of Minor League Baseball in the American South* (2005).

Cohen, Deborah. *Braceros: Migrant Citizens and Transnational Subjects in the Postwar United States and Mexico* (2011).

Crockatt, Richard. *The Fifty Years War: The United States and the Soviet Union in World Politics, 1941–1991* (1996).

Dudziak, Mary L. *Cold War Civil Rights: Race and the Image of American Democracy* (2000).

Finley, Keith M. *Delaying the Dream: Southern Senators and the Fight Against Civil Rights, 1938–1965* (2008).

Gaddis, John Lewis. *The Cold War: A New History* (2006).

Garrow, David. *Bearing the Cross: Martin Luther King and the SCLC (1986)*

Herring, George C. *America's Longest War: The United States and Vietnam, 1950–1975* (2002).

Ransby, Barbara. *Ella Baker and the Black Freedom Movement: A Radical Democratic Vision* (2005).

Suri, Jeremi. *Power and Protest: Global Revolution and the Rise of Détente* (2003).

Titus, Jill Ogline. *Students, Segregationists, and the Struggle for Justice in Prince Edward County, Virginia* (2011).

Westad, Odd Arne. *The Global Cold War: Third World Interventions and the Making of Our Times* (2007).

CHAPTER 11
Vietnam and Civil Disobedience, 1963–1969

The middle and late 1960s were years of progress, protest, prejudice, and renewed hope for peace and racial justice. John F. Kennedy was assassinated, as were Malcolm X, Martin Luther King Jr., and Robert Kennedy. The postwar economic boom continued throughout most of the decade. It was accompanied by heightened fears about the possible growth of Communism abroad and escalating protests at home. The United States had grown accustomed to interpreting the events at home and around the world in terms of the Cold War. In addition, US officials were growing increasingly frustrated with the persistence of Communist forces in Vietnam in the face of military escalation. A growing number of Americans were likewise frustrated by the persistence of poverty and racial injustice. They pressed the federal government to approve meaningful laws and programs that would fulfill the promise of justice and material security. Modern feminism emerged as a force for change, along with the American Indian Movement and activism by other minority groups. Promising a Great Society, President Lyndon Johnson hoped to respond to these demands and promote greater freedom through government. In response, a growing conservative movement revived longstanding traditions that viewed the growth of the federal government as the greatest threat to liberty.

1. FROM NEW FRONTIER TO GREAT SOCIETY

LEARNING OBJECTIVES

1. Few in the early 1960s believed that Congress would approve any significant piece of legislation on civil rights. Explain how the Civil Rights Act of 1964 passed Congress and discuss the significance of the new law.
2. Explain the perspective of conservatives who argued that the powers of the federal government should be limited. Analyze the extent to which opponents of civil rights used the argument of state's rights to mask their own racial prejudice, and the extent to which some conservatives who supported civil rights feared federal interference was a violation of the federal balance between states and the central government.
3. The early 1960s are usually portrayed as a time where women were not politically active. Explain how many women were creating what became known as Second Wave Feminism during this decade. Identify the goals of this movement.

1.1 The Assassination of John F. Kennedy

In 1963, President John F. Kennedy (JFK) once again enjoyed high approval ratings. The economy was prospering, and the ill-conceived Bay of Pigs Invasion was all but forgotten in the wake of Kennedy's successful posturing in Berlin and the resolution of the Cuban Missile Crisis. Kennedy even began to support the limited civil rights initiatives he reluctantly inherited. At the same time, he sought to distance himself from some liberals who desired greater changes than he believed would be politically advantageous to support. His mild support of causes that were unpopular at the moment—such as civil rights—would later be among his most vaunted achievements.

The president's admirers claim that Kennedy would have done more to support meaningful federal intervention to defend civil rights had he not been assassinated in 1963. Some also believe he would have supported the withdrawal of US troops from Vietnam. During his lifetime, Kennedy was restrained by political calculations in these regards. Privately, Kennedy responded to those calling for withdrawal from Vietnam, more support for civil rights, and more aggressive backing for health care reform with the promise that he would address these issues once he had secured a second term.

It was in pursuit of that second term that led Kennedy to Dallas in November 1963. Texas Democrats were in the midst of a political civil war regarding issues such as civil rights. To demonstrate his leadership and ensure his reelection, Kennedy hoped to unite Democrats in one of the most conservative states. He succeeded in this goal but only by becoming a martyr. On November 22, 1963, President Kennedy was shot while parading through Dallas in the back of an open limousine. He was pronounced dead a half hour later in a Dallas hospital. News of the tragedy spread instantly throughout the nation. For the first time, most Americans turned to television news anchors rather than newspaper reporters for information about a major news story. Not only did this result in a deluge of dramatic images but also in a number of reports filed in haste as some of the live television reports featured more speculation than fact. Conspiracy theories spread rapidly in living rooms across the nation as reports about the accused assassin Lee Harvey Oswald circulated. Oswald had planned on traveling to Moscow, leading some Americans to expect that the assassination had been part of a Communist plot.

FIGURE 11.1

Kennedy's vice president Lyndon Baines Johnson being sworn in as president immediately following the Kennedy assassination.

The nature of live television also provided a degree of reassurance that the mechanism of government would continue to function. Millions watched as Vice President Lyndon Johnson took the oath of office while the widowed Jackie Kennedy stood in the background, still wearing a dress that bore the stains of her late husband's blood. The capture of Oswald might have closed the case. However, live television again recorded a killing related to the Kennedy murder. Dallas nightclub owner Jack Ruby jumped out of a crowd and shot Oswald while he was being transferred from one jail to another. Oswald died less than an hour later.

Kennedy's death left Americans with a sense that his vision for the United States might be left unfulfilled, even if few Americans agreed on what that vision entailed. Supreme Court Chief Justice Earl Warren led a six-month investigation, concluding that Oswald had acted alone in killing the president. Many Americans were unconvinced by the Warren committee's report. Even if they disagreed about the circumstances surrounding the Kennedy assassination and the direction the country was headed, Americans agreed that the system of government established by the Constitution was durable.

Throughout history and especially during the 1960s, presidential assassinations usually resulted in chaos and turmoil, perhaps even civil war. In the United States in 1963, the presidency was quietly transferred to former Vice President Lyndon B. Johnson (LBJ) according to the terms set out by the Constitution. As president, Johnson invoked the memory of the slain leader in support of the most significant civil rights legislation since Reconstruction. He also secured passage of Medicare and Medicaid, two federal government–sponsored health care programs for the elderly and the poor. Despite these significant domestic achievements, Johnson's bid for more sweeping reform and possible reelection would be derailed by a seemingly endless war in Southeastern Asia. For Democrats, it seemed as if the history of the Korean War was repeating itself.

1.2   Civil Rights Act of 1964

A New Dealer raised in the cutthroat world of Texas politics, Johnson was a lifelong and ambitious politician who suddenly saw himself elevated to the office he had coveted his entire life. The tragic circumstances that led to his presidency precluded celebration, however, and Johnson somberly accepted the challenge of healing the nation while quietly securing his nomination and victory in the upcoming 1964 election. For Johnson, the key to both was to portray himself as the successor to Kennedy while presenting his policies as the embodiment of the martyred president's will.

Addressing Congress moments after the nation had laid its slain leader to rest, Johnson urged Congress to "let us continue" the work of the Kennedy administration. For Johnson, this meant that an assassin's bullet should not derail the liberal consensus based on tax reduction, federal guarantees of civil rights, and antipoverty programs. Many who had once opposed the former vice president's policies pointed out the unfairness of Johnson equating a martyred president with his own political agenda. At the same time, Johnson skillfully presented previously controversial measures such as the **1964 Civil Rights Act** as a tribute to their fallen leader and the only proper response to an act of violence. As a result, in death, Kennedy became eternally connected to a civil rights bill he had only cautiously supported in life.

African American leaders recognized Johnson's strategy and went along with the charade by eulogizing the former president in ways reminiscent of the historical memory of Lincoln. Civil rights leaders reminded Americans that JFK had promised to eliminate housing discrimination "with the stroke of a pen" while a candidate. In actuality, Kennedy had failed to act on his promise, which had prompted thousands of African Americans to mail pens to the White House to remind him of this promise. However, presenting civil rights as part of an unfulfilled agenda of a martyred president soon became an effective way to secure historic reform legislation.

Black leaders also pointed out that JFK had asked Martin Luther King to draft a second Emancipation Proclamation that he would sign on January 1, 1963, to mark the centennial of the original. Never mind, of course, that the president had also forsaken this promise and even failed to respond to the proclamation King had prepared for the president. Kennedy was a martyred hero, these civil rights leaders reminded themselves, and any connection between the former president and their cause must be promoted regardless of historical accuracy. Perhaps Kennedy would have supported the 1964 Civil Rights bill, they privately counseled one another; after all, the former president had recently addressed the nation on the issue against the counsel of his political advisers who feared any support for the proposed bill would cost him the election.

FIGURE 11.2

The organizers of the 1963 March on Washington lead the march in front of thousands of participants with signs calling for equal employment, voting rights, and the end of segregation. Each of the leading national civil rights organizations was represented on the program, and Martin Luther King Jr. was selected to speak last. Although women were often the most active organizers within these organizations, efforts to recognize their contribution were only belatedly added to the schedule of events.

1964 Civil Rights Act

Perhaps the most significant piece of civil rights legislation in US history, the 1964 Civil Rights Act banned racial discrimination in public accommodations and employment. The law also outlawed gender discrimination and established a federal agency to enforce all of its terms.

FIGURE 11.3

African Americans in Washington, DC, march in response to the bombing of a black church in Birmingham that killed four young girls. One of the victims was a childhood friend of future Secretary of State Condoleezza Rice.

Martin Luther King Jr. recognized that proposing a civil rights bill would not secure its passage in Congress. Even worse, presidents could claim to support the bill only to hide behind its failure each year. This would allow whoever occupied the White House to portray themselves as supporters of civil rights without actually securing any meaningful advances for black voters. King teamed up with veteran organizer A. Phillip Randolph and announced a march on Washington designed to force Congress and President Kennedy (who was still alive at the time) to support the bill. Approximately 300,000 Americans, two thirds of whom were black, converged on the nation's capital for the **March on Washington for Jobs and Freedom** in the summer of 1963. The protest was aimed at publicizing the need for antisegregation laws but also ensuring that all Americans would be given equal political and economic opportunity that would render such laws meaningful.

The march reflected the competing ideas of the six leading civil rights organizations that organized the march. Leaders of the Urban League and A. Phillip Randolph's labor union spoke of the need for economic advancement, while younger leaders such as John Lewis of CORE were more controversial in calling for more radical change. The meetings also reflected the paternalistic orientation of these organizations; a brief acknowledgment of female leaders was only belatedly added to the agenda.

King was given the final spot on the schedule and rose to the stage after a brief announcement that W. E. B. Du Bois had passed away in Ghana. King then rose to the podium and delivered his famous "I Have a Dream" speech. King's address remains an iconic moment in US history. It was also a moment where the mantle of leadership was symbolically passed from the generation of Du Bois to the charismatic young preacher from Montgomery, Alabama. Meanwhile, another young and charismatic clergyman named **Malcolm X** criticized the March on Washington as a pep rally for sycophants and fools who believed they could promote meaningful change through the existing white-dominated system. The next Sunday, a bomb exploded during services in a black church in Birmingham, killing four little girls. In their memory, Democratic leaders and President Johnson rallied behind the 1964 Civil Rights Act the following year.

Virginia congressman and segregationist Howard Smith proposed an amendment to the 1964 Civil Rights Act that added "sex" to the act's existing provisions, guaranteeing equal opportunity in employment regardless of race, creed, color, and national origin. Because he and the other nine Southern congressmen who supported the amendment prohibiting gender discrimination strongly spoke in opposition to and voted against the Civil Rights Act, most historians believe that Smith's amendment was intended to divide supporters and ultimately prevent the law from being passed. Smith understood that the majority of his peers now supported a law banning racial discrimination, but he believed that they considered gender to be a valid consideration among employers and would not pass the Civil Rights Act if it mandated equal treatment of men and women.

If derailing the Civil Rights Act of 1964 was indeed Smith's intent, he was borrowing a strategy used by opponents of civil rights provisions dating from Reconstruction. For example, opponents of black suffrage in the 1860s added women's suffrage to proposed laws that would have permitted black men to vote. These provisions led to the defeat of black suffrage before the passage of the Fifteenth Amendment, as well as the defeat of several civil rights laws throughout the twentieth century. In 1964, however, the Civil Rights Act was passed as amended, outlawing segregation while banning both racial and gender discrimination by employers. The act also created the Equal Employment Opportunity Commission (EEOC), which was charged with enforcing the terms of the new law.

1.3   1964 Election

One of the strongest opponents of the 1964 Civil Rights Act was Arizona Republican senator **Barry Goldwater**. Goldwater represented the conservative wing of the party and secured the Republican presidential nomination shortly after the Civil Rights Law was passed. As a result, the 1964 election was a clear ideological contest between the relatively liberal Johnson against the archconservative Goldwater. The author of *Conscience of a Conservative*, a best-selling autobiography that challenged images of the political right as reactionary and void of positive ideas, Goldwater hoped to reverse the growth of government in every way except national defense. As a candidate, he also promised to replace containment with a more aggressive strategy that would strangle and eliminate communism.

Although many Americans equated conservative ideas, such as states' rights, with the defenders of slavery and racial segregation, Goldwater sought to prove that conservative ideas had positive value for all Americans. He personally approved racial integration in schools but did not believe that the federal government had the power to "force" any state or locality to change the way it did business. More importantly, Goldwater predicted that such attempts would only harden racial prejudice and ensure that well-meaning attempts to integrate schools would fail in ways that harmed all children. For African Americans and many liberal whites, however, Goldwater's advice to be patient and wait until whites of the Deep South sought integration was disingenuous at best. It also did not help that Goldwater had the backing of leading white segregationists such as Alabama governor George Wallace, who had proclaimed "segregation forever" the year before.

Other conservatives developed organizations and started journals such as the *National Review* in hopes of spreading their ideas. One of the leading conservative publications, the *National Review*, had originally supported white Southern intransigence to civil rights in terms that reflected support of white supremacy. By the mid-1960s, however, the journal began to be more critical of arch-segregationists and focused more on the issue of limited federal power. Among intellectuals, the political and economic theories of Friedrich Hayek united most conservatives and increasingly influenced moderates and even some liberals. Hayek posited that increases in governmental power, even under the best of intentions, would inevitably build upon one another until the government had grown so big and so powerful that it controlled nearly every aspect of life.

Other intellectual conservatives offered a spin on Marx's view of historical progression to warn the United States that like other great powers, the US government was in danger of growing too big and squandering its resources at home and abroad. Liberals countered that conservatives only supported limited government when it came to social programs and actually favored increased spending for military and law enforcement. Conservative intellectuals continued to refine their ideas in ways that would lead to a conservative revival by the end of the decade. However, in the early 1960s, most Americans identified themselves as liberal. When these individuals imagined a typical conservative, conspiracy theorists like the **John Birch Society** and militant white segregationists remained the dominant image.

Formed in 1958, followers of the John Birch Society believed they were ideological soldiers in a war against liberals, whose every move was calculated to bring the United States to its knees. By 1963, more than 100,000 Birchers spent much of their time writing letters to editors warning of the dangers of governmental programs and civil rights as harbingers of Socialism and interracial marriage. Even candidate Goldwater was not conservative enough for these on the extreme right, but he spoke to many of the Birchers' fears that the Republican Party had been co-opted by liberals. Why else would President Eisenhower have permitted FDR's programs to continue, he asked, while most leading Republicans in Congress acted as if they were running some kind of "dime-store New Deal"?

Goldwater not only spoke to the fears of many anxious whites who thought society was changing too quickly, but he also spoke without the usual politician's filter. At times, this could be harmful. For example, speaking to a group of Midwesterners, the Republican nominee once asserted that the nation would be better off if the East Coast, a reference to Northeastern liberals, was severed from the nation and sent "out to sea." The Democrats responded by running TV ads throughout the East that featured a cartoon saw slicing off the East Coast while Goldwater's words played in the background. One of LBJ's ads went too far by insinuating that a vote for Goldwater was a vote for nuclear armageddon. Although the ad was immediately recalled, Goldwater's own rhetoric had created the notion that he lacked the patient temperament needed to be a leader of a nuclear power. Johnson won every state outside of the Deep South and Goldwater's home state of Arizona.

Barry Goldwater

A leading conservative and Republican nominee for president in 1964, Goldwater rallied those who believed the federal government was becoming too big and too powerful. Goldwater also opposed the 1964 Civil Rights Act, while personally claiming that he supported the goals of integration. Goldwater was defeated in a landslide in 1964 but continued to be a leading member of the conservative wing of the Republican Party.

FIGURE 11.4

Arizona senator Barry Goldwater sought to distance himself from extremists such as these Klansmen who were demonstrating on his behalf during the election. However, his recent opposition to the Civil Rights Act of 1964 furthered the association between the conservative movement Goldwater represented and those who opposed racial equality.

John Birch Society

A radical conservative organization that opposed the passage of the Civil Rights Act and viewed US participation in the United Nations as part of a radical conspiracy to lessen the sovereignty of the nation until the world was ruled by a single collectivist government.

FIGURE 11.5

Lyndon Johnson defeated the conservative Republican Barry Goldwater in 1964. However, conservative ideas would gain support following Goldwater's landslide defeat.

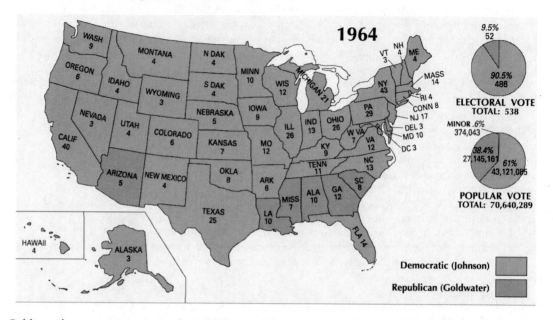

Goldwater's support among Southern whites from Louisiana to South Carolina was largely the result of LBJ's support of legislation forever banning racial segregation. Because of this legislation, black Americans generally supported Johnson's campaign even though they recognized that Johnson shared many of the racial assumptions of many whites. Legendary musician Dizzy Gillespie ran a mock campaign for president that trumpeted many of Johnson's shortcomings. Gillespie promised to support the Democratic candidate when he finally offered genuine support for black Americans. Until then, the trumpet player campaigned promising to end the Vietnam War, poverty, and racial segregation. Gillespie's America would be personified by his replacement of the White House with a "Blues House" where all Americans would be welcome. Gillespie also promised to appoint a number of prominent jazz musicians as cabinet officials and ambassadors, explaining his belief that the improvisational nature of jazz required individuals who intrinsically knew how to work with others to create harmony. The campaign raised money for civil rights causes, but it was more effective in reminding the Democrats that they needed to support civil rights initiatives if they expected the black vote in the next election.

1.4 Massive Resistance and School Integration

massive resistance

A term used to describe the various strategies employed by Southern whites to prevent school integration. Some of these strategies included passing laws mandating that schools be closed if forced to integrate.

One of black voters' leading demands was that their local schools finally be required to comply with the 1954 Supreme Court decision in *Brown v. Board of Education*. The schools of Virginia provided a clear example that the federal government would have to intervene. After the schools of Virginia failed to integrate, black plaintiffs sued and won three separate victories as the federal courts ordered the integration of the schools in Warren County, Charlottesville, and Norfolk. In reaction, the Virginia governor ordered that all of the public schools in these districts close, and state officials required that any school district ordered to integrate must also close its doors. This strategy of thwarting integration at all costs, even if it meant closing schools for white children, was known as **massive resistance**. In 1959, black plaintiffs in Prince Edward County, the same Virginia school district that had been home to one of the original five cases that were consolidated into *Brown v. Board*, sued in federal court. As had been the case in the other Virginia cases, the board was ordered to integrate. However, the all-white school board had already decided that it would close all of the county's public schools if the appeal was lost. In addition, the federal courts had not yet declared that *Brown v. Board* applied to private schools. As a result, board members had devised a plan where public school resources would be used to create a number of "private" schools for white children.

The "privatization" of the Prince Edward County schools in the early 1960s demonstrated a new tactic available for advocates of massive resistance. Publicly owned schools were "leased" to individuals who hired the same white public school teachers to teach in what was now called a "private" school. Although segregationists were able to use a variety of methods to finance their schools with public money, the schools still required some tuition and private donations to function. As a result, many white children were also denied school privileges. As a form of denying racial discrimination, the school board suggested that middle-class African American parents open similar "private" schools for their children. While some black parents pursued this strategy with mixed results, others pointed out that doing so simply perpetuated segregation while shifting more of the financial burden for school funding on parents. Other black parents continued their fight in the courts until they secured a Supreme Court decision ordering the county school board to reopen and integrate the public schools. During the five years that the schools were closed, working-class white and black families drew upon networks of community and kin, pooling money and sending their children to live with out-of-state families.

Photos of angry demonstrations and even violence against the first black children to attend a particular school provide the most poignant images of school integration. However, the greatest obstacle to integration may have been waged by thousands of community groups that defended segregation with the demeanor of a local PTA meeting. Many of these organizations had progressive-sounding names that gave the appearance of defending children or promoting harmony. Others adopted names such as the White Citizens Council (WCC). Each of these groups devised methods to indefinitely postpone school integration through procedural delays, legal challenges, redrawing school boundaries, and creating integration advisory boards that never met.

Groups such as the WCC also sought ways to intimidate black leaders and isolate black families whose children were part of an integration lawsuit. WCC chapters were composed of city officials, business leaders, and middle-class white parents. Some chapters even received city and state tax dollars to fund their operations. The preferred tactic was usually nonviolent, convincing employers to fire any person known to favor integration. If an individual was self-employed, the WCC worked covertly to convince local banks to cut a family's line of credit, even foreclose on mortgages that were in good standing to force integrationists to leave town.

While the WCC officially condemned violence, those black leaders and families that somehow continued their fight for integration were frequently the victims of drive-by shootings and arson. The year following the Brown decision, seven black leaders were murdered or went missing in Mississippi alone. In contrast to Border South states like Virginia and large cities such as Little Rock, few lawsuits were filed to try to force the integration of schools in Mississippi, Alabama, and Georgia. Border South states such as Missouri and West Virginia saw little violence but only piecemeal integration until the late 1950s and early 1960s. School boards in these states typically integrated only one or two grades each year.

The gradual elimination of legal segregation did not remove barriers to meaningful integration. Black students were often barred or heavily discouraged from participating in extracurricular activities they had previously enjoyed. More importantly, the end of segregation also meant that many black teachers were fired rather than permitted to teach in mixed-race schools. Black communities lost control of venerable institutions such as Sumner High in St. Louis and Garnett High in Charleston, West Virginia. These schools were the center of black community life and boasted a teaching corps with more advanced degrees than many colleges. Integration was recognized as an important step toward racial equality, yet for black students who navigated a gauntlet of racism each morning, black teachers who lost their jobs, and black community members who lost control of their local schools, integration continued to place the burden of race squarely on their shoulders.

1.5 Women, Labor, and Second Wave Feminism

Even as more and more Americans supported the idea that race should not be a barrier to employment, most Americans believed that gender was a valid consideration on the job market. Newspapers divided their advertisements for jobs into "Help Wanted (Male)" and "Help Wanted (Female)" sections, and most large businesses kept separate lists of male and female employees for purposes of determining seniority and promotion. Given the assumption that women were provided for by a male breadwinner, few companies provided benefits such as health insurance or pensions for female employees. For those female workers who were married to husbands who received family benefits, these kinds of benefits were less important than fair pay. But for the 40 percent of working women who were single, and for the women who might someday become divorced or widowed, gendered assumptions about wages and benefits were painful reminders that they were not part of the idealized female world of pampered domesticity.

At the same time, many women believed that gender differences should be considered in the workforce. Many states had laws granting time off for pregnancy and child care and other provisions specifically designed to protect women in the workplace. Some of these laws, such as limitations on the number of hours a woman might be required to work, might either benefit a particular female employee or serve as a barrier from obtaining needed overtime pay. In addition, some companies had internal policies granting women longer breaks, days off for child care, and even more days for sick leave. Some women worried about whether laws mandating an end to gender discrimination might lead to the elimination of laws protecting pregnant workers or recognizing the domestic responsibilities of women who worked part time.

The emerging civil rights movement and the experience of many women in labor unions helped to promote ideas about the rights of the individual and the power of collective action. Even as the nation's imagined "ideal woman" took a step away from "Rosie the Riveter" and toward the popularized image of sitcom housewives Donna Reed and June Cleaver, a number of female activists mobilized in favor of greater opportunities for women who worked outside of the home by choice or necessity.

One of the greatest obstacles these women had to overcome was the notion that female employment outside the home was unnatural or undesirable. Many women, as well as men, viewed female labor as a temporary evil that should only be endured during periods of personal financial crisis or war. Many activists tried to show the nation that the idealized image of a dependent housewife within a well-provisioned home not only limited women's freedoms but also ignored the reality of life for many women. Nearly half of working women at this time were single, and 10 percent of children were born out of wedlock throughout the 1950s and 1960s. Others tried a more radical approach using the rhetoric of labor unions about the rights and dignity of all workers combined with the tactics of civil rights activists.

Similar to feminists of previous generations, women's rights activists used both conservative and radical approaches to spread their message. For example, one popular conservative strategy was to liken opponents of equal employment as cowardly assailants of women and mothers, many of whom lacked "male protection." Others sought to connect women's patriotic service against fascism in World War II with the ongoing contest against Communism. Others like **Betty Friedan** became involved in labor unions and exposed corporate wage tables that used gender as a determinative factor. For example, one of Friedan's articles listed the pay rates for male and female laborers in leading companies like General Electric and Westinghouse. The same article revealed that the average black woman earned less than half of the average white woman and that the pay differential between men and women resulted in billions in corporate profits.

Friedan rose to prominence after publishing *The Feminine Mystique*, a book capturing the discontent that many American women felt in a society that minimized their contributions and restricted their options. She and other women of the postwar period helped to create what soon became known as **Second Wave Feminism**. By this definition, previous generations of feminists were part of a First Wave that worked to overturn legal obstacles to equality, such as prohibitions against women's suffrage and property ownership. Women of the postwar period were part of a Second Wave that challenged lasting inequalities, which remained impervious to the repeal of explicitly discriminatory laws. In so doing, these 1960s feminists sought to establish and defend equal rights and opportunities for women. In an era where most women accepted a modified version of the "separate sphere," feminists of the 1960s challenged the notion that gender should predetermine one's role in society.

Most women in the 1960s took a more tactical approach, seeking tangible gains for women in the workforce, including safeguards against termination for life events such as marriage and childbirth. This was important, because employers at this time frequently dismissed female employees when their pregnancies became known. These mothers were generally replaced by younger women who could be paid less and would agree to contracts stipulating that they would resign if they should become pregnant. This practice not only thwarted a woman's ability to achieve seniority and promotion but also reinforced notions that female employment was temporary. Few companies would bother training even the most talented young women for positions beyond the entry level if they believed their ability to serve the company would be interrupted for two or three decades following childbirth and motherhood.

Dozens of industrial nations had provisions guaranteeing time off and some financial compensation for pregnant employees by 1950. In the United States, only Rhode Island had a similar provision at the state level, and it would take nearly three decades for the federal government to pass similar legislation. Women's leaders and organizations in the United States participated in the United Nations International Labor Organization, which, among other things, sought to define and defend the rights of female workers. In 1952, this organization recommended that employers be required to provide medical coverage and twelve weeks of paid leave for pregnant women. Most Americans paid little attention to these recommendations and believed that companies should not be required to provide even unpaid leaves of absence. Even the more radical American women who participated in the 1952 meetings believed that the UN recommendation would result in fewer companies being willing to hire women of child-bearing age. As a result, women's groups in the United States lobbied for provisions guaranteeing that pregnant women could keep their jobs and take unpaid leaves of absence. With the exception of state and local laws, their efforts were not rewarded until the Pregnancy Discrimination Act of 1978.

Second Wave Feminism

A blanket term for the growth of women's rights activism in the late 1950s and 1960s, Second Wave Feminism refers to attempts to eliminate social and economic discrimination against women. The First Wave refers to those who fought for the elimination of legal barriers, such as the rights of women to vote, hold private property, and run for political office. Members of the Second Wave argued that the elimination of legal barriers had not removed all forms of discrimination against women. Although commonly associated with the 1960s and 1970s, the roots of Second Wave Feminism can be seen in the postwar era.

2.   THE GREAT SOCIETY AND THE VIETNAM WAR

LEARNING OBJECTIVES

1. Explain the goals of the LBJ's Great Society, and evaluate his effectiveness in combating racial injustice and poverty.
2. Given the fact that the Fifteenth Amendment banned racial discrimination at the polls, explain the need for the 1965 Voting Rights Act. Summarize the efforts by African Americans to challenge disenfranchisement in the mid-1960s.
3. Martin Luther King said that LBJ's Great Society was derailed by his escalation of the Vietnam War. Explain what King meant, and summarize LBJ's decision between 1964 and 1967 to escalate the war he inherited from Truman, Eisenhower, and Kennedy.

Popular culture soon reflected the movement from the city to the suburbs. Leading sitcom families in 1950s programs such as *I Love Lucy* and *The Honeymooners* were apartment dwellers, but by the 1960s, Americans gathered to watch the daily lives of suburban families in *Leave it to Beaver* and similar programs. While popular culture extolled the virtues of suburban life, a new generation of restless suburban youths continued to embrace counterculture modes of expression. Beneath the façade of conformity and contentedness, the youths of the early 1960s experimented with similar styles of music, literature, and drugs the beatniks had embraced in the previous decade.

Although few beatniks would have appreciated the tribute, 1960 was also the year that a British rock band called themselves *The Beatles* and began their meteoric rise. Offering a middle-class version of the rebellious posturing of the previous generation, *The Beatles* soon embodied the essence of suburban youth culture in the mid-1960s. The final years of the decade, however, featured a culture far more rebellious than the clean-cut teen idols from Liverpool. In 1969, half a million hipsters and fellow travelers converged upon a farm in upstate New York in 1969 to witness rock 'n' roll deliver its own proclamation of emancipation at a concert called Woodstock.

2.1   Poverty in a Land of Plenty

Lyndon Johnson rose to prominence in 1948 after election returns of questionable veracity declared the young man from the hill country of Texas that state's senator by a mere eighty-seven contested votes. Now president, Johnson hoped to put the unfriendly nickname of "Landslide Lyndon" behind him forever by becoming the next Franklin Roosevelt. Although the economy appeared strong, sociologists had produced numerous studies detailing how a fifth of the population lived in squalor. Johnson's supporters believed that the persistence of poverty in the wealthiest nation on the globe was more than a cruel paradox. In response, one of the first initiatives Johnson declared was a "war on poverty." In August 1964, Congress passed Johnson's Economic Opportunity Act. This law provided an average of $1 million for nearly 1,000 locally organized community action agencies around the nation. The president also created the Job Corps, which provided vocational training for young adults in the hopes of breaking the cycle of poverty.

The Great Society

The slogan used by President Lyndon Johnson to promote a variety of proposed domestic legislation aimed at eradicating poverty and racial injustice.

Johnson labeled his sweeping domestic agenda as **The Great Society** and proposed dozens of new laws and new agencies to deal with the problems of poverty and racial injustice. Supporters hailed the programs launched between 1965 and 1967 as a modern-day New Deal complete with a new alphabet soup of federal programs. The Volunteers in Service to America (VISTA) employed young and old Americans to conduct service projects in impoverished cities. Two new cabinet-level agencies, the Department of Transportation (DOT) and the Department of Housing and Urban Development (HUD), were added to the alphabet soup of federal acronyms. Johnson also supported the creation of the National Endowment for the Humanities and the National Endowment for the Arts, provided federal assistance for public broadcasting, and increased federal aid for colleges and students. The most controversial programs, however, were those that provided direct payments to the poor. Food stamps and other programs shifted the burden of poverty relief from cities and states to the federal government. Although some feared that Johnson's welfare programs would encourage dependency and sap the ambitions of the poor, many greeted the program with optimism, believing that it would reduce fraud while providing a more complete security net against poverty.

FIGURE 11.7

This 1968 poster was made by the federal government to inform seniors about Medicare, a program that was part of the Social Security Act of 1965. Medicare is a federal health insurance plan that provides benefits for individuals who are eligible for Social Security.

This optimism was not enough to carry an ambitious plan to provide national health insurance, a plan originally proposed by FDR that continued to stall in Congress throughout the 1960s. Congress and President Johnson instead secured passage of **Medicare** in 1965, a federal system of health insurance for the elderly. Less than half of Americans above the age of sixty-five had any medical insurance, a situation that prevented many older Americans from obtaining medical care. Given the political power of senior citizens, the president quickly approved Congress's plan to fund Medicare through an increase in Social Security taxes. The original plan failed to cover dental care, eyeglasses, certain prescriptions, and a host of other important services and procedures. However, seniors could choose either Plan A, which offset most hospital bills, or Plan B, which functioned much like an employer's health plan with the recipient paying small premiums while the government shouldered the majority of the cost. Congress also approved **Medicaid**, a program providing medical benefits for recipients of welfare and the disabled.

2.2   Voting Rights Act of 1965

Although the federal government had passed numerous laws guaranteeing the right to vote regardless of race, African Americans throughout the South continued to be disenfranchised by a variety of methods. Black leaders throughout the South challenged their exclusion. Thousands had worked quietly to increase voter registration throughout the 1940s and 1950s, yet fewer than 2 percent of eligible black voters were registered and even fewer were able to vote. For example, black and white leaders at the Highlander Folk School in the Appalachian Mountains of Tennessee launched citizenship education schools throughout the South. Under the leadership of civil rights veteran **Septima Clark** and teachers like South Carolina's Bernice Robinson (a beautician with no teaching experience), these schools taught literacy skills needed to pass voter registration exams. Robinson's role as a beautician was important because she was self-employed and her clients were all black. Unlike existing public school teachers, Robinson could not be fired by a white school board member or harassed by a white suprervisor as had occurred so often in the past.

The citizenship school movement expanded rapidly in the early 1960s. Leaders from a variety of civil rights organizations, such as CORE, along with hundreds of Northern college students descended upon Mississippi in 1964 in what became known as the **Mississippi Freedom Summer**. Many of the rural counties in the Delta had black majorities yet did not have a single registered black voter. Whites claimed that this was because black residents cared little for politics, but the reality was that any black person who registered to vote did so at great personal risk. For example, in 1963 Mississippi passed a law requiring the name of any new registrant to be published in the city paper. Allegedly meant to provide fellow citizens an opportunity to identify any nonresident, felon, or otherwise nonqualified voter, any black residents whose names were published soon found themselves fired from their jobs, evicted from their homes, and a handful even went missing.

Medicare

A leading provision of the 1965 Social Security Act, Medicare provides health insurance for Americans age sixty-five and older who meet other eligibility requirements for Social Security benefits.

Medicaid

Created in 1965 as part of Lyndon Johnson's Great Society, Medicaid is a federal program administered by states and provides health insurance to the disabled and low-income Americans who are eligible for federal assistance.

Septima Clark

Known to many as "Freedom's Teacher," Clark innovated the use of citizenship education schools that taught black Americans reading skills that prepared them to pass literacy tests required for voter registration. As director of the Highlander Folk School's outreach program, she trained and recruited teachers of these schools throughout Appalachia and the South.

Mississippi Freedom Summer

A sustained campaign by local African Americans and college students throughout the nation to protest continued disenfranchisement in Mississippi and throughout the South. Students taught reading skills to adults wishing to pass literacy tests while local activists formed their own political party to protest their exclusion from the white-controlled Democratic Party of Mississippi.

FIGURE 11.8

Civil rights leaders Septima Clark (left) and Rosa Parks (right) enjoy a moment together at the Highlander Folk School in Monteagle, Tennessee.

Mississippi law also required any potential registrant to read and interpret a section of the state constitution. A provision officially meant to screen against illiterate voters who might accidentally vote for the wrong party, the test was often used to reject black voters. The exam was a subjective measure administered by white registrars who often failed black attorneys and black professors while approving the applications of illiterate whites. In George County, one white applicant interpreted the phrase "There shall be no imprisonment for debt" to mean "I thank that a Neorger should have two years in collage before voting because he don't under stand." This individual, and tens of thousands of other semiliterate whites, passed the exam. In other areas, however, the laws were used to restrict poor whites with little opportunity for education from voting. As a result, some poor whites joined the Freedom School movement and recognized their common cause with black Southerners.

The Freedom Summer challenged the nearly complete disenfranchisement of African Americans in the Deep South as thousands of black and white college students from throughout the nation converged upon Mississippi and other states to register black voters. Following the methods of Septima Clark's citizenship schools, participants in the Freedom Summer organized classes that prepared potential voters for the registration exam. Robert Moses, a former school teacher who had been working in the state to register voters, helped to train the students and prepare them for the threats and violence they would face. Almost a thousand attended a week-long workshop at Miami University in Ohio where they learned skills such as how to protect their head and vital organs while being clubbed.

> We knew, we knew that to get black people registered to vote…but we also knew that for many of those people who weren't registered, the most important thing to them was often something different. Causing political change through voting was too intangible at first. They wanted to be able to order something out of a catalog, or read a letter from one of their children from out of town without having to take it to a neighbor or their white employer. That meant more to them than a registration certificate at that moment. They just couldn't see that far down the road. So you dealt with them on that level. You had to. The rest followed. That's why those schools worked.
>
> —Bernice Robinson, Highlander Participant and Citizenship School Teacher in Coastal South Carolina

This training proved invaluable as the students dedicated themselves to nonviolent resistance. Hundreds were attacked and arrested, while dozens of churches that were used to hold classes were bombed. Three civil rights workers, James Chaney, Andrew Goodman, and Michael Schwerner, went missing while traveling through Philadelphia, Mississippi, that August. Hundreds of reporters and FBI investigators swarmed Mississippi to join in what many increasingly realized was a recovery operation to find the bodies of the three young men. "We all knew that this search with hundreds of searchers is because Andrew Goodman and my husband are white," Rita Schwerner explained to a shocked nation. "If only Chaney was involved, nothing would have been done." Investigators stumbled upon a half-dozen bodies of local black civil rights workers before finding the three students.

The funeral of James Chaney reflected the anger of many African Americans as they increasingly recognized the second-class status they were given in their own freedom struggle as TV cameras and FBI investigators continued to only report on the actions of white students. But the civil rights movement did not yet fragment along racial lines as it would in the late 1960s. The presence of white students brought TV cameras, which publicized the plight of Southern blacks who recognized that the students were one of the few allies they had. Together, some progress was made even in places like Leflore County where no African Americans had voted in years. A county with a black majority, 1,500 black residents attempted to register, and with the national media present, local registrars could find no reason to disallow 300 of these applications.

Whites in Mississippi prohibited black voters from participating in the Democratic primaries, claiming that this was legal because their organization was private and therefore exempt from the Fifteenth Amendment. African Americans and a handful of white supporters formed the Mississippi Freedom Democratic Party (MFDP) in response. The MFDP challenged the legitimacy of the white-only Mississippi delegation to the 1964 Democratic National Convention. Wishing to keep white Southern voters from supporting a third-party segregationist candidate, the Democratic Party recognized the white-only Mississippi delegation and offered the MFDP only a token number of delegates. MFDP leader Fannie Lou Hamer soon became the public face of the voting rights movement in Mississippi when she explained why her organization could not accept this token offer. Hamer described her own experience of being beaten while in prison for attempting to register black voters in Mississippi, exposing the hypocrisy of Democratic leaders who spoke of the political sacrifices they had made by offering token support to the MFDP. The following year, Democrats hoped to avoid future controversy and approved the **1965 Voting Rights Act**. This law allowed for federal supervision of voter registration and elections when racial discrimination was suspected. "Mississippi has been called 'The Closed Society,'" explained organizer Robert Moses. "We think the key is in the vote."

2.3   The Great Society and Its Limits

President Johnson praised education as the "key which can unlock the door to the Great Society." The president supported the Higher Education Act, which expanded work-study programs and provided loans for tuition and living expenses. These loans would be serviced through private banks but would feature low interest rates because the federal government would guarantee payment. Now all young adults who did not have a wealthy family member to cosign their college loans could turn to their Uncle Sam.

More controversial was Johnson's desire to vastly expand federal aid to K-12 education. Kennedy had attempted a similar measure, but his opposition to funding parochial schools (a provision the Catholic Kennedy supported but feared would prove politically suicidal) derailed the measure. Johnson's bill worked around the controversy by providing subsidies for families with children in private schools (rather than the schools themselves). The primary feature of the Elementary and Secondary Education Act of 1965, however, was the allocation of $1 billion in federal aid for public schools. By bridging the political divide between the supporters of private and public schools, Johnson's bill was the first legislation providing significant funding to K-12 education. Previous laws tied this funding to school integration, which probably did more than *Brown v. Board* to encourage integration in hundreds of school districts. Equally important, the 1965 law began a historic shift in the way public schools were financed. Advocates of federal aid believed that this revenue would compensate for the inequities of locally funded schools. However, poor districts still spent far less per pupil, and federal aid increasingly became an excuse to cut school funding in many districts.

Medicare provided benefits for nearly 20 million Americans but did not cover a host of expenses, such as prescription drugs, leading many to criticize the program for its "gaps" in coverage. In addition, the program quickly became one of the government's leading expenses and required continual increases in taxes. Part of the reason was that the plan was designed to placate lobbyists representing the American Medical Association (AMA), which had derailed two decades of government health insurance proposals that contained cost controls and limits on procedures as "socialized medicine."

Desirous to pass the law without the opposition of the AMA, the plan did little to regulate the costs of medical care or the procedures that might be covered. As a result, medical providers were now paid primarily by insurance companies and the federal government, and they responded by raising their prices an estimated 14 percent per year. Unlike the free market where consumers pay directly and therefore shop for the best prices, recipients of Medicare and Medicaid cared little for the cost of service. Medicaid recipients had previously gone without medical service due to their inability to pay, but once the federal government assumed payment for emergency care, an increasing number of poor Americans went directly to emergency rooms for medical care. In addition, a handful of doctors set up clinics in poor neighborhoods, and these clinics routinely performed unnecessary and expensive tests on Medicaid clients as a way of defrauding the government.

FIGURE 11.9

Fannie Lou Hamer was one of the sharecroppers who registered to vote during the Freedom Summer of 1964. She was fired, evicted, arrested, and beaten while in prison for her efforts to register other black voters. She is pictured here representing the Mississippi Freedom Democratic Party at the 1964 Democratic National Convention in Atlantic City, New Jersey.

Voting Rights Act of 1965

A law intended to enforce the provisions and intent of the Fifteenth Amendment, which barred race as a reason for denying any US citizen the right to vote. The law gave the federal government the power to oversee elections and intervene if it believed that the rights of voters were being infringed.

FIGURE 11.10

Claudia Taylor Johnson, better known as "Lady Bird" Johnson, celebrates a Minnesota Head Start program with some of its students. The First Lady was active on behalf of a number of causes during her husband's administration and was also a successful business leader both before and after her tenure in the White House.

FIGURE 11.11

As a daughter of the Jim Crow South, civil rights leader Ella Baker devoted most of her efforts to challenging racism. However, Baker also believed that racism was a symptom of a larger social illness that kept people and communities from recognizing their common interests and working together to solve common problems.

The nation's increasing standard of living, expanded government programs for the poor, and even the rhetoric of civil rights activism were helping to create a culture of entitlement among many Americans. The notion that a certain minimum standard of living was a "right" that all Americans were entitled to increasingly gained currency throughout the 1960s. Most recipients of government aid in the United States ate meat every day and lived in homes with electricity, running water, and central heating. Each of these was a rare luxury in most nations, while the latter three were relatively new inventions. However, federal programs such as Aid to Families with Dependent Children operated through matching grants to states and therefore failed to provide any benefits to some of the poorest families in states that could not adequately subsidize the program. Still, conservative reservations about providing direct aid to the poor, combined with reported abuses of governmental assistance, led to relative declines in public support for Johnson's war on poverty.

One of the first casualties of the Great Society was the gradual defunding of community action agencies. Inspired by sociologists who identified a "culture of poverty" as the greatest enemy in Johnson's war, federal money was supposed to be directed to these local and autonomous community groups who would then decide how the money would be best spent. The law required that the poor themselves were supposed to lead these groups as much as possible, a provision Johnson hoped would help the poor to learn to help themselves. The provision was both simple and radical. If larger and larger numbers of poor people became engaged in their own welfare, the cycle of poverty might slowly grind to a halt.

Believing that ordinary people who mobilized in an organized, democratic, and meaningful manner might reinvent themselves and their communities, reformers and activists joined with the working poor to create a host of programs such as Head Start, which provided aid for education in poor communities. Many liberals hoped the Office of Economic Opportunity (OEO) would radically challenge the concept of democracy. As civil rights icon and community organizer Ella Baker explained, "In order for us as poor and oppressed people to become a part of a society that is meaningful, the system under which we now exist has to be radically changed." For Baker, this meant that the people must "learn to think in radical terms…getting down to and understanding the root cause" of their problems and "facing a system that does not lend itself to your needs and devising means by which you change that system."

However, those that hoped the OEO might breathe new life into poor neighborhoods and new meaning into the concept of democracy were disappointed by the limited funding that represented less than 1 percent of the federal budget and less than $230 for each of the 35 million poor Americans each year. At the same time, the decentralized nature of the plan also provided ample opportunity for mistakes or even fraud. All the rhetoric about these groups providing a "hand up instead of a handout" for the poor was quickly forgotten when a handful of those hands misappropriated funds. In addition, while the president portrayed himself as a modern-day FDR, Johnson increasingly focused his efforts on events overseas. Just as Truman's social programs were derailed by a war in Asia, efforts to contain the spread of Communism largely determined the outcome of Johnson's presidency after 1965.

2.4   Gulf of Tonkin and Escalation in Vietnam

Although the United States had been actively involved in Vietnam for over two decades, Southeastern Asia was still a peripheral interest to US officials until the mid-1960s when Communist forces under Ho Chi Minh appeared ready to take over the southern portion of the country. The growing power of Communist North Vietnam and the declining position of the US-backed government of South Vietnam led many officials to assume that the North's success was part of a Soviet and/or Chinese plot to spread Communism throughout the globe. In reality, China and the Soviet Union were antagonistic to one another and did not coordinate any substantial action regarding the situation in Vietnam. Ho Chi Minh did receive Soviet aid, but recent scholars have determined that the Soviet strategy was not based on the aggressive and expansionistic worldview US leaders feared. In fact, it appears the Soviets and Americans viewed events in Vietnam in very similar terms.

Americans shared deep reservations about supporting the non-Communist dictatorship of South Vietnam. The Soviets were equally hesitant to support the authoritarian regime led by Ho Chi Minh. Soviet leaders did not believe the North Vietnamese army or the Vietcong were true followers of Marxism and recoiled at the many human rights violations these troops committed. However, the Soviet Union had its own domino theory about what might happen if Communist governments such as Hanoi fell due to Western intervention. If they failed to support Ho Chi Minh as he battled the forces of Capitalism and imperialism, the Soviets asked, what message would this send to Communist leaders around the globe? The United States shared a similar global perspective in backing the South Vietnamese. So, fearing international consequences if they failed to act, both the United States and the Soviet Union backed regimes of which they were not enthusiastic supporters and hoped for the best. As a result, Vietnam turned from a civil war to determine the leadership of a newly independent country to a proxy war between the two superpowers neither wanted to fight.

The United States became increasingly reluctant to support the South Vietnamese after the Catholic Ngo Dinh Diem approved a series of raids against Buddhist monasteries in 1963. Diem believed that the Buddhist majority was hostile to his regime, and instead of seeking mediation, he used US military aid to his army to conduct mass arrests of Buddhist leaders. In response, the Kennedy administration conveyed the message to a handful of South Vietnamese military leaders known to share US reservations about Diem's leadership that the United States would support a coup if it meant removing Diem. Kennedy was personally hurt to find out that the result of the coup, which occurred two months after his message was conveyed, resulted in Diem's assassination.

The leadership of South Vietnam was transferred to the South Vietnamese military, which was equally corrupt and authoritarian. President Johnson continued to provide this government with military aid, largely due to a fear that failure to do so would lead to a North Vietnamese victory and vindicate Republican allegations that he was soft on Communism. The South used this aid to conduct raids on the North. As a result, the North viewed all South Vietnamese and US warships in the adjacent Gulf of Tonkin as enemies. When a handful of small North Vietnamese boats fired at but did not harm a US destroyer in August 1964, President Johnson requested congressional authority to respond militarily.

The actual attack on the US ship was miniscule and a second alleged attack may not have even occurred. However, Congress responded by almost unanimously approving the president's request in what came to be known as the **Gulf of Tonkin Resolution**. The American public was understandably outraged to hear of the "unprovoked" attacks on US servicemen in the Gulf and supported Congress's decision to grant Johnson's sweeping power "to repel (future) attacks…and prevent further aggression."

The public was never made aware that the destroyer in question was involved in an operation against the North Vietnamese. They were also not informed that South Vietnamese forces were launching nightly raids against the North using vessels given to them by the United States. Nor did the public believe that the resolution would later become the basis by which two US presidents would wage a war without a specific congressional declaration. The public did generally approve, however, of President Johnson's immediate actions following congressional approval of the Gulf of Tonkin Resolution. To show US resolve against the perceived threat of Communism in North Vietnam, the president approved aerial attacks against military targets and sent tens of thousands of troops to bases throughout the region.

The United States sent more than 150,000 troops by the end of 1965. Each of these soldiers soon shared complaints about the ineffectiveness of the South Vietnamese army they were sent to support. Consisting of mostly conscripted South Vietnamese troops who had little faith in their own government, the leading priority of these young men was to stay alive rather than confront communists. Even when given superior weapons and support, the South Vietnamese soldiers often dropped their weapons and ran when they confronted the Vietcong. US soldiers soon dubbed these South Vietnamese misadventures "search and evade" missions rather than the official moniker which was "search and destroy."

The Vietcong, in contrast, made up for its lack of equipment with a much stronger resolve to fight. US soldiers soon developed a grudging respect for these "VCs" as they were called. Many of the VC leaders were veterans of the long fight for independence from France and Japan. This core group of an estimated 60,000 guerilla warriors was augmented by 100,000 to 200,000 more civilians who exchanged plowshares for rifles throughout the year and then returned to peasant farming. Known by dozens of inhuman epithets, the Vietcong soon became known by a more human moniker as soldiers using the military alphabet referred to "VC" as "Victor Charlie" and eventually just "Charlie."

The Vietcong and North Vietnamese were generally very familiar with the local terrain, placed thousands of deadly traps throughout the jungle, and utilized hit-and-run guerilla warfare against the US and South Vietnamese troops. They also disguised themselves as local villagers and forced many

FIGURE 11.12

A South Vietnamese soldier guards a young boy who was believed to have participated in an attack against US and South Vietnamese forces. The Vietcong recruited women, children, and the elderly in their guerilla war against the South and the United States.

Gulf of Tonkin Resolution

A nearly unanimous congressional approval of Lyndon Johnson's request to use his authority as commander in chief to escalate military operations in Vietnam. The Resolution was passed after limited debate following a series of reported attacks on US warships in the Gulf of Tonkin.

civilians to join them. Even women and children regularly carried weapons and used them against US and South Vietnamese forces. As a result it was nearly impossible to distinguish between civilians and soldiers in a war where villages became part of the battlefield.

General William Westmoreland recognized all of these challenges, yet believed that more troops, more bombing raids, and more supplies would eventually wear down the enemy. After all, he believed, the United States enjoyed superior technology and possessed immense resources the North Vietnamese army (NVA) could not compete against. Even Ho Chi Minh agreed with this assessment of superior US material resources, but believed that the ideological commitment of his supporters would mitigate the difference. "You can kill ten of our men for every one we kill of yours," Ho allegedly communicated to a French adversary in the 1940s. "But even at those odds, you will lose and we will win."

While it should be mentioned that authenticity of the previous quote cannot be verified, the statement accurately reflects the way both US and Communist forces fought throughout the Vietnam War. General Westmoreland and other US officials focused on exterminating the NVA and VC rather than the more conventional military strategy of taking and holding ground. The NVA and VC, on the other hand, recognized that they would seldom inflict more casualties on the enemy given their disadvantages. They often demonstrated a fatalistic resolve to continue the war, despite heavy losses. Part of this devotion was ideological and reflected an individual's conviction that Ho Chi Minh was leading his nation in a fight for independence from outside influence. At the same time, the VC and NVA used extreme coercion against those who opposed them, including their own recruits. VC and NVA who refused orders, or even civilian villagers who cooperated with the United States and South Vietnamese were often executed.

2.5   Combat in Vietnam

Hoping to demonstrate US resolve and firepower, as well as convince the South Vietnamese that they could defeat the North with US assistance, Johnson ordered a sustained bombing campaign in March 1965. Known as **Operation Rolling Thunder**, the bombing lasted until the fall of 1968. The damage to the North Vietnamese countryside was supposed to be limited to military targets, yet it was difficult to prevent civilian casualties in a nation where the line between civilians and military was impossible to determine from the air. Most historians charge the US military with willful indifference regarding the issue of civilian casualties during Operation Rolling Thunder.

In many respects, US planners made little effort to draw this distinction between civilians and combatants in most of the wars of the twentieth century. Much like the bombing campaigns of the later years of World War II, cities were targeted in a failed effort to crush the will of the North Vietnamese military leaders. Large areas of South Vietnam were also targeted. The US military declared certain areas believed to harbor NVA and VC troops "free fire zones" and used every nonatomic weapon in its arsenal to destroy every living thing in those zones. By the end of the war, 14 billion pounds of explosives had been dropped on Vietnam, roughly 500 pounds of explosives per man, woman, and child. These bombing raids failed in their objective to end North Vietnam's ability to launch attacks on the South. They also failed to win support for the already unpopular South Vietnamese government among the people of Vietnam.

One of the leading reasons for America's aerial strategy was that President Johnson recognized that a land-based offensive against North Vietnam would result in tremendous US casualties. And so the bombing campaigns continued through 1968, and then escalated under President Nixon. Military leaders promised that each new bombing campaign would either convince Hanoi to end its attacks or limit the power of the North. The bombing of cities and villages had historically proven to be an ineffective method of waging war. The only exception to this rule—the use of nuclear weapons—was discussed and rejected by military and civilian leaders throughout the United States. Instead, US commanders hoped that their strategy of combined arms—aerial bombardment and traditional ground forces—would eventually wear down the VC and NVA.

By 1967, Westmoreland commanded half a million troops in Vietnam. The VC and NVA, however, used Fabian tactics of avoiding pitched battles they knew they could not win in a similar effort to wear down their enemy. US commanders responded by waging war on the countryside that was supplying the enemy. The military used napalm, an extremely flammable agent, as well as the chemical defoliant Agent Orange to destroy the 10 million square miles of jungle that provided cover for the VC. The devastation on the ecosystem was tremendous, and agents were also used directly against the fields that both the civilian population and the VC depended upon for food. This destroyed the local economy, a calculated measure that the United States hoped would eliminate the possibility of VC and NVA troops raiding local food supplies.

General William Westmoreland

US Army general and commander of US forces in Vietnam between 1964 and 1968. Westmoreland's strategy was based on his belief that the United States must escalate the war and overwhelm the North Vietnamese and Vietcong through superior firepower and resolve. He believed that the United States was wearing down the enemy and regularly provided exaggerated numbers of enemy killed in battle and underestimated the continued strength of the VC in ways that led many to question his leadership following the Tet Offensive.

Operation Rolling Thunder

A sustained bombing campaign that dropped more ordnance on targets throughout Vietnam between 1965 and 1968 than was delivered by all belligerents through the entire course of World War II.

FIGURE 11.13

A massive B-66 bomber accompanies four F-105s in a July 1966 mission during Operation Rolling Thunder. The F-105 was a fighter jet that could also drop 14,000 pounds of explosives.

Recognizing that napalm and Agent Orange would also eliminate the ability of peasants to grow crops and likely drive many to support Communist North Vietnam, the United States also provided humanitarian aid meant to guarantee the loyalty of villagers. US commanders even considered the possibility of destroying dams and flooding the entire countryside as a means of holding the entire nation hostage and forcing North Vietnamese leaders to end the war on US terms. However, these more bellicose military leaders were overruled, and the United States continued its "limited" campaigns against the North and the free fire zones of the South. The war on the countryside proved ineffective, and humanitarian aid was just as easily smuggled to or captured by the VC as the food that had previously been grown by the peasant majority. In addition, the 3 million Vietnamese in refugee camps recognized the cause of their dependency on US aid and were even more likely to sympathize with the North.

By 1967, the nation was beginning to divide on the question of Vietnam. Antiwar protests attracted only a few hundred supporters throughout 1965, but by 1967, those who opposed the war had created a movement and tens of thousands were attending protests. Most Americans still supported the war effort and viewed these protests as unpatriotic and disrespectful to the US soldiers. Many of these individuals believed that the only logical and honorable solution was to increase troop strength and intensify bombing until North Vietnam was forced to surrender.

Some protesters responded by modifying their message to emphasize their desire to support the troops by bringing them home. Others took the offensive by challenging those who favored escalation to explain how more bombing might lead to surrender and asking exactly to whom they thought the North might surrender. After all, they reminded their opponents, the United States had still not declared war and the South Vietnamese government was viewed by most Vietnamese as illegitimate. Martin Luther King increasingly came to oppose the war as the only consistent position for an advocate of nonviolence. He also feared the war diverted resources that might have been used to aggressively fund antipoverty programs. By the final year of his life, King declared that The Great Society was "shot down on the battlefields of Vietnam."

FIGURE 11.14

President Johnson reacts emotionally to a tape sent to him by his son-in-law, a captain and a commander of a company of US Marines in Vietnam.

3. "MORE THAN A HAMBURGER:" CIVIL RIGHTS AND SOCIAL JUSTICE

LEARNING OBJECTIVES

1. Explain how the civil rights movement was similar and different in the Deep South, Border South, and the North and West. Explain how ethnicity and race were related in the quest for equal rights in the American Southwest.

2. Ella Baker repeatedly tried to explain that the sit-ins of the 1960s were about "more than a hamburger," despite the immediate goal of being served at lunch counters. Explain what she meant and what strategies she and other college students used to achieve their goals.

3. Summarize what Stokely Carmichael meant when he and others spoke of Black Power. Explain how the Black Power movement emerged out of the civil rights movement of the late 1960s.

3.1 Race and the Urban North

In the years following World War II, nearly 5 million African Americans and nearly as many whites migrated from the primarily rural South to Northern cities in search of greater economic opportunity. As was true of previous migration to the North, these families were influenced by both "push" and "pull" factors. The push factors—considerations that induced Southerners to leave the South—included racial segregation for black families and scarce funding for public schools for both whites and blacks. Perhaps more importantly, the invention of a mechanical cotton picker in 1944 had resulted in larger and larger numbers of both white and black sharecroppers being evicted each year from plantations they had lived and worked on for years. The pull factors—those things that attracted migrants to the North—included higher wages, better schools, and for African Americans the absence of legally enforced segregation. In fact, many Northern states had passed laws outlawing racial segregation in schools and public accommodations.

As had been the case with the Great Migration of the 1910s and 1920s, Southern blacks found most housing closed to them. Millions of Southern white sharecroppers likewise found few options they could afford. The government began constructing public housing projects, intending to both relieve overcrowding and provide affordable housing. Yet these projects faced a number of obstacles that limited their effectiveness. The private housing industry recognized that government-subsidized housing would reduce overall demand as many potential homeowners would choose federally subsidized apartments. As a result, people representing the housing industry secured regulations making public housing only eligible for the lowest-income families, meaning that housing projects were occupied exclusively by the urban poor. This stigma led middle-class and suburban neighborhoods to oppose the construction of housing projects in their neighborhoods as harbingers of crime and other urban problems. As a result, public housing was built only in existing poor neighborhoods and concentrated poverty in inner cities.

The increase in minority and poor migration to the city intensified existing patterns of migration out of the city by white and middle-class residents. This phenomenon was labeled "**white flight**" and altered more than the racial composition of America's cities. When the more affluent abandoned the city, the total tax revenue that was previously available to finance the operation of America's largest cities rapidly declined. Suburban governments and school systems were suddenly flush with cash and able to attract new employers to the periphery of the city, further depressing the city core. Suburbanization also hid the problems of the urban and rural poor by insulating residents of affluent suburbs from the decaying schools, unemployment, crime, substance abuse, and other problems that were more prevalent in poverty-stricken areas.

Housing shortages, white flight, and ghettoization were especially felt within the cities of the Midwest and East Coast. The issue affected dozens of minorities, from African Americans and Mexican Americans to new arrivals from Asia and Latin America. For nonwhites of all shades, the North reflected author Gordon Parks's poignant description of his hometown, "where freedom loosed one hand, while custom restrained the other." Parks grew up on a farm near Fort Scott, Kansas, very near the spot where the a black regiment fought Confederates even though the Union had not yet accepted black men in the military. Consistent with the observations of Alexis de Tocqueville long before the Civil War, Parks's 1963 autobiographical novel *The Learning Tree* revealed that racial prejudice was often strongest in the places that had rejected slavery.

In cities throughout the North and the West, ambitious speculators profited from the racial fears of whites and the limited housing options of minorities through a practice known as **blockbusting**. When a minority family successfully purchased a home in a previously all-white neighborhood, blockbusters exploited the anxiety of whites through rumors that many of their neighbors were also selling their homes and moving to the suburbs. Rumors became self-fulfilling prophesies as white residents quickly sold their homes to speculators for a fraction of their value.

Given the lack of decent housing available to African Americans and other minorities, these speculators could charge far more than the original value of the home because they represented the only option for middle-class minority families anxious to move out of the inner cities and segregated barrios. Tens of thousands of minority families purchased these homes each year, escalating white flight to the suburbs. Not all whites fled their neighborhoods, and some even welcomed their new neighbors, resulting in genuine interracial friendships that would have been unlikely to occur a generation earlier. But for thousands of minority families, moving to a primarily white neighborhood meant ostracism and even violence. Hundreds of homes in cities from Baltimore to Los Angeles and even Chicago and Minneapolis burned to the ground each year as a "gentle reminder" that nonwhite families had better know their place.

"Knowing one's place" was a phrase used in the South to describe the acceptable range of low-status occupations and self-effacing attitudes that blacks were expected to maintain. As demonstrated by blockbusting and violence against property, the word "place" demonstrated the demand for geographical separation in the North. Black residents of Northern cities were made to understand that "place" would not be designated by signs barring their entrance to a theater or a restaurant. Instead, they were expected to somehow know where they were and were not welcome. Officially an integrated society, black residents in the North and West faced more pervasive residential segregation, and the resulting separate neighborhoods meant that the schools of these cities were often more segregated than those of the Deep South by 1970. Blacks also faced extreme discrimination on the job market outside of black-owned businesses. Even within primarily black neighborhoods such as Harlem in New York City and Watts in Los Angeles, black men and women could not find employment in many stores located in their all-black neighborhoods. They also faced daily harassment from the majority-white police.

In 1964, an off-duty police officer shot and killed a fifteen-year-old boy who was chasing a white man in Harlem. What should have been a minor affair (the man had sprayed the boy with a water hose) quickly escalated into a race riot when news of the boy's death circulated throughout Harlem, an area that was already angry due to previous incidents and the city's disinclination to hire black officers. The following year, Watts erupted in flames after similar tensions led a simple traffic stop to escalate into a major altercation. More than one hundred race riots erupted in 1967, with black residents venting similar frustrations against racist police, lack of job opportunity, residential segregation, and continued poverty.

Black leaders such as Malcolm X who lived in Northern cities and understood these frustrations became increasingly effective in mobilizing African Americans beyond the South. Born in Omaha, Malcolm Little's earliest memories included his family home having crosses burnt in the yard for his father's leadership in local civil rights organizations and his support of Marcus Garvey. As an adult, Malcolm replaced his given last name with "X" because he recognized that his ancestors were assigned the last name of their master and he wanted to remind himself and others of the family history that was taken from all African Americans in the process. After years of being discouraged by white teachers, Malcolm went from being the most promising student in his otherwise all-white class to the trouble-maker that his teachers expected him to be. While in prison, Malcolm discovered the **Nation of Islam**, a black nationalist religious sect that followed the teachings of Elijah Muhammad. Given the prominence of Islam throughout parts of Africa, Malcolm embraced Muhammad's conservative teachings and believed that Islam was the natural religion of black Americans.

When speaking to black audiences and responding to accusations that he and the Nation of Islam were teaching hate, **Malcolm X** often responded by pointing out that white racism was inherently hateful. He described the way the media, society, and the educational system caused black children to grow up being ashamed of their history, culture, and even their physical appearance. "Who taught you to hate yourself?" Malcolm challenged his audiences. "Before you come asking Mr. Muhammad does he teach hate, you should ask yourself who taught you to hate being what God made you."

In another speech, he discussed the way Africa was misrepresented and marginalized and the way this miseducation led to internalization of racism among people of African descent. "You can't hate the roots of a tree," Malcolm explained, "without hating the tree." For Malcolm X, the roots were the history and culture of Africa that so many African Americans had grown to despise after years of miseducation. Like Carter Woodson and other black educators of previous generations, Malcolm recognized that the failure to teach African subjects in schools led generations of white and black Americans to assume that Africa was void of cultural and historical relevance. Given the media's portrayal of Africa as backward and even savage, Malcolm X explained, it was only natural that black and white children assumed that Africans were inferior to Europeans in ways that reinforced white supremacy in America.

3.2   Black Power and Black Panthers

Following the passage of the 1965 Voting Rights Act, most white Americans reported their belief that problems of racial inequality had been sufficiently addressed. Black leaders countered by chronicling the persistence of de facto segregation in schools and neighborhoods. Even more troubling, they explained, was the continuation of economic inequality. As was usually the case, no one spoke more plainly on this subject than Malcolm X. "I've got a plate in front of me," Malcolm began, "but nothing is on it. Because all of us are sitting at the same table, are all of us diners?"

Malcolm's culinary reference was an intentional jab at those who believed the end of segregated lunch counters had somehow erased centuries of economic inequality. "I'm not a diner until you let me dine. Just being at the table with others who are dining doesn't make me a diner, and this is what you've got to get in your head here in this country. Just because you're in this country doesn't make you an American." Malcolm then discomforted many by likening black America to a colony of the imperialist white America. His economic reference to a people who performed labor for a mere pittance of those in power hit home for many listeners. "You've got to enjoy the fruits of Americanism," he continued. "You haven't enjoyed those fruits. You've enjoyed the thorns. You've enjoyed the thistles. But you have not enjoyed the fruits, no sir. You have fought harder for the fruits than the white man has, you have worked harder for the fruits than the white man has, but you've enjoyed less."

Nation of Islam

A small religious sect under the leadership of Elijah Muhammad, who spread his version of the Muslim faith to African Americans. The sect grew rapidly due to the charisma of NOI leader Malcolm X until Elijah Muhammad expelled him for critical remarks about Muhammad's leadership and his insistence on talking about political matters.

FIGURE 11.15

Martin Luther King Jr. and Malcolm X met only once, on March 26, 1964. The two men briefly exchanged pleasantries and never saw one another again. Although they are often portrayed as opposites, in many ways the more radical approach of Malcolm X assisted King.

Malcolm X

A radical black leader of the Nation of Islam, in the last year of his life Malcolm ended his affiliation with the Nation of Islam and spoke more favorably of the possibility of interracial cooperation; however, he was assassinated by supporters of the Nation of Islam in Harlem in 1965. It is probable that the FBI knew at least some of the details about the planned assassination as they were tracking both Malcolm and the men who killed him.

Most white Americans, including many who considered themselves liberal on issues of civil rights, failed to recognize why Malcolm did not share their belief that the goals of the civil rights movement had been achieved with the passage of the 1964 Civil Rights Act. As a result, the movement started to fracture along racial lines by 1965. In early June 1966, James Meredith began his solitary March Against Fear from Memphis to Jackson, Mississippi, to publicize the persistence of segregation and disenfranchisement despite federal law. Thirty miles into his 220-mile journey, a white supremacist unleashed three volleys from a shotgun that would have killed Meredith had it not been for reporters and FBI agents who were following his march.

Meredith had become a household name four years prior when he integrated the University of Mississippi. As a result, members of the black community along with SCLC, SNCC, the NAACP, and CORE decided to continue Meredith's march. Despite the growing disagreements between some of the leaders of these organizations, they decided to unite in an effort to publicize the attempted murder of James Meredith and remind the United States that most black residents in the Deep South were still denied the ballot and other basic rights. After three emotional weeks, the march concluded successfully and was capped off when a recovering James Meredith joined a crowd that had grown to 12,000 as it arrived in Jackson on June 26.

Divisions had already existed between these four leading civil rights organizations, with the NAACP and the clergy-dominated SCLC being more conservative than the youthful CORE and SNCC. The leaders of the organizations worked hard to compromise with one another during a series of marches and protests throughout Mississippi that summer, but the divisions were becoming more pronounced. During a march of 10,000 to 15,000 participants to Jackson, Mississippi, the group transitioned from singing "We Shall Overcome" to chanting "We Want Black Power" as the demonstrators tired of being tormented and arrested.

While still embracing nonviolence, the change demonstrated the frustrations of black Southerners who were tiring of begging whites for acceptance. Black Power was a slogan seized upon by new SNCC leader **Stokely Carmichael** and reflected a desire to support black candidates rather than beg whites to let them vote for other whites. Black Power reflected a desire to form black-owned companies rather than facing discrimination by the few white bosses that would even consider hiring them at any level. Black Power meant standing up for black institutions rather than praying for the day when whites would permit them to join their own as second-class citizens. Even in Mississippi, the ideas and fiery rhetoric of SNCC's Stokely Carmichael were beginning to eclipse those of King and the SCLC.

Following the march to Jackson, a visibly shaken King explained his belief that without tangible victories, the movement he helped to create might eventually turn away from nonviolence. "The government has got to give me some victories if I'm going to keep people nonviolent," he explained. "I know I'm going to stay nonviolent no matter what happens. But a lot of people are getting hurt and bitter, and they can't see it that way anymore." King also sought to remind listeners that many whites were committed to black freedom while also working to reassure whites that the movement did not threaten them or their interests. King's attempts to bring all sides together made him vulnerable to more militant leaders like Malcolm X and Stokely Carmichael. However, by King's perspective, the internal divisions among various leaders and participants in the march only helped Mississippi "get off the hook" for its continued repression of blacks, regardless of which organizational button they wore.

The year 1966 was also when Bobby Seale and Huey P. Newton formed the Black Panther Party for Self Defense. Named after a black-led political party that had defended the rights of black voters in Lowndes County, Alabama, the **Black Panthers** believed that the black freedom movement needed to be more militant if it was to convince whites to end their racist patterns of behavior. Black men in Oakland rallied to the Panthers due to the irresponsiveness of city leaders to demands for basic services, such as a traffic light at a busy intersection where several black youths had been killed by speeding vehicles. They also demanded an end to police brutality and took the extreme measure of arming themselves and patrolling their own neighborhoods. Citing the Second Amendment and becoming intimately familiar with local gun ordinances, the Panthers marched through black neighborhoods across the nation by 1967, wearing their signature black sunglasses, black leather jackets, and black berets.

Opponents argued that the organization's chief appeal was its aggressive posturing and fiery rhetoric. Organizer Huey P. Newton was arrested in October 1967 for killing a police officer. Citing the police harassment that led to the deadly confrontation, Panther supporters launched a campaign to "Free Huey" that enraged those who already viewed the Panthers as dangerous. Some young men were surely attracted to the Panthers for the wrong reasons, however, Stanford University's Black Panther Party Research Project has identified over sixty community service programs that were organized by local Panther chapters in California alone. One of the most successful Panther projects was the operation of free breakfast programs in nearly every major city. For tens of thousands of inner-city youths, school lunches were the only nutritious meal they could count on receiving. Long before school breakfast programs were established, the Panthers rose early each morning to fix a nutritious breakfast for children in neighborhoods throughout America. As the children ate, the young men sat and talked with them about the importance of black pride and education. For those who opposed the Panthers, the breakfast and afterschool programs seemed little more than indoctrination.

Categorized by the FBI as a "radical" or "subversive" group, the Panthers lost the opportunity to receive federal and state funding that was commonly distributed to other nonprofit organizations that also operated free health clinics and community centers for youths. At the same time, the Panthers' open brandishing of weapons combined with the often-violent rhetoric of some of the more infamous Panther leaders could inflame tensions. The media seized upon each incident where an individual Panther violated the founding principle of being nonviolent with those who were nonviolent as a handful of Panther leaders were found guilty of crimes. However, considering the aggressive efforts of local police and the FBI to monitor the daily activities of each Black Panther, the fact that so few Panthers were arrested and even fewer convicted of any crime challenges one to reconsider the FBI's assumption that this was a subversive group. At the same time, one must also question whether the Panther's often deliberate antagonizing of city officials was also partly to blame for the group's troubles.

Believing the organization to be subversive, the FBI spent hundreds of thousands of dollars to thwart the Panthers' activities. One of the most costly surveillance efforts included the use of paid informants as the FBI hired black men to infiltrate and disrupt the activities of their local Panther chapters. Among the reasons cited as evidence of the Black Panthers' insurrectionary activity was their support of Communist doctrine. Panthers had sold books by Chairman Mao to students attending Berkeley University, but this was largely to raise funds to purchase weapons rather than a reflection of political orientation.

White suburban college students likewise seldom supported the ideas and actions of the belligerent Chinese dictator, but like the Panthers, they sought to cast themselves in the revolutionary image of the era. Both groups also sought authentic experience beyond their insular worlds but never fully grasped what the other might offer their struggle. Berkeley students could hardly claim the mantle of revolutionary when all their friends were white and middle class. Students started carrying Mao's little red book in their pocket to demonstrate their authenticity and hip worldliness, a symbol they had transcended race and class by supporting their "black friends" from the ghetto. Rich in authenticity but lacking access to money and power, black inner-city youths likewise viewed the other as a means to achieve their short-term goal. Had the two groups been able to exchange more than books and currency on the day the Black Panthers went to Berkeley, the goal of both groups to "speak truth to power" might have been realized.

FIGURE 11.17

Many states had no laws against openly carrying and displaying firearms until the Black Panther Party began using weapons in their demonstrations. In this photo, members of a Seattle Black Panther chapter stand on the steps of the statehouse in Olympia, Washington. They are protesting a bill that would make it illegal to openly display firearms.

3.3 SDS and the New Left

In 1962, a small group of college-aged activists met in Port Huron, Michigan, and created an organization called the **Students for a Democratic Society (SDS)**. They issued the Port Huron Statement, which called for greater participation in the process of government. The statement acknowledged the "modest comfort" most of their members enjoyed, which contrasted with the world they were inheriting where poverty was rampant even in wealthy nations like the United States while famine and civil war raged across the globe.

Like the "Old Left" of assorted Marxists, the New Left supported the emerging civil rights movement. However, the New Left believed in free markets and recognized the authoritarian drift of the leading Communist regimes. Instead, the New Left called for "participatory democracy" through increased activism. New Left student activists believed this would lead not only to shared campus governance but also to a federal government that was more responsive to the needs of the common people. Of course, few of the leftists of early twentieth-century America were Communists. In this uniquely American and moderate leftist tradition, the New Left of the 1960s continued the call for increased social spending while adding their own modern challenge to the logic of the Cold War and escalating military budgets. Believing that universities and students had a unique role in spreading this message and promoting participatory democracy, the Port Huron Statement challenged college students to become leaders of grassroots movements for a wide range of causes.

Although a number of SDS chapters were formed throughout the United States, these groups went largely unnoticed until 1964 when students at the University of California in Berkeley launched the Free Speech Movement. Students at Berkeley believed that the administration of their school had betrayed the liberal traditions of the university with its increasing ties to defense contractors. They were even more upset at the way their protests against the Vietnam War had seemingly fallen upon deaf ears. The Vietnam War galvanized many otherwise disparate groups in what would become the New Left, a coalition of organizations and activists who hoped to radicalize the populace beyond the liberal consensus of the late 1950s and 1960s. Whereas liberals accepted the basic premise of the Cold War and agreed with conservatives that Communism must be contained by armed force, if necessary, the New Left called for immediate withdrawal from Vietnam. Liberals supported moderate civil rights

Students for a Democratic Society (SDS)

A controversial student organization that grew in response to its members protests against the Vietnam War. SDS grew to hundreds of chapters but soon divided among themselves regarding issues related to race and civil rights activism.

reform, such as ending segregation and enforcing voting rights for all. The New Left did not believe that laws alone were sufficient to remedy past injustices.

Because New Left groups like SDS were often strongest at elite universities, its adherents were often denigrated by critics as spoiled children of affluence who were ungrateful for the sacrifices of those who had survived the Great Depression and fought in World War II. Despite this image, SDS expanded to smaller universities and community colleges. Members of SDS were often members of SNCC and other civil rights organizations that became more radical in the late 1960s. As a result, SDS chapters moved toward direct confrontations with authority in ways that increasingly led to direct conflict with one another.

SDS members often divided on complex issues and also disagreed about how to best confront the persistence of racism and poverty. Rather than explore these divisions, the group rallied around one message that unified its supporters: end the Vietnam War. SDS held national protests against the war that attracted 20,000 participants in the spring of 1965. By the end of 1967, the SDS had 300 chapters. The SDS-sponsored protests in the nation's capital were attracting nearly 100,000 participants. SDS chapters also held "teach-ins" on hundreds of campuses where students and faculty discussed the history and culture of Vietnam. The intent was usually to find ways to counter the image that Southeastern Asia was little more than a domino or a pawn on a Cold War chessboard.

Many of these teach-ins and other protests were held at universities that refused to recognize the legitimacy of SDS on their campus and threatened to expel its participants. Because LBJ had granted draft deferment to any college student in good academic standing, expulsion meant that an SDS member might be drafted. By October 1967, however, students and other activists expanded their protests. Some even began to shun nonviolence while others engaged in direct confrontations with draft boards. Some SDS members even attempted to take over a military draft induction center in Oakland. The resulting violent confrontation with police galvanized many against the protesters. However, by the end of 1967, support for the war had dropped to 58 percent of the US public.

3.4 Feminism and Civil Rights

In the near term, most feminists celebrated the 1964 Civil Rights Act that banned both racial and gender discrimination in employment and created the EEOC to enforce the law's provisions. Others worried that the scattered provisions that protected women from being fired for pregnancy might become endangered. Still others were concerned that the law would not be enforced at all. As discussed previously, the original version of the act did not include gender until it was amended by Southern congressmen as an attempt to divide the law's supporters. Although several leading members of Congress spoke in favor of this amendment and the act passed with its provisions against gender discrimination, most members of the EEOC believed that enforcing this part of the act would detract from their ability to investigate "more serious cases" dealing with racial discrimination. For the first few years of the EEOC's existence, the organization only half-heartedly pursued complaints regarding gender discrimination, even though they composed over one-third of the cases submitted.

National Organization for Women (NOW)

Formed to enforce the gender equality provisions of the 1964 Civil Rights Act, NOW quickly became one of the leading feminist organizations and sought to eradicate gender discrimination and advance a variety of women's causes.

Many feminists agreed that history of gender discrimination paled in comparison to centuries of racial oppression. "For every discrimination that has been made against a woman in this country," explained Oregon congresswoman Edith Green, "there has been ten times as much discrimination against the Negro." Yet Green and others made it clear that racial discrimination did not lessen the severity of gender discrimination or excuse the federal government for discounting its consequences. Black women added that the EEOC must enforce provisions against gender discrimination to protect their rights because it was impossible to distinguish where one form of discrimination ended and the other began. No law could assure the rights of black women, they explained, unless the practice of categorizing labor in terms of either race or gender were defined as an act of discrimination instead of tolerated on the grounds of tradition. In response to the reluctance of the federal government to enforce the 1964 Civil Rights Act as it related to gender, hundreds of women convened a meeting in 1966 that led to the founding of the **National Organization for Women (NOW)**.

Many women had taken active roles in the civil rights movement and the antiwar protests. Both movements inspired large numbers of women to speak out about their causes, but the movements were generally run by men. These leaders did not think that women could be effective leaders and often just brushed them aside when they wanted to have a voice in the movement's direction. This type of treatment was common. Many women began to band together to discuss their feelings about the way they were being treated. The more these groups networked, the more they found out that other women across the nation shared their experiences and perspectives. Author and activist **Shulamith Firestone** was told by a male antiwar activist, "Move on little girl; we have more important issues to talk about here than women's liberation." Firestone would later publish *The Dialectic of Sex: The Case for Feminist Revolution*, which argued that the paternalism of the traditional American family structure was the foundation of gender oppression.

"There is no overt anti-feminism in our society," wrote feminist scholar Alice Rossi in 1964, "not because sex equality has been achieved, but because there is practically no feminist spark left among American women." Rossi wrote that few if any of even the brightest women she taught in her college classes had plans or even the ambition to pursue a career, instead pinning their hopes on a male suitor who may or may not share their own talent and ambition. The events of the next few years would prove that Rossi's estimation of the women's movement was too pessimistic. At the same time, the revival of the women's movement may have been inspired by Rossi's challenging rhetoric.

The movement was certainly fueled by Rossi's efforts beyond the classroom. She and author Betty Friedan helped to found the National Organization of Women (NOW), with Friedan serving as the group's first president. Like every major women's organization in the past, NOW pursued multiple issues that sought to improve the quality of women's lives in tangible ways while also seeking to promote a more radical agenda.

Some NOW members were initially attracted to the organization by programs such as child care centers and educational programs. Not yet ready to buy into the notion of broad social change, many women joined NOW to share the burdens and obligations of childrearing while networking with other women. Before long, these women were attending meetings and talking about the other obstacles in their lives, such as gender discrimination. Similar to the way that participants in Freedom Schools originally sought tangible goals such as learning to read, members of NOW often joined the women's movement for the tangible benefits offered by child care centers and other programs. In both cases, participants soon began to realize their own empowerment through collective action.

As NOW grew, it also created an infrastructure that was enlisted against the practice of explicit gender segregation and pay differentials. NOW also mobilized to challenge more subtle forms of discrimination from employers and the federal government. NOW lobbied the Equal Employment Opportunity Commission, reminding it of its duty to enforce the terms of the 1964 Civil Rights Act. It also lobbied federal and state governments for support for child-care centers. NOW members also petitioned in favor of laws that would punish employers for practicing discrimination against pregnant employees. While organizing against the termination of pregnant women united NOW members, the issue of terminating pregnancies was divisive in the 1960s. By the 1970s however, the legalization of abortion would be one of the leading issues of many NOW supporters.

Shulamith Firestone

A leading figure in a number of leading feminist organizations, such as the New York Radical Women who launched the famous protest against the 1968 Miss America Pageant. Firestone is the author of the influential book *The Dialectic of Sex*, which served as a theoretical base for many early feminists as well as fodder for those who opposed her ideas. Firestone clearly articulated a connection between male-dominated family structures and gender inequality. Less well-received were some of her theoretical solutions, which included the abolition of natural pregnancy and communal alternatives to the traditional family structure.

FIGURE 11.18

Two of the most famous protests against stereotypical views of women and rigid standards of physical beauty occurred during the 1968 and 1969 Miss America pageants in Atlantic City, New Jersey. Feminists invited women to dump cosmetics, high-heeled shoes, and other objects sold by the beauty industry into a "Freedom Trash Can." Some protesters held signs likening the contest to a livestock competition while others affirmed the beauty of all women.

3.5 Civil Rights Beyond Black and White

Although it was less noticed than many of the mid-1960s civil rights bills, the **Hart-Cellar Act of 1965** would have a tremendous impact on US conceptions of diversity. Immigrants composed only 5 percent of the population at this time. Immigration quotas prior to 1965 heavily favored immigrants from Western European nations. The new law ended these quotas, as well as provisions against Asian immigration.

At the same time, some supporters of the law sought to limit the number of Hispanic immigrants to the United States. The 1965 act placed an annual limit of 20,000 immigrants from any particular nation and capped the permissible immigration of people from the Western Hemisphere at 120,000 per year. The act also placed an annual limit of 170,000 immigrants from the Eastern Hemisphere.

Whereas previous immigration laws banned Communists from coming to the United States, the new law sought to demonstrate the superiority of America's Capitalist system by encouraging an unlimited number of residents of Communist nations to seek "refuge" in America. This law would not result in the predicted immigration of Eastern Europeans, but would frequently be invoked for residents of Southeastern Asia in the following decade. The law also encouraged immigrants with certain valuable skills, such as doctors, nurses, and engineers, to come to the United States. It also provided measures to ease the immigration of family members, even if this meant exceeding the annual quota.

FIGURE 11.19

Cesar Chavez and Dolores Huerta led the United Farm Workers (UFW) in protesting the wages and conditions faced by migrant farm workers. The most effective protests were those that combined strikes (*huelga* in Spanish) with consumer boycotts of lettuce, grapes, and other crops that were grown by employers who refused to work with the UFW.

The law received its first test when Castro ended his prohibition against Cubans leaving the island. Soon, hundreds of thousands of Cubans with American relatives were able to come to the United States. Many experienced prejudice but found strength in family networks and the vast number of fellow Cubans who chose to live in the Miami, Florida, area. The total Hispanic population of the United States tripled during the 1960s from an estimated 3 to 9 million residents. This growing population found inspiration in the community and church orientation of the Black Freedom struggle and common ground with those who experienced discrimination because of their race or ethnicity. In 1967, Latino activists formed the Mexican American Legal Defense and Educational Fund in San Antonio. This organization partnered with the NAACP to support civil rights litigation dealing with equal employment and housing, racial profiling and police brutality, and equal opportunity in education.

One of the most pressing issues in the Southwest was the continued segregation of Mexican American students. In Corpus Christi, Texas, white children were bused out of school districts with large Mexican American populations. The result was that most white and Mexican American children in the city attended schools that were segregated in every way but name. In addition, the "white" schools refused to hire any black or Mexican American faculty. Jose Cisneros and two dozen other Mexican American families sued the school district of Corpus Christi, Texas, in 1968. The court agreed that school officials deliberately sought to maintain separate schools for children of Mexican origin and ordered the school board to reverse strategies that had been used to delay integration.

Poster copyright United Farm Workers

Latino activist **Cesar Chavez** demonstrated the connection between ethnicity and class by exposing the conditions Americans of Mexican origin faced in their new home. The son of a migrant farm family, Chavez was well acquainted with the tribulations of agricultural workers throughout the West. Chavez and Dolores Huerta formed the United Farm Workers (UFW) to unionize migrant workers and demand fair employment contracts. When California growers refused to work with the union, Chavez sought to use the same techniques utilized by the Montgomery Improvement Association to force the growers to work with the union. Recognizing that migrant workers were vulnerable to exploitation precisely because of their lack of economic resources, Chavez organized migrant workers across the nation to influence consumer behavior. It was only when the workers convinced enough US consumers to only purchase wine and grapes from growers who recognized the union that the UFW began to make an impact. By 1970, the combination of labor strikes and consumer boycotts forced two dozen grape growers to recognize the union and sign contracts approved by labor representatives.

Native Americans continued their protests against the federal government's policy of termination, culminating in the 1961 Declaration of Indian Purpose by the National Council of American Indians. This document expressed the desire of tribes to maintain self-determination and the demands for greater economic opportunities. The **American Indian Movement (AIM)** was formed in 1963 to pursue the twin goals of self-determination and greater opportunities, with members wearing red berets and chanting "Red Power" by the mid-1960s in protest of the limited programs led by non-Natives within President Johnson's Great Society. Johnson officially ended the termination of Indian tribes in 1968, and most of the terminated tribes began campaigns to regain their lost status. In California, a group of AIM activists captured the abandoned prison island of Alcatraz in 1969. The occupiers hoped to create a museum and cultural center and unsuccessfully offered to purchase the island for $24 worth of beads and cloth.

Cesar Chavez

A US citizen of Mexican origin, Chavez was a strong believer that union activism would benefit other primarily Latino/Latina migrant workers in California and other Western states who were regularly exploited. By the mid-1970s, Chavez and other activists had unionized 50,000 workers.

American Indian Movement (AIM)

An organization for Native American activists belonging to all tribes, AIM made headlines in the late 1960s and early 1970s due to several direct confrontations with authorities. AIM continues to fight for Native American rights while furthering pan-Indian unity and confronting racial stereotypes.

REVIEW AND CRITICAL THINKING

1. How were African Americans discriminated against in the North and West, and how did leaders such as Malcolm X speak to the frustrations of many urban dwellers who were increasingly losing patience with the tactics and strategies of middle-class leaders like Martin Luther King?

2. Some believe that Ella Baker was equally as important to the civil rights movement as Martin Luther King. Why might many Americans not even know who Baker was? What was her contribution to the civil rights movement?

3. How did the civil rights movement change during the middle and late 1960s? What were the perspectives of leaders such as Stokely Carmichael, and how did more militant leaders win supporters among students and other activists?

4. What might have led to private organizations such as the Panthers creating these kinds of programs when most city, state, and federal governments offered similar programs? Why might the image of the Panthers de-emphasize these efforts in favor of focusing on the posturing and bravado of some Panther leaders?

5. How did the experiences of other minorities reflect the goals and the strategies of the civil rights movement?

4. 1968–1969: UNREST AND UPHEAVAL

LEARNING OBJECTIVES

1. Explain how the Tet Offensive affected the Vietnam War, and describe how the Johnson and Nixon administrations responded to both the military events in Vietnam and the reactions of US civilians back home.

2. Describe the events surrounding Martin Luther King's assassination and how it affected the civil rights movement. Explain the idea behind the 1968 Poor People's Campaign and why it failed in its objectives.

3. Summarize the 1968 election, and explain how the civil rights movement and the Cold War affected the outcome of the election. Explain why Johnson declined to run and how Nixon's election affected the outcome of the Vietnam War.

The year 1968 was a year unlike any other. Beginning with a massive offensive US officials had assured themselves could not happen and ending with the polarization of the US public on a host of issues from Hanoi to Harlem, 1968 was a year of disruption. Women held protests against the paternalism of marriage ceremonies where a father "gave" a bride to another man and likened beauty pageants to judging livestock at a county fair. Students held protests on nearly every major campus in the United States, presenting their views on race, the war, the environment, and nearly every leading social issue. Remembered for both violence and drama, these US protests often paled in comparison to the protests on college campuses throughout the world. Students in Mexico were slaughtered en masse for their protests leading up to the Mexico City Olympics, while workers and students in Paris took to barricades and utilized the rhetoric of the French Revolution to demand broad change. A democratic revolution led by students in Czechoslovakia was crushed by the Soviet Union. In America, a second wave of assassinations and riots angered and polarized the nation, and a new president who alienated many voters and garnered only 43 percent of the vote took office under a promise to bring Americans together.

4.1   Tet Offensive and Vietnam

Given the tendency for US troops to control a village one day and then abandon it to the VC by nightfall, the people of Vietnam found that pretending to support both sides was an important survival tactic. The failure of the VC to recognize the limits of their popular support led to their greatest military defeat during the **Tet Offensive**. All sides had agreed to a week-long ceasefire in observation of the Tet holiday celebrating the lunar New Year. However, on the early morning of January 30, 1968, the Vietcong attacked over one hundred cities and military bases throughout South Vietnam. For a few hours, a small group of guerilla warriors gained control of the US embassy in Saigon. The VC was also able to take control of a handful of military outposts throughout the countryside. However, by the end of the day, nearly half of the estimated 80,000 VC who participated in the Tet Offensive had been killed, captured, or wounded; many were mowed down by automatic weapons after making suicidal runs against fixed US positions.

FIGURE 11.20

This battle map shows the location of major VC and NVA offensives throughout Vietnam during the Tet Offensive. The attacks demonstrated that contrary to the public statements of the military and the president, US forces had not pushed the VC and NVA to the brink of collapse.

The attack surprised the US military, less because of the timing of the attack during the Tet holiday (a similar attack had been launched years before against the French and rumors of a similar attack were rampant) but because a massive offensive against United States and South Vietnamese bases was both contrary to the Fabian tactics used by the VC and NVA and assumed to be beyond the battlefield capacity of these forces. Until this time, Communist forces avoided pitched battles in favor of hit-and-run attacks. For example, US patrols made daily sweeps of the Vietnamese countryside in search of the VC who generally avoided direct confrontations they knew they could not win. The change in tactic puzzled US commanders, some of whom nonetheless celebrated their apparent tactical victory.

The attack also stunned Americans back home who had been told that the VC was near collapse. This apparent gap between what the public was told about the war in Vietnam and the actual situation led to increased scrutiny and criticism by US civilians regarding the war. However, the main reason the VC changed its strategy was not to convince US civilians that their government had overestimated its success or that the Vietnam War was unwinnable. Instead, the VC believed that the people of Vietnam would take up arms and join them in their attack against the South Vietnamese government and overwhelm US forces. The VC failed to recognize that the majority of South Vietnamese simply wanted the war to end.

Although the Tet Offensive failed to rally popular support among the residents of South Vietnam, the massive offensive demonstrated the bankruptcy of the US military's claims that the VC had largely been eliminated. In addition, television coverage showing the carnage and the cruelty of South Vietnamese leaders who executed prisoners led many Americans to call for an immediate withdrawal of US troops. As a result, Tet was both a tactical defeat and a strategic victory for the VC. It resulted in a short-term setback in the Vietcong's ability to counter US forces, but eventually led many Americans to question their nation's presence in Vietnam and led to the eventual decision of President Johnson to try to end the war. Just one month after Tet, a majority of Americans reported their belief that intervention in Vietnam had been a mistake.

On March 31, 1968, President Johnson addressed the nation and announced that he was beginning negotiations with North Vietnam to end the war. He announced an end to aerial attacks on the North, pledged continued military and humanitarian assistance to the South, and intimated his hope that US troops would soon be coming home. Johnson then announced that, to make sure politics stayed out of the peace process, he would neither seek nor accept the nomination of his party for president in the upcoming election.

A shock to many, Johnson's announcement that he would not run for reelection was an acknowledgement of what many believed was inevitable given his low approval ratings. These ratings improved following his announcement, and many viewed his pledge to negotiate an end to the war without political pressure as genuine. However, by this time, Johnson had already lost the support of many Americans, and his military leaders were increasingly losing the support of their troops. Hundreds of "fraggings"—incidents where enlisted men attempted to assassinate their officers using weapons such as grenades—occurred throughout the year. The soldiers who committed these actions were not representative of the majority of troops who followed orders. At the same time, the fraggings demonstrated the tendency of troops to question their orders and even retaliate against commanders they believed unnecessarily risked the lives of their fellow soldiers. Groups such as **Vietnam Veterans Against the War** joined antiwar protests and asked Congress how they could send a young man to die fighting a war that an increasing number of soldiers and civilians began to view as a mistake.

By 1968, a majority of Americans questioned the assumption that the Vietnam War was being fought to preserve the freedoms of the people of Vietnam. Others were beginning to question the importance of Vietnam in the global fight against Communism. By the mid-1960s, there was virtually no cooperation between the Chinese and the Soviets in Vietnam, and total aid to North Vietnam from Communist nations remained negligible, especially when compared to the aid that the United States provided to the South. After 1968, the Soviet Union and China dedicated at least as much effort to combating each other as they did confronting the West. Given the common border between the two nations and a few minor skirmishes in 1969, many predicted that the Chinese and Soviets might engage one another in a deadly war that might destroy Communism. However, US officials still chose to present international Communism as a united front. Although many Americans had paid little attention to the growing rift between China and the Soviet Union, by 1969, the government's insistence that international Communism was a monolithic threat harmed its credibility as more and more Americans became increasingly aware of world affairs.

Still, many Americans continued to support the war because they believed it was crucial to maintaining America's credibility throughout the world. After making so many pronouncements about the importance of fighting Communism and after insisting that Vietnam was the frontline of American freedom, withdrawal from Southeast Asia appeared to many as an admission of US weakness. In addition, withdrawal would seem to indicate that US servicemen and women had fought and died for no reason. After years of presenting each increase in troops and escalation in Vietnam as vital to the defense of the nation, many Americans were understandably reticent to simply reverse course. In addition to the political consequences, people inside the Johnson administration wondered what might happen to the nation's already beleaguered morale if they now admitted that they had long maintained reservations about the wisdom of US intervention in Vietnam. Any admission that the administration had at least partially based its decision to escalate the war on political calculations would surely tear the nation apart, they worried. Even worse would be if it ever came to light that many of the war's decisions were based on the deliberate miscalculations of military advisers who kept promising that victory was inevitable.

Toward the end of 1968, these political consequences were no longer as relevant as Nixon prepared to take office. The outgoing President Johnson began negotiations with the North Vietnamese and prepared the public for the eventual news that US intervention in Vietnam had done little more than maintain a violent status quo. Johnson still hoped that US aid would allow South Vietnam to continue the fight, but made it clear that US forces should be withdrawn. Publicly, Nixon applauded these decisions and made ending the war a leading issue of his presidential candidacy. Privately, however, Nixon still believed the North could be defeated and sought to be the president who turned the war around. As a result, once he won the 1968 election, he secretly derailed Johnson's peace talks by sending messages to the North Vietnamese counseling them to wait until he was president before signing any armistice.

Vietnam Veterans Against the War

An antiwar organization formed by veterans in 1967 in opposition to America's continued military operations in Vietnam. The group quickly recruited more than 20,000 members and held a number of high-profile protests, including John Kerry's testimony to Congress detailing his experiences and the reason he and many others who had experienced combat operations in Vietnam now opposed the war.

FIGURE 11.21

A protest against the Vietnam War in Wichita, Kansas, depicts the government of South Vietnam as a pawn of the United States and an instrument of imperialism.

4.2 King Assassination and the Poor People's Campaign

Poor People's Campaign

An antipoverty protest originated by Martin Luther King, a couple thousand poor Americans of various racial and ethnic backgrounds sought to publicize their plight and push the federal government toward more sweeping antipoverty legislation by establishing a model city run by a diverse group of low-income Americans.

In the fall of 1967, Martin Luther King addressed the annual meeting of the SCLC and announced that he would "dramatize the whole economic problem of the poor" through a new kind of class-based rather than race-based campaign. The ambitious goal of what would soon become the **Poor People's Campaign** was to bring impoverished Americans of all races and regions to Washington, DC, to highlight the common ground between poor Americans of diverse backgrounds and pressure Congress to pass legislation that would alleviate their plight. Previous protests typically marched for a few days or engaged in boycotts or acts of civil disobedience. The organizers of the Poor People's Campaign sought a more ambitious form of protest, attempting to build a functioning interracial community on the National Mall.

In the meantime, King traveled back and forth to Memphis in support of a sanitation worker's strike. The city of Memphis refused to promote black workers to the position of driver and paid the sanitation workers starvation wages. The workers were also not allowed to take a long enough break for lunch that would allow them to sit down or even wash their hands after handling the city's garbage all day. In response to their requests for moderate pay increases and more humane treatment, the mayor threatened to fire the workers. King recognized that Memphis represented a microcosm of the frustrations of black Americans and the dual discrimination of workers that blurred the lines between race and class. Not only were the workers discriminated against because they were black, they were also looked down upon because they were poor and worked in a low-status job.

The sanitation workers in Memphis recognized that they were not on strike to obtain a token raise and began wearing signs that simply read "I AM A MAN." With just three words these workers expressed what the entire Civil Rights Movement was about. King gave the last speech of his life in recognition of their humanity. King declared that black men were no longer going to kowtow to those who treated them with indignity, grin when they were actually offended, stutter when what they wanted to say was plain, or look at the ground when something a white person did upset them. In reference to the threats to his own life, which had grown in recent weeks, King asked the crowd to keep their focus on the goals of the movement. "I may not get there with you," King counseled, "but I want you to know tonight that we as a people will get to the Promised Land." The next day, April 4, 1968, Martin Luther King Jr. was assassinated.

FIGURE 11.22

City and state officials responded to the strike of black Memphis sanitation workers by deploying soldiers with fixed bayonets. Supporters wore signs calling for better pay and an end to the practice of only promoting whites to the position of driver. Many of the workers wore signs that simply read "I Am A Man" to draw attention to the way many of their requests had been disregarded by city officials.

A lifelong advocate of nonviolence who had personally kept a number of demonstrations from denigrating into violence in his final year on Earth, King's assassination led many to question the potential of nonviolent protest. Anger unleashed a series of riots in more than one hundred cities. Black neighborhoods in the nation's capital burned for several days, perhaps the worst scene of destruction out of all the riots. Maryland governor and future vice president of the United States Spiro Agnew met with black leaders in neighboring Baltimore where the rioting was nearly as severe. Rather than ask their advice on how to counter the rioting, Agnew angrily lectured and even insulted these leaders who might have been able to bridge the gap between city hall and the participants. In response to the insult, black leaders walked out of the meeting with their governor and the rioting continued for several days.

White Americans unfamiliar with the long history of similar urban riots questioned why black residents would destroy "their own" neighborhoods. The answer to this loaded question can be found in the histories of many of the afflicted cities. In nearly every major city and many mining communities, workers in the late nineteenth and early twentieth centuries grew tired of peacefully protesting the conditions they faced from employers, landlords, and government, and unleashed violence against the symbols of their oppression. As had been the case with these riots, the buildings and symbols that were targeted were not random during the riots of the late 1960s; black residents singled out stores that refused to hire black workers and the property of slumlords who abused black tenants. Black-owned stores were usually spared, especially those that were known to support the community. Before long, however, fire and destruction became their own tonic as thousands reveled in the cathartic ecstasy of violence for its own sake.

Some black leaders, such as Stokely Carmichael—the civil rights veteran who had endured savage beatings without retaliating—began to question the doctrine of nonviolence. Other black leaders counseled that King's dream must not be deferred by an assassin's bullet. Yet by the time of the scheduled Poor People's March in the summer of 1968, no national figure had risen to assume the mantle of leadership. Even without a strong national leader, a few thousand rural and urban blacks, Appalachian whites, inhabitants of Native American reservations, working-class Asian and Mexican Americans, and poor people of various ethnic backgrounds traveled to the National Mall and established a makeshift camp they called Resurrection City. Over the next month and a half, people of all races erected shanties on the mall and participated in various activities aimed at increasing awareness about the issue of poverty. Intending to show solidarity among the working poor irrespective of race and region, the residents of Resurrection City established their own government that provided free daycares and schools. However, news of these protests quickly descended to the back pages of newspapers before disappearing completely. By the middle of June, most of the protesters had given up and the remaining residents of Resurrection City were forced to leave by mall police, without having achieved any of their goals.

With the death of Martin Luther King, Ralph Abernathy inherited the task of leading the Poor People's Campaign. A seasoned civil rights leader, Abernathy still lacked many of the traits that galvanized people behind King and other fallen civil rights leaders. For example, Abernathy chose to stay in a hotel and commute to Resurrection City. In fairness, few middle-class or wealthy individuals chose to support the Poor People's Campaign by taking up residence on the mall. Even had the movement enjoyed the support of a leader such as King, the Poor People's Campaign faced its most substantial obstacle in that it was generally ignored by the media and was greeted by indifference among most wealthy and middle-class Americans. Whereas Jim Crow was a patent violation of the principles most Americans espoused, the kinds of obstacles facing the poor were less obvious to detect and more difficult to eliminate. Previous marches demanding an end to segregation required little or no expenditures, while the residents of Resurrection City asked for millions to fund government programs. For most Americans, economic inequality was either the consequence of one's own actions or a complex problem deeply woven into the nation's economic structure. For some, the protesters appeared as bohemian transients who expected government handouts. For others, the persistence of poverty seemed to be an intractable problem that no antipoverty program could adequately address.

4.3   Election of 1968

After Johnson announced that he would not seek the Democratic nomination, Vice President **Hubert Humphrey** became the leading candidate for his party's nomination. In 1968, party officials still selected the majority of candidates to national conventions, which rendered the primaries of far less significance than they would later become. In fact, Humphrey, like many past presumptive nominees, made little effort to campaign. Minnesota senator Eugene McCarthy and Massachusetts senator **Robert Kennedy** were the two leading candidates in the Democratic primary, and they hoped they could garner enough grassroots support that party insiders would switch their support from Humphrey to support their candidacies in time for the Democratic National Convention. Eugene McCarthy had opposed the war long before it became politically acceptable to do so, and so he won the affection of many Democrats who believed Humphrey was too connected to LBJ's escalation in Vietnam. Robert Kennedy likewise supported ending the war, but did so in ways that still won him the support of many who questioned the patriotism of war protesters.

Kennedy also won the support of key Democratic groups such as labor unions, most of whom had forgiven him for his aggressive tactics against the popular teamster's leader Jimmy Hoffa. College students, women's rights activists, and nonunion workers likewise favored Kennedy over the other choices, although McCarthy retained an extremely loyal following among the more radical students. Kennedy's support was strongest among the growing numbers of minority voters who had all but abandoned the Republican Party. Kennedy had supported Cesar Chavez and the rights of migrant workers. He had long been popular among African American voters and was the strongest supporter of civil rights within his brother's administration. In fact, Kennedy was one of only a handful of white politicians who African Americans still respected, as evidenced by his ability to speak to inner-city residents in Indianapolis on the night of Martin Luther King's assassination. Bobby Kennedy had just won the primary in California, and many pundits began to believe that he could upset the presumed candidate Hubert Humphrey. However, Bobby Kennedy was assassinated on June 6, 1968.

As the Democratic National Convention approached, antiwar protesters recognized that Eugene McCarthy had little chance and converged on the host city of Chicago to express their displeasure with Humphrey and his refusal to commit to an immediate end to the war. Mayor Richard Daily welcomed the protesters as a challenge to his authority and promised that law and order would be served Chicago style. The mayor called up 6,000 National Guardsmen and more than 7,000 other troops to augment the city police force. Protesters representing major national organizations such as SDS converged with a comical group of anarchist-revolutionaries who promised to "make revolution for the hell of it" and lace the city's water supply with LSD. While TV cameras captured Democrats fighting among themselves over who should be nominated, cameras outside the convention broadcast images of the Chicago police using force against thousands of antiwar protesters. Lost in the images was the nomination of Humphrey for president.

Hubert Humphrey

A native of South Dakota, Humphrey was a long-serving Democrat representing Minnesota in the Senate with a break in service as Lyndon Johnson's vice president. Humphrey attempted to unite Democrats under his own banner in the 1968 election but lost in a landslide to Richard Nixon.

Robert Kennedy

Brother of former president John F. Kennedy, Robert Kennedy served as his brother's attorney general and was the strongest supporter of civil rights in the administration. Elected as a senator representing New York, Kennedy ran for president and was leading in many polls when he was assassinated on June 5, 1968.

FIGURE 11.23

Richard Nixon prevailed over Hubert Humphrey and a divided Democratic Party in 1968. Key to the victory was Nixon's support among white Southerners in the previously Democratic South. The importance of the issue of race among voters is highlighted by the third-party candidacy of segregationist candidate George Wallace.

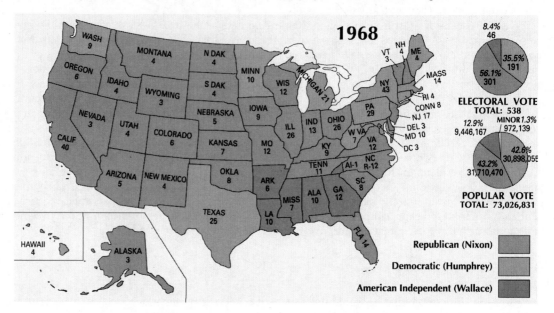

The Republicans countered by nominating Richard Nixon. Many Republicans viewed Nixon as a moderate, especially when compared to Ronald Reagan, the preferred candidate among the party's conservative wing. Nixon had made a name for himself once again (he had lost the presidential election in 1960 and was embarrassed by his subsequent defeat for governor of California two years later) by verbally attacking antiwar protesters. Nixon could not have picked a more opportune moment for his comeback. His campaign promise to restore law and order won the support of older voters. He also deftly appealed to Southern whites by speaking in coded terms that only liberals and minorities recognized as pandering to racism. His promise to achieve "peace with honor" in Vietnam was even more politically evasive and led many who mildly opposed the war to believe that Nixon might share some of their ideas. After all, the war had been almost entirely managed by Democrats, antiwar voters pointed out, and so only Nixon could withdraw US forces without admitting his party's culpability in starting the war. Even the entry of the arch-segregationist and former Alabama governor George Wallace, who won five Southern states, did not derail Nixon. The former vice president prevailed easily over Humphrey's fourteen states and assumed the presidency of a divided nation in 1969.

4.4 Nixon and a Divided Nation

Vietnamization

Nixon's strategy of escalating aerial attacks while increasingly withdrawing US ground troops in hopes that the South Vietnamese army could eventually defeat the North Vietnamese through US military aid.

On July 20, 1969, Kennedy's dream of landing a man on the moon became a reality when astronaut Neil Armstrong declared his small step from a lunar module "a giant leap for mankind." Americans celebrated the achievement as their own and for an evening seemed to forget the myriad issues that divided them. Even NASA failed to unite the nation, and even its greatest triumph could not save its program from being slashed to provide more money for a war in Vietnam Nixon had escalated instead of ending. Nixon explained that his pledge to provide both peace and honor meant doing more to ensure that the fighting was done by South Vietnamese forces. Referring to his plan as **Vietnamization**, Nixon gradually declined US troop levels in the country from 500,000 to 25,000.

Nixon also ended the draft, a decision he denied had any relation to the continuing antiwar movement until revealing in his memoirs that it had everything to do with the protests. Nixon also escalated the number of bombing missions over North Vietnam and even more free-fire zones in the South. He also launched secret bombing campaigns meant to destroy Communist supply networks in Laos and Cambodia, something the Nixon administration vehemently denied until details of the attacks were leaked to the press. Protests against the war escalated as well, and military discipline became a contradiction in terms as tens of thousands of soldiers went absent without leave (AWOL). The nation was so divided that even antiwar protesters attacked one another and the members of SDS disintegrated over internal conflicts by 1970.

"I call it the madman theory," Nixon explained to a trusted aid in regard to his decision to escalate the war into Laos and Cambodia. "I want the North Vietnamese to believe I've reached the point where I might do anything to stop the war. We'll just slip the word to them that 'for God's sake, you know Nixon is obsessed about Communists. We can't restrain him when he's angry—and he has his hand on the nuclear button…'–and Ho Chi Minh himself will be in Paris in two days begging for peace."

In November 1969, news of the **Mai Lai Massacre** was reported by the US press. One of many atrocities committed by both sides against the Vietnamese people, Mai Lai demonstrated the inhumanity of the war and drove many former supporters of the war to reconsider their position. In March 1968, infantrymen in a unit dubbed Charlie Company had faced constant attack from civilians and VC to the point where it was nearly impossible to distinguish between the two. The unit was advised that the village of Mai Lai was a VC stronghold and that all civilians present at that particular moment were either supplying the VC or the kind of civilian guerillas that had been inflicting casualties on US forces like those that had killed their brothers in arms.

After raiding the village, the military discipline of the unit evaporated. The villagers were ordered to line up before being shot one by one by eighteen-year-old men, many of them crying as they fired each round. Others were ordered in a ditch while troops threw grenades into the human pile. "People were diving on top of each other," recalled one GI, describing how mothers tried in vain to shield their children from the deadly shrapnel. Another GI described how a member of Charlie Company distributed candy to the children, then broke down in tears and shot them.

Mai Lai Massacre

According to many veterans, Mai Lai was one of many instances where battle fatigue, the difficulty to distinguish between noncombatants and the Vietcong, and poor military discipline led to a massacre of between three hundred and five hundred villagers by US ground forces. The tragedy in the village of Mai Lai became public information in 1969 and strengthened the antiwar movement.

FIGURE 11.24 Mai Lai Massacre

The military had investigated the incident, which they conceded led to the death of more than three hundred people, most of whom were innocent civilians. The military made some attempts to prevent future occurrences but decided to cover up the incident until US troops began circulating letters and even photos of the massacre. News of the event led to a public trial and conviction of the unit's lowest-ranking officer, who had ordered the men to fire on the civilians. The conviction of Lieutenant William Calley polarized many Americans. Sentenced to life in prison, some believed that he was a callous murderer and should have been executed. Others pointed out that Calley had been ordered to kill any suspected VC—an impossible order that had led to dozens of similar massacres. For these Americans, Calley was being unfairly singled out for a much larger crime perpetrated by thousands of higher-ranking officers who glorified in body counts. Still others saw Mai Lai as an indictment of a war that placed eighteen-year-old men in a no-win situation. Hundreds of returning veterans shared their own stories and testified that brutality was the price of self-preservation, and callousness and even insanity a place of refuge from moral accountability for their actions. For others, morphine and other drugs provided a welcome release from reality.

REVIEW AND CRITICAL THINKING

1. Why did the Tet Offensive, a military debacle for the Vietcong, reduce the confidence of Americans toward their government and help to end the Vietnam War?

2. What was the impact of Martin Luther King's assassination in both the short term and the long term? Had he lived, do you believe that the two disparate wings of the civil rights movement would have been able to resolve their ideological differences?

3. How did college students around the world change history in 1968?

4. Why did President Nixon continue fighting in Vietnam even as he was bringing troops home? Did he or any other leader have an exit strategy?

5. What was Nixon's "Madman Theory," as he explained it to his aide in 1968? Did Nixon follow this theory in practice, or was this merely rhetorical? What impact might this outlook have had upon the way the Vietnam War was fought? Would one expect a similar strategy if the war were being fought in Europe, or would the United States have followed a more limited view of war? What about a war against an enemy with nuclear weapons?

5. FURTHER READING

Bradley, Stefan M. *Harlem vs. Columbia University: Black Student Power in the Late 1960s* (2009).

Carson, Clayborne. *In Struggle: SNCC and the Black Awakening of the 1960s* (1981).

Collier-Thomas, Bettye and V. P. Franklin. *Sisters in Struggle: African American Women in the Civil Rights-Black Power Movement* (2001).

Dallek, Robert. *Flawed Giant: Lyndon Johnson and his Times, 1961–1973* (1998).

Farber, David R. *The Age of Great Dreams: America in the 1960s* (1994).

Gaddis, John Lewis. *We Now Know: Rethinking Cold War History* (1998).

McGerr, Lisa. *Suburban Warriors: The Origins of the New American Right. New Jersey* (2003).

Mezey, Susan Gluck. *In Pursuit of Equality: Women, Public Policy, and the Federal Courts* (1991).

Payne, Charles M. *I've got the Light of Freedom: The Organizing Tradition and the Mississippi Freedom Struggle* (1995).

Rosen, Ruth. *The World Split Open: How the Modern Women's Movement Changed America* (2000).

Schulzinger, Robert. *A Time for War: The United States and Vietnam, 1941–1975* (1997).

Tyson, Timothy. *Radio Free Dixie: Robert F. Williams and the Roots of Black Power* (2001).

CHAPTER 12
The 1970s

The most important achievement of the federal government during the 1960s was the belated achievement of the goals it had declared a century prior during Reconstruction. The Civil Rights Act of 1964 guaranteed equal protection irrespective of race, while the Voting Rights Act of 1965 protected the right of Americans to vote. The 1970s began with the last major expansion of that right, as Congress overwhelmingly approved a constitutional amendment extending suffrage to eighteen-year-olds in March 1971. The Twenty-Sixth Amendment was ratified by the states within a few months with virtually no opposition. Similar amendments had been offered in previous decades, but the 1960s demonstrated as had no other epoch in US history the political activism of college-aged students. It also demonstrated the sacrifice of the younger generation in Vietnam. As that war continued to rage, most Americans agreed someone old enough to be drafted into the military should also have a voice in government.

Despite liberal and conservative support for the amendment, the dominant feature of America in the 1970s continued to be partisan conflict. However, the 1970s were unique from the previous decade in two major ways. First, the most recognizable forms of racial and gender discrimination had been outlawed and a new federal agency had been created to enforce these laws. Most whites believed this was sufficient and hoped that issues of racial equality would cease to occupy a leading place in the public dialogue. Second, the nation experienced political, military, and economic crises at home and abroad that shook the confidence of most Americans.

Americans had grown accustomed to economic and military hegemony throughout the previous three decades. The political upheavals that challenged Soviet rule throughout Eastern Europe during the late 1960s and the rising tensions between China and the Soviet Union suggested that the United States was prevailing in the Cold War. However, the economic and military might of the United States failed to produce victory in Vietnam, insulate the nation from economic decline at home, or guarantee access to Middle Eastern oil. In response to each of these crises, liberals of the **New Left** sought to reassure Americans that the promise of the 1960s might still prevail. Conservatives sought to reinvent themselves by distancing themselves from the racial intolerance of their past while seeking a return to the economic and political hegemony America had once enjoyed.

The New Left was a loose coalition of postwar liberal reformers labeled as "new" to distinguish themselves from the Socialist "old left" of previous generations. Conservatives had rallied behind Republican President Richard Nixon. Eisenhower's former vice president issued a campaign promise to restore "Law and Order," a slogan that appealed to many Americans who were uncomfortable with the rapid changes of the past decade. However, Nixon had also tried to win over moderates and promised to end the war in Vietnam shortly upon taking office. Nixon's pledge of "peace with honor" was vague enough, however, that as president he could still claim that his escalation of the war was exactly what he had promised on the campaign trail.

Nixon hoped that increasing military aid for South Vietnam while escalating the aerial attacks on the rest of the country would allow him to slowly withdraw ground troops without surrendering any more territory to the North. Publicly, Nixon spoke of victory. Privately, even Nixon doubted that the North Vietnamese would ever abandon

New Left

Refers to those who supported liberal causes during the 1960s and 1970s, such as civil rights for women and minorities and the expansion of the welfare state to confront problems faced by the poor. Whereas the "old" left embraced Socialism, the "new" liberal activists generally sought to distance themselves from Marxist ideas in favor of grassroots action within the existing political system.

their campaign to reunite all of Vietnam. Absent of exit strategy, Nixon chose to escalate the war in the hopes of convincing the North to accept an armistice similar to the agreement that ended US participation in the Korean War. Success in this regard, Nixon believed, would make him the most revered commander in chief since Eisenhower. Instead, US forces would belatedly withdraw from Vietnam, which quickly succumbed to Communist forces. Following revelations about some of his secret dealings, Nixon would have the lowest approval rating of any US president and be forced to resign in disgrace.

1. VIETNAM, DÉTENTE, AND WATERGATE

LEARNING OBJECTIVES

1. President Nixon claimed that antiwar protesters and public opinion about the war would not impact his policies regarding Vietnam. Describe those protests and the various opinions and perspectives about the war. Discuss how they likely did impact the president and the rest of the nation.

2. Explain Nixon's strategy regarding the war in Vietnam, and explain why a growing number of Americans opposed his policies. Summarize the process by which the war in Vietnam ended. Explain how the American withdrawal was accomplished and how it affected South Vietnam.

3. Discuss the process by which the Nixon administration came to be involved in illegal operations, and explain how the Watergate break-in became linked to the president.

1.1 Escalation and Protest

FIGURE 12.1

President Nixon points to Cambodia on a map during a press conference in April 1970. Although US forces had been conducting operations in Cambodia prior to this time, the announcement led to renewed protests by antiwar activists.

Almost immediately upon assuming office in early 1969, President Richard Nixon ordered the bombing of the independent and neutral nation of Cambodia. The president hoped to eliminate the supply network that linked North Vietnamese Army (NVA) with Vietcong (VC) fighters in the South. Although destroying these supply networks was a military necessity if the United States hoped to neutralize the VC, bombing a neutral nation violated a host of legal and ethical standards. As a result, the American people were not informed when military operations expanded beyond the Vietnamese border. The people of Cambodia and neighboring Laos had a different perspective, as 70,000 tons of bombs were dropped on their nations during the late 1960s.

In April 1970, Nixon announced that US ground troops would conduct small-scale missions in Cambodia. Antiwar protests increased in the wake of this announcement, and many Americans became concerned that the war might be expanding instead of moving toward the honorable peace Nixon had promised. In reality, Nixon was merely acknowledging what had already been occurring. The delayed protest demonstrates the almost willful complicity of the American media to pass on official military press releases and ignore reports from Laos and Cambodia. International media sources had reported on the bombing of Laos and Cambodia long before Nixon's public announcement, yet only the *New York Times and a handful of other newspapers in the United States reported the story. M*ost Americans wanted to know as little as possible about the Vietnam War—especially if it appeared that defeating the VC and North Vietnam required American troops to fight beyond the borders of Vietnam.

College students proved an exception to this rule as Nixon's announcement was met with a wave of moral indignation. Hundreds of thousands of students participated in protests from Seattle Central Community College to the newly founded Florida International University in Miami. On May 4, 1970, a protest at Kent State University turned violent when Ohio National Guardsmen fired into a crowd and killed four students. The event polarized the nation, with those who still supported the war siding with the soldiers who had previously been attacked by rock-throwing students. Some of these students had even set fire to the Reserve Officer's Training Corps (ROTC) building and then attacked firefighters sent to stop the blaze.

By one perspective, the Kent State tragedy was a "riot" that typified the lack of respect for authority and the rule of law. Those who opposed the war referred to the incident as a "massacre," emphasizing that most of the students were peacefully exercising their constitutional rights of assembly and speech. Ten days later, Mississippi state police shot and killed two students and wounded a dozen others at Jackson State University, a historically black college. Area whites generally believed that the police used a judicious amount of force against the unarmed protesters, while African Americans considered the event to be another massacre. Like the students at Kent State, many had set small fires and were throwing rocks at the police. However, unlike the **Kent State Riot/Massacre**, which polarized the nation, the killings at Jackson State barely made headlines and are seldom included in the historical record.

Historical accounts of the home front also tend to underestimate the diversity of the antiwar movement that quickly expanded beyond activists and scholars like Noam Chomsky to embrace union leaders, Mexican American activists, white factory workers, conservative clergy, and veterans from both wealthy and humble origins Antiwar sentiment was strong in working-class neighborhoods as demonstrated by polls and antiwar protests. This was especially true in minority neighborhoods that provided a disproportionate share of the war's casualties. Martin Luther King Jr. was one of the earliest national figures to publicly condemn the war. He was joined by other African Americans such as **Muhammad Ali** who was drafted but rejected the army's offer to accept a cozy assignment entertaining troops. Refusing induction, the still-undefeated Ali was stripped of his title and was nearly sentenced to a long prison term.

Those who supported the war likewise represented a diverse cross-section of the United States. In fact, even the most liberal universities, such as Berkeley, were host to both antiwar protests and counterprotests by those who supported the war. Antiwar protesters who occupied campus buildings were usually surrounded by even more students who demanded that the protesters abandon their disruptive campaign so that classes could resume. This was especially true among anxious seniors who feared that the protests would disrupt their plans for graduation. Others publicized the atrocities committed by the North Vietnamese and Vietcong. For every Mai Lai Massacre, they argued, there was an instance of equal or greater inhumanity. After taking control of the city of Hue following the Tet Offensive, for example, Vietcong forces tortured and executed thousands of residents whom they believed had aided the United States.

In June 1971, former US Marine Daniel Ellsberg decided to leak a confidential study that detailed the history of escalation in Vietnam. Dubbed the **Pentagon Papers** by the media, the report contained 7,000 pages that revealed the long history of government misinformation dating back to the Kennedy administration. The *New York Times* and the *Washington Post* agreed to publish selections of the leaked documents until the Nixon administration temporarily blocked further publication of the leaked documents. The Supreme Court reviewed the Pentagon Papers and decided that the reports contained nothing that endangered national security, a decision that led to additional releases of the information they contained.

The American public was shocked at the candor of Ellsberg's leaked documents. Each day the *Times* published a new letter from a different commander or military strategist plainly stating that the Vietnam War was unwinnable. The reports clearly indicated that the local population had no confidence in the South Vietnamese government and that no amount of napalm could convince them that this regime was fighting for their liberation. At best, these commanders believed that sending more troops and dropping more bombs might convince the enemy to negotiate a settlement that would preserve the image of American military power. The public was outraged to find how military and civilian leaders had deliberately falsified information to make it appear as though US forces were winning the war. Pentagon officials falsified the numbers of enemy killed, deleted all mention of civilian casualties, and buried information about the breakdown of military discipline among US troops.

Kent State Riot/Massacre

The tragic death of four students on May 4, 1970, after an anti-Vietnam protest escalated into violence on May 4, 1970. Those who opposed the Vietnam War used the phrase "massacre" to describe the event and emphasized that the students were unarmed and exercising their right of free speech. Those who supported the war described the event as a "riot," focusing on the arson and physical violence some of the students had used against the Ohio National Guard.

Muhammad Ali

An outspoken heavyweight boxing champion who became a member of the Nation of Islam, Muhammad Ali was stripped of his title in the aftermath of his refusal to be inducted into the US Army after he was drafted. Perhaps the most famous athlete of his time, Ali based his refusal on his religious and political beliefs. After the military made it clear he would not see combat, Ali's willingness to end his career and go to jail rather than accept an assignment traveling and entertaining troops challenged the image of cowardice that was associated with draft evaders.

Pentagon Papers

A classified report on the US military's actions in Vietnam between 1945 and 1967 that was created by the Department of Defense and leaked to the press by researcher Daniel Ellsberg. This report demonstrated that the military and Johnson administration had sought to mislead the American people regarding the success of their actions in Vietnam.

FIGURE 12.2

As the war continued, an increasing number of Vietnam veterans returned home and contrasted their experiences with the Pentagon's official reports of victories against Communist forces. Protests by veterans, such as this 1967 march, became more common in the final years of the war.

credibility gap

A phrase that came into common usage in the wake of scandals such as the release of the Pentagon Papers. The *gap* was the distance between what federal government officials knew to be true and the official statements of those officials.

George McGovern

A historian who wrote about the labor strikes of the Colorado coalfields, George McGovern became a Progressive Democrat who represented his home state of South Dakota for over two decades. McGovern was defeated by Nixon in the presidential election of 1972, largely because he was viewed as too liberal while Nixon was viewed by many voters as a moderate.

Pundits began using the phrase "**credibility gap**"—a term referring to the difference between what government officials reported about Vietnam and what the Pentagon Papers and other sources revealed the government actually knew to be the truth. The Pentagon Papers combined with previous revelations and the antiwar movement to convince most Americans that their president must direct his efforts to ending the war as quickly as possible. "Peace with honor" now meant withdrawal to a majority of Americans. Nixon responded by ending the draft and reducing the numbers of troops in Vietnam. The troop reductions and end of the draft greatly reduced antiwar activities, which led many to question whether peace activists were more concerned with preventing people like themselves from being sent to war rather than ending the war itself. Young men in need of employment continued to join the military and serve in Vietnam, while the rest of the nation pretended as if the war had ended along with the draft. Others pressed on, hoping to convince the nation that withdrawal from Vietnam was more honorable than maintaining the status quo to avoid the disgrace of surrender.

The Pentagon Papers covered only the years prior to Nixon's election, yet the president became convinced that these documents were released by individuals who were bent on destroying his administration. As a result, Nixon began investigating members of his own staff rather than addressing the important questions that the Pentagon Papers raised about the US presence in Vietnam. Nixon directed his staff to use campaign funds to hire former CIA agents to spy on dozens of the government's own employees. The administration dubbed these men "plumbers" in relation to their mission to investigate and prevent leaks of information that might harm the White House. Before long, these plumbing jobs expanded to a variety of illegal operations meant to spy on and discredit a long list of people the president considered to be his political enemies. One year almost to the day after the Pentagon Papers were leaked, a group of Nixon's plumbers was caught inside the Democratic offices of the Watergate hotel.

1.2 Withdrawal and Fall of Saigon

The North Vietnamese launched another major offensive in the spring of 1972, but Nixon still hoped that he could force the North to accept a cease-fire under his terms. Although Nixon was one of the most knowledgeable US presidents when it came to foreign affairs, he was also one of the least likely to respect the limits of his own authority. While promising the American people that he was working toward peace, Nixon had secretly escalated the war. Nixon approved numerous bombing campaigns and ordered the navy to place mines in every major port of North Vietnam. At the same time, Nixon recognized that these efforts were unlikely to persuade the North to surrender. Nixon simply hoped these actions would help convince the North Vietnamese that US bombing campaigns might never cease, which might lead them to accept US demands regarding American withdrawal. The intense bombing likely had the opposite effect as negotiations stalled throughout 1972. The most contentious issue was the US demand that the North Vietnamese remove all forces from South Vietnam prior to US withdrawal—something that the North viewed as a potential trap.

As election of 1972 neared, over 60 percent of Americans called for an immediate end to the war. An estimated 50,000 to 100,000 draftees had refused to report for induction, many having fled to Canada. Over two hundred army officers had been killed by their own troops, and even veteran soldiers were refusing to follow orders in Vietnam. South Dakota senator **George McGovern** had called for an immediate end of the war in his failed attempt to win the Democratic nomination for president in 1968. His early opposition to the war gave him credibility among the left as he renewed his campaign for the 1972 nomination. His early opposition to the war was also his biggest political liability. To win the general election, the South Dakota senator needed to gain the support of Americans who opposed Nixon but also viewed the antiwar movement with suspicion.

McGovern was challenged by a number of leading Democrats, but the most intriguing aspect of the 1972 Democratic primary was the candidacy of **Shirley Chisholm**. An African American congresswoman from New York, Chisholm won several states of the Deep South that only four years prior had been carried by an archsegregationist. Chisholm never came close to challenging McGovern for the nomination, however, as the liberal South Dakotan also received the support of a diverse group of voters who desired change and an immediate end to the war. However, McGovern's campaign promise to pardon draft evaders alienated many Americans. Recognizing that McGovern's base of support was tied to Vietnam, Nixon maneuvered once again to promise peace while secretly escalating the war. Nixon withdrew his demand of North Vietnamese withdrawal from South Vietnam along with other provisions he knew would convince the North to agree to peace talks. These negotiations were held in private, allowing Nixon to declare that he had prevailed in forcing the North Vietnamese to accept US terms and delivered on the promise to bring "peace with honor."

Nixon's announcement that peace talks were under way deprived McGovern of his leading issue and led to a second Nixon victory. Achieving peace in Vietnam would prove more difficult, and for Nixon, much less honorable. The latest in a long line of military leaders of South Vietnam pointed out what everyone already knew—North Vietnam would resume the offensive once US forces withdrew. The only hope of prevailing against the North absent of US ground forces, argued South Vietnamese leaders, was if US forces continued their bombing campaigns, provided increased military aid, and forced the North Vietnamese to withdraw from the areas of South Vietnam they presently controlled. Nixon understood that achieving all of these objectives was not likely given the political situation in his own country and the military situation in Vietnam. As a result, many view this first round of peace talks as an attempt to secure Nixon's reelection and begin placing a positive spin on the abandonment of an ally the United States had created.

Ho Chi Minh had died in 1969, but his successors shared their former boss's appreciation of the importance of American public opinion. As a result, they recognized that Nixon was under tremendous pressure at home to end the war. If they could simply survive the latest bombing campaign, they believed, Nixon would recognize that accepting North Vietnam's terms for withdrawal was his only politically acceptable option. Once the election was over, however, Nixon brought back his original demand that the North abandon its positions in South Vietnam. He even demanded that the North abandon all efforts at reunification. The North refused these provisions once again, and Nixon responded by escalating the bombing of Southeast Asia.

On Nixon's orders, US warplanes dropped 100,000 bombs in the last two weeks of December alone, pausing only for Christmas. Bombs once again proved poor agents of diplomacy. On January 27, 1973, Nixon returned to the bargaining table, this time accepting a cease-fire that permitted North Vietnam to keep the territory in South Vietnam it had already captured. Thousands of US troops and tens of thousands of Vietnamese died in the three months that Nixon had attempted to negotiate a more favorable end to the war. In the end, even Nixon understood that none of his demands were likely to prevent the North from resuming its offensive against South Vietnam as soon as US troops withdrew.

By April 1973, nearly all US forces had fled South Vietnam and the North launched a major offensive. South Vietnamese leaders made desperate appeals for assistance, but Congress and the American public made it clear that they would not accept any plan to redeploy troops to Southeast Asia. Nixon and his successor Gerald Ford sent military aid to South Vietnam and pleaded for Congress to reconsider. On April 30, 1975, the South Vietnam capital of Saigon was captured by North Vietnamese troops. American embassy staff in Saigon and the thousands of military and support staff that had remained in South Vietnam were airlifted to safety just as the troops entered the city.

FIGURE 12.3

New York congresswoman Shirley Chisholm became the first black candidate to win a state primary in 1972. Chisholm won the Democratic primaries of New Jersey, Louisiana, and Mississippi, partly because many white Southerners had joined the Republican Party by this time. Her victory demonstrates the impact of the 1965 Voting Rights Act as these Southern states had excluded black voters and supported segregationist candidates in recent presidential elections.

FIGURE 12.4

The US military evacuated South Vietnamese officials and their families as Saigon was surrounded by Communist forces. Many of these civilians later migrated to the United States.

post-traumatic stress disorder (PTSD)

An anxiety "disorder" that results after one experiences severe psychological trauma. Post-traumatic stress disorder was common among many American GIs during the Vietnam War, although few were diagnosed or treated by the Veterans Administration in a timely manner. Some believe that the use of the word *disorder* is inappropriate. These individuals argue that the psychological trauma experienced by many veterans is a normal reaction to psychological trauma.

Khmer Rouge

Followers of the Communist Party of Cambodia who seized power following a civil war that coincided with the war in neighboring Vietnam. Led by the brutal dictator Pol Pot, the Khmer Rouge executed between 1 and 2 million people in their effort to purge Cambodia of skilled workers, the educated, and any other person they deemed subversive to their vision of a totally agrarian society.

A war remembered for brutality ended with a demonstration of valor as US military and civilian officials risked their lives to rescue thousands of South Vietnamese officials during the airlift. Because of their support for US efforts, these individuals would have likely been imprisoned or even executed had they been captured by the North. Most were not fortunate enough to escape, and hundreds of thousands of South Vietnamese soldiers and officials were imprisoned. An estimated 1 million Vietnamese fled into neighboring Laos or Cambodia. Others commandeered any craft they could find regardless of seaworthiness and prayed they would be rescued by the US Navy. Tens of thousands of these civilians would eventually find asylum in the United States while the rest became refugees in a region that continued to be plagued by civil war.

1.3   Lessons and Legacies of Vietnam

Many US veterans also felt like refugees when they returned to a nation that was less than grateful for the sacrifices they had made or compassionate regarding the difficulty of adjusting to civilian life. Some 58,000 Americans lost their lives in Vietnam, while 365,000 suffered significant injuries. Not counted among this number were those who suffered from **post-traumatic stress disorder (PTSD)**. The experience of Vietnam veterans, like those of all wars, varied greatly. Infantrymen deployed to forward locations were surrounded by death, and some turned to alcohol and illicit drugs. For some troops stationed in bases throughout the region, the greatest battle was against tedium. When these men returned to the States, many felt that they were ostracized and reverted to their old addictions. Most others simply tried to rebuild their lives, demonstrating a resiliency that was as inspiring as their many selfless actions in combat.

Refugees in Southeast Asia likewise suffered from the lingering scars of war, as well as new ones caused by land mines that remained buried throughout the region and that killed thousands of civilians each year. The war also resulted in the destabilization of neighboring countries. Cambodia descended into civil war. The Communist **Khmer Rouge** under dictator Pol Pot eventually seized power and executed an estimated 2 million Cambodians in the late 1970s. Thanks to the efforts of civil rights veteran Bayard Rustin and countless other activists who publicized the conditions Cambodians faced, tens of thousands of Cambodian and Vietnamese refugees were granted sanctuary in the United States.

Americans differed in their interpretations regarding the outcome of the war. For some, like General William Childs Westmoreland, the war had been lost on the home front where protesters had sapped the will of civilian leaders. For others, the war was based on false assumptions, and protests were needed to call attention to the incongruities and inhumanity that surrounded its execution. Controversy regarding the Vietnam War carries into the classroom where students are more likely to learn about massacres than battles. In sharp contrast to the campaign maps that are presented for previous wars, there is rarely any discussion of tactics and strategy or even a single battle beyond the Tet Offensive. The historic view of the home front during Vietnam is also unique. Students learn about protesters rather than factory production, leaked internal documents take the place of encryption machines, and the returning GI appears as a shadowy figure implicitly juxtaposed against the "Greatest Generation" that saved the world from Hitler.

Recollections of Vietnam veterans reveal both the rationale and the shortcomings of this unique historical memory regarding the military history of the war. Oral histories reveal alienation and despair, the inhuman nature of guerilla warfare, and numerous atrocities committed in the name of survival. They also reveal the valor of American GIs who resolved to never leave a fellow soldier behind against a hidden enemy. Interviews with NVA and VC troops indicate a sort of bewildered respect for the dedication of American GIs toward their brothers in arms, questioning the logic of sending entire platoons to rescue a wounded soldier. Opposing forces were especially mystified that US soldiers would even risk their lives to retrieve the body of their fallen comrades. From the perspective of the GI, however, defending the life and memory of a trusted friend may have been the only part of their service that truly made sense to them. However, American veterans returned to a public that was disinterested in their experiences. After four decades, few historians have sought to collect and preserve these perspectives.

The historical memory of Vietnam is also unique when it comes to the legacy and lessons of the war. Some Americans believe that the lesson of Vietnam is the danger of granting military leaders too much power and the reluctance of civilian officials to respond to popular pressure to end the war. For others, the message for future generations is the danger of permitting politics and politicians from withholding the full range of resources and options from commanders in the field. By this perspective, the overwhelming advantages of the United States in terms of resources and technology made US victory inevitable had it not been for limits placed on military commanders. These individuals believe the United States could have surrounded and eliminated all who opposed their will if only permitted to wage total war as they had in World War II. From the perspective of many Vietnamese, however, the use of napalm and bombing campaigns that dropped a total of five hundred pounds of explosives per resident of Vietnam more closely defined "total war" than any conflict in world history.

Many in Congress at least tacitly agreed with the antiwar perspective and approved the **War Powers Act** over Nixon's veto in November 1973. The new law required the president to notify Congress of any troop deployment within forty-eight hours. It also prohibited the president from using troops in an overseas conflict beyond sixty days without a congressional declaration of war. Those who had protested the Vietnam War celebrated the decision as a vindication of the Constitution and proof of the eventual triumph of democracy. Others argued that the new law permitted the fall of Saigon and doomed many Vietnamese who had supported the United States. Still others feared that the reluctance of the United States to intervene militarily might embolden America's enemies. By this perspective, the War Powers Act aided Communist forces in neighboring Cambodia and discouraged those who were fighting against a left-leaning faction in Angola during subsequent years. For advocates of containment, the legacy of Vietnam was one of second-guessing military commanders and an emasculation of America's commitment to supporting anti-Communist forces around the globe. For others, Vietnam was a reckless intervention that escalated local conflicts and paved the way for the kind of totalitarian regimes that developed in places like Angola and Cambodia.

1.4 Watergate

Nixon had long believed that his political enemies were conspiring against him ever since losing back-to-back elections, first for the presidency in 1960 and then for the governorship of California in 1962. As president, the release of the Pentagon Papers convinced Nixon that enemies inside his own administration were working against him. In response, he hired former CIA and FBI agents to spy on dozens of his own officials in search of "disloyal" employees who might be leaking negative information to the media. Dubbed the "White House Plumbers," these covert operatives illegally tapped phones and eventually expanded their operations to include breaking into the offices of political rivals.

On June 17, 1972, five of the plumbers were caught inside the offices of the Democratic National Committee (DNC) headquarters in the Watergate complex in Washington, DC. The **Watergate break-in** had been authorized by the Committee to Reelect the President (often referred to by the inaccurate but perhaps fitting acronym CREEP). The break-in was conducted with the knowledge of Nixon's attorney general John Mitchell, chief of staff H. R. Haldeman, and chief domestic advisor John Ehrlichman. Most importantly, it had been approved by Nixon himself. Watergate was one of dozens of illegal operations designed to neutralize Nixon's potential opponents. In fact, the June 17 break-in was not the first time Nixon's supporters had targeted the DNC headquarters, and this particular operation was needed to fix the phone taps that were improperly placed in a previous break-in.

FIGURE 12.5

American soldiers refuse to leave wounded and deceased comrades on the battlefield, a practice that has led to both respect and bewilderment among adversaries. Although risking one's life to bring home the remains of another comrade makes little sense to many outsiders, it is one of the defining characteristics of a US soldier.

War Powers Act

A law designed to limit the ability of the president to commit US troops without the authorization of Congress in the wake of the Vietnam War. The law permits the president to send troops without congressional approval in cases of national emergency. However, she or he must notify Congress within forty-eight hours of this action and withdraw US forces within certain time limits without congressional authorization or a declaration of war.

Watergate break-in

A burglary of the Democratic headquarters committed by the supporters of Republican President Richard Nixon in June 1972. Nixon was forced to resign the presidency due to his efforts to cover up the crime.

FIGURE 12.6

Among the evidence used against the White House Plumbers were hidden microphones placed inside ChapStick containers.

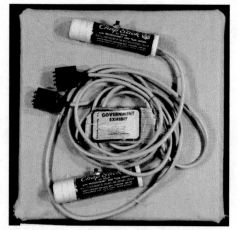

FIGURE 12.7

Nixon's letter of resignation included no statement of guilt or innocence regarding his affiliation with the Watergate Break-In. Nixon was pardoned by President Ford and continued to maintain that he had only acted in the best interests of the nation.

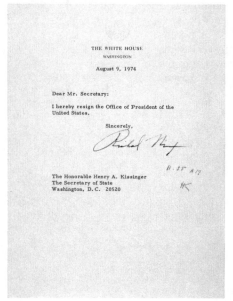

Given Nixon's overwhelming victory over Democratic candidate George McGovern, who won only 17 votes in the Electoral College to Nixon's 520, few suspected that Nixon or any of his top advisers would have ordered the break-in. Given the amateurish methods of the burglars, most Americans assumed Watergate was the effort of some politically motivated fringe group. Secretly, however, Nixon and his top assistants had moved into damage control mode and diverted tens of thousands of dollars in campaign funds to be used as bribes to convince the five arrested men from revealing their connections to the Committee to Reelect the President. These efforts might have succeeded as the prosecutors and press displayed little interest in the initial trial of the five burglars in January 1973. The most piercing questions actually came from the judge. In response, one of the burglars revealed some of what he knew about the conspiracy. This individual was James McCord, a former CIA operative who resented the way the Nixon administration had tried to blame the CIA for a number of unrelated mistakes. Ironically, Nixon would later try to use the CIA to derail the investigation.

By the spring of 1973, *Washington Post* reporters Bob Woodward and Carl Bernstein were chronicling numerous connections between the Watergate break-in and Nixon's most trusted advisers. As they closed in on the truth, Nixon hoped to find someone in his coterie, preferably someone at the lowest level, to admit that he or she had ordered the break-in without consulting the president. There was little honor among thieves and even less among the Watergate burglars. By this point, these men had already been given a combined $75,000 from Nixon's campaign fund to keep quiet. Nixon found that none of his top advisers were willing to fall on their swords to protect him at any price. Many of these men had been conducting illegal or quasi-legal operations for several years, each believing they had enough evidence of the other's dirty tricks that none of the president's men would dare testify against the others. However, due to relentless investigating and the testimony of a few officials outside Nixon's coterie, enough information became known to force the resignation of many of Nixon's top officials by April 1973.

These resignations and the acting FBI director's admission that he had destroyed evidence related to the Watergate break-in led to a high-profile senate investigation in the summer of 1973. One individual testified that the president had known about the break-in and ordered a cover-up. Still others presented the break-in as an operation conducted by people who supported Nixon but were operating without the president's knowledge. It looked to most Americans that Nixon had some connection to the Watergate break-in, but there was still no firm evidence either way until it was discovered that the president had installed a taping system that recorded every conversation in the Oval Office.

Nixon had installed the system believing that only he would have access to the secretly recorded conversations, a resource that could be used to blackmail potential rivals as well as record the events of his administration for his memoirs. Ironically, public knowledge of the tapes proved Nixon's undoing. Nixon tried to stay ahead of events by voluntarily turning over a few tapes that he believed would prove his innocence. However, these tapes had obviously been tampered with. As a result, this led to increased demands that all of the tapes be turned over. Nixon refused, however, citing executive privilege because of the many sensitive conversations that occurred in the White House on various matters unconnected to the Watergate investigation. Nixon also ordered his attorney general to fire the special investigator who had requested the tapes. Instead, both the attorney general and the assistant attorney general resigned in protest.

If Nixon was not guilty of collusion or a cover-up, the American public asked, why was he working so hard to derail the investigation? Nixon's public approval fell to 24 percent—the lowest of any president in US history. As Nixon continued to insist that he was "not a crook," the nation endured an agonizing year of trials and procedural investigations. The investigations culminated with the US Supreme Court case *United States v. Richard M. Nixon*, after which Nixon was ordered to release the White House tapes. Anything dealing with matters of national security remained classified, but the president's conversations regarding Watergate were released. These tapes indicated that Nixon had conspired to use the CIA to cover up the Watergate break-in. These illegal actions were the reason Nixon was impeached and would have been removed from office had he not voluntarily resigned on August 8, 1974. However, the tapes were most shocking in their revelation of secret operations in Cambodia and dozens of illegal spying operations beyond Watergate.

1.5 Resignation and Aftermath

Nixon's resignation would have elevated Vice President Spiro Agnew to the presidency had he not previously been forced to resign after an unrelated investigation revealed the former Maryland governor had accepted bribes from a government contractor. Agnew resigned in October 1973—just as the Watergate investigation was heating up. Nixon appointed Michigan congressman **Gerald Ford** to replace Agnew. As a result, it was the unelected Gerald Ford who became president when Nixon resigned.

As president, Ford disarmed many critics through candor and humility. Ford was the first to point out that he had been appointed rather than elected and promised to lead by consulting others. He also joked that he was a "Ford not a Lincoln," a humble remark and a reference to the reliable and no-frills line of automobiles he implicitly contrasted against the luxury models offered by the same company. He could have called himself a Mercedes, as most Americans were simply relieved that the long national nightmare of Vietnam and Watergate was over. Ford's approval rating stood over 70 percent when he took office. However, the new president may have confused the public's desire to move forward with a willingness to forget all about Watergate. Ford's approval rating dropped 20 percentage points the day he announced a full pardon of ex-President Nixon for any crimes he committed—including ones that might be found in the future. Many Americans believed that Ford was now part of the Watergate cover-up, speculating that he had been appointed in exchange for a promise to pardon Nixon if he was forced to resign.

The Watergate investigation revealed that the CIA had participated in many of Nixon's surveillance operations and had conducted wiretaps and other illegal investigations of antiwar organizations inside the United States. The agency came under fire as the CIA was prohibited from conducting domestic operations. The result was a series of investigations that revealed a litany of CIA assassination plots, secret payments, and even an effort to destabilize Cuba by poisoning livestock in hopes of fomenting revolt against Castro.

It also became clear that the CIA had supported a military coup that led to the death of Chile's elected leader Salvador Allende in September 1973. Allende was a Marxist who the CIA had tried to prevent from being elected in 1970. Once in office, the CIA worked to disrupt Allende's government and recruited Chilean officials who might be interested in using the military to seize power. The US government's exact role in supporting the coup has never been precisely determined, but the Nixon administration welcomed the emergence of coup leader **Augusto Pinochet** as a victory against Communism. Pinochet tortured and executed thousands of Allende's supporters and replaced a left-leaning but democratically elected government with one of the most repressive military dictatorships in Latin America. Once this information became public, Congress decided to curtail the CIA's power to operate with impunity and passed laws demanding closer scrutiny of future operations.

Gerald Ford

The thirty-eighth president of the United States, Gerald Ford had been a long-serving member of Congress representing Grand Rapids, Michigan. Ford was appointed by Nixon to replace Vice President Spiro Agnew after he was forced to resign following a finance scandal. Nixon soon resigned as well due to his role in Watergate, which elevated Ford to the presidency.

Augusto Pinochet

Dictator who ruled Chile after leading a coup against the democratically elected Socialist leader of Chile in 1973. Fearing the spread of Socialism in South America, the United States offered tentative support for Augusto Pinochet's regime despite his brutal repression of dissenters.

REVIEW AND CRITICAL THINKING

1. What did Nixon mean by "peace with honor?" Were his actions as president consistent with this campaign promise? If not, what other options did he have regarding the Vietnam War?

2. How could a candidate such as George McGovern fare so poorly in the general election of 1972, even among those who desired an immediate end to the Vietnam War? Why was Nixon able to present himself as a moderate?

3. How could over two years elapse between the Watergate burglary and the impeachment trial and resignation of President Nixon? Was there any way that Nixon might have prevented the public from discovering his role in the break-in? What would have occurred if Nixon had immediately admitted that there was a connection between his supporters and the break-in?

4. Given his tremendous lead in the polls, few suspected Nixon was behind the Watergate break-in. What led Nixon to approve operations that violated the law? How did his willingness to conduct these kinds of operations outside the law affect his presidency? Why might an American public that expects and even supports the use of these techniques by US intelligence forces abroad react with such indignation to Nixon's use of domestic surveillance?

5. How did Vietnam and Watergate change America?

2. DÉTENTE, DECLINE, AND DOMESTIC POLITICS

LEARNING OBJECTIVES

1. Discuss the connections between the energy crisis and US foreign policy in the Middle East. Analyze the influence of the Cold War on America's actions in the Middle East during the late 1960s and early 1970s. Also, consider the importance of domestic economic and strategic policy concerns as they influenced Middle Eastern affairs at this time.

2. Summarize Nixon's foreign policy regarding the Soviet Union and China. Explain why a cold warrior such as Nixon would decide to simultaneously reach out to China and the Soviet Union during an era in which the relationship between these nations had declined.

3. Summarize the key issues and events surrounding leading domestic issues, such as the economy, environment, welfare, and abortion/reproductive rights in the early 1970s. Present various perspectives on each of these controversial issues in a way that demonstrates an understanding of the way various Americans interpreted each.

2.1 The Energy Crisis

Organization of Petroleum Exporting Countries (OPEC)

A cooperative formed in 1960 by oil-exporting nations whose members seek ways to maximize profits related to oil exports. OPEC demonstrated its power in the 1970s with a series of boycotts against the West that led to a severe energy crisis and increased price for oil. Most OPEC members are located in the Middle East, but other members include Venezuela, Angola, Nigeria, and Ecuador.

Yom Kippur War

October 1973 invasion by Egypt and Syria of the Sinai Peninsula and Golan Heights along their disputed border with Israel. These territories were formerly held by Egypt and Syria, but had been occupied by Israel after Israel repelled a similar invasion in 1967. With Western aid, Israel once again defeated Egypt and Syria.

In the 1960s, the **Organization of Petroleum Exporting Countries (OPEC)** was created as an economic alliance that hoped to work collectively to regulate the global oil market. Oil-producing nations such as Venezuela, Iran, Iraq, Kuwait, and Saudi Arabia believed that the tremendous postwar demand for oil did not match its price, which had remained fairly constant in real dollars for nearly a century. However, OPEC's initial efforts to restrict production stumbled because these nations were so dependent on oil exports for their livelihood—the very factor that had kept supplies high and prices low. The only way to increase the price of oil, OPEC founders recognized, was to reverse the present power structure and make nations that imported oil dependent on the nations that produced oil, rather than the other way around. The challenge was to convince all oil-exporting nations, especially those of the predominantly Arabic Middle East, to restrict production simultaneously.

A failed invasion of Israel by several of oil-producing nations in 1973 spurred the unity OPEC leaders had been hoping for. In response to the West's support of Israel in the **Yom Kippur War**, OPEC's Arabic member states voted to impose an embargo on the United States and Western Europe in October. The war itself was a continuation of the Israeli-Palestinian conflict, as Egypt and Syria reinvaded Israel in hopes of taking back territory it had lost in previous wars. The United States and Western Europe responded with military aid that assisted Israel in its successful defense. This Western intervention resulted in a coordinated effort by religious and secular leaders throughout the Arabic world to force the West to abandon Israel, with the method being the refusal to sell oil to any ally of Israel.

The embargo was not simply about ethnic and religious conflict. For many years, the members of OPEC and even the US-installed shah of Iran had complained that Western nations charged inflated prices for the food and manufactured goods they exported to the Middle East while the oil they purchased remained constant despite growing demand. These complaints were especially relevant in 1973 given recent inflation. The price of Western goods had doubled even as the price the West paid for oil remained about the same.

In the first two decades after World War II, Americans had grown accustomed to the idea that their nation dictated the economic, political, and military terms that other nations (outside of the Soviet sphere) abided by. The oil embargo challenged this confidence and caused an energy crisis that affected all Americans instantly. Fuel prices quadrupled after the start of the embargo in October 1973. An estimated one in five gas stations simply ran out of fuel altogether during the peak of the crisis the following spring. Recognizing that the gulf between supply and demand was so great that the price might continue its upward spiral, the government limited the amount of oil each state received and began printing fuel ration coupons similar to those used in World War II. Although the embargo ended before the federal rationing program took effect, states passed regulations limiting the number of days consumers could purchase fuel. For example, many states utilized a system where a digit in a consumer's license plate determined what days they could purchase gasoline. Speed limits were reduced to fifty-five miles per hour or less, and even NASCAR reduced the distance of its races to conserve fuel.

The US economy was damaged but not disabled by the embargo because domestic oil production still accounted for 70 percent of the nation's consumption in the early 1970s. In addition, domestic production quickly increased once price controls were released, permitting US oil companies to sell their product at market prices, which were substantially higher than the rate the government had set. However, many Western European nations depended almost entirely on the Middle East for oil. North Atlantic Treaty Organization (NATO) members were beginning to reconsider their relationship to Israel, demonstrating the limits of US authority over its own NATO allies. In response, the United States offered millions in aid payments to Israel in exchange for an agreement to withdraw from several areas that were claimed by its Arabic neighbors.

From the perspective of these Arabic nations, the embargo demonstrated that oil could be used to further political objectives. However, business and political leaders in Saudi Arabia and other nations were more impressed by the rapid increase in the price of oil. Saudi Arabia decided to resume sales to the West in the spring of 1974 to take advantage of the dramatic price increase. Other Arab nations likewise placed profits ahead of politics, easing the embargo on nations that still supported Israel. However, the price of oil remained near its 1973 highs because OPEC successfully restricted production and maintained the artificially high price after the initial embargo. Oil did not return to its pre-1973 price (adjusted for inflation) until the 1980s and 1990s when global production increased and the end of the Cold War promoted freer trade. During these later decades, OPEC struggled to dictate production quotas to its members, several of which were at war with one another and in desperate need of revenue.

FIGURE 12.8

Thousands of service stations simply ran out of fuel during the 1973 energy crisis, including this cleverly named service station.

2.2 The Cold War and Détente

Even as America dropped bombs on Communist-controlled areas of Southeast Asia, the Nixon administration was able to almost simultaneously reduce tensions with the Soviet Union and China. Critics of the Vietnam War questioned how the same government that had justified escalation in Vietnam as necessary to roll back Chinese and Soviet aggression could negotiate so freely with both nations while simultaneously requesting more military aid for South Vietnam. From the perspective of the Nixon administration, however, the increased tension between the Soviet Union and China presented an opportunity to drive a wedge in the heart of the Communist world. Others simply hoped diplomacy might be a step toward peaceful coexistence.

The same optimism did not extend to the Middle East, where Cold War tensions and the Israeli-Palestinian conflict mixed with concerns about the flow of oil and control of the Suez Canal. Cold War tensions also continued to intensify local conflicts in Central Asia, Latin America, Africa, and Southeast Asia. In each of these areas, the Cold War expanded postcolonial conflicts into full-scale wars fought by local people armed with US and Soviet weapons. Given the consequences of US escalation in Vietnam, these conflicts remained peripheral to Nixon's diplomatic strategy of **détente** (lessening tensions) with the Soviet Union and China. During his five-and-a-half years in office, Nixon negotiated the most significant arms reduction treaty in world history to that time, restored diplomatic relations with China, and discovered common ground with Soviet leaders based on mutual self-interest and maintenance of the status quo.

détente

The lessening of tensions between adversaries. In this context, détente refers to a reduction of tensions among political leaders and nations.

The Nixon administration's greatest application of détente was the reestablishment of diplomatic relations with the People's Republic of China. Nixon's visit to China was cloaked in secrecy, the culmination of covert meetings arranged by National Security Adviser and future Secretary of State **Henry Kissinger**. Kissinger recognized that if the United States could normalize relations with China, it could further isolate the Soviet Union in world politics. The public's first clue that the two nations might resume diplomatic relations came in the spring of 1971 when China invited the US ping-pong team to Peking. Even this seemingly nonpolitical invitation was part of the secret communications between China and the State Department.

In February 1972, Nixon surprised the world with his unannounced arrival in Peking. Nixon and Mao met and agreed to resume diplomatic relations and work toward mutual trade agreements. Nixon also agreed to withdraw US forces from Taiwan, the non-Communist Chinese government in exile that America had recognized as the legitimate government of China for the past two decades. To the rest of the world, it must have seemed peculiar to witness the former cold warrior, who frequently warned Americans about the dangers of "Red China," shake hands with Chairman Mao. Others were more amazed that conservatives in America raised few objections to Nixon's withdrawal of US forces from anti-Communist Taiwan. But the rapprochement was not necessarily atypical for the pragmatic Nixon or the contrarian nature of Cold War politics. Just as only Eisenhower could have questioned military spending in the midst of the Cold War, Nixon may have been the only politician who could have made such a move without being labeled as "soft" on Communism.

Henry Kissinger

A political scientist who served as Nixon's national security adviser and secretary of state for both the Nixon and Ford administrations. He is best remembered as an advocate of détente between the United States and the Soviet Union and China.

Leonid Brezhnev

The leader of the Soviet Union between 1964 and 1982, Brezhnev greatly increased the power of the Soviet military but also sought to reduce tensions with the West he recognized were hurting his nation economically. Brezhnev notoriously crushed democratic movements in Eastern Europe and invaded Afghanistan under a premise known as the Brezhnev Doctrine that justified intervention if the interests of area Communist nations were endangered by the internal affairs of another nation.

FIGURE 12.9

Richard Nixon meets with China's Mao Tse-tung in February 1972.

Strategic Arms Limitation Treaty (SALT)

Because there were actually two SALT treaties, the 1972 treaty between the United States and Soviet Union that froze the number of nuclear missiles each nation could possess is called SALT I. A treaty in 1979 that sought to build on the arms reductions of SALT I is called SALT II, although the second treaty was never approved by Congress.

Resumption of diplomatic relations with China increased pressure on the Soviet Union to tread carefully as the United States and China moved closer to one another. In fact, one of the leading reasons Nixon visited China was to further détente with the Soviet Union on his terms. Nixon and Soviet premiere **Leonid Brezhnev** communicated frequently, and both agreed that some forms of Cold War competition, such as infinite nuclear proliferation, were mutually self-destructive. Détente was generally welcomed by both sides and is typically praised by historians; but it was not without its own internal contradictions. Détente was predicated on the acceptance of "mutually assured destruction" as a key to stability—a sort of nonviolent hostage taking that discouraged aggression on all sides. Détente also meant that both sides accepted the postwar division of Europe and much of the rest of the globe.

Détente's emphasis on stability appealed to and angered many Americans at the same time. The left was optimistic that détente would lead to arms reductions but was careful to point out that stability did not imply justice for the people of the world struggling under Soviet domination. Those on the political right likewise viewed détente with uncertainty. For conservatives, détente was a tactical victory that also might signal a retreat from earlier commitments to wipe Communism from the map. In contrast to the moral certainties and rhetoric of cold warriors like Nixon in the 1950s, détente also meant the abandonment of clear-cut interpretations of nearly every global and domestic event as related to Communist aggression.

The apex of détente during the Nixon administration occurred in 1972 when the United States and Soviet Union signed the **Strategic Arms Limitation Treaty (SALT)**. The SALT treaty was the culmination of years of negotiations and limited the number and type of nuclear missiles each nation could possess. The Moscow Summit also featured a series of agreements that encouraged trade and cooperation between the two nations. Each of these agreements was soon jeopardized by internal affairs within the Soviet Union and the American response to these changes.

Concerned with the growing number of wealthy and talented people who were leaving the Soviet Union, Moscow added a large monetary fee for visas that prevented most of its citizens who wished to leave the Soviet Union from doing so. Liberals in Congress blasted the provision as a violation of the civil rights of Soviet citizens while conservatives utilized the provision to renew their anti-Soviet rhetoric. Congress responded by passing a law that denied favorable trade relations with any non-Capitalist nation that restricted the movement of its own citizens. Although it did not mention names, the provision was clearly aimed at the Soviet Union. The new law angered Soviet leaders, even those who opposed the emigration restrictions they had just passed as a tacit admission that their nation had yet to become the worker's paradise Karl Marx had predicted. The Nixon administration recognized that pushing for internal Soviet reform would torpedo his efforts at détente and tried to get Congress to reverse course. Ironically, the mines and bombs Nixon had previously ordered against North Vietnam torpedoed his attempts at détente when one of these mines sunk a Soviet ship and caused the deaths of many sailors.

FIGURE 12.10

Soviet Premier Leonid Brezhnev meets with Richard Nixon in June 1973.

Despite increased tensions following this naval tragedy, Nixon and his successor Gerald Ford attempted to keep improving relations between the United States and the Soviet Union. Other than an increase in trade (mostly American grain desperately needed by the Soviet people), détente had peaked in 1972. Ford retained Secretary of State Henry Kissinger, but even the efforts of this brilliant diplomatic tactician failed. A notable exception occurred in August 1975 when both Ford and Brezhnev joined thirty-three other nations in signing the **Helsinki Accords**. Signatories of this declaration agreed to respect the present national boundaries throughout Europe. The agreement effectively meant that the United States, the Soviet Union, and the other nations accepted the postwar division of Europe into eastern and western spheres and agreed to respect existing national borders.

The agreement also contained a pact to abide by the United Nations Universal Declaration of Human Rights that Eleanor Roosevelt had pioneered. This final provision worried the authoritarian leaders of the Soviet Union and Eastern Europe who continued to arrest their own citizens for political dissent. In 1970s America, where dissent was often celebrated, Gerald Ford came under fire from both the left and the right for his participation at Helsinki. Liberals viewed the declaration as an abandonment of those in Eastern Europe who were fighting for democracy and therefore challenging the postwar division of Europe. Conservatives agreed, although they focused their anti-Helsinki rhetoric on what they believed had been another episode of Americans kowtowing to Soviet and other world leaders.

2.3   Cities and the Environment

Many Americans viewed recent world events, especially America's military defeat in Vietnam and its growing dependency on foreign oil, as a symptom of the economic decline that affected their daily lives. Thousands of factories closed each year and the relative wages of industrial workers declined throughout the 1970s. So many Americans migrated in search of work between 1970 and 1990 that the majority of the nation's population growth occurred in the South and the Southwest. By 1980, more Americans lived in these Sunbelt regions than the rest of the nation combined.

FIGURE 12.11

As more and more American factories closed in the 1970s and 1980s, commentators described the emergence of a Rust Belt that featured a net loss of jobs in many of the leading cities of the East and Midwest.

Helsinki Accords

A 1975 treaty signed in Finland intended to reduce Cold War tensions. The United States, Soviet Union, and other nations that signed the treaty agreed to accept the post–World War II division of Europe, including a promise to respect the present borders of nations in Europe. The agreement also committed each nation to honor the UN Declaration of Human Rights.

Rust Belt

The formerly dominant industrial region encompassing the northeastern United States. The term is a reference to the rust that accumulates on the factories after they were abandoned and the wide belt of industrial cities from St. Louis to Chicago and across Ohio to Pittsburgh.

urban renewal

Civic efforts aimed at revitalizing and redeveloping urban areas with various construction projects. Urban renewal plans were often controversial because they involved a municipality claiming privately owned land through eminent domain. Eminent domain required compensation for owners of the land but often made no provision for families that rented homes in the areas that were to be redeveloped.

gentrification

A process that occurs when middle and upper-class residents move into formerly working-class neighborhoods. The process of gentrification often forces neighboring working-class families from their homes as rents and property values rise beyond their ability to pay.

Earth Day

A global holiday instituted by American college students and activists to promote environmental awareness every year on April 22 since 1970.

Portions of the Northeast and the Midwest soon became known as the "**Rust Belt**," a name reflecting the thousands of factories that closed from St. Louis to Milwaukee and across the Great Lakes from Detroit back down to Pittsburgh and the Ohio River valley. The deindustrialization that caused the Rust Belt stretched beyond these borders and affected East Coast cities such as Baltimore and Philadelphia as well as other industrial communities throughout the nation. The demise of these Rust Belt factories that had once employed millions of blue-collar workers was complex. In many cases, employers found it was cheaper to start new factories in areas such as the South where labor unions were weak. Many other companies decided to open factories in other countries where wages were lower and safety and environmental laws did not apply.

With the loss of factory jobs came the decline of union membership and the rise of part-time and contract laborers who were not eligible for benefits and could be fired at any time. Unemployment increased to around 9 percent by 1975, while union membership dropped below 25 percent of nonfarm labor. An unprecedented number of married women entered the workforce in hopes of bolstering family income, mostly accepting low-paying service sector jobs. Cities likewise struggled with the simultaneous loss of middle-class workers and factories.

Downtowns areas responded by launching "**urban renewal**" projects that sought to remove the blight of empty factories and build public works projects. In other cases, urban renewal was simply a euphemism for slum clearance. Minority neighborhoods were demolished to make room for interstate overpasses and other projects designed to connect the suburbs with downtown office buildings. Most urban renewal projects were conducted with little regard for the dispossessed. Although political support for public housing remained low in the 1970s, urban renewal soon required that a growing number of housing projects be built. Seeking to create low-cost units, most cities erected high-rise apartments on cheap land as far away from the middle class as possible. Those who supported the creation of housing projects, simply known as "projects" by many Americans, envisioned these low-cost units as a path toward upward mobility, a sort of halfway house for the working poor. However, these projects concentrated poverty in ways that quickly turned working-class neighborhoods into ghettos that were walled in by interstates and isolated from jobs and public services.

In the 1970s, a new phenomenon related to urban renewal called **gentrification** occurred in many American cities. Property values in older neighborhoods near urban centers had declined; an opportunity for investors who purchased entire city blocks evicted the remaining tenants, bulldozed or renovated older homes, and converted commercial buildings into loft-style condos. Developers also contracted with upscale retailers and bistros that appealed to young urban professionals, known collectively as "yuppies." Racial and ethnic majorities were either evicted or simply priced out of their former neighborhoods, many facing few other housing options beyond the newly constructed projects. Black and ethnic businesses in these neighborhoods were likewise evicted or otherwise forced out, with few options to reestablish their businesses in an urban landscape that had become divided into gentrified downtowns, lily-white suburbs, and ghettoized housing projects.

As developers sought to modify the urban landscape of the 1970s, a different set of Americans became concerned with other aspects of the urban environment. Young adults in the 1960s became increasingly concerned about a variety of social issues such as environmental protection. The environmental movement saw its first major victory when Congress passed the Clean Air Act of 1963, a law that regulated auto and factory emissions. In response to a series of environmental disasters and the increasing political awareness of his constituents, Wisconsin senator Gaylord Nelson suggested that colleges and universities set aside April 22, 1970, as a day of learning and discussion of environmental issues. Utilizing the teach-in strategy of the antiwar movement, students and faculty at the University of Wisconsin and around the nation organized grassroots programs to raise awareness about pollution, toxic waste, and the preservation of natural resources. **Earth Day** has continued to be observed every year on April 22 since its inception in 1970 and is presently celebrated by more than 300 million people around the world.

The colossal success of the first Earth Day in 1970 demonstrated to US politicians that environmental protection had become a leading priority of their constituents. Dozens of environmental protection laws that had been rejected by Congress in previous decades were soon passed by large majorities. President Nixon soon responded by promoting the creation of a federal agency dedicated to environmental issues. Few historians consider Nixon as an environmentalist. As a result, the conservative president's backing of environmental preservation demonstrates the success of grassroots organizers in forcing a pragmatic politician to support their agenda.

During his 1970 State of the Union address, Nixon called on Americans to "make our peace with nature" even as he was secretly working to prolong war in Vietnam. Later that year, Nixon consolidated and expanded existing federal antipollution programs into the **Environmental Protection Agency (EPA)**. The new federal agency was granted authority to create and enforce standards regarding pollution with the guidance of Congress. For example, the EPA pressed Congress to outlaw the pesticide DDT in 1972 because of its toxicity to birds and fish, a danger that had been recognized since the 1950s and popularized by the best-selling novel *Silent Spring*. However, it was only after a lengthy study by the EPA in conjunction with Congress that the chemical was actually banned in the United States.

President Nixon also signed a more stringent Clean Air Act in 1970 that set a five-year deadline for the nation's industries to meet new pollution standards. The law also required automakers to reduce vehicle emissions by 90 percent. Automakers complied with the law by including catalytic converters on every new car, a device that uses catalysts to alter the chemical properties of exhaust. These innovations slightly raised the cost of new automobiles and required consumers to switch to lead-free gasoline. The changes angered muscle-car enthusiasts but also led to a dramatic reduction in the smog that had plagued America's cities since the 1950s.

Congress passed other laws in the early 1970s that limited the use of pesticides, protected endangered species, and required mine operators to limit the pollution that entered neighboring streams and ground water. Although millions of Americans participated in Earth Day celebrations and supported the idea of restricting pollution, many Americans were also concerned that the EPA's new restrictions would raise costs for US businesses in ways that might accelerate the loss of domestic manufacturing jobs. As the economy continued to stagnate in the early and mid-1970s, corporate claims that new regulations were forcing plant closures became more concerning and led to some backlash against the EPA.

One of the biggest domestic controversies of the 1970s pitted corporate interests and the need for low-cost energy against concerns about environmental protection. Alaska was the last great frontier, but in 1968, massive oil reserves were discovered that many believed could reduce the nation's dependence on foreign oil. Environmentalists opposed construction of the eight-hundred-mile Alaska Pipeline that would be necessary to transport oil from the isolated reserves in the Alaskan frontier to the nearest ice-free port in the Northern Pacific. As a compromise, the pipeline was built with a number of features to protect the environment. For example, the pipeline was elevated to allow for the migration of caribou, and hundreds of safety valves allowed engineers to immediately stop the flow of oil in case a leak developed anywhere along the line.

Leaks were an even greater concern when it came to nuclear power plants. Nuclear energy had been greeted by many as a panacea that would solve America's energy crisis by reducing costs and pollution. Dozens of nuclear plants were operated safely until an accident occurred at Pennsylvania's **Three Mile Island** in March 1979. The accident itself was caused by human error, leading to the failure of the reactor's cooling system. As a result, the reactor overheated creating the potential for a meltdown of the containment system that kept radioactive materials from being released into the environment. The actual radiation that had escaped was minimal, but the public was understandably concerned that tens of thousands of people might have died. The accident had cost hundreds of millions of dollars in cleanup operations and curtailed the construction of nuclear reactors in the next few decades. As a result, debates regarding the financial and environmental costs of coal-fired plants remained a leading issue in debates about the environment.

FIGURE 12.12

College students and other young people led the way in promoting Earth Day, which was first celebrated in 1970. Participants conducted service projects, such as these students who are removing trash from the Potomac River.

Environmental Protection Agency (EPA)

A federal agency created in 1970 that conducts research and promotes education regarding the environment and is responsible for enforcing federal standards regarding environmental protection.

Three Mile Island

A nuclear plant near Harrisburg, Pennsylvania that overheated in 1979 and nearly led to a complete nuclear meltdown. The accident led to tougher industry regulations to prevent similar accidents in the future and also discouraged the construction of new nuclear plants.

2.4 Economy and Government

As had been the case with the automobile and other new technologies of the past, the full impact of new technology that aided environmental protections, along with other major innovations of the 1970s such as microcomputers, would not be realized for nearly a decade. These new technologies created jobs in numerous fields throughout the 1970s. However, new technology also allowed companies to do more with fewer employees. For example, new technologies in communications created jobs but also allowed US companies to operate overseas more efficiently. By 1970, hundreds of US firms had become multinational corporations with operations around the globe. Not only did this **globalization** of industry allow manufacturing operations to occur closer to the source of raw materials, but globalization also permitted US-based businesses to hire foreign employees for lower wages and avoid abiding by US labor standards and tax regulations.

Defenders of multinational corporations pointed out that these businesses improved international relations. At the very least, nations that traded with one another seldom went to war. They also claimed that America profited from overseas operations through declining prices for consumer goods and rising corporate dividends for US investors. While offshore operations might have been exempt from US taxation, globalization advocates pointed out that the federal government still received some revenue because the profits of individual stockholders were taxable. Critics countered that these companies were shipping jobs overseas and avoiding their fair share of taxation.

More distressing to many US workers than the details of corporate taxation, it appeared that globalization was an attack on the domestic job market. The United States had produced 40 percent of goods and services worldwide in 1950, but this percentage had declined to 25 percent by the 1970s. Others worried about the military implications of a US economy that lost its manufacturing base. After all, these individuals explained, US victory in World War II was based on the rapid conversion of existing factories to wartime production. By the late 1970s, the United States imported more goods than it exported. Each of these statistics warned of a possible return to America's subordinate role in the global economy. Even more alarming to some, the nations that were making the largest gains in the production of automobiles and aircraft were Japan and Germany. While some Americans resented the fact that the rapid turnaround of these war-torn nations was partially due to US aid, others believed that German and Japanese economic recovery was inevitable. From this perspective, US aid had converted former rivals into two of America's strongest allies in the global war against Communism. Japan and Germany's economic recovery certainly benefited the US and global economy. However, the simultaneous decline of US industry was a bitter pill for World War II veterans, many of whom faced layoffs that may have been the result of international competition.

The late 1970s saw a resumption of economic growth and personal income, although these increases were modest in comparison with the rapid gains of developing economies. All of this added to the perception that the United States was on the decline. Inflation doubled between 1967 and 1973, while unemployment remained high at 8 percent. In the past, unemployment and inflation had usually moved in opposite directions. Prices increased when the economy was doing well but fell during periods of recession. This double whammy of rising inflation and unemployment led economists to create a new label to describe it: **stagflation**.

President Nixon responded in dramatic fashion by abandoning the gold standard in 1971. Prior to this decision, the world's economic system was anchored by the US dollar, which was directly exchangeable for a set amount of gold. Abandoning the gold standard allowed the United States more flexibility to respond to the financial crisis. However, it also furthered the impression that the nation was on the decline. This perception was increasingly strong with industrial workers in the Rust Belt, many of whom experienced significant declines in their real wages as they coped with the consequences of inflation and layoffs. Even those whose wages did not decline often made less money in real terms because of inflation, which exceeded 10 percent by the time Ford took office.

Nixon's domestic policies were guided by an idea he called the **New Federalism**. The core of the president's approach was to share federal tax revenues with states to administer as they saw fit. A pragmatic politician, Nixon actually made few changes—especially when it came to popular federal entitlement programs such as Social Security and Medicare. Nixon actually increased spending for these and other welfare-state initiatives to maintain electoral support and the cooperation of the Democratically controlled Congress. Nixon even supported the creation of the Occupational Safety and Health Administration (OSHA) in 1970, which enforced regulations regarding workplace safety.

However, Nixon also demonstrated his disdain for liberals and their ideas when he tried to remove the funding Congress had set aside for the Office of Economic Opportunity (OEO). When this failed, Nixon appointed a new OEO director who was instructed by the president to destroy the agency. Ultimately, the federal courts ruled that Nixon's efforts to eliminate the OEO represented an unconstitutional effort to thwart the will of Congress. The OEO was spared and continued to administer anti-poverty programs such as Volunteers in Service to America (VISTA) and provide funding for Community Action Agencies (CAA).

CAAs were grassroots community welfare organizations that administered federal antipoverty grants. They legally required the poor to participate in making decisions about how to administer federal funds. In other words, CAAs applied the principles of Nixon's New Federalism to welfare and rewarded initiative rather than simply distributing cash to recipients. Ironically, Nixon hoped to encourage this kind of initiative among the poor during his many attempts to overhaul the welfare system. For example, Nixon's Family Assistance Plan of 1969 would have replaced direct welfare payments with a system requiring job training and other proactive steps before one might receive welfare payments. Nixon's proposed welfare plan also would have provided supplemental income to those who found and accepted employment at a job that failed to provide a federally guaranteed minimum income. Many of Nixon's other domestic policy ideas also failed to pass Congress. During Richard Nixon's 1974 State of the Union speech, for example, the president called on Congress to pass a comprehensive health insurance act. Had the plan passed, it would have required employers to purchase health insurance for all of their employees and would have created a federal health plan that any citizen could have joined.

President Ford's chief domestic priority once he assumed office was to reverse stagflation. Ford began with an ineffective program called "**Whip Inflation Now**," which had the president distributing "WIN" buttons and giving speeches touting voluntary energy reduction and personal savings. Ford's solution was based on the idea that if consumers saved more and purchased less, the laws of supply and demand would slowly reverse inflation. Ford also raised interest rates and reduced federal spending in hopes of tackling inflation. While all of these measures could reduce inflation, they did little to stimulate the economy. The president's Democratic opponents in Congress presented Ford as the next Herbert Hoover, accusing the president of supporting measures that might turn a recession into a depression. Ford's decision to veto dozens of spending bills, including a popular New-Deal-like federal jobs program, did little to bolster his image among working-class voters.

2.5   Feminism and Reproductive Rights

Journalist **Gloria Steinem** described herself as an unlikely convert to feminism. Assigned to cover a feminist rally in 1969, Steinem explained that something inside her "clicked" when she recognized commonalities she shared with the women she interviewed. Steinem recognized that while she had supported civil rights and spoken out against the Vietnam War, years of internalizing negative images of women led her to uncritically accept gendered stereotypes that had been applied to feminists. "I had believed that women couldn't get along with one another, even while my own trusted friends were women," Steinem explained. "It is truly amazing how long we can go on accepting myths that oppose our own lives." Steinem explained how she suddenly realized that stereotypes against feminists served many of the same purpose of sexist jokes and labels that often presented women as caricatures rather than real people. Many of these stereotypes permitted a woman's value to be defined by male perceptions of sexual attraction, which marginalized the ideas and contributions of women. By 1972, Steinem was the publisher of *Ms.*, a new kind of women's magazine that gave voice to many of the same frustrations she had felt.

Steinem's magazine was immediately successful during the socially active prime of the women's movement. *Ms.* also came under heavy criticism by women who hoped it would be more radical and those who felt that the magazine did not adequately represent the experiences of all women. For example, a special issue dedicated to negative self-images of women toward their bodies came under fire after the editors selected a slender white woman for the cover. Readers protested that this cover furthered the kinds of images that judged all women against a single standard of beauty. The editors had actually considered using a larger or nonwhite model, but reconsidered due to fears that the issue's theme of "negative body image" would only reinforce notions that larger and nonwhite women were not beautiful.

The editors also struggled with issues of whether or not to accept advertisements for beauty products and household cleaners—the leading source of income for most other magazines targeted toward women. Always a source of controversy, the articles made *Ms.* unique from other women's magazines even if many of the ads were the same. Writers submitted a variety of articles that brought new perspectives to traditional women's issues. They also demonstrated how national political issues and international affairs affected women's lives. Lampooned by male journalists who predicted *Ms.* would "run out of things to say" in six months, the magazine was a commercial success until the conservative tenor of the 1980s led to lower readership. As revenues declined, the editors became divided regarding the desirability of publishing more popular articles on fashion and celebrities that might attract younger readers.

FIGURE 12.13

President Ford is pictured meeting with Donald Rumsfeld and Dick Cheney, two leading officials in his administration. Cheney replaced Rumsfeld as chief of staff when Ford appointed Rumsfeld as secretary of defense in 1975.

Whip Inflation Now

Gerald Ford's plan to reduce inflation by asking citizens to reduce their discretionary spending thereby using supply and demand to bring down prices.

Gloria Steinem

A journalist who became one of the leading feminist voices of the 1970s, Steinem was the founder of *Ms.* magazine, a supporter of women's reproductive choice, and one of the leading proponents of the Equal Rights Amendment.

One of the lasting consequences of Steinem's magazine was the popularization of the title "Ms." as an alternative to the titles of "Miss" and "Mrs." Given the difficulties married women faced when they went in search of work and the assumption that unmarried women would immediately quit their positions on marriage, it is not surprising that many women in the 1970s embraced the marriage-neutral label. The issue of gender neutrality was one of the many topics discussed when the United Nations sponsored the first World Conference on Women in Mexico City during the summer of 1975. Delegates hailing from 130 different nations helped to draft the World Plan of Action, a document that set goals and standards regarding access to education, employment, political participation, and supported greater access to family planning. The World Plan of Action was ratified by dozens of nations but never considered by the US government. President Jimmy Carter responded by appointing a federal commission to study the matter further. One of the results of the commission was the National Women's Conference, which was held in Houston in November 1977. More than 20,000 women participated in the conference, producing National Plans of Action that was likewise ignored by the government.

The American conference showed that women faced obvious gender discrimination when they sought bank loans. Married women were often required to secure their husband's approval (but never vice versa), and home lenders refused to consider a married woman's income in making loan decisions. Most lenders considered female income as supplemental and subject to change at a moment's notice. This even applied to female veterans applying for Veterans Affairs (VA) home loans. After a lengthy campaign by feminists and consumer activists, Congress passed the **Equal Credit Opportunity Act** in 1974. This law prohibited creditors from using gender along with race, religion, and national origins as factors in making their decisions. While many lenders were still hesitant to market loans to women and minority groups, a growing number of banks began to recognize that minorities and women were part of an underserved market and quickly changed their business practices to comply with the law. As interest rates increased and fewer and fewer consumers were seeking credit, many lenders actively sought the business of the rapidly increasing numbers of career women—both married and single. Some lenders even sought to market loans and other financial products directly to women, producing advertisements that ran in women's magazines that featured images of empowered and independent women.

Women also utilized their consumer power to demand changes at colleges and universities. The number of women in higher education surpassed that of men in the 1970s, yet women still represented a small percentage of faculty and the administration. The Higher Education Act of 1972 amended Title IX of the 1964 Civil Rights Act. As a result, the new law is often simply called **Title IX**. Title IX banned gender discrimination in any educational program or activity that received federal funding. Although the most visible aspect of Title IX has been the requirement of equal opportunities for participation in college athletics, the most significant outcome of the law is likely the vast increase in the numbers of women in professional, medical, and graduate programs. By 2011, women attended law and dental school in roughly equal numbers as men and represented a rapidly growing percentage of faculty and administrators in colleges and universities.

The new law was a product of the experiences of the bill's leading sponsors: Oregon congresswoman **Edith Green** and Hawaii congresswoman **Patsy Takemoto Mink**. Green was the ranking member of the House Committee on Education and had influenced nearly every bill regarding education over the past two decades. Mink was a Japanese American who became the first nonwhite woman in Congress in 1965 and likewise secured a reputation as a leader of her party. Prior to her election by the people of Hawaii, Mink had experienced discrimination as an undergraduate at the University of Nebraska and challenged the racially segregated housing policies of that school. Mink graduated at the top of her class only to find that dozens of her applications to medical schools had been blocked because of her gender.

Equal Credit Opportunity Act

A federal law against using factors such as gender, race, ethnicity, and under some circumstances age in making decisions regarding the extension of credit. The law ended the common practice whereby lenders refused to loan money to married women independently of their husbands or considered only the husband's income when extending credit to a family.

Title IX

The common name for a 1972 amendment to Title IX (section nine) of the 1964 Civil Rights Act. The amendment prohibits the denial of participation in or benefits of any educational program receiving federal funds.

Edith Green

An educator and congresswoman from Oregon who authored and successfully guided several major bills regarding women's rights and education through. Congress. Among these laws were the Equal Pay Act, Title IX, and the Higher Education Act of 1965, which became the basis for popular education programs such as federally subsidized student loans.

Patsy Takemoto Mink

A long-serving congresswoman from Hawaii, Mink was also the first nonwhite woman elected to Congress. She was instrumental in passing a number of laws regarding education, as well as the Title IX Amendment, which now bears her name.

Leading women of color held a prominent role in the National Women's Conference in Houston, but rank-and-file minority women continued to experience discrimination within the movement. Women of color responded by seeking balance between promoting and criticizing the predominantly white feminist movement. At the same time, they challenged white women to really consider what they meant when they spoke of liberation and equality. In 1977, the **Combahee River Collective**, a Boston-based African American feminist organization, issued the "Black Feminist Statement." The women of the Combahee River Collective described the ways that race and gender combined to oppress black women in ways that made their struggle for equality unique from other women. The result of their message was that more and more feminists came to understand that that liberation required a multiplicity of voices.

The feminist movement became more respectful of diversity than the larger society in the 1970s as feminists actively sought the perspectives women that reflected unique experiences based on race, sexual orientation, social class, religion, and ethnicity. The women of the Combahee River Collective labeled this multiplicity of voices "identity politics" and taught that women's liberation could not be achieved by a movement that followed a top-down approach, discounted the perspectives of minorities, sought to minimize the participation of lesbians, or failed to consider the agency of women who held a variety of conservative religious views. Combahee was accompanied by meetings of Latino women and other groups, each agreeing that feminists must embrace a collective of movements rather than one message that was meant to apply to all women.

Differences of opinion regarding abortion and reproductive rights did not emerge suddenly in the late 1960s and early 1970s. For many Americans, however, it may have appeared that the issue had only recently surfaced given the reluctance of Americans in previous generations to discuss the issue publicly. Responses to surveys are always troublesome measures if relied on completely. However, statistics derived from surveys can be helpful in tracking changes in public opinion. For example, 26 percent of respondents in a 1965 survey opposed abortion, even if childbirth represented a threat to the health of the mother. Only 8 percent of respondents felt this way in 1970. Similar surveys indicate that only half of the nation viewed premarital sex as immoral by the early 1970s, whereas three fourths of Americans opposed the practice a decade prior. Other surveys demonstrate that premarital sex and abortion were common prior to the 1970s, even if both had been largely confined to the unspoken fringe beyond polite society.

Because abortion was illegal prior to 1973, women desiring to terminate their pregnancies sometimes physically harmed themselves to induce a miscarriage. Others sought the services of unlicensed practitioners whose methods were often equally harmful. Wealthy women could afford to secure the services of a small number of experienced physicians who were willing to perform safe abortions outside of the law for the right price. The majority of women who sought to end their pregnancies, however, were those who lacked such resources. By the early 1970s, those who sought to legalize abortion were publicizing the tragedy of "back-alley" abortions that often harmed or even killed the pregnant woman.

Opponents of abortion were not unmoved by these tragedies. From their perspective, however, an abortion was not merely a medical procedure that terminated a pregnancy. Opponents of abortion believed that a fetus, even at an early stage of development, was a human life whose rights were equal to the mother. A key indicator of where one stood on the abortion debate was whether one chose to use the term *fetus* or *child* when discussing their beliefs on the subject. A second feature that was unique to the debate surrounding abortion at this time was the level of public participation. In contrast to previous decades when the subject was seldom discussed publicly, the debate surrounding abortion entered American life as never before as the Supreme Court considered its conditional legalization in 1973.

The Supreme Court's ruling in *Roe v. Wade* legalized abortion in the first trimester of pregnancy. The court's ruling, however, was far from the final word on the subject as attempts to overturn *Roe v. Wade* through local restrictions or a direct challenge to the Supreme Court decision itself remains a leading priority among many evangelicals. Given the sensitivities regarding the issue and concerns for both the privacy of women and the rights of unborn children, abortion remains a controversial subject and most politicians try to avoid public discussion of the issue. Scientific advances promoting new ways to conceive children also remain controversial, although the promise of in vitro fertilization for married couples that cannot conceive through natural childbirth has become widely accepted. In 1978 when the first "test tube" baby was born, many feared that natural childbirth would become outdated. This same technology has remained a source of controversy, however, when the conception process has been utilized by unmarried women or same-sex couples.

Combahee River Collective

An African American feminist group formed in Boston that chose their name to commemorate a series of Union army raids that were planned by Harriet Tubman and others. The raids disrupted plantations and freed slaves in coastal South Carolina during the Civil War. In 1977, the groups issued a statement describing the oppression of women as a synthesis of interlocking forms of oppression that encompassed gender but also race, sexual orientation, and other factors.

FIGURE 12.14

Hawaii congresswoman Patsy Takemoto Mink was one of the leaders behind Title IX, a law that forbid gender discrimination in colleges and other educational institutions.

Roe v. Wade

A controversial Supreme Court decision in January 1973 that invalidated a state law in Texas and legalized abortion throughout the United States under certain circumstances.

REVIEW AND CRITICAL THINKING

1. Throughout the 1970s, the United States still produced the majority of the oil it consumed. How did an organization such as OPEC suddenly produce an energy crisis? How did the OPEC embargo affect the United States in the 1970s, and to what degree did the energy crisis change America?

2. What motivated the leaders of the United States, Soviet Union, and China in regard to their relationships with one another during the 1970s? Evaluate the role of détente in terms of Cold War history. Do you think the leaders of these nations were genuine in their desire to reduce Cold War tensions, or were they motivated by other factors?

3. Explain why policies such as urban renewal and the effects of such policies such as gentrification might be controversial. How might the perspectives of different residents of the same city reflect their experiences?

4. How "new" was Nixon's strategy of New Federalism? Evaluate Nixon's domestic policies regarding the welfare state and the environment. Would you consider Nixon to be a liberal or conservative when it comes to the welfare state?

5. Evaluate the response of Nixon and Ford toward the economic crisis of the early and mid-1970s. What dominated their thinking regarding the economy, and what other strategies might they have attempted?

6. What was the message of the Combahee River Collective, and how did this group challenge the feminist movement?

3. EQUALITY AND LIBERATION IN THE NEW AMERICA

LEARNING OBJECTIVES

1. Explain why strategies such as busing and affirmative action were utilized and how these practices led to controversy and backlash. Explain how these strategies were later restricted by the US Supreme Court and the consequences of these court cases.

2. Summarize the civil rights activism of the 1970s as experienced by diverse groups of Americans such as Latinos/Latinas, Native Americans, women, and homosexuals. Explain the connections between these movements and the similarities and differences of their strategies and experiences.

3. Describe the ways that civil rights movements based on race, ethnicity, gender, and sexual orientation inspired other movements. Explain the connection between the consumer movement and the quest for social justice among minorities and women. Also explain the way the consumer movement changed the way people viewed their government and challenged them to look at their role as citizens and consumers in new ways.

The late 1960s was the high tide of the civil rights movement. Many historians also believe the period was the zenith of America's support for greater educational and economic opportunities for African Americans and other minorities. Liberal groups had proliferated in the United States throughout the 1960s, leading to the emergence of greater rights consciousness among African Americans, women, the poor, Native Americans, Latinos, and other groups. However, by the early 1970s, many whites feared that the rising condition of minorities might threaten their own tenuous status. Whites began to display their own theories of rights consciousness that argued that affirmative action and busing violated their civil rights.

Also by the early 1970s, radical groups such as the Students for a Democratic Society (SDS) had self-destructed, mainstream civil rights groups like the National Association for the Advancement of Colored People (NAACP) were mired in hundreds of complicated and expensive court cases, and the once-mighty Student Nonviolent Coordinating Committee (SNCC) was descending into fratricidal conflict. By 1972, SNCC had ceased to exist as an interracial civil rights organization as its leaders chose black nationalism over interracial activism. Meanwhile, existing Black Nationalist groups such as the Black Panthers faced both internal and external pressures. The Panthers sought to balance community service with militancy, while simultaneously fending off the FBI's attempts to destroy their organization. As these institutions struggled to remake civil rights in a post–Jim Crow world, the drama of nonviolent mass resistance was replaced by the technicalities of documenting housing and employment discrimination. What was once a matter of simple justice—eliminating laws requiring segregation and white-only hiring policies—had now become a complex issue involving school redistricting and affirmative action. For many, promise of the 1960s receded into logistical details regarding school desegregation and the tangled roots of economic inequality.

3.1   New Challenges for School Integration

Chief among these logistical challenges was the question of how to achieve racial balance in neighborhood schools when most cities remained racially segregated. Many districts had implemented "freedom of choice plans" that permitted or encouraged black and white parents to send their children to schools where they would be in the minority. Few parents took advantage of these voluntary plans, and the courts decided that something more than voluntary participation would be required to achieve racial balance. Beginning in the late 1960s, urban school districts began reassigning children from minority neighborhoods to school districts with large white majorities. White children were also sent to predominantly nonwhite schools, although this rarely occurred in equal numbers.

Given the need to transport large numbers of children beyond their own communities, this strategy of achieving racial balance became known as "**busing**." Mandatory busing upset many parents on both sides of the racial divide due to the inconvenience it imposed on parents and students. Busing was especially burdensome on large families in inner cities who often found that their children were now attending several different schools throughout the city. Others were upset that busing was destroying the connection between schools and neighborhoods.

Black parents pointed out that these plans were often not implemented equally across the color line. Black parents complained their children usually were the ones who had to wake up hours early each day. Others questioned whether such sacrifice was worth the "privilege" of attending a school outside of one's community where students were often subject to racial prejudice. White parents in working-class urban neighborhoods also questioned the arrangement, pointing out that in the few cases when white children were assigned to inner-city schools, their children rather than wealthy suburban whites were the ones selected.

Defenders of busing recognized these shortcomings and asked critics to come up with alternatives. Short of mandating racial balance in neighborhoods and requiring families to change residences, busing seemed the most practical solution to the persistence of racial segregation in schools. Busing also had many positive attributes, as oral histories of children who participated in these plans often reveal. For example, an administrator who grew up in the predominantly black community of North Omaha recalled that a busing plan in her community led to her first friendships with other white children. Other residents pointed out that busing also connected black and white parents, who would have been unlikely to meet one another had it not been for busing. At the same time, most oral histories reveal that these friendships were usually superficial and schoolchildren rarely spent time at the homes of their new friends.

Charlotte, North Carolina, was even more racially segregated than Omaha, although the pattern of racial segregation that concentrated most of the black population near the center of the city was not unlike that of North Omaha. In Charlotte, children attended schools that were legally open to all races but were still racially segregated in practice—a pattern known as **de facto segregation**. Members of Charlotte's black community sued the school board in 1970, demonstrating that the schools were nearly as segregated as they had been twenty years prior. In response, school officials devised a plan that redrew the city's high school districts to achieve racial balance. The new plan cut the city like a pie, with students in the predominantly black center being assigned to schools throughout the city.

This plan put the burden of desegregation on black students who now had to travel great distances to outlying schools, yet the chief opposition came from white parents. These whites formed their own organization to oppose what they believed was a violation of their civil rights. By 1971 when the US Supreme Court agreed to hear *Swann v. Charlotte-Mecklenburg Board of Education*, the case centered on the question of whether busing was a legal method to achieve desegregation. The Supreme Court decided that in some cases, busing might be the only method to achieve the desegregation required by *Brown v. Board*. The Charlotte case resulted in dozens of lawsuits and the creation of mandating busing plans in cities throughout the United States. For a time, it appeared that legal toleration of de facto segregation had been replaced by a mandate to reverse the last vestiges of segregation, even if it meant transporting children all over America's cities. However, just three years later, a second US Supreme Court decision limited the ways busing might be used in large cities.

busing

The transportation of children to schools beyond their own neighborhood with the goal of achieving racial balance in schools despite the existence of racial imbalance in communities.

de facto segregation

In contrast to de jure segregation (segregation by law), de facto segregation refers to the continued separation of races and ethnicities regardless of laws that are racially neutral. Because of these factors and the persistence of segregated neighborhoods, advocates of school integration believed that it was not enough to simply outlaw segregation.

Milliken v. Bradley

A 1974 Supreme Court decision that forbade schools from busing students across school district lines to achieve racial balance unless it could be proven that those lines were intentionally drawn to segregate schools in violation of *Brown v. Board*. The decision rendered busing to achieve racial balance in many urban areas.

One of the many cities that instituted busing plans in the wake of the *Swann* case was the northern metropolis of Detroit. Decades of white flight resulted in predominantly white suburbs, while most children who lived within the city limits of Detroit were black. After black plaintiffs won a lower court decision in *Milliken v. Bradley*, school officials created an elaborate system that transferred children throughout dozens of school districts within the greater Detroit metropolitan area to achieve racial balance. Affluent whites in suburban communities such as Grosse Point were outraged that their children were being forced to attend urban schools in predominantly black neighborhoods. Other whites in working-class neighborhoods just across the city limit candidly admitted that one of the major reasons they moved was to ensure that their children would not be assigned to the Detroit city schools.

The *Milliken* case reached the Supreme Court in 1974 and resulted in a controversial 5–4 decision barring the use of busing across district lines, unless it could be proven that those lines had been intentionally drawn to segregate students in the first place. In Detroit, school district lines simply corresponded with the many different independent cities that together made up the Detroit metropolitan area. As a result, the city of Detroit once again became its own school district and the only legal remedy to the resulting de facto segregation became a much smaller busing plan that utilized school districts that were just outside the city limits. Because schools are largely funded by local property taxes, the *Milliken* decision was particularly damaging to those who hoped to equalize school funding between suburbs and the increasingly impoverished school districts of inner cities. The decision also reversed busing in many metropolitan areas and confirmed white flight as a method to legally thwart school integration.

FIGURE 12.15

School officials in Charlotte, North Carolina, were able to increase racial diversity in classrooms by transporting children to schools beyond their own neighborhood. This photo was taken in 1973, two years after the Supreme Court upheld the practice of busing children to achieve racial balance in *Swann v. Charlotte-Mecklenburg Board of Education*.

By 1970, urban black voters were often registered in equal or greater numbers than the nationwide average. White flight and black voter registration led to hundreds of black candidates winning election to city offices, and many of America's largest cities elected African American mayors. Many white residents who remained in these cities did so by choice and worked alongside their black neighbors to counter the effects of white flight.

Other whites viewed the rise of black political leaders and busing as an assault on their neighborhoods and their way of life. In Boston, one such group took the name Restore Our Alienated Rights (ROAR) and campaigned to end the "forced busing" of black students into "their" neighborhoods. Most ROAR members insisted they were not racists, a position at least partially supported by some of the arguments made by their more moderate supporters. For example, some ROAR members indicated that they would support busing if plans to achieve racial balance included the wealthy suburbs rather than only the white working-class areas of South Boston.

The actions of many ROAR members reduced the credibility of this message, however, as ROAR rallies often disintegrated into obscenities and violence. In the summer of 1975, ROAR members stoned buses containing black children on their way to predominantly white schools, set fire to symbols of desegregation, and even attacked black children and passersby. The antibusing riots in Boston, Philadelphia, and other cities that summer were often cited as proof that Northerners were no less racist than Southern whites. Other whites joined peaceful counterprotests attended by various racial and ethnic groups that supported busing or at least hoped to find alternative methods to ensure racial diversity in schools. These peaceful counterprotests attracted far more participants in Boston and elsewhere but failed to produce the headlines or notoriety of ROAR. Most whites across the nation expressed disapproval of busing, and the electoral strategies of local and national politicians catered to antibusing sentiment by promising its abolition. Without the support of the US Supreme Court, busing plans were quietly reduced or suspended in most cities by the late 1970s.

3.2 Affirmative Action and Economic Inequality

The civil rights movement demonstrated that there was no singular African American experience or perspective. It also showed that black Americans, like all Americans, were divided by social class. The post–civil rights movement witnessed the extension of this gulf as the black middle class expanded to include more families, while those in poverty languished even further behind. Equality of access to universities and the reduction of employment barriers in business, education, and the professions led to an expansion of the black middle and upper class well beyond the "talented tenth" W. E. B. Du Bois had lauded in the early twentieth century. Whereas only 13 percent of black families earned enough to be considered middle or upper class in 1960, this percentage tripled to include one-third of black families by the 1970s. Equally impressive, by the mid-1970s, more than a million African Americans were enrolled in universities. This represented a 500 percent increase from two decades prior and indicated that blacks and whites were now attending college in roughly the same proportion. Whereas black college graduates found that their degrees mattered little among white employers in the past, this new generation of black graduates found fewer obstacles. For some, new regulations encouraged racial diversity and guaranteed that their applications were given serious consideration in government jobs and large corporations for the first time.

There were four main reasons for this sudden change of heart among predominantly white employers in government and corporate America. The most important was a belated recognition that racial discrimination was contrary to the interests of a particular firm or agency because it robbed that organization of some of the best and brightest applicants. The second was a likewise delayed recognition that a diverse workforce encouraged new perspectives and fostered a positive work environment. The third reason was the negative consequences that companies, which refused to hire black employees, faced given the growing power of black consumers.

The fourth reason for the growth of minority employment was the development of a new remedy intended to proactively counter patterns of historic discrimination. This solution was called **affirmative action** and was implemented by government agencies and a handful of private companies. Supporters of affirmative action recognized that it would not be enough to simply order an end to overt policies that discriminated against minority applicants in the past. Instead, employers must actively recruit minority candidates and consider diversity as a positive attribute when making employment decisions. Hailed by some as the only way to reverse previous behavior, affirmative action was also criticized as reverse discrimination. This backlash against affirmative action was especially aroused when a handful of agencies and universities set apart a number of slots for minority employees or students.

Universities and other organizations that established minimum quotas for minority employment believed such policies were needed to quickly reverse their own historic patterns of discrimination. Supporters of these plans cited statistics and other measures that highlighted the egregious discrimination that had happened in the past and believed that something more than a promise to start taking minority candidates seriously was needed. For example, city police and fire departments in cities with large black populations usually employed only a handful of black firefighters and police among hundreds of whites. White applicants at these departments enjoyed an unfair advantage, advocates of affirmative action pointed out, in that they were often the friends and family of existing members. In addition, without a policy of affirmative action well-qualified minorities might not apply, given the historic injustices practiced by departments in the past. By this perspective, affirmative action leveled the playing field and minimum quotas ensured that a department must employ minority firefighters and police in numbers that were representative of the city's racial demographics. However, from the perspective of a white applicant who was denied employment, affirmative action might have kept them from obtaining a job. In many other cases, the perception that affirmative action might be to blame created a scapegoat that took on a life of its own.

Due to the difficulties of proving whether a white candidate had been rejected because of affirmative action, the nation's attention focused on a handful of cases involving standardized tests where whites with higher scores were still denied employment or admission to a college. In the mid-1970s, a white applicant who was denied admission to the medical school of the University of California Davis sued the college for racial discrimination. A Vietnam veteran with outstanding credentials, Allan Bakke had slightly higher grades and standardized test scores than a few minority applicants. These individuals were admitted as part of a special program to increase diversity by setting aside sixteen places for minority students within each incoming class. The Supreme Court decided *Regents of the University of California v. Bakke* in June 1978. The Supreme Court issued a complicated and split decision that declared racial quotas were legal only in extreme cases. The school was also ordered to admit Mr. Bakke. Similar cases throughout the next decades would reflect the conflict between a color-blind approach and strategies of correcting historic injustices and the persistence of racism without violating the principles of fairness.

affirmative action

Positive steps to increase the number and percentage of minorities and women in employment, education, and other fields where they have been historically discriminated against and underrepresented. Affirmative action plans may include recruitment of minority candidates or more controversial measures that give preference to women and minority candidates.

Regents of the University of California v. Bakke

A landmark Supreme Court decision in 1978 that barred the use of quotas that set aside a certain number of places for minority candidates. The court's complicated split decision supported the continuation of affirmative action plans but believed that government-sponsored racial quotas violated the Civil Rights Act of 1964.

Southern Strategy

An electoral strategy of Richard Nixon to exploit the racism of white voters without explicitly supporting white supremacy. Nixon used this strategy to turn the formerly Democratic states of the South to the Republican Party by appealing to state's rights ideas that had been used in the past to support segregation laws, speaking out against affirmative action and busing, and presenting the Democratic Party as the party of liberals and urban blacks.

Affirmative action affected only a minute fraction of the hundreds of millions of decisions regarding admissions and employment around the country. Yet for many whites, affirmative action came to symbolize a host of frustrations associated with the perception of relative decline that permeated nearly every aspect of life in the 1970s. No one recognized this more than the politically savvy Richard Nixon. Throughout his career, Nixon occasionally took unpopular stands in defense of civil rights. However, by 1972, Nixon's campaign engineered something it called the **Southern Strategy**—an attempt to win the states that had voted for the archsegregationist George Wallace in the last presidential election. Nixon's opposition to busing and affirmative action was part of the strategy and contributed to his electoral victory in Southern states. That the Republican Nixon prevailed throughout the South signified a historic political realignment considering that Southern whites had been voting the Democratic ticket since before the Civil War.

At times, Nixon was able to appeal to white voters while posing as a moderate. "There are those who want instant integration and those who want segregation forever," candidate Nixon exclaimed in a speech expressing his opposition to busing. "I believe we need to have a middle course between those two extremes." However, at other times during his presidency, Richard Nixon made common cause with those who sought to reverse the civil rights movement. For example, Nixon attempted to block the extension of the 1965 Voting Rights Act. Because Nixon knew that Congress would extend the act over his veto, he deliberately chose this symbolic action to win the votes of white Southerners who had opposed the Voting Rights Act under the guise of state's rights.

Nixon recognized that his Southern Strategy risked solidifying the drift of black voters away from the Republican Party. However, he also recognized that sacrificing the black vote was a politically savvy move in the 1972 presidential election due to the winner-take-all system of the Electoral College and the unlikelihood that black voters would pull the lever for Nixon over the liberal George McGovern. Nixon's Southern Strategy led to the portrayal of the Democratic Party as the party of liberals and minorities in the minds of Southerners and many conservatives throughout the nation. The state's rights message of the Nixon campaign was more subtle when it came to race than the rhetoric of archsegregationists such as George Wallace. However, the Southern Strategy had the same effect of further dividing electoral politics along racial lines both within the South and around the nation.

3.3 American Indian Movement

FIGURE 12.16

Members of the American Indian Movement (AIM) held protests throughout the nation, including sit-ins at the headquarters of the Bureau of Indian Affairs in Washington, DC.

In 1972, American Indian Movement (AIM) leader Russell Means organized a protest called the Trail of Broken Treaties. Means sought to publicize and protest the long history of the federal government's dishonest dealings with Native American tribes. Chief among the group's demands was the return of more than 100 million acres of land. AIM activists also demanded the elimination of the Bureau of Indian Affairs, presenting evidence they believed demonstrated over a century of fraud and paternalistic mismanagement.

AIM made headlines later in the year when they held a sit-in at the Bureau of Indian Affairs in Washington, DC. The protesters argued that the bureau had pursued a strategy of token payments to Native Americans for over a century. This strategy permitted the government to appear generous, they argued, but never fully compensated Native tribes for the loss of their land in a way that could lead to independence and self-sufficiency. The small welfare payouts also reduced the likelihood that significant investments would be made in tribal educational and vocational programs. These token payments did little to address the issues that had been caused by hundreds of years of oppression, the protesters argued. In response, AIM called on the government to invest the kinds of resources that would lead to tribal autonomy though educational and economic development programs that would be managed by tribal members themselves.

The sit-ins brought attention to the fact that Native American schools were underfunded and graduates of these schools had few job opportunities. For this reason, the protesters explained, over three-fourths of children dropped out of reservation schools. Natives also protested their exclusion from traditional fishing and hunting grounds by holding "fish-ins" where tribal members "trespassed" onto federal lands to protest the seizure of tribal lands. Members of AIM also followed the example of the Black Panthers by organizing neighborhood patrols aimed at reducing crime and preventing police brutality. Perhaps the most obvious symbol of the connection between the members of AIM and the Panthers was the adoption of the rallying cry of "Red Power" and the wearing of red berets. As the name *AIM* implies, these activists also began to refer to one another as "Indians," embracing a term they believed relayed the unique historical experience of tribal members.

AIM activists protested against discrimination against Native Americans by law enforcement officers. When a white man convicted of killing a Sioux Indian received a light sentence, two hundred Sioux Indians took eleven hostages and seized a church in the small town of Wounded Knee, South Dakota. The planners of the **Siege at Wounded Knee** selected this location to remind Americans of the 1890 massacre that had occurred nearby. Millions of Americans were familiar with the 1890 massacre due to the 1970 bestseller *Bury My Heart at Wounded Knee* by historian Dee Brown. The contrast between the single-shot rifles of the protesters and the automatic weapons of federal marshals and the FBI who surrounded the church rekindled images of the artillery and Gatling guns used by federal forces in 1890. The siege itself led to a seventy-one-day standoff between AIM activists and federal agents. With supplies dwindling, other AIM leaders attempted to resupply their fellow protesters. The FBI intervened, which led to a shootout that injured many on both sides and claimed the lives of one of the AIM members.

In June 1975, a similar shootout occurred at the Pine Ridge Reservation in South Dakota where one Native American and two federal agents were killed. Armed confrontations did little to improve the conditions on reservations and soon led to divisions among Native American activists. Similar to the conflict among the members of the Students for a Democratic Society, SNCC, and other groups, members of the AIM were divided on the question of whether these more aggressive models of self-defense might be counterproductive. In addition, AIM leaders faced the same FBI harassment that had been used against black activists. Between the internal conflicts and outside pressure, AIM soon mirrored the disintegration of SDS and SNCC.

While the armed struggles of AIM activists drew headlines, more subtle protest measures brought positive results for tribal members. Native American leaders went to libraries and archives, chronicling treaty violations of the federal government dating back to the eighteenth century. From Maine to Alaska, native tribes won a variety of court settlements in the 1970s that provided both financial compensation as well as guarantees of legal autonomy. For example, the Taos Indians regained control of nearly 50,000 acres in New Mexico. The settlement included sacred sites such as Blue Lake, which had been seized by the federal government at the turn of the century. Natives also appealed to Congress, leading to the passage of the **Indian Self-Determination and Educational Assistance Act** in 1975. The new law guaranteed that tribes would be able to determine how to spend federal aid as well as administer their own educational programs. The law also gave tribes authority to determine how natural resources on tribal lands would be utilized—an important reform given the large coal, lumber, and oil and gas reserves on many reservations.

Siege at Wounded Knee

A 1973 protest by armed members of the American Indian Movement. AIM members seized hostages near the site of the famous 1890 massacre of Sioux Indians by federal troops. AIM demanded an end to what they believed was harassment of their members, self-determination for the Lakota Sioux, and control of all the lands they believed had been granted to the tribe by previous treaties.

Indian Self-Determination and Educational Assistance Act

Reversed previous government policies and strategies aimed at terminating recognition of Native American tribes. Termination was replaced by the goal of self-determination regarding the affairs and government of native tribes. For example, federal funds for education guaranteed by previous treaties and agreements would now be under the control of native tribes to administer as they saw fit.

3.4 The Chicano Movement

In the mid-1960s, Mexican American activists marched hundreds of miles from the Rio Grande Valley to the Texas state capital of Austin. Similar to the protest marches of African Americans to the state capitals of Mississippi and Alabama, these activists demanded equality. They also demanded that their history and culture be included in college and public school curriculum. The college that is now California State University, Northridge, was the first major university to offer a course on Mexican American history in 1966. Throughout the late 1960s and 1970s, minority students attended college in larger numbers, and their demands for similar courses became essential to those colleges and universities of the Southwest. Students and faculty held teach-ins and began to refer to themselves as Chicanos and Chicanas—labels that predated the formation of the United States and reflected one's pride in their Mexican heritage. The following year Chicano students held protests calling for these informal history and culture courses to become part of the official curriculum in high schools and colleges. Other students joined organizations such as the Mexican American Youth Organization (MAYO), which operated chapters at high schools and colleges.

Chicano students at San Francisco State and Texas State College in San Marcos held protests and threatened to withdraw their tuition if more courses on the history and culture of Chicanos were not included. Students at San Jose State held their own commencement ceremony in protest of the lack of inclusion they faced. Students at the newly created Colorado College of Opportunity (today Metropolitan State College of Denver) may have been the most successful in convincing administrators to respond to their demands. Construction of the college displaced a number of Mexican American families in the neighborhood of Aurora where it was built. In response, the founders of the college had pledged to serve the needs of the local Mexican American community. As a result, administrators were especially compelled to respond to the demands of Chicano students at Metropolitan State, who were also a sizable portion of the student body. Puerto Rican students likewise held a strike against City College in New York in 1969 until administrators agreed to create an ethnic studies program. The result of these protests was that hundreds of colleges created similar programs throughout the country.

The most dramatic manifestation of the Chicano movement was a series of antiwar protests organized by the **Chicano Moratorium**. Chicano men were disproportionately drafted into the armed services during the Vietnam War. They were also disproportionality assigned to infantry units where they died in disproportionately high numbers. Accounting for only 10 percent of the nation's population during these years, Mexican American soldiers accounted for 20 percent of US combat deaths in Vietnam.

An estimated 20,000 to 30,000 people, many wearing the signature brown berets of the Chicano movement, participated in a protest march and meeting in Los Angeles in August 1970. Although this and the dozens of previous antiwar protests launched by the Chicano Moratorium were peaceful, police in Los Angeles used a robbery at a nearby liquor store as a pretext to send hundreds of officers into the crowd. Officially searching for the liquor store bandit, police used clubs and tear gas against those who had been celebrating the morning's march with a concert. The scene quickly disintegrated into violence, and hundreds were injured as helicopters dropped teargas on participants and police alike. A peaceful gathering that had been part celebration and part protest soon turned into a riot when three activists were killed by police. Among the victims was journalist Ruben Salazar who was beloved in the Chicano community for his fearless reports on police violence. Although officials ruled his death an accident, the fact that he died after being hit in the head by a teargas canister while seated at a table led many Chicanos to believe that the police had intentionally targeted Salazar.

The year 1970 was also when activists formed **La Raza Unida**, a political party that sought to represent the growing number of Mexican American voters. The group won few elections in its formative years but succeeded in registering tens of thousands of new voters. La Raza also worked with attorneys who used the legal system to overturn practices such as gerrymandering that had discouraged Mexican Americans from voting in the first place.

Other activists used the courts to challenge the continued segregation of Mexican American schoolchildren following their 1970 victory in *Cisneros v. Corpus Christi Independent School District*. Texas schools had long classified students as either white or black, a system that segregationists had cited in claiming that the city's separate schools for white students and Mexican American students were not actually segregated. After all, the segregationists argued, almost all the students enrolled were either "white" or "other white" according to the official statistics, so how could there be racial discrimination? The court agreed with plaintiffs that Mexican Americans were an identifiable minority and that segregation of these students violated the US Supreme Court's ruling against segregation in *Brown v. Board.*

It was also the year 1970 that **Dolores Huerta**, Cesar Chavez, and the United Farm Workers (UFW) secured their first contracts with California grape producers. Contracts between landowners and agricultural laborers were not covered by federal labor laws. As a result, farm workers could be paid below minimum wage. In addition, federal workplace safety regulations and laws recognizing the rights of workers to organize unions did not apply. The UFW's victory came against tremendous odds and inspired similar protests in citrus and lettuce fields throughout California. It also led to similar movements in the sugar beet fields of the Great Plains and farms and ranches of the American Southwest.

Mexican American culture had long enforced traditional notions of gender but Huerta was able to demonstrate how political activism on behalf of Mexican American families was consistent with the traditional role of women as guardians of the home and family. Huerta was instrumental in enrolling female members. This led to entire families joining the picket lines and handing out literature to consumers at grocery stores. As a result, Huerta became recognized as the leading organizer of UFW boycotts throughout the 1970s. Other leaders such as Esther Padilla testified before Congress about the conditions faced by workers and their families. Through their efforts and the continuing activism of other leaders such as Cesar Chavez, the boycotts and the growing political power of Mexican American communities convinced lawmakers in California to pass a law that required growers to recognize the elected representatives of their workers in 1975.

3.5 Gay Rights Movement

A gay subculture slowly developed in urban districts during the 1950s and 1960s, partially spurred by the experience of homosexual veterans and victims of the Lavender Scare. Dozens of cities were host to formal support networks and gay rights organizations throughout these decades. The Daughters of Bilitis, named after a lesbian in a nineteenth century French poem, was a homosexual women's organization that published newsletters and other periodicals. The largest gay rights organization of this period was the **Mattachine Society**, a group whose name was derived from an Italian word for a jester who was willing to risk punishment for speaking the truth. Together, these organizations gave voice to the growing belief that homosexuality was neither a sin nor an aberration.

These organizations also supported lawsuits to protect the civil rights of their members and other homosexuals. For example, in 1965, the Mattachine Society of Washington, DC, secured an injunction barring employers from firing workers because of their sexual orientation. The success of these early victories led mainstream journalists to acknowledge the existence of homosexuality, as well as the network of support groups and activist organizations. In addition, the taboo against discussion of sexual matters was eroding in the 1960s. Each of these factors predated the most famous event in the gay rights movement. However, nothing brought attention to the emergent gay rights movement these groups were pioneering like the violent protest of homosexual patrons at New York's Stonewall Inn.

The **Stonewall Rebellion** occurred in the Greenwich Village neighborhood of New York City on June 27, 1969. The Stonewall was a bar that had become a popular meeting place for homosexual men in this liberal section of the city. The police arrived late that evening and sought to enforce a handful of outdated laws against public gatherings of homosexuals. Many of those laws had been invalidated by earlier civil rights campaigns by gay rights activists in New York. Ignoring these changes to the law, the New York police launched a raid of the Stonewall and arrested a handful of the patrons. In the past, such raids were routine, and few of those arrested offered much resistance as many gay men and women hid their lifestyle for fear of persecution. A routine arrest might simply be classified as unlawful conduct and attract little attention. Protesting one's arrest meant risking public condemnation. For many, it also meant an end to hiding one's sexual orientation and a beginning of a new life filled with persecution and abandonment by friends and family.

Dolores Huerta

Cofounder of the United Farm Workers, Huerta was an educator and community leader who joined forces with Cesar Chavez to organize farm laborers and advocate their causes to federal and state governments. Huerta directed the successful nationwide boycott of grapes that forced California growers to recognize the UFW.

Mattachine Society

A gay rights organization formed in 1950, the Mattachine Society soon established chapters throughout the nation that served as both a safe social place for homosexuals and a civil rights organization that sought to advance the cause of equal justice regardless of gender orientation.

Stonewall Rebellion

A series of physical protests against police attempting to arrest homosexuals at New York's Stonewall Inn on June 28, 1969. The incident galvanized existing gay rights organizations and led many to acknowledge their homosexuality and support the gay rights movement.

FIGURE 12.18

The Ladder was published by the Daughters of Bilitis beginning in the late 1950s. As this 1957 cover indicates, many homosexuals described the process of hiding one's sexual orientation as wearing a mask.

Harvey Milk

The first openly gay elected official in California, Harvey Milk secured one of the strongest civil rights laws in the 1970s when his fellow city council leaders of San Francisco approved a measure banning discrimination for gender orientation in 1977. On November 27, 1978, Milk and the mayor of San Francisco were both shot by a former city council member. Despite his admission of the crime, the assailant only served five years in prison.

As the police loaded the first arrested patrons into their vehicles, a handful of gay and lesbian patrons began to fight back. Verbal protests against police harassment attracted the attention of gay men and women who were scattered throughout the Greenwich Village neighborhood. These individuals joined the protest, confronting the police with verbal resistance, which eventually escalated to include physical resistance. Before long, beer bottles and other projectiles were being hurled at the police who retreated to the relative safety of the Stonewall Inn. The police were soon barricaded inside the bar and threatened by the growing crowd. With the help of reinforcements, the police withdrew. The participants of the Stonewall Rebellion remained on the street into the morning hours, celebrating the unity and power that came with being unafraid to identify one's self as homosexual and stand up for the rights of others.

The gay rights movement achieved a number of milestones beyond Stonewall during the 1970s. For example, gay rights activists and scholars finally succeeded in their public education efforts and convinced the American Psychiatric Association to remove homosexuality from its list of mental disorders in 1974. This victory coincided with efforts to remove existing stigmas and reflected the emergent gay pride movement. Activists countered existing notions that equated homosexuality with sinfulness and abnormality, celebrating instead same-sex relationships as healthy and normal. Some gay rights activists even posited that homosexuality was as natural of an inclination as heterosexuality but was simply "closeted" at a young age in response to societal norms. Others disagreed, arguing that this notion discounted the unique experiences of gay Americans and distracted from the fight for legal and social equality.

Tragedy struck in November 1978 when San Francisco politician and gay community leader **Harvey Milk** was assassinated. Milk had lived a closeted life while a student at the State University of New York at Albany and during his service in the navy. By the mid-1970s, Harvey Milk became one of the leading gay rights advocates. His transition was prompted by his relocation to a San Francisco neighborhood with a large gay population, which he represented in state and local politics. As a member of the city council, Milk helped pass a 1977 law banning discrimination against anyone in San Francisco because of his or her sexual orientation. A similar law was passed in Miami, Florida, that same year. However, opponents of the measure petitioned to have the new law submitted to the voters of Miami where it was overwhelmingly defeated. Harvey Milk and others were vigilant to make sure the San Francisco law did not meet a similar fate. They also helped to defeat a California ballot initiative that would require school officials to terminate any homosexual or gay rights advocate who was employed by a California school district.

Inspired by deeper meaning of simple slogans such as "Black is Beautiful," homosexual activists like Harvey Milk rallied behind slogans such as "Gay is Good." These slogans recognized the need to counter the dominant society's negative image of other groups. White racism had led African Americans to doubt their own worth, as evidenced by decades of light-skinned beauty pageant winners and destructive skin-bleaching products. The same dynamic had inspired self-loathing in gay women and men. The dominant society, gay rights activists in the 1970s argued, created such a close association between homosexuality and deviance that even activists had internalized these negative images of themselves. If the gay rights movement was to succeed, they concluded, these attitudes had to be replaced by a positive recognition of one's own self-worth.

The self-image of women was especially targeted by dominant societal notions regarding beauty and sexual purity. However, even leading feminists such as Betty Friedan sharply opposed the inclusion of lesbians within the feminist movement. By 1969, however, lesbian activists had convinced the National Organization for Women to reverse course, endorse gay rights, and welcome lesbian members and leaders back into the organization. Given the way opponents of women's rights had fought feminist ideas for generations by equating feminists and lesbians, the endorsement of gay rights by the leading feminist organization signaled a potentially revolutionary change in sentiment.

REVIEW AND CRITICAL THINKING

1. What was busing, and how did it become so controversial? Evaluate the arguments of people of various perspectives who opposed and supported busing. Do you believe that the supporters of ROAR were racists?

2. What was the connection, if any, between those calling for black power, red power, brown power, and even gray power in the 1970s? How were these campaigns different from those who supported white power? What were the strategies used by these different groups? Was the desired outcome of these groups' supremacy and domination or greater equality?

3. Conservatives during the 1970s utilized the violence that erupted in urban ghettos, the Chicano Moratorium, the protests of the American Indian Movement, and the Stonewall Riots as proof that these groups were dangerous. Others sought to point out the parallels between these protests and others throughout history. For example, how different were the causes espoused by Native Americans in the 1970s and those that led to the violent resistance of the 1870s that were now celebrated in US history textbooks? How different was it for black urban dwellers to destroy the perceived symbols of their oppression from other revolts in US history? Did it not make as much sense, they asked, for a community to destroy a store that overcharged them and refused to hire members of their race in 1973 as it had for colonists to destroy tea in protest of a tax forced on them in 1773? Are there parallels between the Stonewall Rebellion and the Boston Massacre? What do you think? Are violent protests ever justified?

FIGURE 12.19

Gay-rights activist Harvey Milk represented a district of San Francisco that was home to a politically active gay community. He was among the speakers listed in this 1978 program for San Francisco Pride's "Gay Freedom Day." Milk's speech was critical of President Carter's silence on the issue but also predicted that gay Americans would someday be granted full recognition of their civil rights. Harvey Milk was murdered four months later.

4.   THE MIDDLE EAST AND MALAISE: AMERICA IN THE LATE 1970S

LEARNING OBJECTIVES

1. Explain the persistence of economic difficulties during the middle and late 1970s and the way the economy affected the United States during these years.
2. Summarize the arguments for and against the Equal Rights Amendment. Explain how competing perspectives led Americans to interpret the amendment differently and how the controversy surrounding the amendment led to its failure.
3. Briefly compare the foreign policies of Carter to those of other presidents during the Cold War. Explain how Carter was able to negotiate an agreement between Egypt and Israel, and why this agreement led many to hope for peace in the Middle East.

4.1   The Economy and the Crisis of Confidence

Jimmy Carter

A naval officer and farmer in Georgia who entered politics and became the thirty-ninth president of the United States after defeating Gerald Ford in the 1976 election. Carter's presidency was marked by economic and international turmoil, and he left office after a landslide defeat to Ronald Reagan. While president, Carter maintained a reputation for diligence and honesty. Although many disagree about his record while in the Oval Office, there is widespread agreement that Carter has become the most successful former president in advancing a variety of important causes after leaving office.

The presidential election of 1976 was a contest between Republican incumbent Gerald Ford and Democrat **Jimmy Carter** of Georgia. Ford had barely survived a challenge in the Republican primary from California's Ronald Reagan, and few gave the president much of a chance to win reelection. Ford's unpopularity began with his pardon of Nixon, even while many of Nixon's aides were serving jail terms for crimes they had committed on behalf of their former boss. Ford then committed a number of blunders, such as mistakenly denying that Eastern Europe was dominated by the Soviet Union in a failed attempt to answer critics who were angered by the Helsinki Accords.

The biggest issue on voter's minds in the fall of 1976 was the economy. Carter enjoyed a tremendous early lead as the economy had only worsened since Ford took office. Democrats portrayed Carter as a "Washington outsider," a populist image that resonated among voters who had grown tired of the daily revelations of political corruption. Carter's own desire for full disclosure almost destroyed this image when the candidate admitted that he had felt lust for women beyond his wife. Although many agreed that Carter was honest, the electorate was not impressed by either candidate. Only half of eligible voters even showed up to the polls. In the end, Carter won 297 votes in the Electoral College to Ford's 240. The Democrats also won nearly two-thirds of Congress, giving Carter an opportunity to enact the legislation he promised would turn the economy around.

Carter began his presidency with high approval ratings, quickly delivering on promises to cut costs by reducing the perks he and his staff received and selling the presidential yacht. His symbolic decision to eschew the customary limousine ride and walk from the capitol to the White House on the day of his inauguration played like a scene from the *Mr. Smith Goes to Washington*. Like the protagonist in that 1940s film—an average citizen suddenly elevated to office—Carter's good intentions and work ethic did not translate to legislative success. The president's method of creating his own panels of experts to draft model legislation alienated key members of Congress because it excluded them from the decision-making process. Carter chastised Congress for failing to recognize that his experts were better equipped to draft policy, a message that further alienated the president from lawmakers.

Americans remained frustrated by continued economic stagnation and high gas prices during the Carter administration. In 1977, the trans-Alaskan pipeline was completed and the Department of Energy was created, but the energy crisis continued. Driving cars with smaller engines and lighter chassis were among many of the adjustments Americans made, yet the nation remained dependent on foreign oil. To make matters worse, the changes made by US automakers came only after foreign competitors entered the market. Chrysler would have been forced into bankruptcy had it not been for a federal bailout of $1.5 billion. Some Americans expressed resentment toward the Middle East and oil companies that had profited from America's economic problems.

In many ways, Carter was better equipped to address these problems than any other president before him. He was an intelligent and detail-oriented workaholic who surrounded himself with experts. He responded to problems directly and avoided the empty platitudes that typified politicians. His speeches made use of scholarly reports and statistics he spent each night reading. And, like Carter himself, these speeches were incredibly forthright and detail oriented. Carter attempted to address each of the challenges he inherited from the energy crisis to deindustrialization, stagflation, budget deficits, and global conflicts including terrorism.

From the perspective of the president's critics, each of these problems had only grown worse under Carter's watch. Some accused the president of using a scattergun approach, trying many measures that actually contradicted one another. Carter's varied attempts to control inflation included voluntary wage and price freezes, modifications of Federal Reserve policy, and reductions in government spending. Carter also deregulated trucking, railroad, and shipping industries by taking away federal controls for rates and fees in hopes of encouraging both competition and profitability.

Although many of President Carter's initiatives received bipartisan support and some likely helped to prevent matters from becoming even worse, each of these decisions came with a political price. For example, Carter's 1979 decision to reduce the money supply helped to reduce inflation, a practical long-term strategy supported by most economists. Carter recognized that years of simply printing more money to mask the country's economic problems would have disastrous long-term consequences. In the near term, however, it reduced the money supply for businesses and consumers. It was a bitter pill, but one Carter decided could not wait. Unemployment jumped from 6 to 8 percent, while the sudden shortage of capital meant that even banks could not obtain loans for less than 15 percent. As the next presidential election approached, the country remained mired in a recession, and even those with steady jobs could not obtain loans for homes or cars with interest rates below 20 percent.

The recession peaked in mid-1979. Carter responded to the growing crisis by inviting various experts and local leaders to the presidential retreat at Camp David to discuss the problems their community faced and brainstorm possible responses. Carter then addressed the nation with a frank overview of the challenges that needed to be addressed. Most Americans initially valued the candor of the president's July 1979 address in which he warned that a "crisis of confidence" had replaced the typical can-do attitude of Americans. Carter outlined areas in which the nation was declining, denounced the irresponsibility of those who allowed private and public debt to spiral out of control, and called on each citizen to accept his or her culpability for their nation's ills. Americans were used to this sort of rhetoric about the threat of America's decline from presidential candidates. But they had never heard such a message from a sitting president. For many, the talk seemed reminiscent of a tough coach's halftime speech to his team, except that he ended the speech without offering a game plan or rousing call for victory.

A half-century of Democratic presidents from Franklin D. Roosevelt to John F. Kennedy had offered inspiring but often-ambiguous speeches in response to the crises of their days. Carter's address contained none of this puffery, but it was also void of the reassurance the American people had come to expect from their president. Even worse, Carter's speech failed to explain how he planned to correct the problems he outlined. Within days, even those who had praised Carter's candor became defensive about the speech. Some even began to perceive it as an indictment of the American people. America was the greatest nation in the world, they exclaimed, precisely because of the very characteristics of hard work and thrift they felt the president had forgotten about. At this moment, one of the president's advisers described the country as descending into "malaise." Given the mood of the nation, it mattered little that Carter himself never used the word *malaise* in his speech. Fairly or not, Americans remembered the address as Carter's "Malaise" speech. Despite the actual content of Carter's message, the collective memory of Carter's presidency began to be that of a leader who accepted the inevitability of the nation's decline.

FIGURE 12.20

President Carter and the shah of Iran together during an official state visit in November 1977. Just over one year later, the shah would be forced out of Iran and seek refuge in the United States. The result was another spike in oil prices and a hostage crisis that would last until the final day of Carter's presidency.

4.2   The Equal Rights Amendment

Women had been pressing for an authoritative and unambiguous federal law banning all forms of gender discrimination ever since Alice Paul first proposed the **Equal Rights Amendment (ERA)** in 1923. This constitutional amendment had been introduced in every Congress since that year and had been endorsed by presidents such as Dwight Eisenhower and John F. Kennedy. However, the amendment did not pass Congress until 1972. Grassroots support for the amendment grew throughout the 1960s, and by 1970, even conservatives such as Nixon gave tentative verbal support to the ERA movement, even if he did little as president to support the amendment.

Equal Rights Amendment (ERA)

Introduced in every session of Congress since 1923, the Equal Rights Amendment stated that "equality of rights under the law shall not be denied or abridged by the United States or by any state on account of sex." The amendment passed Congress in 1972 but fell three states short of ratification.

FIGURE 12.21

The vote regarding the Equal Rights Amendment reveals a regional trend, with the more conservative and evangelical states of the Southwest and Deep South opposing the amendment while most others states supported it.

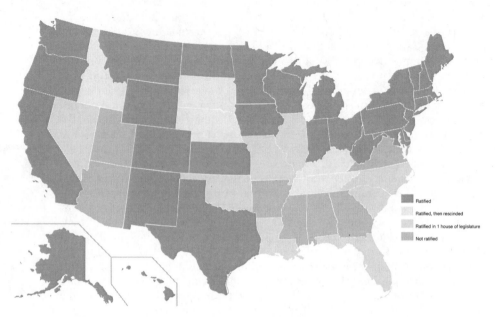

Legend:
- Ratified
- Ratified, then rescinded
- Ratified in 1 house of legislature
- Not ratified

Phyllis Schlafly

A conservative attorney and activist who rose to prominence with her nationwide campaign against the Equal Rights Amendment (ERA). Phyllis Schlafly viewed feminism as a dangerous assault on the family. Her opposition to the ERA succeeded by raising questions regarding the desirability of a government that could make no distinction of gender in its laws.

Dozens of state legislatures had quickly ratified the Equal Rights Amendment when a countermovement led by conservatives such as **Phyllis Schlafly** attracted the attention of the nation. A lifelong anti-Communist crusader, Schlafly argued that the amendment, which guaranteed that "equality of rights under the law shall not be denied or abridged by the United States or by any state on account of sex," would eliminate laws that protected women. Her conservative supporters agreed that mothers would lose preferential treatment in child custody laws if the amendment became law. Women would legally be subject to the draft, they argued, and might also be less likely to collect child support and alimony payments. "Why should we lower ourselves to 'equal rights,'" Schlafly argued, "when we already have the status of special privilege."

Proponents of the ERA disagreed with Schlafly's analysis. They believed that Schlafly and her supporters were part of a reactionary movement that did not take the time to adequately explore the legal issues they raised. Schlafly herself claimed to support the goals of the ERA, yet she had often expressed reactionary views against feminists. She claimed that "women's liberation" was nothing more than a euphemism for "radicals...who are waging a total assault on the family." Despite these polemics against the women's movement, ERA supporters found that Schlafly was gaining support and decided to address the questions she and her supporters raised. Would the ERA invalidate long-standing traditions such as the male-only draft? Would it invalidate recent progressive legislation that protected pregnant women and new mothers in the workplace? And would the amendment legalize practices few Americans in the 1970s supported, such as same-sex marriage?

Supporters of the ERA argued that like all legal decisions, these questions would be decided by the courts. Years later, almost two dozen states passed equal rights amendments to their constitutions without affecting any of the issues Schlafly and her supporters raised during the ERA debate. However, in the absence of simple and absolute answers to these questions, the rapid pace of ratification halted with only thirty-five of the needed thirty-eight states approving the amendment by the end of the seven-year deadline. Congress extended this deadline for another four years but it mattered little as no new states ratified the amendment and some actually reversed their previous support. As a result, the present legal status of the amendment is still debated. Some consider the issue settled by the passing of the deadline while others point out that other amendments have become law after centuries passed between proposal and ratification.

4.3   Foreign Policy

Carter made arms reduction a key part of his presidential campaign, repeatedly criticizing the limits of both Nixon and Ford in this regard. As president, Carter fared little better until a compromise agreement was reached in June 1979. This agreement was known as SALT II (Strategics Arms Limitations Talks of 1979) and reduced the permissible number of long-range missiles and bombers. Ratification of this treaty was delayed as Carter attempted to silence critics who believed that SALT II endangered the

United States by "trusting" the Soviets to follow its unverifiable provisions. Arms reduction was a Soviet trick, some Americans believed, a clever way to get the nation to lower its defenses.

Despite these fears, moderates of both nations appeared to be gaining the upper hand as 1979 was coming to a close. Diplomats slightly modified the SALT II treaty, which was approved and might have passed through Congress had it not been for the Soviet invasion of Afghanistan in December 1979. Anti-Soviet sentiment ran so high following the invasion that no US politician could support an agreement with the Soviet Union without facing backlash at the polls. "Détente," Ronald Reagan explained in a slap at Carter during the 1980 presidential election, "[is] what the farmer has with his turkey—until Thanksgiving Day." Ironically, Reagan would later become one of the strongest proponents of nuclear disarmament in the nation's history. In late 1979 and throughout the first years of the 1980s, however, nuclear disarmament was politically suspect. Although the SALT II treaty was never ratified, Carter's efforts were not completely in vain. Many of the treaty's principles were followed by both sides, and the treaty itself was used as a starting point for subsequent agreements.

President Carter also decided to return the Panama Canal Zone to Panama, a provision that was in the original agreement that he and many others believed was long overdue. However, this decision was also extremely unpopular with many Americans because of the wealth and military power that came with control of the canal. Dozens of conservative groups such as the American Conservative Union keyed into existing images of Carter as "weak" and joined populist anger over the return of the Panama Canal. These conservative organizations attracted hundreds of thousands of members and became a political force in upcoming elections. One of their many arguments was the accusation that Carter had "abandoned" the Panama Canal, believing that this showed an inability to defend the nation's strategic interests.

Carter attempted to deflect criticism that he was naively abandoning the nation's strategic global defense network by backing the development of an elaborate domestic missile defense system. The president's plan called for the creation of an underground rail system that could covertly move intercontinental missiles so that they would be protected from Soviet attack. Carter also sought to disarm his critics by brashly criticizing the Soviets for sending a combat unit to Cuba. However, it was soon discovered that the unit had been stationed in Cuba for decades in accordance with a previous agreement between John F. Kennedy and Nikita Khrushchev. The Soviets recognized that much of this rhetoric was simply posturing, an important part of both US and Soviet politics. Among the more interesting communications between diplomats of both nations during these years were polite requests asking the other side to disregard much of what political leaders of both nations said in order to appease their constituents.

One of the reasons that Carter had been portrayed as "soft" on Communism was his refusal to back certain right-wing regimes that were fighting left-wing groups around the globe. The Ford administration had followed the Cold War philosophy of the Nixon and Johnson administrations, supporting any regime that opposed Communist forces regardless of that regime's own shortcomings. This was certainly the case in Angola where a democratically supported Marxist rebellion had been fighting for independence from Portugal for decades. The Portuguese withdrew from the region in 1975, leading to a civil war between the left-wing Popular Movement for the Liberation of Angola (MPLA) and the Nationalist Front. The Nationalist Front was backed by right-wing dictatorships such as Zaire and the apartheid government of South Africa.

As a result of Cold War alliances, this civil war in Angola became much more destructive. The Soviet Union and Cuba provided military aid for the MPLA while the United States provided aid to the Nationalist Front. Given the recent experience in Vietnam and the unsavory connection between the Nationalists and the repressive regimes that supported them, such as South Africa, Congress eventually withdrew aid to the Nationalist Front. Carter believed that the lesson of Angola and other conflicts in developing nations was that the United States should only back anti-Communist forces that did not have a history of human rights violations. As president, Carter ended the distribution of military aid to dictators in El Salvador, Brazil, and Argentina for this reason. He also created a Bureau of Human Rights within the State Department. However, autocratic leaders in the Middle East continued to receive US aid during the Carter administration due to the nation's dependence on foreign oil. The United States especially backed the shah of Iran despite his growing unpopularity among the people of Iran and his recent support of Organization of the Petroleum Exporting Countries (OPEC)'s embargo against the United States.

FIGURE 12.22

President Nixon meets with Mobutu Sese Seku, the authoritarian dictator of Zaire (today known as the Democratic Republic of the Congo). Mobutu seized power following a coup and the assassination of the democratically elected Patrice Lumumba. Because Mobutu was an opponent of communism, the United States disregarded many of his crimes against the people of Zaire.

Palestine Liberation Organization (PLO)

An organization composed of Palestinian groups that sought the overthrow of Israel and remains dedicated to the creation of a Palestinian homeland. Many Palestinians and world governments consider the Palestine Liberation Organization to be a government in exile, although the United States has been reluctant to extend such recognition and considered the PLO a terrorist front during the 1970s due to the numerous violent attacks its supporters committed against Israel and Israelis. Although the PLO has officially recognized Israel and its right to peacefully exist as a nation, many Americans are reluctant to view the PLO as anything other than a terrorist organization.

Camp David Accords

An agreement between Egypt and Israel that was brokered by President Jimmy Carter over two weeks at Camp David in Maryland and signed at a ceremony at the White House on September 17, 1978. The agreement led to the return of the Sinai Peninsula to Egypt while Egypt became the first Arabic nation to extend official recognition to Israel.

Iranian Revolution

An anti-Western revolution that ousted the US-backed shah of Iran and in favor of the Muslim religious leader Ayatollah Khomeini in January 1979.

Iranian Hostage Crisis

Following the Iranian Revolution a group of armed Iranians laid siege to the US embassy in Tehran and captured fifty-two Americans. The hostages remained in captivity for 444 days until their release on January 20, 1981.

The energy crisis and ongoing conflict in the Middle East dominated Carter's foreign policy agenda. One of President Carter's leading priorities was the resolution of the Israeli-Palestinian conflict. The issue was politically volatile as both anti-Arabic and anti-Jewish backlash was widespread through the United States. Some demagogues blamed the energy crisis on the Carter administration's support for Israel. Others attacked the president for what they perceived to be his failure to take decisive action against Arabic groups such as the **Palestine Liberation Organization (PLO)**. Some even argued that an informal meeting by Carter's ambassador to the United Nations and the UN representative of the PLO was proof that the president supported terrorist organizations. As a result, every action Carter took regarding the Israeli-Palestinian crisis was heavily scrutinized in the US as well as overseas.

During the Ford administration, Secretary of State Henry Kissinger had alternated meetings with Menachem Begin of Israel and Anwar Sadat of Egypt. The process was labeled "shuttle diplomacy" due to the secretary of state's constant travel between the two nations. Partly due to Kissinger's efforts, Israel agreed to return part of the Sinai Peninsula back to Egypt. President Carter followed this détente between Israel and the leader of the Arabic world by persuading both heads of state to travel to the presidential retreat at Maryland's Camp David. Hopes that the meeting might permanently settle the border between Israel and its Arabic neighbors may appear naive in retrospect, but expectations were nonetheless high.

After thirteen days of negotiations in September 1978, the **Camp David Accords** were completed. Israel agreed to completely withdraw from the Sinai Peninsula while Egypt became the first Arabic nation to acknowledge the legitimacy of the Jewish state. As both nations agreed to maintain regular diplomatic relations and continue working toward a permanent solution to the Israeli-Palestinian crisis, Carter's approval ratings rebounded from a low of one in three Americans to about half of the public holding a positive view of their president. This tentative agreement between former enemies would become the most enduring image of Carter's accomplishments as president. The agreement also occurred just prior to another conflict in the Middle East that would help to ensure that Carter would not win a second term as president.

In January 1979, anti-Western sentiment in Iran culminated in the **Iranian Revolution**. Supporters of Ayatollah Khomeini seized power and forced the US-backed shah of Iran to flee for his life. Khomeini sought to nationalize the oil industry in Iran, seizing the assets of Western oil companies that had operated in his country due to agreements between the United States and the shah of Iran in previous decades. Iranian shipments of oil to the United States ended abruptly as a result of Khomeini's seizure of the oil fields, and this intensified the energy crisis throughout 1979. Although Iran produced only a small percentage of the oil Americans consumed, oil prices doubled. The price hike led many to question whether supply and demand was driving US oil prices or if powerful interests were conspiring to use world events as a pretext to increase prices.

The desire for cheap oil and huge profits for Western oil companies had led the American CIA and British Secret Service to help the now-deposed shah of Iran regain power when a similar revolution occurred in 1953. Given this history, many Iranians believed that the United States was sheltering the former dictator in preparation for yet another coup when the shah was granted exile in the United States. In actuality, there were no plans for a coup. The shah had cancer and President Carter decided to allow the shah to enter the United States to undergo medical treatments. Few Iranians were impressed by the president's compassion toward the dictator they had just overthrown. On November 4, 1979, a mob of armed Iranians, many of whom were college students, stormed the US embassy in Tehran and seized fifty-two American hostages. The captors demanded that the shah be returned to Iran where he would face trial and a likely execution. The Iranian rebels also called for a formal apology by the United States for its role in the 1953 coup that had placed the shah in power. Finally, they demanded the return of millions of dollars they believed the shah had stolen from the Iranian people.

Carter responded to the **Iranian Hostage Crisis** by freezing Iranian assets in the United States, placing an embargo on Iranian oil shipments, and deporting college students of Iranian descent who were studying abroad in the United States. The president's supporters believed negotiating with Iran would be tantamount to rewarding terrorists who had taken innocent Americans as hostages. Although most Americans rallied behind Carter initially, the public became increasingly critical of their president as the weeks turned to months without resolution. The hostage crisis received more television coverage than any event prior to the Vietnam War. The American public endured nightly images of Iranian students burning American flags and pundits demanding that their president do something to save the hostages. Carter recognized the near impossibility of a rescue effort. However, political pressure led him to eventually approve a daring but ill-conceived mission to recover the hostages. Poor weather caused a helicopter and a refueling plane to collide before US forces had even entered Iranian airspace. The accident killed eight servicemen. As Iranians celebrated the deaths of these US soldiers, the captors decided to hide the hostages throughout Iran to discourage further rescue attempts.

Carter attempted to resolve the hostage crisis through Khomeini, but the Iranian leader refused to acknowledge the president's communications until September 1980. The reason for Khomeini's sudden willingness to talk in September was the result of an invasion of his country, not by American commandos, but from Iraqi troops. The outbreak of the Iran-Iraq War forced Khomeini to view the hostages as potential bargaining chips with the West. He recognized that America's tentative support for Iraq was reinforced by the hostage crisis. He was also in desperate need for US-made spare parts and ammunition for his military.

Iranian dependency on the US arms industry was the result of prior weapons sales made during the years that the United States and Iran had been allies. In addition, wealthy interests within Iran grew increasingly anxious that their personal assets in the United States remained frozen as a result of the hostage crisis. Because of these concerns, Iranian leaders negotiated the release of the hostages in return for the release of nearly $8 billion of Iranian money that was in US banks or invested in American businesses and real estate.

The agreement was made in the final months of 1980 but did not take effect until the following year. Iran sought to maximize their political leverage with the newly elected president Ronald Reagan by holding the hostages until moments after Reagan had been sworn into office on January 20, 1981. The new president skillfully connected the release of the hostages to his leadership. The deception furthered the image that Carter was to blame for the longevity of the crisis, which had kept the hostages captive for 444 days. To many Americans, the return of the hostages supported Reagan's claim that it was "morning again in America." However, the deal also signaled a new dawn for US enemies willing to commit acts of terror to further their financial interests or political agenda. Reagan himself emboldened these enemies by negotiating covert arms sales with terrorists, spinning a web of deception that spanned several continents and might have led to his impeachment had the details of these arms deals been revealed.

FIGURE 12.23

Students at Miami-Dade Community College participate in one of the many demonstrations against Iran and Iranians who were living in the United States during the hostage crisis.

REVIEW AND CRITICAL THINKING

1. What was Carter's approach to the economic problems that plagued the nation during his presidency? Explain how Carter's "Malaise" speech affected his public perception and why many Americans grew increasingly critical of President Carter's approach.

2. Summarize the rise and fall of the movement to pass the Equal Rights Amendment. Explain the issues and concerns of those who supported and opposed the amendment. What do you think were the concerns raised by Phyllis Schlafly fair criticisms of the amendment?

3. How was Carter's foreign policy different and similar from other presidents during the Cold War? Why were some Americans so critical of Carter's foreign policy? What were there arguments, and what evidence were they able to cite? Contrast these perspectives with those who supported the president.

4. Summarize the reasons given in the textbook for the decline of the New Left and the simultaneous increase in pessimism that occurred during the 1970s. Using specific examples, evaluate these conclusions and consider other possible reasons for the conservative drift of the late 1970s.

5. CONCLUSION

The 1970s saw the end of the Vietnam War, the beginning of a war in the Middle East, and the first president to be removed from office. For residents of Africa, Latin America, and Southeast Asia, a third-rate burglary to wiretap the phones of an opposing political party hardly seemed like crimes compared to the Nixon administration's efforts to topple governments and prolong wars in their countries. But Watergate was different because it used the power of the federal government against a political rival in a way that clearly threatened democracy at home. While the foreign policies of Nixon and his predecessors were often driven by political self-interest, they were also aimed at a goal most Americans identified with—halting the spread of Communism. There was no way to spin the Watergate break-in as anything but an abuse of power driven by personal self-advancement rather than an honest if misguided attempt to fight Communism.

American popular culture mirrored its political culture, shifting away from both the idealism and the excesses of the late 1960s. Cultural icons such as Jimi Hendrix and Janis Joplin both died of drug overdoses in 1970. Vietnam, Watergate, economic stagflation, and the Iranian hostage situation led many to question the assumption that American history was intrinsically tied to progress. The once idealistic youths of the 1960s seemed to disappear, replaced by radicals such as the Weather Underground Organization that advocated violence and other groups that rejected the liberal idealism of Martin Luther King Jr. and Robert Kennedy. These martyred leaders had hoped to use the power of the government to combat poverty and injustice. In many ways, their supporters succeeded in getting the federal government to address both of these issues.

Eager to secure a broad political base, civil rights leaders connected lofty ideals of freedom and equality to measures that simply outlawed discrimination. Desiring to win funding, liberals such as Sargent Shriver predicted that Johnson's War on Poverty would bring economic security to all Americans within a decade. The war in Vietnam limited the funding that might have otherwise been available for these programs. At the same time, the optimistic pronouncements of the New Left also raised expectations beyond what should have been anticipated by the limited actions taken by the federal government. Promised a great society where federal programs eliminated poverty and discrimination, most Americans grew frustrated and blamed some combination of the federal government, minorities, and the underprivileged for the persistence of poverty and racial injustice.

Most of the student activists of the late 1960s and early 1970s graduated from college and found good-paying jobs. If some of these students felt conflicted by working for the same corporate system they had once derided, they soon discovered that mortgages and student loans have a way of changing one's worldview. In short, the "Yippies" that disrupted the 1968 Democratic National Convention with their antiestablishment rhetoric had become the "Yuppies"—a loosely constructed acronym for young urban professionals. As the idealism of the 1960s faded into the crushing realities of the 1970s, the New Left began to fade away as a political force. Perhaps the poor had been given their fair chance, some began to believe, and now it was time to address the sudden avalanche of problems ranging from energy to the economy. Perhaps America suddenly realized that simple justice would not be so simple after all, and the recent converts to liberal causes simply bolted from the movement. Even if the causes of the shifting climate were not clear, it was apparent that the New Left had receded throughout the 1970s and a New Right had emerged by 1980.

6. FURTHER READING

Bauman, Robert. *Race and the War on Poverty: From Watts to East L.A.* (2008).

Cowie, Jefferson. *Stayin' Alive: The 1970s and the Last Days of the Working Class* (2010).

Evans, Sara. *Personal Politics: The Roots of Women's Liberation in the Civil Rights Movement and the New Left* (1980).

Fergus, Devin. *Liberalism, Black Power, and the Making of American Politics, 1965–1980* (2009).

Garcia, Ignacio. *Chicanismo: The Forging of a Militant Ethos Among Mexican Americans* (2000).

Jeffries, Hassan Kwame. *Bloody Lowndes: Civil Rights and Black Power in Alabama's Black Belt* (2010).

Mathews, Donald, and Jane S. Hart. *Sex, Gender, and the Politics of ERA* (1990).

Mieczkowski, Yanek. *Gerald Ford and the Challenges of the 1970s* (2005).

Patterson, James T. *Grand Expectations: The United States, 1945–1974* (1997).

Rosen, Ruth. *The World Split Open: How the Modern Women's Movement Changed America* (2000).

Smith, Paul Chaat, and Robert Allen Warrior. *Like a Hurricane: The Indian Movement from Alcatraz to Wounded Knee* (1997).

CHAPTER 13

The Reagan and Bush Years, 1980–1992

By the summer of 1980, most Americans were deeply concerned about the economy and world events. Stagflation had taken its toll on the economy and unemployment approached 8 percent. Interest rates remained so high that few businesses or consumers could take out loans. The energy crisis continued to remind Americans of their nation's vulnerabilities. Even worse, America seemed helpless in the face of Iranian terrorists who still held fifty-two American hostages. Americans were also concerned that annual budget deficits continued even after the Vietnam War ended. As the 1980 elections arrived, only a third of Americans approved of the job President Jimmy Carter was doing. Only Nixon, at the height of the Watergate scandal, had lower approval ratings.

In response to all of these factors, many Americans supported a growing conservative movement that promised a new direction for the nation based on limiting the size and power of the federal government. Other conservatives lashed out at liberal programs they believed had failed and recipients of welfare, recent immigrants, and supporters of affirmative action. Former actor turned politician **Ronald Reagan** spoke to the concerns of both groups of American conservatives—those who supported the ideas of conservative political and economic theorists and those who believed that America's problems were the result of a parasitical infection on the body politic. Reagan also appealed to the nostalgia of older Americans who longed for the years when US military's might was unchallenged and when US factories produced nearly half of the world's manufactured goods.

Reagan confidently and warmly projected the simple message that he would ensure that American economic power and prestige was restored. Reagan's campaign was upbeat, simple, direct, and for many of his supporters, uplifting. Reagan's fetes also reminded many Americans of an earlier time they hoped to return to. Reagan rallies were as full of patriotic optimism as a Fourth of July parade, while Carter's speeches often felt more like lectures about the problems the nation faced. The message resounded with older whites, especially among white males who were twice as likely to vote for Reagan as nonwhites. For many Americans, however, the way Reagan spoke with and about minorities and the Reagan campaign's cavalier attitude toward their perspectives threatened to reverse the progress the country had made.

Ronald Reagan

A leading Hollywood actor for several decades, Ronald Reagan entered politics after a rousing speech endorsing conservative presidential candidate Barry Goldwater in 1964. Two years later, Reagan became the governor of California. Reagan nearly defeated Ford in the Republican primary of 1976 and would win a landslide election in 1980 to become the fortieth president.

1. CONSERVATISM AND THE "REAGAN REVOLUTION"

LEARNING OBJECTIVES

1. Understand the goals of the New Right and the way this movement represented the concerns of many Americans of different backgrounds during the 1980s. Also, demonstrate understanding of the perspectives of those who opposed the New Right.

2. Explain the priorities of Reagan's administration and how his economic policies affected the nation. Describe "Reaganomics" both from the perspective of the president's supporters and his critics.

3. Describe the impact women had on the conservative movement. Also, summarize the election of 1980. Explain the key issues of the election and the significance of Reagan's victory on US history.

1.1 The New Right

New Right

A coalition of fiscal and social conservatives who supported lower taxes and smaller government while espousing evangelical Christianity. The New Right rose to prominence in the late 1970s and early 1980s and supported political leaders such as Ronald Reagan.

FIGURE 13.1

Ronald Reagan shakes hands with President Gerald Ford at the 1976 Republican National Convention. Reagan had just been narrowly defeated by Ford in the Republican primaries, but Reagan's strong showing against the incumbent president demonstrated the former actor's political appeal to a growing conservative movement.

Many conservatives felt that their perspectives had been marginalized during the 1960s and 1970s. Conservative politicians believed that the shortcomings of liberalism had made many Americans eager for a different approach. These conservative politicians and voters were part of the **New Right** of the 1980s, a group that perceived their nation had been derailed by a liberal agenda in recent years. Conservatives hoped to reduce the size of the federal government beyond the military, decrease taxes and spending on social welfare programs, and find a way to repair the nation's economic strength and global prestige. Most conservatives supported the end of segregation and hoped to end discrimination in employment. However, they disagreed with many of the strategies used to achieve these goals and hoped to reverse programs designed to achieve racial balance through affirmative action.

Just as the New Left sought to distance themselves from the Socialists of the "old left," the New Right attempted to shed its association with the "old right" that had attempted to keep women and minorities "in their place" during previous decades. The New Right hoped to mix compassion and conservatism, assisting the poor but avoiding the direct welfare payments they believed discouraged individual accountability by rewarding those who did not work. They also hoped to replace the nation's progressive tax code that charged wealthier Americans higher rates with a new tax bracket they believed was more balanced. By this perspective, Americans who had demonstrated initiative and entrepreneurial skill should be permitted to keep more of their income as a means of encouraging reinvestment.

The conservatives of the 1980s had learned from the social movements of the 1960s, especially the importance of simple and direct messages appealed to Americans' sense of justice. However, while liberals had looked toward the future in crafting their message, conservatives looked toward the past. This orientation helped the New Right win many supporters during an era of uncertainty about the future. It also offered tremendous appeal to those who feared that traditional values were slipping away. At the same time, the nostalgic orientation of many conservatives encouraged the creation of a sanitized version of the past that neglected America's many failures both at home and abroad. Perhaps unintentionally, the New Right appealed to many of the same people who had opposed the expansion of civil rights. As a result, there remained a tension between those of the New Right that sought both equality and limited government and those who simply wanted to roll back the clock to another era.

What the base of the conservative movement lacked in racial diversity, it sought to make up by representing a number of different backgrounds and perspectives. Evangelical Christians, struggling blue-collar workers, middle-class voters, and disenchanted Democrats united with economic conservatives and business leaders. Together these individuals supported a movement that merged conservative and probusiness economic policies with socially conservative goals such as ending abortion, welfare, and affirmative action. Interest groups affiliated with the Republican Party also stressed a return to moral standards they identified as "family values." These conservative groups increasingly viewed opposition to multiculturalism, gay rights, the feminist movement, abortion, busing, affirmative action, illegal immigration, and welfare as panaceas for the nation's ills.

This new conservative movement advanced a populist rhetoric that appealed to the working and middle classes in ways not seen in US politics since the turn of the century. Unlike the People's Party of the 1890s, which focused primarily on economic issues, the public focus of the new conservative coalition was on social issues. The challenge for the New Right was that modern politics required the mobilization of both wealth and the masses, two groups that had traditionally opposed one another. The strength of the conservative movement was its ability to weld probusiness economic policies with support for conservative social issues in a way that attracted a core group of devoted supporters *and* the backing of wealthy donors.

Without the Evangelical revival of the late 1970s and early 1980s, such a coalition might have never occurred. The United States experienced a period of religious revivalism during the late 1970s and early 1980s. Similar to the Great Awakening of the early eighteenth-century, charismatic religious leaders became national celebrities and attracted legions of loyal followers. The most outspoken of these leaders were a new breed of clergy known as "televangelists" who attracted millions of loyal viewers through religious television programs. Televangelists like Billy Graham, Pat Robertson, and Jim and Tammy Faye Bakker saw their virtual congregations grow as they progressed from old-fashioned revival meetings to radio programs and eventually popular television programs like the *700 Club*—each broadcast on several Christian cable networks.

Evangelical Christian denominations experienced a tremendous surge in membership during these years. Southern Baptists become the nation's largest denomination while the more rigidly structured Christian denominations declined in membership. Christian religions in which membership largely shaped one's daily life, such as the Church of Jesus Christ of Latter-Day Saints (known colloquially as the Mormons), Seventh-Day Adventists, and the Assembly of God also experienced tremendous growth and influence.

While many of these churches avoided direct political affiliations, some televangelists and independent clergy saw political action as part of their mission. These and other religious leaders advocated a host of conservative social issues and recommended political candidates to their followers. Most churches avoided explicit support for a particular candidate or political party for a variety of reasons. Churches were exempt from taxes because of the doctrine of separation of church and state. Many believed sponsoring political candidates threatened that separation and would lead to forfeiture of a church's tax-exempt status. Televangelists like Jerry Falwell challenged that division along with several other leading religious conservatives. Falwell hosted the popular *Old Time Gospel Hour* and solicited his donors to join his political action committee, known as the "**Moral Majority**." These and other political groups claimed responsibility for the election of President Ronald Reagan and a host of other conservative Republicans. The boast was likely a stretch in the case of Reagan, especially given the public's frustration with Carter and the small following these interest groups enjoyed in 1980. However, during the 1982 congressional election, groups such as the Moral Majority enjoyed the support of millions of donors. As a result, the endorsement of these religious-political groups was essential in many congressional districts.

The religious fervor of the 1980s featured aspects of protest against the materialism of the decade, as well as a celebration of it. Just as some Puritans of the colonial era believed that wealth was a sign of God's favor, wealthy individuals during the 1980s were more likely to flaunt their affluence than previous generations. Displays of conspicuous consumption had become regarded as unsavory during the more liberal era of the 1960s and 1970s, but during the 1980s, they were once again celebrated as evidence that one adhered to righteous values such as hard work and prudence. Many of the leading televangelists joined in the decade's celebration of material wealth by purchasing lavish homes and luxury items. The result was a number of high-profile investigations into the possible misuse of donations by televangelists.

Many conservatives, especially white Southerners, inherited traditions of suspicion toward the federal government. This circumspection was magnified by the federal government's legalization of abortion and stricter enforcement of the doctrine of separation of church and state in the public schools. Conservatives also bristled at many of their governmental leaders' growing toleration of homosexuality while mandatory school prayer and state-funded Christmas celebrations were forbidden. From the perspective of social conservatives, each of these occurrences demonstrated that large and powerful government bureaucracies were more likely to support liberal causes. As a result, Evangelicals increasingly supported both social and fiscally conservative causes. Tax breaks, the elimination of welfare programs, and the reduction in the size of the federal government became leading issues of the new Evangelicals. However, most of the new religious right also supported increasing the power of the government to ban behaviors they believed were sinful, while supporting increased authority for law enforcement and larger budgets for national defense.

A variety of conservative intellectuals who were concerned with each of these social issues had developed a number of organizations dedicated to advancing their ideals among the American people. These "think tanks," as they would euphemistically be called, included the American Enterprise Institute and the Heritage Foundation, among others. Each of these groups depended on the donations of both rank-and-file conservatives and a number of wealthy donors. As these groups and the

FIGURE 13.2

Evangelical Christians formed the base of the New Right. Pictured here is a group of fundamentalist Christians in Charleston, West Virginia. Evangelicals made national headlines in 1974 when they protested the use of textbooks they believed contained a liberal agenda to spread ideas such as multiculturalism.

Moral Majority

A political action group consisting of an estimated 4 million evangelical Christians at its peak in the early 1980s. The Moral Majority was led by televangelist Jerry Falwell and supported issues such as legalizing school prayer, teaching creationism rather than evolution, and outlawing abortion.

conservative causes they believed in grew in popularity, conservative politicians won elections by promoting the issues these think tanks supported. Although many conservative politicians tended to subordinate their economic platform in favor of discussing hot button conservative issues that mobilized their supporters, by 1980, many conservative voters also came to believe that lowering taxes for corporations and the wealthy while reducing government spending for social programs would lead to greater prosperity. In other words, the conservative movement succeeded not only by mobilizing voters on social issues but also by altering the perception of the government's proper role in the economy. Whereas middle- and working-class Americans had been more apt to support unions and progressive tax policies during the previous three decades, by the 1980s, a growing number of these same individuals agreed with conservatives about the potential danger of powerful labor unions and feared that higher taxes for corporations and the wealthy might discourage economic growth.

1.2   Election of 1980

Reagan first tapped into the frustrations of the 1970s as a gubernatorial candidate in California promising to cut taxes and prosecute student protesters. As a presidential candidate in 1980, he took every opportunity to remind Americans of the current recession. The Reagan campaign convinced many voters that Carter had made the problem worse by pursuing strategies that tightened the money supply and pushed interest rates as high as 20 percent. Although inflation was the main reason these rates were so high and Carter's actions would reduce inflation over time, the inability of corporations and consumers to borrow money in the short term added to the dire condition of the economy in the summer of 1980. "Are you better off than you were four years ago?" Reagan asked, connecting the nation's economic problems to the Carter administration. The fact that the recession predated Carter's election mattered little. "A recession is when your neighbor loses a job," Reagan later remarked as the election neared. "A depression is when you lose yours." After pausing for effect, the former actor delivered his final line: "and recovery begins when Jimmy Carter loses his."

Candidate Reagan promised to reverse America's declining international prestige and restore its industrial production—two problems many agreed had grown worse under Carter's watch. Reagan also promised to reduce taxes in ways that would spur investment and job creation, reduce the size of the federal government, balance the federal budget, and strengthen national defense. More importantly, he communicated what most Americans believed to be true—that theirs was a strong nation with a noble past. Behind Reagan's populist appeal was one essential message with a long history in American political thought: freedom *from* government rather than freedom *through* government. Reagan preached that the cure for America's ills was to take decision making and power away from Washington and place it in the hands of US businesses and consumers.

FIGURE 13.3

As a Hollywood actor, Ronald Reagan played the character of Notre Dame's George Gipp. In this photo, Reagan is holding a customized jersey bearing the nickname "Gipper" but featuring America's colors instead of the gold and blue of Notre Dame.

Critics of the California movie star claimed that Reagan's rhetoric was hollow and clichéd, even if it was uplifting. They likely missed the point: Reagan was appealing to a nation that felt like it needed a win. Years before, Reagan starred in a film where he played the role of legendary Notre Dame athlete George Gipp. As the nation appeared to be up against the wall, the former actor now assumed the role of Notre Dame coach Knute Rockne, asking America to "win one for the Gipper." Reagan's use of the phrase was out of context, historically inaccurate, and offered nothing in terms of policy or substance. And it was political magic. If presidential elections were popularity contests, Carter did not stand a chance.

With his charisma, charm, and populist appeal, Reagan won the general election by sweeping forty-four states. The Republican Party won control of the Senate for the first time in several decades. The landslide was not as clear as it might appear, however, as voter turnout was so low that only a quarter of Americans of voting age actually cast ballots for Reagan. As some historians often point out, had voter turnout been the same as previous elections and if those voters had followed historical patterns (such as union members supporting the Democratic candidate), Carter would have actually won in a landslide. At the same time, voter apathy is usually a reflection of how many Americans feel about their government. As a result, the low turnout may have been its own kind of referendum on Carter's presidency. The most significant factor in the election was the political power of the New Right. More than 20 percent of self-identified Evangelical Christians who had voted for Carter in 1976 indicated that they voted for Reagan in 1980.

Even Reagan's opponents conceded that the new president was one of the finest public speakers when it came to delivering a scripted oration. Years in front of the camera meant that Reagan instinctively knew where to stand and what camera to look at, much to the chagrin of interns whose job it was to place tape marks and arrows on stages across the country. However, Reagan was often adrift when speaking without a script. He relied heavily on clichés and empty platitudes, and sometimes told stories from popular films as if they were part of history or his own life.

While most of Reagan's tales were anecdotal in nature and some were simply meant to illustrate a point, Reagan's casualness with the truth could also be quite damaging. As a candidate, Reagan aroused populist anger against welfare recipients by fabricating a story about a woman in Chicago's South Side neighborhood. This scam artist reportedly drove a new Cadillac and had received hundreds of thousands of dollars in welfare checks under multiple names. Later investigations demonstrated that Reagan had made up the entire story. Even if Reagan would have offered a retraction, the populist anger against welfare recipients could not be easily reversed. Although the woman was fictional, Reagan played heavily on prejudices against African Americans by describing this "welfare mother" in terms that were clearly meant to imply race.

Many scholars in subsequent decades have questioned whether social conservatives had actually been tricked into voting for politicians who represented the interests of the wealthy and corporations while offering little support for social issues. Reagan had been president of the Screen Actors Guild and could hardly be counted on to support tougher censorship laws. As governor of California, Reagan had supported a reproductive rights law that removed barriers on abortions. Although he relied on the support of pro-life groups, once President, Reagan avoided direct action on the controversial subject of abortion. He also did little beyond offering verbal support for socially conservative causes such as school prayer.

Some observers were surprised that Evangelicals would support a candidate such as Reagan, a divorced Hollywood actor who did not attend church. In contrast, Jimmy Carter was a born-again Christian. However, Evangelicals understood that Carter did not believe that his personal religious ideas should influence policy and he generally supported the more liberal views of his Democratic supporters. In addition, many working-class voters supported Reagan's proposed tax cuts, believing they would result in domestic job creation. Although their reaction confounded many liberals, cuts to welfare were also popular with the working-class voters because welfare had failed to eliminate poverty and seemed in many cases to offer a disincentive to work. Finally, in the wake of scandals involving union leaders such as Jimmy Hoffa, many social conservatives were also hostile toward unions.

Although he did little to further socially conservative causes through legislation, Reagan took immediate action against unions. One of Reagan's first actions as president was to fire more than 10,000 federal air traffic controllers who were part of a union that was striking for a pay increase. Reagan replaced these workers with military personnel on active-duty orders, a move that quickly destroyed the strike and the union. Reagan also supported employers who used similar measures to crush labor activism. And yet 40 percent of union members still voted for Reagan over the Democrat Walter Mondale in 1984. Reagan and other conservatives also supported measures that lowered taxes for corporations and supported free trade policies that made it easier for US companies to open factories in foreign countries. By 1986, Reagan had slashed tax rates for the wealthy by more than 50 percent without similar cuts for the middle and lower classes. Although it confounded many Democrats, Reagan retained the support of many union voters and lower-income Americans through his second term.

1.3 Women and the New Right

Women had composed both the leadership and the rank-and-file of the New Left. The role of women was equally as important to the New Right during the 1980s. Mobilized in opposition to the Equal Rights Amendment (ERA), conservative women mirrored some of the tactics and organizational structure of civil rights activists. Conservative women leaned heavily on the church and other institutions, and also mirrored the organizational structure of previous social movements. The names of conservative women's groups reflected their belief in traditional notions of family and gender. Women Who Want to be Women (WWWW) and Happiness of Motherhood Eternal (HOME) were two such organizations. Conservative women viewed the rapprochement of straight and lesbian activists within the feminist movement, along with recent decisions by the Supreme Court upholding abortion laws and banning school prayer, as proof that they were waging a war against the ungodly forces of both Sodom and Gomorrah.

Reagan's nomination of **Sandra Day O'Connor** encouraged conservative women, less as a symbol of women's advancement as the first woman to join the Supreme Court than the hope that O'Connor would reverse *Roe v. Wade*. Despite her conservatism, O'Connor and other Supreme Court justices upheld the legality of abortion in a number of cases, although they did support an increasing number of restrictions to the procedure. Many conservatives and Evangelicals felt betrayed by the Republican Party and began organizing direct protests against abortion providers.

Sandra Day O'Connor

An attorney originally from El Paso, Texas, Sandra Day O'Connor became the first female Supreme Court justice in 1981.

FIGURE 13.4

Sandra Day O'Connor became the first woman on the US Supreme Court. Because she had a conservative orientation, many of the president's supporters among the New Right hoped she and other Reagan appointees might overturn *Roe v. Wade*.

Thousands of antiabortion activists descended on Wichita, Kansas, under the auspices of a group called Operation Rescue in 1991. The majority of the participants in the self-labeled "Summer of Mercy" were women, many of whom physically blocked the entrances to abortion clinics and were among the 2,000 protesters who were arrested. At the same time, many conservative and evangelical women who opposed abortion also opposed the aggressive tactics of Operation Rescue. This was especially true of the individuals who harassed and even murdered abortion providers that summer. More representative of the conservatism of women during this period were the hundreds of thousands of local women who led community organizations that sought encourage single mothers to consider adoption. Others joined organizations that sought to ameliorate some of the social changes they felt had led to increases in the number of single mothers. Other conservatives sought to prevent drug addiction, crime, and pornography, and to reverse societal toleration for obscenities in Hollywood.

Protests against an increasingly secular popular culture raised questions regarding traditional modes of gender-based divisions of labor in modern families. For millions of women, a life dedicated to family was an important and fulfilling vocation, a dignified calling they feared the feminist movement sought to slander. Books written by conservative homemakers and career women alike proliferated during the 1970s and 1980s. For example, Helen Andelin's *Fascinating Womanhood* sold millions of copies and launched a movement that inspired thousands of women to create and attend neighborhood classes and discussion networks. Andelin believed that the ideal family was one of male leadership and provision alongside female submission and support. Andelin asked her readers to consider what traits made them desirable to their husbands and strengthen their marriages by finding ways to increase this desire and better serve their husband's needs. Although historians might question the accuracy of the author's claims that this patriarchal model was ever typical in any era of American family life, Andelin described a mythical past that most Americans believed had existed. For millions of conservatives seeking a return to a bygone era, it naturally followed that the family should seek a return to traditional arrangements based on paternal leadership.

Other conservative women criticized Andelin as promoting a fiction that more resembled the 1974 novel *The Stepford Wives* than a well-adjusted family. Many conservative women simply sought to counter the image that stay-at-home mothers were somehow naive or victimized. These women agreed that gender discrimination did limit the options of women in the past and believed that women should be free to pursue careers. However, these women also feared that elevating the dignity of women in the workforce had at least unintentionally led many to question the dignity of labor within the home. Not all who espoused a return to traditional modes of gender and family were conservatives or Evangelicals, and many women who had enjoyed successful careers outside the home reported their equal happiness as homemakers. These women hoped to encourage the recognition that many "traditional" couples were genuine partnerships based on mutual respect.

However, for millions of US families, the tradition of women not working outside the home was not economically feasible. By the early 1980s, the majority of married women worked both inside and beyond the home. Many found the experience to be anything but liberating. While these women recognized that gender discrimination limited their career options, they aggressively countered notions that homemaker was a career of last resort. One of the leading criticisms of these women against the idealized superwoman of the 1980s who balanced career and family was related to the sacrifices such balancing required. Sociologists labeled the added burden of career and family the "**second shift**," reflecting the frustration of women who found that their husbands seldom agreed to share domestic responsibilities, even though wives were increasingly likely to work the same number of hours outside of the home.

second shift

A phrase connoting the added burdens of married women with full-time careers who were still expected to fulfill the domestic responsibilities of a homemaker and parent.

1.4 "Reaganomics" and its Critics

Income tax in the United States historically followed the doctrine of progressive taxation, creating tax brackets that increase as an individual earns more money throughout the year. For example, a physician making $200,000 might have the majority of her income taxed at 40 percent, while a firefighter who made $35,000 would be taxed at 20 percent, and a college student working part time who earned only $5,000 might pay no federal income tax at all. For Reagan, the progressive tax structure was responsible for the persistence of America's economic problems. As a Hollywood actor in an era where taxes on those with large salaries was very high, Reagan saw more and more of his income go to taxes as his annual earnings increased. After producing a couple of films each year, any additional money Reagan might make could be taxed at rates approaching 90 percent when adding California's state tax to the federal rate. In response, Reagan chose to make only a handful of films each year.

Reagan drew heavily from his experience as an actor in many aspects of his presidency. In the case of tax policies, the president believed that high tax rates discouraged other talented and successful individuals in their chosen fields from making a maximum effort each year. In his field, it might mean fewer movies. However, if entrepreneurs and financiers followed a similar strategy, then high taxes would constrain economic growth. Believing in a sort of economic Darwinism, Reagan argued that the best way to encourage job creation was to reduce the taxes for high-income Americans because these elites had demonstrated a talent for creating wealth. The wealthy, Reagan argued, could be expected to use their money to produce more wealth through investment and innovation that would spur job growth for everyone else. To this end, Reagan's Economic Recovery Tax Act of 1981 reduced the top tax bracket from 70 to 50 percent while slashing taxes paid by corporations.

The super wealthy were not the only beneficiaries of Reagan's tax cuts, which led to an overall reduction of tax rates by 30 percent throughout his first term. More controversial was the reduction in inheritance taxes. These taxes were not based on earned income, but rather taxed the transfer of wealth from one generation to another. These taxes had inspired many of the richest Americans to donate their fortunes in previous decades. As a result, removing the inheritance tax was much harder to justify in terms of economic stimulus.

FIGURE 13.5

President Reagan discusses a chart that portrays his tax plan as offering substantial savings for the average family. In reality, Reagan's tax policies favored the wealthy and corporations, something the president's supporters believed would result in greater overall economic development.

In his second term, Reagan passed the most sweeping changes to the tax code since the Sixteenth Amendment established the modern system of federal income tax. The **Tax Reform Act of 1986** lowered the highest tax bracket from 50 percent to 28 percent while increasing the minimum rate from 11 percent to 15 percent. The reform also eliminated many of the various tax brackets between these rates, meaning that most Americans either paid 15 percent or 28 percent. A few provisions helped the poor, such as a cost-of-living adjustment to the amount of money that was exempt from taxation so that those living below the federal poverty level no longer received a tax bill. Other reforms eliminated various tax shelters for individuals, although many of these ways of hiding income remained for corporations. The law also required parents to list the social security numbers for each dependent child they claimed for tax purposes, eliminating the ability of individuals to increase their tax deductions through fraudulently listing imaginary dependents. As a popular economist has shown, the reform led to the disappearance of 7 million "children" on April 15, 1987.

Reagan's tax cuts reduced federal revenue by hundreds of billions of dollars each year. This reduction of income could only be offset by equal reductions to the federal budget, borrowing money, or a massive economic boom that created so much taxable wealth that the government still took in more money each year. Reagan promised the latter would occur—the result of an unfettered economy free from aggressive taxation and government regulation. Reagan also proposed significant budget cuts to Social Security and Medicare, just to make sure that the federal budget could be balanced while the nation awaited the economic bonanza he believed his tax cuts would produce. However, cuts to Social Security and Medicare provoked outrage, and Reagan quickly reversed course. In the end, the president approved a budget that was similar to previous years except with massive increases for the military.

Tax Reform Act of 1986

A sweeping tax reform law that simplified the tax code and eliminated some tax shelters and other methods that had been used in the past to hide income or illegally reduce one's tax burden. The law reduced the top tax rates wealthy individuals paid from 50 percent to 28 percent, while raising the minimum tax rate to 15 percent

supply-side economics

An economic theory that suggests government policies should be geared toward keeping revenue and economic decisions in the hands of businesses and consumers. While Keynesian economics suggests using the federal government to stimulate growth through a variety of measures, supply-side economics suggest lowering taxes and regulations on business and trade as ways of stimulating the economy.

Reagan's defense budgets continued to grow each year, doubling the annual budget to an incredible $330 billion by 1985. As a result, many challenged the president to identify exactly how he would fulfill his promise to reduce the nation's indebtedness. Even Reagan's budget director admitted that his administration's economic projections were based on an optimistic faith that reducing taxes for the wealthy would "trickle down" to the middle and lower classes through job creation. This confidence in **supply-side economics** that emphasized government intervention to spur growth and investment through tax reduction was certainly not a new idea. However, because the Reagan administration pursued the principles of supply-side economics with such vigor, the basic theory that increasing the wealth of the wealthy would eventually trickle down to the rest of the nation became known as "Reaganomics." Critics of the president used other monikers such as "voodoo economics" to describe Reagan's theories.

Supporters of Reagan's belief in supply-side economics point out that the Dow Jones Industrial Average—a measurement of the value of the 30 largest companies in the United States—tripled during the 1980s. Inflation fell from over 10 percent when Reagan took office to less than 4 percent, while unemployment fell from 7 percent to just over 5 percent. Critics of Reagan point to the increasing disparity between the rich and the poor that also accelerated during the 1980s as being the real consequence of Reagan's regressive tax policies. They also disagree that tax cuts for the wealthy created jobs, pointing out that the percentage of jobs that paid wages above the poverty level had declined. Critics agree that tax cuts for corporations provided additional revenue for investment, but argue that much of this investment had been used to create manufacturing facilities in other nations.

national debt

The total amount of money that a nation presently owes its creditors.

Although the president's critics usually concede that Reagan's tax cuts and military spending did spur the economy and create some jobs in the short run, they argue that they did so only by borrowing massive sums of money. The size of the **national debt**—the cumulative total of all the money the federal government owes—tripled from $900 billion to nearly $3 trillion in only eight years. Between the start and conclusion of the Reagan administration, the United States had gone from being the leading creditor in the world to the most indebted nation in the world.

deficit spending

This occurs when a government borrows money to finance its operations.

Previous administrations tolerated **deficit spending**—the practice of borrowing money to make up for the amount the government overspent in one particular year. However, the amounts the government borrowed were usually quite small unless the nation was at war. After the 1930s, some government borrowing was also accepted in times of financial crisis as a way to spur the economy. Neither scenario applied to the eight peaceful years of Reagan's presidency, yet the government accumulated a debt that was three times greater than the combined annual deficits of the past two centuries. And contrary to the tradition of repaying the debt, deficits and debt continued to grow at the same pace when former vice president George H. W. Bush took office. The interest on the debt alone quickly became the largest non-defense-related federal expenditure. As a result, any effort to reduce the national debt could only be achieved after balancing the budget and paying hundreds of billions of dollars in interest.

Political candidates are known for making sweeping promises, yet the question of whether Reagan kept his pledge to restore the strength of the US economy remains an item of fierce debate. Democrats are quick to point out that Carter's decision to halt inflationary measures as well as the normal business cycle were part of the reason the economy recovered during the 1980s. Reagan's critics also contrast his promise of fiscal responsibility and smaller government with the tripling of the national debt and the expansion of the federal government, which grew in terms of both budget and the number of federal workers. Furthermore, President Reagan never submitted a balanced budget, and even the debt projections that came from his budget office were too optimistic.

Reagan himself usually deflected the criticisms of his economic policy in a good-humored manner that undermined some of his critics. "You know economists," he would respond, they "see something that works in practice and wonder if it works in theory." Reagan even seemed impervious to an assassin's bullet that ricocheted and lodged near his heart in March 1981. The unfazed president thanked nearby secret servicemen for their service and even joked with surgeons by asking if they were Democrats before they removed the bullet. Most Americans lacked a sophisticated understanding of supply-side economics, but they knew the economy had floundered under Carter and was recovering under Reagan. Questions regarding the long-term wisdom of Reagan's policies continue to engage historians and pundits alike, with responses usually reflecting both economic theory and one's political orientation.

1.5 Wall Street and the S&L Bailout

deregulation

Deregulation is the reduction or elimination of laws previously enforced on a particular industry.

While deficits would not be felt for many years, government **deregulation** of various industries would have a more immediate impact on the economy during the 1980s. Democrats and Republicans alike approved the elimination or reduction of government price controls during the 1970s and 1980s. Nixon removed price controls of oil and natural gas in response to the Organization of the Petroleum Exporting Countries (OPEC) embargo, and Carter eased price controls and regulations governing the transportation industry. Reagan accelerated this trend, believing that most forms of federal regulation, including consumer and environmental protection laws, hampered business growth. In contrast to the Department of Defense, who was told by the president to "spend what you need," Reagan slashed the budgets of federal agencies like the Occupational Safety and Health Administration (OSHA) and the Environmental Protection Agency (EPA). More disturbing to environmentalists, the EPA reinterpreted the Clean Air Act and other laws in a way that was so favorable to industry that an investigation was conducted. The inquiry revealed that twenty administrators in the EPA had each accepted corporate bribes.

Because utility companies were public utilities and had a natural monopoly in the communities they served, these industries had been heavily regulated. However, Reagan reduced these regulations in hopes of increasing competition and reducing prices. Airlines and other common carriers were treated much the same way, with the federal government transferring the control over prices to the executives of these companies and the free market. Energy prices and airfares fluctuated according to market forces following deregulation. These reforms led to mostly lower prices in air travel, but also led to numerous difficulties for utility consumers in some markets.

While the results of deregulation were mixed in most industries, the deregulation of the financial industry led to complete disaster. Banks known as savings and loan institutions (S&Ls) had a reputation for safety because they followed strict rules regarding the ways they could invest their depositors' money. Chief among these rules was the provision that S&L loans be backed by collateral such as a home mortgage. However, interest rates were at record highs during the early 1980s, and the Reagan administration agreed to ease these restrictions and permit S&Ls to make riskier loans. By the late 1980s, hundreds of the S&Ls were facing bankruptcy due to bad loans and a decline in the real estate market.

Because S&Ls were part of the banking system, each depositor's savings accounts were insured by the federal government. As a result, the government was forced to pay more than $150 billion in federal bailouts to make sure families and businesses that deposited their money were protected. Although both parties approved the deregulation of the banking and investment industry, the resulting failure of many leading financial institutions and resulting **Savings and Loan Bailout** of the late 1980s and early 1990s was blamed almost solely on the Republican Party. Given Republican efforts to lower corporate taxes and the tendency for Republicans to be the most enthusiastic supporters of deregulation, it is easy to see why most Americans blamed the party of Reagan when deregulation led to default. However, many of the congressmen who approved the deregulation and were later investigated for accepting illegal donations from members of the banking industry were Democrats.

The Department of the Interior had been insulated from controversy since the Teapot Dome Scandal of the 1920s. However, Reagan appointee and secretary of the Interior James Watt kept his agency in the headlines throughout the 1980s. One of Watt's comments regarding his religious beliefs were regularly quoted out of context by the political left in an attempt to discredit the secretary as well as other religious conservatives. During his Senate confirmation hearing, Watt responded to a question about long-term preservation of resources by stating that he did not know how many generations would pass before the return of Christ but that Americans must shepherd their resources for future generations until that time.

Many on the left at the time reported that Watt had suggested environmental policies did not matter because the end of the world was nigh. Watt himself was fond of misrepresenting the words of his opponents and had earlier declared that there were only two kinds of people in the United States: liberals and Americans. This war of words did not mask the actions of Watt's department for long, as nearly two-dozen high-ranking officials were forced to resign for improper actions. In addition, several officials were convicted of accepting bribes or other ethics violations. Similar to the Teapot Dome Scandal, Department of the Interior officials permitted oil and timber companies to lease, log, mine, drill, and otherwise commercially develop millions of acres of previously protected areas of the federal domain at prices that were often far below estimated market value. One of the most immediate results was the growth of environmental interest groups such as the Sierra Club, whose protests resulted in some areas of the federal domain again being declared off limits to developers.

The Reagan administration also approved a wave of corporate mergers that consolidated vital industries in the hands of a few companies. Critics protested that the government-approved mergers created monopolies. The architects of these deals argued that the mergers created stronger and more efficient businesses. Other practices that were common throughout the 1980s, such as leveraged buyouts, increased the risks to the entire financial system. These leveraged deals permitted a group of investors to purchase a controlling stake in a publicly traded company by using loans to purchase shares. In addition, these investors often secured the loans by using the stock they had just purchased on credit as collateral. As a result, a small drop in the price of any particular stock could bankrupt an entire company and send shockwaves throughout the financial system.

This is precisely what happened on October 19, 1987, when Wall Street experienced the worst crash in its history. Although the market had risen quickly in proceeding years due to speculation, these gains were erased in a single day when the Dow Jones average fell over 20 percent. Companies such as RJR Nabisco that participated in the leveraged buyouts were forced to lay off thousands of

Savings and Loan Bailout

As a result of deregulation and bad investments by banking institutions known as savings and loan institutions, the government paid out at least $150 billion to holders of insured deposit accounts at these institutions.

employees, yet the CEO of the company received over $50 million in compensation. Brokers that facilitated these and other risky strategies, such as junk bond investor Michael Milken, earned over $500 million in 1987 alone. Unlike previous Wall Street financiers, such as JP Morgan, Milken's deals did not support economic growth by matching legitimate entrepreneurs with investors. Instead, Milken's incomes were commission-based, which led him to violate federal laws in order to increase the volume of his transactions. Milken served only two years of a ten-year prison sentence and remains one of the wealthiest men in America.

Accompanying many of these high-stakes mergers was the dreaded news of "restructuring" that often meant the loss of jobs for the employees of the affected corporations. For those in manufacturing, *restructuring* was often a code word for laying off employees to save money. Sometimes restructuring meant that a company was preparing to close a factory in the United States in favor of another country where operating costs were lower. At other times, it simply meant laying off full-time employees with salaries and benefits and replacing them with low-wage hourly workers.

Even privately owned companies that had historically offered high wages to their employees, such as Levi Strauss & Co., soon adopted these strategies. In some cases, these companies had no choice if they wanted to stay competitive. At other times, these measures were simply used to enhance profitability. Levi's blue jeans were the most recognizable American fashion; yet between the early 1980s and 2003, each of the dozens of US Levi's factories was closed. Each announcement resulted in thousands of workers losing jobs that were relatively well paying. Although what was happening at Levi Strauss & Co. was typical of the clothing industry, the fact that the United States no longer produced Levi's came to symbolize the US trade imbalance, which grew to $170 billion by 1987.

REVIEW AND CRITICAL THINKING

1. Why might the political orientation of the nation have become more conservative during the 1980s than other decades? What role did Evangelicals and women play in this transition? How might one argue that the 1980s were actually *not* any more or less conservative than previous eras in US history?

2. Why might Evangelicals support Reagan over Carter? What about union members and blue-collar workers? Were these individuals "fooled" by Reagan's use of social issues, or is this an unfair characterization?

3. What role did women play in the New Right? How did feminism affect the rise of the New Right? What arguments were made in support of and against the introduction of equal rights amendments to state constitutions? Look up the Equal Rights Amendment, and explain your position on the proposed law in relation to these arguments.

4. What was Reaganomics, and how did it differ with other theories, such as Keynesianism? Why did so many Americans support tax breaks for the wealthy and corporations during the 1980s?

5. Were the 1980s a second Gilded Age? Explain your position using specific historical examples.

2. THE END OF THE COLD WAR

LEARNING OBJECTIVES

1. Summarize the Iran-Contra Affair with an explanation of the Reagan administration's intent and the various details of the scandal.

2. Explain the Reagan Doctrine and how it applied to foreign affairs in Latin America, the Middle East, Africa, and Afghanistan.

3. Summarize the diplomatic history of the 1980s as it applies to US-Soviet relations and the fall of Communism. Explain the significance of anti-Communist protest in Eastern Europe and the fall of the Berlin Wall.

Reagan Doctrine

A guiding force in Reagan's foreign policy, the Reagan Doctrine suggested that the United States must support the armed forces of any regime that was waging war against Communist forces.

President Ronald Reagan's top priority while in office was related to international affairs. He was not satisfied with containing Communism, but instead sought to "roll back" its influence throughout the globe. Reagan's style of leadership emphasized leaving the execution of his ideas and policies to others. The president's strategy regarding world affairs, dubbed the **Reagan Doctrine**, likewise relied on finding allies who were willing to support his anti-Communist worldview rather than directly deploying US forces. As a result, the heart of the Reagan Doctrine was the president's announcement that the United States would provide aid to all groups fighting against Communist forces worldwide. Supporters of the Reagan Doctrine pointed out that military aid and covert CIA operations resulted in anti-Communist victories without risking large numbers of US troops or repeating the experiences of Korea and Vietnam. Critics feared that these covert operations may have unintended consequences similar to the Bay of Pigs Invasion and the 1953 coup that placed the shah of Iran in power. Others pointed out that many of the recipients of US military aid, such as the Nicaraguan Contras and the Afghan Mujahedin, used methods and maintained beliefs that many Americans opposed.

2.1   Middle East and Afghanistan

These conflicts and internal contradictions were especially troublesome in the Middle East, where Cold War tensions coexisted with historic rivalries between East and West. The ease with which Egypt was able to play the United States and Soviet Union against one another during the Suez Crisis demonstrated the fragility of détente in the region. Tensions rose even further in the late 1970s as the Soviets hoped to regain influence in the Middle East by supporting a number of Marxist regimes along the Red Sea in East Africa and in neighboring Afghanistan. In the spring of 1978, Communists in Afghanistan temporarily seized power with the aid of the Soviet Union. However, this government proved unpopular with the majority of the Afghan people, partly due to its support for women's rights and other liberal and secular reforms. For the Afghans, this secular and pro-Soviet regime seemed much like the pro-Western government of Iran that had just been overthrown by the Muslim cleric Ayatollah Khomeini.

FIGURE 13.6

President Reagan meets with leaders of Afghan forces opposed to the Soviet Union in 1983.

The Soviets and Americans were stunned. In just one year, religious leaders in Iran had expelled the US-backed shah and Islamic rebels were engaged in a civil war that threatened to overthrow the pro-Soviet government of Afghanistan. If the Islamic Afghan rebels prevailed and started their own government, the Soviets feared, they might also follow the Egyptian model of expelling Soviet military advisers in return for US aid. If this happened, some Soviet leaders feared, Afghanistan might form a deal with the West that might someday lead to the construction of US missile bases along the Soviet border.

Applying their own version of the domino theory, Soviet leaders responded to the growing Afghan Civil War by sending 75,000 troops to support the pro-Soviet regime. With little understanding of the history, geography, religion, or culture of Afghanistan, Soviet leaders predicted that their troops would return within a month after crushing all resistance to the Communist government in Kabul. Instead, the **Soviet Invasion of Afghanistan** resulted in a decade-long war between Soviet troops and Islamic rebels, some of whom were supplied by the United States. US leaders backed a variety of Islamic rebels in hopes of making Afghanistan resemble the quagmire of Vietnam for Soviet forces. In the end, neither the Soviet Union nor the United States made significant efforts to discern the ideas and needs of the Afghan people, spending millions of dollars to arm the enemies of their rival without considering the long-term consequences of a potentially short-sighted action. Just as the US-aligned South Vietnamese government fell shortly after US forces withdrew, the nominal government of Kabul was quickly overrun by **Mujahedin** rebels after Soviet forces withdrew in 1989. Before and after the fall of Kabul, Afghanistan was effectively governed by various rebel forces that became increasingly distrustful of both the Soviet Union and the United States.

As one Soviet political scientist later explained, Moscow's decision to invade Afghanistan was the product of its recent success using the military to sustain corrupt and unpopular Communist regimes in other nations. "In politics if you get away with something and it looks as if you've been successful, you are practically doomed to repeat the policy," Soviet scholar Georgy Arbatov explained. "You do this until you blunder into a really serious mess." Arbatov believed that Soviet leaders became the victims of their own "success" in ways that paralleled the path that led to America's decision to use the CIA to sustain unpopular and corrupt right-wing governments. While the long-term "success" of US covert operations in Latin America and the Middle East might be dubious at best, in the short term, US companies made record profits and US consumers enjoyed low-cost imports of coffee, bananas, and oil. Armed with hindsight, it appears that Soviet military intervention in Afghanistan and Eastern Europe thwarted potential anti-Communist revolutions in the short term. In the long-term, however, it led to costly interventions that bankrupted Moscow and diminished the international prestige of their government in ways that contributed to the fall of Communism and the Soviet Union itself.

Soviet Invasion of Afghanistan

Began on Christmas Day in 1979 and lasted for a full decade. The Soviet Union was attempting to prop up an unpopular Communist government in Afghanistan against the wishes of the majority of the Afghan people. The armed uprising against the Soviet military was led by Islamic fundamentalists who were backed by the United States.

Mujahedin

Islamic guerilla warriors in Afghanistan who fought against and ultimately repelled the Soviet Union's invasion of their country. America's support of the Mujahedin was the result of the Reagan Doctrine's support of any force that was fighting against Communist forces. Because some of the more radical leaders of the Mujahedin later advocated similar confrontation against the West, the decision to provide weapons to Islamic guerillas has been a source of controversy in recent years.

Iraq-Iran War

A war between Iraq and Iran that began with the Iraqi invasion of Iran in September 1980 and lasted until an armistice in 1988. The invasion occurred in the wake of the Iranian Revolution, and as a result, the United States provided tentative support to Iraq due to the belief an Iranian victory would be contrary to America's strategic interests in the Middle East.

terrorism

Using violence or the threat of violence against innocents in an attempt to achieve a certain outcome or spread fear for political purposes.

The Soviets might have reconsidered their decision to invade Afghanistan if they had a more thorough understanding of Afghanistan's own history of resisting conquest. Similar lessons from history might have informed US policy regarding the **Iraq-Iran War**, which erupted in September 1980. Iraqi dictator Saddam Hussein hoped to capitalize on instability in the region following the Iranian Revolution and the declining support of Egypt in the Arabic world following its recognition of Israel. In addition, the Iraqi leader feared that the revolution that had led to the ousting of Iran's secular dictator would spread to his country. Hussein hoped that a quick and successful invasion of Iran—a rival dating back centuries—would lead to renewed Iraqi patriotism and greater popular support of his own regime. Hussein's decision was also calculated on the response of the United States. In the wake of the Iranian hostage crisis, Hussein understood that there was little chance that America would support Iran.

Iran possessed a number of modern weapons systems that it had purchased from the United States during the era when the US-backed shah of Iran was in power. These arms sales ended when the Islamic cleric and fiercely anti-Western Ayatollah Khomeini seized power in 1979. As a result, Iranian forces were in desperate need of US supplies to repair and rearm many of their American-made weapons. However, the possibility of an Iranian victory terrified many Western leaders and led the United States to provide direct and covert aid to Iraq. Reagan sent Donald Rumsfeld to Baghdad in preparation for possible resumption of normal diplomatic relations. The Reagan administration chose to minimize Iraq's use of chemical weapons. It also helped to derail efforts of the United Nations to condemn Hussein for atrocities committed against Kurdish people in Iraq, many of whom were being recruited by the Iranians who hoped to start a popular uprising against Hussein.

Concerns about an Iranian victory led the Reagan administration to ignore many of the atrocities committed by Hussein. The same was not true of Libyan dictator Muammar el-Qaddafi. In 1986, Libyan terrorists planted a bomb that killed two US soldiers in West Berlin. Reagan responded with a series of air raids against military and governmental targets in Libya that killed a number of military personnel and civilians but failed to harm Qaddafi or alter his support of terrorist networks. The use of **terrorism** against the US had become more frequent during the early 1980s. For example, Islamic jihadists bombed a garrison of US Marines in Beirut, Lebanon, in October 1983. This attack instantly killed 241 servicemen who had been acting as peacekeepers in a conflict regarding Lebanon and Israel. Reagan made little effort to retaliate against these Jihadists. Instead, he simply withdrew US forces from Lebanon.

FIGURE 13.7

The remains of the US Marine barracks in Beirut, Lebanon, following a terrorist attack that instantly killed 241 US troops.

In addition, a violent anti-Jewish faction named Hezbollah that was supported by Iran and other Arabic nations captured a number of American hostages. Iranian officials were approached by American operatives who hoped to secure the release of the American hostages. At this point, Reagan violated his own pledge that the United States would never negotiate with terrorists. The Reagan administration brokered a deal whereby the United States agreed to sell arms to Iran to secure release of American hostages held by the Lebanese terrorists. However, only a few hostages were actually released, and the arms sales likely encouraged the subsequent capture of more American hostages.

In 1986, some of the details of these "arms-for-hostages" deals were uncovered and publicly released by Middle Eastern journalists. The Reagan administration initially denied that any deal was made with Iran. However, these journalists uncovered more evidence, which forced a number of high-level US officials to resign in disgrace. Reagan himself denied direct knowledge that the weapons sales were part of any bargain with the terrorists, admitting only that he had failed to detect and prevent members of his administration from carrying out the deals. "I told the American people that I did not trade arms for hostages," Reagan explained in a partial confession. "My heart and best intentions still tell me that is true, but the facts and the evidence tell me it is not." While Reagan's popularity temporarily declined, the confessions of several of his aides prevented special investigators from finding any clear evidence that Reagan had personally ordered the deals. Ironically, the success of Reagan's detractors in creating an image of an aloof president who allowed his staff to make decisions on their own helped to corroborate the president's defense. However, these weapons sales to Iran would soon play a major role in a larger scandal known as the Iran-Contra Affair.

2.2   Latin America and the Iran-Contra Affair

Reagan would earn a reputation as a diplomatic leader who helped to facilitate a peaceful end to the Cold War in Europe. However, the Reagan administration pursued a very different strategy when it came to Latin America. Reagan reversed Carter's policy of only aiding anti-Communist groups that supported democracy, resuming the supply of American military aid to right-wing dictators and paramilitary forces throughout the region. If the risk was small enough, Reagan was even willing to send US forces to directly remove a left-wing government. For example, a left-leaning and pro-Castro government seized power on the tiny Caribbean island of Grenada in 1979. The Reagan administration feared that Soviet missiles might be placed on the island. In 1983, the island's government switched hands and US officials viewed the resulting instability as an opportunity to intervene. Under the pretext of concern for the safety of US students attending a private medical school, thousands of marines landed on the island in October 1983. Within three days, the island and its 100,000 residents were firmly under US control and a new government was formed.

The **Invasion of Grenada** led to international condemnation of the United States. The United Nations Security Council voted 11-1 to condemn the US action, with the American representative casting the single vote in opposition. Reagan's supporters pointed to the fact that only eighteen US troops were killed in the conflict. They also pointed out that the operation had succeeded in its goals to protect US citizens on the island, prevent a possible civil war, and replace a pro-Soviet regime with one that is friendly to the United States. Opponents on the left viewed the action as imperialistic. Others feared that the unilateral action against a member of the British Commonwealth might strain relations with London and other nations because US leaders made no effort to consult with British or Caribbean leaders.

Leaders throughout the region condemned the invasion of Grenada, but many were more concerned with the US intervention in Central America. The Somoza family operated a dictatorial government that operated Nicaragua like a police state. The United States had supported the Somoza dictatorship until the late 1970s when the Carter administration withdrew American support. Without US aid, the Somoza family was ousted by a popular revolution in Nicaragua that was led by a group of Marxist rebels known as the **Sandinistas**. The Sandinistas were generally supported by the people of Nicaragua, but frequently resorted to violence and imprisonment against those who sought a return of the Somoza regime. Reagan and his advisers decided that making distinctions between totalitarian and humanitarian regimes that opposed Communism was a luxury the United States could not afford. This decision simplified US efforts to roll back Communism by encouraging the United States to simply provide weapons to any Latin American dictator or counterrevolutionary regime that opposed the Sandinistas. However, this compromise also led to one of the darkest legacies of the Reagan Doctrine.

FIGURE 13.8

A map showing the routes taken by US troops during the invasion and occupation of the Caribbean island of Grenada.

Invasion of Grenada

On October 25, 1983, 7,000 US soldiers overwhelmed and seized control of the island of Grenada. The invasion was in response to a similar action by Marxist rebels who had earlier seized control of Grenada's government and were perceived by the United States as installing a Communist government aligned with the island of Cuba and the Soviet Union.

Sandinistas

Supporters of the Socialist Party of Nicaragua that controlled the government of that country during the 1980s but were engaged in a civil war with counterrevolutionaries known as "Contras" in the United States.

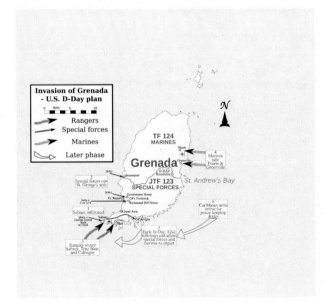

Contras

Guerilla fighters who opposed the Socialist Party of Nicaragua and were aided by the United States. US support of the Contras has remained controversial because of the methods used by the Reagan administration to provide covert aid in violation of US law and because of the connections of many Contra leaders with leading drug traffickers

Iran-Contra Affair

A scandal involving the Reagan administration's covert sale of about 1,500 missiles to Iran in a failed attempt to secure the release of seven hostages. Excess proceeds from the sale were covertly provided to the Contras in Nicaragua. These deals not only violated US laws and constitutional concepts regarding presidential authority, they may have encouraged other terrorist groups to take American hostages.

Under Reagan's leadership, the United States renewed its support for a repressive but anti-Communist dictatorship in neighboring El Salvador. In exchange, the Salvadoran government increased its efforts to eliminate leftist forces in its own country who were backed by Cuba and the Nicaraguan Sandinistas. El Salvador's military government likely used some of this aid to further the work of its notorious "death squads." These units traveled the Salvadoran countryside and killed everyone suspected of being a Marxist or aiding the rebels. The United States also provided massive aid through the CIA to Nicaraguan counterrevolutionaries (nicknamed **Contras**) who sought a return of the Somoza dictatorship. Because of their willingness to fight the pro-Soviet Nicaraguan government, Reagan hailed the Contras as "freedom fighters." Reagan had applied the same label to the anti-Soviet Mujahedin in Afghanistan. Most Americans, unfamiliar with Latin American affairs and supportive of their president, simply accepted Reagan's definition of the Contras as the "good Latin Americans." The US military soon established multiple bases throughout the region. In fact, critics labeled Nicaragua's northern neighbor the USS *Honduras due to the large number of US troops that were present.*

Later revelations would lead many to question the assumption that the Contras were fighting for the freedom of Latin America. In addition, the Reagan administration became increasingly involved in a number of illegal and covert actions that would lead to an investigation of the president and the resignation of several top officials. The entire scandal was labeled the **Iran-Contra Affair**. As the name implies, the Iran-Contra Affair involved events in Nicaragua as well as the Middle East.

The Reagan administration's troubles began in 1982 when Congress refused to continue providing military aid to the Contra rebels in Nicaragua. Many in Congress questioned the assumption that the Sandinistas presented a threat to US security. Others questioned the morality of supporting the oppressive Somoza and Salvador regimes. In September 1982, Congress approved the Boland Amendment, prohibiting US officials from providing aid to the Contras. Aware that US funds were still being covertly funneled to the Contras, Congress approved a second ban on funding the Contras in 1984.

Despite both of these laws, the Reagan administration continued to provide weapons and money to the Contras through a variety of legal and illegal methods. For example, the money the government had earlier received from its secret arms sales to Iran in exchange for the promised release of US hostages had been hidden from Congress and the public. The Reagan administration determined that these funds should be used to covertly supply the Contras with weapons. In addition, the Reagan administration still provided weapons and money to surrounding Latin American dictators. Many of these leaders funneled the American supplies and weapons to the Contras because they feared a Sandinista victory might encourage revolutions in their own nations. Unlike the covert aid that the Reagan administration secured with the proceeds of the Iranian sales, this method of arming the Contras violated the spirit and not the letter of the Boland Amendment.

The Reagan administration also responded to what it viewed as congressional meddling by launching a public relations campaign that sought to present the Contras as freedom fighters and the Sandinistas as anti-American. The government rewarded pliable journalists who agreed to publish a variety of accusations against the Sandinistas. These articles led more and more Americans to agree with the government's position on Nicaragua. In response, Congress eventually agreed to lift its ban on providing the Contras with weapons. However, this aid was quickly rescinded when it was discovered that the Reagan administration had been secretly using government funds to support the Contras all along.

The Reagan administration came under fire in 1984 when it was discovered that the CIA had placed mines in the harbors and rivers of Nicaragua. Even the archconservative Barry Goldwater responded with anger, calling the CIA's actions an unjustifiable act of war. The United Nations condemned the action, and the World Court demanded that the United States apologize and pay reparations. However, the United States was able to use its veto power to thwart any action by the UN Security Council. US Ambassador to the United Nations Jeane Kirkpatrick responded by pointing out that the Sandinistas were likewise guilty of violence in the ongoing civil war.

Kirkpatrick's defense of US actions quickly unraveled in October 1986 when a secret shipment of military supplied was shot down over Nicaragua. A captured crew member and documents on board revealed that these supplies were part of a regular covert operation by the CIA to supply the Contras in violation of US law. Even more damning was the subsequent publication of details about how the administration had used the profits from secret Iranian arms sales to supply the Contras. Three investigations conducted during the late 1980s and early 1990s made it clear that President Reagan was aware of the nefarious details of the weapons sales and secret funding of the Contras.

By the time the US public became aware of the basic details of the weapons sales in November 1986, many officials connected to the scandal had already resigned their posts. Reagan's former National Security Advisor Robert McFarlane even attempted suicide, offering a vague apology to the American people in his note. Most officials were granted immunity for their testimonies, and those convicted of crimes were pardoned when Reagan's vice president **George H. W. Bush** became president. CIA director William Casey passed away before the investigation, and Marine Lieutenant Colonel Oliver North shouldered much of the blame and was fired along with other midlevel officials whose convictions were later reversed or pardoned.

Reagan escaped impeachment by denying any knowledge of the weapons sales. In contrast to the workaholic Carter, who surrounded his office and bedroom with piles of documents, Reagan delegated most every decision to members of his administration. Outside of issues involving taxes, national defense, and the possible spread of Communism, Reagan seemed to regard most issues as details that were best handled by his staff. This orientation allowed Reagan to enjoy daily naps, frequent vacations, and a work schedule that rarely included evenings and weekends. Reagan's critics charged him with being aloof and lazy. Others believed that the president's chief advisor James Baker and a few others in Reagan's inner circle were running the country rather than the man the American people had elected.

Ironically, years of criticism regarding Reagan's hands-off management style helped to convince the American public that the Iran-Contra affair had been conducted in secret behind the president's back. Reagan delivered a series of apparently heartfelt apologies along with a number of testimonies in which he responded, "I don't recall" to nearly every question he was asked. For many Americans, the aging actor appeared as the victim of a partisan attack by individuals who hoped to further their own careers. Critics of the president maintained that even if Reagan was telling the truth, the fact that these criminal deeds were carried out at the highest levels of his administration was evidence that Reagan must step down. Others argued that President Reagan had knowingly funded an illegal war and sold weapons to terrorists.

FIGURE 13.9

This 1985 political cartoon was critical about Reagan's denial of personal culpability regarding the Iran-Contra Affair. In the first panel an actor claims "it didn't happen," which is labeled "Iran-Contra, take 1." In the second panel an actor claims "it happened, but I didn't know," only to later exclaim "I might have known, but I don't remember."

George H. W. Bush

Former CIA director and vice president under Reagan, Bush would become the forty-first president of the United States after defeating Michael Dukakis in the 1988 presidential election.

The investigation effectively ended all aid for the Contras, who quickly agreed to a ceasefire. Once they were no longer engaged against the Contras, popular support for the Sandinistas also declined, and many Sandinista leaders were replaced by a coalition government following a 1990 election. However, the decade-long civil war had spread throughout Latin America and destroyed the region's agricultural economy. This development helped to spur the growth of a number of powerful drug cartels. Because the Contras were also heavily funded by area drug smugglers and because the United States enlisted the services of notorious drug trafficker **Manuel Noriega** to funnel money to the Contras, questions still remain about the complicity of the CIA in the resulting cocaine epidemic of the 1980s. Many residents of inner-city neighborhoods continue to blame the government for the introduction of "crack" cocaine, a highly addictive form of the drug that they believed helped to fund the Contras.

Most scholars agree that the Contras were dependent on drug money, but limit their accusations against the Reagan administration to negligent enforcement and indirect assistance to drug traffickers via US aid to the Contras. Historians who specialize in the history of Latin America have been limited in their access to documents related to the Iran-Contra Affair. As a result, definitive conclusions remain allusive. The Reagan administration's relationship with Noriega and other nefarious individuals with connections to drug traffickers might never be fully understood. At best, these historians argue, the Reagan administration was grossly negligent in assuring that the money funneled to the Contras was actually used to fund an insurgency that Congress had declared the government would no longer support. In the end, the only American to be incarcerated for any crime in connection to the Iran-Contra Affair was an eccentric former minister and peace activist. Bill Breeden stole a sign for an Indiana street named in honor of Admiral John Poindexter, the national security advisor convicted of multiple felonies. Breeden had requested a $30 million ransom for the return of the street sign, the same amount he believed the federal government had transferred to the Contras from the proceeds of the weapons sales. The former minister spent several days in jail, while Poindexter's felonies were dismissed.

2.3   The Soviet Union, Eastern Europe, and China

The Reagan administration was much more cautious when confronting the Soviet Union than developing nations. For example, Reagan barely responded when a Soviet jet shot down a Korean airliner that was carrying a US congressman and had strayed into Soviet airspace in 1983. Reagan's most aggressive move from the Soviet perspective that year was his announcement of the **Strategic Defense Initiative (SDI)**. SDI was a defensive network of satellites that Reagan believed could detect and destroy enemy nuclear missiles with lasers and other countermeasures. Critics of Reagan's plan emphasized the technological challenges in shooting down a single missile from space given current technology. To serve its purpose of deterrence, they pointed out, SDI satellites would have to be able to shoot down hundreds of missiles at once. Even if the United States built thousands of operational SDI satellites, these critics continued, Soviet scientists would simply find ways to build "trickier" missiles with defensive countermeasures of their own that would render the SDI satellites ineffective.

From the Soviet perspective, Reagan's support of SDI was an attempt to upset the strategic status quo that had been based on nuclear deterrence. If SDI proved effective, Soviet leaders feared, the United States would be able to launch a nuclear attack without fear of retribution. For this reason, some conservatives in the United States predicted that a successful SDI program would simply inspire the Soviets to launch a preventive strike before America's "missile shield" was fully operational. Some even feared that SDI technology would be used to create new space-based offensive weapons that would increase the likelihood of nuclear disaster. Believing SDI to be a topic more appropriate for science fiction writers than world leaders, Reagan's critics labeled the plan "Star Wars" after the popular movie that was setting box office records. Others pointed to the billions spent on SDI and other programs as the greatest threat to national defense. By producing crippling deficits that might restrict the nation's ability to fund its military in the future, even some within the military believed that SDI was a poor use of the nation's resources.

Similar to previous administrations dating back to President Eisenhower, the Reagan administration was also cautious when it came to supporting protests against Communism throughout Eastern Europe. These movements gained millions of supporters in Poland and Hungary during the 1970s and 1980s. In 1979, the newly anointed **Pope John Paul II** returned to his native Poland and offered encouragement to those who sought to reform the autocratic Communist government of his homeland. The following year, a new anti-Soviet trade union in Poland named **Solidarity** launched a series of protests that utilized many of the same nonviolent tactics of the American civil rights movement.

The Polish government eventually responded with modest reforms, some of which led to greater economic development. However, Polish authorities initially tried to crush Solidarity and all who supported its movement. Poland declared martial law and imprisoned many of the anti-Communist leaders behind Solidarity. Despite these measures, the protests continued until the spring of 1989 when desperate Polish officials responded to popular demands and permitted a free election. Candidates representing Solidarity and other non-Communist groups won those elections in a landslide, leading to the creation of the first non-Communist government in Eastern Europe since the start of the Cold War. Similar Polish attempts to create independent governments had been crushed by the Soviet Union since 1956, but this time there was no violent response from Moscow.

A series of similar anti-Communist uprisings swept Europe throughout 1989 with relatively little bloodshed. For example, the democratic uprisings in Czechoslovakia became known as the "Velvet Revolution" due to the largely peaceful nature with which power was transferred from the state to the people. That same year, the government of Hungary permitted a commission to investigate its own failed revolution of 1956. In a symbolic gesture that seemed to many a repudiation of the Soviet Union, Hungarian leaders agreed to provide a state funeral for the Hungarian revolutionary leader that Nikita Khrushchev had ordered killed following the failed revolution of 1956. The Hungarian government also declared that its border with Austria was open and dismantled the barbed wire fences and guard posts that had prevented Hungarians from crossing into Western Europe.

Pope John Paul II

The leader of the Catholic Church worldwide between 1978 and his death in 2005, Pope John Paul II was a critic of Soviet Communism who inspired Catholics and non-Catholics throughout his native Poland to support the movement for democracy.

Solidarity

A Polish trade union that opposed Communism and quickly won the support of the majority of Polish workers during the early 1980s.

FIGURE 13.10

This map of Eastern Europe demonstrates the potential impact of Hungary's decision to open their borders. Hungary shared a common border with nations such as Austria that had an open border with the West. It also shared borders with several Communist states of Eastern and Central Europe. The nation to the immediate left of Hungary is Austria, while West Germany is located just north of Austria.

The impact of Hungary's open border with Austria and the West was both immediate and dramatic. Intending only to permit their own citizens to cross into Austria (where they would be able to also cross into West Germany and other non-Communist nations), Hungarian officials were soon confronted with over a 100,000 East Germans who hoped to enter their nation. These hopeful refugees had descended through Czechoslovakia and into Hungary hoping to escape to West Germany via the now open Austria-Hungary border. East German officials rushed to block the growing number of their own citizens who were fleeing their country. Many of these individuals responded by attempting to assure East German officials that they were merely visiting relatives in Hungary. However, these individuals were surprisingly well provisioned for their ostensibly brief vacations and were clearly attempting to escape to the West. The leaders of Czechoslovakia and Hungary recognized that they were powerless to reverse the human tide, but did their best to discourage the migration. By November 1989, none of their efforts would matter as the Berlin Wall came crashing down and East Germans and other Eastern Europeans were allowed to cross into the West by a more direct route.

It is doubtful that anyone living in 1988 could have predicted that the Communist Bloc would cease to exist a year later. Given the history of the region in the past three decades, there were even fewer reasons to believe that democratic revolutions might sweep though Eastern Europe with so little violence. The scenes of students and workers toppling governments and walls occurred much as Karl Marx had predicted a century prior—a mass uprising of intellectuals and proletarians against autocratic regimes. The irony, of course, was that this democratic surge was directed against regimes that were supposed to have created the classless society that Marx's followers had hoped to create.

Marx had underestimated the difficulties of creating a society that was both wealthy and classless. One of the central contradictions of Communism was that it required at least a temporary centralization of government power. The disinclination of the authoritarian governments of Eastern Europe to relinquish these powers led many to fear that the anti-Communist revolutions of the late 1980s would lead to bloody counterrevolutions and civil wars. Instead, most Communist leaders decided the wisest course of action was to permit free elections.

In sharp contrast to the violent response of the Soviet Union during the first three decades after World War II, Mikhail Gorbachev allowed the dialectic of history to progress in a democratic fashion. Rather than send Soviet tanks to resist the will of the people, Gorbachev did not intervene to halt the democratic revolutions that swept Eastern Europe in 1989. Dozens of bloodless coups took the form of free elections and coalition governments. Communist leaders who were once in absolute control now found themselves discredited and on the outside of parliamentary democracies throughout Eastern Europe. Most of these democratic governments were dominated by the same political parties that the Communists had declared illegal and suppressed for decades. However, few of the previous leaders of these nations were imprisoned. Instead of seeking retribution for the crimes of the past, the new governments looked to the future and even permitted Communist parties to enter candidates in free elections.

Not all Communist leaders shared the self-preserving prudence of the Hungarian and Polish leaders in stepping down voluntarily. As a result, not all the revolutions of Eastern Europe were bloodless. Romanian leader Nicolae Ceausescu ordered protesters shot on sight and called for counterdemonstrations by his loyal supporters. This strategy might have worked if Ceausescu had a large number of supporters. It also might have worked if other Communist leaders joined Ceausescu in punishing dissenters. Instead, Ceausescu was all alone. Communist leaders in neighboring Bulgaria voluntarily stepped down, while those in nearby Yugoslavia faced ethnic conflict and civil war.

Soviet leadership made it clear that they would not send their army to prop up Communist governments facing rebellion at home. Hungary, Czechoslovakia, Bulgaria, and Poland were in the midst of peaceful revolutions. With the leading Communist powers abandoning the hard-liner approach of the previous decades or deeply engaged in internal struggles regarding ethnic violence, Nicolae Ceausescu faced the wrath of his own people alone. The government-sponsored counterprotests he ordered were taken over by his opponents. After the government killed a hundred of these protesters, millions of Romanians responded by supporting the martyred revolutionaries. After a failed attempt to flee Romania, Ceausescu and his wife were executed in a scene reminiscent of the Russian Revolution of 1917. This time, however, the departed were avowed supporters of Marx while the executioners opposed Bolshevism. Communist supporters could do little but insist that their ideas had been betrayed by dictators such as Ceausescu as they attempted to win voters in free elections. Democracy had come to Eastern Europe.

2.4   Africa and Apartheid

apartheid

A system of segregation that operated in South Africa between 1948 and 1992. Apartheid was designed to ensure the complete subjugation of the African majority by legally enforcing white supremacy

South Africa was colonized by British and Dutch settlers in the seventeenth century. Rivalry between British settlers and a second group of European colonists of Dutch origins (known as Afrikaners) had led to several wars. By the 1900s, the nonwhite majority of South Africa increasingly challenged the colonial rule of these two groups of Europeans. In response, the rivalry between the Dutch and British in South Africa faded and a common "white" identity emerged. In 1948, the new South African government established a system designed to bring British and Dutch whites together while dividing the nation's various nonwhite groups. The system was labeled **apartheid**, an Afrikaner word meaning "separation."

Under apartheid, racial discrimination became institutionalized and South Africans were classified into categories of white, black, and colored. Whites were people of European heritage, blacks were people of African heritage, and coloreds were those of mixed racial origin. Further divisions were made separating the many South Africans of Asian and Indian descent. In addition, Africans were subclassified according to their tribal origins—a distinction that was especially troublesome as most black South Africans had ceased to define themselves in these terms.

Subsequent legislation forcibly removed millions of South Africans of African descent into government-created "homelands." These homelands were created on the most undesirable lands in South Africa, and residents were denied the rights of citizenship beyond the borders of these government-created slums. Other legislation outlawed political groups that sought to represent people of African descent and made protest against the white-only government a crime. Because whites represented only 15 percent of the population, and because the wealth of South Africa depended on labor-intensive industries such as mining, the government also devised a system to control and exploit non-white labor. A key component of this system was the creation of a passbook system. Nonwhites were forced to carry passbooks at all times. The passes identified who a person was and whether he or she was permitted to work in the mines or in the cities. Without a pass, a person could not leave his or her homeland.

The South African government attempted to present apartheid as a fair system that brought stability through separation. Like Native American reservations, the homelands were independent states within South Africa. Residents of these homelands could vote for their own representatives within those states, but they had no voice in the government of South Africa itself. Few Africans participated in these elections, recognizing that the South African government still maintained authority over the homelands. Instead, South Africans supported numerous protest organizations, such as the **African National Congress (ANC)**.

South Africans were inspired by the nonviolent resistance of the US civil rights movement. However, the protests held in South Africa and other African nations that were struggling for independence from colonial and/or apartheid regimes were more likely to serve as catalysts for activism in the United States. For example, in March 1960 and prior to proliferation of nonviolent protest in the United States, 7,000 South Africans marched to police headquarters near Sharpeville without their passbooks and presented themselves for arrest. Under South African law, any nonwhite citizen could be detained for months without explanation. In addition, those joining dissent movements could be imprisoned for life. The presence of 7,000 South Africans overwhelmed the small police force at Sharpeville. Unable to arrest all of the protesters, the police simply opened fire on the crowd. Over seventy people were killed, and hundreds of others were wounded in what would be known worldwide as the Sharpeville Massacre. Most of the victims of the massacre were shot in the back as they fled for safety.

The US government issued a statement of regret for the unfortunate violence at Sharpeville, which included a mild condemnation of apartheid. Part of the reason for the US reluctance to condemn South Africa was the pervasiveness of racial inequality in the United States in 1960. Even more important, many Cold War scholars believe, was the Marxist orientation of many African independence movements during the 1960s. American political leaders sided with the apartheid government of South Africa until the late 1980s—a result of America's commitment to Britain and its desire to prevent the spread of Marxist ideas. In fact, Robert F. Kennedy (RFK) was the only prominent white American political leader to travel to South Africa during the 1960s. However, his 1966 trip and his lofty rhetoric about democracy and justice failed to include any specific commitment of US support, and RFK was assassinated in 1968.

During the late 1960s, the Johnson administration ordered US companies to sever all ties with apartheid regimes. However, these restrictions were easily evaded by multinational corporations. The Nixon and Ford administrations eased these restrictions and provided aid to European colonial powers such as Portugal that brutally suppressed similar independence movements in its African colonies. Given the close connection between the United States and the nations of Europe that bolstered apartheid regimes in Africa, independence groups such as the ANC drifted toward Moscow and Cuba. And because the ANC received from Cuba and Moscow, the cycle continued and the Nixon and Ford administrations became even stronger supporters of the apartheid government of South Africa. This was especially true after thousands of Africans affiliated with independence movements throughout Africa traveled to the Soviet Union for political and military training in the 1970s.

Marxism's emphasis on proletarian unity against colonial rulers and Capitalists naturally appealed to South Africans because they were treated like colonial subjects. South Africans were denied citizenship rights and forced to work in diamond and gold mines, creating wealth that aided their oppressors. Other ANC leaders such as **Nelson Mandela** discouraged the use of paramilitary tactics, hoping that a nonviolent and class-based movement would bring Africans of various ethnic groups together. He also hoped to unite South African laborers who migrated to Africa from Asia and India. Key to Mandela's plan was convincing the white political and business leaders of South Africa that their nation would become more prosperous if they abandoned apartheid. However, Mandela was arrested by the apartheid government in 1962 and would spend the next twenty-seven years in prison.

African National Congress (ANC)

The national liberation movement of South Africa that led the struggle against the apartheid South African government for four decades. Some ANC leaders used violence, but most sought rapprochement and were able to convince the white leaders of South Africa that ending apartheid would be in the nation's interest.

FIGURE 13.11

Students at Florida State University in Tallahassee participate in a divestment protest. The divestment movement resulted in the economic isolation of the apartheid regime and impelled the South African government to consider democratic reform.

Nelson Mandela

Political leader of the ANC and the antiapartheid movement. Mandela was imprisoned for twenty-seven years, after which he was elected by the South African people to be their first president in the postapartheid era.

The Carter administration was the first to unequivocally condemn apartheid. However, the Reagan administration reversed this position and again allied with the apartheid South African government. The switch was heavily influenced by antiquated intelligence reports that suggested that the ANC was a puppet of Moscow. In actuality, a new generation of ANC leaders had emerged in the 1980s that distanced themselves from the declining Communist Bloc. Instead, they hoped to encourage "black Capitalism" in a new South Africa based on equal opportunity, full citizenship rights, and social justice.

The Reagan administration paid little attention to this change in orientation and continued to back the apartheid regime due to a mistaken fear that an ANC victory would spread Communism throughout South Africa and neighboring Angola and Mozambique. However, college students across the country soon forced the Reagan administration to modify its miseducated position. They also sought to end the complicity of US corporations who sold equipment that was used to enforce apartheid. Students and professors resurrected the teach-ins of the 1960s, leading to a nationwide **divestment** movement on nearly every major college campus. The divestment movement was boosted by early success at Michigan State University where students forced the administration to liquidate all investments within the university's multimillion-dollar endowment fund that were connected to the South African government.

The divestment movement soon spread to dozens of nearby campuses and statewide college systems like the University of California. By the end of the decade, the student movement had led some state legislatures and nearly one hundred cities to ban local and state governments from doing business with any company that did business with the apartheid government of South Africa. The results were dramatic. International Business Machines (IBM) had made millions of dollars by selling computer equipment to South Africa that was used to enforce the passbook system. By 1987, public pressure and the divestment movement forced IBM to end these sales and join other global corporations in severing all relationships with the South African government.

The divestment movement threatened to destroy the economy of South Africa unless it enacted reform. South African antiapartheid leader and Nobel award winner Desmond Tutu indicated that the divestment movement was one of the leading factors in ending apartheid. Most of the credit, of course, belongs to the South African people who demanded reform through their leaders. By the 1980s, the ANC came under the leadership of Thabo Mbeki and others who convinced the white leaders of South Africa that neither they nor their business interests would suffer by ending apartheid. This was no difficult task given the violence against whites advocated by some ANC leaders in the past. In February 1990, Mandela was released from prison after serving twenty-seven years of a life sentence. Two years later, white voters approved reform measures that permitted all South Africans to vote. The first free election in South African history was held in 1994 and resulted in the selection of Nelson Mandela as president. It also resulted in the creation of a coalition government led by the former white leader of South Africa, F. W. de Klerk and ANC leader Thabo Mbeki.

divestment

A strategy of influencing political change by reducing or eliminating investments in a certain company, industry, nation, or other entity. In regard to South Africa, US college students and African Americans used pressure to force colleges and governments to divest their assets in companies that maintained business relationships with the apartheid South African government.

REVIEW AND CRITICAL THINKING

1. One might argue that conservative cold warriors such as Nixon and Reagan experienced much more success in reducing tensions between the United States and the Soviet Union than more liberal presidents such as Johnson and Carter. What do you think? What might have been the domestic reaction if Carter took the same steps to reach out to the Soviet Union as Reagan did with Gorbachev?

2. See if you can summarize the entire Iran-Contra scandal in a single paragraph. Consider the details you were forced to leave out in making this summary, and explain your reasons for including some detail while excluding others. Also, provide your ideas on why Reagan and other high-ranking officials were able to avoid prosecution.

3. In response to UN resolutions condemning the United States for placing mines in the harbors of Nicaragua, America's ambassador to the United Nations pointed out that the Sandinistas had also committed violent acts that harmed civilians. What do you think? Is this a justifiable defense? Is it fair to hold the United States to a higher standard than rival governments? Did the covert nature of US actions add to the perception of wrongdoing?

4. Why might the Reagan administration have provided weapons to Latin American governments fighting left-wing governments while offering little support to the people of Eastern Europe who were in direct confrontation with the Soviet Union? Summarize the history of the fall of Communism in Eastern Europe with an emphasis on specific examples from several different nations.

5. What purpose did apartheid serve for whites and business interests in South Africa? Why would the United States oppose the ANC and its fight to end apartheid? How did the Cold War and international fight for civil rights connect the United States and South Africa? Address these questions with examples from the history of apartheid's demise, including the reluctant support of the ANC within the United States.

3.   AMERICAN LIFE IN THE 1980S

LEARNING OBJECTIVES

1. Explain how the culture of the 1980s reflected economic and political developments as well as new technology. Evaluate the degree to which the 1980s was a "decade of greed" as many suggest.
2. Summarize the history of the "War on Drugs" and the outbreak of the AIDS epidemic. Evaluate the efficacy of the government's response to these crises.
3. Describe the continued challenges faced by women and minorities during the 1980s. Evaluate the leadership of the Reagan administration from the perspective of diverse groups of Americans.

3.1   Technology and Globalization

By the late 1960s, nearly every American home had at least one television and most American families spent several hours watching television programs together. Three major networks had emerged, each with local affiliates. In the 1940s and 1950s, most programs were sponsored by a single advertiser who found ways to incorporate their products into the program. By the 1960s, network programming featured commercial breaks instead of product placement. By the 1980s, cable networks utilizing satellite broadcasts disrupted the monopoly held by the major networks that continued to broadcast over the air. Cable also resulted in specialized channels meant to appeal to specific groups of consumers, such as CSPAN and ESPN, which both debuted in 1979. These specialized channels permitted marketers to more closely focus their advertisements to certain audiences. By the mid-1980s, cable television networks were receiving nearly as much advertising revenue as the major networks. A decade later, new providers launched their own satellites and offered consumers the ability to bypass the cable companies with personal satellite receivers attached to their homes.

The first computer was developed at the end of World War II and filled an entire room. Early computers cost hundreds of thousands of dollars and were designed to assist the military and businesses with record keeping and other applications involving large amounts of data. By the early 1960s, the costs of these computers had been greatly reduced while their utility increased. As a result, an estimated 12,000 computers were in use by government agencies, businesses, and universities by 1970. The development of the space program spurred new research in satellite communication, which used computer technology to send a small amount of voice and data communication around the globe.

The cost of these technologies was still so great that ordinary consumers could not purchase a computer. This situation changed with the invention of the **microchip**, which contained hundreds of circuits that had previously required lots of material and space. The microchip reduced size of a computer to the point that a machine that once filled several rooms could be reduced to the size of a desktop box. Recognizing that the microchip also reduced the cost and increased the flexibility of the machines, Steve Jobs and a few other engineers began building "personal computers." Jobs and his partners formed the Apple Computer company in 1976 and built their first computers in his parent's home. Before long, Apple and IBM were two of the fastest growing companies in the United States and were competing in the production of computers for consumers and businesses alike.

The same microchip technology made possible a number of other consumer products, such as the handheld calculator, the videocassette recorder (VCR), and video arcades, which became popular hangouts for youths. Other technologies led to the development of microwave ovens; these became an instant hit with US households once it was determined that the oven's technique of heating food through radiation was safe. The Sony Walkman, a portable cassette player, made its debut in 1979 and made headphones part of the daily wardrobe of American youths in the 1980s.

Although computer networking would not spread to the general public until the mid-1990s, Department of Defense researchers in partnership with universities developed private communication networks between computers in the 1960s and 1970s. These networks quickly expanded beyond government and academia. The communications protocols became standardized in 1982 and the network of networks known as the Internet was born. By the end of the decade, the Internet had also given birth to a new application of technology. Computer programmers designed a network of interlinked hypertext web pages that hosted data, images, and eventually video and sound through a network called the World Wide Web.

Just as communications were bringing people across the globe together, new technology led to cooperative agreements between researchers in the United States and the Soviet Union. Both nations had dreams of launching a satellite so massive it could host a habitable research facility. The costs and

microchip

Contains a large amount of electronic circuitry within a small chip, usually made of silicon. These circuits allowed the same computer technology that used to fill entire room to fit within a small box, thereby spurring the proliferation of the personal computer.

logistical challenges of such a massive venture inspired cooperation between the two nations, leading to the creation of the International Space Station. The first component of the station was launched in 1998. This station and its laboratories have subsequently grown through a series of modular additions through a multinational cooperative effort. The station remains the largest technological joint venture between nations and has been continuously habituated by scientists from around the globe since 2000.

Wealth, Poverty, and the War on Drugs

The popular culture of the 1980s is infamous for celebrating material affluence. Although the characters in television shows like *Dynasty*, *Dallas*, and *Lifestyles of the Rich and Famous* reveled in conspicuous consumption, the 1980s also saw unprecedented displays of generosity. Corporate and personal donations to charities became commonplace, while the majority of Americans donated to relieve the suffering of flood and famine victims around the globe. For example, a famine in Ethiopia during the mid-1980s inspired a collaborative effort of dozens of celebrities and musicians from Willie Nelson to Michael Jackson who recorded an album and performed in concerts that raised $100 million for famine relief.

Charity was especially needed at home as the gap between the rich and the poor grew and homelessness became an epidemic. While the average salary for a corporate executive was forty times that of a factory worker during the late 1970s, by the end of the 1980s, the leading CEOs made a hundred times more money than their entry-level employees. Adjusted for inflation, the poorest 20 percent of Americans made less money than they had in previous decades. One million Americans lived on the streets, many of them still working at least one job. Although minimum wage had increased incrementally during the 1970s, the pay rate stood unchanged at $3.35/hour throughout the Reagan administration. As a result, a full-time worker made only $134 per week before taxes—an amount that meant a husband and wife working full time with no sick days or vacation lived right at the federal poverty level for a family of four. Twenty percent of children and nearly 50 percent of minority children lived below that level.

The affluent culture of the 1980s and new methods of marketing products meant that these children were frequently reminded of their poverty. By the 1980s, children were not only subjected to television advertisements during popular cartoons; popular cartoons were advertisements themselves. Millions of children tuned in to watch *My Little Ponies*, *Care Bears*, *He-Man*, and *G.I. Joe* each week. Each of these programs and dozens of others were based around preexisting toy lines, thus eliminating what had previously been a blurred line between programming and marketing.

An organization known as Mothers Against Drunk Driving (MADD) emerged to raise awareness about another threat to the welfare of America's youths: intoxicated drivers. MADD lobbied Congress in support of the **National Minimum Drinking Age Act of 1984**, a law that required states to raise their drinking age to twenty-one or face a 10 percent reduction in federal highway funds. The Twenty-First Amendment that had ended prohibition placed the authority to regulate alcohol on the states. As a result, there have often been some differences in interpretation and enforcement of the minimum drinking age from state to state. Some critics of the 1984 law suggest that these state laws actually discourage responsible alcohol consumption among youths. While MADD and other conservatives disagree, some believe that foreign nations with more liberal alcohol laws actually promote more responsible attitudes regarding alcohol. By this perspective, young adults in Europe and Latin America usually enjoy their first drinks in the company of their parents and are thus less likely to hide their alcohol consumption or binge drink once they leave the home.

National Minimum Drinking Age Act of 1984

Required states to lower their minimum drinking age to twenty-one or forfeit a significant amount of federal highway funds.

The conservatism of the decade also inspired efforts to combat illegal drugs. "Crack" was a form of cocaine that was introduced in the 1980s and proved more profitable to drug dealers, even if it was even more addictive and harmful to users than the drug's powder form. The Anti-Drug Abuse Act of 1986 targeted crack dealers, enacting minimum sentencing guidelines that were determined by the amount and type of drug a person possessed when caught. For example, an individual with five grams of crack cocaine would be sentenced to at least five years in federal prison. The sentencing guidelines for crack cocaine were a hundred times more severe than those regarding the powder form of cocaine—a drug that was more likely to be used by middle- and upper-class drug abusers. For example, a person caught with powder cocaine would have to have 500 grams to receive the same sentence as someone with five grams of crack.

Many considered the law to be racially biased against minorities and the poor who were far more likely to be caught with crack cocaine. Defenders of the law suggested that the lower tolerance for crack was justified because of the higher correlation between that form of the drug and addiction, birth defects, and violent crime. Critics of the Reagan administration questioned the effectiveness of the president's "War on Drugs" because it coincided with drastic reductions to antipoverty and job training programs. By this perspective, no amount of law enforcement could prevent young people from dealing drugs if this appeared to be the only way out of poverty. Still others pointed to the fact that individuals like Manuel Noriega had been on the CIA payroll despite his connections to Pablo Escobar and the Medellín Cartel. For these individuals, the covert actions of the Reagan administration in Latin America was evidence that the federal government was not really committed to preventing drugs from entering the country.

Gay Rights and AIDS

In 1983, the state of New York outlawed discrimination against homosexuals. Three years later, New York City became one of the first major cities to pass legislation that included sexual orientation as a category within its nondiscrimination laws. Among those who testified on behalf of New York City's gay rights bill was the civil rights veteran Bayard Rustin. Rustin had been Martin Luther King Jr.'s most trusted adviser and was a leading organizer of the 1963 March on Washington. However, because of his sexual orientation, few within the movement supported Rustin as a candidate for a leadership position. He was even forced to resign from the Southern Christian Leadership Conference (SCLC) because he was gay.

At times, some civil rights leaders even threatened to publicly "out" Rustin. Ironically, Rustin had always been honest about his homosexuality and had agreed to silence regarding his personal life to appease these same civil rights leaders who were concerned that Rustin's sexual orientation would be used by the opponents of the movement. By the early 1980s, however, Rustin was free to speak more openly about the issue of gay rights. He published several candid essays that compared the persecution of African Americans in the 1950s to the contemporary persecution of homosexuals. Despite Rustin's commitment, historians of the civil rights movement generally tread delicately when discussing the issue of homosexuality. For example, most books written on the civil rights movement before the 1990s exclude Rustin's sexual orientation. Rustin's papers were published shortly after his death in 1987. Even though there are dozens of instances where Rustin discussed the subject of homosexuality, there is seldom more than a passing mention of gender orientation in pages written by historians describing Rustin's life.

American physicians became aware of a new virus in 1981 whose symptoms first appeared in a number of gay men. The virus attacked and eventually destroyed the body's ability to fight infection, resulting in fatal diseases that neither the body nor modern medicine could counteract. Researchers quickly determined that sexual orientation had nothing to do with the virus itself and rejected the informal labels given to the disease such as "gay-related immunodeficiency disease." Even if labels such as these were short lived, the casual association between human immunodeficiency virus (HIV) and homosexuality continued in the minds of most Americans for an entire decade.

FIGURE 13.12

First Lady Nancy Reagan speaks at a rally encouraging youths to "Just Say No" to drugs. The Reagan administration was heavily criticized in later years for its connections to some of the most notorious drug smugglers during the Iran-Contra Affair.

FIGURE 13.13

Although he was forced into silence on the subject of his own homosexuality during the 1960s, civil rights activist Bayard Rustin became a leading proponent of gay rights in the 1980s.

acquired immunodeficiency deficiency syndrome (AIDS)

A disease resulting from the HIV virus, AIDS destroys the immune system's ability to combat illness and has led to an estimated 25 million fatalities worldwide.

Ryan White

A young man who contracted the HIV virus during a blood transfusion at age thirteen, Ryan White was castigated by many who did not understand his disease. His life story captured the attention of the nation and led to greater understanding of the way the HIV virus was spread and how it could be prevented, as well as greater compassion for those with HIV and AIDS.

FIGURE 13.14

New York congresswoman Bella Abzug became the first Jewish woman in Congress in 1970. She graduated from Hunter College in New York and worked as an attorney before becoming a politician and women's activist.

Given the antigay climate of the 1980s, the association of HIV and homosexuality led many to disregard the seriousness of the virus and **acquired immunodeficiency deficiency syndrome (AIDS)**, the disease that resulted from HIV. Reagan made no public mention of HIV or AIDS until 1985 and refused to support education or research efforts until political pressure in the late 1980s forced him to reconsider. Many community leaders likewise avoided any mention of the disease. The result was ignorance and misinformation about how HIV was contracted and spread. A small number of religious figures with large television and radio audiences added to the cacophony of miseducation by declaring that AIDS was God's way of punishing homosexuals. With almost no federally supported research into ways to counteract the disease or public education programs, nearly 100,000 Americans lost their lives to AIDS in the 1980s.

One of the reasons for America's eventual acknowledgment of AIDS and belated efforts to counter the misinformation about the disease was the tragic experience of a young man named **Ryan White**. White contracted HIV when he received blood containing the virus during a transfusion—itself a direct result of the failure to spread information about the disease. White was diagnosed with AIDS on December 17, 1984. He was thirteen. Although everyone in the medical field assured community members that his disease could not be spread by casual contact, the misinformation regarding the disease resulted in community-wide outrage when White was readmitted to his school in Kokomo, Indiana. White's family was forced to agree to community demands, including the requirement that Ryan be assigned to a separate restroom and use disposable plates and plastic eating utensils in the cafeteria.

"Because of the lack of education on AIDS, discrimination, fear, panic, and lies surrounded me," White later explained to members of Congress during a hearing on AIDS education. "Some restaurants threw away my dishes…my school locker was vandalized inside and folders were marked FAG and other obscenities…I was not welcome anywhere. People would get up and leave so they would not have to sit anywhere near me. Even at church, people would not shake my hand." By the time White entered high school, AIDS awareness had improved and the student body president worked with area health professionals to assure that parents and students understood AIDS. Although White died in 1990, the change in public education allowed him to enjoy some moments of normal adolescence, such as having a part-time job, learning to drive, and attending the prom.

Women's Rights and the Feminization of Poverty

The conservative tenor of the 1980s led to the creation of a political climate in which fewer women overtly identified themselves as feminists. Some women expressed concerns that the feminist movement had inadvertently produced a stigma affecting women who chose not to pursue careers outside the home. Others believed that the feminist movement had helped to eliminate historic injustices but was no longer needed. Lastly, conservative commentators masquerading as scholars produced "studies" on the misery of feminists who discovered the error of their ways. As single women passed the age of forty, these questionable reports suggested, their chances of marriage were statistically lower than being killed by a terrorist.

While women continued to disagree about the relevance of the feminist movement and what objectives may still need to be reached, there was still widespread agreement that the movement had left a positive legacy that advanced the lives of women. The movement also retained its appeal with minority women, according to a 1989 poll that found 72 percent of Hispanic women and 85 percent of black women approved of the goals of the women's movement, compared with 64 percent of white women.

Gloria Steinem and civil rights veteran Myrlie Evers were among many of the supporters of the **National Women's Political Caucus (NWPC)**, which grew exponentially during the 1980s. New York congresswoman and NWPC founder Bella Abzug quipped that a woman's place was "in the house—the House of Representatives." In this spirit, the NWPC operated as a nonpartisan organization that supported women who desired to run for political office. The organization assisted US congresswomen as well as local officeholders and continues to operate as a support network and information clearinghouse. The success of the NWPC and women everywhere demonstrated that others agreed with Steinem, Evers, and Abzug. Women represented just over three 3 of elected officials in late 1960s, but this number grew to over 20 percent in next three decades.

Women also held important posts within the federal bureaucracy, such as **Eleanor Holmes Norton** who headed the Equal Employment Opportunity Commission (EEOC). An attorney and veteran of the civil rights movement, Norton aggressively sought to implement the mission of the EEOC as it related to women and minorities. Under her administration, the EEOC streamlined its operations so it could more effectively pursue organizations that had shown a pattern of discrimination against women and minorities. For example, the EEOC implemented timetables by which violators of the law must demonstrate that they had taken corrective action. Violators were also compelled to meet agreed-on minimum quotas regarding the employment of the groups they had discriminated against in the past. In addition, the EEOC under Norton established guidelines relating to affirmative action and defined sexual harassment as both a form of discrimination and a violation of an individual's civil rights.

Many of these actions upset conservatives, who believed the EEOC was violating the rights of employers and discriminating against white males. As a result, Ronald Reagan fired Norton shortly after taking office in 1981, replacing her with the conservative Clarence Thomas. Thomas immediately abandoned requirements that federal employers meet certain benchmarks regarding equality in recruitment and employment. In addition, Reagan's cuts to the EEOC meant that a majority of complaints from women and minorities were never investigated.

The attack on the EEOC was particularly troubling as the gap between wealthy and poor women expanded even faster than the general gulf between the rich and the poor. A handful of prominent women made headlines as corporate executives, and the number of women in the professions doubled and then doubled again between the 1960s and the 1980s. These advances masked the reality of life for most female wage earners, the majority of whom were still restricted to a handful of low-paying occupations. More than 80 percent of female laborers were employed within one of twenty occupations out of nearly five hundred different careers listed by the US Census Bureau. Most of these women worked in low-paying service and clerical work. In fact, scholars have demonstrated that if men and women were to be equally represented throughout each occupation, over 50 percent of all employees would have to switch jobs.

Even those women who had jobs in higher-paying occupations such as sales were grouped in hourly work rather than positions where commissions were offered. Old attitudes that suggested that assigning men and women to different tasks was "natural" continued. Employers often defended their hiring practices by explaining that women "did not like competition" or could not understand the products their male staff peddled.

Although women have historically been relegated to the lowest-paid jobs, the consequences of this disparity have increased the suffering of women and children as divorce rates and the numbers of single mothers doubled between 1960 and 1980. The continued inequality of the workplace combined with the increase in female-headed households has led to a phenomenon known as the **feminization of poverty**. During the 1980s, roughly half of single mothers who were employed received salaries that were below the poverty level. The statistics were especially troubling for minority women and those in isolated rural areas where nearly half of all women of childbearing age were single mothers.

Race and the 1980s

The late twentieth century saw a slight increase the number of black Americans joining the ranks of the middle class—a positive legacy of the civil rights movement and policies such as affirmative action. However, the 1980s was also host to a retreat in terms of support for affirmative action. The decade also saw an organized assault on urban black communities through ghettoization, drastic reductions in federal grants for community programs, the loss of jobs, and the introduction of crack cocaine.

The expansion of chain stores into primarily black neighborhoods—a sign of the recognition of black consumer power made possible by the civil rights movement—also displaced thousands of black-owned businesses. Prior to integration, black-owned business received nearly a quarter of all money spent by black consumers. During the 1970s, the proportion of money spent by black consumers at black-owned businesses declined by 50 percent. By the mid-1990s, only 3 percent of African American purchases were from black-owned enterprises. Thousands of independent black hotels, movie theaters, restaurants, and merchandisers that had served black customers with dignity during the era of segregation had closed their doors by this time. Although the decline of independent black business was part of a national trend that saw family-owned businesses displaced by retail chain stores, the effect on the

National Women's Political Caucus (NWPC)

A nonpartisan organization that seeks to increase the level participation of women within the political system as candidates and voters.

Eleanor Holmes Norton

A law professor and civil rights veteran who led the Equal Employment Opportunity Commission before her removal by Ronald Reagan. Norton presently represents the District of Columbia in Congress and has led the fight for full congressional voting representation for the residents of that district, who are presently not represented by a member in Congress who can vote on legislation.

feminization of poverty

Refers to the increase in the number and percentage of women among the nation's poor. The phenomenon is usually associated to the rising number of female-headed households and the increased tendency for these single mothers and their children to fall below the poverty line.

black community was particularly damaging because black entrepreneurs had reinvested in the community and provided jobs. Even black-owned beauty companies, a multimillion-dollar industry that had created tens of thousands of jobs, imploded during the 1970s. Prior to this time, cosmetic makers ignored the black consumer. By the 1980s, three-fourths of black expenditures on health and beauty products went to publicly traded or white-owned businesses.

FIGURE 13.15

Despite the triumph over Jim Crow, integration also coincided with a decline in the number of black-owned businesses. Florida's Frank Butler owned a number of establishments such as this bathhouse near St. Augustine. Ironically, this photo was also taken at a time when this was the only beach between Jacksonville and Daytona that African Americans could use.

The deindustrialization of America was even more distressing as unions and factories were opening their doors to black men and women in significant numbers. As factories closed, fewer and fewer black men could find jobs that paid a family wage. Marriage rates declined but birth rates continued much as they had in the past. The result was that 47 percent of black families were headed by single mothers by the end of the 1980s. Without factory labor in America's cities and with the decline of black-owned businesses, most of the jobs available near black communities were in the service sector. Job training programs and college offered one escape from the cycle of poverty, but federal and state agencies eliminated job training and inner-city high schools had fewer resources to produce students that were prepared for college. In addition, community reinvestment programs and federal aid for urban areas were also reduced or eliminated. For those inside America's inner cities, the only major federal programs that were not reduced were prisons and highway funding, both of which added to the impoverishment of urban communities.

Reagan began his campaign for president with an appearance in Philadelphia, Mississippi. This was no ordinary small town in America. Philadelphia, Mississippi, was the sight of the infamous murder of three civil rights workers in 1964. Reagan was not there to remember the courage of these young people or pay tribute to the cause for which they gave their lives. Instead, Reagan stood next to archsegregationist Strom Thurmond and repeatedly used the phrase "state's rights"—a phrase that had been a code word for white supremacy for over a century. Reagan's white supporters in the 1980s and beyond maintain that Reagan was simply expressing his support for the devolution of government authority from the federal level to the states. African Americans interpreted Reagan's message differently and pointed out that Reagan spent the majority of his presidency expanding the power of the federal government.

As president, Reagan was frequently criticized for marginalizing the perspectives of African Americans. He frequently projected images of black women as "welfare queens" while mistaking the only black appointee to his cabinet as a White House guest. Reagan also fired prominent black leaders such as civil rights veteran Eleanor Holmes Norton from the EEOC. Reagan attempted to fire Civil Rights Commissioner Mary Frances Berry until she challenged the president's decision in federal court and was restored to her post. Although Reagan signed the bill creating a national holiday to honor Martin Luther King Jr., the president did little to support the bill and expressed his belief that observation of the holiday should not be required. He also agreed to speak at a Southern evangelical college that banned black students from its dances during his tenure in office without any acknowledgment of the college's ongoing racial discrimination.

Although the Reagan administration made few efforts to address the subject of South African apartheid, Norton, Barry, and other black leaders joined with the tens of thousands of college students in demanding an end to the racial caste system. These women and thousands of college students waged sit-ins and were voluntarily arrested at the South African embassy in Washington, DC, as part of the antiapartheid movement. By 1986, black and white students and activists held dozens of protests that culminated in the introduction of the Anti-Apartheid Act of 1986, which demanded an end to apartheid and required federal divestment from the South Africa until such an objective was met. The bill passed Congress but was vetoed by Reagan. The coalition of black leaders like Coretta Scott King, black community members, and college students of all backgrounds rallied once again and even convinced a number of conservative republicans to reverse their votes and override Reagan's veto.

One of the most significant cultural movements of the 1980s was the emergence and spread of hip-hop or "rap" music from inner cities to small towns. Hip hop arose from self-taught street musicians that combined elements of 1970s funk with beats and lyrics. Artists such as the *Last Poets* and Gil Scott Heron spoke to the experience of inner-city life in a way that appealed to many outside of the ghettos because of their honesty and intensity. Others used the medium for self-promotion, composing rhymes and beats paired with brash lyrics and posturing bravado. Others such as Chuck D of *Public Enemy* demonstrated the power of the medium with songs such as "Fight the Power" that counseled listeners to aggressively confront racism.

Other black artists such as filmmaker Spike Lee combined rap lyrics throughout his 1989 cinematic masterpiece *Do the Right Thing*, a two-hour tour de force that deconstructed the anatomy of a race riot and started a national dialogue about racial prejudice. Many white politicians tried to seize that dialogue, criticizing *Public Enemy* and other artists instead of the white-owned record companies that hijacked the medium by signing only those rappers wiling to glorify violence and demean women. It was these images of black "thugs and pimps," combined with the buffoonery of previous decades, that typified the media image of black America during the 1980s. "The image of Black people on the tube has not drastically changed over the decades," Chuck D explained in a recent book. "We're either singing, dancing, telling jokes, telling one-liners in a sitcom, talking about a triple-double, touchdown, or stolen base, or getting locked up in a squad car on *Cops*...there's only a few serious Black roles on TV."

Immigration and Hispanic Rights

In 1980, Jimmy Carter signed the 1980 Refugee Act. The statute reformed US laws regarding immigration in a way that allowed quotas to be adjusted annually to provide more flexibility regarding refugees. The 1980 law also adopted the United Nation's definition of the term *refugee* as anyone with a "well-founded fear of persecution" based on politics, religion, race or nationality. The 1980 law added an important stipulation. It barred any individual who had participated in the persecution of others from being considered a refugee themselves.

In the past, individuals applying for asylum in the US were evaluated based on Cold War politics rather than the individual circumstances they faced. For example, a person seeking to leave the right-wing dictatorship of El Salvador in the 1980s would be denied entry into the US because the US maintained formal relations with the Salvadoran government. If a person wished to leave Nicaragua, a neighboring leftist government the US was covertly seeking to topple during the 1980s, they would likely be welcomed. Because their desire to flee from Communist oppression could be used as political capital, people in Communist nations were almost automatically granted asylum. In October 1980, more than 100,000 refugees arrived in the US from Cuba. These individuals were among the estimated 1 million Cuban refugees who were resettled in the United States during the 1980s. Meanwhile, an estimated 10,000 refugees fleeing the militaristic regime of El Salvador were able to enter the US only by walking hundreds of miles and illegally crossing the Rio Grande. Many Salvadorans liken the northbound path of these refugees to that of escaped slaves who illegally crossed the Ohio River and followed the Underground Railroad a century before.

These Salvadorans were among the several million illegal immigrants who arrived in the US during the 1980s. Another 8 million immigrants legally entered the nation between 1975 and 1990. The issue of both legal and illegal immigration continued to spark controversy among Americans. It also revealed division among Hispanics, a term used to describe Americans whose ancestral home was one of the many Spanish-speaking nations in Latin America. Researchers at the University of Texas-Pan American determined that Mexican Americans who had lived in the United States for a number of years generally favored stricter immigration laws. They also found that middle-class Hispanics were more likely to believe that illegal immigration was harmful to US communities than other Hispanics. Some members of these groups joined the growing chorus of predominantly white Americans that called for tougher immigration laws. Employers typically opposed these restrictions, recognizing that the majority of the nation's new immigrants had been skilled workers in their countries of origin.

In the past, undocumented immigrants had been tolerated and even welcomed by many Americans due to the tremendous demand for agricultural and industrial laborers. However, the devaluation of the Mexican currency in the 1980s led to a tremendous surge in the number of undocumented immigrants. Congress responded with the passage of the **Immigration Reform and Control Act of 1986**. The new law required employers to take steps to verify and record the identity of all employees and make sure that each employee was legally entitled to reside and work in the United States. In addition to introducing the I-9 form that all employees must presently complete, the law also introduced fines for employers that knowingly hired undocumented aliens.

The 1986 law also created a guest-worker program and provided amnesty for those who could prove that they had resided in the country for at least five years and were willing to attend federally funded courses in English and US history. The law represented a compromise between numerous interests. As a result, it was criticized by groups representing multiple perspectives on the immigration debate. Hispanic leaders documented the way that the new law was unequally applied to nonwhite immigrants. These groups also believed that the US Border Patrol was beginning to act more like a paramilitary force. Others thought the law did not do enough, citing the ability of the agribusiness lobby to provide an exception for field workers. They were also angered that corporate interests had lobbied for the removal of a provision that would have required employers to determine the validity of a potential employee's identification documents. Without this provision, critics argued, employers could legally hire individuals who provided documents that were obvious counterfeits. Proponents of the law had hoped that it would deter illegal immigration by barring employment for undocumented aliens. Absent stricter regulations for employers, illegal immigration continued to be one of the leading issues of the 1980s and beyond.

Immigration Reform and Control Act of 1986

A law designed to discourage illegal immigration by making it a crime to knowingly hire anyone who was not legally permitted to live and work in the United States. The law also granted amnesty to all illegal residents who arrived in the United States before January 1, 1982.

FIGURE 13.16

San Antonio mayor Henry Cisneros became the second Hispanic mayor of a major US city in 1981. Alfonso Cervantes was elected mayor of St. Louis in 1965.

The Hispanic population of the United States increased to 7 percent of the US population in the 1980s. The total number of Hispanics increased from about 14 million to nearly 20 million and the collective buying power of these individuals represented over $170 billion by the end of the decade. As a result, Hispanic consumer power and the Hispanic vote became increasingly important. For example, a decade-long boycott of Coors resulted in an agreement to hire a certain minimum number of Hispanic workers among Colorado's growing Hispanic population.

Hispanic voters represented 8 percent of registered voters in Texas in 1986, a number that was steadily increasing and would reach 20 percent by 2011. In the mid-1980s, almost half of the nation's 3,000 elected officials of Hispanic origins were from Texas. These political victories were the result of voter registration drives that were made possible by dozens of court challenges in the late 1970s and early 1980s. In these years, the Hispanic vote was often diluted by at-large electoral schemes and gerrymandered districts that prevented Hispanic candidates from winning elections, even in communities with large Hispanic populations. Organizations such as the Mexican American Legal Defense and Education Fund (MALDEF) in the Southwest and the Puerto Rican Legal Defense Fund in Florida and New York demonstrated that these schemes were intended to assure that Anglo candidates continued to win elections and therefore violated the Voting Rights Act of 1965.

A number of Hispanic candidates that were elected as a consequence of court-ordered electoral redistricting would later win the support of Anglos and other groups and win citywide offices. For example, San Antonio elected its first Hispanic mayor since the 1840s when former University of Texas at San Antonio professor Henry Cisneros took office in 1981. Denver also elected a Latino mayor in the 1980s, and New Mexico and Florida voters selected Hispanic governors during these years as well.

Fourteen percent of all public school children dropped out of school in the 1980s. The rate was extremely high among minority students, with 19 percent of black students and over a third of Hispanic students dropping out of school during these same years. Numerous studies suggested that the trend of academic underachievement among non-English speakers could be mitigated through the introduction of bilingual education programs. This was especially true in the lower grades and had been shown to ease the transition into American public schools for children in non-English-speaking homes. However, bilingual education programs were also expensive, and many districts that might benefit from such programs were in low-income areas that relied on a dwindling supply of grants. The limited federal funds for these programs were sharply curtailed during the Reagan administration to the point that only 3 percent of Hispanic children had access to bilingual programs.

One of the justifications for these cuts was the perception that bilingual education might spread from the elementary schools to society at large, discouraging immigrants from learning English and causing the "Quebecization" of the United States. Fears that English and Spanish might become ubiquitous throughout America just as French and English coexist in eastern Canada led to several failed attempts to prohibit languages other than English. It also inspired a failed Constitutional amendment that would have recognized English as the official language of the United States. Over a dozen states passed symbolic legislation to this effect in the following decade. Residents of New Mexico countered this trend in 1989 by passing their own symbolic resolution: "supporting language rights in the United States." Due to a much stronger appreciation for its Spanish heritage, the voters of New Mexico approved a statement recommending all citizens learn English and another language. The nonbinding resolution included a phrase celebrating proficiency in multiple languages as providing both cultural and economic benefits to citizens and the state.

4.   THE PRESIDENCY OF GEORGE BUSH (SR.)

LEARNING OBJECTIVES

1. Summarize the election of 1988, and explain how George H. W. Bush was able to retain the support of voters despite his connection to the Iran-Contra Affair.
2. Provide a brief history of fall of the Berlin Wall and the dissolution of the Soviet Union. Explain how these events, along with the Gulf War, shaped the Bush presidency. Also, explain how George Bush could still lose the election of 1992.
3. Explain the reasons for Saddam Hussein's decision to invade Kuwait and the international response that resulted. Summarize Operation Desert Shield and Desert Storm, and explain how the United States was able to maintain a coalition of diverse nations under its leadership.

4.1   Election of 1988 and Domestic Affairs

The presidential election of 1988 featured a number of scandals and personal attacks against the leading candidates. Colorado senator Gary Hart was the leading Democratic contender, at least until he was photographed with a woman who was not his wife aboard a yacht that was fittingly titled *Monkey Business*. Opponents of Democratic candidate Joe Biden released a tape that made it appear as though the Delaware senator had plagiarized part of one of his speeches. Candidate Jesse Jackson issued a forceful critique of Reagan's policies that won him early supporters. However, many white Americans turned away from the civil rights veteran as he was increasingly hounded by reporters regarding a distant relative's criminal record and his relationship with outspoken leader of the Nation of Islam, Louis Farrakhan. Massachusetts governor Michael Dukakis and Jesse Jackson were even in the early primaries until Dukakis won several large states and carried the momentum and the Democratic nomination.

Republican candidate and Vice President George H. W. Bush faced his own detractors, many of whom viewed the Texas politician as Reagan's lackey. Despite having served as a member of Congress, the director of the CIA, ambassador to the UN, and vice president for eight years, many in the media portrayed Bush as inexperienced and untested. A handful of journalists even labeled the vice president as a "wimp." This particular journalistic expose provided the same level of sophisticated analysis one would expect to find on a grade-school playground where such labels were normally applied. However, similar to the way that nicknames tend to follow school children, the vice president of the United States had to confront this negative image of him else it derail his popularity with voters.

The Bush campaign responded with its own playground antics leading up to the general election. The Bush campaign exaggerated the significance of the governor's veto of a Massachusetts law that mandated the recital of the pledge of allegiance—a law that would have been struck down by the Supreme Court had Dukakis not saved them the trouble. In this and many other ways, the Bush campaign sought to exploit the image of easterners and liberals as unpatriotic. The most notorious attack by the Bush campaign was an ad that tried to connect Dukakis to the rape of a white woman by a black prisoner who had been allowed to leave prison under Massachusetts law.

The Dukakis campaign also waged its own attacks on the character and image of Bush. The Dukakis team was especially malicious in its attempts to slander the intelligence of Bush's vice presidential candidate Dan Quayle. The Dukakis campaign chose to avoid substantive accusations, such as the likely association between Bush and the corruption of the Iran-Contra Affair. As a result, voter turnout was low as the electorate tried to choose between two candidates that had equally destroyed the public's faith in the other. Voters responded by supporting Bush, largely due to a promise to never increase taxes and because of his association with the still-popular Ronald Reagan.

As president, George Bush frequently spoke of a "new world order." Although he never fully defined what form that order should take, the president channeled the image of lasting peace and unrivaled American leadership in global affairs. In such an environment, Bush and his supporters assumed that the reduction of trade barriers would naturally promote US commerce and culture throughout the globe. More specifically, the president worked toward reducing government regulations and taxes between the United States, Mexico, and Canada through an agreement called the North Atlantic Free Trade Agreement (NAFTA). Although labor unions protested that unrestricted commerce with Mexico and Canada would lead to reduction in American jobs, others believed that US companies would profit from NAFTA while the agreement would encourage American companies to develop new fields beyond manufacturing. For example, areas such as California's Silicon Valley could specialize more on developing new technology, while Mexican laborers assembled computers.

Although the idea and the practice were anything but new, globalization accelerated over the past few decades and media sources repeatedly exclaimed that a new era without global boundaries had arrived. Improvements in transportation and the development of satellite communication and the Internet changed the way goods and information flowed across national borders. The fall of Communism inspired corporations and investors around the world to seek new markets in Europe and Asia. The dissolution of the Soviet Union and the liberalization of China's economic policies also convinced world leaders of the merits of free trade and the shortcomings of planned economies and excessive governmental regulations.

President Bush was also faced with the mounting debt of the Reagan years, which threatened to spiral out of control as the economy slowed. As a candidate, he had famously remarked, "Read my lips, no new taxes." The only responsible course of action in response to the mounting debt, Bush believed, was to cut spending and enact small tax increases to at least partially reduce the annual deficits. Bush found little support among his Republican colleagues who were angered by what they perceived as betrayal. Although it harmed his political credibility, President Bush eventually secured a bipartisan agreement that provided small spending cuts and mild tax increases. The national debt continued to grow at a rate comparable to the Reagan years, and Bush was vilified among his own party. The president soon retreated from domestic matters to international affairs, which he preferred, but not before passing the **Americans with Disabilities Act (ADA) of 1990**, which protected the civil rights of disabled Americans.

The rights consciousness that had been spread by the civil rights movement inspired disabled Americans to lobby for protections of their rights throughout the 1970s and 1980s. For example, students demanded and the University of California responded by creating the Center for Independent Living in 1972, one of the first programs for disabled students. The following year, the United States Rehabilitation Act prohibited discrimination on the basis of disability among programs that received federal funds. The American Coalition of Citizens with Disabilities launched a nationwide sit-in in 1977 that protested violations of laws that required federal and state agencies to make reasonable accommodations for disabled persons. The Americans With Disabilities Act of 1990 extended these provisions to all businesses that employed at least fifteen people. The law required employers and government organizations to make certain reasonable modifications to make their facilities accessible for disabled employees and the public. The law also offered tax credits to offset the expenses faced by businesses that sought compliance with the law and fines for violators.

4.2 Berliners Tear Down the Wall

Mikhail Gorbachev had become a symbol of reform for the people of Eastern Europe and was welcomed as a hero when he traveled to East Germany in early October 1989. Gorbachev made no mention of the Berlin Wall during this visit, but tried to impress East German leaders that they must consider reform or face revolution. Impervious to such wisdom, the East German general secretary hoped to use force to quell the protesters until he was forced to resign by members of his own party. The new administration decided to appease protesters by relaxing travel restrictions but maintained the Berlin Wall to prevent a possible flood of defections to the West.

Unfortunately for the new general secretary of East Germany, he did not make his intentions clear to his subordinate. In November 1989, an unwitting press secretary announced that East Germans were free to utilize any border crossing. The people of Germany understandably interpreted this decree to apply to the Berlin Wall. Within less than an hour, thousands of East and West Berliners converged on the wall. Bewildered soldiers assigned to guard the border had of course not been briefed and decided against shooting the joyous crowd that was now dancing and singing on the wall itself. German officials were in a meeting when they found that the miscommunication had inspired Berliners to volunteer their assistance in dismantling the wall with sledgehammers they had brought from home or purchased en route. Gorbachev had already gone to bed and issued his congratulatory message to the wise new leaders of East Germany. The new government demonstrated that wisdom by pretending they had indeed intended the wall to be destroyed.

Americans with Disabilities Act (ADA) of 1990

A 1990 law that required employers of more than fifteen people and government organizations such as colleges and universities to make reasonable accommodations for disabled persons.

FIGURE 13.17

This map of East and West Berlin shows the locations of checkpoints along the Berlin Wall. Before November 1989, residents of the city could only cross into the other section through these checkpoints and with the permission of both governments.

East and West Germans now demanded the political reunification of Germany, an unsettling prospect for many Americans who had survived World War II. It was even more daunting for the Soviets who had twice been invaded by Germany and had long insisted that German reunification was only acceptable if it occurred under the influence of Soviet Communism. President Bush met with Gorbachev in December 1989 to discuss the situation in Germany and Eastern Europe. Bush and most Americans were open to unification largely because they recognized that the Soviets and East Germans were no longer in any position to dictate terms.

The people of East Germany demanded unification as their government and economy were disintegrating. West German chancellor Helmut Kohl likewise favored German unification and proceeded to work toward that goal with French, British, and US support. Having yielded to events throughout Eastern Europe so far, Gorbachev now attempted to prevent the newly unified Germany from joining North Atlantic Treaty Organization (NATO) and continuing to host US military bases. In the end, 300,000 Soviet troops in East Germany departed while the newly unified German nation became one of the leading members of NATO and the headquarters of US forces stationed in Europe. The result led to harsh criticism of Gorbachev among Communist leaders and inspired formerly independent states within the Soviet Union to follow Germany's lead.

The fall of the Berlin Wall in November 1989 was the most dramatic symbol of Communism's decline in Eastern Europe. Like all historical events, government leaders in Europe and the United States had done little more than react wisely to the actions of the people. Reagan's 1987 speech at the Brandenburg Gate in West Germany, where he called on Gorbachev to "tear down this wall," did little to impact the opinions of Berliners who had long protested the wall's existence. In fact, the speech was likely counterproductive because it placed Gorbachev on the defensive. Reagan's supporters played back the speech after the wall was dismantled, however, leading many Americans to casually credit the American President with Europe's transformation.

To his credit, Reagan never made this dubious claim himself. Reagan recognized that he, like the rest of the world, was too surprised by the rapid pace of events to have been the architect of the Berlin Wall's destruction. The Reagan administration's efforts to support West Berlin while working behind the scenes with Gorbachev and European leaders to facilitate political and economic reforms helped to create a situation where Berlin and Germany could be reunited. Without these efforts, the elimination of one wall would have had little historical importance.

In Europe, the fall of Communism was a dramatic conclusion demonstrating the agency of ordinary citizens and the forbearance of political leaders. Chinese leaders beginning with Mao's pragmatic successor Deng Xiaoping also demonstrated forbearance, mixing Communism with free enterprise in ways that enriched the government and many Chinese entrepreneurs. Other leaders embraced Capitalist business practices while maintaining the restrictions against free speech and genuine democracy that were trademarks of the Maoist era.

Students and other protesters inspired by the fall of Communism in Eastern Europe took to the streets in April and May 1989, demanding similar democratic reforms. Protesters erected a miniature Statue of Liberty across from the portrait of the late Chairman Mao in Beijing's Tiananmen Square. Tens of thousands of college students throughout China demonstrated solidarity with the protesters by wearing buttons bearing the image of the Statue of Liberty and other symbols of democracy. These protests continued despite government orders to desist, largely due to the toleration of dissent under the moderate Chinese leader Hu Yaobang. The protests continued after Yaobang died in April 1989. His successors feared that the continued toleration of dissent might result in the Chinese Communist Party sharing the fate of Communists in Eastern Europe. One June 3, 1983, students and other citizens refused the government's order to abandon the protests. The Chinese government responded by sending soldiers and tanks into the streets, a conflict that escalated until hundreds of unarmed protesters were killed. Known today as the **Tiananmen Square Massacre**, the protests demonstrated the reliance on force by Chinese Communist leaders. The massacre continues to serve as an international symbol of the continued fight for democracy in China and around the world.

4.3 The Soviet Union and Panama

The Soviet Union was a collection of states with limited autonomy, although most power was vested in the national government based in Moscow. However, that balance of power was shifting to the states as a result of Gorbachev's reforms. The most dramatic evidence of this transfer of power from the national to the state governments was the declaration of independence by the Soviet states of Estonia, Latvia, and Lithuania in 1988 and 1989. Each of these states had been independent nations before being absorbed by the Soviet Union. Similar to the people of Eastern Europe, many citizens of these areas longed to free themselves from Soviet domination. Alarmed by the apparent dissolution of their nation, Soviet military leaders and Communist hard-liners in Moscow attempted to seize control of the government from Gorbachev in August 1991. They arrested Gorbachev and blamed his toleration of the anti-Communist revolutions in Eastern Europe for the secession of Latvia, Lithuania, and Estonia.

Russia was the largest and most powerful of the Soviet states and was governed by the extremely popular **Boris Yeltsin**. He and other leaders of the remaining Soviet states feared that the coup would reverse their recent autonomy and return the Soviet Union to a hard-line Communist state. Because Moscow was in the middle of Russia, and because most military leaders remained loyal to Yeltsin, the Russian leader's refusal to support the coup led to its undoing and the return of Gorbachev. However, Gorbachev recognized that his authority would never be the same. The Communist Party had been splintering into different factions for many years and the attempted coup represented the way many influential people felt about his leadership.

Gorbachev also recognized that his return to office was only made possible by Yeltsin and other state leaders, most of whom were calling for the dissolution of the Soviet Union and the independence of their own states. Gorbachev could do little to stop the process of devolution he had helped create, both by instituting reforms and by permitting the revolutions. On December 25, 1991, the Soviet Union was replaced by the Commonwealth of Independent States, a loose confederation of eleven independent nations that had formerly been states of the Soviet Union. Boris Yeltsin soon became the leader of the Federation of Russia, the most dominant state of the former Soviet Union. The Commonwealth of Independent States continued to coordinate affairs of most Soviet States, but it was ineffective in preventing a number of military conflicts between members in the following decades.

Panamanian dictator Manuel Noriega was one of the leading money launderers for the international drug trafficking business. In May 1989, Noriega's supporters were defeated by an opposition party by an estimated 3-1 margin. However, Noriega supporters severely beat the winning candidates in front of live television cameras and then declared the entire election a fraud. Several other Panamanian efforts to take control of their nation from Noriega were likewise defeated by the use of violence.

President Bush came under growing pressure to intervene, both as the president of a nation that claimed to protect human rights and democracy and as an outspoken opponent of the drug trade. The problem for Bush was that he had supported the decision to pay Noriega hundreds of thousands of dollars while he was the head of the CIA in the 1970s and continued to support Noriega as vice president during the Iran-Contra Affair. Noriega had been one of the leading CIA contacts in Latin America. Although Noriega had sided with the United States over Soviet agents and even assisted US efforts against certain drug traffickers, Noriega had also sheltered many others and assisted their efforts to traffic narcotics into the United States. Because of his "loyalty" during the Cold War, the federal government overlooked Noriega's connection to drug cartels during the early 1980s. However, they reversed course once reports about Noriega's double-dealing became public information.

The Bush administration attempted to convince Noriega to recognize the election results and step down. When he refused, relations between the Panamanian military and US troops in the Panama Canal Zone grew increasingly tense. After an off-duty US Marine was killed in Panama, President Bush sent more than 25,000 troops into Panama to arrest Noriega. Referred by President Bush as a "police action," the rest of the world called the events that followed the **Panamanian Invasion**. The US used bombs and heavy artillery to crush the surprisingly strong resistance by Panamanian troops who remained loyal to Noriega. Rockets and other explosions led to numerous fires that killed an estimated 2,500 civilians and left many others homeless.

Noriega himself evaded capture by taking refuge in a church, surrendering only after a weeklong siege that included loudspeakers blaring rock music. After his surrender, Noriega was flown to Florida where he was imprisoned on drug charges. The action removed a dictator from office, but the manner in which the operation was conducted led to UN condemnation. In addition to the fires, the aftermath of the attack led to looting that caused millions of dollars of damage. With the exception of the lone US representative, the Organization of American States voted unanimously to condemn the poorly planned operation. In addition, twenty-three US troops perished and several hundred other soldiers were wounded.

FIGURE 13.18

A map of Eastern Europe and the former Soviet Union showing the years in which each nation dissolved its Communist government. In December 1991, eleven of the states that had been part of the Soviet Union were united as the Commonwealth of Independent States. Many of the other states such as Latvia, Lithuania, and Estonia had previously been independent and once again became sovereign nations.

4.4   Desert Shield and Desert Storm

Iraq's failed invasion and prolonged war with Iran resulted in its government becoming indebted to surrounding nations such as Kuwait. Oil producers in Kuwait had enjoyed tremendous profits and improved relations with the West when it went against the designs of Organization of the Petroleum Exporting Countries (OPEC) and raised production. In addition, the border between Iraq and Kuwait was a modern invention created by the British and a boundary that many Iraqis still considered to be illegitimate. Iraqi dictator Saddam Hussein believed that "reclaiming" Kuwait would help his nation escape its debt obligations and give it access to new oil fields and valuable ports. The close relationship between Iraq and the Reagan-Bush administration during the 1980s led Hussein to believe that the United States would not intervene when his military seized Kuwait on August 2, 1990. He was shocked to find instead that the United States led a coalition of dozens of nations that demanded Iraq to withdraw from Kuwait or face military action.

Panamanian Invasion

Dubbed a "police action" by the US government, 25,000 US troops entered Panama on December 20 and seized dictator Manuel Noriega on narcotics charges after several days of fighting and a weeklong siege of a church where Noriega was hiding. Noriega had been soundly defeated in the most recent election but refused to recognize the legitimacy of these elections and the invasion led to the installation of those popularly elected government officials.

Operation Desert Shield

A US-led military operation launched following the invasion of Kuwait by Iraqi forces in August 1990. The purpose of Desert Shield was to prevent further aggression by forces under Iraqi dictator Saddam Hussein. Desert Storm began in August 1990 and ended with the launch of Operation Desert Storm seven months later.

Saudi Arabia recognized that the invasion of Kuwait was likely the first step of many Hussein would attempt in support of his goal of uniting the Middle East under his authority. A number of Arabic nations feared the rise of Hussein would threaten their interests. Leaders of these nations joined the United States and other Western nations in a coalition that deployed troops and surrounded Iraq in **Operation Desert Shield**. By January 1991, ten Islamic nations had dedicated ground forces along with nearly two dozen other nations that had sent troops or some other form of military assistance to prevent Hussein from invading other countries.

Desert Shield soon became more than a defensive operation as Allied forces began staging a planned offensive to enter Iraq and liberate Kuwait unless Hussein surrendered and withdrew from Kuwait. Hussein instead predicted defeat of the Americans and their allies in "the mother of all wars." Although many criticized the Bush administration as being motivated primarily by oil rather than the freedom of the Kuwaiti people, these criticisms were deflected by the diplomatic success of each stage of Desert Shield. Bush secured the support of Congress for each move, including a resolution approving force against Hussein on January 12, 1991. Perhaps more importantly, Bush sought and received the unanimous support of the UN Security Council and most UN members—a marked contrast from the unilateral invasion of Panama two years earlier. The inclusion of Islamic nations was especially important, although it required the United States to distance itself from Israel. The Israelis were forbidden to enter the coalition else America's fragile Middle Eastern alliance fall apart due to the long-standing conflict between the Jewish and Arabic worlds.

FIGURE 13.19

Two US Marines participate in a training exercise during Operation Desert Storm. At the time, many feared that Saddam Hussein would use chemical weapons against US forces.

On January 16, 1991, US and UN forces began pounding Iraqi positions with cruise missiles and fighter jets. Millions of Americans watched the aerial onslaught live on Cable News Network (CNN), complete with reports from journalists and camera crews that had entered Baghdad before the assault. Hussein refused to withdraw, massing his troops in preparation for an amphibious landing on the beaches of Kuwait. Instead, combat operations under the codename **Operation Desert Storm** unleashed armored columns of US forces that crossed the Iraqi border on February 24th and secured control of both Iraq and Kuwait in fewer than one hundred hours. With the exception of a few elite units, most Iraqi troops were conscripts with little loyalty to Hussein and were understandably reluctant to engage the superior military force that quickly encircled their positions.

Hussein launched several SCUD missiles at Israel in hopes of drawing Israeli retaliation that might destroy the alliance between the West and the Islamic states that now opposed him. Israel did not take the bait, and most of these missiles fell harmlessly short of their target or were destroyed in midair by US Patriot missiles. Desert Storm was a resounding victory for US and UN forces, as well as a triumph for the American Special Forces, which utilized techniques of psychological warfare. For example, US aircraft dropped thousands of tons of high explosives that were mixed with pamphlets in Arabic and Kurdish that promised humane treatment to all who surrendered. These and other aspects of psychological warfare, combined with low Iraqi morale and even

Operation Desert Storm

A war waged by the US military with the cooperation of thirty other nations against Iraqi forces in January and February 1991. The US and its allies began their attack on January sixteen following a UN Security Council resolution authorizing the United States to use force against Iraqi forces unless they withdrew from Kuwait by January 15. Ground forces converged on Iraqi positions on February 24, and within four days, Iraqi forces surrendered and agreed to leave Kuwait.

lower chances of successfully defeating US and UN forces, led some Iraqis to surrender to CNN reporters. Estimates of Iraqi fatalities exceeded 30,000, while only 148 American lives were lost. Hussein soon agreed to withdraw from Kuwait, and the small oil-producing nation would remain a US ally in the following decades.

The most pressing question following the rapid success of Operation Desert Storm was whether to withdraw from the region or attempt to remove Saddam Hussein from power. American diplomatic relations with Saudi Arabia and other Middle Eastern nations remained tenuous despite the success of their joint operation. The original objectives of Desert Shield and Desert Storm had been reached, and many feared that expanding the objectives to include the removal of Hussein and transition of Iraq under US authority would anger other nations in the Middle East.

The lightning-quick operation had led to a surge in outward displays of patriotism in the United States, and Bush's approval rating approached an unprecedented 90 percent. Secretary of Defense Dick Cheney explained Bush's decision to withdraw from Iraq as an assessment of the probable costs and casualties that would result from the attempt to occupy Iraq and remove Hussein from power. Cheney and others in the Bush administration agreed in the early 1990s that Hussein did not present a threat to the United States. They also agreed that any attempt to remove Saddam from power might backfire and lead to unacceptably high US casualties.

4.5   The Election of 1992

William Jefferson Clinton, a popular governor of Arkansas, secured the nomination of the Democratic Party by branding himself as a moderate. A shrewd politician, Clinton gave a speech during the 1992 election at the Lyndon Baines Johnson School of Government on the campus of the University of Texas without making any mention of Johnson, the president who was associated with liberal policies such as the War on Poverty. Equally careful to not alienate his Democratic base, Clinton offered cautious support for a number of liberal social issues such as abortion rights. He also expressed a more tolerant view of homosexuals than most leading politicians at that time.

However, Clinton devoted far more time on the campaign trail espousing surprisingly conservative opinions regarding the need to limit the size and power of the federal government and preventing tax increases. Clinton recognized that President Bush was vulnerable on economic and tax issues. The problem became increasingly acute following a minor recession. Just as the costs of Desert Storm mounted, tax receipts dropped, and Bush was forced to increase taxes. These tax hikes violated the president's infamous campaign promise of "no new taxes" and did little to reverse the nation's growing deficit and 7 percent unemployment rate.

More than anything, Clinton was adept at speaking to the economic frustrations faced by "average Americans" who had suffered during the recession and feared losing their jobs. Clinton attacked Republican policies that were favorable to multinational corporations based in the United States as accelerating deindustrialization the loss of American jobs overseas. Bush responded by trying to remind Americans of the prosperity the nation had experienced under the past twelve years of Republican leadership, but Clinton seized this issue by reminding voters at every opportunity that their nation had slipped into a recession during the last four of those years. To highlight the importance of this message to their campaign, Clinton's Little Rock headquarters displayed an internal memo that simply read, "It's the economy, stupid." The sign was intended to remind Clinton supporters to keep talking about how the economy had stumbled once President Bush took office.

Unlike several previous Democratic candidates, Clinton was able to convert popular anger against his opponent into an electoral victory. The unusually high approval rates Bush enjoyed during the height of the Gulf War had dropped rapidly, hitting a low of 30 percent in the months leading up to the election. Bush's support was further eroded by leaders of the religious right, such as Pat Buchanan, who criticized the Bush administration's toleration of homosexuals. Evangelicals were also angered by Bush's failure to pass legislation restricting abortion or furthering other concerns of social conservatives.

Perhaps even more damaging than the criticism of the far right was the third-party candidacy of Texas billionaire **Ross Perot**. Nearly one in five Americans voted for Perot and his promise to run America like one of his successful business enterprises. Perot failed to win any votes in the Electoral College, although he polled well throughout the nation. Perot and his vice presidential candidate James Stockdale, a Congressional Medal of Honor recipient who endured seven years in a Hanoi POW camp, won the support of many Americans who were frustrated by the perceived failures of the two major parties. Given Perot's probusiness and antiestablishment orientation, most historians believe the Perot candidacy cut into Bush's Republican base slightly more than it detracted from Clinton. In the end, Clinton won with nearly 70 percent of the Electoral College. However, Clinton had only received 43 percent of the popular vote to Bush's 38 percent and Ross Perot's 19 percent.

5.   CONCLUSION

Leading conservative politicians often felt the need to defend the political right from charges of insensitivity given its recent history of opposing civil rights and inclination for Cold War saber rattling. The defense of conservatism against charges of callousness was a constant theme from Barry Goldwater's 1960 manifesto *Conscience of a Conservative* to George W. Bush's call for "compassionate conservatism" forty years later. For millions of Evangelicals and social conservatives, a more compassionate form of political conservatism seemed the ideal alternative to the previous two decades of political leadership. Although the Reagan administration spoke the same language of social conservatives, some believe that he failed to represent their values and ideas when it came to legislation or world affairs. Others believe that he failed to rise above the troubled legacy of racial insensitivity at home and continued the short-sighted policies abroad that had plagued his predecessors. At the same time, Reagan was also one of the finest communicators, and it was this skill that led to his greatest achievement—facilitating a peaceful resolution to the end of the Cold War.

The real credit for ending the Cold War, however, lies with those around the globe whose actions influenced the Reagan administration and Soviet Premier Mikhail Gorbachev to work toward rapprochement by starting democratic revolutions. While there are many examples of improved communication and willingness to work toward peace, the two leaders generally followed the tradition of

William Jefferson Clinton

The forty-second president of the United States, Clinton was governor in Arkansas before winning the presidential election of 1992 and reelection in 1996. Clinton was known as a moderate who enjoyed public support during most of his tenure in office due to steady economic growth.

Ross Perot

A wealthy and successful businessman who in 1992 ran what was arguably the most successful third-party campaign for president since Theodore Roosevelt. Perot did not win any electoral votes, unlike a handful of other third-party candidates who ran on platforms of segregation during the civil rights movement. However, Perot won nearly 20 percent of the popular vote with roughly equal support from voters who labeled themselves as either liberal or conservative.

détente. Reagan and Soviet leaders sought to create a safer and more stable Cold War rather than risk the possibility of war or revolution. The end of the Cold War is better understood from a bottom-up approach, exploring the dozens of nonviolent revolutions. Rather than focusing exclusively on the speeches of world leaders, the Cold War must also be understood by exploring the way that ordinary people supported movements, and the failure of violence and intimidation to extinguish their desire for a more democratic society in nations.

If the political leaders of the 1980s later claim that they envisioned and orchestrated a peaceful end to the Cold War, their public speeches and personal correspondence demonstrate otherwise. More importantly, the historical record demonstrates that the fall of Communism was the result of grassroots efforts by an increasingly well-educated global public who exercised unprecedented agency in shaping the history of their nations. In short, attributing the multitude of largely peaceful democratic revolutions that began in the late 1980s to the US president or Soviet Premier suffers from the same analytical shortsightedness as those who maintain that Lincoln freed the slaves. Such assertions ignore the deeper historical context of the era and discount the agency of the people of Eastern Europe and their leaders. It also discredits the importance of US allies such as Britain and its conservative Prime Minister Margaret Thatcher, as well as global leaders such as Pope John Paul II whose opposition to Communism inspired many around the globe.

Reagan's successor George H. W. Bush was less of an ideologue and was willing to sacrifice political expediency to confront the ballooning federal deficit he inherited. He also skillfully assembled an unlikely coalition of Western and Islamic nations in one of the most successful military operations in world history. The election of a Democratic president in 1992 was only a partial repudiation of the conservatism of the White House during the past twelve years; a desire for change, but certainly not a mandate for a return to the more liberal orientation of decades past. The nation approved the laws that had removed the most obvious barriers against women and minorities but most Americans believed that no further actions were necessary to insure equality. If conservatism was on the decline by 1992, it was not because liberals were in the ascendency. In fact, the term "liberal" remained a derisive label. By the time of the 1992 election, so many Americans were self-identified "moderates" that it was difficult to remember exactly what conservatives and liberals stood for. In such a political environment, the candidate who created the first and most convincing brand image as a moderate would surely prevail. In 1992, that candidate was Bill Clinton.

6. FURTHER READING

Critchlow, Donald T. *The Conservative Ascendancy: How the Republican Right Rose to Power in Modern America*, Second Edition (2011).

Hahn, Peter L. *Crisis and Crossfire: The United States and the Middle East Since 1945* (2005).

McGirr, Lisa. *Suburban Warriors: The Origins of the New American Right* (2001).

Patterson, James T. *Restless Giant: The United States from Watergate to Bush v. Gore* (2005).

Rogers, Daniel T. *Age of Fracture* (2011).

Schoenwald, Jonathan M. *A Time for Choosing: The Rise of Modern American Conservatism* (2001).

Smith, Gaddis. *The Last Years of the Monroe Doctrine: 1945–1993* (1994).

Wilentz, Sean. *The Age of Reagan: A History, 1974–2008* (2008).

Williams, Daniel. *God's Own Party: The Making of the Christian Right* (2010).

CHAPTER 14
America in Our Time, 1992–Present

The end of the Cold War and the disintegration of the Soviet Union left the United States as the only military superpower. Some hoped that the nation would respond with massive reductions in military spending, perhaps even an "America first" policy that was similar to the isolationism of earlier periods in US history. Taxpayers had spent $4 trillion building nuclear weapons and trillions more maintaining its military and fighting proxy wars around the globe. Two generations had lost their lives fighting in wars many believed were a mistake and for causes that seemed no longer relevant. Others hoped that America would use its unrivaled military and economic power to promote democracy and human rights around the globe. Still others saw the end of the Cold War as an opportunity for profitable business expansion via globalization.

In many ways, each of these ideas affected US diplomacy in the post–Cold War years. However, even after the fall of Communism, US foreign policy was as much a response to the actions of others throughout the globe as it was an attempt by Americans to shape the world around them. A series of economic crises reminded Americans that their economy and their nation were part of a global system. The cowardice of nineteen terrorists on September 11, 2001, likewise reminded the nation of its vulnerabilities, while the response to this attack demonstrated the character of its people. The attack also awakened the world to the ways that the Cold War had obscured ethnic, religious, and regional conflicts in places such as Central Europe, Africa, and the Middle East. The relationship between the two biggest challenges of the post–Cold War era—global security and economic stability—would shape the US response to the terrorist attacks and define the politics of the next two decades.

1. AMERICA DURING THE CLINTON ADMINISTRATION

LEARNING OBJECTIVES

1. Identify Clinton's top priorities as an incoming president. Explain which of these programs were successful. Discuss the reasons that others were not passed by Congress. Summarize the arguments and methods of those who supported and opposed the Clinton health care plan.

2. Summarize the "Contract with America" and its impact on US history. Explain the main objectives of Republican leaders such as Newt Gingrich and the arguments for and against their leading proposals.

3. Explain the issues of the 1996 presidential election and why Clinton was able to defeat his Republican opponent just two years after the Republicans swept Congress. Explain how Newt Gingrich and the Republicans lost the initiative and how Clinton was able to retain high public approval ratings during his second term even in the wake of scandal.

1.1 Domestic Politics in Clinton's First Two Years

Janet Reno

The first female attorney general and a leading figure in the Clinton administration, Reno was frequently in the public eye due to a number of high-profile crimes and controversies, such as the Branch Davidian siege, the Oklahoma City bombing, and the World Trade Center bombing of 1993.

Earned Income Credit

A tax credit that some low-income wage earners are eligible to receive with the intention of making employment at such a job more financially rewarding and thereby producing a stronger incentive to work rather than seek governmental aid.

Clinton appointed more women and minorities to meaningful positions in the federal government than any president in the past. Madeleine Albright was Clinton's secretary of state while **Janet Reno** served as attorney general. Together, these women led the Clinton administration's efforts to confront domestic and international terrorism. At home, Clinton supported a number of antipoverty programs and proposed a federal plan to extend health care coverage to all citizens. Clinton also sought to maintain his reputation as a moderate. As a result, the president angered many of the more liberal members of his party who had hoped he would reverse the conservative policies of previous administrations and expand the welfare state. Clinton believed the increasing polarization between the political left and right was an opportunity for presidential leadership. If he could steer a course between liberals and conservatives, Clinton believed, he might win support for his health care reform bill while still being perceived as a moderate that united the country.

The president created a few modest programs that won liberal support. One of these programs was AmeriCorps—a federal work program that employs mostly younger people and seniors in a variety of community service fields. After Clinton's health plan floundered, however, it appeared to many liberals that Clinton had decided that the easiest way to be viewed as a moderate was to adopt popular Republican initiatives as his own.

Welfare reform provides one of many examples of Clinton's efforts to steer a middle course between both liberals and conservatives. As a candidate, Clinton had tapped into the suspicion raised by conservative politicians regarding "welfare mothers." Placing stricter limits on direct payments to welfare recipients, the Clinton administration promised to transform welfare into a program that assisted only those who were striving for independence. Toward this goal, Clinton supported stricter regulations on direct payments. He also approved a significant increase of the **Earned Income Credit**, which offered an annual payment to those who worked at low-paying jobs rather than application for welfare. The amount of the credit was based on income and the number of dependents for which a low-income worker was responsible.

Clinton defended the plan as a means to reward those who worked. He pointed out that most individuals on welfare would make only slightly less than a full-time worker at a minimum-wage job unless some adjustment was made. While Clinton also supported a modest increase to the minimum wage, he believed that tax credits for the working poor were necessary to provide incentives for people to get off of welfare. Critics of the plan were angered that those who qualified for the Earned Income Credit paid no federal tax yet would still receive a tax refund under the new plan. This new policy seemed even more unfair to some individuals in the wake of increased tax rates for some families. At the same time, Clinton's support for curtailing direct welfare payments also angered some on the left.

FIGURE 14.1

President Clinton appointed more women to his cabinet and senior staff than any previous president. To the immediate left of President Clinton is Secretary of State Madeleine Albright. In the bottom right corner is Janet Reno, the first woman to hold the position of attorney general.

Clinton's most ambitious domestic initiative was also the most controversial of his entire eight years in office. As a candidate, Clinton seldom missed an opportunity to talk about the rising costs of health care he believed were crippling the economy and bankrupting families. Clinton's supporters pointed out that there were nearly 40 million Americans without health insurance—most of whom were children or full-time workers. If elected president, Clinton promised sweeping legislation that would offer universal health care for all Americans under a federally operated managed-care plan that was similar to the offerings of many private insurance companies. Clinton's supporters argued that because the government would instantly become the largest insurer in the nation, the government would be able to regulate the prices that doctors and hospitals charged. Although a doctor could still charge any amount she wished, the federal government would only pay a certain amount for any particular service. This was similar to the practice of private insurance companies that also established maximum prices they would pay for different procedures and prescriptions. The difference, Clinton believed, was that the federal government would insure so many people that most doctors would have to lower their costs to meet the government rate or else lose the business of numerous patients. Opponents of the plan countered that increased government bureaucracy would either increase the costs of health care or cost taxpayers money.

Clinton's supporters provided numerous statistics in an effort to show that government intervention would save money and improve care. The campaign against Clinton's plan was bankrolled by organizations representing insurers, drug companies, hospitals, and physicians. As a result, most Americans questioned much of the information they were hearing as either politically biased or motivated by the medical industry's own financial interests. However, the plan's opponents were able to raise the specter of "socialized medicine" by connecting suspicion toward bigger government with the fear that regulating prices would reduce the quality of care. Just as government control over prices decreased the incentive for innovation and quality control in Soviet Russia, Clinton's opponents argued, establishing maximum reimbursement rates would reduce competition among physicians and hospitals.

Hillary Clinton

Attorney and wife of President Bill Clinton, Hillary Clinton was the first presidential spouse to have an independent career at the time of her husband's election. As First Lady, Clinton led the effort for health care reform and other initiatives. She was elected to the US Senate in 2000 and was a leading contender for the Democratic presidential nomination in 2008.

Newt Gingrich

The Republican Speaker of the House between 1995 and 1999 and a leading conservative politician, this former historian at the University of West Georgia introduced a platform known as the Contract with America that led to the Republican victory in the congressional elections of 1994.

Contract with America

A platform that united Republican congressional candidates during the 1994 election with its demands for less government, balanced budgets, and support for socially conservative causes.

FIGURE 14.2

President Clinton delivering the 1997 State of the Union address while Vice President Al Gore (left) and House Speaker Newt Gingrich (right) appear in the background.

The comparisons between America's health care system and some of the sensationalized tales of malpractice under Socialism were likely unfair. However, Clinton's plan was complex and few inside or outside of government actually read its provisions. In addition, some Democratic leaders were upset that they had not been consulted in the drafting of the plan. Some Democrats even offered their own competing plans, which led to divisions within Clinton's own party. Other opponents utilized misogynistic imagery against First Lady **Hillary Clinton** and other women who occupied leading roles in the taskforce that drafted the president's plan. These opponents derided the plan as "Hillary Care," creating the image that the president's wife was really in charge of the White House in ways that played upon negative images of powerful women. As a result of all these factors, Congress rejected Clinton's plan. Its failure cast a shadow over the rest of the Clinton administration and reduced the ambition of his future proposals.

1.2 Contract with America

Clinton had directed much of his energy to his failed health care initiative, believing that his electoral victory was a mandate from voters in support of his plan. Although the recession of the early 1990s was fading, symptoms of economic decline lingered and the president had not passed any major legislation in his first two years in office, despite enjoying a Democratic majority in both houses of Congress. That majority soon evaporated following the 1994 midterm elections as Republicans turned the congressional elections into a national referendum on Clinton's first two years in office. United under the leadership of Georgia congressman **Newt Gingrich**, Republicans in congressional districts across the nation ran under the same banner and promised a new "**Contract with America**." The contract itself contained a lofty preamble lauding conservative "family values." It also included a list of resolutions that called for tax breaks, reductions in the size of the federal government, numerous governmental reform measures, and support for socially conservative initiatives.

Democrats countered that the contract was little more than propaganda—a vague collection of clichés and catchphrases aimed at delivering votes rather than guiding policy. However, many of the provisions within the contract were quite specific. For example, one provision required more transparent accounting procedures—while another required full disclosure of the congressional proceedings. Some of the measures resembled the Populist crusade of the century prior, such as term limits for congressional committee chairs and an end to closed-door sessions. Even sweeping provisions such as a Constitutional amendment requiring balanced budgets every year appealed to most Americans as the national debt approached $5 trillion during the 1994 election.

The contract placed Democratic candidates on the defensive and defined the terms of the election in many congressional districts. Democrats responded that many provisions of the contract might sound good in the abstract but were either too vague to represent a clear statement of policy or potentially dangerous because they might lead to unforeseen consequences. For example, most Democrats conceded that the contract's support of the balanced-budget amendment made sense in principle. At the same time, Democrats countered, the amendment might limit the nation's ability to prevail in times of war or economic crisis. However, the Democrats did not have a similar unified platform and were vulnerable to voter frustration after two years of controlling both Congress and the White House. Republicans were able to solidify the association in the minds of many voters between Democrats, higher taxes, bigger government, and the failure of Clinton's health care program. United behind the Contract with America, the Republican Party captured both houses of Congress for the first time since the 1950s.

The Republican Congress proposed dozens of bills inspired by fiscally conservative ideas that aimed to reduce corporate and capital gains taxes. They also sought to reduce government spending on social programs that assisted the poor and promoted education. Federally funded programs in the arts and humanities were especially vulnerable, along with welfare programs such as Aid to Families with Dependent Children (AFDC). Others sought to promote causes supported by social conservatives like eliminating affirmative action, legalizing school prayer, and banning the burning of the US flag. Few of these bills regarding socially conservative causes were ever passed, however, and many historians believe that these measures were more designed to win the support of conservative voters than actually become law.

Other's criticized the Contract with America's avoidance of the issue of abortion as evidence that the Republicans offered only lip service to social conservatives. Although restricting abortion was a leading conservative issue throughout the 1994 election, the contract avoided any mention of the topic. In fact, some critics pointed out the likelihood that the contract's "Personal Responsibility Act" would encourage abortion. This law sought to deny additional welfare support to mothers of multiple children. It also prohibited any federal assistance to mothers under the age of eighteen.

Opponents of abortion were the most loyal supporters of the Republican ascendency and hoped the party would finally reverse *Roe v. Wade* and make abortion illegal once again. However, most within the Republican majority avoided the controversial issue. Laws banning flag-burning passed the

House of Representatives but were defeated in the Senate. These were largely symbolic gestures, however, because the Supreme Court had long maintained that such displays were protected under the Bill of Rights. Social conservatives continued to win supporters through populist appeals against a "liberal" Supreme Court that outlawed school prayer while protecting flag-burning. Many political observers were quick to point out that the majority of justices had been appointed by Republican presidents. Others argued that the Republicans spoke the language of the New Right but were more likely to pursue fiscally conservative policies once in office. As a result, many social conservatives felt betrayed when the Republican Congress did not unite behind legislation outlawing abortion.

When it came to fiscal politics and governmental reform, the Republican majority honored their campaign promises and aggressively promoted the provisions of the Contract with America during the 1995 and 1996 legislative sessions. The most significant of these provisions was the proposed **Balanced Budget Amendment** to the Constitution. This amendment required Congress to submit a balanced budget each year unless three-fifths of both houses of Congress agreed to waive the requirement. The intent of the amendment was to reverse the annual deficits that had accumulated each year. Defenders of the amendment argued that members of the House of Representatives could seldom be counted on to cut popular governmental programs or raise taxes given the realities of the two-year election cycle. Given the measure's popularity among a public that had grown wary of the growing national deficit, the bill passed the House. However, it failed to garner the necessary two-thirds vote in the Senate and was never forwarded to the states for ratification.

A second measure intended to cut government waste gave the president of the United States the authority to sign a bill into law while rejecting certain attached provisions called "riders." Riders were provisions that were frequently attached to a proposed bill in order to secure the support of a specific member of Congress who might have otherwise voted against the bill. For example, a law regulating mine safety might be unpopular with a few members of a particular congressional committee overseeing such matters. To secure their support, a rider providing federal funding for a bridge or other project in each of these members' districts might be added as a rider to win their support. Riders were usually not this overt, but they did result in billions of dollars being spent on "pet" projects that might not have passed Congress on their own merit. The Republican Congress approved a law granting presidential authority to delete riders while approving the law itself through the "line-item veto." However, a subsequent decision by the US Supreme Court declared that a president's use of the line-item veto was an unconstitutional subversion of the powers of the legislative branch. As a result, the line-item veto was a short-lived reform.

Balanced Budget Amendment

A proposed Constitutional amendment that would have prohibited deficit spending by requiring each session of Congress to approve a balanced budget.

1.3   Budget Crisis and the 1996 Election

Although Clinton had championed the role of government in uplifting the poor in 1992, the Republican victory of 1994 demonstrated that reducing welfare spending was still a popular issue among voters. Attempting to chart a course between witch hunts for chimerical "welfare queens" and blaming poverty on the greed of the wealthy, Clinton hoped to promote reform while bolstering his image as a moderate. Clinton promised to "end welfare as we know it" by limiting direct payments and increasing federal funding for job training.

The president's reform policies borrowed heavily from Republican ideas regarding welfare. For example, Clinton supported a provision that would have placed a time limit on the number of months a person could receive benefits. In addition, noncitizens were ineligible for any payments under Clinton's plan, regardless of whether they were legal residents. Clinton also backed an anticrime bill that provided cities and states with $30 billion to hire additional officers. This law passed Congress, and also introduced the standard of three convictions leading to lifetime imprisonment for federal crimes. This "three strikes" rule was soon adopted by many state governments. With existing laws that made the possession of even small quantities of illegal drugs a felony, the prison population that had grown so dramatically during the War on Drugs continued to expand. Clinton also backed an increase to the minimum wage (from $4.25 to $5.15 an hour) that won the support of liberals and the working class.

From the perspective of many House Republicans, Clinton was "stealing" some of their most popular ideas. Republicans responded by making their promise to reduce the size of government and balance the federal budget the cornerstone of their platform. The issue resonated with voters, was consistent with Republican ideas about reducing spending, and supported the conservative goal of liquidating the welfare state. Interpreting their dramatic victory in the congressional elections of 1994 as a mandate to slash government programs, Republicans closed ranks behind a budget and tax plan proposed by House leaders.

Clinton submitted a budget that also enacted significant cuts but retained a $200 billion deficit. The Republicans also submitted a budget. Because their plan included tax breaks and increases for defense spending, the Republicans had to make even deeper cuts to numerous social programs. The Republican plan did not spare popular programs such as Medicare and federally subsidized school lunches, two politically sacred programs that had ruined the political careers of those who opposed them in the past. Clinton and the Democrats responded by hammering away at the apparent support of their opponents for billions of dollars in tax cuts for the wealthy, no tax cuts for the poor and the middle class, and reductions for programs benefitting the neediest children and seniors.

The Republican plan to reduce taxes for the wealthy and corporations while appearing to support plans that would take food from children and medicine from seniors astounded political observers. However, the Democratic Party also appeared to be its own worst enemy and a party divided among itself. Even as the Democrats found some unity in their counteroffensive against the Republican budget, the division between the president and more liberal leaders of his party remained. This gulf was exacerbated by the 1994 election, which had resulted in the defeat of Southern and Midwestern Democrats that had supported the president. These were the regions where the new Republican strategy had worked the best, and they were also the regions where Democrats were more likely to subscribe to Clinton's moderate views. Those Democrats that had survived the 1994 election tended to be from more liberal and urban Congressional districts. These Democrats opposed Clinton's acceptance of deep cuts to social programs. They were especially angered by Clinton's revised budget, which included modest cuts for Medicaid. From their perspective, the president was surrendering a key issue that might have won seniors back to the Democratic fold.

Congress and the president spent the majority of 1995 and 1996 wrangling over budgetary matters. When the Senate and the president refused to approve the House budget, Gingrich and the Republicans refused to compromise, which led to a temporary shutdown of nonessential federal services. National parks and federal offices closed while payments for millions of government employees and recipients of Social Security were delayed. Although the shutdown was caused by a refusal of both sides to compromise, most Americans blamed outspoken Republicans such as Gingrich for the shutdown. The Republicans quickly reversed course and restored Medicare spending, yet many Americans were convinced that Gingrich and his supporters precipitated the standoff as a political calculation rather than an ideological commitment to fiscal responsibility.

Clinton's strategy in the 1996 election was based on appealing to as many voters as possible by portraying himself as a moderate within a polarized system. The strategy required distancing himself from liberals without alienating his liberal base. The key for Clinton was to appeal to moderate conservatives. However, if Clinton strayed too far to the political right, he risked the possibility that a popular liberal candidate might challenge him for the Democratic nomination or run as a third-party candidate. Clinton's ability to chart a middle course on issues such as affirmative action helped convince popular Democrats like Jesse Jackson to support Clinton's bid for reelection rather than entering the race. Had Jackson decided to contend Clinton's reelection, he would have eroded the president's support among many liberal and minority voters. Once Jackson was on board rather than an opponent, Clinton was able to occasionally veer to the right of his own party because there were few other potential Democratic challengers.

Bob Dole

A World War II veteran and senator from Kansas who was defeated in his 1996 bid for the presidency by Democrat and incumbent Bill Clinton.

Defense of Marriage Act

A federal law passed in 1996 that defined marriage as a union between a man and a woman. The law does not prohibit states from performing or recognizing same-sex marriages, but it does not compel a state to recognize the legality of same-sex marriages performed in other states.

Clinton faced the Republican Senator **Bob Dole** in the general election. At age seventy-three, Dole was both an experienced and well-respected leader but also an aging career politician who had failed to inspire voters during the Republican primaries. Dole's brand of conservatism was more moderate than the drift of the Republican Party under Gingrich. The Kansas senator expressed his personal support of the conservative "family values" of the New Right. At the same time, he did not believe that government should accommodate any particular religious views. Dole also believed that the attack led by Gingrich and others upon liberals was both divisive and a distraction from the role of responsible government.

Dole attempted to distance himself from the controversial issue of abortion, but reluctantly embraced an antiabortion provision that was necessary to shore up his support among evangelicals. However, Dole's public opposition to abortion reduced the candidate's appeal among a number of undecided voters, especially female voters, who might have otherwise voted for Dole. Clinton also undercut the potential of Dole's support among undecided voters by supporting a number of socially conservative initiatives. The most controversial of these was the 1996 **Defense of Marriage Act** that legally defined marriage as a union between a man and a woman. Clinton's opposition to same-sex marriage contrasted sharply with his avowed support for gay rights in the past. However, it cost him few votes given the unlikelihood that gay-marriage supporters would vote for a Republican.

Dole seemed noncommittal himself when it came to the budgetary matters. The senator called for a 15 percent tax cut for all Americans while promising to increase defense spending *and* balance the budget. Voters asked how Dole could deliver these seemingly irreconcilable objectives, a question the Republican candidate seemed to dodge as he gave a series of uninspiring speeches across the nation. Clinton matched Dole's travel schedule, tipping the balance between running for president and being the president as he crisscrossed the country and turned every address to the nation into a stump speech.

Clinton's campaign also may have crossed the boundary between fundraising and selling access to the president. Clinton fundraisers allowed dozens of foreign nationals, some with shadowy connections and apparent agendas, to meet with the president for a price. Later investigations would show that Clinton's campaign was even financed by allowing major donors to stay in the White House's famed

Lincoln bedroom. The aggressive fundraising allowed Clinton to approach the massive funding of the traditionally probusiness Republican Party. While Clinton's possible fundraising violations drew the most attention, both campaigns pushed the limits of campaign-finance regulations. For example, recent legislation limited the amount of money an individual or corporation could donate to a particular candidate. However, these same laws permitted unlimited donations of "soft money," which could be used to support a particular issue or party. Both campaigns skirted these restrictions, financing advertisements that implicitly endorsed a candidate. They also made use of political action committees and other proxy organizations to evade the law's funding limits.

The gender gap in presidential elections had historically been almost imperceptible. In 1996, however, Dole polled slightly more votes among men while 16 percent more women voted for Clinton. With this unprecedented support of female voters, Clinton won a decisive victory with 379 votes in the Electoral College to Dole's 159. Even if Dole managed to win all of independent candidate Ross Perot's 8 million votes, Clinton would have still won the popular vote by a slim margin.

1.4 Domestic Affairs in Clinton's Second Term

The 1996 presidential election was about personalities and featured Clinton's ability to adopt popular conservative ideas and programs as his own. Clinton best demonstrated this ability regarding the issue of welfare reform. In 1996, Clinton supported a plan that eliminated Aid to Families with Dependent Children (AFDC), a federal welfare program that had provided cash payouts to poor families since its creation as part of the Social Security Act of 1935. The new law replaced AFDC with **Temporary Assistance for Needy Families (TANF)**. This program contained stricter regulations and a two-year limit that applied to able-bodied adults.

Perhaps ironically, this time limit was specifically mentioned in the 1994 Contract with America. Clinton made only one significant modification to the Republican idea: if an able-bodied adult who had been removed from the welfare rolls drifted back into poverty, the two-year clock would restart and the individual could receive welfare once again. Clinton's plan also capped lifetime benefits at five years, after which an able-bodied person would be completely ineligible for government aid. Clinton's TANF plan even borrowed from the New Federalism of Nixon by having individual states administer the funding for the program. States were granted wide latitude in determining how their TANF programs are administered. Some states placed even shorter limits on the amount of time a person might draw benefits and also required proof that an individual was actively searching for a job.

Liberals felt that Clinton's TANF plan betrayed their party's commitment to providing a safety net for the poor. These individuals pointed out that the vast majority of AFDC recipients were dependent children, as the name of the now-defunct plan suggested. They also reminded voters that 11 percent of the population and 20 percent of children were below the federally established poverty level. Defenders of the plan argued that states would be more effective in administering funds and better able to make sure children were still provided for, even after their parents had used up their eligibility for welfare. Critics of the state-level plan also pointed out that many poor Americans migrated frequently in search of work. They feared that families might "fall through the cracks" of the system as they moved from one state to another and had to reapply and wait for benefits.

Clinton's popularity increased during his second term—largely due to an economic boom and slight tax reductions for the middle class. Real estate and corporate profits grew rapidly and were reflected in rising stock values that benefitted more and more Americans given the popularity of mutual funds and self-service online brokers. The boom was especially evident in the technology-dominated NASDAQ stock exchange, which quadrupled during Clinton's second term. Clinton's popularity defied a series of investigations into his own finances, which began during his first year in office. In 1993, an independent government investigator responded to allegations of malfeasance regarding the Clinton family's real-estate investments in the Whitewater River Valley of Arkansas. Investigator Ken Starr soon expanded the search to include Clinton's fundraising activities, the use of government travel funds, and the disappearance of files related to these investigations. Although each investigation raised questions regarding the character and conduct of the president, the investigations turned up little concrete evidence of wrongdoing.

The investigation may have tarnished the image of the Clinton administration, but most Americans quickly grew tired of the very technical legal questions about what appeared to be at most a minor and complicated violation. Investigations regarding Clinton's personal life, however, quickly became fodder for late-night talk shows and entered conversations around the country. A former Arkansas employee named Paula Jones accused the former governor of both sexual harassment and a consensual extramarital affair. Once again, there was little evidence that Clinton had committed a crime, and Jones failed to collect the hundreds of thousands of dollars she sought.

The Jones affair was closely followed by a more serious revelation of a sexual relationship with a White House intern. For months, the nation largely ignored world events, health care reform, and other budgetary concerns while the sordid details of the Monica Lewinsky scandal came to light. Given the

Temporary Assistance for Needy Families (TANF)

A welfare agency that replaced Aid to Families with Dependent Children, TANF provides grants to individual states to administer their own welfare programs.

relentless and apparently personal nature of independent counsel Ken Starr's previous investigations, many Americans discredited the evidence Starr produced regarding the Lewinsky scandal. However, they also refused to believe the president's denials and were angered when Clinton later revealed that he had lied under oath in an effort to cover up the affair. It was for this crime rather than the affair itself that Clinton was impeached by the House of Representatives. However, the Senate refused to remove the president from office, and most Americans agreed that his indiscretion was neither a high crime nor a misdemeanor. Perhaps unfairly, by the time it was all over, most Americans had a lower opinion of Kenneth Starr, Lewinsky, and even the president's wife than the man who had lied and committed adultery.

Clinton's ability to escape scandal angered conservatives who had hoped the Lewinsky affair would become the Democrat's Watergate. In the preface of his Contract with America, Newt Gingrich and other conservatives had promised to restore the dignity of Congress and end the "cycle of scandal and disgrace" many Americans now associated with high political office. Gingrich was among the president's leading inquisitors and perhaps the loudest voice of those who called for Clinton's resignation or removal. Ironically, a handful of other Republicans who led the charge against Clinton were later convicted of improper sexual relations with underage congressional pages. Gingrich himself was found to be having an extramarital affair with a much younger member of his staff who later became his third wife. Gingrich soon resigned from office after facing ethics charges and criticism for his personal life.

Clinton's continued invincibility to scandal led some to compare the president to the "Teflon" coating that prevented material from sticking to pots and pans. However, Clinton's ability to withstand multiple scandals likely had more to do with the economy than any other factor. The official budgetary surpluses announced by the Clinton administration in its final year were the result of an economic boom that produced increased tax receipts. As a result, Clinton presided over an era of prosperity that allowed the federal government to produce balanced budgets and even a small surplus in Clinton's final years. Despite all of the debate in the early 1990s about the need for sacrifice, the economic boom of the middle and late 1990s created millions of new jobs that allowed the government to balance the budget while lowering taxes and avoiding controversial reductions to popular government programs.

1.5 Violence at Home and Abroad

Attorney General Janet Reno played a much more public role than most attorney generals, beginning in the spring of 1993 with her controversial decision to lay siege to the compound of cult leader David Koresh in Waco, Texas. The compound caught fire during the government raid and ATF agents entered to find that over seventy of Koresh's followers had either been killed or committed suicide. Three years later, two domestic terrorists cited the raid as justification for a deadly attack on a federal building in America's heartland.

Oklahoma City Bombing

The deadliest terrorist attack in the United States until September 11, 2001, the Oklahoma City bombing killed 168 people when a truck bomb exploded next to a federal building on April 19, 1995.

The **Oklahoma City Bombing** of April 19, 1995, claimed 168 lives, making it the most deadly act of terrorism on American soil up to that time. In an era when the nation was politically divided, this cowardly and senseless attack reminded Americans of their commonalities. Millions of complete strangers donated money for the victims' families. Others waited in long lines hoping to donate blood that might aid the hundreds who were wounded in the attack. The president's moving speech also restored his sagging public image and pushed political leaders toward reconciliation. The government responded in unusually bipartisan fashion following the attacks, providing assistance to victims and significantly increasing funding for antiterrorism programs, which helped to thwart a number of similar plots in the coming decade.

FIGURE 14.3

The 1995 Oklahoma City bombing was the deadliest terrorist attack on American soil until the attacks on September 11, 2001.

Americans also donated generously during international crises such as the famines of East Africa during the mid-1980s. By 1990, the East African nation of Somalia was affected by a crisis that could not be solved by bread alone. Somalia had been colonized by Italy a century prior. Somalia secured independence in 1960, but suffered from the same instability that plagued most postcolonial nations. An expanding civil war engulfed the capital city of Mogadishu in 1990 and led to the dissolution of the government. Rival factions declared themselves in power and attempted to assert their will by force while the people of Somalia suffered from the combined effects of famine and civil war. Hundreds of thousands of civilians had died, and the situation was rapidly declining when the United Nations approved the use of troops to restore order and assure that international aid reached civilians.

In 1992, Clinton increased the small contingent of humanitarian forces already in place through Operation Restore Hope. Sending troops to help distribute food and other relief supplies in a time of famine appealed to the sensibilities of most Americans. However, it also threatened the interests of local gangs and profiteers who had risen to power by exploiting the famine and political disorder. Tensions quickly exploded as US troops attempted to locate and capture local warlords who were thwarting humanitarian efforts by stealing most of the food and selling it to purchase more weapons. In the summer of 1993, the most dangerous and powerful Somali warlord killed two dozen UN peacekeepers from Pakistan. The bodies of these humanitarian troops were mutilated by the supporters of this warlord to send a message to any who dared to oppose them.

US Special Forces responded with a message of their own, launching an ambitious raid against this particular warlord in October 1993. The conflict quickly escalated into the **Battle of Mogadishu** when rebel forces shot down two Black Hawk helicopters and disabled several other vehicles with rocket-propelled grenades. US troops under assault and cut off from their base rallied until a rescue operation secured their safety. However, eighteen soldiers had been killed. Absent a clear threat to the security of the United States and shocked by graphic images of rebel soldiers dragging the bodies of US troops through the streets, Clinton and the US public favored withdrawal of US forces.

In the wake of the Battle of Mogadishu, a hasty and precarious ceasefire agreement was reached in the spring of 1994. Clinton's decision to completely withdraw from Somalia following this tenuous "peace" drew heavy criticism. Many recognized that local warlords would simply resume their assault against the people once US forces left the region. These individuals believed that the United States was abandoning its peacekeeping mission and believed Clinton had defaulted on his promise to restore peace and stability in Somalia. However, few American or UN officials were willing to devote the material and human resources required to reach that objective. Armed with hindsight, some critics believe that the hasty withdrawal from Somalia represented a lost opportunity to develop goodwill in the Muslim world. At the very least, these individuals believe that the early exit of US forces emboldened those such as Al Qaeda who had provided support to some of the area warlords.

Ethnic conflict erupted in the African nation of Rwanda in April 1994. The conflict in Rwanda represented the combination of a century of imperialism and decades of ethnic conflict between members of the Tutsi minority and Hutu majority. Seeking stability rather than development, during Rwanda's colonial period, the ruling Germans had placed Tutsi leaders in control. This decision inflamed existing tensions between Tutsi leaders and the majority of Rwandans who were members of the Hutu tribe. The Belgians later controlled Rwanda and continued the German tactic of utilizing existing divisions to administer the colony. Like the Germans, Belgian officials played both ethnic groups against one another.

When the Belgians were finally forced to grant Rwanda its independence in 1962, the sudden departure of the former colonial rulers created a power vacuum that resulted in a series of civil wars that bordered on genocide. In 1994, that border was crossed when a group of Hutu warlords sought to eliminate the Tutsis forever. The United States had no strategic interests in the region and declined intervention. From a distance, the 1994 conflict appeared to be simply another violent episode of ethnic strife in postcolonial East Africa. When ten UN peacekeepers were among the early victims of the violence that broke out in the summer of 1994, the United States responded by calling for the complete removal of UN forces.

Dramatic pleas for help were ignored. For example, a clergy member who had sought refuge within a hospital wrote a desperate letter calling for help. At the time, the hospital was surrounded by Hutus armed with machetes and ordered to kill each person inside. His appeal fell upon deaf ears, and the entire hospital was massacred. The clergyman's plea began with the following words: "we wish to inform you that tomorrow we will be killed with our families." This chilling exhortation later became the title of a powerful and graphic narrative of the killings written from eyewitness descriptions of the 1994 **Rwandan Genocide**. Within one hundred days, approximately 800,000 Rwandans had been murdered, mostly civilians killed by other civilians with machetes and other agricultural tools.

Area African nations intervened, and forces controlled by the Tutsi minority rallied and seized control of the Rwandan government by late summer. This development prompted the mass exodus of Hutus. Even though most Hutu refugees had not participated in the slaughter of the Tutsis, they feared retribution. These Hutu evacuees had no place to go other than cholera-infested refugee camps. Without an understanding of Africa's colonial past, most Americans interpreted the problems of the central African nation in the context of their own miseducation. Desirous for a simple solution for a "backward" nation in the center of a continent they had never learned about in school; most adult Americans continued to marginalize both Africa and Africans by convincing themselves that there was simply nothing that could be done to prevent suffering in every corner of the world.

FIGURE 14.4

Marines search a Mogadishu market for caches of hidden weapons prior to the 1993 Battle of Mogadishu that was popularized by the movie *Black Hawk Down*.

FIGURE 14.5

Following the Rwandan Genocide in 1994, many Hutus fled the country and sought safety in makeshift camps such as this refugee camp in nearby Zaire.

Palestinian Liberation Organization

An organization formed in 1964 with the goal of creating a homeland for the Palestinian people that has sought the elimination of the state of Israel for most of its existence. The PLO had reinvented itself in recent years and is now recognized by the United Nations, although many Americans and people of Jewish descent still consider the PLO to be a terrorist organization.

Oslo Accords

An agreement between Israel and the Palestinian Liberation Organization (PLO) intended to serve as a framework for future negotiations regarding Israeli and Palestinian sovereignty in disputed territories and other matters dealing with relations between Israelis and Palestinians.

FIGURE 14.6

Israeli Prime Minister Yitzhak Rabin shakes hands with Yasser Arafat, leader of the Palestinian Liberation Organization in 1993. Many hoped this meeting and the Oslo Accords would lead to a peaceful settlement of the historic conflict between Palestinians and Israelis.

Clinton later confided that his unwillingness to intervene in Rwanda was his chief regret during his entire eight years as president. Clinton scored high marks in the fall of 1993 when he helped to facilitate a meeting between Israeli Prime Minister Yitzhak Rabin and the leader of the **Palestinian Liberation Organization (PLO)** Yasser Arafat. As had been the case with President Carter's historic rapprochement between the leaders of Israel and Egypt, the simple acknowledgement by Israel and the PLO of each other's legitimacy may have been the most significant outcome of the meeting. The two leaders signed an agreement regarding Palestinian sovereignty within the West Bank and Gaza Strip—two areas that Israel had controlled since the failed 1967 invasion of Israel by Egypt, Syria, and Jordan.

The actual negotiations occurred in Sweden, and the agreement became known as the **Oslo Accords**. The formal acceptance of the Oslo Accords occurred during a White House ceremony attended by Rabin and Arafat in September of 1993. The agreement required Israeli military forces to withdraw from the West Bank and Gaza Strip. It also created an organization to oversee the gradual transfer of authority for these areas to the Palestinian people. Most of the details regarding the transfer were intentionally left vague and were supposed to be decided during future negotiations. At the time, many around the world optimistically believed that the Oslo Accords provided the framework by which a peaceful resolution of the Israeli-Palestinian conflict might be achieved.

However, details matter and neither side appeared willing to trust the other enough to implement even the first steps they had agreed upon. Israel retained its military forces in the Gaza Strip and West Bank, while Palestinian officials proved unable to reduce the violence against Israelis in these and other areas. The Israelis also continued to construct settlements for Jewish settlers in these areas. A vicious cycle of blame emerged where Israelis cited continued Palestinian attacks as justification of their military presence while the Palestinians cited the continued Israeli presence for their actions. Future meetings brokered by President Clinton did little to end the mutual distrust that prevented the first stages of the Oslo Accords from being implemented. The peace process broke down as neither side was willing to disarm or even speak out against supporters who were committing acts of violence in their name. The violence prevented the formation of the interim governmental agencies that were supposed to provide Palestinians with limited sovereignty as a step toward peaceful coexistence and the eventual creation of a Palestinian homeland.

Following the American experience in Somalia, Clinton became cautious in his foreign policy. The president usually denied requests for troops. Instead, he attempted to thwart genocide, famine, and the development of nuclear and chemical weapons through policies of aid and sanctions. For example, Clinton negotiated an agreement with North Korea to halt its attempts to develop nuclear weapons in exchange for food and medicine that were to be distributed among the needy civilian population. Many correctly assumed that much of the aid would be seized by the corrupt government, which would continue its attempts to develop weapons of mass destruction. An uprising in Haiti resulted in the deployment of a small contingent of US soldiers, mostly to reinstall the democratically elected Jean-Bertrand Aristide as president. Once US troops left the impoverished island, Aristide ruled the nation as a dictator, and violence and corruption returned to the island.

The situation was particularly disturbing in the Balkans where nationalist Serbs in Bosnia, with the support of Serbian President Slobodan Milosevic, had been killing Muslim civilians for many years. As a candidate, Clinton had been critical of Bush's refusal to intervene in the Balkans. As president, however, Clinton followed a similar policy. Clinton maintained Bush's arms embargo that was intended to curb violence. This embargo disproportionately hindered the Muslim minority who had fewer weapons to begin with. Clinton recognized the shortcomings of his approach, but he had been deeply affected by the loss of American lives in Somalia. A political pragmatist, he devoted the bulk of his energies to domestic matters that proved politically popular. Even in retrospect, each of Clinton's options regarding North Korea, Somalia, Haiti, and the Balkans might have led to thousands of US casualties and lengthy military occupations, with no guarantee of success.

Despite his attempt to avoid future deployments, the president was forced to take his attention away from the budget debates and other domestic matters in the summer of 1995 when Bosnian Serbs under Milosevic began slaughtering Muslims and other minorities. In July, Bosnian Serbs evicted the women and female children from the town of Srebrenica, which had a Muslim majority, and slaughtered the remaining 7,000 men and boys. By August, Serbian forces under Milosevic began shelling the city of Sarajevo.

The United Nations sent a small force of 6,000 peacekeepers while the United States debated what to do. Muslim fighters and the Croatians tentatively worked together in a successful counteroffensive that forced Milosevic to agree to peace talks that were held in Dayton, Ohio. The Dayton Accords created the new Federation of Bosnia and Herzegovina with a dual government backed by the belated presence of 60,000 NATO troops. From the perspective of the West, the United States had sent its own sons and daughters to protect civilians in a nation where it had little strategic interest. From the perspective of Muslims in Europe and around the world, the West's delayed response occurred only after the bombing of Sarajevo rather than because of years of genocidal acts against the Muslim minority of Southern Europe.

FIGURE 14.7

A US Army engineer directs traffic across a pontoon bridge linking Bosnia-Herzegovina to Croatia, where many supplies and support troops were staged during the 1995–1996 peacekeeping mission in Bosnia. This image demonstrates the importance of engineers and other support troops in modern warfare.

1.6 Free Trade, Globalization, and the Environment

In 1992, many of the nations of Western and Central Europe created the **European Union (EU)**, a confederacy that incrementally grew in its authority to regulate commercial and other international affairs. The United States, Canada, and Mexico responded by forming the **North American Free Trade Agreement (NAFTA)** in 1993. NAFTA had been a leading priority of Republicans and was supported by the incoming Republican President George H. W. Bush. The agreement sought the complete elimination of trade barriers between the three nations. NAFTA angered many Democrats but was still supported by Clinton, who hoped to appear as a moderate and win the support of business leaders.

Environmentalists feared that NAFTA would reduce the effectiveness of protective legislation by encouraging corporations to relocate to Mexico. Labor unions and many individual Americans feared that it would also result in a loss of American jobs for the same reason. NAFTA was unpopular among most voters, partially because some politicians disingenuously equated its limited goals with the European Union. Unlike NAFTA, the EU sought to coordinate most governmental functions and even foresaw joint armies and a common currency. A decade later, the goal of a common currency was achieved when EU member nations adopted the euro as their medium of exchange. However, NAFTA has not expanded to include such collectivist policies but continues to arouse controversy among diverse groups of voters.

Although few nations beyond Europe expressed interest in creating a common currency, major summits were held seeking to reduce global trade restrictions. Many of these summits took place under the auspices of the General Agreement on Trade and Tariffs (GATT), which was signed by two dozen nations shortly after World War II. After four decades of GATT summits, GATT itself was replaced by the **World Trade Organization (WTO)** in 1995. The WTO is an international agency headquartered in Geneva that seeks to encourage free trade and reduce government restrictions regarding international commerce. The WTO is charged with promoting trade and economic development in ways that also protect the economies of member nations. However, many in the United States and around the world have criticized the WTO as a tool of wealthy corporations in developed nations that seek to practice new forms of economic imperialism.

These protests against globalization reached a crescendo in November of 1999 when an estimated 50,000 protesters disrupted the WTO summit in Seattle. A large number of these protesters were college students who joined a diverse movement of citizens who believed that the WTO was fueled by a corporate agenda. Many of the protesters were environmentalists who feared that the WTO would make decisions that would reduce standards and enforcement of environmental protection. Many also believed that developing industries in developing nations would be crushed by international competition. Labor unions were also present in Seattle, fearing globalization would permit corporations in developed nations with higher standards of living to lower wages and benefits or simply relocate their operations abroad. Others feared that unregulated markets would lead to the elimination of smaller companies and promote the growth of multinational corporations they believed operated like cartels.

European Union

An economic and political confederation of independent European nations that choose to utilize a common currency and follow other agreed-upon measures designed to reduce trade barriers between those members and promote trade and diplomacy.

North American Free Trade Agreement (NAFTA)

A trade agreement between Canada, the United States, and Mexico that eliminates trade barriers, such as tariffs, between each nation.

World Trade Organization (WTO)

An organization that seeks to reduce trade barriers between nations, it replaced the Global Agreement on Trades and Tariffs in 1995.

FIGURE 14.8

An estimated 50,000 protesters demonstrated against the 1999 WTO summit held in Seattle. Many of these protesters are dressed as sea turtles due to their belief that globalization doomed many endangered species. The novelty of blue collar union members marching alongside environmental activists in opposition to the WTO led many to refer to the protesters as "teamsters and turtles."

Many Americans viewed the protesters as lacking a positive agenda of their own, opposing globalization but lacking their own alternative. Others believed the protesters were motivated by a misguided and naïve belief in some utopian alternative to Capitalist development. The protesters responded that they had specific solutions and lacked only access to power, rallying behind a brief document circulated by students at the University of Washington and other Seattle-based colleges called the Declaration for Global Democracy. Together, the protesters rallied behind the document's final exhortation of "No Globalization without Representation." The five points of this declaration provided a bit more substance but still appeared vague to the document's critics. They protested the WTO's undemocratic structure and nontransparent methods. The document also challenged world leaders to ensure that human advancement rather than material acquisition would become the standard by which they measured the efficacy of global trade policies.

The students and their supporters also rallied behind something they called sustainable development, a standard that included human rights, worker safety and compensation, environmental protection, and reversal of global inequity. However, the popular image of the 1999 protests does not reflect the progressive tone of these goals. Similar to the labor protests of the late nineteenth century, the message of the protesters soon became moot when a handful of individuals became violent. In response, the police responded with what many considered to be excessive force. Erroneous reports that the protesters had attacked police created or solidified existing negative images of the protesters. The same was true of sensational reports of bystanders being assaulted. Although some news outlets printed retractions, the image of the anti-WTO meeting being dominated by radicals persisted and colored the view of many Americans toward those who protested against globalization.

This concern for maintaining free trade without harming the economies of member nations led to the derailment of several free-trade initiatives within developing countries in the early 2000s. This is especially true in areas such as agriculture, where millions of families depend on agriculture for their livelihood. American grain is often produced much more efficiently due to mechanization. It is also heavily subsidized by the federal government. As a result, many nations fear that the complete elimination of trade restrictions will result in their farmers being forced to compete with inexpensive American grain. While many point out that this development would provide relief for many impoverished urban dwellers, others fear that the competition would destroy the agricultural base of developing nations. If this happened, they argue, the result would be long-term dependency on foreign grain. The WTO launched a major series of conferences in Doha, Qatar, in 2001. The organization continues to meet in related conferences around the globe in hopes of resolving issues regarding agricultural subsidies and other global trade issues.

The WTO and other organizations dedicated to reducing trade barriers have also been derailed by environmental concerns. Environmentalists have shown that certain refrigerants and aerosol sprays deplete the layers of ozone gas in the earth's atmosphere. These ozone layers absorb most of the potentially damaging ultraviolet light that radiates from the sun. Scientists demonstrated that chemical compounds in some refrigerants used in air-conditioning systems were especially dangerous as they neutralized the ability of ozone gas to block ultraviolet rays. As a result, laws were passed in the United States and other nations mandating the use of different refrigerants and regulating the chemicals used in producing aerosol sprays and other manufactured goods. The global nature of environmental concerns such as ozone depletion led to a series of UN initiatives such as the Kyoto Protocol. The result of a global summit on reducing greenhouse gases led by Vice President Al Gore, the Kyoto Protocol produced a binding treaty requiring developed nations to reduce their emission of greenhouse gases. As of 2011, the Unites States is the only developed nation that has not signed the treaty.

1. Describe the way that politics affected Clinton's strategy regarding domestic issues such as welfare reform. How did many of Clinton's more liberal supporters view the president's attempts to be perceived as a moderate regarding welfare and other domestic issues?

2. Clinton believed that his election signified a popular mandate for his ideas regarding health care reform. Explain why his plan failed to pass Congress, being sure to describe the viewpoints of its supporters and its opponents.

3. Explain how Republicans under the leadership of Newt Gingrich rose to challenge President Clinton and the Democrats. Briefly discuss the "Contract with America" and the electoral success of the Republican Party leading up to the election of 1996. Explain why Gingrich and other conservatives failed to maintain this popular support and how Clinton managed to regain high approval ratings in his second term.

4. Explain the source of the conflicts in the Balkans, Rwanda, and Somalia. Discuss America's response to these conflicts and analyze the effectiveness of the Clinton administration in responding to these and other global conflicts.

5. Briefly explain the role of NAFTA and the World Trade Organization (WTO). Explain why many Americans have widely different perspectives regarding these two organizations. Why did students and a variety of other activists demonstrate against the 1999 WTO summit in Seattle?

2. FROM THE CENTER TO THE EDGE: AMERICA DURING THE GEORGE W. BUSH ADMINISTRATION

LEARNING OBJECTIVES

1. **Explain the leading priorities of the Bush administration before the September 11 attack. Summarize the perspective of Democrats and many moderate Republicans in response to the first nine months of the new president's administration.**

2. **Summarize the impact of George Bush's presidency**

3. **Explain how the September 11 attack led to the invasion of Iraq from both the perspective of the Bush administration and the critics of the president. Explain how Bush was able to defeat John Kerry in the 2004 election, despite concerns about Iraq and the huge federal deficits that had increased each year during Bush's first term.**

2.1 The 2000 Election and Aftermath

The primaries leading up to the 2000 election produced few surprises, with Clinton's vice president **Al Gore** and the Republican governor of Texas **George W. Bush** winning the nominations of their parties. The media declared Bush the heir apparent to the Republican Party, and only Arizona senator John McCain came close to challenging this prediction. Bush's campaign hoped that the public would associate Gore with the infidelity of Clinton, a man he so loyally defended throughout the president's impeachment hearings. The risk of this strategy, however, was that the public might also associate the vice president with an administration that had converted budget deficits into surplus during eight prosperous years.

Al Gore

A two-term vice president under Bill Clinton who lost the controversial 2000 presidential election to George W. Bush in 2000 despite receiving more popular votes.

George W. Bush

Son of former President George H. W. Bush, he was the 43rd president of the United States from 2001 to 2009.

Kyoto Global Warming Treaty

A global agreement to reduce greenhouse gas emissions that has been signed by nearly every nation except the United States. The agreement was signed in Japan in 1997 and was largely shaped by representatives of the United States but was strongly opposed by the Bush administration due to concerns that following its provisions would severely harm the economy.

Like Clinton, Al Gore had high approval ratings and experience leading both domestic and foreign initiatives, such as the **Kyoto treaty on global warming**. However, Bush's campaign succeeded in putting Gore on the defensive regarding his relationship with Clinton, even to the point that the vice president sought to distance himself from the administration of which he had been such an integral part. Bush and the Republican Party deftly connected Clinton's extramarital affairs with abortion, gay rights, and liberal opposition to prayer in schools. The strategy had the advantage of playing to verifiable evidence of moral decay in the White House. Rather than point out the flaws in this assessment, Gore chose to run a rather vanilla campaign that avoided controversy. This decision was likely influenced by political observers who predicted that Gore would win the election based on his superior experience and intellect. Early polls agreed, predicting that the Democrats would win a very close race. Given the controversy surrounding the election results, some would argue that these early polls were accurate.

On paper, George W. Bush was hardly the kind of candidate that should worry the Gore campaign. While Al Gore had navigated international treaties, Bush had barely left the country. He was known mostly for his jovial and often juvenile disposition, a self-confessed "party boy" who had found work through his father's connections in the oil industry. Gore had also benefitted from family connections. However, the vice president also had a reputation for intelligence and hard work that was the antithesis of the reputation of the former president's son. In response, the Bush campaign waged an aggressive fundraising campaign and used its unparalleled resources to highlight the affable personality of Texan George Bush in contrast to the allegedly "aristocratic" Al Gore.

The technique was a mainstay of nineteenth century politics and proved equally effective in the new millennium as the Bush campaign slowly chipped away at the Democratic candidate's lead. Meanwhile, Bush seemed warm and genuine in a number of well-conceived appearances and political advertisements. Although the result of campaign disclosure requirements, voters appreciated the apparent straightforwardness of Bush's advertisements, which ended with the phrase, "I'm George Bush, and I approved this message."

On the eve of the election, the polls were too close to predict a winner. Many Democratic leaders urged the progressive third-party candidate Ralph Nader to drop from the race. They believed that the 2 to 3 percent of voters who were predicted to vote for Nader would support their candidate. And they predicted that, without these voters, their candidate might not win key states such as Florida where polls showed Gore and Bush as dead even.

The media portrayed the election as evidence that America had become divided into Democratic "blue" states and Republican "red" states. The phenomenon of a candidate running well in a particular region was as old as the nation itself, yet election returns did seem to validate the idea of a liberal and conservative divide. Metropolitan districts tended to vote for Gore, while rural areas could usually be counted on voting Republican. Gore had received half a million more votes than Bush, but America still abided a system that awarded every electoral vote to the candidate who polled the most votes in a particular state.

The popular vote in most states was very close, a fact that ran counter to the image of polarized "red" and "blue" states. However, in Florida the vote was so close that state officials determined that further investigation of voting procedures and counting methods was necessary. Bush had originally led by about 2,000 votes, but an investigation conducted by the state's predominantly Republican leadership had reduced that margin to 150. The results throughout the rest of the nation were also so close that the winner would be decided by the recount in Florida. However, the Bush campaign won an injunction from the US Supreme Court ordering the recount to stop. As a result, all of Florida's electoral votes went to George Bush, and he became the next president.

The Supreme Court's decision shocked many Americans, including the four Supreme Court justices who dissented and the Florida Supreme Court who had ordered the recount. Later investigations by journalists generally agreed that Bush would have still won the vote in Florida had the recount continued. Others believed that Ralph Nader had been the "spoiler" as the vast majority of his nearly 100,000 votes in Florida alone would have gone to Gore had Nadar's name not been on the ballot. Most Americans agreed it was time to end the Electoral College. However, the indignation of these voters regarding an election that appeared to be decided by attorneys and voting irregularities rather than the will of the people soon subsided. George W. Bush was not the first president to be elected by a minority of voters. In addition, the Electoral College could only be eliminated by passing an amendment to the Constitution. This would require the support of political leaders in large states that benefited from the Electoral College system. Meanwhile, if the new president supported a campaign to eliminate the system that had resulted in his election, it might support detractors who still believed Bush had stolen the election from Gore.

Bush began his presidency with a brilliantly conceived speech in which he humbly promised an inclusive approach. The speech disarmed many of his critics, at least temporarily. Bush's methods and policies soon reanimated the left's objections as the new president moved far to the right of the moderate conservatism that typified his father's administration. Bush proposed and won approval for the largest tax cut in the nation's history, reducing tax receipts by $1.3 trillion. What angered the left most was that nearly all of these reductions benefitted the wealthiest 5 percent of taxpayers who were in the highest tax brackets. Bush also sought to completely eliminate estate taxes—a tax that only affected the heirs of wealthy descendants. Finally, Bush approved reductions in dividend and capital gains tax rates that brought the maximum rate down to 15 percent—a rate even Reagan had rejected as being too low.

Bush differed from Reagan in another important way. Although both utilized the moralistic language of the New Right, Bush made the support of socially conservative views on abortion, homosexuality, birth control, and school prayer a leading priority. He also supported controversial programs, such as private school vouchers. This program encouraged middle and upper-class families to withdraw their children from public schools by using tax dollars to offset some of the tuition charged by private schools. Opponents pointed out that such a system would cripple the nation's public school system, reduce civic participation, and harm the children of less affluent parents who could not afford private school tuition even with federal vouchers.

Bush demonstrated a similar willingness to withdraw from the international community. The Bush administration reversed the postwar tradition of building international coalitions and working through agencies such as NATO and the United Nations. In addition to the sudden refusal to participate in environmental treaties like Kyoto that the United States had actually initiated, Bush also abrogated the antiballistic missile treaty signed by Richard Nixon. Bush also ignored bipartisan support for treaties restricting the use of land mines and testing nuclear weapons. In contrast to the moderate Republican and Democratic leadership of his father and Bill Clinton, George W. Bush had moved the federal government far to the right of center.

Bush also rescinded most of Clinton's executive orders dealing with environmental protection, shocking the world with his declaration that America would not participate in the Kyoto Protocol on global warming. Most of Bush's decisions regarding the environment produced outrage among the left, including his support of a controversial law that would permit oil drilling in national wildlife refuges. Legislation deregulating the oil industry passed only after removing these provisions. Pundits were quick to point out that Bush and Cheney's connections in the oil industry formed the basis of their wealth and political connections. Bush's affable personality and folksy populist appeal insulated him from some of this criticism during his first years in office. More troubling for the president was the growing disapproval of his policies among moderate Republicans, some of whom even left the Republican Party in protest.

2.2   September 11, 2001

On the morning of September 11, 2001, nineteen terrorists seized control of four commercial airliners flying over the East Coast. The hijackers had attended flight schools and had planned a suicide mission that was calculated to cause the greatest physical destruction and psychological terror on the citizens of the United States. Two of the aircraft crashed into the Twin Towers of the World Trade Center in New York City. A third crashed into the Pentagon in Washington, DC. The forth plane was overtaken by passengers before it could reach the destination the terrorists intended to destroy, crashing instead in a field in Pennsylvania. These four plane crashes resulted in the deaths of more than 3,000 people on September 11, including nearly 400 emergency responders. The attack was approximately twenty times more destructive than the Oklahoma City bombing and was greeted by America's enemies as a tremendous success. But whether the attack achieved its objective of terrorizing Americans remained a question that could only be answered by the response of the American people.

Like most life-changing events, September 11 brought out the best and worst in the American people and their government. When the Bush administration identified **Al Qaeda** as the organization responsible for the attack, many Americans responded with rage directed at anyone they suspected might be Muslim or from the Middle East. However, most Americans responded with displays of patriotism and rejected populist anger, choosing instead to donate money to relief efforts and provide for the families of victims. Millions flooded local blood banks, gave generously to the American Red Cross and other relief agencies, and found extra time to volunteer with community organizations or reach out to estranged friends and family members. Military officials feared that volunteer enlistments would end, given the likelihood of mandatory deployments in the future. Instead, they found recruiting offices filled with young people willing to risk everything for an opportunity to serve their country.

Al Qaeda

An international terrorist network responsible for the September 11 attack, Al Qaeda claims to be waging "jihad" (a holy war) against the West and the United States.

FIGURE 14.9

The September 11 attacks led to the deaths of 3,000 innocent people, including 400 emergency workers. This map shows the flight paths of the four hijacked planes used in the terrorist attacks.

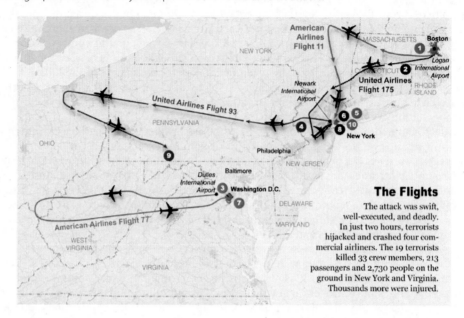

The Flights

The attack was swift, well-executed, and deadly. In just two hours, terrorists hijacked and crashed four commercial airliners. The 19 terrorists killed 33 crew members, 213 passengers and 2,730 people on the ground in New York and Virginia. Thousands more were injured.

One of the most unlikely controversies arose from the outpouring of support for charitable groups, some of which soon found that they had received more donated resources than they could effectively use to aid the victims of the attacks. Other groups sought to aid the city of New York and those who had been only indirectly affected. For example, the economy of New York City was especially vulnerable as tens of thousands of workers were without employment while the city spent millions of dollars dealing with the crisis. The national economy also suffered temporary setbacks. The stock market reopened with dramatic losses as some investors fled in the wake of uncertainty. Other Americans felt it was their patriotic duty to buy stocks or otherwise stimulate the economy through personal spending in support of the millions of employees who worked in the tourist and airline industries that had suffered in the wake of the attacks. Most Americans responded with relative calm, spent a few extra moments with loved ones, donated money and blood to local charities, purchased flags in record numbers, and went back to work.

September 11 was more than a life-changing moment for most Americans; it also defined an era and drove the history of the early twenty-first century more than any other event. Americans of various political persuasions united, at least temporarily, behind their president and his administration's declaration of war against terrorism. An undeclared war in Afghanistan also received popular support, at least initially, as military leaders attempted to find Al Qaeda leader Osama bin Laden and those who had supported his terrorist network. Bin Laden was one of over fifty children born to a billionaire in Yemen whose fortune had been made in construction fields related to the oil industry. Bin Laden inherited much of his father's wealth but turned from his family's secular orientation. Although he had technically fought on the same side as the US-backed Mujahideen who fought against the Soviet occupation of Afghanistan, bin Laden had a deep hatred of the West. Although the West and its financial system was the source of his family's wealth, he believed the West was also responsible for the decline of his version of Islam in the Middle East.

The existence of a well-funded and well-organized terrorist network presented both new opportunities and challenges for America's intelligence and military. In contrast to individual terrorists who were practically impossible to detect until they committed their actions, bin Laden's extensive resources provided US intelligence agents with targets they could track. On the other hand, the existence of a well-funded network operated by men who were often well-educated and from wealthy or middle-class backgrounds made tracking these men more difficult. Bin Laden's network was an interconnected system of terrorist cells averaging five individuals deeply embedded in American society. Usually only one member of the cell even knew the other members and served as the point of contact for other cells. While this individual linked the members of the cell to a larger network, they seldom knew how to contact anyone else in the organization. As a result, communication only flowed downward—a safeguard against one member of the organization revealing the existence of the leaders or other cells. Many of these terrorists had been in the United States for years, waiting until they were contacted with instructions.

As a result, the Bush administration declared that new and more aggressive methods were needed to counter the threat of terrorism. Congress responded in October 2001 by approving the **Patriot Act**. This law expanded the powers of the federal government, permitting the use of covert surveillance against persons suspected of having connections to a terrorist plot or network. Opponents countered that the Patriot Act was an unwarranted intrusion against the right of privacy. Others feared that the Patriot Act was only the first in a series of laws that might restrict the rights of citizens. Some believed that the Patriot Act was a peculiar reaction to counter terrorists, especially as the president repeatedly claimed that the terrorists hated Americans for the freedoms they enjoyed.

While many civil rights violations would surface in later years, there was little curtailment of free speech. For example, only a handful of newspapers refused to print a *Boondocks* comic strip that suggested the Reagan administration's support of the Mujahideen during the 1980s had aided Al Qaeda. Conservative commentators such as Anne Coulter expressed violent and virulent language toward American Muslims but were also not censored. Radical poets such as Amiri Baraka received threats for an uncompromising poem titled *Somebody Blew Up America. Yet neither Baraka nor the right-wing commentators who called for retaliation against Muslims were censored by the government. The first line of Baraka's poem* continues to resonate with Americans as they attempt to balance freedom and security. "All thinking people oppose terrorism—both domestic and international," Baraka exclaimed, "but one should not be used to cover up the other."

2.3 War in Iraq and Afghanistan

Bush demanded that the Taliban, a regime that controlled much of Afghanistan, hand over Al Qaeda leader Osama bin Laden. When this demand was ignored, the United States launched air strikes against Taliban and Al Qaeda strongholds throughout Afghanistan in October of 2001. These attacks were followed by American and British ground forces that quickly overwhelmed Taliban fighters and took control of major cities, such as the Afghan capital of Kabul. However, these troops were unable to capture bin Laden or his supporters as they fled to the remote and mountainous terrain along the Afghan-Pakistan border.

Military resources that might have resulted in the capture of bin Laden and elimination of his terrorist network were soon diverted to Iraq by early 2003. Disregarding the conflicting worldviews and deep distrust between Iraqi dictator Saddam Hussein and Al Qaeda leader Osama bin Laden, the Bush administration became convinced that Hussein was somehow involved with the September 11 plot. Bush also became increasingly convinced that Saddam Hussein was developing or already possessed chemical, biological, or nuclear weapons he would share with terrorist groups such as Al Qaeda. Afghanistan became a holding action where depleted regiments sought to defend a beleaguered Afghan government. US forces in Afghanistan also sought to prevent the growth of the Taliban and Al Qaeda rather than eliminate them, while the Bush administration shifted the bulk of military resources to the invasion and occupation of Iraq.

History provides few reasons to believe that the Iraqi leader was working with Al Qaeda. Saddam Hussein was deeply opposed to the Islamic fundamentalism of bin Laden. In fact, Hussein had led Iraq to the brink of civil war in his efforts to purge the influence of bin Laden's ideology from his nation. Bin Laden viewed Hussein as an "infidel." So deep was bin Laden's dislike of the Iraqi dictator that he had met with Saudi leaders following Iraq's invasion of Kuwait in 1991 and offered to personally lead a crusade of 100,000 Muslim warriors against Hussein.

At the same time, however, history could also offer little to explain or predict the attacks of September 11. Saddam Hussein had long sought weapons of mass destruction the Bush administration worried he might now possess. Even if an alliance with bin Laden was unlikely, Hussein was a danger by himself. The Iraqi dictator had used chemical weapons in the past, harbored anti-American sentiment, and had supported a terrorist plot to assassinate George H. W. Bush when he was president. Iraq was part of "an axis of evil," the younger Bush explained to the American public. For George W. Bush, the lesson of September 11 seemed to be the importance of taking proactive steps against America's enemies. Closely related to this idea was the foreign policy directive that would soon be known as the **Bush Doctrine**: the United States would wage preemptive attacks—with or without the support of the United Nations and its allies—if America's leaders believed such an action was necessary to counter a credible threat to their nation's security.

Patriot Act

Officially known as the Uniting and Strengthening America by Providing Appropriate Tools Required to Intercept and Obstruct Terrorism Act of 2001, the Patriot Act expanded the powers of the federal government to legally use surveillance against any individual suspected of possible involvement in international or domestic terrorism.

FIGURE 14.10

Surrounded by leading Republican congressmen, President George W. Bush signs the controversial Patriot Act into law on October 26, 2011.

Bush Doctrine

Refers to the foreign policy of George W. Bush that supported the use of US military power to prevent perceived threats to national security, even if those possible threats are not immediate and few or no other nation was willing to support these actions.

Donald Rumsfeld

Secretary of Defense under Presidents Gerald Ford and George W. Bush, Rumsfeld was an outspoken supporter of the decision to invade Iraq in 2003. His resignation was demanded by a number of military officials, and Rumsfeld resigned just after the 2006 election.

Dick Cheney

Vice president under George W. Bush from 2001–2009 and Secretary of Defense during the previous Bush administration, Cheney was a leading advocate for the invasion of Iraq in 2003, although he had also supported the decision to withdraw from Iraq following Operation Desert Storm.

Colin Powell

A well-respected general during Operation Desert Storm who was appointed as Secretary of State by George W. Bush, Powell strongly opposed the decision to invade Iraq in 2003, challenging other officials to produce clear objectives and strategies for such an operation while encouraging the president to only consider such a course of action if it were supported by the United Nations.

Operation Iraqi Freedom

Began with the invasion of Iraq in March 2003 and continues to the present. The stated goal of Operation Iraqi Freedom is to replace an autocratic dictator who might have threatened the security of the United States with a peaceful and stable democratic government.

The Bush administration sought to convince a wary nation to apply this doctrine to Iraqi dictator Saddam Hussein. Secretary of Defense **Donald Rumsfeld** had changed his views from 1991 when he had supported the decision to leave Hussein in power rather than face the difficulties of occupation and reconstruction. Vice President **Dick Cheney** was even more determined that Iraq must be invaded, declaring in several press conferences that American intelligence analysts had determined that Hussein possessed weapons of mass destruction (known colloquially as WMDs) when in fact such reports did not exist. Secretary of State and former General **Colin Powell** disagreed, at least at first. He believed that invading Iraq was unwise and branded his own administration's efforts to find evidence that Iraq was a bigger threat than Al Qaeda as "lunacy."

Despite Powell's efforts, Bush's inner circle appears to have already made the decision to invade Iraq. The president ordered Rumsfeld to prepare secret plans for the invasion less than three months after the September 11 attacks. These preliminary plans were created without the input of military leaders or Congress. In fact, the Joint Chiefs of Staff were not even aware the Bush administration was contemplating the invasion of Iraq for the next six months. In the meantime, Bush and Cheney tried to rally public support for the idea of a preemptive strike by creating the connection in the public mind between Hussein's previous bellicosity and his 1998 decision to expel UN weapons inspectors from Iraq. By the end of 2002, the administration had changed its message from one that counseled Iraq *might* have chemical and biological weapons to one that declared Hussein not only possessed these WMDs but was also on the verge of creating a nuclear arsenal. In the wake of the 9/11 attacks, most Americans were still upset at the lack of preemptive action to stop Osama bin Laden. If preemptive action could stop Hussein from launching a devastating attack, Americans asked, what possible argument could be made for doing nothing?

At the same time, reports circulated indicating the unlikelihood that Hussein presented a serious threat to the United States. Some military analysts worried that an American invasion of Iraq might provide Hussein a pretext to use weapons of mass destruction, or any of the modern weapons he was known to possess. An invasion by the world's leading military power might even make it appear that Hussein used these weapons in defense of his beleaguered nation.

Powell might have gone public with his reservations or resigned in protest and hoped that his departure might produce a new sense of caution in the White House. Instead, Powell focused his efforts toward advising the president of the dangers and liabilities he believed Rumsfeld and Cheney were minimizing. The invasion would likely succeed much like it had in 1991, Powell counseled the president. After the invasion, Powell cautioned, "you will be the proud owner" of a nation without a government or infrastructure. The United States would then be responsible for the welfare of the Iraqi people, Powell continued, many of whom harbored deep resentments toward the West. "You break it, you own it," the secretary of state concluded in summation.

Powell also advised the president that the United States should only consider an invasion after first confirming the existence of WMDs and securing the support of the United Nations. The coalition that paired Western and Arabic nations against Hussein in 1991 had been the key to its international legitimacy, Powell argued. Even if WMDs were found to exist, Powell implored, the president must at least follow his father's path of coalition building before considering a second Iraq invasion.

Bush agreed to seek a UN resolution requiring Hussein to submit to an international inspection team that would search for WMDs. The Security Council approved the resolution unanimously, and Hussein agreed to permit the inspectors in the country. The inspectors did not find any evidence of WMDs, a situation that placed the Bush administration in a difficult position after its earlier rhetoric. However, the Iraqi dictator did not cooperate with many of the inspectors' requests as the UN resolution required. As a result, there appeared a high probability that WMDs were hidden in a location the inspectors were forbidden to search. As Bush supporters explained, the absence of positive evidence proving the existence of WMDs was not the same as evidence proving WMDs were not present.

Determined not to allow anything to deter its previous decision, the Bush administration ignored intelligence reports by the United Nations, CIA, and US military; disregarded the advice of Secretary of State Colin Powell; and launched the invasion of Iraq on March 19, 2003. "We can choose to meet this threat now," Bush counseled the nation, "before it can appear suddenly in our skies." The president's rhetoric was clearly meant to connect **Operation Iraqi Freedom** to the September 11 attacks. Most Americans were unaware of the tenuous connections between Hussein and bin Laden, but sensed both uncertainty and déjà vu as they once again watched rockets hit Baghdad on CNN. Still, most Americans supported their president and his decision to remove Saddam from power due to the possibility that he might use WMDs against their nation. At the same time, most also indicated reservations about the long-term consequences of what they were witnessing. Even if there were no weapons of mass destruction, they hoped that removing Saddam Hussein might promote peace and stability in the region.

In stark contrast to the first Gulf War, only Britain provided significant military support. A handful of other nations sent token forces to participate in the American-led "coalition of the willing," but many of these demanded US aid in exchange. The devastating "shock and awe" of US airpower was very similar to the first Gulf War, however. Combined with a rapid deployment of ground forces that converged upon Baghdad, Iraqi troops were once again overwhelmed and surrendered en masse. Others simply threw down their weapons and attempted to blend into the civilian population.

Many Iraqi civilians cheered the Americans as liberators or simply displayed a calculated neutrality to an outcome they knew they could not alter. After six weeks of military operations, 138 US soldiers had lost their lives, but Iraq was firmly under US control. Americans and Iraqis were hopeful that efforts to draft a new constitution and hold democratic elections would usher in a new era of freedom and prosperity for their nation. On May 1, 2003, a jubilant George Bush stood on the deck of an aircraft carrier and declared that "major combat operations in Iraq have ended" in front of a banner that read "Mission Accomplished." For a brief moment, even the president's critics happily concluded that Operation Iraqi Freedom might just be the first step toward stability and democracy in the Middle East.

A few months later, Bush's premature declaration of victory became fodder for those same critics. Rumsfeld's invasion plans failed to prepare for the emergence of an opposition movement and neglected provisions for police and public services. The Bush administration's fateful decision to disband the Iraqi military and police created a power vacuum that the 130,000 US troops struggled to fill. Priceless relics were stolen from museums while the nation's civilian infrastructure was thrown into chaos. Iraqi armories were raided for weapons by insurgents loyal to Saddam Hussein and other anti-US factions, all of whom had managed to evade capture by US forces. Anti-US sentiment rose quickly as food shortages, water and power outages, and looting took its toll on the largely jobless civilian population. Military and state department officials had prepared for each of these problems. However, most of their advice had been disregarded by Bush's inner circle of advisors who equated constructive criticism with disloyalty. Even commonsensical suggestions to protect US soldiers by adding armor to vehicles or ensuring adequate numbers of bulletproof vests went unheeded. Without adequate resources or training, soldiers who did not speak Arabic or Kurdish did their best to act as civil engineers, police, and providers of other vital services.

Despite the lack of material support or adequate training, US troops rallied and eventually stabilized most of the nation. However, insurgents who opposed the US occupation emerged as a major obstacle to the transition between dictatorship and democracy. US military fatalities soon doubled after Bush's declaration of victory. Insurgents used stolen and smuggled rockets and small arms alongside improvised explosive devices (IEDs) that were set to explode on roadsides or in the midst of the civilian population. Recruitment centers for the US-trained Iraqi police were especially targeted. Ironically, the violence against Iraqis prevented the departure of US forces who had hoped to oversee a peaceful and rapid transition toward self-government. Fatalities among large numbers of Iraqi civilians and a few US soldiers became daily occurrences.

A year later, most Americans still supported the decision to invade Iraq. The American public was especially supportive of the men and women of the US armed services who were daily sacrificing their lives for a mission their commander-in-chief explained only in the vaguest terms. A nascent antiwar movement began to emerge, and some even made comparisons between Iraq and Vietnam. However, even those who opposed the war usually phrased their opposition in terms of support for the troops. The respect shown to soldiers demonstrated a marked difference in the way Americans viewed the military in the early twenty-first century compared to previous eras.

Despite the hardships, the troops continued to support one another and the mission they hoped would eventually end with their safe return and peace for the Iraqi people. Others simply rallied around support of one another. With the lack of clear guidance and in a world where the battlefront was all around them, the only thing these troops could trust for sure was each other. Even if their leaders could not agree on why they were there, these men and women shared a soldier's faith that together they could achieve any mission.

2.4 The Economy and the 2004 Election

Bush's tax cuts combined with rising military spending to produce soaring deficits. The President's evasiveness to questions about WMDs and exit strategies following the invasion of Iraq led many to question whether the Bush administration had manipulated facts and led the nation into a war it had not prepared for. Many military leaders quietly opposed the invasion of Iraq because it had weakened the hunt for Al Qaeda in Afghanistan. Uncertainty toward Iraq, which was daily descending into a civil war between Shiites and Sunnis led many voters to conclude that the President failed to prepare its military for the realities of occupation.

The 2004 presidential election pitted Bush against Senator John Kerry of Massachusetts. While questions surfaced about Bush's service in the National Guard, John Kerry was wounded three times and received medals for bravery during the Vietnam War. Kerry also joined the antiwar movement upon his return, believing along with many veterans that the Johnson and Nixon administrations had

FIGURE 14.11

A US soldier and two children walk together down a road in Kirkuk, Iraq, in 2005. Similar to previous US military operations, deployed troops often used their own pay to purchase things that local children needed such as school supplies and sports equipment. Of course, the most popular item among children was candy, as indicated by the large bag (sent by this soldier's family) that is being distributed by one of the children.

deceived the nation regarding Vietnam. In response, the Bush campaign decided to attack Kerry's military record through an elaborate deception.

Leading Texas Republican donors bankrolled a group called Swift Boat Veterans for Truth, which enrolled Vietnam veterans, most of whom had never met Kerry. The group then sponsored numerous television ads that claimed Kerry's honorable service record and medals for courage were based on lies. Kerry and dozens of veterans who served with him attempted to refute the ads, and the SEC later fined the organization. However, because Kerry had been such a prominent antiwar activist, many Americans accepted the image of Kerry's service as less than honorable. The attack on Kerry added a new term to the political lexicon. "Swiftboating" entered the dictionary as a strategy based on spreading negative lies about one's opponents.

One of the consequences of the swift boat deception was that Kerry decided to avoid any discussion of military affairs. This included criticism regarding the administration's handling of the war in Iraq and the hunt for bin Laden. It also meant that Kerry did not challenge Bush with questions about the decision to invade Iraq. Polls once again predicted a close election. Bush advisor Karl Rove and other national Republican leaders counseled GOP supporters in each state to place laws barring gay marriage on state and local ballots as a means to ensure that every conservative in the nation voted in the 2004 election. The strategy proved effective as voter turnout was the highest since the 1960s. Bush prevailed with 286 electoral votes to Kerry's 252.

2.5 Bush's Second Term

On August 29, 2005, Hurricane Katrina devastated New Orleans and dozens of surrounding communities in Mississippi and Louisiana. Around 2,000 people perished throughout the Gulf Coast, with the highest rate of fatalities occurring in New Orleans. The city was almost completely destroyed as the storm crested over the flood walls. Because the city lies below sea level, tens of thousands of New Orleans residents who had been unable to heed the evacuation order were now stranded and without food or drinkable water.

FIGURE 14.12

A New Orleans resident contrasts the use of government money to fund war in Iraq while the city was left without adequate levees that could have prevented the flood. The Bush administration came under heavy criticism for its delayed response to Hurricane Katrina.

For the first several days, emergency services were delayed or so disorganized that they provided little assistance. Because the storm had been forecasted well in advance, the Federal Emergency Management Agency (FEMA) and the Bush administration shouldered much of the blame for the failed preparations and response to the storm. New Orleans residents had long demanded more adequate protection against a hurricane, and the poorest neighborhoods were incredibly vulnerable to flooding. Americans watched in disbelief as news crews showed images of hundreds of stranded citizens. They were especially enraged to see opportunistic criminals who thwarted rescue efforts while other citizens who tried to provide aid were turned back by FEMA officials. Because the majority of those left in New Orleans were poor African Americans, Katrina revealed the continued inequalities of race and class, as well as the cavalier attitude of many in the federal government who belatedly responded.

Similar indifference was displayed by the Bush administration regarding the postcolonial power struggles in Africa. The Republic of the Sudan was host to political unrest, which had combined with ethnic and religious strife for much of the late twentieth century. The isolated region of Darfur in western Sudan suffered from underdevelopment. In addition, a series of wars between area nations and the historic conflict between Muslim and other residents of Darfur brought added suffering to the people of this region. In addition, Sudanese oil profits were funneled to local militias that sought to control the region. The resulting violence led to hundreds of thousands of deaths while 2 to 3 million residents of Darfur became refugees.

Absent a clear strategic or economic interest in the conflict, the United States and the United Nations avoided involvement beyond limited humanitarian aid. Private citizens in America and abroad sought to make up the difference with personal contributions. More importantly, the African Union sent thousands of peacekeepers into the region. The conflict continues to this day. Despite the fact that many rebel groups had vowed to continue fighting, many hoped that a cease-fire signed in 2010 would somehow lead to a restoration of peace in Darfur as well as the rest of the Republic of the Sudan. Many critics of the United States and the West cite Darfur as another example of the failure of the leaders of the developed world to secure the goodwill and support of the Muslim world.

Despite these missed opportunities to promote global stability, nearly all Muslims remain strongly opposed to Al Qaeda and other extremists. In 2004, the 9/11 Commission revealed that the Clinton and Bush administrations had failed to respond to credible reports that a terrorist attack was being planned. It also demonstrated that there was not a meaningful connection between Al Qaeda and Iraq. Other investigations had concluded that there were neither WMDs in Iraq nor credible evidence that Hussein was attempting to obtain such weapons. News of the absence of WMDs surfaced by 2006 just as news that 3,000 US soldiers had died in Iraq. The following year, a controversial surge of US forces increased the number of troops in Iraq from 130,000 back to 160,000 troops.

The surge was heavily criticized by the political left, but appeared to have been successful in reducing violent attacks in Iraq. However, reports of the torture and even rape and murder of Iraqi civilians also surfaced in Bush's second term. In addition, many Americans joined those around the world who protested the US military's indefinite detainment of suspected terrorists without trial in a military prison in Guantanamo Bay, Cuba. Evidence that some of these prisoners were also tortured combined with the unilateral nature of the war to reduce American standing in the world. Critics even claimed that America's wars in Afghanistan, and Iraq, were winning converts to Al Qaeda and other terrorist organizations. Others feared that the deployments reduced the ability of US forces to respond to other global threats. These critics were concerned by the nonresponse of the US military after the former Soviet state of Russia invaded another former Soviet state in the summer of 2008.

REVIEW AND CRITICAL THINKING

1. Explain how George W. Bush was able to come from behind in the polls and win the 2000 presidential election. Describe the controversy regarding disputed votes in Florida and explain how Bush could win the election despite polling fewer votes than his opponent. Offer your own analysis about whether the United States should continue to utilize the electoral college system.

2. Summarize the events of September 11 and describe the way that this terrorist attack affected the nation. Describe the immediate reaction of the nation as well as the federal government's attempts to prevent future terrorist attacks.

3. Given Osama bin Laden's opposition to Saddam Hussein and other leaders of Iraq, why then did the United States decide to use its military to topple Hussein's government after the September 11 attacks? Describe the reasons cited in favor of and against the invasion of Iraq. Explain the ways that the Bush administration led the nation to war.

4. Summarize the election of 2004. How did the Bush administration manage to defeat the candidacy of John Kerry despite its own unpopularity with many voters?

5. Analyze the effectiveness of Bush's second term in office, both at home and abroad. Be sure to discuss the wars in Afghanistan and Iraq as well as domestic issues such as taxes, the budget, and the government's response to Hurricane Katrina.

---

3. DIVERSITY IN THE NEW AMERICA

LEARNING OBJECTIVES

1. Explain what multiculturalism is and why so many Americans had differing views on the benefits of celebrating America's cultural diversity.

2. Summarize the history of controversial state laws in Arizona and California regarding immigration. Analyze the arguments for and against these bills using examples from history.

3. Explain the goals of Third-Wave Feminism and Critical Race Theory. Using specific examples, analyze the legal cases regarding affirmative action and "Don't Ask Don't Tell" in comparison to cases regarding civil rights in previous generations.

3.1 Multiculturalism

As toleration for diversity increased among Americans, many in the United States also became increasingly sensitive to labels used to describe various minority groups. This proved easier in theory than practice given the lack of unanimity among people of various Asian, Middle Eastern, African, South American, and Caribbean peoples. "Asian American" remained a popular moniker, but it was criticized for minimizing the rich diversity of the world's largest continent. African visitors to the United States often wondered why they were called "African Americans," especially in cities like New York where hundreds of thousands of recent immigrants from various African nations resided. In fact, more people of African descent have arrived in America in recent decades than during the centuries of forced immigration and slavery.

New citizens from Asia and Africa usually identify themselves by their country of origin rather than their continent of origin. They view themselves as Laotian, Cambodian, Kenyan, or Ethiopian. Some recent immigrants from Mexico prefer the term "Mexicano" or "Chicano" while those of

Mexican ancestry who were born in the United States often favor "Mexican American," "Hispanic," or simply "American." The new arrivals from the Caribbean and Central and South America likewise identified themselves as Cubans, Dominicans, Brazilians, or other terms depicting nationality. However, they often found themselves grouped along with Mexican Americans. By the 1980s, the term "Latino" gained currency as an all-inclusive label for all people from Spanish-speaking countries and cultures. Older terms such as Hispanic were regarded as offensive to some, largely because of the term's implicit reference to European imperialists from Spain who had enslaved the Indian, African, and Mestizo ancestors of most "Hispanic" people. However, the term continues to be used to refer to people from Spanish-speaking nations and is often interchanged with Latino/Latina and other terms.

multiculturalism

An orientation of support toward various cultures and the people who originate from these cultures, as well as the belief that an organization benefits from diversity.

Some Americans resent the increased sensitivity regarding terms of identity, while many others simply want to be told what term they should use. Most nonwhite, native-born citizens appreciate the new sensitivity regarding their ethnicity but tire of being asked about their origins or even "welcomed" to their own country by strangers. Schools, government organizations, and corporations increasingly required "diversity training" intended to help educate and sensitize their members regarding the values and practices surrounding **multiculturalism**. Because multiculturalism was difficult to define, some criticized these efforts as a way of stereotyping minorities or minimizing the ideas and contributions of nonminorities. Others believe multiculturalism unintentionally perpetuates stereotypical understandings of various groups. As a result, multiculturalism has resulted in greater understanding and appreciation for diversity even as perceptions of multiculturalism have fueled backlash.

On many occasions, backlash against multiculturalism was expressed in ways that clearly demonstrated the pervasiveness of racism in the twenty-first century. At other times, those who expressed anxiety regarding multiculturalism were expressing concerns about changing modes of popular cultural expression. Even more than the previous two generations, many American youths began to appropriate "black" cultural modes of expression. In contrast to suburban environs or the unapologetically old-fashioned rhythms of rural America, many youths came to glorify what they perceived to be a more intense mode of expression through rap music and hip-hop culture. Others were simply attracted to the hypermasculine posturing of gangsta rap. It also didn't hurt that the music, fashion, and slang they adopted drove their parents crazy.

In many ways, these parents and their children were simply repeating cultural history. Norman Mailer's 1957 *White Negro* described the hipster of the 1950s complete with baggy clothes and a suspicion that he was the only authentic article in a world of poseurs. "You can't interview a hipster because his main goal is to keep out of a society [he believes] is trying to make everyone over in its own image," Mailer explained. At the same time Mailer made it clear where the substance of the white hipster came from. "In this wedding of the white and black," Mailer declared, "it was the Negro who brought the cultural dowry." Some modern critics of gangsta rap would argue that most of this dowry had been spent by the turn of the twenty-first century. While many rap traditions survived, some of the most popular artists appealed more to white fantasies and misogyny than authentic black experience and cultural traditions.

3.2 Immigration and Latino Rights

Proposition 187

A controversial ballot initiative that was approved by California voters and would have made it illegal for any undocumented alien to receive the benefit of public programs such as schools and health clinics. A federal court determined the measure was preempted by federal laws regarding the creation and enforcement of immigration law.

Statistics regarding immigrant poverty and education were cited by those on both sides of the immigration debate. By the 1990s, 50 percent of Latino students enrolled in the major cities of California did not graduate high school. Whites perceived these statistics as evidence of a growing and potentially dangerous underclass. Latinos attributed the failure rate to a combination of economic and social issues that the state refused to address. Social conservatives in California united behind a 1994 ballot initiative known as **Proposition 187**. If passed, the proposal would bar noncitizens and undocumented aliens from government-funded services such as public schools and health clinics. Although the law's passage would only exacerbate the problems facing Latino children of undocumented parents, the majority of white voters rallied behind the measure, which became known as the "Save Our State" initiative. In fact, white support for Proposition 187 was so strong that an unpopular Republican governor projected to lose his 1994 reelection bid in a landslide ended up defeating his Democratic opponent because of his outspoken support for Proposition 187.

Minority groups and liberals organized in a failed attempt to defeat the measure, arguing that Proposition 187 was motivated by racism and would not address concerns about illegal immigration. Activists also warned that the law would create a permanent underclass of Californians and was callous toward undocumented children who could not attend school or receive life-saving medical care. Federal courts quickly determined that many provisions in the new law could not be enforced because they conflicted with federal laws regarding immigration. Although the law was deemed unenforceable, the debate surrounding the measure polarized California politics along ethnic and party divisions. Two-thirds of Democrats opposed Proposition 187, while four out of five Republicans supported it. Nearly 80 percent of Latino voters opposed the law, while black voters split evenly and a majority of whites voted in favor of the measure. The law also spurred a renaissance of political activism among Latino voters throughout California and beyond.

FIGURE 14.13

Opponents of Proposition 187 march in Fresno, California.

The debate and subsequent legal action surrounding Proposition 187 led to a heated political debate about federal and state authority regarding immigration. In 2010, the Republican-dominated state legislature of Arizona approved a controversial measure that required state law enforcement officials to request documentation verifying the citizenship of anyone they had reason to suspect might be an illegal alien. All noncitizens were required to maintain documentation of their status, and any person caught without this documentation was subject to immediate deportation.

The strictest immigration law ever passed, Arizona Senate Bill 1070 soon became a subject of nationwide controversy. Although polls indicated wide support throughout the country, many believed that the law's provisions were inspired by xenophobia and encouraged if not required racial profiling by police. As of 2011, many federal officials and even the president of the United States have expressed concerns about the constitutionality of the Arizona law. As a result, some politicians have called for the enactment of a Constitutional amendment that would deny citizenship to children born in America whose parents were not citizens—a provision that has grown in popularity following its proposal in 2005 but conflicts with the Fourteenth Amendment. Others believe the solution is stronger measures against the entry of undocumented aliens. Congress passed the Secure Fence Act of 2006 with bipartisan support. This law authorized the construction of up to 700 miles of fences and other barriers across the 2,000-mile border with Mexico. Areas without a fence were to be monitored by sensors and cameras.

In response to the Fence Act, thousands of students engaged in protests against the wall's construction. The protests became defining features of colleges along the US border from the University of Texas at Brownsville to the University of Texas at El Paso, all the way to Arizona Western College, community colleges in San Diego, and major research institutions such as UCLA and San Diego State University. These students have joined millions of Americans of diverse backgrounds who believe that the wall is an ineffective method of curbing the entry of illegal drugs and immigrants into the county. They also believe that the construction of the wall sends a xenophobic message that violates the history and finest traditions of the American people. Many of these students have studied and adopted the tactics of the civil rights movement to express their views, arguing that the wall is a blight on border communities and a symbol of the second-class citizenship Latinos still hold in the United States.

Local business interests and political leaders joined the students, arguing that the wall and other measures ignore the reality of life along the border, where companies depend on the daily migration of workers to and from their homes in Mexico. Members of the Sierra Club and other environmentalists have also joined the protest, pointing out that many of the barriers violate federal statutes regarding the access to water for migrating animals. Humanitarian groups have expressed even greater outrage at the apathy expressed toward migrating humans. They believe that the fences have led many families to hire criminals to smuggle them into the United States, while others have been forced to take a much riskier path through deserts. As a result, hundreds of bodies have been discovered recently in the Sonoran Desert and other remote areas where there is no wall.

Immigration continues to be a controversial issue that reflects the persistence of cultural and ethnic tensions. Some believe that efforts to build an impassable border between the United States and Mexico is not only xenophobic but also less cost-effective than investing in overseas businesses that would create more jobs in Mexico and thereby removing the leading cause of illegal immigration. Given the recent loss of manufacturing jobs in the United States, such a measure is likely to encounter spirited opposition. One of the only proposed changes to America's immigration policies that has enjoyed bipartisan support was a 2002 law regarding citizenship for soldiers. Republican President George W. Bush approved the measure that simplified and accelerated the process for citizenship for permanent residents (holders of Green Cards) who serve in the US military. Approximately 70,000 soldiers utilized these provisions to become citizens in the decade that followed. As of late 2011, journalists have estimated that 25,000 legal immigrants from all over the globe were serving in the US military and awaiting citizenship.

3.3   Gender Equality and Third-Wave Feminism

One of the most important changes in the last few decades has been the rapid increase in the number of women holding political office. The percentage of women in Congress hovered around 2 to 3 percent from the 1940s to the 1970s. This percentage jumped from 5 percent in 1990 to almost 15 percent by the year 2000, reaching 17 percent after the 2010 elections (a slight decline from the record number of ninety-five representatives and seventeen senators who composed the 111th Congress of 2008–2010). While the number and percentage of women in politics increased rapidly in the past thirty years, it is important to note that the percentage of women in the US legislature remains far below that of most developed nations. As of 2011, the congresses and parliaments of over seventy nations had a higher percentage of female membership than the United States. The global success of women as political leaders in nations as diverse as Norway, Cuba, Rwanda, Argentina, and Mozambique demonstrates the existence and spread of feminism beyond Britain and the United States. In each of the nations listed, women represent around 40 percent of elected representatives in their nation's parliament.

FIGURE 14.14

This chart compares the number and percentages of women in various national legislative bodies around the globe.

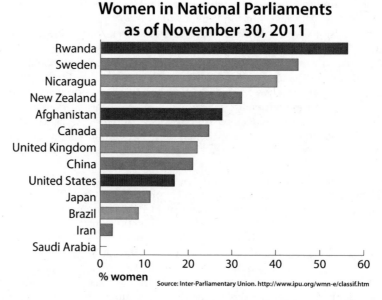

Many scholars believe that feminism, at least feminism as a popular movement, receded slightly after the late 1960s and early 1970s. Many attribute the decline to the conservative political environment of 1980s America. However, the movement flourished internationally during the 1980s in Africa, Asia, South America, the Caribbean, and even some parts of the Middle East. America's role in spreading ideas such as women's suffrage is striking in places like Iraq and Afghanistan. As of 2011, a much higher percentage of women serve in parliament in these nations than within the United States.

Elsewhere, women won the right to vote independent of American influence and have been more progressive in terms of gender equality for many years. The location of the four United Nations Women's Conferences, which have been held in Mexico City, Copenhagen, Nairobi, and Beijing, demonstrate the global nature of the feminist movement of which the United States is a participant rather than a leader. Hillary Clinton was one of the few mainstream American political leaders to even acknowledge the existence of the global feminist movement. As first lady, Clinton attended the 1995 UN Women's Conference in Beijing. Clinton was only the second first lady to attend any UN conference on the status of women, the first being Eleanor Roosevelt who had been appointed to a leadership position within the UN six decades prior.

Some distinguish feminists of the 1990s and early 2000s as belonging to a third wave. Whereas the first wave sought the right to vote and the second sought legal and economic equality, the advocates of **Third-Wave Feminism** define their movement as an effort to permit women to define for themselves what gender justice and feminism means. Born from a recognition that leading feminist organizations often failed to be truly inclusive in terms of race, ethnicity, and social class, the third wave also rejects notions of a single feminist ideal. For example, many feminists of the 1970s and 1980s advanced the notion of a middle-class and presumably white career woman competing in male-dominated fields as the ideal model of women's liberation. Third-Wave Feminists hope to celebrate all women who use their own agency to determine and define what liberation means for themselves. As a result, Third-Wave Feminism is a difficult concept to define. Some feminists believe that the usefulness of labeling "waves" of feminism has passed. For example, **bell hooks** who is among the leading feminists of the modern era, writes about the difficulty and even the inherent contradiction of trying to define something as ubiquitous as feminism.

In recent years, feminist scholars have joined others, such as the late Derrick Bell, who have pioneered a body of scholarship known as **Critical Race Theory (CRT)**. CRT studies the ways that racism and sexism helped to create and reinforce a power structure that historically privileged white males over other Americans. In the past two decades, critical race theorists have used history and other fields to demonstrate how negative images rooted in slave experience have persisted. CRT is a diverse field of study that defies simple definitions or a single representative example. At the same time, the strength of scholars such as Derrick Bell and Darlene Clark Hine is the clarity of the examples they use. Two examples relating to race and gender are instructive: the way CRT scholars demonstrate how slave owners created the "jezebel" and "mammy" stereotypes.

The "jezebel" was a racist image that devalued black womanhood by equating a particular slave with a more primal creature who was unable to control her sexual urges. In so doing, white men who owned slaves transferred the blame for the rapes they committed on the "insatiable lust" of slave women who tempted the otherwise virtuous slave owner. The "mammy" was on the reverse end of the spectrum, a nonsexual, and therefore unthreatening and undesirable, drudge who cheerfully emancipated white women from their daily toil. Critical race theorists explain that these stereotypes led to the elevation of white women because they were contrasted against the negative images of the jezebel and the mammy. As a result, the denigration of black women created the image of white women as both virtuous and desirable. At the same time, these stereotypes allowed elite white men to define a very limited sphere of acceptable female behavior for the idealized woman—a pedestal that elevated and trapped a woman at the same time.

In this and many other ways, recent CRT scholars have shown how racism helped to pit black and white women against one another within a paternalistic society. These scholars argue that aspects of these stereotypes persisted beyond the end of chattel slavery in ways that continued to devalue black womanhood while defining white womanhood in elevated but restricted ways. According to this line of reasoning, issues of race, ethnicity, class, and gender came together in ways that permitted elite white males to define womanhood in racial and gendered terms. As a result, those who identify themselves as Third-Wave Feminists believe that celebrating diversity and encouraging women to define womanhood for themselves is a necessary corrective. In the end, attempting to precisely define Third-Wave Feminism may be an impossible task. Like those who came before them, Third-Wave Feminists are a diverse group of women who seek equality and justice while confidently living life on their own terms.

3.4   Race, Equality, and Law

Some scholars began to refer to America as a "postracial" society at the turn of the twenty-first century. Violent protests that erupted in Los Angeles following the acquittal of police who were videotaped beating the motionless Rodney King in the summer of 1992 demonstrated otherwise. For three days, police and firefighters battled rioters and arsonists. The riots left fifty people dead and caused $1 billion in damages. Three years later, the arrest and subsequent acquittal of the NFL's O. J. Simpson demonstrated that white and black Americans still perceived events differently.

Third-Wave Feminism

A term referring to present-day feminists who are attempting to avoid divisions along racial, ethnic, and class lines of the past in their quest for full gender equality. Third-Wave Feminists seek to remedy the lingering injustices that remain following the success of the first wave, which secured political rights for women, and the second wave's legal victories regarding economic equality.

Critical Race Theory (CRT)

A body of scholarship dedicated to the study of the connection between structures of power and race, although CRT has increasingly come to incorporate gender, ethnicity, and social class. CRT is dedicated to the advancement of social justice and usually incorporates ideas and methods of inquiry from multiple academic disciplines, such as law, history, political science, and sociology.

prison-industrial complex

A phrase conveying both the rapid growth of the US prison population and the idea that its growth is partially due to a collusion between political leaders and corporations within the multibillion-dollar industries that provide products and services used by the criminal justice system, such as private prisons and law enforcement equipment.

FIGURE 14.15

This chart demonstrates the recent increase in the total number of inmates in prisons, jails, and juvenile facilities in the United States between 1920 and 2006.

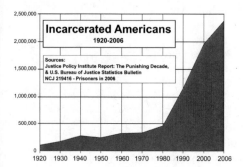

As these incidents demonstrate, perceptions regarding the fairness of the criminal justice system often differed among white and black Americans. Angela Davis is a scholar, Black Panther, and former prisoner who was later acquitted of her alleged crime. Davis spent most of her life as an activist against what she believes are the injustices of the criminal justice system. Davis argues that the term **prison-industrial complex** is a more accurate term for America's law enforcement system. She and others cite a host of studies that use statistics to demonstrate that courts are more prone to dismiss charges against whites and impose stiffer penalties on nonwhites.

Federal statistics show the prison population expanded from 200,000 inmates in 1970 to 2.2 million four decades later. Davis believes that race and poverty continue to play significant factors in this growth and rejects the assumption that the rapid growth of the prison population is simply the result of better law enforcement. "Most people commit crimes," Davis believes, "some people are under much greater surveillance." Davis and others also believe that the growth of the prison system reflects a society that sees incarceration as a simple and immediate way to deal with underlying social problems such as poverty and drug addiction. She and other activists compare the lobbying power of corporations and contractors in the prison industry to the military-industrial complex President Eisenhower described. They argue that just as the armament industry led to the expansion of military spending, the power of a multibillion-dollar law-enforcement industry has fueled the increase in the prison population.

Recent statistics show that one in four black men in their twenties is awaiting trial, in jail, or in some type of parole system. At the same time, one-third of college-aged African Americans have also attended college—a percentage near the US average. Recent policies designed to encourage black enrollment have been heavily scrutinized. For example, a conservative political group challenged the University of Michigan's undergraduate admissions process that ranked candidates by a point system because that system included points for minority candidates. The point system still ensured that a minority candidate had impeccable credentials but would place a minority candidate ahead of a "white" candidate with equal scores.

Gratz v. Bollinger (2003) ruled that colleges could still seek to attract minority applicants and consider race when making admission decisions. However, the Supreme Court argued that Michigan's point system was too rigid and therefore discriminated against white students. In a similar case that same year involving the University of Michigan Law School, the Supreme Court narrowly upheld the legality of an admissions process that considered race as a factor but did not award points or use a quota. The use of quotas had been disallowed by the 1978 *Bakke* decision, while the more recent *Gratz* case prohibited precise mathematical formulas that awarded points for being a member of a minority. The 5–4 split decision of the justices, along with the apparent mixed message permitting schools to use race as a factor in order to increase the diversity of their student body while limiting the use of clear and definable methods of doing so, confused many. The majority decision in the law school case, written by Sandra Day O'Connor, provided context but little specific guidance. O'Connor acknowledged that the present state of race relations was such that affirmative action was still needed to remedy past injustices while looking forward to the day a completely color-blind society might live by completely color-blind policies.

Some Americans believed that day had already come and gone, leaving the nation with policies that discriminated against whites. Two Supreme Court cases decided in June 2007 greatly limited the options for schools seeking racial diversity within cities whose neighborhoods remained racially segregated. In Seattle, a new system of determining school assignments allowed parents to choose any school in the city. When there were more requests than could be accommodated, preference was given to requests that helped encourage racial balance. A similar system operated in Louisville, with the addition of a few measurable standards regarding racial balance. No Louisville school could have fewer than 15 percent or greater than 50 percent black student populations. In *Parents Involved in Community Schools v. Seattle School District No.1* (2007) and *Meredith v. Jefferson County Board of Education* (2007) the Supreme Court ruled that public schools could consider race when making assignments, but that both systems were too rigid. Both cases resulted in split decisions, with four of the nine Justices issuing dissenting opinions. These opinions raised the question of how any school district might create racially diverse schools in America's cities if even the moderate and flexible plans of the Louisville and Seattle public schools were unconstitutional.

The question of governmental power and its limits was also the central issue regarding lawsuits that sought to challenge the proliferation of casinos on Native American reservations. In 1978, the Seminole tribe of Florida opened a bingo parlor on their land near Miami. State officials protested, citing Florida's antigambling laws. The Seminoles filed a lawsuit challenging the state's authority to enforce its prohibition against gambling on tribal land. Federal courts ruled in favor of the Seminoles, arguing that tribal sovereignty prohibited enforcement of state antigambling laws.

In response to the ruling, tribes throughout the nation began developing casinos on their reservations. Within a decade, gambling revenues nationwide exceeded several billion dollars. The proceeds were distributed to individual members as well as tribal governments. For many tribes, these nontaxed revenues have been critical to the construction of schools and small colleges. However, the majority of reservations are too isolated from urban populations to raise significant revenue. In some cases, casinos have led to increased poverty in the isolated communities they serve. In addition, many states have modified their laws to allow the operation of private and state-operated casinos. While these casinos generate millions in revenue for the states, these state-regulated casinos are usually located closer to major cities than most Indian reservations. As a result, some tribes that borrowed money or entered into delayed revenue-sharing agreements with casino operators face a severe budget crisis.

3.5   Gay, Lesbian, Bisexual, and Transgendered (GLBT) Rights

As a candidate, Bill Clinton pledged to end the ban on homosexual service in the United States Armed Forces. Clinton's support of what many believed was an important civil rights initiative won him many supporters on the left during the Democratic primaries. In January of 1993, President Clinton announced that he was putting together a plan that would end all discrimination based on sexual orientation. The announcement drew a firestorm of opposition both within and outside of the military. Even the Chairman of the Joint Chiefs of Staff Colin Powell criticized the new president's plan. In response, Clinton agreed to a compromise measure, a relatively cumbersome standard that was soon labeled **Don't Ask Don't Tell (DADT)**. The new policy still banned homosexuals from joining the military, at least officially, but also banned military officials from requesting any disclosures regarding a member's sexual orientation. It also prevented service members from voluntarily disclosing such information. In effect, Don't Ask Don't Tell permitted homosexuals to join the military so long as they remained "in the closet."

Many gay rights activists were disappointed that the president had compromised his original position. Critics pointed out that the new policy required soldiers to lie about their identity in ways that stigmatized homosexuality. Others recognized that the president's position was still well ahead of public opinion and cost him political support among conservatives and some moderates. Millions within the religious right were appalled by Clinton's new policy. The president's relationship with many conservative military leaders was also strained and would only gradually recover during the final years of his second term. The next seven years of Clinton's presidency demonstrated ideological inconsistencies regarding gay rights that likely reflected political calculations of Clinton's advisors rather than the president's personal views. In 1996, Clinton supported the Defense of Marriage Act that legally defined marriage as a union between a woman and a man. Two years later, and well past the final election of his political career, Clinton signed an executive order that outlawed discrimination against any federal civilian employee because of their sexual orientation.

Don't Ask Don't Tell (DADT)

The commonly used name for the Department of Defense policy regarding the eligibility of homosexuals desiring to serve in the US military. The policy barred military members to inquire about a service member's gender orientation. It also permitted homosexuals who did not reveal their gender orientation to serve in the military, but it required dismissal of any self-acknowledged homosexual. The policy was enacted by President Bill Clinton in December of 1993 until a federal court ruling in July 2011 barred its enforcement.

FIGURE 14.16

A 2001 US Army training aid describing the kinds of information that would be considered as credible evidence that a soldier was homosexual.

In 2003, the US Supreme Court invalidated a Texas law that made same-sex intercourse a crime. Also in 2003, the Massachusetts Supreme Court ruled that same-sex couples were legally entitled to the same privileges and obligations enjoyed by opposite-sex couples who desired marriage. Officials and clergy in cities with large gay populations, such as San Francisco, also began performing marriages. However, the California Supreme Court quickly ruled that these unions had no legal basis. In 2008, the California Supreme Court reversed course, overturning a statewide ban on gay marriage. Despite conservative support, attempts to pass a Constitutional amendment banning gay marriage failed on numerous occasions. However, thirty states have adopted similar prohibitions against gay marriage within their state constitutions.

Because most of these states already prohibited same-sex marriage, few of these measures have had any legal impact upon state law. As a result, many political observers believe that these laws and amendments prohibiting gay marriage were placed on the ballot by conservative politicians as a way to rally their supporters and assure a large conservative turnout at the polls. Others point out that the adoption of a state constitutional amendment banning gay marriage reduces the likelihood that a state would revise existing prohibitions. In addition, these provisions encourage the denial of the health care coverage, survivor benefits, and other protections enjoyed by heterosexual couples. As of 2011, only seven states and the District of Columbia had issued marriage licenses to same-sex couples. A few other states recognize the legality of same-sex marriages performed in other states. Although the 1996 Defense of Marriage Act sought to "protect" states from being compelled to recognize the legality of same-sex unions performed in other states, the fact that states must recognize the legality of heterosexual marriages performed in the United States has led many to question the Constitutionality of the 1996 law.

Candidate Barrack Obama promised to repeal DADT during his 2008 campaign. However, after becoming the president and commander-in-chief, he deferred to military officials, most of whom were opposed or divided on the measure. Gay rights activists, veterans, active soldiers, and progressive military leaders continued to press for the repeal of DADT, even as the president remained silent on the issue. Polls indicated opposition to the repeal of DADT until 2011, when many within the Joint Chiefs of Staff expressed their belief that repeal would not compromise the effectiveness of the US military. In July of 2011, a federal court declared that the provisions of DADT were no longer enforceable. The decision legally opened military service to all Americans regardless of their gender orientation. The military has since revised its policies and now trains personnel that discrimination against a military member because of his or her gender orientation is impermissible.

REVIEW AND CRITICAL THINKING

1. What is multiculturalism, and why would its tenets arouse such strong opposition amongst social conservatives?

2. Describe the controversy regarding the issue of immigration along America's southern border during the past two decades. Explain the history of California's Proposition 187 and Arizona Senate Bill 1070. Describe the way that college students throughout the Borderlands sought to impact the debate regarding immigration.

3. What is Third Wave Feminism and Critical Race Theory? Provide examples of how these ideas might impact a current debate regarding race and gender equality in the United States.

4. Discuss legal cases such as *Gratz v. Bollinger* that have dealt with race and affirmative action. Describe various perspectives regarding these cases and affirmative action.

5. President Clinton revised the ban against homosexuals in the military with a policy known as "Don't Ask, Don't Tell." Explain the history of this policy and discuss the history of gay rights in the military from World War II to the present.

4. CONTINUITY AND CHANGE: THE UNITED STATES AND THE TRANSITION FROM BUSH TO OBAMA

LEARNING OBJECTIVES

1. Explain the ways that the political system continues to marginalize the concept of "one person, one vote." Analyze the obstacles to creating a more democratic electoral process.
2. Summarize the causes and consequences of the economic crisis that arose in 2007–2008. Explain how the crisis affected the 2008 election.
3. Describe the polarization of America's political climate and the cultural war that has emphasized this division. Analyze the modern political climate using examples throughout history.

4.1 Pervasiveness of Inequality

A century and a half after the end of slavery, issues of race and class continued to divide America. In the wake of white flight, the proliferation of private schools, and court decisions that limited busing as a method of achieving racial diversity, America's urban schools were more segregated in the twenty-first century than prior to the 1954 *Brown v. Board* decision. In 1950, the richest 1 percent of Americans controlled 20 percent of the nation's wealth, and top executives usually made between ten and twenty times the average wage of entry-level employees. Five decades later, CEO pay often exceeded 250 times the annual wages of workers, while the wealthiest 1 percent controlled a third to half of the nation's wealth. Poverty rates increased during the same time period, while the working class had increased their wages only when measured against the lower standard of living of much earlier decades. The rich had grown much richer, the poor were more prevalent, and those in between clung to middle-class status by becoming dual-wage households.

Lack of economic equality was reflected in the political system in ways much more difficult to document than the overt disenfranchisement that had given rise to Freedom Schools and Fannie Lou Hamer. Given the importance of securing political donations in modern elections, the poor and middle-class found their interests circumscribed by those who could provide the financial resources a candidate depended upon to be reelected. For several decades, reformers attempted to place limits on the amounts and types of political donations campaigns could accept. These reformers hoped these prohibitions would force political leaders to value the views of voters over interest groups.

Given the decline of labor unions, which had traditionally made large donations to the Democratic Party, and the success of Republicans in soliciting sizable political donations from corporations, leading Democrats made dozens of attempts to place stricter limits on political donations throughout the 1980s and 1990s. Arguing that these limits were politically motivated and a violation of free speech, Republicans mobilized each time to defeat these bills. Several bipartisan attempts to regulate campaign finance were also defeated, such as a 1997 bill sponsored by Arizona Republican **John McCain** and Wisconsin Democrat Russell Feingold.

These measures sought to rein in "**soft money**," a term for donations that are given to a political party or cause rather than directly to an individual politician's campaign. Soft money usually takes the form of union or corporate donations and is generally exempt from limits (presently around $2,500 per candidate per election) that apply to contributions that are made directly to a specific candidate. The 1997 McCain-Feingold bill targeted "soft money" but was defeated by a Republican filibuster. The willingness of Senator McCain to confront the leaders of his own party earned him a reputation as a "maverick."

McCain and Feingold succeeded in passing a campaign finance reform bill in 2002, which placed many limits on soft money. However, many of these provisions were easily circumvented by other methods of political fundraising. In response to the past four decades of campaign-finance reforms, thousands of political organizations were created as part of an effort to further a political agenda without being subject to the rules of the Federal Election Commission. The most common method of evading regulations is for an organization to finance advertisements that sound very similar to a candidate's message but do not explicitly endorse that candidate. For example, an advertisement might suggest that candidate A has a reputation for integrity while candidate B has a criminal record. Other advertisements might connect specific issues or policies with a particular candidate, as long as it does not explicitly counsel its audience to vote for that candidate.

Many restrictions against these kinds of advertisements were considered in each session of Congress at the turn of the twenty-first century. Each restriction weighed the desire to limit corruption and unsavory methods of financing campaigns against concerns regarding the protection of free speech.

John McCain

Arizona senator who took the seat previously occupied by conservative Senator Barry Goldwater. Like Goldwater, McCain would win the Republican nomination for president but lose in the general election to a Democratic candidate.

soft money

Refers to donations that are not regulated by the Federal Election Commission because they cannot be used to support an individual campaign or advocate the election of a particular candidate.

Many Americans recognized that limits on individual campaign contributions were meaningless if unlimited donations might be made to anonymous organizations covertly working to aid a particular campaign. President Barack Obama backed an effort in 2010 that would have required disclosure statements for these kinds of advertisements. It also prohibited foreign entities and recipients of government contracts from making political contributions. Critics of the bill suggested it was politically motivated and violated standards of free speech. Although the bill would have likely passed given its support by the Democratic majority in Congress, the bill was defeated when every Republican senator joined efforts to prevent the measure from reaching the floor for a vote. Later that same year, the Supreme Court reversed prohibitions that had prevented corporations from using unlimited funding to produce and distribute political messages about candidates.

4.2 The Economy

The stock market had rapidly fluctuated during the last three decades, producing record bull and bear markets alike, but generally rising higher at a rate that seemed unnatural to some economists. The value of homes in many urban markets had risen by 10 to 20 percent each year, which caused a boom in real-estate speculation. As had occurred during the 1920s, few Americans were saving money, while others used leverage in dangerous ways. Some families took out multiple mortgages, leveraging their homes to purchase stock on margin or invest in more real estate. Unlike the 1920s, however, consumers were also using credit cards to borrow for everyday purchases, while most college students and their families financed a large portion of their educational expenses with federally backed loans. Other modern financial products, such as second mortgages and home-equity loans, also increased the risk of going into debt.

Perhaps the most remarkable new finance mechanism was the zero-equity home loan. These were loans that did not require a down payment and were increasingly paired with adjustable-rate mortgages (ARMs). These risky types of loans were marketed to those who had dreamed of purchasing a home but had been turned away by traditional lenders. These individuals often did not have a very sophisticated idea of finance and were happy to accept any home loan. They were especially happy to find that they had been approved to buy a brand-new home with no money down. The terms of most ARMs were seldom fully explained by salespeople who were paid on commission. Many of the companies that offered these high-risk loans later sold these loans to other financial companies. The banks that purchased these loans failed to investigate each individual loan or simply believed that any investment backed by a mortgage was safe. Even if home owners defaulted, they reasoned, the bank would get to keep the house, which would have likely increased in value. In some cases, loans were designed to force home buyers to default after a certain number of years, thereby giving the banks ownership of the real estate while keeping all of the payments the family had made up to that time.

It was a fail-proof system for the banks and mortgage companies so long as home prices continued to increase. But in 2005, housing prices stagnated as fewer and fewer buyers entered the market, and by 2007, these prices began tumbling. A family who had purchased a $250,000 home with no money down found they were $250,000 (or more) in debt for a house that was now valued at $150,000. Many chose bankruptcy to this upside-down situation, which left the banks with homes that were worth much less than the money they had originally loaned.

Other home owners tried to fulfill their obligations but found their zero-down adjustable-rate mortgage contained some unpleasant surprises. Although they should have realized at the time, most ARMs came with loan-repayment rates that jumped from a low introductory rate of 4 percent to 6 or even 8 percent. For example, the interest alone on a monthly mortgage payment for a $250,000 home would jump from $833 at 4 percent to $1,458 at 7 percent. Banks that had purchased these risky loans had done so believing that if the family in question could no longer pay their mortgage, the bank would at least be able to take possession of a house that was worth $250,000 or more. Instead, those that defaulted were often abandoning both a bad loan and a home that was worth only a fraction of what they owed.

In the past, home loans were made by local banks that faced the prospect of losing money or even going out of business if they loaned money to families who could not pay. By the early twenty-first century, home loans were made by a variety of financial institutions, but usually ended up in the hands of only a few firms. The government was supposed to regulate the health of this system, but had increasingly reduced the restrictions on lenders due to political pressure and the historic gains of the stock market and real-estate prices.

Critics warned that the health of the nation's economy was directly related to the stability of a handful of banks and investment firms, but until 2007, those firms were making record profits, which masked the symptoms of disaster from all but a few economists no one wanted to hear. Warnings that America's leading financial firms had unwittingly purchased billions of dollars in loans they knew very little about were ignored, while government regulations were regarded as restraints that prevented the economy from reaching its full potential. As a result, the news that venerable New York investment bank Bear Stearns faced bankruptcy sent a wave of panic throughout the system in 2008.

All of a sudden, the United States awoke to the very disturbing reality that nearly all of its leading banks were at risk of default, which threatened to cause the failure of the entire banking system. Because these banks were insured by the federal government, the failure of one major institution like Bank of America might cost taxpayers hundreds of billions of dollars and begin a tidal wave of other banks to fail. The federal government stepped in and negotiated the takeover of Bear Sterns by JPMorgan Chase. IndyMac Bank, the nation's largest mortgage lender soon failed, which was followed by federal bailouts of Freddie Mac and Freddie Mae—two government regulated corporations that bought and sold mortgages from banks. Dozens of other leading institutions were nearing insolvency. AIG was the largest insurance firm in the country and had invested heavily in mortgage-backed investments. Facing the prospect that AIG would no longer be able to pay insurance claims, the Federal Reserve took over AIG's financial obligations by essentially purchasing the heavily indebted company.

The panic spread from banking and insurance to the entire stock market, causing corporations in industries that were already struggling such as auto manufacturing to collapse had it not been for another massive federal bailout. Oil prices skyrocketed, while the latest round of World Trade Organization talks in Doha, Qatar, failed to reduce international trade barriers. A host of states and cities joined California and the former industrial cities of the Rust Belt in reporting that they were in danger of defaulting on the loans they had made to bondholders. Private and public companies responded by downsizing their workforce, while consumers who had money were understandably reluctant to make large purchases, much less invest in stocks or bonds. The Dow Jones average fell from above 14,000 to nearly 8,000 in just over a year. Retirees returned to the labor market, while those who had planned to retire remained at work, resulting in fewer jobs for recent college graduates who lacked the experience of older workers.

The media soon explained that a new and complicated type of investment was partially to blame and had made a handful of speculators and industry insiders very rich. These investments were called derivatives because they derived their value from the occurrence of a certain event—in this case, the failure of thousands of mortgages. These new investments were beyond the understanding of many experts who worked in the financial service industry and beyond the realm of overburdened government officials whose powers to regulate the banking industry had been vastly reduced by both Republicans and Democrats over the past three decades. These derivatives might have reduced risk had they been purchased by the same banks that held the mortgages their value was derived from—a sort of insurance policy that would compensate the banks if the loans they held ever defaulted.

Many derivatives were bought and sold by speculators betting on a market collapse. Given the incredibly shaky foundation upon which the entire housing market had been constructed, it seemed to many as if some in the investment industry had orchestrated the entire debacle. After all, the only way that many of these loans would not default was if home values kept rising at historically unprecedented rates while new home owners could keep paying mortgages that increased each year. As the media and political leaders kept reporting about hedge fund millionaires and bank executives with multimillion-dollar bonuses, the indignation of many Americans who feared the loss of their homes and jobs mixed with fear to form a volatile mixture.

In late September and in the midst of election season, Bush officials in the Treasury Department crafted legislation that would set aside $700 billion to "bail out the nation's largest banks, investment firms, and insurance companies." Debate on the **Emergency Economic Stabilization Act** revealed both the panicked sense that failure to provide these funds would lead to a complete collapse of America's economic system and the fact that few in government really understood that system. Even though many in Congress protested that the bailout bill had never been fully explained, each day the financial headlines grew more dire, and the bill passed with begrudging but bipartisan support.

The bill provided little assistance for smaller banks, and hundreds of these institutions collapsed. Those banks that had acted prudently survived but were not fully rewarded according to free-market principles by the failure of their larger and more irresponsible competitors. Critics pointed out that many aspects of the bailout were Socialistic—by loaning money to some of America's largest businesses, the government was effectively becoming the owner of these enterprises. Others claimed these extreme measures were temporary and necessary to save the free market and prevent a second Great Depression.

Libertarians believed that the businesses that had made poor investments should face the same fate of millions of families that had taken on more debt than they could afford. As thousands faced foreclosure and bankruptcy each day, it seemed unfair to most Americans that the largest banks were getting federal bailouts because the entire economy was so dependent on their survival. Others turned away from positive explanations and toward populist anger. All they knew was that handful of speculators in the derivative market became rich overnight, while bank executives who were seemingly driving the US financial system over a cliff they helped build were still making millions in bonuses. Meanwhile, the stock market was collapsing each day, and millions of US families were one mortgage payment away from homelessness.

Emergency Economic Stabilization Act

A controversial bill authorizing the Treasury Department to use as much as $700 billion to "bail out" banks and investment firms it deemed could have an adverse effect on the national economy if they defaulted on their loans or became insolvent.

4.3 2008 Election

Oprah Winfrey

Entrepreneur, actress, and talk show host who rose to national prominence with her skill in addressing sensitive social issues and uplifting message of personal and community empowerment. Winfrey is one of the wealthiest Americans and perhaps the most independent public figure on television given her ownership of the company that produces her shows, Harpo Productions.

Barack Obama

A charismatic African American politician and former community organizer in Chicago whose improbable career led him to become the 44th president of the United States after only one incomplete term in the US Senate.

FIGURE 14.17

Chicago politician and Illinois Senator Barack Obama became the 44th President of the United States following his 2008 victory over Arizona Senator John McCain.

If one could engineer a perfect economic storm, it would look much like the financial crisis of the late 2000s. The fact that it coincided with an election year increased the drama as both parties searched for an understanding of what had happened and how to fix it. The Democratic primaries promised drama regardless of the financial catastrophe, as New York Senator Hillary Clinton was poised to become the first woman to be nominated by a major political party. The primary election was tightly contested and each candidate sought the endorsement of political leaders. Ironically, the backing of leading talk show host **Oprah Winfrey** may have been the most impartment endorsement of all. The support and publicity of Oprah and other public figures helped a first-term senator from Illinois rise from relative obscurity and secure the Democratic nomination. **Barack Obama** inspired many with his charisma and message of "change" during the primary election. Obama became the first African American to secure the nomination of a major political party. The nomination led many to wonder if racial diversity had finally become a nonissue, or perhaps even a positive attribute in US politics.

Meanwhile, the Bush administration attempted to balance its attempts to promote Republican candidates with managing the financial crisis. The Bush administration fully endorsed the $700 billion bailout plan and supported additional measures to assist General Motors and Ford, along with AIG and many other large corporations. Between each of these bailouts and the increasingly unpopular war in Iraq, the failure to capture bin Laden, and growing sentiment that the Bush administration had jeopardized the economic health of the nation through deficits and deregulation of the financial industry, Bush's approval ratings exceeded the lows of the Nixon administration. As a result, Republican nominee for president John McCain distanced himself from the Bush administration along with most of the rest of his party.

McCain was an Arizona senator with decades of experience, a fact that contrasted sharply with the much younger Obama, who was still serving his first term in the Senate. McCain was also a national hero who had endured years of torture in a prisoner of war camp in Hanoi. At one point during an early debate between a dozen candidates for the Republican nomination, McCain stunned his opponents with his straightforward response to a difficult question. Allegations that the United States had used techniques such as water-boarding to interrogate prisoners at Guantanamo Bay led to a heated discussion among the many candidates regarding the morality of torture to secure information that might derail a terrorist attack. After each candidate seemingly sought to outdo the other with tough talk about what they would do to US enemies, McCain solemnly replied that the United States could not stand for torture. The room went silent.

As a soldier, McCain had endured daily beatings for his refusal to sign his name to enemy propaganda that slandered the United States. As a candidate, he made it clear that his nation must not be guilty of the same crimes. McCain's principled stand in opposition to the nationalistic posturing of his opponents reminded voters of his service to the nation and his willingness to stand up to his own party in the past. McCain had been branded as a "maverick" for his support of campaign finance reform and numerous other measures that were strongly opposed by the Republican establishment. Given the sudden unpopularity of that establishment in 2008, McCain's unorthodox style resonated with voters and gave him an early lead in the polls.

Both candidates ran on a platform of "change." The Obama campaign used the word heavily along with the elusive phrase "hope," which appealed to many, given their frustrations with the Bush administration and what appeared to be the potential collapse of the banking system. As a young senator from Illinois, Obama had warned of the dangers of deregulation, which made him seem prophetic, yet the candidate failed to communicate a specific plan for how he would turn the economy around. The McCain campaign sought to emphasize its candidate's reputation as a maverick to distance the aging senator from the unpopular Bush administration he had usually supported. McCain was most vulnerable on questions regarding the economy because he had supported most of the deregulation efforts that led to the financial collapse. He had also received significant campaign contributions from the director of a failed financial institution that was later arrested for trying to use money to influence government regulators. McCain was cleared on ethics charges in relation to the scandal but admitted that he had acted in a way that created the appearance of impropriety.

The 2008 election would demonstrate that race was still a major issue as Southern whites rallied behind Republican nominee John McCain in far greater percentages than other Republicans or conservatives had enjoyed. McCain's outspoken vice presidential candidate **Sarah Palin** quickly garnered the support of many evangelicals and the extreme right of the Republican Party, but these were not voters that were likely to support Obama's candidacy. Palin's folksy but clichéd polemics and unsubstantiated attacks on her opponent as a "pal" of terrorists soon galvanized the nation, with most moderates turning away from the McCain camp. McCain sought to distance himself from the often racist appeals of some of his supporters, but was perhaps too cautious in his efforts to do so while still profiting from their race baiting. Sarah Palin displayed even less finesse as she combined the tactics of Nixon's early smear campaigns with the former president's Southern Strategy, openly playing to white racial fears by creating the image that nonwhite America was using federally subsidized programs such as ACORN to capture the 2008 election.

The malice of the anti-Obama backlash the McCain-Palin campaign had encouraged soon expanded in ways that harmed the Republican campaign. Despite McCain's belated attempts to correct misinformation about Obama's religious beliefs and citizenship, the American people increasingly viewed the Republican candidates as responsible for the negative turn in the 2008 election. Obama responded to the backlash in such a mild manner that many minorities and liberal whites were disappointed. However, the future president's continued optimism and charisma stood in increasing contrast to the attacks of his detractors. Late in the campaign, Obama delivered a well-received speech in which he asked Americans to make sure that race baiting would fail. "We can let race divide us," Obama exulted, or "we can come together and say, 'Not this time.'" In the end, Americans expressed unfavorable opinions about the techniques used by the McCain-Palin candidacy. The 2008 election also resulted in the first African American president as Obama won with 53 percent of the popular vote. The new president inherited the worst economic crisis since the Great Depression, record deficits, and two wars that defied all military solutions and had sharply divided the American people. Perhaps the president's biggest obstacle, however, was finding a way to translate his lofty rhetoric and the extremely high expectations he had created into support for policies in an extremely polarized political climate.

4.4 Polarization and the Obama Presidency

Obama hoped to pass sweeping legislation that would finally reform the health care system—legislation that had eluded his party for seven decades. But first, Obama focused on the continued economic turmoil of Wall Street and Main Street. In February of 2008, Congress approved a second major stimulus bill. The American Recovery and Reinvestment Act provided nearly $800 billion to ailing state and local governments for a host of projects aimed at providing jobs and bolstering the nation's infrastructure and educational systems. The bill remained controversial, although many believe that it along with previous measures helped to prevent a more serious economic downturn. Several leading Republicans were angered by continued federal spending that exacerbated the national debt, which exceeded $10 trillion.

Obama's health care plan was even more controversial. Many on the political right labeled the plan as "Obamacare" and spread false information about some of the plan's provisions. Some even distorted a section providing coverage for counseling services for terminally ill patients as some sort of mandatory euthanization scheme for senior citizens. A new grassroots movement known as the Tea Party emerged in opposition to the Obama health care bill. Although the health care plan passed the overwhelmingly Democratic Congress, this occurred only after the president removed the most significant reforms, such as a health insurance plan administered by the government. Obama also announced that all combat troops would return from Iraq by 2010, which also concerned many on the right. The president also announced a surge of 30,000 troops in Afghanistan and a renewed effort to target Al Qaeda and the Taliban.

On May 1, 2011, US special forces located and killed Osama bin Laden in Pakistan, raising questions about the extent of Al Qaeda support throughout the region. The news was greeted by most Americans as a hopeful sign that terrorism would decline. Others were alarmed at the degree of revelry that some Americans displayed, which seemed inappropriate to many and likely to embolden America's enemies.

Sarah Palin

John McCain's vice presidential candidate and former governor of Alaska who stepped down from office before her term was complete in order to pursue a career as a national political figure and consultant for Fox News. Palin alienated many moderates but retains a loyal following on the far-right of the Republican Party through organizations such as the Tea Party.

FIGURE 14.18

The Tea Party emerged as a grassroots movement of the political right. Its members generally opposed President Obama and shared the perception that liberals were moving the nation toward Socialism.

FIGURE 14.19

Toward the end of 2011, a grassroots movement opposed to the unequal distribution of wealth in the United States began a protest outside the New York Stock Exchange. The Occupy Wall Street movement quickly spread from New York to local communities, attracting a variety of issues and supporters.

Estimates of the total cost of the wars in Iraq and Afghanistan continued to lead many to question the way the war on terror was being waged. As of 2011, more than 6,000 US soldiers, 2,000 US contractors, and an estimated 130,000 Iraqi and Afghan citizens had perished. The Congressional Budget Office estimates the total cost of the wars at $2 trillion, while researchers at Brown University believe that the long-term costs of caring for the hundreds of thousands of injured veterans will raise the cost to $4 trillion. As Obama announced the return of all American military personnel from Iraq by early 2012, neither Iraq nor Afghanistan appeared to most Americans to be on a clear path toward democracy. Meanwhile, the expenditures of the Department of Homeland Security were continuing to rise, along with the growing threat of terrorism.

The news of bin Laden's death immediately boosted President Obama's approval ratings, but the polarization that divided most Americans remained. Emotional debates ensued that reflected a cultural war between the right and its hypernationalistic rhetoric and the left with its call for greater tolerance of diversity and support for President Obama. That support for the president slowly declined after three years in office that saw the president devote most of his efforts to winning over his conservative critics. Many on the left felt betrayed by the failure of the president to follow through with promises to immediately repeal DADT, close Guantanamo Bay, end the war in Iraq, and enact stricter regulations on banks and investment firms. In addition, the debates during the summer of 2011 regarding the debt ceiling reflect anxieties about the health of the economy and the mounting federal debt that exceeded $14 trillion.

Economic concerns and an ongoing cultural war manifested themselves in numerous ways during the president's final years of his 2011–2013 term. The president's support of a proposed Islamic community in the same Manhattan neighborhood that had been home to the Twin Towers angered many conservatives who began to fear that their president had betrayed the memory of September 11. Others defended the president out of recognition that cherished values of freedom of expression and religion were at stake but still expressed reservations about the legitimacy of the Islamic faith.

Demagogic talk show hosts continued to make hundreds of comparisons between the Obama administration and the methods of Adolf Hitler and Joseph Goebbels. Similar comparisons were made by some on the political left toward conservatives. For most Americans, however, the examples these demagogues used to support their analysis demonstrated both insensitivity to the past and a suspension of critical thinking. Most Americans were disturbed by the crude comparisons of American politicians to these tyrants and the ignorance of world history demonstrated by those who parroted these demagogic pundits. A few within the Tea Party movement such as Sarah Palin revealed and then celebrated a level of historical illiteracy that shocked many Americans and became fodder for late-night talk show hosts.

As Palin demonstrated in 2011 with her assertion that Paul Revere was trying to warn the British, presumably about their own troop movements, interpretations of history continue to reveal a great deal about the present. A June 2011 effort to commemorate the 1921 coal miner's rebellion at Blair Mountain, West Virginia, personifies many of the tensions between the political left and the right and may be useful as a case study to explore the causes and consequences of modern political alignment. Blair Mountain was the site of one of the most violent labor conflicts in history. The land was recently taken off the list of protected historical sights and was scheduled to be developed by mining companies by using explosives to eliminate the top of the mountain. Many working-class West Virginians sided with the coal companies, who presented the protesters as liberals and outsiders with an agenda to eliminate coal jobs in the name of environmental protection. Given the massive layoffs of the past few decades, the desire of many environmentalists to reduce coal consumption, and the way many working-class residents of the state have been caricatured, the defensiveness of this perspective carried its own logic.

At the same time, the loss of relatively high-paying jobs in coal mining and other industries and the assault against the dignity of labor mirrored the cultural and economic issues surrounding the 1921 revolt. Much like their predecessors, modern coal companies were seeking ways of reducing labor costs. Mountaintop removal mining is a technique that utilizes dynamite to blow away the tops of mountains, known euphemistically as "overburden." The technique eliminates the need for skilled miners and engineers who are also more likely to be well-paid and unionized laborers. For this reason, coal companies favor mountaintop removal and other forms of strip-mining because it reduces labor costs.

As a result, many who depend on the coal industry for their livelihood were once again forced to choose between coal operators who they hoped would employ them in the near-term and progressives who viewed labor and capital as hostile toward one another. The progressive vision offers the possibility of better working conditions and environmental protection but has often been expressed in paternalistic ways that alienated many working-class Americans. Similar to those who sought to create a partnership between the liberal reformers and the working class, modern progressives face the challenge of creating partnerships across class lines in a cultural war that continues to polarize America along a liberal-conservative divide.

> ### REVIEW AND CRITICAL THINKING
>
> 1. Discuss the history of campaign finance reform over the past two decades. How have changing laws regarding the ways political campaigns are financed affected the nation?
>
> 2. Summarize the economic history that led to the partial collapse of the real-estate market and the bankruptcy of many leading financial firms. Discuss the response of the federal government to the crisis, including the decision to loan billions of dollars to private businesses that were on the verge of bankruptcy.
>
> 3. Summarize the Republican and Democratic primaries leading up to the 2008 election. How was Barack Obama able to defeat John McCain? Discuss the impact of President Bush's approval ratings, the wars in Iraq and Afghanistan, and the economy. Lastly, discuss the ways that issues of race and gender affected the election.
>
> 4. Explain why many Americans believe that their nation has grown more polarized following the 2008 election than at any time in recent history. Describe the current political climate and the impact of political polarization upon the country.

5. CONCLUSION

The debates regarding environmental protection, globalization, and the distribution of wealth continue to arouse impassioned debate. Issues that were heavily debated during the Clinton administration, such as welfare, continue to revolve around the desire to prevent fraud and dependency while ensuring adequate provisions for children. Both sides cite statistics showing that poverty rates have changed little between 1996 and 2011 to support their own conclusions about the 1996 reforms. Liberals call for more aggressive funding in hopes additional programs might end the cycle of poverty while conservatives claim that welfare itself helps to create a culture of dependency. A similar debate surrounds the issues of taxation and the unequal distribution of wealth that spawned the Occupy Wall Street Movement in the fall of 2011.

The post–Cold War period saw the greatest threats of history replayed throughout the globe. International instability, tyrannical dictators, economic crises, and attempted genocide have continued to shape US policies and identities at home and abroad. For the attentive student of history, the challenges of the past surround the present. America's record regarding international affairs revealed the continuity of challenges and contradictions that had defined America's emergence as a superpower. Aware of the service and sacrifice of those who placed America in a position of global leadership, the youths of this most recent generation continue to balance the priorities of defending those in need with supporting a nation's right to self-determination. For a new generation of Americans, the lessons of generations past resonate in a renewed determination to create an America that lives up to its own lofty ideals. Armed with an understanding of America's past, there is reason to believe that the next generation will arise and lead a nation whose greatest challenges and finest moments are yet to be written.

6. FURTHER READING

Berman, William C. *From the Center to the Edge: The Politics and Policies of the Clinton Administration* (2001).

Chafe, William. *The Unfinished Journey: America Since World War II* (2010).

Eckes, Alfred A. Jr. and Thomas W. Zeiler. *Globalization in the American Century* (2003).

Gidlow, Liette. *Obama, Clinton, Palin: Making History in Elections 2008* (2011).

Johnson, Hayes. *Best of Times: America in the Clinton Years* (2004).

Katz, Michael B. *The Price of Citizenship: Redefining America's Welfare State* (2001).

Lewis, Michael. *The Big Short: Inside the Doomsday Machine* (2010).

Reimers, David. *Unwelcome Strangers: American Identity and the Turn Against Immigration* (1998).

Stiglitz, Joseph. *Globalization and Its Discontents* (2002).

Index